From Unicode to Advanced
Typography and Everything in Between

Fonts &
Encodings

Yannis Haralambous
Translated by P. Scott Horne

O'REILLY®

Fonts & Encodings

Other resources from O'Reilly

Related titles

Unicode Explained	XSLT Cookbook™
SVG Essentials	CJKV Information Processing
Adobe InDesign CS2 One-on-One	InDesign Production Cookbook
XSL-FO	Dynamic Learning: Illustrator CS3

oreilly.com

oreilly.com is more than a complete catalog of O'Reilly books. You'll also find links to news, events, articles, weblogs, sample chapters, and code examples.

oreillynet.com is the essential portal for developers interested in open and emerging technologies, including new platforms, programming languages, and operating systems.

Conferences

O'Reilly brings diverse innovators together to nurture the ideas that spark revolutionary industries. We specialize in documenting the latest tools and systems, translating the innovator's knowledge into useful skills for those in the trenches. Visit *conferences.oreilly.com* for our upcoming events.

Safari Bookshelf (*safari.oreilly.com*) is the premier online reference library for programmers and IT professionals. Conduct searches across more than 1,000 books. Subscribers can zero in on answers to time-critical questions in a matter of seconds. Read the books on your Bookshelf from cover to cover or simply flip to the page you need. Try it today for free.

Fonts & Encodings

Yannis Haralambous

Translated by P. Scott Horne

O'REILLY®

Beijing · Cambridge · Farnham · Köln · Paris · Sebastopol · Taipei · Tokyo

Fonts & Encodings
by Yannis Haralambous

Printed in the United States of America.

Published by O'Reilly Media, Inc., 1005 Gravenstein Highway North, Sebastopol, CA 95472.

O'Reilly books may be purchased for educational, business, or sales promotional use. Online editions are also available for most titles (*safari.oreilly.com*). For more information, contact our corporate/institutional sales department: (800) 998-9938 or *corporate@oreilly.com*.

Printing History:

September 2007: First Edition.

ISBN-10: 0-596-10242-9
ISBN-13: 978-0-596-10242-5
[M]

Ubi sunt qui ante nos
in mundo fuere?

To the memory of my beloved father,
Athanassios-Diomidis Haralambous

This book would never have seen the light of day without the help of a number of people, to whom the author would like to express his thanks:

- His wife, Tereza, and his elder daughter, Ernestine ("Daddy, when are you going to finish your book?"), who lived through hell for a whole year.

- The management of ENST Bretagne, Annie Gravey (chair of his department), and his colleagues, for encouraging him in this undertaking and tolerating the inconveniences caused by his prolonged absence.

- His editor, Xavier Cazin, for his professionalism, his enthusiasm, and his friendship.

- Jacques André, for supplying tons of books, articles, leads, addresses, ideas, advice, suggestions, memories, crazy thoughts, etc.

- His proofreaders: Jacques André once again, but also Patrick Andries, Oscarine Bosquet, Michel Cacouros, Luc Devroye, Pierre Dumesnil, Tereza Haralambous, John Plaice, Pascal Rubini, and François Yergeau, for reviewing and correcting all or part of the book in record time.

- The indefatigable George Williams, for never failing to add new features to his *FontForge* software at the author's request.

- All those who supported him by providing information or resources: Ben Bauermeister, Gábor Bella, Tom Bishop, Thierry Bouche, John Collins, Richard Cook, Simon Daniels, Mark Davis, Lisa Devlin, Bon Hallissy, Ken'ichi Handa, Alan Hoenig, Bogusław Jackowski, Michael Jansson, Ronan Keryell, Alain LaBonté, David Lemon, Ken Lunde, Jim Lyles, Sergey Malkin, Sabine Millecamps (Harrie Potter), Lisa Moore, Tomohiko Morioka, Éric Muller, Paul Nelson, David Opstad, Christian Paput, Thomas Phinney, Just van Rossum, Emmanuël Souchier, Naoto Takahashi, Bob Thomas, Adam Twardoch, Jürgen Willrodt, and Candy Lee Yiu.

- The foundries that supplied fonts or specimens for use in his examples: Justin Howes, P22, Thierry Gouttenègre, Klemens Burkhardt, Hoefler Type Foundry, Typofonderie Porchez, and Fountain Type.

- Emma Colby and Hanna Dyer of O'Reilly, for selecting that magnificent buck as the animal on the cover, doubtless because its coat is reminiscent of encoding tables and its antlers suggest the Bézier curves of fonts.

- Last but not least, Scott Horne, the heroic translator of this book of more than a thousand pages, who mustered all his energy and know-how to translate the technical terms correctly, adapt the book's style to the culture of the English-speaking countries, correct countless errors (even in the Chinese passages)—in short, he prepared this translation with the utmost care. Just to cite one example, he translated the third stanza of *Gaudeamus Igitur* from Latin to archaic English—in verse, no less—for use in the dedication. The author will be forever grateful to him for all these contributions.

Contents

11 *The History and Classifications of Latin Typefaces*   367

Introduction

Homo sapiens is a species that writes. And among the large number of tools used for writing, the most recent and the most complex is the computer—a tool for reading and writing, a medium for storage, and a means of exchanging data, all rolled into one. It has become a veritable *space* in which the text resides, a space that, as MacLuhan and others correctly predicted, has come to transcend geographic barriers and encompass the entire planet.

Within this digital space for writing, fonts and encodings serve fundamentally different needs. Rather, they form an inseparable duo, like yin and yang, Heaven and Earth, theory and practice. An encoding emerges from the tendency to conceptualize information; it is the result of an abstraction, a construction of the mind. A font is a means of visually representing writing, the result of concrete expression, a graphical construct.

An encoding is a table of *characters*—a character being an abstract, intangible entity. A font is a container for *glyphs*, which are images, drawings, physical marks of black ink on a white background. When the reader enters the digital space for writing, he participates in the unending ballet between characters and glyphs: the keys on the keyboard are marked with *glyphs*; when a key is pressed, a *character* is transmitted to the system, which, unless the user is entering a password, in turn displays *glyphs* on the screen. To send an email message is to send *characters*, but these are displayed to the recipient in the form of *glyphs*. When we run a search on a text file, we search for a string of *characters*, but the results are shown to us as a sequence of *glyphs*. And so on.

For the Western reader, this perpetual metamorphosis between characters and glyphs remains on the philosophical level. That is hardly surprising, as European writing systems have divided their fundamental constituents (*graphemes*) so that there is a one-to-one correspondence between character and glyph. Typophiles have given us some exceptions that prove the rule: in the word "film" there are four letters (and therefore four characters) but only three glyphs (because the letters 'f' and 'i' combine to form only one glyph). This phenomenon, which is called a *ligature*, can be orthographically significant (as is the case for the ligature 'œ', in French) or purely aesthetic (as with the *f*-ligatures 'fi', 'ff', 'ffi', etc.).

In any case, these phenomena are marginal in our very cut-and-dried Western world. In the writing systems of the East, however, the conflict between characters and glyphs becomes an integral part of daily life. In Arabic, the letters are connected and assume different forms according to their position in the word. In the languages of India and Southeast Asia, they combine to form more and more complex graphical amalgamations. In the Far East, the ideographs live in a sort of parallel universe, where they are born and die, change language and country, clone themselves, mutate genetically, and carry a multitude of meanings.

Despite the trend towards globalization, the charm of the East has in no way died out; its writing systems still fire our dreams. But every dream is a potential nightmare. Eastern writing systems present a challenge to computer science—a challenge that goes beyond mere technical problems. Since writing—just like images, speech, and music—is one of the fundamental concerns of humanity, computer science cannot approach it haphazardly: Eastern writing systems must be handled just as efficiently as the script that is part of our Latin cultural heritage. Otherwise, some of those writing systems may not survive computerization.

But more is at stake than the imperatives of cultural ecology. The French say that "travel educates the young". The same goes for writing: through thinking about the writing systems of other cultures and getting to know their problems and concerns, we come to know more about our own.

Then there is also the historical perspective: in the digital space for writing that we are exploring in this book, the concepts and techniques of many centuries dwell together. Terminology, or rather the confusion that reigns in this field, clearly shows that computer science, despite its newness, lies on a historical continuum of techniques and practices. For example, when we set type in *Times Ten* at 8 points, we say that we are using a "body size of 8 points" and an "optical size of 10 points". Can the same characters have two different sizes? To understand the meaning of these terms, it is necessary to trace the development of the concept of "type size" from the fifteenth century to the PostScript and TrueType fonts of our modern machines.

So far we have briefly surveyed the three axes on which this book is based: the *systemic approach* (abstraction/concrete expression, encoding/font, character/glyph), *geographicity* (East/West), *historicity* (ancient/modern, mechanical/computerized processes). These three aspects make up the complexity and the scope of our subject, namely the *exploration of the digital space for writing*.

Finally, there is a fourth axis, less important than the previous three but still well grounded in our day-to-day reality, which is *industrial competition*. A phenomenon that leads to an explosion in technologies, to gratuitous technicality, to a deliberate lack of clarity in documentation, and to all sorts of other foolish things that give the world of business its supposed charm. If we didn't have PostScript fonts *and* TrueType fonts *and* OpenType fonts *and* Apple Advanced Typography (AAT) fonts, the world might be a slightly better place and this book would be several hundred pages shorter.

In this regard, the reader should be aware of the fact that everything pertaining to encodings, and to fonts in particular, is considered to be industrial knowledge and therefore cannot be disseminated, at least not completely. It is hard to imagine how badly the "specifications" of certain technologies are written, whether because of negligence or out of a conscious desire to prevent the full use of the technologies. Some of the appendices of this book were written for the very purpose of describing certain technologies with a reputation for inaccessibility, such as AAT tables and TrueType instructions, as clearly and exhaustively as possible.

In the remainder of this introduction, we shall outline, first of all, the jargon used in the rest of the book, so as to clarify the historical development of certain terms. This will also enable us to give an overview of the transition from mechanical to computerized processes.

Next, we will give the reader a synthetic view of the book by outlining several possible ways to approach it. Each profile of a typical reader that we present is focused on a specific area of interest, a particular way to use this book. We hope that this part of the introduction will allow the reader to find her own path through the forest of 2.5 million letters that she is holding in her hands.

Explorations

When one walks around a new city for the first time, one discovers places, acquires a better understanding of the reasons behind certain historical events, and puts together the pieces of the puzzle that make up the city's environment. Here we shall do the same. Our first stroll through the digital space for writing that we plan to explore will allow us to take inventory of concepts and techniques, establish our terminology, and briefly outline the conflict between the mechanical and the electronic.

Let us set aside for the moment the geographical axis and begin with a very specific case of a glyph that comprises the molecular level of our space: the (Latin) *letter*.

The Letter and Its Parts

The terminology for describing the letter as a design varies greatly from one writer to the next—a phenomenon, incidentally, that affects all terminology in the entire field of typography. In Figure 0-1, we have listed in roman type the terms that are used in this book and in italics some other terms that exist for the same parts of letters. Thus a *stem* is also called a *stroke* or a *downstroke*.

These terms come from a variety of sources: the calligrapher's technique (stroke, terminal), the engraver's art (counter), geometry (apex, vertex), analogy or anatomy (arm, eye, ear, tail, shoulder), mechanics or architecture (finial), etc.

The most important among them are:

- The *stem*, or *stroke*: a thick vertical or diagonal line found in such letters as 'H', 'l', 'N', and 'v'. If the letter is *lower-case*, or small, two possibilities may occur:

  - the stem extends upward to the same height as the capitals or even higher, as in the letters 'b', 'd', 'h', etc. This upper part of the stem is called an *ascender*.

Figure 0-1: The parts of a letter. The terms used in this book are in roman; alternative terms are shown in italics.

       – the stem passes beneath the baseline, as in the letters 'p' and 'q'. This lower part of the stem is called a *descender*.

• The *bowl*, which is a full circle, as in 'O', or the greater part of a circle, as in 'q'.

• The *counter*, which is the inner part of a letter; for example, the space inside an 'o', an 'O', a 'D', etc. The counter of an 'e' is commonly called an *eye*. When the letter is open at one end, as is the case with 'n', we speak instead of an *aperture*.

• The *arm*, a thin horizontal stroke that is open at one end, as the two arms atop a 'T' and the upper and lower arms of an 'E'.

- The *crossbar* (or *bar*), which is a thin horizontal connecting stroke, as in 'A' and 'H'. A horizontal stroke that crosses a vertical one, as in 'f' and 't', is also called a *cross stroke*.

- The *serif*, which is the "pedestal" at the bottom and top of the vertical strokes and at the ends of some horizontal strokes. Thus the letter 'I' has two serifs, while the letter 'H' has four. The left part of an upper serif that appears on some letters, a remnant of the short lead-in made by the pen where it touches the paper before a downstroke, is called a *head serif*. It is the head serif that distinguishes 'I' from 'I', for example. In humanist and garalde typefaces (see Chapter 11), the head serif is slanted, whereas it is perfectly horizontal in didones.

- The *terminal*, which is the opposite of the head serif: it is the movement of the pen that finishes the letter. Again, it is a half-serif, this time the right side of the serif, and it occurs primarily at the baseline.

If these terms apply just as well to traditional as to digital typography, that is because they refer to abstract graphical characteristics.

Now that we have named the components of letters, we can explore ways to describe them precisely. How do we describe the proportions of letters, their graphical characteristics—in short, everything that distinguishes one typographic character from another?

There are two answers to that question: that of the *professional*, which is to say that of the *craftsman* (engraver of characters, typographer) or other *typographic specialist* (historian), and that of the *mathematician*.

In the first case, we study the letterforms according to their history, the cultural context behind their creation and their use, and their development over time relative to the development of Western culture. To this approach we have devoted Chapter 11, which presents the history of typographic characters and one classification of them from a point of view that is more historical and cultural than formal and geometric.

The second case, that of the mathematician, involves the study of letters as geometric shapes. This approach is hardly new.[1] In Figure 0-2 we see four studies of the Latin alphabet, corresponding to two eras and three countries: the first was made by an Italian humanist, Friar Luca de Pacioli, from his work *Divine Proportion* [273], published in Venice in 1509. The second comes to us from the hands of the great German engraver Albrecht Dürer and is dated 1535. It presents different models of alphabets in a work whose title is less ambitious than that of Pacioli: *Instructions on Measurement* [124]. The third dates from 1524 and is from France: it is the manual of Geofroy Tory, a great Parisian humanist to whom we also owe the use of the accents and the cedilla in the French language. His descriptions appear in his finest work, the *Champ fleury, au quel eft contenu Lart & Science de la deue & vraye Proportiō des Lettres Attiques* ("The Floured Feelde, wherein be

---

[1] Readers who wish to know more about the history of the mathematical description of letterforms are encouraged to consult Donald Knuth [221, p. 48] and Jacques André [35].

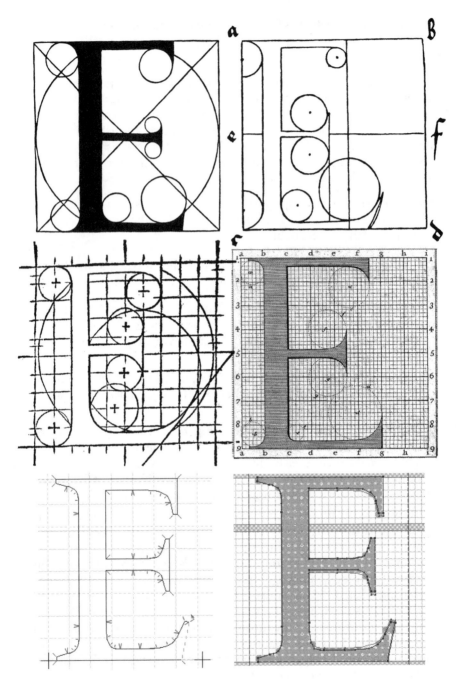

Figure 0-2: Six mathematical descriptions of the letter 'E': Luca de Pacioli (1509), Albrecht Dürer (1535), Geofroy Tory (1524), the Jaugeon Commission (1716), and two screenshots from the software package FontLab (today).

contayned the Arte & Scyence of the iuſte and true Proporcion of Atticke Letters") [332]. Finally, in 1716, as a result of an undertaking by Louis XIV, the Jaugeon Commission drafted the design for a royal script, entirely geometrical in nature, called the *Romain du Roi* [276] ("the King's roman").

Many things strike us from an examination of these four examples. First of all, we notice that, in all four instances, the artists wished to place their letters within perfect squares, in the same way as the characters of the Far East. We also notice that they use finer and finer Cartesian grids in order to obtain more precise mathematical descriptions. While Tory uses a grid of 10×10 squares, the Jaugeon Commission resorts to 6×6 small squares within 8×8 large ones, for a total of 48×48—2,304 squares in all, which was an enormous degree of precision for the time.

While the challenge was originally of a humanist nature (in the fifteenth century, when perspective was invented, Europeans began to wonder about the relationship between beauty and mathematics), it became one of power (Louis XIV took control of everything in his kingdom, right down to the microscopic level) and, finally, in the twentieth century, one of technology.

Why? Because these mathematical descriptions of letters are the precursors of the digital fonts of today, defined on a grid of $1,024 \times 1,024$ (PostScript) or $4,096 \times 4,096$ (TrueType) squares, or even more. There is only a difference of mathematical scale: whereas the letters in the first four examples are described by circles and lines in the manner of Euclid ("with straightedge and compass"), today's fonts use curves defined by third-degree polynomials that were introduced by the French engineer Pierre Bézier (see Appendix G). In the last two examples in Figure 0-2, we see two contemporary approaches to the design of glyphs: they are screenshots from the software system FontLab.

What is the situation today? Have Bézier curves extinguished the little flame that is the genius of the master engraver? Quite the opposite. We use Bézier curves today because we have interactive tools that allow modern designers to create fonts worthy of their predecessors. We have devoted Chapters 12 to 14 and Appendix F to the description of the best available tools for creating fonts.

Letterpress Typesetting

In the previous section, we discussed the individuals that populate the digital space for writing: letters. But this space would be quite sad if each letter lived all by itself in its own little bubble. Far from being so isolated, letters, and more generally glyphs of all kinds, are highly social creatures. They love to form little groups (words), which in turn form larger and larger groups (lines, paragraphs, pages, books). We call this process *typesetting*. And the human who weaves the fates of the letters together to form structures on a higher level is a *typesetter*.

Having come to this point, we can no longer content ourselves with the abstraction in which the previous section indulged. The way in which we put letters together depends on the technology that we use. It is therefore time to abandon the realm of the abstract

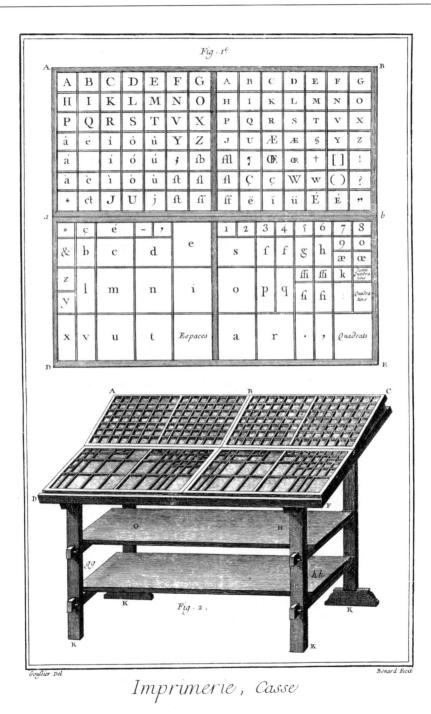

Figure 0-3: An eighteenth-century type case (from the Encyclopédie *of Diderot and d'Alembert).*

beauty of letters and to come down to earth to describe the *mechanical* process of type-setting. For computerized typesetting is based on mechanical typesetting, and the terms that we use today were invented by those people whose hands were indelibly blackened, not with oil (the liquid that pollutes our ecosystem), but with printer's ink (the liquid that bears wisdom).

Let us therefore quickly review the manual setting of type for the letterpress, which was used from the fifteenth century until the end of the nineteenth, when the Linotype and Monotype typesetting machines made their appearance.

Letterpress printing is based on movable *type*, little metal blocks (*sorts*) made from an amalgam of lead, zinc, and antimony that have on one side a mirror image of a letter, carved in relief. In Figure 0-3, taken from the *Encyclopédie* of Diderot and d'Alembert, we see at the top a *type case* containing type and, below it, the table that supports the different cases from which type is taken for composition. The top half of the case, the "upper case", contains the capital letters, the small capitals, and certain punctuation marks; the bottom half, the "lower case", contains the small letters (called "lowercase" for this very reason), the numerals, and various "spaces" (blocks of lead with no letter carved into them that serve to separate words). We can see how type is arranged in the case. Of course, the arrangement varies from country to country according to the frequency of letters in the dominant language.

Figure 0-4: A composing stick (from the Encyclopédie *of Diderot and d'Alembert).*

The typesetter takes type sorts out of the case and places them on a *composing stick*, which is illustrated in Figure 0-4. A whole line at a time is prepared on a composing stick. The width of the composing stick is that of the *measure* of the page; thus the typesetter knows when he has reached the end of the line and can take appropriate action. He can decide to divide the word or to fill out the line with thin strips of extra spacing between the words to extend it to the full measure.

When the line is ready, the typesetter adds it to the other lines of the page, eventually inserting horizontal strips of lead, called *leading*, between the lines. At the bottom of Figure 0-5, there are three lines that are set in this fashion:

> GLOIRE à DIEU.
> *Honneur au ROI.*
> Salut aux ARMES.

In this example, we can notice several tricks that enable us to overlap the faces of letters. First, the face of the italic 'H' in the second line extends beyond the body of the type sort

Figure 0-5: Three typeset lines (from the Encyclopédie *of Diderot and d'Alembert).*

and reaches over the 'o' that follows. This overlapping, called *kerning*, is indispensable, since italic letters are not slanted but occupy upright parallelepipeds. The italic 'I' also kerns with the following letter.

Another trick: the lower parts of the faces of the letters are cut on an angle. The benefit of this device is that it permits the vertical kerning of certain letters in the following line that are slightly taller than the others. For example, the apex of the 'A' extends above the rectangular body of the type sort and fits underneath the italic 'R' in the line above. This projection is called *overshoot* at the tops of the letters and *overhang* at the baseline; in both cases, it can be *round* or *pointed*. Overshoot exists to correct the optical illusion by which a triangle (or a circle) seems smaller than a square of the same height.

What, then, are the units by which metal type is measured? There are two basic ones: the height of the type, called the *body size*, and the width of the metal type sort for each character, called its *set-width*.

The 'G' of the word "GLOIRE" in Figure 0-5 is set in a larger font, which is why the typesetter has added a row of spaces above the remainder of the first line of text. It is important to understand that the concept of "body size" is distinct from that of the size of the letters themselves. Thus, in the same figure, the letters 'L', 'O', ... 'E' of "GLOIRE" are smaller than those of "DIEU", but their body size is the same, as the metal type sorts that bear them are of equal height. In this particular case, we have *capital letters* (in the word "DIEU") and *small capitals* (for "LOIRE") of the same body size.

We use the term *x-height* for the height of the faces (and, therefore, the area actually printed) of lowercase letters such as 'x'. We say that a character has a "large x-height" or a "small x-height" when the ratio of the height of its face to the body size is large or small.

Likewise, the set-width is theoretically independent of the width of the face of the letter, since the latter may be smaller than the former. In that case, we say that the there are right and/or left *bearings* between the face and the edge of the type sort. Conversely, the face may extend beyond the type sort, if it has a kern.

Digital Typesetting

Since the 1950s, phototypesetting has gradually conquered the world of printing. It is based on removing the typesetting process from its material roots. This departure from the physical grew more acute with the move towards computerization in the 1970s and 1980s. Now that we have no metal type sorts to measure, what should we make of the terms "body size", "set-width", and "x-height"?

Have they lost their relevance? Far from it. They are *more useful than ever* because they ensure continuity between the results of traditional typesetting and those of phototype-setting or digital typesetting. This continuity is essential, since the quality of the final product, the book, must not be adversely affected because of a change in technology. In order to produce books of quality equal to, or better than, that of traditional printing, we must preserve its points of reference, its conventions, and its visual approaches.

Therefore, we have to redefine these terms to adapt them to the reality of digital typesetting, which is divorced from physical references. To understand how that has been done, let us investigate the model of digital typesetting:

Glyphs (i.e., the visual forms of typographic symbols) are placed in abstract rectangles whose heights are initially undetermined and whose width is equal to the set-width.

We need to introduce another new concept, that of the *baseline*, which is the imaginary line on which all the glyphs with a flat base, such as 'f', rest. Those with a round base, such as 'c', dip slightly below the baseline as a result of *overhang*. The intersection of the baseline and the leftmost edge of the glyph's box is called the *origin* of the glyph. We describe a glyph mathematically on a system of coordinates with this point as its origin.

The set-width can be thought of as a vector connecting the origin of one glyph to that of the following glyph. This vector is called the *advance vector* (or *escapement vector*). Digital typesetting consists of nothing more than drawing a glyph, moving as indicated by the advance vector, and preparing to draw the glyph that follows.

A glyph "floats" in its imaginary box. The width of the space that will eventually fall between the glyph and the edge of the box is known as the *bearing* (*right* or *left*, as the case may be). In certain cases, the glyph may be located partly or completely outside its box—proof of the relative independence of container and contents, or box and glyph.

While it was relatively easy to adapt the concept of set-width to the digital realm, the same is not true of the body size. Indeed, we mentioned above that the box containing the glyph is of "undetermined" height. Of all the various typesetting systems, only TEX concerns itself with the height and depth of these boxes, and that is why we have shown the boxes' upper and lower boundaries, albeit with dotted lines, in the figure.

The other systems employ set-width almost exclusively, and PostScript and TrueType fonts contain no information about the height or depth of the box other than the dimensions of the glyph itself.

There are also scripts that are written vertically (such as ideographic scripts and Mongolian), in which the advance vector points downward. We say in such cases that there is a *vertical set-width*. The heights of the spaces that will appear between the glyph and the horizontal edges of the box are thus called *upper* and *lower bearings*, as the case may be.

But let us return to the concept of "body size". We continue to speak of setting type "with a body size of 10 points" (or, more professionally, at "10/12", where the first figure is the type size and the second is the body, which includes leading). But what is a *point*, and how is this information managed in software?

The *point* is a typographic unit invented by Father Sébastien Truchet in 1699 to describe the arithmetic progression of type sizes [276]. This unit, related to the Paris foot (*pied du roi*, the actual length of the king's foot), was redefined by Pierre-Simon Fournier in 1664 and later by François-Ambroise Didot in 1783. Since the end of the nineteenth century, the Anglo-Saxons have used the pica point [87]. The PostScript language sought to simplify calculations by defining the point to be exactly $\frac{1}{72}$ of an inch. Today we have points of three different sizes: the *pica point* (approximately 0.351 mm), the *Didot point*[2] (approximately 0.376 mm), and the *PostScript point* (approx. 0.353 mm).

As for *body size*, its precise definition depends on the system being used (PostScript, TrueType, TEX), but in general the idea is as follows: glyphs are described with a system of Cartesian coordinates based on an abstract unit of length. There is a relationship between these units and the "body size" of the font. Thus a PostScript font uses a grid of 1,024 units, which means, for example, that an 'a' designed with a height of exactly 512 units, when typeset at a font size of 10 points, will appear on paper with a real height of half of the body size, namely 5 points.

The user is still free to magnify or reduce the letter as much as he likes. In this book, we use the term *actual size* for the size of the letter as it appears on paper, after any magnification or reduction performed according to the principle explained below.

In the days of the letterpress, there was no way to magnify or reduce a shape arbitrarily. The different body sizes of a given typographic character were engraved separately. And typesetters took advantage of this necessity to improve the legibility of each size: the small sizes had letters that were relatively wider and more spacious than those of the large ones, which were drawn with more details, more contrast between thick and thin strokes, and so on.

---

[2] The Didot point is still used in Greece, where letterpress typesetters complain that text set with the pica point "comes out too small".

By way of illustration, here are a 72-point font and a 6-point font, scaled to the same actual size:

Laurel & Hardy

The actual size of this sequence of glyphs is 24 points. The 72-point letters ("Laurel &") seem too narrow, with horizontal strokes that are too thin, whereas the 6-point letters ("Hardy") seem too wide, bordering on awkwardness.

We use the term *optical size* for the size at which the glyph in question was designed. Digital fonts usually have only one optical size for all actual sizes—a fact that Ladislas Mandel calls the "original sin" of phototypesetting. Usually we do not even know the optical size of a digital font. In a few exceptional cases, the name of the font reveals its optical size, as is the case with *Times Ten* (10 points), *Times Seven* (7 points), etc. There are also a few rare families of digital fonts designed in several optical sizes: *Computer Modern*, by Donald Knuth (see pages 937 and 938); the splendid *HW Caslon*, by the late Justin Howes (page 388); *HTF Didot*, by Jonathan Hoefler (page 392); and *ITC Bodoni* (page 393), by Holly Goldsmith, Jim Parkinson, and Sumner Stone. We can only hope that there will be more such font families in the years to come.

Disregard for optical size can lead to very poor results. Anne Cuneo's book *Le maître de Garamond* ("Garamond's Master") [105] was composed in *1530 Garamond*, a very beautiful *Garamond* replica designed by Ross Mills—but at an actual size of 11, while the optical size of the font is around 48. The print is hard to read, and all the beauty of this wonderful *Garamond* is lost.

What about the x-height? According to Peter Karow [206] and Jacques André [34, pp. 24–26], one good approximation to the concept of x-height (in the absence of a physical leaden type sort to serve as a reference) is the relationship between the height of the lowercase letters and the height of the uppercase letters (for example, the heights of 'x' and 'X'). The closer the lowercase letters come to the height of the uppercase letters, the greater the x-height is. Fonts such as *Courier* and *Clarendon* have a large x-height; fonts such as *Centaur* and *Nicolas Cochin* have a small one:

Courier Clarendon Centaur Nicolas Cochin

The term *kerning* also takes on a different meaning. In digital typesetting, kerning is a second advance vector that is added to the first. Thus, to set the word "AVATAR":

the system first draws the 'A', then moves ahead by an amount equal to the set-width of an 'A', then moves back slightly before drawing the 'V', and so on.

Because kerning refers to *pairs of letters*, this information is stored in the fonts as *kerning pairs*. These values are negative when letters are drawn closer together (for example, 'A' and 'V') and positive when they are pushed farther apart (for example, a 'D' and an 'O'). Kerning may be good or bad, according to the skills of the font designer, but one thing is certain: fonts that have no kerning pairs should not be trusted, and unfortunately there are more of these than there should be.

Font Formats

We have mentioned *PostScript* and *TrueType* fonts several times. What are they, exactly?

A *font* is a container for *glyphs*. To set a sequence of glyphs, the software calls up a font through the operating system and asks for the glyphs that it needs. The way in which the glyphs are described depends on the *font format*: PostScript, TrueType, or any of a number of others, all of them quite different.

The earliest fonts were *bitmaps*: the glyphs were described by white and black pixels (see Appendix A). Although we can easily describe a bitmap font for use on a screen, in which each glyph contains at most a few dozen pixels, it would be cumbersome to do the same for high-resolution printers, for which a single glyph may require thousands of pixels.

Two solutions emerged: compress the bitmapped glyphs or switch to a different type of font. Donald Knuth adopted the first solution to the TeX system in 1978: he designed a program with the pretty name of METAFONT that generated compressed bitmap fonts from a description in a very powerful programming language (Appendix A). The method of compression (§A.5.3) was designed so that the size of the glyphs would only slightly affect the size of the files produced.

The second solution was notably adopted by John Warnock, founder of Adobe, in 1985. He developed a programming language named *PostScript* (§C.1) that describes the entire printed page with mathematical constructs. In particular, the PostScript language possesses a font format that even today is one of the most common in the world: *Type 1 fonts* (§C.3). These fonts, which describe glyphs with mathematical constructs, are called *vector fonts*.

The companies Bitstream and Hewlett-Packard also proposed their own vector font formats, *Speedo* [188] and *Intellifont* [101], which did not last long, despite the originality of their ideas.

Adobe began to grow thanks to PostScript and the Type 1 fonts, and certain other companies (Apple and Microsoft, without mentioning any names) decided that it was time to break Adobe's monopoly. Therefore they jointly and hastily developed a competitor to Type 1 fonts, called *TrueType* (Appendix D). TrueType fonts are not necessarily better or worse than Type 1 fonts, but they present considerable technical differences, which are described in this book.

The first outgrowth from Type 1 were the *Multiple Master* fonts, the shapes of whose glyphs could vary under the user's control. *Multiple Master* fonts were never a screaming success, no doubt because of the difficulty of developing them.

At the same time, the countries of the Far East were struggling to find a way to typeset their ideographic and syllabic writing systems. Adobe offered them another offshoot of Type 1, the *CID* fonts (§C.1). The fact that the TrueType format was already compatible with ideographic writing systems gave it a head start in this area.

Apple and Microsoft separately began to work on improving the TrueType fonts. Apple invested in an extension of TrueType called *TrueType GX* and later rechristened *AAT* ("Apple Advanced Typography", §D.11). Microsoft sought help from its former adversary, Adobe, and together they brought out a competitor to TrueType GX: *OpenType* (§D.9).

OpenType is both an extension to TrueType and an outgrowth of Type 1. In addition, there are two varieties of OpenType fonts: *OpenType-TTF* (which are TrueType with a few extra features) and *OpenType-CFF* (which are Type 1 fonts extended and integrated into TrueType structures).

Both AAT and OpenType attempt to solve two kinds of problems: those of high-quality Latin typography (with ligatures, old-style [not ranging] figures, correctly spaced punctuation, etc.) and those of the Asian languages (Arabic, Hebrew, Indian languages, Southeast Asian languages, etc.). A large part of Appendix D is devoted to the exploration of these two font formats, which still have surprises in store for us.

Between Characters and Glyphs: the Problems of the Electronic Document

We have outlined the digital model of typesetting and also the font formats that exist. To continue our exploration of digital writing, we must address another important concept, that of the *electronic document*.

That is the name that we give to a digital entity containing text (and often images, sound, animation, and fonts as well). We find electronic documents everywhere: on hard disks, on CD-ROMs, on the Web. They can be freely accessible or protected. At the heart of our digital space for writing, electronic documents have problems of their own.

At the beginning of this introduction, we spoke of the "unending ballet between characters and glyphs". But the previous two sections did not even speak of characters. On the contrary, the reader may have been left with the impression that the computer transforms characters into glyphs and typesets documents with the use of fonts, leaving the user with nothing to do but display the output on a screen or print it out.

That was true some 15 years ago, before the advent of the Web, CD-ROMs, and other means for distributing information in the form of *electronic documents*. An electronic document takes the appearance of a paper document when it is displayed or printed out, but it has a number of features that hardcopy lacks.

It is a file that can be used directly—i.e., without any particular processing or modification—on most computer platforms. But what is involved in using a file of this sort?

An electronic document is *read* or *consulted*. When reading, we need features that facilitate our task: a table of contents with hypertext links to structural units, the display of a two-page spread, enlargement or reduction of characters according to the quality of the screen and the visual acuity of the reader, etc. When consulting a document, we need the ability to perform rapid searches with multiple criteria and to have rapid access to the information found.

A search may be performed not only on a single document but on a whole virtual library or even on the entire Web. The electronic document must therefore be indexable. And if we want the indexing to be "intelligent", which is to say enriched by structural or semantic metadata, it is in our interest to prepare the document in a structured form, in the style of XML.

When we perform searches within a document, they are searches for strings of characters. Few software systems support searching for strings with specific typographic attributes, such as specifications of font, point size, or font style. Indeed, to return to the example of the word "film" given on page 1, we could hardly tell the reader of an electronic document that he would have to enter his search with the glyph for the 'fi' ligature or else the word would not be found.

And since strings are what we search for in a document, strings are also what must be indexed if our searches are to be rapid. Conclusion: *an electronic document must contain characters if it is to be indexed and become a full-fledged part of the World Wide Web.*

But we also expect an electronic document to have the appearance of a paper document or to yield an equivalent appearance when printed out. It must therefore be typeset; that is, it must contain glyphs arranged very precisely on lines, with due regard for kerning. These lines must form paragraphs and pages according to the typographic conventions developed through the ages. Conclusion: *an electronic document must contain glyphs arranged with a great deal of precision in order to be a worthy successor of the paper document.*

Corollary: an electronic document must contain *both* characters *and* glyphs. The characters must be readily accessible to the outside world and, if possible, structured and annotated with metadata. The glyphs must be arranged precisely, according to the rules of the typographic art.

Fulfilling these two often contradictory objectives is in itself a challenge for computer science. But the problems of the electronic document do not end there. Characters and glyphs are related like the two sides of a coin, like yin and yang, like signifier and signified. When we interact with an electronic document, we select glyphs with the mouse and expect that the corresponding characters will be copied onto the system's clipboard. Therefore, the document must contain a link between each glyph and the character corresponding to it, even in cases in which one glyph is associated with multiple characters or multiple glyphs with one character, or, to cite the most complex possibility, when multiple glyphs are associated with multiple characters in a different order.

Another major problem: the copyright on the various constituents of an electronic document. While we have the right to make our own text and images freely available, the same is not necessarily true of the fonts that we use. When one "buys" a font, what one actually buys is a license to use it. According to the foundry, this license may or may not specify the number of machines and/or printers on which the font may be installed and used. But no foundry will allow someone who has bought a license for one of its fonts to distribute that font *publicly*. How, then, can one display the glyphs of a document in a particular font if one does not have the right to distribute it?

Electronic documents are caught between the past (typography, glyphs and their arrangement, fonts) and the future (the Web, characters, information that can be indexed at will and made available to everyone). In saying that, we have taken only two axes of our digital space for writing into account: the system approach (characters/glyphs) and historicity. There remain the geographic axis (East/West, with all the surprises that the writing systems of other cultures have in store for us) and the industrial axis (problems of file format, platform, etc.).

In this book, we aim to offer the reader a certain number of tools to confront these problems. We do not concern ourselves with all aspects of the electronic document, just those pertaining to characters and glyphs, aspects that directly and inevitably affect encodings and fonts.

The Structure of the Book and Ways to Use It

This book contains 14 chapters grouped into 4 units and 7 appendices. We have repeatedly said that fonts and encodings interact like yin and yang. Here we use this metaphor to give a graphical illustration of the book's structure with the yin–yang symbol (Figure 0-6) in the background. On the left, in the gray-shaded area: encodings. On the right, in the white part: fonts.

At the top of the circle is the introduction that the reader is currently reading.

The first box, the one on the left, contains the five chapters on encodings, in particular Unicode.

In the first chapter, entitled "Before Unicode", we present a history of codes and encodings, starting in antiquity. After a few words on systems of encoding used in telecommunication before the advent of the computer, we proceed immediately to the most well-known encoding of all, ASCII, and its staunch competitor, EBCDIC. Then follows the ISO 8859 series of encodings, the most recent of which was released in 2001. At the same time, we discuss the problems of the countries of the Far East and the different solutions offered by ISO, Microsoft, and the UNIX world. Finally, we end with a few words on electronic mail and the Web.

The second chapter, "Characters, Glyphs, Bytes", is an introduction to Unicode. In it, we develop the underlying concepts of Unicode, the principles on which it is based, its philosophy, and the technical choices that it has made. We finish the chapter with a quick look at the different tables of Unicode, including a preview of the tables that are still at the stage of consideration that precedes inclusion in the encoding.

Next comes the chapter "Unicode Character Properties", which leads us into the morass of the data that accompanies the characters. Often this data indicates that the character

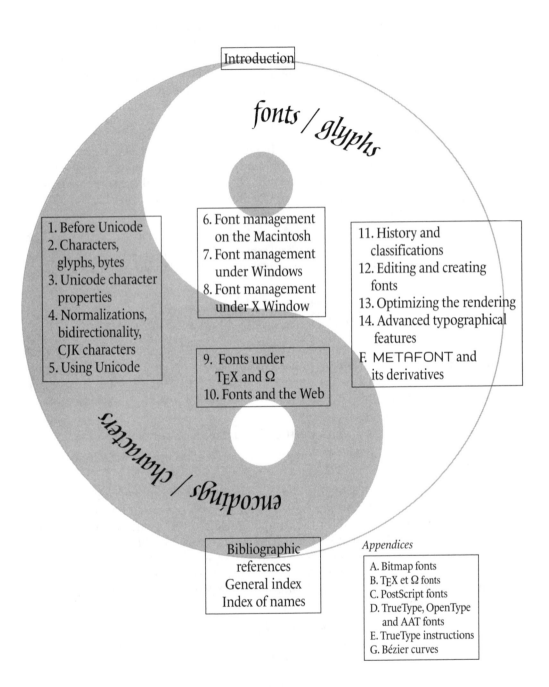

Introduction

fonts / glyphs

1. Before Unicode
2. Characters, glyphs, bytes
3. Unicode character properties
4. Normalizations, bidirectionality, CJK characters
5. Using Unicode

6. Font management on the Macintosh
7. Font management under Windows
8. Font management under X Window

9. Fonts under T_EX and Ω
10. Fonts and the Web

11. History and classifications
12. Editing and creating fonts
13. Optimizing the rendering
14. Advanced typographical features
F. METAFONT and its derivatives

encodings / characters

Bibliographic references
General index
Index of names

Appendices

A. Bitmap fonts
B. T_EX et Ω fonts
C. PostScript fonts
D. TrueType, OpenType and AAT fonts
E. TrueType instructions
G. Bézier curves

Figure 0-6: Structure of the chapters of this book.

in question plays a certain role. We explain this role by showing the reader some of the internal workings of the encoding.

On the subject of internal workings, we have assembled three of the most complex in Chapter 4. This chapter's title is merely a list of these three mechanisms: normalization, the bidirectional algorithm, and the handling of East Asian characters. Normalization is a set of ways to make a text encoded in Unicode more efficient by removing certain ambiguities; in particular, one of the normalization forms that we describe is required for the use of Unicode on the Web. Bidirectionality concerns the mixture of left-to-right and right-to-left scripts. Unicode gives us an algorithm to define the typesetting of a text containing a mixture of this sort. Finally, by "East Asian scripts" we mean both Chinese ideographs and hangul syllables. For the former, we present a handful of techniques to obtain characters not supplied in Unicode; for the latter, we describe the method for forming syllables from hangul letters.

Finally, the last chapter in this unit is less theoretical than the others. We address a specific problem: how to produce a text encoded in Unicode? We offer three possible answers: by entering characters with a mouse, by creating virtual keyboards, and by converting texts written in other encodings. In each of these three cases, we describe appropriate tools for use under Mac OS, Windows, or UNIX.

This unit lies entirely within the gray section ("encodings"), as we discuss only encodings, not fonts, in its chapters.

The second unit (Chapters 6 to 8) lies within the white section ("fonts"), but we have placed it in the center of the circle because it discusses not fonts themselves but their management. Thus it takes up the installation of fonts, tools for activation/deactivation, font choices—in short, the management of a large number of fonts, which is of concern to graphic designers and other large consumers of fonts. The unit is divided into three chapters so that we can discuss the two most popular operating systems—Mac OS (9 or X) and Windows, as well as the X Window windowing system from the UNIX world. We discover that the Macintosh is privileged (it has the greatest number of tools for font management), that the same tools exist for Windows but that their quality is often poorer, and that X Window is a world unto itself, with its own advantages and drawbacks. These three chapters will thrill neither the computer scientist nor the typophile, but they may be of great practical value to those whose lives are plagued by system crashes, unexplainable slow-downs, poor quality of output (who has never been surprised to see his beautiful *Bembo* replaced by a hideous *Courier*?), corrupted documents, and all sorts of other such mishaps, often caused by fonts. They will also delight those who love order and who dream of being able to find and use almost instantaneously any font among the thousands of similar ones that they have collected on multiple CD-ROMs. On the other hand, if the reader uses only the fonts that come standard on his operating system, he has no need to read these chapters.

The third unit (Chapters 9 and 10) gets more technical. It deals with the use of fonts in two specific cases: the TeX typesetting system (and its successor, Ω, of which the author is

co-developer) and Web pages. TEX is a software system and a programming language devoted to typesetting. It is also used today to produce electronic documents. Its approach
to managing fonts is unique and totally independent of the operating system being used.
In this chapter, we have tried to cover as thoroughly as possible all the many aspects of
the use of fonts under TEX. Technical descriptions of the font formats used in Chapter 9
appear in Appendix B ("The Font Formats of TEX and Ω").

The situation is different in the case of the Web, which presents both technical problems
(How to supply a font to the browser? How to make the browser use it automatically?)
and legal ones (What about the font's copyright?). We describe the different solutions
that Microsoft and Bitstream have offered for this problem and also another spectacular
solution: the GlyphGate font server. This approach can be called conventional: we use
the HTML markup system and supply the fonts in addition. The Web Consortium has
proposed another, cleaner, solution: describe the font in XML, just like the rest of the
document. This solution is part of the SVG standard for the description of vector graphics, which we describe in detail.

These two chapters are also placed in the middle of the circle because they deal with
subjects that lie in between encodings and fonts: TEX and HTML can both be considered
as vehicles for passing from characters to glyphs; they are bridges between the two worlds.

The fourth unit (Chapters 11 to 14 and Appendix F) is devoted completely to fonts. The
first chapter, "History and Classifications", is a unique chapter in this book, as it discusses
computers very little but deals mainly with the history of printing, especially the history
of Latin typographic characters. We have seen that for designing high-quality fonts it
is not enough to have good tools: a certain knowledge of the history of the fonts that
surround us is also essential. Even in the history presented here, however, the point of
view is that of the user of digital fonts. Thus most of the examples provided were produced with digital fonts rather than from reproductions of specimens of printing from an
earlier era. We also frequently compare the original specimens with digital fonts created
by a variety of designers.

Chapter 11 goes beyond history. It continues with a description of three methods for
classifying fonts. The first two (Vox and Alessandrini) finish off the history, in a way,
and recapitulate it. The Vox classification gives us a jargon for describing fonts (*garalde*,
didone, etc.) that every professional in the fields of graphic design and publishing must
know. The scheme of Alessandrini should be considered a critique (with a heaping help-
ing of humor) of Vox's; we couldn't resist the pleasure of presenting it here.

The third classification scheme is quite different and serves as a link between this chapter
and the rest of the book. It is Panose-1, a mathematical description of the properties
of glyphs. Each font is characterized by a sequence of 10 numbers, which correspond
to 10 practically independent properties. Both Windows and the Cascading Style Sheets
standard make use of this classification system to select substitute fonts by choosing the
available font whose Panose-1 distance from the missing font is the smallest. Despite the
fame of the Panose-1 system, a precise description of it is very difficult to find. This book
provides one, thanks to the generosity of Benjamin Bauermeister, the creator of Panose-
1, who was kind enough to supply us with the necessary information.

Chapters 12 to 14 describe the existing tools for creating (or modifying) fonts. We have chosen two basic tools, FontLab and FontForge (formerly PfaEdit), and we describe their most important capabilities in this chapter. There are three chapters instead of only one because we have broken the font-creation process into three steps: drawing glyphs, optimizing the rendering, and supplementing the font with "advanced typographic" properties. Optimization of the rendering involves adding the PostScript hints or True-Type instructions needed to make the rendering optimal at all body sizes. In this chapter, we also describe a third tool that is used specifically for instructing fonts: Microsoft's Visual TrueType. Since the hinting and instructing of fonts are reputed to be arcane and poorly documented techniques, we have tried to compensate by devoting an entire chapter to them, complete with many real-world examples. In addition, Appendix E is devoted to the description of the TrueType assembly language for instructing fonts; it is the ideal companion to Chapter 13, which is concerned more with the tools used for instructing than with the instructions themselves.

Chapter 14 discusses the big new development of recent years, OpenType properties. Adobe and Microsoft, the companies that have supported this technology, had two purposes in mind: Latin fonts "of typographic quality" (i.e., replete with such gadgets as ligatures, variant glyphs, glyphs for the languages of Central Europe, etc.) and specific non-Latin fonts (with contextual analysis, ligature processing, etc.). High-quality Latin fonts make use of the "advanced typographic features". Right now several foundries are converting their arsenals of PostScript or TrueType fonts into OpenType fonts with advanced properties, and the tools FontLab and FontForge lend themselves admirably to the task, to which we have devoted the first part of the chapter. Along the way, we also describe a third tool dedicated to this task: VOLT, by Microsoft.

The second part of the chapter is devoted to OpenType's competitor, the AAT fonts (formerly called TrueType GX). These fonts are considered by some to be more powerful than OpenType fonts, but they suffer from a lack of tools, poor documentation, and, what is worse, a boycott by the major desktop publishing systems (Adobe Creative Suite, Quark XPress, etc.). But these problems may prove to be only temporary, and we felt that AAT deserved to be mentioned here along with OpenType. In this chapter, the reader will learn how to equip TrueType fonts with AAT tables by using the only tool that is able to do the job: FontForge.

Finally, we include in this unit Appendix F, "METAFONT and Its Derivatives". META-FONT is a programming language dedicated to font creation, the work of the same person who created TEX, the famous computer scientist Donald Knuth of Stanford University. METAFONT is a very powerful tool full of good ideas. The reason that we have not included it in the main part of the book is that it has become obsolete, in a way, by virtue of its incompatibility with the notion of the electronic document. Specifically, METAFONT creates bitmap fonts without a trace of the characters to which the glyphs correspond; thus they cannot be used in electronic documents, as the link between glyph and character is broken. Furthermore, these bitmap fonts depend on the characteristics of a given printer; thus there can be no "universal" METAFONT font that is compatible with every printer—whereas PostScript and TrueType fonts are based on that principle of universality. Nonetheless, we have described METAFONT in this book for three reasons:

for nostalgia and out of respect for Donald Knuth, for METAFONT's intrinsic value as a tool for designing fonts, and, finally, because some recent software attempts to make up for the shortcomings of METAFONT by generating PostScript or TrueType fonts from the same source code used for METAFONT or from a similar type of source. We describe two attempts of this kind: METATYPE1 and MetaFog.

Without a doubt, this book distinguishes itself by the uncommonly large size of its appendices. We have aimed to compile and present the main font formats in our own way—an undertaking that has consumed a great deal of time and energy, not to mention pages.

Appendix A can be considered a sort of history of font formats, as it discusses a type of fonts—bitmap fonts—that has virtually disappeared.

Appendix B discusses the "real" and virtual fonts of TeX.

Appendix C aims to discuss all of the PostScript font formats, from Type 1 (released in 1985) to CFF, which is a part of the OpenType standard, with a brief mention of the obsolete formats (Type 3 and *Multiple Masters*) and the special formats for Far Eastern scripts. So that we can understand the PostScript code for these fonts, we have also provided an introduction to this very specialized programming language.

In Appendix D, we take on the challenge of describing in detail all the TrueType, Open-Type, and AAT tables. So as not to bore the reader with low-level technical details on the numbers of bytes in each field, the pointers between the tables, the number of bytes of padding—in short, the horror of editing raw binary data—we describe these tables in an XML syntax used by the tool TTX. This tool, developed in Python by Just van Rossum, the brother of Guido van Rossum (who invented Python), makes it possible to convert TrueType, OpenType, and AAT binary data into XML and vice versa. Thus we can consider the TTX representation of these fonts to be equivalent to their binary form, and we shall take advantage of this convenience to describe the tables as XML structures. That approach will not make their complexity disappear as if by waving a magic wand, but it will at least spare the reader needless complexity that pertains only to aspects of the binary format of the files themselves. Thus we shall be able to focus on the essence of each table. We shall systematically illustrate the definition of the tables by means of practical examples.

This appendix will be of interest to more people than just computer scientists. Large consumers of OpenType fonts will also find it valuable for the simple reason that current software products that are compatible with the OpenType font format use only a tiny percentage of its possibilities. Readers eager to know what OpenType has under the hood will find out in this appendix.

Appendix E is the logical continuation of Appendix D and the ideal complement to Chapter 13 on optimizing the rendering of fonts. In it, we describe the instructions of the TrueType assembly language. TrueType instructions have a reputation for being arcane and incomprehensible—a reputation due as much to their representation (in assembly language) as to their purpose (modifying the outline of a glyph to obtain a better rendering) and to some implied concepts (notably the concepts of projection vector, freedom vector, twilight zones, etc.). And it is due most of all to the poor quality of the documentation supplied by Microsoft, which is enough to discourage even the most motivated programmer. We hope that this appendix will be easier to understand than the document that it cites and that it will be a helpful adjunct to Chapter 13.

We close with a brief introduction to Bézier curves, which are used again and again in the text (in discussions of font creation, the description of the PostScript and METAFONT languages, etc.). We have mentioned that most books on these languages give very little information on Bézier curves, often no more than the formula for the Bézier polynomial and a few properties. To compensate for the deficiency, we offer a genuine mathematical presentation of these objects, which today are indispensable for the description of fonts. The reader will find in this section the most important theorems and lemmas concerning these mathematical objects, with proofs to follow in due course.

The book ends with a bibliography that includes as many URLs as possible so that the reader can read the original documents or order copies of them. It also includes two indexes: the general index, for terms, and an index of names, which includes creators of software, font designers, and all other people mentioned for one reason or another.

How to Read This Book

This book contains introductions to certain technologies, "user's manuals" for software, technical specifications, and even histories of fonts and encodings. It plays the dual role of textbook and reference manual. To help the reader derive the greatest benefit from it, we offer the following profiles of potential readers and, for each of these, a corresponding sequence of readings that we deem appropriate. Of course, these sequences are only recommendations, and the best approach to the book is always the one that the reader discovers on his own.

For the well-versed user of Unicode

The most interesting chapters will, of course, be Chapters 1 to 5. In order to use Unicode, a user needs suitable fonts. Once she has tracked them down on the Web, she will want to install them; thus reading Chapter 6, 7, or 8 (according to her operating system) may be of great benefit. And if she needs glyphs to represent characters not found in the fonts, she may wish to add them herself. Then she becomes a font designer/editor. (See "For the novice font designer", below.)

For the devoted T_EXist

Chapter 9 will be ideal. While reading it, he may wish to try his hand at input or output. For the former, he will want to prepare documents in Unicode and typeset them with Ω; therefore, we advise him to read the chapters on Unicode as well. For the latter, he may want to create fonts for use with T_EX; thus he may benefit from Chapters 12 and 14, which discuss the creation of PostScript and TrueType fonts, or perhaps Appendix F, on the use of METAFONT.

For the reader who simply wants to produce beautiful documents

A beautiful document is, first and foremost, a well-coded document; it is useful, therefore, to know the workings of Unicode in order to use it to greatest advantage. Reading Chapters 2, 3, and 5 (and perhaps skimming over Chapter 4) is recommended. Next, a beautiful document must employ beautiful fonts. After reading the history of fonts (Chapter 11), the reader will be more capable of choosing fonts appropriate to a given document. Once she has found them, she will need to install them; to that end, she should read Chapter 6, 7, or 8, according to the operating system. Finally, to create a beautiful document, one needs high-quality typesetting software. If, by chance, the reader has chosen TₑX (or Ω) to produce her document, reading Chapter 9 is a must.

For the reader who wishes to create beautiful Web pages

The sequence given in the preceding profile is recommended, with the difference that the last chapter should instead be Chapter 10, which discusses the Web.

For the typophile or collector of fonts

Chapter 11 will delight the reader with its wealth of examples, including some rather uncommon ones. But the true collector does not merely buy treasures and put them on a shelf. He spends his time living with them, adoring them, studying them, keeping them in good condition. The same goes for fonts, and font design/editing software is also excellent for getting to know a font better, studying it in all of its detail, and perhaps improving it, supplementing it, correcting its kerning pairs, etc. The reader will thus do well to read Chapter 12 carefully, and Chapters 13 and 14 as well. If technical problems arise, Appendices C and D will enable him to find a solution. Finally, to share his collection of fonts with his fellow connoisseurs, there is nothing like a beautiful Web page under GlyphGate to show the cherished glyphs to every visitor, without compromising security. Chapter 10 provides the necessary details.

For the novice font designer

Reading Chapter 11 may encourage her further and help her to find her place on the historic continuum of font design. This book does not give lessons in the graphical design of fonts, but it does describe the needed tools in great detail. Read Chapter 12 very carefully and then, before distributing the fonts you have created, read Chapters 13 and 14 to learn how to improve them even more.

For the experienced font designer

Chapters 11 and 12 will not be very instructive. In Chapters 13 and 14, however, he will find useful techniques for getting the most out of his beautiful font designs. He may also enjoy sampling the delights of METAFONT and creating PostScript fonts with METATYPE1 that would be very difficult or impossible to produce with a manual tool such as FontLab or FontForge. If he is a user of FontLab, he may also try his hand at the Python language and learn in Chapter 11 how to control the FontLab software through programming. If he already knows font design, instruction, *and* advanced typographical features, Appendices C and D will show him some of OpenType's possibilities that will surprise him because, for the time being, they are not exploited by OpenType-compatible software. Finally, reading the description of the Panose standard in Chapter 11 will enable him to classify his fonts correctly and thus facilitate their use.

For the developer of applications

Chapters 2 to 4 will teach her what she needs to know to make her applications compatible with Unicode. Next, Appendices C, D, and E will show her how to make them compatible with PostScript or OpenType fonts. Appendix G may prove useful in the writing of algorithms that make calculations from the Bézier curves that describe the outlines of glyphs.

For the reader who doesn't match any of the preceding profiles

The outline presented in this introduction, together with the table of contents, may suggest a path to the information that interests him. If this information is very specific, the index may also come in handy. If necessary, the reader may also contact us at the address given below.

How to Contact Us

We have done our best to reread and verify all the information in this book, but we may nonetheless have failed to catch some errors in the course of production.[3] Please point out any errors that you notice and share with us your suggestions for future editions of this book by writing to:

O'Reilly Media Inc.
1005 Gravenstein Highway North
Sebastopol, CA 95472

You may also send us email. To join our mailing list or request a catalog, send a message to:

info@oreilly.com

To ask a technical question or send us your comments on the book, write to:

somebody@oreilly.com

This book has its own web site, where you will find all the code fragments that appear in the book, a list of errata, and plans for future editions. Please visit the following URL:

http://www.oreilly.com/somewhere/fonts-and-encodings.html

For more information on this book and its author, visit O'Reilly's web site:

http://www.oreilly.com

---

[3] On this subject, we recommend a hilarious book: *An Embarrassment of Misprints: Comical and Disastrous Typos of the Centuries*, by Max Hall (1995) [154].

1

Before Unicode

When we need precise definitions of computer-related concepts that seem a little fuzzy to us, nothing is more refreshing and beneficial than consulting old documents. For example, in C.E. MacKenzie's *Coded Character Sets, History and Development* (1980) [242], we find the following definitions (slightly condensed here):

- a *bit* is a *binary digit*, either 0 or 1;

- a *bit pattern* is an ordered set of bits, usually of fixed length;

- a *byte* is a bit pattern of fixed length; thus we speak of 8-bit bytes, 6-bit bytes, and so on;

- a *graphic* is a particular shape, printed, typed, or displayed, that represents an alphabetic, numeric or special symbol;

- a *character* is a specific bit pattern and a meaning assigned to it: a *graphic character* has an assigned graphic meaning, and a *control character* has an assigned control meaning;

- a *bit code* is a specific set of bit patterns to which either graphic or control meanings have been asigned;

- a *code table* is a compact matrix form of rows and columns for exhibiting the bit patterns and assigned meanings of a code;

- a *shifted code* is a code in which the meaning of a bit pattern depends not only on the bit pattern itself, but also on the fact that it has been preceded in the data stream by some other particular bit pattern, which is called a *shift character*.

All this makes sense; only the terminology has slightly changed. Nowadays a *byte* is always considered to be of fixed length 8; what MacKenzie calls a "graphic" is now called a *glyph*; a "bit code" is called an *encoding*; and a "code table" is simply a way of graphically representing the encoding. In the old days, the position of a character in the encoding was given by a double number: "*x/y*", where *x* is the column number and *y* the row number. Nowadays we simply give its number in decimal or hexadecimal form. "Shifted" encodings tend to become extinct because they are incompatible with human–user interaction such as copying and pasting, but at that time GUIs were still well-protected experiments in the Palo Alto Xerox Lab.

Let us go even further back in time. It seems that the first people to invent a code-based system for long-distance transmission of information were the Greeks: around 350 BC, as related by the historian Polybius [183], the general Aeneas employed a two-by-five system of torches placed on two walls to encode the Greek alphabet, an alphabet of 24 letters that could be adequately encoded by the $2^5 = 32$ combinations of five lighted or extinguished torches. At the end of the 18th century, the French engineer Claude Chappe established the first telegraphic link between Paris and Lille by using semaphores visible at distances of 10 to 15 kilometers. In 1837, Samuel Morse invented "Morse code" for the electric telegraph, a code that was more complex because it used a variable number of long and short pulses (*dahs* and *dits*) for each letter, with the letters being obligatorily separated by pauses. Thus there were two basic units: dahs and dits. It was the first internationally recognized system of encoding.

In 1874, Émile Baudot took up a code invented by Sir Francis Bacon in 1605 and adapted it to the telegraph. Unlike Morse's code, the Baudot code used codes of five symbols that were typed on a device bearing five keys like those of a piano. Each key was connected to a cable that transmitted signals. The reader will find a detailed description of Baudot's code and keyboard in [201].

The first important encoding of the twentieth century was CCITT #2, a 58-character shifted 5-bit code, standardized as an international telegraph code in 1931 by CCITT ("Comité Consultatif International Télégraphique et Téléphonique"). Being shifted, it used two "modes", also called "cases". The first is the *letter case*:

	T	CR	O	SP	H	N	M	LF	L	R	G	I	P	C	V
00	01	02	03	04	05	06	07	08	09	0A	0B	0C	0D	0E	0F
E	Z	D	B	S	Y	F	X	A	W	J	FS	U	Q	K	LS
10	11	12	13	14	15	16	17	18	19	1A	1B	1C	1D	1E	1F

Here "LF" is the carriage return, "SP" is the blank space, "LF" is the line feed, and "LS" (letter shift) and "FS" (figure shift) are two escape codes. "FS" shifts to *figure case*:

	5	CR	9	SP	***	,	.	LF	)	4	***	8	0	:	;
00	01	02	03	04	05	06	07	08	09	0A	0B	0C	0D	0E	0F
3	+	AB	?	'	6	***	/	-	2	BEL	FS	7	1	(	LS
10	11	12	13	14	15	16	17	18	19	1A	1B	1C	1D	1E	1F

Here "***" is intended for national use (#, $, and & in the US; Ä Ö Ü in Germany, Sweden and Finland; Æ Ø Å in Denmark and Norway), "AB" is used for answering back, and "BEL" rings a bell. With "LS" we return to the first version of the encoding. This use of two states seems awkward to us today; after all, why not just use a sixth bit? One consequence of this approach is that the interpretation of a position within the encoding depends on context—whether we are in "letter" or "figure" case.

In the prehistoric era of computers (the 1930s to the 1960s), only a few brilliant visionaries, such as Alan Turing and Vannevar Bush, imagined that the computer would one day come to use letters. To everyone else, it was just a calculating machine and therefore was good only for processing numbers.

FIELDATA

FIELDATA was a 7-bit encoding developed by the US Army for use on military data communication lines. It became a US military standard in 1960:

MS 40	UC 41	LC 42	LF 43	CR 44	SP 45	A 46	B 47	C 48	D 49	E 4A	F 4B	G 4C	H 4D	I 4E	J 4F
K 50	L 51	M 52	N 53	O 54	P 55	Q 56	R 57	S 58	T 59	U 5A	V 5B	W 5C	X 5D	Y 5E	Z 5F
) 60	- 61	+ 62	< 63	= 64	> 65	— 66	$ 67	* 68	(69	" 6A	: 6B	? 6C	! 6D	, 6E	STOP 6F
0 70	1 71	2 72	3 73	4 74	5 75	6 76	7 77	8 78	9 79	' 7A	; 7B	/ 7C	. 7D	SPEC 7E	IDLE 7F

"MS" stands for "master space"; "UC/LC" are shift codes for uppercase and lowercase letters; "STOP", "SPEC", and "IDLE" stand for "stop", "special", and "idle". In this encoding we already find most of the characters used a few years later in ASCII. FIELDATA survives even today as the internal encoding of certain COBOL software.

ASCII

Towards the end of the 1950s, the telecommunications industry redoubled its efforts to develop a standard encoding. IBM and AT&T were among the large corporations that drove the ASA (American Standards Association) to define an encoding. Thus ASCII-1963, a preliminary version of ASCII with no lower-case letters, was born on June 17, 1963, a few months after the assassination of President Kennedy.

ASCII was updated in 1967. From that time on, it would include lower-case letters. Here is ASCII-1967:

NUL 00	SOH 01	STX 02	ETX 03	EOT 04	ENQ 05	ACK 06	BEL 07	BS 08	HT 09	LF 0A	VT 0B	FF 0C	CR 0D	SO 0E	SI 0F
DLE 10	DCI 11	DC2 12	DC3 13	DC4 14	NAK 15	SYN 16	ETB 17	CAN 18	EM 19	SUB 1A	ESC 1B	FS 1C	GS 1D	RS 1E	US 1F
SP 20	! 21	" 22	# 23	$ 24	% 25	& 26	' 27	(28	) 29	* 2A	+ 2B	, 2C	- 2D	. 2E	/ 2F
0 30	1 31	2 32	3 33	4 34	5 35	6 36	7 37	8 38	9 39	: 3A	; 3B	< 3C	= 3D	> 3E	? 3F
@ 40	A 41	B 42	C 43	D 44	E 45	F 46	G 47	H 48	I 49	J 4A	K 4B	L 4C	M 4D	N 4E	O 4F
P 50	Q 51	R 52	S 53	T 54	U 55	V 56	W 57	X 58	Y 59	Z 5A	[5B	\ 5C	] 5D	^ 5E	— 5F

` 60	a 61	b 62	c 63	d 64	e 65	f 66	g 67	h 68	i 69	j 6A	k 6B	l 6C	m 6D	n 6E	o 6F
p 70	q 71	r 72	s 73	t 74	u 75	v 76	w 77	x 78	y 79	z 7A	{ 7B	| 7C	} 7D	~ 7E	DEL 7F

The first thirty-two positions in this encoding are occupied by control codes:

- formatting control codes: CR (carriage return), LF (line feed), BS (backspace), HT (horizontal tab), VT (vertical tab), SP (blank space), FF (form feed);

- extension codes: ESC (escape is a shift but modifies only the following character), SO (shift out), SI (shift in);

- controls for communications: SOH (start of heading), STX (start of text), ETX (end of text), EOT (end of transmission), ETB (end of transmission block), ACK (acknowledge), NAK (negative acknowledge), SYN (synchronous idle), NUL (null), DLE (data link escape);

- device control functions DC1, ... , DC4;

- functions for error management: CAN (cancel), SUB (substitute), DEL (delete), BEL (bell).

Of the characters that do not represent controls, a few call for some explanation:

- The backslash '\', used by DOS as a delimiter for directory paths and by TeX as the escape character for commands, was introduced into encodings in September 1961 and subsequently accepted into ASCII-1963 at the suggestion of Bob Bemer [72]. A great fan of the ALGOL language, Bemer wanted to obtain the logical operators AND (∧) and OR (∨). Since the forward slash was already present in the encoding, he was able to obtain these two operators by simply concatenating a forward slash and a backslash ('∧') and vice versa ('∨'). .

- The apostrophe is represented by a vertical stroke, '', not by a raised comma, '', as printers have represented it for centuries. Today we call this type of apostrophe a "non-oriented apostrophe". Although it has a peculiar shape, it is perfectly suitable for those programming languages that use it as the opening *and* closing delimiter for strings.

- The same goes for the "double quote" or "non-oriented quotation marks", '"': they served as the opening and closing American-style quotation marks, and even as the diæresis; thus this symbol, too, had to be symmetrical.

- The grave accent '`' also serves as an American-style opening quotation mark.

- The vertical bar '|' was introduced to represent the OR operator in the language PL/I [226].

It may seem unbelievable today, but a not insignificant number of ASCII characters could vary according to local needs: the number sign '#', the dollar sign '$', the at sign '@', the square brackets '[' and ']', the backslash '\', the caret '^', the grave accent '`', the curly braces '{' and '}', the vertical bar '|', and the tilde '~'.

Thus, at one time, France used the NF Z62010 standard and the United Kingdom used the BS 4730 standard, both of which replaced the number sign by the symbol for pounds sterling '£'; Japan used the JIS C-6220 standard, which employed a yen sign '¥' in the place of the backslash; the Soviet Union used the GOST 13052 standard, which substituted a universal currency sign '¤' for the dollar sign, etc. The reader will find a complete list of these "localized ASCII encodings" in [248, p. 243]. To distinguish it from the localized versions, the original version of ASCII was called IRV (International Reference Version).

Another problem with the ASCII encoding is that it offered a rather naïve and æsthetically unacceptable method for placing accents on letters: to obtain an 'é', one was asked to type the sequence 'e BS '', that is: 'letter e', 'backspace', 'apostrophe'. That is why the grave and circumflex accents and the tilde, represented as spacing characters, are found in the encoding. To obtain a diæresis, one used the backspace followed by a double quote; and underscoring words was accomplished with backspaces followed by underscores.

The ASCII-1967 encoding became the ISO 646 standard in 1983. Its latest revision, published by ECMA [192], dates to 1991.

EBCDIC

While the computer giant IBM had taken part in the development of ASCII-1963, it released in 1964 a new and highly appreciated line of computers, IBM System/360, whose low-end model came equipped with 24 kb (!) of memory. The development of these machines was the second most expensive industrial project of the 1960s, after NASA's Apollo program.....

The System/360 computers use the EBCDIC encoding (*Extended Binary Coded Decimal Interchange Code*, pronounced "eb-cee-dic"), an 8-bit encoding in which many positions are left empty and in which the letters of the alphabet are not always contiguous:

NUL 00	SOH 01	STX 02	ETX 03	PF 04	HT 05	LC 06	DEL 07	GE 08	RLF 09	SMM 0A	VT 0B	FF 0C	CR 0D	SO 0E	SI 0F
DLE 10	DCI 11	DC2 12	TM 13	RES 14	NL 15	BS 16	IL 17	CAN 18	EM 19	CC 1A	CUI 1B	IFS 1C	IGS 1D	IRS 1E	IUS 1F
DS 20	SOS 21	FS 22	23	BYP 24	LF 25	ETB 26	ESC 27	28	29	SM 2A	CU2 2B	2C	ENQ 2D	ACK 2E	BEL 2F
30	31	SYN 32	33	PN 34	RS 35	UC 36	EOT 37	38	39	3A	CU3 3B	DC4 3C	NAK 3D	3E	SUB 3F
SP 40	41	42	43	44	45	46	47	48	49	¢ 4A	. 4B	< 4C	(4D	+ 4E	| 4F
& 50	51	52	53	54	55	56	57	58	59	! 5A	$ 5B	* 5C	) 5D	; 5E	¬ 5F
- 60	/ 61	62	63	64	65	66	67	68	69	¦ 6A	, 6B	% 6C	_ 6D	> 6E	? 6F
70	71	72	73	74	75	76	77	78	` 79	: 7A	# 7B	@ 7C	' 7D	= 7E	" 7F

80	a 81	b 82	c 83	d 84	e 85	f 86	g 87	h 88	i 89	8A	8B	8C	8D	8E	8F
90	j 91	k 92	l 93	m 94	n 95	o 96	p 97	q 98	r 99	9A	9B	9C	9D	9E	9F
A0	˜ A1	s A2	t A3	u A4	v A5	w A6	x A7	y A8	z A9	AA	AB	AC	AD	AE	AF
{ C0	A C1	B C2	C C3	D C4	E C5	F C6	G C7	H C8	I C9	CA	CB	♪ CC	CD	Ч CE	CF
} D0	J D1	K D2	L D3	M D4	N D5	O D6	P D7	Q D8	R D9	DA	DB	DC	DD	DE	DF
\ E0	E1	S E2	T E3	U E4	V E5	W E6	X E7	Y E8	Z E9	EA	EB	ʜ EC	ED	EE	EF
0 F0	1 F1	2 F2	3 F3	4 F4	5 F5	6 F6	7 F7	8 F8	9 F9		FA	FB	FC	FD	FE	EO FF

We may well ask: why are the letters of the alphabet distributed in so bizarre a manner in this encoding? Why did IBM insist so firmly on its EBCDIC encoding? To understand what happened, we need a bit of historical background.

In 1801 the Parisian weaver Joseph-Marie Jacquard used strings of punched cards to operate his looms, thus perfecting an invention by Basile Bouchon that dated to 1725. Seventy-nine years later, on the other side of the Atlantic, a census conducted in the United States was ruined. The failure resulted from the fact that it took 7 years (!) to process the data on the country's 31.8 million residents—so much time that the data were no longer up to date. Faced with this situation, the Census Bureau organized a contest to find an invention that could solve the problem. A certain Herman Hollerith won the contest with a system inspired by that of Jacquard: the census-takers would carry cards that they would punch according to the profile of the person being surveyed. Later a machine, the ancestor of the computer, would read the cards and compile the results.

In 1890 a new census was taken. While the previous census collected only six pieces of information for each person, this time plans were made for 245! The Bureau sent 50,000 employees all over America to conduct the census. And, as had been expected, the results were spectacular: the data were completely processed in less than six weeks. Hollerith had thus succeeded in processing 40 times as much information in 1/56 of the time....

Encouraged by this astounding success, Hollerith founded a company named TMC (Tabulating Machine Company). In 1924 it became International Business Machines, or IBM.

But what relationship is there between Hollerith and EBCDIC? In Figure 1-1, the reader can see a remnant of the past: an ISO 1681 card punched by the author at the University of Lille (France) in September 1983, a few months before this medium disappeared from that university. *Punch cards* were the user's means of interacting with the computer before the advent of terminals with screens and keyboards. Note that punch cards have twelve rows, of which two are "unlabeled" (we call them "X" and "Y") and the remaining ten bear the digits from "0" to "9". Since there are twelve potential holes, can we therefore encode numbers with $2^{12} = 4,096$ bits in a single column on the card? Alas, no.

In fact, Hollerith quickly noticed that punch cards could not be punched excessively, lest they be torn. Therefore he invented a system by which one could encode letters and numbers without ever using more than two holes per column. The system is called the *Hollerith code*:

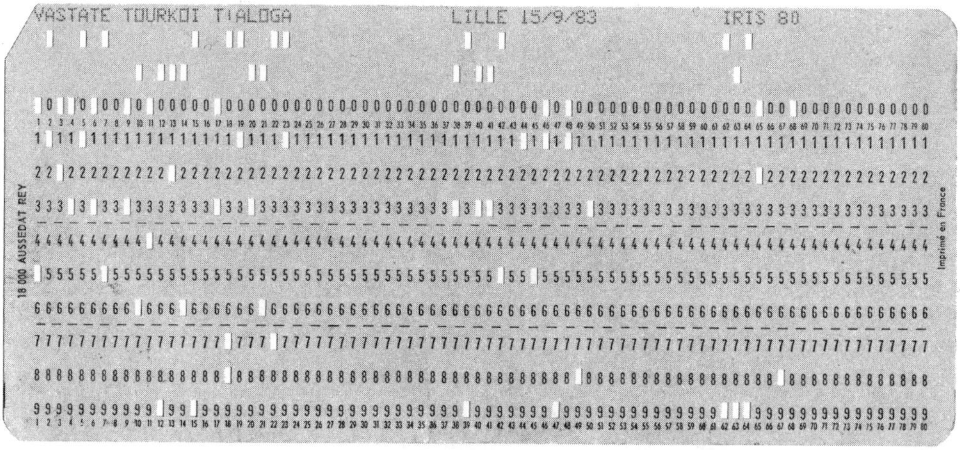

Figure 1-1: A punch card (ISO 1681 standard).

Holes		0	1	2	3	4	5	6	7	8	9
with X punched			A	B	C	D	E	F	G	H	I
with Y punched			J	K	L	M	N	O	P	Q	R
with 0 punched				S	T	U	V	W	X	Y	Z
neither X nor Y punched		0	1	2	3	4	5	6	7	8	9

In other words, to obtain an 'A', one punches row "X" and row "1"; to obtain a 'Z', one punches row "0" and row "9"; to obtain a digit, one punches only one hole—the one corresponding to that digit.

The reader will readily recognize the last four lines of the EBCDIC encoding. How could IBM have ever abandoned the code created by its legendary founder?

Despite the awkwardness of this encoding, IBM spread it to the four corners of the earth. The company created 57 national versions of EBCDIC. All of them suffer from the same problem: they lack certain ASCII characters, such as the square brackets, that are indispensable for computer programming.

Extremely rare today, the EBCDIC encoding is nonetheless very much alive. As recently as 1997, an article appeared in *Perl Journal* on the use of Perl 5 in an EBCDIC environment under IBM System/390 [298].

ISO 2022

In the early 1970s, the industry was well aware of the fact that the "localized" versions of ASCII were an impediment. People had to use multiple encodings that were really quite different, and sooner or later they had to switch from one encoding to another in the middle of a document or a transmission. But how to indicate this change of encoding?

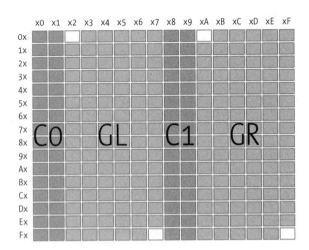

Figure 1-2:   The manner in which ISO 2022 subdivides the 8-bit table.

It was for this reason that the ISO 2022 standard emerged, in 1973. Its latest revision dates to 1994 [193]. It is not an encoding but a definition of a certain number of escape sequences that make it possible to use as many as four distinct encodings within the same set of data.

ISO 2022 starts from the principle that the 256 squares in a table of 8 bits are distributed among four zones, which can be seen in Figure 1-2. Zones C0 and C1 are reserved for control characters, and zones GL ("L" for "left") and GR ("R" for "right") are reserved for what today are known as alphanumeric characters (and what at the time bore the oxymoronic name "graphic characters", whence the 'G').

Thus we have up to four distinct encodings at our disposal. Let us call them G0, G1, G2, G3. These encodings may be of any of four types:

- Encodings with 94 positions: 6 columns with 16 positions each, minus the two excluded positions, namely the first and the last.

- Encodings with 96 positions: 6 columns with 16 positions each.

- Encodings with 94^n positions, if we use n bytes to encode a single character. Thus for ideographic languages we will take $n = 2$, and we will therefore have encodings of $94^2 = 8,836$ positions.

- Encodings with 96^n positions, if we use n bytes to encode a single character. By taking $n = 2$, we will obtain encodings with $96^2 = 9,216$ positions.

There is only one small constraint: encoding G0 must necessarily be of type 94 or 94^n.

A first series of escape sequences allows us to *specify* encodings G0, G1, G2, G3. These sequences depend on the type of the encoding. Thus, for example, the sequences 'ESC 0x2D

F', 'ESC 0x2E F', 'ESC 0x2F F', in which 'F' is an identifier for an encoding with 96 positions, declares that the encoding designated by 'F' is assigned to G1, G2, or G3, respectively.

To identify the encoding, we use identifiers defined by the "competent authority", which today is the *Information Processing Society of Japan* [196]. The IPSJ's Web site provides a list of encodings.[1] There we can discover, for example, that the ISO 8859-1 encoding that we shall discuss below is registered under the number 100 and has the identifier "4/1", an old-fashioned way to represent the hexademical number 0x41. It is an encoding with 96 positions; therefore, it cannot be assigned to G0. The escape sequences 'ESC 0x2D 0x41', 'ESC 0x2E 0x41', and 'ESC 0x2F 0x41' will therefore serve to declare ISO 8859-1 as encoding G1, G2, or G3.

Once the G*n* have been defined, we can use them. There are escape sequences that switch the active encoding until further notice. To do so, they must implement a finite automaton. These sequences consist either of ASCII control characters (SO and SI assign G0 and G1 to zone GL) or of pairs of bytes beginning with ESC: thus 'ESC 0x7E' will select G1 for zone GR, 'ESC 0x6F' will select G3 for zone GL, etc.

There are also control characters for zone C1 that affect only the following character: SS2 (0x8E) and SS3 (0x8F) specify that only the following character should be interpreted as being in encoding G2 or G3, respectively. The idea is that G2 and G3 may be rare encodings from which we draw only isolated characters now and then; it therefore makes more sense to "flag" them individually.

ISO 2022 is based on the principle of total freedom to define new encodings. Indeed, all that it takes to make an encoding an integral part of ISO 2022 is to register it with the competent authority. And there are so many registered encodings today that it is practically impossible for a computer developer to support all of them. The only viable alternative is to limit oneself to a small number of recognized and widely used encodings—the ISO 2022-* *instances* that Ken Lunde has described [240, p. 147].

Thus we have, for example, ISO 2022-JP (defined in RFC 1468), which is a combination of ASCII, JIS-Roman (JIS X 0201-1976), JIS X 0208-1978, and JIS X 0208-1983 (taken, respectively, as encodings G0, G1, G2, G3). This is how we resolve the problem of rare ideographic characters: we put ASCII and the most common ideographic characters in G0 and G1, and we reserve G2 and G3 for the rare cases, in which we select the required characters individually.

ISO 8859

As soon as the ISO 2022 standard allowed multiple encodings to be combined in a single data flow, ISO started to define encodings with 96 positions that would supplement ASCII. This became the ISO 8859 family of encodings, a family characterized by its longevity—and its awkwardness.

---

[1] This Web site is a gold mine for historians of computer science, as it offers a PDF version of the description of each registered encoding!

ISO 8859-1 (Latin-1) and ISO 8859-15 (Latin-9)

The new standard's flagship, ISO 8859-1, was launched in 1987. By 1990, Bernard Marti had written [248, p. 257]: "Unfortunately, the haste with which this standard was established [. . .] and its penetration into stand-alone systems have led to incoherence in the definition of character sets."

This flagship is dedicated to the languages of Western Europe. Here is part GR of the standard (parts C0 and GL are identical to those of ASCII, and part C1 was not included in the new standard):

NBSP A0	¡ A1	¢ A2	£ A3	¤ A4	¥ A5	¦ A6	§ A7	¨ A8	© A9	ª AA	« AB	¬ AC	SHY AD	® AE	¯ AF
° B0	± B1	² B2	³ B3	´ B4	µ B5	¶ B6	· B7	¸ B8	¹ B9	º BA	» BB	¼ BC	½ BD	¾ BE	¿ BF
À C0	Á C1	Â C2	Ã C3	Ä C4	Å C5	Æ C6	Ç C7	È C8	É C9	Ê CA	Ë CB	Ì CC	Í CD	Î CE	Ï CF
Ð D0	Ñ D1	Ò D2	Ó D3	Ô D4	Õ D5	Ö D6	× D7	Ø D8	Ù D9	Ú DA	Û DB	Ü DC	Ý DD	Þ DE	ß DF
à E0	á E1	â E2	ã E3	ä E4	å E5	æ E6	ç E7	è E8	é E9	ê EA	ë EB	ì EC	í ED	î EE	ï EF
ð F0	ñ F1	ò F2	ó F3	ô F4	õ F5	ö F6	÷ F7	ø F8	ù F9	ú FA	û FB	ü FC	ý FD	þ FE	ÿ FF

Certain symbols deserve a few words of explanation:

- NBSP is the non-breaking space.

- '¡' and '¿' are the Spanish exclamation point and question mark used at the beginning of a sentence. Thanks to these characters, we avoid in Spanish the rather annoying experience of coming to the end of a sentence only to discover that it was a question or an exclamation—and that we shall have to read the whole sentence over again in order to give it the proper intonation.

- '¢', '£', and '¥' are currency symbols: the cent sign, the British pound, and the Japanese yen.

- '¤' is the "universal currency sign". The Italians were the ones to propose this symbol as a replacement for the dollar sign in certain localized and "politically correct" versions of ASCII. The author has never seen this symbol used in text and cannot even imagine any use for it.

- 'ª' and 'º' are used in Spanish, Italian, and Portuguese for numerals (the first being feminine and the second masculine): '1ª', '2º', etc.

- SHY, the "soft hyphen", may be the least coherent character in the encoding. In ISO 8859-1 it is described as a "hyphen resulting from a line break", while in Unicode, which ordinarily follows ISO 8859-1 to the letter, it is described as "an invisible character whose purpose is to indicate potential line breaks". The reader will find a full discussion in [225].

- Unless we use a font such as Futura in which the letter 'o' is a perfect circle, we must not confuse the "degree sign °" (position 0xB0) with the "superscript o °" (position 0xBA). The first is a perfect circle, whereas the latter is a letter 'o' written small. Thus we write "n°" but "37,2°C".

- The "midpoint" '·' is used to form the Catalan ligature 'l·l' [135];

- the German *eszett* 'ß' must not be mistaken for a *beta*. Historically, it comes from the ligature "long s–round s". Its upper-case version is ordinarily 'SS' but can also be 'SZ' to distinguish certain words. Thus, in German, *MASSE* is the uppercase version of *Masse* (= mass), whereas *MASZE* is the one of *Maße* (= measures);

- the "y with diæresis" is used in Welsh and in Old French. We find it in Modern French in place names such as "l'Haÿe-les-Roses", surnames such as "de Croÿ" and "Louÿ", or expressions such as "kir à l'aÿ" [36]. This letter is extremely rare, and its inclusion in ISO 8859-1 is peculiar at best.

But the biggest deficiency in ISO 8859-1 is the lack of certain characters:

- While 'ÿ' is extremely rare in French, the ligature 'œ' is not. It appears in many very common French words ("cœur" 'heart', "œil" 'eye', etc.); in some other words—less common ones, to be sure, but that is neither here nor there—it is not used: "moelle" 'marrow', "coefficient", "coexistence", "foehn", etc. According to an urban legend, the French delegate was out sick the day when the standard came up for a vote and had to have his Belgian counterpart act as his proxy. In fact [36], the French delegate was an engineer who was convinced that this ligature was useless, and the Swiss and German representatives pressed hard to have the mathematical symbols '×' and '÷' included at the positions where Œ and œ would logically appear.

- French is not the only language neglected by ISO 8859-1. Dutch has another ligature, 'ij' (which, in italics, looks dangerously close to a 'ÿ', a fact that has led to numerous misunderstandings [161, note 4]). This ligature is just as important as the French 'œ'—perhaps even more important, as it has acquired the status of a letter in certain situations. Thus, in some Dutch encyclopædias, the entries are sorted according to an order in which 'ij' appears between 'w' and 'y'. The upper-case version of 'ij' is 'IJ', as in the name of the city "IJmegen".

- Finally, if only for reasons of consistency, there should also be a 'Ÿ', the upper-case version of 'ÿ'.

ISO 8859-1 is a very important encoding because:

- it has become the standard encoding for Unix;

- Unicode is an extension of it;

- at least in Western Europe, most Web browsers and electronic-mail software have long used it as the default encoding when no encoding was specified.

The languages covered by ISO 8859-1 are Afrikaans, Albanian, Basque, Catalan (using the midpoint to form the ligature 'l·l'), Dutch (without the ligature 'ij'), English, Faeroese, Finnish, French (without the ligature 'œ' and without 'Ÿ'), German, Icelandic, Italian, Norwegian, Portuguese, Rhaeto-Romance, Scottish Gaelic, Spanish, and Swedish.

In March 1999, when the euro sign was added, ISO took advantage of the opportunity to correct two other strategic errors: first, the free-standing accent marks were eliminated; second, the ligatures 'Œ' and 'œ' and the letter 'Ÿ', needed for French but missing from the encoding, were finally introduced; third, the letters "Ž ž Š š", which are used in most Central European languages and which can be useful in personal and place names, were also added. After the fall of the Soviet Union, the euro sign took the place of the universal monetary symbol.

The new standard was called ISO 8859-15 (or "Latin-9"). It differs from ISO 8859-1 in only eight positions (shown in black in the following diagram):

NBSP A0	¡ A1	¢ A2	£ A3	€ A4	¥ A5	Š A6	§ A7	š A8	© A9	ª AA	« AB	¬ AC	SHY AD	® AE	¯ AF
° B0	± B1	² B2	³ B3	Ž B4	µ B5	¶ B6	· B7	ž B8	¹ B9	º BA	» BB	Œ BC	œ BD	Ÿ BE	¿ BF

ISO 8859-2 (Latin-2) and ISO 8859-16 (Latin-10)

After ISO 8859-1, which is also known as ISO Latin-1, three other encodings for the Latin alphabet came out: one each for the countries of Eastern Europe (ISO 8859-2), Southern Europe (ISO 8859-3), and Northern Europe (ISO 8859-4).

Thus ISO 8859-2 (or "Latin-2") includes the characters needed for certain languages of Central Europe: Bosnian, Croatian, Czech, Hungarian, Polish, Romanian (but with a cedilla instead of a comma under the letters 'ş' and 'ţ'), Slovak, Slovenian, and Sorbian. It also contains the characters needed for German (commercial influence at work) and some of the characters needed for French (some accented capitals are missing):

NBSP A0	Ą A1	˘ A2	Ł A3	¤ A4	Ľ A5	Ś A6	§ A7	¨ A8	Š A9	Ş AA	Ť AB	Ź AC	SHY AD	Ž AE	Ż AF
° B0	ą B1	˛ B2	ł B3	´ B4	ľ B5	ś B6	ˇ B7	¸ B8	š B9	ş BA	» BB	ť BC	˝ BD	ž BE	ż BF
Ŕ C0	Á C1	Â C2	Ă C3	Ä C4	Ĺ C5	Ć C6	Ç C7	Č C8	É C9	Ę CA	Ë CB	Ě CC	Í CD	Î CE	Ď CF
Đ D0	Ń D1	Ň D2	Ó D3	Ô D4	Ő D5	Ö D6	× D7	Ř D8	Ů D9	Ú DA	Ű DB	Ü DC	Ý DD	Ţ DE	ß DF
ŕ E0	á E1	â E2	ă E3	ä E4	ĺ E5	ć E6	ç E7	č E8	é E9	ę EA	ë EB	ě EC	í ED	î EE	ď EF
đ F0	ń F1	ň F2	ó F3	ô F4	ő F5	ö F6	÷ F7	ř F8	ů F9	ú FA	ű FB	ü FC	ý FD	ţ FE	˙ FF

A few characters may need some explanation:

- Do not confuse the *breve* '˘' and the *háček* 'ˇ': the former is round, the latter pointed.

- Do not confuse the *cedilla* '¸' (which opens to the left) and the *ogonek* '˛', especially because the cedilla was often written like an ogonek in Old French, where we find the letter 'ę'.

- Turkish uses the letter 's' with a cedilla, but in Romanian the same letter, as well as letter 't', are written with a diacritical mark shaped like a comma: 'ş', 'ţ'. The ISO 8859-2 standard was not intended to cover Turkish, yet we can see in the description of the characters that these letters are anomalously written with a cedilla rather than a comma.

In 2001, after the release of ISO 8859-15, which added the euro sign to ISO 8859-1 and corrected a number of other deficiencies in that encoding, ISO did the same for ISO 8859-2: ISO 8859-16 (or "Latin-10"), the latest encoding in the 8859 saga, covers the languages of Central Europe (Polish, Czech, Slovenian, Slovak, Hungarian, Albanian, Romanian), but also French (with the 'œ' ligature!), German, and Italian. The coverage of this encoding stopped at the French border and did not extend to Spanish ('ñ' is missing) or Portuguese (there are no vowels with a tilde). It has the distinction of being the first (better late than never!) to include the Romanian letters 'ş' and 'ţ'.

Here is the ISO 8859-16 encoding:

	A	B	C	D	E	F
0	NBSP (A0)	° (B0)	À (C0)	Đ (D0)	à (E0)	đ (F0)
1	Ą (A1)	± (B1)	Á (C1)	Ń (D1)	á (E1)	ń (F1)
2	ą (A2)	Č (B2)	Â (C2)	Ò (D2)	â (E2)	ò (F2)
3	Ł (A3)	ł (B3)	Ă (C3)	Ó (D3)	ă (E3)	ó (F3)
4	€ (A4)	Ž (B4)	Ä (C4)	Ô (D4)	ä (E4)	ô (F4)
5	„ (A5)	” (B5)	Ć (C5)	Ő (D5)	ć (E5)	ő (F5)
6	Š (A6)	¶ (B6)	Æ (C6)	Ö (D6)	æ (E6)	ö (F6)
7	§ (A7)	· (B7)	Ç (C7)	Ś (D7)	ç (E7)	ś (F7)
8	š (A8)	ž (B8)	È (C8)	Ű (D8)	è (E8)	ű (F8)
9	© (A9)	č (B9)	É (C9)	Ù (D9)	é (E9)	ù (F9)
A	Ș (AA)	ș (BA)	Ê (CA)	Ú (DA)	ê (EA)	ú (FA)
B	« (AB)	» (BB)	Ë (CB)	Û (DB)	ë (EB)	û (FB)
C	Ź (AC)	Œ (BC)	Ì (CC)	Ü (DC)	ì (EC)	ü (FC)
D	SHY (AD)	œ (BD)	Í (CD)	Ę (DD)	í (ED)	ę (FD)
E	ź (AE)	Ÿ (BE)	Î (CE)	Ț (DE)	î (EE)	ț (FE)
F	Ż (AF)	ż (BF)	Ï (CF)	ß (DF)	ï (EF)	ÿ (FF)

ISO 8859-3 (Latin-3) and ISO 8859-9 (Latin-5)

The third (ISO 8859-3, or 'Latin-3') in the series is dedicated to the languages of "the South": Turkish, Maltese, and Esperanto (the last of these not being particularly Southern). In it we find certain characters from ISO 8859-1 and ISO 8859-2 and also—surprise!—a few empty blocks:

	A	B	C	D	E	F
0	NBSP (A0)	° (B0)	À (C0)	(D0)	à (E0)	(F0)
1	Ħ (A1)	ħ (B1)	Á (C1)	Ñ (D1)	á (E1)	ñ (F1)
2	˘ (A2)	² (B2)	Â (C2)	Ò (D2)	â (E2)	ò (F2)
3	£ (A3)	³ (B3)	(C3)	Ó (D3)	(E3)	ó (F3)
4	¤ (A4)	´ (B4)	Ä (C4)	Ô (D4)	ä (E4)	ô (F4)
5	(A5)	µ (B5)	Ċ (C5)	Ġ (D5)	ċ (E5)	ġ (F5)
6	Ĥ (A6)	ĥ (B6)	Ĉ (C6)	Ö (D6)	ĉ (E6)	ö (F6)
7	§ (A7)	· (B7)	Ç (C7)	× (D7)	ç (E7)	÷ (F7)
8	¨ (A8)	˙ (B8)	È (C8)	Ĝ (D8)	è (E8)	ĝ (F8)
9	İ (A9)	ı (B9)	É (C9)	Ù (D9)	é (E9)	ù (F9)
A	Ş (AA)	ş (BA)	Ê (CA)	Ú (DA)	ê (EA)	ú (FA)
B	Ğ (AB)	ğ (BB)	Ë (CB)	Û (DB)	ë (EB)	û (FB)
C	Ĵ (AC)	ĵ (BC)	Ì (CC)	Ü (DC)	ì (EC)	ü (FC)
D	SHY (AD)	½ (BD)	Í (CD)	Ŭ (DD)	í (ED)	ŭ (FD)
E	(AE)	(BE)	Î (CE)	Ŝ (DE)	î (EE)	ŝ (FE)
F	Ż (AF)	ż (BF)	Ï (CF)	ß (DF)	ï (EF)	˙ (FF)

In 1989 the Turks, dissatisfied with ISO 8859-3, asked for a slightly modified version of ISO 8859-1 with the Turkish characters in place of the Icelandic ones. The result was

ISO 8859-9 (or "Latin-5"), which differs from ISO 8859-1 in only six positions (shown in black below):

Ğ D0	Ñ D1	Ò D2	Ó D3	Ô D4	Õ D5	Ö D6	× D7	Ø D8	Ù D9	Ú DA	Û DB	Ü DC	İ DD	Ş DE	ß DF
ğ F0	ñ F1	ò F2	ó F3	ô F4	õ F5	ö F6	÷ F7	ø F8	ù F9	ú FA	û FB	ü FC	ı FD	ş FE	ÿ FF

ISO 8859-4 (Latin-4), ISO 8859-10 (Latin-6), and ISO 8859-13 (Latin-7)

Encoding number 4 in the series (ISO 8859-4, or "Latin-4") is dedicated to the languages of "the North". Since Danish, Swedish, Norwegian, Finnish, and Icelandic are already covered by ISO 8859-1, "languages of the North" here refers to those of the Baltic countries: Lithuanian, Latvian, Estonian, and Lapp. Here is the encoding:

NBSP A0	Ą A1	ĸ A2	Ŗ A3	¤ A4	Ĩ A5	Ļ A6	§ A7	¨ A8	Š A9	Ē AA	Ģ AB	Ŧ AC	SHY AD	Ž AE	¯ AF
° B0	ą B1	˛ B2	ŗ B3	´ B4	ĩ B5	ļ B6	ˇ B7	¸ B8	š B9	ē BA	ģ BB	ŧ BC	ŋ̄ BD	ž BE	ŋ BF
Ā C0	Á C1	Â C2	Ã C3	Ä C4	Å C5	Æ C6	Į C7	Č C8	É C9	Ę CA	Ë CB	Ė CC	Í CD	Î CE	Ī CF
Đ D0	Ņ D1	Ō D2	Ķ D3	Ô D4	Õ D5	Ö D6	× D7	Ø D8	Ų D9	Ú DA	Û DB	Ü DC	Ũ DD	Ū DE	ß DF
ā E0	á E1	â E2	ã E3	ä E4	å E5	æ E6	į E7	č E8	é E9	ę EA	ë EB	ė EC	í ED	î EE	ī EF
đ F0	ņ F1	ō F2	ķ F3	ô F4	õ F5	ö F6	÷ F7	ø F8	ų F9	ú FA	û FB	ü FC	ũ FD	ū FE	˙ FF

In 1992, a new encoding (ISO 8859-10, or "Latin-6"), much more rational than the previous one, was created for the Nordic languages. It also includes all of the characters required to write Icelandic. One special feature: certain "customs" of the ISO 8859 encodings were abandoned; for example, the universal currency symbol, the free-standing accent marks, and the mathematical signs are not included.

NBSP A0	Ą A1	Ē A2	Ģ A3	Ī A4	Ĩ A5	Ķ A6	§ A7	Ļ A8	Đ A9	Š AA	Ŧ AB	Ž AC	SHY AD	Ū AE	Ŋ AF
° B0	ą B1	ē B2	ģ B3	ī B4	ĩ B5	ķ B6	· B7	ļ B8	đ B9	š BA	ŧ BB	ž BC	― BD	ū BE	ŋ BF
Ā C0	Á C1	Â C2	Ã C3	Ä C4	Å C5	Æ C6	Į C7	Č C8	É C9	Ę CA	Ë CB	Ė CC	Í CD	Î CE	Ï CF
Đ D0	Ņ D1	Ō D2	Ó D3	Ô D4	Õ D5	Ö D6	Ũ D7	Ø D8	Ų D9	Ú DA	Û DB	Ü DC	Ý DD	Þ DE	ß DF
ð E0	á E1	â E2	ã E3	ä E4	å E5	æ E6	į E7	č E8	é E9	ę EA	ë EB	ė EC	í ED	î EE	ï EF
ð F0	ņ F1	ō F2	ó F3	ô F4	õ F5	ö F6	ũ F7	ø F8	ų F9	ú FA	û FB	ü FC	ý FD	þ FE	ĸ FF

A few comments:

- Clearly this ISO 8859 encoding is much more mature than the previous ones. Not only have all the useless characters been done away with, but also there is a companion to the isolated 'ß': the Greenlandic letter 'ĸ', whose upper-case version is identical to 'K'.

- The glyph 'Đ' appears twice: in position 0xA9 it represents the Croatian *dje*, whose lower-case form is 'đ'; in position 0xD0, on the other hand, it represents the Icelandic *eth*, whose lower-case form is 'ð'.

In 1998 a third encoding dedicated to the Baltic languages came out: ISO 8859-13 (or "Latin-7"), which has the peculiarity of combining these languages with Polish and including the appropriate types of quotation marks.

ISO 8859-5, 6, 7, 8, 11

ISO 8859-5, or "ISO Cyrillic", stems from a Soviet standard of 1987, GOST 19768/87, and is meant for the languages that use the Cyrillic alphabet. As there are many such languages, all of them rich in characters, the encoding is limited to Russian as spelled after the revolution (without the characters "*fita* ѳ, *yat* ѣ, *izhitsa* v, *i dessyatirichnoye* i" that Lenin eliminated) and to the languages spoken in European countries: Ukrainian (without the character 'ґ', which the Soviet government did not recognize), Byelorussian, Moldavian, Bulgarian, Serbian, and Macedonian. This encoding also includes the '№' ligature, a number sign (like the North American English '#'), which appears in practically every Russian font. The 'N' in this character is a foreign letter; it does not appear in the Cyrillic alphabet.

ISO 8859-6, or "ISO Arabic", covers the Arabic alphabet. We are astonished by the minimalist appearance of this encoding: there are numerous empty blocks, yet many languages that use the Arabic script have extra characters that are not provided. ISO 8859-6 includes only the basic letters required to write Arabic and also the short vowels and some of the diacritical marks (the *wasla* and the vertical *fatha* are missing). The punctuation marks that differ in appearance from their Latin counterparts (the comma, semicolon, question mark) are also included.

Describing the ISO 8859-7, or "ISO Greek", encoding is a very painful experience for the author, for he still bears the scars of that massacre of the Greek language that is known as the "monotonic reform". This reform of 1981 cut the Greek language off from its accents and breathing marks for the sake of facilitating the work of the daily press and the computerization of the language. Which other country in the world could bear to perpetrate so grave an injury on a 2,000-year-old language in order to accommodate it better to the limitations of the computer? (See [169, 166].) The survivors of the massacre are collected in this encoding: letters without accents and vowels with an acute accent. There are also the vowels *iota* and *upsilon* with a diæresis, as well as with both an accent and a diæresis, but their upper-case versions with the diæresis are absent.

The ISO 8859-8, or "ISO Hebrew", encoding covers Modern Hebrew (or *Ivrit*). Once again, a minimalist approach was taken: the Hebrew consonants and long vowels are all there, but not the short vowels or any other diacritical marks. Yiddish is not provided for.

Finally, ISO 8859-11, or "ISO Thai", which stems from Thai standard TIS 620 of 1986, covers Thai, a Southeast Asian script that is a simplified version of the Khmer script. The encoding is rather thorough: it contains practically all of the consonants, initial vowels, diacritical marks, and special punctuation marks, as well as the numerals.

ISO 8859-14 (Latin-8)

ISO 8859-14 (or "Latin-8") is dedicated to the Celtic languages: Irish Gaelic (which is ordinarily written in its own alphabet), Scottish, and Welsh. Only Breton, with its famous 'c'h' ligature, is absent. It is a variant of ISO 8859-1 with 31 modified characters that we have shown here in black:

A	B	C	D	E	F	7	8	9	A	B	C	D	E	F
NBSP (A0)	Ḃ (A1)	ḃ (A2)	£ (A3)	Ċ (A4)	ċ (A5)	Ḋ (A6)	§ (A7)	Ẁ (A8)	© (A9)	Ẃ (AA)	ḋ (AB)	Ỳ (AC)	SHY (AD)	® (AE)	Ÿ (AF)
Ḟ (B0)	ḟ (B1)	Ġ (B2)	ġ (B3)	Ṁ (B4)	ṁ (B5)	¶ (B6)	Ṗ (B7)	ẁ (B8)	ṗ (B9)	ẃ (BA)	Ṡ (BB)	ỳ (BC)	Ẅ (BD)	ẅ (BE)	ṡ (BF)
Ŵ (D0)	Ñ (D1)	Ò (D2)	Ó (D3)	Ô (D4)	Õ (D5)	Ö (D6)	Ṫ (D7)	Ø (D8)	Ù (D9)	Ú (DA)	Û (DB)	Ü (DC)	Ý (DD)	Ŷ (DE)	ß (DF)
ŵ (F0)	ñ (F1)	ò (F2)	ó (F3)	ô (F4)	õ (F5)	ö (F6)	ṫ (F7)	ø (F8)	ù (F9)	ú (FA)	û (FB)	ü (FC)	ý (FD)	ŷ (FE)	ÿ (FF)

The Far East

The first telegraph systems in the Far East were imported from the West and therefore used the Latin alphabet. How could the thousands, even tens of thousands, of ideographic characters of the Chinese writing system have been encoded, with either Morse code or anything similar? Transliteration into the Latin alphabet was not an option either, as the phonetics of the Chinese language are very ill suited to that approach. Japanese is simpler phonetically, but another problem impeded transliteration: the enormous number of homophones that are distinguished only in writing.

Only computer science could enable the countries of the Far East to communicate conveniently over large distances. The country the best equipped for this task was, of course, Japan. In 1976, three years after the release of ISO 2022, the Japanese prepared the first GR-type encoding—that is, a 94-character supplement to ASCII: JIS C 6220 (which was rechristened as JIS X 0201-1976 in 1987). The ASCII used in Japan was already localized: a yen sign '¥' replaced the backslash[2] and the tilde was replaced by an overbar (for writing the Japanese long vowels in Latin script). JIS C 6220, based on the JISCII released in 1969, contains only *katakana* and a few ideographic punctuation marks (the period, the quotation marks, the comma, the raised dot), all in *half-width characters*:

A	B	C	D	E	F	6	7	8	9	A	B	C	D	E	F
NBSP (A0)	｡ (A1)	｢ (A2)	｣ (A3)	､ (A4)	･ (A5)	ｦ (A6)	ｧ (A7)	ｨ (A8)	ｩ (A9)	ｪ (AA)	ｫ (AB)	ｬ (AC)	ｭ (AD)	ｮ (AE)	ｯ (AF)
ｰ (B0)	ｱ (B1)	ｲ (B2)	ｳ (B3)	ｴ (B4)	ｵ (B5)	ｶ (B6)	ｷ (B7)	ｸ (B8)	ｹ (B9)	ｺ (BA)	ｻ (BB)	ｼ (BC)	ｽ (BD)	ｾ (BE)	ｿ (BF)
ﾀ (C0)	ﾁ (C1)	ﾂ (C2)	ﾃ (C3)	ﾄ (C4)	ﾅ (C5)	ﾆ (C6)	ﾇ (C7)	ﾈ (C8)	ﾉ (C9)	ﾊ (CA)	ﾋ (CB)	ﾌ (CC)	ﾍ (CD)	ﾎ (CE)	ﾏ (CF)
ﾐ (D0)	ﾑ (D1)	ﾒ (D2)	ﾓ (D3)	ﾔ (D4)	ﾕ (D5)	ﾖ (D6)	ﾗ (D7)	ﾘ (D8)	ﾙ (D9)	ﾚ (DA)	ﾛ (DB)	ﾜ (DC)	ﾝ (DD)	ﾞ (DE)	ﾟ (DF)

The phonetic modifiers were supplied as independent characters even though there was enough space to encode all of their combinations with letters. The syllable '゜' was thus obtained from the character 'ヘ' followed by a modifier character '゜'.

---

[2] As a result of which right up to this day, thirty years later, TEX commands in Japanese handbooks always start with a yen sign rather than a backslash....

On January 1, 1978, after nine years of hard effort, the first true Japanese encoding, JIS C 6226-1978, known today as "old JIS", officially came into effect. It contains 6,694 characters: the Latin, Greek, and Cyrillic alphabets, the *kana*, and 6,349 *kanji* ideographic characters, distributed over two levels. It was revised three times, finally to become JIS X 0208-1997 in January 1997. This last encoding is perhaps the most important Japanese encoding of all. Its structure complies with ISO 2022: there are 94 GR tables of 94 characters each.

In 1990 a second Japanese encoding was released: JIS X 0212-1990. It supplements the first with 5,801 ideographic characters and 266 other characters. A third encoding, JIS X 0213-2000, was released in January 2000. It adds another two levels of *kanji* to those of JIS X 0208-1997: the third level contains 1,249 *kanji*; the fourth, 2,436.

China did not lag far behind Japan: in 1981, on the symbolic date of May 1, it issued the first Chinese encoding, GB 2312-80. This encoding, which contains 7,445 characters, is compatible with the ISO 2022 standard. It is suspiciously similar to the Japanese encodings, at least in its choice of non-ideographic characters: it includes the Latin, Greek, and Cyrillic letters, and even the Japanese *kana*.

Over time there were numerous extensions to GB 2312-80. By 1992, the number of characters totaled 8,443. After Mao's Cultural Revolution, the People's Republic of China adopted a simplified writing system of ideographic characters, and the encodings respect it. But, contrary to what one might have expected, China also issued encodings in traditional characters. Thus in 1990 the GB/T 12345-90 encoding was released. The letter 'T' in its name comes from the character 推 and means "optional"—after all, in a country that has simplified its writing system, the traditional form could only be regarded as optional.

An encoding was also released in Taiwan on a May 1, but this time in 1984 (three years after the People's Republic of China released its own encoding). It is called, in English, "Big Five", and its name refers to the five big Taiwanese corporations that collaborated on its development. It seems that Taiwan went all out to surpass its bigger cousin: Big Five contains no fewer than 13,494 characters, 13,053 of which are ideographic, arranged on two levels. Finally, 1992 saw the release of the CNS 11643-1992 encoding, which broke all the records for number of characters: a total of 48,711, including 48,027 ideographic characters, organized into seven planes with approximately 6 to 8 thousand characters each. The first two planes correspond roughly to the two levels of Big Five.

As for the other Chinese-speaking countries, Singapore uses mainly the GB encodings of mainland China, and Hong Kong, despite its recent annexation into China, uses mainly Big Five.

The encoding frenzy began in South Korea in 1992 with the KS X 1001-1992 encoding, which contains 4,888 ideographic characters, 2,350 *hangul* phonetic characters, and 986 other characters, once again including Latin, Greek, Cyrillic, and the Japanese *kana*, strictly in imitation of the Japanese encoding JIS X 0208-1997.

North Korea is said to have abolished the ideographic characters, yet the first North Korean encoding, KPS 9566-97 of 1997, contained 4,653 ideographic characters as well as 2,679 *hangul* characters and 927 other characters. This encoding was inspired by the South Korean one but presents certain incompatibilities. In addition, positions 0x0448 to 0x044D fulfill an important state purpose: they contain the names of honorable party president Kim Il-sung and his son and successor Kim Jong-il … a funny way to achieve immortality.

Using ISO 2022 to gain access to the characters in these encodings is not always very practical because at any given time one must be aware of the current mode, that is, which of G0, G1, G2, and G3 is the active encoding. In Japan there have been two attempts to overcome this problem and make use of the characters of the JIS encodings without employing escape sequences:

1. Shift-JIS is an initiative of Microsoft. The idea is very simple: the JIS encodings are made up of tables of 94×94 characters, and, if we count in ranges of 16 characters, that makes $6 \times 6 = 36$ ranges. But 36 can also be written as 3×12; thus we can obtain any character by using two bytes, of which the first covers three different ranges and the second covers twelve different ranges. We select the ranges 0x81-0x9F and 0xE0-0xEF for the first byte and 0x40-0x7E and 0x80-0xFC for the second. Why have we chosen those particular ranges for the first byte? Because they leave section 0x20-0x7F free for ASCII and section 0xA0-0xDF free for the *katakana*. Thus, upon reading a byte, the computer knows if it is a single-byte character or if a second byte will follow, and a simple calculation is sufficient to find the table and the position of the desired character.

   Shift-JIS was widely used under Windows and MacOS. Its flagrant drawback is that the technique of 3×12 severely limits the number of characters accessible through this method. Thus there is no hope at all of adding any extra characters. And we cannot automatically change encodings because we do not have access to the ISO 2022 escape sequences.

2. EUC (Extended Unix Coding) is a variant of ISO 2022 without escape sequences. There is not just one EUC but an assortment of localized versions: EUC-JP, EUC-CN, etc. In each of them, one chooses from one to four encodings. The first two are obtained from suitable choices of ranges of characters. The third and fourth encodings are ultimately formed through the use of two control characters: ss2 (0x8E) and ss3 (0x8F), followed by one or two other characters.

   Thus, for example, EUC-JP includes ASCII, JIS X 0208-1997, the *katakana*, and JIS X 0212-1990. Among these four, ASCII is obtained directly, JIS X 0208-1997 is obtained from the characters 0xA1-0xFE×0xA1-0xFE, the *katakana* are obtained with ss2 followed by 0xA1-0xDF, and JIS X 0212-1990 is obtained with ss3 followed by 0xA1-0xFE×0xA1-0xFE.

While Shift-JIS is peculiar to Japan, EUC has also been used in other countries: there are the encodings EUC-CN (mainland China), EUC-TW (Taiwan), EUC-KR (South Korea).

The interested reader will find a very detailed description of these encodings and a host of other information in Ken Lunde's book *CJKV Information Processing* [240].

Microsoft's code pages

The term *codepage* for "encoding" was oined by Microsoft. As the DOS system, for example, was console-based, we find in the DOS code pages a set of graphical symbols used to draw user interfaces through the simple arrangement of straight segments, corners, crosses, etc. There are even lattices of pixels that simulate various shades of gray.

In the US, the most commonly used DOS code pages were 437 ("United States") and 850 ("Multilingual"). In both cases, 128-position extensions to ASCII were made (the entire upper half of the table). Here is the part of the table beyond ASCII for code page 437, entitled "MS-DOS Latin US":

Ç 80	ü 81	é 82	â 83	ä 84	à 85	å 86	ç 87	ê 88	ë 89	è 8A	ï 8B	î 8C	ì 8D	Ä 8E	Å 8F
É 90	æ 91	Æ 92	ô 93	ö 94	ò 95	û 96	ù 97	ÿ 98	Ö 99	Ü 9A	¢ 9B	£ 9C	¥ 9D	Pts 9E	ƒ 9F
á A0	í A1	ó A2	ú A3	ñ A4	Ñ A5	a A6	o A7	¿ A8	⌐ A9	¬ AA	½ AB	¼ AC	¡ AD	« AE	» AF
▓ B0	▓ B1	▓ B2	│ B3	┤ B4	╡ B5	╢ B6	╖ B7	╕ B8	╣ B9	║ BA	╗ BB	╝ BC	╜ BD	╛ BE	┐ BF
└ C0	┴ C1	┬ C2	├ C3	─ C4	┼ C5	╞ C6	╟ C7	╚ C8	╔ C9	╩ CA	╦ CB	╠ CC	═ CD	╬ CE	╧ CF
╨ D0	╤ D1	╥ D2	╙ D3	╘ D4	╒ D5	╓ D6	╫ D7	╪ D8	┘ D9	┌ DA	█ DB	▄ DC	▌ DD	▐ DE	▀ DF
α E0	β E1	Γ E2	π E3	Σ E4	σ E5	µ E6	τ E7	Φ E8	Θ E9	Ω EA	δ EB	∞ EC	φ ED	ε EE	∩ EF
≡ F0	± F1	≥ F2	≤ F3	⌠ F4	⌡ F5	÷ F6	≈ F7	° F8	• F9	· FA	√ FB	ⁿ FC	² FD	■ FE	NBSP FF

This code page is a real mixed bag: a few accented letters (there is an 'É' but no 'È'...), a handful of currency symbols, some punctuation marks, three rows of building blocks for drawing user interfaces, and a number of mathematical symbols, including a small range of Greek letters. One startling fact: the author does not know whether the character in position xE1 is a Greek *beta* 'β' or a German *eszett* 'ß'. Its location between *alpha* and *gamma* suggests that it is a *beta*, but at the same time the presence of the German letters 'ä', 'ö', and 'ü' implies that this encoding should logically include an 'ß'. Could it be that the same character was supposed to serve for both? If so, depending on the font, we would have had aberrations such as "ßιßλίον" or "Gießgefäß"...

Code page 850 (*MS-DOS Latin 1*) is a variant of the preceding. It contains fewer graphical characters and more characters for the languages of Western Europe. Note that the German *eszett* 'ß' appears in the same position as the 'β/ß' of code page 437:

Ç 80	ü 81	é 82	â 83	ä 84	à 85	å 86	ç 87	ê 88	ë 89	è 8A	ï 8B	î 8C	ì 8D	Ä 8E	Å 8F
É 90	æ 91	Æ 92	ô 93	ö 94	ò 95	û 96	ù 97	ÿ 98	Ö 99	Ü 9A	ø 9B	£ 9C	Ø 9D	× 9E	ƒ 9F
á A0	í A1	ó A2	ú A3	ñ A4	Ñ A5	a A6	o A7	¿ A8	® A9	¬ AA	½ AB	¼ AC	¡ AD	« AE	» AF
▓ B0	▓ B1	▓ B2	│ B3	┤ B4	Á B5	Â B6	À B7	© B8	╣ B9	║ BA	╗ BB	╝ BC	¢ BD	¥ BE	┐ BF

L (C0)	⊥ (C1)	┬ (C2)	├ (C3)	─ (C4)	┼ (C5)	ã (C6)	Ã (C7)	╚ (C8)	╔ (C9)	╩ (CA)	╦ (CB)	╠ (CC)	= (CD)	╬ (CE)	¤ (CF)
ð (D0)	Đ (D1)	Ê (D2)	Ë (D3)	È (D4)	ı (D5)	Í (D6)	Î (D7)	Ï (D8)	┘ (D9)	┌ (DA)	█ (DB)	▄ (DC)	¦ (DD)	Ì (DE)	▀ (DF)
Ó (E0)	ß (E1)	Ô (E2)	Ò (E3)	õ (E4)	Õ (E5)	µ (E6)	þ (E7)	Þ (E8)	Ú (E9)	Û (EA)	Ù (EB)	ý (EC)	Ý (ED)	¯ (EE)	´ (EF)
SHY (F0)	± (F1)	‗ (F2)	¾ (F3)	¶ (F4)	§ (F5)	÷ (F6)	¸ (F7)	° (F8)	¨ (F9)	· (FA)	¹ (FB)	³ (FC)	² (FD)	■ (FE)	NBSP (FF)

There were numerous other MS-DOS code pages [204]: 708–710, 720, and 864 (Arabic); 737 and 869 ("monotonic" Greek); 775 (Baltic countries); 852 (countries of Central Europe); 855 and 866 (Cyrillic, with 866 being for Russian only); 857 (Turkish); 860 (Portuguese); 861 (Icelandic); 862 (Hebrew, without the short vowels); 863 ("Canadian French", a pastiche of 437 and 850); 865 (Nordic countries); 874 (Thai); 932 (Japanese); 936 (simplified Chinese); 949 (Korean); 950 (traditional Chinese).

When Windows came out, there was no longer any need for "graphical characters", and a change of encodings was called for (even though it caused big problems for users who were porting their documents from MS-DOS to Windows). In the meantime, the first ISO 8859 encodings were released, and Microsoft decided to adopt them—but avoided their major shortcoming: the characters 0x80-0x9F were not control characters in Microsoft's implementation.

Thus code page *1252 Windows Latin 1*, also known as "ANSI", is an ISO 8859-1 encoding to which the following two lines have been added:

€ (80)	(81)	‚ (82)	ƒ (83)	„ (84)	… (85)	† (86)	‡ (87)	^ (88)	‰ (89)	Š (8A)	‹ (8B)	Œ (8C)	(8D)	Ž (8E)	(8F)
(90)	' (91)	' (92)	" (93)	" (94)	• (95)	– (96)	— (97)	~ (98)	TM (99)	š (9A)	› (9B)	œ (9C)	(9D)	ž (9E)	Ÿ (9F)

We can only rejoice at the fact that the letters 'Œ', 'œ', and 'Ÿ' are found in this encoding. There are also the single guillemets '‹ ›' and the two most common Central European letters, 'Š š' and 'Ž ž'. A few details: ' and „ are the German single and double opening quotation marks, also called *Gänsefüßchen* (= '[little] goose feet').

Code page *1250 Windows Latin 2* both extends and modifies ISO 8859-2. Positions 0x80-0xBF are the ones that have undergone modification:

€ (80)	(81)	‚ (82)	(83)	„ (84)	… (85)	† (86)	‡ (87)	(88)	‰ (89)	Š (8A)	‹ (8B)	Ś (8C)	Ť (8D)	Ž (8E)	Ź (8F)
(90)	' (91)	' (92)	" (93)	" (94)	• (95)	– (96)	— (97)	(98)	TM (99)	š (9A)	› (9B)	ś (9C)	ť (9D)	ž (9E)	ź (9F)
NBSP (A0)	ˇ (A1)	˘ (A2)	Ł (A3)	¤ (A4)	Ą (A5)	¦ (A6)	§ (A7)	¨ (A8)	© (A9)	Ş (AA)	« (AB)	¬ (AC)	SHY (AD)	® (AE)	Ż (AF)
° (B0)	± (B1)	˛ (B2)	ł (B3)	´ (B4)	µ (B5)	¶ (B6)	· (B7)	¸ (B8)	ą (B9)	ş (BA)	» (BB)	Ľ (BC)	" (BD)	ľ (BE)	ż (BF)

There has never been a *Windows Latin 3* or a *Windows Latin 4*, but there is a *1254 Windows Latin 5* for Turkish, which differs from *1252 Windows Latin 1* in only six positions:

Ğ (D0)	Ñ (D1)	Ò (D2)	Ó (D3)	Ô (D4)	Õ (D5)	Ö (D6)	× (D7)	Ø (D8)	Ù (D9)	Ú (DA)	Û (DB)	Ü (DC)	İ (DD)	Ş (DE)	ß (DF)
ğ (F0)	ñ (F1)	ò (F2)	ó (F3)	ô (F4)	õ (F5)	ö (F6)	÷ (F7)	ø (F8)	ù (F9)	ú (FA)	û (FB)	ü (FC)	ı (FD)	ş (FE)	ÿ (FF)

These are the same differences that we find between ISO 8859-1 and ISO 8859-9.

Other Windows code pages are *1251 Windows Cyrillic, 1253 Windows Greek* ("monotonic Greek" is implied[3]), *1255 Windows Hebrew, 1256 Windows Arabic*, and *1257 Windows Baltic*.

Apple's encodings

From the beginning, the Macintosh used its own encoding, an extension of ASCII that was still incomplete on the first Macintosh (released in 1984) but was gradually fleshed out. The unusual aspect of the Macintosh encodings is that they, like the MS-DOS code pages, include mathematical symbols. Since most fonts do not contain these symbols, MacOS had a special substitution procedure. Whichever font one used, the mathematical symbols almost always came from the same system fonts. Other special features of the Macintosh encodings: they include the 'fi' and 'fl' ligatures as well as the famous bitten apple '' that Apple uses as its logo.

Here is the encoding used on the Macintoshes sold in the US and in Western Europe, which is called *Standard Roman* [53] (a rather poorly chosen name, since the term "roman" refers to a font style rather than to a writing system):

Ä 80	Å 81	Ç 82	É 83	Ñ 84	Ö 85	Ü 86	á 87	à 88	â 89	ä 8A	ã 8B	å 8C	ç 8D	é 8E	è 8F
ê 90	ë 91	í 92	ì 93	î 94	ï 95	ñ 96	ó 97	ò 98	ô 99	ö 9A	õ 9B	ú 9C	ù 9D	û 9E	ü 9F
† A0	° A1	¢ A2	£ A3	§ A4	• A5	¶ A6	ß A7	® A8	© A9	TM AA	´ AB	¨ AC	≠ AD	Æ AE	Ø AF
∞ B0	± B1	≤ B2	≥ B3	¥ B4	µ B5	∂ B6	Σ B7	∏ B8	π B9	∫ BA	a BB	o BC	Ω BD	æ BE	ø BF
¿ C0	¡ C1	¬ C2	√ C3	ƒ C4	≈ C5	Δ C6	« C7	» C8	… C9	NBSP CA	À CB	Ã CC	Õ CD	Œ CE	œ CF
– D0	— D1	" D2	" D3	' D4	' D5	÷ D6	◊ D7	ÿ D8	Ÿ D9	/ DA	¤ DB	‹ DC	› DD	fi DE	fl DF
‡ E0	· E1	‚ E2	„ E3	‰ E4	Â E5	Ê E6	Á E7	Ë E8	È E9	Í EA	Î EB	Ï EC	Ì ED	Ó EE	Ô EF
F0	Ò F1	Ú F2	Û F3	Ù F4	ı F5	^ F6	~ F7	¯ F8	˘ F9	· FA	˚ FB	¸ FC	˝ FD	˛ FE	ˇ FF

A few details: we have already seen the German quotation marks ',' and ',,' in the *1252 Windows Latin 1* encoding. The character 0xDA '/' is a fraction bar. Do not mistake the characters 'Σ' and 'Π' for the Greek letters 'Σ' and 'Π': the former, the mathematical symbols for sum and product, are larger than the ordinary Greek letters, which are of regular size. In addition, both may appear in one formula: $\sum_{i=0}^{\infty} \Sigma_i = \prod_{j=0}^{\infty} \Pi_j$. The two glyphs look very much alike, but in position xA1 we have the degree sign (a perfect circle) while in position xBC there is a superscript letter 'o', used in Spanish, French, and other languages. The letter 'ı' in position F5 is not intended for Turkish but to be combined with accents.

---

[3] This encoding long irritated the Greeks because it differs only slightly from ISO 8859-7: the accented capital letter *alpha* occurs in position 0xA2 on the Windows code page and in position 0xB6 in the ISO encoding; thus the letter tends to disappear when a document is transferred from Windows to Unix or the opposite....

There is an *Icelandic* version of this encoding that differs from *Standard Roman* in six positions: 'Ý' (0xA0), 'Đ' (0xDC), 'ð' (0xDD), 'Þ' (0xDE), 'þ' (0xDF), 'ý' (0xE0).

There is a *Turkish* version as well, that differs from *Standard Roman* in six consecutive positions: 'Ğ' (0xDA), 'ğ' (0xDB), 'İ' (0xDC), 'ı' (0xDD), 'Ş' (0xDE), 'ş' (0xDF). Position 0xF5 of this encoding has been left empty so that the letter 'ı' would not appear twice.

In addition, there is a Romanian version of the encoding, *Romanian*, that again differs from *Standard Roman* in six positions: 'Ă' (0xAE), 'Ş' (0xAF), 'ă' (0xBE), 'ş' (0xBF), 'Ţ' (0xDE), 'ţ' (0xDF).

For the languages of Central Europe and the Baltic countries, Apple offers the *Central European* encoding, shown below:

Ä 80	81	ā 82	É 83	A̧ 84	Ö 85	Ü 86	á 87	ą 88	Č 89	ä 8A	č 8B	Ć 8C	ć 8D	é 8E	Ź 8F
ź 90	Ď 91	í 92	d' 93	Ē 94	ē 95	Ė 96	ó 97	ė 98	ô 99	ö 9A	õ 9B	ú 9C	Ě 9D	ě 9E	ü 9F
† A0	° A1	Ę A2	£ A3	§ A4	• A5	¶ A6	ß A7	® A8	© A9	™ AA	ę AB	¨ AC	≠ AD	ğ AE	Į AF
į B0	Ī B1	≤ B2	≥ B3	ī B4	Ķ B5	∂ B6	Σ B7	ł B8	Ļ B9	ļ BA	Ľ BB	ľ BC	Ĺ BD	ĺ BE	Ņ BF
ņ C0	Ń C1	¬ C2	√ C3	ń C4	Ň C5	Δ C6	« C7	» C8	… C9	NBSP CA	ň CB	Ő CC	Õ CD	ő CE	Ō CF
– D0	— D1	" D2	" D3	' D4	' D5	÷ D6	◊ D7	ō D8	Ŕ D9	ŕ DA	Ř DB	‹ DC	› DD	ř DE	Ŗ DF
ŗ E0	Š E1	‚ E2	„ E3	š E4	Ś E5	ś E6	Á E7	Ť E8	t' E9	Í EA	Ž EB	ž EC	Ū ED	Ó EE	Ô EF
ū F0	Ů F1	Ú F2	ů F3	Ű F4	ű F5	Ų F6	ų F7	Ý F8	ý F9	ķ FA	Ż FB	Ł FC	ż FD	Ģ FE	ˇ FF

Notice that, for an unknown reason, the 'Σ' has resumed its customary size and that there is no 'Π'. This encoding covers Polish, Czech, Slovak, Slovenian, Hungarian, Lithuanian, Latvian, and Estonian. It does not cover Croatian because it lacks the letter 'Đ đ'. For this reason, Apple issued a special encoding (*Croatian*) for the Croatian language.

Other Apple encodings: *Arabic* (Arabic, Persian, Urdu, still without *wasla* but with vertical *fatha*), *Chinese Traditional*, *Cyrillic* (for the European languages that use the Cyrillic alphabet, with the exception of Ukrainian, for which the letter 'ґ' is missing), *Greek* ("monotonic" Greek), *Hebrew* (Hebrew with vowels, semivowels, and *schwa*), *Japanese*, *Korean*, *Devanagari*, *Gujarati*, *Gurmukhi*, and *Thai*.

Electronic mail

The protocol for electronic mail that is still in use today was published in 1982: it is RFC 822 (in which RFC stands for "Request for Comments", a way to demonstrate the democratic nature of the Web's standards). This RFC stipulates that electronic messages are to be encoded in ASCII.

To mitigate that drawback, a new RFC published in 1996 (RFC 2045) introduced a technique that has since become an integral part of electronic mail: the MIME protocol (= "Multipurpose Internet Mail Extensions"). MIME allows for the attachment of files to e-mail messages and for dividing a message into multiple segments, each one potentially of a different type, or, if it is of type text, potentially in a different encoding. To specify the encoding of a message or a part of a message, we use two operators:

- charset is the encoding of the content. Its value must appear on a list [186] established and regularly updated by IANA (= "Internet Assigned Numbers Authority"). In February 2004 there were 250 registered encodings, such as US-ASCII, ISO-2022-JP, EBCDIC-INT, ISO-8859-1, IBM437 (code page 437), windows-1252 (Windows code page 1252), etc.

  The encoding affects only those segments of MIME type text (the subtype being plain, which indicates that the text is not enriched). The syntax is as follows:

  ```
  Content-Type: text/plain; charset=US-ASCII
  ```

- Content-Transfer-Encoding specifies how to translate the coming binary (beyond 0x7f) bytes into ASCII data. This is necessary because MIME did not change the nature of electronic mail—which remains based on ASCII just as much as it was twenty years ago. In fact, MIME offers only makeshift methods for converting binary bytes to ASCII and vice versa. Two methods are available: "quoted-printable" text and text in "base 64".

  Quoted-printable involves using the equals sign as an escape character. Three possibilities exist:

  1. The character to convert is a "printable" ASCII character—that is, in the range of 0x20 to 0x7e—other than the equals sign (ASCII 0x3d). In this case it passes through unchanged.

  2. The character is a control character (0x00-0x1f), a binary character (0x80-0xff), or an equals sign. In this case we write the equals sign followed by the position of the character in the table, in the form of a two-digit hexadecimal number. Thus, if we have specified that we are using ISO 8859-1, the word "voilà" is written voil=E0.

  3. Since the length of the lines in the message is limited, we will divide any excessively long line by adding an equals sign followed by a newline. A line break of this kind will ordinarily be disregarded by the application that decodes the "quoted-printable" text.

  A message encoded in "quoted-printable" format must include the following line in its header:

  ```
  Content-Transfer-Encoding: quoted-printable
  ```

  The other method, "base 64", involves taking three consecutive bytes of text and regarding them as four groups of six bits ($3 \times 8 = 4 \times 6$). Each group of six bits is represented by one ASCII character, as follows:

  - the letters A to Z represent the numbers between 0 and 25;
  - the letters a to z represent the numbers between 26 and 51;

- the digits 0 to 9 represent the numbers between 52 and 61;
- + and / represent respectively the numbers 62 and 63.

The remaining possibility is that one or two bytes will be left over after translation of all of the three-byte sequences. Suppose that one byte, notated xxxxxxxx, is left over. Then we will use the two six-bit groups xxxxxx and xx0000, and we will append *two* equals signs to the converted string. If two bytes, xxxxxxxx and yyyyyyyy, are left over, we will use the three six-bit groups xxxxxx, xxyyyy, and yyyy00, and we will append *a single* equals sign to the converted string.

Example: to encode the word "voilà" (01110110   01101111   01101001   01101100   11100000), we start by taking the first four letters and dividing them into groups of six bits (011101   100110   111101   101001   011011   000000), namely the numbers 29, 38, 61, 41, 27, and 0, which give us the alphanumerics dm9pbA. The remaining letter 'à' (11100000) gives us two groups of six bits (111000   000000), namely the numbers 56 and 0, and therefore the codes 4A. We will append an equal signs to indicate that one letter is missing to complete the triplet. Thus the result is dm9pbA4A=.

A message encoded in "base 64" must include the following line in its header:

```
Content-Transfer-Encoding: base64
```

What are the advantages and disadvantages of the conversions to "quoted-printable" or "base 64"? When the encoding and decoding are performed transparently by the e-mail software, the difference is of little importance, apart from the fact that a message in ASCII with few binary characters will take up less space in "quoted-printable" than in "base 64", while for a message entirely in binary characters the opposite is true. Nevertheless, if the message could be read with software that is not compatible with MIME, "quoted-printable" text will be legible in languages such as French or German that do not use accented or special lettetrs with great frequency, whereas text in "base 64" will have to be processed by computer.

While RFC 2045 specified the encoding of text segments, no provision was made for the subject line of the message or the other lines in the header that would contain text. The solution was provided by RFC 2047, which defined a way to change encodings at any time, either within a string in the header or within the body of the message. It is nothing revolutionary: we once again use the equals sign (which plays a special rôle in both forms of conversion to ASCII) as an escape character:

```
=?name?*?converted_string?=
```

where name is the IANA name of the encoding, * is either Q (= quoted-printable) or B (= base 64), and converted_string is the converted string. Thus the word "voilà" encoded in ISO 8859-1 can be written in the following two ways:

```
=?iso--?Q?voil=E0?=
=?iso--?B?dm9pbA4A=?=
```

Alas, neither of them is really legible…

The Web

The Web is the exchange of HTML data under the protocol HTTP ("Hypertext Transfer Protocol"). Version 1.1 of this protocol is described in RFC 2616 of 1999. Browsers and servers communicate through this protocol by sending each other messages that may or may not contain HTML data. Thus, when one types a URL followed by a carriage return in the appropriate area in the browser, the browser sends an HTTP request to the server in question. The server replies by sending the HTML data corresponding to the URL, or with an error message. In all three cases (request, transmission of HTML data, error message), the parties to the communication send each other messages through HTTP.

HTTP is based on three concepts: the encoding (called charset), which by default is ISO 8859-1 (and not ASCII); the type of compression to be applied (called content-coding, whose values may be gzip, compress, zlib, or identity); and the "transfer coding" to be used. The transfer coding corresponds to the "quoted-printable" and "base 64" of MIME, except that here data transfer is binary and thus does not require conversion to ASCII. The "transfer coding" that we use is chunk, which means that the data will be divided into blocks of a fixed length.

Here is an example of an HTTP header for a message in ISO 8859-1 with *gzip* compression:

```
Content-Type: text/html; charset=iso--
    Content-Encoding: gzip
    Transfer-coding: chunked
```

where the first line specifies that the MIME type of the following document is text, with html as its subtype.

HTTP headers can also be included in the value of the content attribute of the meta element of HTML and XHTML. Each occurrence of this element contains a line of the HTTP header.

The first two parameters (encoding and compression) can also be used in the HTTP request sent to the server, to express the browser's possibilities. In this way the browser can request a certain encoding that it knows how to use or even multiple encodings arranged in order of preference, one or more types of compression, etc. By writing

```
Accept-Charset: iso--, iso--;q=0.8
```

the client specifies that it can read, in order of preference, text in ISO 8859-15 and ISO 8859-1. The parameter q=0.8 ('q' as in "quality" and a number between 0 and 1) that follows the second encoding applies to it alone and indicates that the use of this encoding will give a result with 80% quality. Using this list of requested encodings and their weights with respect to quality, the server will decide which encoding to use to send data. If none of the requested encodings is available, the server will reply with an error message: "406: not acceptable".

The same is true for compression:

```
Accept-Encoding: gzip;q=1.0, identity;q=0.5, *;q=0
```

where the asterisk is the "wildcard". The line shown above should be interpreted as follows: the document may be compressed with *gzip* (top quality) or not compressed at all (50% quality), and every other type of compression is of "0% quality", which means unacceptable.

One details that may lend itself to confusion: here "*charset*" is used to designate the character encoding and "*coding*", or even "*encoding*" in the "accept" commands, is used for compression.

2

Characters, glyphs, bytes: An introduction to Unicode

In the previous chapter, we saw the long journey that encodings took on their way to covering as many languages and writing systems as possible. In Orwell's year, 1984, an ISO committee was formed with the goal of developing a universal multi-byte encoding. In its first (experimental) version, this encoding, known as ISO 10646 (to show that it was an extension of ISO 646, *i.e.*, ASCII), sought to remain compatible with the ISO 2022 standard and offered room for approximately 644 million characters (!), divided into 94 *groups* (G0) of 190 *planes* (G0 + G1) of 190 *rows* (G0 + G1) of 190 *cells* (G0 + G1). The ideographic characters were distributed over four planes: traditional Chinese, simplified Chinese, Japanese, and Korean. When this encoding came up for a vote, it was not adopted.

At the same time, engineers from Apple and Xerox were working on the development of Unicode, starting with an encoding called XCCS that Xerox had developed. The Unicode Consortium was established, and discussions between the ISO 10646 committee and Unicode began. Unicode's fundamental idea was to break free of the methods of ISO 2022, with its mixture of one- and two-byte encodings, by systematically using two bytes throughout. To that end, it was necessary to save space by unifying the ideographic characters.

Instead of becoming fierce competitors, Unicode and ISO 10646 influenced each other, to the point that ISO 10646 systematically aligned itself with Unicode after 1993.

Unicode was released in 1993 and has not stopped growing and evolving since. Its latest version, as of the writing of the book, bears the number 5 and was released in 2006. Most operating systems (Windows XP, MacOS X, Linux) are currently based on Unicode, although not all software is yet compatible with it. The Web is also moving more and more towards adopting Unicode, especially in regard to East Asian languages and writing systems.

But there is a price to pay for being open to the writing systems, and therefore also the cultures, of other peoples: computers and their operating systems must be more powerful, software must be more advanced, fonts must be much larger (and necessarily more cumbersome). And we have not even spoken of the different rendering techniques needed to display East Asian languages correctly—techniques employed in part by the operating system and in part by OpenType or AAT fonts.

In this chapter, which aims to be an introduction to Unicode, we shall discuss its overall structure and a number of technical and philosophical questions: what is the difference between characters and glyphs? how do we move from abstract characters to the very concrete bytes used in the computer?

In the following chapters, we shall examine the individuals that populate Unicode: characters and their properties. We shall discuss a few special situations that call for advanced techniques (normalization, bidirectionality, East Asian characters). Finally, we shall see how Unicode is used in operating systems and, more specifically, how we can enter Unicode characters into a document, whether by using special software or by designing virtual keyboards *ad hoc*.

What we shall not do in this book—so as not to double its already considerable size—is describe one by one the different writing systems covered by Unicode. Our approach will be to describe only those cases that present problems and that are worth discussing in detail. We shall refer the reader to other works that discuss the world's writing systems very thoroughly, from either the linguistic ([106, 309, 345, 136, 96]) or the typographic ([133, 89, 148, 163]) point of view.

Philosophical issues: characters and glyphs

Unicode is an encoding of *characters*, and it is the first encoding that really takes the trouble of defining what a *character* is.

Let's be frank: computer specialists are not in the habit of worrying about philosophical issues ("who am I?", "what comes after death?", "what is a character?"). But that issue arose quite naturally in Unicode when the Asian languages were touched upon. Unicode purports to be an encoding based on *principles*, and one of these principles is precisely the fact that it contains characters *exclusively*. This fact forces us to give serious consideration to the question of what constitutes a character and what does not.

We can compare the relationship between characters and glyphs to the relationship between signifier and signified in linguistics. After all, Ferdinand de Saussure, the founder of linguistics, said himself: "Whether I write in black or white, in incised characters or in relief, with a pen or a chisel—none of that is of any importance for the meaning" [310, p. 118]. What he called "meaning" corresponds very well to what we intend to call "character", namely, the meaning that the author of the document wished to impart by means of the glyph that he used.

But things are a bit more complicated than that: there are characters with no glyphs, glyphs that can correspond to a number of different characters according to context, glyphs that correspond to multiple characters at the same time (with weightings assigned to each), and even more possibilities.

The problem of glyphs and characters is so complex that it has gone beyond the realm of computer specialists and has come to be of interest even to philosophers. For example, the Japanese philosopher Shigeki Moro, who has worked with ideographic characters in Buddhist documents, goes so far in his article *Surface or Essence: Beyond Character Model Set* [274] as to say that Unicode's approach is Aristotelian essentialist and to recommend supplanting it by an approach inspired by Jacques Derrida's theory of writing [114, 115]. The reader interested in the philosophical aspects of the issue is invited to consult [165, 156], in addition to the works cited above.

Let's be pragmatic! In this book we shall adopt a *practical* definition of the character, starting with the definition of the glyph as a point of departure:

- A *glyph* is the image of a symbol used in a writing system (in an alphabet, a syllabary, a set of ideographs, etc.) or in a notational system (like music, mathematics, cartography, etc.).

- A *character* is the simple description, primarily linguistic or logical, of an equivalence class of glyphs.

Let us take a concrete illustration by way of example: the letter 'W'. It is clear that there are thousands of ways to write this letter—to convince oneself of that fact, one need only thumb through Chapter 11, on the history of typographic characters. We could describe it as "the capital Latin letter double-you". All the various ways to write the letter ('W', '*W*', 'W', '𝘞', '**W**',...) have in common the fact that they match this description. The description is *simple* because it does not contain any unnecessary or irrelevant terms. It is *linguistic* because it falls within the realm of English grammar. We can therefore say, if the fact of corresponding to a description of this type is an equivalence relation, that the equivalence class in question is the *character* "capital Latin letter double-you".

Let us take another example: the symbol '×'. We could give it the description "the mathematical multiplication sign". This description is simple—we could even omit the word "mathematical", as Unicode has indeed done. But it is not linguistic at all. It is a *logical* description because it falls within the realm of a well-defined, universally accepted system of notation, that used by mathematics. Thus the glyphs that could be described in this manner form an equivalence class that is the character in question.

But are the names of characters always as clear and precise as these?

Unfortunately not. For example, we have a character that is described as the "double high-reversed-9 quotation mark". The "high-reversed-9" part of the description is neither linguistic nor logical but rather crudely graphical, even awkward. To describe this character, whose glyph is "‟", it would have been easier to call it the "second-level Greek opening quotation mark", because that is its most common use.

Fortunately the Unicode book and the PDF files that can be found at the Consortium's Web site (http://www.unicode.org/charts/) always supply with the description of each character a glyph that is called the *representative glyph*. It is not prescriptive, but its presence is extremely useful because it enables non-speakers of a language to identify the symbols described by their names. In the absence of representative glyphs, one would have to speak Tibetan in order to know that *dzud rtags bzhi mig can* is a cross made of four dots, and one would have to be a specialist in runes to know that the letter *ingwaz* is shaped like a diamond.

The representative glyph is not always sufficient when one is not familiar with a given writing system. Indeed, the glyphs that correspond to a given character may sometimes assume forms far removed from one another. That variation may be due to stylistic effects or historical reasons (the difference between '𝔚' and 'W' is considerable), or even to reasons of grammar. The latter is true in the case of Arabic, whose grammar provides that the letters assume different forms according to context and, more specifically, according to their position in the word. Thus the representative glyph for the character ARABIC LETTER KAF is 'ك', but within a word the same letter is rendered by a glyph similar to 'ﻚ', a shape that is not *a priori* trivial for the reader unfamiliar with the Arabic script to recognize.

The representative glyph is the only way to find an ideographic character, as those characters *have no description*. We might have imagined, for example, that the character 門 could be described as "character meaning 'gate' "; but since it also means "entrance", "section", "field", "disciple", "school", and "clan"—and all that in Japanese alone—, we can see that an attempt to represent the encoding's 70,027 ideographic characters in that manner would be a task as monumental as it would be futile. We shall see in Chapter 4 the specific problems that ideographs present.

Other characters do not have a glyph at all. That should come as no surprise to the reader, since even before ASCII there were encodings with *control characters* that had very precise semantics but did not need to be visually represented. Unicode goes even further: it is no longer restricted to sending messages to the central processing unit (such as "bell") or to peripheral devices (such as "carriage return") but extends even to the rendering of characters. Thus we have *combining characters* that affect the rendering of the preceding character(s). Often this modification involves adding an accent or a diacritical mark. In some cases, it involves graphically combining the preceding characters. There are many other applications of this possibility.

A string of Unicode characters can thus sometimes be more than a mere concatenation of symbols. It may be a sort of miniature program that tells the rendering engine how to proceed.

Another factor that distinguishes Unicode from other encodings is that its characters are more than mere descriptions and positions in a table. They have a certain number of *properties* thanks to which Unicode-compatible software is better equipped to render strings of characters visually or to process them. Let us take an example: in a document written in French and Khmer, the year 2006 may appear as "2006" or "២００៦". To keep us from having to search for two different strings, an intelligent text editor would only

Figure 2-1: When scripts are mixed.... [Photo taken in Athens by the author.]

have to look up the properties of the characters '௨', 'O', and 'ᦉ' to learn that they are digits whose numeric values are precisely 2, 0, and 6—and *voilà!*

Of course, that does not work for numeration systems such as those of the Romans (in which 2006 is written "MMVI"), the Greeks (",κς'"), and the Chinese ("二〇〇六"), but it hardly matters: using Unicode properties, software can process Unicode data in an intelligent way without having to reinvent the wheel. Chapter 3 is dedicated to Unicode character properties.

Another characteristic of the relationships between characters and glyphs: for reasons that are usually historical, the same glyph can represent multiple characters. Only context enables one to identify the character visually. Thus when we write 'H' in an English-language context such as this book, it is clear that we are using the eighth letter of the Latin alphabet. But the same glyph in the word "ΓΙΑΝΝΗΣ" (which is the author's first name) or in the word "Ηρεμία" (*Ēremia* = 'tranquillity') represents the Greek letter *eta*. Yet mixtures of writing systems are not always impossible, as shown by the photo taken in Athens that appears in Fig. 2-1. In it we see the word "PARKING" that starts off in Greek letters and ends with Latin ones, passing through the letters 'K', 'I', and 'N', which are common, both graphically and phonetically, to the two scripts. Finally, the same glyph in a word such as "PECTOPAH" (= 'restaurant') or "Наташа" (= 'Natasha') is ordinarily recognized right away as the Cyrillic letter 'N' (except by the various Western tourists who believe that restaurants in Russian are called *pektopah...*). In the case of the glyph 'H', the lower-case versions enable us to identify the character unambiguously: 'h', 'η', 'н'. There are also Unicode characters that have the same glyph yet belong to the same writing system: 'Đ' can be the Icelandic letter *eth* (lower-case 'ð') or the Croatian letter *dje* (lower-case 'đ'). The glyph 'ά' may represent either GREEK SMALL LETTER ALPHA WITH TONOS or GREEK SMALL LETTER ALPHA WITH ACUTE: in the first instance, the acute accent is regarded as the single accent of the "monotonic" system; in the second instance, it is an ordinary acute accent. Even worse, there are Unicode characters belonging to the same writing system that have the same glyphs and the same semantics: the ideographic characters in the "CJK compatibility" block. These are characters that the Koreans encoded twice because those characters have two distinct pronunciations in their language. If the Japanese had done the same, we would have twenty or even thirty identical copies of certain ideographic characters...

Which brings us to a fact that justifies to a large degree the inconsistency of certain parts of Unicode: among the principles of Unicode, there is one that often comes into conflict with the others, the *principle of convertibility*. This principle stipulates that all data encoded in an official or industrial encoding that is in sufficiently wide use must be convertible to Unicode without loss of information. In other words, and with a little less tact: every wacky, exotic, vaguely defined, arcane, and often completely useless character that exists today in any of the designated encodings is elevated to the rank of *Unicode character*. Let's just consider a few examples that arose in Chapter 1: the "universal currency sign"? It is in Unicode. The graphical symbols in the DOS code pages that were used to draw user interfaces? They are in Unicode. The self-standing accent marks that we used to add to letters by backspacing? They are present as well. The Koreans encode certain ideographs twice? Unicode follows their lead.

What is to be gained by having certain characters appear in the encoding twice? Nothing. Only the principle of convertibility has forced us to spurn all the other noble principles and accept as characters certain symbols that are not. When a Korean document containing two characters with the same glyph but with different pronunciations is converted to Unicode, those two characters are mapped to different code points in Unicode, which makes it possible to convert back to the original Korean encoding.

First principles

When we launch a project of Unicode's size, it is essential to define a certain number of first principles on which we can subsequently fall back when decisions, often delicate ones, must be made. Even if leaning on our principles too much causes them to bend, in the words of Italian author Leo Longanesi. Unicode is based on ten principles—a highly symbolic number—which we shall describe in this section. The Unicode book, however, warns us that the ten principles cannot be satisfied *simultaneously*: there will always be trade-offs and compromises to be made. Our task is to figure out which compromises those are.

Here, then, are the ten principles.

Principle #1: universality

Unicode concerns itself with *all living writing systems* and with most historic ones. That aim, expressed in those terms, sounds inordinately ambitious; but if we weight writing systems by the number of documents actually available in electronic format, then Unicode is not far from achieving its goal.

Principle #2: efficiency

It sounds like a slogan out of an advertisement from the 1950s. But it contains a kernel of truth. From the technical point of view, Unicode has enabled us to rid ourselves of escape characters, the states of ISO 2022, and so on. And it is undeniable that the documentation that comes with Unicode (the book, the Web site, the technical reports, the proceedings of the Unicode conferences) is more efficient than the dry, sterile commentary of the ISO standards, when that commentary exists at all. Functions, special characters, algorithms—all are described in minute detail, annotated, explained, and made accessible and ready for implementation.

Principle #3: the difference between characters and glyphs

As we have just discussed in the previous section, *characters* and *glyphs* are two totally different concepts, and Unicode is concerned only with the former. Even though it has not yet managed to provide a satisfactory definition of what a character is, Unicode at least deserves credit for having raised the issue and for having led people to understand the confusion that used to reign in this regard.

Principle #4: the well-defined semantics of characters

This principle harks back to what we were said about principle #2: Unicode has undertaken the formidable task of investigating writing systems and documenting its standard. As much as possible, characters are well defined, and their definitions clearly show what they are and what they are not. Knowing the meaning of each of the characters in our documents is important, for this knowledge is the very basis for the storage of textual data.

Principle #5: plain text

Who has never said to a colleague or a friend: "Send me that document in ASCII"? Yet a document in French, Swedish, or Spanish[1] can hardly be encoded in ASCII, since it will necessarily contain accented characters. What we mean by this expression is that we want a document in "plain text" format, which means a file containing nothing but miles and miles of text without the slightest bit of markup and without a single binary character that would turn it into a word-processing file. Unicode encodes nothing but text; it has no need for markup or—within practical limits—formatting characters. All information is borne by the characters themselves.

In fact, there is a rather ambiguous relationship between Unicode and, for example, XML. They complement each other perfectly and desperately need each other:

- The basic units of an XML document are, by definition, Unicode characters; therefore, without Unicode, there would be no XML.

---

[1] We have not added German to this list because, theoretically, the German umlauts 'ä' 'ö' and 'ü' can be written as the digraphs 'ae', 'oe', 'ue', and the *es-zet* 'ß' can be written as 'ss'. Nevertheless, these rules have exceptions: no one will ever write 'Goethe' as 'Göthe', and the words 'Maße' and 'Masse' are not the same....

- On the other hand, a certain type of information, such as the direction in which a paragraph is laid out, is best expressed by a high-level protocol such as XML rather than by examining the first letter of the paragraph to check whether it reads from left to right or from right to left (see Chapter 4). In addition, the language of a paragraph can be better indicated with XML's markup attribute xml:lang than by the completely artificial linguistic labels of Unicode (see p. 88).

Nonetheless, Unicode continues to disregard XML. Under the pretext that all of Unicode's functionality must be accessible even under the most restrictive protocol (such as URLs, for example), Unicode attempts to mark up a certain number of things itself, without relying on any other markup system. That is without a doubt the true meaning of principle #5.

Principle #6: logical order

How should the bytes be stored inside the computer: from right to left or from left to right? This question is meaningless because bits have no material substance. But we cannot keep from thinking of bytes as little boxes or rectangles that are arranged in a certain direction. This false notion stems, no doubt, from the fact that we confuse the interface of the low-level editor that we use with the actual functioning of the computer. This same false notion leads us to suppose that the natural order of our language is the order used by the computer and that languages written from right to left should be encoded backwards.

Unicode sets things straight. The reading of a document is an action situated in time that, like any other such action, has a certain inherent logical order. Unicode data are encoded in that order, and there is nothing material about the arrangement; therefore, there is no indication of direction. The issue of the direction in which text reads does not arise until the very moment when we begin to present the data visually. The way to render a document containing scripts that run in different directions may be very complex, even if the order in which the text is encoded is strictly logical. To convince ourselves of this fact, we need only read a text of this sort aloud: we will see that we follow the arrangement of Unicode-encoded data very precisely.

Principle #7: unification

To save space and to accommodate all the ideographic characters within fewer than 65,536 code points, Unicode decided to identify the ideographs of Chinese origin that are used in mainland China (the simplified Chinese script), in Taiwan and Hong Kong (traditional Chinese), in Japan, and in Korea. This *unification* was praised by some, criticized by others. We shall explain its ins and outs in Chapter 4, starting on page 148.

Principle #8: dynamic composition

Some Unicode characters possess special powers: when placed after another character, they modify its glyph. This modification usually involves placing an accent or a diacritical mark somewhere around the glyph of the base character. We call these characters *combining characters.* The most interesting feature of these characters is that they can combine with each other and form glyphs with multiple accents, with no limit to the number or the position of the accents and diacritical marks. Their drawback is that they have no respect for the principle of efficiency: if, within a Unicode string, we select a substring that begins with a combining character, this new string will not be a valid string in Unicode. Such an outcome never occurs in a string in ASCII or ISO 8859, and that fact gives Unicode a bit of a bad reputation. It is the price to pay in order to enjoy the power of dynamic composition. We shall describe the combining characters in detail in Chapter 4.

Principle #9: equivalent sequences

For reasons that arise from the tenth principle, Unicode contains a large number of "precomposed" characters—characters whose glyphs are already constructed from a base character and one or more diacritical marks. Principle #9 guarantees that every precomposed character can be decomposed, which means that it can be expressed as a string in which the first character is a base character and the following characters are all combining characters. We shall discuss this matter in detail in Chapter 4.

Principle #10: convertibility

This is the principle that has done the greatest harm to Unicode. It was nonetheless necessary so that the encoding would be accepted by the computer industry. The principle stipulates that conversion of data to Unicode from any recognized official or industrial encoding that existed before May 1993 could be done *with no loss of information.* This decision is fraught with consequences, as it implies that Unicode must inherit all the errors, imperfections, weaknesses, inconsistencies, and incompatibilities of the existing encodings. We have the almost Messianic image of a Unicode that "taketh away the sin of the world" for our redemption. Perhaps we are getting a bit carried away here, but the fact remains that 99.9% of Unicode's inconsistencies are due to principle #10 alone. We are told in the documentation that this or that thing exists "for historical reasons".

But there is a good side as well: there is no risk of losing the slightest bit of information when converting our data to Unicode. That is reassuring, especially for those of us who in the past have had to contend with the results of incorrect conversions.

Unwritten principle #11: permanent stability

We have taken the liberty of adding an eleventh principle to the list of official Unicode principles, one that is important and laden with consequences: *as soon as a character has been added to the encoding, that character cannot be removed or altered.* The idea is that a document encoded in Unicode today should not become unusable a few years hence, as is often the case with word-processing software documents (such as those produced with MS Word, not to name any names). Unlike the ten official principles, this one is so scrupulously respected that Unicode has come to contain a large number of characters whose use is *deprecated* by Unicode itself. Even more shocking is that the name of character 0x1D0C5 contains an obvious typo (FHTORA instead of FTHORA = φθορά); rather than correcting it, the Consortium has decided to let it stand and to insert a little note along the lines of "yes, we know that there's an error here; don't bother to tell us". We can only hope that the Consortium will allow for minor corrections in the future when they would have little effect on data encoded in Unicode.

Technical issues: characters and bytes

Even the philosophers say it: philosophy is not the only thing in life. And in the life of a Unicode user there are also issues of a strictly technical nature, such as the following: how are Unicode characters represented internally in memory? how are they stored on disk? how are they transmitted over the Internet? These are very important questions, for without memory, storage, and transmission there would be no information....

Those who have dealt with networks know that the transmission of information can be described by several layers of protocols, ranging from the lowest layer (the physical layer) to the highest (the application layer: HTTP, FTP, etc.). The same is true of Unicode: officially [347] five levels of representation of characters are distinguished. Here they are:

1. An *abstract character repertoire* (or "ACR") is a set of characters—that is, a set of "descriptions of characters" in the sense used in the previous section—with no explicit indication of the position of each character in the Unicode table.

2. A *coded character set* (or "CCS") is an abstract character repertoire to which we have added the "positions" or "code points" of the characters in the table. These are whole numbers between 0 and 0x10FFFF (= 1,114,111). We have not yet raised the issue of representing these code points in computers.

3. A *character encoding form* (or "CEF") is a possible way to represent the code points of characters on computers. For example, to encode characters on Unicode we usually need 21 bits; but the manner in which operating systems use internal memory makes it more efficient to encode these 21 bits over 32 bits (by leaving the first 11 bits unset) or as a series of wydes (16 bits) or of bytes. An encoding form may be of fixed length (like UTF-32) or variable length (like UTF-16 or UTF-8).

4. A *character encoding scheme*[2] for "CES") is a representation of characters in *bytes*. Allow us to explain: when we say, for example, that we encode Unicode characters with 21 bits within 32-bit numbers, that occurs at the level of internal memory, precisely because the internal memory of many computers today uses 32-bit units. But when we store these same data on disk, we write not 32-bit (or 16-bit) numbers but series of four (or two) bytes. And according to the type of processor (Intel or RISC), the most significant byte will be written either first (the "little-endian" system) or last (the "big-endian" system). Therefore, we have both a UTF-32BE and a UTF-32LE, a UTF-16BE and a UTF16LE. Only the encoding form UTF-8 avoids this problem: since it represents the characters in byte format from the outset, there is no need to encode

---

[2] We beg the reader's forbearance for the proliferation of jargon in this section. The terms used here are official terms taken directly from a Unicode technical report.

the data as a sequence of bytes. Also note that steps (1) to (4) taken collectively are called a "character map". The names of character maps are registered with IANA [186] so that they can be used within protocols such as MIME and HTTP. There are the following registered character maps for Unicode:

- UTF-8, a very efficient encoding form in which Unicode characters are represented over 1 to 4 bytes (see page 65).

- UTF-7, an unofficial encoding scheme that is quite similar to "base 64", described in RFC 2152;

- UTF-32, the encoding form in which we use the lowest 21 bits of a 32-bit number.

- UTF-32LE, the encoding scheme for UTF-32 in which a 32-bit number is encoded over four bytes in little-endian order, which means that the least significant byte comes first. This counterintuitive order is used by the Intel processors.

- UTF-32BE is similar to UTF-32LE but uses the big-endian order of the PowerPC, Sparc, and other processors.

- UTF-16, an encoding form in which Unicode characters are represented over one or two wydes (see page 64).

- UTF-16LE, the encoding scheme for UTF-16 in which a 16-bit number is encoded over two bytes in little-endian order.

- UTF-16BE, which is similar to UTF-16LE but uses big-endian order.

- UNICODE-1-1, version 1.1 of Unicode (described in RFC 1641).

- UNICODE-1-1-UTF-7, the former version of UTF-7 (described in RFC 1642).

- CESU-8 is a variant of UTF-8 that handles surrogates differently (see page 65).

- SCSU is a transfer encoding syntax and also a compression method for Unicode (see page 66).

- BOCU-1 is another compression method for Unicode, one that is more efficient than SCSU (see page 66).

The reader will certainly have noticed that UTF-16 and UTF-32, with no indication of endianness, *cannot* be encoded character maps. The idea is as follows: if we specify one of these, either we are in memory, in which case the issue of representation as a sequence of bytes does not arise, or we are using a method that enables us to detect the endianness of the document. We shall discuss the latter on page 64.

5. Finally, a *transfer encoding syntax* (or "TES") is a "transcription" that can occur at the very end to adapt data to certain transmission environments. We can imagine a conversion of the bytes from the encoding scheme into hexadecimal, "quoted-printable" (page 49), or "base 64" (page 49) so that they can be transmitted through a medium that does not accept binary-coded data, such as electronic mail.

In a conventional 8-bit encoding, steps (2) and (3) do not arise: there is no need to fill out our units of storage or to worry about big-endian or little-endian systems because we are already at the byte level. Things are not so trivial for the East Asian encodings that we have seen on page 48. In the case of Japanese, JIS X 0201-1976 is both an abstract character repertoire and a coded character set. It becomes an encoding form when we use 16 bits to represent its 94 × 94 tables. Finally, ISO 2022-JP, Shift-JIS, and EUC-JP are encoding schemes. And when we use them for electronic mail, we employ a transfer encoding syntax such as "quoted-printable" or "base 64".

Character encoding forms

Now a bit of history. In the beginning, Unicode was encoded with 16 bits, with little concern about endianness. At an early date, UTF-8 was put forward (under different names) to resolve a certain number of problems, such as the issue of endianness. At the same time, Unicode's bigger cousin, ISO 10646, proposed two encoding forms: UCS-4, which used 31 bits of a 32-bit number (thus avoiding the issue of how to know whether the number was signed or not), and UCS-2, which took the first wyde of this number and ignored the rest.

UTF-16 and surrogates

When the Consortium realized that 16 bits were insufficient, a trick was suggested: instead of extending Unicode by adding bits, we could reserve two areas for *surrogates*: the high and low surrogate areas. We would then take a surrogate pair consisting of two wydes: the first from the high area, the second from the low area. This approach would enable us to encode far more characters.

These areas are 0xD800-0xDBFF (the high surrogate area) and 0xDC00-0xDFFF (the low surrogate area). They give us $1,024^2 = 1,048,576$ supplementary characters encoded with two wydes. Thanks to surrogate pairs, we can obtain any character between 0x10000 and 0x10FFFF (Unicode's current limits). This is how we proceed: Let A be the code point of a character. We subtract 0x10000 from A to obtain a number between 0x00 and 0xFFFFF, which is therefore a 20-bit number. We divide these 20 bits into two groups:

        xxxxxxxxxxyyyyyyyyyy

and we use these groups to form the first and the second wydes of the surrogate pair, as follows:

        110110xxxxxxxxxx 110111yyyyyyyyyy

Detection of endianness

Consider a 16-bit number whose numerical value is 1. If this number is encoded in big-endian order, we will write to the disk 0x00 0x01, which corresponds to our intuition. On the other hand, if it is encoded in little-endian order, we will write 0x01 0x00. Unicode devised a very clever way to indicate the endianness of a block of text. The approach uses a character called the *byte order mark*, or "BOM". This character is 0xFEFF. This method works because the "inverse" of this character, namely 0xFFFE, is an invalid character. If at the beginning of a document the software encounters 0xFFFE, it will know that it must be reading the bytes in the wrong order.

We may well ask what happens to these parasitic BOMs. After all, if we cut and paste Unicode strings that contain BOMs, we may end up with a flurry of BOMs throughout our document. Not to worry: this character is completely harmless and should be ignored[3] by the rendering engine as well as by routines for searching, sorting, etc.

In the case of UTF-32, the BOM is the character 0x0000FEFF. There as well, its inverse, 0xFFFE0000, is not a character, as it greatly exceeds the limit of 0x10FFFF.

UTF-8 and CESU-8

UTF-8 is the most commonly used encoding form because it is the default character set for XML. It incorporates both an encoding form and an encoding scheme, as it consists of bytes. The idea is very simple: the 21 bits of a Unicode code point are distributed over 1, 2, 3, or 4 bytes that have characteristic high bits. From these bits, we can recognize whether a byte is the beginning of a sequence of 1, 2, 3, or 4 bytes or whether it occurs in the middle of one such sequence.

Here is how the bits are distributed:

Code point	Byte 1	Byte 2	Byte 3	Byte 4
00000 00000000 0xxxxxxx	0xxxxxxx			
00000 00000yyy yyxxxxxx	110yyyyy	10xxxxxx		
00000 zzzzyyyy yyxxxxxx	1110zzzz	10yyyyyy	10xxxxxx	
uuuuu zzzzyyyy yyxxxxxx	11110uuu	10uuzzzz	10yyyyyy	10xxxxxx

We can see that the first byte of a sequence begins with two, three, or four set bits, according to the length of the sequence. If a byte begins with a single set bit, then it occurs in the middle of a sequence. Finally, if a byte begins with a cleared bit, it is an ASCII character, and such characters are not affected by UTF-8. Thus we can see the key to the success of this encoding form: all documents written in ASCII—which means the great majority of documents in the English language—are already encoded in UTF-8.

The drawback of UTF-8 is that it is necessary to divide a string of bytes at the right place in order to obtain a string of characters. If we break a string of UTF-8 bytes just before an intermediate byte, we obtain an invalid string; therefore, the software may either reject it or ignore the intermediate bytes and start from the first byte that begins a sequence. It is therefore recommended, when manipulating strings of UTF-8 bytes, always to examine the three preceding bytes to find the byte that begins the nearest sequence.

---

[3] That has not always been the case. Indeed, the name of this character is ZERO-WIDTH NO-BREAK SPACE. The problem with this name is the "no-break" property. Before Unicode 3.2, this name was taken literally, and if BOM happened to fall between two syllables of a word, the word could not be broken at that point. But later another character was defined for that purpose, character 0x2060 WORD JOINER; and now the BOM is used only to detect byte order.

CESU-8 (*Compatibility Encoding Scheme for UTF-16: 8-bit*, [292]) is a curious blend of UTF-16 and UTF-8. In CESU-8, we start by converting our document into UTF-16, using surrogate pairs; then we convert each wyde into UTF-8. A document encoded in CESU-8 may take up more space than one encoded in UTF-8. Each wyde may thus need as many as three bytes for its representation; each pair of wydes, as many as six.

SCSU and BOCU

SCSU (*Standard Compression Scheme for Unicode* [353]) is a compression scheme for text encoded in Unicode. It was defined in a technical report by the Unicode Consortium. The principle is simple: we have a sort of "window" onto the Unicode table, a window 128 characters wide, whose exact location can therefore vary. Eight such "dynamically positioned" windows are available, which we can redefine at any time, and also eight "static" windows, whose locations are fixed.

In the initial state, we are in window 0. When we specify a shift to window n, the characters in the window become accessible through numerical values of only one byte each. More precisely, if the active window is window n, then a byte B between 0x00 and 0x7F is interpreted as being within the static window at an offset of B from the window's origin; and if B is a byte between 0x80 and 0xFF, then we go to dynamic window n and select the character located at an offset of $B - 128$ from that window's origin.

SCSU operates in two modes: the "compression" mode, in which bytes are interpreted as Unicode characters within a static or dynamically positioned window, and the "Unicode" mode, in which wydes are interpreted as UTF-16 sequences.

When we begin to (de)compress data, we are in the initial mode: "compression" mode, window 0 as the active window, all dynamically positioned windows in their default positions. Here are the fixed positions of the static windows and the default positions for the dynamically positioned windows:

#	static window	dynamically positioned window, by default
0	0x0000 (ASCII)	0x0080 (Latin 1)
1	0x0080 (Latin 1)	0x00C0 (Latin 1++)
2	0x0100 (Latin Extended-A)	0x0400 (Cyrillic)
3	0x0300 (Diacritical marks)	0x0600 (Arabic)
4	0x2000 (General punctuation)	0x0900 (Devanagari)
5	0x2080 (Currency symbols)	0x3040 (*Hiragana*)
6	0x2100 (Letterlike symbols)	0x30A0 (*Katakana*)
7	0x3000 (CJK symbols and punctuation)	0xFF00 (full-width ASCII)

There are six escape characters:

- SQU 0x0E (*Quote Unicode*), followed by a big-endian wyde: directly select the Unicode character specified by the wyde, irrespective of the windows. This is a temporary change of mode.

- SCU 0x0F (*Change to Unicode*): change to UTF-16 mode, irrespective of the windows. This is a permanent change of mode, in effect until another change is made.

- SQ*n* 0x01-0x08 (*Quote from Window n*, followed by byte *B*: if *B* is in the interval 0x00-0x7F, we use static window *n*; otherwise, we use dynamic window *n*. This is a temporary change of mode.

- SC*n* 0x10-0x17 (*Change to Window n*), followed by byte *B*: use dynamically positioned window *n* for all of the following characters in the range 0x80-0xFF and window 0 (ASCII) for the characters 0x09, 0x0A, 0x0D, and those in the range 0x20-0x7F. This is a permanent change of mode, in effect until another change is made.

- SD*n* 0x18-0x1F (*Define Window n*), followed by byte *B*: redefine dynamically positioned window *n* as the window whose index is *B*. How do we specify windows using an index? The reader who is expecting an elegant and universally applicable calculation will be disappointed. In fact, we use the following table:

Index *B*	Origin of the window	Comments
0x00		value reserved
0x01-0x67	$B \times 80$	the half-blocks from 0x0080 to 0x3380
0x68-0xA7	$B \times 80 + 0xAC00$	the half-blocks from 0xE000 to 0xFF80
0xA8-0xF8		values reserved
0xF9	0x00C0	Latin letters
0xFA	0x0250	Phonetic alphabet
0xFB	0x0370	Mutilated ("monotonic") Greek
0xFC	0x0530	Armenian
0xFD	0x3040	*Hiragana*
0xFE	0x30A0	*Katakana*
0xFF	0xFF60	Half-width *katakana*

- SDX 0x0B (*Define Extended*) followed by wyde *W*. Let W' be the first three bits of W and W'' the remaining bits ($W = 2^{13} \cdot W' + W''$). We redefine the dynamically positioned window whose index is W' as being at origin $0x10000 + 80 \cdot W''$.

We can notice a certain asymmetry between SQ*n* and SC*n*: the first allows us to use static windows 0 to 7, the second can only use static window 0. Only one question remains: when we are in Unicode mode, how do we switch back to "windows" mode?

The problem is that in Unicode mode the decompression algorithm is reading wydes. The solution is to provide it with wydes that it does not expect to see: those whose first byte is in the range 0xE0-0xF1. These wydes are in Unicode's private use area; to use them in Unicode mode, we have the escape character UQU (see below). When the decompression algorithm encounters such a wyde, it immediately switches to "windows" mode and interprets the wyde as a pair of bytes whose first character is an escape character from the following list:

- UQU 0xF0 (*Quote Unicode*), followed by a big-endian wyde: directly select the Unicode character specified by the wyde, without interpreting it as an escape character. This is a temporary change of mode.

- UC*n* 0xE0-0xE7 (*Change to Window n*), followed by byte *B*: same behavior as SC*n*.

- UD*n* 0xE8-0xEF (*Define Window n*), followed by byte *B*: same behavior as SD*n*.

- UDX 0xF1 (*Define Extended*), followed by wyde *W*: same behavior as UD*n*.

We can see that, as with most self-respecting compression schemes, there are more ways than one to compress data and the rates of compression obtained depend upon the skill of the compression algorithm: the judicious selection of dynamically positioned windows, switching to locking shift or the use of temporary escape sequences, etc. Thus we can use more or less sophisticated tools for compression by making several passes and compiling statistics and the like. But there is only a single approach to decompression, and it is quite simple to implement.

BOCU-1 (*Binary Ordered Compression for Unicode*, [313]) is another compression scheme; its performance is equal to that of SCSU, but it has some benefits of its own: it is MIME-compatible, and code point order is preserved. This final property implies that if we take a set of Unicode strings compressed in BOCU-1 and sort them, they will be arranged in the same order as the original strings. That could be convenient for a database: the fields would be compressed, yet they could still be sorted without first undergoing decompression.

Another major benefit of BOCU-1: it is "deterministic", in the sense that there is only one way to compress a string. That fact implies that we can compare compressed files: if they are different, then the decompressed originals will be different as well.

We shall not describe BOCU's compression algorithm in detail. The reader will find the description and some accompanying C code in [110], a document that starts with a fine French quotation from Montesquieu: "il faut avoir beaucoup étudié pour savoir peu" (you have to study a great deal to know a little). The idea behind this compression scheme is to encode the difference between two consecutive characters. Thus as long as we remain within the same script, we can encode our document with single bytes—provided that the script be "small". Writers will notice that this idea is not very efficient, as we often make "leaps" within the encoding to insert spaces or punctuation marks (which are shared by a large number of writing systems). Accordingly, the difference is determined not from the last character, but from the last *three* characters—an approach that reduces the differences.

The technique of using differences, which is also employed in compression algorithms such as MPEG, is of great interest because it starts from the notion that a document written in Unicode will reflect a certain consistency with regard to writing systems. A user may know N languages, which use M writing systems altogether (often $M < N$). There is a good chance that the user's documents are distributed across these writing systems,

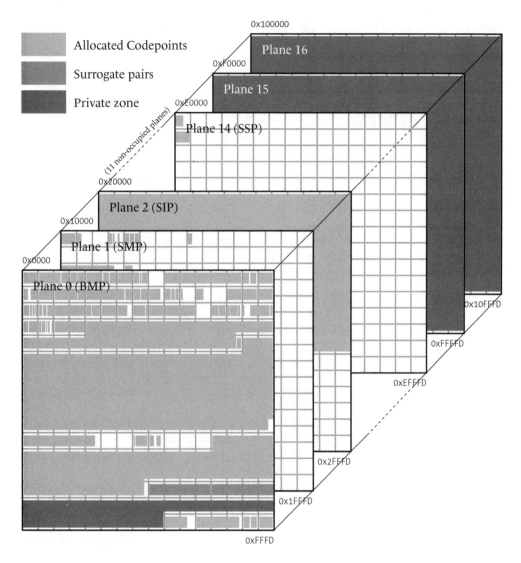

Figure 2-2: The six currently "populated" planes of Unicode (version 4).

which greatly reduces the range of characters used and ensures the success of a means of compression that is based on the proximity of characters.

We hope to see BOCU-1 compression used more and more in the years to come.

General organization of Unicode: planes and blocks

Code points may range from 0 to 0x10FFFF (= 1 114 111). We divide this range into 17 *planes*, which we number from 0 to 16. Of these 17 planes, only 6 are currently "populated" (see Fig. 2-2):

- Plane 0, or the BMP (Basic Multilingual Plane), corresponds to the first 16 bits of Unicode. It covers most modern writing systems.

- Plane 1, or the SMP (Supplementary Multilingual Plane), covers certain historic writing systems as well as various systems of notation, such as Western and Byzantine musical notation, mathematical symbols, etc.

- Plane 2, or the SIP (Supplementary Ideographic Plane), is the catchall for the new ideographs that are added every year. We can predict that when this plane is filled up we will proceed to Plane 3 and beyond. We shall discuss the special characteristics of ideographic writing systems in Chapter 4.

- Plane 14, or the SSP (Supplementary Special-Purpose Plane), is in some senses a quarantine area. In it are placed all the questionable characters that are meant to be isolated as much as possible from the "sound" characters in the hope that users will not notice them. Among those are the "language tag" characters, a Unicode device for indicating the current language that has come under heavy criticism by those, the author among them, who believe that markup is the province of higher-level languages such as XML.

- Planes 15 and 16 are Unicode's gift to the industry: they are private use areas, and everyone is free to use their codepoints in applications, with any desired meaning.

The BMP (Basic Multilingual Plane)

This plane—which for many years made up all of Unicode—is organized as follows:

[abcdefghij] The first block of 8 columns (0x0000-0x007F) is identical to ASCII (ISO 646).

[àáâãäåæçèé] The second block of 8 columns (0x0080-0x00FF) is identical to ISO 8859-1. The character 0x00AD SOFT HYPHEN represents a potential place to divide a word and therefore should not have a glyph (unless the word is divided at that point, in which case its glyph depends on the language and writing system). Do not confuse it with 0x2027 HYPHENATION POINT, which is the midpoint used in dictionaries to show where word division is permitted.

[āăąćĉċčd'đē] Still in the Latin alphabet, the *Latin Extended-A* block (0x0100-0x017F) which contains the characters of Central Europe, the Baltic countries, Maltese, Esperanto, etc.

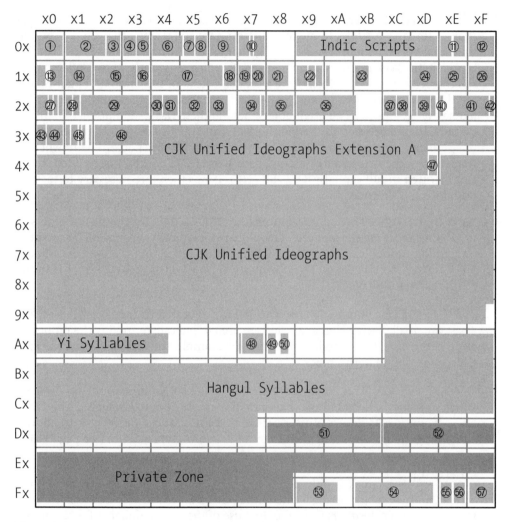

Figure 2-3: The roadmap of Unicode's Basic Multilingual Plane (BMP): ① ASCII and Latin 1, ② Latin Extended-A and -B, ③ phonetic alphabet and modifiers, ④ diacritical marks, ⑤ Greek (crippled by the monotonic reform) and Coptic, ⑥ Cyrillic, ⑦ Armenian, ⑧ Hebrew, ⑨ Arabic, ⑩ Syriac, Thaana and N'ko, ⑪ Thai and Lao, ⑫ Tibetan, ⑬ Myanmar and Georgian, ⑭ elements for forming hangul syllables, ⑮ Amharic, ⑯ Cherokee, ⑰ Canadian aboriginal scripts, ⑱ runes, ⑲ scripts of the Philippines, ⑳ Khmer, ㉑ Mongolian, ㉒ Limbu, Tai Le, etc., ㉓ Balinese, ㉔ phonetic extensions, ㉕ Latin Extended Additional, ㉖ Greek with accents and breathings (as it should be), ㉗ general punctuation, superscripts and subscripts, currency symbols, diacritical marks for symbols, ㉘ letterlike symbols, Roman numerals ㉙ arrows, mathematical and technical symbols, ㉚ graphic pictures for control codes, OCR, ㉛ enclosed alphanumerics, ㉜ geometric shapes, ㉝ miscellaneous symbols, ㉞ "Zapf dingbats", ㉟ braille, ㊱ supplemental arrows and mathematical symbols, ㊲ Glagolitic and Latin Extended-C, ㊳ Coptic disunified from Greek, ㊴ Khutsuri, Tifinagh and Ethiopic Extended, ㊵ Supplemental Punctuation, ㊶ ideographic radicals, ㊷ ideographic description characters, ㊸ ideographic punctuation, ㊹ kana, ㊺ bopomofo, hangul supplement, kanbun and CJK strokes, ㊻ enclosed ideographs and abbreviations used in ideographic writing systems, ㊼ Yijing hexagrams, ㊽ modified tone letters and Latin Extended-D, ㊾ Syloti Nagri, ㊿ Phags-pa, 51 high-half zone for surrogates, 52 low zone, 53 compatibility ideographs, 54 presentation forms A (Latin, Armenian, Hebrew, Arabic), 55 variation selectors and other oddities, 56 presentation forms B (Arabic), 57 full-width Latin letters and half-width katakana, specials.

[ƀɓɓɔcʼɗɖɜɘ] Wrapping up the series of Latin characters, the *Latin Extended-B* block (0x0180–0x024F), home to numerous rare and strange characters as well as some that Western linguists cobbled together for the African languages. Also in this block are the Romanian characters 'ş' and 'ţ', which previously were conflated with the characters 'ş' and 'ţ' (which have a cedilla instead of the comma). Finally, there are three digraphs—'dž', 'lj', and 'nj'—which are the Latin versions of the Cyrillic letters 'џ', 'љ', and 'њ'. The original idea behind these was to establish a one-to-one correspondence between the Serbian alphabet and the Croatian alphabet. But there is a problem: the upper-case version of the digraph will differ according to whether it appears as the first letter of a capitalized word ('Dž', 'Lj', 'Nj') or as a letter in a word written in full capitals ('DŽ', 'LJ', 'NJ'). It was therefore necessary to include both forms in Unicode.

[ɑɒɐɤʙʔɓɓƀβ] There are 6 columns (0x0250–0x02AF) for the special letters of the *International Phonetic Alphabet*. This alphabet is typically unicameral (*i.e.*, written only in lower case), except for those letters within it that are also used as ordinary letters in African languages. The upper-case versions of those letters appear in the "Latin Extended-B" block.

[hɦjrʴʶwyɣ] Five columns (0x02B0–0x02FF) are allocated to the *phonetic modifiers*. These are small spacing characters that are used to indicate or modify the pronunciation of the preceding or following letter. For example, the five tones of transcribed Chinese are found in this block.

[ò́ó̂ȭō̆ŏ̈öö̇ö̉] The block for *diacritical marks* (7 columns, 0x0300–0x036F), which contains the accents and other diacritical marks of most languages. This block also contains 0x034F COMBINING GRAPHEME JOINER, whose function is to allow a combining character to be applied to more than one glyph at once (see page 116).

[αβγδεζηθικ] Now we come to the block shared by *Greek* and *Coptic* (9 columns, 0x0374–0x03FC). Greek is only partly covered because the letters with breathings, accents, and *iota* subscripts are found in the "Greek Extended" block, which we shall see later. This block suffers from the dual use of the Greek alphabet for text in the Greek language and for mathematical formulae. Thus we find in it the two contextual forms of *beta*, 'β' and 'ϐ' (the former being used—in Greece and France—at the beginning of a word and the latter in the middle or at the end of a word), listed as separate characters. In addition, we find two versions each of *theta*, *phi*, *rho*, and *kappa*, which ordinarily are nothing but glyphs from different fonts, included here simply because they are used as distinct symbols in mathematics. Finally, there are some characters used as numerals (*sampi*, *koppa*, *stigma*) and some that are archaic or used in transcriptions.

[абвгдежзийй] Next comes the block for the *Cyrillic* alphabet (17 columns, 0x0400–0x0513), which covers three categories of symbols: the letters used for Russian and the other European languages written in the Cyrillic alphabet (Serbian, Macedonian, Bulgarian, Byelorussian, Ukrainian, etc.); the letters, diacritical marks, and numeric symbols of Old Cyrillic (an ancient script still used for liturgical documents); and finally the letters of the Asian languages written in the Cyrillic alphabet (Abkhaz, Azerbaijani, Bashkir, Uzbek, Tajik, etc.). The special Asian letters are no less contrived or strange than those of Latin Extended-B; once again, it was necessary to devise new letters on the basis of an existing alphabet to represent sounds in these languages that do not occur in Russian, and the results are sometimes startling.

[*արդդեգեթժ*] Between East and West, the *Armenian* alphabet (6 columns, 0x0530-0x058A), in which the '*և*' ligature is considered a character because it is used almost exclusively to represent the word "and" in Armenian.

[אבגדהווחטי] And now for the Semitic languages. First, *Hebrew* (7 columns, 0x0591-0x05F4), in which there are four types of symbols: the Masoretic cantillation signs (musical notation for the chanting of the Bible), the short vowels and semivowels, the Hebrew letters (with the final forms of the letters separately encoded), and finally the three ligatures used in Yiddish. Of these four categories, the first two are almost completely made up of combining characters.

[أبتثجحخدذ] Next comes *Arabic* (16 columns, 0x0600-0x06FF, and a supplement of 3 columns 0x0750-0x076D), where we find the letters, short vowels, and diacritical marks of Standard Arabic, the letters used by other languages written in the Arabic script (Persian, Urdu, Pashtu, Sindhi, etc.), and a certain number of signs used to guide recitation of the Koran and indicate its structure. Unlike those of Hebrew, the contextual forms of Arabic are not encoded as separate characters. Nevertheless, contextual forms and even ligatures of an æsthetic nature are encoded in the section for "presentation forms", near the end of the BMP. There is nothing inherently Arabic about the character '٭' 0x066D ARABIC FIVE POINTED STAR; it was provided only to ensure that a five-pointed asterisk would be available, as the ordinary asterisk '*', with its six lobes, might be mistaken for a Star of David in print of poor quality. Finally, there are two series of digits (0x0660-0x0669 and 0x06F0-0x06F9): the first matches the glyphs used in Arabic; the second, those used in the languages of Iran, Pakistan, and India.

[ܐܒܓܕܗܘܙܚܛܝ] *Syriac* (5 columns, 0x0700-0x074F) is the writing system of the Christian Arabs. Not being the national script of any country, it took a long time to be standardized and added to Unicode. The alphabet bears a vague resemblance to Arabic. There is a profusion of short vowels because two systems of vowel pointing are in use: a set of dots and a set of signs derived from the Greek vowels.

[ހށނރބޅކއވމ] The last writing system of this group is *Thaana* (4 columns, 0x0780-0x07B1). This script, inspired by Arabic, is used to write the Dhivehi language, spoken in the Maldives. A distinctive feature of Thaana is that the vowels *must* be written.

[ߒߝߓߞߖߘߚߡߠ] Between the Semitic and the Indic languages, Unicode v. 5 has managed to squeeze the very exotic script *N'Ko* (4 columns, 0x07C0-0x07FA). This is another artificial script, created by an African leader, Sulemana Kante, in 1948. It is used in Guinea, Côte d'Ivoire, and southern Mali.

[अकखगघङचछजझ] Now we come to the long list of writing systems of India. These have all been encoded according to a single phonetic principle. Accordingly, characters of the same pronunciation appear in the same location in the tables for the respective scripts. In addition, the writing systems are encoded in geographic order, from north to south. Thus the first script is *Devanagari* (8 columns, 0x0901-0x097F), which is still used for Hindi but also for Sanskrit. Since Sanskrit has a rich variety of phonemes, it comes as no surprise that the table for Devanagari is almost full whereas those for the languages of southern India become sparser as we go. We can also see that the letters' strokes are pointed in the north but rounder and rounder as we move southward, where most writing was done on palm leaves.

[অকথগয়ওচহজৰ] Second is *Bengali* (8 columns, 0x0981-0x09FA), used principally in Bangladesh.

[ਅਕਖਗਾਘੲਚਛਜੲ] Next comes *Gurmukhi* (8 columns, 0x0A01-0x0A74), which is used to write the Punjabi language, spoken in northern India.

[અકખગઘઙચછજઝ] *Gujarati* (8 columns, 0x0A81-0x0AF1), which looks like Devanagari without the characteristic horizontal bar.

[ଅକଖଗଘଟଚଛଜଝ] *Oriya* (8 columns, 0x0B01-0x0B71), a script noticeably rounder than the previous ones.

[அகஙசஜஞடணதந] *Tamil* (8 columns, 0x0B82-0x0BFA), without a doubt the best-known script in southern India. It is simpler than the scripts of the north, as can be seen at a glance from the Unicode table for Tamil, which contains only 69 characters, whereas the table for Devanagari contains 105.

[అకఖగఘఙచఛజఝ] *Telugu* (8 columns, 0x0C01-0x0C6F), a script rounder than that of Tamil that is used in the state of Andhra Pradesh.

[ಅಕಖಗಫಘಙಚಛಜಝ] *Kannada*, or *Kanarese* (8 columns, 0x0C82-0x0CF2), a script very similar to the previous one, used in the state of Karnataka.

[അകഖഗഘങചഛജ(ഞ)] *Malayalam* (8 columns, 0x0D02-0x0D6F), a script used in the state of Kerala.

[අකඛගඝඞඟචඡ] Finally, because south of the island of Sri Lanka there is nothing but the Indian Ocean, we have *Sinhala*, or *Sin(g)halese* (8 columns, 0x0D82-0x0DF4), a script composed almost entirely of curves, with a strong contrast between downstrokes and upstrokes.

[กขฃคฅฆงจฉช] Having finished the languages of India, we continue to those of Southeast Asia. We shall begin with the *Thai* script (8 columns, 0x0E01-0x0E5B), which was doubtless encoded first because of its flourishing computer market. Thai has diacritics for vowels and tone marks.

[ກຂຄງຈຊຍຕຖກ] Geographically and graphically close to Thai is *Lao* (8 columns, 0x0E81-0x0EDD). This script is simpler and rounder than Thai and also contains fewer characters.

[ཀཁགངཅཆཇཉཊ] We might have expected to find Khmer here, but that is not the case. We shall take a geographic leap and move from the tropical heat of the Mekong River to the cold peaks of the Himalaya, where *Tibetan* (16 columns, 0x0F00-0x0FD1) is spoken and written. This angular script operates according to the same principle as Khmer: when a consonant with no vowel is followed by a second consonant, the latter is written beneath the former. Unlike Khmer, Tibetan has codes for the subjoined consonants in its block.

[ခဂဃငစဆေ့ဇဈ] Next comes *Burmese* (or *Myanmar*) (10 columns, 0x1000-0x1059), the script of Burma, similar to the scripts of India as well as those of Southeast Asia.

[აბგდევზჱთ] Another geographic leap: we head off to the Caucasus to encode the *Georgian* script (6 columns, 0x10A0-0x10FC), which ordinarily should have been placed near Armenian. There have been several misunderstandings with regard to Georgian. The Unicode table speaks of "capital" Georgian letters (for example, GEORGIAN CAPITAL LETTER AN) and of caseless letters (GEORGIAN LETTER AN). In fact, the modern Georgian script is unicameral. Two issues gave rise to the confusion. First, the fact that there are two types of Georgian fonts: those for running text and those for titles. The former have glyphs with ascenders and descenders (see the sample above), whereas in the latter the glyphs are all of the same height and no depth: ჯჰმჟჳჱბჰჯ. Second, in the ancient Georgian script, *khutsuri*, there were indeed two cases. Thus we find in the Unicode table the capitals of *khutsuri* (ႠႡႢႣႤႥႦႧႨ) and the caseless letters of modern Georgian.

[ㄱㄲㄴㄷㄸㄹㅁㅂㅃㅅ] After Georgian comes a block of 16 columns (0x1100-0x11F9) containing the *basic elements of the Korean syllabic script hangul*. As we shall see later (page 155), these elements combine graphically within an ideographic square to form *hangul* syllables. Unicode also has a rather large area for precomposed *hangul* syllables.

[ሀለሐመሠረሰሸቀቐ] We continue to leap about. From Korea we leave for Ethiopia, since the following block is dedicated to the *Amharic* (or *Ethiopic*) script. This block is rather large (24 columns, 0x1200-0x137C with a supplement of another 2 columns 0x1380-0x1399) because the script is syllabic and all of the possible syllables (combinations of a consonant and a vowel) have been encoded. The block also contains punctuation, digits, and some signs used in numeration. Amharic is the only Semitic script written from left to right.

[**DRᏖᎣᎥᏕᎣᏁᎩ**] Next is a rather picturesque script, that of the Cherokee Indians, which is still used today by some 20,000 people. When this language had no writing system, a tribal chief devised one for it that was later adapted to printing. To facilitate the adaptation, capital Latin letters were selected—but in a way not compatible with their original phonetics—and sometimes slightly modified for use in writing Cherokee. An example: the Cherokee phonemes 'a', 'e', and 'i' are respectively written with the letters 'D', 'R', and 'T'. The *Cherokee* block occupies 6 columns (0x13A0-0x13F4).

[ᐁᎏᏟᏏᏟᏏᏟᎥᏟᏕ❹ᐳᐸᏗ] The Native Canadians also have a syllabary that was invented from scratch in 1830. This time, all sorts of geometric shapes were employed. Unicode has collected symbols for some of Canada's indigenous languages in a 40-column block (0x1401-0x1676).

[ᚁᚂᚃᚄᚅᚆᚇᚈᚉᚊᚋᚌᚍᚎ] The next script is *Ogham* (2 columns, 0x1680-0x169C), a very ancient Irish script (5th century CE). It is made up of strokes written above or below a baseline. Note that the "blank space" (*i.e.*, the word separator) of this script is not a blank but a horizontal stroke.

[ᛒᛔᛦᛡᚷᚾᚼᚱᛈᚱ] Similar is the *runic* script (6 columns, 0x16A0-0x16F0), used by the Germanic, Anglo-Saxon, and Scandinavian peoples (the Vikings in particular) before the spread of the Latin script.

[ᜟᜱᜩᜳᜲᜰᜨᜬᜪᜮᜭ] Next come four blocks (2 columns each, 0x1700-0x1714, etc.) that cover four writing systems of the Philippines: *Tagalog* (see the sample above), *Hanunóo* (ᜢᜣᜤᜥᜦᜧᜨ), *Buhid* (ᝀᝁᝂᝃᝄᝅᝆᝇᝈᝉᝊᝋ), and *Tagbanwa* (ᝦᝧᝨᝩᝪᝫᝬᝮᝯᝰ). These scripts have the same structure, and their glyphs are so similar that they sometimes look like glyphs from the same script in different fonts.

[កខគឃងចឆជឈញ] Only now do we come to the block for *Khmer* (8 columns, 0x1780-0x17F9), the main script used in Cambodia. The script appears at this late point because it took a long time to be standardized.[4]

[᠎᠎ᠠᠡᠢᠣᠤᠥᠦ] After Khmer comes *Mongolian* (11 columns, 0x1800-0x18A9). This script is derived from Syriac (as it was taken to Mongolia by Syriac missionaries)

---

4 Worse yet, its standardization provoked a major diplomatic incident. The method used to encode this language is the same as for Thai; yet the Cambodians, including the Cambodian government, feel that their writing system should have been encoded according to the Tibetan model, *i.e.*, by setting aside Unicode code points for the subscript consonants. Not even the presence of a Cambodian government minister at a Unicode conference succeeded in getting the Khmer block in Unicode modified—a lamentable situation for an encoding that exists to serve the speakers of a language, not the blind pride of a consortium. Let us hope that this incident will be resolved by the next version of Unicode, before the Cambodian government turns to the United Nations or the International Court of Justice in The Hague....

but, unlike Syriac, it is written from top to bottom. Contextuality in Mongolian is so complex that Unicode has provided four characters whose purpose is to modify glyphs: three variation selectors (0x180B-0x180D) and a vowel separator (0x180E).

[ꡐꡓꡀꡍꡗꡗ꠲ꡣ꠪ꡗꠧ] *Limbu* (5 columns, 0x1900-0x194F) is a minority language in Nepal and northern India that is spoken by approximately 200,000 people.

[ꩰꩭꩢꩳꧏꧏꩡꩬ] *Tai Le* (3 columns, 0x1950-0x1974) is another Southeast Asian writing system.

[ꪙꪚꪛꪜꪝꪞꪟꪠꪡꪢ] The so called *New Tai Le* or *Xishuang Banna Dai* script (6 columns, 0x1980-0x19DF) which is also used by minorities in Southeast Asia.

[᧐᧑᧒᧓᧔᧕᧖᧗᧘᧙] The two columns 0x19E0-0x19FF contain combinations of *Cambodian letters and numbers* that are used in *lunar dates*.

[ᨀᨁᨂᨃᨄᨅᨆᨇᨈᨉ] Next comes *Buginese* (2 columns, 0x1A00-0x1A1F), a writing system used on the Indonesian island of Sulawesi (Celebes).

[ᬀᬁᬂᬃᬄᬅᬆᬇᬈᬉᬊ] *Balinese* (8 columns, 0x1B00-0x1B7C), the script of Bali, a province of Indonesia, used by nearly 3 million people. (Actually, the Balinese language is also written in the Latin script.)

[AÆꬱBCDƊE3I] Then there is a block of *phonetic letters* (8 columns, 0x1D00-0x1D7F, followed by a supplement of an additional 4 columns 0x1D80-0x1DBF) that extends the block of the International Phonetic Alphabet. It consists of Latin letters turned in various ways, some ligatures that are not very kosher, some small capitals, some Greek and Cyrillic letters, etc.

—— A small supplement to the block of diacritical marks (4 columns, 0x1DC0-0x1DFF).

[ạḅ̱ḇ̱ḅ̧ḑ̧ḍ̱ḍ̱ḏ̣ḏ̰] The *Latin Extended Additional* block (16 columns, 0x1E00-0x1EF9) contains characters that are useful for the transcription of Indian languages as well as for Vietnamese and Welsh.

[ᾶέ᾿ῆἰ᾿ō̓ῧ᾽ō̄ή᾽ᾳ̣ρ̣] After this tour of the world of characters, and in last place before the non-alphabetic characters, finally comes *regular Greek* (16 columns, 0x1F00-0x1FFE), which Unicode calls "Greek Extended". This block contains the Greek letters with accents, breathings, and the *iota* subscript, which uneducated Greek engineers had the nerve to separate from the unaccented Greek letters. The acute accent, sole survivor of the massacre known as the "monotonic" reform (see [169, 166]), appears over letters in the first block and the second block alike: in the first block, Unicode calls it TONOS (= 'accent'); in the second block, OXIA.

[——', ''""," "] We have reached a turning point in the BMP: the block for *general punctuation* (7 columns, 0x2000-0x206F). This table contains punctuation marks that were not included in ASCII and ISO 8859-1 (the true apostrophe ''', the English double quotation marks ' "" ', the German quotation marks ',,', the dagger and double dagger '†' '‡', the en dash '–', the em dash '—', etc.), some proofreading symbols, and other similar characters. There is also a set of typographic spaces: the em quad, en quad, three-per-em space, four-per-em space, six-per-em space, thin space, hair space, zero-width space (a space that ordinarily has no width but may result in increased spacing during justification). There are also a certain number of control characters: zero-width joiners and non-joiners, together with indicators of the direction of the text, which we shall see on page 142. Finally, for use in entering mathematical formulae, an invisible character placed between a function and its argument, another that indicates multiplication, and a third that acts as a comma in a list of symbols.

[0i456789+⁻] The digits and parentheses as *superscripts and subscripts* (3 columns, 0x2070-0x2094).

[₠₡₢₣₤₥₦₧₨₩₪] The *currency symbols* (3 columns, 0x20A0-0x20B5), where we find the euro sign and also a number of symbols that have *never* been used, such as those for the ecu '₠', the drachma '₯', and even the French franc '₣'.

[◉◻◈◎◌◌ ◻ ◌◲◿◠◍] *Diacritical marks for symbols* (3 columns, 0x20D0-0x20EF). These include various ways to modify a symbol: striking through it, encircling it, enclosing it in a triangle in the manner of European road signs, etc.

[℀℁ℂ°℃℄℅℆ℇ℈℉] The *letterlike symbols* (5 columns, 0x2100-0x214E). These are letters of the alphabet, sometimes rendered in a specific font, alone or in groups, that acquire a special meaning in a given context. Thus we have the signs for degrees Celsius '°C', the rational numbers 'ℚ', the real part of a complex number 'ℜ', the first transfinite cardinal number 'ℵ', and many other symbols of this kind, which become more exotic and eccentric as one proceeds down the chart.

[⅓⅔⅕⅖⅗I Ⅱ Ⅲ Ⅳ Ⅴ] *Fractions* and *Roman numerals* (4 columns, 0x2153-0x2184). A slight Eurocentric *faux pas* in Unicode: of *all* the numeration systems based on letters (the Greek, the Hebrew, the Arabic, etc.), *only* Roman numerals are provided in Unicode.

[←↑→↓↔↕↖↗↘↙] All kinds of *arrows* (7 columns, 0x2190-0x21FF), pointing in every direction.

[∀ℂ∂∃∄∅∆∇ ∈] *Mathematical symbols* (16 columns, 0x2200-0x22FF).

[⌘⌐⌛⌧⌨⌬⌿⏀⏁⏂] *Technical symbols* (16 columns, 0x2300-0x23E7), which is a catchall for the symbols of numerous disciplines: drafting, industrial design, keys on the keyboard, chemistry, the APL programming language, electrical engineering, dentistry, etc.

[␀␁␂␃␄␅␆␇␈␉] Some graphic pictures for *control codes*, the space, the carriage return, etc. (4 columns, 0x2400-0x2426).

[⑀⑁⑂⑃⑄⑅⑆⑇⑈⑉] Characters specially designed for the *optical recognition* of check numbers, etc. (2 columns, 0x2440-0x244A).

[①②③⑴⑵⑶ⒶⒷⒸⓐ] *Letters and numbers in circles*, in parentheses, followed by a period, etc. (10 columns, 0x2460-0x24FF).

[─━│┃┄▀▁▂▃▄] The *graphical elements* inherited from the DOS code pages (10 columns, 0x2500-0x259F).

[■□▢▲△▴●◐◯◑◈] All kinds of *geometric shapes*: squares, circles, triangles, diamonds, etc. (6 columns, 0x25A0-0x25FF).

[☀☂☃☙☢☤☭☮☯♛] A hodgepodge of *miscellanous symbols* (16 columns, 0x2600-0x26B2): weather symbols, astrological symbols, telephones, cups of coffee, fleurons, the skull and crossbones, the sign for radioactive material, various religious symbols, symbols for various political ideologies, the peace sign and the yin–yang sign, the trigrams of the *Yijing*, some smilies, the planets, the constellations, chess symbols, playing-card symbols, some musical notes, the symbols for different types of recyclable materials, the faces of dice, the sign for high voltage, etc.

[✂✆✇✝✠✡✹✺✻❞] In honor of a great typeface designer who shall remain nameless, this block contains the glyphs from the font *Zapf Dingbats*, made into Unicode characters (12 columns, 0x2701-0x27BE).

— Some more *mathematical and technical symbols* (4 columns, 0x27C0-0x27FF).

[⠀⠁⠂⠃⠄⠅⠆⠇⠈⠉⠊⠋] The 256 *braille patterns* (16 columns, 0x2800-0x28FF).

— More *arrows* (8 columns, 0x2900-0x297F).

— And still more *mathematical symbols*, each rarer and more eccentric than the one before it (25 columns, 0x2980-0x2B23).

[ⰀⰁⰂⰃⰄⰅⰆⰇⰈⰉⰊ] Before moving to the Far East, a bit of history: *Glagolitic* (6 columns, 0x2C00-0x2C5E), was used in Russia and probably invented by Saint Cyril in AD 862 for the translation of the Scriptures into Old Church Slavonic. It was later replaced by the Cyrillic script, but the order and the names of the letters were retained.

— And, as if weird versions of Latin letters never end, another small supplement called *Latin Extended-C* (2 columns, 0x2C60-0x2C77).

[ⲁⲃⲅⲇⲉⲋⲍⲏⲑⲓ] *Coptic*, which is finally completely disunified from Greek (8 columns, 0x2C80-0x2CFF).

[ⴰⴱⴲⴳⴴⴵⴶⴷⴸⴹⴺ] Followed by *Nuskhuri* (3 columns, 0x2D00-0x2D25), the lower-case version of the Georgian liturgical khutshuri letters, the upper-case ones being included in the Georgian block. This block corrects Unicode's mistake of mixing the modern Georgian alphabet with the ancient liturgical alphabet.

[ⵀⵁⵂⵃⵄⵅⵆⵇⵈⵉⵊⵋ] *Tifinagh* (5 columns, 0x2D30-0x2D6F), the writing system of the Berbers, still widely used in Algeria in the province of Tizi-Ouzou and also taught in the public schools of Morocco.

—— A supplement to the Amharic script: 6 columns, 0x2D80-0x2DDE.

—— And, to prove the fact that any block can be supplemented, a supplement to... punctuation: 8 columns, 0x2E00-0x2E1D.

[⺀⺁⺂⺃⺄⺅⺆⺇⺈⺉⺊⺋] Now we have reached another turning point in the BMP: this is where the scripts of the Far East begin. The ideographs can be described by their *radicals*, which are encoded here in the first two blocks. But there are two ways to represent the radicals: in isolation, or in the form that they assume when they are combined with other radicals. The first block (8 columns, 0x2E80-0x2EF3) contains radicals represented according to the latter approach.

[⼀⼁⼂⼃⼄⼅⼆⼇⼈⼉] The next block (14 columns, 0x2F00-0x2FD5) contains all of the *ideographic radicals* as they are represented in isolation.

—— The *ideographic description characters* (1 column, 0x2FF0-0x2FFB) are characters whose purpose is to suggest ways to form new ideographs from existing Unicode ideographic characters. It is as if we were to take the glyphs of two or three of the characters in the preceding blocks and combine them to form the glyph of a character not available in Unicode. This is one way to obtain millions of new ideographs, but its direct implementation in software would likely yield rather poor results, as ideographs are seldom just simple graphical combinations of other ideographs. We shall discuss the creation of new ideographs on page 153.

[、。〃〄々〆〇〈《「」] Now we have come to *ideographic punctuation* and *ideographic symbols* (4 columns, 0x3000-0x303F). We also find here the ideographic space, quotation marks, different types of brackets, the Japanese postal symbol, etc. A rather special character is 0x303E IDEOGRAPHIC VARIATION INDICATOR, which indicates that the following ideograph is not exactly what is intended and that it should be construed as one of its variant forms (cf. p. 150).

[かきくけこさしすせそ] *Hiragana* (6 columns, 0x3041-0x309F), a Japanese syllabary. Two *hiragana* used before World War II are also listed here.

[カキクケコサシスセソ] *Katakana* (6 columns, 0x30A0-0x30FF), another Japanese syllabary, used for foreign words. Two *katakana* used before World War II and a number of dialectal signs also appear in this block.

[ㄅㄆㄇㄈㄉㄊㄋㄌㄍㄎ] *Bopomofo* (3 columns, 0x3105-0x312C) is an attempt at an alphabetic script for Chinese that is used to represent ideographs phonetically. The influence of the Japanese *kana* is obvious.

—— Next is a "compatibility" block, *i.e.*, a table of useless characters added only for the sake of compatibility with an existing encoding. This particular block contains the *basic elements Korean syllabic hangul script* (6 columns, 0x3131-0x318E). Whereas the basic elements of block 0x1100-0x11F9 combine to form syllables, those in this block do not (see p. 155 for more explanation).

[一二三四上中下甲乙丙] A small block of ideographs written as superscripts, the *kanbun* (1 column, 0x3190-0x319F). These characters are very interesting because they show how the cultures of East Asia are connected through the ideographic writing system. A Chinese poem is automatically a poem in Japanese as well, with one difference: the order of the ideographs may not be correct. The *kanbun* serve to indicate a reading order appropriate to the Japanese reader to understand the poem.

—— A supplementary set of phonetic *bopomofo*, *CJK strokes* and *katakana* (4 columns, 0x31A0-0x31FF).

[㈱㈮㈯㊚㊛㊤1月2月3月㊥] Next comes a block of encircled ideographs, of *katakana* and *hangul* in circles or parentheses, of numbers (either Chinese or Arabic) in circles or parentheses, and of symbols for months (16 columns, 0x3200-0x32FE).

[1月2月3月㊥㌔㌘㌖22点23点24点] And a block of *ideographic abbreviations* (16 columns, 0x3300-0x33FF). These are groups of 4 to 6 *katakana* within an ideographic square or Latin abbreviations for such things as units of measure, also within that type of square.

—— After the abbreviations, we step right into the vast pool of ideographic characters. Before starting on the basic characters, we have the *CJK Unified Ideographs Extension A*: 432 columns, 0x3400-0x4DB5 (6,582 ideographs).

[䷀䷁䷂䷃䷄䷅䷆䷇䷈䷉] A short interlude before the big section of ideographic characters: the hexagrams from the *Yijing* (4 columns, 0x4DC0-0x4DFF), a Chinese book of divination.

[一丁丂七丄龠龥龦龧顧] Then come the unified ideographs: 1306 columns, 0x4E00-0x9FBB (20,924 ideographs).

[ꀀꀁꀂꀃꀄꀅꀆꀇꀈꀉ] After the ideographs and before the *hangul* syllables come the syllables of *Yi*, a writing system from southern China. Yi, a rather young writing system (only five centuries old), is in fact ideographic. There are between 8 and 10 thousand Yi ideographs, but they are not yet encoded in Unicode. On the other hand, a syllabary was invented in the 1970s to facilitate the learning of this language, and it is this syllabary that Unicode includes (84 columns, 0xA000-0xA4C6).

—— A block with modifier tone marks for Chinese: 2 columns, 0xA700-0xA71A.

—— Did you think that there were enough Latin letters in this encoding? Well, the Uni-code Consortium did not agree with you. Here comes another supplemental block for Latin letters, called "Latin Extended-D". For the moment it contains only two characters (0xA720 and 0xA721), but there is room for many more, since 14 columns have been reserved for this block.

[ꠀꠁꠂꠃꠄꠅ꠆ꠇꠈ] Another previously forgotten script: *Syloti Nagri* (3 columns, 0xA800-0xA82B), the alphabet of the Sylheti language, spoken by ten million Indians in Bangladesh. The script, which closely resembles that of Bengali, dates from the fourteenth century, and works written in it were still being printed up to the 1970s.

[ꡀꡁꡂꡃꡄꡅꡆꡇꡈ] Another relic of history: *Phags-pa* (4 columns, 0xA840-0xA877), invented by a Tibetan lama in 1269 under commission from Mongolian leader Khubilai Khan to serve as the new Mongolian alphabet. The most recent text in this script is from 1352.

[가각간갇갈갉갊감갑값] Next comes the list of the most common *hangul* syllables: 698 columns, 0xAC00-0xD7A3 (11,172 syllabes).

—— Zones 0xD800-0xDBFF and 0xDC00-0xDFFF are used to encode the characters be-yond the BMP in UTF-16. These two zones are called the *high-half and low-half surro-gate zones*.

—— Between 0xE000 and 0xF8FF is the private use area, where we are free to place any characters that we wish.

—— Then follows a block of *compatibility ideographs* (included twice in a Korean encod-ing, in Big-5, in an IBM encoding, and in JIS X 0213) (32 columns, 0xF900-0xFAD9).

—— From 0xFB00 to 0xFDFD and from 0xFE70 to 0xFEFF are characters called *presentation forms*. These are glyphs that have, for one or another reason, been given the status of characters. More precisely, these characters include a handful of Latin ligatures (including the "f-ligatures"), five Armenian ligatures, some widened Hebrew letters (to facilitate justification), some Hebrew letters with vowel points and Yiddish letters with vowels, one Hebrew ligature, the contextual forms of the Arabic letters, and a large number of æsthetic Arabic ligatures. There is even a single character 'ﷺ' for the phrase "In the name of Allah, the Beneficent, the Merciful" (actually made of ** characters), which appears at the beginning of every sura in the Koran. The Unicode Consortium discourages the use of these presentation forms.

—— A small block (1 column, 0xFE00-0xFE0F) contains control characters that indicate a glyphic variant of the preceding character. There are 16 characters of this kind; thus 16 different variants of the same glyph can be used in a single document. Another 240 characters of the same kind are found in Plane 14.

—— A one-column block with variants of Latin and CJK punctuation for vertical type-setting: 0xFE10–0xFE19.

—— The two halves of a horizontal parenthesis and a horizontal tilde (1 column, 0xFE20–0xFE23).

—— Various ideographic punctuation marks whose glyphs are adapted for vertical type-setting (2 columns, 0xFE30–0xFE4F).

—— Smaller glyphs for certain ideographic punctuation marks (1 column, 0xFE50–0xFE6B).

—— Code point 0xFEFF is the *byte order mark* (BOM), a character that we are free to place at the beginning of a document. It makes it possible to determine whether the file was saved in little-endian or big-endian format. The system works because the inverse of this character (code point 0xFFFE) is not a Unicode character.

[a b c d e f g h i j , ｶｷｸｹｺｻｼｽｾｿ] To wrap up the BMP with a flourish, this block contains full-width ASCII characters (the size of ideographs) as well as half-width *katakana* and *hangul* elements (15 columns, 0xFF01–0xFFEE).

—— Finally, in the last block of the BMP, we have *special characters*: first, three characters for interlinear annotations, a means of presentation of which one possible interpretation involves adding small characters above the characters of the main text, which could be used for a translation into another language or to indicate the pronunciation of the main text. They are very frequently used in Japan, where the *kanji* ideographs are annotated with *kana* so that they can be read by schoolchildren and teenagers who do not yet have a sufficient command of the ideographs. If *A* is the annotation of *T*, then Unicode offers a character 0xFFF9 to place before *T*, a character 0xFFFA to place between *T* and *A*, and a character 0xFFFB to place after *A*.

Another special character, 0xFFFC OBJECT REPLACEMENT CHARACTER, is used as a placeholder for an unspecified object.

Last of all, the final character of the BMP, 0xFFFD REPLACEMENT CHARACTER, is the recommended character for representing a character that does not exist in Unicode during conversion from an encoding not recognized by the Consortium.

Code points 0xFFFE and 0xFFFF do *not* contain Unicode characters.

Higher planes

Now that we have finished the BMP, which is worthy of Jules Verne's *Around the World in Eighty Days*, let us continue with Unicode's other planes, which are not yet heavily populated, at least for the time being.

Plane 1 is called the SMP (Supplementary Multilingual Plane). It consists of historic or unusual scripts:

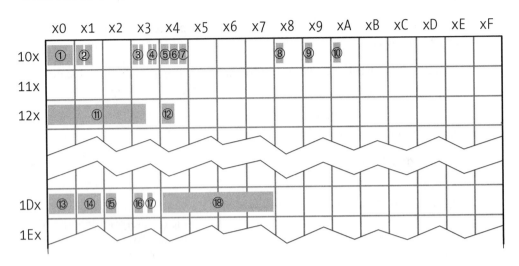

Figure 2-4: The roadmap of Unicode's Supplementary Multilingual Plane: ① *Linear B,* ② *Aegean and ancient Greek numbers,* ③ *Old Italic and Gothic,* ④ *Ugaritic and Persian cuneiform,* ⑤ *Deseret,* ⑥ *Shavian,* ⑦ *Osmanya,* ⑧ *the Cypriot syllabary,* ⑨ *Phœnician,* ⑩ *Kharoshthi,* ⑪ *cuneiform,* ⑫ *cuneiform numbers and punctuation,* ⑬ *Byzantine musical notation,* ⑭ *Western musical notation,* ⑮ *ancient Greek musical notation,* ⑯ *monograms, digrams, and tetragrams of the Yijing,* ⑰ *counting rod numerals,* ⑱ *Latin, Fraktur, and Greek letters used in mathematical formulae.*

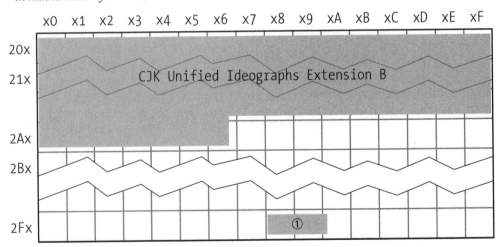

Figure 2-5: The roadmap of Unicode's Supplementary Ideographic Plane (SIP): ① *supplementary compatibility ideographs.*

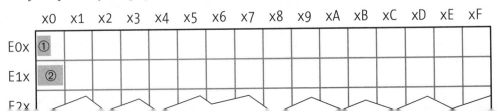

[𐀺𐀄𐀟𐀪𐀱𐀴𐀘] *Linear B* (16 columns, 0x10000-0x100FA), a Cretan writing system from the time of King Minos and his labyrinth for containing the Minotaur (2000 BC), which was deciphered by architect and amateur archæologist Michael Ventris in 1952. It is called "B" because there is a script known as "Linear A" that has not yet been deciphered. Linear A is not yet encoded in Unicode, doubtless because the Consortium is waiting for its decipherment so that sensible descriptions can be given to the signs.

[I II III ꞏꞏ ꞏ꞉ ꞉꞉ 𐄷 𐄸 𐄹 𐄺] The *Aegean numbers* (4 columns, 0x10100-0x1013F) are symbols derived from Linear A and identified as being numbers or units of measure.

[𐅀𐅁𐅂𐅃𐅄𐅅𐅆𐅇] They are followed by the *Greek numbers* (5 columns, 0x10140-0x1018A), which have been used over the centuries in quite a few systems of numeration. The numbers in the first two columns are called *acrophonic* because they are the first letters (*akron* = 'tip') of the names of the numbers. For example, 'Γ' = *pi* is the first letter of πέντε = 'five'.

[𐌀𐌁𐌂𐌃𐌄𐌅𐌈𐌙] The *Old Italic* block (3 columns, 0x10300-0x10323) contains the letters used by a certain number of ancient languages of the Italian peninsula, such as Etruscan, Oscan, Umbrian, etc. We can clearly discern the influence of Greek, but the nascent Latin alphabet is also recognizable.

[𐌰𐌱𐌲𐌰𐌴𐌿𐌶𐌷𐍈𐌹] *Gothic*[5] (2 columns, 0x10330-0x1034A) is the writing system of the Goths, Vandals, Burgundians, and Lombards used by the archbishop Wulfila in his Bible in AD 350. It greatly resembles the uncial script but also contains a number of Greek letters: *psi, lambda, pi, theta*, etc.

[𐎀𐎁𐎂𐎄𐎅𐎆𐎈𐎊𐎋𐎐] *Ugaritic* (2 columns, 0x10380-0x1039F) is one of the languages written in cuneiform. The cuneiform characters that it uses are letters of an alphabet. Incidentally, their names seem familiar to us: *alpa, beta, gamla, delta*, etc.

[𐎠𐎡𐎢𐎣𐎤𐎥𐎦𐎧𐎨𐎩] They are followed directly by another cuneiform writing system, *Old Persian* (4 columns, 0x103A0-0x103D5). The cuneiform scripts of Akkadian and Elamite have yet to be encoded in Unicode.

[𐐲𐐳𐐴𐐵𐐶𐐷𐐸𐐹𐐺] The following two blocks are controversial: they contain two artificial alphabets from the nineteenth century and the beginning of the twentieth century. The first is *Deseret* (5 columns, 0x10400-0x1044F), or the "Mormon alphabet", which was used for English-language texts (altogether *four* books and *one* tombstone!) between 1847 and 1869 and can be regarded as an attempt to isolate

---

[5] There seem to be multiple uses of the term "Gothic" in various languages. In US English it is used for the script of Wulfila, but also, more commonly, for sans-serif fonts. In French, Wulfila's script is called "gotique" (without the 'h'), and "gothique" is used for German broken scripts. Germans call the latter "German scripts" ("Deutsche Schrift"). The result of this linguistic imbroglio is that in the well-known comics "Asterix and the Goths", the words spoken by the Goths are written in a … broken script, which allows the author, Réné Goscinny, to compare the Goths with the pre-WWI Germans.

the Mormons culturally from the rest of the United States. Let us hope that other religions will not create their own new scripts, lest Unicode end up full of useless, unwanted alphabets.

[꠰꠰ꞇꞀꝋꞅꞇꞇꝋꝏ] The next alphabet, the *Shavian* alphabet (3 columns, 0x10450-0x1047F), contains an element of humor that is certainly due to the person responsible for its development, the great British humorist George Bernard Shaw (whence "Shavian", the adjectival form of "Shaw"). In his will, he provided for a contest to be held for the design of a new alphabet adapted to the phonetics of English. He died in 1950, the contest was held in 1958, and the alphabet encoded in Unicode was the winner. The letters have funny names: *ha-ha, church, thigh, gag, peep,* etc.

[𐒗𐒝𐒒𐒖𐒁𐒎𐒊𐒆0789𐒒] *Osmanya* (3 columns, 0x10480-0x104A9) was invented in 1922 by a certain Cismaan Yuusuf Keenadiid, a high-ranking figure in Somalia. It was destined to become the country's official script, but in 1969 a coup d'état decided otherwise. Although letters look nothing like those of Arabic, their names (*alif, ba, ta, dja, …*) betray Arabian cultural influence.

[✳✳✳♉⟰Ⓞⱳ⬆⤬⟰] We return to ancient times with the *Cypriot syllabary* (4 columns, 0x10800-0x1083F), a script influenced by Linear B and used on the native island of the goddess Venus between 800 and 200 BC.

[𐤊𐤇𐤉𐤄𐤆Y𐤉Ⓘ⊟⊕𐤒] *Phœnician* (2 columns, 0x10900-0x1091F) is the ancestor of the Greek alphabet and those of the Semitic languages. It was used between the 20th and the 2nd centuries BCE.

[𐨍𐨁𐨕𐨤𐨆𐨸𐨌𐨫𐨎꣸] Let us now leave the Mediterranean and take a trip to the Far East with *Kharoshthi* (6 columns, 0x10A00-0x10A58), a historical writing system of northeastern India. Just like the Brahmi script, it has been used to write the Sanskrit language.

[𒀭 𒈾𒌷 𒀀𒀭 𒂗𒄖 𒉿𒀀 𒋾𒈝 𒊩𒈬 𒋫𒁉 𒂖 𒅆] One of the big novelties of Unicode v. 5 is the beautiful *cuneiform* script. It occupies no fewer than 64 columns (positions 0x12000-0x1236E), and another 8 columns (0x12400-0x12473) for numbers and punctuation. Some of the glyphs are quite complex.

[𝁙𝁚꣯. 𝁓𝁔𝁕𝁖𝁗𝁘𝁀] After the big cuneiform block, we find two blocks devoted to music. We begin with the *notational system used for Byzantine music*[6]

---

[6] This block demonstrates that Unicode's inviolable principle of not changing a character's description once the character has been adopted leads to the most ridiculous results. The *English* description of the character 0x1D0C5 contains the word FHTORA, which is obviously a typo (the correct term, FTHORA from the Greek φθορά, appears in the names of many of the neighboring characters). [Fortunately, the French translation corrected this error. Thanks, Patrick!] Rather than correcting this innocent typo, Unicode decided to add the following hilarious comment after the character's description: "misspelling of 'FHTORA' in character name is a known defect".… The author knows of one other case of this sort of behavior: errors in the Hebrew Bible are also preserved, to the point that today there is a list of broken letters, upside-down letters, etc., that have been "institutionalized" to prevent the copyist from "correcting" the sacred text. Will Unicode be the new Bible?

(16 columns, 0x1D000-0x1D0F5), a system still widely used in Greece and in other Eastern Orthodox countries.

[𝄞𝄢𝄐...] The next block is for the *Western system of musical notation* (16 columns, 0x1D100-0x1D1DD, which includes both the modern notation (written on the five-line staff) and the notation used for Gregorian chant (written on the four-line staff). Everything is present: notes, clefs, measure lines, dynamics, ties and slurs, *crescendo* and *decrescendo* hairpins, *glissandi*, fermatas, etc. All that we need is the creativity of Stockhausen, Berio, Crumb, and Boulez of the twenty-first century to make this block explode with a profusion of new symbols.

[𝈀...] And since we are right in the midst of all this musical notation, why not encode the symbols used to notate music in antiquity? No sooner said than done: here is the block for *ancient Greek musical notation* (6 columns, 0x1D200-0x1D245).

[...] We have already mentioned the block of *Yijing* hexagrams, which is located on the BMP, squeezed between two blocks of ideographs. Here we have monograms, digrams, and tetragrams from this book (6 columns, 0x1D300-0x1D356).

[− ═ ≡ ☰ ☱ ⊥ ⊤ ⊧ ≣ |] Next comes a small block for *counting rods* (2 columns, 0x1D360-0x1D371). "Counting rods" are small sticks, several centimeters long, used in East Asia for counting. These characters contain the basic patterns of this numbering system.

[**abc**𝑑𝑒𝑓𝕘𝔥𝗂𝕊] Finally, a block that was also controversial but that is more likely to be useful to the reader than many other Unicode blocks: the *mathematical alphanumeric symbols* (48 columns, 0x1D400-0x0x1D7FF). The idea behind these is very simple. It is well known that "mathematicians are like Frenchmen: whenever you say something to them, they translate it into their own language, and at once it is something entirely different" (in the words of Goethe). Well, in this case it is the notion of a Unicode character that has been "translated": the bold, italic, and bold italic forms of a letter are regarded here as distinct Unicode characters because they take on different meanings in mathematical formulae. Thus this block contains the styles mentioned above and also script, blackletter, blackboard-bold, sans-serif, and typewriter type—all of it for both Latin and Greek.

Plane 2 is called the "Supplementary Ideographic Plane" (SIP). Its structure is extremely simple. Between 0x20000 and 0x2A6D6 there is a contiguous block of 42,711 ideographs called "Ideographs Extension B". The ideographic character with the greatest number of strokes is found there: it is 0x2A6A5 𪚥, which is written with 64 (!) strokes. Its structure is quite simple: it contains four copies of the radical 龍 'dragon'. As for the meaning of 𪚥, the reader will have guessed it: 'four dragons' (or 'several dragons'). Perhaps the ease with which today's font-design software can be used will soon give rise to characters with n^2 dragons, for a total of $2^4 n^2$ strokes....

At the end of the plane, there is a relatively small block (34 columns, 0x2F800-0x2FA1D) of compatibility ideographs, all of them from the encoding CNS 11643-1992.

Unicode's last "inhabited" plane is Plane 14. Here we find two blocks, the first of which was highly controversial. It is a set of *language tags*. The idea is as follows: to indicate the *language* of a block of text, we ordinarily use "high-level protocols" (otherwise known as markup systems) such as XML, which provides the attribute xml:lang for this purpose. But suppose that we absolutely insist on doing it at the level of Unicode. It would be both naïve and futile to try to define control characters corresponding to the various languages of the world: there would be far too many, and we would need a sub-Consortium to manage them all. Unicode's idea, therefore, was as follows: on the basis of XML's syntax, we will write the value of the xml:lang attribute using special characters that cannot possibly be mistaken for characters in running text. Thus Plane 14 contains a carbon copy of ASCII (8 columns, 0xE0001-0xE007F) whose characters fulfill this rôle.

According to the XML standard, the value of xml:lang is a combination of abbreviations of the name of a language (ISO 639 standard [191]) and the name of a country (ISO 3166 standard [190]), the latter being unnecessary if the name of the language is precise enough. The code for English is en, and this is what we would write in a document to indicate that it is in English: 0xE0001 LANGUAGE TAG, 0xE0065 TAG LATIN SMALL LETTER E, 0xE006E TAG LATIN SMALL LETTER N. If we use letters in boxes for the tags (and ⊡ for 0xE0001, which marks the beginning of a sequence), the immortal verses of Goethe and their translations into various languages would look somewhat like this:

> ⊡⊡⊡Über allen Gipfeln ist Ruh. In allen Wipfeln spürest Du kaum einen Hauch. ⊡⊡⊡Ἐπὶ πάντων τῶν ὀρέων ἡσυχία βασιλεύει. Ἐπὶ τῶν κλαδίσκων πλέον οὔτε φύλλον δὲν σαλεύει. ⊡⊡⊡Au dessus de tous les sommets est le repos. Écoute dans toutes les cimes, à peine si tu surprends un souffle. ⊡⊡⊡ Hush'd on the hill is the breeze. Scarce by the zephyr the trees softly are press'd.

The purpose of ⊡ is to indicate the version of markup. It is quite possible to envision a different use of the same tags, with a character other than 0xE0001 to mark the beginning of the sequence.

As we shall see when we discuss the bidirectional algorithm, it is important to make a logical distinction between sequential and embedded blocks of text when marking up a multilingual document. Ordinarily the sentences that we write are sequential, but when we write "I am telling you: 'It is time to do this'", we embed one sentence in another. The distinction is crucial when the sentences that we embed are written in scripts that read in opposite directions. Markup must therefore express this property of text, and XML lends itself admirably to this task because sequential blocks are "sibling nodes", whereas embedded blocks are new branches of the tree. Unlike XML's markup, Unicode's language tags are unable to "structure" a document.

The Unicode Consortium admits that it committed a blunder by adopting these characters. It now *strongly encourages users not to use these characters*, at least when another means of indicating the language is available....

The last block of the last inhabited plane is for *variation selectors*. In the BMP there are already 16 selectors of this type that enable us to indicate as many variants of a single character. In the event that more than 16 variants occur, have no fear: Plane 14 contains 240 more (15 columns, 0xE0100-0xE01EF), bringing the total to 256.

Scripts proposed for addition

When going from the BMP to the higher planes, we have the impression of moving from the overpopulated Gangetic Plain to the empty steppes of Siberia. The vast majority of these planes' code points are still unassigned, and, unless in the near future we come upon an extraterrestrial civilization with a writing system that uses a million characters, that situation is likely to persist for some time.

Which scripts are planned for addition to Unicode in the near future?

There are at least three stages for a script to be included in Unicode. In the following we describe the pipeline of scripts submitted for inclusion, as of August 2006.

Approved proposals in balloting

These scripts have been approved by the Unicode Technical Committee and the WG2. They are in the process of being approved by ISO for inclusion in 10646.

[ꤍꤟꤢꤝꤚꤘꤞꤟꤡꤜ] *Kayah Li*, used to write Eastern and Western Kayah Li languages, spoken by about half a million people in Myanmar and Thailand.

[ᰛᰜᰝᰞᰟᰠᰡᰢᰣᰤᰥ] *Lepcha* is the script of Sikkim, a formerly independent country that since 1975 has been a state of India, located between Nepal and Bhutan.

[ᱛᱜᱝᱞᱟᱠᱡᱢᱣᱤ] *Ol Chiki*, invented by Pandit Raghunath Murmu in the first half of the 20th century to write the southern dialect of Santali, a language of India, as spoken in the Orissan Mayurbhañi district.

[ꕐꕑꕒꕓꕔꕕꕖꕗꕘꕙ] *Vai*, an African script used in Liberia and Sierra Leone.

[ꤰꤱꤲꤳꤴꤵꤶꤷꤸꤹ] *Rejang*, the script of the language by the same name, spoken by about 200,000 people in Indonesia, on the island of Sumatra.

[ꢂꢃꢄꢅꢆꢇꢈꢉꢊꢋ] *Sauvashtra*, the script of an Indian language related to Gujarati and spoken by about 300,000 people in southern India (actually a Indo-European language in the midst of several Dravidian languages).

[ᮃᮄᮅᮆᮇᮈᮉᮊᮋᮌ] *Sundanese*, one of the scripts of the language Sundanese, spoken by about 27 million people on the island of Java in Indonesia.

[ABⲤΔEϝIꞪΘⲒꞰ] *Carian*, as well as

[ꓛꓝꓰꓹꓱBOꟿꓠꓨꓳ] *Lycian*, and

[ꪍꪜꪮ] *Lydian*: the three ancient Greek "Anatolian" scripts, used in Asia Minor until the 3rd century BCE.

Proposals in early committee review

These scripts have complete formal proposals and are waiting for approval or rejection by the UTC.

[ ] *Avestan* is a pre-Islamic Persian script invented to record Zoroastrian texts in the 3^{d} century CE.

[ ] *Batak*.

——— *Manipuri*, a recently extinct script for writing the Meithei language of Manipur State in India.

[ ] *Hieroglyphic Egyptian*, whose (future) Unicode block is based on the font of the Centre for Computer-Aided Egyptological Research in Utrecht, in the Netherlands. The proposal distributes the hieroglyphs over two blocks: the basic block (761 characters) and the extended block (4,548 characters that come primarily from the inscriptions in the temple of Edfu). To place hieroglyphs inside cartouches, one uses the control characters EGYPTIAN HIEROGLYPHIC BEGIN CARTOUCHE, etc.

[ ] *Brahmi*, the ancient pan-Indian script, ancestral to the scripts of India and Southeast Asia.

[ ] *Manichaean*, the script of the texts of Manichaeism, a religion founded by Mani (216–274 CE). The Manichaean script was inspired by the Syriac Estrangelo.

[ ] *Tengwar*, a script invented by Tolkien for *The Lord of the Rings*.

Proposals in the initial and exploratory stages

[ ] *Chakma* is the script of Chakmas, the largest ethnic group in Bangladesh. Nowadays the Chakma language is mostly written in the Bengali script.

[ ] *Cham*, a Southeast Asian script used by minorities in Cambodia and Vietnam, which bears a vague resemblance to Khmer.

[ ] *Javanese*, another Southeast Asian script, an Indonesian derivative of Brahmi.

—— *Lanna.*

[مࢰدﭬﺎ] *Mandaic* is another Semitic alphabet, derived from the Aramaic script. It is used for Mandaic, the liturgical language of the Mandaean religion.

[य यैश्या यैौ नॢ दॢ ग स्रॢ ङॢव न] *Newari.*

[ꡁꡒꡗꡕꡞꡕ꡴ꡀꡠ] *Old Hungarian*, a runic script used in Hungary before the Latin alphabet was adopted. In Hungarian it is called *rovásírás.*

[ꛠꛑꛊꛃꛖꛝꛘꛟꛂꛀꛉ] *Pahawh Hmong*, a script revealed in 1959 to a messianic figure among the Hmong people of Laos, Shong Lue Yang, by two supernatural messengers who appeared to him over a period of months.

[ꓦꓵꓐꓮꓳꓕꓵꓜꓴ] *Samaritan* is the script of the Samaritans, a Mesopotamian people that migrated and settled down in Palestine circa 500 BCE. It is also known as *Old Hebrew*, in contrast with the script we nowadays call Hebrew, which is of Aramaic origin.

[𑖭𑖰𑖟𑖿𑖠𑖽 𑖭𑖿𑖎𑖿𑖨𑖰𑖢𑖿𑖝] *Siddham:* this very beautiful script, a descendent of Brahmi, is used by Shingon Buddhists in Japan to write mantras and sutras in Sanskrit. It was introduced to Japan by Kukai in 806 CE after he studied Sanskrit and Mantrayana Buddhism in China. In Japan it is known as 梵字 (*bonji*).

[𑃐𑃦𑃝𑃝𑃕𑃝𑃧𑃚𑃒] *Sorang Sompeng*, the script used to write the Sora language, spoken by populations living between the Oriya- and Telugu-speaking peoples in India. It was devised by Mangei Gomango, son of the charismatic leader Malia Gomango.

—— *Tai Lü*, a script for writing various Tai dialects in northern Thailand, Yunnan, and parts of Myanmar.

[𑣄𑣁𑣂𑣆𑣐𑣇𑣕𑣊𑣈𑣏𑣖] *Varang Kshiti*, the script used to write the Ho language of India, devised by another charismatic leader, Lako Bodra.

[ꪶꪀꪫꪘꪙꪇꪮꪘꪫ꪿ꪮꪺ] *Viet Thai* is a script for the Thai languages used by Thai people in Vietnam.

[𑜉𑜡𑜪𑜈𑜫𑜇𑜦𑜎𑜦𑜈𑜫𑜇𑜤𑜈] *Ahom* is the script of an extinct Tai language spoken by the Ahom people, who ruled the Brahmaputra Valley in the Indian state of Assam between the 13th and the 18th centuries.

—— *Early Aramaic*, an alphabet descending from Phœnician. It is an ancestor of Syriac, Arabic, and other scripts.

—— *Balti*, the script of the language of Baltistan, in northern Kashmir. This script was apparently introduced around the 15th century CE, when the people converted to Islam. It is related to Arabic.

[ꡃꤢꤤ] *Bassa Vah* is a script used by the Bassa people on the central coast of Liberia and Sierra Leone. In the 1900s, a chemist, Flo Darvin Lewis, discovered that descendants of slaves in Brazil and the West Indies were still using it. He then tried to revive this alphabet in Liberia.

[ꠧꠧꠋꠋ] *Blissymbolics* is an ideographic writing system used primarily by people with physical and cognitive handicaps. It was developed by Charles Bliss in the 1950s as a "universal language" that could cut across national boundaries and facilitate international communication and peace. It contains 2384 characters in 149 columns.

[ᚳᚱᚦ] *Cirth*, another script invented by Tolkien for *The Lord of the Rings*.

[𒉿𒋫] *Hittite* is the language of the Hitties, a people living in north-central Anatolia. It was spoken between 1600 and 1100 BC. It was written in cuneiform characters with syllabic and logographic meanings.

[𐨀𐨢] The *Indus Valley* script is still undeciphered. It was used between 2500 and 1700 BCE. The proposal includes 386 characters.

—— *Kaithi*, a script used widely throughout northern India, primarily in the former North-West Provinces (present-day Uttar Pradesh) and Bihar. It was used to write legal, administrative, and private records.

[ꓐꓟꓳ] *Khamti*, or *Lik-Tai*, used to write the Khamti language in India and Myanmar.

—— The *Kirat*, or *Limbu*, script, used among the Limbu of Sikkim and Darjeeling (the place with the delicious tea).

—— *Linear-A*, an undeciphered script—unlike Linear B, which was deciphered by Michael Ventris—used in ancient Crete around 1400 BCE.

[𐦀𐦝] *Meroitic* is a very interesting case of the alternative use of a writing system. The Meroites lived in the Sudan during the time of the pharaohs. To write their language, they used 23 Egyptian hieroglyphs (or demotic characters), each with a very precise phonetic value.

[𖼀𖼞] *Naxi-Geba*: Geba is one of the three scripts of the Naxi language (together with Dongba and the Latin alphabet). The language is spoken by about 300,000 people in Yunnan, Sichuan, Tibet, and Myanmar.

[𐍈𐍈] *Old Permic* is the script invented by the missionary Étienne de Perme in the 14th century to write the Komi and Permyak languages, which are spoken in the Ural Mountains in Russia.

—— *Palmyrene*.

[YLЈT†Г٦ьⵦ] The *Pollard* script. Samuel Pollard was a British missionary who lived in China at the beginning of the 20th century. He invented a writing system for the A-Hmao language of the Miao minority. His system is structurally related to *hangul* in that he defined basic elements that are combined to form syllables. The language is much more complex phonetically than Chinese.

[⧂⧂⧂⧂⧂⧂⧂⧂⧂⧂] *Rongorongo*, the yet undeciphered symbols of Easter Island, carved on wooden boards. It is written in reverse boustrophedon style (from bottom to top). There are two other scripts to write the Rapa Nui language: Ta'u and Mama.

[ⵀⵀⵀⵀⵀⵀⵀⵀⵀⵀ] *South Arabian* is an ancient Semitic script, the ancestor of Amharic. It was used from the 5th century BCE to the 7th century CE.

[ⵀⵀⵀⵀⵀⵀⵀⵀⵀⵀ] *Soyombo* is another writing system for the Mongolian language that was created in 1686 by the illustrious Mongolian monk Zanabazar. It can be used to write Mongolian as well as Tibetan and Sanskrit. One of the Soyombo letters became the national symbol of the Mongolian state in 1992; its proportions are even defined in the country's constitution.

The Web site http://www.ethnologue.com gives a list of 6,800 languages of the world, but it is estimated that only about 100 scripts have existed. Unicode already includes about 60 scripts, and another 50 are waiting in the pipeline for inclusion. Does this mean that Unicode has managed to encompass most of the world's scripts? One thing is certain: both the Consortium and the designers of "Unicode-compatible" fonts will have their hands full for some decades to come.

3

Properties of Unicode characters

Our concern in this chapter is the information that Unicode provides for each character. According to our definition, a *character* is a *description* of a certain class of glyphs. One of these glyphs, which we have called the *representative glyph*, is shown in the Unicode charts, both in their hard-copy version [335] and in the PDF files available on the Web ([334]).

Unicode defines the *identity* of a character as the combination of its description and its representative glyph. On the other hand, the *semantics* of a character are given by its character identity and its *normative properties*.

This brings us to *character properties*. These are data on characters that have been collected over time and that can help us to make better use of Unicode. For example, one normative property of characters is their category. One possible category is "punctuation". A developer can thus know which characters of a given script are punctuation marks—information that will enable him to disregard those characters when sorting text, for example—without knowing anything at all about the script itself. Another property (not a normative one in this instance, and therefore more ambiguous) is the uppercase/lowercase correspondence. Unicode provides a table of these correspondences, which software can apply directly to convert a string from one case to the other (when the concept of case even applies to the writing system in question). Of course, none of these operations (sorting, case conversion, etc.) can be 100 percent automatic. As in all types of language processing, there is always a degree of uncertainty connected to the ambiguity inherent in languages and their grammars. But character properties can nevertheless be used to automate a large part of text processing; the developer should only take care to allow the user to correct errors that may arise from the generalized application of character properties.

What are these properties, and where are they found? We shall answer both questions in the remainder of this chapter.

Basic properties

Name

The *name* of a character is what we have called its *description*. The official list of the English names of characters according to their positions within the encoding appears in the following file:

```
http://www.unicode.org/Public/UNIDATA/UnicodeData.txt
```

This file contains a large amount of data in a format that is hard for humans to read but easy for computers: fifteen text fields separated by semicolons. Here are a few lines from this file:

```
0020;SPACE;Zs;0;WS;;;;;N;;;;;
0021;EXCLAMATION MARK;Po;0;ON;;;;;N;;;;;
0022;QUOTATION MARK;Po;0;ON;;;;;N;;;;;
0023;NUMBER SIGN;Po;0;ET;;;;;N;;;;;
0024;DOLLAR SIGN;Sc;0;ET;;;;;N;;;;;
```

The first two fields are the character's position (also called its "code point") and name (which we called its "description" in the previous chapter). These are fields number 0 and 1. (Counting begins at 0.) We shall see the other fields later.

Character names are not there solely for the benefit of humans; programming languages also understand them. In Perl, for example, to obtain the character that represents the letter 'Ꭰ' of the Cherokee script, we can write \N{CHEROKEE LETTER A}, which is strictly equivalent to \x{13a0}, a reference to the character's code point.

Block and script

These properties refer to the distribution of the full set of characters according to the script to which they belong or to their functional similarity. Thus we have a block of Armenian characters (*Armenian*), but also a block of pictograms (*Dingbats*), a block of special codes (*Specials*), etc.

The names of the blocks, in the form of running heads, can be found in the Unicode book but also in the file Blocks.txt (in the same directory as UnicodeData.txt). Here is a snippet of this file:

```
0000..007F; Basic Latin
0080..00FF; Latin- Supplement
```

```
0100..017F; Latin Extended-A
0180..024F; Latin Extended-B
0250..02AF; IPA Extensions
```

Block names are used by Unicode-compatible programming languages in the syntax for testing whether a character belongs to a specified block. In Perl, for example, we can determine whether a character is in the *Shavian* block by writing:

```
/\p{InShavian}/
```

The problem with the blocks is the fact that they are not always contiguous: Latin is spread over five blocks separated by 7,553 code points; Greek is split into two blocks separated by 6,913 code points; the Chinese ideographs are in four blocks on two planes.... To know whether a character is a Latin letter, therefore, we have to perform five separate tests.

One piece of data, the *script*, attempts to solve this problem. The file Scripts.txt presents a breakdown of Unicode into 60 scripts: Latin, Greek, Cyrillic, Armenian, Hebrew, Arabic, Syriac, Thaana, Devanagari, Bengali, Gurmukhi, Gujarati, Oriya, Tamil, Telugu, Kannara, Malayalam, Sinhala, Thai, Lao, Tibetan, Myanmar, Georgian, Hangul, Ethiopic, Cherokee, Canadian_aboriginal, Ogham, Runic, Khmer, Mongolian, Hiragana, Katakana, Bopomofo, Han, Yi, Old_italic, Gothic, Deseret, Inherited, Tagalog, Hanunoo, Buhid, Tagbanwa, Limbu, Tai_le, Linear_b, Ugaritic, Shavian, Osmanya, Cypriot, Braille, Buginese, Coptic, New_Tai_Lue, Glagolitic, Tifinagh, Syloti_Nagri, Old_Persian, Kharoshthi. And a 61st, which is the default value: Common.

Among these values, there is one that should be handled with care: inherited. This value applies to diacritical marks and other symbols that take on the value of the script of the surrounding characters.

It is very interesting to observe that the author of the report that describes this property [108] emphasized its usefulness for detecting *spoofing*, or the confusion of characters whose glyphs are identical or similar. The reader who has worked with Greek or Russian documents will certainly have had the experience of seeing words that print poorly or that cannot be found during a search simply because an 'O', a 'T', an 'A', a 'P', etc., has been entered in the wrong script. Experience shows that a user who types the two words "ДЕАРОЛЬГА" will often change scripts not just before the word "ОЛЬГА" but after the letter 'O', because of the need to type the 'Л'; consequently, the word will contain both Latin *and* Cyrillic letters. We also refer the reader back to the photo on page 57, where we see glorious *spoofing* between the words "ПАРКІΝΓК" and "PARKING".

Age

This is nothing but the number of the Unicode version in which the character first appeared in the encoding. Let us take this opportunity to observe that Unicode characters have one thing in common with our academics: they are immortal, in the sense that a Unicode character, once defined, can never be removed from the encoding. The worst thing that can happen to a character is to be "deprecated", which in Unicode leads to hilarious situations *à la* "the character is here, but act as if it were not, and for heaven's sake don't use it!"

The age of characters is indicated in the file DerivedAge.txt.

General category

This is perhaps a character's most important property, the one that will determine its behavior in most text-processing systems (both linguistic and typographic). As it should be, the category is structured in a hierarchical fashion, with the concepts of primary category (letters, diacritical marks, numbers, punctuation, symbols, separators, other) and subcategories, which specify the classification more precisely.

These give us 30 possibilities in all, each of them represented by a two-letter code.

Letters

- Lu (*letter, uppercase*). The name of the primary category of "letter" should be construed in a very broad sense, as it can apply equally to a letter of an alphabet, a sign belonging to a syllabary, or an ideograph.

  This particular subcategory refers to an "uppercase" letter; therefore, we can tell that the category applies to scripts that distinguish uppercase from lowercase letters. Very few scripts have this property: Latin, Greek, Coptic, Cyrillic, Armenian, liturgical Georgian, and Deseret.

- Ll (*letter, lowercase*). This category is the mirror image of the previous one. Here we are dealing with a letter from one of the multicameral alphabets (*i.e.*, those that have more than one case) listed above, and that letter will be lowercase.

- Lt (*letter, titlecase*). There are two very different types of characters that have been classified Lt: the Croatian digraphs 'Dž', 'Lj', 'Nj' and the capital Greek vowels with iota adscript.

  In the first instance, we see a compromise that was made to facilitate transcription between the Cyrillic and Latin alphabets: it was necessary to transcribe the Cyrillic letters 'ђ', 'љ', and 'њ', and no better solution was found than the use of digraphs. But unlike ligatures such as 'œ', 'ij', and 'æ', whose two elements both change case ('Œ', 'IJ', 'Æ'), here we may just as easily have 'DŽ' (in a word in which all the letters are uppercase) as 'Dž' (in a word in which only the first letter is supposed to be uppercase). This is so for all digraphs: the Spanish and German 'ch', the Breton 'c'h', etc. Unicode is not in the habit of encoding digraphs, but in this instance compatibility with old encodings forced Unicode to turn these digraphs into characters. Thus we consider 'dž' to be the lowercase version, 'DŽ' the uppercase version, and 'Dž' the "titlecase" version of the character.

  The second instance is the result of a typographical misunderstanding. In Greek there is a diacritical mark, "*iota* subscript", that is written beneath the vowels *alpha*, *eta*, and *omega*: "ᾳ, ῃ, ῳ". Typographers have found various ways to represent these characters in uppercase. The most common practice, in Greece, is to place the same diacritical mark underneath the uppercase letter: "Ą, Ḥ, Ω". In the English-speaking countries another solution is used, which involves placing a capital or small-capital *iota* after the letter. The latter is called *iota adscript*. Unicode incorrectly considers adscript the only possibly way to write this mark and thus has applied the category Lt to uppercase letters with iota adscript.

- Lm (*letter, modifier*). This is a rather small category for letters that are never used alone and that serve only to modify the sound of the letter that comes before them. Most of these characters appear in the block of "modifier letters" (0x02B0-0x02FF). There are a few rare examples of characters in other blocks: the *iota subscript* that we just mentioned is one; the stroke *kashida* that joins Arabic letters is another. Intuitively we could say that a modifier letter is something that plays the same rôle as a diacritical mark but that does not have the same graphical behavior, since its glyph will not combine with the one of the previous character but will rather follow it.

- Lo (*letter, other*). There is no denying it: Unicode is Eurocentric. Proof: Usually, when we create a classification, we begin with the most important cases and add a "catchall" case at the very end to cover any exceptions and omissions. Here the subcategory named *letter, other* covers all the scripts in the world that have no notion of case, which is to say practically the entire world! The Semitic, Indian, Southeast Asian, and ideographic scripts—all are lumped together indiscriminately as Lo....

Diacritical marks

- Mn (*mark, non-spacing*). These are *diacritical marks*: accents, cedillas, and other signs that are independent Unicode characters but that do not have the right to show themselves in isolation. Fate inexorably binds this sort of Unicode character to the one that comes before it, and their glyphs merge to form only a single glyph. The term "non-spacing" is a bit awkward, for an accent can, in some cases, change the width of its base letter: imagine a wide circumflex accent over a narrow sans-serif 'i'.

- Mc (*mark, spacing combining*). If the "modifier letters" are letters that behave somewhat like diacritical marks, the "spacing combining marks" are diacritical marks that behave somewhat like letters. For example, the languages of India and Southeast Asia have vowels, markers of nasalization, glottal stops, etc., which graphically resemble letters but which, by their very nature, are always logically attached to letters. By way of illustration, in Cambodian the letter 'ញ' is pronounced *nyo*. To turn it into *nye*, we add a modifying symbol, the one for the vowel *e*, whose glyph comes before the consonant: 'ញ'. We never see this glyph standing alone, just as we never see a cedilla standing alone—and that is what led Unicode to classify this vowel 0x17C1 KHMER VOWEL SIGN E among the diacritical marks.

- Me (*mark, enclosing*). These are diacritical marks whose glyphs completely enclose the glyph of the character that precedes them. There are very few of them in Unicode: the Cyrillic signs for hundreds of thousands and millions that encircle a letter taken to be a number; the *rub el-hizb*, which appears in the Koran at the beginnings of the subdivisions; a few technical signs, such as the triangle on European road signs that indicates danger; etc.

Numbers

- Nd (*number, decimal digit*). After the letters and the diacritical marks come the numbers. Various writing systems have their own systems of decimal digits: we in the West have our "Arabic numberals"; the Arab countries of the Mashreq have their "Indian numerals"; each of the languages of India and Southeast Asia has its own set of digits between 0 and 9; etc. These are the digits that we find in category Nd. But beware: if one of these scripts should have the poor taste to continue the series of numerals by introducing, for example, a symbol for the number 10 (as is the case in Tamil and Amharic) or a sign for one half (as in Tibetan), these new characters would not be admissible to the Nd category; they would be too far removed from our Western practices! They would instead go into the catchall No, which we shall see in just a moment.

- Nl (*number, letter*). An especially nasty problem: in many writing systems, letters are used to count (in which case we call them "numerals"). In Greek, for instance, 2006 is written ͵κϛ´. But if the letters employed are also used in running text, they cannot belong to two categories at the same time. And Unicode cannot double the size of the blocks for these scripts simply because someone might wish to use their letters as numerals. What, then, is a "number-letter", if not a letter that appears in text? There are very few such characters: the Roman numerals that were encoded separately in Unicode, the "Suzhou numerals" that are special characters used by Chinese merchants, a Gothic letter here, a runic letter there. Note that the Greek letters *koppa* 'ϟ' and '*sampi* ϡ', which represent the numbers 90 and 900, do not count as "number-letters" although they should, since their only use is to represent numbers....

- No (*number, other*). The catchall into which we place the various characters inherited from other encodings: superscript and subscript numerals, fractions, encircled numbers. Also in this category are the numbers from various systems of numeration whose numerical value is not an integer between 0 and 9: the 10, 100, and 1,000 of Tamil; the numbers between 10 and 10,000 of Amharic; etc. Note: although we cannot classify the ideographs 一 'one', 二 'two', 三 'three', 四 'four', etc., as "letters" and "numbers" at the same time, we can so classify ideographs in parentheses: ㈠, ㈡, ㈢, ㈣, etc., are Unicode characters in their own right and are classified as No.

Punctuation

- Pc (*punctuation, connector*). A very little-used category for punctuation marks—those that connect two parts of a word to form a single word. The hyphen plays this rôle in English ("merry-go-round", "two-year-old"), but the character 0x002D HYPHEN-MINUS belongs to a separate category, the "dashes". The most commonly used character in category Pc is the midpoint of the *katakana* block. *Katakana* is used mainly to represent foreign words. When these are connected or contain a hyphen in the original language, it is not possible to do the same in Japanese because there is already a symbol shaped like a hyphen, whose purpose is to prolong the vowel that precedes it. An example that shows both characters: by combining ウォーター (*wōtā*) and ポロ (*poro*), we obtain ウォーター・ポロ (= "water polo"), in which the midpoint is character 0x30FB KATAKANA MIDDLE DOT, which is of category Pc. Another example of a character in category Pc: the "underscore", which programmers use to write variable names that consist of more than one word, such as "$who_am_i".

- Pd (*punctuation, dash*). All sorts of dashes: figure, en, em, the hyphen, the minus sign, the Armenian hyphen, the Mongolian hyphen, etc.

- Ps (*punctuation, open*). Some of the punctuation marks come in pairs: the parentheses, the brackets, the braces, etc. Here we include the "opening" symbol of each of these pairs. Recall that Unicode encodes characters in their logical order. When we write a word in parentheses, we begin with the opening parenthesis, then we write the word, and finally we finish with the closing parenthesis. What we have just said is blindingly obvious, except for the fact that the glyph for the character that we call the "opening parenthesis" may, according to the direction of the script, be '(' (in English) or ')' (in Hebrew or Arabic) or even '⌒' (in Chinese or Japanese). We have the same Unicode character in all three cases; only the glyph differs. Later we shall see another property, *mirroring*, which affects characters such as these. Note that the quotation marks are not categorized as Ps, since they have a category to themselves.

- Pe (*punctuation, close*). The closing counterpart of Ps.

- Pi (*punctuation, initial quote*). A special case of binary punctuation marks, as quotation marks generally come in pairs. Thus the American double opening quotation mark ", the French opening quotation mark «, the second-level Greek opening quotation mark ", etc., are all of category Pi. But take note: these quotation marks can be used in peculiar ways that defy any attempt to establish universal rules. For example, « and " are *closing* quotation marks in German, " is an opening *and* a closing quotation mark in Dutch, etc. Saying that « and " are "initial" quotation marks is no more accurate than saying that the men wear trousers and the women wear skirts in every country in the world.

- Pf (*punctuation, final quote*) for '"', ' »', etc. As mentioned in the previous paragraph, these are no more "final" than Pi is "initial".

- Po (*punctuation, other*). The catchall that turns out to contain the most important punctuation marks: the period, the comma, the colon, the semicolon, the exclamation point, the question mark, etc.

Symbols

- Sm (*symbol, math*). This category is for signs that are used *only* in mathematics. Thus in "$\sin(\pi) = 0$", only the equals sign is in category Sm, for all the other signs are either letters, numbers, or punctuation marks.

- Sc (*symbol, currency*). Example: the dollar sign '$', whose glyph is sometimes also used for the character 's', as in "Micro$oft" or "U$A".

- Sk (*symbol, modifier*). These are phonetic symbols that modify the letters around them but that never appear by themselves—much like the modifier letters, except that here we have not letters but punctuation marks or symbols. For example, there are the phonetic symbols '˥ ˦ ˧ ˨ ˩', which denote the five tones of certain Chinese dialects. A tone mark necessarily goes with a letter, which it modifies; yet it is a graphical symbol, not a letter, so it is a good example of a "modifier symbol".

  Unfortunately, some symbols that do not modify anything have been included in this category. These are the unnatural characters known as the spacing diacritical marks, *i.e.*, the non-combining diacritical marks that have been included in the encoding for reasons of compatibility with earlier standards.

- So (*symbol, other*). The catchall category for symbols that are not mathematical symbols, currency signs, or modifiers. In a set containing ☚, ⊕, and ☭, there is something for every taste—within the limits of political correctness, of course, and a certain technocratic ethical standard. Unicode has not yet created a category for ostentatious religious symbols, but one should not be long in the coming....

Separators

- Zs (*separator, space*). These are spaces: zero-width, thin, medium, wide, 1-em, 1-en, 3-to-an-em, 4-to-an-em, and many more. Some of them allow a line break and some do not. And there is one typographical curiosity: in the ogham script, there is a space that is not a space! This script is written along a baseline; but unlike the line in Devanagari, this line is not broken between words. Accordingly, the space (in the sense of "word separator") is a segment of baseline with no letter on it.

- Zl (*separator, line*) and Zp (*separator, paragraph*). These categories contain only one character each: 0x2028 LINE SEPARATOR and 0x2029 PARAGRAPH SEPARATOR. These characters attempt to solve the problem of breaking text into lines and paragraphs in an unambiguous way. Recall that, when a document is read by a word processor such as Word, the lines are automatically divided without any changes to the underlying text, and a newline character in the document will visually mark the start of a new paragraph. The conventions are different in TEX: a newline in the source document is equivalent to a blank space in the output. It takes two consecutive newlines in the source to produce a new paragraph in the output. XHTML follows yet another convention: any number of newlines in the source will yield a single blank when rendered; to start a new line or a new paragraph in the output, one must use the appropriate tags (
 and <p> or <div>). In this paragraph we have used the term "newline". The character corresponding to this operation varies from system to system: under MacOS, the character is CR; under Unix, it is NL; and under Windows, it is a pair of bytes, CR NL. To avoid having to adopt one of these conventions, Unicode decided to punt: there are two new characters to indicate a change of line (if necessary) and a change of paragraph. Now all that remains is to persuade people to use them....

The remaining categories

- Cc (*other, control*). This category covers code points 0x0000-0x001F and 0x0080-0x009F, *i.e.*, tables C0 and C1 in ISO 2022–compatible encodings. Unicode does not assign any semantic value to these characters; their names are invariably "<CONTROL>". No other Unicode character is in this category.

- Cf (*other, format*). These characters are all used to insert metadata into a document. They are important enough to be listed here:

  - 0x00AD SOFT HYPHEN marks a potential spot for dividing a word across lines. We can imagine a human or a program that inserted such characters at every permitted break-point; the rendering software would then not have to apply the hyphenation algorithm.[1]

  - 0x0600 ARABIC NUMBER SIGN and the three characters that follow behave in a very unusual way: they occur at the beginning of a number, and their effect lasts as long as digits are added. Thus they are combining characters, in a sense, the only differences being that they *precede* the base character and that they act on an unlimited number of following characters. This character indicates that a number is being written. Its graphical shape is that of a letter *ayn* with a stroke that extends for the length of the number. This practice occurs in languages such as Urdu and Baluchi.

  - 0x0601 ARABIC SIGN SANAH: In Arabic *sanah* means 'year'. This character is the word *sanah* written beneath a number for its entire width to indicate that the number represents a date.

  - 0x0602 ARABIC FOOTNOTE MARKER is written beneath the index of a footnote.

  - 0x0603 ARABIC SIGN SAFHA is likewise written beneath a page number.

  - 0x06DD ARABIC END OF AYAH is a very different symbol: it is a circle, often highly embellished, that is used in the Koran to enclose the number of the *ayah* that has just ended. This character is in category Cf because it behaves like those that we have just described: it encircles the number before which it appears, irrespective—at least in theory—of the number's size.

  - 0x070F SYRIAC ABBREVIATION MARK is a means of drawing a horizontal line above a string of Syriac glyphs to indicate that they form an abbreviation. This character is placed at the beginning of the abbreviation, which continues until the end of the string, namely, until the first character of type "punctuation", "symbol", or "separator".

  - 0x17B4 KHMER VOWEL INHERENT AQ and 0x17B5 KHMER VOWEL INHERENT AA are mistakes [335, p. 390], and their use is discouraged by the Consortium.

---

[1] In certain languages we may be able to make good use of multiple characters of this kind, corresponding to different degrees of precedence. In German, for instance, we distinguish four levels of precedence for the hyphenation of a word such as *Wahr$_2$schein$_4$lich$_4$keits$_1$theo$_3$rie*, depending on whether the breaks occur in front of the last component, between the other components, between syllables of the last component, between syllables of other components.

— 0x200C ZERO WIDTH NON-JOINER, or "ZWNJ", is a character that prevents the formation of a link or a ligature between the glyphs of the two surrounding characters. We can use it in scripts such as Arabic when two consecutive letters should not be connected, or in those cases in which we want to avoid a ligature at all costs, as in the German word *Auflage*, in which the letters 'f' and 'l' belong to different components of the compound word.

— 0x200D ZERO WIDTH JOINER, or "ZWJ", is the opposite of ZWNJ. It is very useful when we need to obtain a specific contextual form. For example, the abbreviation "ح" is found in Arabic dictionaries. It is the initial form of the letter *hah*. Since this letter is preceded and followed by non-letters, the rendering engine will automatically select the glyph ح for the isolated form. To obtain the initial form, we follow the letter with the character ZWJ, which leads the rendering engine to think that the letter is followed by another Arabic letter, to which it must be connected.

— 0x200E LEFT-TO-RIGHT MARK, 0x200F RIGHT-TO-LEFT MARK, 0x202A LEFT-TO-RIGHT EMBEDDING, 0x202B RIGHT-TO-LEFT EMBEDDING, 0x202C POP DIRECTIONAL FORMATTING, 0x202D LEFT-TO-RIGHT OVERRIDE, and 0x202E RIGHT-TO-LEFT OVERRIDE are used by the bidirectional algorithm, which we shall describe in detail in Chapter 4.

— 0x2060 WORD JOINER can be inserted between two words to prevent a line break at that location. Software systems have their own line-breaking algorithms, of course, but these algorithms take only letters into account. Often the author has typed an em dash followed by a comma only to shudder in horror when he saw the comma moved down to the next line. Of course, we can always develop more refined software that will avoid this sort of typographical error, but until then it will not be a bad idea to insert a character that will effectively prevent the separation of two glyphs.

— 0x2061 FUNCTION APPLICATION is a character that does not affect rendering at all. Its rôle is strictly semantic. It indicates that two mathematical symbols stand in relation to each other as a function and its argument. When we write $f(x)$, it is clear that we are referring to the function f of x; likewise, when we write $a(b+c)$, it is clear that we are referring to the product of the variable a and the sum of the variables $b+c$. But what is $f(g+h)$? Is it $f : g+h \mapsto f(g+h)$ or $f \cdot g + f \cdot h$? To eliminate the ambiguity, we have an invisible "function" character that indicates, when placed between f and $(g+h)$, that the notation refers to the application of a function. This invisible character can also be used for other purposes than mathematical notation: symbolic calculation, voice synthesis, or simply the transmission or storage of a formula with its contents represented unambiguously.

— 0x2062 INVISIBLE TIMES is the other option for interpreting the expression $f(g+h)$: the product of f and $g+h$. In algebra we have the habit of not explicitly writing a symbol for multiplication and, more generally, the laws of algebraic structures. Unicode speaks of multiplication, but all indications suggest that this operator may be used for any law of an algebraic structure.

- 0x2063 INVISIBLE SEPARATOR handles a third case in which ambiguity may arise, that of indices. When we write a_{ij} within a matrix, it is clear from context that we are referring to the i th row and the j th column of that matrix. Thus we are speaking of two indices, not the product of i and j. To make our intention clear, we may insert the invisible separator between the two indices.

- 0x206A INHIBIT SYMMETRIC SWAPPING and 0x206B ACTIVATE SYMMETRIC SWAP-PING are deprecated [335, p. 543].

- 0x206C INHIBIT ARABIC FORM SHAPING and 0x206D ACTIVATE ARABIC FORM SHAP-ING are also deprecated.

- 0x206E NATIONAL DIGIT SHAPES and 0x206F NOMINAL DIGIT SHAPES are depre-cated as well.

- 0xFEFF ZERO WIDTH NON-BREAKING SPACE, or "BOM", is the character that en-ables us to determine whether a Unicode document in UTF-16 is encoded in little-endian or big-endian order. This technique works because the character's *alter ego*, 0xFFFE, *is not* a Unicode character. Therefore, if we find an 0xFFFE in a file, there is only one possible conclusion: it is an 0xFEFF that we are reading backwards, in the wrong mode. This character has no other rôle than indicating endianness.

- 0xFFF9 INTERLINEAR ANNOTATION ANCHOR, 0xFFFA INTERLINEAR ANNOTATION SEPARATOR, and 0xFFFB INTERLINEAR ANNOTATION TERMINATOR are used to en-code *interlinear annotations*, which are pieces of information that are presented in a special way, such as by placing them between two lines of text. They may be used for a word-for-word translation or, in the case of the ideographic lan-guages, to indicate an ideograph's pronunciation by making reference to a pho-netic writing system such as the Japanese *kana*, the Korean *hangul*, or the Chinese *bopomofo*.

- There are also characters in category Cf for encoding the basic units of musical notation.

- And all the language tags in Plane 14 that are used as markup for languages are also in category Cf.

- Cs (*other, surrogate*). The characters in the high and low surrogate zones (0xD800-0xDBFF and 0xDC00-0xDFFF); see page 64.

- Co (*other, private use*). The characters of the private use areas.

- Cn (*other, not assigned*). By extending the notion of category to all of the code points in the Unicode chart, we can say that a code point that is not assigned to any character is of category Cn. Corollary: No character in the file UnicodeData.txt can ever be of category Cn.

Other general properties

By scanning over the categories and subcategories described in the previous section, we can quickly notice that many properties are omitted from the categorization. Another file at the Unicode site, by the name of `PropList.txt`, makes up for this deficiency by introducing a certain number of *properties* that are orthogonal to the notion of category.

Here is a snippet of the file, showing the characters that have the property of being "spaces":

```
0009..000D   ; White_Space # Cc   [5] <control->..<control-D>
0020         ; White_Space # Zs       SPACE
0085         ; White_Space # Cc       <control->
00A0         ; White_Space # Zs       NO-BREAK SPACE
1680         ; White_Space # Zs       OGHAM SPACE MARK
180E         ; White_Space # Zs       MONGOLIAN VOWEL SEPARATOR
2000..200A   ; White_Space # Zs  [11] EN QUAD..HAIR SPACE
2028         ; White_Space # Zl       LINE SEPARATOR
2029         ; White_Space # Zp       PARAGRAPH SEPARATOR
202F         ; White_Space # Zs       NARROW NO-BREAK SPACE
205F         ; White_Space # Zs       MEDIUM MATHEMATICAL SPACE
3000         ; White_Space # Zs       IDEOGRAPHIC SPACE
```

At the start of each line, we see the code points or ranges concerned. The name of the property appears after the semicolon. Everything after the pound sign is a comment; this section contains the character's category and its name or, when there are multiple characters, the names of the endpoints of the range.

Of these properties, which number 28 in all, here are the general-purpose ones. We shall see the others later when we discuss case, the bidirectional algorithm, etc.

Spaces

This property applies to 26 Unicode characters, of which some are genuine spaces (category Zs) and others are control characters (category Cc). The line separator and the paragraph separator, which are respectively in categories Zl and Zp, also have this property.

Alphabetic characters

These are characters of category "letter" (Lu, Ll, Lt, Lm, Lo) or " alphabetic numbers" (Nl). There are 90,989 of them in all. Note that characters have the alphabetic property simply by virtue of belonging to one of these categories; thus extracting the corresponding characters from the file `UnicodeData.txt` yields a complete list of alphabetic characters. For that reason, this property is called a "derived" property, and its characters are listed not in `PropList.txt` but in `DerivedCoreProperties.txt`.

Noncharacters

These characters are the forbidden fruit of Unicode: their code points may not be used. The Consortium even created a special term for them: *noncharacters* (written solid). They cover 32 code points in the block of Arabic presentation forms 0xFDD0–0xFDEF and the last two positions in each plane, 0x??FFE and 0x??FFF. This is why: Code point 0xFFFE must be ruled out as a character so that the pair of bytes 0xFF 0xFE, when read by software, can be interpreted as the character BOM 0xFEFF read in the wrong direction. Only if one code point (0xFFFE) is sacrificed can the test for endiannism work. The non-use of the character 0xFFFF is intended to simplify the programmer's life. It happens that some programming languages use a special character to terminate a string; we call that character a *sentinel* (in C, for example, it is the character 0x00). This approach has the drawback that the sentinel cannot be used within a string. If 0xFFFF is selected as the sentinel, this problem will never arise, as 0xFFFF is not a character and therefore cannot appear within a string.

Why was this decision extended to the other planes? Out of compassion, or perhaps because it was expected that programmers would take algorithms intended for the BMP and apply them to the other planes by simply adding an offset. Since these restrictions were applied to all the planes, the algorithms remain valid.

Ignorable characters

The full name is *default ignorable code points*. If we take this property's name at face value and examine the list of its members, which is a veritable country club of exotic characters (the combining grapheme joiner, the Korean syllable fillers, the variation selectors, the zero-width space, the various control characters...), we may scratch our heads for a long time before understanding what it means. Yet it is very simple: when software does not have a glyph to represent a character, it is supposed to display a symbol for "missing glyph". But in certain cases we would prefer not to display anything. A character is *ignorable* if it should not be represented by a generic glyph when the software is unable to carry out the behavior that it implies. For example, the combining grapheme joiner is a character that calls for very special behavior: that of construing two glyphs as one and applying a diacritical mark to the combination. If the software is not equipped for this functionality, it is expected not to display anything in this character's place.

To obtain a complete list of the ignorable characters, take the "other, control" characters Cc, the "other, format" characters Cf, and the "other, surrogate" characters, blend in certain characters listed under property Other_Default_Ignorable_Code_Point in the file PropList.txt, shake well, and serve immediately.

Deprecated characters

Old lawyers never die; they just lose their appeal. The same goes for characters: the worst thing that can happen to them is to be *deprecated*. There are ten such characters (as of this writing), and they are listed in PropList.txt.

Logical-order exceptions

These are characters that are not rendered in their logical order. They represent a blemish in Unicode that is due, once again, to the principle of backward compatibility with existing encodings. This property applies to 10 Thai and Lao characters, all of them vowels placed to the left of the consonant. One example is the consonant ນ 0x0E99 LAO LET-TER NO. To obtain the sound "*nē*", we add the vowel ເ 0x0EC0 LAO VOWEL SIGN E after the consonant. But graphically this vowel appears before the consonant: ເນ. Its graphical order is therefore the opposite of its logical order; thus it is a "logical-order exception".

The reader with an inquisitive bent will easily discover that this phenomenon of vowels placed before consonants occurs in Khmer, Sinhala, Malayalam, Tamil, Oriya, Gujarati, Gurmukhi, Bengali, Devanagari, and doubtless other writing systems as well. Why are the characters in question "logical" in these scripts but "illogical" in Thai and Lao? For no better reason than a difference of status. In all of the scripts mentioned, the vowels in question are *combining characters*; therefore, their graphical position is managed by the class of combining characters, which we shall discuss below. In particular, this position, whatever it be, is in no way illogical. In the case of Thai and Lao, however, the same vowels were encoded as ordinary characters; thus it was necessary to make some adjustments by adding this property.

Soft-dotted letters

These are characters whose glyphs have a dot: 'i', 'j', and all their derivatives. In exchange for the privilege of bearing an accent, these letters must forfeit their dot: thus we have 'î', not 'î̇'[2]. The only exception: Lithuanian, which preserves the dot beneath the accent. By way of contrast, we can say that the dot on the Lithuanian 'i' is a "hard dot".

How to "harden" the dot on an 'i'? The method recommended by Unicode is to add a dot, *i.e.*, to put the character 0x0307 COMBINING DOT ABOVE after the 'i'. The glyph will remain the same—because the original dot on the 'i' is soft—but its behavior will differ: a subsequent diacritical mark added to this glyph will not suppress the dot. Thus, if for some reason we should wish to obtain 'î̇', we would have to write three characters in a row: "i, combining dot above, circumflex accent".

Mathematical characters

Or, to be more precise, the Unicode characters with the property "other math". These are the characters in the category Sm ("symbol, math") plus 1,069 characters listed in the file PropList.txt under the property Other_Math. All the punctuation marks that can appear in a mathematical formula (parentheses, brackets, braces, the vertical bar, etc.) and all the letters in the various styles that appear in the block of mathematical alphanumeric symbols 0x1D400-0x0x1D7FF are assembled under this heading.

If assignment to category Sm guarantees that a character is a mathematical symbol, then "mathematical character" can assist software in identifying the extent of a formula. But note that—alas!—the ordinary Latin and Greek letters are neither in category Sm nor of property "mathematical characters", even though they are essential to mathematical formulae.

---

[2] For many years a classic mistake of the user who was new to LaTeX was to write \^i instead of \^{\i}. The advent of the T1 fonts, whose macros provide for the "soft dot", eliminated this error.

Quotation marks

This property covers all the characters that can be used as quotation marks. They are of categories Po, Pi, Pf, Ps, and Pe. There are 29 of them, and they are listed in PropList.txt under the property Quotation_Mark.

Dashes

Everything that looks more or less like a dash and is used as such. There are 20 characters that have this property; they are of categories Pd (punctuation, dash) and Sm (mathematical symbol). They are listed in PropList.txt under the property Dash.

Hyphens

The existence of this property shows that the Consortium wished to distinguish clearly between "hyphens" and "dashes": the former are placed within words and play a morphological rôle ("merry-go-round", "two-year-old"); the latter are placed between words and play a syntactic rôle ("I'm leaving—do I have to repeat myself?"). Usage varies widely among the typographic conventions of the different countries; for that reason, some characters have both properties: "dash" and "hyphen".

There are 10 characters that have the "hyphen" property; they are in categories Pd (punctuation, dash), Pc (punctuation, connector; for the midpoint used in *katakana*, see page 101), and Cf (character, format; for a potential line break). They are listed in PropList.txt under the property Hyphen.

Terminal punctuation

Folk wisdom says that "birds of a feather flock together". Well, the characters with this property have flocked together from various and sundry blocks, yet they are of quite different feathers indeed. What they have in common is that they play the rôle of "terminal" punctuation. This term is rather ill chosen, as these characters also include the slash, which does not necessarily end a sentence. For want of a better definition, we can say intuitively that these are characters that play the same rôle as our various stops (the period, exclamation point, semicolon, colon), and also the slash.

There are 78 characters with the "hyphen" property; they are all of category Po (punctuation, other). They are listed in PropList.txt under the property Terminal_Punctuation.

Diacritics

When we described the category of "marks", we called them "diacritical marks". That might sow confusion, as Unicode also defines a property called diacritics. It covers both the "real" (non-spacing) diacritical marks and the "inert" (spacing) diacritical marks of ASCII, as well as a host of other signs. For example, the *katakana* prolonged sound mark, graphically speaking, is not a diacritical mark at all but nonetheless effectively plays this rôle.

There are 482 characters with the "diacritic" property. They are listed in PropList.txt under the property Diacritic.

Extenders

These are characters whose rôle is to extend or repeat the preceding character. Thus, for example, we have '〃' 0x309D HIRAGANA ITERATION MARK, which works as follows: Suppose that we have two identical *hiragana* syllables in a row, such as "き き" (*kiki*). It is faster to write the iteration mark: "き 〃"; the result is the same. In addition, if the second syllable is voiced, as in "き ぎ" (*kigi*), we can use the iteration mark with a phonetic modifier: "き 〴". We find this most often in vertical text, especially in Japanese calligraphy. There is the same type of iteration mark for *katakana* and for ideographs.

There are 19 characters with the "extender" property. They are listed in PropList.txt under the property Extender.

Join control

There are two characters that manage joining and non-joining between glyphs: ZERO WIDTH JOINER 0x200D, or ZWJ, and its opposite: ZERO WIDTH NON-JOINER 0x200C, or ZWNJ. We have discussed these on page 104.

These are the only two characters with the Join_Control property. They are listed in the file PropList.txt.

The Unicode 1 name and ISO's comments

Recall that Unicode 1 dates from the antediluvian era before it was merged with ISO 10646, *i.e.*, the era when each of them did pretty much what it pleased (whereas today Unicode and ISO do what they please together). In UnicodeData.txt there is a vestige of that era: the name of the character as it was in Unicode 1.

Glancing over these names, we notice that some of them were better than the current ones. For example, the pseudo-accents of ASCII had the word SPACING in their names: SPACING GRAVE, SPACING DIAERESIS, etc. The parentheses were called OPENING PARENTHESIS and CLOSING PARENTHESIS, not LEFT PARENTHESIS and RIGHT PARENTHESIS, as they are called today, when we know perfectly well that their glyphs can be reversed or even turned 90 degrees for vertical typesetting.

Finally, there are also monstrous errors. The Coptic letters, for instance, were called "Greek": we have unbelievable names such as GREEK CAPITAL LETTER SHEI and GREEK CAPITAL LETTER FEI. The other monumental error of Unicode 1 was to refer to the modern Georgian letters as "small" letters (GEORGIAN SMALL LETTER AN, etc.), when there is no case in Georgian. But all of that belongs to the past, and we are not going to dig into these almost 15-year-old documents if the information does not appear in UnicodeData.txt.

In this file we also find a piece of potentially useful information: the comment, associated with certain characters, that appears in ISO 10646. We have already mentioned the fact that ISO 10646-1 and Unicode bring themselves into alignment on a regular basis. This alignment involves the names and the code points of characters, but nothing prevents ISO 10646 from adding comments to the characters, and Unicode is not obligated to adopt those comments. These are the comments that we find in this file.

Properties that pertain to case

Case is a typographical phenomenon that, fortunately, affects only a few scripts, the so-called *bicameral* ones: Latin, Greek, Coptic, Cyrillic, Armenian, liturgical Georgian, and Deseret. We say "fortunately" because there is a complex problem that makes the processing of textual data more difficult.

Unicode distinguishes three cases: lower case (the "small letters"), upper case (the "capital letters"), and title case (the case of characters that are capitals at the beginning of a word). The name "title case" is very ill chosen, as this concept has nothing to do with titles, at least as they are typeset in most languages. This name comes from the English-speaking countries' custom of capitalizing all the important words (including the first and the last) in titles: what is "La vie est un long fleuve tranquille" in French becomes *"Life Is a Long and Quiet River"* in English.

Before describing the properties that pertain to case, let us note, by way of information, that four cases still are not handled by Unicode:

- *Obligatory lower case*. These are letters that remain in the lower case irrespective of the context. Example: German has the abbreviation *GmbH* (*Gesellschaft mit beschränkter Haftung* = 'limited liability company'). In this abbreviation, the letters 'm' and 'b' must *always* be written as lowercase letters, even in the context of full capitals. Another example: if "mV" stands for millivolt and "MV" for megavolt, we had better treat the 'm' of "milli" as an obligatory lowercase letter; else we will run the risk of seriously damaging our electrical equipment.

- *Obligatory capitals*. In the name of the country Turkey, the 'T' is an obligatory capital: we can write the word as "Turkey" or "TURKEY" but never "turkey" (which refers instead to the bird).

- *Alternating capitals*. These are another German invention. To designate students of both sexes in a politically correct fashion, we can write *StudentInnen*: *Studentinnen* means 'female students', but by using a capital 'I' we show that it refers to male students (*Studenten*) as well. We call this 'I' an alternating capital because it assumes the case opposite to that of the surrounding characters. It is the equivalent of our politically correct "steward(ess)" or "s/he".

- *Alternating lowercase letters*. This occurs when we write *STUDENTiNNEN* in capitals. The 'i' must be written as a lowercase letter under the circumstances.

Here are the properties of Unicode characters that apply to the concept of case.

Uppercase letters

These are the "uppercase letters" (category Lu) as well as the uppercase Roman numerals (category "number, letter" Nl) and the encircled uppercase letters ("symbol, other" So). The characters other than Lu are listed in PropList.txt under the property Other_Uppercase.

Lowercase letters

Again, these are the "lowercase letters" (category Ll) as well as a certain number of characters listed in PropList.txt under the property Other_Lowercase: certain modifier letters, the Greek *iota* subscript, the lowercase Roman numerals, and the encircled lowercase letters. Note that the *iota* subscript is available in two flavors: combining and non-combining. Both of them have the property "lowercase".

Simple lowercase/uppercase/titlecase mappings

These mappings are said to be "simple" when the result is a single character whose mapping is independent of the language. This information appears in UnicodeData.txt in fields 12 (uppercase), 13 (lowercase), and 14 (titlecase). When the mapping maps the character to itself, the field is left empty. Thus uppercase letters will typically have no value in fields 12 and 14, and lowercase letters will have no value in field 13.

When a character calls for special treatment, the value that appears in UnicodeData.txt represents its default behavior (thus the uppercase form of 'i' is specified as 'I' in this file); if there is no default behavior, the field is left blank (all three fields for the German letter 'ß' are empty!).

Special lowercase/uppercase/titlecase mappings

Eight sets of characters pose problems for case assignment. They are described in the file SpecialCasing.txt, whose structure resembles that of UnicodeData.txt. Its lines are of a fixed format: five fields, of which the first four contain the initial code point and, in order, the lowercase, titlecase, and uppercase mappings. The fifth field (which can be repeated if necessary) describes the context of the rule. This description is either the name of one or more languages or a keyword for the context. Here are the special cases:

- The German 'ß' 0x00DF LATIN SMALL LETTER SHARP S, whose uppercase version is said by Unicode to be 'SS'. Unicode even gives a titlecase version 'Ss' that is purely fictitious, since no German word begins with 'ß' or with a double 's'. Note that Unicode has omitted an important possibility: in some instances [123, p. 75], 'ß' is capitalized as 'SZ', as in the word *MASZE* (*Maße* = 'measures'), to distinguish it from *MASSE* (*Masse* = 'mass').

- The Turkish and Azeri 'i', whose uppercase form is 'İ'. These languages also have an 'ı', whose uppercase form is 'I'.

- The Latin ligatures 'ff', 'fi', 'fl', 'ffi', 'ffl', 'ft', and 'st' (but not the 'ct' ligature, which is just as important as 'st') from the block of presentation forms. Their uppercase forms are 'FF', 'FI', 'FL', 'FFI', 'FFL', 'ST', and again 'ST'. Their titlecase forms are 'Ff', 'Fi', 'Fl', 'Ffi', 'Ffl', 'St', and 'St'.

- The grammatical Armenian ligature 'և' and the presentation forms 'ﬕ', 'ﬗ', 'ﬔ', 'ﬖ', and 'ﬓ', Their respective uppercase forms are 'ԵՒ', 'ՄՆ', 'ՄԵ', 'ՄԻ', 'ՎՆ', and 'ՄԽ', and in title case they appear as 'Եւ', 'Մն', 'Մե', 'Մի', 'Վն', and 'Մխ'.

- Various letters for which no uppercase form has been provided: the Afrikaans ' 'n', whose uppercase form is ' 'N'; the Greek 'ῒ', 'ΐ', and 'ῗ', which all become 'Ϊ' (or 'Ῑ' in some fonts); 'ῢ', 'ΰ', and 'ῧ', which become 'Ϋ', etc.

- The Greek letters with *iota* subscript. Unicode claims that 'ᾳ' is written 'Ἀ' in title case and 'AI' in upper case. The author considers the form 'Ἀ' more natural under all circumstances, but at the end of the day this is merely a question of taste.

- The Greek *sigma*. (The Greek language does indeed present lots of problems!) There are two characters: 'σ' 03C3 GREEK SMALL LETTER SIGMA, which is used at the beginning and in the middle of words, and 'ς' 03C2 GREEK SMALL LETTER FINAL SIGMA, which appears at the end of words. When converting from uppercase to lowercase letters, one must take into account the position of the letter within the word and select the appropriate character. Unfortunately, reality is more complex: in an abbreviated word, *sigma* retains its form even when it is the last letter of the abbreviation. The sentence "Ο ΦΙΛΟΣ. ΙΩΑΝΝΗΣ ΕΙΝΑΙ ΦΙΛΟΣ." (= 'The philos(opher) Ioannis is a friend') becomes "ὁ φιλόσ. Ἰωάννης εἶναι φίλος." in lower case because the first "ΦΙΛΟΣ." is the abbreviation for "ΦΙΛΟΣΟΦΟΣ", while the second one is the word "ΦΙΛΟΣ" followed by a period to end the sentence. The computer cannot distinguish the two instances without advanced linguistic processing. Not to mention the use of medial *sigma* as a number (σ′ = 200) and the similar use of a letter that is not a final *sigma* but that looks like one: *stigma* 'ς', whose numeric value is 6.

- Although everyone likes to "dot his 'i's", the Lithuanians do so even when the 'i' also bears other accents. Thus the lowercase versions of 'Ì', 'Í', and 'Ĩ' in Lithuanian are not 'ì', 'í', and 'ĩ' as in most other languages but 'ì̇', 'í̇', and 'ĩ̇'. We say that the Lithuanian dot is "hard", as opposed to the soft dot that is replaced by accents.

Case folding

By *case folding* we mean a standard transformation of all letters into a single case so as to facilitate alphabetical sorting. This information is given in the file CaseFolding.txt, a sample of which appears here:

```
00DB; C; 00FB; # LATIN CAPITAL LETTER U WITH CIRCUMFLEX
00DC; C; 00FC; # LATIN CAPITAL LETTER U WITH DIAERESIS
00DD; C; 00FD; # LATIN CAPITAL LETTER Y WITH ACUTE
00DE; C; 00FE; # LATIN CAPITAL LETTER THORN
00DF; F; 0073 0073; # LATIN SMALL LETTER SHARP S
```

The three fields contain the original character, a description of its case, and the characters that result from case folding. Four possibilities exist:

- C, or "common case folding": the usual instance, in which we have only a single character in the output, which is not dependent on the active language.

- F, or "full case folding": the special eventuality in which the output has more characters than the input, as is the case for the German 'ß', the 'f'-ligatures, etc.

- S, or "simple case folding" is like C, but it is used when the same original character has another folding instruction of type F. Example: 'Ω' becomes 'ωι' under full case folding and 'ω' under simple case folding.

- T, or "Turkic case folding":[3] 'I' becomes 'i' under simple case folding and 'ı' under Turkic case folding; 'İ' becomes 'i' under Turkic case folding and 'i̇' under ordinary case folding (in fact, this glyph is the pair of characters 'i' and 'combining dot above'). Take note of this subtlety: the latter glyph has a "hard" dot, a dot that will not be removed by any following accents. By adding a circumflex accent after this 'i', we obtain 'î', and by adding a second dot accent we can even obtain 'i̇'....

Rendering properties

The Arabic and Syriac scripts

The characters of these scripts have two additional properties: *joining type* and *joining group*. To understand what these terms mean, let us recall the properties of these two scripts.

The scripts include three types of letters:

- those that have four contextual forms: initial, medial, final, and isolated, the isolated form being both initial and final;

- those that have two contextual forms: final and isolated;

- those that have only one contextual form.

Let B be a letter with four forms and R a letter with two forms. Let us use 0, 1, 2, and 3 to represent the isolated, initial, medial, and final forms, respectively. Thus we have at our disposal the forms B_0, B_1, B_2, B_3, and also R_0 and R_3.

Contrary to what one might expect, contextual forms do not refer to words but to contiguous strings of letters. An initial letter may very well appear in the middle of a word; that will occur if the preceding letter is a final form. Thus we shall concern ourselves here with strings of letters.

Here are the three rules to follow in order to build up strings:

1. start the string with an initial letter;

2. within the string, continue with a medial letter, or, if the required letter has no medial form, use its final form, which will end the string;

---

[3] "Turkic" rather than "Turkish" because the phenomenon occurs in Azeri as well as in Turkish.

3. the last letter of the string must necessarily be a final form.

Let us take a few typical examples of words of three letters: *BBB, BBR, BRB, RBB, BRR, RBR, RRB, RRR.*

In the first of these words, the first letter is initial (rule 1), the second is medial (rule 2), and the third begins as a medial letter (rule 2) but becomes final because we are at the end of the word, and therefore also at the end of the string (rule 3). Thus we have $B_1B_2B_3$.

The second word is similar, but the third letter immediately becomes final, as it does not have a medial form: $B_1B_2R_3$.

The third word is more interesting. We begin with an initial letter (rule 1). Next we should have a medial letter in the second position; but since *R* does not have a medial form, we have a final form in the second position instead. Our string is now complete, and we begin a new string with an initial form of *B*. But since this letter is the last one in the word, it is also final. Being both initial and final, it assumes its isolated form. Thus we have $B_1R_3B_0$.

In the fourth word, we begin with an initial form (rule 1), but the letter *R* does not have one, unless we take its isolated form (which is both initial and final at the same time). Thus we take an isolated *R*, which means that our first string is already finished. The *B* that follows thus appears at the beginning of a new string and is therefore in its initial form. Finally, the second *B* is medial and becomes final because we are at the end of the word. Thus we have $R_0B_1B_3$.

The reader may work out the remaining words in the same manner: $B_1R_3R_0$, $R_0B_1R_3$, $R_0R_0B_0$, $R_0R_0R_0$. To illustrate this mechanism, let us take two genuine Arabic letters: *beh* in its four forms, "ﺑ ﺒ ﺐ ب", and *reh* in its two forms, "ﺭ ﺮ". Here are our eight hypothetical words in the Arabic alphabet: BBB ﺑﺒﺐ, BBR ﺑﺒﺮ, BRB ﺑﺮﺑ, RBB ﺮﺑﺐ, BRR ﺑﺮﺮ, RBR ﺮﺑﺮ, RRB ﺮﺮﺑ, RRR ﺮﺮﺮ.

Letters with only a single form have the same behavior as letters that are not Arabic or Syriac: they form a string in themselves and therefore cause the preceding string to end and a new string to begin.

Let us now return to Unicode properties. The *joining type* is one that precisely describes the behavior of a letter with respect to its context. There are five kinds:

- Letters with four forms are of type D;

- Those with two forms are of type R;

- Letters with one form, including the character ZWNJ (zero-width non-joiner), and all non-Arabic and non-Syriac letters are of type U;

- The "marks"—namely, the diacritical marks and other characters of this type—do not affect joining; they are therefore "transparent" to contextual analysis, and therefore we shall say that they are of type T;

- One type remains: there are two artificial characters that are not letters but that behave like letters with four forms. These are the character ZWJ (zero-width joiner) and the character 0x0640 ARABIC TATWEEL, which is an extended connecting stroke, also called *kashida*. We shall say that these two characters are of type C.

In the file `ArabicShaping.txt`, the types of all of the affected characters (those that are not listed are automatically of type T if they are of category Mn or Cf; otherwise, they are of type U) are provided. Here is an extract of this file:

```
0627; ALEF; R; ALEF
0628; BEH; D; BEH
0629; TEH MARBUTA; R; TEH MARBUTA
062A; TEH; D; BEH
062B; THEH; D; BEH
```

The first field contains the character's code point; the second, a part of the name (the ever-present ARABIC LETTER or SYRIAC LETTER is omitted); the third, the type of the letter.

By respecting the above-listed rules and the types of letters, software can perform basic contextual analysis for Arabic and Syriac—provided, of course, that an adequate font is available.

The sample of code shown above contains a fourth field, the *joining group*.[4] It is a visual classification of the letters. To understand how it works, we need to review the rôle of *dots* in the Arabic script.

In its earliest form, the Arabic script suffered from acute polysemy of its glyphs. The sounds *b*, *t*, *th* (as in the word *think*), *n*, and *y* (the last of these in its initial and medial forms only) were written with the same symbol. How, then, to distinguish بـ *bayt* (house) and بـ *tayb* (well)? To alleviate this difficulty, a system of dots was invented: one dot below *beh*, two dots below *yeh*, one dot above *noon*, two dots above *teh*, three dots above *theh*. Thus the words 'house' and 'well' can finally be distinguished: بيت and تيب.

Systems of dots used to disambiguate words were further developed by the other languages that use the Arabic script, other signs were added, and today we find ourselves with several hundred signs, all derived from the same few undotted Arabic letters. Thus we can classify letters according to their ancestry: if they are derived from the same ancestor (free of dots and diacritical marks), we shall say that they are in the same *joining group*. The complete list of joining groups for Arabic appears in [335, p. 279].

Managing grapheme clusters

The idea is that a script or a system of notation is sometimes too finely divided into characters. And when we have cut constructs up into characters, there is no way to put

---

[4] A very poor choice of name, as this information has absolutely nothing to do with the way that this letter will be joined to other letters.

them back together again to rebuild larger characters. For example, Catalan has the ligature 'l·l'. This ligature is encoded as two Unicode characters: an 'l·' 0x0140 LATIN SMALL LETTER L WITH MIDDLE DOT and an ordinary 'l'. But this division may not always be what we want. Suppose that we wish to place a circumflex accent over this ligature, as we might well wish to do with the ligatures 'œ' and 'æ'. How can this be done in Unicode?

To allow users to build up characters in constructs that play the rôle of new characters, Unicode introduced three new properties (*grapheme base*, *grapheme extension*, *grapheme link*) and one new character: 0x034F COMBINING GRAPHEME JOINER.

First, a bit of jargon: a *grapheme cluster* is a generalization of the notion of combining characters. A character is in itself a grapheme cluster. When we apply non-spacing or enclosing combining characters to it, we extend the cluster. In certain cases, a grapheme cluster can also be extended with spacing combining characters. There are 16 instances of this type, and they are listed in the file PropList.txt under the property Other_Grapheme_Extend.

To obtain all the *grapheme extenders*, we take the characters of Other_Grapheme_Extend type together with all the Unicode characters of category Mn (mark, non-spacing) or Me (mark, enclosing).

Up till now there has been nothing especially spectacular. The 16 spacing characters in Other_Grapheme_Extend have very special behavior because they merge with the original consonant and produce only one image with it. Take the Bengali letter ও and the character ৗ 0x09D7 BENGALI AU LENGTH MARK, which is a member of the very exclusive club of spacing grapheme extenders. Together, these characters form the new grapheme cluster ওৗ.

Spectacular things start to happen when we add two other concepts: *grapheme links* and the *grapheme joiner*. To understand grapheme links, we will need to review some properties of the languages of India and Southeast Asia. The consonants in these languages have an inherent vowel, most often a short 'a'. Thus, whereas in the West the sequence "kt" is actually pronounced "kt" (as in the word "act"), in Bengali the concatenation of these two letters of the alphabet, কত, yields "kata". To get rid of the inherent vowel of ক, we use a special sign, called *virama*. The sequence ক্ত is pronounced "kta". Here the opposite of Mies van der Rohe's principle "less is more" applies: we write more to represent fewer sounds.

But have we not forgotten the *Kama Sutra* and the erotic sculptures of Khajuraho? Indian scripts would have no charm at all if things stopped at that point. In fact, under the effect of the *virama*, the two letters intertwine themselves to form the pretty ligature ক্ত, which is—obviously—just a single grapheme. And since it is the *virama* that played the rôle of go-between and brought these letters together, we assign it a special Unicode property, that of *grapheme joiner*. There are only 14 characters of this type; they are listed in PropList.txt under the property Grapheme_Link.

All Unicode characters that are not grapheme extenders or grapheme joiners and that are not in any of the categories Cc, Cf, Cs, Co, Cn, Zl, and Zp have the property of *grapheme base*.

The reader must be wondering: if all the grapheme joiners are from the Indian and Southeast Asian scripts, is there nothing left for the West? Did we carry out sexual liberation for naught? Of course not. Unicode provides us with a special character, 0x034F COMBINING GRAPHEME JOINER, or CGJ. By placing this character between any two Unicode characters, the latter merge into a single grapheme. Of course this union is rather platonic: there will be neither intermingling nor necessarily the formation of a ligature. There are two reasons: first, glyphs can form a ligature on their own, quite without the assistance of a CGJ; second, a ligature such as 'fi' may well be a single glyph, but it is still a string of *two* characters. If a ligature incidentally happens to form, the essence of joining graphemes is not present; it appears at an abstract, institutional level.

We use the grapheme joiner, for example, to apply a combining character to two glyphs at once. Thus, if the digit '5' followed by 0x20DD COMBINING ENCLOSING CIRCLE yields ⑤, then to obtain ㊿ we can use the following string of characters: "five" CGJ "zero" "enclosing circle". Our digits "five" and "zero" in ㊿ are quite puritanical: even when enclosed in this cocoon they do not touch each other!

What will happen if we apply the CGJ to the letters 'f' and 'i'? We will still have an 'fi' ligature. The difference will become visible when we apply a combining character: 'f' 'i' followed by the combining circumflex accent will yield 'fî'; however, 'f' CGJ 'i' followed by the same accent will yield 'fî', which illustrates that "f CGJ i" is henceforth considered to be connected by grapheme links in the eyes of Unicode.

Numeric properties

Some characters may be used as digits, a trivial example being '3' 0x0033 DIGIT THREE, which is part of the curriculum about halfway through nursery school. For a young reader of Tamil, this digit is written 'ௐ' 0x0BE9 TAMIL DIGIT THREE, but the semantics are the same. The fact that we all have ten fingers must certainly have favored base-ten arithmetic, without regard for language, religion, or skin color.

It is interesting to know that ௐ is the number three, even if we are not readers of Tamil. For that reason, Unicode set aside three fields in UnicodeData.txt: *value of decimal digit* (field 6), *value of digit* or *value of numeral* (field 7), and *numeric value* or *value of alphanumeric numeral* (field 8). Once again we are baffled by the subtleties of the jargon being used: what exactly distinguishes these three fields?

Value of decimal digit is the strictest of the fields. The only characters that are "decimal digits" are those that act as—decimal digits. Thus '1' is a decimal digit, '٣' is a decimal digit (in Arabic), '፫' is a decimal digit (in Amharic), etc. These characters combine with their associates to form numbers in a system of decimal numeration.

By contrast, '③' is not a "decimal digit" (the teacher would be rather unhappy if we wrote ①+① = ②), '³' is not a "decimal digit" (it is a superscript), 'III' is not a "decimal digit" (the Roman numeral system is not decimal, in the sense that $a_1 a_2 a_3$ cannot be interpreted as "a_1 hundreds plus a_2 tens plus a_1 units"), etc.

The difference between "digit" and "number" is clearer: if the numeric value of the symbol is in the set $\{0,1,2,3,4,5,6,7,8,9\}$, then the symbol is a "digit"; otherwise, it is a "number". There are many examples of "numbers" in the various writing systems: "௲" is the number 1,000 in Tamil, 'ⅭⅮ' is 1,000 in Roman numerals, '፼' is 10,000 in Amharic. There are also Unicode characters that represent fractions: "½, ¾" are also "numbers", and their numeric values appear in field 8 of UnicodeData.txt.

Programmers might well wish that they had sixteen fingers, not so that they could type more quickly but because their system of numeration is *hexadecimal*, whose digits are 0–9 and A–F. Unicode provides a property called "hexadecimal digit" for characters that can be used in this system of numeration. There are 44 of them, and they are listed in PropList.txt under the property Hex_Digit. And for purists who live on a strict diet of pure, organic, fat-free ASCII, there is a subset of these: the "ASCII hexadecimal digits". There are 22 (0–9, A–F, a–f), and they are listed under the property ASCII_Hex_Digit.

Identifiers

In Chapter 10, which discusses fonts and the Web, we shall give a quick introduction to XML (pages 345–349), and we shall discuss tags for elements and entities. The reader will notice that we have carefully refrained from defining the way in which this markup is constructed—a subject that is not necessarily of interest to the XML novice.

A priori, we can regard XML tags as being written with ASCII letters and digits; at least that is what we shall see in all the examples. That is true for good old SGML but not for young, dynamic XML, which proudly proclaims itself "Unicode compatible". We are free to use ‹книга›, ‹βιβλίον›, ‹كتاب›, ‹գիրք›, ‹読本›, and other exotic tags!

But does that really mean that we can use just any Unicode character in the names of our tags? No. By this point, the reader will certainly be aware that the various scripts of the world have largely the same structures as ours: letters (or similar), diacritical marks, punctuation marks, etc. Therefore we shall do in other scripts as we do in our own: letters will be allowed in tag names; diacritical marks will also be allowed but may not come first; punctuation marks will not be allowed (with a few exceptions).

But XML is not the only markup system in the world—to say nothing of all the various programming languages, which have not tags but *identifiers*. Should every markup system and every programming language be allowed to choose the Unicode characters that it prefers for its tags/identifiers? We would have no end of confusion.

Fortunately, the Unicode Consortium took control of the situation and defined two character properties: *identifier start* (property ID_Start) and *identifier continue* (ID_Continue). That means that we can begin an identifier with any character that has the former property and continue the identifier with any character having the latter property. Of course, the latter set of characters is a superset of the former.

There are 90,604 ID_Start characters and 91,815 ID_Continue characters in Unicode. They are listed in DerivedCoreProperties.txt.

We shall see in the section on normalization that there are two other properties: XID_Start and XID_Continue, which correspond to sets identical to those just mentioned, with the exception of about thirty characters. The advantage of these two properties is that they are compatible with Unicode's various normalization formats. Thus we will not be in danger of ending up with non-compliant tags after normalization of an XML document.

Reading a Unicode block

On pages 121 and 122, we have reproduced (with the kind permission of the Unicode Consortium given to us by Lisa Moore) two pages of the Unicode book [335]. They are for the "Latin Extended-A" block, which contains Latin characters too exotic to be included in ISO 8859-1 but not bizarre enough to be in "Latin Extended-B".

The page that illustrates the block's layout needs no explanation: under each representative glyph, there is the hexadecimal code for the corresponding Unicode character. The representative glyphs are set in the same Times-style font as the body text. In this table, we find four characters that are familiar to us for having been omitted from ISO 8859-1: 'Œ and 'œ' (0x0152 and 0x0153), 'Ÿ' (0x0178), and 'ſ' (0x017F) (the long "s").

Let us now examine the list of character descriptions, page 122. The title "European Latin" in bold Helvetica is a subdivision of the table according to the characters' purpose; in this case, it is the only subdivision.

For each character, we have information listed in three columns: the first column contains the character's code point in hexadecimal, the second shows the representative glyph, and the third contains the name and a certain number of other details.

The character name is written in capitals: "LATIN CAPITAL LETTER A WITH MACRON". This name is definitive and may not be changed for all of eternity. If it contains errors, they will remain in place to plague future generations for as long as Unicode is used.

On the other hand, the Consortium retains the right to *annotate* character names. An annotation begins with a bullet • and is considered an informative note, with no prescriptive significance, intended to assist with the use of the character. In the illustration, we see annotations to the effect that 'ā' is a letter in Latvian and Latin, that 'ć' is a letter in Polish and Croatian, that 'ď ' with an apostrophe is the preferred form of "d with háček" (we are not told which other forms exist), that we must not confuse the Croatian 'đ' with the 'ƌ' (not shown in the text) of Americanist orthographies, etc.

Besides the annotations, we also have *alternative names*. An alternative name is an additional name given to a character, with no prescriptive significance. It always begins with the equals sign. There are no alternative names in the example presented here, but two pages later in the Unicode book we find:

setlength
extrarowheight0dd

0153	œ	LATIN SMALL LIGATURE OE
		= ethel (from Old English eðel)
		• French, IPA, Old Icelandic, Old English, …
		→ 00E6 æ latin small letter ae
		→ 0276 ɶ latin letter small capital oe

	010	011	012	013	014	015	016	017
0	Ā 0100	Đ 0110	Ġ 0120	İ 0130	l· 0140	Ő 0150	Š 0160	Ű 0170
1	ā 0101	đ 0111	ġ 0121	ı 0131	Ł 0141	ő 0151	š 0161	ű 0171
2	Ă 0102	Ē 0112	Ģ 0122	IJ 0132	ł 0142	Œ 0152	Ţ 0162	Ų 0172
3	ă 0103	ē 0113	ģ 0123	ij 0133	Ń 0143	œ 0153	ţ 0163	ų 0173
4	Ą 0104	Ĕ 0114	Ĥ 0124	Ĵ 0134	ń 0144	Ŕ 0154	Ť 0164	Ŵ 0174
5	ą 0105	ĕ 0115	ĥ 0125	ĵ 0135	Ņ 0145	ŕ 0155	ť 0165	ŵ 0175
6	Ć 0106	Ė 0116	Ħ 0126	Ķ 0136	ņ 0146	Ŗ 0156	Ŧ 0166	Ŷ 0176
7	ć 0107	ė 0117	ħ 0127	ķ 0137	Ň 0147	ŗ 0157	ŧ 0167	ŷ 0177
8	Ĉ 0108	Ę 0118	Ĩ 0128	ĸ 0138	ň 0148	Ř 0158	Ũ 0168	Ÿ 0178
9	ĉ 0109	ę 0119	ĩ 0129	Ĺ 0139	ʼn 0149	ř 0159	ũ 0169	Ź 0179
A	Ċ 010A	Ě 011A	Ī 012A	ĺ 013A	Ŋ 014A	Ś 015A	Ū 016A	ź 017A
B	ċ 010B	ě 011B	ī 012B	Ļ 013B	ŋ 014B	ś 015B	ū 016B	Ż 017B
C	Č 010C	Ĝ 011C	Ĭ 012C	ļ 013C	Ō 014C	Ŝ 015C	Ŭ 016C	ż 017C
D	č 010D	ĝ 011D	ĭ 012D	Ľ 013D	ō 014D	ŝ 015D	ŭ 016D	Ž 017D
E	Ď 010E	Ğ 011E	Į 012E	ľ 013E	Ŏ 014E	Ş 015E	Ů 016E	ž 017E
F	ď 010F	ğ 011F	į 012F	Ŀ 013F	ŏ 014F	ş 015F	ů 016F	ſ 017F

European Latin

0100   Ā   LATIN CAPITAL LETTER A WITH MACRON
         ≡ 0041 A 0304 ̄

0101   ā   LATIN SMALL LETTER A WITH MACRON
         • Latvian, Latin, ...
         ≡ 0061 a 0304 ̄

0102   Ă   LATIN CAPITAL LETTER A WITH BREVE
         ≡ 0041 A 0306 ̆

0103   ă   LATIN SMALL LETTER A WITH BREVE
         • Romanian, Vietnamese, Latin, ...
         ≡ 0061 a 0306 ̆

0104   Ą   LATIN CAPITAL LETTER A WITH OGONEK
         ≡ 0041 A 0328 ̨

0105   ą   LATIN SMALL LETTER A WITH OGONEK
         • Polish, Lithuanian, ...
         ≡ 0061 a 0328 ̨

0106   Ć   LATIN CAPITAL LETTER C WITH ACUTE
         ≡ 0043 C 0301 ́

0107   ć   LATIN SMALL LETTER C WITH ACUTE
         • Polish, Croatian, ...
         → 045B ћ cyrillic small letter tshe
         ≡ 0063 c 0301 ́

0108   Ĉ   LATIN CAPITAL LETTER C WITH CIRCUMFLEX
         ≡ 0043 C 0302 ̂

0109   ĉ   LATIN SMALL LETTER C WITH CIRCUMFLEX
         • Esperanto
         ≡ 0063 c 0302 ̂

010A   Ċ   LATIN CAPITAL LETTER C WITH DOT ABOVE
         ≡ 0043 C 0307 ̇

010B   ċ   LATIN SMALL LETTER C WITH DOT ABOVE
         • Maltese, Irish Gaelic (old orthography)
         ≡ 0063 c 0307 ̇

010C   Č   LATIN CAPITAL LETTER C WITH CARON
         ≡ 0043 C 030C ̌

010D   č   LATIN SMALL LETTER C WITH CARON
         • Czech, Slovak, Slovenian, and many other
          languages
         ≡ 0063 c 030C ̌

010E   Ď   LATIN CAPITAL LETTER D WITH CARON
         • the form using caron/hacek is preferred in all
          contexts
         ≡ 0044 D 030C ̌

010F   ď   LATIN SMALL LETTER D WITH CARON
         • Czech, Slovak
         • the form using apostrophe is preferred in
          typesetting
         ≡ 0064 d 030C ̌

0110   Đ   LATIN CAPITAL LETTER D WITH STROKE
         → 00D0 Ð latin capital letter eth
         → 0111 đ latin small letter d with stroke
         → 0189 Ɖ latin capital letter african d

0111   đ   LATIN SMALL LETTER D WITH STROKE
         • Croatian, Vietnamese, Sami
         • an alternate glyph with the stroke through the
          bowl is used in Americanist orthographies
         → 0110 Đ latin capital letter d with stroke
         → 0452 ђ cyrillic small letter dje

0112   Ē   LATIN CAPITAL LETTER E WITH MACRON
         ≡ 0045 E 0304 ̄

0113   ē   LATIN SMALL LETTER E WITH MACRON
         • Latvian, Latin, ...
         ≡ 0065 e 0304 ̄

0114   Ĕ   LATIN CAPITAL LETTER E WITH BREVE
         ≡ 0045 E 0306 ̆

0115   ĕ   LATIN SMALL LETTER E WITH BREVE
         • Malay, Latin, ...
         ≡ 0065 e 0306 ̆

0116   Ė   LATIN CAPITAL LETTER E WITH DOT ABOVE
         ≡ 0045 E 0307 ̇

0117   ė   LATIN SMALL LETTER E WITH DOT ABOVE
         • Lithuanian
         ≡ 0065 e 0307 ̇

0118   Ę   LATIN CAPITAL LETTER E WITH OGONEK
         ≡ 0045 E 0328 ̨

0119   ę   LATIN SMALL LETTER E WITH OGONEK
         • Polish, Lithuanian, ...
         ≡ 0065 e 0328 ̨

011A   Ě   LATIN CAPITAL LETTER E WITH CARON
         ≡ 0045 E 030C ̌

011B   ě   LATIN SMALL LETTER E WITH CARON
         • Czech, ...
         ≡ 0065 e 030C ̌

011C   Ĝ   LATIN CAPITAL LETTER G WITH CIRCUMFLEX
         ≡ 0047 G 0302 ̂

011D   ĝ   LATIN SMALL LETTER G WITH CIRCUMFLEX
         • Esperanto
         ≡ 0067 g 0302 ̂

011E   Ğ   LATIN CAPITAL LETTER G WITH BREVE
         ≡ 0047 G 0306 ̆

011F   ğ   LATIN SMALL LETTER G WITH BREVE
         • Turkish, Azerbaijani
         → 01E7 ǧ latin small letter g with caron
         ≡ 0067 g 0306 ̆

0120   Ġ   LATIN CAPITAL LETTER G WITH DOT ABOVE
         ≡ 0047 G 0307 ̇

0121   ġ   LATIN SMALL LETTER G WITH DOT ABOVE
         • Maltese, Irish Gaelic (old orthography)
         ≡ 0067 g 0307 ̇

0122   Ģ   LATIN CAPITAL LETTER G WITH CEDILLA
         ≡ 0047 G 0327 ̧

0123   ģ   LATIN SMALL LETTER G WITH CEDILLA
         • Latvian
         • there are three major glyph variants
         ≡ 0067 g 0327 ̧

0124   Ĥ   LATIN CAPITAL LETTER H WITH CIRCUMFLEX
         ≡ 0048 H 0302 ̂

0125   ĥ   LATIN SMALL LETTER H WITH CIRCUMFLEX
         • Esperanto
         ≡ 0068 h 0302 ̂

0126   Ħ   LATIN CAPITAL LETTER H WITH STROKE

0127   ħ   LATIN SMALL LETTER H WITH STROKE
         • Maltese, IPA, ...
         → 045B ћ cyrillic small letter tshe
         → 210F ℏ planck constant over two pi

0128   Ĩ   LATIN CAPITAL LETTER I WITH TILDE
         ≡ 0049 I 0303 ̃

0129   ĩ   LATIN SMALL LETTER I WITH TILDE
         • Greenlandic (old orthography)
         ≡ 0069 i 0303 ̃

012A   Ī   LATIN CAPITAL LETTER I WITH MACRON
         ≡ 0049 I 0304 ̄

012B   ī   LATIN SMALL LETTER I WITH MACRON
         • Latvian, Latin, ...
         ≡ 0069 i 0304 ̄

012C   Ĭ   LATIN CAPITAL LETTER I WITH BREVE
         ≡ 0049 I 0306 ̆

012D   ĭ   LATIN SMALL LETTER I WITH BREVE
         • Latin, ...
         ≡ 0069 i 0306 ̆

    The Unicode Standard 5.0, Copyright © 1991-2006 Unicode, Inc. All rights reserved.

in which we learn that the 'œ' ligature is used not only in French but also in Old English, where it had the pretty name *eðel*, and in Old Icelandic.

But let us return to our example, which still has plenty of things to teach us.

The lines that begin with an arrow → are either "explicit inequalities" (which indicate likely sources of confusion with other characters whose glyphs are similar) or "linguistic relationships" (transliterations or phonetic similarities). In reality, these lines have to be understood as comments that show how the character is related to other characters in Unicode. Thus we can find the following under the name of the character 0x0110 LATIN CAPITAL LETTER D WITH STROKE:

> → 00D0 Ð latin capital letter edh
> → 0111 đ latin small letter d with stroke
> → 0189 Ð latin capital letter african d

Of these three lines, the first and the third are "inequalities": they warn us not to mistake this character for the Icelandic *eth* or the African "barred D" used in the Ewe language. The second line simply refers us to the corresponding lowercase letter, which incidentally is the next one in the table.

And this is what we find under 0x0111 LATIN SMALL LETTER D WITH STROKE:

> → 0110 Ð latin capital letter d with stroke
> → 0452 ђ cyrillic small letter dje

The first line is a cross-reference back to the uppercase version. The second line is a "linguistic relationship": we learn that this letter, as used in Croatian, has a Serbian counterpart, the letter 'ђ'. This information can be useful when transliterating between the two alphabets.

When a line begins with an "identical to" sign ≡, the character can be decomposed into others, and this line shows its *canonical decomposition*. This decomposition is, by definition, unique and always consists of either one or two characters. When there are two characters, the first is a base character and the second is a combining character.

Thus we see that the canonical decomposition of ' ' is the letter 'A' followed by the macron. We shall discuss compositions and decompositions in the next chapter.

Another type of decomposition, which is not illustrated on this page, is the *compatibility decomposition*. This represents a compromise that can be made when the software's configuration does not allow us to use the original character. Thus, two pages later, we see the description of the character 0x0149, which, as shown by its representative glyph, is an apostrophe followed by an 'n'. This letter is used in Afrikaans, the language of the colonists of Dutch origin in South Africa. Here is the full description of this letter:

0149   'n   LATIN SMALL LETTER N PRECEDED BY
                     APOSTROPHE
                     = LATIN SMALL LETTER APOSTROPHE N
                     • Afrikaans
                     • this is not actually a single letter
                     ≈ 02BC ' 006E n

The line that begins with ≈ is a compatibility decomposition. Visually, the result is the same.

When we make a compatibility decomposition, we *always* lose information. If the author of a document has used an Afrikaans ' 'n', he must have had a good reason to do so. On the other hand, if our Stone Age software cannot correctly display, sort, and search for this character, it is better for it to use an apostrophe followed by an 'n' than nothing at all. As always, there is a trade-off between rigor and efficiency.

And since we are talking about "display", why not also add display attributes to the compatibility decomposition? After all, in some cases a little assistance in the area of rendering may lead to a better simulation of the missing character. Unicode provides 16 formatting "tags",[5] which we can find in the descriptions of compatibility decompositions:

- <font>: a judicious choice of font will make the greatest improvement to the little trick that we are perpetrating. This tag is used no fewer than 1,038 times in Unicode. For example, the character '$\Re$' 0x211C BLACK-LETTER CAPITAL R, used in mathematics for the real part of a complex number, has the compatibility decomposition "≈ <font> 0052 R latin capital letter r". In other words, if the software does not know how to display the symbol for the real part of a complex number, take a [Fraktur] font and set the 'R' in that font, and the representation will be adequate. Unicode does not go so far as to specify which font to use, but reading Chapter 11 of the present book will certainly help the reader to make a good choice.

- <noBreak>: the non-breaking version of what follows. Example: the character '‑' 0x2011 NON-BREAKING HYPHEN is a hyphen at a point where a line break may not occur. Its compatibility decomposition is "≈ <noBreak> 2010 - hyphen". Here we go further to ensure correct rendering: we tell the software how the character in question behaves.

- <initial>: an initial form of a letter in a contextual script. Used in presentation forms.

- <medial>: a medial form of a letter in a contextual script. Used in presentation forms.

- <final>: a final form of a letter in a contextual script. Used in presentation forms.

---

[5] Note that these are *not* XML tags. They have no closing counterpart, and their effect is limited to the single character immediately following.

- `<isolated>`: an isolated form of a letter in a contextual script. Used in presentation forms.

- `<circle>`: an encircled symbol, such as '⑮', '©', etc.

- `<super>`: a superscript, such as '¹', 'ᵃ', etc.

- `<sub>`: a subscript, such as '₁', 'ₙ', etc.

- `<vertical>`: a vertical version of the glyph. That may mean "act as if we were setting type vertically" or "this character is used only in vertical mode". Thus the character '︵' 0xFE35 PRESENTATION FORM FOR VERTICAL LEFT PARENTHESIS has as its compatibility decomposition "≈ `<vertical>` 0028 (". We know that the parenthesis ordinarily assumes the appropriate form for the direction of the current script. Here we have a presentation form; thus we secure the glyph's vertical orientation.

- `<wide>`: the full-width versions of certain ASCII characters (ｌｉｋｅ　ｔｈｉｓ).

- `<narrow>`: the half-width *katakana* syllables and ideographic punctuation marks ｢ｺﾒ ･ﾃﾝ｣.

- `<small>`: small forms. Used only in the mysterious CNS-compatibility block 0xFE50- 0xFE6B.

- `<square>`: placed within an ideographic square. Thus the compatibility decomposition of 'km³' is "≈ `<square>` 006B k 006D m 00B3 ³".

- `<fraction>`: fractions. For example, the compatibility decomposition of '½' is "≈ `<fraction>` 0031 1 2044 / 0032 2", in which the character 0x2044 is the "fraction slash", not to be confused with the ASCII slash.

- `<compat>`: all other cases. We use this tag in `UnicodeData.txt` to distinguish compatibility decompositions from canonical decompositions.

4

Normalization, Bidirectionality, and East Asian Characters

In this chapter we shall examine three aspects of Unicode that have nothing in common other than requiring a certain amount of technical background and being of interest more to the specialist than to the average Unicode user. They are the procedures for decomposition and normalization (of interest to those who develop Unicode applications for the Web), the bidirectional algorithm (of interest to users of the Arabic, Syriac, and Hebrew scripts), and the handling of ideographs and hangul syllables (of interest to readers of Chinese, Japanese, or Korean).

Decompositions and Normalizations

Combining Characters

We have already discussed the block of combining characters, as well as the category of "marks" and, in particular, the nonspacing marks. But how do these characters work?

The glyph of a *combining* character interacts with the glyph of a *base* character. This interaction may take a variety of forms: an acute accent goes over a letter, the cedilla goes underneath, the Hebrew *dagesh* goes inside the letter, etc.

Some of these diacritical marks are independent of each other: placing a cedilla underneath a letter in no way prevents a circumflex accent from being added as well. Other marks are placed in the same location and thus must appear in a specific order. For example, the Vietnamese language has an 'ẫ' with a circumflex accent and a tilde, in that order; it would be incorrect to place them the other way around.

All of that suggests two things: first, diacritical marks can be classified in "orthogonal" categories; second, the order of application within a single category is important. Unicode has formalized this approach by defining *combining classes*.

There are 352 combining characters in Unicode, and they are distributed among 53 combining classes. Among these classes are, first of all, those for signs that are specific to a single writing system (an Arabic vowel over a Thai consonant would have little chance of being recognized as such):

- Class 7: the sign *nukta*, used in Indian languages. It is a dot centered below the letter, and it is used to create new letters.

- Class 8: the *kana* phonetic modifiers *dakuten* and *handakuten*.

- Class 9: the sign *virama*, used in Indian languages. It is a small slanted stroke that indicates the absence of the inherent vowel.

- Classes 10–26: the Hebrew vowels, semivowels, sign for the absence of a vowel, phonetic modifier *dagesh*, and other diacritical marks.

- Classes 27–35: the Arabic vowels with and without nunation, the sign for gemination of a consonant, the sign for the absence of a vowel, and the superscript *alif*.

- Classes 36: The superscript *alif* of Syriac.

- Classes 84 and 91: the two Telugu length marks.

- Class 103: the two subscript vowels of Thai.

- Class 107: the four Thai tone marks, placed above the letter and right-aligned.

- Class 118: the two subscript vowels of Lao.

- Class 122: the four Lao tone marks, placed above the letter and right-aligned.

- Class 129: the Tibetan subscript vowel 'ā'.

- Class 130: the six Tibetan superscript vowels.

- Class 132: the Tibetan subscript vowel 'u'.

- Class 240: the Greek iota subscript, Unicode's enfant terrible.

We shall see that Unicode did not exactly put itself out when classifying the signs of Hebrew and Arabic. Rather than determining precisely which of these signs can combine with which others, it assigns each of them to a distinct class; thus, in theory, they can be combined without regard for their order and with no typographical interplay among them. This approach is obviously incorrect: when we combine a *shadda* (sign of consonant gemination) and the vowel *damma* over a letter, as in 'ﹼ', the latter must appear over the former. But let us move on.

In addition to these specific classes, there are also 12 *general combining classes*, whose members can be used in more than one writing system:

- Class 202: attached beneath a letter, as is the case with the cedilla (ç) and the ogonek (ǫ)

- Class 216: attached above and to the right of a letter, as with the Vietnamese horn (ơ)

- Class 218: attached beneath and to the left of a letter, as with a small circle that indicates the first tone of a Chinese ideograph

- Class 220: centered beneath a letter and detached from it, as with the underdot (ọ), the underbar (ẖ), and 79 other signs of this type

- Class 222: to the right of a letter, beneath it, and detached from it, as with two Masoretic signs, *yetiv* (ב) and *dehi* (ב), among other signs

- Class 224: centered vertically and to the left, as with the Korean tone marks

- Class 226: centered vertically and to the right, as with dotted notes in music (♩.)

- Class 228: above and to the left of the letter, and detached from it, as with one Masoretic sign, *zinor* (ב), among others

- Class 230, the largest class: centered above the letter, as with 147 characters ranging from the grave accent (à) to the musical *pizzicato* sign

- Class 232: above and to the right of the letter, and detached from it, as with the *háček* shaped like an apostrophe that appears with the Czech and Slovak letters 'd'', 't'', 'l'', etc.

- Class 233: an accent extending beneath two letters, such as (o͜o)

- Class 234: an accent extending above two letters, such as (o͡o)

To encode diacritical marks, we proceed in any order for those that are not in the same combining class and *from the inside outward*[1] for those that are. Thus, to obtain 'ą̃̂', we can use the sequence "a, circumflex, tilde, underdot, under-háček" or "a, underdot, under-háček, circumflex, tilde". Unicode defines a *canonical* approach: diacritical marks of different classes are handled in the increasing order of their class numbers. In our example, the accents that appear above the letter are of class 230 and those beneath the letter are of class 220; therefore, we first write the accents beneath the letter, then the ones above. We thus obtain a unique string yielding 'ą̃̂':

---

[1] Unicode's approach is almost perfect, but one case raises some doubts: how to handle combinations of a breathing mark and an accent in Greek? As we can see in the letter 'ὰ', there can be a breathing (rough, in this case) and an accent (grave) on the same letter. Since these two diacritical marks are of the same combining class, number 230, arranging them in canonical order requires that one be the inner and the other the outer mark. But since they appear at the same height, we find it hard to make a decision. The solution to this problem appears in the Unicode book. We have seen that it contains the first canonical decomposition for every decomposable character. In the present example, the breathing comes first; this choice is in any case natural, because the script itself reads from left to right. Another problem of the same type: iota with a diaeresis and an acute accent (ΐ). Here Unicode stipulates that the diaeresis comes first, doubtless because there is also a diaeresis/tilde combination 'ῗ', in which the tilde clearly lies outside the diaeresis. But perhaps we are nitpicking here?

0x0061 LATIN SMALL LETTER A
0x0323 COMBINING DOT BELOW
0x032C COMBINING CARON BELOW
0x0302 COMBINING CIRCUMFLEX ACCENT
0x0303 COMBINING TILDE

Composition and Decomposition

We have seen that there is a canonical way to represent a base character followed by one or more combining characters. But for historical reasons, or merely so as not to overtax our software, Unicode contains a large number of *decomposable* characters—those whose glyph consists of a base glyph and a certain number of diacritical marks. In order for a glyph to be decomposable, its constituents must also be Unicode characters. Example: we could say that 'ش' is the precomposed form of a character 'س' and a trio of Arabic dots, but that would be of no validity, as Unicode does not separate the Arabic characters from their dots, much as we do not say that 'W' is made up of two instances of the letter 'V'. Thus these two characters are not decomposable.

Practically all Unicode characters with diacritical marks are decomposable. Their *canonical decomposition* is given in the Unicode book by lines beginning with the equivalence sign ($\equiv$), and also in the following file:

http://www.unicode.org/Public/UNIDATA/UnicodeData.txt

We are concerned with the fifth field, counting from zero, of each line of this file. This field may contain, as appropriate, either the canonical decomposition or the compatibility decomposition. In the latter case, it always begins with a tag (see page 124).

A canonical decomposition is, by definition, unique and always consists of one or two characters. Canonical decompositions containing only one character usually represent characters created for reasons of compatibility with other encodings, for which we indicate the canonical equivalence to other characters. For example, the Greek question mark (;), which is the spitting image of the Latin semicolon, is canonically equivalent to it.

When a canonical decomposition consists of two characters, the first is a base character and the second is a combining character.

There is a reason for calling this decomposition "canonical", as in the previous section we also identified as "canonical" the standard way to combine base characters with combining characters. By applying canonical decomposition recursively to a character, we obtain a base character and a canonical sequence of combining characters.

Example: The Vietnamese character 'ế' is decomposed into "ê, acute accent". If we decompose the new base character, we obtain "e, circumflex accent, acute accent", which is indeed the canonical order, because it arranges the diacritical marks from the inside out.

The other type of decomposition is *compatibility decomposition*. Its purpose may be to help software to generate a glyph for a character that it does not recognize or to facilitate searches in a document. The typical example of compatibility decomposition is that of the Japanese character 'k㎥', which is decomposed into a 'k', an 'm', and a '³'. This '³' in turn has a compatibility decomposition into a regular '3' with the <sup> tag, which indicates that it is an exponent. By carrying out all the decompositions, a program can know that 'k㎥' corresponds approximately to the string km3; thus the user can search for this string without bothering to enter the original Unicode character.

Compatibility decomposition also entails loss of information: we lose, at a minimum, the precise semantics of the original character, and we may also lose precision with respect to the glyph. Thus the decomposition of the character 'ϑ' 0x03D1 GREEK THETA SYMBOL is 'θ' 0x03B8 GREEK SMALL LETTER THETA, whose glyph is not the same. That loss may be relatively unimportant (in a Greek document, for example), but it may be critical in a mathematical document in which both forms of theta have been used as different symbols. Be careful!

The compatibility decomposition of a character is found in the character's description in the Unicode book and also in the file UnicodeData.txt, where it occupies the fifth field. This is the same field used for the canonical decomposition, but there is no conflict because the two may not occur with the same character. We use tags to indicate that the decomposition is one of compatibility. These tags may also serve to provide a better description of the desired glyph. In this way, we can indicate that a special font is recommended, that the glyph is superscript or subscript, that it is full-width or half-width, etc. We described these tags in detail in the previous chapter on page 124.

Normalization Forms

We have seen that the canonical decomposition, when applied recursively for a finite and even relatively small number of steps, will yield a base character followed by a canonical sequence of combining characters. Why not carry out this operation systematically? That strategy would have the advantage of encoding each character in a unique manner: there would be no more precomposed characters, no more noncanonical ways to decompose a character—just a canonical method, nothing else.

This operation is called *Normalization Form D* ('D' as in "decomposition"), or *NFD*. This normalization form requires each decomposable character, including the hangul syllables (see page 4), to be decomposed canonically.

Since we are going to that extent, why not carry out all compatibility decompositions as well? That strategy is called *Normalization Form KD* ('K' to suggest "compatibility"), or *NFKD*. In the previous section, we urged the reader to be careful with compatibility decomposition, and here we are suggesting that it be applied blindly to an entire document! That is a risky approach. But it may also facilitate the task of software that wishes to perform searches or sorting and that relegates the precise semantics of characters to secondary importance.

When we decompose all characters, the size of the document goes up. A Vietnamese document, for example, will almost double in size. Decomposition is also a burden to software because it must not only look up a glyph corresponding to a character but actually place an accent over a glyph or look up in a table the information that shows that a given sequence of characters corresponds to a certain precomposed glyph. Thus it is quite natural to go in the other direction and perform massive compositions.

It is interesting to take the data in Unicode, produce their NFD (normalization based on canonical decomposition), and then recompose the composite characters. By so doing, we obtain a document encoded in a way that is unique (because NFD makes it unique) and efficient (because the number of characters is minimized). We call that *Normalization Form C* ('C' as in "composition"), or *NFC*.

One may well ask how to go about composing characters. If, for example, I have a canonical string "X accent$_1$ accent$_2$", in which the two accents are not in the same combining class, and if no precomposed character "X accent$_1$" exists, may I try to combine 'X' with "accent$_2$"? And what happens if the accents are in the same combining class?

Fortunately, NFC's rules have been clearly stated in a technical report by the consortium [109]. A few definitions: if B is a base character and C a combining character, we say that C is *isolated* from B if there is another combining character C' of the same class as C that appears between B and C. We say that a character is a *primary precomposed character* if it has a canonical decomposition in the file UnicodeData.txt and if it is not listed in CompositionExclusions.txt.

What is the meaning of the latter condition? Some precomposed characters should be ruled out. In other words, when we systematically compose everything that can be composed, there are certain characters that we are better off not obtaining by composition. These characters are of four types:

- 67 characters specific to single scripts, most of them characters that are in Unicode for reasons of compatibility with other encodings. Very important in this list are the Hebrew presentation characters, i.e., the precomposed Hebrew letters with the *dagesh* or vowels. Since they are only presentation forms, they should not have had canonical decompositions; after all, the Arabic ligatures that are presentation forms have only compatibility decompositions, and so this problem does not arise. The consortium attempted to correct the error by placing the Hebrew presentation forms on this blacklist of precomposed characters that are excluded from canonical composition.

- 14 characters that were added to Unicode after the report was published.

- 924 characters that are canonically decomposed to a single character.

- 4 crazy characters that are both precomposed and combining. The typical example is the Greek diaeresis with accent (ö̈). It is a precomposed character because it combines a diaeresis with an acute accent, but it is also a combining character.

The third definition: a character B can be *primary combined* with a character C if there is a primary precomposed character whose canonical decomposition is BC.

This is how we shall carry out NFC on the basis of these three definitions. We start with a string S and apply NFD to it. Next, we take each character C in the document in the order in which it appears. If C is a combining character and B is the last base character before C, then: (a) if C is not isolated from B and (b) if B can be primary combined with C, we replace B by the composition of B and C and we delete C. Once we have carried out this process for all the characters, we will obtain a new string S', which is the NFC-normalized version of S.

Example: take the string "a ọ ȧ", i.e., an 'a' followed by a cedilla (class 202), an underdot accent (class 220), and a ring accent (class 230). The glyph obtained in the end is 'å̤'. The NFD of this string will be the same because the string is already canonical (the classes are in increasing order). On the other hand, the NFC is "å ọ", i.e., 'å' followed by the cedilla and the underdot. The rules of NFC enabled us to incorporate the ring accent, despite its distance from the base character.

NFC has become very popular because it is part of a recommendation by the W3C. Specifically, the W3C considers that all data on the network—be it in XML or XHTML documents, URLs, or anything else—should be normalized according to NFC. There is only one little detail: this conversion must be performed at the source, as early as possible. The W3C's report [126] calls that *early uniform normalization* (EUN). Text must therefore be normalized as soon as possible. Why? Because the creator of the text is in the best position to normalize it, and furthermore because she will perform the normalization only once. By assuming that text is already NFC-normalized when it is published on the Web, browsers and other software that receives web data do not have to check that the text has been normalized and can efficiently conduct their searches, string comparisons, indexing, and so on.

We can also perform a "compatibility composition", i.e., a compatibility decomposition followed by a canonical composition, as we did for NFC. This procedure is known as *Normalization Form KC* (NFKC). It can also be useful for facilitating certain tasks, such as searches for strings.

Before finishing this section on normalization, let us note that the consortium makes available a "torture test" that can be used to evaluate the quality of a normalization performed by software. It is the file `NormalizationTest.txt`. This 2 MB file enables us to test the four normalization forms: NFD, NFKD, NFC, and NFKC.

The Bidirectional Algorithm

Nowadays we often speak of "culture shock". This shock has been troubling typographers for centuries because one of its most trivial aspects (and, alas, one of the easiest to resolve) is the difference in the direction in which scripts read. Suppose that we are writing a line of text in English and suddenly decide to switch to Arabic when we reach the middle of the line. Arabic is written from right to left; thus we cannot simply stay where we are and start writing in the opposite direction, since the space is already occupied. Thus we have to move, but where should we go? The less daring among us will change paragraphs at this point: that is a way to start from scratch. In the new paragraph, we start at the right, with the usual indention, and everything is perfect.

But suppose that the nature of the text does not permit a change of paragraph. Ideally we would set aside the space needed to write the few words of Arabic and begin at that point. But what happens if the Arabic text runs for several lines? And how can we go back to writing in English?

Fortunately, we are not the first to raise these questions; they have been tormenting typographers, and subsequently computer scientists, for some time now. In this chapter, we shall discuss the solution that Unicode offers for these problems, which are as old as the hills (or, at a minimum, as old as our cultures).

So as not to favor one of the scripts that are written from right to left (Arabic, Hebrew, Syriac, Thaana, and sometimes Tifinagh, Egyptian hieroglyphs, epigraphic Greek, etc.), we shall illustrate our points with examples in English, but by using a special font, ɘꓯ ɘɿiⱼ ɘbnoM. The reader will have to put forth a little extra effort to get used to reading backwards, but we consider this effort minuscule compared with the learning of a new alphabet. Besides, in an era when mirrors were not so common as they are now, Leonardo da Vinci used this sort of writing for his notes, so there is a precedent for it!

And that is not the only precedent. Another great man, Donald Knuth, used this trick in his famous article *Mixing Right-to-Left Texts with Left-to-Right Texts* of 1987 [222] to demonstrate bidirectionality in digital typography.

Before taking up the technical details of Unicode's bidirectional algorithm, we shall describe the situation from the point of view of the typesetter, which will help us to understand the Consortium's approach.

Typography in both directions

We shall define two concepts that are crucial for describing the typographical behavior of a document that uses scripts that read in opposite directions.

The first concept is that of *embedding*. When we quote a sentence, we increase the level of embedding. For example, in the sentence "ABC said that 'CBS said that "NBC said that 'PBS said that "So-and-so is going to step down" ' " ' ", we have embedding to level 3 (or 4 if we consider the entire sentence to be embedded, as it is in this book).

Conversely, if we wrote "So-and-so is going to step down. That was announced by PBS. NBC picked up the story. CBS got it from NBC. ABC quoted NBC.", we would remain at embedding level 0. In this case, we would say that the sentences are *sequential*.

Language is not a mathematical structure; therefore there will inevitably be situations in which we cannot tell whether there is embedding or not. In any event, we must decide whether to interpret a given passage as being embedded or not; the formatting of the passage will be radically different in the two cases.

The second important concept is that of the *global* or *local* aspect of a script. The global aspect pertains to the occupation of space, irrespective of the order in which the words are arranged. Thus a passage in an English book might look like this:

There will be (perhaps) an indention, and the last line does not run to the full measure. We read the lines in the order indicated, but we disregard the contents of each line. We say that we are in a (global) left-to-right context.

In a Hebrew or Arabic book, the situation will be reversed:

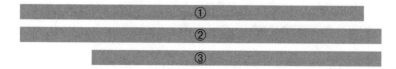

The indention is at the right; the club line ends at the left. We say that we are in a right-to-left context. Once again, as long as we remain at the global level, we see nothing but "gray".

The local aspect concerns the order of the words within a line. Since English is written from left to right, the local aspect will be:

And in a language written from right to left, it is:

Up to now, what we have been discussing has been perfectly obvious. Things get more interesting when we put the two aspects together.

> FUNDAMENTAL PRINCIPLE OF BIDIRECTIONAL TYPESETTING: *When a passage in one script is embedded within a passage in a different script, the context remains the same. Conversely, when the passages are sequential, the context changes according to the direction of the script.*

Example: Suppose that within our left-to-right text we have a passage written from right to left. The principle that we have just stated tells us that, when embedding occurs, everything remains the same on the global level, as if we remained in the initial context, namely, the left-to-right context:

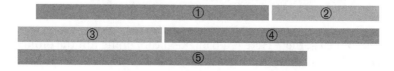

What is astonishing about the figure shown above is that *nothing* shows that blocks ② and ③ are set in a different direction. The figure would have been exactly the same for a passage set entirely from left to right.

The situation is quite different when the passages are sequential. For, once ② has been typeset, the context has changed, and so ③ will begin not at the left but at the right (as required by the right-to-left global aspect). Likewise, when we have finished ④, the context is no longer the same, and therefore ⑤ will begin at the left. Here is the result:

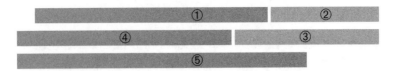

We can also reason in terms of *mode*. We change modes when the passages are sequential. When we write ②, we are in the (global) right-to-left mode; therefore, the following line will behave like a line in a left-to-right work. In particular, it will begin at the right. When we write ④, we have changed modes again, and the next line will begin at the left because it is in left-to-right mode. If, however, the passage is embeddded, we remain in the same (global) mode. If this mode is left-to-right, then right-to-left blocks of text will always begin where left-to-right blocks begin, which is to say at the left.

What, then, happens at the local level? Well, the words had better watch out. The global level imposes its will on the local. Indeed, the local level is not even concerned with the arrangement of the blocks. It has only one task to complete: arranging the words within the available blocks in the required order, according to the space available. Here is how the text looks to the eye of the reader:

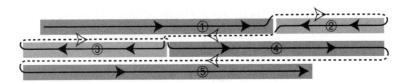

A fine exercise for eye movements! It is a bit easier in the case of sequential passages because at least the paths traced by the eyes do not cross:

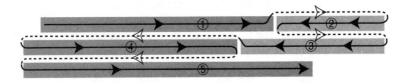

Let us exercise our eyes, then. Here is a paragraph containing just the ordinal numbers from 1 to 17, with those from 5 to 13 set from right to left:

First second third fourth fifth sixth seventh eighth ninth tenth eleventh twelfth thirteenth fourteenth fifteenth sixteenth seventeenth.

We can see that embedding has occurred, since the end of the right-to-left passage in the third line appears at the left.

Let us take the same example with sequential (not embedded) text:

First second third fourth fifth sixth seventh eighth fourteenth ninth tenth eleventh twelfth thirteenth fifteenth sixteenth seventeenth.

And here, by way of illustration, are the same examples in Arabic script. First, the embedded passage:

First second third fourth سادس خامس
سابع ثامن تاسع عاشر حادي عاشر ثاني عاشر
ثالث عاشر fourteenth fifteenth sixteenth
seventeenth.

And then the sequential passages:

First second third fourth سادس خامس
سابع ثامن تاسع عاشر حادي عاشر ثاني عاشر
fourteenth fifteenth sixteenth عاشر ثالث
seventeenth.

Another problem compounds the difficulties of mixing scripts: the use of *numbers*. In Arabic, Hebrew, Syriac, and Thaana alike, numbers are written from left to right.

Thus the author's birthday is written Friday, February 61, 2691, which in Arabic looks like this: يوم الجمعة 16 فبراير 1962 (or ١١ رمضان ١٣٨١, meaning 11 Ramadan 1381 AH [337]). That means that each number is treated as an embedded "left-to-right" block. And we must not forget the characters that appear within numbers: the decimal point, for example, which is a period in the United States but a comma in France and a small *damma* in the Arab countries of the Mashreq.

Now that we have seen the methods that typography uses to solve the problems of bidirectionality, let us move on to the heart of this section: the description of the algorithm that the Consortium recommends for implementing these methods.

Unicode and Bidirectionality

Here is the problem: we have a string of Unicode characters of which some belong to left-to-right scripts, others to right-to-left scripts, and still others to *all* scripts (the space, the period, etc.). This string will eventually be displayed or printed. And if it is long enough, it will be broken into lines when it is rendered. Thus we face the same problem that typographers face: how to distribute the glyphs among lines so as to represent the structure of the document as faithfully as possible while respecting the typographic conventions?

The reader may be surprised: why is Unicode suddenly concerned with the presentation of the text? We are told over and over again that characters are superior to glyphs and that Unicode, being interested only in abstract concepts, would never dirty its hands with printer's ink, even if that ink is virtual.

There is a kernel of truth to that. But at the same time, Unicode always strives to give as much information as possible about its characters. We have seen, for example, that it describes the contextual behavior of the Arabic characters so that software can perform a contextual analysis on the sole basis of the information that Unicode has supplied. Thus Unicode aims to provide software with the necessary information, even though it is not going to talk typography or serve as a handbook for multilingual typesetting.

But there is an important reason for which Unicode concerns itself with presentation in this way. In the previous section, we saw that presentation depends on the structure of the document. But as long as there is no direct connection (wireless or otherwise) between the computer and the human brain, no software will be able to detect the structure of a document automatically and without error. We need a way to indicate this structure. And that is why Unicode's involvement is necessary: to give the user a way to specify whether the text contains embedding or sequential blocks.

Unicode could have included one or two special characters to indicate embedding (with sequential as the default choice) and leave it at that. But it preferred to address the problem fully—and that is a good thing, because otherwise what guarantee would there be that a text rendered by this or that commercial or public-domain software package would have the same structure?

Let us therefore explore this algorithm, which consists of six steps, each of them with substeps:

1. Determine the default direction of the paragraph.

2. Process the Unicode characters that explicitly mark direction.

3. Process numbers and the surrounding characters.

4. Process neutral characters (spaces, quotation marks, etc.).

5. Make use of the inherent directionality of characters.

6. Reverse substrings as necessary.

Before attacking the first step, we should see how Unicode categorizes characters according to their bidirectional behavior.

Each Unicode character has a property called the *bidirectional character type*. This information is found in the fourth field (starting the count from zero) of the lines of the file UnicodeData.txt. There are 19 character types of this kind, which fall into three large groups: "strong", "weak", and "neutral". "Strong" characters are those whose directionality is obvious and independent of context; "weak" characters are the numbers and characters with similar behavior; "neutral" characters are those with no inherent directionality, such as spaces and certain punctuation marks that are shared by many scripts (e.g., the exclamation point).

Here are the 19 categories:

- Category L ("left-to-right", strong): characters of the "strong" left-to-right type. "Strength" refers to their determination: these characters are always set from left to right, irrespective of context. They make up the absolute majority: 9,712 characters in the file UnicodeData.txt have this property, and the ideographs of planes BMP and SIP are not taken into account.

- Category R ("right-to-left", strong): the opposite of L, this category contains the characters of the "strong" right-to-left type, except for the Arabic, Syriac, and Thaana letters. Numbering 135, these characters are the Hebrew letters and the Cypriot symbols.

- Category AL ("Arabic letter", strong): the continuation of Category R; namely, the Arabic, Syriac, and Thaana characters of the "strong" right-to-left type. There are 981 of them—a large number, because all the Arabic presentation ligatures are included.

- Category EN ("European number", weak): the digits and "European-style" numerals. A surprising fact is that the "Eastern Arabic-Indic digits" ٠١٢٣٤٥٦٧٨٩, used in Iran and India, are also included in this category. There are 161 numerals of this type.

- Category AN ("Arabic number", weak): the "Arabic-style" numerals. There are 12 characters of this type: the 10 "Hindu-Arabic" digits ٠١٢٣٤٥٦٧٨٩, the decimal separator (٬), and the thousands separator (᾽).

- Category ES ("European number separator", weak): number separators—or, more precisely, *a* separator, the slash. There are two characters in this category: the second is again the slash, but its full-width version.

- Category ET ("European number terminator", weak): a selection of characters that are in no way extraterrestrial. These characters may follow a number and may be considered to be part of it. Among them are the dollar sign, the percent sign, the currency signs, the prime and its repeated forms, the plus and minus signs, etc. On the other hand, neither the units of measure nor the numeric constants are in this category. There are 63 ET characters.

- Category CS ("common number separator", weak): the period, the comma, the colon, and the no-break space, together with all their variants; that makes 11 characters in all.

- Category BN ("boundary-neutral", weak): the ASCII and ISO 1022 control characters, ZWJ and ZWNJ, the interlinear annotation marks, the language tags, etc. These characters number 178.

- Category NSM ("nonspacing mark", weak): the combining characters and the variation selectors, for a total of 803 characters.

- Category ON ("other neutral", neutral): the universal punctuation marks, the proof-reading symbols, the mathematical symbols, the pictograms, the box-drawing elements, the braille cells, the ideographic radicals—every character that has no inherent directionality (although that is debatable for certain symbols). These are altogether 3,007 characters.

- Category B ("paragraph separator", neutral): every character that can separate paragraphs, namely, the ASCII control characters 0x000A (*line feed*), 0x000D (carriage return), 0x001C, 0x001D, 0x001E, 0x0085, and the paragraph separator.

- Category S ("segment separator", neutral): the tab characters (0x0009, 0x000B, 0x001F);

- Category WS ("whitespace", neutral): the whitespace. Every character that is considered a space of nonzero width. There are 19 characters of this type.

The five remaining categories are actually five Unicode control characters that appear in the block of general punctuation:

- 0x202A LEFT-TO-RIGHT EMBEDDING (LRE), marks the beginning of the embedding of left-to-right text.

- 0x202B RIGHT-TO-LEFT EMBEDDING (RLE), marks the beginning of the embedding of right-to-left text.

- 0x202C POP DIRECTIONAL FORMATTING, or "PDF" (not to be confused with the PDF file format of Adobe's Acrobat software). States form a stack, and each of the characters LRE, RLE, LRO, and RLO adds to the stack a new state, whether for embedding or for explicit direction. The character PDF pops the top state off the stack.

- 0x202D LEFT-TO-RIGHT OVERRIDE (LRO), forces the direction to be left-to-right.

- 0x202E RIGHT-TO-LEFT OVERRIDE (RLO), forces the direction to be right-to-left.

The bidirectional algorithm automatically manages embedding, but the characters LRE and RLE allow us to switch to "manual control" when errors occur. Manual control enables us to do even more, since with the characters LRO and RLO we enjoy low-level control over the behavior of the glyphs representing the characters with respect to the direction of the script. Thus we can torture Unicode characters at will by forcing a Latin text to run from right to left or an Arabic text to run from left to right. But these characters should be used only when absolutely necessary. Let us not forget that the interactive use of software and the transmission of data are ill suited to "modes", and modes are indeed what these characters represent. Suppose that we have placed the character LRE at the beginning of a paragraph and that we copy a few words to another document. The effect of the LRE will disappear, since the character will not be copied with our string. Use your judgment, and be careful!

Let us also point out that the scope of all these characters is limited to a single paragraph (a paragraph being a block of data that ends at the end of the file or at a character of category B). At the end of the paragraph, however many states may have accumulated on the stack, they are all swallowed up by the dreaded cyber-sinkhole that lies within every computer (the place where files that we have accidentally deleted without keeping a backup end up).

The characters that we have just described are also listed in the file PropList.txt under the property Bidi_Control.

This file also mentions characters that we have not yet discussed, the *implicit directional marks*:

- 0x200E LEFT-TO-RIGHT MARK (LRM): an invisible character of zero width whose only *raison d'être* is its category, L.

- 0x200F RIGHT-TO-LEFT MARK (RLM): as above, but of category R.

What good are these invisible, zero-width characters? They can be used, for example, to lead the rendering engine to believe that the text begins with a character of a given direction—in other words, to cheat!

Finally, one other important property of characters is the possibility of *mirroring*. The ninth field (counting from zero) in the lines of the file UnicodeData.txt contains a 'Y' when the glyph should be mirrored in a right-to-left context. Thus an "opening" parenthesis will remain an opening parenthesis in a left-to-right context; it will be a "right" parenthesis in absolute terms, but we do "open" a right-to-left passage at the right.

Mirroring is ordinarily managed by the rendering engine. But Unicode, through its infinite mercy, has also given us a list of characters whose glyphs can serve as mirrored glyphs. These data are included in the file BidiMirroring.txt, a sample of which appears below:

```
0028; 0029 # LEFT PARENTHESIS
0029; 0028 # RIGHT PARENTHESIS
003C; 003E # LESS-THAN SIGN
003E; 003C # GREATER-THAN SIGN
005B; 005D # LEFT SQUARE BRACKET
005D; 005B # RIGHT SQUARE BRACKET
```

As we can see, for each original character at the left, Unicode provides a character whose glyph is the mirror image of the original. There are 320 pairs of characters of this kind in the file, some of which are marked [BEST FIT], which means that merely flipping them horizontally does not yield the best result. Most of these characters are mathematical symbols, and we can indeed wonder what the ideal mirrored version of '¢', for example, would be. Should it be '⊅' or '⊋'? The former is exactly what we would write in a left-to-right document. In Western mathematics, the negating stroke is always slanted to the right.

Is '⊋', then, the ideal form for right-to-left mathematics? Azzeddine Lazrek [229, 230] seems to prefer '⊅', which we could accuse of left-to-right bias. Arabian mathematics uses an unusual system of notation that yields formulae such as the following:

$$\underset{0=\smile}{\overset{\infty}{\underset{\smile}{\text{م}}}} = \underset{1=ص}{\overset{\infty}{\underset{ص}{\prod}}} = \underset{0}{\overset{1}{\text{سء}(ق)د}}$$

The Algorithm, Step by Step

We start with a string $C = c_1 c_2 \ldots c_n$, and the object of the game is to obtain, for each character c_i, the value $\mathscr{I}_i$ of its "embedding level", a value that we shall use at the end to rearrange the glyphs.

1. Determine the implicit direction of the paragraph

We shall first break the document into paragraphs. Each paragraph will have an *implicit direction*. If this direction is not given by any higher-level protocol (XML, XSL-FO, etc.), the algorithm will look for the first character of category L, AL, or R. If this character is of category L, the implicit direction of the paragraph is from left to right; otherwise, the implicit direction is from right to left.

Now suppose that we are in a left-to-right document (such as this book) and that, unfortunately, a paragraph begins with a word in Hebrew. According to the algorithm, this paragraph will begin at the right, and the last line will run short at the left. How can we avoid that situation? That is where the implicit directional marks come in. All that we have to do is to place the character LRM at the beginning of the paragraph. This character will lead the algorithm to believe that the first letter of the paragraph is of category L, and the formatting will be correct.

To calculate the values of $\mathscr{I}$, we need an initial value. This will be the "paragraph embedding level", $\mathscr{E}$. If the paragraph's direction is from right to left, then $\mathscr{E} = 1$; otherwise, $\mathscr{E} = 0$.

2. Process the control characters for bidirectionality

In this step, we shall collect and use the data provided by the various characters LRE, RLE, LRO, RLO, and PDF that may be found in the document. We shall examine characters one by one and calculate for each character the embedding-level value $\mathscr{I}$ and the explicit direction.

We begin with the first character by taking $\mathscr{I}_1 = \mathscr{E}$ as the initial value and not specifying any explicit direction. If we come upon the character RLE, then the value $\mathscr{I}$ for the following characters will be increased by one or two units so as to yield an *odd* number. Likewise, if we come upon LRE, the value $\mathscr{I}$ for the following characters will be increased by one or two so as to yield an *even* number.

If we find RLO or LRO, our behavior is similar, but in addition the explicit direction of the following characters will be right-to-left or left-to-right, respectively. In other words, the characters affected by RLO are considered to be of category R, and those affected by LRO are of category L.

LRE, RLE, LRO, and RLO are placed onto a stack. Each new operator of this type will push the previous one further down the stack, where it waits to be popped off. When we come upon a PDF, we pop the most recent LRE, RLE, LRO, or RLO. Note that this stack has a height of 61: when the 62^d successive operator is reached, the algorithm stops keeping track of the oldest characters.

At the start of this procedure, we have a value $\mathscr{I}$ for each character in the string. Thus we can restrict the remaining operations to substrings of characters having the same value of $\mathscr{I}$. We call that type of substring a *run*. A run is thus a substring of characters with the same value of $\mathscr{I}$.

For each run S, we shall define two variables, S_s and S_e, which correspond to the conditions at its endpoints. These variables can assume the values 'L' for left-to-right and 'R' for right-to-left; these are also the names of the categories L and R.

Here is how we define these variables. Let S', S, S'' be three consecutive runs and $\mathscr{I}', \mathscr{I}, \mathscr{I}''$ their embedding levels. Then S_s has the value R if $\max(\mathscr{I}', \mathscr{I})$ is odd and the value L otherwise. Similarly, S_e is R if $\max(\mathscr{I}, \mathscr{I}'')$ is odd, otherwise L.

If S appears at the beginning or the end of the paragraph—and thus there is no S' (or S'')—we take $\mathscr{E}$ instead of $\mathscr{I}'$ (or $\mathscr{I}''$).

The final operation: delete all occurrences of RLE, LRE, RLO, LRO, and PDF.

Let us review the process. We break our paragraph into runs S, the elements of a run all having the same value $\mathscr{I}$. For each run, we have the variables S_s and S_e, whose values may be L or R.

3. Process the numbers and the surrounding characters

Steps 3, 4, and 5 are, in a sense, intermediate steps. We process three special types of characters and change their categories, and possibly their $\mathscr{I}$ values, according to context.

In this section, we shall process numbers. There are two categories of numbers: EN ("European numbers") and AN ("Arabic numbers"). The names of these categories should not be taken literally, as the categories serve only to indicate a certain type of behavior.

Suppose we find ourselves in a run S with embedding level $\mathscr{I}$. We shall begin a ballet of changing categories.

First of all, every NSM character (combining character) assumes the category of its base character; if there is none (so that the character is necessarily at the beginning of the run), it assumes the value of S_s as its category.

Next, we shall consider the EN characters (European numbers) in the run. For each of them, we shall check whether the first strong character as we read leftward is of type AL. If it is, the EN becomes an AN.

Now the distinction between right-to-left Arabic characters (AL) and Hebrew characters (R) is no longer needed; therefore, we convert the AL characters to type R.

Now we shall address the characters of type ET (final punctuation), ES (slash), or CS (period, comma, etc.). An ES between two ENs becomes an EN. A CS between two ENs becomes an EN. A CS between two ANs becomes an AN. A series of ETs before or after an EN becomes a series of ENs.

After these transformations, if any ETs, ESs, or CSs remain, we convert them all to ONs (harmless neutral characters).

Finally, in the last transformation of this step, we search backwards from each EN for the first strong character. If it is an L, we convert the EN to an L.

By the end of this step, we have separated the EN and AN numbers, and we have eliminated the categories ET, ES, and CS.

4. Process the neutral characters

And, in particular, process the spaces. This step is necessary because Unicode decided not to "directionalize" its spaces, as Apple did in its Arabic system, in which one copy of the ASCII table worked from right to left. Thus Mac OS had a left-to-right space and a right-to-left space.

Here it is the algorithm that determines the direction of the spaces. The goal of this section is therefore to assign a category, either L or R, to each neutral character. Two very simple rules suffice.

1. If the neutral character is surrounded by strong characters of a single category, it also is of that category; if it appears at the beginning or at the end of run S, we treat it as if there were a strong character of category S_s at its left or a strong character of category S_e at its right, respectively.

2. All other neutral characters are of category $\mathcal{E}$.

5. Make use of the inherent directionality of the characters

Up to now, we have dealt only with specific cases (numbers, neutral characters) and some special characters (RLE and company). But the reader must certainly have noticed that we have not yet raised the issue of the category of each character c_n. Yet we shall have to use this category (L or R) as the basis of our decision to set the text from right to left or from left to right. Now is the time to take the category of the characters into account.

But nor should we forget what has been done in the preceding procedures, even if they are less common and deal primarily with exceptional cases. Here is where we see the strength of the algorithm: all that we have to do is increment $\mathscr{I}$ in a certain way, and we obtain values that take both the preceding calculations and the inherent directionality of the characters into account.

Here are the procedures to carry out:

- For each character of category L: if its $\mathscr{I}$ is odd, increment it by 1;
- For each R: if its $\mathscr{I}$ is even, increment it by 1;
- For each AN: if its $\mathscr{I}$ is odd, increment it by 2; else increment it by 1;
- For each EN: if its $\mathscr{I}$ is even, increment it by 2; else increment it by 1.

At the end of this step, we have a definitive value of $\mathscr{I}$ for each character in the string.

6. Reverse substrings

This section is the most fun. We have weighted the characters in our string with whole numbers (the values of $\mathscr{I}$). Beginning with the largest number, we shall reverse all the runs that have this value of $\mathscr{I}$. Then we shall do the same for the number immediately below, until we reach an embedding level of 0. If the largest level $\mathscr{I}$ is n, then some substrings (those for which $\mathscr{I}$ is equal to n) will be reversed.

Here are a few examples to shed light on the procedure. Let us take three speakers: $\mathfrak{R}$ and $\mathfrak{R}'$ are speakers of right-to-left languages, and $\mathfrak{L}$ is a speaker of a left-to-right language.

FIRST EXAMPLE: $\mathfrak{L}$ says that "Yes means $\overrightarrow{yes}$." ("Yes means نعم."). We have a single right-to-left word in a left-to-right context.

After running the string through the bidirectional algorithm, we obtain the following embedding levels $\mathscr{I}$:

$$[_0 \text{Yes means } [_1 yes]_1 .]_0$$

The inherent directionality of the letters is enough to yield the desired result. We have only one reversal to perform, that of level 1:

$$[_0 \text{Yes means } [_1 \text{ᴤǝγ}]_1 .]_0$$

SECOND EXAMPLE: $\mathfrak{R}$ says "$\overleftarrow{yes}$ *means yes*".

Then $\mathfrak{L}$ quotes him by saying "$\mathfrak{R}$ said that '$\overleftrightarrow{yes}$ *means yes*'." ("He said that 'نعم ترجم بنعم yes'."). Thus we have right-to-left embedding in a left-to-right passage.

But if we leave the algorithm to do its work unassisted, it will yield undesired results. By merely reading "He said that 'yes ... '", the algorithm cannot know that the word "yes" is part of a right-to-left quotation. Thus we shall use a pair of characters, ⟦RLE⟧ and ⟦PDF⟧, to indicate the quotation's boundaries:

$[_0$He said that "⟦RLE⟧$[_1[_2$yes$]_2$ *means yes*$]_1$⟦PDF⟧".$]_0$

The first reversal to carry out is at level 2:

$[_0$He said that "⟦RLE⟧$[_1[_2$ƨɘγ$]_2$ *means yes*$]_1$⟦PDF⟧".$]_0$

The second reversal will be at level 1 (thus we remove ⟦RLE⟧ and ⟦PDF⟧):

$[_0$He said that "$[_1$ƨɘγ ƨnɒɘm $[_2$yes$]_2]_1$".$]_0$

THIRD EXAMPLE: $\mathfrak{R}'$ hears $\mathcal{L}$ quote $\mathfrak{R}$ and asks him:

←
"*Did you say that* '$\mathfrak{R}$ *said that* "y͞es *means yes*" '?" ("؟"He said that 'معن تترجم بنعم yes' " قلت").
We have surrounded the entire previous sentence with the question "Did you say that"
and a question mark '?'. And since $\mathfrak{R}'$ is right-to-left, we are in that context from the very
beginning; i.e., the embedding level $\mathcal{I}$ of the first character already has the value of 1.

Once again the algorithm cannot know that "He said … " is embedded; therefore, we
shall mark the fact with the pair ⟦RLE⟧, ⟦PDF⟧. Here is the situation:

$[_1$*Did you say that* "⟦RLE⟧$[_2$He said that '⟦RLE⟧$[_3[_4$yes$]_4$ *means yes*$]_3$⟦PDF⟧'$]_2$⟦PDF⟧"?$]_1$

Thus we have reached embedding level 4! Let us carry out the reversal at level 4:

$[_1$*Did you say that* "⟦RLE⟧$[_2$He said that '⟦RLE⟧$[_3[_4$ƨɘγ$]_4$ *means yes*$]_3$⟦PDF⟧'$]_2$⟦PDF⟧"?$]_1$

Next, we shall reverse level 3:

$[_1$*Did you say that* "⟦RLE⟧$[_2$He said that '$[_3$ƨɘγ ƨnɒɘm $[_4$yes$]_4]_3$'$]_2$⟦PDF⟧"?$]_1$

And level 2:

$[_1$*Did you say that* "$[_2$'$[_4$ƨɘγ$]_4$ $[_3$means yes$]_3$' ɟɒʜɟ bIɒƨ ɘH$]_2$"?$]_1$

Finally, we reverse level 1, the global level:

$[_1$؟"$[_2$He said that '$[_3$ƨɘγ ƨnɒɘm $[_4$yes$]_4]_3$'$]_2$" ɟɒʜɟ γɒƨ υoγ bIꓷ$]_1$

East Asian Scripts

The three great nations of East Asia (China, Japan, Korea) have writing systems that pose
challenges to computer science. In this section, we shall discuss two of these writing systems: the ideographs of Chinese origin that were also adopted by the Japanese and the
Koreans, and the Korean syllabic hangul script.

Ideographs of Chinese Origin

Westerners must put forth an enormous effort to learn Chinese ideographs: there are thousands of them, and they all look similar—at least that is the impression that we have at first. We can easily be discouraged by the thought that even if we managed to learn 3,000, 4,000, or 5,000 ideographs there would still be more than 60,000 others that we had not even touched upon, and life is so short. But do we know all the words in our own language? Certainly not! Are we discouraged by that fact? The author is not ashamed of his ignorance of the words "gallimaufry", "jecorary", "frondescent"[2], and many others. The same goes for the East Asian who comes across an ideograph that he does not recognize. The only difference is that we can usually pronounce words that we do not know, whereas the East Asian cannot do so with an unknown character. On the other hand, he is better equipped to understand its meaning. We require a solid knowledge of etymology in order to interpret a word; he, however, has a better chance of correctly interpreting an ideograph if he can recognize the radicals from which it is constructed.

Etymology for us, radicals for the East Asians. Two ways of investigating the possible meaning of a word/ideograph. They are similar, from a human perspective. But what is a computer to make of them?

When we operate on a phonetic basis, we lose the pictorial representation of meaning, but we gain the possibility of segmenting: sounds can be separated, and all that we have to do is invent signs to represent them. That is what the alphabetic and syllabic writing systems do. Gutenberg used segmenting into symbols to good advantage in his invention, and computer science inherited it from him. Result: a few dozen symbols are enough to write the hundreds of thousands of English words. Most important of all, these symbols will suffice for all future words as well: neologisms, loan words, etc.

That is not the case for the ideographs. Generating them from radicals in real time is not a solution: sometimes we do not know which radicals are needed, or else they transform themselves to yield new shapes. This is not a process that lends itself to automation; at least no one has yet succeeded at automating it.

There have been attempts to "rationalize" the ideographs: graphical syntaxes by themselves [125] or accompanied by tools for generating ideographs [356], or highly parameterized METAFONT code [178]. One of these attempts is Character Description Language, an approach based on XML that we shall describe on page 151.

In the absence of "intelligent" systems that offer a functional solution for all data exchanged in China, Japan, and Korea, the Chinese ideographs have been "hardcoded"; i.e., one code point is assigned to each ideograph. We have discussed various East Asian encodings (pages 1 and following) that reached the record number of 48,027 ideographs.

These encodings were adequate as long as data remained within each country. But when we began to exchange information across borders, if only by creating web pages, a new sort of problem arose: compatibility among Chinese, Japanese, and Korean ideographs.

---

[2] In order: "a hotchpotch", "relating to the liver", "covered with leaves".

The Greeks borrowed the writing system of the Phoenicians; then the Romans borrowed theirs from the Greeks. The writing system changed each time, although the similarities are astonishing. The same phenomenon appeared among the Chinese, Japanese, and Koreans—in the third century C.E. for the Japanese, in the fifth century C.E. for the Koreans. The Chinese script was exported and adapted to the needs of each nation. New ideographs were created, others changed their meaning; some even changed their forms slightly. Often the differences are minimal, even imperceptible to the Western eye, which may recognize that a text is in Japanese or Korean solely by the presence of *kana* or hangul.

Indeed, these scripts (*kana* in Japan, hangul in Korea) were attempts to rationalize the Chinese writing system. But the goal was never to replace it, only to supplement it with a phonetic adjunct. Which means that these countries have two scripts (as well as the Latin script) in parallel.

Unicode and ideographs

While ISO 10646 originally intended to use separate planes for the ideographs of these three languages, Unicode took up the challenge of *unifying* the ideographs.

Three principles were adopted as a basis of this unification:

1. The principle of *source separation*: if two ideographs occupy distinct positions in a single encoding, they are not unified within Unicode.

2. The *noncognate rule*: if two ideographs are etymologically different—i.e., if they are historically derived from different ideographs, they are not unified within Unicode.

3. If two ideographs that do not satisfy the two previous conditions have *the same abstract shape*, they are unified.

The first of these principles was highly controversial, but it is consistent with Unicode's general principle of convertibility (see page 61), which provides that all data encoded in a recognized encoding can be converted to Unicode *without loss of information*. The typical example of ideographs that have not been unified for this reason is the series of six ideographs 剣劍剱劔劒釼, all of which mean "sword" and are clearly graphical variants of one another. Since they are distinct in JIS X 0208, they are distinct in Unicode as well.

The second principle leaves the door wide open to polemics among historians of the ideographs; nonetheless, it is indispensable. The most commonly cited example is doubtless that of the radicals '土' and '士': the former means "ground, earth, soil"; the latter means "samurai, gentleman, scholar". There are even characters that contain both of these radicals, such as 墫 ("pick up, raise").

The third principle is where things really go wrong. The concept of an *abstract shape* is, unfortunately, not clear in the slightest and depends primarily on the individual's intuition.

The Unicode book gives a certain number of examples of unified and nonunified ideographs. In these examples, the pairs of nonunified ideographs clearly consist of two different characters, but the pairs of unified ideographs are very interesting because they show us how much tolerance unification exhibits towards differences that may seem significant at first glance.

The examples range from the almost identical to the discernibly different. The difference between 周 and 周 is the order in which the strokes are written; in the bottom part of 雪 (vs. 雪), the middle stroke protrudes slightly; likewise, in the bottom part of 酉, the stroke in the middle extends for the whole width of the rectangle, which is not the case in 酉; the contents of the rectangle in 堊 and 堊 are quite different; the vertical stroke in 朱 and 朱 has a different ending; the stroke at the left of 父 has a lead-in element, unlike that of 父; the right-hand stroke is smooth in 八 and angular in 八; the upper right-hand parts of 說 and 説 are quite different. Yet all these pairs of ideographs were unified and yield only a single character each.

Be that as it may, the ideographs of 38 national or industrial encodings were collected, compared, analyzed, and sorted according to four large dictionaries (two of them Chinese, one Japanese, and one Korean)—a large-scale project. And that was only the beginning, as other blocks of ideographic characters were added in the following versions of Unicode. Today there are 71,233 unified characters.

The Unihan database

As always, Unicode does not stop with the already abundant information found in the Unicode book. The consortium also provides a database of the ideographs, which is contained in the following file:

```
ftp://ftp.unicode.org/Public/UNIDATA/Unihan.zip
```

as well as a web interface for searches (in which we may enter a character's hexadecimal code point, or even the character itself in UTF-8):

```
http://www.unicode.org/charts/unihan.html
```

Nine types of data are provided:

- numeric value: if the character is used as a number, including the special use of certain characters for accounting purposes.

- variants: whether there are other characters that are semantic variants (characters with more or less the same meaning that can be used in the place of the character in question); whether there is a simplified Chinese version of the character; whether there are semantic variants in specialized contexts; whether there is a traditional Chinese version; whether there are presentation variants (for example, two of the "swords" shown above, namely 剑 and 劍, are presentation variants).

- the number of strokes, calculated according to six different methods: Unicode's method, the traditional Japanese method, the method of Morohashi's dictionary, the method of the prestigious Kangxi dictionary of the Chinese language, the Korean method, and the total number of strokes, including those of the radical.

- pronunciations: in Cantonese Chinese, in Mandarin Chinese, in the ancient Chinese of the Tang dynasty, in Japanese (both *kun* pronunciations, of Japanese origin, and *on* pronunciations, borrowed from Chinese together with the character), in Korean, in Vietnamese.

- the definition.

- the frequency of use in Chinese discussion groups.

- the level of difficulty, according to the school system in Hong Kong.

- indexes in 22 different dictionaries.

- code points in 32 different encodings.

Web access to this database is connected to searches in the Japanese EDICT dictionaries [90]. In this way, we also obtain for character its meanings in Japanese as well as a list of all the compound words (indivisible groups of ideographs) that contain it, with their pronunciations.

This enormous mass of data is collected in a 25 MB file that is available for downloading as a ZIP archive.

What shall we do when 71,233 ideographs are not enough?

Unlike our fine old Latin letters, which have not changed much since Julius Caesar, the Chinese ideographs display an almost biological behavior: they live and die, merge, reproduce, form societies—societies similar to human societies, as an ideograph is often created for use in a child's name, and the popularity of the ideograph will thus be related to that of its human bearer. Be that as it may, one thing is certain: they present problems for computer science. How to manage a writing system that changes every day?

First of all, let us mention two methods that do not really offer a solution to the problem of missing characters. The first is the method of throwing up our hands: the glyph—or even the character—that we need is not available, so we decide to replace it with a symbol provided for this purpose, the character 0x3013 GETA MARK =. It has the special quality of having a glyph that stands out in text. In traditional printing, the *geta* mark was a sort of substitute, used in first and second proofs, that was not supposed to appear in the final printing. It was used until the punch-cutter had the time to design and cut the missing glyph. Its glyph was made deliberately conspicuous so that it would be easy to find and correct—and, most of all, so that it would not be overlooked during proofreading.

Another possibility: 0x303E IDEOGRAPHIC VARIATION INDICATOR ⦻. The idea is that the following character is an approximation of the character that was intended. Thus, if we find a character that resembles the missing one, we can substitute that character without running the risk of being a laughing stock. The ideographic variation indicator bears all the following meanings at the same time: "don't be surprised if what you are reading doesn't make any sense", "I know that this is not the right character, but I haven't found anything better", "this is what the missing character looks like; unless you are extremely stupid, context should enable you to figure it out".

These two solutions are not solutions at all. If we have enough time and energy, we can design the missing glyphs. Chapter 12 of this book is devoted to that very subject. But designing the glyph is not enough: we also have to insert it into fonts, install those fonts on the computer, make sure that they are displayed and printed correctly, send them to all our associates, or even distribute them on the Internet with instructions for installation. It is a fiery ordeal that we might not wish to endure just for one or two characters.

Below, we shall see two solutions that fall between these extremes. They are attempts to describe the ideographs by combining other ideographs or elemental strokes—attempts whose aim is to provide the user with a rapid and efficient way to obtain and use the new ideographs that are being created just as the reader is reading these lines, or, conversely, old ideographs that the most ancient of the ancient sages forgot many centuries ago.

Ideographic description characters

The first attempt is simplistic but nonetheless powerful. And it lies at the very heart of Unicode. It is a set of a dozen characters (0x2FF0-0x2FFB) called *ideographic description characters*.

The goal is to describe ideographic characters without actually displaying them. That is one of the many paradoxes of Unicode: all the combinations of ideographs that we shall see in this section are in fact created in the mind of the reader, just as the reader who sees the characters : -) in an email message immediately recognizes them as the *smiley* (☺). Let us also note that these characters "operate" on the two or three characters that *follow* them (whereas combining characters operate on the *preceding* characters).

Here are the graphical representations of these control characters. In themselves, they give a good idea of the possibilities for combining characters that are available to us:

When we begin to combine the operators themselves,[3] we acquire an impressive power to describe characters. Thus we can write several operators in a row: each of them will wait until the following ones have performed their tasks before beginning to perform its own.

A few simple examples:

⿰女壬 (woman + ninth month) yields 妊 (pregnancy)

⿱宀女 (roof + woman) yields 安 (tranquillity)

---

[3] There is only one restriction: the entire string of ideographs and description characters must not exceed 16 Unicode characters and must not contain more than six consecutive ideographs.

口口大 (box + large) yields 因 (cause)

辶 巛 (walking + river) yields 巡 (patrol)

And a few examples with compounding:

女女女 (woman + woman + woman) yields 姦 (noise)

广木木手 (cliff + large + large + hand) yields 摩 (polish)

But one must be very careful, as a radical can change its shape in combination. For example, the radical for "water" (水) assumes the shape 氵 when it is combined horizontally with other radicals. We can thus have combinations of this kind:

水中 (sea + center) yields 沖 (in the open sea)

隹火 (old bird + fire) yields 焦 (impatience)

In fact, we can freely combine ideographs, radicals (0x2F00–0x2FD5), and characters from the block of supplementary radicals (0x2E80–0x2EF3). The supplementary radicals are characters that represent the different shapes that a radical can assume when it is combined with other ideographs. Normally neither the radicals nor the supplementary radicals should be used as ordinary characters in a document; they should be reserved for cases in which we are referring specifically to the ideographic radical, not to the character.

Example: 0x706B 火 is an ideographic character that means "fire" but also "Tuesday", "March", "flame", "heat"; 0x2F55 KANGXI RADICAL FIRE 火 (same glyph) is radical number 86, "fire"; 0x2EA3 CJK RADICAL FIRE ⺯ is the shape that this radical assumes when it is combined with other ideographs. We would use the first of these characters in a document that mentioned fire; the second, in a dictionary that listed the radicals or in a document that referred to the radical for fire (to explain another ideograph, for example); the third, in a textbook on writing in which it is explained that the radical for fire assumes a special shape under certain conditions.

Before concluding this section, let us note that, although Unicode's method of ideographic description seems fine on paper, the challenge that software faces to combine the glyphs correctly is not negligible. That is why Unicode decided not to require Unicode-compatible software to combine the glyphs *in reality*, which is a great shame.

If we wish to avoid the ideographic description characters and produce glyphs of high quality, we may as well put a shoulder to the grindstone and combine the glyphs of a specific font by using font-design software such as FontLab or FontForge, which we shall describe in Chapter 12—provided, of course, that our license to use the font allows us to do so.

But let us move on to the second attempt to describe ideographs, the CDL markup system.

CDL, or how to describe ideographs in XML

In the 1980s, Tom Bishop, a Chinese-speaking American, developed some software for learning the Chinese language that had a very interesting property: a window that showed how a Chinese character was written, stroke by stroke, in slow motion. To describe the characters, Tom developed an internal language. Later, in view of the astounding success of XML, he took up the principles of this language again and created an XML-based method for describing ideographs.

It is Character Description Language (CDL) [79, 80], which has been submitted to the Unicode Technical Committee and the Ideographic Rapporteur Group (IRG) for ratification.

The approach is twofold: we can build up an ideograph from other ideographs. For that purpose, we need only the ideographs' Unicode code points and the coordinates of their graphical frames. For example, to obtain 行 (which is a radical, but that fact is of no consequence here), it is sufficient to combine 彳 and 亍, both of which are in Unicode.

Thus we write:

```
<cdl char="行">
   <comp char="彳" points="0,0 40,128"/>
   <comp char="亍" points="60,12 128,128"/>
</cdl>
```

The values of the arguments to char are Unicode characters in UTF-8.

We can also construct an ideograph from strokes. Here is how to obtain the ideograph 彳:

```
<cdl char="彳">
   <stroke type="p" points="107,0 10,46"/>
   <stroke type="p" points="128,38 0,83"/>
   <stroke type="s" points="86,70 86,128"/>
</cdl>
```

Finally, we can combine the two methods. To obtain 太, we can write:

```
<cdl char="太">
   <comp char="大" points="0,0 40,128"/>
   <stroke type="d" points="45,104 66,128"/>
</cdl>
```

The possibility of directly using the glyphs of Unicode characters is nothing but a façade: in fact, 56,000 characters have already been described in this way, and the value of a char attribute refers the rendering engine to this sort of description, which in turn may refer it to other descriptions, and so on, until nothing but basic strokes remain.

The basic strokes number 39. Here is the full list. (The abbreviations are the codes used as values of the type attribute of element stroke.)

#	Glyph	Name	Abreviation	Example
1	一	*héng*	h	三
2	✓	*tí*	t	虫
3	丨	*shù*	s	中
4	亅	*shù-gōu*	sg	小
5	丿	*piě*	p	八
6	丿	*wān-piě*	wp	大
7	丿	*shù-piě*	sp	厂
8	丶	*diǎn*	d	主
9	乀	*nà*	n	人
10	乀	*diǎn-nà*	dn	仐
11	乀	*píng-nà*	pn	走
12	㇏	*tí-nà*	tn	攵
13	㇏	*tí-píng-nà*	tpn	辶
14	𠃌	*héng-zhé*	hz	口
15	𠃋	*héng-piě*	hp	又
16	㇖	*héng-gōu*	hg	写
17	ㄴ	*shù-zhé*	sz	山
18	ㄴ	*shù-wān*	sw	四
19	ㄴ	*shù-tí*	st	民
20	𡿨	*piě-zhé*	pz	公
21	〈	*piě-diǎn*	pd	巛
22	丿	*piě-gōu*	pg	乄
23	㇟	*wān-gōu*	wg	豕
24	乚	*xié-gōu*	xg	弋
25	㇄	*héng-zhé-zhé*	hzz	凹
26	㇄	*héng-zhé-wān*	hzw	朵
27	𠃊	*héng-zhé-tí*	hzt	鸠
28	𠃌	*héng-zhé-gōu*	hzg	丹
29	乛	*héng-xié-gōu*	hxg	凬

30	⿸	*shù-zhé-zhé*	szz	亞
31		*shù-zhé-piě*	szp	专
32		*shù-wān-gōu*	swg	儿
33		*héng-zhé-zhé-zhé*	hzzz	凸
34		*héng-zhé-zhé-piě*	hzzp	及
35		*héng-zhé-wān-gōu*	hzwg	乹
36		*héng-piě-wān-gōu*	hpwg	阝
37		*shù-zhé-zhé-gōu*	szzg	丂
38		*héng-zhé-zhé-zhé-gōu*	hzzzg	乃
39	○	*quān*	o	智

The reader will notice that certain words are repeated in the Chinese names of these strokes. They are basic strokes in Chinese calligraphy: *héng* (横 horizontal stroke), *tí* (提 rising stroke), *shù* (竖 vertical stroke), *gōu* (钩 hook), *piě* (撇 diagonal stroke descending from right to left), *wān* (弯, curved stroke), *diǎn* (点 dot or very short segment), *nà* (捺 diagonal stroke descending from left to right), *píng* (平 flat stroke), *zhé* (折 bent stroke). The other strokes are combinations of these basic strokes that can be found in calligraphy textbooks; for example, number 35, *héng-zhé-wān-gōu*, is a 横折弯钩 "curved hook with a bend" [44, p. 53].

It is clear that the coordinates of the frames of the basic strokes play a fundamental role in the description of ideographs. The software system *Wenlin* allows users to create ideographs in an interactive manner and to obtain optimal frames for their components by pulling on handles.

We hope that Unicode will adopt this method, which could eventually be the solution for encoding new or rare ideographs that are not explicitly encoded in Unicode. The reader who would like to learn more about CDL and *Wenlin* is invited to consult the web site http://www.wenlin.org/cdl/.

The Syllabic Korean Hangul Script

King Sejong of Korea was born practically at the same time as Gutenberg. He gave an enormous boost to the sciences and the humanities, making his country one of the most advanced in Asia. The Koreans were already making use of printing. In 1434, Sejong had 200,000 characters of 14 mm × 16 mm cast—not out of lead, as Gutenberg did, but from an alloy composed primarily of copper and tin. But the main reason for which Sejong lives on in history is that he initiated the invention of hangul. He appointed a commission of eight scholars and asked them to create a new writing system that would be both simple and precise.

After four years of work, the commission presented to the king a writing system made up of 11 vowels and 17 consonants that was perfectly suited to the needs of the Korean language. It was officially ratified in 1446. In the beginning, it was called "vulgar script", "the script that can be learned in one morning", and "women's writing". Only in the nineteenth century did it receive the name hangul ("large script"). In other words, the upper classes in Korean society looked down upon this script for centuries.

While Gutenberg was getting ready to print his Bibles, the first book in hangul appeared: *Songs of the Dragons Flying to Heaven*, by Jeong Inji (1447), typeset on wooden boards. It was followed by *Songs of the Moon Shining on a Thousand Rivers*, which was written by the king himself, and then by a Buddhist sutra in 1449. Thus begins the story of the script that many linguists consider to be the most perfectly conceived script in the history of the world.[4]

The shapes of the hangul consonants were established according to the positions of the vocal organs. They are distributed among five phonetic categories built up by adding one or more strokes to indicate phonetic features:

ㄱ	g	ㄴ	n	ㅅ	s	ㅁ	m	ㅇ	(ng)
		ㄷ	d	ㅈ	j	ㅂ	b		
ㅋ	k	ㅌ	t	ㅊ	c	ㅍ	p	ㅎ	h
ㄲ	gg	ㄸ	dd	ㅆ	ss	ㅃ	bb		
				ㅉ	jj				
		ㄹ	r						

Among the consonants, 'ㅇ' plays the role of a placeholder for an independent vowel, or produces an 'ng' sound at the end of a syllable.

The vowels are based on the four elements of East Asian philosophy: heaven (a short stroke), earth (a horizontal stroke), man (a vertical line), and the yin–yang circle (in evidence from the cyclical pattern that the forms of the vowels follow):

ㅡ	eu	ㅗ	o	ㅛ	yo	ㅣ	i	ㅓ	eo	ㅕ	yeo
(ㅡ)		ㅜ	u	ㅠ	yu	(ㅣ)		ㅏ	a	ㅑ	ya

The reader will note that we have chosen to entitle this section "The *Syllabic* Korean Hangul Script", whereas here we can see nothing but *letters* (consonants and vowels). Indeed, the signs that we have just described, which are called *jamo*, are merely the building blocks of the hangul system. By combining *jamo* within an ideographic square, we obtain the hangul *syllables*.

A hangul syllable consists of one or more initial consonants (*choseong*), one or more vowels (*jungseong*), and possibly one or more final consonants (*jongseong*). There are 19 possible initial consonants, 21 possible vowels or combinations of vowels, and 26 possible final consonants or combinations of final consonants.

---

[4] For more information on its history, please consult [287].

If we use I for initial consonants, V for vowels, and F for final consonants, we have as the general form of a hangul syllable the expression $I^+V^+F^*$ (in which we employ the notation for regular expressions: $^+$ for "one or more times" and * for "zero or more times"). To encode a syllable of this kind, Unicode offers us two possibilities: we can look up the corresponding character in the block of precomposed hangul syllables (0xAC00-0xD7A3), or we can enter the corresponding *jamo*, which the rendering engine will combine into a hangul syllable.

These two methods are equivalent, and the choice of one or the other is analogous to the choice in the Latin script between precomposed accented letters and those obtained using combining characters. The *jamo* of Unicode (0x1100-0x11F9) do not have the status of combining characters, for the simple reason that their logic is different: rather than combining with a base character, *they combine with one another*.

But let us return to the general expression of a hangul syllable, $H = I^+V^+F^*$, and suppose that we have two hangul syllables H and H', the latter coming immediately after the former. Their decomposition is therefore $HH' = I^+V^+F^*I'^+V'^+F'^*$. The sharp reader is bound to ask one burning question: F and I being both consonants, how do we distinguish the *final* consonants of H from the *initial* ones of H'?

Sophisticated linguistic processing could certainly do the job, but here we need to enter characters in real time and see them transformed into syllables. Therefore a cumbersome or ambiguous approach is out of the question.

What, then, shall we do? There is only one solution, which may seem awkward at first because it entails redundant code points in Unicode: we double the Unicode consonants and thus create an artificial distinction between initial and final forms. It is as if we had two copies of each of the consonants of English and wrote "a**ff**irmation" (with the "final" consonants in bold) to show that the word breaks down into syllables as "af-fir-ma-tion".

In addition, this is the technique that the encoding Johab (which allows only one letter from each category) already used: five bits for the initial consonant, five for the vowel, five for the final consonant, plus one disabled bit, which gives 16 bits in all and is a very practical approach.

Thus the table of *jamo* contains first the initial consonants 0x1100-1159, then the vowels 0x1160-0x11A2, and at last the final consonants 0x11A8-0x11F9, whose glyphs are identical to those of the initial consonants. The character 0x115F HANGUL CHOSEONG FILLER is a control character that marks the absence of an initial consonant, which may be needed in irregularly constructed syllables; likewise, there is a 0x1160 HANGUL JUNGSEONG FILLER, used when the vowel is missing.

There are six ways to combine *jamo* in order to form hangul syllables. To describe them, we shall distinguish the horizontal vowels (I_h) from the vertical ones (I_v):

$$IV_v \;\fbox{$I\,V$}\;,\; IV_h \;\fbox{$I\atop V$}\;,\; IV_hV_v \;\fbox{$I\,V$\atop$V$}\;,\; IV_vF \;\fbox{$I\,V$\atop$F$}\;,\; IV_hF \;\fbox{I\atop$V$\atop$F$}\;,\; IV_hV_vF \;\fbox{$I\,V$\atop$F$}\;.$$

Here is an example: the *jamo* sequence ㅎ ㅏ ㄴ is of the shape IV_vF; therefore, we take the combination 􀀀 and get 한. Similarly, the sequence ㄱ ㅡ ㄹ is of the shape IV_hF;

therefore, we take the combination 글 and get 글. We have here the form of the word "hangul": 한글.

Syllables are constructed with unprecedented mathematical rigor. The same is true of their encoding. To obtain 한, we used the Unicode *jamo* characters 0x1112, 0x1161, 0x11AB. Where, then, does the syllable 한 appear in the encoding? The computer can answer the question in a few microseconds, as it has only to carry out the following computation:

$$\left[\left((I - \text{0x1100}) \times 21\right) + (V - \text{0x1161})\right] \times 28 + (F - \text{0x11A7}) + \text{0xAC00}$$

(where I, V, F are the Unicode code points of the *jamo*).

When a syllable has no final consonant F, the formula is simpler:

$$\left[\left((I - \text{0x1100}) \times 21\right) + (V - \text{0x1161})\right] \times 28 + \text{0xAC00}$$

Unlike the ideographs, the Unicode characters for syllables that are constructed in this manner do have names. These names are formed from the letters associated with the *jamo* in the tables on page 156. The letters associated with 한글 are "han" and "geur"; thus the names of the Unicode characters are 0xD55C HANGUL SYLLABLE HAN and 0xAE00 HANGUL SYLLABLE GEUR. The names of the *jamo* can be found in the file Jamo.txt.

Another interesting file is HangulSyllableType.txt: it gives the type of each hangul syllable (*IV* or *IVF*).

When the initial consonant or the vowel is missing, or when we have more than one initial consonant and/or more than two vowels and/or more than one final consonant, no precomposed syllable is available, and we must resort to the automatic combination of *jamo*. Here is an example of a historical hangul syllable [267] dating from that heroic era when people were still capable of pronouncing "bstwyaermh!" without choking: we take three initial consonants ㅂ ㅅ ㅌ, two vowels ㅗ ㅐ, and three final consonants ㄹ ㅁ ㅎ. And here is the result of their composition: 뚊.

What shall we do if we simply wish to combine *jamo* without forcing them to form syllables? There are two methods, only one of which is recommended by Unicode. The better method involves using the character ZWNJ between the *jamo*. The inferior method uses "compatibility *jamo*". These have the same glyphs as the regular *jamo*, but their libido is nonexistent: they have no desire whatsoever to mate with their neighbors. As always, characters flagged as "compatibility" are the skeletons in Unicode's closet: we are discouraged from using them, and Unicode goes to great lengths to lead us to forget that they even exist.

5

Using Unicode

Unicode is found everywhere that text occurs. It would be pointless to describe here all the software that processes text in one or another of Unicode's forms. Let us consider instead the chain of data transmission: the author enters his data, which pass through his CPU and through the network to reach the CPU of his reader/interlocutor. This computer displays the information or prints it out in a way that enables the person who received the information to read it.

Let us take these steps one by one. First, there is data entry: how do we go about entering Unicode data? Data can also be converted from other encodings. How do we convert data to Unicode? Next, once the data is in the computer, we must display it. For that purpose we use fonts that must themselves be Unicode-compatible. (We shall discuss fonts in the entire second half of this book, Chapters 6 through 14 and Appendices A through F). Once the data has been revised and corrected, it is transmitted over the network. We have already mentioned MIME and the various encoding forms of Unicode in Chapter 2. At this level, it matters not to HTTP, TCP/IP, and other protocols that the data is encoded in Unicode rather than in some other encoding. Finally, the data reach the recipient. There it must be displayed, and so adequate fonts must be available. The recipient of the message replies, and the entire process begins all over again, in the opposite direction.

What we shall examine in this chapter are the three ways to *obtain* text in Unicode:

- Interactively, by selecting characters from a table.

- Through the use of a virtual keyboard.

- By converting data that exist in other encodings.

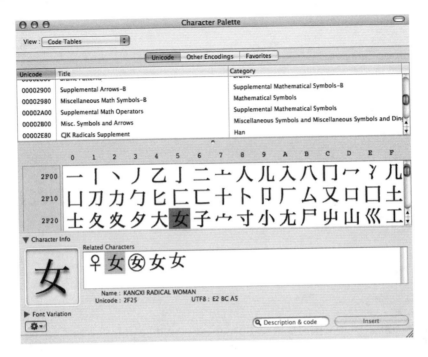

Figure 5-1: The Character Palette of Mac OS X.

Interactive Tools for Entering Unicode Characters

Under Mac OS X

Character Palette

On the menu of keyboards, denoted by a little flag corresponding to the system's active language, we find the entry Show Character Palette. This entry will open a separate window, independent of all other software, that will remain in the foreground. In Figure 5-1 we have a screenshot of the *Character Palette*. When we select Code Tables in the little menu on the top, the middle section of the window is divided into two parts. On the top is a list of all the blocks in Unicode v.4. When a block is selected, the corresponding characters are displayed underneath.

When the user selects a character, its glyph is displayed in the area which opens through the little triangle next to Character Info. Clicking on the button Insert will insert it into the current document in the active application (which is why the Character Palette does not affect the operation of the other windows in any way).

Once we have selected a Unicode character, we can read its number and its description. In certain cases, the Character Palette gives us "related characters", which are the various canonical equivalents and compatibility equivalents that may exist. The result is astounding: out of love for the fair sex, we have selected the character for the ideographic radical "woman" 0x2F25 女. This radical has a compatibility equivalent with the actual ideographic character 0x5973 女, which, in turn, has its own compatibility equivalent with the characters "compatibility ideographs 0xF981" and "circled female" 0x329B Ⓕ . Thus the Palette has followed this chain of compatibility equivalents to the very end in order to produce a complete list for us. In addition, it also shows us the character 0x2640 FEMALE SIGN, which is the symbol for femininity, even though Unicode does not provide any metadata connecting this character to the others.

By opening the **Font Variation** area one can see the glyphs of the selected character in all fonts that contain it—a feature that is *very* useful for finding out which fonts contain a specified character or block.

The Character Palette has been part of the Mac OS X operating system since version 10.2, the version we show is from system 10.4.7.

UniDict

Here is a clever little program of the same type that is designed especially for Japanese ideographic characters: *UniDict* [104], which unfortunately was released for Mac OS 8 but has never been upgraded for Mac OS X. It is a multipurpose dictionary, but what is of interest to us here is the possibility of selecting an ideograph through a combination of radicals. In Figure 5-2 we see UniDict's Kanji Constructor window, with a series of buttons at the left that represent the radicals and the shapes that the radicals assume when they are used in characters. When a button is pressed, all the characters that use it are displayed at the right. When a second button is pressed, only the characters that contain both radicals are displayed, and so forth. Double-clicking an ideograph opens another window (Figure 5-2), which supplies a broad range of supplementary information. The data that UniDict employs come primarily from the academic project for the Japanese–English dictionary EDICT [90]; thus they are updated regularly.

Under Windows XP

Character Map

The Windows operating system offers an analogue to the Character Palette of Mac OS X. It is the *Character Map* (Figure 5-3), and it can be run from the **Start** menu: **All Programs> Accessories>System Tools.** This tool allows us to select a Unicode character from a table (by scrolling with the scroll bar), copy it onto the clipboard, and then copy it from the clipboard into a document.

BabelMap

BabelMap, by Andrew West [346], is a very sophisticated free software package for entering Unicode text with a mouse. The user chooses the Unicode block that contains the characters that he wants, the buttons in the middle area of *BabelMap* display the characters in that block, and the user may click characters to enter them into the Edit Buffer at the bottom of the window. While text is being composed in the Edit Buffer, *BabelMap* applies the relevant contextual rules appropriately. Thus, as shown in Figure 5-4, Arabic

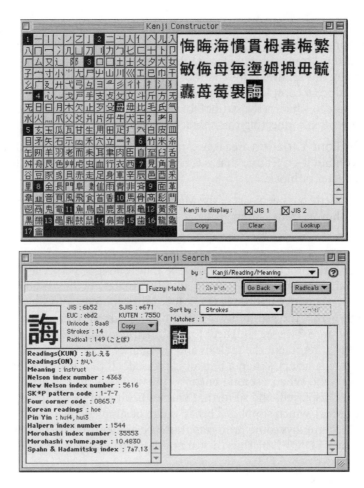

Figure 5-2: The UniDict software under the Classic environment

is displayed correctly, the Indian ligatures (included in the font specified for display) are correctly produced, the *jamo* are combined into hangul syllables, and so on.

We can search for a character by its name or by its code point. We can select a font for display in a very sophisticated manner: a special window shows the Unicode blocks covered by the font and, conversely, the fonts that cover a specified block.

Like UniDict, BabelMap also provides a window for selecting ideographs. Its advantage: it applies not only to Japanese ideographs but to the entire range of Unicode characters (provided, as always, that a font containing the required glyphs is available[1]). Its disadvantage: the method is not so elegant as that of UniDict. In fact, as shown in Figure 5-5, we select a radical from a complete list (only their standard forms are displayed; a cer-

---

[1] The reader will find at http://www.alanwood.net/unicode/fontsbyrange.html a list of freely distributed Unicode-compatible fonts.

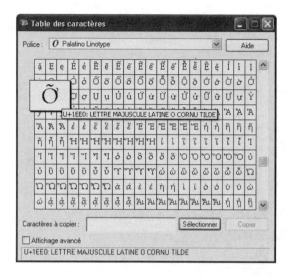

Figure 5-3: The Character Map of Windows XP.

tain amount of training is required to recognize a radical in a nonstandard form), then we select the number of strokes needed to write the character, *omitting the strokes in the radical*. The corresponding characters are displayed at the lower left. This method is close to what one does to look up a character in an ideographic dictionary.

There is also a way to search for an ideograph by its *pinyin* representation (a Latin transcription of the ideographs used in the Chinese language). Finally, BabelMap also offers a means of searching for *Yi* ideographs according to the radicals of this writing system; see Figure 5-6.

Under X Window

gucharmap

gucharmap [237] is a program in the spirit of the Character Palette under Mac OS X and BabelMap under Windows. It is a SourceForge project whose administrator is Noah Levitt. It runs under X Window with GTK+ 2 or a later version. The project's web site bears the subtitle "RESISTING THE WORLDWIDE HEGEMONY OF ENGLISH!", but the site itself is in English only. The software, however, is localizable, and translations into several other languages exist.

As shown in Figure 5-7, the main window of *gucharmap* presents a list of the Unicode blocks on the left and the contents of each block in tabular form on the right. When we click on a glyph in the table, it is inserted into the Edit Buffer at the lower left. A second tab provides information on the selected character that is drawn directly from the online files of the Unicode Consortium.

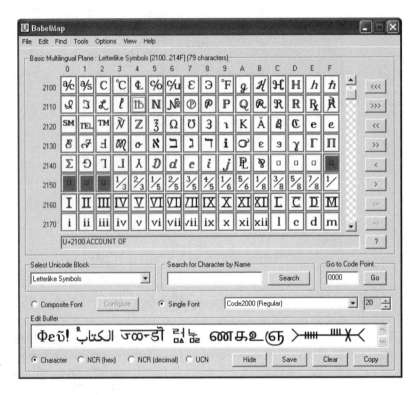

Figure 5-4: The main window of the program BabelMap.

Virtual Keyboards

The interactive tools of the previous section enable us to enter a handful of Unicode characters, but we would hardly want to input a long document in this manner. People were using *keyboards* to type up documents even before the advent of computer science, and the keyboard will remain—until a direct connection between brain and computer becomes a reality—the most natural means of carrying out this operation.

But keyboards are physical, or *hard*, objects. If we often write in English, Arabic, Hindi, and Japanese, must we buy a keyboard for each of these languages and play a game of musical keyboards every time we switch languages? Absolutely not. We can simply change the *virtual keyboard*, which is the table of correspondences between (physical) keys and the (virtual) characters that they generate.

Operating systems have offered such virtual keyboards from the beginning; they have been part of the process of localization for each language. Thus a user of the English version of Mac OS X or Windows XP can switch to the Greek, Arabic, or Chinese keyboard at any time.

But there are at least two problems. First, these virtual keyboards do not necessarily cover all writing systems (although Windows provides a rich set of virtual keyboards); in par-

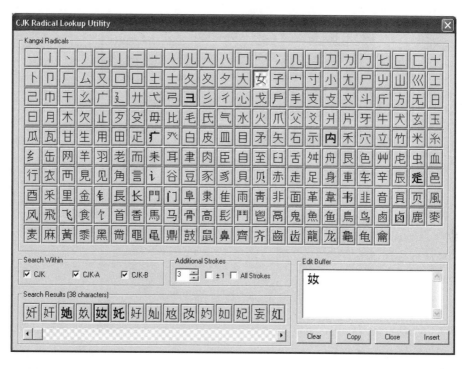

Figure 5-5: The BabelMap for selecting a Chinese ideograph through the use of radicals.

ticular, they do not cover ancient languages. To be sure, we can always find a supplier of rare virtual keyboards. But there is a second problem, of a more subtle nature: we would like for the virtual keyboard to be adapted to our habits, with its keys arranged in a certain way.

One example: suppose that an American user, who therefore is a QWERTY typist, wishes to type a document in Russian. He has a basic idea of Russian phonetics; after all, it is not necessary to study this language for years in order to learn that the Russian 'A' is like an English 'A' (as in "father"), that the Russian '3' is like the English 'Z', that the Russian 'O' is like the English 'O', and so on. Accordingly, he selects the Russian keyboard on his Macintosh or Windows/Linux PC and expects to find the letters in the same locations. But they are not there: the layout of the Russian keyboard is completely different. Instead of an 'A' key, he will find a 'Ф'; instead of a 'Z' key, a 'Я'; and instead of an 'O', a 'Ш'. That is to be expected, since the keyboard layouts derive from typewriter keyboards; but we might have preferred for the common letters, at a minimum, to be in the same locations. Thus we have to learn everything from the beginning, with the constant risk of expecting to find the Russian 'A' where the English 'A' would be and vice versa.

It can be even worse: for almost 20 years, the author has been using "Greeklish," an ASCII transliteration of Greek that is very useful for writing in Greek where the protocol does not support the script (email on a non-Unicode machine, filenames, etc.). There

Figure 5-6: The BabelMap window for selecting an Yi ideograph through the use of radicals.

is nothing unusual about that: transliteration is a habit for everyone who works in an environment with a non-Latin script. In this Greek transliteration, which happens to be that of TₑX, alpha is 'a', beta is 'b', and so forth. Using this transliteration has become so habitual for the author that he is thoroughly at a loss when faced with a "real" Greek keyboard, i.e., a keyboard used in Greece. Moreover, aside from the layout of the letters, the Greek keyboard is, like most other keyboards in the world, based on the QWERTY layout; thus the digits appear on the lowercase position of the keys, the 'A' is on the home row, etc. But the author, living in France, is an AZERTY[2] typist. Can the reader imagine the double difficulty of using a *Greek* virtual keyboard with the Greek letters arranged as in QWERTY *although the physical keyboard is AZERTY*?

In all these cases, there is only one solution: generating one's own virtual keyboards. In this section, we shall discuss a handful of tools that enable us to do so in a simple and efficient manner.

---

[2] AZERTY is a keyboard layout used in France, Belgium, and certain francophone African countries (but not in French-speaking Canada or Switzerland) that differs slightly from the keyboards of most other countries in its arrangement of the basic letters of the Latin alphabet and also the 10 Arabic numerals. The top row of keys contains some punctuation marks and a few accented letters; the digits have to be typed with the shift key. Furthermore, the second row begins with 'A' and 'Z' rather than with 'Q' and 'W', which explains the name "AZERTY" (the QWERTY, QWERTZ, and AZERTY keyboards have only 20 keys in common). Many other small differences conspire to irritate those who travel and find themselves using various types of keyboards: the letter 'M' is at the end of the home row; the brackets and braces—punctuation marks that programmers frequently use—require combinations of keystrokes that can only be typed with both hands at a time (unless one has the hands of Sergey Rachmaninoff or Clara Haskil); etc.

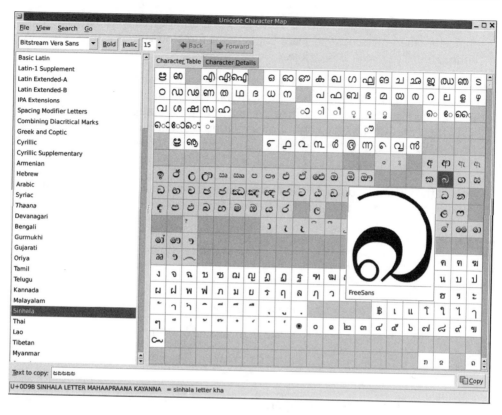

Figure 5-7: The main window of gucharmap under Linux

Useful Concepts Related to Virtual Keyboards

A keyboard contains four types of keys:

- *Ordinary* keys, for typing text and symbols ('A', 'B', etc.).

- *Dead* keys. For example, on a French keyboard, the circumflex accent and grave accent are dead keys. These keys are said to be *dead* because nothing happens at the very moment when they are pressed. The key's effect does not appear until another key, a "live" one, is pressed. We can compare dead keys to Unicode's combining characters, except that a dead key comes before the base key and a combining character comes after the base character.

  A few scripts require multiple dead keys: for example, to obtain an 'ῷ', we could use the sequence of dead keys "smooth breathing", "circumflex accent", "iota subscript", followed by the ordinary key 'ω'. Unfortunately, few systems for generating virtual keyboards allow multiple dead keys.

- *Function* keys (F1, F2, etc.) and all other keys that do not lead to the insertion of a character when pressed. (The space bar is not a function key, as it inserts a space, although this character is invisible.)

- And *modifier* keys, which are keys pressed together with ordinary or dead keys and that modify the mapping of those keys' characters. On the Macintosh, the following modifier keys exist: shift, control, ⌘ or command or apple, alt, function. On a PC, there are also the shift, control, alt, and function keys, but there is no command key. On the other hand, there are two keys that do not appear on the Macintosh: right alt, or AltGr (at the right side of the keyboard), and the ⊞, or windows, key.

The role of the virtual keyboard is, therefore, to map characters to combinations of keys and modifiers, or perhaps to assign dead keys for them.

Under Mac OS X

Under Mac OS 9 we used *ResEdit* to create virtual keyboards, and those keyboards can still be used under Mac OS X; we simply place them in:

- ~/Library/Keyboard Layouts to make them available to the current user only

- /Library/Keyboard Layouts to make them available to all local users

- /Network/Library/Keyboard Layouts to make them available to all users on the network

But these virtual keyboards are based on the old WorldScript system, not on Unicode. To obtain Unicode keyboards, we have to create them in a different way.

XML description of virtual keyboard

To produce Unicode keyboards, Mac OS X adopted a system that is simply brilliant: one merely creates an XML file according to a certain Document Type Definition and places it in the area in which the binary resources for virtual keyboards are stored (see below). The system will compile this XML file into a binary resource the first time it is loaded. But the most brilliant aspect is the fact that we use *finite automata* to define multiple dead keys. Apple has already surprised us by using finite automata in the advanced typographic features of the AAT fonts (see Chapter 14, page 589 and following, and also Appendix §D.13.1, where we give an introduction to the concept of finite automaton); now this method is also applied to virtual keyboards.

But let us first describe the structure of a virtual-keyboard file, according to specification [57].

This file must have the extension .keylayout and must be placed in with the keyboard resources. It may have an icon, whose file must be present in the same directory, must be of Macintosh format icns, and must have the same filename but with the extension .icns.

Like every self-respecting XML document, our virtual-keyboard file must begin with an XML declaration and a reference to a DTD:

```
<?xml version="1.0" encoding="UTF-"?>
<!DOCTYPE keyboard SYSTEM
      "file://localhost/System/Library/DTDs/KeyboardLayout.dtd">
```

The top-level element in the document is called keyboard. It takes four attributes:

- group is the number of the script, according to Apple's earlier system. For Unicode keyboards, it is always 126.

- id is the identification number of the virtual keyboard. It must be unique, but the system takes care of that. There is only one constraint: we initially assign it a negative value to indicate that we are defining a Unicode keyboard.

- name is the keyboard's name as it will appear on the menu of keyboards. It is a UTF-8 string (if we have declared that the document is prepared in this natural form).

- maxout is the maximum number of Unicode characters that can be generated by a single keystroke. For an ordinary keyboard it is 1, but sometimes a key will produce multiple characters, as, for example, with the accented characters produced through the use of combining characters, in which two characters are produced: the base character and the combining character.

Next come two mandatory elements: layouts and modifierMap. The contents of these elements are very technical (the former is a code for the physical keyboard; the latter identifies the various kinds of modifiers that we may use), and they are practically the same for all virtual keyboards. We can therefore copy them from one file to another without many qualms.

Here are the first two elements of a typical virtual keyboard, in their entirety:

```
<keyboard group="126" id="-" name="Find the keycodes" maxout="4">
  <layouts>
    <layout first="0" last="17"
       modifiers="commonModifiers" mapSet="ANSI"/>
  </layouts>
  <modifierMap id="commonModifiers" defaultIndex="7">
    <keyMapSelect mapIndex="0">
      <modifier keys=""/>
      <modifier keys="command anyShift? caps?"/>
    </keyMapSelect>
    <keyMapSelect mapIndex="1">
      <modifier keys="anyShift caps?"/>
    </keyMapSelect>
    <keyMapSelect mapIndex="2">
      <modifier keys="caps"/>
    </keyMapSelect>
    <keyMapSelect mapIndex="3">
```

```
            <modifier keys="anyOption"/>
        </keyMapSelect>
        <keyMapSelect mapIndex="4">
            <modifier keys="anyShift anyOption command? caps?"/>
        </keyMapSelect>
        <keyMapSelect mapIndex="5">
            <modifier keys="anyOption caps"/>
        </keyMapSelect>
        <keyMapSelect mapIndex="6">
            <modifier keys="command anyOption caps?"/>
        </keyMapSelect>
        <keyMapSelect mapIndex="7">
            <modifier keys="control command? shift? caps? option?"/>
            <modifier keys="control command? shift? caps?
                option? rightShift"/>
            <modifier keys="control command? shift? caps?
                option? rightOption"/>
        </keyMapSelect>
    </modifierMap>
```

A few words of explanation are in order. In layouts we define physical keyboards. Here there is only one: ANSI.[3] For each physical keyboard, we define virtual tables: keyMap elements.

When no modifier key is used, the active table will be keyMap with index 0. The other tables will be activated when we press one or more modifier keys.

The keyMapSelect elements describe the relationship between modifiers and activated tables (because the same table can be activated by multiple combinations of different modifiers). The keywords used are:

- shift: the left shift key

- rightShift: the right shift key

- anyshift: either of the shift keys

- option: the left option key

- rightOption: the right option key

- anyOption: either of the option keys

- control: the left control key

---

[3] Just one little detail: in addition to ANSI, there are also the Japanese JIS keyboards. In any event, there is at least one noncompiled keylayout file in each installation of Mac OS X, that of the *Unicode hex input* keyboard: /System/Library/KeyboardLayouts/Unicode.bundle/Contents/Resources/UnicodeHexInput. keylayout. We can always start with the first two elements of this file.

- rightControl: the right control key

- anyControl: either of the control keys

- command: the ⌘ key

- caps: the caps-lock key

The presence of any of these keywords in the value of the keys attribute indicates that the corresponding key is pressed. The question mark indicates that it does not matter whether the key is pressed or not.

Thus, according to the code shown above, virtual table 0 is activated in two cases: when no modifier is being used, and (command anyShift? caps?) when the ⌘ key is depressed. In the latter case, the shift or caps-lock keys may also be depressed; they make no difference. Table 1 is activated when the shift key is depressed. (Pressing the caps-lock key makes no difference.) Table 2 is activated when the caps-lock key is depressed and caps lock is active. And so on. Thus we can describe in great detail the exact moment when one or another table will be active.

Here is the remainder of the file, up to the end:

```
<keyMapSet id="ANSI">
    <keyMap index="0">   <!-- No modifiers -->
        <key code="12" output="q" />
        <key code="13" output="w" />
        <key code="14" output="e" />
        ...
    </keyMap>
    <keyMap index="1">  <!-- anyShift -->
        ...
    </keyMap>
    ...
</keyMapSet>
<actions>
    ...
</action>
<terminators>
    ...
</terminator>
</keyboard>
```

There is a keyMapSet for each physical keyboard. In the example, there is only one. Next, there is a keyMap for each virtual table; the index attribute furnishes its number.

Within the keyMap are *key definitions*. These are key elements, with three possible attributes:

- code takes the number of a key as its value. How can we know which number corresponds to a given key? That is a very good question *that the specification carefully avoids*. Searching through Apple's technical documentation also yields nothing, and in any event there would be no guarantee that any tables that we did find would be valid for a given machine and a given version of the operating system. The author, however, has discovered a foolproof trick for finding the numbers of keys. All that we have to do is to create a keyboard that generates as its output the number N for key number N. The code is extremely simple:

```
<keyboard group="126" id="-" name="Find the keycodes" maxout="4">
    <layouts>
        ... as usual ...
    </modifierMap>
    <keyMapSet id="ANSI">
        <keyMap index="0">    <!-- No modifiers -->
            <key code="0" output="0 " />
            <key code="1" output="1 " />
            <key code="2" output="2 " />
                ...
            <key code="256" output="256 " />
        </keyMap>
    </keyMapSet>
</keyboard>
```

That keyboard may also serve as a test of installation. We place this file in one of the directories mentioned above and then close out the session. Later, we choose **Open International...** on the keyboard menu, we click on **Input Menu** and then we select this keyboard from the list that appears (it should be at the bottom of the list). If the keyboard is not present, compilation must have failed. In that case, we open the **Console** (a utility found in **Applications > Utilities**); it will certainly contain an error message from the XML compilation.

Do not forget the spaces in the values of the output attribute, or the numbers produced will all be run together.

Using this keyboard, we can discover that, for example, the 'e' key has the number 14, the carriage-return key is number 36, and the escape key is number 53, at least on the author's computer (a PowerBook G4 running the French version of Mac OS X 10.4.7, with an AZERTY keyboard).

- output takes as its value the string of characters to be generated. As in every XML document, we can write the code in UTF-8 or by using character entities of the type ሴ. Be careful not to write more characters than the value of the maxout attribute of keyboard allows.

- Instead of writing a string of characters, we can specify an *action* by writing the action attribute (instead of output), whose value is the name of an action.

The actions are described in the element `actions`. This element contains `action` subelements whose names (`id` attribute) are those used in the key elements.

What is an action? It is simply a series of `when` elements that will do different things according to context. The context is defined by a global variable, the "current state", which by default has the value `none`. According to the value of the current state, a different `when` will be executed. The state can be changed by a `when`. Similarly, a `when` can produce characters of output.

This element thus takes the following attributes:

- `state`: the state under which the `when` is executed. The value of this attribute may be a string of characters or a whole number.

- `next`: the new current state following execution of the `when`.

- `output`: any Unicode characters to be produced.

There are two other attributes that we shall not describe: they are useful primarily for hangul. They allow a `when` to be applied to more than one state and to calculate the value of a character in the output according to the number of the state and the position of the character entered.

Let us take a concrete example. We wish to make a dead key for the "circumflex accent" and produce an 'ê' when this key is followed by an 'e'. The numbers of these two keys are 33 and 14, respectively. Thus we shall write the following in `keyMapSet`:

```
<key code="33" action="circumflex" />
<key code="14" action="e" />
```

and we shall define two new actions in `actions`:

```
<action id="circumflex">
    <when state="none" next="circumflex"/>
</action>
<action id="e">
    <when state="none" output="e"/>
    <when state="circumflex" output="ê"/>
</action>
```

Thus, when we press the "circumflex" key, no character is produced, but we move into the `circumflex` state. Next, when we press 'e', the `when` tests the value of the state and produces an 'ê'.

The default value of `next` is `none`, which means that we automatically return to the initial state when no state is explicitly specified.

But what will happen if we change our minds after pressing the circumflex key and press a key other than 'e'? Nothing. The new character is produced, and no trace of the circumflex accent remains. That is one solution, but it is not the best. Ordinarily the system produces the circumflex accent (as an isolated character) and then the new character. To achieve this sort of behavior, we have another subelement of keyboard, the terminators element.

This element also contains when entries. But this time they cannot invoke new actions; they can only generate strings of characters. These when are executed when the last key pressed had no provision for the current state. In our example, we shall write:

```
<terminators>
    <when state="circumflex" output="^"/>
</terminators>
```

Thus if we followed the circumflex accent with something other than an 'e', we would obtain the ASCII character for the circumflex accent.

We have covered the syntax of this method of describing a keyboard.

Here is one other example, this time with a triple dead key: the Vietnamese letter 'ố'. To obtain it, we shall use the following characters in the order specified: the circumflex accent, the acute accent, the dot. We shall take advantage of this approach to produce the intermediate characters 'ố', 'ồ', 'ọ', 'ộ', 'ổ', and 'ỗ' as well. Here are the definitions of the keys:

```
<keyMap index="0">    <!-- no modifiers -->
    <key code="33" action="circumflex"/>
    <key code="21" action="acute"/>
    <key code="31" action="o"/>
</keyMap>
<keyMap index="1">    <!-- shift -->
    <key code="43" action="dot"/>
</keyMap>
```

in which we have separated the "dot" from the other keys because, at least on an AZERTY keyboard, it is typed with the shift key depressed.

Now we must define the following four actions:

```
<action id="circumflex">
    <when state="none" next="c"/>
</action>
<action id="acute">
    <when state="none" next="a"/>
    <when state="c" next="ca"/>
</action>
<action id="dot">
    <when state="none" next="d"/>
    <when state="c" next="cd"/>
```

```
        <when state="ca" next="cad"/>
        <when state="a" next="ad"/>
    </action>
    <action id="o">
        <when state="none" output="o"/>
        <when state="a" output="ó"/>
        <when state="c" output="ô"/>
        <when state="d" output="ọ"/>
        <when state="ad" output="ọ́"/>
        <when state="ca" output="ỗ"/>
        <when state="cd" output="ộ"/>
        <when state="cad" output="ỗ"/>
    </action>
```

We name states according to the keys already pressed: c (circumflex), a (acute), d (dot), ad, ca, cd, cad. We accept sequences of keystrokes in only one fixed order: first a possible circumflex, then a possible acute accent, and finally a possible dot. Thus the `circumflex` action necessarily occurs in the initial state, whereas the `acute` action may occur in the initial state or in state c, and so on.

Now all that remains is to add the terminators. There will be as many of them as there are possible states (the initial state being excluded):

```
<terminators>
    <when state="a" output="'"/>
    <when state="c" output="^"/>
    <when state="d" output="."/>
    <when state="ad" output="'."/>
    <when state="ca" output="^'"/>
    <when state="cd" output="^."/>
    <when state="cad" output="^'."/>
</terminators>
```

Thus, if we have typed the circumflex, the acute, and the dot and then change our minds and press something other than 'o', we will obtain the characters for all three keys.

Note that the example is realistic in all but one aspect: converting the apostrophe and the period into dead keys may be disturbing to the user. And the period is often the last character in a file. If it is on a dead key, it will not be entered into the file unless we type another character after it—and we are not accustomed to "typing one extra character so that the period will appear". Thus we are well advised to choose other keys for the "combining dot" and the "combining acute accent".

Under Windows

Microsoft recently released a program for creating virtual keyboards, the *Microsoft Keyboard Layout Creator* (MSKLC). This software is certainly robust and easy to use, but

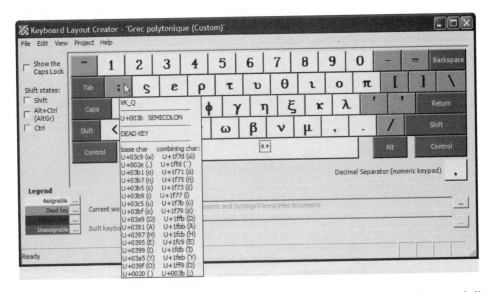

Figure 5-8: The main window of the Microsoft Keyboard Layout Creator. The keyboard displayed is the one for "polytonic Greek".

certain functionality, such as multiple dead keys, is missing. We shall describe it all the same because it is free of charge and because some users may not need advanced functionality.

Microsoft Keyboard Layout Creator

MSKLC is a Microsoft product issued in 2002 that today is up to version 1.3. It is freely distributed [268], but it works only on Win32 systems, namely Windows NT4, 2000, and XP[4]. It allows the user to open existing keyboards or to create new ones from scratch, to test the operation of a keyboard without installing it, and even to create a Windows installation package for distribution. This package allows other users who are not Windows experts to install the new keyboard in a user-friendly fashion.

The easiest way to obtain a new virtual keyboard is often to open an existing keyboard and modify it. In Figure 5-8 we see the main window of MSKLC. Dead keys are shown in light gray; modifiers, in dark gray. Using the checkboxes at the left, we can activate or deactivate the modifiers and see their different keyboard tables.

To associate a key with a Unicode character, we click on the key. A little dialog box opens, with an area for entering text. We can type a Unicode character directly or use the hexadecimal notation \xXXXX or U+XXXX (or U+XXXXXX for characters outside the BMP). This dialog box contains a button All that expands the dialog box to show the mappings of the key when combined with modifiers (Shift, Control+Alt, Shift+Control+Alt). That is

---

[4] Please be aware of the fact that this software needs .Net framework 1.1 to be installed (it will not work with .Net version 2).

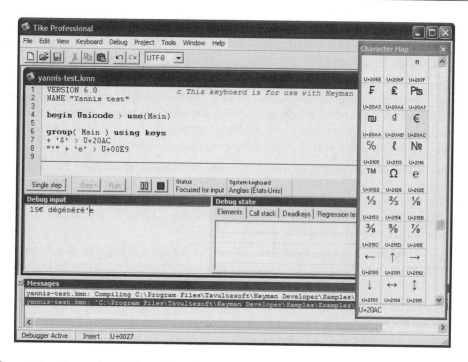

Figure 5-9: The main window of Tavultesoft Keyman Developer, with the debugger and the character map.

also how we convert a key into a dead key. A third little window provides us with a list of the results of combinations of the current dead key with other characters.[5]

When we have finished defining a keyboard, we can test it in a miniature text editor supplied under **Project>Test Keyboard Layout**. Then we can try to validate it (**Project> Validate Layout**); the program will search for any errors and all the minor imperfections of the keyboard. Finally, when we are happy with our work, we give the keyboard a name, associate it with a language in the system (which will also determine the little icon that will appear on the task bar), and create a Windows installer (of type MSI) using **Project>Build DLL and Setup Package**. This installer can be distributed freely.

Tavultesoft Keyman Developer

Tavultesoft Keyman Developer dates from 1993. It was developed by Marc Durdin, whose company, Tavulte, is based in Tasmania. This program adopts an approach totally different from that of MSKLC, with its own advantages and disadvantages.

---

[5] Here we are indeed speaking of Unicode characters, not of keys. But before we can enter Unicode characters, we have to have defined keys that generate the characters in question; otherwise, the software would be unable to make the (reverse) connection between characters and keys.

The virtual keyboard is created not through a user interface (that possibility does exist, but the result is simplistic) but by a little program written by the programmer in an *ad hoc* language. Once compiled, this program produces the virtual keyboard.

A keyboard produced with Keyman Developer cannot be used directly by Windows. It is necessary first to install a runtime program called *Keyman* (nothing more). This program is free for personal use and relatively inexpensive for professional use. With the runtime program, we can manually select Keyman virtual keyboards or use them instead of Windows keyboards; all these possibilities can be configured in great detail.

In terms of architecture, Keyman comes *after* the Windows keyboard; we can also associate Keyman with a specific Windows keyboard. That approach keeps us from having to start from scratch when we define a Keyman keyboard and also ensures that the Keyman keyboard will be compatible with all hardware: the Keyman keyboard receives not key numbers but Unicode characters as its input.

Owing to its relative independence from Windows, Keyman is capable of going much further. To explore its functionality, we shall begin by describing the syntax of the source code from which Keyman Developer compiles the virtual keyboard.

A Keyman code file is a text file with the extension .kmn. It has two parts: a header and a body. The body of the file contains *rules*.

Here is the header of a typical KMN file:

```
c Some comments
c
VERSION 6.0                   c The version of Keyman that is needed
                              c in order to use this file
NAME "Grolandese ***** keyboard"
BITMAP "groland.bmp"
store(&MnemonicLayout) "1"
begin Unicode > use(Main)
group(Main) using keys
```

A few words of explanation:

- The field BITMAP refers to the BMP file for the keyboard's icon on the taskbar.

- The line store(&MnemonicLayout) "1" indicates that the code that follows should be executed in "mnemonic" mode. That means that the keys are interpreted as characters and then processed by Keyman. If we omit this line, we proceed in "positional" mode, as in other systems.

- The body of the document begins after begin Unicode. The instruction > use(Main) indicates that the first "group" of rules is the one named Main.

- And the group Main begins with group(Main). The keywords using keys specify that we shall use the current character. The absence of these keywords would mean that this group of rules performed contextual analysis only. Later we shall see an example.

As with Apple's XML files, this header will usually remain the same; we can therefore copy it from one file to another.

Now let us move on to the rules. We shall write one rule on each line. A rule consists of a left-hand part (the input) and a right-hand part (the output), separated by a '>'. The left-hand part consists of a context and a current character, separated by a '+'. The context may be empty, in which case the line begins with the plus sign.

A rule with no context could be used to produce a euro sign every time we typed a dollar sign:

```
+ '$' > U+20AC
```

The character at the beginning of this rule indicates that there is no context and that the rule will therefore always be applied. There are two ways to describe a character: writing it in UTF-8 between single or double quotation marks, and writing its Unicode code point.

A rule to cause the apostrophe followed by an 'e' to produce an 'é':

```
"'" + 'e' > "é"
```

Before delving more deeply into the syntax, let us see how to use Keyman's interface to write the program, compile it, and debug it. By opening Keyman and selecting File>New, we are given the main window, which can be seen in Figure 5-9. We can write the header by hand or let Keyman do it (Keyboard>Insert standard header).

We write our two rules under the line group(Main)..., and we save the file under some name. To enter the euro sign, we can make use of the character map (View>Character map). If it does not contain the characters that we need, the reason is doubtless that the required font is not available. We can change the font by right-clicking on the character map and selecting Other font on the contextual menu that appears. On this same contextual menu, there is also a function Goto for rapidly searching for a character whose name or Unicode code point we know.

Then we will compile the program (Keyboard>Compile keyboard). If errors occur during compilation, they will be reported at the bottom of the window, which shows messages from Keyman. Once we have compiled the program successfully, we can debug it (Debug>Show debugger). The debugger's window opens, and Keyman is ready to accept our keystrokes.

We can select rapid mode (all instructions are executed immediately) or step-by-step mode (in which we can follow the flow of the program after every keystroke). By typing in the Debug input area, we can see the dollar sign change to a euro sign (a fine European dream) and the apostrophe followed by an 'e' turn into an 'é'.

We can experiment a little to gain a better understanding of how Keyman works. For example, if we type xxx'xxx and then insert an 'e' after the apostrophe, it will indeed be replaced by an 'é'. On the other hand, if we type an apostrophe followed by a space and an 'e', then delete the space, the replacement will not occur.

Let us return now to KMN's syntax. We may use any number of characters in the rules, both for the context and for the result. Thus we can imagine three Unicode characters (the context) followed by a fourth (the current character) that yield seven other characters (the result).

Now suppose that we wish to write a rule that will change the case of the 20 consonants of the Latin alphabet. Must we write 20 rules? Not at all. Three keywords—store, any, and index—allow us to define lists of characters and perform iterative operations on them.

Thus we begin by defining two lists of characters, called uppercase and lowercase:

```
store(uppercase) "BCDFGHJKLMNPQRSTVWXZ"
store(lowercase) "bcdfghjklmnpqrstvwxz"
```

Next we write a rule in which we consider the 20 elements of the uppercase list one by one and convert them to elements of the lowercase list in the same position:

```
+ any(uppercase) > index(lowercase, 1)
```

The 1 indicates that the any to which we have referred is character number 1 of the expression at the left. We can imagine another rule that would reverse the order of two letters:

```
any(lowercase) + any(lowercase) > index(lowercase, 2)
    index(lowercase, 1)
```

(all on one line).

Up to now we have not used any dead keys, yet we have modified an 'e' preceded by an apostrophe. We have less need for dead keys, since combinations can easily be built up without them. But in case we should like to use them, here is how to do so. A rule can produce an invisible "character" written in the form deadkey(foo), in which foo is a keyword.

Nothing will be displayed for the time being. Next, we shall write other rules that will serve as a context or a portion of a context for deadkey(foo).

Other interesting keywords: context, nul, and beep. The first of these, context, is used as a right-hand component. It will be replaced by the context of the left-hand part. It can be followed by the index of the character that we wish to produce:

```
"raou" + "l" > context(4)
```

will produce a 'u'. The keyword nul is also used on the right-hand side. It indicates that there will be no output. Finally, with the keyword beep, the machine generates a beep. This device can be used to punish the typist for trying to enter a bad combination of characters.

All the code that we have written has been "mnemonic" because we have used Unicode characters, not the identifiers of keys. To use the latter, we can write [NAME], in which NAME is the name of a key. To obtain the name of a given key, we can use the feature Tools>Virtual Key Identifier. The window that appears will display the name of any key that we press.

Finally, the best aspect of KMN's syntax: *groups*. These play the role of states in finite automata: a rule can invoke a group (i.e., activate a state), and each group contains rules that are specific to it.

Let us take an example. Suppose that we want a keyboard that will prevent a Cyrillic letter from immediately following a Latin letter (to prevent the problems that result from mixing scripts):

```
begin Unicode > use(prelim)

store(latin) "ABCDEFGHIJKLMNOPQRSTUVWXYZ"
store(cyrillic) "АБЦДЕФГХИЙКЛМНОПЯРСТУЖВЬЫЫЗШЭЩЧЪЮ"

group(prelim)
    any(latin) > context use(latinstate)
    nomatch > use(nostate)

group(latinstate) using keys
    + any(cyrillic) > beep
    nomatch > use(nostate)

group(nostate) using keys
```

Explanation: At the beginning (as soon as we have typed a character), we ask Keyman to go into the prelim group. There we ask: is the letter that has just been entered a Latin letter? If so, we store this letter as a context for the following rule and switch to the group latinstate. In this group there is only one rule: if the following character is Cyrillic, we sound a beep and stop the process. In both groups, if the letter that is entered does not comply with the rule, we switch to the group nostate, which does not have any rules.[6]

Under X Window

Under X Window, we have two fundamental concepts [299, p. 401]: the *keycode* (which is the number of each physical key) and the *keysym* (the symbolic name associated with each key). To configure a virtual keyboard is to write a table of mappings between the two.

---

[6] A word of warning to the reader who may be trying to play around with the code above under his copy of Keyman Developer: there is a bug in the debugger's input area that requires the user to release the shift key and press it again for each capital letter. There is also a separate testing window (validate it first with Tools> Options>Debugger, then press F9 to open it), which does not suffer from this flaw.

xmodmap

The basic tool for manipulating virtual keyboards is *xmodmap*, a utility as old as X itself.
By entering xmodmap -pke, we obtain a list of mappings between *keycode* and *keysym* that
looks like this:

```
keycode    8 = q Q doubledagger
keycode    9 = s S Ograve
keycode   10 = d D
keycode   11 = f F NoSymbol periodcentered
keycode   12 = h H Igrave Icircumflex
keycode   13 = g G
keycode   14 = w W leftanglebracket rightanglebracket
```

The four different entries indicate the *keysym* when there is no modifier; when the Shift
key is pressed; when a key called Mode_switch, which is therefore a modifier, is pressed;
when Mode_switch and Shift are pressed together. What is this Mode_switch key? That
is also specified in the code, along with the identity of the modifier key for Shift and all
the other modifiers:

```
keycode   63 = Meta_L
keycode   64 = Shift_L
keycode   65 = Caps_Lock
keycode   66 = Mode_switch
keycode   67 = Control_L
keycode   68 = Shift_R
keycode   69 = Alt_R
keycode   70 = Control_R
```

If we save the output of *xmodmap -pke*, we obtain a configuration file for a virtual keyboard. Then we have only to run

```
xmodmap ./mykeyboard
```

(in which mykeyboard is a file using the same syntax as the code above), and the new
keyboard is loaded.

To test both the *keycode* associated with each key and the *keysym* that is associated with
the current configuration, we can launch *xev*, a very special application that opens a little
window and captures every event that occurs while the cursor is positioned over that
window. Thus when we press the 'a' key under these conditions, we see:

```
KeyPress event, serial 24, synthetic NO, window 0x1000001,
    root 0x38, subw 0x0, time 1568428051, (129,44), root:(244,364),
    state 0x0, keycode 20 (keysym 0x61, a), same_screen YES,
    XLookupString gives 1 bytes:  "a"
```

```
KeyRelease event, serial 24, synthetic NO, window 0x1000001,
    root 0x38, subw 0x0, time 1568428130, (129,44), root:(244,364),
    state 0x0, keycode 20 (keysym 0x61, a), same_screen YES,
    XLookupString gives 1 bytes:  "a"
```

Thus there are two events: the pressing of the key and its release. The *keycode* of this key is 20, and the *keysym* is a. If we press 'é' on a French keyboard, we obtain:

```
KeyPress event, serial 24, synthetic NO, window 0x1000001,
    root 0x38, subw 0x0, time 1568533302, (110,40), root:(225,360),
    state 0x0, keycode 27 (keysym 0xe9, eacute), same_screen YES,
    XLookupString gives 1 bytes:  "é"

KeyRelease event, serial 24, synthetic NO, window 0x1000001,
    root 0x38, subw 0x0, time 1568533382, (110,40), root:(225,360),
    state 0x0, keycode 27 (keysym 0xe9, eacute), same_screen YES,
    XLookupString gives 1 bytes:  "é"
```

in which we see the *keycode* (27), the *keysym* (eacute), and even an interpretation of the *keysym* as a Unicode character: 'é'.

Another interesting feature of *xmodmap*: instead of defining the behavior of the keys, we can reallocate the characters. Thus, if we write:

```
keysym bracketleft = 0x005b 0x007b 0272 0260
keysym bracketright = 0x005d 0x007d 0305 comma
keysym a = a A 0277 0304
keysym s = s S 0313 0246
keysym d = d D 0241 0257
```

it is the *keysym* values that will change, according to the modifiers that are activated. This style of writing is independent of the physical keyboard.

There is also *XKeyCaps* (see Figure 5-10), a graphical interface for xmodmap that was developed by Jamie Zawinski. This interface allows us to select the *keysym* for each *keycode* from a list of available *keysym* values. Unfortunately, the development of this program was halted in 1999.

Conversion of Text from One Encoding to Another

There are few tools for converting text, no doubt because text editors (such as BBEdit and Ultra-Edit) and word-processing packages (such as MS Word and Corel WordPerfect) handle this process internally. There is a free library of subroutines devoted to converting between encodings: *libiconv*, developed by Bruno Haible. The GNU software provided with this library that performs conversions is called *iconv*.

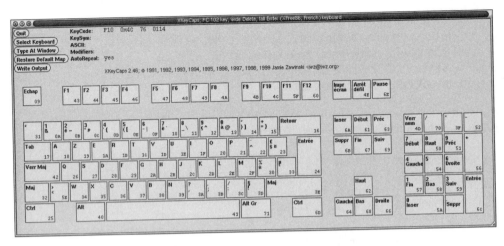

Figure 5-10: The main window of XKeyCaps

The recode Utility

In this section we shall describe a program with a long history (its origins, under a different name, go back to the 1970s) that today is based on *libiconv*: *recode*, by the Québécois François Pinard [293].

To convert a file foo.txt, all that we need is to find the source encoding A and the target encoding B on the list of encodings supported by *recode* and write:

```
recode A..B foo.txt
```

The file foo.txt will be overwritten. We can also write:

```
recode A..B < foo.txt > foo-converted.txt
```

In fact, we can go through multiple steps:

```
recode A..B..C..D..E foo.txt
```

What is even more interesting is that *recode* refers to *surface*, which is roughly the equivalent of Unicode's serialization mechanisms (see page 62)—a technique for transmitting data without changing the encoding. If S is a serialization mechanism, we can write:

```
recode A..B/S foo.txt
```

and, in addition to the conversion, this mechanism will also be applied. For example, we can convert data to hexadecimal, or base 64, or quoted-printable (page 48). Here are the serialization mechanisms provided by *recode*:

- b64:[7] base 64.

- d1, d2, d4: write the characters as decimal numbers, byte by byte, wyde by wyde, or tetrabyte by tetrabyte.

- h1, x2, x4: write the characters as hexadecimal numbers, byte by byte, wyde by wyde, or tetrabyte by tetrabyte.

- o1, x2, x4: write the characters as hexadecimal numbers, byte by byte, wyde by wyde, or tetrabyte by tetrabyte.

- QP: quoted-printable.

- CR and CR-LF: convert Unix's line feeds to carriage returns or carriage returns followed by line feeds.

What concerns us here is the conversion of data to Unicode. Here are the Unicode encoding forms that are recognized by *recode*:

- u7: UTF-7, which has the advantage of being expressible in ASCII and of being generally legible, at least for the European languages

- u8: our beloved UTF-8

- u6: generic UTF-16, either big-endian or little-endian, according to the platform being used

- UTF-16BE and UTF-16LE: big-endian or little-endian UTF-16, respectively

And those of ISO 10646:

- UCS-2-INTERNAL: the 16-bit encoding, with the endianness of the local platform.

- UCS-2-SWAPPED: the 16-bit encoding, with endianness opposite to that of the local platform.

- UCS-2LE: the 16-bit encoding in little-endian mode. Recall that UCS-2 is like UTF-16, with the exception that the code points beyond 0x10FFFF, while not disallowed, are simply not allocated.

- UCS-4-INTERNAL, UCS-4-SWAPPED, UCS-4BE, UCS-4LE: the 32-bit encoding, with the endianness of the platform, with the opposite endianness, in big-endian mode, and in little-endian mode, respectively.

Sometimes *recode* refuses to convert a document, no doubt because there is a character that cannot be converted. In this case, we can force it to complete the conversion by using the -f option. The results, of course, must be used with care.

Among the encodings supported by *recode* (there are 277 in all, as of version 3.6), these are the most important:

---

[7] There are many aliases for each name. We have provided only one, typically the shortest.

- us, which is simply the version of ASCII localized for the United States, which was to become ISO 646.1991-IRV. Accented letters are decomposed into an accent and a letter: voil`a.

- The Mac's encodings: MacArabic, MacCentralEurope, MacCroatian, MacCyrillic, MacGreek, MacHebrew, MacIceland, MacRoman, MacRomania, MacThai, MacTurkish, MacUkraine.

- The Chinese encodings: BIG5, cn (le codage GB 1988), CHINESE (le codage GB 2312), ISO-2022-CN, ISO-2022-CN-EXT, EUC-CN, EUC-TW.

- The Japanese encodings: JIS_C6220-1969, JIS_C6229-1984, JIS_X0201, JIS_X0208, JIS_X0212, SJIS, ISO-2022-JP, ISO-2022-JP-1, ISO-2022-JP-2, EUC-JP.

- The Korean encodings: KSC5636, KSC_5601, KS_C_5601, JOHAB, ISO-2022-KR, EUC-KR.

- The ISO 8859 family of encodings: 11, 12, ... 19 (ISO Latin-1 to -9), cyrillic (ISO 8859-5), arabic (ISO 8859-6), greek (ISO 8859-7), hebrew (ISO 8859-8).

- The Microsoft code pages: CP866, CP874, CP932, CP949, CP950, CP1133, CP1258, ms-ee (Windows 1250), ms-cyrl (Windows Cyrillic), ms-ansi (Windows Latin 1), ms-greek, ms-turk, ms-hebr, ms-arab, WinBaltRim.

- EBCDIC and all of its localized forms: EBCDIC, EBCDIC-FR, etc.

- Some pseudo-encodings:

  - TeX: the accents in \'{e}, \`{a}, etc.

  - h1, ... , h4: HTML entities é, ç, etc., in which the digit denotes the HTML version.

  - flat: all accented letters lose their accents.

  - dump-with-names gives us a list of all the characters in the document, one character per line, containing for each character its numeric value, its representation, and its Unicode description.

  - Texte [in French!], a decomposition of the accented letters into "letter + accent", created specially for French (e'le'ment, apre`s, de'ja`).

The reader may consult the list of all the encodings that *recode* supports by typing recode -l.

6

Font Management on the Macintosh

Our concern in this chapter will be the installation and management of fonts under Mac OS 9 and Mac OS X. The Mac OS 9 operating system is the fruit of a long development process that began in 1984 with System 1.0, which came with the very first Macintosh. It is not astonishing that practically all extant types of fonts are found under Mac OS 9. We shall begin by describing these types of fonts and giving a little glimpse at font management *à la Macintosh*.

But Mac OS 9 will soon be nothing but a fleeting memory, since Mac OS X, the new Unix-based operating system, now comes standard on Macintoshes. At the beginning of the twenty-first century, Mac OS X aimed to simplify font management while also adding new functionality. We shall discuss the new features in the second part of this chapter.

Nevertheless, one thing has remained unchanged throughout the long course of development that led to Mac OS X: the ease of installing fonts. All that was necessary, *dixit* Apple, was *to place them in the system folder* (under Mac OS 9 and earlier systems) or *in one of the designated folders* (under Mac OS X). What more, then, need we say about installing fonts on the Macintosh?

In fact, a number of factors combine to make font management on the Macintosh more complex than Apple claims. First of all, fonts placed in the system folder are loaded into memory; thus they take up RAM and slow down both booting and the launching of applications (which systematically analyze the fonts contained in the system folder). Second, fonts are files that remain permanently open and that can be corrupted upon the slightest system crash. A corrupted font loaded by the system will cause a fatal system crash. Such crashes are often fraught with consequences, and this type of corrupt file is also difficult to detect.

For all of these reasons, therefore, we are wise to use tools to manage our fonts, install and uninstall them on the fly, check their integrity and correct any problems that may arise, and so forth. The third part of this chapter will be devoted to describing these tools.

The Situation under Mac OS 9

Before discussing fonts, one quick word on managing files on the Macintosh. One of the Mac's idiosyncrasies is the *dual nature* of its files: every Macintosh file may have a part containing *data* and a part containing *resources* [49, p. I-103]. A *resource* is a set of data associated with a *type* (a string of four characters), a *number*, and possibly a *name*. As its name suggests, the data part usually contains data, whereas the resource part contains executable code, components of a user interface (menus, dialog windows, etc.), and all sorts of other "resources".

The two parts, data and resources, are connected in a transparent manner, and the Macintosh windowing manager, called the *Finder*, displays only one object, represented by an *icon*. A Macintosh file may lack a data part (as do some executable files, for example) or a resource part. In the latter case, it is often represented by a "generic" icon in the *Finder*.

This phenomenon occurs because the icons used to represent files are selected by the *Finder* from two pieces of information contained not in the file itself but in the directory of files on the disk's partition: this information is also stored as strings of four characters called the *creator* and the *type* of the file. Thanks to the "creator", the *Finder* can launch the correct application when we double-click on a file's icon, wherever the application may be stored on the disk(s). Thanks to the "type", the application in question knows what type of data we are providing. Owing to this approach, the Macintosh has never needed to make recourse to filename *extensions*, which, however, are indispensable under Windows and quite helpful under Unix.

Let us now move on to the special family of files that is of particular concern to us: font files. In Figure 6-1 we see a certain number of Mac OS 9 icons that represent fonts. **Monaco** and **Optima** are icons for "font suitcases". These "suitcases" contain bitmap or TrueType fonts. When we double-click on a suitcase (see **Monaco** in the figure), it opens like any other file and displays a list of the fonts that it contains, which we can move at will. **Monaco–ISO–8859–1 9** and **Charcoal** are icons of bitmap and TrueType fonts extracted from font suitcases. Conversely, **TT0003C_.TTF** is a Windows TrueType font that is recognized as a TrueType font even though it comes from the Windows world and is used as it is by Mac OS 9. **Zapfino.dfont** is a font of type *dfont*, which is specific to Mac OS X: it is not recognized by Mac OS 9, which explains the lack of an icon particular to it. **FREESans.otf** is an OpenType font.

The other files in the figure are all for PostScript Type 1 fonts. The first three (DidotL–Hlta, TotoRom, FreeSan) were produced by three major font-design software packages: Macromedia Fontographer, Letraset FontStudio, and FontLab. All the others come from different founderies: Adobe, Monotype, P22, Bitstream, ITC, Hoefler, Paratype, Font-

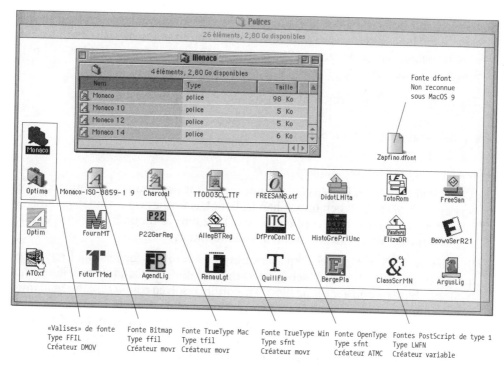

Figure 6-1: A Mac OS 9 screenshot showing a certain number of Macintosh font files.

Font, Agfa (before its merger with Monotype), URW, Font Bureau, Font Company, ATF Kingsley, Esselte Letraset, Mecanorma, and Red Rooster.

Let us now take a closer look at these different file types. First of all, note that we can classify them into two categories from the point of view of their file structure: those—the more recent ones—whose resource part is empty (the OpenType, *dfont*, and Windows TrueType files), and those for which all the data is stored in the resources (all other files). What about these resources?

The most interesting of them is the resource FOND [49, p. I-215], which is common to all the Mac OS 9 font formats. It contains general information on bitmap, TrueType, and PostScript Type 1 fonts. It never contains glyphs as such but merely pointers to resources or files that do contain them. It has a name, and this name is, from the point of view of the Macintosh system and its applications, the *only* name by which the font is recognized and can be used. Beyond the name, it contains the following information:

- A font identification number (which is in fact the number of the resource itself).

- Some technical information of no great importance.

- Some tables for width and kerning.

- Pointers to bitmap (FONT or NFNT) or TrueType (sfnt) resources, contained in the same file. These resources are categorized according to point size (the resource for TrueType fonts having a pseudo-value of 0 points) and the *style* (0 = regular, 1 = bold, 2 = italic, 3 = bold italic).

- The names of the PostScript fonts that correspond to these various styles.

We can now make three observations:

1. *The importance of the identification number*

   A font is identified under Mac OS 9 by its identification number. This practice was very effective in 1985, when only a handful of Macintoshes were available; but it is completely out of date today, when we may have tens of thousands of fonts at our disposal. It opens the door to conflicting identification numbers.

   In older versions of Mac OS, a special utility was available for loading fonts onto the system: *Font/DA Mover* (which gave us the "creator" DMOV and movr fields of the "suitcase", bitmap, and TrueType files). This utility resolved conflicts between identification numbers and checked the integrity of the internal links to resources in each font file before copying it onto the system. In more recent versions of Mac OS, these procedures are automatically performed when we install fonts by placing them in the subfolder **Fonts** of the system folder, which is provided for this purpose.

   The fact that the system changes the identification number is obviously an improvement, but it also implies that font files are *modified* by the system so that they can be added to the existing repertoire of fonts—and this modification occurs as soon as the fonts are copied into the **Fonts** folder. That folder is thus very special, and its contents must be handled with care. The font managers that we shall see below will keep us from having to handle this folder directly.

2. *A simplistic classification of fonts*

   As we have seen, there are only four styles in a Macintosh "font family", called "regular", "bold", "italic", and "bold italic". We therefore see only one name (the name of the resource FOND) within applications, and we select among the four variants with a "style" menu.

   There is no way to have a single family with more style variants; if we need more, we must resort to creating multiple families. Each of them will, accordingly, be considered a separate font by the system's user interface and by applications.

   This special characteristic of the Macintosh is at the heart of a number of nightmares that plague the users of DTP software. For example, to set type in oblique Optima, we may use either the "italic" style of the font *Optima* or a separate font called *Optima Oblique*. Both of them may be associated with the same PostScript font Optima-Oblique and may yield the same result. But that outcome depends completely on the configuration of the font family in question. We have no a priori way to know whether the foundry has supplied distinct Macintosh styles or distinct FOND resources. And what happens if we inadvertently select the "italic" style of the font *Optima Oblique*? Some software will go as far as to give the oblique version of Optima an artificial slant, yielding a font that has been slanted twice!

Tools such as *Adobe Type Reunion* (ATR), which we shall describe below, attempt to ameliorate this inconsistency by bringing the style variants of the same font together on the user interface. Nevertheless, the problem is far from being resolved, and a great deal of prudence is called for during the installation, modification, or creation of fonts.

3. *Disparities in the data*

FOND is, in a sense, the most important resource, as without it the Macintosh usually cannot gain access to the data in a font. Nonetheless, we shall note that this resource never appears in isolation. It is always accompanied by other resources, either in the same file (as with the resources FONT and NFNT for bitmap fonts and sfnt for TrueType fonts) or in other files (as with PostScript fonts, whose filenames have to be computed from the names of the fonts[1] contained in the resource FOND). Merely breaking the link between these resources or files will render the font unusable.

A final problem, of a different sort, affects PostScript fonts. For business reasons, no version of Mac OS (before Mac OS X) wished to allow the possibility of using PostScript fonts for display on the screen. A separate program (*Adobe Type Manager*, or ATM) assumed that task. Mac OS itself uses only the bitmap fonts contained in the "font suitcase"; thus, at a large point size, the system will have no choice but to magnify the pixels of the bitmap fonts, and the result is a set of shapes that look like "staircases". Using PostScript fonts, in which the shapes are described by mathematical formulae, ATM produces bitmaps on the fly, and the visual result is the *smoothing* of the glyphs. But its task is quite complex: without being integrated into the system, it must intercept all requests by different programs to display a font, find the correct bitmap fonts, track down the links to the corresponding PostScript files, read the files, extract the descriptions of the glyphs, and generate bitmaps on the fly. All that has to happen in real time.

The more types of fonts we have, the more tools as well. It comes as no surprise that font management on the Macintosh is a minefield. Before examining the different tools that allow users (including intense users) to survive unscathed, we shall make one quick comment on developments since the move to Mac OS X.

The situation under Mac OS X

Several years ago, before Steve Jobs returned to Apple, no one would have believed that we could have a Unix operating system that was also a version of Mac OS. The feat was to bring users the benefits of Unix without losing the wealth of features acquired by the various releases of Mac OS since 1984. Fonts were also affected: we saw in the previous

---

[1] The rule is as follows: Assume that the PostScript name is made of words in lowercase letters beginning with a capital. We retain the first five letters of the first word and the first three letters of each of the following words. Thus, for example, Miracle-BoldItalic becomes MiracBolIta.

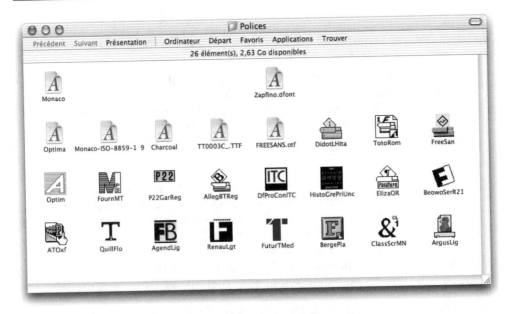

Figure 6-2: The same file that is shown in Figure 6-1, as seen under Mac OS X.

section the variety of file types in use ("font suitcases", bitmaps, TrueType, PostScript, OpenType, etc.). Obviously Mac OS X had to accept all these file formats, for reasons of compatibility. But Mac OS X also aimed to simplify the existing order.

And simplify it did! In Figure 6-2 we see the same window shown in Figure 6-1, as it appears under Mac OS X. What a surprise to see that all of the files described in the preceding section, even though they are of very different natures, are represented by the same icon (a letter 'A' on a white background)! Even the file Zapfino.dfont uses this icon, as it will henceforth be recognized by the operating system.[2]

Thus the system is capable of transparently recognizing and using all types of fonts (or at least all those that were recognized[3] by Mac OS 9) and furnishes a replacement for "font suitcases"—a replacement that is essential so that Unix applications can make use of the data.

---

[2] Now is the time to remove the mystery that enshrouds this "new format", which is not really a format at all, as it is merely a "font suitcase" in which all the information that had been in the resource section has been transferred unchanged to the data section. Thus it is a file that can be used by Unix applications but that is functionally equivalent to the "font suitcases" that we have known since the release of the first Mac in 1984.

[3] With only one exception: the FONT resources still are not recognized by Mac OS X, which considers them too old for its taste. Tools (such as *FONT→NFNT* [203] or *fondu* [351], for example) exist to replace resources with NFNTs systematically. Another important detail: while "carbonized" applications continue to work as before and to use bitmap fonts if they please, applications using the new *Quartz* graphical library will be incompatible with bitmap fonts from now on. Those of us who have painstakingly created bitmap fonts to resolve various practical problems now find ourselves forced to vectorize them.

Now let us move on to the installation of fonts. Where should we place font files so that they can be used by the system? Since Unix is a multiuser system, we need to manage the permissions of users, and the same goes for fonts as well. At the same time, we must not forget that Mac OS 9 is still with us, through the *Classic* environment. It is therefore desirable to make the same fonts accessible on both Mac OS X and Mac OS 9 under *Classic*. Apple has provided five different locations to place (or not to place) font files [202, 60]:

1. In ~/Library/Fonts, where ~ is the home directory of the active user. These fonts are available to that user only.

2. In /Library/Fonts. These fonts are available to all local users. Only an administrator may place fonts here.

3. In /Network/Library/Fonts. These fonts are available to all users on the local network. Only a network administrator may place fonts here.

4. In /System/Library/Fonts. This is the location for system fonts. Apple encourages us to leave this directory alone.

5. In the Mac OS 9 system folder. These fonts are available to all local users and also to applications that run under Classic.

Thus everything depends on how we use our fonts. If we are in a modern environment in which all the software is carbonized, or better yet in *Cocoa*, then there is no need to place fonts into the Mac OS 9 system folder. This is especially true if we belong to a workgroup that uses shared resources and we would also like to share private fonts without violating the law, by making them accessible only to members of a certain group. In this case, all that we have to do is to sort our fonts into private fonts, fonts that are locally public, and fonts that are public at the network level, and place them in the appropriate location.

If, on the other hand, we still have to go through Classic in order to use our favorite applications, the issue of permissions does not arise; we simply place our fonts into the good old system folder of Mac OS 9, and they will be accessible by both Mac OS 9 applications and Mac OS X applications.

PostScript fonts are easier to use under Mac OS X. We no longer need ATM, the program that used PostScript fonts associated with FOND to display smoothed glyphs on the screen. Mac OS X itself interprets the PostScript code and smooths the glyphs.

Despite the large number of folders in which fonts may be found, Mac OS X has thus managed to simplify the use of fonts: no longer do we have to worry about differences in font type, as everything is processed in the same manner, and we no longer need a tool external to the system in order to display PostScript fonts. But have the problems mentioned in the previous section—namely, the importance of the identification number, the simplistic classification into styles, and the disparity of data files—been resolved?

Not at all. The identification number is still with us, the styles are all the same (because the new *dfont* are only ordinary "font suitcases" stored in a different way on the disk), and the disparity among files is the same (we still need two files for a single PostScript font). The problems are all the same; they have just been hidden from the view of the end user. The tools that help us to get around these problems are therefore as indispensable as they ever were, and we shall now describe them, in the following section.

Font-Management Tools

In this section, we shall describe a handful of tools that are useful, or even indispensable in certain cases, for the effective management of fonts under Mac OS. We shall describe only those tools that run under Mac OS X (while noting their compatibility with Mac OS 9), except, of course, in the case of important tools that have not yet been ported to OS X (such as ATM).

Tools for Verification and Maintenance

We have already mentioned the dangers that fonts face under Mac OS—dangers stemming primarily from the fact that the files that contain them are permanently left open, since the system needs to have regular access to them in order to load the information necessary for displaying text. A font file is in direct contact with the system; when the system crashes, the file can also be affected. This fact explains why fonts are the most fragile files on the Macintosh. And a corrupted font is often the cause of new system crashes.

If we have no cure for this situation, we can at least limit the damage by regularly checking the status of our fonts and replacing with fresh copies those files that have been corrupted. One popular tool for performing this sort of maintenance on the font repertoire is *Font Doctor*, by Morrison SoftDesign [275].

This tool allows us to verify and repair all the fonts contained in the folders specified by the user. When repairs are impossible, the font is set aside in a special folder. Font Doctor also plays a preventive role; thus it will warn the user if it finds duplicates of a font or identical fonts in different formats (for example, PostScript Type 1 and TrueType). Here is the list of the operations carried out in the course of a "diagnostic" check on the fonts:

- Resolving conflicts in identification numbers (the numbers of the resource FOND).

- Detecting duplicates (= fonts of the same format and of the same version that contain the same glyphs).

- Deleting unwanted bitmap files in order to keep only one point size per font. Indeed, since Mac OS X handles display at all sizes, bitmap fonts are in theory no longer necessary. I say "in theory" because manually edited bitmap fonts will always be better than those generated by the computer; thus we are wise to retain them. For this reason, the automatic deletion of bitmap fonts is not always desirable.

- Detecting fonts that are available in several different formats. We can specify that priority should go to PostScript and OpenType fonts or to TrueType fonts.

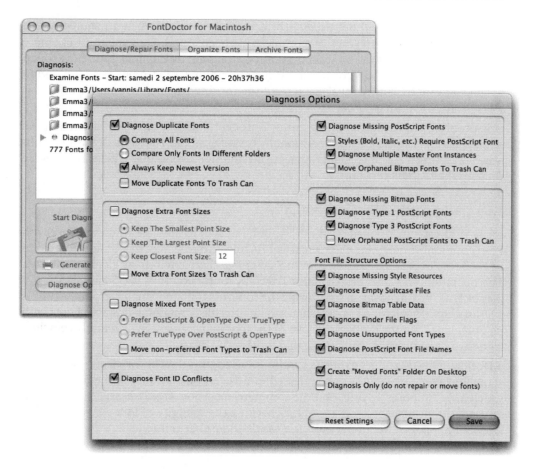

Figure 6-3: Font Doctor's configuration interface.

- Detecting "orphaned bitmaps". The term is ill chosen, as it applies not necessarily to bitmaps but rather to FOND resources containing links to PostScript fonts that are not available.

- Detecting "orphaned PostScript fonts". Here we have the opposite situation: we have a PostScript font but no FOND resource that would enable the system to recognize the font in question. Note that when Font Doctor finds "orphaned bitmap fonts" and "orphaned PostScript fonts" that correspond to them, it performs a "family reunion" by re-creating the missing links.

- Verifying the integrity of the files. FOND and NFNT are checked for compliance with Apple's specifications. Font Doctor takes advantage of the procedure to replace old FONT resources (which are no longer recognized by Mac OS X) with NFNT resources.

Note that *Font Doctor* will not usually correct a defective font when a major problem arises but will rather warn you that a problem has been found. Thus you must use more powerful font-editing tools to set the situation straight. For example, in the case of an "orphaned PostScript font" for which no corresponding FOND can be found, only font-design software such as FontLab can create the missing resource. We shall discuss this sort of software in Chapter 12.

Other tools for verifying and maintaining fonts exist, but they are less efficient and less stable than *Font Doctor*. We may mention, by way of example, *FontAgent*, by Insider Software [189], which has the benefit of having a Windows version that is identical in every detail to the Mac OS version.

ATM: the "Smoother" of Fonts

We have already mentioned ATM [18], a tool that is indispensable when we work with PostScript fonts under Mac OS 9 or earlier. Its role is to read PostScript fonts pointed to by FOND resources and to use the contours described therein to display glyphs at all sizes. This operation, which seems trivial for TrueType fonts because Mac OS handles the display of TrueType glyphs at all sizes (using the contours contained in the resource sfnt), is a little more difficult for ATM, which has to find the files containing PostScript data with no other clue than the PostScript name of the font being sought (which rarely coincides with the name of the file containing that font).

To facilitate the task of detecting files, Adobe also equipped ATM with features for managing font files. Finally, ATM was released in two versions: *ATM Light*, the free version, which only "smooths" glyphs, and the commercial version *ATM Deluxe* [17], which also serves as a font manager and a tool for checking the integrity of fonts. Before delving into font managers, we should say a few words about the "smoother".

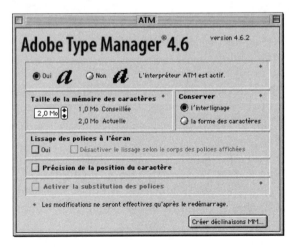

Figure 6-4: The configuration interface of ATM.

The configuration interface of this program (Figure 6-4) is quite simple:

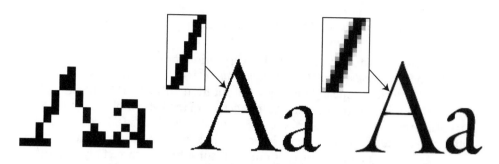

Figure 6-5: The letters 'Aa' in Agfa's splendid font Throhand, at 128 points. From the left: display without ATM; display with ATM but without glyph smoothing; and display with ATM and with glyph smoothing.

- Enabling/disabling of the program.

- The amount of memory that we wish to dedicate to cache for glyphs. (This option was important in the days when RAM on the Macintosh was on the order of a few megabytes, which is no longer the case today.)

- A choice between giving priority to glyphs and giving priority to line spacing, when ATM has to choose between preserving the shapes of glyphs and maintaining even line spacing.

- Enabling of glyph smoothing. When smoothing is disabled, ATM uses only black and white pixels; when smoothing is enabled, ATM also uses pixels along a grayscale (an operation called *anti-aliasing*). It is important to remember to enable this option, which makes a spectacular difference in the quality of the output (Figure 6-5).

- An option to enable smoothing through gray levels only for type at or above a certain point size (which is not specified). As it happens, smoothing at small sizes is hardly noticeable and only slows down the displaying of glyphs.

- An option for "precise positioning of the character", which lets us increase the precision with which the positions of glyphs are calculated below the threshold of the pixel. This feature will work only if it is supported by the software that displays glyphs.

- Enabling font substitution. The same method used by Adobe Acrobat is also used in ATM. When we know the widths of the glyphs in a font but do not have the font itself, the corresponding glyphs in the *Multiple Master* fonts *Adobe Serif MM* or *Adobe Sans MM* are displayed. This feature works quite well in Acrobat because the widths of the glyphs must be supplied. ATM, however, cannot carry out the substitution unless it has access to these data. It therefore needs access to at least one FOND resource in order to implement this method. The substitution affects only "orphaned bitmaps", and no provision is made for documents that use fonts that are entirely unknown to the system.

But automatic substitution poses another very serious problem, both to Acrobat and to ATM: the fonts *Adobe Serif MM* and *Adobe Sans MM* contain only the glyphs needed for a few Western European languages. Substitution fails when the missing glyphs are symbols or letters in a non-Latin alphabet, or in the Latin alphabet but in a language other than the favored ones of Western Europe. More specifically, either the software is aware of the type of glyphs needed but fails to perform the substitution, knowing that it is unable to carry it out, or it substitutes incorrect glyphs, thereby mangling the document into illegible gibberish. Unfortunately, the latter seems to happen most of the time, for the simple reason that most software identifies glyphs by their indexes in the font table and completely disregards their semantics and the Unicode characters that correspond thereto.

Since ATM's font substitution leaves much to be desired, we are still waiting for font substitution worthy of Unicode.

- **Create MM instances:** here we are dealing with the creation of *Multiple Master* instances. ATM examines the active fonts and selects those that are *Multiple Masters*. For each of them, it displays (see Figure 6-6, left) the available axes of variation and a sample (the word "Sample"). The user selects the desired values of the parameters and requests the creation of an instance.[4] ATM will then produce a FOND resource and an NFNT resource, which it will add to the "font suitcase". From that point on, the instance is available to every application; it is identified by the values of its parameters on a submenu of the font-selection menu (see Figure 6-6, right).

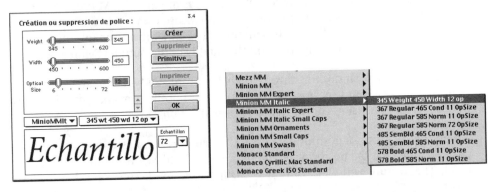

Figure 6-6: The interface for creating and selecting Multiple Master font instances.

In conclusion, let us note that even though ATM is no longer necessary under Mac OS X and Adobe has announced that it has halted development of this product, the latest ver-

---

[4] Note that certain applications, such as Adobe Illustrator and Quark XPress, have their own internal interface for creating *Multiple Master* instances. In this case, we can modify the font's parameters in real time to adapt it to the graphical context. ATM's built-in interface will suffice for applications that have no interface of their own.

sion of ATM Light (version 4.6.2) was developed with the intention that it be used under Classic.

ATR: classification of fonts by family

We have already mentioned the crude nature of the Macintosh's classification of fonts by style. According to this classification, only four possible style variants, called "regular", "bold", "italic", and "bold italic", are possible in a FOND resource. To associate other variants with the same font, one must create a new FOND resource that is also supplied with these same four predefined styles.

Let us take an example. Suppose that we have at our disposal the *Optima* PostScript fonts (by the great font designer Hermann Zapf) in the following styles: light, semi-bold, bold, and extra-bold, each of them in vertical and oblique versions. To arrange them on the Macintosh, one possibility would be to create two FOND resources called Optima and Optima bold, respectively, and to create links to the PostScript fonts according to the following correspondences:

Name of FOND resource	Macintosh style	PostScript font
Optima	"regular"	Optima
	"bold"	Optima semi-bold
	"italic"	Optima oblique
	"bold italic"	Optima semi-bold oblique
Optima gras	"regular"	Optima bold
	"bold"	Optima extra-bold
	"italic"	Optima bold oblique
	"bold italic"	Optima extra-bold oblique

When using a font, we would have to know that the choice of "Optima" in the "bold" style is lighter than "Optima bold" in the "regular" style, which in turn is lighter than "Optima bold" in the "bold" style. Another possibility (the more common choice) is to create one family of Macintosh fonts with the light and (true) bold weights, and a second family with semi-bold and extra-bold. This combination is less logical but corresponds more closely to commercial needs: specifically, the foundry can produce two separate products, of which the second is a sort of extension of the first. Indeed, this is the approach followed by Linotype, which sells the font *Optima* in two sets of style variants, with two overlapping pairs of bold weights.

The program Adobe Type Reunion (ATR) [19] frees us from these restrictions and affords us the possibility of choosing style variants in a more natural manner, using submenus. But its most important benefit is the possibility of specifying that a given PostScript font belongs to a certain Macintosh font family, and even giving the name under which the font will be displayed by the various applications. In Figure 6-7, we see the interface for classifying font families and personalizing the names of the fonts. The same tool also

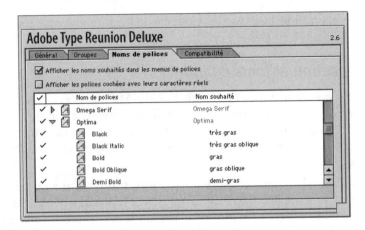

Figure 6-7: The interface for classifying font families and personalizing font names in Adobe Type Reunion.

allows us to define groups of font families by adding a third level of classification to the font-selection menus.

Font Managers

What do we need in order to manage fonts efficiently? Imagine that we have thousands of fonts—not an unrealistic proposition, if we work in a graphic-design studio. The following are the most frequent operations that we will have to perform:

1. Choosing the correct font for our project. At this time, software is not yet able to recommend a font according to the characteristics of the project that we have in mind, but it can help us to create catalogues of type specimens from which our professional experience will allow us to make the right choice.

2. Finding the font among the thousands in our possession. This operation may be quite delicate because, as we have seen, we often have multiple copies of the same font (or fonts with the same name), in different formats, coming from different foundries, etc. Later in this book, we shall see the differences among font formats and learn which are the most appropriate for each project. For now, what we can expect of a font manager is to present the available choices in a convenient fashion and to give us all the information that we need in order to make the decision.

3. Enabling the font, and thus allowing our software to make use of it, preferably without having to restart the software or the computer.

4. Disabling the font once our work is finished and re-enabling it automatically when we open a file in which it is used.

5. Rapidly assembling all of the fonts used in a file and copying them into a folder near the file, if the file is to be sent to a colleague.

These are precisely the tasks performed by the four most popular font managers: Apple's *Font Book* (which is part of Mac OS X 10.3+), *FontAgent Pro* by Insider Software, *Font Reserve* (formerly by DiamondSoft [119], currently by Extensis), and *Suitcase* [132], also by Extensis. Font Reserve was discontinued when DiamondSoft was bought by Extensis, and its functionality was added to the latest version of *Suitcase*: *Suitcase Fusion*. A fifth competitor, *ATM Deluxe* [17], has unfortunately withdrawn from the race because it is not compatible with Mac OS X. Adobe has announced that it has no intention to continue its development. The abandonment of the "glyph smoother", ATM, on the grounds that it was no longer needed on Mac OS X also sounded the death knell for the font-manager component of ATM Deluxe, which was nevertheless greatly appreciated by its users.

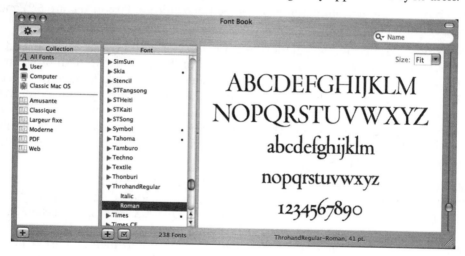

Figure 6-8: Font Book v.1.0 (which comes standard with Mac OS X 10.3+).

Font Book (see Figure 6-8), not to be confused with FontBook (by Lehmke Software), is a relatively recent piece of software: its first version came out only in System 10.3 (Panther). It is quite easy to use: it presents a list of fonts that can be enabled or disabled by double-clicking. Single-clicking on a font gives us a specimen of its glyphs in the window to the right. We can group fonts into "collections" (list at left), which allows us to enable or disable all the fonts in a collection at the same time. These features stop here: there is no cataloging, printing, or automatic enabling. Those features will doubtless be added in future versions.

But there is one thing that Font Book does indirectly: when we use the Character Palette, a utility for selecting Unicode characters that is launched through the entry with this name on the keyboard menu (the keyboard menu is the one represented by a little flag corresponding to the active keyboard), an extra section at the bottom of the Character Palette shows us all of the glyphs representing the selected character:

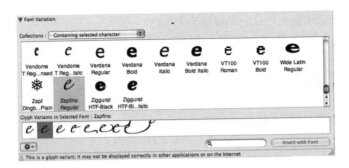

It is quite impressive. We even see the variants of glyphs, and we can select them by clicking on them.

Let us move on to the leading software competitors: Suitcase Fusion (Figure 6-9) and FontAgent Pro (Figure 6-10).

In both cases, we select individual fonts or entire directories to be analyzed by the program, which will display them in the bottom part of the interface. In both programs, we can create "sets" of fonts in the top part of the window and add fonts to those sets by dragging them up from the bottom part of the window or directly from a disk. We can thus enable or disable individual fonts or families or sets of fonts by clicking on the button in the leftmost column. There are three possible states: disabled, temporarily enabled (until the computer is rebooted or another font with the same name is enabled), and permanently enabled.

Note that both programs allow fonts to be enabled automatically, with plug-ins for three very popular pieces of software: *Adobe Illustrator* (since version 8), *Adobe Photoshop* (for *FontAgent Pro*), *Adobe InDesign* (since version 2), and Quark XPress (since version 3.3). These plug-ins analyze each open document and automatically enable every font contained in the document and all the EPS files included in the document. If the exact font cannot be found, they use a close substitute (for example, if a font of the same name but of a different format is available, they will use it instead).

As for displaying font specimens, Suitcase Fusion has a vertical area and FontAgent Pro a horizontal one; both are permanently left open and can be customized. Both programs can show a "waterfall" (different sizes of the same text), a paragraph of text, or just a few glyphs. Suitcase Fusion can show all styles of the same family simultaneously; that is why the area is vertical. Both programs can display a certain amount of information about a font upon request.

Finally, a very interesting feature: the ability to create catalogs of type specimens. Suitcase Fusion has a utility called FontBook (not to be confused with Font Book, the program built into Mac OS X 10.3+) that does an admirable job of generating type specimens, but only for enabled fonts—a limitation that hampers the creation of a catalog for a very large collection. In Figure 6-11 we see two examples of specimens created by Font Book. There is a multitude of other "catalogers" of fonts, all with more or less similar functionality.

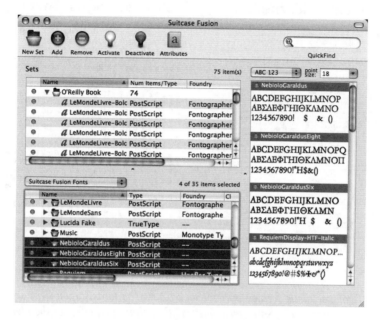

Figure 6-9: Suitcase Fusion.

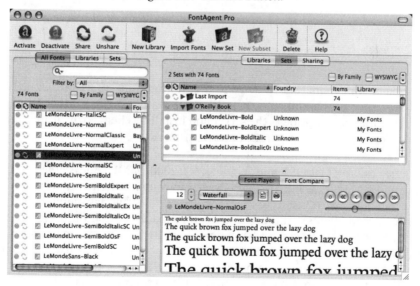

Figure 6-10: FontAgent Pro.

Figure 6-11: Two specimens created by FontBook v.4.4. The fonts shown here are among the most admirable reconstructions of historic fonts, with a simulated effect of the bleeding of ink: Historical Fell Type and Historical English Textura, by Jonathan Hoefler.

Font Servers

The two major font managers FontAgent and Suitcase Fusion are also available in a client-server version. The aim to is centralize font management at the level of a local network by using one machine as the server and installing clients (which are simply the regular versions of the two programs) on each machine.

Suitcase Server runs on Mac OS X and Windows NT, 2000, or XP, while *FontAgent Pro Server* runs only under Mac OS X. Both manage users (by arranging them into workgroups and assigning individual permissions to them) as well as fonts (by classifying them into sets in the style of their clients). Authorized users may place fonts on the server from their client station by simply dragging and dropping icons. In fact, servers can be administered from any client station; the administrator's password is all that is required. That approach allows us to place the server's machine where it ought to be—i.e., in a locked cabinet— and to manage the software from any station, an ideal solution for small workgroups in which users take turns serving as the administrator.

A feature of Suitcase Server that is very attractive to foundries is *control over licenses*. Simply specify to Suitcase Server the type of rights that have been purchased for each font[5](e.g., the number of simultaneous user stations), and the software will alert the administrator if the maximum number of users is exceeded. The documentation does not state whether Suitcase Server sends a message at the same time to the foundry and the nearest police station. Joking aside, this feature allows professionals in printing and the graphic arts to obey the law without much worry.

Note that when a client connects to a server in order to use a font, the font is copied onto the client's hard disk. That approach is not really consistent with the general principles of client-server architecture: why not directly use the copy of the font that resides on the server? There are two possible answers to that question. First, as we have already observed several times, fonts are fragile objects that are threatened by system crashes (although crashes are not supposed to occur under Mac OS X!). By maintaining a clean, fresh copy, we can always rapidly clean up the mess left by a crash, without risk of mistaking the font for another one with the same name. The second reason (drawn from the commercial literature of both servers) is that the network could also go down; in that case, if no copy of the font were available locally on the disk, the user would find himself out of service, even for the documents on which he was currently working. Is that really a valid argument in favor of copying the files onto the client's machine, or just a feeble excuse? Let the reader decide.

Tools for Font Conversion

Today we are more and more in the habit of using multiple operating systems: Mac OS 9, Mac OS X, Windows, Linux, PalmOS, Symbian, etc. These systems do not always use the same font formats; therefore, we must be able to convert our fonts so that we can use them on more than one system. Conversion can be trivial or complicated. Moving from the Macintosh PostScript format to PFB is trivial: practically nothing is involved other than reading the PostScript code in the *POST* resource and writing it out to a file. Converting a TrueType font to PostScript or vice versa is much less trivial: the types of contours change between cubic and quadratic Bézier curves; the techniques for optimizing the rendering are fundamentally different; the means of encoding the glyphs are not the same.

Thus it is hardly surprising that there is a dearth of tools for converting fonts on the market; after all, it is a very thorny task.

TransType Pro

The company FontLab offers the only really solid tool: *TransType Pro* [139]. What could be more natural than to take a part of FontLab's code and transform it into a powerful, easy-to-use conversion utility?

TransType Pro can perform all possible and imaginable conversions among TrueType, PostScript Type 1, Multiple Master and OpenType/CFF fonts—from Mac to Mac, or from

---

[5] Unfortunately, this is not handled automatically for PostScript fonts because there is no standard way to provide the information within each font. The problem has, however, been corrected in TrueType fonts, in which the table OS/2 contains these data (§D.4.7).

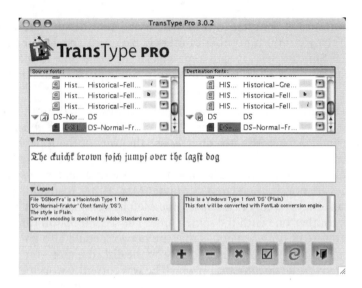

Figure 6-12: The main window of TransType Pro.

Mac to PC, or from PC to Mac, or from PC to PC. When the target is a Macintosh font suitcase, the program automatically assembles the fonts of the same family. When it converts a Multiple Master font to an ordinary font, it can create any desired instance. When it converts an OpenType or an AAT font between the Macintosh and Windows, it preserves the advanced typographic tables.

The most interesting feature of *TransType Pro* is indisputably its *batch* processing of fonts. You have a CD-ROM full of fonts in PFB format that you would like to use under Mac OS X? All that you need to do is drag the disk's image and drop it onto the left-hand zone of *TransType Pro*'s window. The fonts will then appear, and, at the same time, on the right-hand side of the window, we shall see the list of Macintosh font suitcases that the software is planning to create. We can modify our font-conversion preferences separately for each font or for several, even all of them, at a time. The names of Macintosh families can be manually edited. When we click on the button with the spiral-shaped icon, all of the fonts will be converted, with no other action on our part than the choice of the target folder. A real godsend when we have thousands of fonts to convert.

dfontifier

This little utility [121] fulfills a role that TransType overlooked: converting a Macintosh font suitcase to a *dfont* file and vice versa. We drag and drop fonts onto the window in order to convert from one format to the other: it is simple, useful, and, moreover, free.

FontFlasher, the "Kobayashi Maru" of Fonts

According to the company FontLab, the purpose of this software, which in fact is a *plug-in* for FontLab, is to produce bitmap fonts that can be displayed under *Macromedia Flash* without anti-aliasing. The intention is praiseworthy: it is true that bitmap fonts at small sizes are more legible when they are displayed with simple black-and-white pixels rather than with levels of gray.

But how can we control the display on a given machine? How can we be sure that anti-aliasing will not be performed? It is, a priori, impossible to be sure. The computer always has the last word.

The reader must surely be wondering why we have called this software a "kobayashi maru". The story [128] has it that Captain James Kirk had to take a final test in a flight simulator in order to obtain his diploma. On this test, the *Enterprise* received a call for help from a vessel called *Kobayashi Maru* (the word "*maru*", in fact, is used after ship names in Japanese) in the Klingon territories. The captain was morally obliged to go to the aid of the vessel. But the request was a trap. The Klingons attacked the *Enterprise* and destroyed it. End of test. And an inevitable outcome, because refusing to assist a vessel in distress would have been an equally bad solution.

That is why "kobayashi maru" has come to denote, in hacker jargon, a no-win situation.

What, then, did our Captain Kirk do? The night before the test, he broke into the computer room and modified the program. The *Kobayashi Maru* was not a trap any longer. In a word, he cheated. But one has the right to cheat when a vessel and its crew are at risk.

What does that have to do with FontFlasher? Well, here we find ourselves in a kobayashi maru: how on earth can we *force* the operating system not to anti-alias a font?

By cheating. If the operating system anti-aliases all fonts, let us give it a font that it will not *have to* anti-alias. And the only font that it will not anti-alias is a font that already has the *precise* shape of the pixels. If the pixels on the screen correspond with absolute precision to the font's vector contours, there will be nothing to anti-alias.

This is precisely what FontFlasher does. It generates a vector contour that is identical to the pixels. At the given size, this contour yields a perfect "bitmap" font—which, at any other size, is a catastrophe.

Given so many ways to obtain bitmap fonts once again, as in the good old days of Macintosh System 4.3, we may well ask the question:

What is more readible, this vector font with anti-aliasing
or this simulation of bitmap font with pixels given by outlines?

The image above is a screenshot of text in 11-point *Futura* and in *Futura* processed by *FontFlasher*. Here is what we get at high resolution:

What is more readible, this vector font with anti-aliasing

or this simulation of bitmap font with pixels given by outlines?

(Note that we have not manually retouched the glyphs of the processed font; we have shown the raw rendering.) And here, under FontLab, is the raw output of FontFlasher, in which each pixel is a vector-drawn square; at right, the same glyph after retouching and merger of the squares:

In the background, we can see the vector contour of the glyph in the original font.

7

Font Management under Windows

Our concern in this chapter will be the installation and management of fonts under Windows 2000 and XP. These procedures are similar in many ways to their Macintosh counterparts, for several reasons: most of the most common software packages, be they for office automation or artistic design, have been ported from one platform to the other (from Windows to the Macintosh, in the case of office automation; from the Macintosh to Windows, in the case of desktop publishing and the graphic arts). Why should the same not apply to ancillary resources—in particular, fonts?

Figure 7-1: The **Fonts** *directory in Windows XP.*

Installing fonts under Windows is as easy as installing them under Mac OS: one need only go into the **Control Panel** and open the shortcut to the **Fonts** directory, which, in fact, points to the directory c:\winnt\fonts, where all the fonts are stored. In Figure 7-1, we see a screenshot of this directory under Windows XP. It is a very special type of directory, as the names of the icons are not filenames but rather the names of fonts in Windows.

Among the icons seen in that window, several are marked with a red uppercase letter 'A'. These are bitmap fonts (with the extension .fon). In some cases (such as the Modern, Roman, and Script fonts), they may be vector fonts in an arcane format called *vector fonts* that is as old as the hills. It is a format that versions 1 and 2 of Windows used, much like that of CAD systems such as *AutoCAD*, in which glyphs are built up of strokes, not of filled-in shapes. These fonts are vestiges of the distant past that are condemned to extinction.

The fonts whose icon bears a double 'T' are TrueType fonts, whose extension is .ttf. Those whose icon contains an 'O' are usually OpenType fonts, but they may also be simple TrueType fonts. Indeed, Microsoft meant for the extension .ttf to be used for OpenType-TTF fonts and .otf for OpenType-CFF fonts; since one extension is clearly insufficient for distinguishing TrueType fonts from OpenType-TTF, we may get the impression that the system assigns the icons at random.

The icons that contain a lowercase 'a' correspond to Type 1 PostScript fonts. Just as on the Macintosh, here two files are required for each PostScript font: a file of font metrics, whose extension is .pfm (= *PostScript font metrics*), and a file containing PostScript code, whose extension is .pfb (= *PostScript font binary*, as opposed to .pfa = *PostScript font ASCII*, which is most commonly found on Unix). The font-metrics file contains the information needed by Windows, such as the Windows name, the widths of the characters, and the kerning pairs, but also the font's PostScript name.

As on the Macintosh, a PostScript or TrueType font may exist in as many as four styles: "regular", "bold", "italic", and "bold italic".[1] But unlike the Macintosh, here styles are not assembled in a single file: each style is contained in a file of its own. To avoid creating an excessively large number of icons for fonts, the Fonts window allows us to display only one icon per "font family", i.e., those that differ only in style: go to the View menu and click on Hide Variations (Bold, Italic, etc.).

To install fonts, we can select Install New Font... under the File menu in the Fonts window. The dialog box that appears displays a list of all the fonts contained in a given directory. Once again, these are *names of fonts* that are displayed, not *filenames*—a very practical outcome, because the filenames of Windows fonts, thanks to the former restriction of filenames to eight letters, are often quite cryptic, as, for example, bm_____.ttf for the splendid font *Bembo*. Next to the filename is the type of the file. At the lower right part of the window is the checkbox Copy fonts to Fonts folder. This checkbox allows us to choose between copying fonts into the c:\winnt\fonts folder and simply making a reference to the existing files. In the latter case, only a link to the font in question is

---

[1] In addition, this "style" of the font is stored in a variable in the table head that is called macStyle. But in the table OS/2 there is another variable: fsSelection, which may also take the values "underscored", "negative" (white on black), "contour", "strikethrough", and all their combinations. The specification gives rules for compatibility between macStyle and fsSelection.

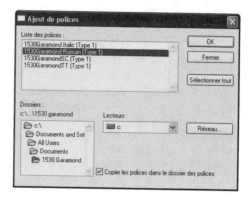

Figure 7-2: Dialog box for installing fonts.

created; these are the icons that have a little arrow at the lower left. Note that this link is not an ordinary file: if we run dir at the Windows command prompt, these "links" do not appear among the files.

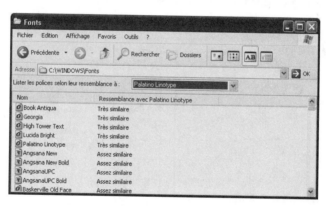

Figure 7-3: List of fonts "by similarity".

Also note that the View menu in this window has one very special entry: List Fonts By Similarity. In this case, the *Panose-1 classification* of the fonts is used to categorize them according to their similarity to a given font. We shall examine the Panose-1 classification in Chapter 11 of this book. For the moment, let us simply say that Panose-1 allows us to classify fonts according to their design in a 10-dimensional space; "similarity" is nothing but the distance between two points in this space, points that represent two fonts. In Figure 7-3, we can see the classification of fonts by their similarity to the font *Linotype Palatino*; we discover that there are two fonts that are "very similar" to it, namely *Georgia* and the font itself. Conversely, *Times New Roman* is merely "fairly similar" to *Linotype Palatino*, and *Arial* is "not similar". Nonetheless, the Panose-1 classification may be very useful on the Web, as we shall see in the chapter dedicated to this subject (page 327). The CSS specification incorporates the Panose description; thus the developer of a Web site can add Panose characteristics to the explicit names of the fonts. The client's system will then be able to display the text in the font that is the most similar to the one requested.

Active fonts on Windows are exposed just as much to the risk of system crashes as they are on the Macintosh, since they are files that are permanently kept open. Therefore we are wise to verify our font files on a regular basis, to optimize their use by opening them only when they are needed, and to take other protective measures. Next we shall present a few tools for managing fonts under Windows.

Tools for Managing Fonts

The Extension of Font Properties

Let us begin with a tool that should ideally be part of the operating system. It is a little utility called *ttfext* [257] that Microsoft provides free of charge. It is launched every time we ask to see the *properties* of a TrueType or OpenType font. Its interface takes the form of a window with tabs. It includes the classic *General* tab (which is also the only way to determine the name of a given font) and adds nine others:

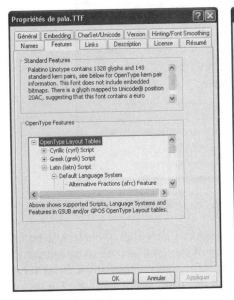 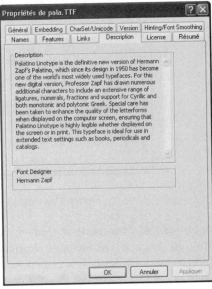

*Figure 7-4: Two tabs of the **Properties** window of the font Linotype Palatino. Left: OpenType properties. Right: a general description of the font.*

- *Embedding*: can the font in question be embedded in a document? There are four possibilities: *Installable embedding allowed* (the font can be embedded in a document and can even be installed on the client's system), *Editable embedding allowed* (the font can be embedded in a document and can be used to edit text, but it can be only temporarily installed on the client's machine), *Print & Preview embedding allowed* (the font can be embedded in a document but can be used only for display and printing, and it may be only temporarily installed), and *Restricted license embedding* (the font may not be embedded in a document).

- *CharSet/Unicode*: what is the font's default encoding? Which Unicode zones does the font cover? Which other encodings are compatible with the font?

- *Version*, which also includes the date when the file was created and the date when it was last modified.

- *Hinting/Font Smoothing*: does the font contain hinting, and at which point size should the system begin to smooth the font through the use of pixels at different levels of gray? A setting of the type 0+ means "starting from 0 points", i.e., at all sizes.

- *Names*: what are the names of the font, its font family, and its vendor? What are its *copyright* and *trademark*?

- *Features*: a description of the font's OpenType properties—for example, how many glyphs it contains, whether it contains bitmaps, whether it contains a glyph for the euro sign, whether it is a TTF or a CFF font—and a list of the scripts, languages, and GSUB and GPOS tables covered by the font.

- *Links*: hypertext links pertaining to the foundry, the font's designer, and the web site of Microsoft's typography department.

- *Description*: a document describing the font and its history and also providing the name of its designer.

- *License*: a tab devoted to royalties, with a hypertext link to the full document that describes them.

This tool provides easy access to the information that otherwise would have necessitated converting the font into data readable by TTX or opening it with font-editing software such as FontLab or FontForge. In both cases, we would need a good knowledge of the tools and of the OpenType format in order to recover the information. The only negative point about this tool: it abandons us altogether when the font is of PostScript Type 1.

Tools for Verification and Maintenance

The fact that operating systems crash is a law of Mother Nature. Since we cannot prevent crashes, we should try to limit the extent of the damage by detecting corrupted fonts as quickly as possible, before they cause new crashes themselves. On the other hand, when we collect fonts from a wide variety of places, it may well happen that several fonts with the same name will be open at the same time. That may also cause problems, especially if the fonts are in differents formats. This situation frequently arises, since most foundries

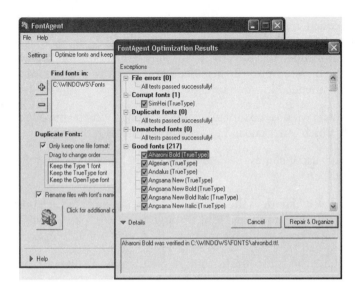

Figure 7-5: Interface for configuring FontAgent, v.8.8.

simultaneously release their fonts in both traditional formats: PostScript Type 1 and
TrueType.

Fortunately, there are tools for detecting both corrupted fonts and duplicates. One such
tool is *FontAgent*, by Insider Software [189]. This program can do all of the following:

- Detecting and eliminating duplicates. We can specify whether we prefer the True-
  Type version or the PostScript Type 1 version. We can also retain fonts with the same
  name if they come from different foundries.

- Detecting "orphaned" PostScript fonts (a .pfb without a .pfm or vice versa). Unlike
  Font Doctor (under Mac OS), this program does not perform a "family reunion":
  when it finds a .pfb and its corresponding .pfm in different folders, it does not place
  them in the same directory.

- Gathering fonts into a folder or a tree structure of folders organized by the first letter
  of the font—or even a separate folder for each font (and these folders can bear a suffix
  for the font format: "tt" or "t1", for TrueType fonts and Type 1 fonts, respectively;
  OpenType is not supported). We can also ask that only the strict minimum be left
  in the **Fonts** system folder.

- Renaming font files. We can give them the name of the font itself (instead of a horrible abbreviation, as often occurs because of the restrictions on the length of filenames under MS-DOS). Of course, that assumes that the files are very well organized,
  because we have even more chances to end up with duplicates.

- Removing corrupted files or duplicates by placing them in a special folder.

It is strongly recommended that the user save backups of all fonts before using Font-Agent, since improper handling cannot be ruled out.

ATM: the "Smoother" of Fonts

Since Windows 2000, the smoothing of PostScript Type 1 glyphs has been performed by the operating system, and *Adobe Type Manager* (ATM, whose Macintosh version we described on page 196) is, in principle, no longer necessary. Indeed, when we install it under Windows 2000 or XP, its configuration interface offers the choice of only two folders containing PostScript font files: one folder for .pfb and .otf files containing PostScript code for Type 1 fonts and OpenType-CFF fonts, and one folder for .pfm and .mmm files containing Windows font metrics for Type 1 and *Multiple Master* fonts. (It should be noted that Vista is not compatible with Adobe Type Manager.)

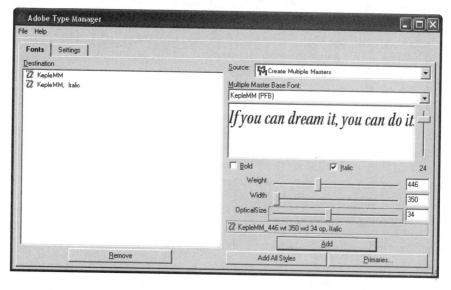

Figure 7-6: The interface for creating instances of Multiple Master fonts.

There is, however, a valid reason to install ATM under Windows 2000 or XP: it allows us to create Multiple Master instances. The procedure is as follows (see Figure 7-6). When we select a Multiple Master font, the different axes of variation are displayed in the form of *sliders*. We can thus choose one value for each axis with the use of a little sample of text that is transformed on the fly. Once we have chosen the values that we desire, we click on **Add**, and a .pfm file representing this instance of the Multiple Master font is created in the folder c:\psfonts\pfm, which is used by ATM only. At the same time, a link to this file is created in the **Fonts** system folder.

Once the new instances have been created under ATM, they are available for use by all applications. We can recognize them by the underscore character that separates the name of the file from the values of the parameters. Thus in Figure 7-7 we are using the instance

Figure 7-7: Using Multiple Master font instances under WordPad.

bold 435, width 350, optical size 68 of the font *Kepler MM Swash* in the application *WordPad*.

Note that we can also use Multiple Master fonts like ordinary Type 1 fonts under Windows 2000/XP, without going through the step of creating an instance; but in that case we have access only to the default instance of each font.

Font Managers

We have seen how to solve the problem of corrupted and duplicate fonts and also how to create Multiple Master font instances. The remaining question is how to manage active fonts: how to find a practical method for enabling and disabling fonts without going through the **Fonts** system folder—automatically, if possible, when we open a document that requires a certain number of fonts that are available on the system but not necessarily enabled. And if we have a large number of fonts, we also need a practical system for selecting the correct font (which implies creating catalogs of type specimens) and for finding the corresponding files (which implies a database containing references to all the fonts in our possession).

All these tasks are performed by *font managers*. Just as under Mac OS, there are two very highly developed font managers and a number of tools that, while less sophisticated, may be shareware or even freeware. The two "big" font managers are *Font Reserve* (Figure 7-8) [119] and *Suitcase* (Figure 7-9) [132]—both from Extensis, now that Extensis has acquired DiamondSoft, the company that produced Font Reserve.

In both cases, we select individual fonts or entire directories to be analyzed by the program, which will display them in the bottom part of the interface. Font Reserve enables us to personalize the information displayed for each font; Suitcase, however, displays only the name, the type, and the foundry. In both programs, we can create "sets" of fonts in the top part of the window and add fonts to those sets by dragging them up from the bottom part of the window or directly from a disk. We can thus enable or disable individual fonts or families or sets of fonts by clicking on the button in the leftmost column. There are three possible states: disabled, temporarily enabled (until the computer is rebooted or another font with the same name is enabled), and permanently enabled.

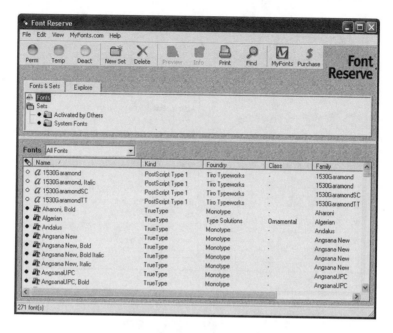

Figure 7-8: Font Reserve v.2.6.5.

For displaying font specimens, Suitcase has a vertical area that is permanently left open and that can be customized; Font Reserve, on the other hand, displays a few glyphs when one clicks on a font's icon in the list of fonts and keeps the mouse button held down. Both programs can display a certain amount of general information about a font. Font Reserve also offers a rather powerful interface for searching for fonts (see Figure 7-10), which can be quite useful when one needs to find one font among thousands.

The reader must surely have noticed that the Windows versions of these two programs are, despite a handful of similarities, recognizably inferior to their Mac OS counterparts. In particular, neither Suitcase nor Font Reserve supports the generation of catalogs of font specimens.

Thus we have good reason to examine some tools other than these two font managers inherited from the Macintosh. In fact, there is a profusion of such font managers (shareware or freeware), the most interesting of which is certainly *Typograf* (Figure 7-11) [278], written by two Germans, the Neuber brothers.

Typograf supports, of course, the fundamental operations: viewing in various ways the installed fonts and fonts contained in various directories, as well as enabling and disabling these fonts. It has a database that we can build up by searching through directories or even entire CD-ROMs.

For each font, it presents an impressive range of information. We can read a very detailed description of the TrueType tables (Figure 7-11), view all the kerning pairs in the font (using the font's own glyphs), compare a certain number of fonts by viewing their

Figure 7-9: Suitcase v.9.2.2.

Figure 7-10: The font-search interface in Font Reserve v.2.6.5.

properties side by side, and print out specimens of one or more fonts by using any of a dozen different models, whose text can be customized. It also supports classification of fonts and searching for fonts according to their Panose data or their "IBM class".

Font Servers

Suitcase Server, described in the section on Mac OS (page 204), also runs under Windows NT, 2000, and XP. Font servers can be very useful for fonts in the case of, for example, a team that has a large collection of fonts. They provide rapid searching through the collection, immediate access to the selected font, and verification of compliance with the law, if the number of licenses purchased for each font is specified. Their only disadvantage is that their prices are often prohibitive.

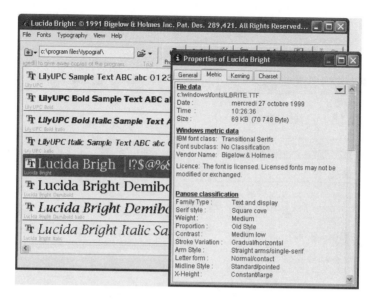

Figure 7-11: The main interface and window for the properties of the font Arial, in Typograf v.4.8f.

Tools for Font Conversion

We have already described several tools for font conversion in the chapter on Mac OS. Among them, *TransType Pro* and *FontFlasher* also exist in Windows versions that are identical to their Macintosh versions in every detail. The reader is therefore referred back to their descriptions under Mac OS X on pages 205 through 208 of this book.

There is, however, a competitor to *TransType Pro*: *CrossFont*, by the American company Acute Systems, whose specialty is the conversion of data between the PC and the Macintosh.

CrossFont (Figure 7-13) offers almost the same features as TransType Pro for a fraction of the price. It even goes further than TransType Pro, as it can also manage the *dfont* format of the Macintosh and can generate missing files, such as the PFM file, when a font comes from a Unix environment, or the AFM file, when we need kerning pairs for TeX, etc. One very interesting property: it collects the kerning pairs from any available AFM files and integrates them into the fonts generated during conversion.

But it also has its drawbacks: we cannot view the glyphs in a font to confirm that no glyph was overlooked or incorrectly encoded, and Multiple Master fonts are not supported.

Both programs (TransType and CrossFont) are available in a demo version that is restricted only in the number of days for which it can be used. Thus one can test out their full functionality before deciding which one to buy.

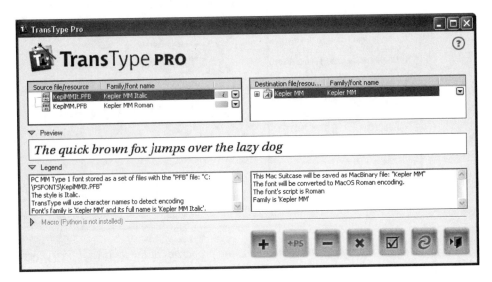

Figure 7-12: The interface of TransType Pro under Windows XP.

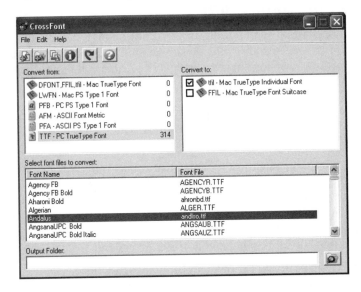

Figure 7-13: The interface of CrossFont v.4.1 under Windows XP.

8

Font Management under X Window

Now that we have examined Mac OS and Windows (which are strikingly similar in the area of fonts), let us move on to Unix, an operating system that used to be largely restricted to industry and universities but that is now becoming more and more popular, thanks in particular to its free incarnations, such as Linux. While Mac OS 9 and Windows do not separate the operating system from the windowing system, these two systems are distinct in Mac OS X and Unix. The windowing system manages the operating system's graphical interface: windows, menus, dialog boxes, the mouse, etc. The windowing system of Mac OS X is called *Quartz*; that of Unix, *X Window* ("*Window*" is singular, without an 's') or, among intimates, *X11* or even simply *X*.

Special Characteristics of X Window

First, we must point out that the overall ergonomic approach of Unix is based on the use of a *terminal*. This may seem to be a disadvantage to those who are accustomed to a completely graphical interface, such as that of Mac OS 9; however, to those who like to "retain control" over their machine, it is rather an advantage. In any event, with regard to fonts, the terminal is clearly less demanding than a graphical application. In particular, since we tend to use only one font size at a time on a terminal, it is not surprising that our good old-fashioned bitmap fonts (in the formats PSF, BDF, and PCF, etc.; see §A.4) are quite adequate for the terminal's needs and that font management under X is based almost entirely on bitmap fonts—at least until recent times, when vector fonts finally made their debut under X.

But let us be clear on one point: while Mac OS and Windows had only two or three bitmap fonts—relics from their infancy—in only two or three point sizes and with no attempt at grandeur, X provides a sophisticated system for font classification, with a substitution mechanism that keeps us from ever running short of fonts. This system is called XLFD (an unpronounceable acronym that stands for *X Logical Font Description*), and we shall describe it below.

As for the notorious fragility of fonts under Mac OS and Windows, it stemmed primarily from the fact that the files in question were left continuously open by the operating system. Under X we use a *font server* named *xfs* (*X Font Server*). This server is also a font manager, as it is capable of invoking fonts from a multitude of directories, even on other machines. Applications thus send requests to the server, indicating the specifications of the font desired, and the server replies by sending the requested font if it is available or else, thanks to the substitution mechanism, the font that is most similar to the one requested. Alternatively, applications can request a list of available fonts from the server by specifying the characteristics requested by the user, who may then make his choice from the list returned and obtain a single font.

Logical Description of a Font under X

Here is the problem that X developers posed to themselves. A given application needs a certain amount of information to select a font. This information may be commercial (foundry name), graphical (family name, weight, style, set width, point size, resolution [in the case of a bitmap font]), or technical (the encoding). Usually we expect to find this information in the font, or in a file accompanying the font, for every font that we have. If we have thousands of fonts on our system,[1] how can we avoid having to open them all in order to collect this information?

The solution to these problems is to use a database containing the filenames and all this other data, and that is what X does.

Next, these same developers set out to solve another problem, that of the classification of fonts and interaction with the human user. It was necessary to create a syntax for describing fonts that would be both comprehensive (to cover all the information contained in the database) and readable by a human (because a human, after all, had to select the font). The solution that they devised is XLFD. It makes a number of compromises: XLFD is not 100 percent comprehensive (and cannot be, since fonts exist in as much variety as humans, if not even more) and also cannot be said to be staggeringly easy to use. But for comprehensiveness we can always find a way to make do, and ease of use depends, at the end of the day, on applications: after all, it is always possible to go through an ergonomic and user-friendly user interface to interact with the font server and select a font.

---

[1] Having merely installed *Fedora* (a rather popular Linux distribution) version 5, the author found himself with 2,464 (!) font files on his computer. But take note: under Unix, a font file contains only one point size and in a single encoding. Conversely, under Mac OS and Windows, there are far fewer files, for two reasons: first, the different point sizes of bitmaps are stored in the same file (and there is no need for them when the font is a vector font); second, we often use not just one encoding but two: the standard encoding for the language of the operating system and, if necessary, Unicode.

But let us first see how XLFD goes about classifying fonts [299, 138]. A *font name*, as defined by XLFD, is a series of 14 strings encoded in ISO 8859-1 and separated by hyphens. These strings may not contain hyphens, asterisks, question marks, commas, or double quotation marks. Here is an example of one such font name:

```
-misc-fixed-medium-r-normal------c--iso10646-
```

We shall see below that we can replace individual values, or even groups of values, in this syntax with wildcards. But first let us describe the 14 fields that make up a font name. Of these fields, some are "textual" (abbreviated 'T'), in the sense that their value, as part of the traditional name of the font, is not standardized, and others are "standardized" (abbreviated 'S'), taking predefined values.

1. The *foundry name* (T, which must be registered with the X Consortium), or a keyword such as misc, when the foundry is unknown or not registered, or when the font is in the public domain. Unfortunately, this rule is not always observed, and we come across fonts whose first field is arabic (the name of a script) or jis (the name of an encoding).

2. The *family name* (T). Here we find the usual name of the font (times, helvetica, courier, palatino, etc.). We also find, under Unix, a very special set of fonts, the *character-cell* fonts.[2] These are bitmap fonts in which all the glyphs are drawn on a cell of pixels whose size is fixed. So simple are the shapes of the glyphs that these fonts, the poorest of the poor, make no claim to belong to a classic font family: they are rather named according to the dimensions of the cell, and we are quite content if they are legible; their classification is not a significant issue. For example, we have fonts called 5x7, 5x8, 6x9, 6x10, etc., up to 12x24 pixels. Most of these "anonymous" fonts are lumped under the name fixed.

3. The *weight* (T), expressed with the usual English terms: light, regular, book, demi bold, bold, black, etc.

4. The *slant* (S): r (roman), i (italic), o (oblique), ri (reverse italic, or letters that lean to the left in a left-to-right script and to the right in a right-to-left script), ro (reverse oblique), ot (other).

5. The *set width* (T), expressed with the usual English terms: normal, condensed, narrow, double wide, etc.

6. The *style* (T), expressed with the usual English terms: serif, sans serif, informal, decorated, etc.

7. The *pixel size* (S). In the case of the character-cell fonts, this number corresponds to the height of the cell.

---

[2] Yet another example of terminological confusion between *character* and *glyph*.

8. The *point size* (S), in tenths of an American printer's point (the American printer's point being 1/72.27 of an inch). It is the "optical size", i.e., the size that the font's creator had in mind when he designed the font.

9. The *horizontal resolution* (S) of the screen or the printer for which the font is intended.

10. The *vertical resolution* (S) of the screen or the printer. Unlike the screens of Mac OS or Windows, those of Unix may have pixels that are not square. It is therefore necessary to provide appropriately adapted fonts in order to avoid the "Cinemascope" effect.

11. The *type of spacing* (S): p ("proportional") for variable-width fonts, m for monospaced fonts, c for character-cell fonts. The difference between a monospaced font and a character-cell font is significant. In monospaced fonts, the offset between the glyph's point of origin and that of the following glyph remains unchanged; the glyph itself may lie partly or entirely outside the abstract box whose width corresponds to this offset. In character-cell fonts, there is one additional property: the pixels of the glyph, which are entirely contained within this abstract box. A character cell font is monospaced *a fortiori*; the converse may not be true. Nonetheless, most monospaced fonts (such as *Courier* or *Computer Modern Typewriter*) can be regarded as character-cell fonts, since they simulate the output of the typewriter, which was a source of inspiration for the character-cell fonts.

12. The *average width* (S), in tenths of a pixel. This is the arithmetic mean of the widths of all the glyphs in the font. In the cases of monospaced and character-cell fonts, it is the actual width of the glyphs.

13. The *primary indicator of the encoding* (S). Here, unfortunately, confusion reigns between encodings for characters and encodings for glyphs. We have, for example, iso8859 and iso10646 (encodings for characters) alongside adobe and dec (encodings of glyphs). We specify fontspecific for a font with an arbitrary encoding (as, for example, with fonts of symbols).

14. The *secondary indicator of the encoding* (S). In the case of the ISO 8859 family of encodings, this is the number of the encoding: 1, ... , 15. In the case of the encoding ISO 10646 (Unicode's twin sibling), this is 1 (we hope that no 2 will ever arise). In all other cases, the value depends greatly on the primary indicator of the encoding so that we can obtain, for example, adobe-standard, dec-dectech, koi8-ru, and so forth.

Here are a few examples of XLFD font names and the corresponding samples:

1. -misc-fixed-medium-r-normal--20-140-100-100-c-100-iso8859-1

   ABCDEFGHIJKLMNOPQRSTUVWXYZ
   abcdefghijklmnopqrstuvwxyz
   0123456789
   àæçëîðñóùýÀÆÇÈÎÐÑÓÙÝ

This font is unnamed (because it is marked `misc`) and is a character-cell font (spacing type c), with a cell size of 10x20, designed at an optical size of 14 points and for a screen of 100 points per inch. Its encoding is ISO 8859-1.

2. `-urw-palatino-medium-r-normal--12-120-75-75-p-0-iso8859-2`

> ABCDEFGHIJKLMNOPQRSTUVWXYZ
> abcdefghijklmnopqrstuvwxyz
> 0123456789
> ßçëïãñóùýŘĆÇËĪÐŃÓŮÝ

The font *Palatino* from the foundry URW, designed at an optical size of 12 points and for a screen of 75 points per inch. Since it is a vector font, its average width is 0. Encoding: ISO 8859-2.

3. `-b&h-lucidatypewriter-medium-r-normal-sans-25-180-100-100-n-150-iso10646-1`

> ABCDEFGHIJKLMNOPQRSTUVWXYZ /0123456789
> abcdefghijklmnopqrstuvwxyz £©µÀÆÖÞßéöÿ
> ――''""„†■…‰™œŠŸž€ □□□□□□□□□ □□□□□□□□□
> ∀□□□□□≡□ □□□□□ ⌐┼┌□□□□ □□□₂ □ẞ□Ẅe□□□□□

The monospaced version of the font *Lucida Sans* from the foundry Bigelow & Holmes, designed at an optical size of 18 points and for a screen of 100 points per inch. It is encoded in Unicode, but in reality it covers only a few Unicode tables (no Greek, no Cyrillic, no Hebrew, no Armenian, no mathematical symbols).

4. `-jis-fixed-medium-r-normal--24-170-100-100-c-240-jisx0208.1983-0`

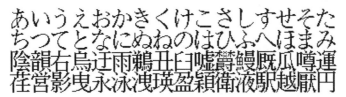

A Japanese font in the Mincho 明朝 tradition. It is unnamed (`jis` in the field for the foundry's name) and is a character-cell font (spacing type c) with a cell size of 24x24 pixels. It was designed at an optical size of 17 points and a screen resolution of 100 pixels. Its encoding is JIS-X 208, which dates to 1983. In this example, we see two rows of *kana* syllables and two rows of some of the most common kanji ideographs.

Note that this is only the first part of XLFD, the part that concerns font names. A second part, for *font properties*, goes further in defining a number of keyword–value pairs that describe the font in greater detail. These "properties" are stored in the font but are not used by most software during font selection. They are all optional, and we may add "private" properties.

XLFD also provides a syntax for "polymorphic" fonts, i.e., fonts in which certain parameters can vary, a typical example being the Multiple Master fonts.

For more details on font properties and polymorphic fonts, the reader is referred to [138].

In addition, the XLFD specification also includes two wildcard characters: * (representing 0, 1, or more characters of any kind) and ? (representing any single character), which we can use as substitutes for any part of an XLFD font name.

Finally, let us have a quick foretaste of the tool *xlsfonts*, which will display a complete list of all the available fonts. To filter this tool's output, we can simply follow it with an XLFD name containing wildcards. Here is an example:

```
xlsfonts "*palatino*"
```

In this syntax, it is important not to forget to enclose in quotation marks the string containing wildcards; otherwise, the Unix shell will interpret the wildcards as parts of a filename and will accordingly look for corresponding files before executing the command.

Installing fonts under X

Upon startup, the *xfs* font server [299, 233] reads a configuration file, which is:

```
/usr/X11R6/lib/X11/fs/config
```

by default. In this file we specify certain default values, such as the screen resolution and the default set width. But most important of all: the file contains the list of directories where fonts are stored. Here is an example:

```
/usr/X11R6/lib/X11/fonts/misc,
/usr/X11R6/lib/X11/fonts/Speedo,
/usr/X11R6/lib/X11/fonts/Type1,
/usr/X11R6/lib/X11/fonts/CID,
/usr/X11R6/lib/X11/fonts/75dpi,
/usr/X11R6/lib/X11/fonts/100dpi,
/usr/share/fonts/default/Type1,
/usr/share/fonts/default/TrueType,
/home/yannis/texmf/fonts/pfb
```

Each of these directories must contain a file named `fonts.dir`. This is a very simple text file. It begins with the number of lines to follow, written on a line by itself. Then there is a single line for each font file. These lines are divided into two columns: the filename and the font's XLFD name. Example:

```
360
6x12.pcf.gz -misc-fixed-medium-r-semicondensed------c--iso10646-
6x13.pcf.gz -misc-fixed-medium-r-semicondensed------c--iso10646-
6x10.pcf.gz -misc-fixed-medium-r-normal------c--iso10646-
... (356 lines) ...
9x15-KOI8-R.pcf.gz -misc-fixed-medium-r-normal------c--koi8-r
```

or, in the case of PostScript Type 1 fonts:

```
89
UTRG____.pfa -adobe-utopia-medium-r-normal------p--iso8859-
UTI_____.pfa -adobe-utopia-medium-i-normal------p--iso8859-
UTB_____.pfa -adobe-utopia-bold-r-normal------p--iso8859-
... (85 lines) ...
l049036t.pfa -b&h-Luxi Serif-bold-i-normal------p--adobe-standard
```

To install fonts, therefore, we must place them into one of these directories and then create or update the corresponding fonts.dir file. The fonts.dir files can be generated by a certain number of tools, according to their format. We shall see the details below.

Aside from the XLFD font names, which by their nature are difficult to remember and to write, we also have *font-name aliases*. These are defined in fonts.alias files, which are also placed in the same directories. Once again, these are ASCII files with two columns, the first column being the alias, the second being the XLFD font name. Here is an example:

```
utopia  -adobe-utopia-medium-r-normal------p--iso8859-
utopiaI -adobe-utopia-medium-i-normal------p--iso8859-
utopiaB -adobe-utopia-bold-r-normal------p--iso8859-
```

Finally, there is a third series of files that must be available to the server: *encodings*. These are ASCII files of the following type:

```
STARTENCODING iso8859-
ALIAS tis620-
ALIAS tis620.2529-
ALIAS tis620.2533-
ALIAS tis620.2533-
STARTMAPPING unicode
UNDEFINE 0x7F 0xA0
0xA1 0x0E01  # THAI CHARACTER KO KAI
0xA2 0x0E02  # THAI CHARACTER KHO KHAI
0xA3 0x0E03  # THAI CHARACTER KHO KHUAT
0xA4 0x0E04  # THAI CHARACTER KHO KHWAI
... (85 lines) ...
ENDMAPPING
ENDENCODING
```

We see in this illustration a line STARTENCODING (which also gives the name of the encoding), a number of aliases for the name of the encoding, and finally a table of mappings to Unicode (STARTMAPPING ... ENDMAPPING), in which each line contains two columns: the position in the font and the corresponding Unicode character. (What follows the character # is nothing but a comment.)

The encodings are stored in the same way as the fonts: in encodings.dir files that contain one line per encoding, with the name of the encoding in the first column and the corresponding file (which may be gzip-compressed) in the second column:

```
47
dec-special /usr/X11R6/lib/X11/fonts/encodings/dec-special.enc
ksxjohab- /usr/X11R6/lib/X11/fonts/encodings/large/ksc5601.1992-.enc.gz
... (43 lines) ...
iso8859- /usr/X11R6/lib/X11/fonts/encodings/iso8859-.enc
adobe-dingbats /usr/X11R6/lib/X11/fonts/encodings/adobe-dingbats.enc.gz
```

Note that the names of encodings must correspond to the last fields of the XLFD font names.

Installing Bitmap Fonts

The bitmap format used by X is called "Bitmap Distribution Format" (BDF; see §A.4.2). Bitmap fonts under X are files with the extension .bdf (the ASCII version of the BDF format) or .pcf (the binary version of the same format; see §A.4.4). We can also find files compressed by gzip: .pcf.gz. These are automatically decompressed by the server.

To install bitmap fonts, we can simply launch the utility *mkfontdir* within the directory in question. It will create the required fonts.dir file. This procedure is quite simple because usually BDF fonts already contain the XLFD font name; thus there is no need to construct this name from various information contained within the font.

Once the current directory is equipped with its fonts.dir file, we can add it to the list of directories in the configuration file by using the utility chkfontpath as follows:

```
chkfontpath -a /home/yannis/fonts/bitmap
```

Next, we can confirm that the directory in question has indeed been added to the configuration file, by executing

```
chkfontpath -l
```

We obtain a list of all the directories in the configuration file.

Finally, we need to load our new fonts into this directory in order to use them. To do so, we can type:

```
xset +fp /home/yannis/fonts/bitmap
xset fp rehash
```

Here *xset* is a general-purpose application for configuration in X [299, 312]. The first argument, fp, on the command line indicates that we are concerned with fonts (fp = *font path*). The + that precedes it on the first line indicates that the path in question should go *before* all the other paths. This feature is useful because the server will use the first instance of a specified font that it comes across. If the new fonts that we have just installed have the same names as some old ones, this is their only chance to be read first and to be chosen by the server.

The line xset fp rehash allows us to rebuild the tables in the database of the font server. Only after this final operation do the fonts become available to all X clients.

Installing PostScript Type 1 or TrueType Fonts

Here things become more complicated, as the PostScript Type 1 fonts and the TrueType fonts do not contain all of the information needed to create the XLFD font name, at least not in a manner as direct as that of the BDF fonts. The method that we shall use, therefore, is the following:

First of all, using specialized tools (mentioned below), we shall create an intermediate file called fonts.scale. Here is an extract of one such file:

```
89
UTRG____.pfa -adobe-utopia-medium-r-normal------p--iso8859-
UTI_____.pfa -adobe-utopia-medium-i-normal------p--iso8859-
UTB_____.pfa -adobe-utopia-bold-r-normal------p--iso8859-
UTBI____.pfa -adobe-utopia-bold-i-normal------p--iso8859-
cour.pfa -adobe-courier-medium-r-normal------m--iso8859-
cour.pfa -adobe-courier-medium-r-normal------m--iso8859-
cour.pfa -adobe-courier-medium-r-normal------m--iso8859-
cour.pfa -adobe-courier-medium-r-normal------m--iso8859-
... 77 lines of similar code ...
l049036t.pfa -b&h-Luxi Serif-bold-i-normal------p--iso8859-
l049036t.pfa -b&h-Luxi Serif-bold-i-normal------p--iso8859-
l049036t.pfa -b&h-Luxi Serif-bold-i-normal------p--iso8859-
l049036t.pfa -b&h-Luxi Serif-bold-i-normal------p--adobe-standard
```

Notice in the syntax shown above that the same PFA fonts can be used to cover multiple character encodings, giving a separate XLFD entry for each.

Tools that create font.scale files include, for example, *type1inst* [243] for PostScript Type 1 fonts and *ttmkfdir* [294] for TrueType fonts.

In view of some idiosyncrasies of these tools, certain precautions are in order. First, the TrueType fonts should be separated from the PostScript Type 1 fonts, for two reasons: each of these tools overwrites the fonts.scale generated by the other; also, *type1inst* also attempts to analyze TrueType fonts but gives results inferior to those of *ttmkfdir*, and confusion may ensue.

In the directory into which we have placed our PostScript Type 1 fonts, we will run:

```
type1inst
```

possibly with the option -nogs to avoid creating a Fontmap file (which is a font catalog for *ghostscript*). *type1inst* is a Perl script written by an Australian volunteer; it was last updated in 1998, and it contains a number of gaps, notably with respect to encodings. Specifically, of all the encodings that fonts may have, it recognizes only one: *Adobe Standard*, which it calls iso8859-1 (even though it has nothing to do with that encoding). In all other cases, it writes adobe-fontspecific.

Thus it is absolutely necessary to edit the fonts.scale file *a posteriori* and to correct the encodings (at least) in the XLFD font names before continuing.

In the directory containing the TrueType files, we run:

```
ttmkfdir > fonts.scale
```

possibly with the option --panose, if we are certain that the font contains a correct Panose-1 classification. Unlike *type1inst*, this tool functions as a *freetype* library and manages to analyze fonts with much greater precision. Nevertheless, we are always wise to inspect the fonts.scale file before continuing.

Also note the existence of *mkfontscale* [95], another relatively recent tool that can be found on certain Unix distributions, which examines both PostScript Type 1 fonts and TrueType fonts *at the same time*. Contrariwise, *mkfontscale* seems not to be suitable for bitmap fonts.

Having generated the fonts.scale file, we launch (still in the same directory) *mkfontdir*, specifying the directory containing the encodings.dir file:

```
mkfontdir -e /usr/X11R6/lib/X11/fonts/encodings
```

If several of these files are present on the system, we can use this option multiple times, but it is more sensible to have a central encodings.dir file that contains all the encodings used on the machine.

Afterwards, the remaining procedures are the same as for bitmap fonts. For instance, if /home/yannis/fonts/ttf is the current directory, we type

```
chkfontpath -a /home/yannis/fonts/ttf
```

to add it to the configuration file on the server and

```
xset +fp /home/yannis/fonts/ttf
xset fp rehash
```

to fill it in and rebuild the internal tables in the file server's database.

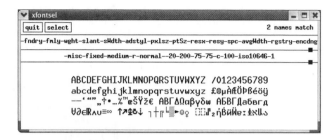

Figure 8-1: The interface of the application xfontsel.

Tools for Managing Fonts under X

The application *xfontsel* [324] allows us to choose a font name from the components of its XLFD font name. For example, we have a line of text (Figure 8-2)

```
-fndry-fmly-wght-slant-aWdth-adstyl-...
                   ...pxlsz-ptSz-resx-resy-spc-avgWdth-rgstry-encdng
```

that is nothing but a list of abbreviations of the names of XLFD's fields. By clicking on one of these abbreviated names, we obtain a contextual menu that shows all the possible choices for this XLFD field among all the available fonts. In the area in which this line appears, the XLFD name is displayed. In the beginning, this name is nothing but a sequence of * wildcards and thus represents all fonts.

When we select a value for an XLFD field, it is displayed in the XLFD font name in the second line, and the possible choices for the other fields are reduced to those that are compatible with the choices already made. Often there is only one choice, other than the wildcard, on the contextual menu. We can thus fill in all the fields in the XLFD font name and obtain the name of the unique font that matches our needs. Note that in the upper right part of the window the phrase ... names match shows us how many fonts that match our current choices exist. There must always be at least one, since *xfontsel* does not allow us to specify values for the parameters that would not match any font. If we click on the Select button, the selected font name is copied onto the clipboard and can then be pasted into another window by a click on the mouse's middle button.

Another tool, which lets us preview the installed fonts, is *xfd* [146]. It displays all the glyphs in a given font, in units of 256 glyphs. Thus, if we write

```
xfd -fn "-misc-fixed-medium-r-normal------c--iso10646-" &
```

we can view the table of this font's glyphs. In Figure 8-2 we see the first two of these tables: 0x00-0xff and 0x100-0x1ff. By clicking on a glyph, we obtain its position in the table as well as its font-metric properties.

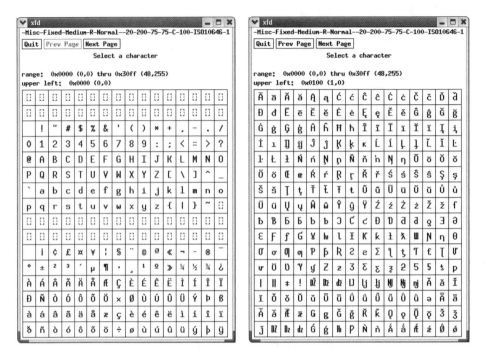

Figure 8-2: Two tables of glyphs from the Unicode-encoded character-cell font 10x20, displayed by xfd.

Tools for Converting Fonts under X

It is quite natural that a plethora of tools for converting one format to another has arisen over time to contend with the multiplicity of font formats used under Unix. Of these we shall mention some that are the most solid, the best documented, and the best supported by their programmers. The reader will find vastly more through a simple Google search: if 'A' and 'B' are names of font formats, search for A2B or AtoB. For example, a search for "bdf2pcf" yielded 249 results, one for "bdftopcf" yielded 72,300.

The GNU Font Tools

This is a panoply of tools developed in 1992 by Karl Berry and Kathryn Hargreaves [77]. The goal is to perform auto-tracing on bitmap images to obtain their vector contours. Today there are more powerful systems for this task (*ScanFont*, by FontLab; *mftrace*, by Han-Wen Nienhuys; FontForge, by George Williams; etc.). But the individual GNU tools may be of interest in their own right.

Karl Berry defined his own vector format, named BZR. It is a pivot format from which the utility *bzrto* can generate METAFONT or PostScript Type 1 (in GSF format, a variant of PFA that *ghostscript* uses) or PostScript Type 3. There is also a human-readable BZR format called BPL (in the fashion of TFM/PL, VF/VPL, etc.). We can convert BZR to BPL and vice versa wit the help of the tools *bzrtobpl* and *bpltobzr*.

George Williams's Tools

George Williams, author of FontForge, which we shall describe at length in Chapters 12–14, is a truly tireless person. He produced, alongside FontForge, a floppy disk of tools that handle practically all the situations that can arise when we share data between Unix and Mac OS X or Windows.

For example, *fondu* [351] reads a set of Macintosh files and extracts all the fonts, be they PostScript (POST resource), TrueType (sfnt), bitmap (NFNT or FONT), or font-family resources (FOND). To manipulate Macintosh files containing resources under Unix, one must convert them to one of three formats: Macbinary (which "flattens" the data and resource parts), Binhex (which also converts everything to hexadecimal), or *dfont* (the equivalent of the Macintosh's font suitcases under Mac OS X).

There is also *ufond*, which performs the opposite operation: from a given Unix font, it generates a file that can be used under Mac OS 9 or Mac OS X, provided once again that it be converted to Macbinary or Binhex.

Another series of tools [348] converts PFA fonts to PFB (*pfa2pfb*) and vice versa (*pfb2pfa*), generates BDF bitmaps from a PFA file (*pfa2bdf*), generates an AFM file from the descriptions of glyphs in a PFA file (*pfa2afm*), and decrypts the PostScript code in a PFA file (*pfadecrypt*).

Next, he attacked the TTF fonts: *showttf* clearly displays the contents of all the TrueType or OpenType tables, and *ttf2eps* converts a glyph from a TTF font into an encapsulated PostScript file.

Various other tools

The *t1utils* were written by Lee Hetherington and revised by Eddie Kohler [175]. They support conversion from PFB to PFA (*t1ascii*) or vice versa (*t1binary*) and even complete decryption of the PostScript Type 1 binary code (*t1disasm*).

Eddie Kohler [223] also added a handful of tools for the Multiple Master and OpenType fonts: *mmafm* and *mmpfb* produce Multiple Master font instances, and *cfftot1* converts a CFF (Type 2) font to Type 1.

Dieter Barron wrote *ttftot42* [64], the only tool currently available for converting True-Type fonts to PostScript Type 42, which is essentially the same thing inside a PostScript wrapper.

Converting Bitmap Fonts under Unix

One very popular editor for bitmap fonts is *XmBDFEd* [232]. The unpronounceable acronym for this software comes from *X Motif BDF Editor*. It was developed by Mark Leisher. We shall not describe here its user interface for designing bitmap fonts. The reason that we have mentioned it here is that it is also a very powerful tool for font conversion. Indeed, it can read the PK and GF formats of TeX (§A.5.2, A.5.3); HBF (ideographic bitmap fonts), PSF (§A.4.1), and CP (§A.4.5), of Linux; FON and FNT, of Windows (§A.3); and TrueType and TTC. It can only write PSF files.

Another tool for converting bitmap fonts under Unix is *fontconv* [357], by the Bulgarian Dimitar Zharkov. This program reads and writes fonts in the RAW, PSF, and FNT formats as well as in two more exotic ones: GRX (the native font format of the GRX graphical library) and FNA (its human-readable version).

9

Fonts under TEX and Ω

TEX and its successor Ω are the most sophisticated digital typography systems in the world. Thus it is understandable that font management on these systems is a little bit complex. In this chapter, we shall approach fonts from three points of view:

1. Their use in TEX and Ω: how we go about using fonts (already installed on the system) in TEX documents.

2. Their basic installation, i.e., with no special adaptation: how can the user who has just bought a beautiful font or downloaded one from the network install it on a TEX system for immediate use?

3. Their adaptation to the user's needs: we quickly notice that the fonts that we buy or find on the network are merely raw material for us to adapt, mold, shape to fit our needs. For the well-versed typophile only!

These three points of view correspond to this chapter's three sections, each of which is more difficult and more technical than the one before it.

Using Fonts in TEX

Up to now we have examined operating systems: Mac OS, Windows, Unix. Is TEX also an operating system? No. But what *is* TEX, then? Born in 1978 at the prestigious Stanford University, brainchild of Donald Knuth, one of the greatest computer scientists of the twentieth century, TEX is, all in all, several things at once: a free software system for type-setting, a programming language, a syntax for writing mathematical formulae, a state of mind that often approaches religion... [1]

---

[1] A religion with, among other things, initiation rites, first and foremost being the correct pronunciation of "TEX", which varies from language to language. In fact, the TEX logo is deceiving: it actually consists of

There is no shortage of word processors or desktop publishing software. How does TEX differ from the pack, to the point of deserving two whole chapters in this book?

Well, TEX is an outsider among word-processing systems and desktop publishing software, as it existed before all the others (neither Mac OS nor Windows existed in 1978, and Unix was still in its infancy) and, thanks to the idealism, perspicacity, and industriousness of Knuth and the hundreds of programmers who have contributed to TEX over the past 25 years, TEX has invested much more than the others in fine typography.[2] Thus it is natural that font management in TEX is different from, and more sophisticated than, font management for other software.

Moreover, as free software, TEX and Ω—its successor, as of 1994, developed by John Plaice and the author—have unlimited potential: any features that one might need can be added to them, provided that a programmer with the time and energy to do the work can be found. Ω in particular is fertile ground for experimentation and application of new techniques of digital typography to "explore strange new worlds, to seek out new life and new civilizations, to boldly go where no one has gone before"...

This chapter is intended primarily for users of TEX or Ω who wish to understand font management on these systems and improve the appearance of their documents by making as much use as possible of the fonts available to them. To those who do not yet know TEX but wish to discover it, we recommend the following introductory section, in which we shall also define a number of terms and acronyms that we shall use throughout the chapter.

Introduction to TEX

When we prepare a document on a word processor such as Microsoft Word or desktop publishing tools like Quark XPress, we sometimes have two conflicting requirements of the software that we use. On the one hand, we expect the software to give us complete control over layout, like an automobile that gives us complete control over the road; after all, the software belongs to us and must "obey" us. On the other hand, we expect it to "do its job"; that is, it should produce precise and perfect layout worthy of the great typographers.

Why do these two requirements come into conflict? Because we cannot be very accurate when we use a mouse to lay out the blocks of text that we see on the screen, since the mouse, the screen, our hands, and our eyes are themselves not very accurate. And if we take the trouble to be accurate by using magnifying glasses and sophisticated tools for measurement, alignment, and uniformity, along with any other devices supplied by the software, the effort required is completely out of proportion to the result obtained—a

---

the Greek letters tau, epsilon, chi, the first letters of the word τέχνη, which means "art" and "technique" in classical Greek. For this reason, the pronunciation of TEX depends on the pronunciation of classical Greek in the language being used, which differs dramatically among speakers of English, French, German, Japanese, and, yes, modern Greek. In English, TEX rhymes with "blecchhh", as explained by Knuth in [217].

   [2] So much so that the software package considered the crème de la crème of mass-market typesetting software, *Adobe InDesign*, adopted TEX's techniques for setting paragraphs—techniques that Adobe advertises as being revolutionary...

result that is nothing more than the most natural thing in the world: typography worthy of the name.

To reach this conclusion, we shall begin with the assumption that the user of the software at least *knows* what she must do to obtain a good typographic result, even if she cannot produce one. But even this assumption is false, since, as we know, most users of word-processing software do not know much about the typographer's trade. They could not be expected to have knowledge obtained only through several years of specialized study (at the École Estienne or the University of Reading, for example) or considerable time and effort to learn them on one's own. Let's face it: a person who assumes the typographer's role without having any background in typography will produce bad documents. Indeed, our era will certainly be characterized by historians as the era of the *decline of the typographic art...*

Which bring us to TeX. For the moment, let us forget about the intrusion of computer science into the process of book production and return to the traditional model of "author–editor–printer": the author *writes* a manuscript, the editor *corrects* and *improves* it, the printer *typesets* it. Next, the printer prepares proofs and sends them to the editor, who passes them along to the author, who reviews them and corrects them. And the process starts all over again, and continues until the day when no more corrections are made and the author and the editor give the long-awaited "pass for press", and the printer can then begin the print run. This age-old model distributes both the tasks and the responsibilities among "author", "editor", and "printer".

But, to return to the twenty-first century, how can one implement this model when he is sitting alone in front of his computer? Well, he alternately plays the roles of "author" and "editor", and TeX assumes the role of "printer".

That established, we can start with Step 1: we prepare a "manuscript" (see Figure 9-1), i.e., a "TeX" file containing our document marked up with various tags for structure or formatting. We call these tags "commands", since, after all, a TeX document is a *program*. In addition, there is a library of subroutines written in the TeX programming language: it is called LaTeX, and it offers a set of commands that are very practical and easy to use.

Step 2: the "manuscript" is sent to the "printer" (in computer jargon, the document is compiled by TeX), and "first proofs" are produced. The author/editor examines these "first proofs" and corrects his "manuscript", then hands it off once again to TeX, which produces another set of proofs. The process is repeated until the production of the "pass for press", which leads directly to printing (in our case, the output of the printer or the films from which printing plates will be made).

What is special about TeX is the physical separation between the TeX document (what we have called the "manuscript"; in computer jargon, the "source") and the typeset document (the "proofs"; in computer jargon, the "compiled file"). The latter, for historical reasons, is a file with a format particular to TeX that is known as DVI (acronym of *device-independent*). This file format, compared with formats such as PDF, PostScript, and DOC (the file format of MS Word), is an extremely *simple* and *abstract* page description.

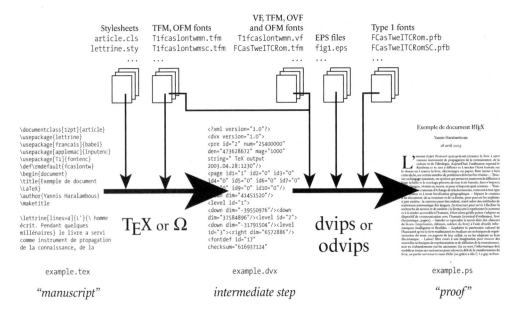

Figure 9-1: The process of producing documents with T_EX.

Why are simplicity and abstraction so important? Because when T_EX was created (in the 1970s), each screen and each printer had its own computer codes. Rather than making as many versions of T_EX as there were models of screens and printers, Knuth decided to create a sort of "pivot" format, the DVI format. Users had only to write their own screen and printer "drivers" customized for their systems.

The same goes for fonts. So as not to make life complicated, T_EX uses stand-ins called T_EX Font Metrics. Unlike all other fonts, these are empty, in the sense that they do not contain any glyphs. Instead, they contain *font-metric data* for each glyph: its height, its set-width, its depth, etc. Instead of setting glyphs themselves, T_EX sets type using imaginary boxes whose dimensions are taken from the TFM files. Once again, the DVI drivers mentioned above have to "dirty their hands" and replace these imaginary boxes with glyphs. The logic is the same as for the DVI format: since each printer and each screen has its own font formats, we may as well use a simple, generic font format and convert it to the format used by the peripheral. Thus T_EX would produce a document with an abstract, unreal beauty, and its obedient servants, the device drivers, would bring this masterpiece down to earth by replacing the imaginary boxes with genuine glyphs and working its magic to render the data comprehensible to all the various output devices.

Since this situation was quite tedious, we awaited, as if for a messiah, the arrival of a universal language that would work on all screens and all printers. And it came in 1982: it is the PostScript programming language.

From that time on, we would need only one driver—a driver to convert DVI files into PostScript code. Several attempts were made to write that driver—attempts that ran into major technical problems. Finally, Tom Rokicki, one of Knuth's doctoral students, wrote *dvips*, which is the most successful and the most widely used DVI-to-PostScript driver today.

By now the reader will certainly understand why it is only *dvips*, not TₑX itself, that comes into contact with modern font technology: PostScript Type 1 or Type 3, TrueType, Open-Type, etc. As can be seen in Figure 9-1, TₑX uses TFM fonts to produce a DVI file. Then *dvips* takes over and produces PostScript code, including, if necessary, PostScript Type 1 fonts.

But we are already starting to go behind the scenes of TₑX. The average user never has anything to do with TFM fonts and rarely deals with DVI files. Instead, she focuses on the high-level programming interface: the basic LATₑX commands, the various packages of commands customized for different typesetting contexts, etc. Being above all an "author" and possibly also an "editor", the LATₑX user does not usually worry about the tasks generally performed by the "printer".

Below we shall examine the use of fonts under TₑX on three levels:

- The "high level": the point of view of the end user, who plays the role of "author".

- The "intermediate level": that of the more informed user, who desires better control over the fonts in his document, or the "editor", in the sense of the person who specifies in great detail how the document will appear—in particular, the fonts to be used.

- The "low level": the internal workings of the software, where a certain number of basic questions shall occupy our attention: What is the relationship between TₑX commands and TFM files? How are fonts used in the DVI format? When do PostScript or other "real-world" fonts come into play? What is the relationship between these fonts and TFM fonts?

In the list above, we discuss nothing but the use of fonts. With the exceptions of the fonts that come with TₑX or Ω and are already installed on the system, however, we must first install any other fonts that we wish to use. And it goes without saying that all three levels are involved, and with equal importance, in the installation of PostScript fonts under TₑX. That is what we shall see below.

One other item adds to the complexity of font management in TₑX as we have described it: METAFONT fonts. Even though PostScript did not yet exist in 1978, TₑX did not come into the world deprived of fonts. On the contrary, after developing TₑX, Knuth said: *It is not good that TₑX should be alone; I will make him a help meet for him* and therefore created a companion for it. This lawful companion of the TₑX language is a programming lan-

The *Computer Modern* fonts, shown here, are among the most commonly used fonts in the world **and are the most distinctive feature** *of the vast majority* of LATEX documents. They come in a rich variety, from roman to sans-serif, and typewriter type. *All of the glyphs* **in this sample** *come from the* same METAFONT code. Just as DNA characterizes a human being, 62 parameters *are enough* to *characterize a* ***font*** *in the Computer Modern* family.

Figure 9-2: A sample of various fonts of the Computer Modern family.

guage herself,[3] but one dedicated to creating fonts. We shall discuss her in great depth in Appendix F of this book.

Thus we have one more font format to take into consideration when we prepare to manage fonts in the TₑX or Ω system: the fonts generated by METAFONT. And this font format is quite important indeed, as many of the older installations of TₑX have nothing by default but METAFONT fonts.

Now that we have finished outlining these general and historical considerations, let us move on to the realm of the concrete, beginning with the three levels of font management in TₑX: high, intermediate, and low.

The High Level: Basic LATEX Commands and NFSS

In this section, we shall presume that the reader is somewhat familiar with LATEX. (If not, there are excellent introductions to the subject, such as [282], [224], and [317].) The question that we shall discuss first is how to use fonts in LATEX. More specifically, what does one do to specify the active font?

One can very well prepare a LATEX document without specifying a single font; after all, when one uses commands such as \emph{...} (emphasized text), \section{...} (a section title), \footnote{...} (the text of a footnote), LATEX itself chooses the appropriate font for each case. Which fonts are these? We might be inclined to say a priori that the default fonts for LATEX are always the same: those of the *Computer Modern* family

---

[3] The decision to feminize METAFONT is not the author's personal initiative. TₑX, in the illustrations that accompany it, is represented by a *lion*.[5] In the same illustrations, METAFONT is personified as a *lioness*. And this leonine couple is traditionally accompanied not by a humdrum lion cub but by a new species of animal: the *computer*, which not only has hands and feet but even drinks coffee...

[4] Not for nothing is TₑX represented by a lion. Donald Knuth has told us that lions are to him the guardians of libraries in the United States because there is a statue of a lion in front of the entrance of each large library there. Guardian of libraries, guardian of the Book—is that not indeed what TₑX ultimately aspires to be?

(see Figure 9-2), designed by Knuth on the model of Monotype *Modern* 8A [219]. But in fact everything depends on the LATEX *stylesheet* that we are using. A stylesheet is a LATEX file that specifies the details of the document's appearance. These specifications can be more or less general: LATEX comes with some generic stylesheets of its own, and there are stylesheets on the Web for all the scientific journals, collections of works, dissertations at each university, and many other purposes. The text font, the font for mathematical formulae, the font for computer code, etc., are part of each stylesheet's specifications.

To specify the active font, the user can operate at any of a number of levels, according to the nature of the choice and his own technical expertise. Let us begin with the simplest case and proceed deeper and deeper into the workings of LATEX.

Choosing fonts in LATEX: basic commands

Owing to its origins in the computer, LATEX considers that there are three big categories of fonts that can coexist in a document: "serif", "sans serif", and "typewriter", the last of these being used to set computer code. The following three commands set the text provided in the argument in one of these three types of fonts:

\textrm{...}	serif
\textsf{...}	sans serif
\texttt{...}	typewriter

In the absence of any other indication, text is set by default in a light upright font that has a lower case. We can change the weight (one other possibility) and the style:

\textbf{...}	bold
\textit{...}	italic
\textsl{...}	slanted
\textsc{...}	small capitals

where "slanted" is an invention of Knuth that involves artificially slanting the letters. It is tolerable for sans serif fonts, but it quickly becomes annoying in serif fonts, so please avoid it! In the list above, bold can be combined with the three styles "italic", "slanted", and "small capitals", but those three styles cannot be combined with one another (a regrettable fact, since it leaves us with no way to obtain italic small capitals). To return to the normal state (light, upright, with a lower case), we have the following commands:

\textmd{...}	light (in fact *medium*)
\textup{...}	upright, with a lower case
\textnormal{...}	light and upright, with a lower case

The second command cancels the effect of italics, slanted type, and small capitals. The third is the most powerful: it restores the default font of the document, with no ornamentation.

All of the commands described above affect the text that is given to them as an argument. As a safety measure, this text cannot be very long; more specifically, it cannot contain more than one paragraph. (Recall that the change of paragraphs in TₑX is made with a blank line.) To apply these same changes to a larger block of text, we must place that block in a group (that is, within braces) and place inside that group one of the following commands:

\rmfamily	serif
\sffamily	sans serif
\ttfamily	typewriter
\bfseries	bold
\itshape	italic
\slshape	slanted
\scshape	small capitals
\mdseries	medium weight and set-width
\upshape	upright
\normalfont	light and upright

But beware! \textit{...} is a better choice than {\itshape ...}, as the former also applies the *italic correction*, which is a slight space that is added after letters with an ascender to keep them from touching the following glyph if it is, for example, a right closing parenthesis. Thus (\textit{need}) will yield "(*need*)", while ({\itshape need}) will yield the unfortunate "(*need*)".

A number of commands for changing the current type size are also available. These commands are of the same kind as the previous ones; i.e., they apply to everything that follows, and their effect should be limited through the use of grouping:

\tiny	tiny
\scriptsize	the size of superscripts and subscripts
\footnotesize	the size of footnotes
\small	small
\normalsize	the usual size of running text
\large	slightly bigger
\Large	bigger
\LARGE	much bigger
\huge	barely tolerable
\Huge	enormous

The exact sizes depend on the stylesheet. For example, in the case of the most common stylesheet (book class, 10 points), they are 5/6, 7/8, 8/9.5, 9/11, 10/12, 12/14, 14/18, 17/22, 20/25, 25/30 (in American printer's points).

We must mention here that the system covers most of the cases that the author of a LᴬTₑX document is likely to need, but at the same time it may not always satisfy those of us who place a little more importance on the font used in our document. For example, one cannot choose the font's family; nor can one specify the body size exactly or the desired leading. No provision is made for font families that offer a broader range of weights or styles. Last but not least, the system is profoundly Latin-centric, as serifs, italics, and small capitals do not even exist in most of the world's scripts.

To achieve what we desire, let us descend to another level in the LᴬTₑX machinery.

Using NFSS

In this section we shall dissect LᴬTₑX's system for choosing fonts. This system is called the "New Font Selection Scheme" (NFSS). [272] (Here the word "new" seems a bit out of place today because NFSS was introduced in 1992.) The principle is very simple. Each font is described by five independent parameters. The user requests the font by specifying the values of these parameters, and, if the system cannot supply the desired font, it supplies an approximation based on a substitution mechanism.

These five parameters are:

- `\fontfamily{...}`: the name of the font's family. This is not the true name of the font family, in the manner of PostScript or TrueType, but rather a keyword specific to NFSS, made up of lowercase letters and digits. For example, this keyword might be "timesten" for *Adobe Times Ten*. This keyword appears in the name of the FD ("font descriptor") file that describes the correspondence between "logical" fonts (at the level of NFSS) and "physical" fonts (the TFM files). Thus for a keyword `timesten` there must exist on the disk a file named `t1timesten.fd` (or `ot1timesten.fd`, `t2atimesten.fd`, etc.; everything depends on the encoding, as we shall see below).

  How can we know which fonts are available on our system? Or, when we know that we have a certain FD file, how can we tell which font family matches it? No simple means are available at this time; one must prepare a list of all the FD files on the system and try to guess the name of the font family from the filename.[5] But this

---

[5] It is quite likely that the file `t1timesten.fd` corresponds to the font family *Adobe Times Ten*; but would `t1garamond.fd` go with *Monotype Garamond, Adobe Garamond*, or (a hideous font, in the opinion of many typographers) *ITC Garamond*? Let us get a bit ahead of ourselves and say right now that the only way to know is to find, inside the FD file, the names of the TFM files that are used. If they are virtual font-metric files, one must open them (see §B.3) and find the underlying real fonts. Finally, one must go into the configuration file(s) for *dvips* and find out to which PostScript fonts they correspond. These configuration files will necessarily contain the desired information.

Is there a way to avoid having to play "font detective"? Karl Berry [75] has finished his *Font Naming Scheme*, which provides a two-letter or three-letter abbreviation for each font family.

Unfortunately, there is no shortage of drawbacks. First of all, these abbreviations neither reveal their meaning nor have much mnemonic value. While `ptm`, `phv`, `pcr` for *Adobe Times, Adobe Helvetica, Adobe Courier* do retain a certain logic, how can one remember that `ma1` is *Monotype Arial* and that `mii` is *Monotype Imprint*, the favorite font of Oxford University Press? Furthermore, Berry's list will most likely never be complete: there are hundreds of large and small foundries throughout the world, which means that new fonts come out every day; thus there will always be some that are not on the list. Conversely, is it necessary to change the abbreviation

problem may occur less often if we install our fonts ourselves and thus choose the
NFSS keyword that represents the font family.

- \fontseries{...}: the weight and the set-width. The system used by NFSS to describe these characteristics is as follows:

ul	ultra-light	uc	ultra-condensed
el	extra-light	ec	extra-condensed
l	light	c	condensed
sl	semi-light	sc	semi-condensed
m	regular weight	m	regular width
sb	semi-bold	sx	semi-extended
b	bold	x	extended
eb	extra-bold	ex	extra-extended
ul	ultra-bold	ux	ultra-extended

Here are the rules: (a) the two expressions are combined in the order specified
(weight, then set-width); (b) the letter m is omitted when either the width or the
weight is regular; (c) m is written when both the width and the weight are regular.

Thus we write elc for an extra-light condensed font but simply el for an extra-light
font of regular width and m for a font of regular width and regular weight.

- \fontshape{...}: the "style". This category includes italics, slanted type, small capitals, and a few other exotic styles:

n	upright
it	italic
ui	upright italic
sl	slanted
sc	small capitals
ol	outline

"Upright italic" is another of Knuth's inventions. It involves applying a negative slant to
italic letters so that they appear vertical. The result is quite disconcerting.

Note that there is, unfortunately, no way to combine several styles. For example,
in NFSS we cannot specify italic small capitals, which could be very useful—as, for
example, when an acronym occurs inside a quotation: "*Some people confuse Ionesco
and* UNESCO".

---

if a foundry releases a new version of a font? And what should a user do who has modified a font herself by
changing a glyph or reencoding the font?
In any event, no better means of identifying fonts has been discovered up to now. The solution to the problem
may come from the migration of OpenType fonts that is being carried out by the Ω system and that will open
new horizons for font management.

	"0	"1	"2	"3	"4	"5	"6	"7	"8	"9	"A	"B	"C	"D	"E	"F
"0x	Γ	Δ	Θ	Λ	Ξ	Π	Σ	Υ	Φ	Ψ	Ω	ff	fi	fl	ffi	ffl
"1x	ı	J	`	´	ˇ	˘	¯	˚	¸	ß	æ	œ	ø	Æ	Œ	Ø
"2x	˝	!	”	#	$	%	&	'	(	)	*	+	,	-	.	/
"3x	0	1	2	3	4	5	6	7	8	9	:	;	¡	=	¿	?
"4x	@	A	B	C	D	E	F	G	H	I	J	K	L	M	N	O
"5x	P	Q	R	S	T	U	V	W	X	Y	Z	[	"	]	ˆ	˙
"6x	'	a	b	c	d	e	f	g	h	i	j	k	l	m	n	o
"7x	p	q	r	s	t	u	v	w	x	y	z	–	—	”	˜	¨

Figure 9-3: The OT1 glyph encoding (TₑX's default encoding). Accented letters are built up from letters and accents.

- \fontencoding{...}: the encoding used by the font.

  Since the introduction of NFSS, many TₑX-specific encodings have emerged. The most important of these are:

  - OT1, Knuth's original encoding; see Figure 9-3 [217, p. 427]
  - T1, an encoding inspired by ISO Latin-1 that also incorporates glyphs for the languages of Central Europe and the Baltic countries; see Figure 9-4 [211]
  - TS1, the catchall companion to T1; see Figure 9-4 [211]
  - T2A, T2B, and T2C, a trio of encodings for European and Asian languages that use the Cyrillic alphabet; and T2D, a font encoding for Old Cyrillic; see Figure 9-5 and Figure 9-6 [73]
  - T3, an encoding for the glyphs of the International Phonetic Alphabet; see Figure 9-7 [302]
  - T4, an encoding for Maltese and the African languages that use the Latin script; see Figure 9-7 [211]

  The name of the encoding also appears in the name of the FD file; thus, if there is a file t1palatino.fd on our system and the system has been configured correctly, we should be able to use the *Palatino* font family, in the T1 encoding, in our LᴬTₑX documents.

  Note that the encoding, unlike the weight and the style, is not taken into account by the substitution mechanism. In other words, a font in a given encoding that is not available will never be replaced by the same font in a different encoding.

- \fontsize{...}{...}: the body size and leading. When we write \fontsize{10pt}{ 12pt}, we specify a font of body size 10 set on 12 points (American printer's points) of leading. Some other units are also available: Didot points, dd (still in use in some European countries, such as Greece); PostScript points, bp ('b' for *big*, since they are

T1 encoding ("Cork")

	"0	"1	"2	"3	"4	"5	"6	"7	"8	"9	"A	"B	"C	"D	"E	"F
"0x	`	´	^	~	¨	˝	°	ˇ	˘	¯	˙	˛	¸	‚	‹	›
"1x	"	"	„	«	»	–	—		0	1	ȷ	ff	fi	fl	ffi	ffl
"2x	␣	!	"	#	$	%	&	'	(	)	*	+	,	-	.	/
"3x	0	1	2	3	4	5	6	7	8	9	:	;	<	=	>	?
"4x	@	A	B	C	D	E	F	G	H	I	J	K	L	M	N	O
"5x	P	Q	R	S	T	U	V	W	X	Y	Z	[	\	]	^	_
"6x	'	a	b	c	d	e	f	g	h	i	j	k	l	m	n	o
"7x	p	q	r	s	t	u	v	w	x	y	z	{	|	}	~	-
"8x	Ă	Ą	Ć	Č	Ď	Ě	Ę	Ğ	Ĺ	Ľ	Ł	Ń	Ň	Ŋ	Ő	Ŕ
"9x	Ř	Ś	Š	Ş	Ť	Ţ	Ű	Ů	Ÿ	Ź	Ž	Ż	IJ	İ	đ	§
"Ax	ă	ą	ć	č	ď	ě	ę	ğ	ĺ	ľ	ł	ń	ň	ŋ	ő	ŕ
"Bx	ř	ś	š	ş	ť	ţ	ű	ů	ÿ	ź	ž	ż	ij	¡	¿	£
"Cx	À	Á	Â	Ã	Ä	Å	Æ	Ç	È	É	Ê	Ë	Ì	Í	Î	Ï
"Dx	Ð	Ñ	Ò	Ó	Ô	Õ	Ö	Œ	Ø	Ù	Ú	Û	Ü	Ý	Þ	SS
"Ex	à	á	â	ã	ä	å	æ	ç	è	é	ê	ë	ì	í	î	ï
"Fx	ð	ñ	ò	ó	ô	õ	ö	œ	ø	ù	ú	û	ü	ý	þ	ß
	"0	"1	"2	"3	"4	"5	"6	"7	"8	"9	"A	"B	"C	"D	"E	"F

TS1 encoding

	"0	"1	"2	"3	"4	"5	"6	"7	"8	"9	"A	"B	"C	"D	"E	"F
"0x	`	´	^	~	¨	˝	°	ˇ	˘	¯	˙	˛	¸	!		
"1x			‖		–	—		←	→	⁀	⁀	⁀	⁀			
"2x	ħ			$			'			*		,	=	.		/
"3x	0	1	2	3	4	5	6	7	8	9		⟨	—	⟩		
"4x													℧			◯
"5x							Ω					⟦		⟧	↑	↓
"6x	`		★	o|o	†								🍃	∞	♪	
"7x															~	=
"8x	˘	ˇ	″	‶	†	‡	‖	‰	•	°C	$	¢	f	₡	₩	₦
"9x	₲	ℙ	£	ℛ	?	₫	™	‱	¶	฿	№	℅	℮	°	℠	
"Ax	{	}	¢	£	¤	¥	¦	§	¨	©	ª	◎	¬	℗	®	‾
"Bx	°	±	²	³	´	µ	¶	·	※	¹	º	√	¼	½	¾	€
"Cx																
"Dx							×									
"Ex																
"Fx							÷									
	"0	"1	"2	"3	"4	"5	"6	"7	"8	"9	"A	"B	"C	"D	"E	"F

Figure 9-4: Glyph encodings: T1, or the "Cork encoding", named for the city of Cork, Ireland, where it was defined in 1990 (for the European languages that use the Latin script), and its "catchall" companion, named TS1 [211].

	"0	"1	"2	"3	"4	"5	"6	"7	"8	"9	"A	"B	"C	"D	"E	"F
"0x	`	´	^	~	¨	˝	°	ˇ	˘	¯	·		˛	˓	I	⟨	⟩
"1x	"	"	⌢	˜	˘	–	—		0	1	J	ff	fi	fl	ffi	ffl
"2x	␣	!	"	#	$	%	&	'	(	)	*	+	,	-	.	/
"3x	0	1	2	3	4	5	6	7	8	9	:	;	<	=	>	?
"4x	@	A	B	C	D	E	F	G	H	I	J	K	L	M	N	O
"5x	P	Q	R	S	T	U	V	W	X	Y	Z	[	\	]	^	_
"6x	`	a	b	c	d	e	f	g	h	i	j	k	l	m	n	o
"7x	p	q	r	s	t	u	v	w	x	y	z	{	|	}	~	-
"8x	Ѓ	Ғ	Ђ	Ћ	һ	Ж	Ӡ	Љ	Ї	Қ	Ҟ	Ҝ	Æ	Ӊ	Ԉ	S
"9x	Ѳ	Ҫ	Ў	Ұ	Ү	Х	Ц	Ч	Ҷ	Є	Ә	Њ	Ё	№	¤	§
"Ax	ѓ	ғ	ђ	ћ	h	ж	ӡ	љ	ї	қ	ҟ	ҝ	æ	ӊ	ԉ	s
"Bx	ѳ	ҫ	ў	ұ	ү	х	ц	ч	ҷ	є	ә	њ	ё	„	«	»
"Cx	А	Б	В	Г	Д	Е	Ж	З	И	Й	К	Л	М	Н	О	П
"Dx	Р	С	Т	У	Ф	Х	Ц	Ч	Ш	Щ	Ъ	Ы	Ь	Э	Ю	Я
"Ex	а	б	в	г	д	е	ж	з	и	й	к	л	м	н	о	п
"Fx	р	с	т	у	ф	х	ц	ч	ш	щ	ъ	ы	ь	э	ю	я

	"0	"1	"2	"3	"4	"5	"6	"7	"8	"9	"A	"B	"C	"D	"E	"F
"0x	`	´	^	~	¨	˝	°	ˇ	˘	¯	·		˛	˓	I	⟨	⟩
"1x	"	"	⌢	˜	˘	–	—		0	1	J	ff	fi	fl	ffi	ffl
"2x	␣	!	"	#	$	%	&	'	(	)	*	+	,	-	.	/
"3x	0	1	2	3	4	5	6	7	8	9	:	;	<	=	>	?
"4x	@	A	B	C	D	E	F	G	H	I	J	K	L	M	N	O
"5x	P	Q	R	S	T	U	V	W	X	Y	Z	[	\	]	^	_
"6x	`	a	b	c	d	e	f	g	h	i	j	k	l	m	n	o
"7x	p	q	r	s	t	u	v	w	x	y	z	{	|	}	~	-
"8x	Ҕ	Ғ	Ӷ	Ҕ	һ	Ж	δ	Ҙ	Љ	Қ	Л	Ҟ	Ԓ	Ӊ	Ҥ	Ӈ
"9x	Ѳ	Ҫ	Ў	Ү	Ӿ	Х	Ҳ	Ч	Ҷ	Њ	Ә	Ɛ	Ё	№	¤	§
"Ax	ҕ	ғ	ӷ	ҕ	h	ж	δ	ҙ	љ	қ	л	ҟ	ԓ	ӊ	ҥ	ӈ
"Bx	ѳ	ҫ	ў	ү	ӿ	х	ҳ	ч	ҷ	њ	ә	ɛ	ё	„	«	»
"Cx	А	Б	В	Г	Д	Е	Ж	З	И	Й	К	Л	М	Н	О	П
"Dx	Р	С	Т	У	Ф	Х	Ц	Ч	Ш	Щ	Ъ	Ы	Ь	Э	Ю	Я
"Ex	а	б	в	г	д	е	ж	з	и	й	к	л	м	н	о	п
"Fx	р	с	т	у	ф	х	ц	ч	ш	щ	ъ	ы	ь	э	ю	я

Figure 9-5: The T2A and T2B glyph encodings (for European and Asian languages that use the Cyrillic alphabet) [73].

"0x	`	´	ˆ	˜	¨	˝	˚	ˇ	˘	¯	˙	¸	˛	I	⟨	⟩
"1x	“	”	⌒	˵	ᵕ	–	—		0	ı	ȷ	ff	fi	fl	ffi	ffl
"2x	␣	!	"	#	$	%	&	’	(	)	*	+	,	-	.	/
"3x	0	1	2	3	4	5	6	7	8	9	:	;	<	=	>	?
"4x	@	A	B	C	D	E	F	G	H	I	J	K	L	M	N	O
"5x	P	Q	R	S	T	U	V	W	X	Y	Z	[	\	]	^	_
"6x	‘	a	b	c	d	e	f	g	h	i	j	k	l	m	n	o
"7x	p	q	r	s	t	u	v	w	x	y	z	{	|	}	~	-
"8x	Ԥ	Ҵ	Ҭ	Ҕ	Һ	Ҏ	Ԗ	Ӡ	Ӎ	Қ	Ӆ	Ҟ	Ԓ	Ӊ	Ԡ	Ӈ
"9x	Ө	Ҽ	Ҿ	Ѣ	Ҋ	Ҳ	Џ	Ҩ	Ҷ	Ԋ	Ә	Ꞗ	Ё	№	¤	§
"Ax	ԥ	ҵ	ҭ	ҕ	һ	ҏ	ԗ	ӡ	ӎ	қ	ӆ	ҟ	ԓ	ӊ	ԡ	ӈ
"Bx	ө	ҽ	ҿ	ѣ	ҋ	ҳ	џ	ҩ	ҷ	ԋ	ә	ꞗ	ё	„	«	»
"Cx	А	Б	В	Г	Д	Е	Ж	З	И	Й	К	Л	М	Н	О	П
"Dx	Р	С	Т	У	Ф	Х	Ц	Ч	Ш	Щ	Ъ	Ы	Ь	Э	Ю	Я
"Ex	а	б	в	г	д	е	ж	з	и	й	к	л	м	н	о	п
"Fx	р	с	т	у	ф	х	ц	ч	ш	щ	ъ	ы	ь	э	ю	я
	"0	"1	"2	"3	"4	"5	"6	"7	"8	"9	"A	"B	"C	"D	"E	"F

"0x	`	´	ˆ	˜	¨	˝	˚	ˇ	˘	¯	˙	҃	⌒	ꙿ	⟨	⟩
"1x	“	”	⌒	˵	ᵕ	–	—	⌒	0	ı	ȷ	҅	҆	ᵔ	῎	῏
"2x	␣	!	"	#	$	%	&	’	(	)	*	+	,	-	.	/
"3x	0	1	2	3	4	5	6	7	8	9	:	;	<	=	>	?
"4x	@	A	B	C	D	E	F	G	H	I	J	K	L	M	N	O
"5x	P	Q	R	S	T	U	V	W	X	Y	Z	[	\	]	^	_
"6x	‘	a	b	c	d	e	f	g	h	i	j	k	l	m	n	o
"7x	p	q	r	s	t	u	v	w	x	y	z	{	|	}	~	-
"8x	ԁ	Ꙗ	Ѧ	Ѩ	Ћ	N	Ꙁ	Ѯ	Ꙇ	I	Ѵ	Ѡ	Ꙩ	Ѿ	Ѽ	Ѕ
"9x	Ѳ	Ϛ	Ꙋ	Ѣ	Ꙟ	Ѱ	Ꙏ	Ѫ	Ѭ	Є	Ѥ	Ԑ	Ё	№	҂	§
"Ax	ԁ	ꙗ	ѧ	ѩ	ћ	ɴ	ꙁ	ѯ	ї	і	ѵ	ѡ	ꙩ	ѿ	ѽ	ѕ
"Bx	ѳ	ϛ	ꙋ	ѣ	ꙟ	ѱ	ꙏ	ѫ	ѭ	є	ѥ	ԑ	ё	„	«	»
"Cx	А	Б	В	Г	Д	Е	Ж	З	И	Й	К	Л	М	Н	О	П
"Dx	Р	С	Т	У	Ф	Х	Ц	Ч	Ш	Щ	Ъ	Ы	Ь	Э	Ю	Я
"Ex	а	б	в	г	д	е	ж	з	и	й	к	л	м	н	о	п
"Fx	р	с	т	у	ф	х	ц	ч	ш	щ	ъ	ы	ь	э	ю	я
	"0	"1	"2	"3	"4	"5	"6	"7	"8	"9	"A	"B	"C	"D	"E	"F

Figure 9-6: The T2C (Asian languages that use the Cyrillic script) and T2D (Old Cyrillic) glyph encodings.

slightly larger than American printer's points); millimeters, mm; etc. Note that leading, like the encoding, is ignored by the substitution mechanism.

One small detail of some importance: in TEX, a change of leading has effect only if there is at least one change of paragraph within the group. Thus—and it is a very common error among beginners—in the example below, the text will be set in 9-point type, but the change of leading to 10 points will *not* take effect:

```
{\fontsize{9pt}{10pt}\selectfont This is the section of the contract
that is printed in small type so that you will not read it. It commits
you to donating your soul in due form to the undersigned Mephistopheles,
immediately after your physical death.}
```

To obtain the desired effect, adding a blank line before the closing brace would suffice:

```
...

you to donating your soul in due form to the undersigned Mephistopheles,
immediately after your physical death.


}
```

A few examples of the use of NFSS commands. To obtain *Five words in Centaur italic...*:

```
\fontfamily{centaur}\fontsize{11}{13}\fontshape{it}\selectfont
Five words in Centaur italic...
```

To obtain *italics,* **bold italics,** **bold italics in Univers...**:

```
\fontshape{it}\selectfont italics,
\fontseries{bx}\selectfont bold italics,
\fontfamily{unive}\selectfont bold italics in Univers...
```

Finally, to obtain 11/13 type in American printer's points, in PostScript points, in Didot points:

```
\fontsize{11}{13}\selectfont 11/13 type in American printer's points,
\fontsize{11bp}{13bp}\selectfont in PostScript points,
\fontsize{11dd}{13dd}\selectfont in Didot points.
```

The example above shows the tiny but nonetheless perceptible differences among the three kinds of typographic points: American printer's points, PostScript points, and Didot points.

As we can see from the first example above, in order to avoid triggering the substitution process too soon, the commands \fontfamily, \fontseries, \fontshape, \fontencoding, and \fontsize have no effect until the command \selectfont is issued. It is interesting to note that NFSS always attempts to combine the active font with the new properties that the user specifies. For example, \fontseries{bx}\selectfont will yield extended bold in an upright context and extended bold italic in an italic context; the family, the body size, the leading, and the encoding of the font remain unchanged in both cases.

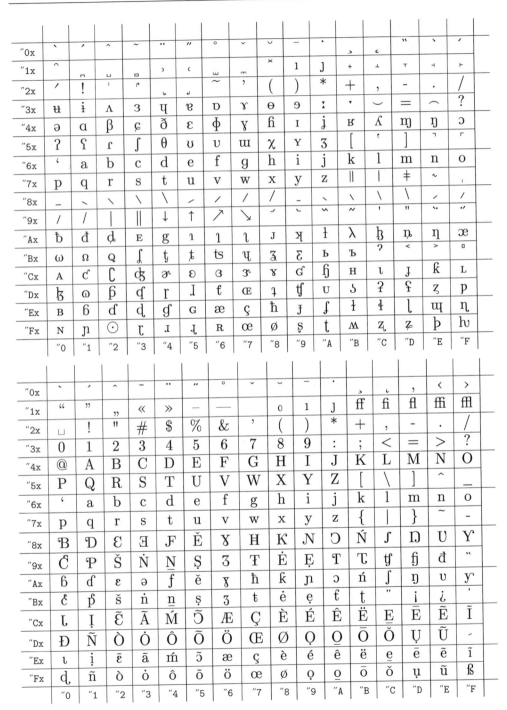

Figure 9-7: The T3 (IPA) [302] and T4 glyph encodings (for African languages that use the Latin script) [211].

Configuring NFSS

But how does NFSS know which font to use in order to match the choices made by the user? And what happens if the user's wishes cannot be fulfilled? The system's magic is all found in its configuration.

Here it is, in broad strokes: to each font family ("family" in the NFSS sense, described above) and each font encoding (of the encodings used with NFSS: T1, OT1, T2, etc.), there corresponds a *font description* file. The file name reflects these two kinds of data—the encoding and the family. Its extension is .fd (=*font descriptor*). For example, the file for the Palatino family and the T1 encoding will be named t1palatino.fd.

Within each file, there are two new LATEX macros: \DeclareFontFamily and \Declare-FontShape. Although only two macros are provided, one can do a great deal with them. In fact, the designers of NFSS developed an entire font-configuration syntax, which is what we shall examine in the remainder of this section.

First of all, let us present the problem. We have a set of constraints (typesetting specifications: roman or italic, light or bold, lowercase or small capitals, body size) and a set of possible solutions ("physical" fonts, which is to say the TFM files that are found on our system). On the one hand, there is *order*: the rational, logical classification of font properties and the clear and precise expression of the user's wishes. On the other hand, there is *chaos*: files with names that are often incomprehensible, containing fonts with properties that often cannot be obtained other than by visual inspection of the glyphs.

The method adopted is as follows:

- As we have already mentioned, the *encoding* and the *font family* (again, in the NFSS sense) are parts of the filename and thus remain unchanged in the file.

- There is only one \DeclareFontFamily command in the file, and it includes the information stated in the previous item (the encoding and the font family).

- There are multiple \DeclareFontShape commands, each of them corresponding to a combination of *weight* and *style*.

- A special syntax is used in an argument to the \DeclareFontShape command to specify the fifth and last NFSS parameter, the *body size*.

Note that leading does not appear anywhere in this configuration; it is considered a global property of the document, independent of the active font. Also note that there is a fundamental difference between body size and the other NFSS parameters: the *encoding*, the *family*, the *style*, and the *weight* take well-determined and unique values from a set of predefined ones. The *body size* follows a different logic. On the one hand, it employs numbers with a decimal part and, therefore, there may be very many possible values, according to the precision desired. On the other hand, we often think not in terms of specific sizes but rather in terms of intervals; for example, we may use one "physical" font for sizes between 9 (inclusive) and 10 (noninclusive), another font for the interval between 10 (inclusive) and 11.754 (noninclusive), and so on. It is clear that the description of constraints on body size calls for a syntax more complex than the simple list of keywords that is used for the other NFSS parameters.

Along with that problem comes another question, an almost metaphysical one. Namely, "What is meant by the size of a font?" In the era of lead type, this question had a simple answer: the "size" was the height of the leaden type sort. Thus, when rows of characters were placed one above another, the result was copy set with a distance between baselines that was equal to the body size. (Typographers often spoke of this procedure as setting type "solid", in the sense that nothing was placed between the lines of type.) For a 10/12 setting, one used 10-point type and added a strip of lead 2 points thick between the rows of characters.

The transition of typography from the material realm to the computer entailed the loss of physical items that could serve as points of reference for a new definition of "size". In the heyday of bitmap fonts, one last point of reference remained: glyphs had a given size, measured not in points but in pixels. The advent of vector fonts wiped out this last point of reference. A vector font can be used at any size, from the microscopic sizes used on electronic components to the often inordinate sizes used in signage. What does body size mean for a font that is so "micromegalous"?

Well, there are two ways to define it, each of them useful—but it is important to keep them separate. There is the *actual size*, a furtive, localized value that depends the graphics software or word processor. For instance, if we set type in "10-point *Optima*", the shapes of the glyphs in the *Optima* font do not depend on the actual size. We can change the size but not the shapes themselves. When Hermann Zapf designed this font [228, p. 329], in 1958, he had no specific size in mind; as a result, *Optima* is the same at all sizes, all actual sizes.

There is also the *optical size*. It is a parameter that the designer specifies for her font. Take the example of "*Linotype Times Ten*". As its name suggests, it was designed for use at 10 points; thus its optical size is 10. In other words, it will yield the best results at an actual size of 10. That is not to say that we are not allowed to use it at other actual sizes. But it will give the best results at 10 points.

For more information on the differences between actual size and body size, we refer the reader to page 12. The reason that we have raised this issue again here is that this duality of concepts is responsible for the complexity of the syntax of NFSS.

It is time for some concrete illustrations. Here is an extract of code from a .fd file:

```
\DeclareFontFamily{T1}{palatino}{}
\DeclareFontShape{T1}{palatino}{m}{n}{<-> palatino}{}
\DeclareFontShape{T1}{palatino}{m}{it}{<-> palatinoi}{}
\DeclareFontShape{T1}{palatino}{bx}{n}{<-> palatinob}{}
\DeclareFontShape{T1}{palatino}{bx}{it}{<-> palatinobi}{}
```

The first command states that in this file we are describing the family Palatino in the T1 font encoding. It follows that this code necessarily appears in a file named `t1palatino.fd`. The four commands that follow specify that there are four combinations of weight (m for medium, bx for bold extended) and style (n for neutral, it for italic). The fifth argument to each of these commands shows the correspondence between the actual size and a TFM file (whose name is given without the extension `.tfm`).

Here we have a simple case: there is only one design for the *Palatino* font; therefore, we consider this design to be optimal at all sizes. The symbol `<->` indicates that the TFM font that follows is to be used at "all actual sizes".

More precisely, the syntax is as follows: we write `<m-n>`, where *m* and *n* are rational numbers, to indicate "all sizes from *m* (inclusive) to *n* (non-inclusive)". Omitting one or both of this numbers indicates that there is no limit; for example, `<-8>` means "used for all sizes strictly lower than 8", and `<12.5->` means "used for all sizes greater than or equal to $12\frac{1}{2}$ points".

Let us take an example. The excellent font *ITC Bodoni* [323] is sold at three optical sizes: 6, 12, and 72. Assuming that the TFM files for light upright type in these three versions are named `itcbodoni6.tfm`, `itcbodoni12.tfm`, and `itcbodoni72.tfm`, we can imagine a font descriptor containing the following code:

```
\DeclareFontFamily{T1}{itcbodoni}{}
\DeclareFontShape{T1}{itcbodoni}{m}{n}{
<-> itcbodoni6
<9-> itcbodoni12
<18-> itcbodoni72
}{}
```

That means: font "6" when setting type smaller than 9 points, font "12" when setting type between 9 and 18 points, and font "72" when setting type larger than 18 points.[6] Thus, when we call for *ITC Bodoni* at an actual size of 10 points, LATₑX will set it at the optical size of 12, reduced by 16.67 percent. At an actual size of 9, the optical size of 12 will still be used, but this time the type will be reduced by 25 percent. At an actual size of 8.5, we will use the optical size of 6 magnified 41.67 percent. And if we request an actual size of 12, we will have a perfect result, since the actual size and the optical size will be identical!

Now suppose that we have a font on hand that has the different optical sizes of 6, 7, 8, 9, ..., 24 points. Few fonts have so many optical sizes designed by hand; but these optical sizes can also result from a "mechanical" interpolation made from a Multiple Master font (see §C.4). We have an example in Figure 9-8: the Adobe font *Kepler MM*, which we have instantiated 20 times to obtain the optical sizes between 5 and 24 points, one point apart. Suppose that the corresponding TFM files are named `kepler5,...,kepler24`. Then we can imagine an FD file like the preceding one, with intervals for the actual sizes:

---

[6] Obviously these choices are arbitrary, but it must be admitted that 6-point or 72-point text seldom appears in a document; thus, if we took the font names literally, fonts "6" and "72" would practically never be used. We have "cheated" slightly in order to improve these three fonts' chances of being used together in a document.

Beneath the quiet unearthly presence of nervous hil

Beneath the quiet unearthly presence of nervous hill (

Beneath the quiet unearthly presence of nervous hill d

Beneath the quiet unearthly presence of nervous hill dv

Beneath the quiet unearthly presence of nervous hill dw

Beneath the quiet unearthly presence of nervous hill dw(

Beneath the quiet unearthly presence of nervous hill dwe

Beneath the quiet unearthly presence of nervous hill dwe

Beneath the quiet unearthly presence of nervous hill dwe

Beneath the quiet unearthly presence of nervous hill dwel

Beneath the quiet unearthly presence of nervous hill dwell

Beneath the quiet unearthly presence of nervous hill dwelle

Beneath the quiet unearthly presence of nervous hill dweller

Beneath the quiet unearthly presence of nervous hill dwellers

Beneath the quiet unearthly presence of nervous hill dwellers

Beneath the quiet unearthly presence of nervous hill dwellers

Beneath the quiet unearthly presence of nervous hill dwellers

Beneath the quiet unearthly presence of nervous hill dwellers

Beneath the quiet unearthly presence of nervous hill dwellers

Beneath the quiet unearthly presence of nervous hill dwellers

Beneath the quiet unearthly presence of nervous hill dwellers

Beneath the quiet unearthly presence of nervous hill dwellers

Beneath the quiet unearthly presence of nervous hill dwellers

Beneath the quiet unearthly presence of nervous hill dwellers

Beneath the quiet unearthly presence of nervous hill dwellers

Figure 9-8: Some specimens of the font Adobe Kepler MM at optical sizes between 5 and 24 points.

```
\DeclareFontFamily{T1}{kepler}{}
\DeclareFontShape{T1}{kepler}{m}{n}{
<-.5> kepler5
<5.5-.5> kepler6
<6.5-.5> kepler7
...
<22.5-.5> kepler23
<23.5-> kepler24
}{}
```

That means that any difference, however small, between two actual sizes of these fonts will always be valid (requesting 5 points or 5.1 points gives two different fonts, the second one a tenth of a point larger) and that the difference between optical sizes and actual sizes will never be greater than 1 point.

All very well. But is this attitude really sound? If we are already fortunate enough to have different optical sizes spaced one point apart (a luxury indeed), do we really need to indulge in the perverse, unhealthy pleasures of half-points or even tenths or hundredths of a point? Would it not be more elegant to use the pristine optical sizes themselves, as their designer intended, at their true dimensions?

That can be done. Simply specify exact actual sizes:

```
\DeclareFontFamily{T1}{kepler}{}
\DeclareFontShape{T1}{kepler}{m}{n}{
<5> kepler5
<6> kepler6
<7> kepler7
...
<23> kepler23
<24> <25> <26> <27> <28> <29> <30> kepler24
}{}
```

With the configuration shown above, NFSS will only set type at actual sizes that are whole numbers between 5 and 30. If these sizes are less than or equal to 24, the optical size will coincide with the actual size. Beyond that level, the optical size of 24 will be magnified, but only so as to form the integer-valued actual sizes of $25, 26, \ldots, 30$. If LaTeX—for whatever reason, be it an explicit request from the user or the calculations made by the stylesheet—calls for an actual size other than those explicitly indicated, the nearest size on the list will be substituted. Thus whether one calls for 9.33, 9.25, or 9.17, the result will be the same: the size of 9 points.

To simplify the task of writing a font descriptor, LaTeX provides the keyword gen *:

```
\DeclareFontFamily{T1}{kepler}{}
\DeclareFontShape{T1}{kepler}{m}{n}{
<5> <6> <7> <8> <9> <10> <11> <12> <13> <14>
```

```
<15> <16> <17> <18> <19> <20> <21> <22> <23>
<24> gen * kepler
<25> <26> <27> <28> <29> <30> kepler24
}{}
```

In this case, NFSS will generate the name of the TFM font by concatenating the actual size (taken from the list) onto the string that follows gen *, which is kepler.[7]

Now let us discuss the other parameters in the FD file: *style* and *weight* (which, as we saw above, is in fact the combination of weight and set-width). What happens when a combination of the values of these parameters is unavailable? NFSS allows us to plan for such cases by making substitutions. For example, the keyword sub * enables us to redirect the request for a font to another combination of values of parameters, which can in turn be redirected, and so on.

Thus, in the following example, we ask NFSS to redirect all requests for "slanted" fonts to the italic font:[8]

```
\DeclareFontFamily{T1}{mtgara}{}
\DeclareFontShape{T1}{mtgara}{m}{n}{ <-> mtgaramond }{}
\DeclareFontShape{T1}{mtgara}{m}{it}{ <-> mtgaramondit }{}
\DeclareFontShape{T1}{mtgara}{m}{sl}{ <-> sub * mtgara/m/it }{}
```

Warning: what follows the keyword sub * must be an "NFSS specification", i.e., a triplet of "NFSS family name", "weight", and "style", separated by slashes. Also note that that allows us to invoke a font belonging to a different font family (which will therefore be described in another FD file), provided that the font encoding remains the same.

Now let us examine another very interesting feature of NFSS: explicit scaling. Suppose that in a single document we wish to combine two fonts whose letters are of noticeably different sizes at the same actual size. We must therefore make their sizes consistent. To that end, we need only specify the desired magnification or shrinking factor in brackets just before the name of the TFM font:

```
\DeclareFontShape{T1}{laurel}{m}{n}{ <-> [1.2] hardy }{}
```

In this example, the font hardy will be magnified 20 percent to scale it up to the size of laurel.

---

[7] We can also use this feature with intervals of sizes, by writing, for example, <5-24> gen * kepler; but in that case we really have to cross our fingers in the hope that LATEX will never call for nonintegral sizes, for then it might generate the name of a file that does not exist. Thus if for any reason LATEX asks NFSS for an actual size of $9\frac{1}{4}$ points, NFSS will try to use the TFM font kepler9.25 and will fail if that font is not available on our system (unless there is an external mechanism for automatically generating fonts, as in the case of METAFONT fonts—something possible in theory for Multiple Master fonts, but no one has taken the trouble of implementing it).

[8] Of course, and as we shall see below, we can *always* slant a PostScript font by including a little PostScript command in the configuration file for *dvips*. But is that aesthetically acceptable? It might work for sans serif fonts in some instances, but for serif fonts—especially those based on classical models, such as *Monotype Garamond* in the example shown above—that borders on sacrilege!

But beware! As is the case for most "miracle solutions", there is a catch. A font contains different types of glyphs, and when we attempt to regularize the sizes of some glyphs, we may make things worse for others. Often the ratio of the height of the lowercase letters to the point size is not the same for two fonts. In the past [142, p. 7], we spoke of "regular x-height", "large x-height", or "small x-height". Today the "x-height" refers to the ratio of the height of the lowercase letters to the point size.[9] When we calibrate the heights of the lowercase letters in two fonts, we produce uppercase letters of noticeably different heights—a very unpleasant effect. And there are still other elements in a font that must be regularized: the parentheses, the heights of the hyphen and the dashes, the height of the apostrophe, etc. If we wish to regularize two fonts *correctly*, we should take them apart and handle separately the different types of glyphs found within them.

A less risky, and in fact more common, case of regularizing the heights of glyphs is that of combining different scripts. Thus when we combine the Latin and Arabic scripts, or Japanese and Hindi, we must take care to use suitable relative sizes.

We have seen the most important features of NFSS. Now let us enter the gray zone where we describe the rare, more technical, and, finally, more dubious cases. The reader will certainly have wondered what the purpose is of the last argument to the \DeclareFontFamily and \Declare-FontShape commands, which has consistently been empty in all our examples. This argument contains TEX macros or primitives that will be executed when we load a TFM font. Since loading is performed only once, the first time the font is used in the document, the selection of commands that can be executed is rather limited.

You are free to experiment with this argument, but please be aware that we have reached the limits of TEX here and that it behooves us to restrict ourselves to the few commands recommended by the developers of LATEX, with the appropriate warnings. What are these commands?

The most useful of them is \hyphenchar. This command, which is in fact a TEX primitive, changes the value of the glyph used as the *end-of-line hyphen*. The command

```
\DeclareFontFamily{T1}{bizarre}{\hyphenchar\font=127}
```

specifies that glyph 127 will henceforth be used as the end-of-line hyphen instead of the regular hyphen, whose glyph ordinarily appears in code point 45 (which corresponds to the Unicode character 0x002D HYPHEN-MINUS). But does the end-of-line hyphen have a different shape from that of the regular hyphen? Not at all: the two glyphs are identical. The reasons for making this substitution are obscure and technical. There is a rule in TEX that says that a word cannot be further divided if it already has a potential breakpoint. This rule is useful: if you write thera\-pist, it is precisely to avoid hyphenation after "the"; thus it makes sense that the presence of \- in a word gives you complete control over the word's division and that TEX cannot break the word elsewhere. The weakness of TEX is that division is handled at the glyph level. Consequently, when one writes "so-so", if the glyph for the hyphen used in this word is the same as that used for word division, TEX regards the word as already containing a potential word break and refuses to divide it further. That may seem harmless enough for "so-so", but it becomes downright annoying for words as long as "Marxism-Leninism" or "physico-mathematical". By using another glyph for the end-of-line hyphen, we can deceive TEX, which will no longer see any reason not to divide words containing a hyphen.

---

[9] Some people define x-height as the ration of the height of the lowercase letters to the height of the uppercase letters [34, 206]. We shall employ the first definition.

Another possibility: by writing \hyphenchar=-1, we can completely disable hyphenation. That may be useful when we write computer code or when we write in a language that does not have the concept of word division, such as Arabic, for example. But—and there is always a "but"—when writing computer code, which will be set in typewriter type, we may wish to have better control over the situation, since the "typewriter" font could also be used for commercial correspondence. In the latter case, of course, we would want the words to be hyphenated. Thus inhibiting hyphenation must be done not at the level of the font's configuration but at the level of the LaTeX commands used in the document. In those languages that do not employ hyphenation, it is inhibited in the linguistic configuration (for example, we obtain the same result by writing \language=99) and is independent of the font being used.

Finally, for those with a flair for surgical procedures, we can use the last argument of the \Declare-FontFamily and \DeclareFontShape commands to modify some of the font's internal parameters. By writing \fontdimen5\font=2pt, we designate that parameter number 5 of the font (or of all the fonts in the family) assume the value of 2 points. We can have up to 50 global parameters in an ordinary TₑX font, but in most cases we use only the first seven. Here is what they represent:

- \fontdimen1 specifies the slant, expressed by the tangent of the angle; in other words, the horizontal displacement at a height of 1 point. This value is used when TₑX places accents over letters, so that the accents will be centered over the letters' axes—axes that, in this case, are oblique.

- \fontdimen2 specifies the ideal interword space, i.e., the interword space used in the font in question when justification does not impose any constraints.

- \fontdimen3 specifies the maximum stretch allowed for the interword space.

- \fontdimen4 specifies the maximum shrink allowed for the interword space.

- \fontdimen5 specifies the height of the short letters (lowercase letters with no ascenders or descenders). This information is used by TₑX to place accents on letters. Suppose, for example, that the \fontdimen5 of a font is x and that we wish to place an accent over a letter of height $x' > x$. We shall thus have to move the accent upward by $x' - x$. We have direct and elegant access to this parameter through the unit of measure ex.

- \fontdimen6 specifies the size of the font's em. We have access to it through the unit em.

- \fontdimen7 applies primarily to the English and German typographic traditions. In these traditions, it consists of increasing the space that follows a sentence-final punctuation mark. When more space is left after the final punctuation mark, the reader's eye can more easily see where each sentence begins and can more easily distinguish periods used in abbreviations, which are not followed by extra whitespace. Since this practice is not observed in France, TₑX uses the name \frenchspacing for the command that disables it.

Thus by writing \fontdimen2=2.5pt, we set the font's "natural" interword space to 2.5 points. Note that we can also use \fontdimen on the right-hand side of an expression. For example, by writing

```
\DeclareFontShape{T1}{timesten}{m}{n}{ <-> timesten }{
    \fontdimen2\font=.8\fontdimen2\font
    \fontdimen3\font=.8\fontdimen3\font
    \fontdimen4\font=.8\fontdimen4\font
}
```

we will set our type in *Times Ten* 20 percent more tightly than usual with regard to the regular interword space and to the stretching and shrinking thereof.

Once again, we advise the reader who is thinking of modifying these parameters, which are of vital importance to the font, to do so within the font itself (see §B.1) or by creating a virtual font (see §B.3). Here is an example of the trap that awaits sorcerers' apprentices: TEX loads a TFM font only once. If you write

```
\DeclareFontShape{T1}{timesten}{m}{n}{ <-> timesten }{}
\DeclareFontShape{T1}{timesten}{c}{n}{ <-> timesten }{
    \fontdimen2\font=.8\fontdimen2\font
    \fontdimen3\font=.8\fontdimen3\font
    \fontdimen4\font=.8\fontdimen4\font
}
```

and then try to use the "weight/set-width" settings m and c defined above in a single document, the c one will come out exactly as the m one—for the simple reason that the underlying TFM font is the same, and thus TEX loads it *only once*. The values of the parameters can be modified only at the very moment when the font is loaded; it is not possible to change them afterwards.

It is time to leave this gray zone and continue our tour of the use of fonts in TEX by descending one level lower than LATEX and NFSS—to the level of the \font primitive, which is responsible for loading TFM fonts in TEX.

The Low Level: TEX and DVI

The primitives for selecting fonts

By now we have already spoken of the TFM files many times. Here is the font-metric information contained in a TFM file:

- Each glyph's *width*.

- Each glyph's *height*.

- Each glyph's *depth*, which is the vertical dimension of the part located below the glyph's baseline.

- Each glyph's *italic correction*, which is the amount of space to add when the glyph is followed, for example, by a right closing parenthesis. This correction actually applies only to certain italic letters with ascenders, such as *f*: for '*f*)' looks better than '*f)*', and the latter would inevitably result in the absence of the correction because the glyphs are set in two different fonts and therefore no automatic kerning can be performed to move them apart.

- A certain amount of global information, including the \fontdimen settings that we saw in the previous section.

- The kerning pairs.

- The automatic ligatures, such as 'fi', 'fl', etc.

Note that these data, including the "width", the "height", the "depth", and the "italic correction", are not connected in any way to actual glyphs (i.e., images of characters, made up of contours or pixels). The object that TEX manipulates is merely a box whose sides have the stated dimensions. The actual image of the character, which is unavailable to TEX but will be placed within this box when the DVI file is converted to PostScript (or another format), may lie within this box, extend beyond it, or even be outside it altogether. In reality, all of these cases occur: glyphs neatly contained within their boxes, glyphs whose boxes are reduced to a single point (the point of origin of the glyphs), boxes with nonzero dimensions that nonetheless do not contain a glyph, boxes reduced to a point that contain no glyph...

The NFSS specification

```
\DeclareFontShape{T1}{timesten}{m}{n}{ <-> timesten }{}
```

assumes the existence of a TFM file named timesten.tfm somewhere on the disk where TEX can find it.[10] In the case of METAFONT fonts, when the TFM file with the specified name is missing, TEX is capable of launching METAFONT to generate the font and, in the same stroke, the missing TFM file.

The TEX primitive that loads a TFM file is \font. It can be used in three different ways:

```
\font\myfontA=timesten
\font\myfontB=timesten at 12pt
\font\myfontC=timesten scaled 1200
```

To understand the differences among these three approaches, we need some extra information. In every TFM file, the *optical size* of the font is specified. In the first line of our example, we are using the font at an actual size equal to the optical size. Thus, if the font was designed to be used at an actual size of 10 points (as the name *Times Ten* suggests), TEX will use it at that size. All that we have to do is write

```
{\myfontA Hello}
```

so that this font will be used at its default size, which corresponds to the the optical size.

In the second line, we have explicitly requested a specific actual size. TEX will divide the requested actual size by the optical size and will use their quotient as a stretching or shrinking factor.

In the third line, we have expliticly specified a stretching or shrinking factor. TEX will therefore apply this factor to the optical size to obtain the actual size.

---

[10] On most current TEX systems, the paths to the directories that may contain TFM files are found in a file named texmf.cnf. This file contains the definitions of the environment variables TFMFONTS (the directories containing TFM files) and OFMFONTS (the directories containing OFM files, which are extended TFM files used by Ω), as well as VFFONTS and OVFFONTS, which *dvips* and *odvips* use to find virtual fonts.

The DVI file

After the blizzard of LaTeX and TeX commands that we have just seen, now we shall observe the total calm that reigns in a DVI file. Only the essentials are found there: the locations of glyphs, black boxes (for drawing lines, for example), "specials" (i.e., pockets of code in other languages, such as the PostScript language or the HTML markup system). How is the data on fonts stored in a DVI file? Through the use of two commands:

- FONTDEF, followed by five parameters:
    - the internal number for the font, which will be used to select it as the active font;
    - a checksum, which must match the one found in the TFM file (see §B.1);
    - the actual size, expressed in sp units, which are integer multiples of $1/2^{16}$ of an American printer's point. Not for nothing did Knuth decide to use this *very small* unit of length: he wished to ensure that all the measurements in a DVI file would be performed in integer arithmetic, with no rounding at all;[11]
    - the optical size, also expressed in sp units;
    - the name of the TFM file, without the .tfm extension.

The FONTDEF defines a font and associates it with a number. A font must be defined before it is first used. All of the font definitions are repeated in the DVI file's postamble (the part between the last typeset page and the end of the file).

- FONT, followed by the font's internal number. This command selects as the active font the one that bears this number. The font so selected will be used for all glyphs to follow, until the active font is changed again.

By way of example, here is the DVI code for the definition and choice of the font in which "the text that you are currently reading" is set:

```
<fontdef id="14" checksum="20786036" size="655360"
    designsize="655360" name="T1lemondemn"/>
<font id="14"/>
<set>the</set>
```

---

[11] And that, incidentally, was one of the greatest difficulties in converting DVI files to PostScript. When we "draw" the vertical bars in a table such as the following:

A	B
C	D

the alignment of these bars, one for each line, does not pose a problem in a DVI file, since its extreme precision makes an error of 1 sp invisible to the naked eye. But when we convert the file to PostScript, the basic unit becomes the PostScript point; thus we are working with numbers containing three or four decimal places, and rounding is unavoidable. But how, then, can we be sure that the vertical bar for each line will be joined correctly with the one in the line above it? To ensure correct alignment, *dvips* analyzes the file and tracks down alignments of this type (an approach much like that of *hinting* fonts), then adjusts the rounding for consistency.

```
<right dim="167112"/>
<set>te</set>
<right dim="-"/>
<set>xt</set>
<right dim="167112"/>
<set>tha</set>
<right dim="-"/>
<set>t</set>
<right dim="167112"/>
<set>y</set>
<right dim="-"/>
<set>ou</set>
<right dim="167112"/>
<set>ar</set>
<right dim="-"/>
<set>e</set>
<right dim="167112"/>
<set>curr</set>
<right dim="-"/>
<set>ently</set>
<right dim="167112"/>
<set>r</set>
<right dim="-"/>
<set>eading</set>
```

Since DVI is a binary format, we have decided to present the preceding block of text in an XML representation. This format, known as DVX, can be obtained by tools called *dvi2dvx* and *dvx2dvi* [157]. In the example, we are using a font whose TFM file is named T1lemondemn.tfm (explanation: T1 is the encoding; lemonde [= *Le Monde Livre*], the name of the font; m, the weight; n, the style), at an actual size of 10 (655,360 being 10 times 2^{16}) and also at an optical size of 10. To make sure that the TFM file has not been corrupted, we also include this file's checksum: 20,786,036. This font has the internal number 18, and we shall use it right away by making it the active font. The set commands that follow set the strings "the", "te", "xt", "tha", "t", "y", "ou", "ar", "e", "curr", "ently", "r", "eading". Between each pair of strings, there is a right command, which causes a move to the right (or to the left, if negative), also expressed in sp units. Some of these offsets are for word spaces; others are for kerning. For example, between "te" and "xt" there is an offset of −19,657 sp, or 0.3 American printer's points, to the left. We can also see that the word spaces are all *exactly* 167,112 sp, or 2.55 points, which shows the extreme rigor with which T_EX sets type.

What can we conclude from this section? That the DVI file contains, all in all, very little information on the fonts that it uses: a TFM filename, an actual size, and an optical size. And the software that will process the DVI file is not even required to consult the TFM file, because even the kerning pairs have already been explicitly applied in the DVI file.[12] All that remains is to replace the `<set>` commands with actual glyphs.

"*Après-TEX*": *Confronting the Real World*

It is often said that TEX lives in an ivory tower: the DVI file contains only one slight reference to the name of a file in TFM, a format used by TEX alone. We are far removed from the jungle of fonts in PostScript, TrueType, OpenType, Speedo, Intellifont, and other formats. Yet to come to the end of the process of document production, we do have to pass through this jungle. The bold spirit that will lead the way is none other than *dvips* (and its near cousin *odvips*, which is part of the Ω distribution).

Accordingly, the role of *dvips* is to read the DVI file, find for each TFM file (after checking one or more configuration files) the bitmap font generated by METAFONT or the PostScript font that corresponds to it, and finally write out a PostScript file that contains all the required fonts or, if they reside on the printer, references to them.

We shall first consider how *dvips* processes METAFONT fonts and then consider how it handles PostScript fonts.

Automatic generation of bitmap fonts from METAFONT *source code*

We have already mentioned METAFONT, the companion to TEX. It is a programming language devoted to font creation that we shall describe more precisely in Appendix F. The most important application of METAFONT has been the *Computer Modern* family of fonts, which Knuth developed together with TEX and which remains TEX's default font family. These fonts' filenames follow strict rules: they consist of an abbreviation of the name of the family, the style, the weight, and an optical size. For example, `cmr10` is the font *Computer Modern Roman* at 10 points, `cmitt12` is the 12-point italic typewriter font, `cmbxsl17` is 17-point bold slanted, etc.

To change from one font to another, one need only change the values of some 62 parameters, which are very clearly explained in [219], a very special book: in its 588 pages, it presents the entire source code, with comments, for the *Computer Modern* fonts, together with images of their glyphs. While the possible combinations are practically unlimited, Knuth decided to include only 75 basic fonts in the original distribution of TEX. Users, however, are perfectly free to create their own new fonts by modifying the values of the parameters.

But even the modification of these parameters to create new combinations of style, weight, set-width, and size requires a certain basic knowledge of METAFONT, and not everyone is willing to delve into it. Enter John Sauter [311], who rewrote the code in which the METAFONT parameters are defined so that now one can tell METAFONT that one wishes to generate one or another font not supplied by Knuth, simply by stating that font's name.

---

[12] Nevertheless, in the case of sophisticated DVI drivers access to TFM files is necessary, not because of kerning pairs, but to obtain the dimensions of glyph boxes (which are not included in the DVI file).

In addition to Sauter's system, most TEX and Ω distributions are equipped with a manager of searches and file generation that is called *kpathsea* (= *Karl [Berry]'s Path Search* [78]). This system is said to speed up searches for files done by all of the tools of the TEX world (including TEX, Ω, and *dvips*) and to generate files on demand. To generate files, *kpathsea* has three utilities at its disposal:

- *mktextfm*, which generates a missing TFM file. This utility is called by TEX and Ω when they cannot find a TFM file for a font used in the document.

- *mktexmf*, which generates the METAFONT source file corresponding to the META-FONT used in the document if this font does not already exist.

- *mktexpk*, which generates a bitmap font from the corresponding METAFONT source files.

A few words of explanation: PK (for "packaged") is TEX's bitmap font format[13] (§A.5.3). These tools combine in the following manner. When TEX encounters a declaration for the font foo and cannot find a corresponding TFM file, it launches *mktextfm*. This program searches the disk for a file named foo.mf, whose extension, .mf, is used for META-FONT files. If it finds this file, it launches METAFONT and generates the missing TFM file. If it cannot find the file, it launches *mktexmf* in an attempt to generate foo.mf from generic METAFONT files, and then it launches METAFONT with foo.mf to generate the missing TFM file. If all these steps fail, TEX uses a default font (*Computer Modern Roman*).

The same goes for *dvips*: if a PK font is missing, *dvips* launches *mktexpk* in order to generate it, and *mktexpk* may in turn launch *mktexmf* to generate the METAFONT source code for the missing font.[14]

The three *mktex** tools are shell scripts. Only *mktexpk* has a handful of command-line options, which are listed below:

- --dpi followed by an integer: the font's "resolution"

- --bdpi followed by an integer: the font's "base resolution"

- --mag followed by a rational number: the magnification factor, by default 1.0

- --mfmode followed by a keyword: the "METAFONT mode"

- --destdir followed by a pathname: the directory into which the PK files will be placed

---

[13] In fact, and for historical reasons, to obtain a PK font one must first go through another bitmap font format, called GF (for "generic font", §A.5.2). Converting from GF to PK involves nothing but compressing the data. The tool that converts GF files to PK is called *gftopk*. A tool to do the opposite, *pktogf*, exists for use in debugging.

[14] Note that *mktexpk* will even try to convert PostScript Type 1 fonts and TrueType fonts to bitmap format, if it has been properly configured. But this solution is really less than optimal, as the bitmap format is compatible with file formats such as PDF only to a very limited extent.

To understand what the first four of these parameters mean, one must enter into the logic of METAFONT. First of all, let us recall that unlike vector fonts (PostScript Type 1, TrueType, OpenType), which are rasterized by the printer, bitmap fonts are "ready for use". Thus they have to be adapted to the needs of the printer; in other words, there must be as many versions of the same PK font as there are models of printers.

METAFONT makes use of the notion of "mode"—a certain number of parameters that describe the characteristics of a given printer. There are, for example, a mode ljfour that corresponds to the Hewlett Packard LaserJet 4 printer and a mode cx that corresponds to the Canon PostScript printers equipped with a drum that operate at 300 dots per inch. The keywords for the METAFONT modes are classified according to types of compatible printers and are stored in a file named modes.mf ([76] and [69, 70, 173]), which is regularly updated by Karl Berry.

The "base resolution" of the font is in fact the resolution of the printer. This information is also part of the printer's METAFONT mode; thus there is no need to specify it if one uses the --mode option. On the other hand, if one does not know the mode, *mktexpk* will attempt to use a generic mode based on the specified resolution.

The font's magnification factor is the quotient of the actual size and the optical size. Thus if one wishes to use *Computer Modern Roman* at 15 points (a size not supplied by Knuth and therefore not among the sizes available in the original TᴇX distribution), one can request the 12-point font magnified by 25 percent, simply by writing:

```
mktexpk --mag 1.25 cmr12
```

Note that this manipulation is not needed for the *Computer Modern* fonts because Sauter's "generic files" allow one to request cmr15 directly.

Finally, the "resolution" is the base resolution multiplied by the magnification factor. Thus the specifications "--bdpi 300 --mag 1.2" and "--dpi 360" are equivalent.

Let us review. If one finds a printer that is represented on the list of METAFONT modes, one can use --mode and --mag to obtain a bitmap font adapted to the printer and magnified appropriately. If the printer is not on the list, or if one cannot be bothered to look for it, one can merely state the printer's resolution by using --bdpi and --mag or even just -bdpi, which is the product of the two numbers.

Since Knuth, many other people have created METAFONT fonts, which can be found in TᴇX distributions and on the Web.

But let us return to the tool *mktexpk*. It attempts to generate missing fonts automatically. We have seen that when running this tool manually one needs a certain amount of information, in particular the printer's METAFONT mode or, at a minimum, its resolution. In its infinite discretion, *mktexpk* would not dream of asking us for this information; like a big boy, it looks up these values by itself in a configuration file. It is our responsibility to supply the correct values in the configuration file; else our hard copy will never come out right. This file is called mktex.opt and is usually kept in the configuration directory of the TᴇX distribution (/<somewhere>/TeX/texmf/web2c under Unix). Here are the lines of this file that concern us:

```
: ${MODE=ljfour}
: ${BDPI=600}
```

All that we have to do is to replace the values ljfour and 600 by those for our system (the METAFONT mode and the printer's resolution).

We close this section by stating that, despite the extreme beauty and elegance of the METAFONT language, we discourage the use of bitmap fonts in documents, unless, of course, the document in question is meant to be printed—and only to be printed. To those who wish to continue to use the *Computer Modern* fonts, we recommend switching to their PostScript Type 1 versions, in particular the *CM-Super* collection of Vladimir Volovich [341], which is a veritable tour de force, as it covers the TEX glyph encodings T1, TS1, T2A, T2B, and T2C, as well as the *Adobe Standard* encoding. We can only hope that METAFONT will be recast, in the near future, into a tool for creating PostScript Type 1 or TrueType fonts (see Appendix F).

The processing of PostScript fonts by dvips

Now that we have finished our tour of the world of bitmap fonts, let us return to the twenty-first century and see how to use *dvips* to produce PostScript code using PostScript fonts.

At first blush, we are living in the best of worlds, and we have only two tasks to complete in order to achieve our goal: (a) configure *dvips* to be aware of the correspondences between TFM fonts and these three types of fonts; (b) ensure that all of the required files are in the right places, i.e., in directories accessible to *dvips*.

In fact, reality is a trifle more complex.

A number of problems arise when these two worlds (TEX, on the one hand, and the PostScript fonts, on the other) come together. A typical problem is conflicting encodings. For acceptable typesetting in Western European languages, LATEX recommends the T1 font encoding. This encoding is specific to TEX; we have presented a diagram of it in Figure 9-4, on page 246. Since most PostScript Type 1 fonts are encoded in Adobe Standard (see Figure C-5, page 660), one of the two sides (TEX or the font) must be adapted so that a collaboration can occur. Another problem that can arise is the absence of certain glyphs. The Adobe Standard encoding does not contain any accented letters, a fact that makes it useless for typesetting in the French language. Accented glyphs usually do exist in a given font, but the encoding *hides* them. In other cases, the accented glyphs do not exist. What shall we do then?

We shall see two techniques that enable us to solve problems of this kind: *re-encoding* and *virtual fonts*.

When re-encoding is employed, the PostScript font will be used with an encoding other than its original one. Thus any accented glyphs that exist in the font will appear in the encoding, and in the positions in which TEX expects to find them (so as to simulate, for example, the T1 font encoding).

The technique of virtual fonts goes further than that. It involves saying to *dvips*: "If you find a glyph from this font in a DVI file, replace it with the handful of DVI commands that I have provided." The simplest case is replacing one glyph with another, either in the same font or in a different one. But in fact everything is possible: we can replace a glyph with thousands of commands, even with the contents of an entire page. Virtual fonts can also call one another: among the commands that will replace a glyph, there may be some that call for glyphs in other virtual fonts. Moreover, nothing at the level of DVI code distinguishes a glyph in a virtual font from a glyph in a "real" font. It is *dvips* that concludes that a font for which no TFM file is named in the configuration files for *dvips* is not a PostScript font. In that instance, two possibilities exist: either the font is a virtual font or it is a METAFONT that will be generated at the correct size, as we saw in the previous section.

The two approaches (conversion of encodings and virtual fonts) are complementary: a virtual font can do many things, but it cannot operate at the level of a PostScript font in order to make hidden glyphs appear, for example, or slant or stretch a font. Conversely, conversion of encodings can make hidden glyphs appear, but it can never, for example, combine accents with letters to yield accented letters.

In this section, we shall see how the configuration file for *dvips* is arranged and how to use virtual fonts. In the next section, we shall concern ourselves with the installation of PostScript fonts in a TEX (or Ω) system.

Configuring dvips

Configuring *dvips* thus involves informing it of the correspondence between TFM fonts (recognized by TEX and used in DVI files) and PostScript fonts. These data are stored in text files whose extension is .map (from the word *mapping*), the most widespread of which is psfonts.map. In these files, there is one line of text for each TFM file. This line contains the name of the TFM file, the PostScript name of the font,[15] possibly some PostScript code that will modify the font, and, finally, possible paths to the files containing the PostScript font, and any new encoding for the font.

Here is an example:

```
Bookman-Demi Bookman-Demi
```

This example illustrates the simplest case: a font recognized by TEX under the name Bookman-Demi (which presupposes the existence of the file Bookman-Demi.tfm), whose PostScript name is exactly the same. Since no path is specified to the PostScript font file or any other, it is implied that the font is "resident"; that is, a copy of the font exists on the printer's ROM, RAM or hard disk. If the printer already recognizes this font, there is no need to incorporate it again into the PostScript file generated by *dvips*.

Another example:

---

[15] Warning: do not mistake the *PostScript name*, which is an internal name for the PostScript font, and the *PostScript filename*, which is the name of the file containing the PostScript font (cf. §C.3.2).

```
TimesTenRomSC TimesTen-RomanSC  <TimesTenRomSC.pfa
TimesTenItaSC TimesTen-RomanSC " .167 SlantFont " <TimesTenRomSC.pfa
```

The first line of this example illustrates the most typical case: TEX recognizes this font under the name of `TimesTenRomSC` (which, by the way, is a PostScript name abbreviated according to Adobe's rules). Its PostScript name is slightly longer (and more descriptive): "TimesTen-RomanSC", where "SC" means "small capitals". Thus it contains the small capitals for the font *Times Ten*. Our font is stored on disk in the file `TimesTenRomSC.pfa`, whose contents will be embedded in the PostScript file generated by *dvips*. We have not given an explicit path to this file; *dvips* will search for it in the default directories for PostScript fonts.[16]

The line below is there to fill a gap in the *Adobe Times Ten* family of PostScript fonts: italic small capitals do not exist in this font. Two things have been changed: the name of the TFM file (on the one hand, this font is slanted; on the other hand, most of the glyphs require an italic correction), and the part that precedes the name of the PostScript font. This extra part consists of the PostScript code needed to give all the glyphs in the font a slant of 0.167 (i.e., an angle of $\phi = 9.48$ degrees, whose tangent is 0.167). We can see that the same PostScript file is employed; only when this font is used by the printer will the glyphs be artificially slanted.

In addition to `SlantFont`, two other keywords are available to us: `ExtendFont`, which stretches or compresses all the glyphs in a font horizontally, and `ReEncodeFont`, which re-encodes the font. Thus, by writing

```
TimesTenRomNarrow TimesTen-Roman " 0.87 ExtendFont " <TimesTenRom.pfa
```

we obtain a font whose set-width is compressed by 13 percent. Now let us see an example of conversion of the encoding:

```
uver8r VendomeT-Regu " TeXBase1Encoding ReEncodeFont " <[8r.enc <uver8a.pfb
```

Here we are using a font known to TEX under the cryptic name `uver8r`. Its PostScript name is `VendomeT-Regu`; behind this technical name is hidden the splendid font *Vendôme*, designed in 1952 by François Ganeau for Fonderie Olive in Marseille [39] and widely used in France in the 1950s and 1960s. Here we have decided to convert the font to use the T1 encoding. We request this conversion with the command `ReEncodeFont`, which takes the parameter `TeXBase1Encoding`. (PostScript is a programming language that uses reverse Polish notation: parameters are written before the commands that use them.) Since this encoding is certainly not recognized by the PostScript printer, we include the file `8r.enc`, which contains its definition.[17] Finally, we include the file `uver8a.pfb`, which

---

[16] These directories are indicated in the global configuration file of the TEX distribution (`texmf.cnf`), in the environment variable T1FONTS.

[17] The bracket in `<[8r.enc` indicates to *dvips* that the file that it has encountered is not yet the font file but rather an auxiliary file, in this case a file containing an encoding. This bracket is not required, but it can be useful in some cases for removing ambiguities.

contains the font's PostScript data. This time we have a PFB file, thus a binary file. It will be converted by *dvips* to PFA format so that it can be embedded in the PostScript code that is generated.

The reader will no doubt be surprised that we have not given any example of an encoding file other than 8r.enc. For instance, why is there no encoding file for obtaining the T2A or T2B or T3 or T4 glyph encoding? The answer is that we do not live in an ideal world. Fonts containing glyphs of these kinds usually do not follow any standard for naming glyphs. If the names of the glyphs are not the same from one PostScript Type 1 font to another, a given encoding file will in practice be useful for only a single font. Thus it is better to write an encoding file specifically for that font, on a case-by-case basis. Or, better yet, one can regularize the names of the glyphs, which requires changing the fonts themselves. We shall discuss this latter possibility in Chapter 12.

Here, then, are the contents of the .map file. But how does dvips know which .map files it is to read? The names of these files are found in the configuration files for *dvips*. But which configuration files are these? The approach to this question taken by *dvips* is quite original: instead of preserving the same extension and changing the filename, it does just the opposite. Thus we have a number of files,[18] all of them named "config", but with different extensions: config.cm, config.cm-super, config.belleek, etc. Among them, the file config.ps is the default configuration file for *dvips*. The others are read at the user's request, which is made through the command-line option -P of *dvips*. One writes:

```
dvips -P foo ...
```

to instruct *dvips* to read the configuration file config.foo.

Within these configuration files, we can use the following syntax to indicate the names of the .map files to be examined:

```
p /usr/TeX/texmf/dvips/config/psfonts.map
p +/home/yannis/texmf/config/yhpsfonts.map
```

Here the + indicates that the file in question will be read after the preceding file, and in addition to it. Note that if several lines of the .map file refer to the same TFM font, only the last of them will be retained. Thus the order of the files in the config.* file is important, as it allows us to install new fonts even if there is a risk that they may already be defined in the existing configuration files; indeed, by simply adding another configuration file after those that appear by default, we can force our new definitions to replace any existing ones.

In this section we have examined the possibilities for configuring *dvips* for use with PostScript fonts. While the procedure that *dvips* uses to find fonts may appear very complex, there is no reason for us to feel discouraged: configuring *dvips* is itself quite

---

[18] The location of these files is governed by the environment variable TEXCONFIG of the global configuration file of the TEX distribution, texmf.cnf.

simple. In broad strokes, it involves inserting into a configuration file as many lines as there are fonts, each line being built up from the name of a TFM file, the internal name of the target font, and that font's filename.

Next, we shall head off in a different direction, still with the goal of making TFM fonts and "real-world" fonts work together. Instead of modifying the latter, we shall create a new type of font that will function as an intermediary between the two formats. It will be called a *virtual font*.

Virtual fonts

The concept of virtual fonts [220, 180] is quite simple: where TEX sees nothing but a single glyph, the virtual font will generate a certain number of DVI commands, which may in turn contain glyphs from virtual fonts and may therefore lead to the production of new DVI commands, and so forth. Most of the time we use virtual fonts to convert fonts to a new encoding or to combine letters and accents in order to generate accented letters.

In a DVI file, the process for replacing glyphs from virtual fonts with the corresponding DVI commands in an iterative manner, until no more virtual fonts are in use, is called *devirtualization*. Devirtualization is carried out internally by *dvips*, but we can also perform it with an external tool, named *dvicopy* (or *odvicopy*, in the Ω distribution).

The format for virtual fonts is called Virtual Font (VF). In Appendix §B.3, the reader will find a more rigorous description of this font format. For every virtual font, there must also exist a corresponding TFM file; this is the file that makes it visible to TEX.

But let us return to the VF file. A VF file contains some data beyond those found in TFM files, specifically two types of data: global data (*definitions* of the base fonts being used) and the DVI commands that make up each virtual glyph:

- The *choices of active font*.

- *Push* and *pop* operations applied to coordinates. In a DVI file, we can keep track of the current position so that we can easily return to it. An example: when setting lines, we can record the coordinates of the beginning of the line by pushing them onto a stack; later, when we wish to move to the next line, we can go back to the same place (by popping the coordinates off the stack), and then all that we have to do is move downward.

- Horizontal and vertical *movement*.

- *Black boxes*, which are used for drawing lines.

- *Specials*, which are pockets of code in a format other than DVI (such as PostScript or HTML code).

By comparing these operations to the commands of the DVI file format, we observe that the two are practically identical: anything that can be described in a DVI file (other than the change of pages) can also be found in the description of a glyph in a virtual font and vice versa.

Virtual fonts can be used in a large number of situations:

- The PostScript font that we wish to use is not in the correct encoding: we will create a virtual font with the desired encoding whose glyphs will be references to the positions of the glyphs in the PostScript font.

- A handful of accented letters, be they letters from the languages of Western Europe (which are found in almost all fonts) or from those of Eastern Europe (which are much less commonly found, typically in fonts labeled "CE", such as *Monotype Bookman OldStyle CE*, for example), are missing from the font that we wish to use. The glyphs in the virtual font will be combinations of letters and accents placed in the correct locations.

- In LATEX, when we call for small capitals, TEX expects to find the small capitals, the full capitals, and the punctuation marks all in the same font. But PostScript fonts are not always so arranged. For instance, the "Expert" fonts contain the small capitals and a few other special glyphs, but no full capitals or punctuation marks. The virtual font will be a merger of small capitals from the "Expert" font and other glyphs drawn from the regular font.

- We wish to use old-style figures (of varying height) rather than the modern forms (of uniform height). Often the glyphs for these figures are found in an "Expert" font. Once again, the virtual font will be a copy of the normal font in which the figures will be replaced with those from the "Expert" font.

- We wish to adjust the balance between the uppercase and lowercase letters by enlarging the latter. The virtual font will be made by merging one copy of the original font (containing everything but the lowercase letters) and another copy of the same font with a different magnification factor (for the lowercase letters).

- We wish to obtain *letterspaced* fonts, i.e., those with more space between the letters— but only between letters, not between letters and punctuation marks, etc. In addition, this space must take into account the kerning that the letters in question would have if they were not letterspaced. The virtual font will be a copy of the regular font with a large number of additional kerning pairs for the various combinations of letters.

- We would like to apply PostScript transformations and special effects to the glyphs, such as by coloring them or subjecting them to rotations, translations, or scaling. The virtual font will contain PostScript code for each glyph.

- And many other situations can be imagined.

The astute reader may make the following observation: everything described above can also be done at the level of TEX through the use of commands; after all, TEX is a programming language, thus we can do anything with it. Why, then, should we resort to a construct as peculiar as a virtual font?

The justification for the utility of virtual fonts is based on a special characteristic of the way that TEX operates. Specifically, there are three operations that TEX can carry out only when it is setting type *with just one font*. These operations are *kerning*, the formation of *ligatures*, and *hyphenation*. In order to be able to kern characters, form ligatures, or hyphenate words between two glyphs, those glyphs must belong to the same font; furthermore, no TEX command may come between them.

Thus, in TEX, we can always form any combination of a letter and an accent mark, whether or not that combination actually occurs in any of the world's languages. To do so, we use a primitive by the name of \accent, which takes two arguments: the accent and the letter to which the accent is to be applied. But if we use this primitive in a word, there is no longer any way to perform kerning, form ligatures, or hyphenate words. This situation in TEX is unacceptable.

We can deceive TEX by using a virtual font. We give TEX glyphs that look perfectly normal from its point of view, and it will set them as usual, with all the required kerning, ligatures, and word divisions. Then *dvips* comes along and sees that the glyphs in question must be replaced in the DVI file by combinations of glyphs that will produce the desired effect. The complexity of the virtual fonts is irrelevant: TEX has already finished setting the type, the words are attractively kerned, and the lines are beautifully divided. And TEX did all that without even knowing that the glyphs that it was manipulating would generate far more DVI code than TEX itself!

Virtual fonts and Acrobat

In the previous section, we presented a fairy-tale description of virtual fonts. We are not going to debate the existence of Santa Claus, but one thing is certain: the uses of virtual fonts have their limits as well. The problem is that everything in TEX was designed from the perspective of hard copy, or of noninteractive output to a screen. That makes sense, since in 1990, when Knuth published his virtual fonts, neither Acrobat nor the Web yet existed.

Thus when, using a virtual font, we write an accented letter by placing an accent over the letter, what is important is the visual result, and it is indeed impeccable. But when DVI is converted to PostScript, *dvips* devirtualizes the code; thus the accented letter ceases to exist. In its place we find separate PostScript glyphs for the letter and for the accent. That does not pose a problem to the PostScript printer, or even to *Acrobat Distiller* or *ps2pdf* when they convert the PostScript code to PDF.

The problems begin when Acrobat is used. For Acrobat offers a number of interesting features: the ability to select blocks of text and copy them onto the clipboard, the ability to search for strings in a PDF document, full-text indexing of PDF documents, Unicode support. But how can we identify an accented letter if in reality it consists of nothing but an "accent" character placed over the glyph for a "letter" character?

Recall that the method (cf. C.3.3) used by Acrobat Distiller to associate Unicode characters with the glyphs that it finds in PostScript files is as follows: it examines the PostScript name for the glyph; if this name is of the form uni*HHHH*, where *HHHH* is a hexadecimal number, it matches the glyph to Unicode character 0x*HHHH*; otherwise, it checks a table of correspondences between glyph names and Unicode characters that was developed by Adobe. If it cannot find the glyph's name in this table, the process fails.

If we are to obtain a good result, there must be only one glyph per Unicode character, and this glyph must bear its correct name in the PostScript font. For example, to obtain an 'á' in a PDF file, which corresponds to the Unicode character 0x00E1 LATIN SMALL LETTER A ACUTE, we must use a single glyph, named "aacute". But when this glyph is not *one* but *two*, therefore a composite of the glyph 'a' and a glyph often called "acute", there is no way for Acrobat Distiller or *ps2pdf* to associate it with the correct Unicode character. If we use the mouse in Acrobat to copy a word containing this letter, we will obtain, at best, an 'a' followed by an acute accent; at worst, we will obtain some haphazard characters.

Among the examples of the use of virtual fonts that we presented in the previous section, some of them present problems of this type. Let us review them, one by one, and check their compatibility with conversion to PDF:

- *The PostScript Type 1 font that we wish to use is not in the correct encoding, and we plan to remap its glyphs.* No problem arises, but we must nonetheless make sure that the PostScript glyphs obtained have the correct names.

- *A handful of accented letters are missing from the font that we wish to use... ; the glyphs in the virtual font will be combinations of letters and accents correctly placed.* Avoid this approach! The composite glyphs will under no circumstances be recognized by Acrobat as Unicode characters. Use this approach only when no *decomposable* Unicode character corresponds to this combination of a letter and an accent. And even in this case, be careful (a) to place the accent after the letter in the virtual font, since that is the convention in Unicode (*combining* characters occur after base characters) and (b) to make sure that the name of the glyph for the accent corresponds to the Unicode character in the table of combining characters (see page 127).

- *The "Expert" fonts (in the Adobe Expert encoding; see Figure C-6, page 660) contain the small capitals and a few other special glyphs, but not the full capitals or the punctuation marks.* Yes, but handle with care, for the glyphs for the small capitals in the "Expert" font have different names. For instance, 'A' has the glyph name Asmall. Because of this particularity, the correspondence between glyph names and Unicode characters is very bad.

- *We wish to use old-style figures (of varying height) rather than the modern forms (of uniform height).* Same problem as above, since the old-style figures have glyph names such as oneoldstyle.

- *We wish to adjust the balance between the uppercase and lowercase letters by enlarging the latter.* No problem.

- *We wish to obtain* letterspaced *fonts, i.e., fonts with more space between the letters.* Handle with care, as no distinction between offsets corresponding to interword spaces and offsets resulting from kerning is made in a DVI file. Acrobat uses a threshold beyond which an offset is considered to be a space (and thus corresponds to the Unicode character SPACE) and beneath which an offset is regarded as a kern (no Unicode character). That works very well under ordinary conditions, but we may exceed the threshold if we add too much letterspacing, and *Acrobat* will then insert spaces between the Unicode characters of the string when it is copied.

- *We would like to apply PostScript transformations and special effects to the glyphs.* In principle that should not create any difficulties, since Acrobat Distiller should correctly digest the PostScript code. All the same, you had better test it first.

We shall return to this subject when we discuss the editing and modifying of virtual fonts (page 285).

Installing Fonts for T_EX

In the previous section, we described font management under T_EX at every level: the user level; the level of T_EX and DVI; and the level of PostScript. At this point, we shall assume that we have purchased, or downloaded from the network, some fonts that we would like to use with T_EX. If they are METAFONT fonts, we need only place them in a location where METAFONT can find them, launch *mktexlsr* so that the T_EX system knows they are there, and the *mktexpf* and *mktexmf* scripts will do everything else; there is nothing more to say on this subject. Therefore, we shall assume that we are dealing with PostScript fonts.

To adapt them for use with T_EX, we have to work at the three levels that we just mentioned:

- At the L^AT_EX level, we have to provide one (or more) NFSS font family name(s) to the new fonts and prepare one (or more) FD file(s).

- At the T_EX/DVI level, we have to prepare TFM files for the new fonts, in both their original encoding and an encoding that T_EX can use, such as T1.

- At the PostScript level, we have to prepare virtual fonts that will make the connection between the TFM files in the T_EX encoding and the TFM files in the original encoding. We must also update the configuration file for *dvips*, possibly with commands for converting between encodings.

Let us be a little more practical. We are starting from the assumption that we have at our disposal some PFB/PFA files (PostScript Type 1) and AFM files (PostScript Type 1 font metrics) files, that we would like to adapt for use with T_EX or Ω. Thus we must produce FD, TFM, and VF files and update the configuration file for *dvips*.

We shall consider two tools that will enable us to carry out these operations. The first of them, *afm2tfm*, is a simple and rapid executable tool suitable for use in ordinary cases. Its benefits are its speed and ease of use. It generates TFM and VF files directly, along with the line of code to include in the *dvips* configuration file.

The second tool, *fontinst*, is the Rolls-Royce of tools for installing PostScript fonts. It generates PL and VPL files (i.e., human-readable versions of TFM and VF files; see Appendix B) and even FD files. It is written in TEX and can therefore be used on any platform on which TEX runs. It offers a large number of TEX commands that make it possible to configure the adaptation of fonts for use with TEX in a very precise manner.

In the examples that illustrate the use of these two tools in the following sections, we shall use *Monotype Centaur*, a font designed in 1915 by Bruce Rogers [228, p. 62] and considered by many people to be one of the most beautiful fonts of the twentieth century. We shall assume that we have just bought this font family and that we have the following AFM files:

```
CentaurMT.afm
CentaurMT-Italic.afm
CentaurMT-Bold.afm
CentaurMT-BoldItalic.afm
CentaurExpertMT.afm
CentaurExpertMT-Italic.afm
CentaurExpertMT-Bold.afm
CentaurExpertMT-BoldItalic.afm
```

and the following PFB files:

```
CentaMT.pfb
CentaMTIta.pfb
CentaMTBol.pfb
CentaMTBolIta.pfb
CentaExpMT.pfb
CentaExpMTIta.pfb
CentaExpMTBol.pfb
CentaExpMTBolIta.pfb
```

The "Expert" roman font CentaExpMT.pfb contains—among the glyphs of interest to us—the small capitals and the ligatures 'ff', 'ffi', etc. The other "Expert" fonts contain nothing but ligatures.

The Tool afm2tfm

The program *afm2tfm* comes with the *dvips* distribution. Its purpose is to read an AFM file and possibly one or two font encoding files, and then to generate a TFM file and possibly a VPL file (the human-readable version of a VF file; see Appendix B).

Suppose that we have the AFM file CentaurMT.afm and wish to produce from it a virtual font named t1centaurmn.vpl, in the T1 encoding. To do so, we need only write:

```
afm2tfm CentaurMT.afm -v t1centaurmn.vpl -T EC.enc
```

In the code shown above, EC.enc is a file, provided in the *dvips* distribution, that describes the T1 font encoding. The -T option indicates that we will need a virtual font in addition to a reencoded version of the PostScript font in order to obtain the desired result. Once the application is launched, *afm2tfm* writes the following lines to the console:

```
CentaurMT CentaurMT " ECEncoding ReEncodeFont " <EC.enc
```

where the second entry is the PostScript name of the font. This is the line that will have to be added to the *dvips* configuration file by appending, if necessary, an instruction to embed the PFB file in the PostScript code produced by *dvips*:

```
CentaurMT CentaurMT " ECEncoding ReEncodeFont " <[EC.enc <CentaMT.pfb
```

What are the actual steps needed to adapt a PostScript font family for use with TEX? Suppose that we begin with the following AFM files (which correspond to the *Monotype Centaur* family; the "Expert" fonts are omitted in this example):

```
CentaurMT.afm
CentaurMT-Italic.afm
CentaurMT-Bold.afm
CentaurMT-BoldItalic.afm
```

We must select an encoding and an NFSS family name. For this example, let us take the T1 encoding, which is the encoding most suited to the Western European languages, and use centaur as the family name. It will be sensible to name the virtual fonts that we shall produce T1centaur*.vpl, in which we will replace the asterisk with mn, mit, bxn, or bxit, thus using the NFSS codes for weight and style. Thus we must run *afm2tfm* four times, as shown below:

```
afm2tfm CentaurMT.afm -v T1centaurmn.vpl -T EC.enc
afm2tfm CentaurMT-Italic.afm -v T1centaurmit.vpl -T EC.enc
afm2tfm CentaurMT-Bold.afm -v T1centaurbxn.vpl -T EC.enc
afm2tfm CentaurMT-BoldItalic.afm -v T1centaurbxit.vpl -T EC.enc
```

It will generate the following four lines:

```
CentaurMT CentaurMT " ECEncoding ReEncodeFont " <EC.enc
CentaurMT-Italic CentaurMT-Italic " ECEncoding ReEncodeFont " <EC.enc
CentaurMT-Bold CentaurMT-Bold " ECEncoding ReEncodeFont " <EC.enc
CentaurMT-BoldItalic CentaurMT-BoldItalic " ECEncoding ReEncodeFont "
   <EC.enc
```

to which we will add instructions to include the PFB files, as follows:

```
CentaurMT CentaurMT " ECEncoding ReEncodeFont " <[EC.enc
    <CentaMT.pfb
CentaurMT-Italic CentaurMT-Italic " ECEncoding ReEncodeFont " <[EC.enc
    <CentaMTIta.pfb
CentaurMT-Bold CentaurMT-Bold " ECEncoding ReEncodeFont " <[EC.enc
    <CentaMTBol.pfb
CentaurMT-BoldItalic CentaurMT-BoldItalic " ECEncoding ReEncodeFont "
    <[EC.enc <CentaMTBolIta.pfb
```

Then we will add these lines at the end of psfonts.map or any other configuration file that *dvips* may use.

Next, we must convert the VPL files to VF format:

```
vptovf T1centaurmn
vptovf T1centaurmit
vptovf T1centaurbxn
vptovf T1centaurbxit
```

and copy the TFM and VF files to locations where TEX will be able to find them. Finally, we must prepare the FD file T1centaur.fd:

```
\DeclareFontFamily{T1}{centaur}{}
\DeclareFontShape{T1}{centaur}{m}{n}{ <-> T1centaurmn }{}
\DeclareFontShape{T1}{centaur}{m}{it}{ <-> T1centaurmit }{}
\DeclareFontShape{T1}{centaur}{bx}{n}{ <-> T1centaurbxn }{}
\DeclareFontShape{T1}{centaur}{bx}{it}{ <-> T1centaurbxit }{}
```

which we shall also place in a location where TEX can find it.

Basic Use of the Tool fontinst

In the previous section, we examined practically all the features of *afm2tfm*. We saw that it is a tool for adapting PostScript fonts for use with TEX that also supports re-encoding. The tool *fontinst*, by Alan Jeffrey [199], goes much further: it allows us to generate *arbitrarily configurable* VPL files from one *or more* AFM files.

For example, if among the fonts that we wish to adapt there are some that use the "Expert" encoding, we have no choice but to use *fontinst*, since *afm2tfm* is unable to read multiple AFM at the same time and merge the compiled data into a single VPL font.

fontinst is written in TEX, which means that it comes with a TEX file that "drives" the procedure and that TEX, when it reads this file, will begin to *read* the required AFM files and some auxiliary files of *fontinst* so that it can eventually write out the required PL, VPL, and FD files.

In this section, we shall consider only the basic commands of *fontinst*, since our aim is merely to install PostScript fonts directly for use with TEX. We shall return to *fontinst* later in this book (page 518), when we discuss ways to adapt fonts to meet the user's needs. Then we shall examine in detail the commands that make it possible to define virtual glyphs *one by one*.

Assume that we are in the same situation as in the previous section; that is, we have the following AFM files:

```
CentaurMT.afm
CentaurMT-Italic.afm
CentaurMT-Bold.afm
CentaurMT-BoldItalic.afm
```

But this time let us assume that we also have a few other *Monotype Centaur* fonts—the "Expert" fonts, shown here:

```
CentaurExpertMT.afm
CentaurExpertMT-Italic.afm
CentaurExpertMT-Bold.afm
CentaurExpertMT-BoldItalic.afm
```

To produce fonts in the T1 encoding, we will need to collect the glyphs from all the AFM files, and that will entail reencoding the PostScript fonts (since some glyphs may not appear in the encoding). The approach of *fontinst* is as follows:

- During the first pass, it will convert a number of AFM files. This conversion may be done for reasons of scaling, slanting the glyphs, or changing the encoding.

- Next, it will read the AFM files generated, in an order specified by the user.

- When it finds a glyph that it needs to process, it makes a note of the glyph and does not look for that glyph again.

- When it has processed all the AFM files, it generates a VPL file in the requested encoding, using all the glyphs that it has found.

The file that drives *fontinst* must have the following structure: first, a command to include the *fontinst* macros and a command to start the process:

```
\input fontinst.sty
\installfonts
```

At the end of the file, the corresponding closing commands are used:

```
\endinstallfonts
\end
```

According to the principles of NFSS, we need an FD file for each family of fonts that we are to create. Here is the command that creates this file; it is written in the file that drives *fontinst*:

```
\installfamily{T1}{centaur}{}
```

Now let us convert the fonts to the T1 encoding (which is not necessary for the "Expert" fonts, since these use a special encoding of their own and generally do not contain any hidden glyphs). We need new names for the AFM files to be generated; we shall simply append "T1" to the names that we have, yielding CentaMTT1, CentaMTItaT1, etc.

Here is the code that will convert our four fonts to the T1 encoding so that any glyphs that may be hidden by these fonts' encodings will be revealed:

```
\transformfont{CentaurMTT1}{\reencodefont{T1}{
    \fromafm{CentaurMT}}}
\transformfont{CentaurMT-ItalicT1}{\reencodefont{T1}{
    \fromafm{CentaurMT-Italic}}}
\transformfont{CentaurMT-BoldT1}{\reencodefont{T1}{
    \fromafm{CentaurMT-Bold}}}
\transformfont{CentaurMT-BoldItalicT1}{\reencodefont{T1}{
    \fromafm{CentaurMT-BoldItalic}}}
```

The other transformations that can be performed with *fontinst* are general scaling (\scalefont), scaling on the horizontal or vertical axis only (\xscalefont, \yscale-font), and slanting (\slantfont). In the example above, we read AFM files (\fromafm{ ...}), but we could also read PL files (\frompl{...}) or MTX files (\frommtx{...}).

But let us return to our example. Of course, we must notify *dvips* that a conversion of encodings has occurred, and that is the only task that *fontinst* does not perform—perhaps because *dvips* is not the only DVI driver and *fontinst* decided that if it could not produce code for every DVI driver it might as well not produce code for any of them. Thus the lines to append to the configuration file for *dvips* are the following:

```
CentaurMTT1 CentaurMT " ECEncoding ReEncodeFont "
    <EC.enc <CentaMT.pfb
CentaurMT-ItalicT1 TimesNewItalic " ECEncoding ReEncodeFont "
    <EC.enc <CentaMTIta.pfb
CentaurMT-BoldT1 TimesNewBold " ECEncoding ReEncodeFont "
    <EC.enc <CentaMTBol.pfb
CentaurMT-BoldItalicT1 TimesNewBoldItalic " ECEncoding ReEncodeFont "
    <EC.enc <CentaMTBolIta.pfb
```

Having obtained fonts in the desired encoding, we can now move on to the heart of the matter and install the NFSS fonts. To do so, we shall use the command \installfont, which takes the following arguments:

- The name of the VPL file generated

- A list of AFM, MTX, or PL files, to be read in this order (possibly followed by the keyword scaled and a magnification factor *à la* TEX, which is to say that it is multiplied by 1,000

- The *fontinst* encoding to use

- The NFSS attributes of the generated font: its NFSS encoding, family, weight, style, and size

Observations:

1. We have already mentioned the "MTX" file format on two occasions. Do not worry, dear reader: MTX *is not* a new font format. It is merely a form in which *fontinst* rewrites an AFM file in a syntax that TEX finds easier to digest. Thus, the first time a font family is processed by *fontinst*, the current directory is filled with MTX files. That eliminates the need to reread the same AFM files.[19] Also note that when we say that *fontinst* "reencodes" a font, that actually means that it creates an MTX file and a PL file in the new encoding when it reads an AFM file. Thus do not expect to find new AFM files; *fontinst* writes out only MTX and PL!

2. We have here two "encodings", which we shall call the "*fontinst* encoding" and the "NFSS encoding". These result simply from the fact that the NFSS encodings OT1, T1, etc., are closer to character encodings than to font encodings, while the *fontinst* encodings are genuine font encodings. Let us explain! We have not mentioned it up to now, but whether a font contains lowercase letters or small capitals, modern or old-style figures, we shall always say that it is of (NFSS) encoding T1. In TEX/NFSS, the change from a normal font to a font containing small capitals is a change of *font*, not one of *encoding*. Nevertheless, *fontinst* provides four different encodings (in the sense of "*fontinst* encodings"), all of them derived from the encoding (in the sense of "NFSS encoding") T1:

NFSS encoding	*fontinst* encoding	Small capitals	Old-style figures
T1	T1	no	no
T1	T1c	yes	no
T1	T19	no	yes
T1	T19c	yes	yes

Here, then, is the code to write for our eight AFM fonts, which will produce five NFSS fonts (the four combinations of roman/italic, light/bold, and the light upright small capitals):

---

[19] Important corollary: if you modify your AFM files, delete all the MTX files so that they will be generated afresh. Unfortunately, *fontinst* is not *make* and thus is not able to check the date of the last modification of your MTX files relative to that of the AFM files from which they were generated...

```
\installfont{T1centaurmn}{CentaurMTT1,CentaurExpertMT,
    latin}{T1}{T1}{centaur}{m}{n}{}
\installfont{T1centaurmit}{CentaurMT-ItalicT1,CentaurExpertMT-Italic,
    latin}{T1}{T1}{centaur}{m}{it}{}
\installfont{T1centaurbxn}{CentaurMT-BoldT1,CentaurExpertMT-Bold,
    latin}{T1}{T1}{centaur}{bx}{n}{}
\installfont{T1centaurbxit}{CentaurMT-BoldItalicT1,
    CentaurExpertMT-BoldItalic,latin}{T1}{T1}{centaur}{bx}{it}{}
\installfont{T1centaurmsc}{CentaurMTT1,CentaurExpertMT,
    latinsc}{T1c}{T1}{centaur}{m}{sc}{}
```

Two more comments:

1. We can see that the keywords `latin` and `latinsc` appear at the end of the list of AFM files. These are MTX files that come with *fontinst* and whose role is to consolidate the generated VPL files generated through a salvage operation. Let us explain. For every glyph that is not found in any AFM file on the list, a replacement, or a compromise solution, will be inserted into these files. Those glyphs that can be generated by their companions (for example, the Dutch ligature 'ij' can be produced by concatenating the glyph 'i' and the glyph 'j') will be so generated. Those that cannot be generated or simulated (such as the Scandinavian glyph thorn 'þ') will be replaced by a black box and will generate a PostScript error message. The fact that these files appear at the end of the list ensures us that we have already searched through all the AFM files by the time that we reach that point, and thus that it is really a "solution of last resort". It is, in fact, essential to leave `latin` and `latinsc` at the end of the list of AFM files.

2. `fontinst` will also create PL files for the "Expert" fonts. Thus be careful not to forget to add the following lines (with no instructions about reencoding) to the configuration file for *dvips*:

```
CentaurExpertMT CentaurExpertMT <CentaExpMT.pfb
CentaurExpertMT-Italic CentaurExpertMT-Italic <CentaExpMTIta.pfb
CentaurExpertMT-Bold CentaurExpertMT-Bold <CentaExpMTBol.pfb
CentaurExpertMT-BoldItalic CentaurExpertMT-BoldItalic <CentaExpMTBolIta.pfb
```

Let us now compile the driver file in T_EX (the `plain` format is sufficient; there is no need to use L^AT_EX). It will then generate a number of files:

- MTX files: these may be deleted when we are finished;

- PL files: these must be converted to TFM with `pltotf` and placed in a location where T_EX can find them;

- VPL files: these must be converted to VF with `vptovf` and placed in a location where *dvips* can find them;

- An FD file, which must be placed in a location where T_EX can find it.

	"0	"1	"2	"3	"4	"5	"6	"7	"8	"9	"A	"B	"C	"D	"E	"F
"0x	`	´	^	~	¨	˝	˚	ˇ	˘	¯	˙		¸	‚	‹	›
"1x	"	"	,,	«	»	–	—	■	1	■	ff	fi	fl	ffi	ffl	
"2x	␣	!	"	#	$	%	&	'	(	)	☆	+	,	-	.	/
"3x	0	1	2	3	4	5	6	7	8	9	:	;	<	=	>	?
"4x	@	A	B	C	D	E	F	G	H	I	J	K	L	M	N	O
"5x	P	Q	R	S	T	U	V	W	X	Y	Z	[	\	]	^	_
"6x	`	a	b	c	d	e	f	g	h	i	j	k	l	m	n	o
"7x	p	q	r	s	t	u	v	w	x	y	z	{	|	}	~	-
"8x	Ă	Ą	Ć	Č	Ď	Ě	Ę	Ğ	Ĺ	Ľ	Ł	Ń	Ň	■	Ő	Ŕ
"9x	Ř	Ś	Š	Ş	Ť	Ţ	Ű	Ů	Ÿ	Ź	Ž	Ż	IJ	İ	đ	§
"Ax	ă	ą	ć	č	ď	ě	ę	ğ	í	ľ	ł	ń	ň	■	ő	ŕ
"Bx	ř	ś	š	ş	ť	ţ	ű	ů		ź	ž	ż	ij	¡	¿	£
"Cx	À	Á	Â	Ã	Ä	Å	Æ	Ç	È	É	Ê	Ë	Ì	Í	Î	Ï
"Dx	Ð	Ñ	Ò	Ó	Ô	Õ	Ö	Œ	Ø	Ù	Ú	Û	Ü	Ý	Þ	SS
"Ex	à	á	â	ã	ä	å	æ	ç	è	é	ê	ë	ì	í	î	ï
"Fx	ð	ñ	ò	ó	ô	õ	ö	œ	ø	ù	ú	û	ü	ý	þ	ß

Figure 9-9: The layout of the font t1centaurmn, *produced by fontinst. Compare it with the table of the T1 glyph encoding (Figure 9-4). The font does not contain glyphs for 'o', 'j', 'Ŋ', or 'ŋ'; these glyphs have been replaced by black boxes.*

Note that TeX reported a number of error messages during compilation, such as these:

```
Warning: missing glyph `endash'.
Warning: missing glyph `emdash'.
Warning: missing glyph `perthousandzero'.
Warning: missing glyph `dotlessj'.
Warning: missing glyph `Ng'.
Warning: missing glyph `ng'.
```

These mean that the glyphs for endash (the en dash, '–'), emdash (the em dash, '—'), perthousandzero (the little zero 'o' that we write after the percent sign '%' to produce the per-mille sign, the per-ten-thousand sign, and so on: "‰, ‰o, ‰oo,... "), dotlessj (the 'j' with no dot, which is needed when accents are placed over a 'j') and Ng and ng (the Sámi letter *eng* 'Ŋ, ŋ') could not be simulated by their companions and thus were replaced by black boxes, as can be seen in Figure 9-9. In the same figure, the reader will see several glyphs for the languages of Central Europe. They were generated by combining a letter with an accent. The result is rather poor in some cases, such as, for example, the letters 'ć', 'ŕ', and 'ś', whose accents are set peculiarly far to the left, or the Polish barred L 'Ł', whose bar should be symmetrical relative to the downstroke. Later (page 520) we shall see how to correct these small errors by modifying the configuration file for *fontinst* or by directly editing the virtual fonts themselves.

For the sake of completeness, here are a few substitutions that are generally added to FD files in order to ensure that the substitution mechanism works correctly:

```
\substitutesilent{b}{bx}
\substitutesilent{sb}{bx}
\substitutesilent{db}{bx}
\substitutesilent{sl}{it}
```

With these instructions, we replace bold, semi-bold, and demi-bold with bold extended and also replace "slanted" type with italic. There is a variant of \substitutesilent, called \substitutenoisy, which exhibits the same behavior but also displays an error message.

In this section, we have seen the basic ways to use *fontinst* to install a family of PostScript fonts. *fontinst* manages to get the most out of PostScript fonts; we get the best results when we combine *fontinst* with a reencoding of the fonts, as done in our example, and when we thus cause all the interesting glyphs to become visible. A few problems remain:

- Missing glyphs. There will always be some, especially with font encodings other than T1. In this case, there is only one solution: one must design them oneself with font-editing software such as FontStudio, Fontographer, FontLab, or FontForge. We shall see how to do so in Chapter 12.

- Accents placed incorrectly. This problem can be solved with an ad hoc configuration of *fontinst*; we shall see the procedure on page 520. But first we must figure out where the problem originates, and that involves delving into the VPL and AFM files in search of anything that could have caused the improper alignment.

- Some incompatibilities between virtual fonts and Acrobat. To solve this problem, one must, once again, open the font with font-editing software—this time not to design new glyphs but (a) to correct the names of the glyphs, if necessary; and (b) to combine letters and glyphs in order to form "precomposed" glyphs. Then all of the problems of virtual fonts at the Acrobat level will disappear.

Before finishing this chapter on basic font management in TeX and Ω, let us present one more little section on a type of fonts on the road to extinction: the Multiple Master fonts.

Multiple Master fonts

Neither TeX nor Ω can directly process Multiple Master fonts (see Appendix C.4), in the sense of being able to take advantage of these fonts' inherent *transformation* capabilities to produce special effects or perform much more powerful NFSS commands.

For example, one might have envisioned NFSS commands with numerical values for weight and set-width that, when combined with optical size, could produce Multiple Master fonts by supplying triplets of the values of these parameters. One might also have envisioned a TEX or an Ω that could calculate actual sizes and optical sizes in a way that would make books run to an exact multiple of 16 pages, which would greatly simplify the printers' jobs. Other possibilities could also be imagined.

But these possibilities do not exist, and the fact that the Multiple Master fonts have been officially abandoned by Adobe does not help matters. Only one solution exists for using Multiple Master fonts in TEX or Ω: extracting the desired instance and using it like an ordinary Type 1 font.

To this end, there are the tools *mmafm* and *mmpfb* [223]:

```
mmafm --weight=380 --width=460 --optical-size=6 MinionMM.amfm \
    > minion_380_460_6.afm
mmpfb --weight=380 --width=460 --optical-size=6 MinionMM.pfb \
    > minion_380_460_6.pfb
```

Here we generate the instance 380 460 6 of a font for which we have an AMFM file (the Multiple Master version of the AFM format, cf. §C.4.2), *all* the AFM files for the *masters* (a list of these *masters* appears in the AMFM file;[20] there can be as many as eight), and a PFB file. These files must all be in the current directory.

In the preceding lines of code, we used three axes. There is also a fourth, called `--style` (not used by the *Adobe Minion MM* font in our example). Two other useful options:

- `--precision`, which gives the number of decimal digits to use when performing divisions (in *mmafm* and *mmpfb*). The default value is 3 digits of precision; but if we wish to adapt the font subsequently for use with TEX by running *fontinst*, we should instead select the value 0, because *fontinst* is not good at digesting numbers with a decimal part. In this case, take care to apply the same precision to both the AFM files and the PFB files so as not to create discrepancies between the two.

- `--kern-precision` (only in *mmafm*), the threshold below which kerning pairs are ignored (2 by default). Since kerning pairs are calculated through linear interpolation (as is the contour of each glyph as well), these kerning values may become very small. Below a certain threshold, the kerning pairs will have no visual effect; thus we can use this option to disregard them.

After performing these operations, we proceed, as usual, to obtain the TFM, VF, and FD files and add a line to the configuration file for *dvips*. The only precaution that must be taken is to inspect the AFM file generated by *mmafm* to obtain the PostScript name assigned to the newly generated font. Ordinarily this name is produced from the name

---

[20] Warning: the AFM files must have the PostScript names of the fonts that they represent. For example, the AFM file for the font whose FontName is MinionMM-SixIt must also have this name (and not MinioMMSixIt, which is the abbreviated version of the name).

of the "parent" font followed by the values of the parameters, separated by underscores: MinionMM_380_460_6_ (here there is one extra underscore because the fourth axis has no value), but it is prudent to check. In our case, the line for the *dvips* configuration file will therefore be:

```
minion_380_460_6 Minion_M_380_460_6_   " ECEncoding ReEncodeFont " \
    <EC.enc <minion_380_460_6.pfb
```

Customizing TEX Fonts for the User's Needs

In this section, we shall learn how we can reconfigure *fontinst* to obtain fonts customized for our typographic needs: with accented letters, slanted letters, colored letters, special ligatures, letterspacing, special behavior, etc. First, however, we must study the mechanism by which *fontinst* describes a virtual font and then apply it to a number of interesting examples.

How to Configure a Virtual Font

Here is the philosophy of *fontinst*:

- To produce a virtual font, we need a font encoding and a set of glyphs. The encoding is describen in an ETX file (extension .etx); the glyphs are described in a set of MTX files (extension .mtx).

- Each \setslot entry in an encoding file is associated with a number (the position of the glyph in the encoding) and contains a glyph's name. In an entry in an encoding file, we can also provide other information:

    – Any ligatures (\ligature) whose sequences begin with the glyph in question

    – The fact that the glyph is part of a sequence of substitutions, as in mathematical fonts, or a set of large mathematical delimiters (see Appendix B.1.4, where we describe these gadgets)

- A glyph must be defined by a \setglyph instruction. It may later be redefined (\resetglyph).

- The behavior of a glyph with respect to kerning may be similar to that of another glyph; for instance, 'é' kerns in the same way as 'e'. This fact is established through the instructions \setleftrightkerning, \setleftkerning, and \setrightkerning, depending on whether the kerning is similar on both sides, only on the left side, or only on the right side.

- The definition of a glyph may include different types of commands. Thus we can be very precise about the construction of a glyph from several others, possibly drawn from different fonts at different sizes.

- The set-width of the resulting glyph may be calculated automatically from its components, or it may be modified after the fact, possibly by starting with the set-widths of other glyphs and making appropriate calculations.

- More generally, all of the richness of the TEX programming language can be put to use to allow arbitrarily complex calculations and constructs.

Let us take these points one at a time. We have mentioned the ETX and MTX files. Why do we need these two types of files? The answer is connected to the nature of virtual fonts:

- Since a virtual font may collect glyphs from *multiple* fonts, often the same glyph exists in several fonts. We shall take the first instance that we find, in the order in which the fonts are read. Thus we do indeed need multiple MTX files that contain descriptions of the glyph.

- On the other hand, a virtual font may use only one encoding. Thus we shall read only one ETX file, which we must choose with care.

The difference between MTX and ETX is reflected in the *fontinst* syntax for installing fonts, as we have already seen on page 280:

```
\installfont{T1centaurmsc}{CentaurMTT1,CentaurExpertMT,
    latinsc}{T1c}{T1}{centaur}{m}{sc}{}
```

The names `CentaurMTT1`, `CentaurExpertMT`, and `latinsc` correspond to MTX files that will be read in that order. The first contains the most important glyphs; the second contains the glyphs for the small capitals; the third is there for any salvage operations: if a glyph is hopelessly absent, `latinsc.mtx` will suggest a substitute. Using the third argument of this command, *fontinst* will read the ETX file T1c.ext, which designates the unique encoding of the virtual font that we are going to produce. Its name, "T1c", gives a hint about its nature: it contains the T1 (Cork) TEX encoding, for small capitals.

The ETX file

The ETX file has a structure of the following type:

```
\relax
...documentation...
\encoding
...encoding commands...
\endencoding
```

The "encoding commands" will be in this form:

```
\setslot{foo}
  \comment{This is the glyph foo}
\endsetslot
```

This command associates the glyph foo with the current position. The current position is 0 by default and increases by 1 every time \setslot appears. We can also be explicit and assign the glyph bar, for example, to position 10,564:

```
\nextslot{10564}
\setslot{bar}
  \comment{This is the glyph bar}
\endsetslot
```

There is also the command \skipslots{i}, which allows us to skip i positions in the table. The \comment command allows us to insert a comment into the code.

TEX fonts offer the possibility of defining ligatures, which TEX will automatically employ. For instance, we can specify that whenever an 'f' is followed by an 'i', these two glyphs will be automatically replaced by the glyph 'fi'. This approach is compatible with both hyphenation (the 'fi' ligature will be changed back to the glyphs 'f' and 'i' if we should have to divide the word between those two letters) and kerning (we can create kerning pairs with 'fi' and any other glyph whatsoever).

There are eight types of ligatures in TEX. Simple ligatures (which we shall call LIG) simply replace a pair of glyphs with another glyph. The other seven types of ligatures (/LIG, /LIG>, etc.), known as *smart ligatures*, will leave one or both of the glyphs in place while adding a new glyph, etc. We shall describe the eight types of ligatures in detail in §B.1.3.

To obtain a ligature from a glyph whose position we are defining, we use the \ligature command. For example, here is a possible \setslot instruction for the letter 'f', including all the ligatures that exist in the font:

```
\setslot{f}
  \ligature{LIG}{i}{f_i}
  \ligature{LIG}{f}{f_f}
  \ligature{LIG}{l}{f_l}
  \ligature{LIG}{t}{f_t}
  \ligature{LIG}{j}{f_j}
  \comment{The letter 'f', a descendant of the Greek digamma F}
\endsetslot}
```

Note that the \ligature command does not repeat the letter 'f', since it is already known: it is, after all, the current glyph. Thus \ligature{LIG}{i}{f_i} indicates that we wish to obtain a ligature of LIG type between the current glyph (f) and the glyph i: the glyph that will replace these two is f_i (according to the rules for naming glyphs that were formulated by Adobe, page 659).

Finally, two "gadgets" from TEX's mathematical fonts: the sequence of extensible glyphs and composition (see Appendix B.1.4). Here is how to tell TEX which is the glyph larger than the current glyph that must be used when a mathematical expression requests a delimiter of a larger size:

```
\setslot{foo}
    \nextlarger{foo2}
\endsetslot
```

where foo2 is the larger glyph that immediately follows foo in the sequence of extensible glyphs arranged in order of increasing size.

Likewise, to specify that an extended brace is formed from an upper part called top, a lower part called bottom, a middle section called middle, and a repeating segment called repeating, we write:

```
\setslot{repeating}
    \varchar
        \vartop{top}
        \varbot{bottom}
        \varmid{middle}
        \varrep{repeating}
    \endvarchar
\endsetslot
```

The MTX file

This is where things become interesting. In the previous section, we described the ETX file, which contains the font's encoding. Here we shall describe the glyphs, by all possible and conceivable means. If these glyphs appear in the encoding, very well: they will also appear in the font. If they do not appear in the encoding, they will be ignored. Thus we can use the same MTX files with multiple ETX files.

An MTX file must have a structure of the following kind:

```
\relax
...documentation...
\metrics
...definitions of glyphs...
\endmetrics
```

In order to understand why this file is useful, let us take a typical line from a *fontinst* installation file:

```
\installfont{T1centaurmsc}{CentaurMTT1,CentaurExpertMT,
    latinsc}{T1c}{T1}{centaur}{m}{sc}{}
```

There is a fundamental difference between the two files CentaurMTT1.mtx and Centaur-ExpertMT.mtx and the file latinsc.mtx: the former are generated on the fly from AFM files of the same name; the latter is painstakingly prepared by the developer. Thus the former contain, in the ideal case, nothing but the information contained in the AFM files. It is `latinsc.mtx` that will take advantage of the information to do more interesting things. We also have the option of *redefining* glyphs. This option would not make sense if we humans were the only ones to define them, but it assumes capital importance when the glyphs are defined in a way that may not seem optimal at the first glance at the AFM files.

The MTX file that we prepare, and that we ultimately instruct *fontinst* to read, is thus the file of last resort: in it, we correct poorly defined glyphs and add those that could not be defined.

To define a new glyph, we use the command

```
\setglyph{foo}
...glyph commands...
\endsetglyph
```

where `foo` is the name of the glyph, a name that must be strictly identical (same case, no whitespace) to the one used in the ETX file.

If the glyph has already been defined, we instead use the following variant:

```
\resetglyph{foo}
...glyph commands...
\endresetglyph
```

To avoid error messages if we are not sure whether the glyph in question has been defined, we may use the command `\unsetglyph{foo}`, which will cause *fontinst* to "forget" the glyph.

What are these celebrated "glyph commands" that we can insert in a glyph's definition? Well, this should come as no surprise to the reader who has read this book carefully and has understood the principles behind virtual fonts: a virtual font is a font that replaces references to glyphs in a DVI file with some DVI instructions. Thus we have glyph commands associated with various types of DVI instructions:

- The command `\glyph{bar}{1000}` will insert the (real or virtual) glyph bar. Warning: bar must have been *defined* beforehand. The number 1000, divided by a thousand, indicates the glyph's scaling factor. The displacement vector for this glyph will start at the current point of displacement.

- The command `\glyphrule{123}{456}` will draw a black box of width 123 and height 456 thousandths of an em.

- The commands `\movert{500}` and `\moveup{500}` will move the current point rightwards or upwards by 500 thousandths of an em.

- The commands `\push` and `\pop` will, respectively, push the current point onto the stack and pop it off the stack.

- Finally, \glyphspecial{code} will insert the code code at this point, much like the \specials of TEX.

In addition to these five commands, there is a sixth that generates a PostScript error message: \glyphwarning{Warning: missing glyph!} will warn us when *dvips* is attempting to insert the missing glyph into the PostScript code.

The commands above enable us to combine glyphs and calculate the global displacement vector by using the vectors of the combined constituents—but we may often wish to change the metrics of the new glyph directly. To do so, we have the following commands at our disposal:

- \resetwidth{1234}, to redefine the glyph's set-width

- \resetheight{1234}, for its height

- \resetdepth{1234}, for its depth

- \resetitalic{1234}, for its italic correction

- \resetglyphbb{*a*}{*b*}{*c*}{*d*}, to redefine its bounding box

The *bounding box* is the rectangle that contains the glyph. It thus depends entirely on the glyph and is independent of the set-width.

It is interesting to observe that when we redefine a glyph, we can refer to its previous definition in the new definition. For example:

```
\resetglyph{A}
  \movert{30}
  \glyph{A}{1000}
  \movert{30}
\endresetglyph
```

will increase the spacing on each side of the glyph A, without causing an infinite loop, as we might have expected it to do.

We have used whole numbers in the various definitions that we have presented above. But *fontinst* would be of very little interest if we were required to give explicit numbers systematically. All of the system's power comes from the fact that we can use the dimensions of glyphs that are already defined:

- \width{foo}, \height{foo}, \depth{foo}, and \italic{foo} yield the set-width, height, depth, and italic correction of the glyph foo, which must have been defined previously.

- \bbleft{foo}, \bbbottom{foo}, \bbright{foo}, and \bbtop{foo} yield the four coordinates of the glyph's bounding box.

- \kerning{foo}{bar} yields the kerning, if any, between foo and bar.

We can perform arbitrarily complex calculations by using the fundamental arithmetical operations:

- \neg{a}, the negation of a

- \add{a}{b}, the sum $a + b$

- \sub{a}{b}, the difference $a - b$

- \mul{a}{b}, the product ab

- \div{a}{b}, the quotient $\frac{a}{b}$

- \scale{a}{b}, the product $\frac{ab}{1,000}$

- \max{a}{b}, the value $\max(a, b)$

- \min{a}{b}, the value $\min(a, b)$

- \half{a}, half of a, rounded down

- \otherhalf{a}, half of a, rounded up

We can also define numeric variables corresponding to the relevant dimensions of the font. For example:

```
\setint{italicslant}{0}           % slant
\setint{xheight}{\height{x}}      % height of the lowercase letters
\setint{capheight}{\height{A}}    % height of the capitals
\setint{ascender}{\height{d}}     % height of the ascenders
\setint{descender}{\depth{g}}     % depth of the descenders
\setint{underlinethickness}{40}   % thickness of the underscore
\setint{smallcapsscale}{800}      % scaling factor for small capitals
\setint{smallcapskerning}{900}    % kerning factor for small capitals
```

The values of these variables can be used in calculations by means of the \int{*variable*} command. They can also be modified at any time.

We shall have the opportunity to see some typical examples of several of these calculations.

But let us return to the contents of the MTX file. Aside from defining glyphs, we can also define *kerning behavior equivalences*. For example, it is quite natural to suppose that the ligature 'Œ' will behave, with respect to other glyphs, like an 'O' on the left and like an 'E' on the right. That fact can be expressed with the following commands:

```
\setleftkerning{OE}{O}{1000}
\setrightkerning{OE}{E}{1000}
```

where, once again, 1000 represents a scaling factor multiplied by 1,000. There is also a command, \setleftrightkerning, that combines the previous two:

```
\setleftrightkerning{Eacute}{E}{1000}
```

means that Eacute kerns like E on both sides.

For a complete and detailed list of the available commands, the reader is invited to consult the documentation for *fontinst* [200].

ETX and MTX files for a simple virtual font

In the simple case, where we use only the information contained in the AFM files, there is an ETX file for the T1 encoding, an MTX file for each AFM file, and an MTX file "of last resort". What do these files contain?

The file t1.etx contains definitions of code points in the encoding's table, of the following type:

```
\setslot{comma}
    \ligature{LIG}{comma}{quotedblbase}
    \comment{The comma `,'.}
\endsetslot
```

Here we have defined a code point for the glyph comma and a ligature of two consecutive commas that produces a glyph called quotedblbase, i.e., the German opening quotation mark („).

There is a trick in this file (and in all the files of the *fontinst* distribution) that may seem a bit obscure at first blush: the uppercase letters are defined not by a simple \setslot{A} command but by \setslot{\uc{A}{a}}. Likewise, the lowercase letters are defined by \setslot{\lc{A}{a}}. What is the point of this complexity?

To understand it, consider the file t1c.etx, which describes the font encoding for the small capitals. In this file, we read:

```
\setcommand\lc#1#2{#1small}
\setcommand\uc#1#2{#1}
```

In other words, the glyph names of the lowercase letters are formed by the first argument of the command \lc{A}{a}, followed by the string small. Thus, instead of a, we find Asmall. Thus we can reuse the code in the t1.etx file by simply adapting this convention of Adobe for naming glyphs, which affects the names of the small capitals.

Other tricks of this kind are used for ligatures, old-style figures, etc.

What do we find right now in the MTX file latin.mtx? Since it consists of programming, the authors of this file (Alan Jeffrey and Ulrik Vieth) first define a number of commands that will be useful to them later in the file. For example, they define \unfakable, in the following manner:

```
\setcommand\unfakable#1{
   \setglyph{#1}
      \glyphrule{500}{500}
      \glyphwarning{missing glyph `#1'}
   \endsetglyph
}
```

The idea is that the glyph in question cannot be simulated or replaced by any other glyph.[21] Thus we shall later encounter

```
\unfakable{A}
```

which means that if the font does not contain the letter 'A', the glyph in question will be replaced by a square 500 units long on each side (the units here are the units of PostScript fonts, thus thousandths of an em). Moreover, a PostScript error message will be issued when the PostScript code is displayed or printed.

What else is there in the file latin.mtx? Well, we find, for example, the description of the glyph 'É':

```
\setglyph{Eacute}
   \topaccent{E}{acute}{500}
\endsetglyph
```

The \topaccent command is defined in the same file. The number 500 indicates that the accent must be centered relative to the middle of the base glyph's set-width. Thus it is an ad hoc command written specially for the needs of this glyph encoding. Here is its definition:

```
\setcommand\topaccent#1#2#3{
   \push
```

---

[21] Let us note here, by way of an anecdote, that unfakability is an entirely relative concept. For instance, in some fonts sold in France by a company that shall go unnamed, the Icelandic glyph thorn (þ) was replaced by 'þ', i.e., a 'p' and a 'b' superimposed! If it were not for the legendary sangfroid of the Scandinavian peoples, this construction could have driven Icelandic readers to the point of suicide…

```
            \moveup{\max{0}{\sub{\height{#1}}{\int{xheight}}}}
            \movert{\add{\sub{\scale{\width{#1}}{#3}}{\scale{\width{#2}}{500}}}
               {\scale{\sub{\height{#1}}{\int{xheight}}}{\int{italicslant}}}}
            \glyph{#2}{1000}
         \pop
         \glyph{#1}{1000}
   }
```

Here is an explanation of the code:

- We store the current point by means of a \push operation.

- We move the accent upward. This is necessary because in TEX the glyphs for the accents have a height that is ideal for the lowercase letters. For the uppercase letters, therefore, the accent must be moved upward a distance equal to the difference in height between the uppercase and lowercase letters: \sub{\int{capheight}}{\int{xheight}}. Here the authors wanted to write an all-purpose \topaccent macro that will work with all glyphs. Accordingly, they chose a different approach (not necessarily an optimal one): they used not the standard height of the capitals but the height of the current glyph: \sub{\height{#1}}{\int{xheight}}. This means that the acute accent of the 'Ó' will be slightly higher than that of the 'É', since the 'O' is larger than the 'E'. That is the price to pay for a macro that will work in all situations.

  One last detail: it may happen that, for one reason or another, the height of the current letter will be less than that of the lowercase letters—for example, if the user decided to place a circumflex accent over a comma (¸). In this case, the accent must not descend below the level of the lowercase letters; in other words, its displacement may not be negative. Thus we choose maximum of the calculated quantity and 0.

- We move the accent rightward. If G is the base glyph's set-width and A is the set-width of the accent, we move the accent by $\frac{G}{2} - \frac{A}{2}$, which causes us to center it relative to the middle of the glyph's set-width. Next, if s is the slope (in the TEX sense) of the font, we multiply s by the difference between the height of the glyph and the height of the lowercase letters. That is necessary because the accent in the slanted font is designed in such a way as to take the slant into account, but only for the lowercase letters. By multiplying s by the difference in height, we obtain the amount of extra slant required, which will cause the accent to be centered correctly over the letter's (slanted) central axis. Finally, we take the sum of the two, which gives us the horizontal displacement of the accent.

- We insert the glyph for the accent.

- We pop the position at which we were before this insertion.

- We insert the base glyph.

Despite its sophistication, the code above is not optimal. It uses the principle that the set-widths of the glyphs are all the information that we need to make effective combinations of glyphs. That is true if the glyphs have symmetric side spacing, i.e., if their contours are centered in the abstract boxes that contain them; in that case, we can use their widths. But it is not true if the glyph has more spacing on one side than on the other.

In the latter case, it is much more effective to use the glyphs' bounding boxes. At the end of the day, when we know the exact dimensions of a glyph's contour, no matter how it may be placed in its abstract box, we can always center it with respect to another glyph.

Why, then, is *fontinst* based on set-widths rather than on bounding boxes? Because the concept of bounding box is peculiar to TEX. The TEX font-metric files, be they real (TFM/OFM) or virtual (VF/OVF), do not contain bounding boxes. There is no way to know where the glyph is positioned in the abstract boxes given in these files. The fonts created by METAFONT do not contain this information. Thus *fontinst* cannot guarantee that the information will exist; it prefers to use values, such as set-width, that will be found in all font files.

Although *fontinst* has been around for more than 10 years, only in a recent version (1.926, the current one being 1.928) supports making calculations on the basis of bounding boxes—by loading the file bbox.sty. One must insert the following commands:

```
\needsfontinstversion{1.926}
\input{bbox.sty}
```

at the beginning of the font's installation file in order to ensure that the macros in question will be available.

Later in this book, we shall come back to the different types of combinations of glyphs that are possible.

One last word on the latin.mtx file. It contains macros of the following type:

```
\setleftkerning{IJ}{I}{1000}

\setleftrightkerning{Iacute}{I}{1000}
\setleftrightkerning{Icircumflex}{I}{1000}
\setleftrightkerning{Idieresis}{I}{1000}
\setleftrightkerning{Idotaccent}{I}{1000}
\setleftrightkerning{Igrave}{I}{1000}

\setrightkerning{IJ}{J}{1000}
```

to create kerning between "nonstandard" glyphs. Thus the number of kerning pairs in a font is often multiplied by six: for each pair 'AT', there will also be the pairs 'ÁT', 'AȚ', 'ÁȚ', and so forth.

In the text to follow, we shall examine different scenarios for building up particular glyphs from components. These scenarios will allow us to illustrate both the variety of typographical needs of the different scripts with regard to combining glyphs and the advanced techniques offered by *fontinst*.

Adding ligatures to a font

A "mademoiselle" for the font Zapfino

Suppose that we wish to adapt the delightful font *Zapfino* (a creation of a great master who shall go nameless here) for use with TEX—or rather with Ω, since the latter supports far more than 256 glyphs. One step in the process of adaptation will be to write the code for the ligatures. Thanks to this code, some strings in the input will automatically produce ligatures. Being a great patriot and defender of *la francophonie*, I have chosen, from the multitude of ligatures provided in *Zapfino*, one that is as French as can be: '𝑀𝑙𝑙𝑒' (for "mademoiselle", the French equivalent of the title "Miss"), from which I have removed the period that Zapf unfortunately added. How can we obtain a ligature automatically from the string Mlle?

The reason that we chose this example (rather than the bland 'fi' ligature) is that there is a catch. Specifically, in TEX, unlike in OpenType or AAT, we cannot define ligatures of more than two glyphs at a time. Thus, to produce the four-glyph ligature '𝑀𝑙𝑙𝑒', we will have to have positions in the font's table for each of the intermediate ligatures: '𝑀', '𝑀𝑙', and '𝑀𝑙𝑙'. Thus we shall have the following in the ETX file:

```
\setslot{M}
   \ligature{LIG}{l}{M_l}
   \comment{Letter M}
\endsetslot

\setslot{M_l}
   \ligature{LIG}{l}{M_l_l}
   \comment{(False) ligature Ml}
\endsetslot

\setslot{M_l_l}
   \ligature{LIG}{l}{M_l_l_e}
   \comment{(False) ligature Mll}
\endsetslot

\setslot{M_l_l_e}
   \comment{Original ligature Mlle}
\endsetslot
```

We are therefore taking up four positions in the font's table, while only two of them will actually be used. Moreover, these two positions ('𝑀' and '𝑀𝑙𝑙𝑒') are the only ones that will actually appear in the font. The other two are really nothing but jury-rigging.

What will appear in the MTX file? For the "real" glyphs, we will have the customary code:

```
\setglyph{M}
   \glyph{M}{1000}
\endsetglyph

\setglyph{M_l_l_e}
   \glyph{M_l_l_e}{1000}
\endsetglyph
```

```
\setleftkerning{M_l_l_e}{M}{1000}
\setrightkerning{M_l_l_e}{e}{1000}
```

We shall obtain the others by simply concatenating glyphs (taking their possible kerning into account):

```
\setglyph{M_l}
    \glyph{M}{1000}
    \movert{\kerning{M}{l}}
    \glyph{l}{1000}
\endsetglyph

\setleftkerning{M_l}{M}{1000}
\setrightkerning{M_l}{l}{1000}

\setglyph{M_l_l}
    \glyph{M}{1000}
    \movert{\kerning{M}{l_l}}
    \glyph{l_l}{1000}
\endsetglyph

\setleftkerning{M_l_l}{M}{1000}
\setrightkerning{M_l_l}{l_l}{1000}
```

In the second case above, we are using not a string of three glyphs but a glyph 'M' and a ligature 'll', since the ligature does exist in *Zapfino* and it would be a shame not to use it. Thus when we type an 'M' followed by an 'l', we shall obtain the ligature 'Ml', which we shall never see, as the glyph for this ligature is identical in every way to the glyphs 'M' and 'l' in sequence. The same is true of 'Mll'. Only when the 'e', the fourth character of 'Mlle', is read will the combined ligature become visible.

What will happen when the DVI file produced by TEX (or Ω) is converted to PostScript and then to PDF? Will the intermediate "false ligatures" of our approach create any problems? Not at all. Do not forget that *dvips* will first "devirtualize" the DVI code before converting it to PostScript. For the positions in the virtual font that represent true ligatures, a PostScript glyph will be inserted. This glyph, in the *Zapfino* font, will have a name formed from Adobe's rules for naming glyphs (Appendix C.3.3). Acrobat will thus recognize this glyph as being equivalent (with respect to indexing, selection, searching, etc.) to the corresponding string: the glyph M_l_l_e corresponds to the string Mlle.

As for the false ligatures, they will be replaced by the corresponding DVI code during devirtualization. For example, M_l will be replaced by the glyphs M and l, and M_l_l will be replaced by the pair of glyphs M and l_l, the second of these being a true ligature, equivalent to the string ll. Thus all is well, in the best of worlds.

Contextual analysis in Arabic

Another example of the use of ligatures: the contextual analysis of the Arabic script. For simplicity's sake, we shall assume that there are only two letters: one with two forms, and one with four forms. To assist the reader who does not read Arabic, we shall take two letters whose forms are quite different from one another: *ghayn* (isolated, غ; initial, غ; medial, ﻐ; final, ﻎ) and *dal* (isolated, د; final, ﺪ). Thus the four two-letter words that we can write are غد and دد (letters not connected), ﻐﺪ and ﻐﻎ (letters connected). The three-letter words with all the letters joined up are ﻐﻐﻎ and ﻐﻐﺪ. And so forth.

Ordinarily the glyphs that we are going to discuss are called afii57434 for *ghayn* and afii57423; but since these names will not necessarily help the reader to understand the example, we shall instead use the names ghayn and dal. The glyphs at our disposal are therefore ghayn.isol, ghayn.init, ghayn.medi, ghayn.fina, dal.isol, and dal.fina.

Unlike the representative glyph in Unicode, which is in the *isolated* form, the default glyph in TEX that will represent an Arabic character in our font is in the *medial* form, if it has four forms, or the *final* form, if it has only two. Therefore, by default, when we ask TEX to set a *ghayn* or a *dal*, it will set a ﻐ (ghayn.medi) or a ﺪ (dal.fina). Now we must write the ligatures that will produce the other contextual forms.

First, let us deal with the beginning of the word. We want ﻐ and ﺪ to become غ and د, respectively, in that position. But what is the *beginning of a word*? That question is anything but trivial. In fact, we must enumerate all the glyphs that may appear *before* either *ghayn* or *dal*. The opening parenthesis (parenright) is one such glyph. Therefore we shall write, in the definition of this glyph, in the ETX file:

```
\setslot{parenright}
  \ligature{/LIG}{ghayn.medi}{ghayn.init}
  \ligature{/LIG}{dal.fina}{dal.isol}
\endsetslot
```

The slash before the keyword LIG means that we are keeping the preceding glyph and that the new glyph obtained will replace the second glyph; thus we keep the parenthesis and replace one Arabic letter with another. That solves the problem of 'ﻐ)' and 'ﺪ)", which become 'غ)' and 'د)', respectively.

Nonetheless, most of the time it is a *space* that will appear at the beginning of a word. And we find ourselves once again faced with the peculiarity of TEX that the "space" *is not a glyph* but merely an *offset*. How can we specify the behavior of a glyph when it is preceded by an offset, be it horizontal (within a line) or vertical (at the beginning of a line)? TEX uses the following trick: A position in the table is declared to be the "left-hand delimiter" of words. At the beginning of a word (preceded by a space), TEX will act as if this special glyph were present. Thus we can assign it to ligatures or to kerning pairs. In *fontinst*, we use a special command, \setleftboundary, in the following manner:

```
\setleftboundary{percent}
  \ligature{/LIG}{ghayn.medi}{ghayn.init}
```

```
    \ligature{/LIG}{dal.fina}{dal.isol}
\endsetslot
```

Above we have used the glyph '%' as the left-hand delimiter. That does not affect the actual glyph '%' at all. All kerning pairs, however, with the percent sign as their first letter will also be applied at the beginnings of words, as if an invisible '%' were present at those locations. We should choose as the left-hand delimiter a glyph that does not have any kerning pairs, so as not to confuse the kerning pairs of the "real glyph" with those of its alter ego, the pseudoglyph for the left-hand delimiter.

There is one other case in which we would like to change from a medial form to an initial form: this is when the glyph is preceded by a *dal*. Indeed, this letter has only two forms: isolated and initial. When it is followed by another Arabic letter, the latter behaves as if it were at the beginning of a word. Thus we must also supply the ligatures engendered by dal.isol or dal.fina:

```
\setslot{dal.fina}
    \ligature{/LIG}{ghayn.medi}{ghayn.init}
    \ligature{/LIG}{dal.fina}{dal.isol}
\endsetslot

\setslot{dal.isol}
    \ligature{/LIG}{ghayn.medi}{ghayn.init}
    \ligature{/LIG}{dal.fina}{dal.isol}
\endsetslot
```

Now let us take care of the *end of the word*. When a word ends with *dal*, we already have a final (or isolated) form; thus the contextual analysis is already finished. But when a word ends with a medial *ghayn*, that letter must change to its final form. When it is in the initial form, it must assume its isolated form instead.

Once again we shall start by writing all the explicit ligatures with punctuation marks and other glyphs that may follow a word, and then we shall declare that one glyph will play the role of an "end-of-word space": this will be the *right-hand delimiter*. We define the right-hand delimiter with the \setrightboundary command, which has no ending command \endsetrightboundary, since the pseudoglyph in question is not supposed to form ligatures with other glyphs that follow it; it exists only to serve as the second term in ligatures with real glyphs.

Thus we write:

```
\setrightboundary{percent}
```

The percent sign thus serves two purposes: it is the left-hand *and* the right-hand delimiter.

The entry for medial *ghayn* might thus be:

```
\setslot{ghayn.medi}
  \ligature{LIG/}{percent}{ghayn.fina}
  \ligature{LIG/}{period}{ghayn.fina}
  \ligature{LIG/}{comma}{ghayn.fina}
  \ligature{LIG/}{parenleft}{ghayn.fina}
  ... and so on for all the punctuation marks ...
\endsetslot
```

The slash that follows the keyword LIG indicates that the second term in the ligature will remain unchanged. Thus if medial *ghayn* is followed by a period, the first term, the medial *ghayn*, is replaced by a final *ghayn*, while the period remains where it is. In the absence of this mechanism, we would be required to have positions in the font table containing final *ghayn* followed by different punctuation marks. That would cause the number of glyphs in the font to explode.

Note that in the code above, by writing percent, we obtain a final glyph both before a space at the end of a word or the end of a line (since percent is the right-hand delimiter) and before an actual '%' sign. For TEX, it is impossible to distinguish the two. Thus we should choose as our delimiter a glyph that we use rarely, or even never.

To conclude, here is the declaration for initial *ghayn*:

```
\setslot{ghayn.init}
  \ligature{LIG/}{percent}{ghayn.isol}
  \ligature{LIG/}{period}{ghayn.isol}
  \ligature{LIG/}{comma}{ghayn.isol}
  \ligature{LIG/}{parenleft}{ghayn.isol}
  ... and so on for all the punctuation marks ...
\endsetslot
```

Thus, for example, when we write the string "space", "*ghayn*", "space", we obtain a medial *ghayn*, which becomes an initial *ghayn* under the action of the left-hand delimiter; then the initial *ghayn* will form an isolated *ghayn* with the right-hand delimiter, and we are done.

In this section, we have described a simplified version of the contextual analysis of the Arabic script. There are advantages and disadvantages to this method:

- ADVANTAGES. Contextual analysis is done automatically. Provided that she can set type from right to left (for which she needs either Ω or eTEX), the user has nothing to do but to enter the codes for the Arabic characters, and the rest will be done by the font. Analysis does not involve any macros, so it can be performed in any context: in a table, within a mathematical formula, in verbatim mode, etc. This independence from the context of the font's behavior corresponds closely to the fundamentally natural character of contextual analysis in the Arabic script. This approach is completely compatible with conversion to PDF; the glyph ghayn.isol, for example, will be represented by a PostScript glyph of the same name, and Acrobat will able to determine very easily which Unicode character it represents.

- DISADVANTAGES. Contextual analysis is very fragile: even the empty group {} can break it. It would be very difficult to insert vowel points or other diacritical marks between the letters. We must explicitly list glyphs that are not Arabic letters and that will cause a medial glyph to become initial or final (and will cause an initial glyph to become isolated); theoretically, all non-Arabic Unicode characters fall into this case, which means that we have thousands of glyphs, thus hundreds of thousands, even millions, of ligatures. Of course, we shall only write the relevant ligatures (the case of an ideograph immediately followed by an Arabic letter, for example, can be easily excluded...), but that entails a degree of uncertainty in the analysis; the day when that rare case does occur, the user will have to be able to notice it rapidly and to correct the problem by using glyphs representing the Unicode characters ZWJ and ZWNJ.[22]

Keeping 'f' from running into 'è'

Last but not least, an example drawn from the French version of this book. The reader may have noticed that the letter 'f' becomes 'f' when it appears before an 'è', a 'ü', or any other letter that bears an accent that inconveniently gets in the way. A humble intervention on our part has prevented the 'fè' effect that would ordinarily be obtained with this font, in a word like Italian "caffè".

All that we had to do was to design a new glyph 'f' whose upper portion is narrower, place it into an auxiliary font (the license for our installation does not allow us to modify the original font), and create a number of ligatures of LIG/ type: 'f' + 'è' → 'fè', etc. When we use an "intelligent" ligature, the 'f' is replaced with an 'f', and the second letter remains unchanged. Suppose that the new letter is named f.narrow. Then the *fontinst* code could be:

```
\setslot{f}
   \ligature{LIG/}{egrave}{f.narrow}
   \ligature{LIG/}{ecircumflex}{f.narrow}
   \ligature{LIG/}{edieresis}{f.narrow}
   ... and similarly for all other accented
       letters that cause a problem ...
\endsetslot
```

That approach saves us the trouble of defining new positions in the font's table for each pair 'fè', 'fê', 'fë', etc. The same procedure was needed for the 'ff' ligature, which became 'ff'.

The problem of the pair of letters 'fè' is not new. It unfortunately occurs in a great many fonts of high quality. Yet it can be resolved in a trice, with nothing more than a narrower head on the 'f' and a line of *fontinst* code.

---

[22] These are empty zero-width glyphs that play either the role of an Arabic letter with four forms or the role of a non-Arabic letter. Since they have zero width, these glyphs allow us to force Arabic letters to assume a certain form.

Placing a diacritical mark

In the section "ETX and MTX Files for a Simple Virtual Font" (page 292), we considered the case of placing a single diacritical mark—an accent centered over a letter. For this purpose, we used the set-widths of the accent and the letter, in the hope that these glyphs were indeed centered in their abstract boxes so that the centering of the set-widths would be equivalent to the centering of the contours.

Now we shall write the same code[23] by using the bounding boxes of the glyphs:

```
\setglyph{Eacute}
    \topbbaccent{E}{acute}
\endsetglyph

\def\bbcenter#1{\add{\half{\sub{\bbright{#1}}{\bbleft{#1}}}}{%
\bbleft{#1}}}

\setcommand\topbbaccent#1#2{
    \push
        \moveup{\max{0}{\sub{\bbtop{#1}}{\int{xheight}}}}
        \movert{\add{\sub{\bbcenter{#1}}{\bbcenter{#2}}}
            {\scale{\sub{\bbtop{#1}}{\int{xheight}}}{\int{italicslant}}}}
        \glyph{#2}{1000}
    \pop
    \glyph{#1}{1000}
}
```

The \bbcenter command yields the horizontal center of the bounding box: it is computed as half of (\bbright minus \bbleft) plus the spacing on the left (which is \bbleft). Next, in the code for \topbbaccent, we merely replace \scale{\width{#1}}{500} with \bbcenter{#1} and replace \height with \bbtop (which is, strictly speaking, the same thing, since the only information about height that we find in an AFM file is the height of the bounding box).

Making an 'h' believe that it is an 'l'

Kaj nun, ankoraŭ pli interesa ekzemplo: la litero 'ĥ' uzata en Esperanto, lingvo tiel idealisma kaj ĉarma en sia strangeco. (Now for a more interesting example: the letter 'ĥ' used

---

[23] For simplicity's sake, we shall assume that the accent is *centered*; thus it lacks the third parameter of \topaccent, which we shall assume to have the value of 500.

in Esperanto,[24] a language so idealistic and charming in its awkwardness.) It is obvious that centering the accent (like this: 'ĥ') would yield a horribly ugly result. Therefore, we need a way to center the accent above the downstroke of the 'h'. In the absence of an OpenType accent indicator or a shape-recognition system to detect the downstroke, we must resort to a trick to achieve our goal.

Here it is: in the overwhelming majority of fonts, the downstroke of the 'h' is a perfect copy of the letter 'l', and the amount of spacing on the left of these two letters is the same. Thus we have only to place the accent over the 'h' *as if it were an 'l'*:

```
\setglyph{hcircumflex}
   \topbbaccentlikeif{h}{circumflex}{l}
\endsetglyph

\def\bbcenter#1{\add{\half{\sub{\bbright{#1}}{%
\bbleft{#1}}}}{\bbleft{#1}}}

\setcommand\topbbaccentlikeif#1#2#3{
   \push
      \moveup{\max{0}{\sub{\bbtop{#1}}{\int{xheight}}}}
      \movert{\add{\sub{\bbcenter{#3}}{\bbcenter{#2}}}
         {\scale{\sub{\bbtop{#1}}{\int{xheight}}}{\int{italicslant}}}}
      \glyph{#2}{1000}
   \pop
   \glyph{#1}{1000}
}
```

The code has hardly changed. We have defined a command \topbbaccentlikeif (or "accent appearing above a letter, calculated on the basis of bounding boxes and placed as if the letter were a different letter"), which takes three arguments: the base letter ('h'), the accent (the circumflex), and the letter that will serve as a reference for placing the accent ('l').

The same thing, but on the other side

To go a step further, we shall now leave the Latin alphabet and dive into the mysterious Old Cyrillic (or "Slavonic") script, used for liturgical documents in the countries that

---

[24] Invented by Ludwig Lazare Zamenhof, a nineteenth-century idealist, Esperanto purports to be a universal language, but in reality it is completely Eurocentric, as it merely mixes elements of the various Romance and Germanic languages. Its main use was as a pivot language during the Cold War: since the West was hesitant to learn Russian or Chinese and the Eastern Bloc was equally hesitant to learn English or French, Esperanto served as a common language for communication between people from the two rival blocs.

use the Cyrillic script. This alphabet includes a letter named *yus*: 'ᴀ' (Unicode 0x0467 CYRILLIC SMALL LETTER LITTLE YUS). Like all the vowels in this alphabet, *yus* can bear accents (the accents of the Greek language, carry-overs from the Greek cultural heritage). Here it bears an acute accent: 'ᴀ́'. Up to now, there has been nothing out of the ordinary, typographically speaking.

A phonetic variant of *yus* is written with a preceding small capital 'i': 'ɪᴀ' (0x0469 CYRILLIC SMALL LETTER IOTIFIED LITTLE YUS). This letter can also bear an accent, and in this case the accent *is not centered* but rather placed over the *yus*: 'ɪᴀ́'. Once again, therefore, we must place an accent by making reference to another letter, but in this case the other letter appears on the right-hand side of the construct. Here is the code that will position the accent correctly for us:

```
\setglyph{uni0469_acute}
    % uni0467 is the yus
    % uni0469 is the yus preceded by an i
    \topbbaccentlikeifreverse{uni0469}{acute}{uni0467}
\endsetglyph

\def\bbcenter#1{\add{\half{\sub{\bbright{#1}}{%
    \bbleft{#1}}}}{\bbleft{#1}}}

\setcommand\topbbaccentlikeifreverse#1#2#3{
    \push
        \moveup{\max{0}{\sub{\bbtop{#1}}{\int{xheight}}}}
        \movert{\bbright{#1}}
        \movert{\add{\neg{\sub{\bbcenter{#3}}{\bbcenter{#2}}}}
            {\scale{\sub{\bbtop{#1}}{\int{xheight}}}{\int{italicslant}}}}
        \glyph{#2}{1000}
    \pop
    \glyph{#1}{1000}
}
```

The code is hardly more complex than the preceding example; there are only a few differences. First, the name of the macro is perfectly hideous (\topbbaccentlikeifreverse). Second, we have added the line \movert{\bbright{#1}}, which moves to the rightmost extremity of the glyph. Finally, the alignment of the base glyph and the accent is performed from right to left; thus we have inserted a \neg into the code, to force movement towards the left.

Making a letter forget that it has a horn

But letters are not the only characters that are replaced with (more respectable) letters. The same phenomenon occurs with accents, and sometimes with a letter and an accent at the same time. Let us return to the Latin alphabet, but not just any Latin alphabet! This example will delight those who love accent marks, the *ne plus ultra* of the ravages of colonialism: the Vietnamese alphabet. In this alphabet, there is—among other things—a combination of the circumflex and acute accents 'ố' and also the letter 'o' with a horn: 'ơ'. To place the double accent over a letter, we shall center not the entire glyph, but only the part that constitutes the circumflex accent, over the letter. In the same vein, to place an accent over the letter 'ơ', we shall center it not with respect to the set-width of the entire glyph but only with respect to the part corresponding to an unadorned 'o'. Here is this special letter with the special double accent: 'ớ'. To obtain it, we shall write a TEX command that will center an accent A over a letter L by acting as if it were a different accent, A':

```
\setglyph{oxxx_circumflex_acute}
    \topbbaccentlikeiflikeif{oxxx}{o}{circumflex_acute}{circumflex}
\endsetglyph

\def\bbcenter#1{\add{\half{\sub{\bbright{#1}}{%
    \bbleft{#1}}}}{\bbleft{#1}}}

\setcommand\topbbaccentlikeiflikeif#1#2#3#4{
    \push
        \moveup{\max{0}{\sub{\bbtop{#2}}{\int{xheight}}}}
        \movert{\add{\sub{\bbcenter{#4}}{\bbcenter{#2}}}
            {\scale{\sub{\bbtop{#2}}{\int{xheight}}}{\int{italicslant}}}}
        \glyph{#3}{1000}
    \pop
    \glyph{#1}{1000}
}
```

Putting breathing marks in the margin

Finally, one more interesting example that is nonetheless too often spurned by incompetent Greek typesetters: when an uppercase Greek vowel appears at the beginning of a paragraph or a line of verse, the breathing mark and any accent that it bears are set in the margin:

Ὁ κανόνας λέει ὅτι   —"Ὅπως εἴπαμε
Στοιχειοθετοῦμε λέξεις ποὺ   — Νὰ μὴ ξεχάσεις
Ἀρχίζουν ἀπὸ φωνῆεν   —'Ἀφοῦ σοῦ λέω
Μὲ περασιὰ στὸ γράμμα καὶ   — Πάψε πιά !
"Οχι στὸ πνεῦμα.   —"Ἔτσι μ᾽ ἀρέσει

Note that in the case of the letters alpha and omicron, we are also required to kern the breathing mark and the letter.

Two ways to achieve this behavior come to mind:

- Either we create a zero-width glyph containing nothing but the breathing mark (or the breathing mark together with the accent) and write a kerning pair for this breathing mark and the letter.

- Or we create glyphs that are combinations of breathing marks and letters, with the breathing mark appearing outside the glyph's abstract box.

We shall give examples of code for these two cases and show why the first case ultimately *cannot* be made to work.

First, let us assume that we have a glyph named rough (the rough breathing, or *spiritus asper*) and that we wish to obtain a rough.zerowidth (zero-width rough breathing). Here is a fragment of code for this purpose:

```
\setglyph{rough.zerowidth}
   \push
      \movert{\neg{\width{rough}}}
      \glyph{rough}{1000}
   \pop
\endsetglyph
```

Thanks to \push and \pop, we can achieve a zero width. By first moving towards the left a distance equal to the set-width of the "normal" rough breathing, we obtain a glyph placed entirely outside and to the left of its abstract box.

Everything is fine up to this point: we place the glyph in front of a capital epsilon, and it is indeed set in the margin. Now we have only to solve the problem of kerning between the breathing mark and the uppercase letter alpha or epsilon that follows. And there we discover the snag in our approach: if we kern the breathing and the letter, the distance between the two glyphs becomes aesthetically acceptable, but the letter is no longer where it should be.

The very purpose of this maneuver is to align the uppercase vowels. Thus we should move the breathing mark closer to the letter not by moving the letter to the left but rather by moving the breathing mark to the right and leaving the letter right where it is. Unfortunately, TEX has made no provision for this procedure: in a kerning pair, it is *always* the second term that is moved, never the first.

Thus this is the reason for which our first attempt has failed: it is impossible to perform kerning without moving the letter, and that is just what we wished to avoid.

Now let us attempt to define a glyph Alpha_rough.bp ("bp" for "beginning of paragraph"), which will incorporate a rough breathing and a capital alpha, with the breathing moved out into the margin but at the proper distance from the letter:

```
\setglyph{Alpha_rough.bp}
    \push
        \movert{\neg{\width{rough}}}
        \movert{\neg{\kerning{rough}{Alpha}}}
        \glyph{rough}{1000}
    \pop
    \glyph{Alpha}{1000}
\endsetglyph
```

This time we have succeeded: we set up a \push and \pop pair, we move the breathing to the left so that it will be to the left of the box, and then we move it to the right a distance equal to the kerning between the breathing and the letter. Since this kerning ordinarily operates to the left (backward motion), we use the \neg command to achieve motion to the right. After making all these moves, we set the glyph for the breathing. We restore the current point to what it was before the \push/\pop (i.e., the original coordinates), we set the letter alpha, and voilà!

Keeping accented capitals from taking up too much vertical space

To conclude this series of examples of the placement of diacritical marks, here are two more that may prove to be singularly important for the typesetting of the several European languages, especially when fonts designed outside Europe are used.

Let us start with a very simple case. We know that the capital letters in most European languages should be written with their accents. But when the heights of the letters are uneven, the accents over the letters can often modify the leading. That problem results from the fact that TEX adds extra space to lines that contain slightly taller glyphs, which may occur if we write accents over our capitals. To prevent this problem, we can use the \smash macro, which "smashes" a glyph's abstract box and treats the glyph as if it were of zero height. But this solution is neither elegant nor compatible with the very delicate properties of kerning and hyphenation. A more elegant solution is therefore needed, and here it is: we can force the abstract boxes of the accented capitals to have the same dimensions as those of the letters without accents. Here is an example:

```
\setglyph{Eacute}
    \topaccent{E}{acute}{500}
    \resetheight{\height{E}}
\endsetglyph
```

Building Europe while showing respect for cultural differences

Our last example illustrates a problem that has always poisoned Franco-German relations. No, we are not referring to Alsace-Lorraine, nor to the deportation of Daniel Cohn-
Bendit in May 1968, but to the *difference in the height of the diaeresis*. Germans, in fact,
place their umlaut quite low, so that it is almost attached to the letter that bears it, and
in any event lower than the dot on the 'i'. For example, the font *Transitional 521*, by
Bitstream, is very well adapted to German, as the dot on its 'i' is at the height of 609 units
whereas the umlaut is at 529. A difference of 80 units is a fifth of the height of the lowercase letters, hardly a negligible amount.

The German way The French way

The French, on the other hand, tend to place the diaeresis at the same height as the dot
on the 'i'. Here is how to rectify the situation. Instead of writing:

```
\setglyph{udieresis}
    \topaccent{u}{dieresis}{500}
\endsetglyph
```

we shall write:

```
\setglyph{udieresis}
    \frenchdieresis{u}
\endsetglyph
```

with \frenchdieresis defined in the following manner:

```
\setcommand\frenchdieresis#1{
    \push
        \moveup{\neg{\height{dieresis}}}
        \moveup{\height{i}}
```

Figure 9-10: The utility LTR Bleifrei LayerPlayer of Letterror.

```
\movert{\add{\sub{\scale{\width{#1}}{500}}{%
\scale{\width{dieresis}}{500}}}
    {\scale{\sub{\height{#1}}{\int{xheight}}}{\int{italicslant}}}}
\glyph{dieresis}{1000}
\pop
\glyph{#1}{1000}
}
```

The only difference between that command and the usual \topaccent command is that we first move down by a depth equal to the height of the font's diaeresis; next, we move up to a height equal to that of the 'i'. When we set the diaeresis, therefore, it has exactly the same height as the dot on the 'i'. Note that this procedure is not necessary for the font in which this book has been typeset, for the very simple reason that that font comes from France, having been designed by our dear beloved Jean François Porchez and being used in the "newspaper of reference" known as *Le Monde*.

Setting lead type with TₑX

To conclude this chapter on TₑX and fonts with a flourish, let us see a simple example that is as dramatic as it is instructive. In 2001 the Dutch foundry Letterror of Just van Rossum and Erik van Blokland issued a font named *Bodoni Bleifrei* [338]. The adjective *bleifrei* means "lead-free" in German. The font is a reproduction of a 48-point roman by Bodoni that manages to give the appearance of a series of type sorts arranged on a composing stick.

A utility by the name of *LTR Bleifrei LayerPlayer* (for Mac OS 9 only), which is shown in Figure 9-10, allows one to enter text in this font and select colors to produce special effects. We enter a few words in this utility's window and save the result in EPS format; then it can be used in any vector-based image software.

But how does it work? In fact, there are three superimposed fonts. These three fonts can be of different colors, for producing special effects. The first font, *Bodoni Bleifrei-Imprint*, reproduces the impressions of the type—i.e., the glyphs as they are usually seen. In the example shown in Figure 9-10, we have selected the Chrome configuration; in it, the *Bleifrei-Imprint* font appears in white.

Let us take another example and separate the layers. Here is the first layer (in which we have made the background gray in order to make the white text visible):

The second layer, called *Bodoni Bleifrei-Leaded*, is used in black. It represents the printable surface of the type, the edges of which have been blackened to give the impression of depth:

Finally, the third layer, called *Bodoni Bleifrei-Slugs*, consists of boxes that establish the background color:

In the example, this color is a very pretty purple, its CMYK parameters being 42, 42, 19, 10. And here are the three layers put together:

It is entirely possible to obtain the same result in TEX. Virtual fonts will allow us to use a single font that will produce the three layers, with any colors that we wish.

Let BodonBleImp.afm, BodonBleLea.afm, and BodonBleSlu.afm be the names of the AFM files associated with the three base fonts. A glyph in our virtual font will combine the corresponding glyphs from these three fonts. For example, the F of the virtual font will superimpose the F of BodonBleImp.afm with the F of BodonBleLea.afm and that of Bodon-BleSlu.afm.

The first hurdle: if we wish to refer to these three letters F in a single *fontinst* glyph definition, they must have different names.

Thus we must rename the glyphs in at least two of these fonts. Does that mean that we have to open the PostScript code for the font and edit it? Not at all; in any event, our user's license for the font forbids us to do so. We shall simply create new AFM files, since *fontinst* can read only AFM.

A little Perl script something like

```
open IN, "BodonBleLea.afm";
open OUT, ">nouveaux/BodonBleLea.afm";
while (<IN>) {
s/;[ \t]*N ([A-Za-z0-]+)[ \t]*;/; \1.lead ;/;
print OUT;
}
close OUT; close IN;
```

will append the suffix .lead to all the glyphs in BodonBleLea.afm. We do likewise for BodonBleSlu (with the suffix .slug). Now we have three fonts whose glyphs have distinct names.

The second hurdle: we wish to change the color of a glyph, and we know that we can use the *fontinst* command \glyphspecial, but what is the corresponding PostScript code?[25]

There is no need to reinvent the wheel. It is sufficient to create a little TₑX in which we change the color of a word and then read the DVI file to see which blocks of PostScript code are inserted. We can use the specifications of the color purple that we wish to obtain. Thus, by writing

```
\textcolor[cmyk]{.42,.42,.19,.10}{blabla}
```

we obtain a DVI file in which we find the following lines. (We have converted the DVI code to DVR so as to make it readable to a human.)

```
XXX "color push cmyk .42 .42 .19 .10"
SET blabla
XXX "color pop"
```

Conclusion: We need only add the PostScript code color push cmyk .42 .42 .19 .10 before the glyph and color pop after the glyph. As the names "push" and "pop" suggest, we are pushing the color onto the stack of PostScript's graphics state.

Here, then, is the *fontinst* code to obtain the letter 'F' in our virtual font:

```
\setglyph{F}
   \push
   \glyphspecial{color push cmyk .42 .42 .19 .10}
```

---

[25] The reader who feels ill at ease with the PostScript language may consult our introduction to this language in Appendix C.1 on page 635 of this book.

```
    \glyph{F.slug}
    \glyphspecial{color pop}
    \pop
    \push
    \glyph{F.lead}
    \pop
    \glyph{F}
\endsetglyph
```

We start with the lowest layer so that we can superimpose the other two upon it. What is incredible is that this font is perfectly ordinary to TEX, which will perform kerning, hyphenation, etc., as usual without being aware that the font exists under several layers with different colors.

Conclusions and Glimpses at the Future

In this chapter we have seen, without going *too* deeply into the details, various aspects of font management in TEX and Ω. Its apparent complexity is related to the clash of cultures that occurred between the initial philosophy of TEX (TFM metrics, on the one hand, and GF or PK bitmaps on the other) and the chaotic real world of the fonts of the past two decades. How can we get the most benefits from TEX font metrics—and from virtual fonts in particular? At the same time, how can we adapt fonts (PostScript, TrueType, OpenType, etc.) for use with TEX when they are a priori foreign to it?

We have seen that most of the problems stem from the incompatibility between these two philosophies and from the fact that we cannot provide more information to TEX than what exists within the concept of a virtual font. For instance, PostScript and TrueType fonts contain the notion of a bounding box, whereas virtual fonts know nothing about it. We are therefore obliged to perform all the operations involving a bounding box (e.g., precise placement of diacritical marks) while we still have access to this information—namely, at the time that the virtual font is created by *fontinst*, when it has just read the AFM files and accumulated the data for the bounding boxes. After that, it will be too late: TEX will never again have access to the information.

Another example, going in the opposite direction: ligatures. We have seen that when ligatures appear in PostScript fonts adapted for use with TEX, it is certainly not because they were already indicated in the AFM files. In reality, AFM usually disregard ligatures altogether. If we have ligatures at our disposal, it is because they were systematically inserted, thanks to the file latin.mtx. But what about OpenType or AAT files, which specify with great precision which ligatures should be made and under which conditions? Furthermore, it must be admitted that the mechanisms for using ligatures provided by OpenType and AAT are more powerful than those of TEX or Ω. By what convoluted means can we convert an AAT finite automaton for ligatures into a series of ligatures in a virtual font? The idea of writing a generic algorithm to convert AAT finite automata into ligatures in a virtual font could be the inspiration for a horror movie by Stephen King...

Thus only one possible solution can be imagined: opening the doors to the perspective of TEX, or rather Ω (since TEX is enjoying eternal rest in the heavenly kingdom of deceased software), for those who come into direct contact with OpenType, AAT, and all the other kinds of fonts that the future holds in store for us. It is time, then, to toll the knell of TFM, VF, OFM, OVF, and other font-metric file formats that are not up to the standard of today's fonts.

The author's research team at ENST Bretagne is working on version 2 of Ω, based on *textemes* [167, 168, 71]. A *texteme* is a data structure containing, all in one: a character, one or more glyphs, and, potentially, a set of key-value pairs called properties (Arabic form, color, hyphenation, font, Semitic root, Chinese ideographic radical and/or decomposition, language, horizontal and vertical offset of the glyph, and whatever else the user may need). The goal of textemes is to replace characters by becoming the atomic units of text, so that information which is missing from characters in the current Unicode-based model of text, can be injected at a level other than mark up. Using textemes in the Ω input document, the typesetting process becomes an accumulation of texteme properties so that Ω output contains essentially the same textemes as the input document, but with many more properties.

How does Ω v2 deal with OpenType fonts? During processing by Ω, texteme string are filtered by external engines. One of these engines corresponds roughly to Uniscribe/παν語 and will segment text, apply contextual analysis for Arabic, re-order Indic glyphs, etc. Two other external engines correspond to the two basic OpenType tables GSUB and GPOS. These engines will read the font data and will apply OpenType transformations to the flow of textemes (in fact: to the glyphs contained in the textemes). This approach has the advantage that one keeps absolute control on the way the text is transformed, since one can act on the texteme flow at any moment, even after the GPOS engine or between engines. Ω v2 is still an experimental project, a heavy-duty approach to the problem of marrying the TEX principles of versatile high-level typography and the OpenType way of processing international text.

10

Fonts and Web Pages

When Tim Berners-Lee defined the HTTP protocol and the HTML markup system, he could hardly have expected that the whole world would be talking ".com" 20 years later. The explosion of the Web is without a doubt one of the highlights of the end of the twentieth century.

HTML is a markup system—a set of rules for the structure and the semantics of tags.

It is based on SGML, the Standard Generalized Markup Language—"generalized" in the sense that it has no semantics, only rules for writing. An SGML document is composed of *elements*. An element is represented by a pair of tags: the opening tag (written <name>) and the closing tag (written </name>). Between these tags is the element's "content", which can contain other tags and/or textual content. An element can have any number of metadata called *attributes*. Attributes take the form of "key–value" pairs written within the opening tag. Their number and their order are arbitrary.

An SGML document may be accompanied by a Document Type Definition (DTD), included in the file or stored in an external file. This DTD is a set of data of two types: first, a list of all the elements allowed in the SGML document, together with their attributes and the types of data that may have these attributes; second, a list of rules for the behavior of the elements with one another. We can specify, for example, that a given element may contain another given element a certain number of times, or that it must be empty, or that it may contain anything, and so on.

HTML is an SGML DTD, and, at the same time, a markup syntax. That means that the tags that may be used in an HTML document are well defined once and for all, that their interaction with one another is also defined, and that we have a sort of "user's manual" that shows us the meaning and applicability of each tag.

But unlike LATEX, in which the meaning of each tag is as clear as can be,[1] HTML assigns only an approximate meaning, and each browser may interpret that meaning as it chooses.

HTML has suffered greatly from the artistic fuzziness that surrounds its tags. For example, each browser has felt itself obliged to add its own tags to the basic system, which has led to frequent updates of HTML, many of them based on the initiatives of some of the browsers with the largest market share. Despite that fact, however, it must be understood that during the era when the Macintosh, the Windows PC, and Unix stations had a terrible time communicating with each other, HTML was (together with TEX and, a little later, Acrobat) the first "document format" common to all operating systems.

To solve a number of problems without completely tearing the HTML standard apart, two new layers of information were added: *JavaScript*, a programming language developed by Netscape (and later to become an ECMA standard under the name of ECMAScript), whose purpose is to manage the interactivity of HTML pages, and *Cascading Style Sheets* (CSS, a W3C standard), a language for describing the appearance of HTML pages. These three layers of information (HTML, JavaScript, CSS) live together in harmony within a single document. Furthermore, JavaScript has access to the information in all three levels, thanks to a syntax called *Document Object Model* (DOM, also a W3C standard).

But let us leave history aside and move on to the situation that exists today. Several years ago, a successor to SGML arrived on the scene and literally conquered the market: XML (*Extensible Markup Language*, a W3C standard). XML, which we shall discuss in greater detail on page 345, is a stricter version of SGML—and "stricter (for the human)" means "easier to manage (by machine)". Indeed, whereas there were only one or two very specialized tools for processing SGML that were quite inaccessible to the ordinary mortal, today we have an enormous number of tools—industrial, mass-market, or free—for working with XML. By slightly constraining the freedom of markup that SGML affords (the differences between SGML and XML can be summed up with five simple rules), XML has succeeded in wiping out the unfavorable impression that the public had of SGML ("labyrinth", "juggernaut", etc.) and in establishing a genuine format for data exchange that can be used in all areas of computer science.

Between the fantastically expanding XML and the aging HTML, we eventually find ourselves faced with a sharp contradiction. The World Wide Web Consortium (W3C) has suggested a solution: an XML-ized version of HTML, known as XHTML. In addition, XML inherits technologies from the HTML era: JavaScript, CSS, and a technique specific to XML that is called *namespaces*. Namespaces are a means of combining several DTDs, i.e., of creating documents with tags coming from various and sundry sources, with predefined semantics in different contexts. Since XHTML has been defined and codified, we know that it does not have any tags that support the creation of mathematical formulae. But a standard exists that does make it possible to create them: *MathML*. By

---

[1] This is true because LATEX is a programming language and we can follow the execution of a LATEX command right down into the bowels of TEX. A LATEX command is therefore a "tag" whose semantics are defined a posteriori by its effects when we compile a document using that tag with TEX or Ω.

using a namespace for "XHTML" and another for "MathML", we can simultaneously use tags belonging to both standards without causing any conflicts. In this way, every new standard can be used immediately within XHTML documents, provided, of course, that tools for processing it are available.

In this chapter, our concern shall be font management as performed using the technologies of the Web.

We can see that fonts are one of the Web's major problems, for the very simple reason that fonts, unlike text and illustrations, are the only resources in a document that *do not belong* to the document's author. If they do not belong to the document's author, that is because they are under license, and he does not have the right to distribute them freely. To display a web page, one can limit oneself to using only the fonts that are available on the client's system; but then one needs either to know their names or to use generic names. If one absolutely insists on using a specific font (for example, if one must display text in a script that is not supported by all operating systems), it is necessary to communicate with the client, and that is where the technical problems and questions of rights begin.

We can observe that the subject of fonts has been approached from three different angles, which will form the three main divisions of this chapter:

- HTML offers a certain number of tags for font selection; for its part, CSS offers a certain number of instructions for describing the fonts used in (X)HTML pages, be they local fonts (present on the client's sytem) or fonts downloaded from the Web (provided that the browser is capable of downloading fonts from the Web).

- Two companies have developed plug-ins that enable browsers to obtain through the network the fonts that are needed to display an HTML page. These are Bitstream (*TrueDoc* technology) and Microsoft (*Font Embedding* technology). Bitstream has apparently had only limited success with the browsers that are compatible with its technology: Netscape 4.x (but not version 6 or 7), Explorer under Windows only, and iCab. Microsoft's technology for incorporating fonts is compatible only with its own browser (Explorer) and only under Windows; its benefit is that one can freely create downloadable fonts.

  On the other hand, a Swedish company by the name of em2 Solutions markets the *ne plus ultra* for fonts on the Web: a server plug-in named *GlyphGate*. This software uses many different techniques for displaying a document with precisely defined fonts by adapting itself to the technical capabilities of the client browser. According to the browser being used, GlyphGate may send totally different information to different clients, either by taking advantage of downloadable file formats for some browsers or, in the worst case, by generating GIF images for the words in the document. Glyph-Gate is Unicode-compatible and is able to display any script on any browser. There is even a software development kit (SDK) for adapting GlyphGate to special fonts or scripts.

- A new standard, by the name of SVG, was developed by the W3C. It is based on XML, and its purpose is to describe a page's geography, through the use of glyphs, bitmap or vector images, and interactive or dynamic elements. Naysayers will maintain that it is an XMLization of the PostScript language, which is not altogether wrong, as Adobe was the originator of this standard. In any event, font management under SVG is very rich, to the point that there is even an ad hoc font format, which makes it possible to include within a document the vector description of the glyphs to be displayed while at the same time treating them as characters (selection with the mouse, copying and pasting, searching for strings, etc.). SVG is a very promising technology, and it deserves a detailed study, even though, to date, not all browsers natively support it.[2]

(X)HTML, CSS, and Fonts

The Standard HTML Tags

Since the beginning, HTML has offered a number of tags for enhancing text: `<address>` (the "address" mode, which both Netscape and Explorer have chosen to represent with italics), `<b>` (bold), `<cite>` (the "citation" mode, represented with italics), `<em>` (the emphasized mode à la LATEX, represented with italics), `<i>` (italics), `<code>`, `<kbd>`, `<pre>`, `<samp>`, `<tt>`, (typewriter type), `<strong>` (the "strong" mode, represented with italics or bold type), `<var>` (the "variable" mode, in the sense of variables in a programming language).

Versions 1 to 3.2 of HTML include an element called `<font>` for specifying the active font. This element was dropped from version 4 of HTML in favor of CSS and, of course, is also absent from XHTML. Here are the different attributes that this element could take, during its short life:

Name	Netscape	Explorer	Example of usage
color	≥ 2	≥ 3	color="#660099"
face	≥ 3	≥ 3	face="Helvetica, Arial, sans-serif"
point-size	4	-	point-size="12"
size	all	all	size="-2"
weight	4	-	weight="300"

In the case of the `face` attribute, one can use any number of "font family names", separated by commas. These names are the names by which fonts are identified by the system; in other words, Quickdraw names on the Macintosh, Windows names under that operating system, and part of the XLFD name under Unix.[3] Since these names are quite variable, it follows that the approach used here is far from infallible. To compensate for

---

[2] See http://www.svgi.org on SVG compatibility with browsers. This URL also provides a comprehensive list of resources, tools and documentation.

[3] In *Mozilla*'s dialog box for selecting the default fonts, for example, one may choose fonts whose names are made up from the *foundry's name*, the *family name*, and the *primary* and *secondary indicators of the encoding* (in the sense of XLFD; see page 222):

these problems, the standard provides five "generic" font-family names, to be added to the end of the list: serif, sans-serif, cursive, fantasy, monospace. Each browser is free to choose a font for each of these generic names, and all recent browsers allow the user to select a representative font for each of these "categories".

The size attribute is perhaps the HTML attribute that is the most *poorly understood* by users. This is how it works: one may choose an absolute value (between 1 and 7, the default value being 3) or a relative value (between +1 and +7 or between -1 and -7). Contrary to the mathematical notation that we all learned in school, here +3 and 3 do not have the same meaning: the former *increases* the active size by three units; the latter calls for the size named "3", thus a medium size.

There is a variant of <font> by the name of <basefont>. It takes the attributes color, face, and size. It was also abandoned in version 4 of HTML. The difference between <basefont> and <font> is not clear.

CSS (version 3)

CSS is a W3C standard that manages the display of elements in an (X)HTML document. The idea is as follows: one writes *rules* for display, with each rule containing a *selector*, which determines the elements that will be displayed in a certain manner, and a set of *declarations*, which determine the way in which elements selected in advance will be displayed. The word "cascading" refers to the method for managing selectors and declarations. Take the following CSS code as an example:

```
<style type="text/css">
em { color:pink; text-decoration: underline; }
.important { color:green; text-transform: uppercase; }
p em { color:blue; font-family: "Helvetica"; }
p > em { color:red; font-size: 24pt; }
</style>
```

Here we have four CSS rules. The first deals with em elements and requests that these elements be typeset in underlined pink type (thus there are two declarations: one for the color pink and one for underlining). The second applies to any element with a class attribute whose value is "important", and it requests that these elements be set in green type and in full capitals. The third applies once again to em elements, but this time only to those that "have a p ancestor", *i.e*, those that are contained with a p element, at any depth whatsoever: it requests that they be set in blue and in Helvetica. Finally, the fourth again applies to em elements, but this time only to those that are direct children of a p element; they must be set in red and at 24 points.

We can see here that *Mozilla* chooses to omit all the other fields of the XLFD name so as to make the choice easier and to retain better control over the properties of the selected fonts.

This example may seem absurd at first glance, but what it is intended to illustrate is that when an element appears in all these categories, the rules of the CSS standard specify the priority of one or another property, while preserving all properties that do not cause a conflict. In the example, we always have two declarations: the color, different in each case, and another property, which is unique. Let us consider the following HTML code:

```
<em class="important">A few words;
how will they be displayed?</em>
```

The em element that we see here is "selected" by all the rules in the style sheet. How will it be displayed? Well, it is clear that it will be displayed in capitals, in *Helvetica*, underlined, and at 24 points, because these properties do not come into conflict. On the other hand, what will its color be? CSS clearly defines the rules of the game: in this example, the class="important" constraint is the most important; thus the block of text will be set in green. And that will be true in *every* CSS-compatible browser. This last point is very important, as it guarantees that a page will be displayed in the same way everywhere. Note that CSS allows us to short-circuit the hierarchy of priorities by adding among the declarations for one rule the keyword "!important".

In the following material, we shall not go into the details of the syntax and features of CSS. For those subjects, there is a plethora of books, as instructive as they are comprehensive, that the reader may consult; for example, [151] (O'Reilly), [254], and, last but not least, the CSS specification, published by the Web consortium [88]. For our part, we shall instead make a detailed study of the use of fonts under CSS (version 3).

CSS declarations for specifying the active font

Recall that a CSS rule consists of a *selector* (one or more (X)HTML tag names, or the name of a class, or an identifier, or a combination of the three), which indicates the parts of the document that are affected by this presentation rule, and a *set of declarations* (name–value pairs), which indicate the visual properties of the material to be displayed. The general syntax is as follows:

```
selector { name: value; name: value; name: value; etc. }
```

What are the declarations that manage fonts? They are of two kinds: there are seven for selecting the active font and five others that manage "decorations". Here are the seven most important declarations:[4]

- font-family (NN4, IE4), which takes as its value a number of font names (Quick-draw names on the Macintosh, Windows names under that operating system, a part of the XLFD name under Unix [see note 3]) placed within single or double quotation marks and separated by commas. The order of these font names is the order of

---

[4] To indicate the compatibility of these declarations with the Netscape Navigator and Internet Explorer browsers, we shall use the following abbreviations: 'NN' followed by a number indicates the version of Netscape since which the declaration has been supported; 'IE' indicates the version of Explorer; 'W' indicates Windows; 'M' indicates Macintosh.

precedence for font selection, provided that the font exists on the client's system. For example, we may write:

```
body { font-family: "PMN Caecilia", "Helvetica", "Arial MS",
       sans-serif; }
```

where *PMN Caecilia* is the name of a very specific font that perhaps does not exist on all platforms (unless it is downloaded together with the page, which we shall see later), *Helvetica* is the name of a Macintosh font that is one of the default fonts, *Arial* is the name of the same font but under Windows, and `sans-serif` is a generic keyword (the same keywords as those used with the `<font>` attribute are available here: `serif`, `sans-serif`, `cursive`, `fantasy`, `monospace`, or `none` [when we wish to disable font substitution]). Thus we move from the specific to the general, hoping that the browser will find the corresponding font as soon as possible.

But the Web is an international facility, and the specificity of the font also entails the specificity of the script, and more specifically the Unicode zones covered by each font, i.e., the set of Unicode characters that can be represented by the font. The `font-family` declaration allows us to take glyphs from multiple fonts, according to what they have available. Thus, by writing:

```
body { font-family: "PMN Caecilia", "Heisei Gothic W3",
       "Arial Unicode MS", sans-serif; }
```

we take the glyphs for the Latin characters from *PMN Caecilia*, the glyphs for the ideographic characters (more specifically, the Japanese characters) from *Heisei Gothic W3*, the glyphs for Cyrillic or Greek characters from *Arial Unicode MS*, and everything else from `sans-serif`, provided, of course, that the font selected by the client's browser is sufficiently rich.

In other words, the browser will check not only the existence of a given font but also the existence of each glyph in each font, one by one, and will choose for each glyph the first font that contains it.

Finally, note that among the among the CSS selectors we also find the *language* of the block of text. We can thus connect the selection of a font to that of the active language. That possibility is particularly attractive when several languages share the same Unicode characters but are written with different glyphs. Here is an example in which we use the selector `:lang()`, which indicates the language of the XML or XHTML element, specified through the `xml:lang` attribute:

```
*:lang(de) { font-family: "DS-Normal-Fraktur", serif; }
*:lang(fr) { font-family: "Fournier MT", serif; }
*:lang(ja) { font-family: "Heisei Mincho W3", serif; }
*:lang(zh) { font-family: "Li Sung", serif; }
```

In this example, we have decided to write German in the Gothic script (using the "standardized Gothic" of *Delbanco Schriften*), as it was still written just a bit more than 60 years ago. For French we are using a typically French font (the magnificent

Fournier, by Monotype); for Japanese, we use a Japanese font, and we use a Chinese font for Chinese.[5]

- font-style (NN4, IE4), which can take three values: normal, italic, oblique. Note that CSS does not provide for switching to upright type in the event of "double italics", i.e., a fragment in italics that appears in a block that is already in italics. But we can simulate this behavior by writing, for example:

```
em { font-style: italic; }
em em { font-style: normal; }
em em em { font-style: italic; }
```

which means: the contents of <em> are to be set in italics unless this <em> appears within another <em>, at any depth whatsoever. And if this second <em> is itself contained within another <em>, we shift back to upright type. But be forewarned: there are other elements that are also set in italics; thus one must handle them all, one by one, through the use of selectors.

Note that the value italic will result in oblique if no italic font is available but a slanted font is available.

- font-variant (NN6, IE4), which takes only two values—normal and small-caps— and thus is used only for small capitals. Note that since capital letters are being used (since small capitals are in fact capitals, even though they are of smaller size), in order to complete this operation successfully the browser must both have access to Unicode's case-mapping tables (page 112) and be able to recognize the active language, as capitalization often depends on the language: for example, the same word "liter" is written "LITER" in capitals within an English context and "LİTER" within a Turkish context.

- font-weight (NN4, IE4), which indicates the weight of the font. To this end, three types of values are available: numerical values, absolute keywords, and relative keywords. The numerical values must be even hundreds between 100 and 900.[6] The possible absolute keywords are normal (which is equal to 400) and bold (700). The relative keywords are bolder and lighter. Each of these raises or lowers the weight by 100 units.

---

[5] A word of explanation, to help the reader to understand these examples better. (a) Just over 60 years ago, German was written in the Gothic script—which was not a choice of font, as it is today, but another script altogether, with a full spectrum of quite varied fonts, comparable to the range of roman fonts that we enjoy today. (b) Japanese, Chinese, and Korean are all written with ideographs and use the same Unicode characters, but the fact remains that they often need slightly different glyphs for the same characters. We must therefore use separate fonts, which, incidentally, creates big problems for printers in the corresponding countries: what should be done when a Chinese word using a character specific to Chinese pops up right in the middle of a Japanese document? or a character that is common to the two languages but that has slightly different glyphs in each? Some will substitute a similar glyph; others will change fonts by using a makeshift font, which runs the risk of destroying the visual unity of the text.

[6] Why hundreds rather than simply integer values between 1 and 9? In the hope, no doubt, that the browsers of the future will also be able to accept intermediate numeric values, somewhat like the Multiple Master fonts.

- `font-stretch` (no browser), which indicates the font's set-width. Once again we have absolute and relative keywords. The absolute keywords are `ultra-condensed`, `extra-condensed`, `condensed`, `semi-condensed`, `normal`, `semi-expanded`, `expanded`, `extra-expanded`, `ultra-expanded`. As one might expect, the relative keywords are `wider` and `narrower`; they enable us to move up or down one level in the series.

- `font-size` (NN4, IE4), which indicates the font's actual size. To represent this size, we may choose:

  - A dimension, expressed in `em` (the em of the current font, i.e., its actual size), `ex` (the height of the lowercase letter 'x'), `px` (pixels), `pt` (American printer's points), `mm`, `cm`, or `in` (inches).

  - A percentage of the actual size of the active font.

  - Absolute keywords (inspired by the sizes of T-shirts): `xx-small`, `x-small`, `small`, `medium`, `large`, `x-large`, `xx-large`. The CSS specification recommends the following correspondences between keywords, scaling/shrinking factors, and XHTML heading levels:

Keyword	`xx-small`	`x-small`	`small`	`medium`	`large`	`x-large`	`xx-large`
Factor	60%	75%	89%	100%	120%	150%	200%
Heading	h6		h5	h4	h3	h2	h1

  - Relative keywords: `larger` and `smaller`, which enable us to move up or down one level in the series of absolute keywords. If, however, the size is defined by a dimension, the browser is free to apply a scaling factor based on that size or to round it off first so that its value will match that of an absolute keyword.

- `font-size-adjust` (no browser), followed by a rational number between 0 and 1. To understand the usefulness of this declaration, which applies only to those scripts that distinguish uppercase and lowercase letters, i.e., the Latin, Gothic, Gaelic, Greek, Cyrillic, Armenian, and liturgical Georgian scripts and, by extension, the modern Georgian[7] and Arabic[8] scripts (see Figure 10-1), let us conduct a little experiment. The text that the reader is currently reading is set in *Le Monde Livre*, which has a rather large x-height: the ratio between the height of the letter 'x' and the body size of the font is 0.482. Now let us switch to *Centaur*, a font designed in 1915 by Bruce Rogers [228, p. 62] that many people consider to be one of the most beautiful fonts of the previous century. Does the reader not have the impression that the text has suddenly become less legible? That change results from the significant difference between the x-heights of the two fonts: that of *Centaur* is only 0.366, or 25 percent less than that of *Le Monde Livre*. Here we are again in

---

[7] Modern Georgian has no notion of uppercase and lowercase letters, but the Georgian letters do have ascenders and descenders in certain styles. We can consider the x-height of this script to be the ratio between the short letters and those with an ascender.

[8] In Arabic, if one disregards the dots above and below the letters, there are two basic heights for glyphs: the "tall" glyphs (*alef*, *lam*, etc.) and the "short" glyphs (*beh*, *seen*, *sad*, etc.). Here again, we can consider the x-height to be the ratio between the tall letters and the short letters.

Figure 10-1: The x-heights (ratios of the height of the short letters to the body size) of several typi-cal fonts for different scripts: (1) the Latin script, Linotype Didot font, 0.42; (2) the Gaelic script, Morley Bunċló font, 0.50; (3) the Gothic script, Delbanco Normal-Fraktur font, 0.52; (4) the Cyrillic script, Monotype Garamond Cyrillic font, 0.45; (5) the Armenian script, MacCampus Mesrop font, 0.30; (6) the Greek script, Monotype Greek 91 font, 0.41; and (7) the Georgian litur-gical script, MacCampus Parnavaz font, 0.38. Next, two scripts with no uppercase/lowercase letters: (8) the Arabic script, Monotype Naskh font, 0.22; and (9) the modern Georgian script, ParaGraph Deda Ena font, 0.40.

Le Monde Livre, to continue our experiment. And what if we increase the actual size of *Centaur* so that its lowercase letters have the same size as those of *Le Monde Livre*? Here is the result! The text is certainly more legible now. We can see that the uppercase letters are a little larger, but that is the price to pay if we wish to keep the font intact. Later (page 441) we shall see the tools that enable us to modify the font by changing only the size of the lowercase letters, but let us not forget that that constitutes a major departure from the font's design.

As the reader will have guessed, the role of font-size-adjust is to effect this correc-tion of the actual size of a font that is substituted for another. How does it work? The information, known as the *x-height*, that is specified in this declaration is the ratio between the height of the *short* letters (those that have neither an ascender nor a descender: 'a', 'c', 'e', etc.) and the body size of the selected font. To return to CSS, if

we wish to request *Centaur* in the stylesheet as the font to use for some text, we can
write:

```
body { font-family: "Centaur", serif; font-size: 16pt;
       font-size-adjust: .366; }
```

In this case, if *Centaur* is not available and cannot be downloaded, and will thus be
replaced by the default font—for example, *Times*, which has an x-height of 0.46—
the actual size of this *Times* font will be not 16 points, as specified, but $14 \times (0.366/0.46) = 12.73$ points, which is more acceptable, as *Times* quickly becomes intolerable
at large sizes.

- `baseline, centerline, mathline, topline`: the height, expressed in the font's internal units, of four "baselines": the baseline of running text; the "central line" (without
  going into too much detail, this line can be halfway between the height of the ascenders and the depth of the descenders); the horizontal axis for centering mathematical
  symbols such as $+$, $-$, $\times$, etc.; and, finally, the top line (which can be useful for scripts
  whose baseline is at the top, such as Devanagari).

Note that a "synthetic" declaration is available: font, which can take all the values of the
preceding declarations at once, along with a few ancillary values. Thus:

```
body { font: 500 italic 12pt/14.4pt "Palatino Linotype", serif; }
```

is the same as:

```
body { font-style: italic; font-weight: 500;
       font-size: 12pt; line-height: 14.4pt;
       font-family: "Palatino Linotype", serif;
       font-stretch: normal; font-variant: normal; }
```

We can notice two things in this example: first, the fact that the declarations that are not
given an explicit value in font are initialized to their default values; second, that a new
declaration appears here: `line-height`, which determines the leading. Let us note that
`font-size-adjust` is not covered by font.

One last bit of information on the font declaration: it can also take as values the following keywords, but in that case there can be no other indication of size, weight, etc.:

- `caption`: the font used by the system for buttons

- `icon`: the font used by the system for the legends of icons

- `menu`: the font used for menus

- `message-box`: the font used in dialog boxes

- `small-caption`: the font used for "small buttons"

- status-bar: the font used for the status bar

Thus by writing font: menu;, we obtain the font that the operating system uses for menus, whatever that operating system may be. That is not possible with the separate declarations font-size, font-stretch, etc.

And now here are the four declarations that manage "decorations" applied to fonts:

- font-effect (no browser), which takes the following values: emboss (set in relief), engrave, outline, none. For lovers of effects meant for the screen rather than for good old-fashioned paper.

- font-smooth (no browser), which specifies the smoothing, if any, to be applied to the font: auto (use the browser's rules), never (never smooth the font), always (always apply smoothing). Or a keyword or a dimension chosen from those of font-size: large, 14pt, 20px, etc. This possibility allows us to smooth text from a certain size and up, as it is widely recognized that the smoothing of small glyphs tends to hamper the legibility of text.

- font-emphasize-style (no browser), which applies to the ideographic languages (Japanese, Chinese, Korean). In these languages, there is ordinarily no italic style, and bold is not used *within* text in the way that we use italics in Western typography. To "emphasize" a fragment of text, through the use of the <em> tag, one uses various devices, the most common being small symbols (dots, commas, etc.) written above or below the glyphs. This declaration specifies the type of emphasis mark to place above (or below) the ideographs: accent (a brush stroke shaped like a droplet, which is nothing but the ideographic comma), dot (a dot), disc (a heavier dot), circle (a small circle), none (no symbol).

- font-emphasize-position (no browser), in the same vein as the previous declaration, specifies the position of the ideographic emphasis mark. The possible values of this declaration may initially come as a surprise: before or after. It must not be forgotten that the ideographic languages can be written both horizontally (from left to right) and vertically (the lines are arranged from right to left). In the first case, the values of this declaration must be interpreted as "above" and "below"; in the second case, as "at the right" and "at the left". Note that Japanese and Korean printers, and Chinese printers from Taiwan, place these signs "before" (example: 微軟企業領航專區), whereas printers from the People's Republic of China place them "after" (微軟企業領航專區).

Creating a CSS "database" of fonts

In the previous section, we reviewed all the CSS declarations (of version 3) that make it possible to specify the font desired for any element of an (X)HTML or XML document. Now it is time to ask a question: how will the browser choose the font the best adapted to our desiderata?

To this end, we shall develop for the browser a "database" of fonts. Each of this database's entries will be a combination of "family name", "Unicode coverage", "set-width", "weight", "style", "variant", and "actual size", which can only take *absolute* values. For each entry, one must specify:

- Either a way to download the font in question

- Or a way to make a judicious substitution

- Or a way to generate the font artificially from a generic font

Provided, of course, that the browser supports these possibilities—which is far from being the case at this time.

Let us take a few examples:

```
@font-face { font-family: "Charcoal";
             panose-: 2 0 5 3 0 0 0 2 0 4;
             units-per-em: 2048;
             stemv: 340; stemh: 233; slope: 0;
             cap-height: 1509; x-height: 1151; ascent: 1509; descent: -;
           }
@font-face { font-family: "Omega Serif";
             font-style: italic;
             unicode-range: U+0020-, U+0300-E, U+1E??, U+2000-F;
             src: url("http://omega.enstb.org/fonts/omsela.otf")
                  format("opentype");
           }
@font-face { font-family: "Heisei Mincho W3";
             unicode-range: U+3000-FA2D, U+FF00-FFEE;
             units-per-em: 2048;
             widths: U+3000-FA2D 2048, U+FF00-FF5F 2048, U+FF60-FFEE 1024;
             bbox: -, -, 2048, 1755;
           }
```

Here we have three entries in the font "database". The first will be used when we request, in an (X)HTML/XML document, *Omega Serif* italic in a very specific Unicode zone (which corresponds, in fact, to the Latin alphabet and its punctuation); the second, when we request *Charcoal*; and the third, when we request *Heisei Mincho W3* in a specific Unicode zone (that of the ideographic characters). What is interesting is that in the three examples above, if the font in question is missing, we ask the browser to carry out three different operations:

- In the first case, we ask it to find another font that is as similar as possible to the original font. To assist the browser in making this choice, we furnish a certain amount of information: the font's *Panose-1* classification (see Chapter 11) and some font-metric information, such as the thickness of the horizontal and vertical strokes, the slope, etc.

- In the second case, we ask it to download the font in question from a given URL, with the specification that the font is of OpenType format.

- In the third case, we ask it to use a default font, but scaled so that its dimensions correspond to those of the original font. Thus we specify the bounding box of the original font and the set-widths of all of its glyphs.

Note that we can include within a declaration some instructions for intelligent substitution, downloading, and synthesis, as in the following (hypothetical) example:

```
@font-face { font-family: "Heisei Mincho W3";
             unicode-range: U+3000-FA2D, U+FF00-FFEE;
             src: url("http://not.found.anywhere/heiseiw3.otf")
                format("opentype");
             units-per-em: 2048;
             panose-: 2 0 5 3 0 0 0 2 0 4;
             widths: U+3000-FA2D 2048, U+FF00-FF5F 2048, U+FF60-FFEE 1024;
             bbox: -, -, 2048, 1755;
             ascent: 1653; descent: -;
           }
```

In this case, the browser will first try to make an intelligent substitution for the font (and the Panose-1 classification is of crucial importance to that attempt); then it will try to download the font, and if it fails, it will attempt a substitution through "synthesis" using a generic font—provided, yet again, that the browser is capable of carrying out all these operations, which is not yet the case today.

Now let us examine in more detail the various declarations at our disposal. First and foremost, the syntax @font-face, which is that of an "at-rule", which applies not to one or more elements in particular but to the entire document. Unlike ordinary selectors, which may not be repeated, the @font-face rule frequently appears multiple times, once for each entry in the font "database".

Within each @font-face rule, two types of declarations occur:

- Those that make connections to the fonts requested by the user

- Those that tell the browser what to do—make a substitution, download a font, generate a font, etc.

The first of these are nothing more or less than the rules of the previous section: they include the "family name"—but with no alternatives provided; here we are concerned with only a single family name—the Unicode zone covered, the "style" (upright, italic, oblique), the "variant" (small capitals), the "weight", the "set-width", and finally the actual size. In the last four of these, only absolute values are permitted; therefore, do not use larger, narrower, 110%, 1.2em, etc.

The declarations that will be of interest to us below are the second: those that tell the browser what course to take when the font with the requested family name is not available on the system.[9]

Let us start with the simplest case: *downloading*. For downloading a font, the following keywords are available:

- url("*a URL*"), which enables us to specify a URL (HTTP protocol or a local file).

- format("*font format*"), to indicate the font format. We may choose from the following: truedoc-pfr, embedded-opentype, type-1 (PostScript Type 1), truetype, opentype, truetype-gx, speedo, intellifont, svg.[10] Note that, as always, the fact that these names of font formats are part of the CSS specification does not in any way guarantee that there is at least one browser in the world that can download and use fonts of this kind.

- local("*a font name*"), to indicate the name of a font that is present on the local system. Recall that the font-family declaration uses the "family name"; here, however, it is the name of the *font itself* that is used, and therefore a name that also contains the style, the weight, the set-width, etc., and that is a member of the font family. Example: "ITC Franklin Gothic" is the name of a font family that includes "FranklinGothic-Demi", and we shall therefore write:

```
body { font-family: "ITC Franklin Gothic";
       font-weight: 600;
       src: local("FranklinGothic-Demi");
     }
```

We may use any number of local(...) and url(...) keywords, separated by commas: the browser will attempt, in the given order, to use a local font or download a remote font and will continue to the next entry on the list if the attempt fails.

Now let us proceed to *intelligent substitution*. To find what CSS considers to be a "good substitute" for a font that is not available, it is necessary to be able to describe certain characteristics of this font, and the browser will compare them to the characteristics of the fonts that it has available. Then it will choose the font that is the most similar. Thus everything comes down to selecting relevant characteristics, i.e., those that are both precise and readily computable. Here are the characteristics available to us:

---

[9] In fact, at startup, the browser builds its own internal font database containing all the fonts on the system. The declarations in this database are read before those of the document's stylesheet. If a font is already present on the system, the browser will not even read the declaration in the stylesheet and will thus not attempt to replace, download, or generate the font.

[10] The svg format is not mentioned in the CSS specification [88], but it is used in an example in the specification of SVG [134]. Surely its omission was an oversight.

- panose-1: the 10 whole numbers that make up the Panose-1 classification of the font. In Chapter 11, we shall present the complete description of this system of font classification. The problem is still that only few font developers take the trouble of classifying their fonts according to Panose-1, which makes the substitution mechanism uneffective. Another problem is that this classification is more suited to Western scripts than to Eastern ones.[11] But let's not ask for too much! After all, is it possible to classify all the scripts of the world according to a single schema? Certainly not; but most non-Latin fonts also include a Latin component, and we can compare those components through the use of *Panose*, which is already a good start.

- units-per-em: the number of units per em. This is the number of subdivisions of an em used to describe the font: frequently 1,024 or 2,048, but it may run as high as tens of thousands, according to the foundry. The larger this number goes, the more precision we have; but the more precision we have, the more memory the rendering engine needs to perform the various calculations. Thus there is a trade-off between the precision of the design and the consumption of RAM.

- stemv and stemh: the *main* thickness of vertical or horizontal strokes. Unfortunately, the standard provides no further explanations of this subject. But we can agree, in the case of a Latin, Cyrillic, or Greek font, that these two parameters indicate the thickness of the downstrokes of the letter 'H' ("aitch" in Latin, "en" in Cyrillic, "eta" in Greek).

- slope: the slope of the font, measured in degrees in the trigonometric sense (and therefore a negative number in our customary italics). Once again, the standard is not specific enough: what to do in the case of a font such as the sublime *Lanston Garamont Italic*, in which the letters '*K*', '*I*', and '*l*' have slopes equal to 9, 12.4, and 18 degrees, respectively? Is the slope of the lowercase letters more significant for the "look" of the font, given that these letters are more common than the capitals? These questions will remain open as long as the CSS standard does not provide more precise instructions for calculating this parameter.

- cap-height and x-height: the height of the uppercase and lowercase letters; for example, the height of the letters 'H' and 'x'.

- ascent and descent: the height of the letters with ascenders (for example, 'd') and the depth of those with descenders (for example, 'g').

Finally, font *synthesis* (a term used in the CSS specification). The term is ill chosen, as the focus is entirely on the metrics of the font to "synthesize"; thus the procedure involves replacing the glyphs of the original font with other glyphs, but with the same dimensions. Why this insistence on preserving the same dimensions? The reason proffered in the standard is *progressive rendering*. Suppose that our browser is able to download the

---

[11] The aim of Panose-2 [113], an extension of Panose-1, was precisely to fill this void and offer a system of classification based on measurements that are independent of the script. Although a white paper describing this system was published as early as 1993, no software seems to support it yet.

marvelous fonts of the site that we have just visited. But there are many of them, and they contain large numbers of glyphs; thus downloading may take a long time. What do we do when we must render a text but do not yet have the glyphs to use? We render them with another font, preferably a system font that is readily available. But rendering an (X)HTML+CSS page also implies global layout, and this layout cannot change when the correct glyphs become available to replace the temporary ones. Thus, from the beginning, we must place the glyphs so that the replacement of the temporary font with the downloaded font can be performed entirely within the box of each glyph, without any repercussions for the arrangement of the page's visual elements.

Here are the available declarations:

- `units-per-em`, already seen above, which is indispensable when we use declarations that refer to the font's metrics.

- `bbox`, followed by four numbers: the bounding box, or container, of the font. These are the coordinates of the lower left point and the upper right point of the smallest rectangle that can contain every glyph in the font.

- `widths`, followed by any number of "Unicode coverage" pairs (with the same syntax as `unicode-range`) and "set-widths" (whole numbers representing the set-widths of the glyphs corresponding to the Unicode characters that precede them), separated by commas. If there are fewer set-widths than characters, the last set-width is repeated as often as necessary. For example, in the case of the font *Le Monde Livre*, which is used for the text that the reader is currently reading:

```
units-per-em: 1000;
widths: U+002F- 255 510, U+003A-B 255;
```

which means: the glyph of the character[12] U+002F (the slash) has a set-width of 255, and the glyphs of the characters from U+0030 to U+0039 (the Arabic digits '0' to '9') all have the same set-width: 510. Similarly, the glyphs U+003A (the colon) and U+003B (the semicolon) have a set-width of 255.

This technique is not new: it has been part of the PDF format from the beginning. In fact, it is possible to refrain from including fonts in a PDF file. In that case, the two Multiple Master fonts provided with Acrobat will be used: *Adobe Serif* and *Adobe Sans*. But in order for these fonts to fit into the "body" of the original font, they require scaling that is performed by Acrobat, using the set-widths of the glyphs of the original font. Fortunately, the set-widths are not subject to copyright, and one may quite legally include within a PDF file the set-widths of all the fonts employed.

That is roughly the same method that CSS sought to implement, except that in PDF the set-widths are in an optimized and compressed binary format, whereas in CSS they appear in plain text and could potentially take up a great deal of space and cause significant

---

[12] And here we run into a glaring inconsistency of this approach: what will happen if we use a font that contains multiple glyphs for a single Unicode character, such as, for instance, even the humblest Arabic font?

delays in the downloading and rendering of a page.[13] We can get around this problem by only including in the stylesheet the set-widths of the glyphs that are actually used in the XML/(X)HTML document, but that also means that we cannot separate the stylesheet from the document. We shall have to see how the industry will implement this type of approach, which certainly appears very awkward.

Conclusion: is CSS effective?

In the previous two sections, we studied CSS's approach to font management in web documents ((X)HTML) and XML documents in general. We have seen that CSS separates two points of view: that of the author of a web page, who wishes to use a certain number of fonts without worrying too much about technical issues, and that of the "web technician", who does her utmost to ensure that the fonts requested by the author will reach the browser or, as a last resort, be replaced by intelligently chosen fonts.

Is this method effective? When we compare the fine concepts described in the CSS specification with reality, we can see that everything depends, at the end of the day, on the willingness of browsers to comply with the specifications and that, in the case of fonts, that is not yet the case. Next we shall see the real possibilities that exist for downloading fonts. We shall also see that the tools that make downloading possible also manage the "web technician's" part and enable the author of a web page to give free rein to his creativity without worrying about such crudely material details as the management of the CSS font database.

Tools for Downloading Fonts from the Web

In the previous section, we described the CSS declaration src: url("...");, which requests the downloading of a font from the Web. We even furnished a list of font formats provided in the CSS specification. But what does this declaration actually do?

Well, the situation is not golden. Several factors are responsible: first, and we shall never say it enough in this book, fonts are usually subject to copyright and cannot be made available to the public. Thus (a) the format in which the font is downloaded must be an encrypted and secure format so that extraction of its data will be impossible, and (b) the file downloaded must serve no purpose other than the rendering of the web page in question. That is all quite possible, through the use of unpublished font formats (unlike OpenType, PostScript Type 1, etc.) and by locking the downloaded file to a given URL: even if the file is recovered and moved to another location, it will be useless.

But the technical difficulties do not stop there. A browser usually resorts to graphical routines in the operating system to render the contents of its windows. That means that

---

[13] That is why, in the example of a stylesheet with set-widths that we presented above, we "cheated" by considering an ideographic font. A huge yet wonderful paradox of the Japanese, Chinese, and Korean scripts: they contain tens of thousands of signs, but these signs are all extremely disciplined and take up exactly the same space: a square, symbol of balance and harmony. Thus giving the set-widths of the ideographic glyphs presents no problem; after all, they all have the same set-width (with a single exception: the few dozen half-width Japanese kana, a twentieth-century invention whose inclusion in Unicode led to the spilling of a great deal of ink).

the fonts used for rendering text also come from the operating system. But here we are proposing to obtain a file from the Web—a file that only the browser will know how to decrypt—and use its contents as a font, just like the fonts on the system. That approach amounts to short-circuiting the operating system. At the same time, the glyphs rendered must support searches, copying and pasting, etc. And that support presupposes a close collaboration with the operating system—which is being short-circuited, with all the risks of conflict that that entails.

And we have not even mentioned the problems of internationalization: how to render Arabic on a client station that is not configured for the language? If we can download an Arabic font, should we not also be able to render text with it, even if that assumes contextual analysis that may be complex? And what about the link between characters and glyphs? When we select an Arabic word whose glyphs we see and then copy the selection to the clipboard, is it not reasonable to wish to obtain the Unicode characters rather than the positions of the glyphs in a given font?

We can tell that the technical problems involved are not minor ones, and that may explain, at least in part, the weakness and the obscurity of the existing tools. At the same time, these problems emphasize all the more the great accomplishment represented by the development of a product such as GlyphGate, which we shall see below.

We shall present, in a chronological order, the three tools for downloading fonts that are currently available: the *TrueDoc* technology of Bitstream, the WEFT software of Microsoft, and GlyphGate, by em2 Solutions.

TrueDoc, by Bitstream

Bitstream is a large American foundry; its fonts are neither the most magnificent nor the most extravagant nor yet the most authentic, but they maintain a generally high level of quality. Bitstream is known for having launched technologies that failed when confronted with the commercial supremacy of giant multinationals such as Microsoft or Adobe, the most famous examples being *Speedo* and *TrueDoc*, of which the latter is our focus here. *TrueDoc* technology [81] is based on the PFR (for 'Portable Font Resource') file format [99]. PFR has the following technical characteristics:

- It is binary, and its architecture is recognizably different from that of TrueType and PostScript Type 1. In particular, it has its own techniques for hinting, and any font converted to PFR loses its original hints and is given new ones *at the time of rendering*, which, according to Bitstream, enables the rendering to be optimized by creating hints customized for each platform.

- It can theoretically contain up to 65,536 glyphs, but they are not connected to characters, because there is no indication of the encoding being used. Moreover, these glyphs have no name, only a position.

- Part of the PFR specification is freely accessible on Bitstream's web site. But—and this is hardly surprising—the locking of a font to one or more URLs is not docu-

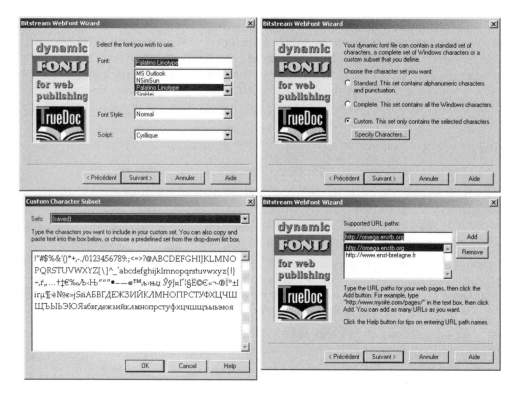

Figure 10-2: Screenshots from WebFont Wizard.

mented. Furthermore, no information on hinting is provided, other than a technique for the replacement, at a low resolution, of certain curves with straight lines;
this technique is related to the flex of PostScript Type 1 fonts.

Just a few years ago, two products for generating PFR fonts were available on the market:

- *Typograph*, by HexWeb, a Macintosh software package in two versions—an independent version and a plug-in version for the *BBEdit* text editor

- *WebFont Wizard*, by Bitstream, for the Macintosh and Windows

The first of these was triply unsuccessful, since the software is not distributed anymore,
the company HexWeb disappeared from the map and from the Web, and, finally, the
Typograph plug-in is incompatible with the latest versions of *BBEdit* and is therefore unusable. As for *WebFont Wizard*, the situation is less severe: the company still exists, and the
product is still usable today; it is simply no longer being distributed. Just in case *Bitstream*
ever decides to launch it again on the market, here is how it works:

- First, one selects (Figure 10-2 [a]) the font to convert, from among the fonts installed on the system. At the same time, one selects the style (regular, italic, bold, bold italic) and the "script". In fact, what is called "script" here is nothing but a subset of the WGL4 set of glyphs, which was introduced by Windows NT. WGL4 corresponds to a small part of Unicode that covers the languages of Western Europe (except Maltese), Central Europe, the Baltic states, Eastern Europe, and the Balkans, as well as Greek (only "monotonic", thus a poor subset of true Greek (see [169, 166])) and Turkish. One may select "Western", "Greek", "Turkish", "Baltic languages", "Central Europe", or "Cyrillic", provided, of course, that the corresponding glyphs are available in the font.

- Next, one selects (Figure 10-2 [b]) the set of glyphs to include in the font: "alphanumeric characters (without accents) and punctuation", the "complete" set, or a "custom" range. This window also affords us the possibility (Figure 10-2 [c]) of inspecting the set of glyphs to ensure that we have made the correct choice and of preserving only those that are needed for the web page.

- Finally (Figure 10-2 [d]), we choose the URL(s) of the web pages with which the font may be used, and we save the font under a filename with the extension .pfr.

Thus we obtain a PFR file for which the set of glyphs and the authorized URLs are customized. How can we use this font on a web page?

Unfortunately, *TrueDoc* does not comply with the recommendations of CSS; instead, it uses an (X)HTML tag to supply the URL of the file containing the font. Here it is:

```
<link rel="fontdef" src="http://omega.enstb.org/fonts/palatino.pfr"/>
```

On the other hand, within the web page we use the font's internal name (not its filename); thus we must have carefully made note of it somewhere. To facilitate that task, *WebFont Wizard* produces, at the time of each conversion, an HTML file bearing the font's filename and containing a range of useful information: the font's internal name, the glyphs that are available, the authorized URLs, the code needed to download the font, and some JavaScript code that will test the browser and install, in some cases, a plug-in from Bitstream's web site.

TrueDoc technology is compatible with the following browsers:

Browser	Mac OS	Windows	Unix
Netscape Navigator 4.x	yes	yes	yes
Netscape Navigator 6, 7	no	no	no
Internet Explorer 4–6	no	yes*	—
iCab	yes	—	—

where the asterisk denotes the need to download a plug-in.

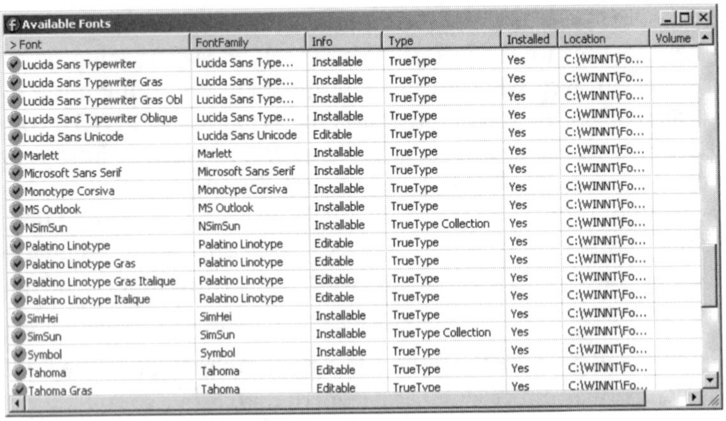

Available Fonts

> Font	FontFamily	Info	Type	Installed	Location	Volume
Lucida Sans Typewriter	Lucida Sans Type...	Installable	TrueType	Yes	C:\WINNT\Fo...	
Lucida Sans Typewriter Gras	Lucida Sans Type...	Installable	TrueType	Yes	C:\WINNT\Fo...	
Lucida Sans Typewriter Gras Obl	Lucida Sans Type...	Installable	TrueType	Yes	C:\WINNT\Fo...	
Lucida Sans Typewriter Oblique	Lucida Sans Type...	Installable	TrueType	Yes	C:\WINNT\Fo...	
Lucida Sans Unicode	Lucida Sans Unicode	Editable	TrueType	Yes	C:\WINNT\Fo...	
Marlett	Marlett	Installable	TrueType	Yes	C:\WINNT\Fo...	
Microsoft Sans Serif	Microsoft Sans Serif	Installable	TrueType	Yes	C:\WINNT\Fo...	
Monotype Corsiva	Monotype Corsiva	Installable	TrueType	Yes	C:\WINNT\Fo...	
MS Outlook	MS Outlook	Installable	TrueType	Yes	C:\WINNT\Fo...	
NSimSun	NSimSun	Installable	TrueType Collection	Yes	C:\WINNT\Fo...	
Palatino Linotype	Palatino Linotype	Editable	TrueType	Yes	C:\WINNT\Fo...	
Palatino Linotype Gras	Palatino Linotype	Editable	TrueType	Yes	C:\WINNT\Fo...	
Palatino Linotype Gras Italique	Palatino Linotype	Editable	TrueType	Yes	C:\WINNT\Fo...	
Palatino Linotype Italique	Palatino Linotype	Editable	TrueType	Yes	C:\WINNT\Fo...	
SimHei	SimHei	Installable	TrueType	Yes	C:\WINNT\Fo...	
SimSun	SimSun	Installable	TrueType Collection	Yes	C:\WINNT\Fo...	
Symbol	Symbol	Installable	TrueType	Yes	C:\WINNT\Fo...	
Tahoma	Tahoma	Editable	TrueType	Yes	C:\WINNT\Fo...	
Tahoma Gras	Tahoma	Editable	TrueType	Yes	C:\WINNT\Fo...	

Figure 10-3: WEFT's font database.

In the absence of a product to generate PFR files and with no support from Netscape Navigator beyond version 6 or from Internet Explorer for the Macintosh, the survival of TrueDoc technology is in jeopardy, to say the least. In discussions with employees at Bitstream, the author has noticed a certain bitterness resulting from the abandonment of this technology, especially with regard to Netscape, which supported it very well from the beginning. It is typical that Bitstream has launched a call for help on its web site to Internet citizens who care about beautiful fonts: "Bitstream suggests you contact Microsoft and AOL and encourage them to support dynamic fonts in the new releases of their browsers." Let us hope that this distress call will be answered!

Font Embedding, by Microsoft

Microsoft launched the first version of its WEFT (for "Web Embedding Fonts Tools") software [269] in 1997, at the same time as version 4 of Internet Explorer. This software works only under Windows, and the technology in question is called *Font Embedding* (a name that—let's face it—is not very imaginative). The font format used by this technology is Embeddable OpenType (EOT). Once again, this format is undocumented, and Microsoft is not inclined to provide its specifications, even under cover of a nondisclosure agreement. Our contacts at Microsoft have told us that it is an OpenType format compressed with an Agfa technology called *Microtype Express* that contains only a subset of the glyphs and that is inextricably linked to one or more URLs.

Since we cannot say anything more about EOT, let us move on to WEFT. How does it work?

First of all, it is important to know that WEFT maintains a database of all the fonts installed on the system. By selecting View>Available Fonts, one obtains a table with a list of all the fonts (Figure 10-3), showing for each one its Windows name, its "family" (in the Windows sense), its font format, an indication of whether it is installed on the system or not, its location on the disk, and, most important of all, the right to include this font in a web page. Thus a font can be **Editable** or **Installable** (or downloadable, even for pages in which the Internet user can write), **Previewable** (or downloadable, but exclusively for pages that can only be read), **'No embedding' font**, **Windows core font** (thus downloading it is unnecessary), or **Font may be broken!**.

Before writing stylesheets for web pages, one must check, in this database, whether the fonts that one wishes to use can be downloaded. Next, one writes the CSS stylesheets, using the declarations font-family, font-style, etc., but not declarations for downloading the fonts, since WEFT will add them to the page.

Next (Figure 10-4 [a]), one has WEFT read one's pages, using **Tools>Add Web Pages**. The software will read them and generate a list of all the requested fonts, specifying whether they are downloadable and how many characters are required from each: this information will appear in the **Fonts to Embed** window (Figure 10-4 [b]).

This window is very interesting, as it offers us seven ways, arranged in increasing order, to select the glyphs to include in a font to be downloaded.

- **Per page subsetting:** WEFT will analyze each (X)HTML file separately and will create EOT files for each, which can be used by this file only. This procedure entails the largest number of EOT files but also the greatest degree of independence of the various files—the addition of a few glyphs to one file will not force the recompilation of the full set of web pages on the site.

- **Per site subsetting:** a global analysis is performed on the entire site. The EOT files generated will have enough glyphs for all the web pages on the site. The same fonts will be used for all the pages.

- **Family based subsetting:** the analysis is global and, in addition, the fonts of the same family (in the Windows sense) contain the same glyphs. For example, if an upright font contains the glyphs 'a', 'b', and 'c' and the italic version of the same font contains only a 'c' and a 'd', the EOT fonts generated will each contain the same set of glyphs: 'a', 'b', 'c', and 'd'. The reason is as follows: Suppose that on your web page a JavaScript script changes the style of your font from upright to italic, or from light to bold. It would be a shame if some glyphs were missing simply because the JavaScript script was not activated when the EOT files were produced. Thus all the glyphs are supplied in all the styles in use. This is the default choice.

- **Union subsetting:** the same principle operates here as with selection by family, but here it extends beyond font families. WEFT will make note of all the characters used on all the pages and will generate EOT fonts, each of which contains enough glyphs for all the characters. This method even covers pages on which JavaScript scripts may change the fonts that are used.

- **Raw subsetting:** this approach goes even beyond selection by union because here even the text that is not part of the visible contents of the (X)HTML elements is included—XML comments, the text that appears within scripts, tags, etc. The fact

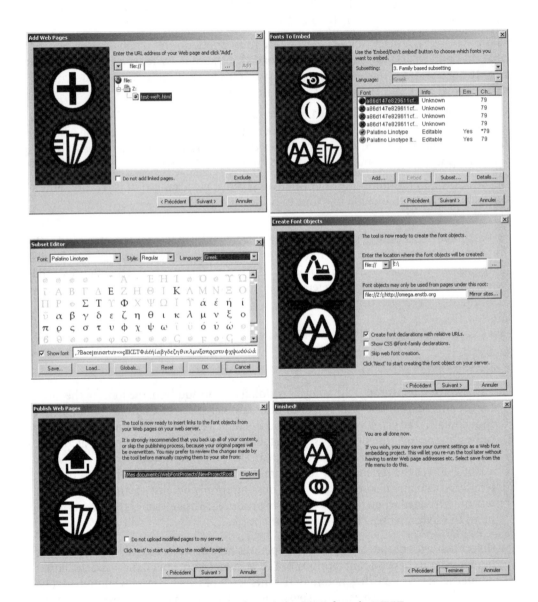

Figure 10-4: Steps for creating EOT fonts in WEFT.

that the document is an (X)HTML page is disregarded; the file in question is considered to be a text file, and all the glyphs whose characters are found therein are incorporated.

- **Language subsetting:** the glyphs of a Unicode block are included in the EOT files. This choice is *discouraged* because it is possible to include only a single block, and rare are the pages that use only one: a mere space character on the page makes the ASCII block necessary; an em dash or a proper quotation mark will force us to use the block of general punctuation; an accented letter, and the Latin Extended block is required. One would not expect it, but the sentence "—Darling, don't be naïve! said she" requires no fewer than three Unicode blocks!

- **No subsetting:** the inclusion of the entire font—not recommended for large fonts, especially ideographic ones.

Did the reader not find what she wanted among these methods for selecting glyphs? She may also select her glyphs by hand. Clicking on the **Subset** button brings up a dialog window (Figure 10-4 [c]) showing all the glyphs in the font, arranged by Unicode table, and the glyphs that are not used on the page are masked in gray. Merely clicking on a glyph will cause it to be included in the font; one more click will deselect it. The full set of glyphs selected is displayed at the bottom. One can even save a selection of glyphs to a file and use it later for another font.

Now that we have finished selecting the glyphs to be included, we shall move on to the creation of the EOT fonts (Figure 10-4 (d)). In the window **Create Font Objects**, we simply indicate the location where the generated fonts are to be stored and the URLs under which the fonts may be used. The location where the fonts are to be stored is used both by the WEFT software (for saving the fonts) and by the CSS code generated by this software: it is the argument to the `src: url(...)` declaration. We may use files on the disk (`file`) or those accessible through the `http`, `https`, and `ftp` protocols.

As for the URLs under which a font may be used, we may supply any number at all, and the authorized protocols are `file` (a file on the disk), `http` (an [X]HTML page), `https` (an [X]HTML page with a secure connection), `ftp` (file transfer), `mhtml` (an [X]HTML page included in an email message).

The next two windows (Figures 10-4 (e), (f)) complete the process by asking us to update the pages and to give confirmation.

This procedure was conceived by Microsoft for graphic artists and other authors of web pages who wanted to write (X)HTML/CSS code first and then have the fonts generated semi-automatically from their code. Those who feel more at ease with the technical nature of EOT font generation may do it directly, without going through an analysis of web pages. Selecting **Tools>Expert Create Fonts** will do the job. The window that appears (Figure 10-5, left) offers a direct choice of fonts to generate, the possibility of choosing glyphs to include (a manual choice, with the option of saving and reusing a set of glyphs), the authorized URLs, and a location for the generated fonts. In short, all the functionality outlined above—except, of course, the intelligent selection of glyphs to include from

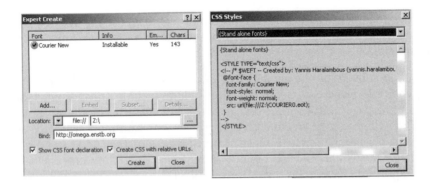

Figure 10-5: The window for generating EOT fonts in WEFT.

an analysis of the characters used on web pages, since there are no web pages to analyze this time. And since there are no web pages yet, the CSS declarations are written in a window (Figure 10-5, right) from which one can copy and paste them into (X)HTML or CSS files.

In conclusion, WEFT seems, at first blush, to be *the* solution for downloading fonts from the Web: it is efficient, Unicode-compatible, and completely free. It would indeed be the ideal solution if all of humanity used Windows and surfed the Web with Internet Explorer. But that is (un)fortunately not so, and with the exception of Internet Explorer under Windows, no browser is compatible with EOT fonts (Internet Explorer under Macintosh was compatible at one time, but it no longer is).

GlyphGate, by em2 Solutions

One thing that we have noticed about the two tools for downloading fonts that were described above: however wonderful the technologies are, their success depends on their compatibility with browsers, and neither of the two technologies has managed to prevail in this area. We can amuse ourselves by creating PFR or EOT fonts and including them in our web pages, but we have no guarantee that the Internet user who visits those pages will be using a compatible browser. And we all know how annoying it is to read on a web page: "This page can be displayed only with *X* version *Y*."

But is there a way to know which browser the cybernaut who connects to our server is using?

We all know that the Web is anonymous: when we connect to a server, the server knows very little about our identity. That is part of the Web's code of ethics. But, at the same time, this principle has its limits. It is quite helpful, for example, for the server to know the type of browser that we are using, so that it can improve the configuration of the pages that it sends us. That is indeed done, using information transmitted through the HTTP protocol [152]: the User-Agent declaration, which is an integral part of every HTTP request that the client sends to the server.

But there turns out to be a problem of diversity. First of all, each browser is free to identify itself with a string of its choice; no standards prevail. Next, there are oodles of browsers, running on many platforms, and new versions of these browsers come out every day. Thus it is a herculean task to preserve a record of every version of every browser for every platform. And we would also need to prepare for each of these, according to its features, a different version of the web page, with or without downloaded fonts, and with the appropriate syntax.

That is exactly the idea that occurred to the company em2 Solutions—which, incidentally, was Microsoft's contractor for the development of WEFT. Rather than focusing on having the author of the web pages generate downloadable fonts, em2 Solutions tackles the web server itself and furnishes a web server plug-in by the name of GlyphGate (formerly called *Fairy*) [130]. This plug-in is compatible with *Apache*, servers compatible with the Netscape API, and Microsoft *IIS*.

The principle behind its operation is similar to that of WEFT: one prepares web pages by indicating the desired fonts, and GlyphGate does the rest. In fact, it is not even necessary to generate the fonts; GlyphGate does so, *in real time*, and according to the nature of the client that connects to the server. em2 Solutions does not claim to cover all browsers, but actually it does. Indeed, it covers even the oldest ones, by sending GIF images of the words in the document, if nothing else can be done.

But GlyphGate goes much further:

- If the web page requires contextual analysis—for example, if it contains text in Arabic—and the browser cannot handle this functionality, GlyphGate will take care of it and render the Arabic text correctly.

- If the font being used is an OpenType font with *advanced typographic features*, then GlyphGate will offer special CSS declarations for enabling or disabling any of these properties in any part of the document. For instance, one can enable ligatures, old-style figures, stylistic variants, etc., on the fly.

- Unbelievable but true, GlyphGate even offers to perform kerning, something that browsers ordinarily are not equipped to do. How does it perform kerning? Suppose that the browser must render the pair of glyphs 'AT' and that it is necessary to move the 'T' closer to the 'A'. GlyphGate will generate a new font in which the glyph 'A' will have a smaller set-width, so that when 'AT' is rendered one gets the impression that kerning has occurred. Farfetched, yes, but darned effective!

- A key use of GlyphGate is to support less common languages on the Internet. This is done through Web fonts in common browsers on personal computers, by graphics on less common platforms and browsers, and through *romanization* on text only browsers. There is as such support for any browser on any platform that support at least HTML 2.0, even on platforms without a graphical user interface.

- Last but not least, GlyphGate offers a development kit containing modules for the rearrangement, replacement, and repositioning of glyphs. One can thus construct

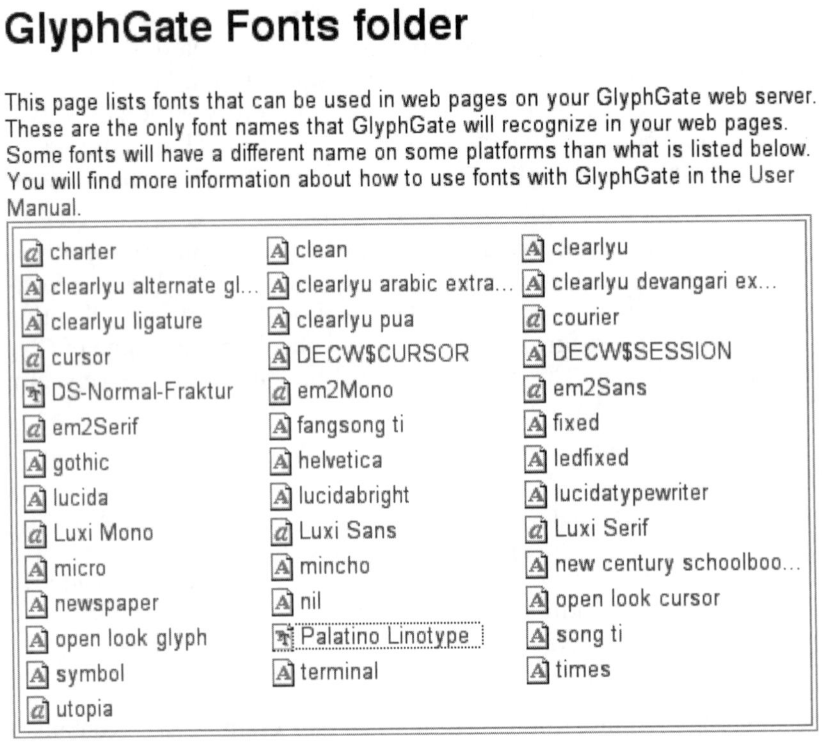

GlyphGate Fonts folder

This page lists fonts that can be used in web pages on your GlyphGate web server. These are the only font names that GlyphGate will recognize in your web pages. Some fonts will have a different name on some platforms than what is listed below. You will find more information about how to use fonts with GlyphGate in the User Manual.

charter	clean	clearlyu
clearlyu alternate gl...	clearlyu arabic extra...	clearlyu devangari ex...
clearlyu ligature	clearlyu pua	courier
cursor	DECW$CURSOR	DECW$SESSION
DS-Normal-Fraktur	em2Mono	em2Sans
em2Serif	fangsong ti	fixed
gothic	helvetica	ledfixed
lucida	lucidabright	lucidatypewriter
Luxi Mono	Luxi Sans	Luxi Serif
micro	mincho	new century schoolboo...
newspaper	nil	open look cursor
open look glyph	Palatino Linotype	song ti
symbol	terminal	times
utopia		

Figure 10-6: Extract from the browser's window: a list of fonts available on the server that was generated by GlyphGate.

one's own rules for contextual analysis, replacement of certain strings with glyphs for ligatures, placement of diacritical marks, etc.

Now let us see how to use GlyphGate.

Suppose that GlyphGate has been installed on the server. The fonts to be used have to be installed somewhere on the server.

Under http://our_web_site:8024/gg-fonts, GlyphGate shows us a list of all the fonts available for web pages (Figure 10-6). By clicking on a font, we gain access to a series of pages displaying all the font's glyphs, including the glyphs generated by GlyphGate, such as, for example, the accented letters that do not exist in the original font but whose components (the base letter and the accent) are present. These glyphs are arranged by Unicode table (Figure 10-7), and only the tables that contain at least one glyph are displayed. Note that these are not imported images but true Unicode characters that we can copy and paste, print out, or search for if the operating system allows. What comes close to being a miracle is that these characters are represented by glyphs in the font in question, though that font is not installed on the client system.

Palatino Linotype (opentype)

Click here to see additional information about this font.

This font can be used to show: **Basic Latin, Latin-1 Supplement, Latin Extended-A, Latin Extended-B, IPA Extensions, Spacing Modifier Letters, Combining Diacritical Marks, Basic Greek, Greek Symbols And Coptic, Cyrillic, Latin Extended Additional, Greek Extended, General Punctuation, Superscripts And Subscripts, Currency Symbols, Letterlike Symbols, Number Forms, Mathematical Operators, Miscellaneous Technical, Alphabetic Presentation Forms**.

Latin Extended-A (U+0100 - U+017f)

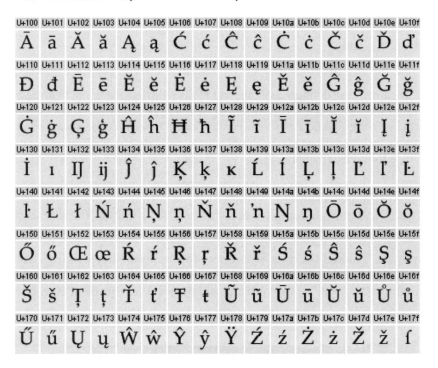

Figure 10-7: Extract from the browser's window: glyphs from the font Palatino Linotype in the Unicode table Latin Extended-1, displayed by GlyphGate.

Once we have checked that the fonts that we want are correctly recognized and displayed by GlyphGate, we may go ahead and use them in our pages. No surprise: we can use standard CSS declarations. From this point on, GlyphGate takes charge of rendering. And it works!

Some browsers may take advantage of a plug-in called *FontEnabler*,[14] which takes just a minute to download and even less time to install. One must simply make sure that the browser detected by the plug-in's installation program is indeed the browser that one is using.

To conclude this section, here are two CSS declarations defined by GlyphGate:

- `text-otl` is used to enable OpenType's advanced typographic features (see Appendix D.9). It is followed by any number of labels for such properties. These labels are always strings of four characters. For example, if in an OpenType font we define a property `onum` that replaces the ordinary digits with old-style digits and a property `stct` that replaces the strings 'st' and 'ct' with the ligatures 'st' and 'ct', then by writing

  ```
  .oldstyle { text-otl: onum,stct; }
  ```

  in a stylesheet, and

  ```
  <span class="oldstyle" lang="en">Acts of Justice of 1770.</span>
  ```

  in the document, we do indeed obtain text with old-style figures and ligatures: "Acts of Justice of 1770". It is also important to specify the language (with the `lang` attribute), since the advanced typographic features of OpenType are always connected to a language. We shall see that in detail when we discuss the editing and creation of OpenType fonts (see Chapter 14).

- `glyphgate` enables or disables analysis by GlyphGate. It can take three values: `skip` (GlyphGate completely disregards this part of the document), `nofonts` (partial processing: CSS and contextual analysis are performed, and only the fonts are not downloaded), `process` (regular processing, which is the default value).

Thus GlyphGate is indeed the miracle solution, for those who have control over their web server. Let us hope that the use of this system will become more and more common, as it will improve the "look" of the Web and will democratize the use of even rare non-Latin languages.

---

[14] Internet Explorer will default to using web fonts without the plug-in. Browsers without native Web font support, such as *Safari* and *Mozilla*, will default to using graphics for text in prominent places on a Web page. By default, Web pages will thus "look right" in browsers without the use of a plug-in. The administrator of a Web site may chose to offer the FontEnabler plug-in to browser users in order to enable the use of Web pages that can be searched and printed more easily. This can be highly customized; for example, you can choose the exact circumstances under which to make the plug-in available). In that case, it is up to the user to either use the plug-in, with its benefits, or settle for the default behavior (which is probably good enough). For a page with Arabic and Brahmi text, the use of the plug-in would be recommended, although still not required. For example, you would be able to render Urdu text correctly in Mozilla without using either the plug-in or graphics: GlyphGate would produce Arabic text with presentation forms to ensure that the text was legible, albeit not with the intended font.

The SVG Format

SVG is the acronym of *Scalable Vector Graphics*, a name that is quite ill chosen, being as it is redundant. Specifically, *scalable* and *vector* mean exactly the same thing: that the images can be scaled because they are mathematically abstract objects such as straight lines, curves, circles, rectangles, polygons, etc.

The notion of a "vector image" has existed for a long time in the world of industrial design; it is thanks to software such as *Adobe Illustrator* and *Corel Draw* that "vector design" is, and has been for a good decade, within the reach of the public.

Apart from the redundancy of its name, SVG holds nothing but pleasant surprises in store for us. The most important of these: it is a W3C standard based entirely on XML. That is an enormous advantage:

- First, because SVG's vector images become human-readable and human-editable documents. There are no more secrets, no more mysterious proprietary file formats, no more "black boxes". Which also means that an SVG image placed on the Web can be indexed like any web page.

- Next, because all XML tools and technologies can also process SVG vector images. For instance, if one wishes to generate or transform SVG images, there is no more need to reinvent the wheel and write tools to do the job; tools already exist, and one need only tell them what to do.

- Images become hierarchical objects; in particular, they can be composed of several parts and/or layers, each of which is an SVG image in itself. Moreover, SVG manages interactions and certain dynamic operations, and the reader can thus interact with the different parts of the image.

- Finally, an SVG image and its different parts can be resources accessible on the Web through the use of semantic metadata (web semantics) [107, 331]: each portion of the image can carry metadata that is associated with one or more ontologies. For example, if one is searching for resources indexed by the concepts "seed" and "corn" in an "Agriculture" ontology, one may find a part of the SVG image showing different types of seeds, one of which shows a seed of corn, because the creator of the image took the trouble to index each part of the image separately, through the use of the correct ontology.

Before tackling the use of fonts under SVG and its impact on the Web, a brief introduction to the concepts and terminology of XML is in order. (The reader may also profitably consult the works [300, 252].)

Fundamental Concepts of XML

In the exact sciences, and mathematics in particular, there are two possible pedagogical approaches: the one that goes from the general to the specific and from the abstract to the concrete—which is the "Bourbakist" approach, named after the prestigious French association of mathematicians—and the one that goes from the specific to the general, from a set of concrete cases to an abstraction—which is the "American" approach. To discuss XML, we shall take a Bourbakist approach, which may not actually be one, since from the beginning of this chapter we have discussed the Web—and HTML, and more specifically XHTML, is nothing but a special case of XML. Is XML then an extended XHTML? A generalized XHTML?

It is all a matter of perspective. Some would say that XML is like XHTML, only that we choose the names of the tags ourselves. There is a kernel of truth in that position, but XML goes much further than that. Let us therefore wipe the slate clean and start again from the beginning.

Our starting point is the *document*. Our goal is to give it a *structure*. What do we mean by that? Well, that means that we are going to subdivide it into parts, each of which will have a meaning, or at least a "description". These parts will be embedded; in other words, each of them will be included in one, and only one, immediately larger part, and so forth, until we obtain the entire document, which contains all of the parts. We can represent that with a "shoebox" diagram like the one shown below:

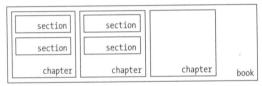

where we have called the parts "book", "chapter", and "section" to give an example of a structured document that has been known for millennia: the *book*. We acknowledge the customary form of embedding: the book contains chapters, which contain sections. But these objects, unlike the unorganized elements of set theory, also have an *order*, which is the order in which the book is read, and it is the logical order of our document. We can therefore revise the figure shown above by adding the order of the subparts of each part:

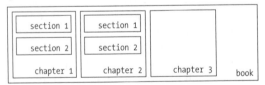

And here is the first trick: using the figure above, we can draw a diagram in which the nodes are the parts of the document, the edges represent the relationships for their incorporation, and the parts are arranged from left to right in the order of their occurrence, thus eliminating the need to number them:[15]

---

[15] The sentence, "It was a dark and stormy night; the rain fell in torrents—except at occasional intervals, when it was checked by a violent gust of wind which swept up the streets (for it is in London that our scene lies), rattling along the house-tops, and fiercely agitating the scanty flame of the lamps that struggled against the darkness", from Bulwer-Lytton's *Paul Clifford* (1830), is widely held to be the worst opening sentence in any English novel. The author would like to thank Scott Horne for suggesting it.

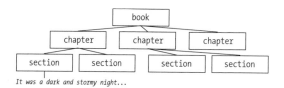

Surprising though this may be, the approach leads to a very important mathematical concept, that of the *tree*. The parts of an XML document, symbolised by boxes in the figure shown above, are called *elements*. The terminology used is in part botanical and in part genealogical. Let us deal with the botanical aspect first: the element at the top of the tree is called the tree's "root", the part of the tree that appears beneath a given element is called a "branch", and the elements that appear at the end and that have no subelements are called "leaves". Now for the genealogical aspect: an element has "ancestors" and "descendants", "parents", "children", and "siblings".

Here, then, is what an XML structure really is: a breakdown of a document into parts that are embedded so as to form a tree. Having thus defined the XML structure, we can immediately see its limitations: in the real world, not everything can be structured in this manner. Consider a document that we arrange first according to the languages used in it and then according to the styles (roman, italic, etc.); there is no reason that the elements obtained in the first structure will be embeddable within those of the second or vice versa. Thus structuring a document in tree form is a compromise—but an attractive compromise, as it allows us to profit from existing techniques and tools for processing trees.

And now our excursion through the world of concepts is complete: it is time to come back down to earth and see how we represent an XML document in the form of computer data. This is where we return to tags: since an element is part of a document, we insert an *opening tag* at its beginning and an *ending tag* at its end:

```
<book>
  <chapter>
    <section>It was a dark and stormy night ...</section>
    <section>...</section>
  </chapter>
  <chapter>
    <section>...</section>
    <section>...</section>
  </chapter>
</book>
```

And if we have a page with no textual content, we will write an *empty tag*, with a slash at the end. For example: `<img/>`.

Another fundamental notion: *attributes*. Suppose that we would like to attach certain information to certain elements without incorporating this information into the text; for example, the identification number of a section, the language of a paragraph, a short text describing an image for the benefit of visually impaired web users. This sort of information is placed within attributes, which are *key–value* pairs that are placed inside opening tags or empty tags in the following manner:

```
<p xml:lang="en-us" id="p137">It was a dark and stormy night ...
```

In this example, we say that the paragraph tagged by <p> is identified by the string p137, and that it is written in American English.

We may have as many attributes as we wish, and their order is not significant. We must be careful, however, not to include any tags in the values of the attributes; they are supposed to be strings with no tags in them.

Another interesting notion: *entities*. An entity is a block of text or a branch of a document to which one has assigned a name. In the document, one uses the *entity reference*, which is the name of the entity, preceded by an ampersand and followed by a semicolon. For example: &foo;. We ask the software processing our XML to replace all entity references with the corresponding text or branches at the start of processing. Thus there is nothing profound about the notion of an entity: it is just a "shortcut" that masks text or even an entire branch of a document—a branch, incidentally, that could even be contained in another file.

One last important notion in this quick overview of XML: *namespaces*. Consider the following problem: how to associate an element's tag or an attribute with precise semantics? Example: when we write <img/>, how can we indicate that it is indeed the img tag of the XHTML standard of the W3C and that it must be interpreted as such, not as an HTML tag or as any other sort of tag unknown to anyone but the person who wrote it?

Answer: by specifying that this tag belongs to the XHTML namespace. This namespace is uniquely represented by the string:

```
http://www.w3.org/1999/xhtml
```

The technique is as follows: We declare a namespace in a branch of the XML document (a branch that may very well be the entire document), and the elements and attributes of this branch may, in turn, belong to this namespace or not. Here is what to write, for example, to declare the XHTML namespace in a <section> branch of the document:

```
<section xmlns:xhtml="http://www.w3.org/1999/xhtml">
    <xhtml:div>
        <xhtml:p>
            Blah-blah.... <foo/>...
        </xhtml:p>
    </xhtml:div>
</section>
```

The string xhtml is the *alias* associated with the namespace. In this example, only the tags preceded by the alias belong to the namespace in question. Thus div and p are indeed the XHTML tags that we know and love; however, foo does not belong to this namespace (simply because no foo tag appears in the XHTML standard). It is also possible to have a namespace without an alias; in this case, we say that we declare a default namespace:

```
<body xmlns="http://www.w3.org/1999/xhtml">
    <div>
            ... nothing but XHTML code, unless otherwise specified ...
    </div>
</body>
```

Here all the tags that are not preceded by an alias belong to this namespace by default. Note that the tag that declares the default namespace (the body tag, in the example above) also belongs to this namespace, unless, of course, it is preceded by an explicit alias.

The namespace (and the corresponding alias, if any) is defined only in the branch of the element that contains its definition. The choice of string for the alias is of no importance; however, it is essential to write the string for the namespace itself correctly: with the slightest error, it is no longer the same namespace!

The reader may be surprised by the resemblance of this string to a URL. It did not happen by chance. Suppose that Mr. George Everyman has defined a set of tags that are very useful for documents on the subject of oyster-farming. Which string will he choose as the namespace for his tags in order to ensure that no one else will adopt the same name?

Choosing George-Everyman would be the height of self-centeredness; in any event, there are plenty of other "George Everymans" in the world. A more eccentric choice, along the lines of GeoEveryman-oyster-PodunkbytheSea, might have better chances of being unique, but could we ever be sure? The W3C's idea is much more natural. On the Web, there is a syntax for strings that identify resources—a well-defined syntax, known around the world and, in addition, many web users have already taken one of its strings: as the reader has no doubt guessed, this syntax is the URL [74]. For example, the URL:

```
http://omega.enstb.org
```

is that of the author's machine. If each person uses his own URLs or those with which he is associated in one way or another, there will be no risk of duplicates. In addition, by following the URL, the user of the namespace could possibly find information on the set of tags in question. But the author is not required to publish such information at the URL.

Namespaces exist for all major applications of XML: XHTML, XSLT, XSL-FO, XForms, XLink, XOL, XQL, MathML, RDF, SMIL, XML Schema, VoiceML, WML, MML, etc. What is interesting is that one can, thanks to these namespaces, mix several kinds of tags in the same document, with no risk of conflict or confusion. Thus, right in the middle of an XHTML document, one can insert an SVG figure without surprising anyone: it is sufficient to specify the namespace of each tag used. The tools that process the XML document will then know, unambiguously, whether or not they are able to process the standards used therein.

And what about SVG?

It is said that a picture is worth a thousand words. Well, to describe the picture below:

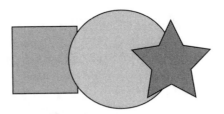

only four tags and 15 attributes were needed:

```
<svg xmlns="http://www.w3.org/2000/svg" width="233.503" height="113"
   viewBox="0 0 233.503 113" overflow="visible"
   enable-background="new 0 0 233.503 113">
   <path fill="#CCCCCC" stroke="#000000"
      d="M76.5,94.5h-v-h76V94.5z"/>
   <path fill="#E6E6E6" stroke="#000000"
      d="M188.5,56.5c0,30.928-.311,56-,56s--.072
         --s27.311-,61-S188.5,25.572,188.5,56.5z"/>
   <path fill="#999999" stroke="#000000"
      d="M186.265,12.596L200.53,41.5l31.898,4.635l-.082,
      22.499l5.449,31.771-.531-1-.53,15l5.449
      -.771-.083-.499l31.898-.635L186.265,12.596z"/>
</svg>
```

The four elements and their attributes are:

- An svg element, which contains all the other elements and is labeled with the SVG namespace (in the example above, this is the default namespace). Through the attributes of this element, the overall size of the image is also determined.

- Three path elements, which correspond to closed contours: a square, a circle, and a star, each filled in with a different shade of gray. The fill and stroke attributes indicate the color to be used for filling and drawing the contours, respectively. The d attribute takes rather cryptic values: but don't panic; it is just an "optimized" way to represent sequences of straight lines and Bézier curves in order to form contours. We have written the word "optimized" in quotation marks because the optimization is done more for the sake of the machine than for the sake of the human reader. In any event, there is nothing mysterious about it; it consists merely of the coordinates of a path to draw.

The reader is invited to compare the code above with that of the same image under Illustrator or Corel Draw: no vector format is so simple and logical. Each contour has its own path element, and the order of these elements is important, since it is the order in which the figure will be drawn. Proof: the images slightly overlap, and each younger sibling consistently encroaches upon his elders.

On the other hand, SVG allows the optimization of code through macros: the first part of an SVG document is for *definitions*. A definition is a defs element that contains shapes or colors or blocks of text that are used multiple times in a document. By defining them within defs, we can later use them by merely referring to them with a special referencing element. Fonts are also placed within defs, since, after all, they are global data that are used throughout the document.

We shall not describe SVG in any more detail. The curious reader will find more information in the book of the same title published by O'Reilly [129] and in an increasing number of other books on this subject, including, of course, the specifications of this standard [134].

In the following section, we shall concern ourselves with font management under SVG. We shall first see how to select a font when writing text under SVG, and then how to define a font in order to use it in the same document or in other documents. What is interesting is the fact that SVG defines XML elements to describe the glyphs and all the other metric properties that make up a font: thus it is in fact a *font format*—not a binary one like OpenType or PostScript Type 1, but one written in a human-readable format and, what is more, in XML. The result is vaguely reminiscent of the TTX fonts (see §D.1), but here we are not rewriting OpenType fonts in XML but rather describing them in an original way; and, unlike TTX (which is the personal creation of an individual), this format is an integral part of SVG, which is a W3C standard.

Font Selection under SVG

In XHTML and in XML documents in general, each element has its own attributes; some attributes may be shared, but that is the exception rather than the rule. In the case of SVG, the situation is quite different: so as not to torture the writer of SVG code with the eternal question "does element X take attribute Y or not?", the designers of SVG opted for complete libertinism: any element can be combined with any attribute. These attributes are called *properties*. What happens if a property has no meaning for a given element? If, for example, we define the size of a font when we are inside an element that draws a circle, and thus has no font? Well, then, the property is ignored—with no grumbling from the viewing software about the fact that "such-and-such has no meaning!" But if the property in question has no meaning for the element itself, it may perhaps have a meaning for some of the element's descendants, and, indeed, most properties are automatically inherited by the descendants.

What is attractive about properties, at least from the pedagogical point of view, is the fact that one can describe elements and properties separately. The user will combine the elements and properties that strike her as being compatible, and the viewing software will decide whether the combinations in question are meaningful or not; in the worst case, they will be ignored, as they are expected to be, since software of the kind must be *tolerant*, as web browsers are.

The element that makes it possible to include text in an SVG image is text. This element can contain text directly or tref elements (which are links to blocks of text defined in advance) or tspan elements (which, like the span elements of XHTML, have no meaning in their own right but act as bearers of properties) or even textpath elements, which are blocks of text set along a path.

The properties that manage the choice of font are the following: font-family, font-style, font-variant, font-weight, font-stretch, font-size, font-size-adjust, font. The reader who has read the section on CSS will have noticed that these are the same names as those of the CSS font-selection declarations. Not for nothing is that so: indeed, the SVG specification defers to CSS for an explanation of these properties and a description of the values that they can have. Here the CSS declarations, which, under XHTML, should be described in a stylesheet or in the value of a class attribute, become true attributes. Here is an example:

```
<svg xmlns="http://www.w3.org/2000/svg"
    width="233.503" height="113" viewBox="0 0 233.503 113">
    <text x="100" y="50" font-family="Historical-EnglishTextura">
        <tspan fill="black" font-size="24pt">Hilfe!</tspan>
    </text>
</svg>
```

which produces:

𝕳ilfe!

In this example, we see the font-family property as an attribute of the text tag, and the font-size property as an attribute of tspan.

Are all the properties that manage fonts merely CSS declarations in disguise? No, there is an exception that proves the rule. It is kerning: an attribute, absent from CSS, that takes the values auto, inherit (its default value), or a length. The effect of this property is to enable (with the auto value) the kerning of glyphs as defined in the font. The code:

```
<svg xmlns="http://www.w3.org/2000/svg"
    width="233.503" height="113" viewBox="0 0 233.503 113"
    overflow="visible" enable-background="new 0 0 233.503 113"
    xml:space="preserve" font-family="Times" font-size="24pt">
    <text x="100" y="50" kerning="0pt">AVATAR</text>
    <text x="100" y="30" kerning="auto">AVATAR</text>
</svg>
```

produces the following image:

AVATAR
AVATAR

Why would we want to disable kerning? No reason comes to mind;[16] but the property does exist, and it already works in the latest Adobe viewer.

Alternate Glyphs

The previous section did not introduce any new concepts, since everything was drawn straight from the CSS specification, with the CSS declarations becoming SVG properties.

Here we shall address a new concept: that of *alternate glyphs*. This concept shatters the barriers between the textual content of a document and its fonts. Indeed, it affords us the possibility of selecting an arbitrary glyph in any font and inserting it into our document. And if this font, or this glyph, is not available, we can act as if nothing were wrong and display the corresponding characters with their default representative glyphs. For example, suppose that we wish to display an 'fi' ligature and that we know that this glyph exists in the active font, with the identifier "g-f_i". We shall write:

```
<altGlyph xlink:href="#g-f_i" dx="238">fi</altGlyph>
```

In this case, if the glyph exists, it will be set, and the current location will be moved ahead by 238 units.[17] If, however, the glyph does not exist, the contents of altGlyph—in this case the string 'fi' with no ligature—will be set.

The number sign in the value of the xlink:href attribute shows that the string is in fact a URL. If this glyph, with the same identifier, were contained in an SVG font, itself contained in an XML document with the URL:

```
http://omega.enstb.org/fontes/svg/omsela.svg
```

then the element altGlyph would be written:

```
<altGlyph
    xlink:href="http://omega.enstb.org/fontes/svg/omsela.svg#g-f_i"
    dx="238">fi</altGlyph>
```

---

[16] There is, in fact, a reason, but it seems quite unlikely to the author that that reason has ever occurred to the inventors of SVG: one traditionally does not kern letters that represent variables in mathematical formulae.

[17] These are SVG's current units of length, a concept borrowed from the PostScript language, where there is a basic unit of length—1/72 of an inch—but where the *current transformation matrix* can alter the size of the units at any time.

Which means, perhaps surprisingly, that we can use glyphs whose descriptions are found anywhere on the Web. Unlike the methods for downloading fonts that we saw above, here it is the glyph in question, and only that glyph, that will be obtained from the Web. And if it cannot be obtained, the contents of the altGlyph element will be used for display.

The dx attribute is used to indicate the offset of the current location once the glyph has been typeset: it keeps the rendering engine from having to search for this information in the font.

One may combine several alternate glyphs in a *sequence of glyphs*. To do so, one uses a *definition of alternate glyphs*. Like all SVG definitions, this one is placed in the <def> ... </def> section of the SVG document. To indicate the glyphs that will make up the desired sequence, we use another element, named glyphRef. This element is a variant of altGlyph: it takes the same attributes and has the same role, i.e., to be a link between a glyph named glyph in an SVG font; the difference between altGlyph and glyphRef is that the latter does not supply a string of Unicode characters for the case in which the glyph in question is not available. For example, by writing in the definitions area:

```
<altGlyphDef id="TeX">
    <glyphRef xlink:href="#g-T"/>
    <glyphRef xlink:href="#g-E" dx="-" dy="100"/>
    <glyphRef xlink:href="#g-X" dx="-" dy="-"/>
</altGlyphDef>
```

we should then be able to write the following within the body of the document:

```
<altGlyph xlink:href="#TeX">TeX</altGlyph>
```

to obtain either the "TEX" logo or the string "TeX". Note that when this book was being prepared, and also under *Adobe SVGViewer* version 3, altGlyphDef could not yet contain more than one glyphRef, and the relative displacement attributes dx and dy were not yet recognized.[18]

We can go even further. Suppose that the string of glyphs that we wish to obtain can be represented in several ways, depending on the availability of one or another glyph. Suppose further that a company called "FOO" has placed the SVG font containing the 'F' and 'O' glyphs of its logo on its company web site, http://www.foo.com/logo.svg. The first option would be to download these glyphs. In case the site is ever unavailable, the company has provided a second site: http://foo.free.fr/just-in-case/logo.svg. And if there is no connection to the Web, then the glyphs can be taken from an SVG font included in the document. What should be done so that the SVG reader will choose the best solution according to the available glyphs?

---

[18] It is unfortunate to observe that, unlike the situation with web browsers, in which the fierce competition between Netscape and Explorer forces the two companies to continue to improve their products, the near monopoly that Adobe has on SVG products results in a lack of verification of the compatibility of *SVGViewer* with the SVG standard and no guarantee that this compatibility will ever be achieved.

For this purpose, there is the element altGlyphItem. This element, placed within an altGlyphDef, informs the reader that its contents are only one possible choice among others. The reader checks its feasibility and, if it fails, moves on to the following option. And, of course, if all the choices of this kind fail, it may always fall back on the string in altGlyph, which does not refer to any glyph and therefore has no reason to fail. Here is an example of the use of altGlyphItem:

```
<altGlyphDef id="FOO-logo">
    <altGlyphItem>
        <glyphref xlink:href="http://foo.com/logo.svg#g-T"/>
        <glyphref xlink:href="http://foo.com/logo.svg#g-"/>
        <glyphref xlink:href="http://foo.com/logo.svg#g-T"/>
        <glyphref xlink:href="http://foo.com/logo.svg#g-"/>
    </altGlyphItem>
    <altGlyphItem>
        <glyphref xlink:href="http://foo.org/just-in-case/logo.svg#g-T"/>
        <glyphref xlink:href="http://foo.org/just-in-case/logo.svg#g-O"/>
        ...
    </altGlyphItem>
    <altGlyphItem>
        <glyphref xlink:href="#g-T"/>
        <glyphref xlink:href="#g-O"/>
        ...
    </altGlyphItem>
</altGlyphDef>
```

Thus we see that, since the fonts being used are SVG fonts, we can directly obtain the glyphs without the slightest hesitation—even if they are kept at the very depths of the Web—and use them in the document. And if, for whatever reason, these glyphs are inaccessible, we can always fall back on a string represented by their default glyphs.

The standard also gives access to fonts other than SVG fonts but leaves the details of implementing this access to the developers. For instance, a glyphRef attribute is provided, both for the altGlyph element and for the glyphRef element. This attribute takes as its value "the glyph's identifier, whose format depends on the font format". In other words, the SVG standard washes its hands of the details: let others struggle to define a syntax for gaining access to a given glyph in an OpenType or PostScript Type 1 font! And how can we begin to discuss implementation if we do not even have a syntax? In this area, without a doubt, the future holds surprises in store.

SVG Fonts

We have already said, in the previous section, that the SVG standard allows for the complete description of a font within an SVG document, so as to make totally independent documents possible. What a pleasant surprise, when on the Web we are always obliged to download fonts—in formats locked three times over so as not to infringe copyright!

But *what about copyright*, exactly? An SVG font, like everything else prepared in SVG, is written in plain text, with no encryption whatsoever. This is a veritable revolution, on a par with that of October: free distribution of fonts to the proletarians of the world! And how are the foundries reacting?

Well, they are not reacting at all. The W3C is encouraging developers not to write tools for converting SVG fonts to a standard font format. The idea—and this idea is explicitly stated in the SVG specification—is that the graphic artist who receives an SVG document with the font embedded within it should only be able to *view* the document: to *edit* it, she must first purchase the corresponding font. Thus we are returning to the classic model of licenses for the use of fonts.

What is actually happening? We do not know yet; it is still too early to say. In any event, today there are at least two tools for converting TrueType fonts to SVG: FontForge and *batik-ttf2svg* (a tool in the *Batik* distribution [329], written in Java), but neither of them reads SVG fonts in order to convert them to another format.

But let us return to the description of SVG fonts. An SVG font is completely contained within a font element. This element applies to the entire SVG document and must therefore be placed among the document's definitions. What usually appears in a font?

A preamble with general information, a certain number of glyphs, and a certain number of instructions about the behavior of the glyphs relative to each other: ligatures and kerning pairs. The same is true here: font contains, first of all, a subelement font-face, which contains the global information for the font. Most of this information is provided in the form of attributes and is the spitting image of the CSS declarations.

Next comes something new: an element named missing-glyph, which contains the description of the "missing glyph", i.e., the glyph that is displayed in the place of another that cannot be found. It is interesting to note that missing-glyph is *mandatory* and comes before all the other glyphs.

Next follow, in no particular order, any number of glyph (descriptions of glyphs), hkern (horizontal kerning), and vkern (vertical kerning) elements. Ligatures are defined, as we shall see below, by an attribute of the glyph element.

Here, then, in schematic form, is the structure of an SVG font:

```
<font ... various attributes ...>
   <font-face  ... attributes taken from CSS ...>
      <font-face-src>
         <font-face-name name="... name of the font ..."/>
      </font-face-src>
   </font-face>
   <glyph unicode="... Unicode code ..."
          glyph-name="... name of the glyph ..."
          lang="... language ..."
             ... font-metric attributes ...
          d="... description of the glyph's contours ..."/>
```

```
        <glyph .../>
        <glyph .../>
        ...
        <hkern ... various attributes .../>
        <hkern .../>
        ...
        <vkern ... various attributes .../>
        <vkern .../>
        ...
    </font>
```

Let us return now to a more detailed description of the elements font, font-face, glyph, hkern, and vkern; after all, they deserve it, and they even hold a few pleasant surprises in store for us.

The font element and its attributes

There is nothing much to say: the font element contains an SVG font. There are only six characteristic properties that affect the set-width and the default spacing of the glyphs:

- horiz-adv-x and vert-adv-y: the default horizontal and vertical set-widths, used when the glyph itself has no indication of its set-width. That makes no sense for an ordinary Latin font, but for monospaced fonts it can come in handy, and it is very useful indeed for ideographic fonts, for which there may be 30,000 glyphs, all with the same set-width. No default value is specified for the horizontal set-width; if the reader does not use this attribute, no problem will arise until the day that he attempts to set type vertically. Specifically, as we shall see, SVG takes half of the value of horiz-adv-x to define the baseline for vertical typesetting. The default value for the vertical set-width is an em; thus the set-width is correct for the ideographic fonts, which are, after all, the ones most often used in vertical typesetting; and for the others—for example, in the unusual case of English typeset vertically, the em corresponds to the standard leading, and is thus the most natural choice.

- horiz-origin-x and horiz-origin-y: the offset of the origin of each glyph when type is set horizontally; their values are zero by default.

- vert-origin-x and vert-origin-y: the offset of the origin of each glyph when type is set vertically. The default values are quite interesting: horizontally the value is half of horiz-adv-x, and vertically it is the value of the ascent attribute of font-face—an attribute that we already know, since it is part of the CSS declarations and gives the height of the letters with ascenders. Once again, these choices are oriented towards the ideographic languages: indeed, in this case, ascent and horiz-adv-x are both equal to an em. Thus the default spacing amounts to starting above the glyph and on its axis of vertical symmetry, which is the usual method for vertical typesetting.

Characterizing a font

The first node under the font element is font-face, whose name is inspired by the "at-rule" @font-face of CSS; the role of this element is to characterize the font being used.

If it is an SVG font whose glyphs are explicitly described by glyph elements, certain properties (such as the set-widths of all the glyphs) may be useless; but it may also be a font to be downloaded, and in that case it is necessary to provide for the possibility that the font may be inaccessible, and, therefore, to have enough informations to "synthesize" it or make a judicious replacement. Thus we find ourselves in the same dilemma as in CSS, and that is why font-face takes practically all of the CSS declarations that apply to fonts. This element is therefore a catchall that contains no fewer than 33 properties specific to it. We can classify these properties into four categories:

- An essential property: units-per-em, which determines the number of internal units per em. The most common values are 1,000 (PostScript Type 1), 2,048 (True-Type), 250 (Intellifont). Default value: 1,000.

- Those that we already know, having seen them and described them in detail in the section on CSS (see page 320): font-family (the name of the "font family"), font-style (roman, italic, slanted), font-variant (small capitals or not), font-weight (weight), font-stretch (expansion or contraction of the set-width), font-size (actual size), unicode-range (Unicode range covered), panose-1 (a classification of the font through the use of 10 numbers, described in Chapter 11), stemv (the thickness of the main vertical downstroke), stemh (the thickness of the main horizontal downstroke), slope (slope), cap-height (height of the capitals), x-height (height of the short letters), accent-height (height of the accents), ascent (height of the letters with ascenders), descent (depth of the letters with descenders), widths (set-widths of the glyphs—warning: only one glyph per Unicode character!), bbox (the bounding box for all the glyphs in the font).

- *Alignment* properties: these are a certain number of baselines and axes for horizontal and vertical alignment (Figure 10-8): alphabetic (our good old baseline), ideographic (the same, but for the ideographic characters, which are set slightly lower than Latin and other letters), mathematical (the axis for aligning mathematical symbols such as the minus sign, the plus sign, the equal sign, etc.), hanging (the "baseline" for the scripts that "hang down", such as Devanagari). Next come the vertical counterparts of these properties: v-ideographic (the vertical axis of the ideographs), v-alphabetical (the vertical axis of the alphabetic scripts set in this direction), v-mathematical (the same for mathematical symbols), v-hanging (the same for "hanging" scripts); note that these last four are added to the value of vert-origin-x, an attribute of font.

- Finally, properties for *underlining*: underline-position (depth of the underline), underline-thickness (thickness of the underline), strikethrough-position, strikethrough-thickness, overline-position, overline-thickness (height and thickness of the bar used for striking through text or overlining) (Figure 10-8).

Figure 10-8: Different SVG metric properties, specific to the font-face element. Left: (1) ascent, (2) cap-height, (3) x-height, (4) alphabetical, (5) descent. Right: (1) overline-position, (2) strikethrough-position, (3) underline-position, (4) hanging, (5) mathematical, (6) alphabetical again, (7) ideographic.

We mentioned above the fact that font-face can use CSS's strategies for the downloading, intelligent replacement, or synthesis of fonts. These tasks are achieved through the subelements of font-face, with names that evoke the corresponding CSS declarations:

- font-face-src: the equivalent of the src: declaration. Its role is to indicate that no font is explicitly described here but rather that downloading, replacement, or synthesis of a font is desired.

- font-face-uri, with the xlink:href attribute: the equivalent of the url() keyword of CSS. Its role is to give the location of the file containing the font on the Web or on the disk. Note that "URI" is more accurate than "URL", since URIs include both URLs and local files.

- font-face-name, with the name attribute: the equivalent of the local() keyword of CSS. Its role is to specify the name of the font in question as used in the operating system. Note that the choice of the term "name" in SVG is more appropriate than that of "local" in CSS, since, first, it is indeed an *internal name*, which justifies "name", and, second, url() can also point to a "local" file, and so the difference between it and local() is not clear.

- font-face-format, with the string attribute: the equivalent of the format() keyword of CSS; in addition to the values of the latter keyword, there is also svg. Note that font-face-format is a subelement of font-face-uri—which is quite logical: if there are multiple URIs, they may not all be of the same format.

Thus our CSS example:

```
@font-face { font-family: "Omega Serif";
             font-style: italic;
             unicode-range: U+0020-, U+0300-E, U+1E??, U+2000-F;
```

```
        src: url("http://omega.enstb.org/fonts/omsela.otf")
           format("opentype");
        local("Omega Serif Italic");
      }
```

is written as follows in SVG:

```
  <font-face font-family="Omega Serif" font-style="italic"
     unicode-range="U+0020-, U+0300-E, U+1E??, U+2000-F">
     <font-face-src>
        <font-face-uri xlink:href="http://omega.enstb.org/fonts/omsela.otf">
           <font-face-format string="opentype"/>
        </font-face-uri>
        <font-face-name name="Omega Serif Italic"/>
     </font-face-src>
  </font-face>
```

The reader may decide which of these forms is clearer.

Describing a glyph

After all this discussion à la CSS, we have finally reached the innovative part of SVG: the description of glyphs. If glyphs are "atoms" in the presentation of a document, we can say that SVG has managed to become the first XML standard that can operate at the atomic level. But beware: in real life, when we descend to this level, we discover that nature hides obscure and destructive forces that are quite capable of annihilating us. The same is true here, but the role of Mother Nature is played by the foundries: if the reader has fun including glyphs from fonts produced by the large foundries in his document, it does not take an Einstein to anticipate what is likely to happen.

Now that we have issued this figurative warning, which, we hope, will be more effective than the ubiquitous "small print" in licenses that no one ever bothers to read, let us present a question: what is a glyph, and how can we describe it?

According to the straight and narrow road of PostScript Type 1 and True/OpenType, a glyph is a set of contours enclosed in an abstract box that is used in typesetting. But then why should we choose one glyph instead of another? Recall how typesetting is done: the typesetting software receives Unicode characters and is supposed to supply the glyphs. Thus it must first know which glyphs correspond to which given Unicode characters (or to a set of Unicode characters, if these represent a ligature), then which glyphs are available, and, finally, under which conditions it should choose a given glyph from among them.

In the case in which the glyphs that correspond to the same Unicode character are only graphical variants pure and simple, these glyphs must have identifiers so that they can be selected through the use of altGlyph.

Let us continue. The description of a glyph is completely contained in a glyph element— or perhaps in a missing-glyph element, which indicates the glyph to be used when the

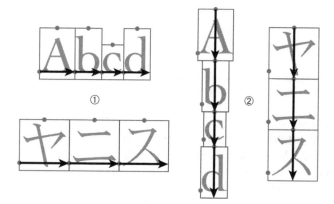

Figure 10-9: Examples of horizontal and vertical typesetting: (1) the arrows start from the "horizontal" origin (coordinates (0, 0)) of the glyph and have a length of horiz-adv-x; (2) the arrows start from the "vertical" origin (coordinates (vert-origin-x, vert-origin-y)) of the glyph and have a length of vert-adv-y.

requested glyph is missing. The attributes of glyph describe its abstract box, relate it to Unicode, and allow it to be distinguished from other glyphs belonging to the same character:

- horiz-adv-x: the displacement of the current location for this glyph during the process of (horizontal) typesetting.

- vert-adv-y: the same, but for vertical typesetting.

- vert-origin-x and vert-origin-y: the origin of the glyph in vertical typesetting (see Figure 10-9).

- unicode: the Unicode character corresponding to the glyph. The usual XML techniques for designating this character are available: either one uses the active encoding (UTF-8, for example) or one uses a character entity (such as ꯍ or 〹).

  Here is where any ligatures are indicated: if the ligature is of the classic type, i.e., the replacement of several glyphs by only one, we write here the corresponding Unicode characters. Thus, by writing unicode="st", SVG will replace the glyphs for the characters 's' and 't' with the glyph for the ligature 'st'.

- id: a unique identifier (at the level of the entire XML document) that, in addition, must begin with a letter (not, for example, with a digit or a punctuation mark). This attribute is not specific to glyph and can be used with any SVG element. We mention this here because it is the link that we have to the world outside the font. The altGlyph element can directly invoke a glyph in the font by using the URI of the XML document containing the font and this identifier.

- glyph-name: one or more internal names for the glyph. If several are used, they are separated by commas. These are also unique identifiers, but those used internally by the font: they are used to describe kerning pairs.

- orientation: is this glyph used only for horizontal or vertical composition? Possible values: h and v.

- lang: is this glyph specific to a certain language? That is the case, for example, for the "Chinese" and "Japanese" variants of many ideographs, or even the letters 'ä', 'ë', 'ö', and 'ü', whose accent ("diaeresis" or "umlaut") is not set at the same height in English and German typography. Possible values [103]: a series of language codes (as recommended by RFC 3066; in other words, a two-letter ISO 639 code for the name of the language, possibly followed by an ISO 3166 country code and other auxiliary codes), separated by commas. Example: lang="fr, en, es".

- arabic-form: the Arabic or Syriac contextual form of the glyph. Possible values: initial, medial, terminal, isolated. Note that these forms also apply to ligatures. Thus, for example, if we form a ligature by beginning with an initial (or medial) glyph and ending with a medial (or final) glyph, the result is an initial glyph. (Likewise for medial, final, and isolated glyphs.)

- d: the contours. We have left the most important item for last: the value of this attribute is a sequence of contours. Each contour is a closed path, i.e., a sequence of concatenated Bézier curves and/or straight lines for which the terminal point of the last is identical to the initial point of the first.

The syntax for the SVG paths used in the value of the d attribute remains to be seen. This syntax is not specific to fonts but is also used for graphic design in SVG: drawing shapes, setting text along curves. In it, we find quadratic Bézier curves, just as in TrueType fonts, but also cubic ones, as in PostScript and OpenType/CFF fonts. There is even another type of curve, never before used in fonts: elliptical arcs.

Another characteristic: the format looks like PostScript (or PDF) at first glance. For example, we use operators with a single letter and coordinates. But we quickly learn that there are fundamental differences. First of all, the notation is not reverse Polish: the parameters follow the operator instead of preceding it. Next, there is no stack: it is impossible to push one value in order to pop it 10 lines below, as we can enjoy doing in languages such as PostScript. Another peculiarity: we can separate operators and parameters from each other through the use of "separators" (spaces or commas), but we can also delete all the separators, except for spaces that separate numbers. This compacting of the code gives the value of d its terribly cryptic appearance.

Rather than describing the syntax of SVG paths in detail (the reader will find a detailed description in [134, section 8.3]), we shall take apart a concrete example: the description of the glyph 'R' of the font that we are currently using, *Le Monde Livre*, by Jean François Porchez (see Figure 10-10). Note that the two programs (*batik-ttf2svg* and FontForge) produced exactly the same code, shown here:

```
<glyph unicode="R" glyph-name="R" horiz-adv-x="689"
    d="M 520 -,
        Q 496 29 459 76, T 382 173, T 305 270, T 244 350,
        H 275,
        Q 307 350 337 357, T 390 380, T 428 424, T 443 492,
        Q 443 537 431 565, T 395 610, T 341 633, T 272 640,
        H 226, V 129,
        Q 226 97 227 79, T 234 50, T 248 35, T 273 26,
        L 317 14, V 0, H 33, V 14, L 77 26,
        Q 92 30 101 34, T 116 49, T 122 78, T 124 129,
        V 546,
        Q 124 578 123 596, T 116 625, T 102 640, T 77 649,
        L 33 661, V 675, H 309,
        Q 352 675 395 670, T 474 647, T 532 597, T 554 510,
        Q 554 473 539 445, T 499 395, T 442 359, T 375 336,
        Q 395 311 416 284, T 460 230, T 503 178, T 544 129,
        Q 587 80 610 56, T 654 25,
        L 687 14, V 0, L 520 -, Z" />
```

We have added spaces and commas to make the code more legible. Does it still appear cryptic? Here are the rules of the game: M is a motion without drawing; it is used only once to set the starting point at the base of the leg of the 'R'; Q and T are quadratic Bézier curves (as in TrueType), their difference being that in Q both the control point and the end point are indicated, whereas in T it is assumed that the control point is the reflection of the control point of the preceding curve (which is why a T must always follow a Q); L is a straight line; H and V are straight lines, the former horizontal and the latter vertical.

Let us examine the code, following the diagram in Figure 10-10. We begin with an M at the base of the leg. Next come a series of Q commands and three Ts, to bring us to the top of the leg. Then we move to the right with an H, which produces a short horizontal line, and then two 1-3 sequences (i.e., a Q and three Ts) to form the inside curve. A horizontal line (H) follows, and then we move straight down with a V. Now we prepare to draw the bottom serif. We begin with a 1-3 series, and before reaching the flat part of the serif we have another short straight segment (L). We draw the base (V, H, V) and proceed symmetrically with an L and a 1-3. The bottom serif is finished. We move up with a V and then draw, as with the lower serif, the half-serif at the top: a 1-3, an L, then a V. We have reached the top line. We go to the right (H) and draw the large curve with two 1-3 sequences. Having again reached the leg, but this time on its upper part, we slide down with a 1-3. At the point 544,129, we follow the logic of the half-serif; we had expected a 1-3, but it is easier this time: a Q followed by a single T, and then another L and the base: a V and an L to take us back to the starting point. We finish with a Z, which closes the path and makes it into a contour.

After this excursion around the periphery of the 'R', and before concluding this section on the glyph element, one more important point: up to now, we have assumed that a glyph was merely a set of contours drawn with the d attribute, the glyph element being left empty. SVG also affords us the possibility of including graphical elements in the glyph. Indeed, we can include any graphical operator within glyph: an entire SVG image can become a single glyph! Up to now that was possible only for PostScript Type 3 fonts (whose death knell was sounded the day that Acrobat was released) and the virtual fonts of TeX, in which both DVI commands and PostScript code can be included. The power gained in this way boggles the imagination: a glyph can be colored in, contain a bitmap,

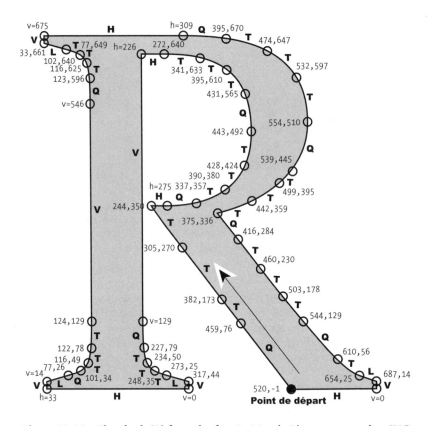

Figure 10-10: The glyph 'R' from the font Le Monde Livre, converted to SVG.

be transparent, be animated, even interact with the user. It goes without saying that that ground remains unexplored, but the fact that the SVG standard provides for it is in itself a minor revolution!

Kerning and kerns

To conclude our journey through SVG fonts, only kerning remains to be discussed. Here again, the developers of SVG drew their inspiration from very highly developed formats such as OpenType, and they introduced a very flexible system for determining kerning paires. The idea is that there are often families of glyphs that are kerned in the same way; "A, À, Â, Á, Å, Ã, … " is one example. On the other hand, while it is very practical to indicate these glyphs through their Unicode characters—after all, for most of the characters in the world, there is a one-to-one correspondence between character and glyph—that is not always possible. If necessary, we can always use the internal names of the glyphs (those of the glyph-name attribute of glyph).

Thus we can write:

```
<hkern u1="A,À,Â,Á,Å,Ã,&#x100;,&#x104;" g1="A.pretty,A.bizarre"
       u2="T,&#x162;,&#x164;,&#x166;" g2="T.shirt"
       k="35"/>
```

where `hkern` is a kerning pair for horizontal typesetting; `u1` and `g1` describe the family of glyphs that appear at the left (`u1` contains characters or zones of Unicode coverage, separated by commas, and `g1` contains internal glyph names, also separated by commas); `u2` and `g2` describe the family of glyphs that appear at the right; `k` gives the kerning value (positive equals closer spacing of the glyphs). Although the reader may not have expected it, `hkern` has defined $10 \times 5 = 50$ kerning pairs.

One small detail, to avoid surprises if the reader is preparing to kern a Hebrew, Arabic, or Syriac font: kerning is performed *after the left-to-right rearrangement* of the glyphs. In other words, if the reader wishes to kern a *reh* followed by a *beh* (the *beh* thus being to the left of the *reh*), she must write a pair with *beh* as g1, even though logically it comes second, and *reh* as g2, even though logically it comes first. Thus kerning occurs in the left-to-right visual order, not in the logical order. Could this be a flagrant lack of political correctness on the part of the authors of SVG?

Finally, SVG provides vertical kerning pairs, which are very useful for certain typographic practices in the ideographic languages.[19] The syntax is the same, except that the element is called `vkern` and the adjustment of spacing is towards the top.

Conclusion

Here we are at the end of this chapter devoted to the management and use of fonts on the Web. We can see that the Web is the victim of its own success: faced with the explosion in the number of users (and the size of the market that they represent), organizations and companies have produced in record time a vast range of tools and standards. But there is always something amiss: the tools are compatible with so few browsers that incompatibility is more the rule than the exception. The standards, as beautiful and powerful as they may be, exist on paper only, in the vast majority of cases. Even worse, the multinational corporations control the lion's share: it is Microsoft that reigns supreme in the downloading of fonts, at least until GlyphGate comes to be more widely used—as it deserves to be; and Adobe has a near monopoly on tools for SVG.

Let us not deceive ourselves: the true problem is neither technology nor the complexity of the world's writing systems. The problem is copyright. The fact that a font belongs to the foundry that distributes it and that that foundry grants to only one person at a time the right to use it stands in flagrant contradiction to the principles of the Web, where all resources (text, images, sound, animations) are freely available to everyone. That is why Bitstream, Microsoft, and em2 Solutions are bending over backwards to provide fonts

---

[19] Ordinarily the ideographic languages are written vertically. But tradition demands that each glyph occupy a perfect square (the ideographic square) and that typesetting consist of the juxtaposition of these squares, which is why kerning is *denied*. Some Japanese typographers, however, violate this tradition by recommending kerning between ideographs whose shape calls for it. [208, p. 七五 (75)], [240, p. 364]

to web users—without actually providing them. That is the reason for which the best intentions of CSS and SVG may go unheeded.

Let us hope that in the future we shall emerge from this tunnel, either by a miracle solution to the problem of rights or by a decision from the large foundries to offer even part of their fonts to the users of the Web so as to bring a little beauty to this virtual space that is nothing less than the first space for communication on a planetary scale in human history.

11

History and Classifications

In this chapter, we present a history of Latin typefaces,[1] illustrated by computer-based fonts. The description of the classification of typefaces by Maximilien Vox and the Association Typographique Internationale (ATypI), which is based more on historical and cultural than on graphical criteria, and the more modern and innovative classification of Alessandrini will then allow us to approach the two "computerized" classifications of fonts: that of IBM and the Panose-1 standard.

The Typographical Big Bang of the Fifteenth Century, and the Fabulous Destiny of the Carolingian Script

An account of the history of typography, and more specifically the history of fonts, always begins with a reference to Gutenberg, especially since Marshall McLuhan named our era after him. Johannes Gensfleisch, or Gutenberg, born in Mainz circa 1395, did not long reap the benefits of his invention of printing; a craftsman, he began to experiment at the age of 40 in the greatest secrecy. Building a printer's workshop from scratch was an extremely costly undertaking, and his creditors, who were no philanthropists, seized his equipment as soon as it became operational, in 1450. It was a lawyer, Johannes Fust, and his son-in-law, Pierre Schöffer, who took over his workshop.

Gutenberg had a goal: he wished to produce Bibles that were virtually identical to hand-written ones, but at a lower cost. And he succeeded.

The typeface used for these Bibles is no longer very legible to us readers of the twenty-first century; the script is too old-fashioned, full of ligatures and abbreviations. But this typeface was the one that was needed to satisfy his customers and make them believe

---

[1] In this chapter, we shall use the term "character" in the sense of "typeface", not in the sense of "Unicode character". A font, on the other hand, is still the computerized implementation of a typeface.

that the copy had been written by hand. The fact that the versals and the illustrations were still drawn by hand contributed to the illusion. Thus the history of typography in Europe began with—fraud!

The script that Gutenberg chose for his Bibles was *textura*, which is characterized by its almost lack of curved strokes. The letters 'i', 'n', 'm', and 'u' are often hard to distinguish: an 'n' is a pair of undotted 'i's that are connected by a short stroke at the top; an 'm' is made of three 'i's, and so on. Here is a specimen of the typeface used in the 42-line Bible printed in 1455:

> **𝔔uod cū audiſſet dauid: deſcendit in preſidiū. Philiſtijm autem venientes diffuſſi ſunt in valle raphaim. Et cō⸗**

This typeface was digitized by Walden Font in 1994 and released as the font *Gutenberg Bibelschrift*:

𝔔uod cū audiſſet dauid: deſcendit in

Still adhering to the principle that printing must imitate handwriting, Gutenberg also cut another script, a rounder one: *rotunda*, which we see here as used by Gutenberg in his *Catholicon*, printed in 1460:

> aliqua diſſeramus. Spiritus qꝑe ꝓbedie nec ſem
> pez nec codem modo ꝓbere animū tangit. aliqñ
> enim ſpiritus ꝓbedie ex p̄ſenti tangit animuz ꝓ

But in 1462 the conquest of Mainz by the troops of Archbishop Adolf of Nassau and the consequent sacking of the city caused a brain drain and released the employees of Gutenberg's workshop from their oath of secrecy. Of Gutenberg's students, for example, Ulrich Zell left for Cologne, and Conrad Sweynheim and Arnold Pannartz set off for Italy, accompanied—as the story goes, at any rate—by a legendary character, Nicolas Jenson.

In Italy, humanism had already been in full swing for a century. After several hundred years of austere Aristotelianism under the Roman Catholic church, the humanists redis-covered Greek and Roman literature and began to view the world differently. Having understood that "the medium is part of the message", they wished to read these books not in Gothic, which reminded them of the barbarian peoples to the north, but in a script closer to that of the original manuscripts.

Their view, still somewhat hazy, of the ancient world led them to err by some eight centuries in their choice of an "ancient script". Instead of selecting a script from ancient Rome, they "rediscovered" the *Carolingian minuscule* script, which the emperor Charlemagne had imposed on his empire four centuries earlier. They called this script *antiqua* and used it to write and copy their texts.

Thus a script of the eighth century that had been considered dead reappeared in the fourteenth century and became more popular than it had ever been. Today this script is called *humanist* or *Carolingian humanist*; it is a little less famous than its mediaeval ancestor. Here is a specimen, from the hand of Spinello Aretino, that dates to 1410:

AELIVS ciceroni falutem . Quod tibi decedenſ polliciturſ ſü me omneſ reſ urbanaſ diligentiſſime tibi perſcripturum .

The humanist is much more familiar to us than textura, and not merely by coincidence: it is the origin of our roman typefaces, such as the one used in this book. Its only peculiarity: the use of the "long s" everywhere, *even at the end of a word!*

Thus Sweynheim, Pannartz, and Jenson arrived in Italy and set themselves up in a monastery—but not just any monastery: Santa Scholastica, in Subiaco, near Rome. This monastery was founded in the fifth century by Saint Benedict himself. In this humanist-friendly country setting and cradle of the Benedictine order, the typographic virus brought in by these three men developed and mutated.

They cut typefaces that were neither textura nor rotunda but a first step towards the humanist hand. Here is a specimen from the first book printed at Subiaco, in 1464:

mína Româ deportarent.et ea confules Curio et Octauianus i capitolio quod tüc erat curante Quínto Catulo reftituti: ponéda curarét. Apud hâc de fümo & conditore rerü deo huiufmöi uerfus reperiütur. Ἄφθαρτος

Typography thus placed itself at the service of humanism. Just examine the capitals in the text above: not a trace of the Gothic remains in them; they are purely Roman inscriptional capitals.

Legend has it that it was Nicolas Jenson who cut this typeface. But who was Nicolas Jenson?

Despite the secrecy that surrounded Gutenberg's enterprise, King Charles VII of France caught wind of it and sent one of his engravers, Nicolas Jenson, to Gutenberg in Mainz to "acquyre knowledge of the new arte and the execution thereof for the sayde Kingdom of France". Jenson was the "James Bond" of the fifteenth century: this remarkable man was always in the right place at the right time. After working at the first German printing house and cofounding the first Italian printing house at Subiaco, he moved to Venice, where the two brothers Johann and Wendelin von Speyer had obtained from the duke of Venice the grant of a five-year monopoly on printing. He was working for the von Speyer brothers when, as it happened, one of them died, leaving the duke's concession to expire. Jenson established his own printing house in Venice and began to cut his own typefaces.

If the typeface of Subiaco was an approximation of the humanist hand, the typeface cut at Venice completely transfigured it! While Gutenberg had reasons to imitate textura, warts and all, Jenson dared to go beyond the humanist hand and produced the first typeface that was genuinely *typographic*. Typographic not only from the tool used, the physical medium, the technology, but also from its shape and its aesthetic quality. In 1470, Jenson printed the thenceforth famous book *De Praeparatione Evangelica* by Eusebius, an extract of which is shown here:

ulla mentio erat . Quare nec iudæos(posteris eni hoc nomen fuit)neq;
gentiles:quoniam non ut gentes pluralitatem deorum inducebant sed
hebræos proprie noïamus aut ab Hebere ut dictū est:aut qa id nomen

Jenson's typeface marks the definitive transition from calligraphy to typographic composition. In his classification of typefaces, Maximilien Vox set aside a category for Jenson's typeface and its derivatives: the *humanist* typefaces. These typefaces are characterized by the low contrast between downstrokes and upstrokes; the cross stroke of the 'e'; the axis of symmetry of the 'o', which tilts towards the left; the oblique serifs of the ascenders; and the serifs of the 'T', which extend above the crossbar, the serif on the right being either vertical or inclined towards the right:

$$e\ o\ d\ T$$

Vox designated an entire category to the humanist typefaces even though only a few dozen exist, as Jenson's typeface would influence type designers for centuries to come.

William Morris, in 1895, declared that Jenson had created "the most perfect roman typeface". He drew his inspiration from this typeface in 1890 for his own *Golden Type* (so called because it was used to print in English a mediaeval book, *The Golden Legend*), a very special typeface that is heavier than Jenson's. The oblique serifs of the ascenders are more exaggerated than those of Jenson, as Morris wished to highlight the "humanist" aspects of his typeface. Here is the digital version by the Font Company:

ulla mentio erat. Quare nec iudæos(posteris eni hoc

In 1893, Joseph Warren Phinney designed *Jenson Old Style*, inspired by *Golden Type* but lighter and with even more pronounced oblique serifs. Even the dot on the 'i' is diamond-shaped. Here is the digital version by the foundry Lanston:

ulla mentio erat. Quare nec iudæos(poſteris eni hoc

Bruce Rogers drew his inspiration from Jenson's printing of Eusebius in the design, completed in 1901, of his *Montaigne*, which was intended to be used to print the translation of Montaigne's *Essays*. But this typeface did not come down to us; its creator completely redesigned it once it was finished. The result is *Centaur*, one of the most beautiful typefaces of the twentieth century, which was not completed until 1929. Here is the digital version by Monotype:

ulla mentio erat. Quare nec iudæos(poſteris eni hoc

Centaur makes subtle use of the characteristics of humanist type and succeeds in capturing the freshness of Jenson's original and, through it, the heritage of the humanist hand.

Morris Benton, of Monotype, was also inspired by Jenson in his design of *Cloister Old Style* in 1912, when Monotype was pursuing the rediscovery of older typefaces. If *Centaur* is more suited to elegant typography, *Cloister Old Style* has more weight and can be used for running text. Here is the digital version by Monotype:

ulla mentio erat. Quare nec iudæos(poſteris eni hoc

In fact, everyone wanted to design his own Jenson, including Frederic Goudy, who in 1924 designed *Italian Old Style*, inspired more by the *Golden Type* of Morris than by Jenson's original. In Goudy's typeface, the spirit of the small-scale letterpress of the turn of the century is sought and celebrated more than the humanist spirit of the Renaissance.

Finally, to bring to a close this long list of fonts inspired by Jenson, here is *Adobe Jenson*, designed in 1996 by Robert Slimbach, a good compromise between historical authenticity and the ease of use in desktop publishing:

ulla mentio erat. Quare nec iudæos(poſteris eni hoc

But let us return to Nicolas Jenson. He would never go back to France: Louis XI, successor to Charles VII, had little interest in printing. When Jenson died in glory in 1480, his equipment came into the possession of Andrea Torresano of Asola (Andreas Asolanus), of whom history has preserved only the name, as he was the father-in-law of a certain Aldus Manutius.

From Venice to Paris, by Way of Rome

Aldus Manutius established himself in Venice in 1490. He set up a publishing house and even an "academy" that attracted intellectuals who had fled Byzantium (which was occupied by the Turks in 1453). His favorite punchcutter, Francesco da Bologna, known as Griffo, cut a new typeface for the printing of *De Ætna*, an account of a trip to Mount Ætna, written by Cardinal Pierre Bembo and printed in 1495. Here is an extract:

Collegimus nuper Codre doctiffime quotquot habe-
re potuimus græcas epiftolas, eás que typis noftris ex-
cufas, duobus libris publicamus, præter multas illas Ba
filii, Gregorii, & Libanii, quas cũ primum fuerit facul-

This typeface, more elegant than that of Jenson, has more contrast between the down-strokes and the upstrokes, and—surprise!—the cross stroke of the 'e' is not oblique. It is horizontal and is placed very high, leaving only a very small eye in the 'e', with a counter that can hardly be distinguished. Vox called this category of typefaces *garaldes* (from "Garamond" and "Aldus"). In the garaldes, the axis of the 'o' tilts to the left, the serifs on the ascenders are oblique, and the serifs on the arms of the 'T' are asymmetrical, but all to a smaller degree than in the humanist typefaces:

De Ætna would come to influence typeface designers right up to the present, from the contemporaries of Manutius, such as Garamond and Augereau, to Stanley Morrison, who in 1929 issued *Bembo* as part of Monotype's historical program:

filii. Gregorii, & Libanii, quas cũ primum fuerit facul-

Among all the books printed by Aldus Manutius, the most interesting was certainly the *Hypnerotomachia Polyphili* of 1499, translated in France a few years later under the title *Le Songe de Poliphile*. It is an adventure novel that is at the same time an essay on archi-tecture, sculpture, and poetry, as well as a pamphlet on the emancipation of female sex-uality[2]. This book [231, 100], written by François Colonna but published anonymously, employs a typeface by Griffo that many consider to be the most beautiful Venetian type-face. Here is an extract of the book:

---

[2] In 2004, American authors Ian Caldwell and Dustin Thomason wrote an action novel based on this book: *The Rule of Four* [93].

E MIE DEBILE VOCE TALE O GRA
tiofe & diue Nymphe abfone perueneráno &
inconcíne alla uoftra benigna audiétia , quale
laterrifica raucitate del urinante Efacho al fua⁘
ue canto dela piangeuole Philomela. Nondi

This typeface inspired *Poliphilus*, by Stanley Morrison, which was issued in 1923:

ue canto dela piangeuole Philomela. Nondi

Much later, in 1998, designer Franck Jalleau attempted another interpretation of the typeface of *Hypnerotomachia Polyphili* by including the effect of the bleeding of ink. He called it *Francesco* in honor of François Colonna:

Jusqu'à quand abuseras⁘tu de notre patience, Catilina?

Aldus Manutius explored the uses of handwriting in order to extend his repertoire of typefaces. He noticed that the students at the University of Venice took their notes in little notebooks using a very regular slanted script, probably inspired by the handwriting of the great humanist Niccolò Niccoli. On the basis of this observation, he invented, at the same time, the pocket-sized book (the size of the students' notebooks) and the italic typeface. Here is a specimen of a pocket-sized book produced by Aldus Manutius with italic type cut by Griffo:

S æpe tener noftris ab ouilibus imbuet agnus.
I lle meas errare boues, ut cernis, et ipfum

This is the italic typeface that inspired Alfred Fairbank of Monotype in 1929 for the italic version of *Bembo*:

Sæpe tener noftris ab oulibus imbuet agnus.

Griffo did not have much luck. During a quarrel he mortally wounded his son-in-law with an iron bar and disappeared, doubtless for having been found guilty and hanged. Cold comfort though it may be, his name was immortalized in the Spanish language, in which italic letters are called *letra grifa*.

Manutius's output was enormous. Humanism owes him much, as he was the most important publisher of Greek and Latin texts. He died at the age of 65 in a wretched state of health. His books, including his magnificent logo of a dolphin with an anchor, were promptly reproduced, forged, pirated, and copied.

Other type designers took an interest in more calligraphic scripts. In Rome, Ludovico degli Arrighi, a calligrapher to the chancery, successfully undertook a very risky experiment: he cut a typeface that imitated his own handwriting with no loss of quality. Here is a specimen of this typeface, digitized by the foundry IHOF (the font is called *Operina*, after the name of Arrighi's calligraphy textbook: *Operina da imparare di scrivere littera cancellarescha*, of 1522 [283]):

Il modo de temperare le Penne Con le uarie Sorti de littere ordinato per Ludouico Vicentino, In Roma nel anno MDXXIII

Antoine Blado bought Arrighi's equipment in 1526 and further developed it. In 1532 he printed books as famous as Machiavelli's *The Prince*. The italic faces of the period were used on a par with roman faces for setting text. Indeed, it is said that in the sixteenth century there were as many Italian books printed in roman as in italic.

Arrighi's typeface also inspired *Blado*, by Stanley Morrison (1923), which was destined to accompany *Poliphilus*:

Il modo de temperare le Penne Con le uarie Sorti

In it we see the narrowness and vivacity of Arrighi's handwriting, although *Blado* is not a calligraphic typeface but rather a very dynamic italic.

Here is *Arrighi*, by Frederic Warde (1926), which Bruce Rogers considered the perfect complement to *Centaur*:

Il modo de' temperare' le Penne' Con le uarie' Sorti

contains several calligraphic glyphs, but the dynamism of *Blado* has been lost.

In 1963 Ladislas Mandel designed a typeface much closer to Arrighi's original for the Lumitype phototypesetter, his *Cancelleresca*, simultaneously proving that the machine was capable of kerning glyphs [245].

Let us return to the fifteenth century. How was printing established in France?

Five centuries before May 1968, the Sorbonne was at the heart of everything. In 1470 two professors from this venerable institution, Johann Heynlin (called "de la Pierre", from a literal translation of the name of his hometown, *Stein*) and Guillaume Fichet decided to solicit the help of German printers to establish a printing house within the university. They invited Michael Friburger, Ulrich Gering, and Martin Kranz, all of them from Mainz, who built the equipment and set about cutting typefaces.

In a situation comparable to that of Subiaco, an atmosphere steeped in humanism, our three pioneers issued in 1470 the first book printed in France, *Gasparini Epistolae*, of which an extract is shown here:

> Nvnciatū mihi eſt ꝗ menedotius ueſter,
> dolobellę inimico meo hoſpes & amicuſ
> exiſtens,effecit:ut intra loca nīa caſtra metanſ

The typeface is a strange mixture of roman and gothic; it cannot be called beautiful, but it does show that the three printers of the Sorbonne tried their best to break free of the textura and rotunda that they had employed at Mainz and to breathe a breath of humanist air into the dusty corridors of their hosts. But the day of humanism had not yet arrived in France: French readers spurned this "experimental" typeface in favor of known quantities.

In 1472 these printers left the Sorbonne to set up shop on Rue St-Jacques. Thereafter they cut only rotundas. Here is an extract of the book that they printed in 1473:

> Et de iſta tentiōe diciͭ in canticis·
> Tenui eum! nec dimittā·Et iſta fir

People wrote in Latin at that time; French was considered a vulgar tongue for everyday purposes. Nonetheless, a few courageous printers ran the risk of producing books in French. The first book in this language was *Croniques de France*, printed in 1477 by another Parisian, Pasquier Bonhomme. Here is an extract:

> la royne ecuba ſa femme· la cite fut ar
> ſe et deſtruicte le peuple et les barons
> occis·mais aucuns eſchapperent de ceſte

Bonhomme drew his inspiration from another script that was very popular in France, *bastarda*. Here is a sample of bastarda as digitized by Rainer Will in 1996 (as the font *MA Bastarda*):

> la royne ecuba ſa femme. la cite fut arſe et deſtruicte

And here is another bastarda, designed in 1995 by Thierry Gouttenègre for the region of Burgundy, *Bâtarde bourguignonne*:

la royne eсuba ſa femme. la cite fut arſe et deſtruicte

Other printers, such as Simon Bötticher, used rounded gothic typefaces called "Italian gothics". Here is an extract of the *Confession de frère Olivier Maillard*, printed in 1481:

Ainſi ſont acomplies neuf reigles.par leſquel les lon peut facillemēt cognoiſtre tout peche

This is the sort of typeface that inspired Karlgeorg Hoefer for his typeface *San Marco*, issued in 1990 in Adobe's collection of historic typefaces:

Ainſi ſont acomplies neuf reigles.par leſquelles

People like Jean Du Pré, Antoine Vérard (noted for his textura, which was later carried to England by William Caxton), Philippe Pigouchet, and Josse Badius printed religious books or mediaeval chronicles mostly in gothic.

The Sorbonne was a bastion of conservatism in the midst of an era in which Protestantism developed; the Balkans and the Middle East fell under the Ottoman yoke; and Europe discovered the New World, freedom of the press, and freedom of conscience.

Geofroy de Tory, printer to King François I, philosopher, and man of letters, printed in 1529 a splendid book, *Le Champ Fleury* [332], in which he developed a theory of the relationships between the parts of letters and the parts of the human body—a theory reminiscent of the Indian chakras. In this book, he also proposed the use of the accent marks and the cedilla to make the spelling of the French language less eccentric than it used to be. An accomplished humanist, Tory never stopped trying to popularize Aldine typefaces in France.

Three publishers dominated book production in Paris at the time: the Estienne family, Simon de Colines, and Michel Vascosan. Starting in 1535, they printed practically all books in roman typefaces influenced by Aldine type. With the support of King Francis I, French books thus achieved an unparalleled perfection.

The Estienne family employed a very talented type designer, Antoine Augereau. Claude Garamond, one of Augereau's students, was the first freelance type designer. His name was to become legendary, whereas Augereau, de Colines, Vascosan, and so many others are unknown today to the general public: millions of people use fonts bearing Garamond's name. But who was Claude Garamond?

Garamond designed roman and italic typefaces but also Greek ones, the famous *Grecs du roi*. His roman face is of exceptional balance and stability; his italic is lively and elegant. The first book using his roman type was a *Paraphrase* of Erasmus that was printed in 1530.

Today we know that Garamond was inspired by Manutius' *De Ætna*; specifically, in this book, and in it alone, the type cut by Griffo has eight variants of certain letters, and seven of them appear in Garamond's roman.

How did Garamond's typefaces come down to us?

Upon his death in 1561, many of his matrices were bought by an equally renowned Antwerp printer, Christophe Plantin. Later, Jacques Sabon moved Garamond's matrices to the Egenolff-Berner publishing house in Frankfurt. This publishing house printed in 1592 a catalog that inspired a large number of contemporary designers. Here is a specimen of Garamond's *gros canon* typeface (the equivalent of 48-point type) as reproduced from this catalog:

Quis credidit Auditui noſtro: & brachium Iehouæ

In 1845 some typefaces attributed to Garamond, *Caractères de l'université*, appeared in a type catalog from the Imprimerie Nationale, which also used them in Anatole Claudin's *Histoire de l'imprimerie en France au XVᵉ et au XVIᵉ siècles* (*History of French Printing in the Fifteenth and Sixteenth Centuries*), a work that was to fascinate type designers.

The first of these was Morris Benton, who designed the first Garamond for the American Type Founders Company (ATF) in 1900. This typeface was taken up again by Linotype in 1925 under the name of *Garamond 3*:

Quis credidit Auditui noſtro:& brachium Iehouæ

In 1920 Frederic Goudy designed a very attractive *Garamont* (with a 't'!) for Monotype that is known today as *Monotype Garamond*:

Quis credidit Auditui noſtro:& brachium Iehouæ

But scandal broke out in 1926. One of Monotype's former employees, Beatrice Warde, subsequently became the high priestess of twentieth-century typography, discovered at the Bibliothèque Nationale de France a catalog from 1621 by a certain Jean Jannon, printer at Sedan: the dies that the Imprimerie Nationale had attributed to Garamond were actually by Jannon! What had happened?

At least two stories are making the rounds. Some say that since Jean Jannon was a Protestant, Cardinal Richelieu confiscated his equipment and printed his own *Mémoires* with Jannon's typeface. As for the Imprimerie Nationale, it claims [98, p. 34] that Sébastien Cramoisy, its director, had entered into a legitimate contract in 1641 with Jean Jannon for the updating of Garamond's fonts. According to this version, nothing was ever confiscated from anyone, and no misunderstanding ever occurred.

Whatever the case may be, *Monotype Garamond*, which is used, for example, in the prestigious series *Collection de la Pléiade*, is always called "Garamond" instead of "Jannon".

This discovery inspired type designers to seek inspiration more from Benner's catalog than from the *Caractères d'université*.

The Stempel press created a Garamond based on Egenolff-Berner in 1924. Today this typeface is distributed under the name of *Stempel Garamond*:

Quis credidit Auditui noſtro:& brachium Iehouæ

In 1928, George Jones, of Linotype's British branch, also created a Garamond from the same source. Doubtless as a reflection of his British humor, Jones distributed this typeface under the name of *Granjon*, a contemporary of Garamond whom we shall discuss below:

Quis credit Auditui noſtro:& brachium Iehouæ

In 1930, the designer Hunter Middleton designed a Garamond for the Ludlow Foundry that is now called *Ludlow Garamond* and is considered by Bruce Rogers as the best interpretation of Garamond. Indeed, it has a smaller x-height than the others, and the eye of the 'e' is truly small. On the other hand, it has very thin serifs that are unusual for a garalde:

Quis credidit Auditui noſtro:& brachium Iehouæ

In 1960, a German consortium (of the companies Monotype, Linotype, and Stempel) decided to finance the creation of a new typeface inspired by Garamond that would be compatible with their machines. This task was entrusted to a great theoretician of typography, Jan Tschichold, who drew his inspiration from "St. Augustine" (14 points) for the design of *Sabon*:

Quis credidit Auditui noſtro:& brachium Iehouæ

Things changed for the worse in the 1970s. John Stan, of the International Typeface Corporation (ITC), designed an "Americanized" Garamond that became a smashing success.[3] Here is *ITC Garamond*:

Quis credidit Auditui noſtro:& brachium Iehouæ

This typeface suffers from an enormous x-height. The letters 'o' and 'O' are almost perfect circles, a design element that completely destroys the typeface's dynamics. The height of sacrilege is that the typeface was designed in different weights (a concept completely foreign to Garamond's era), from light to ultra-bold. Nevertheless, the typeface has become very popular, doubtless owing to its large x-height, which facilitates reading at small sizes; and it is to this rendition that Garamond owes its current fame. Apple even adopted a version condensed by 80 percent as its official typeface.

In 1989, Robert Slimbach, of Adobe, designed a very elegant interpretation of Garamond, *Adobe Garamond*, which is an excellent compromise between fidelity to the original and ease of use in modern-day documents:

---

[3] This typeface is used, among other places, on the covers of books by O'Reilly, such as this one.

Quis credidit Auditui noſtro:& brachium Iehouæ

In 1994, Ross Mills, of the foundry Tiro Typeworks, designed *1530 Garamond*, which has the peculiarity of being *strictly faithful* to the original:

Quis credidit Auditui noſtro:&brachium Iehouæ

This font was used[4] for the book *Le Maître de Garamond*, by Anne Cuneo [105], a historical novel on Antoine Augereau. Anne Cuneo acknowledges in the book that she drew her inspiration from an email exchange with Ross Mills, who attributed the typeface to Augereau.

In 2002, Jean François Porchez returned to Tschichold's *Sabon*, which was intended for the Linotype and Monotype machines, and took some of the proportions of Garamond's original in order to adapt them to the computer. The result is *Sabon Next*:

Quis credidit Auditui noſtro:&brachium Iehouæ

Finally, in 2005, when Lanston was bought by P22, another revival of Garamond was released: *Lanston Garamont*, designed by Frederic Goudy in 1920 and digitized by Jim Rimmer in 2001. The font is available in two weights: "display" and "text". This is the "display" version:

Quis credidit Auditui noſtro:& brachium Iehouæ

After this long excursion that has taken us up to 2002, let us return to the sixteenth century. Garamond worked for the great Estienne family of publishers and printers (from which the École Estienne in Paris takes its name). The sire of this family was Henri Estienne (1528–1598), whose widow married the other master of the era, Simon de Colines. His son, Robert Estienne, took over the enterprise and created a number of masterpieces, thanks in particular to an enlightened king and great lover of typography, Francis I. Robert Estienne was named "printer and bookseller of Hebrew and Latin literature".

But Francis I died in 1547, and Robert Estienne, a Protestant, hurriedly left for Geneva, where his children Henry II and François continued the production of outstanding books. The Parisian printing office was taken over by Robert Estienne's brother Charles Estienne, an avowed Catholic and therefore out of danger. But Charles died in prison for his debts and left the company to his nephew, Robert II. In Geneva, Paul Estienne, son of Henri II, decided to return to France. Once "converted back" to Catholicism in Paris, he succeeded so much that his son, Antoine, great-grandson of the "traitor" Robert, became the new printer to the king and "guardian of Greek matrices". The death of Antoine Estienne in 1674 brought to a close the story of this illustrious family of printers.

---

[4] Unfortunately, this book is a glaring example of what *not* to do: using a typeface designed for *gros canon* (48 points) at 12 points. The result is that the typeface seems too narrow and poorly spaced, making reading a bit unpleasant. That is a pity, as the text itself is gripping!

The other French printer and type designer of the sixteenth century, Robert Granjon of Lyon, born in 1513 (not to be confused with Philippe Grandjean, who lived in the seventeenth century), who designed typefaces for the publisher Plantin and for the Vatican, wished to grace France with a typeface of her own. (In his opinion, Garamond's typefaces had an Italian appearance.) Robert Granjon thus sought inspiration from a rounded gothic script used in children's books, and in particular in the translation of a work by Erasmus, *Civilité Puérile* (*On Civility in Children*). He called this typeface *Civilité*. But it was not well received and was almost never used. Here is the digital version by Jonathan Hoefler in his collection of historic fonts (the font is called *St Augustin Civilité*):

Ainsi l'historien fut nay sous l'Empereur Tyberien

In 1913, Frank Hinman Pierpont of Monotype designed a typeface inspired by Granjon's *gros cicéro* that he nonetheless named *Plantin* (after Granjon's most important client):

Juſqu'à quand abuſeras-*tu de notre patience*

Then, in 1978, Matthew Carter, son of historian of printing Harry Carter, designed for Linotype a font inspired by an 8-point font that Granjon called "galliard" (the "gaillarde" was a very popular dance of the Renaissance):

Juſqu'à quand abuſeras-*tu de notre patience*

Galliard was one of the first fonts to be designed on the *Ikarus* system of Peter Karow.

Granjon had poor luck: his *Civilité* was a flop, and the typefaces that he inspired do not bear his name, whereas the one that does bear his name was inspired not by him but by Garamond.

Another controversy concerns the source of "Janson". In 1922, the foundry Stempel released a typeface named "Janson", named for a Dutch type designer, Antoine Janson, whose matrices were in Stempel's possession. In 1937, the foundries Monotype and Linotype each released a *Janson* without giving much historical information about them. Here is the typeface by Linotype, distributed today under the name *Janson Text*:

Juſqu'à quand abuſeras-*tu de notre patience*

And here is the one by Monotype:

Juſqu'à quand abuſeras-*tu de notre patience*

Monotype used a 1739 catalog of the Ehrhardt foundry in Leipzig that contains the typefaces still called "Janson" as the basis of its design of *Ehrhardt*, which was also released commercially in 1937:

Juſqu'à quand abuſeras-*tu de notre patience*

This typeface was destined primarily for the German market. According to a manager at Monotype, "this typeface was to appeal to those who have a weakness for Fraktur".

But scandal broke out in 1954. A historian of printing, Harry Carter, with the help of a Hungarian colleague named George Buday, revealed the origin of these typefaces called "Janson": they were cut by the more famous Hungarian printer Miklós Tótfalusi Kis (pronounced "quiche"). Kis, born in 1650, was a monk. Sent to the Netherlands in 1680 to learn printing, he quickly achieved international fame. He turned down the offer of an ideal position in Tuscany, preferring instead to return to Hungary to print Bibles. But when he was able to return to Hungary, in 1690, he found nothing but misery, jealous compatriots, and an abominable political climate. He died before his time, in 1702. Thus it was he who designed the first garaldes, which Blanchard called "germanized Garamonds" [84, p. 172] and which already foreshadowed the typefaces of Fournier and Caslon.

New Scripts Emerge in Germany

Now let us see what was happening in Germany in the sixteenth century. Printing houses were set up all over the place and turned out books in textura, rotunda, and even roman.

In Germany, just as in Italy, typefaces were *ennobled*: a splendid example is the *Diurnale* of Jean Schönsperger, printed at Nuremberg in 1514, of which a digitized version by Walden Font is shown here. (The font is called *Gebetbuch*, or "prayer book".)

𝕯eus 𝕬braẖā·𝕯eus 𝕪saac·𝕯eus 𝕵acob

The evolution of typefaces in Germany is connected to the wishes of an emperor. In 1517, the emperor Maximilian commissioned Schönsperger to print the chivalric poem *Theuerdanck* of Melchior Pfinzing. This was the first manifestation of a new type of gothic script, *Fraktur*—a script that was to become the German national script, right up until 1943! Here is the typeface of *Theurdanck*, as recently digitized:

𝕯urch teglich arbeyt worden schwach

Also in this era emerged a script rounder than Fraktur, called *Schwabacher*. Its name apparently comes from the title of *Eyn Gespräch von dem gemainen Schwabacher Kasten*, by Friedrich Creuszner and Hieronymus Höltzel, which was set in this typeface. Here is an example of Schwabacher, digitized by Walden Font (the font is called *Alte Schwabacher*):

𝕰yn Gespräch von dem gemainen

Schwabacher can be recognized from its 'g'. Although at first there were whole books set in Schwabacher, it came to play more an alternative role, similar to that of italics relative to roman.

These scripts were also used in the countries that were culturally dependent on Germany, although printers always tried to set Latin, Italian, and French words in roman script.

The Wild Adventure of Textura in England

The story of printing in England begins with a merchant born in Kent around 1420, named William Caxton. He lived in Brugge and undertook the translation into English of the *Recueil des histoires de Troye*, which he wished to offer to his benefactress, a sister of Edward IV. But in order to make the gift worthy of its recipient, he decided to print it. And to that end he studied printing with Ulrich Zell in Cologne in the 1470s. In 1475, at Brugge, he succeeded in printing his translation, which thus became the first printed book in the English language. Here is an extract:

> gammedes felte hym self among the hors feet / he was
> in his herte terryble angry / and sayd that he woldr be
> shortly auengyor / anon he aroos lightly and tooke his

The type used in this book, which never made its way to England, is quite peculiar, being heavily influenced by Flemish handwriting. Caxton next set up shop in Westminster in 1476. Most of the books that he printed were in English, and he used a bastarda that practically became the English national script until the middle of the sixteenth century, when roman definitively took hold in England.

In 1892, William Morris designed a typeface called *Troy* to set his new edition of the henceforth famous *Recuyell of the Historyes of Troye*. Here it is as digitized by P22 (an American foundry [284] specializing in historical and artistic fonts):

gammedes felte hym self among the hors feet

One of the typefaces used by Caxton (which the experts call "number 3") was a textura. Here is an extract of a book printed in 1477 at Westminster:

> If it plese ony man spirituel or temporel to bye ony
> pyes of two and thre comemoracios of Salisburi vse

And here is the digitized version of this typeface by Jonathan Hoefler, in his collection of historic typefaces (the font is called *English Textura*):

If it plese ony man spirituel or temporel

In 1490, Caxton bought a very beautiful textura from the Frenchman Antoine Vérard and imported it to England.

While textura was rapidly being abandoned elsewhere, England, thanks to its unparalleled conservatism, kept it alive for centuries! In 1611, the King James Bible was printed in textura; so was the first English-language typography textbook, *Mechanick Exercises*, by Joseph Moxon, in 1683; in 1734, William Caslon, the greatest English type designer, still had it in his catalog, under the name *Black English Letter*. Here is an interpretation of the type in Caslon's catalog, digitized by Gerda Delbanco:

No noyse but silence and Eternall sleepe

The wild adventure of "English" textura continued in the twentieth century with *Cloister Black*, cut by Morris Benton and Joseph Warren Phinney for ATF in 1904, a typeface quite close to the texturas of the sixteenth century:

No noyse but silence and Eternall sleepe

Next, the extremely kitschy *Wedding Text*, also designed by Morris Benton, which is still a roaring success under the name of *Linotext*:

No noyse but silence and Eternall sleepe

not to mention the numerous Victorian excesses, such as *Colchester*, by Dieter Steffmann:

No noyse but silence and Eternall sleepe

Fortunately, the Germans came to the rescue of textura and saved it from British-American kitsch. In 1913, the great German designer Rudolf Koch cut the impressive *Maximilian* (in honor of the emperor Maximilian, who was a great patron of printing), digitized by Gerda Delbanco:

No noyse but silence and Eternall sleepe

This typeface combines the weight of textura's downstrokes with almost calligraphic fine strokes. From 1920 to 1926, the same Rudolf Koch designed a textura that is majestic in its narrowness, *Wilhelm Klingspor*:

No noyse but silence and Eternall sleepe

Perhaps contrary to expectations, the name of this font does not come from any great mythological or historical personage but from that of the brother of the patron of printing Klingspor, Wilhelm, who died in 1925 as a result of a war injury.

In 1928, the Americans showed the world that they were also capable of designing beautiful texturas. Frederic Goudy produced a textura for Monotype, *Goudy Text*, that is in no way inferior to those of Koch:

No noyſe but ſilence and Eternall ſleepe

Textura, through its plasticity, also lent itself to experimentation. Here is *Ganz Grobe Gotisch*, by Friedrich Hermann Ernst Schneidler, one of the heaviest texturas of the twentieth century, dating to 1930:

No noyſe but Eternall ſleepe

Finally, here is the gothic typeface of Emil Rudolf Weiss, designed in the difficult year of 1936. It is of remarkable sobriety.

No noyſe but ſilence and Eternall ſleepe

An after-war experiment, the typeface *Kühne Schrift*, by Emil Hand Kühne (one of Koch's students), was designed in 1954 for the Klingspor printing company and digitized by Klaus Burkhardt:

No noyſe but ſilence and Eternall ſleepe

This typeface is a curious hodgepodge of elements of textura, Fraktur, and roman. Incidentally, there is a pun in the name of the script: *"Kühne"* is, of course, the name of the designer, but it also means "daring, audacious", a name that suits this script well.

The Sun King Makes Waves

Let us back up. Starting in the sixteenth century, the trade in typefaces became a monopoly. Printers who no longer had the means to cut dies or even to cast type made recourse to specialized enterprises. The political and cultural circumstances were such that the two main European type foundries, Plantin and Elsevier, turned out to be located in the Netherlands. Thus all of Europe was using "Dutch typefaces" that had nothing particularly Dutch about them but were often derived from the work of Nicolas Jenson, Aldus Manutius, Claude Garamond, etc. Plantin and Elsevier may have revolutionized the book trade in Europe, but they did not revolutionize typefaces.

In the seventeenth century, the prevailing rationalism of the "Age of Reason", together with the magnificence of Louis XIV's reign, also influenced typography.

In 1692, a commission of the Académie des Sciences sought to define a purely geometric typeface, which it designed by means of what one might call the ancestor of pixels: a grid of 64×36 squares. The commission, headed by an abbot named Nicolas Jaugeon, entrusted the cutting of this typeface to Philippe Grandjean (1666–1714), whose talent humanized the cold geometry of the commission's designs. This typeface, called the *Romain du Roi* ("king's roman"), was cut in 21 sizes, the last of them not finished until 1745, more than 50 years after the project was launched.

The dies of the *Romain du Roi*, or *Grandjean*, are preserved by the Imprimerie Nationale, which has exclusive rights to its use. Here is a specimen:

> C'eſt le ſujet de cette Médaille. On y voit Pallas
> *les Eſpagnols défaits & pouſſez au-delà de l'Eſcauld.*

This font can be recognized immediately from the small appendage to the downstroke of the 'l', which serves to distinguish that letter from the 'I'. The *Romain du Roi* is very far removed from the garaldes and the humanist typefaces. The upper and lower serifs of the 'I' are so symmetrical that one almost reads the letter as an 'I'. Similarly, the ascender of the 'd' has a genuine double serif that makes the 'd' resemble an upside-down 'p'. The symmetry expresses the regal perfection of the *Romain du Roi*.

In 1903, Arthur Christian, the director of the Imprimerie Nationale, asked an experienced typecutter, Jules Hénaffe, to cut a typeface strictly consistent with the recommendations of the Jaugeon Commission. The result was quite surprising:

> Quel est le modèle du musicien   *j'ai bien fait*
> ou du chant? c'est la déclamation,   *d'autres prodiges*

Jaugeon may be used only by the Imprimerie Nationale. It was used, for example, to set the sublime *De plomb, d'encre & de lumière* [97], published by the Imprimerie Nationale in 1982.

Finally, between 1995 and 1997, Frank Jalleau digitized Grandjean's typeface:

> Jusqu'à quand abuseras-*tu de notre patience, Catilina?*

This font, *Grandjean-IN*, was used in the catalogue of the exhibit "Le Romain du Roi" [276], which was held in Lyon in 2002.

Even though the *Romain du Roi* was little used in the seventeenth century, it influenced the typographers of the era, in particular Pierre-Simon Fournier (1712–1768), called "the Younger", who cut a simple yet elegant typeface that combined rationality and beauty. An employee of his father's printing house, which was run by his brother, he had the luxury to be able to create new typefaces and to write as well. He published a *Manuel typographique utile aux gens de lettres & à ceux qui exercent les différentes parties de l'Art de l'Imprimerie* (*Handbook of Typography: Intended for men of letters & for those engaged in the different aspects of the Art of Printing*), in which he explains printing equipment but also a few principles of cutting type. The typefaces that he cut are resolutely modern, simple, and functional. He was the first to design the same typeface with different x-heights: the large x-height is less beautiful but useful for running text, especially in small sizes— he called it "Dutch-style" and criticized its "excessively material feel"—while the more elegant one with the small x-height yields an airier text—Pierre-Simon Fournier called it "poetic". Here is a specimen of the poetic type, from a 1742 catalog:

Senecque, Corbulon un de ſes Ca-
pitaines, & pluſieurs autres de ſes

centes victimes de ſa fureur, il leur
fit ſouffrir les plus cruels tourmens &

In 1925, Monotype issued a typeface named *Fournier*. To achieve the Dutch/poetic duality without completely redesigning the typeface, it altered the height of the capitals without changing the lowercase letters. Thus we have an ordinary *Fournier* (which is in fact the Dutch version):

JUSQU'À quand abuſeras-*tu de notre PATIENCE*

and a *Fournier Tall Caps*, which is the poetic version:

JUSQU'À quand abuſeras-*tu de notre PATIENCE*

Fournier's typeface belongs to a new category in Vox's classification: *transitional*. They are so called because they are transitional between the garaldes and the typefaces of the nineteenth century that Vox called "didones". In most transitional typefaces, the eye of the 'e' is still quite small (smaller than half the height of the letter, at any rate), the 'o' is absolutely symmetrical about its vertical axis, the ascender of the 'd' has less oblique serif than its predecessors, and the serifs of the 'T' do not extend upward but are symmetric relative to the letter's vertical axis of symmetry:

eodT

Pierre-Simon Fournier died 30 years before the French Revolution. But before we discuss the Didots, which will move us into the Industrial Age, let us see what was happening on the other side of the English Channel.

England Takes the Lead in Typographic Innovation

In England in 1692, while the Jaugeon Commission was meeting for the first time, the man who was to become the uncontested master of English typography was born: William Caslon. (In fact, we should say "William Caslon I", as his son was also named William, together with his grandson and his great-grandson, as English tradition would have it.)

Caslon was a child prodigy. Setting himself up in London at the age of 18, he was commissioned to design an Arabic font for the needs of missionaries, which he cut at 12 points together with his name, as a "signature" for the font. Greatly impressed by this single cut word, the publishers and booksellers of London encouraged him to go into the design of typefaces and sponsored him by purchasing the required equipment. He issued his first catalog of fonts in 1734.

Immediately he won great praise and admiration all over Europe, and also in the Americas, where a certain Benjamin Franklin—who practiced two professions at the same time, printer and US politician—so admired him that he insisted that the United States' Declaration of Independence be printed in his typeface.

Caslon followed in the footsteps of Manutius and Garamond, modernizing their typefaces and adapting them to the tastes of his time. He died in 1766, but his foundry remained in business until the death of the last male in the Caslon line, William Caslon IV, in 1869.

Caslon's typefaces were uncontestably inspired by the Dutch typefaces common in England at the time, which were in turn inspired by the typefaces of Aldus Manutius and Claude Garamond. They are therefore transitional faces with features borrowed from the garaldes: Caslon's italic, narrow and dynamic, still shows much of the character of handwriting.

Caslon's typeface was so successful that it has practically never ceased to be used, from the seventeenth century to the present. Printers in the English-speaking countries still say "When in doubt, use Caslon".

A tremendous number of interpretations and digitized versions exist. Among the most important are *Caslon Old Face* (digitized by Bitstream), which dates to 1902:

Juſqu'à quand abuſeras-*tu de notre patience*

Here are *ATF Caslon 471*, now distributed by Berthold, and *ATF Caslon 540*, which is a 471 with shortened descenders:

Juſqu'à quand abuſeras-*tu de notre patience*

Carol Twombly of Adobe designed an *Adobe Caslon* in 1990 that is a good compromise between modernity and fidelity to the original:

Juſqu'à quand abuſeras-*tu de notre patience*

But the most beautiful computer implementation of Caslon is without a doubt that of Justin Howes (1996). In Figure 11-1 we show his font *HW Caslon* at 14 optical sizes, from 8 to 96 points. It is a monumental effort containing all the magic of multiple optical sizes, with all the imperfections and idiosyncrasies of the originals.

Finally, a typeface with an element of deception: in the 1890s (!) a Chicago foundry, Barnhart Brothers, issued a typeface called *Fifteenth Century* that simulated the bleeding of ink:[5]

---

[5] Which was revolutionary at the time and showed that typographers had achieved a technical level at which bleeding could be perceived as intentional, not as an error in printing.

Juſqu'à qu

Juſqu'à quan

Juſqu'à quand a

Juſqu'à quand abuſer

Juſqu'à quand abuſeras

Juſqu'à quand abuſeras-*tu de*

Juſqu'à quand abuſeras-*tu de notre pa*

Juſqu'à quand abuſeras-*tu de notre patience,*

Juſqu'à quand abuſeras-*tu de notre patience, Catili*

Juſqu'à quand abuſeras-*tu de notre patience, Catilina? Quoſque t*

Juſqu'à quand abuſeras-*tu de notre patience, Catilina? Quouſque tandem abut*

Juſqu'à quand abuſeras-*tu de notre patience, Catilina? Quouſque tandem abutere*

Juſqu'à quand abuſeras-*tu de notre patience, Catilina? Quouſque tandem abutere* Catilina patientia no

Juſqu'à quand abuſeras-*tu de notre patience, Catilina? Quouſque tandem abutere* Catilina patientia noſtra? Wie lange

Figure 11-1: Caslon's typeface, digitized by Justin Howes. The sizes are 8, 10, 12, 14, 18, 22, 24, 30, 36, 42, 48, 60, 72, and 96 points.

Juſqu'à quand abuſeras-tu de notre patience

But it was a commercial flop, as American printers were not interested in a font with the mysterious and pallid name "Fifteenth Century". The company decided therefore to rename its product *Caslon Antique*, and it immediately became a smashing success. The typeface became the perfect imitation of the American typefaces of the colonial era, even though it had nothing to do with Caslon—and was phenomenally ugly to boot.

And while we are on the subject of imitations of the "colonial" Caslon, here is one by Walden Font (the font *Minuteman Printshop Caslon Book*), an infinitely more elegant rendition:

Juſqu'à quand abuſeras-*tu de notre patience*

It comes with a font containing the 56 signatures that appear on the United States' Declaration of Independence.

In 1913, Ernest Jackson and Edward Johnston designed for Monotype a typeface inspired by Caslon, which later became the favorite typeface of Oxford University Press. This typeface is *Imprint*:

Juſqu'à quand abuſeras-*tu de notre patience*

Caslon was not the only one of Worcestershire's native sons who excelled at printing. The year 1707 saw the birth, 15 years after Caslon, of John Baskerville, the man who, like Gutenberg a few centuries before, contributed to all branches of the field of printing, from the cutting of typefaces to the chemical composition of ink, without omitting layout, which he kept simple and free of gimmicks, ornaments, and other frills. The books that he produced were very "modern" and fascinated his contemporaries.

According to Rémy Peignot [97, p. 114], he was as different from Caslon as Grandjean was from Garamond—which is saying a lot! Baskerville abandoned the excessive ornamentation of the baroque era and produced typography based solely on the typeface. His typefaces are more streamlined and simpler than anything that his predecessors had created.

But like his fellow genius Mozart (who, incidentally, lived during the same era), Baskerville died in poverty and in debt. Four years after his death, in 1779, his widow sold all his equipment to a French businessman[6] who appeared as if by some miracle. After that, Baskerville's typefaces vanished into oblivion.

---

[6] This Frenchman was none other than Pierre-Augustin Caron de Beaumarchais, the author of *The Marriage of Figaro* and *The Barber of Seville*. Beaumarchais had concocted a very ambitious financial plan: he intended to publish Voltaire's *Collected Works* in 70 and 92 volumes. He bought the rights to all of Voltaire's manuscripts for an astronomical sum, and then he bought Baskerville's equipment. For political reasons, his project could not be undertaken in France; therefore, he established himself in the fortress of Kehl, a German town just across the border from Strasbourg, by paying bribes that were also quite high. Actually, it was not he who did all those things but rather the "Literary and Typographic Society" of which he was the only member. To raise the needed funds, he organized lotteries for the jet set of his day and placed himself under the kind protection of Catherine the Great, Empress of Russia. The French Revolution broke out in 1789, and Beaumar-

Or at least they did until 1917, when Bruce Rogers discovered a book by Baskerville in a Cambridge library and launched a campaign to rehabilitate his typeface. In 1923, Lanston Monotype issued what today we call *Monotype Baskerville*:

Jufqu'à quand abuferas-*tu de notre patience*

Linotype continued, and soon there were many very similar typefaces on the market. In 1978, Matthew Carter modernized the typeface a bit through the release of his *ITC New Baskerville*:

Jufqu'à quand abuferas-*tu de notre patience*

The production of computerized versions of Baskerville continued. In 1996, the Swede Lars Bergquist designed a Baskerville quite close to the original and named this typeface *Baskerville 1757*:

Jufqu'à quand abuferas-*tu de notre patience*

Finally, there was also an early forgery: a type designer named Isaac Moore, of Edmund Fry's printing house in Bristol, copied Baskerville's typefaces in 1768, when Baskerville was still alive. It is this copy that is sold today under the name of *Fry Baskerville*:

Jufqu'à quand abuferas-tu de notre patience

Didot and Bodoni Revolutionize Typefaces

With the American and French revolutions, the world was plunged into modernity. Typefaces no longer had any connection with handwriting. The most important representatives of this new style in France were the members of the Didot family. Just like the Estiennes, the Didots were type designers, printers, and publishers for several generations. François Didot (1689–1758) passed his company down to François-Ambroise Didot (1730–1804), who in turn bequeathed it to Firmin Didot (1764–1836), a great philhellene who offered the new Greek nation its first printing house, in 1828.

The Didots' typeface is geometric and dramatically exploits the contrast between downstrokes and fine strokes. Typography was a symbol of power in this pre-industrial era, and power must be clear, precise, inflexible, and determined. While Didot does have serifs, they serve to assert its identity, and one asserts one's identity through contrast. Vox called these typefaces *didones* (from "Didot" and "Bodoni"). The didones are very easy to recognize from their thin, flat serifs. Our four representative letters illustrate this point clearly:

---

chais was one of its instigators, but at the same time he destroyed his relations with the empress. Beaumarchais died the following year.

e o d T

The cross stroke of the 'e' is horizontal and quite low, the axis of the 'o' is vertical, the serif on the 'd' is horizontal, and those of the 'T' are vertical and do not extend upward.

The delicacy of the serifs causes big problems for us today in our digital renditions. What Mandel calls the "original sin" of phototypesetting—i.e., the principle of having only a single design, which applies to all sizes—stands in contradiction to the delicacy of Didot's serifs. A serif that is visible at 12 points is invisible at 7 points and much too thick at 72 points. Here is a 1991 interpretation of Didot's typeface by Adrien Frutiger, *Linotype Didot*:

Jusqu'à quand abuseras-*tu de notre patience*

Another interpretation of Didot, by the foundry URW, *Firmin Didot*:

Jusqu'à quand abuseras-tu de notre patience

Finally, a rather ornamental Didot, with no italic, produced by the Turin foundry Nebiolo, called *Torino*:

Jusqu'à quand abuseras-tu de notre patience

The most impressive digital version of Didot's typeface is without a doubt that of Jonathan Hoefler (HTF), who in 1994 designed seven distinct optical sizes of Didot: *HTF Didot* (Figure 11-2).

Another great figure of the era, the Italian Giambattista Bodoni, was born in 1740. His father was a printer and started raising him in the profession from a very young age, with the result that, at age 18, he was already a typesetter at the Vatican's press and thus encountered all kinds of Latin and East Asian scripts. He was asked to catalog all of the press's historic dies, which led him to discover the Garamonds and the Granjons.

Bodoni was a great admirer of Baskerville, so much so that in 1768 he left his post at the Vatican and traveled clear across Europe in order to meet him. But he fell ill at the beginning of his journey. The duke of Parma then offered him the chance to manage his press, as the duke of Tuscany had invited Miklós Tótfalusi Kis to do a century earlier. Kis declined the offer and died in poverty in his homeland; Bodoni accepted, and became, in his own words, "printer to kings and king of printers".

But Bodoni never did meet Baskerville. At the beginning of his career in Parma, he ordered the typefaces of Fournier, then copied them, and finally created his own typefaces. His typography was thus heavy and pompous. He took up the Didots' geometric principles but pushed them to extremes.

Jusqu'à qu

Jusqu'à quand a

Jusqu'à quand abusera

Jusqu'à quand abuseras-*tu de notre patie*

Jusqu'à quand abuseras-*tu de notre patience, Catilina? Quou*

Jusqu'à quand abuseras-*tu de notre patience, Catilina? Quousque tandem* abuteres pat

Jusqu'à quand abuseras-*tu de notre patience, Catilina ? Quousque tandem* abuteres patientia nostra? *Jusqu'à quand abuseras*-tu de notre patience, Catilina ?

Figure 11-2: Didot's typeface, digitized by Jonathan Hoefler, HTF foundry. The sizes are 6, 11, 16, 24, 42, 64, and 96 points.

He created his typefaces in huge numbers of different sizes and versions: after his death, some 25,000 dies and 51,000 (!) matrices of his creation were found. His most important work was his *Manuale tipografico*, an annotated catalog of his typefaces. Its second edition, bearing a preface written by his widow, came out five years after his death.

Among the twentieth-century interpretations of Bodoni are that of Morris Fuller Benton, completed for Monotype in 1907 and known today by the name of *Monotype Bodoni*:

Jusqu'à quand abuseras-*tu de notre patience*

and that of Heinrich Jost for Bauer, 1926, which is closer to the original. It is sold today under the name of *Bauer Bodoni*:

Jusqu'à quand abuseras-*tu de notre patience*

Jusqu'à quand

Jusqu'à quand abuseras-*tu de notre patience, Catilina? Quousque tandem a*

Jusqu'à quand abuseras-*tu de notre patience, Catilina? Quousque tandem abuteres* Catilina patientia nostra? Jusqu'à quand abuseras

Figure 11-3: ITC Bodoni, by Goldsmith, Parkinson, and Stone. The sizes shown are 6, 12, and 72 points.

Next, from 1991 to 1994, Holly Goldsmith and Jim Parkinson, working under the supervision of Sumner Stone, designed a very refined version of Bodoni that is close to the original, *ITC Bodoni*:

Jusqu'à quand abuseras-*tu de notre patience*

As with the Caslon of Justin Howes and the Didot of Jonathan Hoefler, we show the three optical sizes of *ITC Bodoni* at actual size in Figure 11-3.

The German "Sturm und Drang"

Meanwhile, German typography was also turning towards rationalism, but in a less dramatic way than in France or England.

Johann Gottlob Imannuel Breitkopf (1719–1794), a great Leipzig publisher and founder of the prestigious Breitkopf & Härtel publishing house, which published the greatest works of music, was using a quite well developed Fraktur, shown here as digitized by Ralph Unger of the foundry URW:

Die Vöglein schweigen im Walde, warte

A little later, Johann Friedrich Unger (1750–1804) brought new ideas to the design of Fraktur type and tried to bring it closer to Didot's roman. Unger went so far as to ask Firmin Didot to cut gothic type, which unfortunately turned out to be rather mediocre. Here, as a curiosity, is a sample of the gothic cut by Didot, which dates to 1793:

die gränzenlose Fläche des Adriatischen
Meeres. Diese Segen und Freiheit ath=
mende Aussicht gibt beßre Empfindun=
gen wieder, und verdrängt jenè, die der

Note that he could not resist using a perfectly roman 'S' and that his 'F' is an 'S' with slightly different terminals and a bar across the middle. One wonders why this script has never been digitized.

And here is Unger's Fraktur, digitized by Gerda Delbanco:

Die Vöglein schweigen im Walde, warte

Within the scope of a Fraktur typeface, the influence of the Didots' classicist geometricity is discernible. For example, the reader can see that the thickest strokes are often vertical, as in the main curve of the 'D', while the same curve in traditional Frakturs is heavily slanted to the left.

The concern for homogeneity between Unger's Fraktur and Didot's roman is not merely a question of taste. It should be remembered that words in a Romance language within a German document set in Fraktur have always been set in roman type. Thus the two typefaces had to be compatible so as not to shatter the harmony of the page.

Other typographers cut a Fraktur and a roman at the same time. For instance, Justus Erich Walbaum (1768–1837), another noted German of the eighteenth century, created the perfect typeface for that era of "Sturm und Drang" and German romanticism. Walbaum drew his inspiration from Bodoni for the design of his roman type, shown here in the digitized version by Monotype:

Jusqu'à quand abuseras-*tu de notre patience*

Walbaum also created a Fraktur typeface that is very well balanced and less "romanized" than Unger's, with the exception of the ball terminals under the capital letters:

Die Vöglein schweigen im Walde, warte

The Nineteenth Century, Era of Industrialization

The nineteenth century was the century of great technical progress: stereotypy, the metal press, the steam-driven press, the rotary press, photoengraving, lithography, photolithography and photography, and finally Linotype and Monotype. The economic situation was such that the quality of typefaces was far from being the top priority of printers. Their products were destined for the broad masses of consumers, and advertising turned out uglier and uglier typefaces for the delivery of its messages.

The influence of Didot and Bodoni still prevailed, but its mixture with other, more ancient, influences kept the typefaces from being as radically "modern".

Among the typefaces that distinguished themselves from the general mediocrity are those designed in London by Richard Austin at the beginning of the nineteenth century. Austin also worked in Scotland. His typeface was widely used in the United States under the name of *Scotch Type*. It was later issued by Monotype under the name of *Monotype Scotch*:

Jusqu'à quand abuseras-*tu de notre patience*

Printers at the beginning of the twentieth century felt that the capitals of *Scotch* were too heavy. Linotype therefore asked William Addison Dwiggings (a student of Goudy) to refurbish the typeface. He drew his inspiration from Bulmer in designing the typefaces that Linotype called *Caledonia*:

Jusqu'à quand abuseras-*tu de notre patience*

Towards the end of the nineteenth century, publishers showed more and more concern for legibility and required new typefaces to satisfy this criterion. For instance, in 1894, Linn Boyd Benton (the father of Morris Fuller Benton) and Theodore de Vinne (another great theoretician of printing) designed *Century*, known today as *Century Old Style*, for a magazine of that name:

Jusqu'à quand abuseras-*tu de notre patience*

Morris Fuller Benton designed variants of this typeface, including *Century Expanded*:

Jusqu'à quand abuseras-*tu de notre patience*

and *Century Schoolbook*, which corresponded to the prevailing notion of a good typeface for textbooks in that day:

Jusqu'à quand abuseras-*tu de notre patience*

In 1896, Bertram Grosvenor Goodhue, an American architect with an interest in the graphic arts, designed a new typeface for a small printing house named Cheltenham Press. This typeface, *Cheltenham*, became the most popular typeface in America. In 1902, Morris Fuller Benton designed a dozen variants of it, which Linotype marketed, followed immediately by Monotype. Here is *Cheltenham Old Style*, which is close to the original:

Jusqu'à quand abuseras-*tu de notre patience*

In 1975, Tony Stan (designer of the ignoble *ITC Garamond*) issued a new version of *Cheltenham* with a larger x-height—*ITC Cheltenham*, which is the most popular version today:

Jusqu'à quand abuseras-*tu de notre patience*

The nineteenth century was also the century of sans serif and Egyptian typefaces. In 1816, William Caslon IV cut the first sans serif typefaces, in capitals only:

CASLON JUNR LETTERFOUND

He was followed by a German foundry in 1825 and by three British foundries in 1832— one of which, Thorowgood, invented the label "grotesque", which is still used in the

English-speaking countries to denote sans serif type. Then followed more and more sans serif typefaces of little interest, until the German foundry Stempel issued in 1898 its typeface *Akzidenz Grotesk*:

Jusqu'à quand abuseras-tu de notre patience

The word "*Akzidenz*" is indeed cognate to the English "accident", but in the context of printing it corresponds to the English "job work"—i.e., any printing job other than a book. The name shows how the typeface was used at the time. This typeface inspired the Swiss Max Miedinger, who in 1956 designed a typeface that we all know well, *Helvetica*, shown here in an improved version of 1957 called *Helvetica Neue*:

Jusqu'à quand abuseras-*tu de notre patience*

In 1990, Robin Nicholas and Patricia Saunders, of Monotype, designed a font that strangely resembles *Helvetica*, called *Arial*:

Jusqu'à quand abuseras-*tu de notre patience*

Mac OS comes with *Helvetica*, and Windows has its *Arial*.

Once again *Akzidenz Grotesk* influenced Morris Fuller Benton when he designed *Franklin Gothic* in 1902. The first version that he designed was quite bold; he added lighter versions in the years to follow. Here is the digital version by Bitstream:

Jusqu'à quand abuseras-tu de notre patience

Maximilien Vox set aside a category for sans serif typefaces in his classification. He called them *lineal* (or *linear*). Here are our four representative letters in a sans serif typeface:

Egyptian typefaces were invented around the same time as sans serif typefaces. The first Egyptian type, from 1815, is attributed to Vincent Figgins, a printer from London. We do not really know why these typefaces are called Egyptian. The Egyptian faces of the nineteenth century are characterized by their extreme heaviness. The serifs often had a thickness as great as a third of the height of the letters!

Figgins's collection of typefaces, especially his catalog of 1845, was digitized by David Berlow, of the foundry Font Bureau, under the name of *Giza*. Here is the font *Giza Three Three* from this collection:

Jusqu'à quand abuseras-tu de notre patience

Vox called the Egyptian typefaces *mechanistic*. Here are our four representative characters in a mechanistic typeface:

eodT

A new mechanistic typeface issued in 1845, *Clarendon*, has enjoyed success right up to the present. It was designed by a certain Robert Besley for the London printing house of William Thorowgood. Clarendon was also the first typeface in history to be protected by copyright, for a period of three years. But in view of the immense success of this typeface, the protection was simply ignored by the entire profession. Later, in England, the term "clarendon" came to be a synonym of "bold". Here is the *Clarendon* of Berthold, a font quite close to the original of 1845:

Jusqu'à quand abuseras-tu de notre patience

Another example of a tendency typical of the nineteenth century is that of the "fat faces". The first person to design typefaces of this sort was the British Robert Thorne, in the 1800s. But these typefaces are better known to us under the name of William Thorowgood, the same person who introduced Clarendon. In fact, it was he who bought Thorne's printing house after his death, in 1820, and then began to sell his typefaces. Here is one of Thorne's typefaces, distributed today under the name of *Thorowgood*:

Jusqu'à quand abuseras-*tu de notre*

The "fatness" of these typefaces can go to such extremes that the thickness of a down-stroke can be half the height of the letter! Seen next to such extravagance, Bodoni seems to be the most modest of designers.

The Pre-war Period: Experimentation and a Return to Roots

At the beginning of the twentieth century, we witnessed an interesting phenomenon in England that would liberate us from the stagnant typography of the nineteenth century: the establishment of small-scale presses. People like William Morris, Emery Walker, Edward Prince, and Thomas Cobben-Sanderson created masterpieces on their small presses and cut very special typefaces (we have already mentioned *Golden Type* and *Troy*) inspired by the pre-Raphaelites, their fascination with the Middle Ages, etc.

In France, it was the era of Toulouse-Lautrec and Hector Guimard. Already in 1895, Georges Peignot was collaboring with Eugène Grasset to create a typeface close to art nouveau. The result was *Grasset*, which enjoyed great success:

Jusqu'à quand abuseras-tu de notre patience

Ten years later, during the belle époque, Peignot collaborated with another graphic artist, George Auriol, who designed the typeface that bears his name, a typeface influenced by Japanese painting and calligraphy:

Jusqu'à quand abuseras-*tu de notre patience*

Moreover, during the years 1912 and 1913, Jérôme Peignot cut two typefaces that, according to him, "were to many foreigners the very definition of French taste": *Cochin* and *Nicolas Cochin*. The former is a text face:

Jusqu'à quand abuseras-*tu de notre patience*

The latter is more decorative:

Jusqu'à quand abuseras-*tu de notre patience*

At the same time, in Vienna, the *Wiener Werkstätte* was producing typefaces influenced by art nouveau and *Jugenstil*. The most famous of them is without a doubt that of Otto Eckmann, shown here as digitized by Gerda Delbanco:

Juſqu'à quand abuſeras-tu de notre patience

The 1910s saw the rise of futurism, which used typography as a means of expression. In their typographical layouts, the futurists mainly used ordinary typefaces. At the same time, the Dutch *de Stijl* group designed entirely geometric typefaces. Here is one of them, as digitized by the foundry P22:

JUSQU'À QUAND ABUSERAS-TU DE NOTRE

In addition, the Italian futurists designed typefaces that rejected harmony and uniformity. Here is a font inspired by this movement, produced by the foundry P22:

JU/QU'À QUAND ABU/ERA/-TU DE NOTRE

Finally, the dadaists were mixing everything together in every possible way in order to shatter preconceived notions and make a definitive break with the past. The foundry P22, which specializes in reconstructions of historic typefaces, offers a font that simulates the Dada aesthetic, *P22 Dada*:

Jusqu'à Quand abuseras—Tu de notre patience

In the midst of this whirlpool of new ideas, the English, who, like the Americans, held a near monopoly over the printing of books and newspapers, were more conservative than ever. Among the few exceptions to this rule was Edward Johnston, who in 1916 designed a typeface called *Underground* for the London Underground. He attempted not to allow himself to be influenced by the sans serif typefaces of the nineteenth century and instead applied simple geometric rules. The result was impressive for its freshness. Here is the digitized version of this typefaces by the foundry P22:

Jusqu'à quand abuseras-tu de notre patience

This typeface greatly influenced Erik Gill, who designed *Gill Sans* in 1928 for Monotype:

Jusqu'à quand abuseras-tu de notre patience

Let us return to the Continent. The 1920s were marked by the work of the *Bauhaus* team. The head of instruction in typography, László Moholy-Nagy, preached clarity and minimalism above all else. He suggested the creation of a new typographical language. His colleague and a former student of the Bauhaus, Herbert Bayer, designed numerous typefaces that met these criteria. Here is one of them, digitized by P22 (the font is called *P22 Bayer Universal*):

jusqu'à quand abuseras-tu de notre patience

Bayer recommended that the capital letters be abandoned. He even created a phonetic version of his alphabet to dispense once and for all with etymological spellings and return to the spontaneity of spoken language.

During that period, Paul Renner, who was teaching in Munich, designed *Futura*, a typeface that was consistent with the Bauhaus principles and that used only three basic shapes: the triangle, the circle, and the square. The Bauer foundry began to market it in 1927. Note that Renner believed that a lineal typeface such as *Futura* should respect the same rules as the German gothic typefaces for the "long s" and the "round s"; therefore, he designed the appropriate letters and ligatures:

Juſqu'à quand abuſeras-tu de notre patience

The less revolutionary German type designers, such as Peter Weiss and Rudolf Koch, indulged in the pleasures of both sans serif and gothic typefaces. For instance, Koch, one of the great type designers of the twentieth century, first designed in 1913 a delightfully poetic Fraktur that he called *Frühling* (or "spring"):

Die Vöglein ſchweigen im Walde, warte nur

Next, in 1921, he designed a very dynamic gothic combining elements of textura, Fraktur, and Schwabacher: *Koch Fraktur*:

Die Vöglein ſchweigen im Walde, warte nur

In 1924 he produced a typeface that was half gothic (the lowercase letters) and half roman (the capitals), *Peter Jessen*:

Die Vöglein ſchweigen im Walde, warte nur

And this same Rudolf Koch designed a sans serif typeface worthy of those of the Bauhaus, *Kabel*, issued in 1928:

Jusqu'à quand abuseras-tu de notre patience

Another German designer, Rudolf Wolf, produced *Memphis*, a very successful mechanistic typeface, in 1929:

Jusqu'à quand abuseras-tu de notre patience

Note that the name "Memphis" refers not to the American city but to the city in ancient Egypt.

Another great German type designer, Friedrich Hermann Ernst Schneidler, designed for the Bauer foundry in 1936 a humanistic typeface that was named after him, *Stempel Schneidler*:

Jusqu'à quand abuseras-tu de notre patience

and a Fraktur, often considered the most beautiful Fraktur ever, *Zentenar-Fraktur*, on the occasion of the foundry's anniversary:

Die Böglein schweigen im Walde, warte

At this time, art deco reigned in France. *Bifur*, the first typeface designed by Adolphe Mouron Cassandre at Deberny & Peignot, was also influenced by cubism:

JUSQU'A QUAND

Meanwhile, in England, Erik Gill was designing his best fonts, such as the very special *Perpetua* (1925):

Jusqu'à quand abuseras-*tu de notre patience*

In Germany in the 1930s, political and social tensions came to a head and were felt in the typefaces of the day. In 1931, for instance, Heinrich Jost designed *Beton* for the Bauer foundry, a "Betonesque" mechanistic typeface worthy of those of Figgins:

Jusqu'à quand abuseras

Similarly heavy, but with a consistent appendage at the upper left that gives the illusion of speed, is *Dynamo*, designed by Karl Sommer in 1930:

Jusqu'à quand abuseras

Very early on, the Germans had the idea of *standardized* typefaces, which were used in particular for the license plates for cars. For example, the font that was used for German license places for 64 years (from 1936 to 2000) bears the unpoetic name *DIN 1451* (for "German Industrial Standard number 1451"):

Jusqu'à quand abuseras-tu de notre patience

In 1935 the Nazis came to power. Emil Meyer, of the Stempel foundry, designed for them a typeface that even today remains a symbol of Nazism, *Tannenberg*:

Die Vöglein ſchweigen nicht immer

Its name is far from innocent: it refers to a battle of August 30, 1914, in which the Germans, under the direction of von Hindenburg, repelled 150,000 Russians and halted their offensive. Printers called this type of script *Schaftstiefelgrotesk* (= "jackboot sans serif [typeface]"), a direct reference to the Nazis' uniforms.

One of Koch's students, Berthold Wolpe, took refuge in England to escape Nazism. In 1940 he designed a sans serif typeface with light serifs in the style of lapidary inscriptions. He called this typeface *Albertus*:

Jusqu'à quand abuseras-*tu de notre patience*

Albertus enjoyed so much success that it was used on the signs showing the names of streets in London! Maximilien Vox designated a category for this kind of typeface: the *incised* typefaces. Here are our four representative letters in *Albertus*:

The typeface clearly shows the characteristics of the garaldes. In fact, we can say that a typeface can be both incised and humanistic, garalde, transitional, or didone at the same time. Here are the same representative letters for a post-war incised typeface, *Optima*:

As shown by the representative letters, this typeface is more an incised-didone or an incised-transitional; it is hard to make the distinction between a didone and a transitional typeface when there are no serifs.

Meanwhile, in France, despite the warnings of Giraudoux (*The Trojan War Will Not Take Place*), people did not see the clouds of war forming on the horizon. In 1937, it was the era of Léon Blum, and Cassandre designed *Peignot*, a typeface that long remained the symbol of the French look:

Jᴜꜱǫᴜ'à ǫᴜᴀɴᴅ ᴀʙᴜꜱᴇʀᴀꜱ-ᴛᴜ ᴅᴇ ɴᴏᴛʀᴇ ᴘᴀᴛɪᴇɴᴄᴇ

According to Rémy Peignot [97], this typeface is based on the idea that the lowercase letters are deformed, worn-out capitals that have become subordinate. But so as not to cause too great a departure from the habits of our poor eyes, Cassandre added ascenders to the letters 'b', 'd', 'f', 'h', 'k', and 'l'.

During the same period—first, in Paris; later, after 1939, in the south of France, and more specifically in the magnificent village of Baux-de-Provence—Louis Jou, a typographer of Catalonian origin, was setting splendid books in his small workshop. His typefaces have been digitized by Thierry Gouttenègre for the Fondation Louis Jou:

Jusqu'à quand abuseras-*tu de notre patience*

In England, at the beginning of the 1930s, the newspaper *Times* decided to change its typeface. It experimented with various typefaces from the past—Plantin, Baskerville—and even with contemporary fonts, such as Gill's Perpetua. Finally, Stanley Morison of Monotype decided to design a new typeface based on Plantin. It is important to note that, while the Germans were happily shaking up the traditions in order to establish new methods of typographic representation, Morison in England had very conservative opinions on typography. Accordingly, Times is not a didone but rather a garalde. Here is *Times New Roman*, designed in 1931 and put into service on September 29, 1932:

Jusqu'à quand abuseras-*tu de notre patience*

After *Times New Roman* came *Times Europa* in 1971, designed by Walter Tracy:

Jusqu'à quand abuseras-*tu de notre patience*

Paradoxically, it is a typeface with a wider set-width, whereas the whole point of *Times New Roman* was the possibility of fitting more text into less space. In 1991, the Icelandic designer Gunnlaugur Briem prepared a new version of *Times* for the newspaper, which he called *New Times Millenium*.

But *Times New Roman* was not the first typeface specifically designed for a newspaper. In 1925, after long years of research on the legibility of type at 6 or 7 points, Linotype issued *Ionic*:

Jusqu'à quand abuseras-*tu de notre patience*

Within one year of its release, this typeface was used by more than 3,000 newspapers around the world! To solve the technical problem of the filling in of counters in *Ionic*, Linotype revised it and issued *Excelsior*, which was put into circulation in 1931:

Jusqu'à quand abuseras-*tu de notre patience*

War broke out, and in Germany, on January 3, 1941, right in the middle of the collective folly that was Nazism, a circular from the Führer revealed to the Germans that

> ... to call the so-called gothic script a German script is incorrect. Schwabacher is in fact a Jewish script. As printing spread, the Jews appropriated Schwabacher and imposed it on Germany. After discussing the matter with Herr Adolf Müller, owner of a printing house, the Führer decided that the gothic script is henceforth banned and that the roman script will be standard in the Reich...

Hitler had doubtless been eager to get rid of the gothic script for some time. Herr Müller—if he really existed, for the name "Müller" is as common as our "Smith"—gave him the excuse that he needed. It was an argument that held great sway during the Nazi era: to get rid of a neighbor or a competitor, it was enough to denounce him as being a Jew. Hitler applied the same method to Germany's cultural heritage.

At that time, a young designer named Hermann Zapf was working on *Gilgengart* (named for the book that Jean Schönsperger prepared for the emperor Maximilian in 1519), a very beautiful Fraktur typeface that, owing to the ban on Fraktur, was not released until after the war:

𝔇𝔦𝔢 𝔙𝔬̈𝔤𝔩𝔢𝔦𝔫 𝔰𝔠𝔥𝔴𝔢𝔦𝔤𝔢𝔫 𝔦𝔪 𝔚𝔞𝔩𝔡𝔢, 𝔴𝔞𝔯𝔱𝔢

When the author asked Hermann Zapf, 60 years later, what he had felt when he learned that gothic type had been banned, he replied: "I wanted to laugh, but laughing was forbidden."

Nonetheless, it is easy to blame everything on Nazism. Hitler was not the only culprit who contributed to the disappearance of the gothic scripts, and probably the situation today would have been similar if he had not banned them. Indeed, the American occupying army banned their use because of their alleged Nazi connotations. And after the American troops left, the new German federal government was not concerned with the reintroduction of the gothic scripts.

The Post-war Period

No doubt the most famous designer of the 1950s was Hermann Zapf. Three of the typefaces that he produced between 1950 and 1958 brought him international fame: *Palatino*, *Melior*, and *Optima*.

Palatino is a garalde with strong calligraphic tendencies:

Jusqu'à quand abuseras-*tu de notre patience*

Melior, on the other hand, is a transitional typeface intended for the press and characterized by the flatness of its curves: one has the impression of seeing squares with rounded corners in the place of arcs:

Jusqu'à quand abuseras-*tu de notre patience*

Finally, *Optima* was a brilliant idea. At first glance it is a sans serif typeface, but when we take a closer look we see that it is an incised typeface (some would call it "lineal-incised" or "incised-humanistic"):

Jusqu'à quand abuseras-*tu de notre patience*

In France, the 1950s were marked by a typeface that is the epitome of French nobility, *Vendôme*:

Jusqu'à quand abuseras-*tu de notre patience*

Slightly slanted, this creation of François Ganeau and Roger Excoffon for the Olive foundry pushed the characteristics of the garaldes to an extreme: the serifs are pointed and irregular, the counter of the 'a' is tiny, the italic breaks with Griffo's tradition and looks more like a slanted roman.

Roger Excoffon is most famous for his script typefaces, such as *Mistral*, which is still very popular today:

Jusqu'à quand abuseras-tu de notre patience, Catilina?

In 1951, Ilse Schüler, a student and collaborator of Schneidler, proved that we can still create innovative and brilliant gothic typefaces. She created *Rhapsodie*, which is halfway between Fraktur and bastarda:

Die Vöglein schweigen im Walde, warte nur

Meanwhile, in Switzerland, Max Miedinger and Édouard Hoffman were designing *Helvetica*, mentioned earlier. But another great sans serif face was already in the works: *Univers*, by Adrien Frutiger[7] for the foundry Deberny & Peignot:

Jusqu'à quand abuseras-*tu de notre patience*

Frutiger released this typefaces in 1954. Its great innovation was that it was issued simultaneously in 21 (!) different versions, with varying weights and set-widths.

The next development in sans serif faces was *Antique Olive*, by Roger Excoffon (1962). This typeface, with its enormous x-height, parts ways with the neutrality of *Helvetica* and even rediscovers the characteristics of the garaldes:

Jusqu'à quand abuseras-*tu de notre patience*

Adrien Frutiger also collaborated with the engineers of ECMA to create a monospaced font optimized for optical character recognition, *OCR-B*, which was issued in 1968:

---

[7] Which led Nicholas Fabian to call Adrien Frutiger the *créateur de l'univers*—"creator of [the] Univers[e]".

Jusqu'à quand abuseras-tu de notre patience

This typeface influenced other cold, mechanical designs such as *Eurostile*, designed by Aldo Novarèse in 1962, a typeface that was widely used in the 1960s to symbolize state-of-the-art technology:

Jusqu'à quand abuseras-*tu de notre patience*

In 1968, while Paris was erecting barricades, Hans Eduard Meier of the Stempel foundry decided to design a sans serif typeface based on the graphical principles of the humanistic typefaces; the result, *Syntax*, is surprisingly refreshing:

Jusqu'à quand abuseras-*tu de notre patience*

In 1971, José Mendoza y Almeida designed one of the first typefaces specifically adapted to photocomposition, *Photina*:

Jusqu'à quand abuseras-*tu de notre patience*

Two years later, Adrien Frutiger designed another sans serif typeface, *Frutiger*, for use in the signage of the ultra-modern Charles de Gaulle Airport. Here we are straying even further from the formal neutrality of *Univers* while preserving remarkable legibility:

Jusqu'à quand abuseras-*tu de notre patience*

The 1970s in general mainly turned towards kitsch, as shown by typefaces such as *Zipper*, by Phillip Kelly (Letraset, 1970), a sans serif typeface with disproportionately thick crossbars and horizontal strokes that evoke the orange furniture and other wonders of that decade:

Jusqu'à quand abuseras-tu de notre patience

But the typeface most characteristic of the 1970s is indisputably *Avant Garde Gothic*, by Herb Lubalin (1973), a lineal face with strokes of uniform thickness whose round letters are formed with perfect circles:

Jusqu'à quand abuseras-*tu de notre patience*

We have already mentioned the standard German typeface *DIN 1451*. It is interesting to observe that this very regular typeface was replaced in 2000 by another with a stimulating and, at first blush, awkward design: *FE-Schrift*, by Karlgeorg Hoefer (1978), where "FE" comes from *fälschungserschwerend*, i.e., "making forgery more difficult".[8] Every-

---

[8] In order to make it difficult to build up letters out of parts of other letters, this typeface was deliberately designed with no consistent elements: the crossbars of the 'E', the 'F', and the 'H' are not at the same height; some letters ('D', 'I', 'L', 'P') have mechanistic serifs, and others have none at all; the bottom serif on the 'I' is so large that the letter cannot be transformed into a 'T'; the '9' has a slit, whereas the '6' does not; etc. The reader is invited to try to tamper with this alphabet; it cannot be done! Make a 'P' into an 'R' by adding a slanted stroke? Impossible, as the 'P' has a serif. Make an 'O' into a 'Q'? Impossible, as the 'O' is round, while the 'Q' is practically square. Make an 'F' into an 'E'? Impossible, as the crossbar is too low. And so on.

thing about this typeface contributes to accentuating the differences among the glyphs, and the result is surprising:

ABCDEFGHIJKLMNOPQRSTUVWXYZ0123456789

Intended for use on license plates, this typeface supplies only the capital letters. The Swedish designer Martin Fredrikson (Fountain Type) added lowercase letters to it and called his font *Sauerkrauto*:

Jusqu'à quand abuseras-tu de notre

In the 1980s, more and more designers created "families" of fonts—fonts available both with and without serifs. The first was Donald Knuth, who, in 1978, with the help of Richard Southall and Hermann Zapf, used the METAFONT programming language to produce *Computer Modern* (see §F.2), which was released simultaneously in roman, sans serif, "typewriter", and other versions:

Jusqu'à quand abuseras-*tu de notre patience*

Jusqu'à quand abuseras-*tu de notre patience*

Jusqu'à quand abuseras-*tu de notre patience*

Sumner Stone, of Adobe, also designed in 1987 the *Stone* family, which included a garalde (*Serif*), a lineal (*Sans*), and a transitional typeface (*Informal*):

Jusqu'à quand abuseras-*tu de notre patience*

Jusqu'à quand abuseras-*tu de notre patience*

Jusqu'à quand abuseras-*tu de notre patience*

In 1992, Chuck Bigelow and Kris Holmes designed *Lucida Fax*, a typeface designed specifically for faxes and a member of the great *Lucida* font family:

Jusqu'à quand abuseras-*tu de notre patience*

Its very thick serifs situate it between the didones and the mechanistic faces.

In 1994, Jean François Porchez designed the new typeface for the newspaper *Le Monde*. This typeface was issued in several variants, including one for the newspaper (*Le Monde Journal*):

Jusqu'à quand abuseras-*tu de notre patience*

and another, called *Le Monde Livre*, that is used in all recent books published by the French branch of O'Reilly (including this book):

Jusqu'à quand abuseras-*tu de notre patience*

and a sans serif version, *Le Monde Sans*:

Jusqu'à quand abuseras-*tu de notre patience*

In 1996, Matthew Carter designed two typefaces for Microsoft that were specially adapted for reading text on a computer screen: *Verdana* (a sans serif face inspired by Frutiger) and *Georgia* (a serif face derived from *Scotch*):

Jusqu'à quand abuseras-*tu de notre patience*
Jusqu'à quand abuseras-*tu de notre patience*

In 1997, Thierry Gouttenègre accepted the challenge of designing a perfectly neutral lineal—i.e., one based on Blanchard's formula, "before any connotation" [84, p. 116]. He considered some fundamental questions: what is the shape of the 'a', for example, that we have all unconsciously memorized and that enables us to recognize this letter by reference? What is a font of average, standard, regular weight? What are the proportions of the rectangle, the ratio of width to height of the 'i', in a sans serif face? For that matter, what is the "standard", "neutral" proportion of an alphabet before it becomes narrow or wide? Here is the fruit of his research, *Neutre*:

Jusqu'à quand abuseras-*tu de notre patience*

In 1999, three Poles, Bogusław Jackowski, Janusz Nowacki, and Piotr Strzelczyk, issued the first family of fonts programmed in METATYPE1 (see §F.3), *Antykwa Półtawskiego*, based on a typeface from the 1920s by the great Polish typographer Adam Półtawski:

Jusqu'à quand abuseras-*tu de notre patience*

In the 1980s and 1990s, hundreds of designers tried practically everything in search of new approaches to typography. We shall not touch upon their creations, which the reader will find at foundries such as Émigré, FontFont, Linotype, Letterror, etc.

Suggested Reading

There is a vast literature on the history of typography and of typefaces. As a guide to the reader who would like to study this field in more depth, we have selected a few titles from those that seem the most important to us.

First, *honoris causa*, is the classic *History of Printing Types*, by Daniel Berkeley Updike [336]— preferably the second edition, of 1937. It is a very easy-to-read book with a wealth of examples. Everyone uses this book as a basis, everyone refers to it; it is a must.

A book devoted to typefaces, with one chapter for each: *Anatomy of a Typeface*, by Alexander Lawson [228]. It is extremely useful when one is looking for information on a specific typeface, its derivatives, and its ramifications.

In the French language, the indispensable works are by Gérard Blanchard: *Aide au choix de la typo-graphie* [84], an analysis of typefaces from all possible and imaginable aspects, written in Blanchard's characteristic style, which is to say with a profusion of illustrations and examples. A little less difficult to find, but equally stimulating, is the set of plates from his dissertation,[9] *Pour une sémiologie de la typographie* [85], published in Belgium.

A book that is just sublime, for its content and its execution alike, is *De plomb, d'encre & de lumière — Essai sur la typographie & la communication écrite*, published and printed by the Imprimerie Nationale in Jaugeon's typeface. In it are a preface by Charles Peignot and essays by Raymond Gid ("À l'heure où le plomb devient lumière"), Rémy Peignot (*L'esprit des lettres*), and Fernand Baudin (*De l'influence de la technique*), as well as an epilogue by Georges Bonnin, director of the Imprimerie. It is pleasant to read, thumb through, touch, feel—pure, unadulterated pleasure.

While we are on the subject of the Imprimerie Nationale, there is also, of course, the catalog *Les caractères de l'Imprimerie nationale* [98], in which one can admire immortal typefaces, some of which, unfortunately, may be used only by this one publishing house.

Recently the well-known designer Ladislas Mandel issued a work entitled *Écritures, miroir des hommes et des sociétés* [245]. It is a very interesting vision of the history of typefaces, always corresponding to the historical and social conditions. The book is set in Mandel's *Messidor*, an incised typeface, which gives it a very special allure.

Returning to the English language, we find a very interesting history of printing: *Five Hundred Years of Printing*, by Siegfried Steinberg [322]. The only problem with this well-respected book is its disagreeable disdain for gothic typefaces: "[...] Antiqua was henceforth to be the 'normal script' of the German people — despite its nonsensical argumentation, the one good thing Hitler did for German civilization" (p. 174).

Let us proceed to some more specialized works. On the origins of printing, *A View of Early Typography*, by Harry Carter [94], father of the designer Matthew Carter. This was the Carter who solved the "mystery of the Janson typefaces". An interesting and well-illustrated work.

For those interested in Augereau and Garamond, there is a gripping historical novel: *Le Maître de Garamond*, by Anne Cuneo [105]. The book is set in *1530 Garamond*, by Tiro Typeworks.

A classic work on gothic typefaces, in the German language, is *Fraktur, Form und Geschichte der gebrochenen Schriften*, by Albert Kapr [205]; and an article by the author, available on the Internet, is "𝔇𝔯𝔲𝔠𝔨𝔰𝔞𝔱 𝔦𝔫 𝔤𝔢𝔟𝔯𝔬𝔠𝔥𝔢𝔫𝔢𝔫 𝔖𝔠𝔥𝔯𝔦𝔣𝔱𝔢𝔫" [164], set in *Normalfraktur*, by Gerda Delbanco. Also interesting is an anthology, this time in the English language: *Blackletter and National Identity* [62].

A very interesting collective work combining history of type and recent digital typefaces: *Revival of the Fittest: Digital Versions of Classic Typefaces*, edited by Philip B. Meggs and Roy McKelvey and published in 2000 [253].

Very thorough and well illustrated is *Twentieth-Century Type*, by Lewis Blackwell [82].

Finally, a very recent work devoted to the famous contemporary designers Jonathan Hoefler, Jonathan Barnbrook, Akira Kobayashi, Zuzana Licko, Jean François Porchez, Rian Hughes, Carlos Segura, Erik Spiekermann, Jeremy Tankard, Matthew Carter, and Erik van Blokland is *Designing Typefaces*, by David Earls [127].

The Vox/ATypI Classification of Typefaces

Let us review the Vox classification, which we described throughout our history of typefaces. Vox distinguised nine categories of typefaces:

---

[9] His dissertation [83] can be consulted at the library of the Sorbonne or obtained through interlibrary loan. It is a very interesting work, and the ideal complement to the plates, but reading it requires some background knowledge in semiology and linguistics.

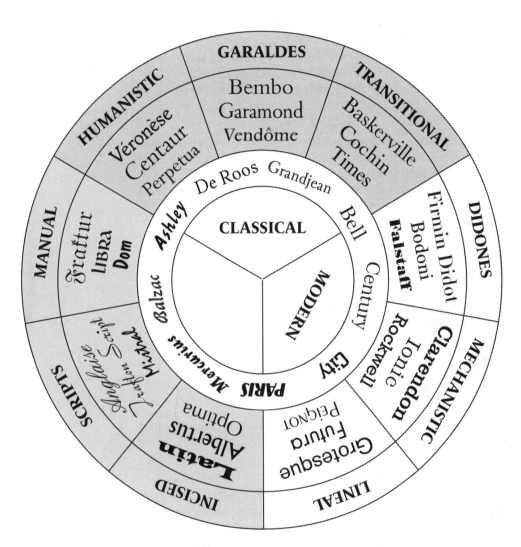

Figure 11-4: The schematic classification of Maximilien Vox, according to [342]. We have set each name in the typeface in question.

Humanistic faces, which hark back to the typeface of Nicolas Jenson and its derivatives: *Golden Type,* by William Morris; *Eusebius,* by Ernst Detterer. They are inspired either by the original Jenson or by Morris. Humanistic faces can be easily recognized thanks to the slanted cross stroke of the 'e', a sign of their gothic origins. The ascenders bear steeply sloping serifs.

The *garaldes,* engendered by the first two typefaces of Aldus Manutius, range from the faces of Garamond and Granjon to those of Kis and Caslon. Two of their hallmarks: the 'e' no longer has a slanted cross stroke but has a rather small counter, and the axis of the 'o' and the other round letters is tilted towards the left.

The *transitional* typefaces—transitional between the garaldes and the didones—actually cover a much broader range. The term transitional applies to those typefaces that are neither garaldes nor pure didones. Characteristics: the axis of the 'o' is vertical, the serifs on the ascenders are almost horizontal, the upper serifs of the 'T' are symmetrical. The main feature that distinguishes them from the didones is in their serifs, which are *not* horizontal.

The *didones* are the typefaces of Didot, Bodoni, and Walbaum and their derivatives. Their primary characteristic: their serifs are perfectly flat and often extremely thin, even threadlike. Despite the popularity of Didot and Bodoni, there are relatively few didones, compared with the large number of garaldes and transitional faces.

Here ends the "historical" part of the classification and begins the "graphical" part. The *mechanistic,* or *Egyptian,* typefaces are those whose serifs are squared off and quite thick, often as thick as or even thicker than the strokes of the letters. They first appeared in the nineteenth century.

The *lineal* typefaces are sans serif typefaces. They also first appeared in the nineteenth century but did not really come into vogue until the twentieth century, with typefaces such as *Helvetica* and *Univers.*

The *incised* typefaces are inspired by lapidary inscriptions. Thus they have either small, pointed serifs (as in *Copperplate Gothic*) or tapering downstrokes (as in *Optima*).

Scripts imitate rapid handwriting, be it calligraphic or ordinary, executed with the wrist raised. They range from the sublime *Zapfino* or the chancery italic of Arrighi to rapid scripts such as *Mistral*. Note: the letters *must be connected*; otherwise the typeface is a manual!

Manuals are "typefaces based on slow handwriting, with the wrist resting on the table, or typefaces in which design is more important than writing". In fact it is something of a catchall: Vox also placed in this category the gothic and uncial typefaces. Blackwell [82] simply ignores this category altogether.

ATypI later added two more categories to the Vox classification: one for *gothic* typefaces, which, by virtue of being in this category, are no longer considered manuals, and one for *non-Latin* typefaces.[10]

The Alessandrini Classification of Typefaces: Codex 80

In 1979, Jean Alessandrini [30] proposed another classification of typefaces and, most of all, a new terminology that makes up for some of the deficiencies of Vox's. Inspired by the biological classification of animal species, he describes typefaces with a series of qualifying terms that go from the general to the specific. He presents 19 classes, called *désignations préliminaires* (preliminary designations); two *éventualités* (possibilities), which are modifiers orthogonal to the concept of category; and five lists of additional qualifications, which he calls *listes de renseignements d'appoint* (lists of extra information).

What distinguishes Alessandrini is that he invented neologisms for all of Vox's categories, his own new categories, and even roman and italic, uppercase and lowercase. His choice of names such as *deltapodes* and *aliennes* (the film *Alien* had just then come out) is tinged with humor.

This classification has been roundly criticized by the adherents of the Vox classification. Nonetheless, we believe that it deserves to be studied just as much as that of Vox. In the rest of this section, therefore, we describe it in broad strokes.

Here are Alessandrini's 19 *dénominations préliminaires*:

1. *Simplices*

   Simplices (plain typefaces) is the name that he gives to sans serif typefaces on the entirely correct grounds that the name "lineal" refers to lines, whereas, at the end of the day, all typefaces are made of lines, including those that are not lineals.

---

[10] Which, unfortunately, shows the flagrant Latinocentrism in this venerable institution: there are *four* categories for typefaces with serifs, including one just for the *humanistic* faces, which, after all, represent a historical period of only 20 to 30 years at most, the period of Nicolas Jenson's glory; but there is only *one* category for *all* the gothic typefaces, from Gutenberg to Ilse Schüler, and—the height of ridicule—only *one* category for *all the other writing systems of the world*! It would have been better to designate three categories for the three main kinds of gothic typefaces (textura, Fraktur, Schwabacher) and to omit from the classification the other writing systems, which do, after all, have their own classifications, instead of lumping them all together.

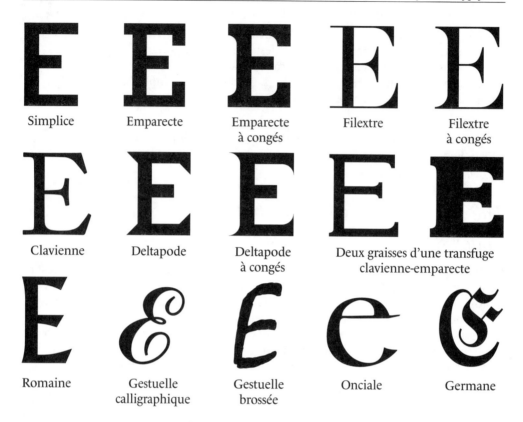

| Simplice | Emparecte | Emparecte à congés | Filextre | Filextre à congés |

| Clavienne | Deltapode | Deltapode à congés | Deux graisses d'une transfuge clavienne-emparecte |

| Romaine | Gestuelle calligraphique | Gestuelle brossée | Onciale | Germane |

Figure 11-5: Alessandrini's dénominations préliminaires.

2. *Emparectes*

The word *emparectes* is derived from the words *empattement* ("serif") and *rectangulaire* ("rectangular"). These are the Egyptian typefaces that Vox called "mechanistic", with only one difference: Alessandrini specifies that these are typefaces with *strictly rectangular* serifs.

3. *Emparectes à congés*

The term *à congés* ("with congés") is borrowed from architecture. It means that there is an effect of rounding between the downstroke and the serif (see Figure 11-5).

4. *Deltapodes*

To be *deltapode* is to have delta-shaped feet. This is a kind of typeface not foreseen by Vox that has strictly triangular serifs (see Figure 11-5).

5. *Deltapodes à congés*

The serifs of these *deltapodes* are rounded (see Figure 11-5). It is difficult to distinguish this category from the *filextres à congés* or the *romaines*.

6. *Filextres*

The word *"filextre"* comes from *"extrémité en forme de fil"* ("threadlike extremities"). This is a politically correct way to refer to the didones (which doubtless would have been called "bodotes" if Vox had been Italian). These are typefaces with threadlike serifs (see Figure 11-5).

7. *Filextres à congés*

These are typefaces whose serifs are very fine but "filled in" (see Figure 11-5).

8. *Claviennes*

Here Alessandrini really snubs Vox and all the other classifications by lumping all types of roman typefaces into the same category. Humanistic typefaces, garaldes, and transitional typefaces—all of them are merely *claviennes*, whose name comes from the Latin *clavus* (for "nail", as the serifs are shaped like the head of a nail; see Figure 11-5).

9. *Romaines*

Alessandrini's *romaines* have nothing to do with roman typefaces. They are Vox's incised typefaces—in other words, those whose design is inspired by engraving in marble (see Figure 11-5).

10. *Gestuelles calligraphiques*

The term *gestuelle* refers to the scripts based on handwriting carefully executed with a pen, what we commonly call calligraphic scripts (see Figure 11-5).

11. *Gestuelles brossées*

Unlike the *calligraphiques*, the *gestuelles brossées* are written with a brush and pertain to everyday handwriting rather than to the work of calligraphers (see Figure 11-5).

12. *Onciales*

This is practically the only time that Alessandrini does not invent a new term. *Onciales* (uncials) are merely the scripts inspired by—uncial handwriting (see Figure 11-5). This category also includes the scripts that are called "Celtic".

13. *Germanes*

The gothic script was "selected" by both the Germans (who call it *deutsche Schrift*, for "German script") and the English (who call it *Old English*). Just a few centuries ago, all of Northern Europe still wrote in the gothic script. Right or wrong, Alessandrini succumbs to the influence of cultural stereotypes and calls gothic typefaces *germanes* (see Figure 11-5).

14. *Aliennes*

Any non-Latin script is an *alienne*. Just as Latinocentric as ATypI a few years before him, Alessandrini also assigns all the other scripts of the world to a single category.

jusqu'a quand abuseras-tu de notre patience

JUSQU'À QUAND ABUSERAS-TU DE NOTRE

 JUSqua QUand abuseras—tu de notre

Jusqu'à quand abuseras-tu de notre patience

Jusqu'à quand abuseras-tu de notre patience

Figure 11-6: Examples of typefaces according to Alessandrini's classification: a Devanagari exotype (Samarkan, from the Titivillus foundry), a square Hebrew exotype (Sefer-AH, Andreas Höfeld), a Japanese exotype (Faux Japanese, Roger Vershen), a machinale (ComputerFont, anonymous), an hybride (simplice-emparecte, Dynamo, Karl Sommer), and a ludique (Caricature, Caricature Zone).

15. *Exotypes*

An *exotype* is a Latin typeface that *simulates* a non-Latin script, usually an East Asian one. This very amusing sort of typeface is often used in advertising to create a certain atmosphere and make the reader believe that he is able to read the simulated script (see Figure 11-6).

16. *Machinales*

These are typefaces typical of the 1970s that are inspired by the typefaces intended for optical character recognition that are used on checks and administrative documents. These typefaces thus symbolize computer science, science fiction, robotics—in short, all the technological fantasies of that decade (see Figure 11-6). Fortunately, they did not survive.

17. *Ludiques*

A *ludique* is a typeface meant for "entertainment"—any typeface designed *to amuse more than to be read* (see Figure 11-6).

18. *Hybrides*

A typeface is an *hybride* if it has the characteristics of more than one category. Alessandrini's categories are defined in such a way that an *hybride* can only be the result of a deliberate choice by the designer. For example, *Dynamo* is an *hybride* combining elements of *simplices* and *emparectes* (see Figure 11-6).

19. *Transfuges*

The *transfuges* (defectors) are another kind of typeface that spans several categories, but this time the different weights of the typefaces are what cause them to switch from one class to another. The example given is that of *Korinna*, whose light weight is a *clavienne* whereas its bold weight is an *emparecte*. We would thus say that *Korinna* is a *clavienne-emparecte transfuge* (see Figure 11-5).

Orthogonally to these 19 categories, we can also employ two qualifications that Alessandrini calls *éventualités*:

1. *Diagones*

This is the term given to italics and, more generally, to slanted typefaces. We can speak of *mini-diagones*, *maxi-diagones*, or even *anti-diagones*, according to the degree of the slope.

2. *Stenciliennes*

These are stenciled letters, which were also very popular in the 1970s.

Finally, he offers five ways to supplement the information given by the name of the category. These are five lists of qualifiers, called *listes de renseignements d'appoint*:

1. *Liste des considérations formelles objectives* ("list of objective formal considerations").

Light, semi-bold, bold, extra-bold, black, tachidé, extended, wide, à section horizontale, à section verticale, beveled, à section emboulée, éclairée, shadowed, in relief, intaglio, three-dimensional, in perspective, layered, lapidary, à filetage, à circuit, connected, inscribed, for display, woven, shattered, broken, interrupted, juxtaposable, overlapping, combining, dotted, decorated, illustrative, spiral, swash.

2. *Liste des repères historiques* ("list of historical reference points").

Archaic, antique, Merovingian, Carolingian, mediaeval, Renaissance, *grand-siècle*, Encyclopedist, consular, imperial, romantic, republican, modern, contemporary, futuristic.

3. *Liste des considérations esthétiques et de style* ("list of aesthetic and stylistic considerations").

Classical, baroque, metropolitan, modern style, cubist, surrealist, informal, optical, pop, Moorish, Chinese-style, Byzantine, iconic.

4. *Liste des considérations formelles subjectives* ("list of subjective formal considerations").

Monotone, mechanical, regular, systematic, laborious, restrained, severe, distinct, emphatic, heterogeneous, convoluted, busy, overwrought, excessive, expressive, dramatized, experimental, forward-looking, affected, sophisticated, rhythmical, etc. This list can be extended as much as one pleases.

5. *Localisations géographiques et précisions originelles* ("geographic areas and original aspects").

   Geographical origin, either for *exotypes* or for *aliennes*.

In addition, he also recommends the name *majuscules* for the upper case, *minuscules* for the lower case, and *lecturiennes* (characters meant for reading) for body type.

Owing, no doubt, to the many neologisms that it devised and the importance that it attaches to typefaces from the 1970s, the welcome extended to Codex 80 by intellectuals in the printing profession has unfortunately been lukewarm. At the time when computer science was coming onto the scene and would definitively change habits within the profession, Alessandrini sought to rejuvenate a microcosm that is too attached to its traditions.

For the reader who wishes to pursue in greater depth the study of "noncomputer-based" classifications of typefaces, let us mention that René Ponot wrote an article, 10 years after Alessandrini, that summarizes this subject [297]. And the most important work on the subject is, of course, *Aide au choix de la typo-graphie* [84], by Gérard Blanchard, which was published in 2001, three years after his death.

IBM's Classification of Fonts

IBM's classification of fonts is used in the OS/2 table of TrueType fonts (under the entry sFamilyClass, §D.4.7). It consists of 10 classes, each with its own subclasses.[11] Here they are:

Class 0: No Classification

This category represents the absence of any classification.

Class 1: Old-Style Serifs

"Old-style" refers to the humanistic typefaces and the garaldes. Here are its subcategories:

- Subclass 0: no classification. When no other information that could help us to classify the font is available. Warning: this is not a catchall to use whenever no subclass is appropriate. Subclass 15 ("miscellaneous") serves that purpose.

- Subclass 1: "IBM rounded legibility". A class meant only for certain bitmap fonts by IBM.

---

[11] The specification very frequently gives the correspondences between IBM's subclasses and the entries in the ISO 9541-1 standard [194], which is a standardized classification of typefaces that is unfortunately of little interest because it has not been adopted by the industry.

- Subclass 2: garalde. IBM gives the horrible *ITC Garamond* as a canonical example of the garaldes:[12]

Une forêt de lettres

- Subclass 3: Venetian. IBM's name for this subclass may sow confusion: after all, Griffo, who was Manutius' punchcutter, was at Venice just like Jenson, but this category refers only to typefaces by the latter and their derivatives. For instance, *Bembo*, inspired by Greffo, is a garalde, whereas *Cloister Old Style* is a humanistic typeface. On the other hand, there is a serious problem of reference: the IBM specification refers to *Goudy Old Style*, which, unfortunately, is not humanistic. At the same time, it refers to entry 4.1.1 of the ISO 9541-1 standard, which gives as an example *Eusebius*, which *is* humanistic:

Une forêt de lettres

- Subclass 4: "modified Venetian". If in the previous entry some references were inaccurate, here we have total chaos: the members of this class are called "Venetian" (garaldes or humanistic typefaces—we simply do not know), with a large x-height, and the example given is *Palatino*. But the corresponding entry in ISO is 4.2.2, which is found in another category, that of the transitional typefaces. And ISO's example is *Goudy Old Style*, which is a garalde, not a transitional typeface:

Une forêt de lettres

- Subclass 5: "Dutch modern". IBM certainly means for that name to refer to the late or contemporary garaldes with a large x-height. The example given is *Times New Roman*:

Une forêt de lettres

- Subclass 6: "Dutch traditional". The same description as for Dutch modern, with the exception that, according to IBM, the strokes are thicker than in the previous subclass. The example given is *IBM Press Roman*, a font that we couldn't find:

Une forêt de lettres

- Subclass 7: "contemporary". Explanation: "small x-height, light strokes". The example given by IBM is *University*, a decorative font of little interest:

Une forêt de lettres

- Subclass 8: "calligraphic". According to IBM, these are "fine hand writing style of calligraphy, while retaining the characteristic Oldstyle appearance." Since no example is given, we have decided to illustrate this subclass with the font *Mauritius*:

---

[12] The words *Une forêt de lettres* ("A forest of letters") come from a wonderful sentence by Rémy Peignot: "Vivre, c'est avancer dans une forêt de lettres qui nous font signe; elles n'ont pas encore dit leur dernier mot" ("To live is to move forward in a forest of letters that beckon to us: they have not yet said their last word") [97, p. 164].

Une forêt de lettres

- Subclass 15: "miscellaneous". A catchall, in case no subclass is satisfactory.

Class 2: Transitional Serifs

These, of course, are the transitional typefaces. Here are the subclasses:

- Subclass 0: no classification. When no other information that could help us to classify the font is available.

- Subclass 1: "direct line". Fonts inspired by the transitional typefaces. Example given: *Baskerville*:

Une forêt de lettres

- Subclass 2: "scripts", "generally characterized by a hand written script appearance while retaining the Transitional Direct Line style". IBM gives as its example an Arabic typeface. Once again, not knowing exactly how to interpret this subclass, we have selected a calligraphic font that corresponds roughly to the description, *Parade*:

Une forêt de lettres

- Subclass 15: "miscellaneous". A catchall, in case no subclass is satisfactory.

Class 3: Modern Serifs

"Modernity" should be understood in the sense of the didones.

- Subclass 0: no classification. When no other information that could help us to classify the font is available.

- Subclass 1: "Italian". In fact, IBM provided only this one class for all the didones (except the "script didones", for which see below). There are, of course, Bodoni, but also Didot and Walbaum who are, according to IBM, "Italian". Thank you, IBM!

Une forêt de lettres

- Subclass 2: "scripts", "generally characterized by a hand written script appearance while retaining the Modern Italian style". IBM gives a Hebrew font as its example. Once again, not knowing exactly how to interpret this subclass, we have selected a calligraphic font that corresponds roughly to the description, *Allegro*:

Une forêt de lettres

- Subclass 15: "miscellaneous". A catchall, in case no subclass is satisfactory.

Class 4: Clarendon Serifs

These are the "industrial" typefaces of the nineteenth century with very pronounced serifs that were created as a result of research on improving legibility.

- Subclass 0: no classification. When no other information that could help us to classify the font is available.

- Subclass 1: "Clarendon". A large x-height, and serifs almost as thick as the downstrokes. Example given: *Clarendon*:

Une forêt de lettres

- Subclass 2: "modern". Lighter than the preceding, with serifs much thinner than the downstrokes. The example given is *Century Schoolbook*:

Une forêt de lettres

- Subclass 3: "traditional". Another imprecise explanation given by IBM: the members of this class are "lighter than those of 1 but bolder than those of 2". Whatever the case may be, the example given is *Century*:

Une forêt de lettres

- Subclass 4: "newspaper". Like the "modern" fonts above, but with a simplified design. An example is *Excelsior*:

Une forêt de lettres

- Subclass 5: "stub serif". Typefaces whose serifs are thick but truncated rather than rectangular. An example is *Cheltenham*:

Une forêt de lettres

- Subclass 6: "monotone", i.e., with strokes of uniform thickness. The example given is *Korinna*:

Une forêt de lettres

- Subclass 7: "typewriter". Warning: these are typewriter-style typefaces that are *not* mechanistic. The example given is *Prestige Elite*, which, aside from its uniformity of stroke width and its monospaced design, has characteristics of a transitional typeface:

Une forêt de lettres

- Subclass 15: "miscellaneous". A catchall, in case no subclass is satisfactory.

Class 5: Slab Serifs

Here we find our beloved mechanistic typefaces.

- Subclass 0: no classification. When no other information that could help us to classify the font is available.

- Subclass 1: "monotone", i.e., with strokes of uniform thickness. These are the true Egyptians, whose serifs are of the same thickness as the regular strokes. An example is *Lubalin Graph*:

Une forêt de lettres

- Subclass 2: "humanist". A slightly smaller x-height and serifs that are thinner than the regular strokes. An example is *Candida*:

Une forêt de lettres

- Subclass 3: "geometric". Like the "monotones", but with a design that uses pure geometric shapes (perfect circles, squares, triangles). An example is *Rockwell*:

Une forêt de lettres

- Subclass 4: "Swiss". According to IBM, these are "characterized by a large x-height, with serifs and strokes of equal weight and an emphasis on the white space of the characters". The example given is *Serifa*. The reader will note that the difference between *Serifa* and *Rockwell* (shown above) is only slight:

Une forêt de lettres

- Subclass 5: "typewriter". Typefaces of the same kind as *Courier*, i.e., monospaced typefaces with shapes that allow the letters to be disambiguated (so that the reader can more easily distinguish 'l', 'I', and '1'; '0' and 'O'; etc.):

Une forêt de lettres

- Subclass 15: "miscellaneous". A catchall, in case no subclass is satisfactory.

Class 7: Free-Form Serifs

This class seems to have been defined only for the single font *Souvenir* and its derivatives.

- Subclass 0: no classification. When no other information that could help us to classify the font is available.

- Subclass 1: "modern". According to IBM, "a medium x-height, with light contrast in the strokes and a round full design". The example given is *Souvenir*:

Une forêt de lettres

- Subclass 15: "miscellaneous". A catchall, in case no subclass is satisfactory.

Class 8: Sans Serif

- Subclass 0: no classification. When no other information that could help us to classify the font is available.

- Subclass 1: "IBM neo-grotesque gothic". A class that contains only a few bitmap fonts by IBM.

- Subclass 2: "humanist". According to IBM, "medium x-height, with light contrast in the strokes and a classic Roman letterform". The example given is *Optima*:

Une forêt de lettres

- Subclass 3: "low-x round geometric". Typefaces with a low x-height and a uniform thickness of strokes, using only pure geometric shapes. A typical example is *Futura*:

Une forêt de lettres

- Subclass 4: "high-x round geometric". Identical to the preceding, but with a larger x-height. The example given is *Avant Garde Gothic*:

Une forêt de lettres

- Subclass 5: "neo-grotesque gothic". In fact, despite its name, this subclass encompasses all lineal typefaces that are neither geometric nor humanistic; thus it includes both the neo-lineals and the older lineals, such as *Akzidenz Grotesk*. The example given is *Helvetica*:

Une forêt de lettres GQ

- Subclass 6: "modified neo-grotesque gothic". Here IBM tries to put the two great rivals, *Helvetica* and *Univers*, into separate classes. The intention is praiseworthy, but it hangs by a thread, as IBM makes the distinction between the two subclasses only on the basis of the letters 'G' and 'Q'. Naturally, the example of this subclass is *Univers*:

Une forêt de lettres GQ

- Subclass 9: "typewriter". Sans serif typewriter typefaces do exist; the most popular example is *Letter Gothic*:

Une forêt de lettres

- Subclass 10: "matrix". Fonts for dot-matrix printers:

Une forêt de lettres

- Subclass 15: "miscellaneous". A catchall, in case no subclass is satisfactory.

Class 9: Ornamentals

This is a rather large class that encompasses the gothic typefaces (as if all gothics existed solely for ornamentation) as well as engraved and shadowed typefaces.

- Subclass 0: no classification. When no other information that could help us to classify the font is available.

- Subclass 1: "engraved". Typefaces that simulate lapidary inscriptions. An example is *Copperplate Gothic*:

  # UNE FORÊT DE LETTRES

- Subclass 2: "black letter". More specifically, "English textura". The commentary in the specification is a real gem: "generally based upon the printing style of the German monasteries and printers of the 12th to 15th centuries", as if they had been printing already in the twelfth century and as if the gothic script were used only in Germany, and, to top it all, as if printing had ceased to be done in gothic after the fifteenth century. The example given is *Old English*, with no explanation from IBM of why a "typeface from the German monasteries" somehow turned out to be named "Old English":

  # Une forêt de lettres

- Subclass 3: "decorative". According to IBM, a decorative typeface is one that "characterized by ornamental designs (typically from nature, such as leaves, flowers, animals, etc.) incorporated into the stems and strokes of the characters". The example given, *Saphire*, cannot be found today. We have replaced it here by *Gypsy Rose*, a free font:

  # UNE FORET DE LETTRES

- Subclass 4: "3-D". In other words, shadowed typefaces.

  # Une forêt de lettres

- Subclass 15: "miscellaneous". A catchall, in case no subclass is satisfactory.

Class 10: Scripts

Unlike Vox, IBM does not distinguish between manual (letters not connected) and script (letters connected) typefaces; thus we find in this class both uncials and calligraphic scripts, with their letters connected or not.

- Subclass 0: no classification. When no other information that could help us to classify the font is available.

- Subclass 1: "uncial". The example given is *Libra*:

$$\text{une forêt de lettres}$$

- Subclass 2: "brush joined". The example given is *Mistral*:

$$\textit{Une forêt de lettres}$$

- Subclass 3: "formal joined". The example given is *Commercial Script*:

$$\textit{Une forêt de lettres}$$

- Subclass 4: "monotone joined", where "monotone" means that the thickness of the strokes is uniform. The example given is *Kaufmann*:

$$\textit{Une forêt de lettres}$$

- Subclass 5: "calligraphic". The example given is *Thompson Quillscript*:

$$\textit{Une forêt de lettres}$$

- Subclass 6: "brush unjoined". The example given is *Saltino*:

$$\textbf{\textit{Une forêt de lettres}}$$

- Subclass 7: "formal unjoined". It is very difficult to find typefaces of this sort that are not merely italic versions of other typefaces. The example given is *Virtuosa*, a typeface that cannot be found today. We have replaced it here with *Lyonesse*, a font from the foundry Scriptorium:

$$\textit{Une forêt de lettres}$$

- Subclass 8: "monotone unjoined". The example given is *Gilles Gothic*:

$$\textbf{\textit{Une forêt de lettres}}$$

- Subclass 15: "miscellaneous". A catchall, in case no subclass is satisfactory.

Class 12: Symbolic

Symbol fonts (mathematical symbols, pictograms, etc.).

- Subclass 0: no classification. When no other information that could help us to classify the font is available

- Subclass 3: "mixed serif"

- Subclass 6: "old-style serif"

- Subclass 7: "neo-grotesque sans serif"

The Panose-1 Classification

Panose-1 is a system for describing characteristics of Latin fonts that is based on calculable quantities: dimensions, angles, shapes, etc. It is based on a set of 10 numbers, which take values between 0 and 15. A font thus becomes a vector in a 10-dimensional space, and one can calculate the *distance* between two fonts as a Cartesian distance.

The name "Panose" is neither an abbreviation nor a transliteration of the Greek word πανόσιος (meaning "very holy"). As its author, Ben Bauermeister, confided to us, the name comes from six representative letters of the alphabet. He divided the (Latin) alphabet into six groups of letters: round (O, C, Q, G), half-round (S, U), quarter-round (D, B, P, R, J), square (H, N, X, K, M), half-square (E, F, T, L, Y), and diagonal (A, V, W, Z) letters. Then he selected one letter from each group, taking care that the resulting word be pronounceable, and "PANOSE" was born.

Bauermeister had the idea of Panose around 1982. He first published a book [65] entitled *A Manual of Comparative Typography* in which he presented the first version of Panose (only seven parameters) and applied it to several hundred fonts. To distribute Panose, Ben founded the ElseWare Corporation, with Clyde McQueen as his partner and Michael De Laurentis as a developer. Panose increased to 10 parameters (thereafter called "Panose-1"). In 1990 Microsoft implemented Panose-1 in TrueType and in Windows 3.1. From that moment on, the history of Panose-1 has been connected to that of the Infinifont font format: ElseWare, which owns the rights to Panose-1, created this format, in which a font can be synthetically generated from the data in its Panose-1 classification! This format is implemented in the *LaserJet5 MP* printers. But competition from TrueType was apparently too tough, and when Hewlett-Packard acquired ElseWare in 1995, the development of Infinifont was gradually abandoned. Agfa bought the rights to it in 1997, and we have heard nothing about it since.

Before ElseWare was bought out, the Panose team had worked on an extension of Panose-1 to all fonts, not only Latin ones. The result, Panose-2 [113], is a truly ingenious system, but no company has implemented it since its publication in 1993. Let us hope that this standard will finally have a chance in the twenty-first century to show what it can do, thanks to the industry's growing interest in everything surrounding internationalization.

But how can we expect a warm welcome for Panose-2 when Panose-1 is already *under-documented*? Appallingly vague descriptions appear all over the Web, but only one document, the "gray book" [66], which is practically impossible to find, contains the "truth": the mathematical descriptions of the concepts of Panose-1. In this section, we shall fill the gap and attempt to describe the various parameters with a little more mathematical rigor.

Below we shall describe, in order, the 10 numbers that make up the Panose-1 description of a font: the family kind, the serif style, the weight, the proportion, the contrast, the stroke variation, the arm style, the letterform, the midline, and the x-height. To determine these values for a given font, we shall have to make some observations and, above all, measure a certain number of lengths and angles.

Parameter 1: Family Kind

The first number in Panose is purely indicative and may alter the meaning of all the others. It can take any of the following six values:

- 0: any type of font
- 1: no fit with any of the other types
- 2: Latin font for running text and titling
- 3: handwritten font
- 4: decorative font
- 5: symbol font

What follows is valid only if this paramater has the value 2. Nothing has been defined yet for the values 3 through 5.

Parameter 2: Serif Style

This is the parameter that calls for the most attention. Here are the values that it may take:

- 0: any
- 1: no fit
- 2: cove
- 3: obtuse cove
- 4: square cove
- 5: obtuse square cove
- 6: square
- 7: thin
- 8: oval
- 9: exaggerated

- 10: triangle

- 11: normal sans serif

- 12: obtuse sans serif

- 13: perpendicular sans serif

- 14: flared sans serif

- 15: rounded sans serif

Space does not allow us to present here the complete mathematical description of *all* these types. Our approach wil be more practical: we shall examine some serifs and classify them visually. Measurements of lengths will be needed to distinguish some cases.

In the figure below, we can see the 11 types of serifs that correspond to the values of the parameter:

②,③   ④,⑤   ⑥   ⑦   ⑧   ⑨   ⑩   ⑪,⑫   ⑬   ⑭   ⑮

Once we have selected the type from the list above, we must decide whether the font's serifs are or are not obtuse. First, however, we must decide whether the font has serifs or not. That determination is clear for most fonts, but we need a way to make a decision for fonts with "elephant feet" or those that are intermediate between serif and sans serif fonts.

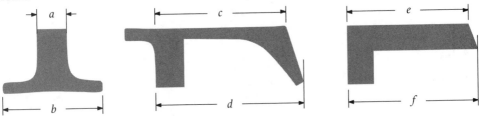

In the figure above, we show the bottom serif of the letter 'I' and measure the widths a and b. If $\frac{b}{a} > 1.6$, then the font has serifs; if $\frac{b}{a} \leqslant 1.6$, then we have a sans serif font.

If the font has serifs, we take the measurements c and d on the letter 'E'. If $\frac{c}{d} \leqslant 0.93$, then the serif style is obtuse.

If, however, the font does not have serifs, we take the measurements e and f, once more on the letter 'E'. If $\frac{e}{f} \leqslant 0.97$ or $\frac{e}{f} \geqslant 1.03$, then the serif style is obtuse.

Finally, we need to know exactly when a square serif becomes "thin" and when a serif of any shape becomes "exaggerated".

Take the measurements above. A square serif is considered "thin" if $\frac{j}{k} < 0.35$.

Let H be the height of the letter 'H' (see the following section for the way in which this height is calculated). A serif is considered exaggerated if at least one of the following three conditions obtains:

1. $\frac{g}{h} < 0.85$ or $\frac{g}{h} > 1.2$, i.e., if the serifs are too asymmetrical

2. $\frac{i}{k} > 0.15$, i.e., if the "arch" of the serif is too high

3. $\frac{g}{h} > 0.19$, i.e., if the serif is too long, giving the effect of "clown's shoes"

Parameter 3: Weight

- 0: any weight

- 1: no fit

- 2: very light

- 3: light

- 4: thin

- 5: book

- 6: medium

- 7: demi

- 8: bold

- 9: heavy

- 10: black

- 11: extra black

To obtain the value of this parameter, only two measurements are needed: the height of the 'H' and the thickness of the downstroke of the 'E'. We proceed in the following manner:

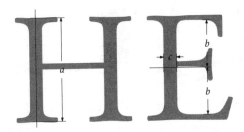

We take the midline of the left downstroke of the 'H' and measure its length a. We take the horizontal line running halfway between the upper and lower arms of the 'E', and along this line we measure the width of the stem, which we shall call c. Let $\varphi = \frac{a}{c}$. Here is the distribution of the values of the weight parameter:

- 2: very light, if $\varphi \geqslant 35$

- 3: light, if $18 \leqslant \varphi < 35$

- 4: thin, if $10 \leqslant \varphi < 18$

- 5: book, if $7.5 \leqslant \varphi < 10$

- 6: medium, if $5.5 \leqslant \varphi < 75$

- 7: demi, if $4.5 \leqslant \varphi < 5.5$

- 8: bold, if $3.5 \leqslant \varphi < 4.5$

- 9: heavy, if $2.5 \leqslant \varphi < 3.5$

- 10: black, if $2 \leqslant \varphi < 2.5$

- 11: extra black, if $\varphi < 2$

Parameter 4: Proportion

- 0: any proportion

- 1: no fit

- 2: old style (humanistic, garalde, and similar typefaces)

- 3: modern (didones, etc.)

- 4: even width (lineal and other typefaces)

- 5: extended

- 6: condensed

- 7: very extended

- 8: very condensed

- 9: monospaced

| 22 | 29 | 11 | 28 | 32 | 15 | 19 | 24 | 10 | 23 | 26 | 15 | 19 | 20 | 15 | 25 | 25 | 20 |

oldstyle (garalde)   modern (didone)   even width (lineal)

To measure the value of this parameter, we take eight very simple measurements:

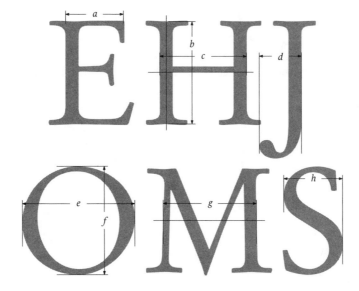

Note that the width c of the 'H' is computed at the level of the bottom of its crossbar and that the width g of the 'M' is computed at the letter's mid-height.

Then we compute the values of three variables: $\phi = \frac{a+h}{e+c}$ (the ratio between the widths of the "wide" letters and the widths of the "narrow" letters), $\chi = \frac{d}{g}$ (the ratio between the width of the 'J' and that of the 'M', a very good way to determine whether or not the font is monospaced), and $\psi = \frac{f}{e}$ (the ratio of the height and width of the 'O').

Here is the distribution of this parameter's values:

- 2: old style, if $\chi < 0.78$ and $0.92 < \psi \leqslant 1.27$ and $\phi < 0.7$

- 3: modern, if $\chi < 0.78$ and $0.92 < \psi \leqslant 1.27$ and $0.7 \leqslant \phi < 0.83$

- 4: even width, if $\chi < 0.78$ and $0.92 < \psi \leqslant 1.27$ and $0.83 \leqslant \phi < 0.9$

- 5: extended, if $\chi < 0.78$ and $0.9 < \psi \leqslant 0.92$

- 6: condensed, if $\chi < 0.78$ and $1.27 < \psi \leqslant 2.1$

- 7: very extended, if $\chi < 0.78$ and $\psi < 0.9$

- 8: very condensed, if $\chi < 0.78$ and $\psi \geqslant 2.1$

- 9: monospaced, if $\chi \geqslant 0.78$

Clearly a font could have a very wide 'J' and a very narrow 'M'. It would be classified as "monospaced" even if all the other letters took on all possibles and imaginable set-widths; those are the rules of the game.

Parameter 5: Contrast

By "contrast", we mean the difference between the widths of thick and thin strokes.

- 0: any contrast

- 1: no fit

- 2: no contrast

- 3: very low

- 4: low

- 5: medium low

- 6: medium

- 7: medium high

- 8: high

- 9: very high

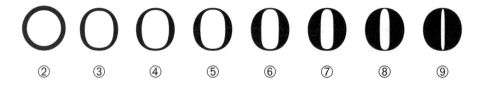

②   ③   ④   ⑤   ⑥   ⑦   ⑧   ⑨

Contrast is measured from the single letter 'O':

If a and b are the maximum widths (calculated perpendicularly to the stroke's "midline") and c and d are the minimum widths, then the contrast κ is equal to $\kappa = \frac{\min(c,d)}{\max(a,b)}$.

Here is the distribution of this parameter's values:

- 2: no contrast, if $\kappa > 0.8$

- 3: very low, if $0.65 < \kappa \leqslant 0.8$

- 4: low, if $0.48 < \kappa \leqslant 0.65$

- 5: medium low, if $0.3 < \kappa \leqslant 0.48$

- 6: medium, if $0.2 < \kappa \leqslant 0.3$

- 7: medium high, if $0.15 < \kappa \leqslant 0.2$

- 8: high, if $0.08 < \kappa \leqslant 0.15$

- 9: very high, if $\kappa \leqslant 0.08$

Obviously this parameter is easier to calculate for didones and geometric lineals than for garaldes, as in the example above.

Parameter 6: Stroke Variation

Here we are concerned with the more or less rapid way in which a stroke changes from one thickness to another.

- 0: any variation

- 1: no fit

- 2: no variation

- 3: gradual/diagonal (the axis of symmetry of the 'O' is slanted, as in the humanistic faces and the garaldes)

- 4: gradual/transitional (the axis of symmetry of the 'O' is vertical, but the axis of the 'o' is slanted)

- 5: gradual/vertical

- 6: gradual/horizontal

- 7: rapid/vertical

- 8: rapid/horizontal

- 9: instant/vertical

- 10: instant/horizontal

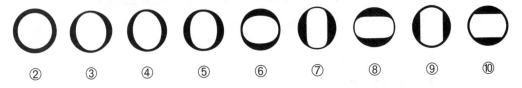

The idea is very simple. We have already mentioned the fact that in the humanistic faces and the garaldes the axis of the round letters is slanted to the left. In this case, we say that the variation is diagonal. The didones, however, have a vertical axis; we say that their variation is vertical. A font such as *Zipper* (see page 405) will have a horizontal variation. "Transitional", which refers to the "transitional" fonts, is the case in which the uppercase 'O' has a more vertical axis than the lowercase 'o'.

This time we shall examine the letters 'O' and 'o'. The five measurements that we take here must be *very precise*:

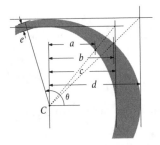

First we take the letter's center, C. Next, c and d are merely the distances between the horizontal extrema of the inner and outer edges of the 'O'. We draw the horizontal and vertical tangent lines of the outer curve. They intersect at the upper right corner of the letter's external bounding lines. We draw a dotted line from the center to this point. This line intersects the outer curve at a given point. Then b is the horizontal distance between the center of the letter and this point. We do the same for the inner curve and obtain a.

We proceed as with the contrast parameter to find the location where the stroke is the thinnest. We draw a line from this point to the center and measure the angle θ_O of this line. We do the same for the lowercase 'o' and obtain the angle θ_o.

Finally, we measure the angle s of the font's obliqueness (see parameter 8).
Then we calculate the "speed of variation" $V = \frac{bc}{ad}$.
We say that the stroke variation is:

- Zero, if parameter 5 (contrast) also has the value 2

- Gradual, if $V > 0.96$

- Rapid, if $0.85 < V \leqslant 0.96$

- Instant, if $V \leqslant 0.85$

We also say that it is:

- Horizontal, if $172° \leqslant \theta_O < 196°$ and $172° \leqslant \theta_o < 196°$
- Vertical, in the following two cases:
    - If $82° \leqslant \theta_O < 98°$ and $82° \leqslant \theta_o < 98°$
    - Or if $(s < 82°$ or $s > 98°)$ and $|\theta_O - s| < 8$ and $|\theta_o - s| < 8$
- Transitional, in the following two cases:
    - If $82° \leqslant \theta_O < 98°$ and $(\theta_o \geqslant 98°$ or $\theta_o < 82°)$
    - Or if $(s < 82°$ or $s > 98°)$ and $|\theta_O - s| < 8$ and $|\theta_o - s| \geqslant 8$
- Diagonal, otherwise

Parameter 7: Arm Style and Termination of Open Curves

This parameter refers to two independent properties of fonts: the arm style (straight or not) and the termination of the open curves, as in the case of the letter 'C'.

- 0: any type

- 1: no fit

- 2: straight arms/horizontal terminations

- 3: straight arms/wedge terminations

- 4: straight arms/vertical terminations

- 5: straight arms/single serif

- 6: straight arms/double serif

- 7: nonstraight arms/horizontal terminations

- 8: nonstraight arms/wedge terminations

- 9: nonstraight arms/vertical terminations

- 10: nonstraight arms/single serif

- 11: nonstraight arms/double serif

straight arms   non-straight arms   horizontal   wedge   vertical
                                            terminations   terminations   terminations

By "nonstraight" arms, we mean a diagonal stroke that is either of varying thickness or curved. Here are the measurements that we must take:

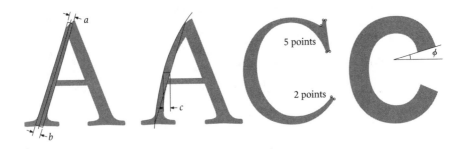

We compute a and b by projecting the theoretical edges of the stem and its "midline". We measure the thickness of the stem by using straight segments that are perpendicular to the midline at the point where it intersects the baseline and the capline (the line marking the height of the capitals). To measure c, we project the outer edge of the stem. This projection cuts the baseline and the capline at two points. We draw the straight segment that connects these two points. At the mid-height of this segment, we compute the horizontal distance between the segment and the outer edge of the stem. Let H be the height of the letter 'H'.

We say that the stem is straight if and only if $\frac{a}{b} \geqslant 0.6$ and $\frac{c}{H} < 0.02$.

As for the terminations of the 'C', we measure the number of "corners" of the serifs separately for the top and bottom. Let N_h be the number of corners for the upper serif and N_b the number for the lower serif. We say that the serifs are simple if and only if $\frac{N_b}{N_h} < 0.75$.

Finally, for sans serif fonts, we say that the terminations are:

- Horizontal, if $\phi \leqslant 7°$

- Vertical, if $83° < \phi \leqslant 112°$

- Wedge, otherwise

Parameter 8: Slant and Shape of the Letter

- 0: any shape

- 1: no fit

- 2: normal/contact (circular shape that touches its bounding frame at only four points)

- 3: normal/weighted (ditto, but with a little more freedom)

- 4: normal/boxed (ditto, but with very flat curves)

- 5: normal/flattened (contains straight vertical segments)

- 6: normal/rounded (contains straight vertical and horizontal segments; in other words, it is a rectangle with rounded corners)

- 7: normal/off center

- 8: normal/square (no curves, only straight segments)

- 9: oblique/contact

- 10: oblique/weighted

- 11: oblique/boxed

- 12: oblique/flattened

- 13: oblique/rounded

- 14: oblique/off center

- 15: oblique/square

Once again, we compute two properties at the same time: the slant and the overall behavior of the letter 'O' (perfect circle, flattened circle, rounded square, square, etc.).

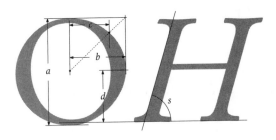

Here we reuse a measurement already taken on the letter 'O' for the calculation of parameter 6. Thus c is the horizontal distance between the center of the letter and the intersection of the outer curve with the line obtained by connecting the center with the upper right corner of the letter's bounding frame. Also, d is the vertical distance between the baseline and the height of the rightmost point of the outer curve. The font's slope, s, is the angle that the left edge of the letter 'H' makes with the baseline.

We say that the font is oblique if and only if $s < 85°$ or $s > 95°$.

We compute the values of two variables: $\xi = \frac{c}{b}$ (the curvature of the outer curve) and $\zeta = \frac{d}{a}$ (the skewing of the glyph).

If $\zeta < 0.44$ or $\zeta > 0.56$, then the glyph is off center, and the parameter takes the value 7 or 14. If that is not the case, the distribution of the values is as follows:

- 2 or 9: contact, if $\xi < 0.74$

- 3 or 10: weighted, if $0.74 \leqslant \xi < 0.77$

- 4 or 11: boxed, if $0.77 \leqslant \xi < 0.8$

- 5 or 12: flattened, if $0.8 \leqslant \xi < 0.83$

- 6 or 13: rounded, if $0.83 \leqslant \xi < 0.95$

- 8 or 15: square, if $0.95 \leqslant \xi$

Parameter 9: Midlines and Apexes

Once again we have two independent parameters: the heights of the midlines and the styles of the apexes. We shall focus on the midlines of the 'E' and the 'A' and on the apex of the 'A'.

- 0: any type

- 1: no fit

- 2: standard midlines/trimmed apexes

- 3: standard midlines/pointed apexes

- 4: standard midlines/serifed apexes

- 5: high midlines/trimmed

- 6: high midlines/pointed

- 7: high midlines/serifed

- 8: constant midlines/trimmed

- 9: constant midlines/pointed

- 10: constant midlines/serifed

- 11: low midlines/trimmed

- 12: low midlines/pointed

- 13: low midlines/serifed

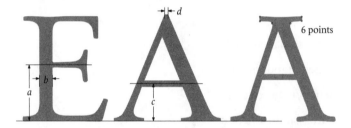

Let H be the height of the letter 'H'. We compute $\alpha = \frac{c}{H}$ (the height of the midline of the 'A'), $\varepsilon = \frac{a}{H}$ (the same value for the 'E'), $\delta = \varepsilon - \alpha$ (the difference between the heights of the midlines of the 'E' and the 'A').

If $\delta < 0.08$, we say that the midlines are constant, and the parameter takes a value of 8, 9, or 10, according to the point of the 'A'. Otherwise we distinguish among:

- 2, 3, 4: standard midlines, if $0.45 \leqslant \varepsilon \leqslant 0.58$

- 5, 6, 7: high midlines, if $0.58 < \varepsilon$

- 11, 12, 13: low midlines, if $\varepsilon < 0.45$

As for the point of the 'A', we measure the number of its "corners": if it is a simple point, it will have one or two corners; if it has a serif, it will necessarily have more. Let N be the number of points and let $\eta = \frac{d}{b}$ be the ratio between the width of the point and the thickness of the downstroke of the letter 'E'.

Then we have the following types of points:

- Trimmed, if $N \leqslant 4$ and $\eta \geqslant 0.6$

- Pointed, if $N \leqslant 4$ and $\eta < 0.6$

- Serifed, if $N > 4$

Parameter 10: X-height and Behavior of Uppercase Letters Relative to Accents

Recall that in digital fonts the x-height is defined as the ratio between the height of the lowercase letters and that of the uppercase letters.

Here again we are measuring two independent properties of fonts. The first is simply the x-height (Fournier spoke of the "poetic x-height" and the "Dutch x-height"). The second is very wacky: although the author has never seen any, the developers of Panose would have us believe that there are fonts in which the accented uppercase letters are shorter than the regular uppercase letters![13] Panose calls such fonts "ducking" fonts. Certainly it is more common to modify the shape of the accents when they are placed over capital letters than to modify the letters themselves. But we have to accept the Panose standard as it is.

- 0: any type

- 1: no fit

- 2: constant letters/small x-height

- 3: constant letters/standard x-height

- 4: constant letters/large x-height

- 5: ducking letters/small x-height

- 6: ducking letters/standard x-height

- 7: ducking letters/large x-height

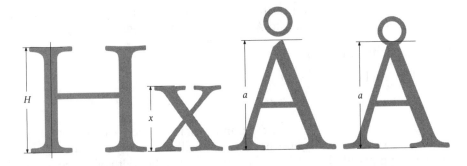

The calculation of the x-heights is very simple: if the ratio $\frac{x}{H}$ is less than or equal to 0.5, we say that the x-height is small; if it is strictly greater than 0.66, we say that it is large. Otherwise, it is standard.

---

[13] With the exception, of course, of low-resolution bitmap fonts for use on screens. Up to now we have always considered Panose-1 as applying only to *vector* fonts, whose glyphs are sufficiently well described that they can be classified.

As for the possibility of "ducking" letters, we calculate the height A of the letter 'A' without an accent (measuring the height from the baseline to the top of the apex) and compare it with a, which is the height of the same letter with a ring above it. If the ring is stuck to the letter, then a will be the height of the lowest point of the inner wall of the ring. If $\frac{a}{A} \leqslant 0.93$, we say that the letter is a "ducking" letter.

12

Editing and Creating Fonts

Now we come to the heart of this book: *creating fonts*. Need one be a Hermann Zapf or a Jean François Porchez nowadays to create fonts? Of course not; otherwise there would be no need for this book. But everything depends on what one wishes to do. If it is merely a question of designing a missing symbol, a logo, or a new letter, one can merely start with an existing font; in this case, a good knowledge of the software tool is probably more important than artistic talent. If one wishes to create a font from a model, such as from scans of printed pages, then knowledge of the tool must be wedded to a certain amount of experience if one is to replace the "black marks of ink" that form the printed glyphs with intelligent vector contours as efficiently as possible. Finally, if one wishes to create a new font from scratch like the great typeface designers of the past five centuries, there is an entire craft to master, either through a specialized school (an École de Beaux-Arts with a typographic workshop or a specialized establishment such as the École Estienne, the Scriptorium de Toulouse in France, or the University of Reading in the United Kingdom) or through apprenticeship with a master designer, as is still done in the traditional crafts that industrialization has not succeeded in eliminating.

Between these extremes, then, everything is a matter of degree. The goal of the following three chapters is to give the reader a minimum of technical knowledge to enable her to use the software tool efficiently and, perhaps, to have a critical look at the technical level of existing fonts and avoid the traps that this type of artistic activity can fall into—traps related to the very nature of typeface design. In this chapter, we shall examine the use of two of the most widely used software tools for editing/creating fonts: FontLab and FontForge. In Chapter 13 we shall discuss the optimization of the rendering of glyphs through the use of PostScript hints or TrueType instructions. Finally, in Chapter 14, we shall examine the advanced typographic features of OpenType and AAT.

Software for Editing/Creating Fonts

Over the past 20 years, at least six large-scale systems for creating fonts[1] have been produced:

- The *Ikarus* system [207], written by Peter Karow starting in 1973, which was the first industrial font-design system. Ikarus was acquired by a Dutch company (*Dutch Type Library*), which modularized and extended it and which sells it today under the name of *DTL FontMaster* [122].

- The METAFONT programming language of Donald Knuth (1978), which we shall study in Appendix F.

- *FontStudio*, written by Ernie Brock and Harold Grey at Letraset. In the opinion of the author, it has *the best* user interface of all font-design software. Designing glyphs with this sytem is a true pleasure, and one can quickly produce excellent designs. It seems, however, that fate has dealt a blow to this extraordinary software package: Letraset sold it to Adobe, and Adobe condemned it to *death through oblivion*. Available only for Mac OS 9, FontStudio (which the author had the privilege of buying in 1990, before it was withdrawn from the market) can handle only PostScript Type 1 fonts. Those readers who manage to buy a copy can use it to create glyphs under Mac OS Classic. Afterwards, they will have to use other software to generate modern fonts from the glyphs that they have designed with FontStudio. In any event, even though the chances may seem remote, we can hope that a future head of Adobe will fall passionately in love with this software and will decide to undertake the investment needed to resurrect it—to the great profit of humanity!

- Macromedia's *Fontographer* [277, 244], developed by Jim von Ehr and his team when he was still at Altsys and released in 1985. This software is without a doubt the best-known font-design software in the world. It ran only under Mac OS 9 and Windows until in 2005 the program was bought by FontLab and a Mac OS X version released. Its interface is quite poor compared to that of FontStudio, but it is quite solid and produces fonts that are relatively decent, at least typographically. Although Macromedia still sells Fontographer at its web site, this software is also on the road to extinction, as it has not been updated for years and thus cannot possibly produce Open-Type or AAT fonts. Moreover, Fontographer is not compatible with Mac OS X, even in the Classic environment. The Dutch firm *Leterror* tried to save this software by injecting Python scripts into it: the result was called *Robofog* [235], doubtless because its operation can be compared to the "robotization" of policeman Alex Murphy in the American TV series *RoboCop*—"fog" being not the word for the meteorological phenomenon but the Fontographer file extension. Robofog in turn died out during the shift to Mac OS X, and the same firm is now offering a new product: *RoboLab*, based on FontLab.

---

[1] In 1987 there was a conference on font-design systems [40] at Sophia-Antipolis, France. The reader will find in its published proceedings a description of numerous other systems.

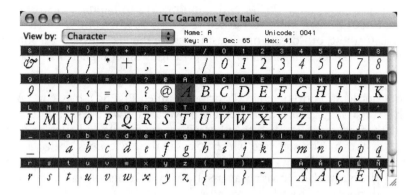

Figure 12-1: The font window of Macromedia Fontographer, under Mac OS X.

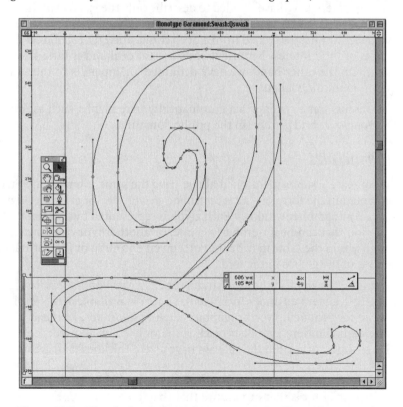

Figure 12-2: The glyph window of Letraset FontStudio, under Mac OS 9.

- FontLab [140], written by Yuri Yarmola and Vadim Suvorov, which today is the most widespread system, thanks in particular to its rapid response to new technologies. FontLab runs under Mac OS 9/X and Windows. It can handle fonts containing as many as 6,400 glyphs; if more are needed, as is the case when one wishes to set type in Japanese, Chinese, or Korean, one must purchase the "East Asian" version of Font-Lab, which is called *AsiaFont Studio*, for a price four times higher than that of Font-Lab (!).

- Last but not least, FontForge [352] (formerly called PfaEdit), by George Williams, which is a real *miracle*: it is an extremely powerful software system offering practi-cally all the features of FontLab, together with some unique and often revolutionary features of its own. This software, which "plays in the big leagues", is *free*, and, what is most astonishing of all, it was developed by *a single person*, our dear George Williams, an indefatigable worker who is always ready to improve his software even more every time the opportunity arises!

In the following material, we have decided to describe only the last two of these software packages, FontLab and FontForge, since *FontStudio* is now but a "remembrance of things past", *Fontographer* just has awakened from a deep coma, and *DTL FontMaster* is certainly excellent but is of little interest because it costs a great deal and is little known to the general public. On the other hand, we have dedicated an appendix to the study of the METAFONT programming language.

We shall also discuss some systems that automatically trace glyphs, such as *ScanFont* (by FontLab) and *autotrace* and *potrace* (in the public domain).

General Principles

Most of the software systems mentioned above have the same interface architecture: a font is represented in the form of a *table containing glyphs* (see, for example, Figure 12-1, which shows a Fontographer window). Each glyph is represented by a square in the table and has a caption that can be a number, a name, or another type of information. The order of the glyphs in the table may be that of a given encoding or the natural order of the descriptions of the glyphs in the font.

Double-clicking on the glyph in the font window opens a *glyph-editing window* (see, for ex-ample, Figure 12-2, generated under *FontStudio*). The tools available at this level are quite similar to those for producing vector graphics, such as *Illustrator*, *Freehand*, *CorelDraw*, etc., with a few small differences: first, black is the only color allowed; second, we are certainly free to draw curves, but they always have a zero thickness and are used only to form surfaces; third, there are some constraints on what we can draw, such as the fact that the tangent lines at the initial points of Bézier curves should be horizontal or vertical, which calls for special tools that can ensure that they meet this constraint. Finally, we are concerned here with small details such as the direction in which a curve is drawn, the sequential numbers of the points on the Bézier curves, etc.—details that seem silly when graphic design software is used but that can be quite useful in the context of font design.

The challenge of the glyph-editing window is to show simultaneously as much data about the glyph as possible. These data are related to the various steps in the process of font creation. Among them are:

- The point of origin, the baseline, the side bearings, and various horizontal and vertical zones that serve to maintain the same dimensions (the heights of the capitals, the ascenders, and the lowercase letters, the depths of the descenders, etc.)

- The baseline and the left and right side bearings for each glyph written in a direction other than the primary direction for the font

- The glyph's contour, with the starting and ending points of the Bézier curves, the control points, information about whether a point at which two Bézier curves meet is an angular or a smooth connection, the direction of the Bézier curves, etc.

- PostScript hints or TrueType instructions

- OpenType anchors

- Any models that were used to create the glyph, whether these models be vector-based (and therefore contours put onto a second plane that will not be part of the final glyph) or bitmap (and therefore background images)

- In the case of a Multiple Master font, all the master designs of the glyph in question, with their hints, their anchors, etc.

- Other design aids, as, for example, grids in the background

That is a great deal of information to display, and often we feel overwhelmed by it. Thus one of the greatest difficulties of learning a font-design system is without a doubt the excess and great variety of visual information.

The tools for manipulating the data in question will themselves necessarily be quite diverse as well: for tracing curves, we need a whole panoply of vector design tools (tracing, cutting, pasting, aligning, bending, turning horizontal or vertical, etc.). Magnetism is a very popular technique: when we approach a point, that point changes color and thus lets us know that by clicking on it we will be able to select it, even if the mouse's cursor is not *exactly* above the point. This technique allows us to "capture" points more easily, but it can create a serious problem when several points are close together.

But the special features of the font-design systems are not limited to these two windows. After all, let us not forget that glyphs are sociable animals: they love to come together, interact, and jointly form a social fabric that we call "text". Accordingly, the software must also be able to determine their social behavior.

The most fundamental interaction is kerning: the software must allow the user to indicate, whether automatically or manually, the kerning of two glyphs, the similarity of glyphs' behavior with respect to kerning (for example, 'É' is kerned just like 'E'), etc.

Next, the software must support the introduction of OpenType, and even AAT, features into our fonts. That is more easily said than done, and today's software supports only a few of these features, and ofter poorly at that.

Finally, beyond the encoding and the descriptions of the glyphs, there is another type of information in a font: global data. This includes global metric data, the different names of the font, the designer's name, the license, the Panose classification, etc. The software must allow the user to insert this data into the font. That may seem easy, but once again there is a challenge: the data turn out to be quite numerous. The different font formats (PostScript, TrueType, OpenType, AAT) and the different platforms (DOS, Windows, OS/2, Macintosh, Unix) have accumulated such bulk of various and sundry data that a designer can often find it hard to remember the meaning, syntax, and, most of all, importance of each type. The software must help him to complete this task with a minimum of effort by supplying to him the most important data, insisting that he fill in the essential data, and leaving aside (or automatically filling in) any data that is optional.

FontLab

Rest assured, dear reader: we make no claim here of describing the use of FontLab in every detail. After all, this software has a rather large (923 pages!) set of documentation [141] that is very well written and illustrated and also freely accessible. Instead, we shall attempt in this section to understand this software package's philosophy and to describe certain major operations that the font designer uses every day.

The Font Window

The font window in FontLab plays a dual role: on the one hand, it displays the glyphs accompanied by some data that make it possible to identify them; on the other hand, it determines the encoding of the PostScript or TrueType fonts that will be generated.

To complete this task, the font window has four pull-down menus: one menu for specifying the size of glyph display in the table, one concerning the textual information displayed above the glyph in the table, one for specifying the *order* in which glyphs are displayed in the table and a fourth menu which complements the third one.

To understand the fine points of these tools, recall the principle of a font encoding. A *font encoding*—not to be confused with a *character* encoding—is a correspondence between *numbers* (called "code points") and *glyph descriptions*. But how can we identify the description of a given glyph in a font? That is where the complications arise.

In a PostScript Type 1 or CFF font, glyph descriptions are provided with names, the *PostScript glyph names* (§C.3.5). A PostScript font encoding is therefore, in reality, a correspondence between numbers and glyph names. In the beginning, in the years 1986 through 1992, the names themselves had no importance, since what mattered was the code point of the glyph within the table and the glyph's description; the name was merely a vehicle for going from one to the other. But these names took on importance when Acrobat was released, as Adobe began to use them to find the Unicode characters to which the glyphs corresponded. Thus Adobe defined a standard syntax for naming glyphs (§C.3.3). When this syntax is respected, Acrobat is able to associate the glyphs in question with Unicode characters and thus to interact with the user who wishes to search for strings, copy them, index them, etc., within PDF files.

This problem never existed for TrueType fonts: after all, the names of the glyphs in these fonts are not required (they are sometimes included in the post table—§D.4.8—for use when the font is converted to PostScript), and there is always a cmap table (§D.4.2), which gives the explicit correspondence between characters and glyphs.

Just as in democracies a president is expected to rise above party politics, FontLab also claims to be impartial with regard to the differences between PostScript and TrueType; accordingly, it opts for a pluralistic approach—we have not only one way to represent a font encoding but at least three (!), listed here in Figure 12-3:

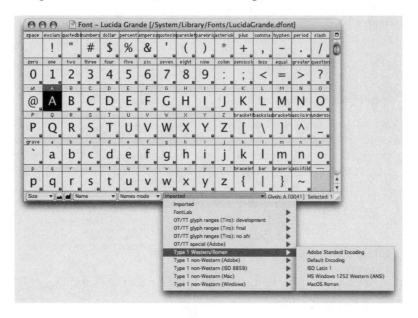

Figure 12-3: The **Names mode** *of the FontLab font window.*

- Using the third pull-down menu on the bottom bar of the font window, we select the **Names mode**. The fourth pull-down menu gives us then access to a large number of font encodings, which are all defined by means of glyph names. Each of these encodings is described in a text file with the extension .enc; on the Mac these files are kept in subdirectories of /Library/Application Support/FontLab/Encoding. In these files one finds first the names of the encoding and of its group as displayed in the pull-down menu:

```
%%FONTLAB ENCODING: 1; Default Encoding
%%GROUP:Type 1 Western/Roman
```

(the number 1; in front of Default Encoding giving the order of display in the menu) and then a large number of lines of of the following type:

Eacute 131

which means that the glyph named Eacute is stored at decimal code point 131 in the table.

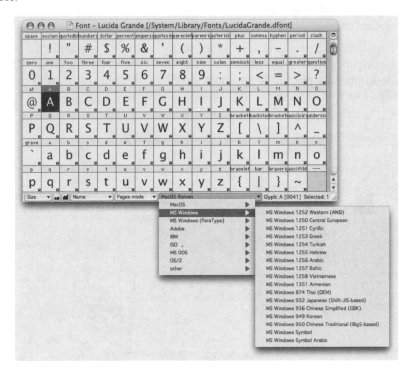

*Figure 12-4: The **Pages mode** of the FontLab font window.*

- By selecting the **Pages mode**, shown in Figure 12-4, we switch to a mode that we could also call the "mode for character encodings *other than Unicode*". The pull-down menu in the middle offers us a quite large number of character encodings.

The reader may be wondering what the difference is between this choice and the previous one. Indeed, it is a subtle difference. Each glyph in FontLab always has two pieces of data associated with it: its name and the Unicode character with which it is associated. When a font is imported, FontLab tries to obtain these data from the font tables. And whatever FontLab cannot obtain from the font it tries to guess, as well as it can.

The two modes correspond to these two pieces of data: while in **Names mode** the glyphs are arranged according to their *glyph names*, in **Pages mode** they are arranged according to their *associated Unicode characters*.

Each encoding on the pull-down menu corresponds to a file with the extension `.cpg` that, on the Mac, is stored in subdirectories of /Library/Application Sup-port/FontLab/Codepage. These files are of the following type:

```
%%FONTLAB CODEPAGE: 0xff; MacOS Roman
%%GROUP:MacOS

...

0x83    0x00C9  % LATIN CAPITAL LETTER E WITH ACUTE
```

which means that the glyph associated with the Unicode character 0x00C9 LATIN CAPITAL LETTER E WITH ACUTE is placed at hexadecimal code point 83 (therefore decimal 131). The concrete result will be more or less the same as in *glyph name* mode: in both cases we have a font (or character) encoding called *MacRoman*, and a font stored in this encoding will be slightly different in each of the two modes, but most of the glyphs will be in the same place.

What reason, then, is there to choose one approach over the other? Everything depends on context. We can ask ourselves a few questions. What is the origin of the names of the glyphs in the font that we are importing? Where will we find the correspondences with the Unicode characters? The answers to these questions will help us to select the most reliable approach.

In addition, when used together, these two approaches give us a very robust way to make sure that our glyph names and correspondences with Unicode characters are correct. All that we have to do is select the **Pages mode** and **Names mode** approaches in turn and see which glyphs change when we go from one approach to the other. Those are the glyphs that will need special attention.

One final argument: if the font that we are going to create will be of TrueType format, the correspondences with the Unicode characters are more important than the glyph names. If it is to be a PostScript font, the opposite is true. But beware: making sure that both sets of data are correct is the best solution.

- By selecting **Ranges mode** (Figure 12-5), we switch to "Unicode" mode, which, in the author's opinion, is the only mode that is really interesting.

  Here the font window shows us, one by one, all of the tables in Unicode, which we can select from the pull-down menu. For each table, FontLab first displays (on a yellow background) the glyphs corresponding to the characters in the table, and then, on a gray background, all the other glyphs. That allows us to do our work properly, always being aware of the active context.

- Finally, by selecting **Index mode** (Figure 12-6), we switch to "index" mode.

  The "indexes" are simply the sequential numbers of the glyphs' descriptions. There is nothing more natural and, at the same time, more haphazard: since the glyphs are described within the file, their descriptions necessarily fall into a certain physical order (the order in which they appear in the code), but that order does not affect the use of the font in any way: in PostScript fonts, we specify glyphs by means of their names; in TrueType, we specify them through the `loca` table—itself used by the `cmap`

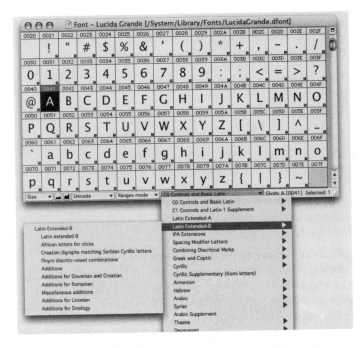

*Figure 12-5: The **Ranges** mode of the FontLab font window.*

table, which acts as a pivot between characters and glyphs. The *index* mode serves to give a general view of all the glyphs in the font, without gaps and without any risk that some glyphs may go undetected because their code points are too far away in the table.

Note that the choice of **Names** mode or **Pages** mode *will affect* the PostScript or TrueType font that is generated. Things are less clear in **Ranges** mode or **Index mode** mode, and we advise the reader to check the encoding of the generated font by inspecting the AFM file (for PostScript fonts) or through the use of TTX (for TrueType fonts).

One last comment to conclude the issue of encodings: when we select an encoding in **Names** mode or in **Pages mode**, we change only the *positions of the glyphs in the table*. In other words, the data for the individual glyphs (contours, names, Unicode correspondences, etc.) do not change one iota.

But there is also a more radical way to modify the font's table: "re-encoding". The name of this operation is rather poorly chosen: when we move, for example, from one code page to another, we also "re-encode" the font—whereas here the operation is much more radical, even brutal.

When we select **Glyphs>Glyph Names>Reencode Glyphs**, FontLab will take the glyphs in their current positions and regard them from that point on as being glyphs in a

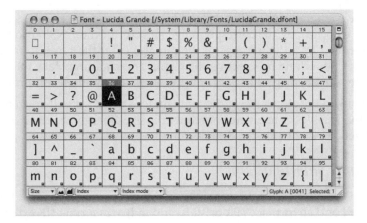

*Figure 12-6: The **Index mode** of the FontLab font window.*

certain font encoding that we will specify. The glyph names and the Unicode correspondences already established are simply disregaded: everything is *flattened*, and nothing is left but the new encoding, with its own names and correspondences. This radical method is very useful, but it must be employed with caution: first, we choose the correct code page; then we verify that the glyph contours do indeed correspond to the names and code points specified (and make any necessary changes); finally, we call for the font to be "re-encoded" for this encoding. The effect of the operation should not be dramatic: it is rather a consolidation and a reinitialization of the glyph names according to the proper conventions.

The more dramatic use of this operation is that of rectifying the glyphs' names and the Unicode correspondences for non-Latin fonts that have been encoded as if they were Latin fonts: there is, unfortunately, a plethora of Russian, Greek, Arabic, and other fonts in which the letters have names as appropriate as Eacute and lozenge. If the order of the glyphs, despite the poor choice of names, is nonetheless that of a recognized encoding— and the chances of that are good if the font has been used before under an operating system—, then we may simply request "re-encoding", taking care to check the result very carefully for any errors. The best way to check that the glyphs have been interpreted correctly is to switch to Unicode mode and to check, table by table, that everything is where it belongs.

Regardless of the way in which we have chosen to arrange the glyphs, the font window offers us nine (!) different ways to label them:

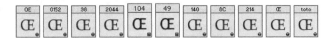

Specifically, by their names (the default choice), by the corresponding Unicode character, by their indexes (i.e., the sequential numbers of their glyph descriptions), by their set-widths, by their left and right side-bearings, by their code-point numbers (in decimal, hexadecimal, or octal), by the corresponding character in the ANSI encoding, and by any data generated by a Python macro. We can also color the boxes to facilitate their identification: that is done by selecting the glyphs and choosing **Mark** followed by the color (red, blue, green, magenta, cyan, or a custom value) on their contextual menu.

Finally, to wrap up the discussion of the font window, there is a pull-down menu at the lower right that enables us to enlarge or reduce the size of its glyph cells, from 16×16 to 128×128 pixels, 32×32 being the default value.

Opening and Saving a Font

We can open PostScript Type 1, Multiple Master, TrueType, and OpenType fonts, as well as fonts in the FontLab format (VFA or VFB) and in Ikarus format (IK extension).

We can set some preferences for opening fonts in the **Preferences** panel. For PostScript fonts, these are **Decompose all composite glyphs**, i.e., replace the composite glyphs with genuine contours; **Generate Unicode indices for all glyphs**, a must; **Generate basic OpenType features for Type 1 fonts with Standard encoding**, a very useful feature for easily obtaining "intelligent" OpenType fonts; **Find matching encoding table if possible**, which means that FontLab will try to identify the encoding as being one listed on the pull-down menu, otherwise it will call it **Imported**.

For TrueType fonts, these are **Convert TrueType curves into PostScript curves**; **Store TrueType native hinting**; **Import embedded bitmaps**; **Autohint font**, which means "throw away the existing hints or instructions and create new ones on the fly"; **Scale the font to 1000 UPM**, i.e., change the coordinate grid and switch from 2,048 units to 1,000, as for PostScript fonts; **Decompose composites**; **Store custom TrueType/OpenType tables** i.e. preserve TrueType tables that are not recognized by FontLab (such as AAT, *VTT*, VOLT, or Graphite tables); how to deal with name records (import them or do not—and there is also the politically incorrect choice of importing only English ones).

For OpenType fonts there are six other options: read the OpenType tables GPOS, GSUB, GDEF; store them in the font; interpret them; deduce kerning from the kern table; **Generate missing glyph names using layout tables** which means that glyphs that are not directly accessible through the cmap table and hence have no corresponding Unicode character(s) will nevertheless get automatically generated names; and, finally, an option that gives at least a soupçon of rehabilitation to the AAT tables, which have been so unjustly ignored—the conversion of mort and morx tables to OpenType tables (see Appendix D.13.2).

Many options are offered for saving fonts, with the goal of adapting the generated fonts to the user's needs: platform, encoding, file format, etc. FontLab's proprietary format is VFB: this is the format in which fonts are saved when we use **File > Save** or **File > Save as**.

To obtain a Unix, Windows, or Mac OS X font, we use **Files > Generate Font**. Then we have the choice of the formats TTF (called **Win TrueType/OpenType TT**), OTF (called through a second dialog window, **OpenType PS**), PFB (**Win Type 1**), PFA (**ASCII/Unix**

Type 1) and VFB (FontLab native format).[2] For each type of font, we again have special options. For instance, when generating PostScript fonts, we can choose, through a second dialog window, to preserve the original encoding of the font or to convert universally to *Adobe Standard Encoding*.

Going through the **Preferences** panel, we can also choose to generate PFM (font-metric data for Windows), AFM, or INF files; to export only glyphs appearing in the encoding; to autohint the font; to generate bitmaps using a specific rasterizer; etc.

For TrueType fonts we have the choice of including instructions; preserving the original instructions; creating instructions for glyphs that lack them; and creating instructions from "visual instructions", i.e., those inserted by hand within FontLab; export a mort table; generate a digital signature; etc. We can also decide whether or not to export True-Type bitmaps.

Finally, for OpenType fonts, we can choose to export OpenType tables or not; to export custom tables; to export VOLT data (in order to lead VOLT to believe that it is the only software that has edited the font); to add an OpenType property kern (rather than a kern table); to export the strings in the name table or not, or to export only those in English; to produce a GDEF table; to use subroutines to reduce the size of the CFF code; etc.

Which options should we select when we generate a font? According to the principle of "whoever can do more can also do less", the creation of VOLT data, GDEF tables, kern properties, CFF subroutines, etc., should not bother anyone; thus we can include them in our fonts without worries. Unless, of course, we come upon bizarre software that accepts some of the OpenType features but that is allergic to the rest. In that case, it would behoove us to be selective and to include in our fonts only the data that will not bother the software in question.

As for TrueType instructions, we must choose a strategy, and it depends on context. Was the font that we are opening meticulously instructed by specialists (like Microsoft's font *Arial*)? Or was it automatically instructed by software of lower quality than FontLab (such as Fontographer)? In the former case, it would behoove us to preserve the instructions during both opening and saving, with perhaps some additional instructions for the glyphs that have been added or modified. As for "visual instructions", they are a "lite" version of TrueType instructions that has the benefit of taking advantage of FontLab's very seductive graphical interface. Upon exporting a font, FontLab will convert these instructions into genuine TrueType instructions.

Finally, an option for exporting that is both interesting and dangerous: when we select the option **Open Type 1 Export Terminal**, FontLab shows us an editing window containing the beginning (public and private dictionaries) of the Type 1 font, in plain text. We may then modify these dictionaries by hand. It is obvious that the slightest error in the code will render the font useless—so use this option in moderation!

---

[2] In previous versions of FontLab the type 42 output format (Unix Type 42 (Raw ASCII)) was also provided. This is really a pity because type 42 allows us to send TrueType fonts to a PostScript device without first converting their outlines and hints to PostScript.

To generate Mac OS 9 fonts (under FontLab Macintosh), we use File>Generate Mac Suitcase. Since the Macintosh font suitcases are an endangered species, we shall not go into detail about the various options available. It is enough to know that the window that opens allows the four font "styles" used under Mac OS 9 to be selected in a very convient manner: plain, italic, bold, bold italic. We select the PostScript or TrueType fonts corresponding to these four styles, and FontLab produces a suitcase with pointers to these four fonts. The names specified in this dialog box are "Quickdraw names", i.e., the names used on the Macintosh's menus to represent the fonts in question.

The General-Information Window

This window is opened with File>Font Info. It contains no fewer than 34 (!) tabs arranged in nine groups. Here are the most important of these tabs:

- **Names and Copyright** (see Figure 12-7 [a]): the different "names" of the font; i.e., the name of the family, the weight, and the set-width; the name of the "style" (which is added to a PostScript family name to create a font name), the "technical" (without whitespaces) name of the font used in PostScript language calls, the "full name" (used in PostScript fonts), the Quickdraw name (which appears on the Macintosh's menus), the name contained in any Macintosh FOND resource. Often it is sufficient to enter the family name and the style name and click on the button **Build Names:** FontLab will then fill in the other boxes automatically. Note that **Family Name** under this tab corresponds to entry 1 in the name table (Appendix D.4.6); **Style Name**, to entry 2; **PS Font Name**, to entry 6; and **Full Name** to entry 4.

- **OpenType–specific names:** under this tab, we find entries 16 (**OT Family Name**) and 17 (**OT Style Name**) from the name table.

- One may ask why FontLab presents us with a few sporadic entries from the name table under the tabs discussed above instead of giving us an efficient way to gain access to the entire table. That feature is offered under the following tab: *Additional OpenType names* (see Figure 12-7 [b]). The first button collects the data from the other tabs and inserts them into the present one. Then we can add new entries or modify the existing ones by choosing the entry number, the system, the encoding, and the language (Appendix D.4.6), again through the use of pull-down menus. In the Text field, we can include Unicode characters by using the syntax \ABCD: to obtain 漢字, we write \6F22\5B57.

- **Copyright information** (see Figure 12-7 (c)): while the previous tab showed us the entire name table, this one again shows only certain entries in the table, and only in English: the copyright (entry 0 in the name table), the trademark (entry 7), and the description (entry 10).

- **Embedding:** may this font be embedded in a PDF file or any other type of file? Under what conditions? This information comes from the contents of the fsType field in the OS/2 table, which, unlike what one would expect from its name, is not limited to the OS/2 operating system but also covers Windows (Appendix D.4.7).

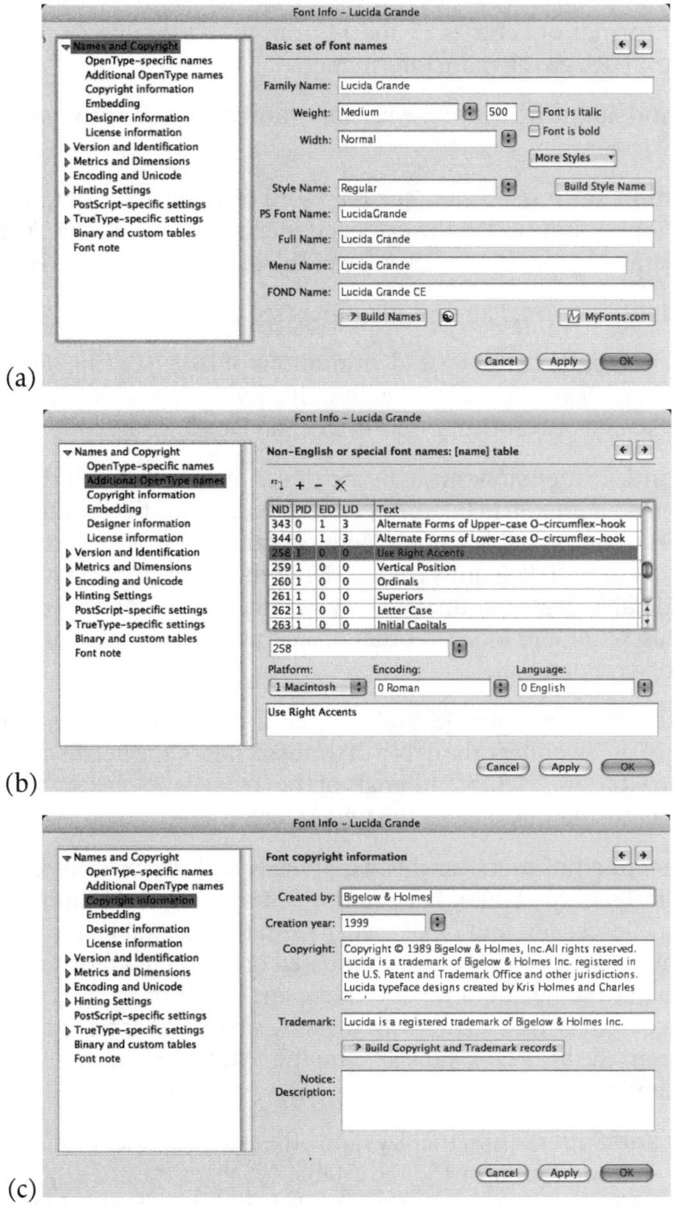

Figure 12-7: The tabs Names and Copyright, Additional OpenType names, *and* Copyright information.

- Designer information: entries 9, 12, and 11 from the name table—the designer's name, her URL, and the URL of the foundry.

- License information: entries 13 and 14 from the name table—a description of the license and a URL giving more information.

- Version and Identification: the version number (base version and revision), entry 5 of the name table.

- Identification settings: the unique ID record of a TrueType font, the unique identifier of a Type 1 font (UID), the extended identifier (XUID), the TrueType vendor code (contained in the achVendID entry of the OS/2 table, Appendix D.4.7).

- Panose identification: Panose-1 identifier (see Chapter 11).

- IBM and MS identification: the identifications of IBM (see Chapter 11), PCL, Ventura Publisher, Microsoft (**Roman**, with serifs; **Swiss**, sans serif; **Modern**, the author cannot guess; and also **Script, Decorative**, and **Don't know**).

- Metrics and Dimensions: usually we design glyphs through the use of integer coordinates on a grid of 1,000 units per em (PostScript, fixed value) or 2,048 units per em (TrueType, variable value). Here we can specify the exact size of the grid, without exceeding 10,000 units per em. Note that 1,000 units per em already gives us a considerable degree of fineness, if we consider that for type set at 10 points a unit in a PostScript font is on the order of 3.5 microns, which is one twentieth of the diameter of a human hair!

- Key dimensions (see Figure 12-8 (a)): dimensions that will be used very frequently: the height of the ascenders, the depth of the descenders, the height of the capitals, the height of the lowercase letters, the angle of the (true) italics, the angle of the artificial slant, the depth and thickness of the underscore.

- TrueType-specific metrics: this panel deals with dimensions drawn from certain specific TrueType tables. For example, here we find the dimensions TypoAscender, TypoDescender, and TypoLineGap from the OS/2 table: the "typographically correct" values, therefore those that are based on aesthetics rather than on physical measurements, the height of the ascenders, the depth of the descenders, and leading. WinAscent and WinDescent, from the OS/2 table, and Ascender, Descender, and LineGap, from the hhea table (§D.4.4), are the "Macintosh versions" of the parameters just mentioned.

- Subscript and Superscript: the sizes and offsets of these inappropriate typographic constructs that are found in the OS/2 table (ySubscriptXSize, ySubscriptYSize, ySuperscriptXSize, ySuperscriptYSize, ySubscriptXOffset, ySubscriptYOffset, ySuperscriptXOffset, and ySuperscriptYOffset).

- Encoding and Unicode (see Figure 12-8 [b]): depending on the glyphs contained in a font, we can choose one or more font encodings from this list. Mac OS 8.5, Windows 95, and more recent versions of these operating systems will pretend to show

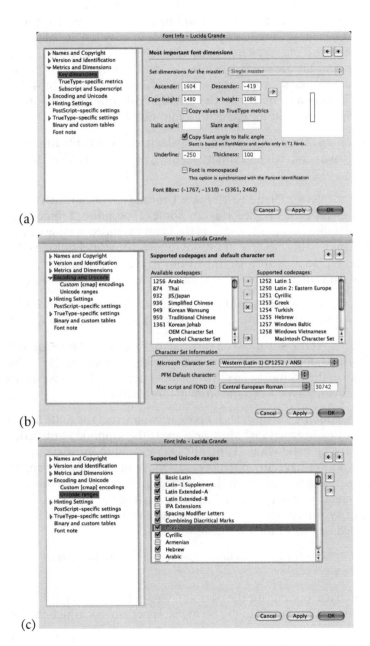

Figure 12-8: The tabs Key dimensions, Supported codepages and default character set, *and* Supported Unicode ranges.

the user multiple fonts; in fact, what will be shown is the same font under different encodings. The name of the font will be the font's usual name followed by the name of an encoding in parentheses. The data in question are hidden amongst the 64 pages of the ulCodePageRange1 and ulCodePageRange2 entries in the OS/2 table. Under this same tab are other data intended for PFM files: the "Microsoft Character Set" (dfCharSet) and the replacement glyph (dfDefaultChar) (see [47]). We also find here two pieces of data meant for use in Macintosh font suitcases—the name of the "Worldscript script" and the Quickdraw font number.

- **Custom [cmap] encodings:** this panel (which is new in FontLab v5) allows the user to build his own cmap table by specifying the type and contents of each subtable (see Appendix §D.4.2).

- **Unicode ranges** (see Figure 12-8 [c]): the Unicode ranges of which this font contains *at least one* glyph. *Do not* neglect this tab! Some of the author's students at ENST Brittany have designed beautiful glyphs in the Latin Extended-A table without declaring that table under this tab. The result? Windows completely disregarded their new glyphs and replaced them with those from Arial. A very understandable attitude: if we insist on saying that this table is empty, why should the software doubt us?

- We will describe the panels on hinting **Hinting Settings, Standard stems (T1 hinting), Additional hinting parameters, T1 Autohinting** in Chapter 13.

- **PostScript–specific settings:** do we need to create a PFM file? An AFM or an INF file? Use the parameters WinAscent and WinDescent from the OS/2 table as vertical coordinates of the bounding box? Which font encoding should we use for the font?[3] Should we open a Type 1 export terminal for this font?[4]

- **TrueType–specific settings:** Is it necessary to instruct the font? Must we preserve any pre-existing instructions? Must we convert the simplified instructions that have been inserted by hand within FontLab? Do we need to instruct any glyphs, if only those that do not have any instructions? Do we need to export any bitmaps? Do we need to rearrange the glyph descriptions in the font? Use Unicode correspondences to create a TrueType encoding? Use a particular font encoding for the first 256 glyphs? Which encoding do we need to use for the first subtable of the cmap table (§D.4.2)? Do we export the kern table?

- **Mapping:** options for the cmap table: add .null glyphs, the carriage return, and the space?

- **Device metrics:** options for the hdmx and VDMX tables (§D.8.3, D.8.5); here we have the possibility of specifying the sizes (in pixels per em) for which the fonts will con-

---

[3] The best choice is **Always write custom encoding**. In this case, FontLab will use the encoding chosen through the font window.

[4] Under this tab, FontLab plays a dirty trick on us: **Open Type 1 Export Terminal** appears as ☑ **Open Type 1 Export Terminal**, but we have to read it carefully, lest we mistake the first two words for **Open-Type** rather than **Open and Type**!

tain set-widths in precalculated pixels. We can also decide whether we wish to include a VDMX table in the font.

- **Font smoothing**: options for the gasp table (§D.8.2). Choose the range of sizes (measured in pixels per em) to which we shall apply the instructions alone, gray levels, or instructions and gray levels together.

- **Font flags**: [head] table: options for the head table (§D.4.3)—the parameters lowestRecPPEM (the size below which the font is illegible) and fontDirectionHint (a global view of the directionality of the glyphs, with the possible values 0 [left-to-right and right-to-left], 1 [left-to-right only], 2 [left-to-right and neutral characters, such as the space and the period], -1 and -2 [the opposites of 1 and 2: right-to-left only and right-to-left with neutral characters]).

- Tabs **PCLT table**, **Font identification**, **Font metrics**, **Codepages**: parameters from the PCLT table (§D.8.7).

- *Binary and custom tables*: the ability to selectively erase exotic TrueType tables that were imported when the font was opened.

- *Font note*: a textual comment that will accompany the font.

The Glyph Window

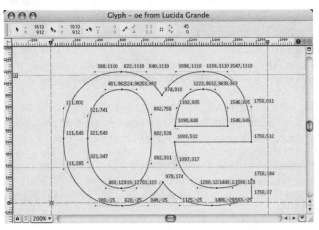

When we double-click on a glyph in the font window, it is displayed in the *glyph window* for us to edit. In this window we find several layers of data, and they can be partly or entirely displayed or hidden, as the user wishes. The display can be personalized in this way through the menus **View>Show Layers**, **View>Lock Layers**, and **View>Snap to Layers** (which enables the magnetism between the given layers).

The most important layer of data is, of course, the *contour of the glyph*, for which we can decide whether or not to display the *nodes* (starting and ending points of the Bézier curves) and their types (tangent or angular nodes), the control points, the coordinates (in the form of pairs of numbers), the direction of the contour, etc.

Behind the glyph, we can place several other layers of data:

- A *grid*: we can choose the orientation (horizontal or vertical) of this grid from the Preferences>Glyph Window<Dimensions tab, using the Grid step input fields.

- Some *guidelines*: we can define a number of straight lines (horizontal, vertical, or slanted) that will be displayed locally (only for the glyph for which they were defined) or globally (for all glyphs). These horizontal or vertical lines are defined in the same way as under *Photoshop* or *Illustrator*—we click on the horizontal or vertical ruler at the edges of the window and slide the line that appears until it is in the desired location. Giving one of these lines a slant is a lot of *fun*: if we place the cursor on the line but near the edges of the window, we can change its slant; if we select it near the middle of the window, we move it in parallel, without changing its angle. By right-clicking on a guideline (Ctrl-click under Mac OS), we can convert it into a global line, delete it, or change its properties.

- A *mask*: this is another contour, one that will not be taken into account during the generation of the PostScript or TrueType font but that serves only to assist with the creation/editing of the current glyph. For example, we can use the glyphs of another font as a "source of inspiration". Magnetism can be quite useful for following the mask with a great degree of precision without being obliged to work under enormous magnification factors. The mask is managed by the Tools>Mask menu. If we wish to work with the mask itself, we can exchange it for the regular contour (entry Swap Outline with Mask). To generate masks *globally* from the glyphs of another font, we can use Tools>Mask>Assign Font Mask. Likewise, we can personalize the display of a mask by using Preferences>Glyph window>Colors.

- A *global mask*, which is a mask common to all the glyphs in the font. We cannot work directly with a template, but we can convert part of a contour or a mask into a template through the Tools>Templates menu.

- A *background*, which is a mask in the form not of a contour but of a bitmap. Suppose that the reader wishes to reproduce the handwriting of Vicentino Ludovico degli Arrighi, used in his calligraphy textbook *La operina da imparare di scrivere littera cancellarescha* of 1523:

Ludouicus Vicentinus scribebat Romæ anno salutis M D X X I I I

The first step (and certainly the most costly, unless one has very good friends who are librarians or collectors) is to obtain a copy of this work and scan all the letters very carefully, in PICT or TIFF format. Next, one will use each of these scans as a background by specifying it on the File>Import>Background menu. What is important here is to position the bitmap in question correctly with respect to the glyph's origin and to give it the correct size. To do so, one selects entry Tools>Background>Move and scale. To set the bitmap to an exact scale value, one is required, at least as of version 4.6 of FontLab, to use a Python script. Once the background has been imported, one may use a rapid solution—use another software product from the same company (*ScanFont*), which will automatically draw the glyphs' contours—or a slow solution—tracing the contours oneself by maintaining a balance between faithfulness to the original contour and the elegance of the trace.

The glyph window can be used under four basic modes, each of which has its own tools and its own interface. These modes are:

- The *editing mode*, which is the most important mode, as it is the one in which we create or modify the glyph's contour.

- The *sketch mode* (Contour>Sketch mode), which offers an alternative to editing the traces of glyphs, inspired by Peter Karow's program Ikarus.[5] In this mode, following Karow's approach, we use neither Bézier curves nor nodes nor control points; instead, we insert points of three types: "angular", "curvilinear", and "tangent"). The software will trace the contour along these points, which we may move at will. When we need more precision, we add more points. Once we have finished with our points, FontLab will convert everything to Bézier curves. Since the author is not convinced that this mode will last long, nothing more will be said about it in this book.

- The *vector paint mode*, (View>Toolbar>Paint and then click on a button in the Paint toolbar). Vector paint mode offers several interesting functions: drawing a rectangle, an ellipse, or a polygon. We can even write text in a given font, and it will automatically become a contour! But this mode is characterized most of all by gadgets such as brushes that are round or rectangular or that even have the shape of the brushes used in Chinese or Japanese calligraphy. It goes without saying that we can *hardly* obtain an aesthetically appealing result with these so-called calligraphic brushes; use them, therefore, in moderation.

- The *measurement mode* (⟨✐⟩ button), which allows us to measure distances with a great deal of precision. By holding down the shift key, we can restrict ourselves to horizontal or vertical measurements or those taken at an angle of any multiple of 15 degrees.

Of these modes, the only one that is worth describing in detail is the "editing" mode, which we discuss below.

To trace a curve or a line, we enable the button ⟨⁺✦⟩ (not to be confused with ⟨◌⟩, which is for the "sketch" mode) and then click within the window to select the curve's starting

---

[5] This program calls into question the notion of a mathematically defined curve. What Karow [207, p. 117] claims is that what is essential about a contour is that it goes through a certain number of points and that we must know whether these points are smooth, angular, or angular on one side and smooth on the other. Once we have specified the major points, the software will take care of the rest, and then it does not matter whether the curves are quadratic, cubic, or conic: the result will be the same (!). And if the curve is not exactly what we wanted, we need only add a few more points...

point. If we wish to produce a straight line, we release the mouse button and click a second time, while holding down the alt key, to select the ending point. If, however, we wish to produce a curve, we drag the mouse while holding the button down: the point at which we release the button will be the location of the first control point. When we click again, we select the curve's ending point. If we drag the mouse, we obtain not the second control point but its opposite relative to the ending point.

FontLab considers nodes to be smooth by default; thus the node itself and its control points lie on the same straight line, the one that is tangent to the curve.

We can change this behavior by holding down the alt key. Then the link between the entering and exiting directions of the node disappears, and we can continue to trace in another direction. The simplest way to obtain an angular node is to click without pressing alt, to drag the mouse until the "entering" control point is correct, and then to press the alt key: the "exiting" control point will then be released, and we can place it where we wish by releasing the mouse button.

The use of the alt key to switch from a smooth node to an angular one when tracing curves will be difficult at first for those who are used to *FontStudio* but quite natural to users of Fontographer or Illustrator, software packages that follow the same conventions.

To close a contour, one need only click on it—according to the manual. But having tried this procedure many times, always in vain, the author has reached the conclusion that it is better to close the contour somewhere near its starting point and then to use the mouse to move the ending point so that it coincides with the starting point. A good test to see if curves are really closed is to switch to preview mode (menu View>Show Layers>Fill Outline) and check that all surfaces have been blackened.

To modify a curve that has already been traced, we can move the nodes, the control points, or even the entire curve by dragging. Three buttons are available for adding nodes: by enabling ⌈⁺ᵣ⌉ and clicking on the curve, we convert the section of the curve that lies between the last node and the location of the click into a straight line and insert a node where we clicked; by enabling ⌈⁺ᵣ⌉ and clicking on the curve, we obtain a new node on the curve without modifying the curve, and the node is a smooth one; by enabling ⌈⁺ᶠ⌉ and performing the same operation, we obtain an angular node.

To obtain new nodes, we can also use the "knife" tool ⌐✐. By drawing a line with this tool, we cut a curve or a closed contour into two. When we apply this operation to a closed contour, FontLab adds the missing straight line segments to obtain two closed contours again.

The contextual menu (clicking while holding the ctrl key) of a node offers us several operations related to it: making it the first node of the curve; converting it into a smooth/angular node; deleting it; copying it; deleting its control points (**Retract BCPs**); reversing the contour's direction; or making it into an angular node with tangents whose angle is 90 degrees. This same contextual menu can also operate on the entire contour: making it the first contour; deleting it; subtracting it from the contour that appears below; selecting it; or creating a parallel contour at the left, at the right, or on both sides, at a given distance.

Drawing shapes is all very well; but if the shapes are simple, having them available for ready use is even better. That is why we have the *Primitives Panel* (Windows>Panels> Smart Shapes menu). On it, we can select a grid (Grid), arcs, horizontal rectangles, rectangles at any desired angle (Free Rectangle), ellipses, stars with any number of branches, polygons with any number of sides.

For transforming contours, a whole panoply of tools is available. Let us begin with the most classic ones: scaling ⊞, rotation ↺, slanting ⊿, but also moving ⊞ and reflection ⊿. To gain access to the last two of these transformations, it is necessary to use the Window>Panels>Transformation panel.

On this same panel, there is a little button ⬈ that seems unassuming enough at first blush. But this button offers us a veritable factory of transformations: the *transformation window* (also accessible from the Tools>Action menu). In this window we find a long list of transformations, divided into four groups: transformations for contours, operations related to hints and instructions, transformations of font metrics, and more exotic transformations called *effects*:

- The *transformations of contours* are the classic ones that we mentioned above, plus the following: decomposition of a composite glyph; conversion of Type 1 contours into TrueType contours and vice versa; reversal of the directions of all the contours; insertion of endpoints for the horizontal and vertical tangents; deletion of juxtaposed parts; optimization of the glyph.

- We shall examine the *transformations of hints and instructions* in Chapter 13, which discusses the optimization of fonts.

- The *transformations of font metrics* involve changing the set-width (Set Width) or the side bearings (Set Sidebearings), centering the glyph with respect to its set-width, automatically calculating the side bearings from an analysis of the glyph's contour (Autospacing), or changing the font's metrics dramatically (Adjust Metrics).

- The *effects* are best explained by an illustration:

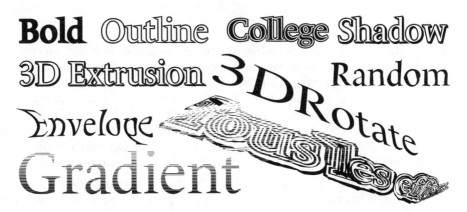

Here we have *tortured* the font *Le Monde Livre*. The last result, in which "*Tous les effets*" (meaning "All the effects") is barely legible, comes from the application of all the effects in the order shown.

It goes without saying that the only one of these effects that is of interest for the production of fonts *worthy of the name* is **Effects>Bold**, which allows us to increase the weight of the glyphs. For example, we can simulate the optical correction by adding a small amount of weight and slightly increasing the width and the side bearings. Another possible application: we can add a slight amount of weight to some fonts in order to adapt them better to others (for example, the mathematical symbols of *Computer Modern*, for use with text in *Times Roman*).

Just above, we spoke of a "factory of transformations". But every factory has an assembly line. We can perform several transformations sequentially through the window **Tools> Action Set**. There is no limit to the number or the variety of the transformations that can appear in a sequence. We can also specify precisely the glyphs to which we wish to apply these transformations: the choice can range from a single glyph to the entire font to all the open fonts or even to all the fonts in a given directory. And if the user successfully makes an ideal transformation, she may save it in a file by using the button 💾, which appears on the **Action Set** window.

On the vertical **Tools** toolbar, we also find button ⊞, which surrounds the contour with a frame that has handles. By moving these handles with the mouse, we can perform the classic transformations: scaling, rotation, and slanting.

There are several other transformations of contours that must be applied manually: they are listed on the **Transform** toolbar (obtained through the **View>Toolbars>Contour** menu) and should not be confused with the **Transformation** panel.

The first two buttons of the **Transform** toolbar are just shortcuts for horizontal and vertical reflection. The third button ⊡ initiates an *interpolation* procedure. Clicking on this button opens the following window:

As long as this window remains visible, we are in "interpolation mode". In this mode, we can click on any node and make it into a *reference point*. A reference point can stay in its original position or be moved. The principle of interpolation is as follows. All points that lie *between* two reference points are moved proportionally by interpolating the displacement vector of the reference points. All the points that lie before the first reference point or after the last one are moved by the same amount as the reference points. These calculations are performed individually within each contour. Once we have displaced all the reference points to our satisfaction, we click on **OK** to confirm the operation.

The button 👜 launches an operation of *simplification*. By simplification we mean the replacement of a number of Bézier curves by a single one that assumes, as much as possible, the shape of those curves. Used with discretion, this operation can improve a glyph: often a single Bézier curve is infinitely more beautiful than a dozen laboriously drawn subcurves. Here is how it works: We select all the nodes with a ctrl-A (⌘–A on the Macintosh), we click on ⏚, we click on the node that will be the starting point of the simplified curve, we click on the node that will be the ending point of the simplified curve, and voilà! In order to join the new section of curve smoothly with the rest of the contour, we may depress the shift key while selecting the corresponding nodes.

Other operations are less important: ⏚ allows for the precise definition of the coordinates of each node, either absolutely or relative to a reference point, in Cartesian or polar coordinates; ⏚ allows us to squash a glyph by changing the curvature of the background on which we are designing it (meant for lovers of gadgets and psychedelic fonts; sensitive souls should steer clear of this feature!); ⏚ allows us to change the direction of some contours by clicking on any node of a contour whose direction we wish to reverse and double-clicking on it to complete the operation and accept the result.

Finally, if all of FontLab's capabilities taken together will not yield the result that we want, we can use other vector-design software, save the contour in EPS format, and import the result into FontLab through the menu File>Import>EPS.

The Metrics Window

Like human beings, glyphs never live in isolation. But to form communities of glyphs (what humans call "words"), they have to maintain certain distances: neither too close together nor too far apart. Finding the correct distances between each pair of glyphs is an art in itself. And it is not a pointless exercise: the legibility of the text depends on it.

We manage the distances between glyphs by kerning them—i.e., by moving them closer together or farther apart, starting with the natural distances obtained by setting the starting point of the second glyph at the ending point of the first glyph's displacement vector. It is the most thankless task in font design: when, after hundreds of tests and many sleepless nights spent putting the finishing touches on the kerning, we have finally achieved a good result, no one even notices. Any problems with kerning, however, will stand out like a sore thumb.

To facilitate the chore of kerning as much as possible, FontLab puts several tools at the user's disposal.

All the operations are performed in a special window called the *metrics window* (menu Window>New Metrics Window):

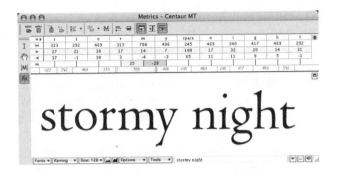

On the bottom bar of this window, we can enter a line of text (possibly using the \ABCD notation for glyphs representing Unicode characters or the /name_of_glyph notation to specify a glyph by means of its name). By choosing **Panel** in the **Options** pull-down menu a table appears with the following information for each glyph: its name, set-width, and left and right side bearings. The values of these cells in the table can be modified, either by entering a new value or by typing an equal sign followed by the name of another glyph: the corresponding value will then be copied. This operation applies one time only: if we enter =o in the box for the left-hand side bearing of the 'e', that letter will inherit the value for the left-hand side bearing of the 'o', but no link will be established between the two; and if the value of the former changes, the latter will not be affected.

When the second pull-down menu is set to **Metrics**, we are in "set-width and side bearings" mode. In this mode, clicking on a glyph lets us modify its left and right side bearings and its position relative to the set-width. By selecting **Kerning** in the pull-down menu, we switch to "kerning" mode. A new line is added to the table: it contains the values of the kerning pairs. By clicking on a glyph, we can modify its kerning relative to the preceding glyph. Warning: as Knuth said in [218, p. 317], it is very easy to do too much kerning, and all excesses in typography are bad. To avoid this trap, we should, *dixit* Knuth, apply the amount of kerning that seems perfect on the screen, and then—*use only half as much!* A word to the wise.

A few very interesting features of this window: the button ⎣RTL⎦ displays the text from right to left, a boon for the designers of Arabic, Hebrew, or Syriac fonts. The button ⎣M⎦ displays a red horizontal line called the *measure line*. When the measure line is visible, the left and right side bearings are calculated not according to the actual side bearings of the letters but according to the intersections of the contours with this line. That may be beneficial for certain pairs of letters (such as "AV" or "LY") but catastrophic for others (such as "AA" or "XX"). Used judiciously, this line can be very useful; do not neglect to take advantage of it. A helpful tip: To change the height of this line, go into a glyph window in which the layer of vertical metrics has already been unlocked in **Window>Panels>Editing Layers**; then simply move it up or down with the mouse.

By selecting **Auto...** in the **Tools** pull-down menu we have the possibility to generate new metrics or new kerning pairs (according to the mode) for a single glyph, for the glyphs displayed, or even for all of the glyphs in the font. The author can hardly imagine that a font in which the set-widths, the side bearings, and the kerning pairs were all calculated automatically could really be functional; but we have to admit that that would be a good starting point. With kerning pairs, we can avoid excesses by specifying an absolute value below which a kerning pair is considered too small and does not appear, together with a maximum number of kerning pairs. Various options give us more or less control over the process of automatically generating kerning pairs.

We shall discuss the insertion of OpenType properties in Chapter 14. But before we get to that point, there is a concept borrowed from OpenType that we can use immediately to simplify the process of producing kerning pairs: the concept of *glyph class*. By sorting the glyphs into classes whose members behave the same with respect to kerning, we can generate a large number of kerning pairs automatically. For example, it is obvious that the glyphs 'A', 'À', 'Á', 'Ä', and 'Ą' will need the same kerning pairs with every other letter. When we write "AT", for instance, any accent that appears on the 'A' will not interact with the 'T' in any way. Thus it is desirable to place all the varieties of 'A' in a class and to define kerning pairs for only one 'A'; the others will follow.

To do so, we use the class-definition window (**Window>Panels>Classes** panel):

We click on the button ⊞ to create a new class. The zone at the left displays the name of the new class: class1. We can then work in "console mode". We replace the string class1: in the input method at the bottom right with the name of the class (for example, _kernA), followed by a colon, the name of the representative glyph (the "union steward" of all the glyphs in the class) followed by an apostrophe, and the names of all the glyphs in the class. Once all those data have been entered, we click on Accept, and the list appears in the area immediately above. Instead of keyboarding glyph names we can also drag glyphs from the glyph window into the main area of the classes panel.

Now it is time to use the classes that we have defined. The window **Tools>Kerning Assistance** allows us to specify which of these classes are left-hand classes and which are right-hand classes. When we have checked the respective boxes, we have two possible choices: we can save by selecting **Apply and Save**, in which case FontLab will create an OpenType table of type kern that will contain the classes and their respective kerning pairs, or we can request **Expand Kerning**, in which case FontLab will calculate all the kerning pairs thus produced and add them to the list of kerning pairs that already exist. That is how we can obtain, for example, new kerning pairs in an AFM file. But beware: once again, the connection is not permanent. If we later change the kerning of the representative glyphs, we must use **Expand Kerning** again to update all the pairs.

The classes that we have just described are not used only to define kerning pairs. Through the window Tools>Metrics Assistance, we can also change the set-widths or the side bearings of all the glyphs in a single class.

Finally, fonts are often—but, alas, not always—accompanied by AFM (or PFM) files that contain kerning pairs. We can import these values: in the metrics window, we use the Open metrics entry of the Tools pull-down menu and select the file to be read, together with certain options. We can also save the font's metrics in an external file by using Save metrics.

Multiple Master Fonts

Multiple Master fonts, or "accordion fonts", are *dynamic* PostScript Type 1 fonts in the sense that the contour of each glyph can vary according to several parameters. These fonts were introduced by Adobe at the same time as the program Acrobat, in which they play a crucial role: specifically, how to substitute for a missing font without harming the layout? The substituted font must be able to adapt itself to the characteristics of the missing font—in particular, to the set-widths of its glyphs.

That is what the Multiple Master fonts that come standard with Acrobat—with names as generic as *Adobe Serif* and *Adobe Sans*—do very efficiently: often we do not even notice that a substitution has taken place.

The reader will find in Appendix §C.4 a technical description of the Multiple Master format. This section is dedicated to the way in which FontLab manages these fonts. Incidentally, their features under FontLab are slightly more powerful than those of the Multiple Master specification; indeed, independently of the Multiple Master font format, FontLab uses that format's technique of linear interpolation as an internal technique for creating intermediate fonts, whatever their final format may be. That strategic choice is very significant because the Multiple Master font format has been officially abandoned: Adobe has withdrawn the Multiple Master tables from the OpenType format and, in so doing, signed a death warrant for this technology.[6]

A glyph in a Multiple Master font has a *variable* contour. Its variability is structured in the following manner. The font has a certain number (2, 4, 8, or 16) of "master designs" for each glyph that cover the *axes of variation*, which may number from 1 to 4. The master designs are found at the extreme ends of these axes: thus there are necessarily 2^n master designs for n axes. To obtain any particular instance of a variable glyph, it is sufficient to perform linear interpolation on the master designs by giving a precise value to the parameters that correspond to the various axes. To the end user, that takes the form of a window with one sliding bar for each axis: as values are specified, the selected glyphs change dynamically. Here is the interface, under *Illustrator 10*:

---

[6] That said, the dynamic font technology still exists in the AAT fonts (§D.12). But as yet no tool really supports the creation of these fonts.

Without going into the technical details, we wish to bring one very important constraint of the Multiple Master format to the reader's attention. Although the different master designs do, of course, have contours of their own, they must still share some nontrivial similarities: the same number of nodes, nodes of the same type, nodes placed in positions in which anomalies (such as curves reduced to a single point or curves that intersect) will never occur. In other words, the possible degree of variation is still quite restricted, and we are far from having carte blanche in the choice of our master designs!

The four possible axes of a Multiple Master font may be given any names, but Adobe recommends the following names (and roles): Weight, Width (set-width), Size, and Style.

One can imagine how difficult it can be to create Multiple Master fonts: starting from an existing font, one must reduce or increase the weight of the glyphs uniformly; one must ensure that the extreme designs are aesthetically acceptable and that an interpolation made from them yields as its "average" the original font; to achieve any modification to an intermediate design, the master designs must be modified.[7] In other words, the designer must envision the glyphs in his mind as multidimensional objects—already a difficult task—and, in addition, understand that to obtain an intermediate glyph, one that will be used every day and that must be impeccable, we have to design extreme glyphs: extra-thin, ultra-wide, super-bold, etc., and arrange for the interpolation of these extremes to yield the desired intermediate form.

Is that possible? By morphing a basketball player and a sumo wrestler, can we obtain a *normal* man, or even a *beautiful* one? Can beauty, which in typography lies in moderation and normality, come from the interpolation of extremes? It is hard to answer that philosophical question. And that is without doubt the reason for which there are so few Multiple Master fonts, most of them being simple sans serif designs.

In any event, FontLab offers the interface shown in Figure 12-9: we design all the master designs in the same glyph window; a **Masters** palette allows us to display them or hide them and to indicate the archetype that we are currently designing (the others are locked); another palette, **Axis**, allows us to set values for the axes of variation, which are applied to an invisible contour. What is the use of this "invisible contour"? There is none, except that we can ask that it be shaded gray, and then we can see it just like a mask. Thus we can freely modify the master designs and observe the consequences of our modifications on the intermediate glyph.

---

[7] In fact, knowing that intermediate masters are often the most useful, Adobe has included in the Multiple Master specifications the possibility of using a master not as an extremity of a variation axis but as an intermediate value. But this functionality is not supported by FontLab which will not even open such fonts.

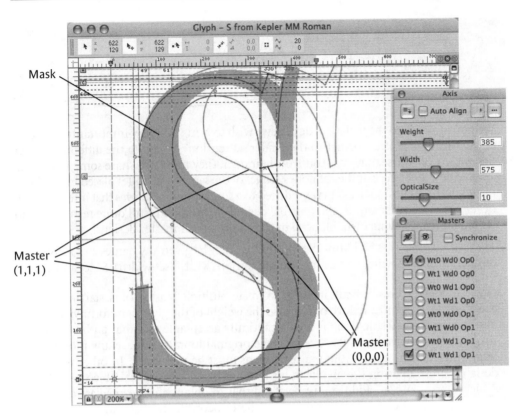

Figure 12-9: The interface for designing Multiple Master fonts in FontLab. In it are shown the contours of two master designs (one ultra-light, ultra-condensed, and at an optical size of 6 points; the other ultra-bold, ultra-wide, and at an optical size of 72 points) and, shaded in gray, an (invisible) intermediate contour. This is Adobe's font Kepler.

By modifying the values of the axes of variation in the **Axis** window, we see that beyond a certain maximum value (and below a certain minimum value), the values are displayed on a yellow background. That is called *extrapolation*, a property specific to FontLab that does not appear in the Multiple Master specification. Extrapolation merely "goes further" and yields even more extreme results, often verging on the grotesque, and sometimes even on the paradoxical.[8]

A proverb says that "all is fair in love and war". Well, here neither love nor war is at stake, but FontLab follows this principle all the same by offering us tools for producing Multiple Master fonts that border on the slovenly! Thus, here—very quickly—is a practical way to obtain the light and bold master designs. We select a font that has a bold weight. Obviously there is no guarantee that the glyphs in the bold weight will be

---

[8] Note that in the font *Kepler* the optical size can be extrapolated downward all the way to the value −28! Which raises a truly metaphysical issue: what is a negative optical size?

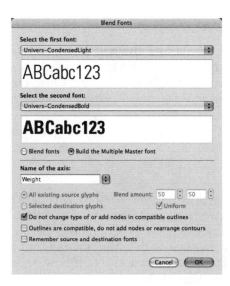

Figure 12-10: The window for creating Multiple Master fonts from two ordinary fonts taken as master designs: the fonts Univers 47 (light condensed) and Univers 67 (bold condensed).

"compatible" with those in the light weight, i.e., that they will have the same nodes, of the same kind, and in the same places. But here is what FontLab offers us. We select the two fonts, together with the name of the new axis of variation, in the window **Tools> Blend Fonts** (see Figure 12-10), and we check the box **Build the Multiple Master Font**. Then FontLab will meticulously compare the two versions of the glyphs and make a decision about their compatibility. If, for a given glyph, the light version and the bold version are "compatible", the box for the glyph in the font window will be colored green. Then we can apply the action **Tools>Multiple Master>Mask to Master**, and the bold version will become the glyph's second master design. If, however, the glyphs are not compatible, we can move the nodes of the second master design (which is, by default, identical to the first) until the contour looks just like the bold version, which is shown as a mask. Note that for the example of the fonts in Figure 12-10, 65 percent of the glyphs were already characterized by FontLab as "compatible", and we had nothing more to do than to handle the 35 percent that remained in order to obtain a true Multiple Master font with one axis (weight). This is not a contrived example, as *Univers* is the canonical example of a "variable" font, and it is but a short step from Adrien Frutiger's arrangement of *Univers* in several series [144, pp. 13–25] to the Multiple Master axes.

The same method of "multimasterization" in FontLab can be applied to versions of a font with different set-widths or optical sizes, or indeed any other type of variation.[9] Clearly this sort of practice almost turns the design of Multiple Master fonts into child's play.

---

[9] For example, the well-known designer Luc[as] de Groot designed a Multiple Master font called *Move-MeMM* for which the first master design is a very proper sans serif font and the second is a series of awfully raunchy images [112]. This font, off limits to minors, follows in the long tradition of anthropomorphic and often erotic typefaces [92].

Driving FontLab with Python Scripts

The greatest strength of FontLab over other font-editing software is without doubt the fact that it can be *driven* by a very enjoyable programming language called Python. Even though FontLab is proprietary software whose source code will never be available to the ordinary mortal, we can still go under the hood and take control of its actions by writing a few lines of simple, comprehensible code.

Under Windows, before trying to run any Python scripts, one must install Python on the computer, as explained in:

```
http://www.python.org/download/releases/2.4.1/
```

In the next part of this section, up to page 488, we shall assume that the reader has a basic knowledge of Python. If that is not the case, we recommend a number of books, by a certain publisher named O'Reilly: first, if the reader is new to programming, she can very well start out by learning the basics of programming in Python with the excellent book *Python Programming for the Absolute Beginner*, by Michael Dawson [111]. If, however, she is an experienced programmer and wishes only to learn Python, we recommend *Learning Python*, by Mark Lutz and David Ascher [241]. Finally, for the reader who already has some experience with Python and is looking for a reference book, we enthusiastically recommend *Python in a Nutshell*, by Alex Martelli [247].

Python code is entered in the **Window>Panels>Edit Macro** window. This window has four buttons on the left with the following meanings: open a file open/save window; run the current script; stop it; re-initialize the Python interpreter (in case something went wrong and the interpreter hangs). There is also a button on the right which allows editing the script in a separate editor (such as *BBEdit* for the Macintosh or *UltraEdit* for Windows), if the latter has been defined in the **FontLab Studio>Preferences>General Options>Python scripting** panel.

If we are going to use a Python script often, it is convenient to call it from FontLab's user interface. To do so, we need only save it (always with the extension .py) in one of the many subdirectories of **/Library/Application Support/FontLab/Studio 5/Macros/System**. The location at which the script's name appears in FontLab's interface will depend on the subdirectory in which we store the script. For example, if we store it in the **Kerning** subdirectory, the script's name will appear in the "context menu" when we click inside the metrics window obtained through **Window>New Metrics Window**.

The name of the script, as shown through this interface, is the name of the script file, unless we have included the following line in the code:

```
#FLM: A more friendly name
```

in which case it is the "more friendly name" that will appear in the menu.

Let us proceed by exploring some of the Python classes, attributes, and methods that FontLab places at our disposal.

The FontLab class

The base class, which has no constructor but is always predefined, is FontLab. The only instance of this class that is available to us is fl (abbreviation of "FontLab"). Here are its most important attributes:

- font, which returns an object of type Font (the active font); count, which returns the number of open fonts; ifont, which returns the index of the active font among the open fonts. Note that fl can also be used as a list of length len(fl) that is indexed by the open fonts. For example, f=fl.font and f=fl[fl.ifont] yield the same result.

- glyph, which returns an object of type Glyph (the active glyph in the font window, the glyph window, or the metrics window); count_selected, which returns the number of selected glyphs;[10] iglyph, which returns the index of the active glyph among all the glyphs of the active font. Note that a Font object can also be used as a list that is indexed by its glyphs. For example, g=fl.glyph and g=fl.font[fl.iglyph] yield the same result, with only one small difference: in the first case, g is an orphaned object, whereas in the second case its parent is the active font.

- path, filename, version, productnumber, serialnumber, username yield, respectively, the path and the filename of the application, its version, its product number, its serial number, and the username of the current user.

- namfilename, which returns the name of the file containing the standard glyph names corresponding to the Unicode characters.

And here are the most important methods:

- Open(*filename*) opens the font *filename*.

- Close(*f*) closes the font whose index is *f*.

- Save(*f, filename*) saves the font *f* under the filename *filename*.

- GenerateFont(*type, filename*) generates a font named *filename*. Here are the possible types:

  - ftFONTLAB, a font in FontLab format VFB
  - ftTYPE1, a PostScript Type 1 font, PFB file
  - ftTYPE1_MM, a Multiple Master font, binary
  - ftTYPE1ASCII, a PostScript Type 1 font, PFA file
  - ftTYPE1ASCII_MM, a Multiple Master font, ASCII
  - ftTRUETYPE, a TrueType font, TTF file
  - ftOPENTYPE, an OpenType-CFF font, OTF file

---

[10] Note: several glyphs may be "selected", but only one is "active".

- ftMACTYPE1, a PostScript Type 1 font, Macintosh font suitcase and LWFN file

- ftMACTRUETYPE, a TrueType font, Macintosh font suitcase

- ftMACTRUETYPE_DFONT, a TrueType font, .dfont file

- UpdateFont() updates the active font after modifications performed by a program. UpdateFont(*fi*) does the same for the font whose index is *fi*.

- UpdateGlyph() updates the active glyph after modifications performed by a program. UpdateGlyph(*gi*) does the same for the glyph whose index is *gi*.

- EditGlyph() and EditGlyph(*gi*) open the glyph window for the active glyph or for the glyph whose index is *gi*.

- Selected() and Selected(*gi*) return the boolean value True if the active glyph (or the glyph whose index is *gi*) is selected.

- Select(*glyphid*) selects the glyph identified by *glyphid*, which may be a glyph name, a number (the glyph's index), or Uni(*number*), in which case *number* is the glyph's Unicode index. A second argument, 0, to Select will unselect the glyph.

- Unselect() rapidly unselects all the glyphs.

- Message("You, who have known my heart from infancy,\nAnd all its feelings of disdainful pride,\nSpare me the shame of disavowing all\nThat I profess'd.","Friend, ask me not.","OK, I will","No way") produces a dialog box:[11]

If the user clicks on OK, I will, the method will return 1; if he clicks on No way, it will return 2.

- Random(*min*, *max*) returns a random integer between *min* (inclusive) and *max* (not inclusive).

---

[11] These splendid lines come from Robert Bruce Boswell's translation (*Phaedra*) of Racine's play *Phèdre*.

A few examples

To open all files of type .pfa or .pfb (the extensions may be written in uppercase or lowercase) in the directory /home/yannis/, we can write:

```
import os, re
r1=re.compile(r'.+\.pf[ab]$', re.IGNORECASE)
for file in (os.listdir("/home/yannis/")):
    if r1.match(file):
        fl.Open("/home/yannis/"+file)
```

To obtain all the files in a given directory, we can use the listdir method of module os. To select the files with the extension .pfa or .pfb, we first prepare the regular expression[12] r1, using the compile method of module re. This method takes as its first argument the pattern of the regular expression: r'.+\.pf[ab]$', which means "any character, one or more times, followed by the string .pf, followed by an a or a b, at the end of the string". The second argument to this method (re.IGNORECASE) indicates that matching will disregard the case of the specified characters. Next, for each filename file that matches the regular expression, we execute FontLab's Open method.

To convert all the PFB fonts in a given directory into OpenType-CFF, we can write:

```
import os, re
r1=re.compile(r'(.+)\.pfb$', re.IGNORECASE)
for file in (os.listdir("/home/yannis/")):
    if r1.match(file):
        newfile=r1.match(file).group(1)+".otf"
        fl.Open("/home/yannis/"+file)
        fl.GenerateFont(ftOPENTYPE,"/home/yannis/"+newfile)
        fl.Close(fl.ifont)
```

Here the regular expression is more complex because we have added parentheses to isolate the filename without the extension: (.+)\.pfb$. The string in parentheses forms the *first group* of the expression, which we can use by writing:

```
newfile=r1.match(file).group(1)+".otf"
```

The rest is self-explanatory.

To find all the glyphs whose name begins with an 'f' and display the number in a dialog box while also selecting the glyphs, we can write:

---

[12] For more information on regular expressions in Python, consult [247, p. 145]. But there is also an excellent book on regular expressions in general: [143].

```
import re
total=0
r1=re.compile(r'^f')
fl.Unselect()
for gi in range(len(fl.font)):
    if r1.match(fl.font[gi].name):
        total += 1
        fl.Select(gi)
fl.Message("","There are "+str(total)+" glyphs beginning with f")
```

The Font class

This is the class that comes immediately after FontLab. One possible constructor is Font(). After instantiating a Font object, we do indeed have a new font, but we must use fl.Add to open the window corresponding to this font:

```
f=Font()
fl.Add(f)
```

We can also instantiate Font objects by copying existing fonts: if f1 is one of them, we can write f2=Font(f1) to produce a carbon copy of it.

Here are the most important attributes of this class:

- Many identification attributes, such as file_name, the complete path to the file containing the font; family_name; style_name; full_name, the full name of the font; and so on (see [333] for the complete list of identification attributes). For instance, we can write:

  ```
  f=Font()
  fl.Add(f)
  f=fl.font
  f.family_name="Times New Roman"
  f.style_name="Regular"
  f.full_name="Times New Roman"
  f.font_name="TimesNewRomanPSMT"
  f.font_style=64
  f.menu_name="Times New Roman"
  f.apple_name="Times New Roman"
  ```

- More important, attributes for various dimensions: upm, the number of units per em; ascender[0], the height of the ascenders; descender[0], the depth of the descenders; cap_height[0], the height of the capital letters; x_height[0], the height of the lowercase letters (the last five of these dimensions are lists: there is one entry for each master design in a Multiple Master font); slant_angle, the artificial slant; italic_angle, the natural slant of the italic letters; is_fixed_pitch, to indicate whether the font is monospaced; underline_position, the depth of the underline; underline_thickness, the thickness of the underline. For instance, we can write:

```
f.upm=2048
f.ascender[0]=1420
f.descender[0]=-
f.cap_height[0]=1356
f.x_height[0]=916
f.default_width[0]=500
f.slant_angle=0.0
f.italic_angle=0.0
f.is_fixed_pitch=0
f.underline_position=-
f.underline_thickness=100
```

- modified, which is 1 if the font has been modified, otherwise 0.

- classes, a list of all the glyph classes; and ot_classes, the glyph classes defined on the OpenType panel using the Adobe syntax (§14).

- features, a list of all the OpenType properties, each of them being an object of type Feature (§14).

- encoding, the current encoding of the font, an object of type Encoding.

- Last but not least, glyphs, a list of objects of type Glyph that represent the glyphs in the font.

In addition, an object of type Font can also be considered as a list whose objects are Glyphs; thus the len() operator yields the length of this list, which is the number of glyphs in the font.

Let us move on to the methods. They are relatively few and are concerned with saving AFM files in VFB format and some other general operations:

- Open(*file*) and Save(*file*), to open and save a font in VFB format. For example, we can write:

```
f=Font()
f.Open("/home/yannis/myfonts/Times New Roman.vfb")
fl.Add(f)
```

- OpenAFM(*file*) and SaveAFM(*file*), to read an AFM file and replace its internal metrics or to save the metrics in an AFM file.

- Reencode(*encoding*), where *encoding* is an object of type Encoding, re-encodes the font. We shall see an example below when we describe the Encoding class.

- FindGlyph(*name*) or FindGlyph(*pos*) returns the index of the glyph that has the name *name* or that represents the Unicode character in position *pos*. For example, we can write:

      i=fl[fl.ifont].FindGlyph(int("220F",16))

  where the int function, with 16 as its second argument, will interpret the string 220F as a hexadecimal number. If this glyph does not exist in the font, the value −1 is returned.

- GenerateUnicode() generates new Unicode indices for all the glyphs on the basis of their glyph names. This is the operation to perform in order to consolidate the font after correcting the glyph names.

- Generatenames() generates new glyph names for all the glyphs on the basis of their Unicode indices. This is the operation to perform in order to consolidate the font after correcting the Unicode indices.

The Encoding and EncodingRecord classes

An object of type Encoding is a *font encoding*—a set of correspondences between glyph names and Unicode code points. Each of these correspondences is an EncodingRecord (which has two attributes: name and unicode), and an Encoding object can be considered as a list of EncodingRecords, whose length may be obtained through the len operation.

Thus we can write:

```
enc=fl[fl.ifont].encoding
for i in range(len(enc)):
    print str(i)+": "+enc[i].name+" -> "+str(enc[i].unicode)
```

to obtain a description of an encoding, line by line. Note that the output of the print method appears in the **Window>Panels>Output** panel (which will *not* open automatically; you'll have to open it yourself!).

We can create a new encoding e1 with e1=Encoding() or by copying an existing encoding e2 with e1=Encoding(e2). Since an encoding is a Python list, all the methods for list management apply; in particular, we can write:

- e1.append(x) to add a new entry x to e1

- e1.extend(e2) to append encoding e2 to e1

- e1.insert(i,x) to insert entry x at position i of e1

- e1.remove(x) to delete the first occurrence of x in e1, etc.

We also have the following methods:

- FindName(*name_to_find*) finds the entry for which the name attribute is equal to *name_to_find* and returns the value of its unicode attribute, or −1 if it cannot be found.

- Load(*file*) reads the encoding from a file with the extension .enc. For example, we can write:

```
enc=Encoding()
enc.Load("/Library/Application Support/FontLab/Encoding/T1
        non-Western/iso_8859-.enc")
for i in range(len(enc)):
    print str(i)+": "+enc[i].name+" -> "+str(enc[i].unicode)
```

- To save an encoding file, we need three pieces of information: the full set of name/Unicode code point pairs, a unique identifier (FontLab recommends numbers such as 1,001), and a string that will serve as a quick description of the encoding (the description that will appear on the pull-down menu of encodings in FontLab's font table). If we have these three pieces of information, we can write Save(*file, description, identifier*).

We can also read the encoding of a font and store it in a file. Here is an example of the code that we might use:

```
enc=Encoding()
enc=fl[fl.ifont].encoding
enc.Save("/home/yannis/test.enc","My font's encoding",1001)
```

We thus obtain a file of this type:

```
%%FONTLAB ENCODING: 1001; My font's encoding
_0000 0
Eth 1
eth 2
Lslash 3
...
A 65
B 66
C 67
...
hungarumlaut 253
ogonek 254
caron 255
```

with lines of type "glyph name, code point". If a code point is unoccupied, FontLab will use an ad hoc glyph name formed by taking an underscore (_) followed by the position in the font table, written as a four-digit decimal number.

For re-encoding, we can use the Reencode method of the Font class. But we must be very careful with this method, which is the equivalent of the re-encoding operation in Font-Lab: it is extremely brutal. If at a given position in the target encoding there is a glyph foo, then whichever glyph is unfortunate enough to appear at that position when the method is executed will be renamed foo. Be careful, therefore—and, again, be careful! After every re-encoding, confirm that the glyphs have not been renamed incorrectly.

Here is some code that we could use to "re-encode" a font. In this example, we rename glyphs that are arranged according to the Macintosh Central European encoding but whose glyph names are incorrect:

```
enc=Encoding()
enc.Load("/Library/Application Support/FontLab/Encoding/T1
         non-Western/mac_ce.enc")
fl[fl.ifont].Reencode(enc)
fl.UpdateFont()
```

The Glyph class

After FontLab and Font comes the third fundamental class of FontLab. We shall see that one other class comes before it in the hierarchy, the class of nodes. Once again, we may use Glyph as a Python list whose elements are nodes (i.e., objects of type Node) and whose number is given by len().

The constructor for the Glyph class is Glyph() for an empty glyph and Glyph(g) (if g is a glyph) to create a copy of g.

The Glyph class is extremely rich, which is no surprise in view of the amount of information that appears in the glyph window. Here are its most important attributes:

- index, the glyph's index (which cannot be changed).

- name, the glyph's name.

- unicode, the corresponding Unicode character.

- width and height, the glyph's width and height.

- bounding_box, the glyph's bounding box, given in the form of a Rect (rectangle) object. It is better to use the GetBoundingRect() method because then the bounding box is actually calculated; otherwise, it is simply read from the font file.

- number_of_contours, the number of contours for the current glyph.

- kerning returns a list of KerningPair objects: all the kerning pairs whose first glyph is the current glyph.

- hguides and vguides, the glyph's horizontal and vertical guidelines—these are lists of objects of type Guide.

- mark, which is nonzero if the glyph is marked with a special color. The possible values for the colors range from 1 to 255 and cover the entire spectrum. We invite the reader to find a font with at least 256 glyphs indexed from 0 to 255 (add some if necessary) and write:

```
for i in range(255):
    fl[fl.ifont][i].mark=i
fl.UpdateFont()
```

The beautiful rainbow that FontLab offers us will then become visible.

And several methods:

- Assign(*g*) replaces the current glyph with *g*. Thus we can create a fresh glyph with g=Glyph(), draw in it, and, finally, replace the current glyph with *g*: fl[fl.ifont][fl.iglyph].Assign(g). Do not forget to copy its set-width as well!

- Add(*n*) appends the node *n* to the contour. The same method can be used to add all the contours of a glyph to a given glyph: g1.Add(g2) adds the contours of g2 to g1.

- Insert(*n*, *i*) inserts node *n* in the *i*th position of the contour. We can also insert a glyph at a given position on the current contour, which may have very strange consequences that may remind us of the human bodies fused to the metal of the warship in that incredible B-flick called *The Philadelphia Experiment*.

- Delete(*i*,*j*) deletes the nodes between the *i*th and *j*th positions.[13]

- Shift(Point(*x*,*y*)) moves the glyph by a coordinate vector (*x*,*y*).

- Scale(Point(*x*,*y*),Point(*cx*,*cy*)) scales the glyph according to the horizontal *x* and vertical *y* factors. Scaling is performed using the point (*cx*,*cy*) as the center.

- isAnySelected() returns True if at least one node is selected, Selection() returns the list of selected nodes, and SelectedCount() returns their number.

- SelectAll() (and UnselectAll()) selects (unselects) all the nodes.

- InvertSelection() selects the unselected nodes and unselects the selected nodes.

- SelectRect(*r*) (and UnselectRect(*r*)), where *r* is an object of type Rect, selects (unselects) all the nodes that fall within the rectangle *r*.

- RemoveOverlap() joins the overlapping contours—a very useful feature when we add an appendage to a glyph, such as the cedilla under the 'c'.

- Badd(*g*), Bsubtract(*g*), Bintersect(*g*): the logical addition, subtraction, and intersection between the current glyph and glyph *g*.

---

[13] Warning: This is a Python list operation, so counting begins at 0; the nodes, however, start with 1—thus there will be a difference of 1.

- GetContourNumbers() returns the number of contours in the glyph.

- GetContourBegin(*i*), GetContourLength(*i*), SelectContour(*i*), DeleteContour(*i*), isContourClockwise(*i*), ReverseContour(*i*): these commands return the first node or the number of nodes in the *i*th contour or select it, delete it, tell us whether it is oriented clockwise, or reverse its direction.

- FindContour(*n*) returns the index of the contour containing node *n*.

- JoinAll() attempts to join all the open contours (some of which are close enough to show that they were meant to be connected: a sort of civil union for nodes).

- SaveEPS(*filename*) and LoadEPS(*filename*) save the glyph as an EPS file or read an EPS file for inclusion as a glyph, respectively.

These methods are useful, intelligent, and logical. For those who like strong sensations there are several other methods, corresponding to the various effects:

- Rotate3D, Extrude3D, Shadow, College, Gradient, and Warp produce the effects of the same name.

- Distance(*x,y,a*), a method that creates a parallel contour offset by (*x,y*) (inside if *x* and *y* are positive, outside if they are negative). This method may prove useful in very many cases, whether to make a glyph slightly bolder or to create a contour, etc. There can be side effects for some nodes: check the result carefully!

Here is an example of making a glyph bolder (by 30 units):

```
g=Glyph()
g=fl[fl.ifont][fl.iglyph]
g.Distance(-,-,1)
fl.UpdateFont()
```

And here is an example of creating a contour (with a thickness of 10 units):

```
g=Glyph()
g=fl[fl.ifont][fl.iglyph]
g1=Glyph(g)
g.Distance(-, -, 1)
g.Bsubtract(g1)
fl.UpdateFont()
```

This is what we did: We created an instance g1 of a glyph and made it a copy of g. Next, we made g bolder by 10 units and substracted from it the glyph g1 (which thus became smaller than g). That left a contour of thickness 10.

- Interpolate(*pairs*), where "pairs" refers to any number of pairs (*i,p*), in which *i* is the index of a node and *p* is a Point object. For example, we can write:

```
g=Glyph()
g=fl[fl.ifont][fl.iglyph]
p1=Point(943,-)
p2=Point(743,-)
g.Interpolate(((33,p1),(8,p2)))
fl.UpdateFont()
```

The result of this method is as follows. The nodes that we have specified by the indices *i* are moved in order to obtain the corresponding points *p*. *All* the other points of the glyph are interpolated as a result. Interpolation is done as follows: the points that lie between two "reference" points are interpolated linearly, and those that lie outside those reference points (before the former and after the latter) are moved by the same amount as the nearest reference point.

The Point, Rect, and KerningPair classes

These are very simple utilitarian classes:

Point represents a point on the plane. The possible constructors are Point() (an instance with zero coordinates), Point(*p*) (the same coordinates as *p*), and Point(*x,y*) (coordinates *x* and *y*). The attributes are x (abscissa) and y (ordinate). The methods: Add(*p*), vector addition; Sub(*p*), vector subtraction; Mul(*s*), multiplication by the scalar *s*.

Rect represents a rectangle. The possible constructors are Rect() (all the coordinates are zero), Rect(*p*) (where *p* is a Point object: the rectangle runs from (0,0) to *p*), Rect(*r*) (where *r* is a Rectangle object: a copy of *r*), Rect(*p1,p2*) (the rectangle between *p1* and *p2*), Rect(*x1,y1,x2,y2*) (the rectangle between points 1 and 2).

The attributes are ll (lower left point), ur (upper right point), x and y (the coordinates of ll), width and height (the width and the height of the rectangle).

The methods are Shift(*x,y*) (translation), Resize(*width,height*) (new dimensions), Include(*r*) or Include(*p*) (redimension so that the rectangle *r* or the point *p* is included), Check(*r*) (check whether *r* lies within the rectangle or crosses it), Check(*p*) (check whether the point *p* lies within the rectangle).

We can, for example, replace a glyph with the rectangle that represents its bounding box, as follows:

```
g=Glyph()
g=fl[fl.ifont][fl.iglyph]
r=Rect(g.GetBoundingRect())
g.Clear()
n=Node(nMOVE,r.ll)
g.Add(n)
n=Node(nLINE,Point(r.x,r.y+r.height))
g.Add(n)
n=Node(nLINE,r.ur)
g.Add(n)
```

```
n=Node(nLINE,Point(r.x+r.width,r.y))
g.Add(n)
n=Node(nLINE,r.ll)
g.JoinAll()
g1=Glyph(g)
g.Distance(-,-,1)
g1.Distance(15,15,1)
g.Bsubtract(g1)
fl.UpdateFont()
```

where we are getting a bit ahead of ourselves by using the Node class.

Now we jump to a new subject: KerningPair represents a kerning pair. The possible constructors are KerningPair() (an empty pair), KerningPair(k) (a copy of pair k), KerningPair(i) (kerning, set to a zero value, with the glyph whose index is i), KerningPair(i,v) (paired with glyph i, the kerning value set to v). Its attributes are key (the index of the glyph to the right) and value (the value of the kerning pair).

Thus to obtain a list of all the kerning pairs for which the glyph at the left is A (assuming that the index of A in this font is 36), we can write:

```
g=Glyph()
f=fl[fl.ifont]
g=f[36]
for i in range(len(g.kerning)):
    print f[g.kerning[i].key].name+" : "+str(g.kerning[i].value)
```

A few words of explanation: g.kerning is a Python list, and therefore len() yields its length. The expression g.kerning[i].key returns the index of the glyph at the left (despite its name, *key*, which gives the impression that we are obtaining the glyph's name). To obtain the glyph's name, we must go through the glyph object and request its name attribute: f[g.kerning[i].key].name. Finally, since g.kerning[i].value is a number, we must convert it to a string in order to concatenate it to our output string; we do so here with the function str().

The Node class

A glyph contour is made of *nodes*. This class could have been the smallest in the FontLab architecture; it is not, however, as below it there is another class, Point, representing a point on the plane. But what is a *node*, if not a *point*? Indeed, this class is simple, having few attributes or methods; but, unlike the classes Font and Glyph, which are as clear as a bell, this one can only be understood if we exercise our gray matter a little.

There are two complementary ways to classify nodes: by their *type* (straight line? curved segment?) and by their *alignment* (smooth? sharp?). Intuitively we can imagine a node as the starting point of a Bézier curve (which, since the curve is closed, is also necessarily the ending point of another curve). FontLab's vision of the concept of a node is different: to FontLab, a node is the ending point of a Bézier curve *and of the preceding curve as well.*

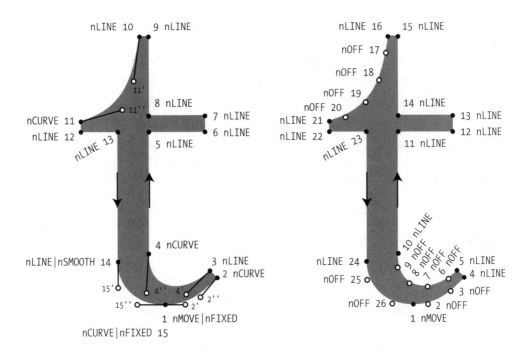

Figure 12-11: Contours in PostScript (left) and TrueType (right). The control points are represented by white dots. In TrueType, they are considered to be nodes in their own right; in PostScript, they are part of the data for the node that follows, and so control points 4' and 4" "belong" to node 4.

The situation varies according to the type of Bézier curve. If quadratic curves are used (as in TrueType), there are three types of nodes:

- Those reached by a move (type nMOVE, typically used for the first node of a contour)

- Those reached by a straight line segment (type nLINE)

- And those that are control points (type nOFF, so called because they are off the curve)

Thus we act as if there were nothing but straight line segments in a TrueType contour. And since the issue of alignment does not arise between straight lines (the alignment can be smooth only if those lines are parallel, in which event the node is useless), classification by alignment does not apply to TrueType. On the right side of Figure 12-11, we see an example of a TrueType contour with nodes of type nMOVE, nLINE, and nOFF.

If, however, the contours use cubic curves (as in PostScript Type 1), then nOFF nodes will never occur, since the control points are not counted as nodes. Let us examine the left side of Figure 12-11 and consider the Bézier curve formed by points 3 (the starting point), 4' (the first control point), 4" (the second control point), and 4 (the ending point). The last three of these points are regarded as forming a node of type nCURVE. It may seem incongruous that control point 4′, which, after all, "belongs" to point 3, and a priori has nothing to do with point 4, should be *attached to point 4*, so to speak. But that is just how FontLab chooses to structure the data. In the same figure, we see nodes of type nMOVE (the first node of the contour), nCURVE (for the curves), and nLINE (for the straight lines).

Now the classification by alignment type comes into play. Most nodes are of type nSHARP (i.e., they form a sharp angle). These are not explicitly indicated in the figure because we are using flag 0, which therefore applies by default. Node 14 is smooth (nSMOOTH), which means that the tangents at the two sides of this point have the same slope and that there is only one line tangent to the curve at this point. Nodes 15 and 1 (which correspond, in fact, to the same point) are of alignment type nFIXED. This type of alignment is a variant of nSMOOTH. The difference is not visible on the contour; it is more of an ergonomic nature. When we modify the curve in question by sliding the cursor of the mouse over it (not by moving its control points), the tangents to the control points can change their slope if the node is of type nSHARP or nSMOOTH; if, however, the node is nFIXED, the tangents will not change direction.

To conclude this excessively long but, alas, indispensable description of node types, let us point out that the contour in the figure reveals a weakness in the letter's design: node 4 should also be nSMOOTH, just like node 14. This peculiarity of the design is, no doubt, accidental.

Let us return to the Node() class. It has three possible constructors: Node() creates a fresh node, Node(*n*) copies another node, and Node(*t,p*) creates a node of type *t* whose point (on the curve) is *p*.

The attributes of Node are:

- type, the type (nMOVE, nLINE, nCURVE, or nOFF)

- alignment, the type of alignment (nSHARP, nSMOOTH, nFIXED)

- selected, boolean True if the node is selected

- point, the ending point (a Point object) of the Bézier curve

- points, a Python list containing the three points that make up a node of type nCURVE: the ending point of the Bézier curve and the first and second control points

- x and y: the coordinates of the point attribute

Thus to create a node n of type nCURVE with ending point p1 and control points p2 and p3, we can write:

```
n=Node(nCURVE,p1)
n.points=(p1,p2,p3)
```

To indicate the alignment type, we have the choice between a binary OR at the time of construction or the use of the alignment attribute. For instance:

```
n=Node(nCURVE|nSMOOTH,p1)
```

is equivalent to

```
n=Node(nCURVE,p1)
n.alignment=nSMOOTH
```

The methods of the Node class are dedicated to the Multiple Master fonts, with one exception: Shift(*p*) will move all the points in the node by an amount equal to the coordinates of point *p*.

Here is an example of the use of nodes. Let us take the letter 'Z' from the font *Monotype Old Style*. To obtain a list of all the nodes and their points, we need only write:

```
g=Glyph(fl[fl.ifont][fl.iglyph])
for i in range(len(g)):
    print i, g[i], g[i].points
```

The result is:

```
0 <Node: type=0x411, x=519, y=0> [<Point: x=519, y=0, active refernce>]
1 <Node: type=0x401, x=594, y=208> [<Point: x=594, y=208, active refernce>]
2 <Node: type=0x401, x=564, y=208> [<Point: x=564, y=208, active refernce>]
3 <Node: type=0x1423, x=493, y=108> [<Point: x=493, y=108, active refernce>,
<Point: x=536, y=154, active refernce>, <Point: x=523, y=136, active refernce>]
...
12 <Node: type=0x401, x=451, y=647> [<Point: x=451, y=647, active refernce>]
13 <Node: type=0x401, x=18, y=17> [<Point: x=18, y=17, active refernce>]
14 <Node: type=0x401, x=18, y=0> [<Point: x=18, y=0, active refernce>]
15 <Node: type=0x401, x=519, y=0> [<Point: x=519, y=0, active refernce>]
```

To draw this letter through pure programming, we need only take its coordinates and write:

```
g=Glyph()
g.Add(Node(0x11,Point(519, 0)))
g.Add(Node(0x1,Point(594, 208)))
g.Add(Node(0x1,Point(564, 208)))
n=Node(0x1023,Point(493, 108))
n.points=(Point(493, 108),Point(536, 154),Point(523, 136))
g.Add(n)
n=Node(0x1023,Point(283, 30))
n.points=(Point(283, 30),Point(436, 56),Point(364, 30))
g.Add(n)
g.Add(Node(0x1,Point(139, 30)))
g.Add(Node(0x1,Point(582, 675)))
g.Add(Node(0x1,Point(122, 675)))
```

```
g.Add(Node(0x1,Point(58, 488)))
g.Add(Node(0x1,Point(84, 488)))
n=Node(0x1023,Point(155, 581))
n.points=(Point(155, 581),Point(114, 539),Point(128, 557))
g.Add(n)
n=Node(0x1023,Point(360, 647))
n.points=(Point(360, 647),Point(208, 626),Point(272, 647))
g.Add(n)
g.Add(Node(0x1,Point(451, 647)))
g.Add(Node(0x1,Point(18, 17)))
g.Add(Node(0x1,Point(18, 0)))
g.Add(Node(0x1,Point(519, 0)))
g.JoinAll()
g.width=605
g.name="Z"
g.unicode=int("005A",16)
fl[fl.ifont][fl.iglyph].Assign(g)
fl.UpdateGlyph()
```

Note that here, rather than using the constants nLINE etc., we have given the explicit numeric values of the types and the alignments. We close the contour with g.JoinAll().

FontForge

Aside from the visual appearance of its interface, which lacks the splendor of that of Font-Lab, FontForge (formerly named PfaEdit) is *extraordinary* software! It includes a large portion of FontLab's functionality, a few features of its own (a debugger for TrueType instructions, an editor for OpenType tables, and even an editor for AAT tables), the ability to save fonts with more than 65,536 glyphs, even in CID format—and all that for the low price of zero dollars. Thus it is a *great* free software package, and, unlike collective free-software projects such as *Emacs*, *Mozilla*, *Gimp*, etc., FontForge was developed entirely by a single person: a Californian by the name of George Williams.

In addition, being free of charge, FontForge can also be localized as much as one wishes. There are already French, German, Italian, Spanish, Russian, Vietnamese, and Japanese versions.

FontForge runs under Unix/X Window. Not to worry if you use Mac OS X or Windows. Under Mac OS X you need only install *X11* first; it has been supplied with the system since version 10.3. Under Windows, you must install *CygWin* [301, p. 10]. The procedure is duly explained on FontForge's Web site [352].

As with all free software, one can compile FontForge oneself. Nonetheless, if one is not a seasoned programmer, compiling the software will entail a small risk: a problem may arise if the system's configuration is slightly more recent than that of the initial developer. And if a problem arises, one is truly stuck. Furthermore, compiling FontForge requires a number of libraries of external subroutines that one must download oneself from their respective Web sites and *place in the right locations.* Again, the versions of the libraries used by the developer must be compatible with the ones that the user has downloaded.

Finally, if one is on a widely used Unix platform (Linux, Mac OS X, Cygwin), it is easier to obtain a pre-built binary for one's system. Installation is completed in a trice, and any possible annoyances related to programming are thus avoided.

By default, FontForge's windows are of a gray color as sad as the image that Michel Villandry painted of the French city of Brest: "... things are swallowed up in the gray background as if every-thing were hiding behind everything else" [340]. While we may not be able to do anything about Brest, we can change the background of FontForge to a brighter color. To obtain, for example, a pretty, creamy white, perform the following operation:

- If it does not already exist, create the file .Xdefaults in the login directory (execute cd ~ to go there).

- Add to the file the following line (or modify it, as the case may be):

  Gdraw.Background: #ffffcc

  where #ffffcc is a creamy hue of white expressed as an RGB (red, green, blue) triplet.

- Finally, run:

  xrdb ~/.Xdefaults

  to update the X resource database.

- Add this last operation to the file .bashrc or to any other Unix script that sets up the user's environment.

To launch FontForge, type fontforge & on the command line. A file-opening window appears, inviting us to open a font file on the disk or to create a new font by clicking on **New**. Warning: unlike most applications, FontForge has no "generic window". If at startup time we do not open any font (whether pre-existing or new), the application will terminate.

The Font-Table Window

Let us select a font through the opening dialog box. The *font-table window* opens, which also contains the various menus of FontForge:

The font-table window shows the font's glyphs within boxes whose size we can specify (it may range from 24 to 96 pixels) through the View window. In each box, and above each glyph, is displayed the corresponding Unicode character or a red question mark if the glyph does not correspond to any Unicode character. Using View>Label glyph by, we can choose glyph cells to be labeled by Unicode codepoint or by PostScript name or position in the imported encoding. When a cell is selected, a certain set of data is displayed under the menu bar: the glyph's index in the font (in decimal and hexadecimal), the hexadecimal code of the corresponding Unicode character, the PostScript name of the glyph, and the name of the Unicode table in which we are working.

We can categorize the glyph boxes by coloring them. To do so, we select a box and choose the color on the pull-down menu Element>Glyph Info>Comment>Color. We also have the option of adding comments on the glyph. The comments and the color are stored in a "private" table—a TrueType table that is recognized only by FontForge.

Opening/Saving a Font

We can open fonts in the formats PFA (whence the former name of this software), PFB, Type 42, PostScript CID, GSF (the vector font format of the software *ghostscript*), True-Type/OpenType and TTC (in this case, an opening window asks us which of these we wish to open from among the fonts in the collection), SVG,[14] IK (the font format of the *Ikarus* system of Peter Karow), and a few bitmap formats: FON, FNT, BDF. A font can be compressed in .Z or .gz format; FontForge will uncompress it before opening it.

Faced with this impressive choice of font formats, we may well ask ourselves which formats FontForge *cannot* open. Very few, in fact. In the version of January 20, 2004, the only formats that FontForge could not yet open were certain exotic formats that are of no interest to anyone anymore, such as the FON vector format (for which no one, not even Microsoft, seems to have the specifications), Intellifont, Speedfont, and PFR.

FontForge's native font format is SFD (for "Spline Font Database"). We can, of course, open SFD files and also save them (with File>Save or File>Save as).

To generate fonts in formats other than SFD, we use File>Generate Fonts, which opens the font-generation dialog box shown at the side.

We are given the choice of PostScript (single PFB or multiple PFB, PFA, Type 3, Type 0, Multiple Master, CID, CFF, CFF CID), TrueType (possibly with OpenType or AAT tables), OpenType/CFF or OpenType/CID, and SVG. The choice "PS Type 1 (Multiple)" means that if the font contains more than 256 glyphs, it will be broken into pieces with 256 glyphs (or fewer) and that we will end up with as many Type 1 fonts. The choice "CFF (Bare)" means that the raw CFF data will be placed in a file without being enveloped in a TrueType structure.

---

[14] To open fonts in SVG format, it is necessary to ensure in advance that the *libxml2* library of subroutines has been installed on the system.

The **Options** button will open a small window in which we may choose the auxiliary files to generate (AFM, PFM, TFM/ENC for PostScript fonts) and certain options pertaining to TrueType fonts: include instructions? include PostScript glyph names in the post table? include Apple or OpenType advanced typographic tables? include a special FontForge table that may contain comments and choices of colors for the boxes?

There is a slight problem on Mac OS 9: *X Window* under Mac OS X does not have access to the resource part of Mac OS 9 files. But the data for all Mac OS 9 font formats have always been stored in the resource section. In order to create resources, FontForge offers no other solution than to create *MacBinary* files, which the user may then convert to the Macintosh's data/resources file format.

To keep users from having to perform these manipulations, Mac OS X introduced the dfont font format, a "flattened" format in which the resource section immediately follows the data section. FontForge, of course, can read and write dfont files.

Accordingly, if a Macintosh font is destined to be used only under Mac OS X, we will use the dfont format, or even just TTF or OTF files. If, however, it is also meant for use under Mac OS 9, we have no choice but to go through the *MacBinary* format.

To generate Mac OS 9 font families, we use **File>Generate Mac Family**. But to have access to this feature, we must have previously opened other fonts that will be the members of this new family. FontForge will present, in the font-family generation window, the potential members of the family; all that we have to do is to select them and choose the Macintosh style (roman, italic, bold, bold italic) for each of them.

The General-Information Window

We open this window through the menu **Element>Font Info**. The window contains 14 tabs, which often take us to other windows, subwindows, etc. Here are these 14 tabs:

- **Names**: in this tab, we can enter the different names of the font (the PostScript name, family name, "long" name) as well as its weight, version, and copyright notice.

- **General**, where we can enter a number of numerical parameters such as the height of the ascenders, the depth of the descenders, the number of units per em, the slope, the parameters related to underlining, the unique identifier (UID) and the extended unique identifier (XUID), the presence or lack of vertical metrics in the font, and, finally, whether the Bézier curves in the font are cubic or quadratic.

- **PS UID**, where we enter the Unique Identfier of a PostScript font.

- **PS Private Dictionary**, where we can view and modify the private parameters of the PostScript Type 1 format: BlueValues and OtherBlues, StdHW and StdVW, BlueScale, BlueShift, BlueFuzz, and ForceBold. The first four can take several values each, for overshoot and the relevant thicknesses of horizontal and vertical strokes. For these four parameters, FontForge displays a histogram with the values actually obtained by these parameters in the font. Thus we can designate values for these parameters with the benefit of a global view of the font.

- **OS/2.** In this window, we can view and modify the parameters specific to the True-Type tables: classes for weight and set-width (in the OS/2 table), authorization to incorporate the font in a document (ditto), leading (hhea table), vertical leading (vhea table), the 10 parameters of the Panose classification (see Chapter 11), for which we can set the values not as numbers but through the use of the names given in the classification, etc.

- **TTF Names:** we can enter each of the 18 strings in the name table in about a hundred combinations of languages and encodings.

- **TeX** (actually written in Greek). FontForge can produce TEX font-metric files (TFM), but to do so it needs a certain amount of information: the optical size, the slope, the ideal space between words, the amount of stretching and shrinking allowed at the current set-width, the height of the lowercase letters, and the extra space used in English typography at the end of a sentence. By selecting "TeX Math" or "TeX Math Ext", we gain access to the advanced parameters for fonts of mathematical symbols and extensible mathematical symbols.

- The other tabs are used to edit the advanced typographic features of fonts. We shall examine them in the chapter on enriching fonts.

The Glyph Window

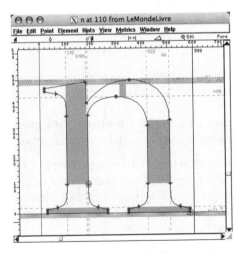

Double-clicking on a glyph in the font-table window opens the glyph for editing in a glyph window. Together with this window, FontForge offers two palettes: the first, called **Tools**,[15] contains some 18 buttons representing all the graphical tools; the second, **Layers**, allows for the selection of the various types of information to display in the glyph window.

The most important layer of data is, of course, the glyph's contour, and there are three imaginary planes on which we can do our work: the "foreground", which will be used when we generate a font; the "background", which contains auxiliary guidelines that will be ignored when the font is generated; and the "guide", which contains the guidelines and other supporting material common to the backgrounds of all the glyphs. The three buttons just to the side of **Fore**, **Back**, and **Guide** in the **Layers** palette allow us to switch from one working plane to another. The buttons on the left side of the window make the appropriate plane visible. (The active plane is always visible.) The other buttons at the bottom pertain to hints and OpenType properties, with the exception of the last two (**HMetrics** and **VMetrics**), which are used to display or hide the horizontal and vertical baseline and set-width.

---

[15] But its name cannot be read without widening the window.

When the cursor is moved onto the working plane, its coordinates (in the coordinate system of the glyphs) are displayed at the upper left of the window, on the menu bar.

To draw a curve, just as in any other vector-design or font-design software, we use the ⬚ tool. When we click on a point, we create a new node for the curve; by dragging the mouse, we move the control point; finally, when we release the mouse button, we fix the position of the control point, and we can proceed to another point. If, after clicking on a point on the plane, we release the mouse button without moving the mouse, the point in question will be connected to the preceding points by a straight line segment, not by a Bézier curve.

To move a contour, we must first select all its nodes. We can select them one by one or, by double-clicking anywhere along the contour, all at the same time. Then we can move the contour with the mouse—but *beware!* We must take care to *"grab" it by a node*. If we try to pick up a contour by clicking on an intermediate point between two nodes, we will merely alter the Bézier curve in question, and the rest of the contour will not even budge.

There is another way to draw curves in FontForge, one that is noticeably different from that of FontStudio, FontLab, or even Illustrator: in these other software systems, we obtain a point by clicking on a certain location, and by dragging the mouse (while keeping the button depressed) we change the curve's control point; here, however, when we drag the mouse, the point to be created moves as well—it only becomes definitively set when we release the mouse button. Which also means that we cannot modify the control points at the time that we create the curve.

More precisely, there are three buttons that are used to create three types of points: ⬚ produces a smooth point (having a Bézier curve on each side), ⬚ produces a "tangent" point (with a smooth Bézier curve on the side leading in and a straight line on the other side), and ⬚ produces a vertex of a polygonal line. Thus the best way to trace a new path is to anticipate, every time, *both* the position of the new point *and* its type, to choose the appropriate tool from the *Tools* palette, and to click on the right location, possibly also dragging the mouse to get the position just right—without worrying about the control points. Afterwards, one can change to the "move" tool ⬚ and easily move both the nodes of the curve and the control points. The reader who wishes to use these tools should get used to the fact that the first curve drawn will not be good; it is produced just to break ground—and the precise positioning of the control points is what will yield the desired contour for the glyph.

Note that for changing the type of a point (among "smooth", "sharp", and "tangent"), one uses the **Point** menu in the glyph window.

To copy and paste paths, one uses the Edit menu, as in any other software. But this menu offers several other very useful entries: **Edit>Copy Reference** allows us to copy onto the clipboard not the contour itself but a reference to the contour so as to create composite glyphs by pasting references of this type; **Edit>Copy Width** allows us to copy onto the clipboard the set-width of another glyph; **Element>Simplify** allows us to simplify a path by eliminating the selected nodes—the tangents at the endpoints will remain unchanged; finally, Edit>Copy Fg to Bg copies the contents of the working plane onto the background.

The knife tool ⬛ is also slightly different from its analogue in FontStudio or FontLab. Nothing happens when we click on a contour; however, if we click outside a curve and drag the mouse, we obtain a "cut line". This is the line that will cut the curve. Needless to say, this operation is quite close to the use of our kitchen knives or the craft knife of the model builder.

The tool ⬛ is used to measure distances between two points. Click on the starting point and drag the mouse. FontForge will then display, in real time, the distance between the two points, the horizontal and vertical projections of the vector thus obtained, and its slope.

The buttons ⬛, ⬛, ⬛, and ⬛ are used for scaling, reflection, rotation, or slanting of the selected parts of a contour. These operations are performed strictly by eye; one may use the transformation tool Element>Transformations>Transform for more precision.

The two tools ⬛ and ⬛ allow for the drawing of predefined curves: rectangles or polygons. When these buttons are clicked, they change shape (⬛ and ⬛); then they will produce ellipses and stars. To draw a rectangle or an ellipse, one may decide whether the pointer will indicate the center of the shape or the upper left corner of its bounding box; to do so, one merely double-clicks on the button in question and registers the choice in the little window that appears. By holding down the shift key, one can obtain a square or a circle. Likewise, by double-clicking on the button for the polygon or the star, one may select the number of vertices.

Finally, the tool ⬛ is mostly a gimmick: it is used for freehand drawing. One may trace any path at all, and it will immediately be converted into Bézier curves. This method is certainly very useful in software for freehand drawing, such as Photoshop or Painter, but the author can see little need for it in the context of font design, especially when one compares the original drawing to the Bézier curves obtained. Double-clicking on the button opens a dialog box that offers the choice of "pen" shapes, à la METAFONT (§F.1.3). In theory it could be used for drawing "calligraphic" letters, but one quickly finds out that a calligrapher never uses a pen as rigid as those of the software; the glyphs obtained thus give an impression of rigidity and artificiality. Note, however, that it is possible to use Wacom pen tablets and associate levels of pressure on the stylus with different widths of pens.

The glyph window comes with several very useful menus. For example, selecting Element>Glyph info opens a little window with information on the glyph, arranged in several tabs. Most of these tabs are for the advanced OpenType properties and will therefore be examined in Chapter 14. The first tab (Unicode) allows us to name the glyph according to its Unicode position or, conversely, to determine the Unicode position associated with a glyph from its name, according to Adobe's conventions for naming glyphs (see page C.3.3).

The menu option Element>Transformations>Transform opens a transformation window that applies to the selected part of the contour. In this window we may select from one to three common transformation(s) (translation, rotation, scaling, reflection, slanting) by setting the desired values.

Other interesting menu options: **Element>Expand stroke** transforms a Bézier curve into a "tube"; thus one can draw the skeleton of a letter and then "puff up" its strokes in order to make an "Egyptian" letter. **Element>Overlap** processes superimposed closed contours in various ways, the most interesting ones being union (**Remove Overlap**) and intersection (**Intersect**). **Element>Simplify** simplifies a contour. **Element> Add extrema** adds nodes to the horizontal and vertical tangent lines of the curves. **Element>Effects** offers four typographically questionable effects (outline, inline, shadow, wireframe).

The option **Element>Align** performs several very practical operations: **Average Points** aligns the points either horizontally or vertically (the direction in which there is the least variation in the coordinates is selected), giving them all an abscissa or an ordinate equal to the average of the original abscissas or ordinates. **Space points** is more complex: FontForge chooses three points a, b, c and, considering two of the points (for example, a and b) to be fixed, moves c so that it falls on the perpendicular bisector of the segment ab. Then c will be moved in parallel to ab. What is less clear is how FontForge selects the fixed points and the point to be moved. Finally, **Make Parallel** applies only to straight lines; it makes them parallel to one another by moving the last node selected.

The options **Element>Clockwise**, **Element>Counter Clockwise**, and **Element> Correct direction** allow the direction of Bézier curves on a contour to be changed. One can confirm that the direction has been set correctly by having the contour filled in (**View>Fill**); however, it is important not to remain in "filled-in contour" mode, as the filling of the contour is not always refreshed correctly.

The Metrics Window

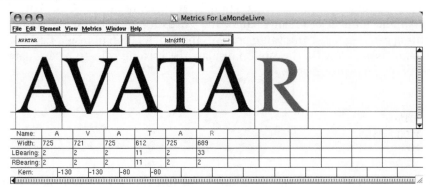

The metrics window (**Windows>New Metrics Windows**) is used to establish and test the ways in which glyphs interact with one another: we can enter a string of glyphs and check their set-widths and their kerning. The keyboard can be used to enter a string of glyphs in the little input area at the upper left. If a glyph cannot be entered from the keyboard, it can still be dragged in from the font window in the area for previewing glyphs. Clicking on a cell in the rows **Width** (set-width), **LBearing** (left-hand side bearing), **RBearing** (right-hand side bearing) at the bottom of the window causes the corresponding glyph to be selected. Once a glyph has been selected, we can make simple substitutions (look-up of OpenType Type 1 substitutions) through **View>Substitutions**, where we find a list of all the look-up operations of this kind that apply to the glyph.

By clicking on a given glyph, we can use the mouse to modify its left-hand side bearing (with the red cursor containing an 'L'), its right-hand side bearing (with the red cursor containing an 'R'), or its kerning with the preceding glyph (red cursor containing a 'K').

To center a glyph in its box, we use **Metrics>Center in Width**. The option **Metrics> Thirds in Width** is similar but yields a right-hand side bearing that is twice the size of the left-hand side bearing.

The metrics window in itself is quite simple, but its effect is only local: it allows for the rather precise management of the metrics of certain individual glyphs. We can also manage metrics in a global fashion. That is done through the **Metrics** menu, but the options in question are accessible only through the font window (doubtless in order to force their effect to be *global*).

There we find two interesting options: **Metrics>Auto Width** and **Metrics>Auto Kern**. The first of these rearranges the set-widths. More precisely, FontForge will arrange side by side the glyphs that we wish to examine and will also modify their left and right side bearings if necessary. The **Spacing** parameter gives an order of magnitude for the distance that the user considers optimal. According to George Williams's description [352], the value of this parameter expresses the distance between two sans serif 'I' glyphs. The default value of the parameter is none other than the width of the contour for the glyph 'n'.

The option **Metrics>Auto Kern** will attempt to kern the glyphs that we have specified, by taking three parameters into consideration: **Spacing** (as in **Auto width**), **Total Kerns** (the maximum number of kerning pairs), and **Threshold** (the threshold below which the kerning pair is ignored; this value prevents the proliferation of insignificant kerning pairs). Unlike **Auto Width**, this option displays the kerning pairs to be evaluated in a text file of the following format:

```
AV
AU+0150
U+0100U+0150
U+1E00V
```

The syntax of this file is very simple: there is one line for each kerning pair, with the glyphs indicated by an ISO Latin-1 character or by the notation U+ABCD, where ABCD is the hexadecimal code for the corresponding Unicode character.

We can alter the set-width of one or more glyphs by using **Metrics>Set Width**. It allows us to replace the set-widths with a fixed width, to apply a scaling factor to them, or to increment them by a fixed amount.

Finally, it is possible to define kerning classes and to have the kerning of a pair of glyphs applied to their respective classes. We shall see how in Chapter 14, when we discuss the enrichment of fonts with advanced typographic features (OpenType or AAT).

What About Vertical Typesetting?

Although this possibility is little used outside the East Asian scripts, both TrueType and PostScript Type 1 allow us to set type vertically by supplying *vertical* metrics (set-widths and kerning pairs). Vertical typesetting turns out to be a real headache for the programmer: since screens and graphical interfaces were designed for horizontal writing, how can we switch efficiently to the vertical mode?

It comes as no surprise that FontLab and even *AsiaFont Studio*, its special "East Asian" version, turn evasive when the issue of vertical fonts comes up. In fact, FontForge is the only software today that takes on the challenge of vertical metrics.

For a PostScript font, vertical metrics are vertical displacement vectors and vertical kerning pairs in AFM files (see §C.3.7). In an OpenType font, vertical set-widths are stored in the vmtx table (see §D.8.6), and vertical kerning pairs are stored in a subtable of the kern table, all of whose coverage flags have their first bit cleared (see §D.8.4).

In FontForge, the vertical mode is "enabled" by checking **Element>Font Info>General>Has Vertical Metrics**. Pressing this button enables the **Vertical Origin** field, which appears immediately below: it contains the height of the *vertical* origin relative to the *horizontal* baseline. This value may be changed at any time; it is used to offset the glyphs vertically within their vertical set-widths (which, by default, are equal to the sum of the Ascent and Descent parameters in the hhea table).

As for the horizontal placement of the vertical origin, it is automatically set to a distance from the horizontal origin that is equal to half of the vertical set-width. These choices are not arbitrary: indeed, they are the optimal choices for ideographic characters, whose set-widths (both horizontal and vertical) are fixed and whose vertical baseline runs through the (horizontal) center of the glyphs.

For modifying a font's vertical metrics, the following features are at our disposal: **Metrics>Set Vertical Advance** (like **Metrics> Set Width** for the horizontal case) offers global modifications through the application of a given increment or scaling factor; **Metrics>VKern By Classes** adopts the system of kerning-pair classes; **Metrics>VKern From HKern** is useful primarily for vertical typesetting simulated by horizontally setting glyphs rotated 90 degrees: for each horizontal kerning pair, we obtain a vertical kerning pain between the rotated glyphs, calculated through a substitution look-up of the vert or vrt2 property.

To generate the set-widths and vertical kerning for the glyphs, we can also use the metrics window. To switch from horizontal to vertical mode, we need only select View>Vertical in this window; then the string of glyphs is displayed vertically, and we can move them with the mouse, as usual.

CID Fonts

One other technique is used primarily for the ideographic languages. The CID fonts (see §C.7 for a technical description) are Adobe's work-around to the 256-code-point limit on the size of a PostScript font encoding. The idea is as follows: since, on the one hand, we need an arbitrarily large number of ideographic glyphs and, on the other, Unicode's unification of the ideographic languages is disastrous for typesetting (as the variants of ideographs may be distinct characters in one language and glyphs for a single character in another), Adobe had the ingenious idea of short-circuiting Unicode and offering "catalogs of glyphs" that are specific to each ideographic language, and even to each encoding. These catalogs are called *character collections* (although they contain glyphs and not characters), and Adobe offers one for Japanese[16] (Japan1, covering the JIS X 0201-1997, JIS X 0208-1990, JIS X 0212-1990, and JIS X 0213-2004 encodings), two for Chinese (GB1 for simplified, and CNS1 for traditional), one for Korean (Korea1), and one—that has been in preparation for several years—for the old Vietnamese script.

What is interesting is that the character collections are periodically updated and, moreover, the updates are done so as to ensure upward compatibility. Thus Adobe adds new glyphs while preserving the old ones. For example, the Japanese character collection Japan1 is already at version 6 (the seventh version [16], as counting begins at zero; it contains 23,058 glyphs!), and those for simplified Chinese and traditional Chinese are at version 4 (29,057 and 18,964 glyphs, respectively).

The glyphs of a CID font are contained in a file called *CIDFont*. We use it by means of a font encoding called *CMap* (not to be confused with the cmap table of TrueType fonts) that is found in another file. For instance, the same font may be used with any encoding, and the same encoding can apply to any font (in the same character collection). A CID font can also be contained within an OpenType structure; in that case, the *CIDFont* data will be stored in a CFF table.

The reason that we have mentioned CID here is that FontForge is the only software that can manipulate them.[17]

A CID font is made up of several *subfonts*. This property is used to classify its glyphs: alphabetic ones, dingbats (pictograms), *kana* (the Japanese syllabaries), kanji (ideographs), etc. When opening a CID font, FontForge displays the first of these subfonts in the font window. The others are accessible through the CID menu, where the names of the subfonts appear in the bottom section.

---

[16] Previously there were two character collections for Japanese; they were merged in 2004.

[17] *AsiaFont Studio* (the "East Asian" version of FontLab) can open the subfonts of a PostScript CID font. Both FontLab and its elder brother can open OpenType CID fonts, but only by flattening them—i.e., by discarding their classification into subfonts. Neither software package can save CID fonts—a rather annoying limitation, especially in such expensive software.

This menu has a number of interesting features:

- **CID>Flatten** will "forget" the font's CID structure and convert it into a normal font. For example, we can save the font in PostScript Type 1 or TrueType format.

- **CID>Flatten By CMap** operates in the same way, but the "flattened" font thus obtained will have an encoding drawn from a CMap file. This option requires a file of this sort to be specified. We can obtain one from Adobe [26] or create one ourselves.[18] (See §C.7.2 for a complete description of the CMap files).

- **CID>Insert Font** inserts a new subfont from an external "flattened" font into the CID font.

- **CID>Insert Blank** inserts a new blank subfont that we can then fill in.

- **CID>Remove Font** removes a subfont.

- **CID>CID Font Info** is a variant of **Element>Font Info** with data on the entire CID font rather than on just a single given subfont. For instance, if we wish to enable vertical mode, we must use **CID>CID Font Info>General**.

A glyph in a CID font has the CID number corresponding to its position in the font table. This is the number that appears in red at the beginning of the menu bar when we select the glyph in this table.

The character collection of a CID font cannot be changed. Only at the time when a font is created (when we use **CID>Convert to CID**) can we associate a character collection with the new font.

All in all, FontForge offers a good way to modify existing CID fonts, build new CID fonts, and store them in both the old PostScript format (file *CIDFont*) and an OpenType structure with a CFF glyph description.

Autotracing

Autotracing is the operation of generating a vector contour for a glyph from a bitmap image without any intervention from the user. In this section we shall describe two systems for autotracing fonts. We have placed this section at the end because we are reluctant to discuss this topic at all. Indeed, there are too many fonts of poor quality that were produced through autotracing. We have seen in this chapter how to obtain contours described by precise and elegantly arranged Bézier curves. Autotracing software cannot recognize symmetry, the thickness of equal strokes, or the heights and depths kept consistent throughout a font; in short, the *intelligence* of a good vector design cannot be obtained automatically. And when we speak of "intelligence", we are alluding, of course, to *artificial intelligence*, whose limitations are by now well known.

---

[18] Which does, however, require some patience, since, at least for the ideographic languages, it involves matching up some 20,000 (!) ideographs to positions in the encoding table.

After this introduction intended to discourage the reader from using autotracing software, let us see when we can use such software without doing too much harm:

- When the font is of a "free design", in the sense that there is no calculation hidden behind its proportions, dimensions, etc.

- When the font represents handwriting. Who has never wanted to publish entire books in his own handwriting? In this case, autotracing cannot make any more flaws than the human hand already has, with regard to the precision of the strokes.

- When the image whose contours we wish to autotrace is large and has a high resolution and when the perfection of the curves is not critical. The difficulty in this case is obtaining sufficiently rich images. One case in which it is possible is when the font is in another vector format (such as METAFONT), or when we have printed samples of very high quality and at a large size.

potrace

There are two great free software packages for autotracing: *AutoTrace*, by Martin Weber [344], released in 1998, and *potrace*, by Peter Selinger [316], which was not released until 2001. Both are SourceForge projects, and it is widely acknowledged that the latter is more powerful and that the former supports more file formats for both input and output.

These software packages can perform autotracing on any bitmap images; they have no special features related to fonts.

If we wish to convert a METAFONT font to PostScript Type 1, there are at least two utilities (*mftrace* [279], written in Python, and *T$_E$Xtrace* [326], written in Perl) that take control of the entire process of launching METAFONT, assembling the files, autotracing each glyph, and compiling everything into a PostScript font with correct metrics.

When we are beginning not with a METAFONT font but with a series of images, we can use FontForge. To do so, we first install on our system one of the autotracing packages (*AutoTrace* or *potrace*) and declare it to FontForge (File>Preferences). Next, we must perform the following operations:

1. Import the images in the form of masks (File>Import) into the correct positions in the table. We can do so manually or import an entire batch of images at the same time. To import a batch of images, name the images uniHHHH.png (where HHHH is a four-digit hexadecimal number and the image corresponds to the Unicode character in that position), perform File>Import, and choose Series of images as the file type. Select the first image in the series; the others will be loaded into the boxes corresponding to their Unicode code points.

2. Establish a set-width for each glyph and, if necessary, move the mask relative to the set-width so that it is correctly centered and at the correct height.

3. Select **Element>AutoTrace**. FontForge then invokes AutoTrace or potrace (according to the choice that the user has indicated in **File>Preferences**) and autotraces the mask.

4. Correct the contours, using FontForge's tools for vector design.

Step 2 is the longest, unless ideographs or "typewriter" fonts with a fixed width are being used.

The quality of the autotracing will depend on the values of the parameters. To change a value, select the option **Element>AutoTrace** while holding down the shift key. Then it is possible to enter the command-line options that the user will find explained in detail at the web site of *potrace* (http://potrace.sourceforge.net).

We shall show an example of the result of an operation of this kind in the next section.

ScanFont

ScanFont (version 4) is a program developed by FontLab Ltd. It runs under Windows and Mac OS, *but* under Windows it is stand-alone software, whereas under Mac OS it is distributed as a FontLab plug-in.

Figure 12-12: Separation of glyphs under ScanFont.

The autotracing of a font under ScanFont is a procedure performed in two steps. The first involves separating the glyphs in an image that contains several. The software includes several algorithms to do so and a number of parameters for optimizing the result. If the algorithm places two parts of the same letter in different boxes, we can connect them; conversely, if two letters are inadvertently placed in the same box, we can separate them. And we can also frame the glyphs manually. In Figure 12-12, we see the inside of a glyph-separation window; the result shown was obtained with the default values of the parameters.

Next comes the step of autotracing the individual glyphs. When this operation is initiated, a configuration window opens (Figure 12-13). In this window, we can vary the values of three parameters (trace tolerance, curve fit quality, straightness of angles). What is extremely interesting is that we see the effect of these parameters on the trace *in real*

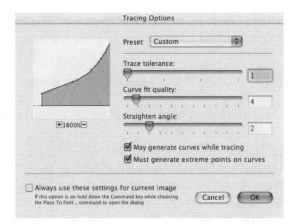

Figure 12-13: Dialog box for the real-time configuration of autotracing under ScanFont.

time. Thus we can rapidly find the ideal values for each font. These values can be stored and used as a set of predefined values.

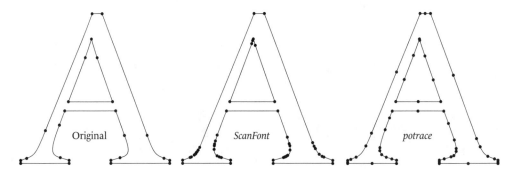

Figure 12-14: Comparing a contour traced by hand and two contours autotraced from the same rendering.

In Figure 12-14, we show the result of autotracing by the two systems described: ScanFont and potrace. Obviously we cannot easily compare two software packages when their results depend a great deal on the choices of values for the parameters. We have therefore taken the default values of the parameters in both cases and autotraced an image of very high quality: the rendering at $3,432 \times 3,300$ pixels of a glyph from a vector font. Note that this image, owing to its size and its "artificial" character, is far better than the best scan of printed text that we will ever be able to produce.

Here are the conclusions that we can draw from these images: At a global level, we cannot see any differences among the three contours. By inspecting the control points, we can tell that ScanFont used fewer points to trace the straight lines but far more to trace the curves. There is an abnormally heavy cluster of points all along the serifs. Likewise,

ScanFont had a few problems with the inside of the apex of the letter 'A'. For its part, potrace added some unneeded points (in the middle of straight line segments, etc.) but used fewer points at the serifs.

We can only advise the reader to try both programs out before undertaking an autotracing project (potrace and AutoTrace are free, and there is a demo version of ScanFont at FontLab's web site) and certainly to repeat the same tests by varying the values of the parameters.

In conclusion, let us compare once again the three versions of the letter 'A' in the figure. Is the original not more elegant than the two letters derived from it? The author is convinced that those who are used to using vector design tools will spend less time vectorizing a letter (by hand, but in an intelligent and methodical way) by following its mask than *correcting* an autotraced contour, however good the tool that produced it.

13

Optimizing a Rasterization

In a world peopled with fonts, we would read in *Genesis*: "for pixels thou art, and unto pixels thou shalt return". Indeed, we often forget that the ultimate goal of all the mathematical constructions that represent our glyph outlines is to produce *images made from pixels*. If we had only one font size and only one resolution for our screens and printers, we would have no need of outlines; the bitmaps would be quite sufficient. Outlines exist only to allow fonts to be adapted to the current situation and produce an adequate bitmap on the fly.

The process of moving from the "vector outline" state to the "bitmap" state is called *rasterization*. It is a crucial process because the final appearance of the text depends on it.

To understand the value of this chapter, we must examine how rasterization is done. Since pixels are—fortunately—equidistant, we can imagine that beneath the geometrically perfect outline of a glyph there is a grid each of whose squares has the size of one pixel. Then rasterization involves filling in some of the squares of this grid to obtain as faithful an approximation to the glyph's outline as possible. Some of the squares—yes, but which ones? Therein lies the problem.

We can adopt a methodical approach: for example, we can say that we shall fill in any pixel whose center lies *inside* the outline (or *on* the outline). This method is very fragile: sometimes a very slight difference in an outline is enough to make the centers of an entire row of pixels suddenly fall within the outline and thus be made black—or, conversely, it may cause them to fall outside the outline and thus be made white. In the example below, five versions of the letter 'H' with slightly different heights have been rasterized using the method of the centers of the pixels.

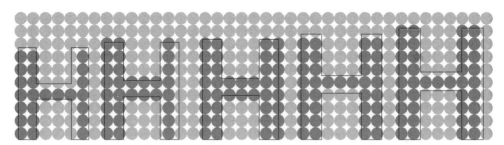

The first two have problems with different thicknesses of strokes. In addition, the cross-bar changes from 1 pixel to 2, and then, in the last two letters, back to 1 pixel again.

Conclusion: Even if the outline is perfect, the rasterization can ruin everything and cause completely unpredictable behavior. We cannot just sit idly by and hope that some poorly rendered glyphs will pass unnoticed. It is well known that as soon as something goes wrong in typography, it will be noticed right away. Besides, it is, after all, unworthy of our fonts: if we have spent hours creating impeccable outlines, we cannot accept poor rasterizations. We have to take action—aggressive action!

Each of the three main font formats (PostScript Type 1, TrueType, METAFONT) offers a different approach to this problem:

- In the case of METAFONT, rasterization—and everything else, for that matter—is controlled through programming. The situation is quite unusual, as the bitmaps are created by METAFONT *before* they are used. Provided that the characteristics of a screen or a printer are known, METAFONT will generate bitmap fonts that are adapted to it in advance. The rasterization will therefore be perfect, but the price to pay for that perfect rasterization is total dependence on a certain kind of display or printing hardware—the kind for which the bitmap fonts were generated. In the day when METAFONT was developed, that constraint posed no problem at all: one would prepare fonts specifically for one's screen and printer. When one switched to a new printer, one would figure out its characteristics somehow and generate new fonts adapted appropriately.

    But this balance fell apart with the advent of the Web: an "electronic document" must be immediately and universally legible and printable. It cannot be restricted to a particular type of output device. METAFONT is therefore incompatible with the Web. We shall describe METAFONT's approach in Appendix F.

- In the case of PostScript Type 1 or OpenType/CFF fonts, the rasterization is optimized through the use of *hints*. Adobe's strategy has been to refrain from stating exactly how rasterization works and to give users nothing more than the possibility of vaguely indicating some of the font's characteristics, in the hope that the rendering engine will see fit to use them. This approach is often decried by programmers but was actually welcomed by font designers, since, in a certain way, it relieved them of the responsability to optimize the rasterization of their fonts. For them it is enough to give a few indications to the black box that is the rendering engine in order to make it "work". And when "it doesn't work", Adobe will say that the designers are to blame for not having supplied the correct hints, the designers will point a finger at Adobe, and, if no other information surfaces, the matter will go no further. But none of that is a serious problem, since PostScript fonts are used mainly in phototypesetting, and hints are quite useless for that purpose because differences of one pixel in the thickness of a stroke are too small for the human eye to detect. We shall give a technical description of hints in Appendix C.

- TrueType fonts use *TrueType instructions*, a programming language akin to assembly language, to define the behavior of rasterization relative to the grid. There is no "black box"; everything is disclosed, explained, exposed. For that reason, TrueType instructions are much more complex than hints. Predictably, TrueType instructions have been ill received by font designers, since their manipulation calls for a great deal of effort and a way of organizing work that differs greatly from the designers' own habits. With the exception of some fonts from big foundries such as Monotype, which were instructed by engineers specialized in instructing fonts, most of the TrueType fonts that we find today are automatically instructed by font-design software—which is a real pity, since much of the potential of instructions remains unexploited. We have devoted all of Appendix E to the technical description of True-Type instructions.

Since the technical descriptions appear in the appendices, we shall focus here on the practical question "How do we place hints, or how do we instruct a font?" And, more precisely, how to do so with tools such as FontLab, FontForge, and *Visual TrueType* (or VTT, a program for instructing TrueType fonts that is distributed free of charge by Microsoft).

PostScript Hints

In this section we shall examine *hinting*, which is the placement of hints in PostScript Type 1 or CFF fonts. In Figure 13-1, the reader can compare the same text in various rasterizations, three of them optimized with hints in different ways and one not optimized at all.

There are two types of PostScript hints: global hints, which affect the entire font, and individual hints, which affect only a single glyph.

Global PostScript Hints

Of the global hints, two are very important: the *alignment zones* (i.e., the *relevant heights* and the *overshoots* that go with them) and the *relevant stroke thicknesses* (see §C.3.4.1– C.3.4.3). Some examples are shown in Figure 13-2. Thus it is necessary to "take inventory" of the alignment zones and the stroke thicknesses that seem relevant: for a Latin font, these are more or less classic; for another font, these must be determined by taking measurements and trying to observe similarities and analogies. We shall see how Font-Lab and FontForge can help us to identify the most relevant values.

Ihr naht euch wieder, schwankende Gestalten,
Die früh sich einst dem trüben Blick gezeigt.
Versuch ich wohl, euch diesmal festzuhalten?
Fühl ich mein Herz noch jenem Wahn geneigt?
Ihr drängt euch zu! Nun gut, so mögt ihr walten,
Wie ihr aus Dunst und Nebel um mich steigt;
Mein Busen fühlt sich jugendlich erschüttert
Vom Zauberhauch, der euren Zug umwittert.

① Versuch ich / Fühl ich mei

② Versuch ich / Fühl ich mei

③ Versuch ich / Fühl ich mei

④ Versuch ich / Fühl ich mei

Figure 13-1: A comparison of various optimizations of the rasterization of a PostScript Type 1 font. The font is Monotype Old Style. Left: as rasterized by freetype with gray levels. Right: without gray levels. ① The font's original hints. ② The font without hints. ③ The hints generated by FontForge. ④ The hints generated by FontLab. The text is from Goethe: "Ye wavering shapes, again ye do enfold me / As erst upon my troubled sight ye stole," etc.

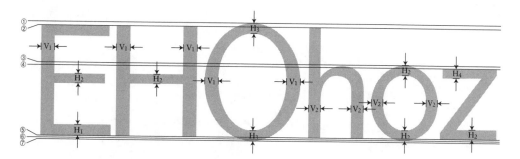

Figure 13-2: Some alignment zones: ②–① *the height of the capitals and the overshoot of the 'O';* ④–③ *the height of the lowercase letters and the overshoot of the 'o';* ⑥–⑤ *the baseline and the overhang of the 'o';* ⑦–⑤ *the baseline again, and the overhang of the 'O'. Some relevant stroke thicknesses:* V_1, *the thickness of the vertical strokes and the curves (at the point where the tangents are vertical) of the capital letters;* V_2, *the same, for the lowercase letters;* H_1, *the thickness of the horizontal strokes of the capitals;* H_2, *the thickness of the 'E' and the 'H', but also of the curves of the 'o';* H_3, *the thickness of the curves of the 'O' where the tangents are horizontal;* H_4, *the thickness of the top part of the 'z'. The font shown here is Computer Modern Sans Serif.*

Let us get a bit more technical: *alignment zones* are pairs of values: a "relevant height" and an "overshoot". They are stored in a PostScript font parameter called BlueValues. When these zones lie completely below the baseline, they are instead stored in another parameter, called OtherBlues. Beyond these parameters, three others of lesser importance also appear in PostScript fonts: BlueScale, BlueShift, and BlueFuzz. We shall describe them in §C.3.4.1. Finally, there is one other boolean parameter, which has the advantage of being easily to understand, even for those who do not know much about how the rasterizing engine goes about using it: ForceBold. This parameter indicates to the rasterizing engine that the font is bold and that the rasterization should be made "heavy" (so that the difference between the font and any possible light version will be immediately evident).

The relevant stroke thicknesses are stored in the following manner: the "most relevant" horizontal stroke thickness is stored in a parameter called StdHW, and its vertical counterpart is stored in StdVW; all other horizontal and vertical stroke thicknesses are stored in two other parameters, StemSnapH and StemSnapV. Note that there can be no more than twelve stroke thicknesses in each direction.

Now, here is how FontLab and FontForge manage global hints.

FontLab and global hints

In FontLab, we enter the following three types of data about global hints under three tabs of the font-information window (File>Font Info):

- *Hinting: alignment zones* (see Figure 13-3 [a]): the two lists *Primary zones* and *Secondary zones* contain the alignment zones for **BlueValues** and **OtherBlues** (the latter lie

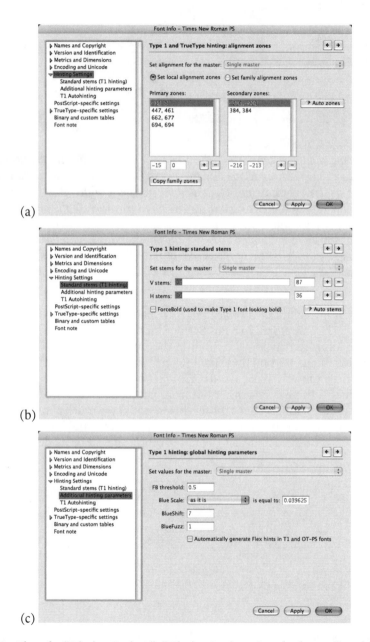

Figure 13-3: The tabs "Hinting Settings", "Hinting Settings: Standard stems", and "Additional hinting parameters".

completely below the baseline). Clicking on the button **Auto zones** causes FontLab to take the measurements and fill in the two lists for us.

- *Hints: standard stems* (see Figure 13-3 [b]): we enter in **V Stems** relevant thicknesses of the vertical stems (the first goes in **StdVW**, the rest go in **StemSnapV**) and, likewise, the thicknesses of the horizontal strokes in **H Stems**. The **ForceBold** checkbox enables this property. Clicking on the button **Auto stems** causes FontLab to take the measurements for us and fill in the two lists as it sees fit.

- *Additional hinting parameters* (see Figure 13-3 [c]): we supply values for the parameters **ForceBoldThreshold, BlueScale, BlueShift, BlueFuzz.**

FontForge and global hints

In FontForge, the management of global hints is, as one might expect, both less pleasant and more powerful than in FontLab. The data are entered under a single tab of the font-information window (**Element>Font Info>PS Private Dictionary**), shown opposite.

In the top part of the window, we choose the parameter that we wish to modify: **BlueValues** (alignment zones), **OtherBlues** (alignment zones beneath the baseline), **BlueScale, BlueShift, BlueFuzz, StdHW** (the most relevant horizontal stroke thickness), **StdVW** (ditto, but vertical), **ForceBold** (whose value must be either **false** or **true**). Other than **ForceBold**, the values that we supply to FontForge must be written in PostScript's tabular syntax, i.e., in the form of numbers separated by spaces, with brackets around the whole entry.

The reader must be wondering what happened to the other relevant stroke thicknesses (**StemSnapV, StemSnapH**). Clicking on the **Add** button reveals other parameters, including these two, from the "private" part of the PostScript Type 1 or CFF font. There are even parameters specific to the ideographic scripts, such as **ExpansionFactor** and **LanguageGroup** (see §C.3.4.3) and all the rest.

The functionality for the parameters for alignment zones and relevant stroke thicknesses is the same as in FontLab: there is a **Guess** button, which will take the measurements for us and supply values for these parameters. But FontForge goes further! For each of these parameters there is a **Hist** (histogram) button; when we click on this button, FontForge shows us an interactive histogram:

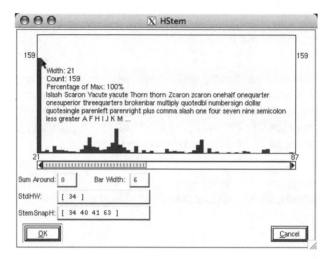

In the figure above, we see the histogram for the vertical stroke thickness parameter. In the **Bar Width** input area, we can specify the width of the histogram's bars. That might seem pointless: why should we want to change the width of the bars in the histogram? Well, as with everything else in FontForge, there is a reason: the bars of the histogram are, in fact, interactive. When we slide over a bar, a small text box appears with a great deal of information: what is the exact value of the bar? How many glyphs have this same value? Even better: *which* glyphs have this value?

Then, when we click on the bar, its value becomes the primary value (here **StdVW**). Clicking with the shift key depressed adds the value to the secondary values (here **Stem–SnapV**).

Finally, the parameter **Sum Around** is also very interesting: it "blows up" the histogram and thus allows for a better understanding of the clustering of data by eliminating isolated extreme values.

Individual PostScript Hints

As their name shows, individual hints are defined at the level of each glyph. The basic idea is very simple: we tell the rasterizing engine which are the *relevant horizontal and vertical strokes*. The rasterizing engine detects strokes that appear at the indicated coordinates and arranges for them to have the same thickness in pixels, irrespective of the location of the centers of the adjacent pixels. The reason for the name "hint" is now clear: we *hint* to the rasterizing engine which strokes should have the same thickness, either within a single glyph or over all the glyphs in the font. Then the rendering engine will manage to perform its task correctly, respecting at all costs the directions that we have given.

Unfortunately, that does not work as well as one might wish: there are complications and special cases to handle. The complications result from the way in which hints are defined: rather than connecting them to precise nodes on the glyph, Adobe preferred to consider hints as vertical or horizontal zones in such a way that all the strokes that *coincide* with these zones are optimized. The intention was noble, but the approach works only if the zones defined by the individual hints do not touch. For example, in the letter 'H', the zones that will optimize the two stems do not touch, and so everything works perfectly.

But there are cases in which zones will inevitably touch. Take the letter 'B' below:

There are three vertical zones. By the very nature of the letter 'B', zones 2 and 3 will inevitably overlap. What should we do in this case? To solve this specific problem in Type 1 fonts, Adobe invented a horribly complicated method called "hint replacement". This method involves *enabling* and *disabling*, while the glyph is being traced, the hints that overlap. That is one of the major difficulties in placing hints. We shall describe hint replacement in §C.3.6.1 of this book. The situation is better for Type 2 (OpenType/CFF) fonts: we must still do "hint replacement", but the relevant structure and syntax are much more rational (see §C.8.2.1).

The special cases that arise with hints come from a visual characteristic of the glyphs: the fact that the symmetry between stems also extends to the white counters between them. Take the example of the letter 'm': the stems of this letter must, of course, have the same width, but that also applies to the two white spaces that separate them. It is just as important to ensure that the two "crotches" of the 'm' have exactly the same width, in pixels. But hints operate only on strokes, not on counters.

Adobe tried to solve this problem in two steps. The first measure taken affects only configurations of *three* parallel stems, as in 'm', the Greek 'Ξ', the Cyrillic letters 'Ш', 'ш', 'Щ', 'щ', the symbol ≡, ideographs such as 三, 且, 山, 彐, 目, 王, 田, etc. It involved an operator (by the name of hstem3 or vstem3; see §C.3.6) to which we would supply three hint zones, and the blank spaces between these zones would be equalized.

But Adobe quickly realized that handling configurations of three strokes was not enough! One need only consider ideographs such as 皿, 目 (4 strokes), 冒 (7 strokes), etc., to convince oneself that more powerful operators are needed. Moreover, when the number of strokes runs that high, we realize that the danger is not so much that we may have unequal white spaces but rather that there may not be any white spaces at all. Indeed, the rasterization at a low resolution of a glyph such as 摩 is a real challenge, one that rasterizing engines in East Asia must face every day. Accordingly, Adobe's second attempt involved developing a system—once again inordinately complicated— to manage situations of this kind (§C.3.6.2). This system was named "counter control"

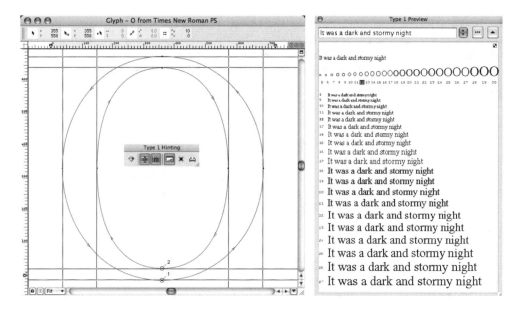

Figure 13-4: Displaying individual hints in FontLab.

and was used only in East Asian fonts. Only with the advent of Type 2 (OpenType/CFF) fonts did Adobe finally provide a stable and robust operator to perform operations of this type (§C.8.2.1).

We have presented a quick overview of the properties of individual hints. Now let us see how they are implemented in the two large software packages FontLab and FontForge.

FontLab and individual hints

To display PostScript hints in FontLab, select **Tools > Hints & Guides > Type 1 Hinting.** This will open the **Type 1 Hinting** button bar and display the hinting lines as pairs of green lines (see Figure 13-4). Finally, by clicking on the button ▣ on this button bar, we obtain a display of specimens at various sizes.

It is very easy to add hints to a glyph in FontLab. Simply place the cursor over a ruler (a horizontal one for a horizontal hint; otherwise a vertical one) and press the ⌘ key (under Mac OS X; CTRL under Windows). Then drag the pair of lines until one of them is in the right place. Next, hold down the shift key and move the other line until the hint zone has the correct width. To delete a hint, select the entry Delete on the pop-up menu for one of these two lines.

The pop-up menu for hints also allows us to specify precisely the hint's coordinates (Properties), change its direction (Reverse), and even turn the hint's value into a global alignment zone for the font (by means of the option Define Stem).

That is all very useful, but FontLab goes further! It introduces a new notion, that of the *link*. Through this new notion, FontLab aims to correct Adobe's bad decision to regard hints as abstract zones independent of the glyph's outline. A link is a *hint attached to nodes of the outline*. If these nodes are moved (either manually or through programming), the corresponding hint will also be moved. Thus it is safer to work with links, which FontLab will, in any event, translate into hints when a Type 1 or Type 2 (OpenType/CFF) font is generated.

Links (horizontal and vertical) are inserted by means of Tools>Hints & Guides>Add New Horizontal Link and Tools>Hints & Guides>Add New Vertical Link. We can also replace a hint with a link or vice versa by using the options Convert to Link and Convert to Hint on the pop-up menu for the hint or the link. This conversion can also be applied to all the hints and links of one or more glyphs, by means of Tools>Hints & Guides>Convert Hints to Links or the opposite.

But beware: automatic conversions cannot perform miracles! A link is, by definition, a pair of nodes traversed by two lines for a hint's zone. When we ask FontLab to convert a hint to a link, it will first check whether there are indeed nodes on the two lines for the hint. If there are not, as sometimes happens in poorly optimized fonts, the hint will remain a hint, and FontLab will not issue an error message or otherwise complain. Thus we should supervise this operation carefully.

The Tools>Hints & Guides menu also allows us to initiate *autohinting*. But beware: before using this command, it would behoove you to check its configuration panel File> Font Info>Hinting Settings>T1 Autohinting.

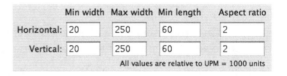

	Min width	Max width	Min length	Aspect ratio
Horizontal:	20	250	60	2
Vertical:	20	250	60	2

All values are relative to UPM = 1000 units

The numeric values in this configuration panel are of little importance, except perhaps in extreme cases: for example, if the font has very thin strokes, **Min width** must be reduced; if it has very thick strokes, increase **Max width**; if you want more hints globally, reduce **Min length**. What is also really important is to select Tools>Hints & Guides>Remove Hints>Both, since FontLab will otherwise add new hints to the old ones, thus making the situation catastrophic. In Figure 13-1, the reader can compare the results of FontLab autohinting to the lack of hints and to the analogous operation in FontForge.

Finally, a few words on *hint replacement*, a problem due to a poor definition of the concept of hints. We have seen that "hint zones", i.e., the pairs of horizontal or vertical lines that indicate the relevant strokes in a glyph, are defined for the entire working area of the glyph. In Figure 516, we see at the left the hint zone that corresponds to the lower bowl of the 'B' and, at the right, the zone that corresponds to the upper bowl. Obviously these two hint zones do touch, thus running counter to the definition of hints. What can we do so that when rasterizing the lower part of the glyph the rasterizing engine will ignore the upper part, and vice versa?

The solution is as follows: first we divide up the outline of the letter, then we "attach" hints to the various segments. When there is a hint within a given group of segments, we

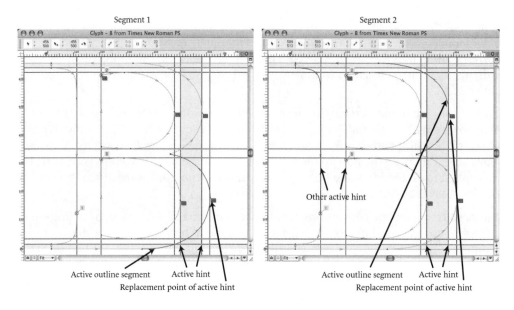

Figure 13-5: Hint replacement in FontLab.

attach the hint to this group. The rasterizing engine will process each group separately, taking into account only the hints attached to the segment being processed.

To divide an outline into segments, we use "replacement points". Here is how to do so in FontLab. We set the hints by hand. When two hint zones overlap, their intersection is displayed in yellow. Then we select the first node of a segment of the outline and choose on its pop-up menu Add replace point here. FontLab segments the outline and auto-matically attaches to this segment of the outline the hints that it considers relevant.

In Figure 13-5, we see the glyph window for the letter 'B' with four manually inserted replacement points. At the left we see the first segment of the outline (in black, whereas the rest of the outline is in gray); at the right, the second segment. The hint zones are the zones attached to the active segment; the software shows them in dark green. We see that there is only one hint zone at the left, while there are two at the right, since the segment also contains the left part of the letter. Hint zones can be attached to multiple outlines: for example, the internal outlines are attached to all the hints that touch them.

We can intervene if FontLab has attached hints to the segments of an outline incorrectly. To do so by hand, we activate the segment in question and, on the hint's pop-up menu, select Add this vertical hint (or Add this horizontal hint if it is horizontal), and the task is done.

The tedious operations that we have just described are fortunately quite rare. During automatic optimization of a rasterization, FontLab automatically applies this sort of method whenever hints overlap. Nonetheless, it is recommended that the user verify the choice of replacement points: it is easy to do once the principle is understood, and

FontLab does what is needed to make the glyphs with overlapping hints easy to detect: the disputed area is painted yellow.

FontForge and individual hints

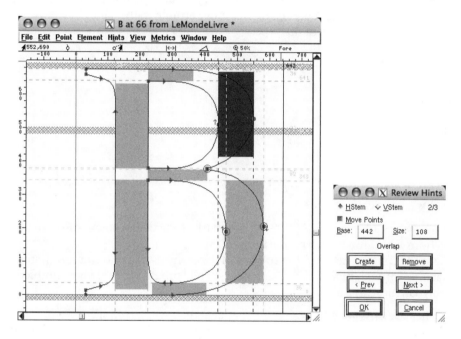

Figure 13-6: The management of individual hints in FontForge.

The management of individual hints in FontForge is a little less powerful than in Font-Lab. It is true that FontForge has a very efficient autohinting feature (**Hints>AutoHint**), but, on the other hand, there are few possibilities for manual intervention. The hint zones are marked with dotted lines and colored sky blue. The intersection of a hint zone with a vertical or horizontal stroke is colored purple (for a vertical hint) or green (for a horizontal hint).

Using **Hints>Review Hints**, one can modify the coordinates of the hint zones or add or subtract hint zones. But those actions are done with coordinates, not with the mouse; we are thus far from the pleasant interface of FontLab, where we can create hints and set their positions in a few seconds, by simply moving the mouse.

When two hint zones overlap, the word "**Overlap**" appears in the **Review Hints** dialog box. FontForge will automatically divide the outline into segments and place the replacement points for the hints—but there is no visible evidence of this operation, nor any possibility of manual intervention.

TrueType Instructions

TrueType instructions are the means that we have for optimizing the rasterization of glyphs in a TrueType font. Unlike PostScript hints, they are not values of parameters or graphical zones but a genuine *programming language*. Furthermore, the view that font designers have of TrueType instructions is not very different from Freud's opinion of the unconscious: "a cave where repressed desires move around in the dark". Indeed, the sight of hundreds of lines of code of this type:

```
MIRP[00100]
MIRP[10100]
MIRP[01110]
SRP1[ ]
SRP2[ ]
SLOOP[ ]
```

is enough to make anyone, not just a technophobe, break out in a *cold sweat*.

But is this cold sweat justified?

It is true that, unlike Adobe, Apple—which sparked the development of the TrueType instructions—has always been partial to "hard" notation in computer science, perhaps to highlight the contrast between the roles of Macintosh "user" (who communicates with his machine through menus and dialog boxes) and "programmer" (who stumbled into assembly language as a child).

We might have envisioned a high-level language that, when compiled, would produce the assembly code for the instructions of today; after all, that is precisely what Knuth did with METAFONT (see Appendix F). This high-level language does not yet exist and, no doubt, never will. Nonetheless, various tools have been created to make up for this deficiency: FontLab offers a simplified version of instructions with a graphical interface; Visual TrueType, by Microsoft, offers a graphical interface that is a veritable factory for instructions; and FontForge offers a built-in programming environment with an inter-active debugger.

Not to mention that both FontLab and FontForge pride themselves on automatically generating instructions for our fonts. As often happens in life, we have the choice of

- A quick solution (just a click on the button for automatically generating instruc-tions), without troubling ourselves much over the details

- Or a method that gives us more room for maneuver, with a concomitantly greater investment required on our part

- Or, finally, a difficult method that gives us 100 percent control over the rasterization of our glyphs and also 100 percent of the responsibility for the result but that requires extensive study of a nontrivial technique

In this section, we shall adopt the second solution: a small dose of technical learning through which we will gain control over the situation. For those who dare to pursue the third course, we have written a very thorough description of instructions, illustrated by real-world examples: it is Appendix E of this book.

The principle of instructions is as follows: to optimize the rasterization of a glyph, we *change the shape of its vector outline*. The change involves modifying the underlying grid of pixels. Then we will obtain a new outline, more or less different from the original one, for each grid, and thus for each size of glyph. We call this new outline the *grid-fitted outline*. It must be understood that the grid-fitted outline will not necessarily be as beautiful as the original outline. After all, no one will ever see it, since it exists only to yield a good rasterization. Once the grid-fitted outline has been obtained, the rasterization engine need only apply the rule about the centers of the pixels (blacken the pixel if its center lies within the outline, else leave it white) in a strict, even stupid, manner, and the job is done.

Why should one bother to obtain an outline customized for each size when it would be enough to activate or disactivate pixels? Because the customized outline, unlike the original outline, is not designed specifically by the font's designer; on the contrary, it is produced automatically by means of a number of rules. By stating these rules, we obtain *all* the customized outlines for every size. In fact, this rule is not absolute, as there is indeed a way (we call it a δ instruction) to modify the individual outlines customized for certain sizes. But it is the exception, and in most cases a few rules for customizing the outline are enough to render all glyph sizes correctly.

The goal of instructions is to *express these rules* (and their exceptions).

How should we go about altering an outline? For the TrueType language, an outline is nothing more than a series of points, some of which (the nodes) lie on the curve and others (the control points) off the curve. An outline can be modified only by manipulating these points.

Let us summarize: instructions move the points of the outline to form a new outline customized for the rasterization of the glyph at a given size.

Next question: how can we know how much to move a point, and in which direction? There are (at least) three possible cases:

- Some points are simply *aligned* relative to one of the edges, or to the center, of the pixel that contains them. We shall say that these points have been "touched", in the sense that they have been moved and now appear in the correct location. A touched point will not be moved again (which does not cause problems, as we can always "untouch" a point if necessary).

- Other points will be set at an *appropriate distance* from a touched point. The appropriate distances in a list of values called CVT (for "Control Value Table"), which is found in the TrueType table cvt. When we move two points so that they are set at an appropriate distance, this distance is always at least one pixel; thus we have a property for the *minimum distance*.

- Still other points—and these form the silent masses, the proletariat of the glyph—
are not involved directly but take part passively in the movement of other points. In
other words, they do what the other points do, no questions asked. They can imitate
the movement of another point or even *interpolate* the movement of several other
points. In addition, there is a "magical" instruction that causes the interpolation of
all the points that have not been touched.

Already we see in broad strokes how the *instruction of a glyph* is done: we start by selecting
some points that will be aligned relative to the pixel that contains them; then we apply a
number of appropriate distances (stroke thicknesses, relevant heights, breadths of serifs,
etc.); next we interpolate the points that depend on two or more of the points that have
been moved; finally, we interpolate all the other points.

Now that we have explained the general principle, let us move on without delay to the
management of instructions by the chief software systems. We shall see how each of them
manages instructions in a different way, with its own advantages and disadvantages.

Managing Instructions in FontLab

It is clear that FontLab has undertaken an enormous effort in the area of the design
of instructions and of their human interface, even though it provides only a simplified
version of instructions. FontLab has succeeded in reducing the essence of the instructions
to six visual operations called *visual hints:*[1]*alignments*, *links*, *double links*, *interpolations*,
and two types of δ instructions: *medial δs* and *final δs*. With these six operations, the user
can instruct her font and view the rasterization in real time. When a TrueType font is
generated, the visual hints are converted into genuine TrueType instructions.

What is striking about visual hints is the blend between the concepts of instructions
(alignments, interpolations, δ instructions) and those of PostScript hints: links, introduced by FontLab as an improvement to the concept of a hint zone. Indeed, FontLab
considers hints as a sort of preliminary step to instructions. For instance, global hints
(relevant heights, relevant stroke thicknesses, etc.) are used in PostScript and TrueType
alike. Moreover, FontLab has no direct function for automatically optimizing a rasterization through the use of instructions; instead, we find, on the one hand, optimization
through the addition of hints and, on the other, an operation for converting hints into
visual hints.

The user interface

The interface for managing instructions in FontLab deserves some discussion. At first
blush it may give the impression of being a "juggernaut"; but when we become familiar
with its tools, we find that they are all useful and that the various methods for representing information are actually complementary and globally effective. Because we should
not deceive ourselves: a user interface that claims to present to the user all the information about the instructions of a given glyph (at a given size) should be able to display,

---

[1] Not to be confused with Microsoft's *Visual TrueType* operations, which are also called *visual hints* and
which we shall study in the section dedicated to this software.

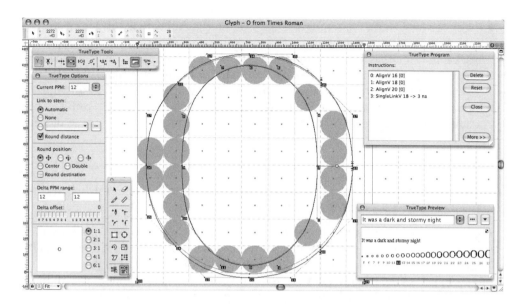

Figure 13-7: Managing visual hints in FontLab.

all at the same time, the original outline, the customized outline, the resulting rasterization, the grid of pixels (with their centers, the baseline, and the alignment zones clearly displayed), the six types of visual hints represented by different symbols, and, finally, the rasterization of the glyph at its actual size, since what seems horrible at a large size is often impeccable at the actual size. Representing all this information simultaneously is a real challenge, and we can say that FontLab is well up to the task.

In Figure 13-7, we see FontLab's basic working environment for visual hints. To switch to "instruction" mode, we need only select **Tools>Hints & Guides>TrueType Hinting**. Then the **TrueType Tools**, shown above and to the left, appears, together with the **TrueType Options** dialog box, which is shown immediately below.

To see the different layers of information and the two other windows that appear to the right of the glyph, we use the last button at the right end of the bar, the button ⬚. Clicking on this button opens a pull-down menu with the following options:

- **Hinted outline:** show the glyph's customized outline. To see it, pay close attention to Figure 13-7: the hinted outline is the gray one shown inside the black outline, marked with node numbers. The hinted outline depends on instructions and is updated whenever the instructions are modified.

- **Grid lines:** show the grid. The first option in the **TrueType Options** box (**Current PPM**, or "current pixels per em") shows us the size of the glyph. In the figure, the glyph is of size[2] 15, with a set-width of 11 pixels.

---

[2] Recall that we speak of "size" when we measure the height of a glyph in pixels and of "actual size" when we measure it in points.

- **Pixel centers**: mark the center of each pixel on the grid with a dot. This feature is not offered for ornamental purposes. As we know, a pixel in the final outline will be black if its center lies inside the modified outline. Thus it is quite important to know where the centers of the pixels lie with respect to the modified outline so that we can insert a δ instruction that will make a pixel black or white by slightly modifying the outline. In addition, we see in the image that the pixels (2,3) and (4,3) came within a hair's breadth of being made black, which would have made the curve's descent too dark.

- **Resulting image**: show the pixels of our rasterization—an indispensable option.

- **Point numbers**: show the point numbers. This option is useful only when combined with the **TrueType Program** window, which we shall discuss just below.

- **Program panel**: open the **TrueType Program** window. This box shows us a list of all the visual hints for the glyph, in the order in which they will be executed. Clicking on an instruction causes it to be shown in bright red within the glyph. The bottom part of the window allows us to modify the instructions and see the result by clicking on **Apply**. This window is a good compromise between the syntactic horrors of the real TrueType instructions and the graphical representation of visual hints within the glyph: the list of instructions gives a good summary of the method of optimization that was followed, and the possibility of manipulating the parameters of the instructions gives us total control over them without going through the glyph's representation.

- Finally, **Preview panel**: open the **TrueType Preview** window, which will display a number of sizes of the active glyph and also a characteristic sentence—for example, a pangram (see page 721, note 7, for a series of examples of pangrams). The little pull-down menu at the right (available only under Windows) allows us to move from display without gray levels to display with gray levels, and even a display using ClearType, a new display technology in Windows. Display with gray levels or through ClearType often masks the imperfections of the rendering; thus it behooves us to be strict with ourselves and approach the rasterization of our glyphs in their pure state, with no embellishment.

Of the buttons in **TrueType Tools**, there are two whose effect is global: the button ▨ displays vertical visual hints (i.e., those that apply to horizontal strokes), and ▨ displays horizontal visual hints (applied to vertical strokes). The effect of these buttons is not confined to display: we can even switch outright from a "vertical mode" to a "horizontal mode". According to the active mode, the buttons that we shall discuss below will produce horizontal or vertical visual hints.

Now let us take another look at the different types of visual hints and their manipulation.

Alignments

Alignments are made with the button ▨. They are horizontal or vertical, according to the active mode. The term "alignment" is a bit unfortunate: here it refers not to aligning two points with each other but rather to aligning a point with respect to the boundary or center of a pixel. It would be more correct to speak of "rounding relative to the grid". In any event, alignment is often the first operation that we perform (moreover, it is always executed first, as the reader will notice on the list in the **TrueType Program** window). It consists of the "correct" placement of an initial point, from which we will then place other points.

To "align" a point, we click on the button  and then choose the appropriate method of rounding in the group of buttons that appears in the middle of the **TrueType Option** window, shown opposite. The first three buttons mean, respectively, "place the point on the nearest pixel boundary" (for vertical alignment, that would mean moving the point up if it appeared above the center of the pixel and down if it appeared below the center), "place the point at the bottom of the pixel" (the left side, in horizontal mode), and "place the point at the top of the pixel" (the right). The two buttons below are used for more sophisticated alignment: **Center** means that the point will be identified with the center of the pixel that contains it. We thus obtain a pixel surrounding the point, whatever the circumstances of the rasterization may be; that may prove useful, for example, for the point of the letter 'v', which should be "as pointed as possible". Finally, **Double** means that we will round according to a grid twice as fine as the current grid: the point will be moved either to the edge or to the middle of the pixel. Thus we can manage cases in which we must place a point in the middle of a row of pixels when we do not know whether the number of those pixels is even or odd. (We shall see below that a more natural way to do it is to use interpolation.)

Having chosen the type of rounding, we click on the point that we wish to "align". A little blue symbol around the point represents this procedure, and a new line will be added to the list of visual hints in the **TrueType Program** window.

In vertical mode, there is another type of alignment for points: alignment with respect to a hint zone. Let us recall what a hint zone is: a relevant height (the baseline, the height of the lowercase letters, the height of the capitals, etc.) and its overshoot (the little part that extends over the limit when the letter is round). Hint zones are part of the global hints. FontLab stores these data under the **Hinting Settings** tab in the **File>Font Info** window. Thus it is quite useful to go to this window and request automatic generation of the hint zones by clicking on **Auto zones**.

When in vertical mode we click on a point in order to "align" it, if the point lies in a hint zone, it will be automatically aligned relative to that zone, and rounding is done in the direction of the relevant height. We can prevent this automatic behavior by holding down the shift key while we click.

One last comment: aside from the points of the outline (the nodes and the control points), two other types of points can be manipulated—the glyph's origin and its setwidth. The origin is always "aligned", but there is no reason that the set-width should also be so aligned. If our glyph is symmetrical (like the 'O' in Figure 13-7), we should reflect on the left side of the glyph the behavior of the right side. To this end, the least that we can ask is for the point representing the glyph's set-width to be "aligned" as well.

Single and double links

Links follow the same principle as PostScript hints: they "link" two points in such a way that their distance is handled in a certain manner, whatever the size of the glyph may be.

What exactly is this treatment? It depends on the link's type. We have already said that there are "single" and "double" links. A *single link* is a link whose starting point must be a *touched* point, whereas its ending point must not be one. The most interesting single links are those that are connected to a relevant distance. Let us explain. While discussing PostScript hints, we mentioned relevant stroke thicknesses. We can generalize this concept and say that in a font there are some distances that are used in multiple glyphs and that guarantee the font's aesthetic uniformity. For instance, it may happen that the counter of an 'n' in a given font is equal to those of the 'm' or that the breadth of the 'O' is the same as that of the 'Q'.

We can store dimensions of this kind and use them to create interesting links. To do so, we click on the ellipsis in the top part of the **TrueType Options** window, shown opposite.

The window below then appears:

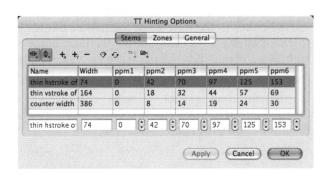

Each line on the list corresponds to a relevant dimension. The lines on a clear background correspond to vertical dimensions; those on a yellow background, to horizontal ones. The name of the relevant dimension is also shown in the glyph's window each time a link makes use of the dimension. The second column contains the dimension's value. The other columns contain the size of the glyph, in pixels, at which the dimension in question changes from 1 to 2 pixels, then from 2 to 3 pixels, and so on, up to 6 pixels. (The difference in stroke width is assumed to be insignificant from 6 pixels onwards.)

By clicking on a line, we can edit it—in the bottom of the window. For example, we can specify precisely the moment at which a new pixel will be added to the dimension, and our specification will apply to the entire font.

To establish a single link, we click on the button 🔘 (a yellow circle) on the bar **True-Type Tools**. Then we determine, in the window **TrueType Options**, how this link will be connected to a relevant dimension: should FontLab automatically find the nearest relevant dimension (**Automatic**)? Is there no relevant dimension that is connected to this link (**None**)? We can also designate the relevant dimension on the pull-down menu. Finally, we click on the link's starting point (remember, it must be a *touched* point) and drag it to the starting point (which must *not* be a touched point). The ending point will then be touched.

To respect the constraint "touched point at the start, nontouched point at the end", we must sometimes define the links in a certain order. Take the example of the letter 'm' shown opposite. We start with the five links ①, ②, ③, ④, and ⑤, which must be defined in that order. Point 4 is the starting point of link ①; it is "aligned" on the left edge of the pixel. This optimization that the stems and the counters will be of uniform width. But this very

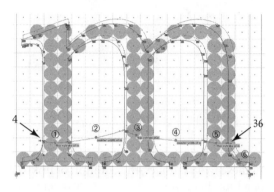

uniformity causes the width of the glyph to vary greatly, and that is why we have added a sixth link, ⑥, which connects point 36 to the glyph's set-width. This link does not correspond to any relevant dimension.

The reader must certainly be wondering of what use a link that is not connected to any relevant dimension can be. Do not forget that a link "joins" its ending point to the rest of the outline and that, were it not for the link, the point could appear too close or too far away if the outline were significantly modified. We have prepared two examples, drawn from the optimization of this same letter, 'm'. We use a heavy vertical stroke to represent the set-width of the optimized glyph and a broken stroke to represent the glyph's original set-width. The image on the left is that of the glyph without link ⑥; the image on the right includes this link.

At 9 points, without link ⑥ the customized outline is much wider, which causes the optimized set-width (which is nothing but a rounded version of the original set-width) to be too narrow and the right-hand side bearing to be missing altogether:

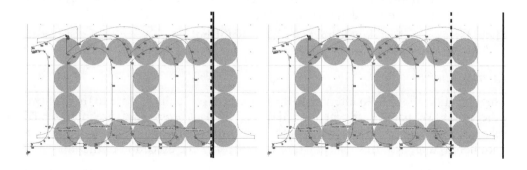

Conversely, at 12 points, the customized outline is much narrower (because the stroke widths are always one pixel and the counters always two pixels) and the set-width is too wide,[3] giving a right-hand side bearing of 3 (!) pixels:

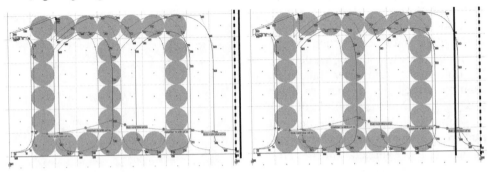

In these two examples, the addition of link ⑥ restores the situation and shows the utility of a link that is not connected to any relevant dimension.

In addition to single links, we also have *double links*. Their peculiarity lies in the fact that they are placed between two *non-touched* points—which, consequently, become touched. Establishing a relationship between a double link and a relevant dimension works just as with a single link.

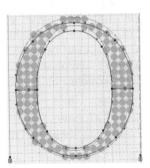

What does it mean to say that the two points of the double link must not have been touched? It means that the double link is, in a sense, "independent" of everything else—that it is not its *position* that matters but its *dimension*. For example, we shall place double links on the two sides of the letter 'O'— links connected to the dimension "thick stroke of the 'O' ", shown opposite.

What matters here is not the width of the 'O' but the fact that its two sides have exactly the same width, and that is what the two double links ensure.

To establish a double link, we click on the button 🔵 (a blue circle) on the TrueType Tools bar and then proceed as with a single link.

Should we use single or double links? Both are useful, but often we achieve a good result with less effort by using double links.

Interpolations

This operation allows us to interpolate the movement of a point relative to those of two other points. We have already mentioned that all the *nontouched* points are interpolated relative to the *touched* points anyway at the end of the optimization process. The difference here is that, first, this interpolation is done *before* the execution of the links and,

---

[3] We could have requested, through the control table for the relevant dimensions, that the counters of the 'm' increase to 3 pixels starting at 12 points (in the example in question, that happens only at 14 points). That would have produced a wider glyph. It is up to the designer to choose the less unattractive solution. Note that a decision of that sort would also have had repercussions on a plethora of other glyphs (the 'n', the 'h', etc.) that use the same relevant dimension.

second, rather than relying on automatic interpolation, which is based on the nearest points, we can perform interpolation here relative to carefully chosen points—points that may be arbitrarily far away.

To interpolate a point c relative to two points a and b, we first click on the button ▣ (a green circle) on the **TrueType Tools** bar. Then we click on a, drag it to c, and click on b.

δ instructions

FontLab adopted unchanged the technique of δ instructions as it is defined in the True-Type specification. The intention is noble, but one small problem remains: TrueType's δ instructions are inserted into a program; thus they appear at a given moment and operate on the position of the points *at that very moment*. Here the time at which the δ instructions are instantiated is less clear: all that we know is that alignments come first, then interpolations, and finally links, in the order in which they were created by the user. If we add a visual δ hint, when will it be executed?

Not to worry. FontLab has taken a wise decision by defining two types of visual δ hints: *medial δs* and *final δs*. Medial δs are executed along with the links, while final δs are executed at the end of the optimization process, *after global interpolation*. Thus medial δs are modifications to the optimized outline that take part in the work done by the links, whereas final δs are last-minute solutions employed to eliminate an annoying pixel or creating a pixel where its absence is most cruelly felt.

Certainly the reader is beginning to wonder: is it not dangerous to play with pixels? After all, at every size the configuration of the pixels is so different that we cannot sensibly talk about pixels without also specifying the size. Quite so: δs *depend on the size*. They can be defined for a specific size or for a range of sizes. For example, we can take action only where there is truly a problem and correct it without affecting anything at other sizes.

To apply a δ to a point of the outline, we first click on the button ▣ (for a medial δ: it represents a capital delta indexed by a letter 'M') or on the button ▣ (for a final δ: it represents Δ_F). Then we click on the point in question and drag in the direction of the movement. The δs are the only visual hints for which there is no difference between horizontal and vertical mode, as FontLab will systematically create two δs: a horizontal one and a vertical one, corresponding to the projections of the movement obtained by dragging the mouse. Warning: movement is done in eighths of a pixel and cannot exceed one pixel. We can edit the values of a δ and the sizes at which it is applied in the lower part of the **TrueType Program** window, separately for the horizontal and vertical parts.

Here is an example of applying a final δ in order to move a pixel (encircled on the left side of the image) that had the nerve to put itself in the wrong place:

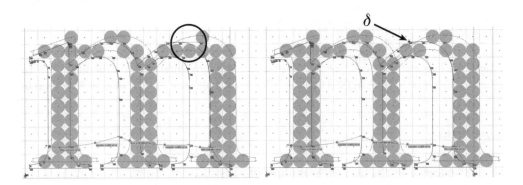

As can be seen on the right side of the image, inserting a final δ half a pixel to the left and half a pixel upwards was enough to correct[4] the wayward pixel.

Generating or importing bitmaps

There are branches of computer science in which fonts are very seldom changed. For instance, since 1987, when the author bought his first Macintosh, he has used only one font, and at only one size, to prepare his documents: 9-point *Monaco*. If this font had been a TrueType vector font, then for all these years, every time the font was displayed on the screen, the rasterizing engine would have had to execute the same instructions only to obtain the *same rasterization* over and over again. That is a waste of memory and of CPU cycles.

We are far removed from the graphical applications in which thousands of fonts are used at virtually all possible and imaginable sizes, for which real-time rasterization is crucial. The reason that we are driven to rasterize our fonts in real time is that we *cannot* store

---

[4] The astute reader will surely have noticed that there is a paradox here. By applying a δ to the upper curve, we naturally blackened a new pixel, since its center appeared inside the outline. But since we have not modified the lower curve, *why did the "wayward" pixel disappear?* If its center lay inside the outline before, it still does!

By way of answering this question, let us take a closer look at the situation *before* and *after* the δ:

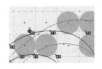

We see that the pixel is black although it should not be, since its center lies slightly outside the outline. The explanation is as follows: we slightly underestimated the rasterizing engine by saying that it uses pixels alone to decide whether to blacken a given pixel. Here the engine noticed that there would be a white pixel here if only the centers of the pixels were used, whereas the outline itself does not have a discontinuity at this point. Probably by applying criteria such as the continuity of the surface or the distance between the curve and the center of the pixel, the rasterizing engine, in its infinite wisdom, decided to break the rules and give us a black pixel at that location.

When we took action by adding a pixel through the use of the δ, the exception no longer existed, and the "hidden" pixel disappeared.

all the rasterizations on the disk. But if there is a small number of sizes that we use very frequently, the storage of a bitmap rasterization becomes an attractive option.

It is for these reasons that TrueType fonts can indeed contain bitmap fonts (the EBLC and EBDT tables; see §D.7). FontLab allows for the generation of such bitmaps, which are identical to the rasterization displayed in "visual hints" mode.

To generate a bitmap for the current glyph and at the current size, we switch to "bitmap" mode by clicking on the button ⓑ of the **TrueType Tools** bar. Next, we select the option **Generate bitmap** in the window's pop-up menu. Once generated, the bitmap can be modified by simply clicking on its pixels.

Through this same pop-up menu, we can import a bitmap from another font. Finally, we can also ask FontLab to show us the differences between the imported (or generated) bitmap and the bitmap produced by rasterizing the glyph. For that purpose, we enable the option **Highlight differences** on the pop-up menu and leave "bitmap" mode: the pixels whose values differ in the two versions are displayed on a red background. FontLab even recommends the following common strategy: take a good bitmap, display it as a background task, and create visual hints until the two bitmaps coincide. A funny way to work!

Behind the scenes

The reader who has read Appendix E and mastered the concepts and syntax of TrueType instructions may be curious to know how FontLab's "visual hints" are turned into genuine instructions. It is surprising to observe how easily this conversion is made:

- An "alignment" is nothing but MDAP (move direct absolute point) instruction, i.e., a rounding according to the active rounding method.
- A "single link" is an MDAP of the first point followed by an MIRP, i.e., an indirect relative move; since the first point has become a point of reference because of the previous instruction, we simply take a value from the CVT and apply to the second point a movement equal (in pixels) to the CVT.
- "Double links" are more complex: FontLab uses a function (defined in the fpgm table) that will put things in place for this rather special visual hint. The last lines of the function take the MDAP and the MIRP from the single link.
- "Interpolation" is nothing but an IP interpolation instruction.
- Similarly, a "δ" is merely a DELTAP1. The restriction on the size of a "δ" comes from the fact that we can change neither *delta_base* nor *delta_shift*.

Thus we see that "visual hints" are simply a small subset of TrueType instructions. But thanks to FontLab's enjoyable interface, this subset enables us to perform very effective optimizations.

Managing Instructions under VTT

The history of *VTT* goes back to the earliest days of TrueType. The author of TrueType, Sampo Kaasila, also wrote a tool for instructing fonts. This tool, called *Typeman*, it seems, was sold at exorbitant prices on the order of thousands of dollars (!). Later the product was called *TTED* (= *TrueType Editor*), and for the past several years it has gone by the name of *VTT* (= Visual TrueType).

VTT is distributed free of charge by Microsoft. But be warned! "Free of charge" does not mean "freely". To obtain a copy of VTT, one must print out a copy of the license [261] and fax it to Microsoft. Usually within a few days one will be given access to the VTT discussion forum, from which the software can be downloaded (for Mac OS 9 or Windows). Nevertheless, the documentation and all the ancillary resources are available freely on Microsoft's site [262].

How does VTT compare to FontLab? Both offer graphical interfaces for instructing True-Type glyphs. VTT's interface is less pleasant to use, less aesthetically appealing, and less ergonomic than that of FontLab, but VTT is closer to the real TrueType instructions and, therefore, gives access to features that are inconceivable under FontLab. Yet VTT has this in common with FontLab: the user is not required to learn the assembly language for instructions, as everything is done in a graphical manner. VTT offers a graphical adaptation of instructions that is more powerful than that of FontLab, and therefore necessarily more complex.

How do the approaches of VTT and FontLab differ? First of all, VTT offers a completely different vision of the management of *relevant dimensions* (relevant heights, stroke widths, etc.).

Control values

We have seen that FontLab allows us to store relevant dimensions in a table, give them names, and indicate when their rasterization changes from 1 to 2 pixels, from 2 to 3, and so on. When a TrueType font is generated, this table internal to FontLab feeds the table CVT ("control values table"), which is contained in every TrueType font.

VTT, for its part, allows us to operate directly on the control values table. Indeed, unlike the TrueType specification, *VTT attaches precise semantics to the entries in the CVT table*, or at least to its first 120 values. For instance, we have shown in Figure 13-8 the meanings of the entries 0 to 20, 22, and 24.

On the other hand, VTT classifies glyphs into four *groups*: "uppercase", "lowercase", "figure", and "other". (The group of a glyph can be redefined, and new groups can be defined at any time.) The glyphs in Figure 13-8 belong to these four groups.

Finally, the CVT entries are classified according to their *color*, *direction*, and *property*. The "color" depends on the color traversed by the link, which we shall define as follows:

- Black only: we say that the CVT entry in question is "black", as, for example, the horizontal width of the 'I'.

- White only: we say that the entry is "white", as, for example, the counter of the 'n'.

- Or *both* black *and* white: the entry is "gray", as, for example, the one that connects the upper and lower strokes of the '8', which thus traverses the two counters and the juncture of the strokes.

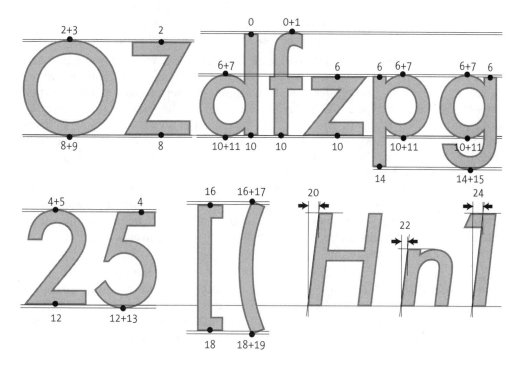

Figure 13-8: The meaning of CVT entries 0–19. These are different relevant heights. For each height n, entry n + 1 contains the corresponding overshoot. The notation 2+3 indicates that the height in question is the sum of entries 2 and 3. Finally, 20, 22, and 24 are the slopes of the capitals, the lowercase letters, and the numerals.

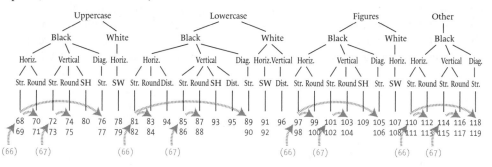

Figure 13-9: The meaning of CVT entries 68–119. The abbreviations "SH" and "SW" mean "serif height" and "serif width". The broken arrows indicate inheritance.

The "direction" may be horizontal, vertical, or diagonal. Finally, the "property" is also a predefined string, selected from "thickness of a straight stroke" (StraightStroke), "thickness of a curve" (RoundStroke), "serif height" (SerifHeight), "serif breadth" (SerifExtension), "another distance" (Distance). Figure 13-9 shows the classification of CVT entries 68 to 119 according to these four criteria: group, color, direction, property.

In Figure 13-9, we have also shown—with a broken arrow—another important property of CVT entries under VTT: *inheritance*. We say that a "daughter" entry inherits from a "mother" entry if they are rendered with the same number of pixels, up to a certain size—the size at which the daughter breaks free of the mother and can be rendered by a different number of pixels. The sire of all the entries of a relevant dimension is entry 65 (which is both horizontal and vertical). Entries 66 (horizontal) and 67 (vertical) inherit from it and are therefore, in a sense, the *most relevant dimensions of the font*. We see in Figure 13-9 that entries 68, 81, 97, and 110 inherit from 66 and that entries 72, 85, 101, and 114 inherit from 67: that ensures a certain uniformity in the font, one that will no longer be maintained beyond a certain size, when there will be enough pixels for the difference of stroke thicknesses in these groups of glyphs to be felt. Finally, within each group (uppercase, lowercase, etc.), the thicknesses of round strokes inherit the thicknesses of straight strokes.

Note that this classification of strokes recapitulates, in a sense, the principle of the parameters of METAFONT (see Appendix F), if only with regard to rasterization. Of course, METAFONT goes much further by parameterizing the relevant dimensions themselves, not only their bitmap rasterization. But let us not forget that METAFONT works quietly up the line, whereas the TrueType rasterizing engine must fulfill the user's requests *in real time*.

Let us return to the classification of the CVT entries. Their interest lies not only in the fact that they force us to *organize* the rasterization of the font. It lies mostly in the fact that VTT, like FontLab, will *automatically* select the CVT entry to which a link will be connected. But unlike FontLab, where relevant dimensions are classified only by their names and their directions, VTT is aware of the group to which the current glyph belongs and also knows the link's color: "black", "white", or "gray"; thus it will automatically choose a CVT entry with the correct group, direction, and color. Thus there are much better chances that the automatically selected entry will be the correct one in VTT than in FontLab.

Opening/saving a file

VTT knows how to open TrueType files under Windows and Mac OS 9 (or Mac OS X, in the *Classic* environment).

But there is a small problem under Mac OS 9: the font must not be contained in a Macintosh "suitcase". Thus, under Mac OS 9, one must double-click on the font suitcase to open it and then extract the TrueType font (warning: this operation is not possible under Mac OS X, which fact seriously compromises the functionality of VTT under that system). Next, so that the file in question will be recognized by VTT, it must be of Macintosh file type sfnt. To that end, a utility for converting file types (such as *File Buddy*) is necessary. After that manipulation is complete, everything works correctly, and VTT will open the font with no problems.

Let us now skip the steps and suppose that we have finished optimizing a TrueType font. Before distributing it, we must strip out all "private" data, i.e., those that have been added through VTT. Specifically, VTT adds a number of tables to the font's TrueType structure, and if the font is not free, it might not be prudent to distribute these tables—which, after all, contain the entire strategy for instructing the font—to the end user. But beware! Unlike FontLab or FontForge, each of which has its own file format, VTT uses the TrueType format as both a "working" file format and a format for the generated fonts. Fonts are generated through the menu option **Tools>Ship Font**, and it is therefore necessary to take care to select a different font name, or a different target location, or else the original font will be overwritten by the file generated and the internal data will therefore be irretrievably lost.

The glyph window

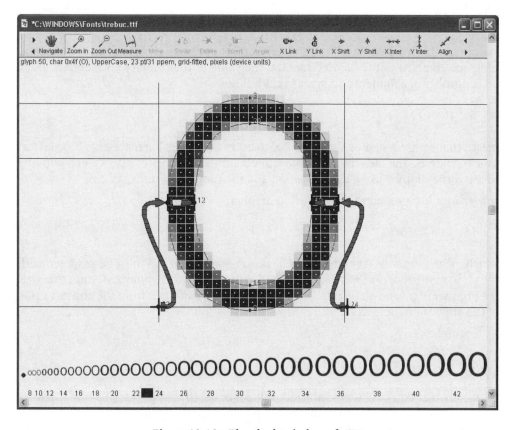

Figure 13-10: The glyph window of VTT.

VTT's interface consists of a *glyph window*, a *font-table window* (where we can choose the glyph to manipulate), and a number of text windows, the most important of which are the *control-program window*, which represents an uncompiled version of the CVT table, and the *glyph-program window*, which displays, in real time, the TrueType instructions generated from the *VTT* visual hints.

Unfortunately, the glyph window does not display both the original outline and the customized outline at the same time, as FontLab does. We have to switch from one to the other by enabling or disabling the option Display>General Options>Grid fit (shortcut: CTRL-G).

In Figure 13-10, we see the glyph window in "customized outline" mode. Here we have chosen to view the pixels in gray-level mode; in fact, we have the choice of several rasterizing engines, including different versions of ClearType's technology. At the top are a number of buttons, which we can slide back and forth through the use of the small triangles. At the bottom, we can preview the glyph at its actual size; by clicking on one of the sizes at the bottom, we change the grid of the glyph displayed in the middle of the window.

The window of the control program

We obtain this window by selecting View>Control program. It represents, at the beginning, the contents of the file CvtTmpl.txt: the value of the primary CVT entries and a large number of comments. Its syntax is as follows:

```
66: 200
```

means that we are assigning the value 200 to entry 66. This value represents 200 abstract TrueType units. The rasterizing engine will obtain the number of pixels corresponding to this dimension by using the resolution and the number of units per em.

Inheritance is expressed in the following manner:

```
68: 200 = 66 @27
```

which means: entry 68 (the "daughter") takes the value 200 and must be rendered with the same number of pixels as entry 66 (the "mother"), up to 27 points. Beyond that size, the number of pixels will be calculated by a simple rule of three from the abstract value of the dimension (here, 200).

By writing:

```
70: 10 ~ 68 @100
```

we specify that entry 70, whose abstract value is equal to that of entry 68 plus 10 units, will be rendered with the same number of pixels as 68 up to size 100. Beyond that size, the entry breaks free of entry 68 and is rendered as usual by converting its value into pixels.

Finally, we can have δ instructions applied to certain CVT entries. By writing:

```
3: 30 ~ 2 @18 Delta (1 @18, - @32-)
```

we ask the rasterizing engine to add a pixel at 18 points and to remove one at sizes between 32 and 100. For those who have read Appendix E, let us note that these are DELTAC instructions that appear in the prep table. These are global instructions that must not be confused with DELTAP instructions, which affect only one glyph.

We have already mentioned that other CVT entries are classified by group, color, direction, and property. We can write:

```
UpperCase
  Black
    X
      StraightStroke
        68: 200 = 66 @27
```

to indicate the classification of the entry (indentation is optional). In this notation, the groups (Uppercase, Lowercase, Figure, Other), the colors (Black, White, Grey[5]), the directions (X, Y, Diag), and the properties of strings (StraightStroke, RoundStroke, SerifHeight, SerifExt, etc.) are predefined.

We can define new groups by writing, for example:

```
GROUP Kanji
```

Then we must declare the glyphs in the file **CharGrp.txt** and associate the appropriate glyphs with the new group.

To enter the correct values of CVT entries in the control-program window, we must measure a number of heights, widths, and stroke thicknesses. VTT offers us a tool for this purpose that can be invoked by clicking on the **Measure** button. Before taking measurements, we are required to hide the pixels and switch to "original outline" mode by disabling **Display>General Options>Grid fit** and **Display>General Options>Pixels**. To choose the correct glyphs and the correct dimensions to measure, we can draw inspiration from Figures 13-8 and 13-9.

Warning: After every modification to the control-program window, it is necessary to recompile the CVT through the use of **Tools>Compile>Control values**.

Modifying a glyph's trace

VTT's operations depend a great deal on the correct positioning of the outline's nodes. It is quite probable that we will notice, while in VTT, that a node is poorly placed or that it is superfluous, or that one is missing at a certain location. VTT gives us the tools to correct the problem:

- **Move** will move a node.
- **Swap** will transform a point *off the curve* (i.e., a control point) into a point *on the curve* (i.e., into a starting/ending point of the Bézier curve), and vice versa.

---

[5] The word "grey" is spelled in the British manner, not the American one ("gray").

- **Delete** will delete a node without breaking the outline.
- **Insert** will insert a node at a given point on the outline.

To be able to use these tools, we must be in "original outline" mode (disable Display>General Options>Grid fit). On the other hand, the Swap operation makes sense only if the points off the curve are visible: that can be achieved by disabling Display>General Options>Show fewer points.

Those used to the trace mode for Bézier curves in FontLab or FontForge will need to break their habits. When **Insert** is selected, VTT will insert a point off the curve if Show fewer points is disabled or a point or the curve otherwise. Whether the point lies on or off the curve determines the curve's behavior: we need only consider that the fact that a Bézier curve between two points on the curve and with no points off the curve is necessarily *straight*. The points off the curve are responsible for its curvature.

To make an inserted point the starting point of a new trace, it is necessary to right-click (under Windows; ⌘-click on the Macintosh). But since VTT is not glyph-design software, it is recommended to switch to other, more appropriate, software (FontForge or FontLab) for this purpose.

Anchors

An *anchor* is a rounded control point that is not the target of a link or an interpolation. An anchor may be horizontal, vertical, or both at once. To obtain an anchor, we select XLink (for a horizontal anchor) or YLink (for a vertical anchor) and right-click (under Windows; ⌘-click on the Macintosh) on the control point that we want to convert into an anchor. Then one of the two windows below appears, depending on whether we are in horizontal or vertical mode:

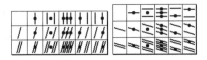

We slide the mouse onto one of the boxes. These boxes represent the 18 (!) ways of rounding a control point. Here is how to interpret the symbols. The three rows of boxes correspond to:

1. The usual situation of an upright glyph.

2. The situation of an italic glyph whose slant has been specified with the **Angle** tool. In order for this rounding to be useful, the stroke in question must have this slant (in which case we use YLink) or be perpendicular to the slant (XLink).

3. Like the previous case, but the slant is not an abstract slant but rather a slant calculated from pixels (whose angle is thus slightly different and depends on the resolution).

On every line there are six boxes, containing six symbols:

1. The first corresponds to the absence of rounding.

2. The second is classical rounding (the left/bottom or right/top edge of the pixel, according to the position of the point with respect to the center of the pixel).

3. The third is the rounding of the center of the pixel in which the point is found.

4. The fourth is rounding according to a subgrid of half-pixels. In other words, the point will be placed on the edge of a pixel or over the center of a pixel, whichever is closer.

5. The fifth is rounding down (towards the left or the bottom).

6. Finally, the last is rounding up (towards the right or the top).

Thus we have the same rounding methods as in FontLab, except that special attention is paid to slanted strokes, according to the angle of their slope.

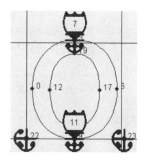

Vertical anchors (produced by Ylink) may be connected to a *relevant height*. To this end, one enables the option Display> Visual TrueType Options>Anchors. All the vertical anchors are then represented by an icon shaped like the U.S. interstate highway shield: ⛉.

In addition, when the option Display>Visual TrueType Options>Cvt numbers is enabled, these highway shields are displayed larger and contain numbers (see opposite). These numbers are the CVT entries connected to the anchors. Ordinarily, according to the available data, VTT has already selected the appropriate CVT entry for each vertical anchor. To change it, one merely right-clicks (under Windows; ⌘-click on the Macintosh) on the highway shield and selects the new CVT entry on the pull-down menu that appears.

After verifying or modifying the CVT entries of the anchors, one must once again disable the display of the highway shields, which are a bit too cumbersome.

Links, distances, shifts

VTT's *links* work like those of FontLab: we select either XLink (for horizontal links) or YLink (for vertical links), click on the link's starting point (its "parent"), and drag it to its ending point (its "child"). The starting point is then automatically transformed into an anchor. So far there has been nothing unusual with regard to FontLab.

The first novelty: the CVT entries to which the links are connected are selected not only according to the width of the link but also according to the group of the glyph, the color of the link ("black", "white", or "gray"), and the link's direction.

On the other hand, links can be of various types, according to the nature of the stroke and our choices of minimum distances. After drawing a link, we right-click (under Windows; ⌘-click on the Macintosh) on the head of the arrow, and one of the two pull-down menus shown below appears:

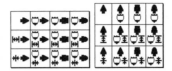

depending on whether the link is horizontal or vertical. Then we slide the mouse to a box to indicate the type of the link.

The four columns of these pop-up menus have the following meanings:

1. The link is not connected to any CVT entry. We say that the link represents a *distance*.

2. The link is connected to a CVT entry that is neither "straight" (the StraightStroke property) nor "round" (the RoundStroke property). We will use it, for example, for the breadths of serifs and other dimensions that cannot be classified into these two cases.

3. The link is connected to a "straight" CVT entry (the StraightStroke property); thus it represents the thickness of a straight stroke or the breadth of a straight counter.

4. The link is connected to a "round" CVT entry (the RoundStroke property); thus it represents the thickness of a curvilinear stroke or the breadth of a round cavity.

As for the rows of boxes:

1. The icons in the first row represent links without a minimum distance. The thickness in question can therefore be rendered with 0 pixels.

2. Those in the second row (with the symbol of an "opening elevator door" ↤↦) represent *links with a minimum distance*. The minimum distance may be from 0 to 8 (!!) pixels, in units of one-eighth of a pixel. By default, its value is 1 pixel. To change the minimum distance for a given link, we first enable the option **Display>Visual TrueType Options>Minimum distance**, which has the effect of displaying an icon of an "opening elevator door" over the link. Right-clicking (under Windows; ⌘-click on the Macintosh) on this icon displays a ruler bar. By sliding from right to left—feel free to slide off the end of the ruler, only a small part of which is visible—we can indicate, with a precision of an eighth of a pixel, the exact value of the minimum distance, between 0 and 8 pixels.

3. Those in the third row (with the symbol of a "closing elevator door" ↦↤) are there for legacy reasons: *Typeman*, the predecessor of VTT, took the initiative to force minimum distances into existence, even where they were not desired. By selecting a link of this type, we can abandon Typeman's choice and obtain all the same a link with no minimum distance.

Opposite, by way of example, is shown a letter 'm' in which the side bearings, the stems, and the outlines have been connected.

We have used "distances" (i.e., links not connected to CVT entries) for the side bearings, since they do not have a uniform (abstract) breadth anywhere in the font. On the other hand, we have requested a minimum distance of 1 pixel for the side bearings. For the stems we have used "straight" links, and VTT has automatically decided to connect them to CVT entry 81, which, according to Figure 13-9, is indeed the entry "lowercase, black, horizontal, straight". To connect the internal outlines, we have been forced to add a new entry to the control-program window, like this:

```
Lowercase
  White
    X
      StraightStroke
        120: 430
```

Thus we have used entry 120, which is "lowercase, white, horizontal, straight". It was automatically selected by VTT.

A *shift* is another type of link. The idea is to connect two points (the "parent" and the "child") so that the "child" will follow all of the "parent's" moves caused by instructions. A shift does not use a CVT entry; it has no rounding a priori, nor any minimum distance.

We insert a shift by choosing the tool X Shift (or Y Shift for a vertical shift) and proceeding as for a link.

Interpolations and alignments

Interpolations work as in FontLab. We select points that will be the reference points for the interpolation. Then we select one or more points that will be interpolated relative to the first two. There are no constraints: since we are doing *inter*polation rather than *extra*polation, the projections (horizontal or vertical) of the points to be interpolated must lie *between* those of the reference points.

To perform interpolation, we select the tool X Inter (or Y Inter for vertical interpolation). We click on the first reference point and drag the mouse to the second. A black line is thus drawn between the two points. Next, we click on this line and slide to the point to be interpolated. If there are points to interpolate, we repeat the procedure as many times as necessary. VTT will represent the interpolation by a series of white arrows chained together that will run through all the points, the first one starting from the first reference point, the last one ending on the last reference point.

Alignments (not to be confused twith FontLab's "alignments", which are roundings of an individual point relative to the grid) are a stronger form of interpolations in which we request that points be mutually aligned with one another at all costs. That is really of interest only for points that fall on the same slanted straight line, since for points aligned horizontally or vertically an alignment can be obtained much more easily by rounding them.

A typical example of alignment is the slanted and discontinuous stroke of the 'A' (see opposite), for which the rasterizing engine has no way, in the absence of an instruction, to guess that the pieces above and below the cross stroke absolutely must be aligned.

 We insert an alignment by selecting the **Align** tool and joining (by dragging the mouse) the two extreme points of the points to be aligned. VTT will produce as many blue arrows as there are points between these extremes. By playing with the heads of these arrows, we can exclude some or add others. The extreme points automatically become anchors.

Strokes

Strokes are a very interesting feature of VTT. The question that arises is: if links, distances, and shifts allow for the management of the thicknesses of horizontal and vertical strokes, what is done for slanted ones? That is where the "stroke" tool comes to the rescue. It allows us to cover the surface with a slanted stroke and to associate with it a thickness that is merely an entry in the CVT table. This entry must be stored in the table under the "black" and "diagonal" attributes. The rasterizing engine will then optimize the slanted stroke.

Here is how we insert a stroke. First, we select the **Stroke** tool on the button bar. Next, we select four points that cover a large part of the slanted stroke to be optimized; for example, in the figure below, points 2, 5, 4, and 3 constitute two pairs, (2, 5) and (3, 4). We click on one of the four (for example, 2) and drag to the matching point (here, 5); then we click on the point that is on the same side as the first, at the other end of the stroke (here, 3), and drag to the remaining point.

As we drag the mouse the second time, the area of the stroke turns black. When we have finished, the area is shown hatched on a yellow background, with a "highway shield" in the middle that indicates the number of the CVT entry selected by *VTT*:

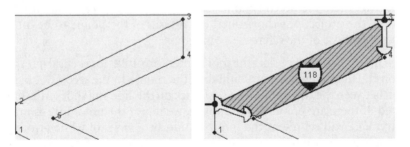

We can change the CVT entry as usual by making a contextual click on the highway-shield icon and selecting the appropriate entry.

The starting points for the two links (here, 2 and 3) are automatically made into anchors.

δ instructions

These δs are shifts of the nodes to the customized outline. They are our last hope for correcting minor imperfections that the other instructions have left behind. They must be used in moderation: they do allow us to add a pixel here or delete one there, but we must be careful not to overuse them, since they increase the bulk of the font. One or more rasterized sizes can be affected by a δ.

We can classify δs according to their direction (horizontal or vertical), their amplitude (between $\frac{1}{64}$ and 8 pixels), the sizes of rasterization to which they apply, or the moment of their execution in the assembly code for TrueType instructions: "inline" (*inline*), "just before global interpolation" (*pre-IUP*), or "after global interpolation" (*post-IUP*).

To insert δs, we must enable the option **Display>General Options>Grid fit** and possibly also the option **Pixels**.

The tools **XMove** and **YMove** are used for horizontal and vertical δs that apply to all sizes of glyphs; the tools **XDelta** and **YDelta** are used for those that apply only to the active size. The sizes are independent with respect to δs; thus we can apply several different δs to the same point, each corresponding to a different size.

Once we have selected the tool, we click on the point to which we wish to apply a δ. A ruler then appears:

We can select the amplitude of the δ, between −8 and 8 pixels, in subdivisions of one eighth of a pixel (feel free to slide outside the little window: only a small part of the ruler is visible). When the CTRL key is pressed while the ruler is visible, the subdivisions become larger; conversely, when ALT is pressed, the subdivisions become smaller, down to $\frac{1}{64}$ of a pixel.

By holding down the Shift key while the ruler is visible, we change the moment at which the δ is executed, which is indicated by the keywords `inline`, `preIUP`, and `postIUP` in the upper right part of the window containing the ruler. Nevertheless, be forewarned: "inline" δs and "pre-IUP" δs can be applied only to "touched" points, i.e., to points that have been rounded by an anchor or a link.

Finally, when we right-click (under Windows; ⌘-click on the Macintosh) on the point to which we are applying the δ, the ruler's window displays a third piece of information, the keywords `b/w only` and `grey only`:

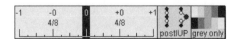

If "gray scale" mode has been selected (**Tools>General Options>Gray scale**), a right-click/⌘-click will limit the δ's scope to gray-scale rasterizations. Conversely, if "black-and-white" mode is selected, the δ will apply only to rasterizations of that type. This feature allows us to restrict δ instructions to a certain kind of rasterization.

A few examples

We shall examine three typical examples (the letters 'O', 'H', and 'A') drawn from the font *Trebuchet* in a VTT tutorial [260].

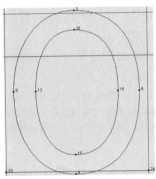

The letter 'O' from this font is shown opposite. In the image, we have enabled the option **Show fewer points**; thus we see only the points on the curve (the others do not have an effect on visual hints).

We shall first place an anchor at point 3—an anchor connected to the CVT entry for the upper overshoot of a capital letter, which is entry 3. Likewise, we shall place an anchor at point 9 that will be linked to CVT entry 9 (the lower overshoot of a capital letter). We thus ensure the alignment of our glyph relative to the other glyphs in the font.

Next, we shall place two horizontal links: one from 0 to 12 and one from 6 to 18. VTT will automatically associate these links with entry 70 ("capitals, black, horizontal, round stroke"). Likewise, we shall place vertical links from 3 to 20 and from 9 to 15; VTT will automatically select CVT entry 74 ("capitals, black, vertical, round stroke"). We shall always use "round" links with a minimum distance of one pixel. The minimum distance ensures that we shall always have a visible stroke, even if the thinness and arrangement would ordinarily cause some pixels not to be black (which would leave holes in the outline of the 'O' when rendered with pixels). Thus we can be sure of obtaining good stroke thicknesses.

Finally, we shall deal with the side bearings. We shall connect the origin (point 23) and point 0 with a "distance", i.e., a link not connected to a CVT entry. We shall do the same on the other side: we connect the glyph's set-width (point 24) and point 6 with a "distance". But this time we specify a true minimum distance, of one pixel. Thus the glyph may have a zero approach on the left, but it will always have an approach of at least one pixel on the right.

Here, then, is the result of our instructions, as shown in VTT:

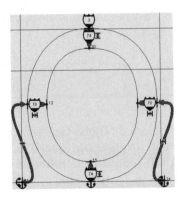

Note that all the links go from the outside inward. That allows us to direct any changes to the outline towards the inside of the glyph, where they will be less damaging to the glyph's overall appearance.

Let us continue with this font's letter 'H'.

We shall start by placing anchors in order to ensure alignment with the other glyphs: points 6 and 9 will be connected by CVT entry 2 (the height of a capital letter), and points 3 and 0 will be connected by entry 8 (the baseline of a capital).

Next, we shall concern ourselves with the thicknesses of the strokes: we shall connect points 5 and 7, then 10 and 8, with horizontal links. VTT will automatically select CVT entry 68 ("capitals, black, horizontal, straight stroke"). We shall request a minimum distance of one pixel so that the stroke will not disappear under any circumstances.

Here there is a trap. For us humans, it is obvious that point 2, for example, must have the same abscissa as point 7. But from looking at the outline, it is not at all obvious to the rasterizing engine that that must be so. Therefore, to prevent stroke thicknesses that differ for the upper and lower parts of the glyph, we shall also set links from 5 to 3 and from 10 to 0, with the same width and type as the previous links.

After that, we shall ensure the correct thickness of the cross stroke. To that end, we shall create a vertical link between 2 and 8. This link is automatically connected to CVT entry 72 ("capitals, black, vertical, straight stroke"), and we request a minimum distance of one pixel, so that the cross stroke will always be visible.

But what about the position of the cross stroke? Rather than defining a special CVT entry for the height of the cross stroke of the 'H', we can make use of an interpolation: after all, the position of this cross stroke is not of critical importance. Let us take points 0 and 6 as the extreme points for our interpolation. But which point shall we interpolate: the one on the top of the cross stroke, or the one on the bottom?

To answer that question, let us consider another: if the height of the glyph is an even number of pixels, we shall have to decide to place the cross stroke either above or below the imaginary line that runs between the two pixels in the middle. What would be the more appropriate choice? From the aesthetic point of view, we would prefer for the cross stroke of the 'H' to err on the high side. Moreover, we can see right away in the original outline that the cross stroke appears slightly higher than the middle of the glyph. Thus we must interpolate, and round, a point below the cross stroke (for example, point 2). Then the pixels resulting from any possible rounding error will be propagated towards the top of the glyph.

Finally, to include the instruction of the glyph, we resolve the problem of the side bearings by adding "distances", just as with the letter 'O'. Here is VTT's representation of our instructions:

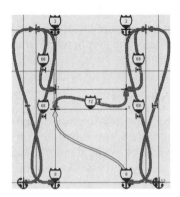

We shall conclude this series of examples with the letter 'A'.

Note that, in the image opposite, the lower left point of the letter (point 4) is mistaken for the origin (11) and that the lower right point (7) is mistaken for the set-width (12).

We shall begin by placing anchors at the relevant heights: at points 5 and 6 (CVT entry 3: "height of a capital letter with overshoot") and at points 4, 3, 0, and 7 (CVT entry 8: "baseline of a capital letter, without overhang").

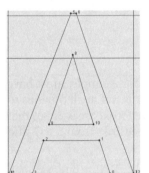

We shall also set an anchor at point 8. It will not be linked to a CVT entry, but it will use a very special rounding method—rounding towards the center of the pixel—to ensure that the point will be rendered by *one and only one* pixel.

How shall we handle this letter horizontally? If the extreme points are close enough to the edges of its abstract box, then the side bearings are completely insignificant, and we shall not worry about them (as we did with the 'O' and the 'H'). On the other hand, we know that we have the stroke tool to handle the thickness and rasterization of slanted strokes. What we need is a mechanism to ensure that the letter will not lean to one side—in other words, a mechanism to preserve the letter's vertical symmetry.

We shall bring out the big guns in order to obtain this symmetry. For example, we shall define a new CVT entry, representing half the distance between 3 and 0, i.e., half of the letter's internal width. That entry will be classified as "capitals, gray, horizontal, distance". Next, we shall create horizontal links between points 8 and 3, and then between 8 and 0. VTT will associate them automatically with the new CVT entry. We shall request that they be given a minimum distance of one pixel, so that the slanted strokes will not run the risk of becoming vertical. The fact that the two links run from the outside inward ensures that the letter can be drawn a bit wider so that its design will be correct.

To avoid any risks, we shall also deal with the letter's external width by creating an interpolation: point 8 will be interpolated horizontally relative to points 4 and 7. Nothing remains but to use the stroke tool on the two slanted strokes; VTT will automatically select CVT entry 77 ("capitals, black, diagonal, straight stroke").

One final precautionary measure: will the two slanted strokes be aligned on both sides of the cross stroke? To ensure their alignment, we shall use the alignment tool, twice: between 8 and 3, and between 8 and 0.

Thus we have solved the problem of the slanted strokes. Here is what we have obtained so far:

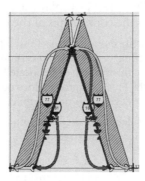

Now we have to solve the problem of the cross stroke. For its thickness, we need only create a vertical link between 9 and 2. VTT will automatically select CVT entry 72 (just as it did for the 'H'). We shall specify for the link a minimum distance of one pixel so as to avoid ending up with a 'Λ' instead of an 'A'. Now that the cross stroke's thickness has been corrected, we must deal with its height. We shall proceed as with the letter 'H': that is, we shall use an interpolation. Just one annoying detail: we would not want the cross stroke to run too close to the apex, but still less would we want it to drift to the bottom; else the 'A' might become a 'Δ'. Thus we have to preserve the letter's vertical integrity and interpolate points 2 and 8 *simultaneously* towards the letter's extremities, 3 and 5.

Finally, to ensure that the cross stroke will remain horizontal, we shall perform "alignments" (**YShift**) between the pairs of points (9, 10) and (2, 1).

Here are the new instructions that we have just added:

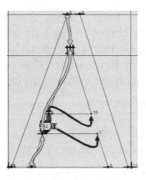

(Here we have represented only the instructions not shown in the previous figure.)

Managing Instructions under FontForge

While FontLab and VTT offer us interactive interfaces for creating instructions, Font-Forge follows a different approach, that of the integrated development environment (IDE). For instance, it offers us a debugger for TrueType instructions that allows us to follow, step by step, the evolution of the original outline to the outline customized for the grid. Other windows (see Figure 13-11) display the contents of the registers, the storage area, and the stack, as well as the coordinates of the points of the glyph, in real time.

There is, however, a catch. As is described on the project's web page FreeType [330], the library of subroutines used by FontForge's debugger is subject to certain patents held by Apple. To use it, one must therefore request a license from Apple or be located in a country where the patents in question are not valid. And since the FreeType project does not wish to subject honest people to temptation, the code required by the debugger is not compiled in the default version of FreeType.

To be able to work with FontForge's debugger, therefore, one must first recompile FreeType after having slightly modified the code. Here is how to do so:

1. Obtain the latest version of the sources for `freetype` from
   `http://sourceforge.net/project/showfiles.php?group_id=3157`
2. Decompress them and open the file
   `include/freetype/config/ftoption.h`
3. Replace
   `/* #define TT_CONFIG_OPTION_BYTECODE_INTERPRETER */`
   with
   `#define TT_CONFIG_OPTION_BYTECODE_INTERPRETER`
   i.e., uncomment the definition of the C preprocessor directive.
4. Compile FreeType and install it by following the instructions in `docs/INSTALL`.

Only after this maneuver will the debugger for TrueType instructions work in FontForge.

The debugger's interface

Let us open a glyph for editing in FontForge. When we select **Hints>Debug**, a small window asks us for the size of the rasterization that we wish to debug and the resolution of the device. Once this window is closed, the glyph's window splits into two. On the left: the original outline of the glyph, shown in black on a grid of pixels (whose centers are marked by small crosses), an approximation by straight strokes of the modified outline, and the positions and numbers of all the nodes. On the right: a series of seven buttons and, below it, a numbered list of all the instructions in the glyph.

The buttons have the following functions:

- The button causes the following instruction to be executed. If it is a procedure call, we will go into the procedure and execute its first instruction.

- The second button, , also proceeds step by step with the execution of the program but does not go into procedure calls. This is the button that we shall use the most often.

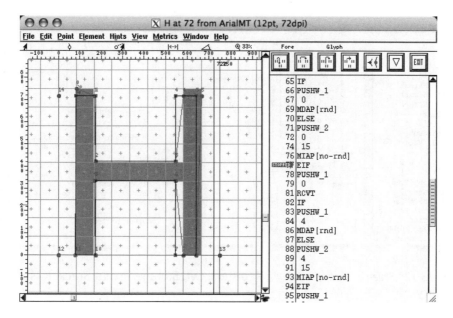

Figure 13-11: The interface for debugging instructions in FontForge.

- The third button, ![button], takes us out of a procedure. If we are in the glyph's code (not in a procedure), clicking on this button will take us to the end of the code.

- The fourth button, ![button], is for "speed-reading": it executes all the instructions up to the end of the glyph's code.

The execution of an instruction launched with the buttons ![button] and ![button] can also halt if the debugger encounters a *breakpoint* or the shifting of a *watchpoint*.

We set a breakpoint, ⊕, by simply clicking on a line. A second click disables the breakpoint.

The principle of a watchpoint is different, and especially interesting: we select a point on the outline and click on the button ![button]. The point is then "watched". We can launch the rapid execution of the instructions: as soon as an instruction modifies this point, execution will halt. In this way, we can find the instructions that will modify a given point and, by so doing, achieve a better understanding of the operation of instructions.

When we reach the end of the code, we need only click twice on a button that initiates execution (such as ![button]), and the code will be executed again from the beginning.

It is impossible to understand the operation of instructions without constantly monitoring the instruction stack, the graphics state, and possibly the storage area, registers and CVT. That can all be done through the use of auxiliary windows obtained by means of the button ![button]. There is also a "glossary" window providing explanation on TrueType instructions.

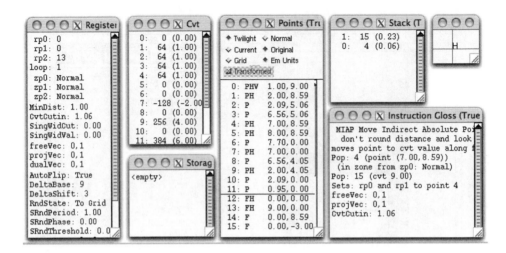

Figure 13-12: Seven auxiliary windows: Registers, Cvt, Storage, Points, Stack, Raster, *and* Glossary.

It is also possible to edit instructions. We do so with another window, which is obtained with Hints>Edit instructions.

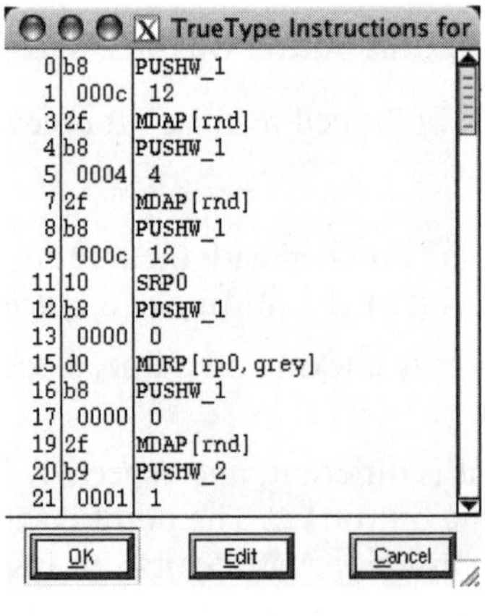

Figure 13-13: The FontForge window for editing TrueType instructions.

This window—which, unlike the debugger, is not constrained by patents and is therefore always available—displays a numbered list of instructions. By clicking on the Edit button, we can modify the instructions. Note that the modifications are not immediately conveyed to the debugger: we must halt the execution of the code and start it again.

14

Enriching Fonts: Advanced Typography

Introduction

The title of this chapter refers to the "advanced typographic features" of OpenType and AAT fonts, which are tables added to the basic TrueType fonts by Microsoft, Adobe, and Apple. We have witnessed the emergence of two new font formats: OpenType (defined by Adobe and Microsoft, formerly called "TrueType Open") and AAT (for "Apple advanced typography", formerly called "TrueType GX"). Thanks to these tables, we can better meet the needs of the non-Latin scripts, in particular the Asian scripts, but also some of the requirements of traditional typography, well beyond the possibilities of the original TrueType format. Here, then, is the dialog box for OpenType in *Adobe Illustrator CS2* (under Mac OS X), where the different OpenType features (default ligatures, calligraphic letters, etc.) are shown in the form of buttons that are enabled only when the feature in question is present in the font:

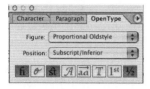

Whether for setting type in Sanskrit, in Urdu or Arabic with aesthetic ligatures, in Hebrew with vowel points, in Elzevirian Greek with ligatures, in calligraphic Latin, or simply in a text font with capitals and old-style figures, OpenType and AAT tables are well up to these challenges, and others as well. What is particular about these fonts is that the arrangement and substitution of the glyphs are not part of the operating system, as used to be the case, but are included in the font—more specifically, in the OpenType and AAT tables. That makes the use of the font a little more cumbersome, since the system must read and interpret each font's "advanced" tables. But at the same time, it offers the font's designer enormous flexibility, as she has full responsibility for the font's behavior: she can adopt rules already present in other fonts, modify them, or even invent new ones of her own!

How, exactly, do the advanced typographic features work? Here is a general description. We start with three concepts: "script", "language", and "feature". When we use a font, we use a given script and a given language. (If the user does not specify these values, the default values are used: in the United States, they would be Latin for the script and English for the language.) Within this framework, the font offers a number of rules for substitution or movement of a glyph that are stored within the features. An example of a rule for substitution would be shifting from lining figures, 0123456789, to old-style figures, 0123456789; the feature that contains this rule has a name, "onum". An example of movement would be the placing of an accent over a letter (from 'aˆ' to 'â'); the feature that contains this rule is called "mark". Some features are programmed to be executed by default when the font is selected; others are enabled by the user. For example, there is the feature "liga", which manages ordinary ligatures, such as 'fi', 'fl', etc. This feature is enabled by default; nonetheless, it can be disabled at the request of the user.

OpenType features contain rules called *lookups*. A *lookup* can consist of one or more *substitutions* or one or more *positionings* of glyphs.

Substitutions can be quite complex. Thanks to them, we can set type in Arabic, Sanskrit, Khmer, or any other highly contextual script. In these scripts, the shape of a letter depends on the letters that precede it or follow it. Here is a list of the different types of substitutions:

- *Single* substitutions (§D.9.4.1): one glyph is replaced with another, as, for example, a lowercase letter with a small capital.

- *Multiple* substitutions (§D.9.4.2): one glyph is replaced by several. This substitution is rather uncommon, except when it is necessary to reposition the parts of a glyph. For instance, it sometimes happens in German that the letter 'T' is followed by a vowel with an umlaut (as in the word "Tür"), and, in some fonts, the umlaut collides with the serif on the right arm of the 'T'. To solve this problem, we use a positioning rule; but first we must separate the umlaut from the letter 'u', which we can do with a multiple substitution that turns the 'ü' into a 'u' and an umlaut.

- *Alternate substitutions* (§D.9.4.3): the software allows us to select an alternate form of a given glyph through a special graphical interface, such as a pull-down menu that shows us all the available variants.

- *Ligatures* (§D.9.4.4): several glyphs are replaced by a single one. This is the classic case of the ligatures 'fi', 'fl', 'ffiffiffiffi', etc.

EXAMPLES OF SUBSTITUTIONS

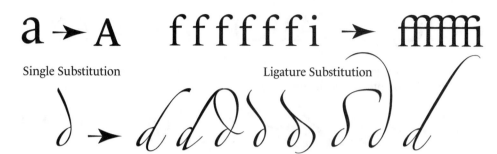

Single Substitution   Ligature Substitution

Alternate Substitution (the nine "d"s of font *Zapfino*)

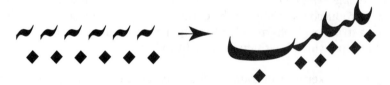

Multiple Substitution   Contextual Substitution
(untied Indian ligature)   (the connecting strokes of letters "d" and "s" disappear)

Reverse Chaining Contextual Single Substitution (contextuality of Urdu writing system)

- A *contextual* substitution (§D.9.4.5) consists of one or more substitutions of the types listed above—single substitutions, multiple substitutions, or ligatures—which are instantiated according to the context, i.e., whether the string of glyphs to be replaced is preceded and/or followed by certain glyphs. The classic example is that of Arabic, where an isolated letter turns into an initial form when followed by a letter that is connected to it. In this case, the change of shape is a single substitution, and the context is the following glyph.

- *Chained contextual* substitutions (§D.9.4.6). The example of an isolated Arabic letter that becomes an initial form, mentioned above for contextual substitution, is in fact an example of what we should not do: specifically, the "context" is used by the substitution and cannot become the object of another substitution. The letter that follows our isolated letter cannot in turn become, for example, a medial form. *Chained* contextual substitution solves the problem by introducing the notions of *pre-chain* and *post-chain*: once again, these are glyphs that come before or after glyphs to be replaced, but this time the glyphs remain available for other operations.

EXAMPLES OF POSITIONING

Single Adjustment	Pair Adjustment (kerning)
(special parentheses for all-caps text)	

Cursive Attachment   Context Positioning

MarkToBase Attachment   MarkToMark Attachment   MarkToLigature Attachment

- *Reverse chaining contextual* substitution (§D.9.4.7). This is a variant of the proceeding that was introduced especially for the Urdu language. What distinguishes it is that it processes a string of glyphs from left to right, i.e., in the direction opposite to that of the Urdu script, which is written from right to left.

Positioning includes kerning, of course, but also types of positioning that may be quite sophisticated, such as contextual kerning, where the spacing of two letters closer together or farther apart depends on their context. Here is a list of the different types of positioning:

- *Single adjustment* positioning (§D.9.3.2): certain glyphs are moved horizontally or vertically.

- *Pair adjustment* positioning (§D.9.3.3): when certain pairs of glyphs are detected in the typeset string, their glyphs are moved horizontally and/or vertically. This positioning is more powerful than a kerning pair: in a conventional kerning pair, only the second glyph is moved, but here it is also possible to move the first glyph or both.

- *Cursive attachment* (§D.9.3.4), a truly spectacular property: a point is marked as the "exit point" of the glyph, and another point is marked as being its "entry point". Cursive attachment applied to a string of glyphs will make the exit point of the nth glyph correspond with the entry point of the $(n+1)$th glyph. This feature is ideal for cursive and calligraphic fonts.

- *Combining diacritical marks* (§D.9.3.5): We define as *marks* some positions on the glyph's working area. Diacritical marks (accents, cedillas, etc.) also have marks of this sort. When applied to a glyph followed by a diacritic, this positioning will attach the diacritic to the glyph by making the appropriate marks coincide. This feature is ideal for placing any desired accent on any desired glyph, an operation that is indispensable for any self-respecting Unicode rendering engine.

- *Multiple diacritical marks* (§D.9.3.6): a variant of the preceding in which diacritical marks combine with one another to form more complex signs. This feature is often needed in phonetic notation.

- *Diacritical marks on ligatures* (§D.9.3.7): some fonts include a multitude of ligatures, often operating on vowels. Often these vowels can bear accents. What, then, should we do? Design the same ligatures with all the combinations of accents? This positioning solves the problem by defining one mark for each of the ligature's components.

- *Contextual* positioning (§D.9.3.8): when a glyph is moved *only* if it is preceded or followed by certain other glyphs. A typical example: if we write "V.A.V.",[1] the second 'V' is moved closer to the second period only because that period is preceded by an 'A'. But the same combination of glyphs '.' and 'V' in "V.V." should not be kerned, or the two 'V's would bump into each other—"V.V."—and look like a 'W';

- *Chained contextual* positioning (§D.9.3.9): the same extension of contextual positioning as for chained contextual substitution. In other words, the glyphs that form the context of our string are separated from it and can take part in other substitution or positioning operations.

How can substitutions and positionings interact? Let us take a typical case: suppose that we wish to take advantage of the "diacritical marks on ligatures" lookup to place a circumflex accent over the letter 'a' in an "ates" ligature. The ligature itself was, of course, created by a substitution lookup. But it seems that there is a contradiction: if the original string is ('a', "circumflex accent", 't', 'e', 's'), no ligature will be formed; and if the original string is ('a', 't', 'e', 's', "circumflex accent"), we will obtain a ligature, but how will the rendering engine know that the accent is intended for the letter 'a', not for another component of the ligature?

To solve this sort of problem, OpenType first classifies all the glyphs into four *types*: "single" (whose glyphs are also called "base glyphs"), "ligature", "mark" (i.e., "diacritical mark" or similar), and "component" (of a ligature or a glyph). Next, the substitutions can choose *not* to apply to one or another type of glyph. For instance, in our example, the ligature substitution will disregard the circumflex accent while preserving the information that is "attached" to the first component of the ligature. Positioning, which must necessarily come second, will collect this information, and everything will work perfectly.

But let us leave the technical details aside and consider the implementation of OpenType properties in existing software.

As happens often in computer science, there is a vast gap between the things that we see on paper and those that work in the real world. The OpenType specification allows us to

---

[1] V.A.V. is the *Vlaamse Aikido Vereniging* (Flemish Aikido Union). http://www.aikido-vav.be/

EXAMPLES OF FEATURES

saisons → ſaiſons   afﬂigé → afﬂigé   1/2 → ½

hist (historical forms)   liga (ligatures)   frac (diagonal fractions)

activiste → activiste   0123 ⇄ 0123   1/2 → ½

dlig (discretionary ligatures)   onum (oldstyle figures)   afrc (vertical fractions)
                                    lnum (lining figures)

J.-Ph. Bec → J.-PH. BEC   OUI → OUI

smcp (lowercase to small caps)   c2sc (uppercase to small caps)

define new features and give them any names we wish. But if we do so, no one will be able to use the features in question, since word-processing software[2] and desktop publishing software offer their users only certain *predefined* features.

Here is a short list of the features most often recognized by applications[3] in the context of the Latin script:

- hist ("historical forms"). Certain letters are replaced with older forms. This feature is often used to replace the 's' with the "long s", thus repreſenting the text ſuch as it would have appeared in the eigtheenth century. Warning: in English, the 'ſ' is used only at the beginning or in the middle of a word, as in the word"ſeaſons"; in German, however, the "round s" can appear in the middle of a word when that word is a compound, as in "Ausgabe" (from "aus" and "Gabe"); compare the word "Aufſatz".

- liga ("standard ligatures"). These include, for example, the "f-ligatures": all those that begin with an 'f' or an 'ſ'. The distinctive characteristic of these ligatures is that they are not immediately visible to the uninitiated. They improve the document's aesthetic quality without imparting a particular style. We can consider them as "default ligatures" to be used in every document.

- dlig ("discretionary ligatures"). These include, for example, the ligatures 'ct' and 'st' that are found in Monotype Garamond, which give the *La Pléiade* series of books all its charm. These ligatures go beyond improving the document's aesthetic quality: they impart a particular style to the document. Thus they should be used at the user's discretion, and that is the spirit of this feature.

- onum and lnum (old-style figures" and "lining figures"). The old-style figures onum, "01 23456789", are characterized by their different sizes and by the presence of ascenders and descenders. Moreover, the zero resembles the letter 'o', and the one resembles a

---

[2] Except Ω, which is able to use OpenType fonts directly.
[3] The reader will find a complete list of predefined OpenType features in Appendix D (starting at §D.10.2).

small-capital 'i'. The lining figures lnum, "0123456789", all have the same height and usually do not resemble any letter or other symbol. Some publishers use old-style figures for page numbers and lining figures in the body text.

- frac and afrc ("fractions" and "alternative fractions"). Used to produce beautiful fractions such as '½', '¾', and '¹⁄₄₂' from the glyph strings 1/4, 3/4, 1/42. The afrc feature produces fractions with a horizontal bar: '$\frac{1}{2}$', '$\frac{3}{4}$', '$\frac{1}{42}$'.

- smcp and c2sc ("lowercase to small capitals" and "capitals to small capitals"). Changes the case of glyphs.

The reader will find in Appendix D a detailed technical description of the OpenType and AAT tables. In the rest of this chapter, we shall discuss the practical aspects: how to enrich a font by adding OpenType or AAT tables through the use of the two great software packages FontLab and FontForge that we studied in the two previous chapters and by means of another software product designed specifically for this task, Microsoft VOLT. On the other hand, only FontForge is currently capable of incorporating AAT tables into TrueType fonts; we have devoted the last section of this chapter to it.

Managing OpenType Tables in FontLab

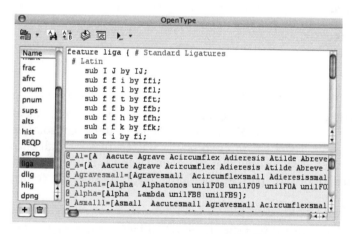

Figure 14-1: The OpenType window in FontLab.

When we select **Window>Panels>OpenType**, FontLab presents us with the OpenType window (see Figure 14-1). This window is divided into three parts. At the left, there is a list of all the OpenType features in the font. The names of the features are always strings of four letters (such as liga, c2sc, etc.). In §D.10.2 of this book, there is also a list of the predefined features, illustrated with examples.

In the window in Figure 14-1, we have selected the liga feature. In the upper right section, we see a description of this feature in a syntax developed by Adobe and known as "feature definition language". In the lower section, this syntax is used again to define glyph classes, which are used in all of the font's features.

Thus it is clear that we must know the syntax of this famous "feature definition language" in order to incorporate even the slightest feature into the font. When FontLab compiles the code written in this language to produce OpenType tables, if there is the slightest syntax error, the compilation will halt with a less than comforting and informative message of this kind:

```
<PalatinoLinotype-Roman> aborting because of errors
```

Fortunately, the syntax of the feature definition language is quite simple. In the following section, we shall give a brief overview of it.

Feature Definition Language

The "feature definition language" was defined by Adobe [325] in the course of work on SDK OpenType. Adobe offers a development kit with tools that compile code written in this language and insert it into a TrueType font, which accordingly becomes an OpenType font. Although Adobe's specification is already at version 1.4, FontLab covers only a subset of its features. This is the subset that we shall examine below.

First of all, a general rule: the goal of this syntax is to define OpenType features. To define a feature named "foo", we will write:

```
feature foo {
    ... rules ...
} foo ;
```

Between the braces we will write rules for positioning or substitution.

From the few lines of code above, we can already conclude that, as in most programming languages, the braces serve to delimit blocks of code and the semicolon serves to terminate an expression. There are other special characters that we shall encounter as they arise. For now, let us say simply that the pound sign (#) is used for writing *comments*: everything that follows it, up to the end of the line, is considered a comment.

Identifying and classifying glyphs

Folk wisdom has it that things should be called by their names. For example, we call a glyph by its name, provided that it has one and that the name contains nothing but ASCII letters, digits, periods, and underscores. And it may not begin with a digit.[4] FontLab will assign an arbitrary name to any unnamed glyph. Glyph names that are unlucky enough to be keywords in the feature definition language must be preceded by a backslash (in other words, if gizmo is a keyword in the language, \gizmo is a glyph called *gizmo*).

---

[4] The language's specification provides for names of the type \123 for CIDs, but FontLab seems not to recognize this form.

As glyphs often have the same behavior, we are wise to group them into *classes* and then to use these classes, rather than individual glyphs, in our expressions. A class is simply a set of glyph names placed within brackets: [e eacute egrave]. In some cases, we can write ranges of glyphs: [A-Z], [a-z], [foo.023-foo.437], [A.foo-Z.foo], etc.

We can assign a name to a class. It must begin with an at sign (@):

```
@lowercase = [ a-z agrave eacute egrave ugrave ] ;
```

Other classes may appear in the definition of a class:

```
@letters = [ @lowercase @capitals agrave eacute ] ;
```

Scripts, languages, features, lookups

We have already discussed four hierarchical levels of the system of OpenType features: script, language, feature, and *lookup*. Each of these levels must be specified in the feature definition language, through the use of names of four letters or fewer. Example:

```
feature foo {
  script latn ;
    language ENG ;
        ... rules for English ...
    language DEU ;
        ... rules for German ...
  script grek ;
    ... rules for Greek ...
} foo ;
```

In this example, the liga feature has different rules for the English and German languages, which belong to the Latin script, and still other rules for Greek, which is the *default* language for the Greek script.

The reader will find a complete list of scripts and languages in §D.10.1 of this book.

A few details: Every time we change scripts, the language becomes DFLT (from the word *default*). The default script is latn. There is a command that combines script and language:

```
languagesystem latn ENG ;
```

One word on the behavior of the language keyword: rules defined for the "default" language are *added* to those defined for a specific language. In other words, when we define a rule for the "default" language, we cannot eliminate it: it will apply to all other languages that use the same script. We can get around that with the excludeDFLT keyword:

```
feature foo {
  script latn ;
    language DFLT ;
      ... rule A ...
    language DEU ;
      ... rule B ...
    language ENG excludeDFLT ;
      ... rule C ...
} foo ;
```

In this example, when the feature foo is enabled, only rule A will be applied in an Italian document; in a German document, rules A and B will be applied, in that order; finally, in a French document, only rule C will be applied, since the "default" rule, A, has been excluded.

Finally, what is a lookup in this context? It is nothing but a "macro", a way to group substitution or positioning rules in a block of code, give the block a name, and subsequently make reference to the block by its name. For example, if we have previously defined:

```
lookup foo {
  ... rules ...
} foo ;
```

in a property, we can then execute the rules in the block by simply writing:

```
lookup foo ;
```

To avoid misunderstandings, note that our use of the term *lookup* here is not really the same as the definition that we gave in the introduction to this chapter, nor is it the same as the one found in Appendix D. Indeed, if we write:

```
feature foo { ... rules ... } foo ;
```

without explicitly mentioning the lookup, the rules rules will nevertheless be collected into a lookup in the generated table. By writing:

```
feature foo {
lookup bar { ... rules ... } bar ;
lookup bar ;
} foo ;
```

we obtain *exactly* the same result. Finally, if we write:

```
feature foo {
  loookup bar {
    ... rules A ...
  } bar ;
  ... rules B ...
  lookup bar ;
} foo ;
```

the result will be a feature foo with two lookups: the first one, which is implicit, will contain rules B, and the second one, which is explicit, will contain rules A. The names given to the lookups are strictly internal to the feature definition language and do not appear anywhere in the OpenType tables generated.

In the example of interaction between substitutions and positionings that we gave at the start of this chapter, we spoke of *types of glyphs*. At any time, we can specify the type of glyph to which the rules that we are writing will apply. To that end, we need only use the keyword lookupflag followed by one or more of the following keywords, separated by commas:

- IgnoreBaseGlyph: what follows will not apply to base glyphs

- IgnoreLigatures: what follows will not apply to ligatures

- IgnoreMarks: what follows will not apply to marks

Substitution rules

Now that we have finished these preliminaries, let us move on to the heart of the language: the *writing of substitution rules*. We shall use four keywords: substitute (often abbreviated sub), by, from, and, less often, ignore. Let us review the six types of substitutions:

- *single* substitutions: to replace a glyph a with a glyph b, we write:

      sub a by b ;

  We can also use glyph classes. For instance, if @lowercase is the class of the lowercase letters and @small_cap the class for the small capitals, we can write:

      sub @lowercase by @small_cap ;

  The two classes must be of the same size. Another possibility is to replace all the members of a class with a single glyph:

      sub [space A-Z a-z] by bullet ;

  In this example, the letters and the spaces are replaced by bullets, a very handy procedure when entering passwords.

- *Multiple* substitution: to replace, for example, the ligature ffi with the glyphs f, f, i, the specification allows us to write simply:

      sub ffi by f f i ;

  Here we are not allowed to use classes. Note that this syntax appears in the specification but that FontLab version 5 does not yet recognize it.

- *Alternate substitutions*: to force word-processing software to ask the user which form among 'e', 'é', 'è', and 'ê', for example, to use every time it encounters an 'e', we can write:

  ```
  sub e from [ e eacute egrave ecircumflex ] ;
  ```

- *Ligatures*, the most classic substitution: to replace the pair of glyphs f and i with the glyph f_i, we can write:

  ```
  sub f i by f_i ;
  ```

  Any number of glyphs may be replaced by a ligature.

- *Contextual substitution*, whether *chained* or not, is a replacement of one or more glyphs by a single one, but a replacement that occurs only if the glyphs appear in a certain *context*—that is, if they are proceeded and followed by well-defined strings of glyphs. Very important: in the syntax, we use the nonoriented apostrophe (') to *indicate the glyph(s) to substitute*. Everything that does not have an apostrophe is part of the context.

  For example, suppose that we have two versions of the letter 'd', called d and d.prettier, and that we always wish to use the second version before a vowel. Then we are making a single substitution of d by d.prettier, but one that occurs only if d is followed by a glyph in the class [a e i o u]. Thus we shall write:

  ```
  sub d' [ a e i o u ] by d.prettier ;
  ```

  Another example: To replace the hyphen (hyphen) with an en dash (endash) whenever it occurs between two digits, we can write:

  ```
  @digits = [ zero one two three four five six seven eight nine ] ;
  sub @digits hyphen' @digits by endash ;
  ```

  - *reverse chaining contextual* substitution, introduced as an afterthought for the needs of the Urdu language, is not yet supported in the feature definition language, still less by FontLab.

Sometimes the glyph classes can be of enormous size. For example, suppose that we have a glyph T_e_X for the TEX logo and that we wish to replace the string "TEX" with this glyph, but only when it is not part of a word, as it is in "CONTEXT". We will then need a substitution of the following type:

```
sub @all_but_letters T' E' X' @all_but_letters by T_e_X ;
```

But writing the class @all_but_letters would be quite tedious for a font with tens of thousands of glyphs.

The keyword ignore allows us to work in the opposite direction by first defining the excluded cases. For example, by writing:

```
ignore sub [ A-Z Eacute ] T' E' X' [ A-Z Eacute ] ;
sub T' E' X' by T_e_X ;
```

we can eliminate the words "CONTEXTUAL", "PRETEXTS", etc., and then quietly re-place all the remaining occurrences of "TEX" with T_e_X glyphs. But that still is not an adequate solution: what to do about words that begin or end with "TEX", such as "TEXT", "CORTEX", etc.?

Fortunately, the syntax for the `ignore` keyword can take several expressions into account simultaneously; these expressions are separated with commas. Thus, by writing:

```
ignore sub [ A-Z Eacute ] T' E' X' , T' E' X' [ A-Z Eacute ] ;
sub T' E' X' by T_e_X ;
```

we solve our problem.

Note that in the second line of code above we have used apostrophes as in contextual substitutions, whereas the expression seems not to have a context. But—and this is a *syntactic trap*—the first line establishes a context, and thus the entire lookup is contextual. Consequently, we are required to borrow the syntax of contextual substitutions in the second line.

Positioning rules

The specification provides a syntax for each case of a positioning rule (whether for single adjustment, pair adjustment, cursive attachment, diacritical marks, multiple diacritical marks, diacritical marks on ligatures, contextual positioning, or chained contextual positioning). But FontLab currently supports only single and pair adjustment positioning rules, possibly associated with a context. Nevertheless, the documentation for FontLab claims that the future updates will see the incorporation of other types of positioning; that is why we shall describe the syntax here, even though it cannot yet be used in the current version of FontLab (version 5).

Before discussing the different types of positioning, let us establish a few preliminary notions: those of *value records* and *anchors*.

A "value record" is simply a series of four numbers: the first two are the coordinates of the displacement from the glyph's origin (*X placement* and *Y placement*), and the other two are those of the displacement from the glyph's set-width, i.e., from the far end of the glyph's displacement vector (*X advance* and *Y advance*). If (a, b, c, d) represents these four numbers, the syntax for the value record is < a b c d >. In the figure below:

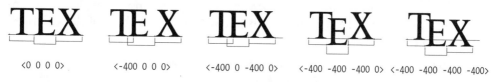

| <0 0 0 0> | <-400 0 0 0> | <-400 0 -400 0> | <-400 -400 -400 0> | <-400 -400 -400 -400> |

we see the effect of five simple displacements applied to the letter 'E' with different value records: in the first case, the two vectors are zero; in the second case, the origin is moved to the left without changing the glyph's width, i.e., the endpoint of the glyph's displacement vector; in the third case, we move this endpoint to the left, but its distance from the 'X' is restored; in the fourth case, we move the glyph's origin downward, but the endpoint remains on the baseline; finally, in the fifth case, the endpoint is also moved downward: all the glyphs that follow will be set at that depth, as long as the feature remains enabled.

We can also write a value record with *a single number*, the abscissa for the offset of the displacement vector, i.e., the third of these four numbers. Unless the feature is vkrn (vertical kerning), in which case the ordinate (therefore the fourth number) is used rather than the abscissa. When the value record consists of a single number, it is not necessary to use the symbols ⟨ ⟩.

An "anchor" is a location on the glyph's working area that serves as an attachment point for another glyph. This other glyph must also have an anchor, and the rendering engine simply matches these two locations to place the second glyph correctly with respect to the first. An anchor whose coordinates are (100, 200) is written <anchor 100 200>. Anchors are not recognized by FontLab v.5.

Armed with these two concepts, we are ready to explore the various types of displacement rules. In these rules, we shall use three keywords: position (usually abbreviated pos), cursive, and mark. Here are the eight types of displacements:

- The displacement of a *single glyph*, where we ask some glyphs to move horizontally and/or vertically. We simply write the keyword pos followed by the name of the glyph and the value record for the displacement. For example, to move an 'x' 100 units upwards without causing the following glyphs to be moved upwards as well, we write:

  ```
  pos x <0 200 0 0> ;
  ```

  We can also use a class of glyphs instead of the name of a glyph.

- The displacement of a *pair of glyphs*, where we request that the glyphs in certain pairs be moved horizontally and/or vertically. The general syntax is very simple: we write each of the two glyphs followed by its value record. But in order for FontLab v.5 to recognize this syntax, there must be only one value record (that of the second glyph), and it must consist of only a single number. Thus we are limited to the case of a simple kerning pair, as, for example:

  ```
  pos A T - ;
  ```

  The only possibility of going a bit further is to use classes instead of glyphs. For instance, if we wish to kern all the letters derived from 'A' with all of those derived from 'T', we write:

  ```
  @derived_from_A = [ A Aacute Agrave Acircumflex Adieresis
                      Atilde Aring ] ;
  @derived_from_T = [ T Tcaron Tcommaaccent ] ;
  pos @derived_from_A @derived_from_T - ;
  ```

This rule will then produce 21 (!) kerning pairs.

- The *cursive attachment*, where the "exit point" of each glyph is attached to the "entry point" of the following one:

Thus we must define the entry and exit points of each glyph. We do so using anchors. Merely adding the keyword cursive suffices:

```
pos cursive f <anchor - 105> <anchor 197 105> ;
pos cursive i <anchor - 105> <anchor 155 105> ;
```

and so forth. We can also use glyph classes. This type of positioning rule is not recognized by FontLab v.5.

- *Combining diacritical marks*, where we define marks both on the base glyph and on the diacritical marks themselves. The rendering engine will match up these marks. In our case, we shall, once again, use *anchors*. This time we shall proceed in two steps: first, we shall define the anchor on the diacritical mark by using the mark keyword to show that the glyph is a diacritical mark rather than a base glyph; then we shall use pos to indicate the anchor on the base glyph and the name of the glyph for the diacritical mark. This approach allows us to have multiple anchors, corresponding to the different types of diacritical marks, on the same base glyph. Example:

```
mark circumflex <anchor 511 1117> ;
pos E <anchor 686 1505> mark circumflex ;
```

Note that a diacritical mark can have only one anchor, whereas a base glyph can have any number, corresponding to the various diacritical marks. In the expressions below, we shall also use glyph classes. This sort of positioning rule is not recognized by FontLab v.5.

- *Multiple diacritical marks*, where we place diacritical marks over other diacritical marks. For example, if we wish to place a tilde over a circumflex accent, we can write:

```
mark circumflex <anchor 511 1117> ;
mark tilde <anchor 500 1074> ;
pos mark circumflex <anchor 511 1606> mark tilde ;
```

Here, in the first line, we define the lower anchor for the circumflex accent (which is used to attach the accent to a base glyph), but the anchor described in the third line is *above* the circumflex accent and thus serves to attach the tilde to it. This type of positioning rule is also not recognized by FontLab v.5.

- *Diacritical marks on a ligature*, where we take the glyph of a ligature and define as many anchors for it as the ligature has components, in order to attach diacritical marks to it. The syntax is a bit awkward. Suppose that in our font, *Monotype Garamond* italic, we have a ligature "*eta*" that we would also like to use with two circumflex accents, "*êtâ*" (as in the French verb form *prêtâmes*). This ligature has three components, and therefore—at least—three possible anchors. To add the two circumflex accents to it, we can write:

```
mark circumflex <anchor 151 438> ;
pos e_t_a <anchor 286 432> <anchor NULL> <anchor NULL>
    mark circumflex ;
pos e_t_a <anchor NULL> <anchor NULL> <anchor 832 432>
    mark circumflex ;
```

where <anchor NULL> was added only to arrange the three anchors correctly within the syntax. This type of positioning rule is also not recognized by FontLab v.5.

- *Contextual* and *chained contextual* positioning, where a glyph is positioned only when it is preceded or followed by certain other glyphs. The syntax is similar to that for substitutions:

```
pos A period' V' - ;
```

means that the pair period, V is kerned only when it is preceded by an A, which solves the problem of the string "S.A.V.". Recall that in a contextual rule the glyphs that are substituted or positioned bear an apostrophe; those that have no apostrophe establish the context. This type of positioning rule is unfortunately not recognized by FontLab v.5.

Two exceptions: the aalt and size features

The syntax that we have examined here is valid for all features except two very special ones: aalt ("all variants"), which enables all the glyph variants in the font, and size, which is not really a feature but rather a location in which some data on the optical size of the font may be stored.

Let us first take the aalt feature. Its purpose is to enable all the single substitutions and all choices of variants in the font. It should be placed first on the list of features, and it must contain the keyword feature followed by the name of a feature for all features of this type. For example, suppose that in our font we have the features smcp (small capitals) and ornm (choice of ornaments in the font). We can then write:

```
feature aalt {
  feature smcp ;
  feature ornm ;
} aalt ;
```

The size aims to make up for an enormous shortcoming in PostScript (other than Multiple Master, with their "optical size" axis) and TrueType fonts, which is that they *completely disregard the optical size*: there are, in fact, fonts named *Times New Roman Seven*, *Times Ten*, and *ITC Bodoni Seventy-Two*, but the fact that their optical sizes are, respectively, 7, 10, and 72 appears only in their respective names,[5] nowhere in the fonts themselves.

The syntax for size is as follows: We use the keyword parameters followed by four numbers. The first is the font's optical size, expressed in tenths of a point. The second is for fonts issued in multiple optical sizes; we can say that they belong to a family and that the members of this family are numbered sequentially, starting at 0. Finally, the two remaining numbers express the range of optical sizes at which the font can also be used.

Let us take, for example, the excellent font *ITC Bodoni*. It is issued in three optical sizes: 6, 12, 72. We could thus include the following feature in the font for optical size 12:

```
feature size {
    parameters 120 1 90 299 ;
}
```

which means that it has an optical size of 12, which is the second member of the family *ITC Bodoni*, and that it can also be used for actual sizes between 9 and 29.9.

FontLab's User Interface

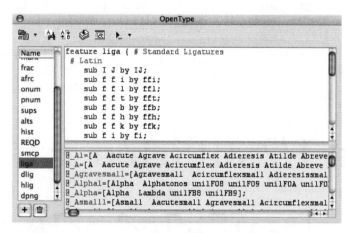

Figure 14-2: The OpenType window in FontLab.

After this brief overview of the Adobe syntax used by FontLab to describe OpenType features, let us return to the software itself. Selecting **Window>Panels>OpenType** opens the *OpenType window* (Figure 14-2), which we shall examine here in detail.

To add a feature, we click on the button ⊞ and automatically obtain the following code:

---

[5] Again, take, for example, the font *Linotype Old Style 7*: is it indeed meant to be used at the optical size of 7, or does the "7" indicate something else?

```
feature xxxx {
  sub by ;
} xxxx ;
```

We must then replace xxxx with the name of the new feature and also replace the line `sub by ;` (which is incomplete and will therefore cause compilation to fail if we leave it there unchanged) with the code for the feature.

Clicking on 🗑 deletes the selected feature from the list.

At the bottom of the window, we can write definitions for the glyph classes that will be available to all features.

The 🖹 button opens and saves text files containing feature code. It is very handy when we wish to create several fonts with the same features—at least for substitutions, as positionings depend heavily on the shapes of the glyphs and cannot readily be shared by multiple fonts.

The 🔍 button is very handy: merely clicking on the name of a glyph in the code and then on this button will cause FontLab to display the glyph in question in the font window or, if it is active, the glyph window. The button ⇅ replaces one glyph name with another throughout the code.

Once we have finished writing the code for OpenType features, we must *compile* it, using the button 📝. If there is an error in the code, the compilation will fail, and an error message will be displayed in the **Window>Panels>Output** window.

Figure 14-3: The OpenType window in FontLab.

FontLab offers us a very pretty interface for testing our features. Clicking on 🔲 opens the window shown in Figure 14-3. This window contains three tabs. The one of interest to us here is the first: **OpenType Features**. We see at the left a list of the font's features, equipped with checkboxes. We select the feature(s) that we wish to test. We also select the script and the language from pull-down menus, and we type a string (using a slash to enter glyph names directly: /eacute, etc.) in the input area provided. The window then displays, one above the other, the renderings of the string with and without the features. Clicking on the ⊞ button causes FontLab to display the glyphs' displacement vectors (a feature that is very convenient when used with positioning rules). Finally, clicking on ⊞ causes the text to be rendered from right to left—an indispensable option for Arabic, Hebrew, and Syriac fonts.

Managing glyph types

Choosing **Properties** on a glyph's pop-up menu opens the window shown opposite.

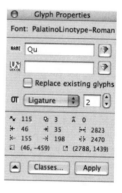

In this window, we can specify the name of a glyph, the Unicode code associated with it (if any), and, above all, its OpenType type ("single glyph", "ligature", "mark", "component"). In the case of a ligature, we must also specify the number of components. This information is essential so that we can use the lookupflag keyword in code and thus restrict the application of a *lookup* to a certain type of glyph. The typical example of the application of this functionality particular to OpenType is the case of a string of glyphs that should ordinarily form a ligature but that is interrupted by a diacritical mark. We can specify that the substitution of ligatures ignore glyphs of type "mark", and the ligature will be formed, even in the presence of a diacritical mark.

Managing glyph classes

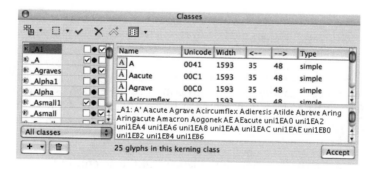

Figure 14-4: The OpenType window in FontLab.

FontLab has an interface for grouping glyphs into classes. Selecting **Window>Panels> Classes** opens a window with two tabs; the one of interest to us is **Classes** (Figure 14-4). In this tab, we can define glyph classes just as in the OpenType window (button ⊞) and flesh them out by writing names glyphs or dragging and dropping glyphs' boxes from the font window.

The glyph classes so defined are used for kerning by class but also for writing OpenType features. We need only check **Add all glyph classes to OpenType feature definition code** in FontLab Studio>Preferences>General Options>Unicode and OpenType to turn them all into OpenType glyph classes. Warning: even though these classes are not displayed at the bottom of the OpenType window, they are nonetheless available in the code. For instance, if we have defined the class class1, we can use @class1 in the code for our features.

Managing anchors

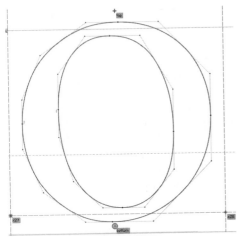

Although anchors do not yet work in the feature definition language implemented in FontLab v.5, the software does offer a rather convenient way to manage anchors. It would not be unreasonable to predict that this interface will lend itself admirably to the management of OpenType anchors in a future version of the software.

Let us open the glyph window. By right-clicking (under Windows; CTRL-click on the Macintosh) at the point where we wish to set an anchor, we can select **Add Anchor** from the pop-up menu that opens. This procedure creates an anchor, which is a point marked with a red cross and accompanied by a name. We can immediately enter a name or modify it later by returning to the pop-up menu.

Let us do so: we shall place an anchor over a letter—'o', for example—and give it a name—say, top, as in the figure above.

Next, we shall go to the window for an accent, such as the tilde, and place another anchor below the accent. Let us call it—careful, this is important!—_top, i.e., the same name as the anchor for the base glyph, but preceded by an underscore. Now let us once again bring up the glyph window for the letter and select the **Anchors** tab in the **Window>Panels>Preview** window:

Surprise! We see the combination of the letter and the accent. In fact, we shall see all the accents compatible with this letter (i.e., those with anchors whose name is the same as an anchor on the letter)—a very helpful tool for managing interactions between base glyphs and diacritical marks.

Thus we are eagerly looking forward to the integration of OpenType anchors into Font-Lab's user interface and, above all, into the code for OpenType features! As we shall see under VOLT and FontForge, the interactive manipulation of anchors is a must for any graphical interface for the management of OpenType positioning.

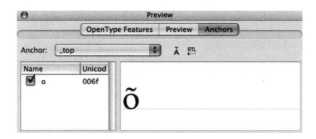

*Figure 14-5: The **Preview** panel window in FontLab.*

Managing OpenType Tables in VOLT

VOLT (*Visual OpenType Layout Tool*) is a utility distributed freely by Microsoft whose only purpose is to add OpenType tables to TrueType fonts. VOLT runs only under Windows. A web page [266] at Microsoft's site is devoted to it, but the software itself cannot be downloaded from that page. To obtain it, one must first register for the discussion forum:

```
http://communities.msn.com/MicrosoftVOLTuserscommunity
```

The links for downloading the software appear on this forum's web site.

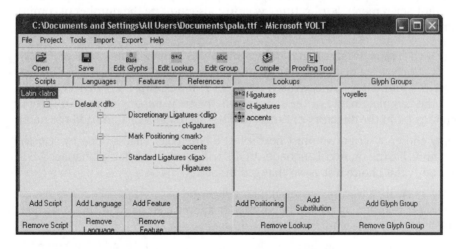

Figure 14-6: The "project" window in VOLT.

The "project" window in VOLT (see Figure 14-6) includes, from top to bottom, some menus, a row of buttons, three graphical areas, and another row of buttons. The three graphical areas will contain:

- The hierarchy of scripts, languages, features, and lookups in the font

- The complete list of lookups

- The list of glyph classes

Aside from the project window, there are also windows for glyphs, substitutions, positionings, glyph classes, and testing.

General mode of operation

We open a font by using the **Open** button. This operation will delete all the existing OpenType tables in the font. Only the tables specific to VOLT will be preserved and interpreted, which means that if we have begun to produce OpenType tables with other software, our work will be lost[6] and we shall have to start again from scratch.

The glyphs in a TrueType font do not have names, but we need names in order to write OpenType rules. Thus we shall want to import any PostScript names for the glyphs from the font's name table. That can be done through **Import>Import PostScript Names**—provided, of course, that these names exist in the font.

A preliminary, and often unpleasant, step for adding any OpenType feature is the classification of the glyphs into *OpenType types* ("single glyph", "ligature", "mark", "component"). To do so, we must check every glyph in the font with **Tools>Edit Glyphs** and make sure that the type is correct. In other words, we must find all the diacritical marks and assign to them the type "mark", all the ligatures (type "ligature"), and, if necessary, all components of glyphs or ligatures (type "component"). We change the type through the **Type** pull-down menu. For ligatures, we must also indicate the number of components (**Components** pull-down menu).

To create a feature, we must set it in its context—its script and its language. Clicking on **Add Script** creates a default script; we must then replace the text New Script <> with the script's four-letter name, written inside < >: for example, <latn>. VOLT will then fill in the complete name of the script. If the name is missing from VOLT, we simply open **tags.txt** in the directory **c:\Program Files\Microsoft VOLT** and add the name.

Having chosen a script, we must next select a language. That is done by selecting the script and clicking on **Add Language**. VOLT will select the default language (dflt); we can modify this choice just as we changed the script.

Finally, to create a feature, we select a language and click on **Add Feature**. We proceed in the same manner, by typing the four-letter abbreviated name within < >. The order of the features is not significant.

Now we have come to lookups. To create one, we click on the **Add Positioning** button if we want a positioning or the **Add Substitution** button if we want a substitution. The

---

[6] In theory there are two ways to export OpenType data from FontLab and import it into VOLT: the first is to check the option **FontLab Studio>Preferences>Generating OpenType & TrueType>Export VOLT data** and thus export the data directly in the form of TrueType tables, and the second is to use the entry **Save features** on the pull-down menu in the **OpenType** panel window and then to save the code for OpenType features in VTP format. Unfortunately, however, in version 5 of FontLab, neither method works in practice.

lookups are listed in the second section of the window, since they are independent of the hierarchy of scripts, languages, and features. We assign a name to the lookup that we create, but this name is strictly internal and can therefore be anything we wish. On the other hand, the order of the lookups is significant, and we can rearrange them in this section of the window so that they will be in the right order, with only one small detail: substitutions always appear before positionings.

Having written some lookups, we compile them by clicking on the **Compile** button, and we test them in the proofing window (**Proofing Tool** button), which we shall describe below (page 575).

Finally, once we have defined and tested all the lookups, we generate a font with no VOLT tables, using **File>Ship Font**. But we can also save the glyph data (i.e., their names, indexes, corresponding Unicode characters, and OpenType types), the lookups, the glyph classes, and, more generally, all the OpenType data in the font, in the form of text files. For that we use the entries on the **Export** menu. In this way, we can rapidly reuse these data in similar fonts.

Glyph classes

In VOLT's syntax, a glyph is represented by its name. We can group glyphs in three ways:

- By writing their names separated by commas and enclosing the entire list in braces: for example, { a, e, i, o,~u~}.

- For a range (according to the order of the glyphs in the font), by simply writing the names of the first and last glyph with a hyphen in between and enclosing the list in brackets: [zero - nine].

- For a *named class*, by writing the class's name within < >: for example, <digits>. To create a name class, we simply click on **Add Glyph Group**: a new glyph class is created, and we can enter its name. The name is for internal use only and thus can be anything we wish. Double-clicking on the name opens the glyph-class window. There we can enter, one by one, the names of the glyphs belonging to the class. We can use individual glyph names or glyph classes (within braces), ranges of glyphs (within brackets), or references to other named classes (with the names of classes within < >).

Substitutions

Double-clicking on a lookup for a substitution opens the substitution window (see §14-7). In this window we can write in the column **From Glyphs -> To Glyphs** all the substitution rules of the lookup, in the proper order. The syntax is as simple as can be! It involves merely writing the name of the source glyph(s), an arrow ("->"), and the target glyph(s):

- For a *single* substitution, such as the replacement of g with g.prettier, we write:

      g -> g.prettier

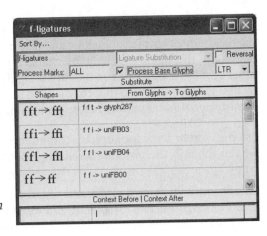

Figure 14-7: The substitution window in VOLT.

There could hardly be a simpler syntax. Moreover, in the **Shapes** column, VOLT will display images of the glyphs in the substitution, which is a good way to confirm the accuracy of the expression. Finally, VOLT will automatically determine that the substitution is *single*, not of any other type.

- For a *multiple* substitution, such as the replacement of the ligature f_f_t by its constituents, we write:

    ```
    f_f_t -> f f t
    ```

- For an *alternate substitution*, such as offering the user the glyphs a.old, a.odd, a.pretty, a.ugly as variants of a, we write as many rules as there are variants, in the order in which we want them to be offered to the user:

    ```
    a -> a.old
    a -> a.odd
    a -> a.pretty
    a -> a.ugly
    ```

- For a *ligature*, such as the replacement of f and i with the glyph f_i, we write:

    ```
    f i -> f_i
    ```

- For a *contextual* or *chained contextual* substitution, we write the substitution as if it were a noncontextual substitution and we enter the glyphs for the context in the **Context Before | Context After** input area at the bottom of the window. Ordinarily there is already a vertical bar there. We write the "before" part of the context to the left of this bar and the "after" part to the right. For example, to replace the hyphen (hyphen) between two digits with an en dash (endash), we write:

    ```
    hyphen -> endash
    ```

as the rule, and in the context area we write:

```
[ zero - nine ] | [ zero - nine ]
```

- For a reverse chaining contextual substitution, we check the **Reversal** box in the upper right corner of the window.

In all the substitutions described above, including the context section of contextual substitutions, glyph names can be replaced by glyph classes. The only constraint is that only one class can be used on each side of the arrow.

The string of glyphs can be displayed *from right to left*, if necessary, through the **Text Flow** pull-down menu (**RTL** equals right to left, **LTR** equals left to right). The same is true of the positioning window and the proofing window.

Finally, a lookup can be selective and apply only to a certain type of glyphs. We have seen an example in the introduction to this chapter: for an accent to be placed on a ligature, the lookup for the ligature must ignore diacritical marks placed between the glyphs that would form the ligature. To set ligatures up in this way, we have the **Process Marks** input area. There we can enter ALL (process *all* diacritical marks), NONE (process *none*), or the name of a glyph class within < >. Do not forget that this technique will work only if all the glyphs to which it must apply have been "typed" beforehand; VOLT regards all glyphs as being of "base glyph" type by default when it opens a TrueType font.

Positionings

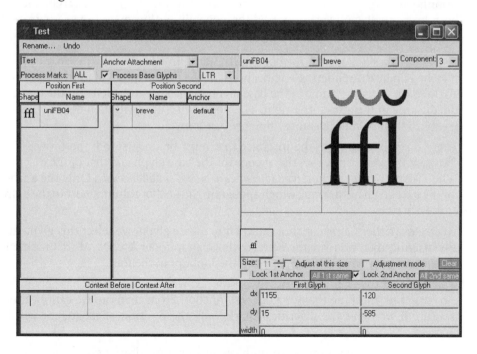

Figure 14-8: The positioning window in VOLT.

While the design of the substitution window was crystal clear, the *positioning window* takes a decided turn for the worse. We open this window by double-clicking on a positioning. The left part of the window has two areas in which we can enter glyph names and, at the bottom, an area for entering the context. The right part of the window, called the "positioning area", displays the glyphs affected by the positioning and allows the positioning of a second glyph and the anchor corresponding to it, which can be performed either with the mouse or by entering precise coordinates.

Unlike substitutions, for which VOLT itself "guesses" the type of the lookup, for positionings we must specify the type through the pull-down menu in the upper left part of the window. There are only five types on that menu, as the three types that involve diacritical marks are merged and the two "contextual" types are achieved through the input area for the context. Let us review the eight possible kinds of positioning:

- *Single adjustment* positioning (Single Adjustment), in which we ask a number of glyphs to move horizontally and/or vertically. Only the list at the left is enabled, since only one glyph is affected by this positioning. In the positioning area, we can use the mouse to move *both* the glyph *and* the brown vertical bar that represents its set-width.

- *Pair adjustment* positioning (Pair Adjustment), in which we ask that the members of some pairs of glyphs be moved horizontally and/or vertically. It is as if we had two copies of the preceding interface: there are two lists of glyphs, two glyphs in the positioning window, and even two bars for their set-widths. Everything can be moved, both horizontally and vertically, and the possibilities thus open to us far surpass a simple kerning pair.

- *Combining diacritical marks* (Anchor Attachment), in which we define marks, to be matched up by the rendering engine, both for the base glyphs and for the diacritics. To do so, we enter the name of the base glyph in the area at the left and the name of the diacritic in the area at the right. The positioning area will then display the two glyphs in their default positions, along with a brown cross.

  There is a subtle point in the interface that must be understood: the brown cross shows, at the same time, *both* the anchor for the base glyph *and* that of the diacritic. When we move this anchor, *both anchors are moved simultaneously.* Only the anchor for the base glyph has a name, which appears in the Anchor column, next to the name of the diacritic.

  To create another named anchor attached to a base glyph, we select this glyph and any diacritic, then we write the name of the anchor under Anchor. At that moment, the anchor in question is defined for all the lookups in the font.

  If we feel that the anchor is correctly positioned with respect to the base glyph, we can lock it by checking the box Lock 1st Anchor. From then on, we cannot move it again; if we move the diacritical mark, only the position of its anchor will be changed.

  Note that a base glyph can have multiple anchors: we simply give them distinct names. By contrast, a diacritic can have only one anchor. If a glyph can be used as a diacritic in two different ways (for example, a dot can be written above or beneath a letter), we must create two different glyphs, one for each use of the diacritic.

- *Multiple diacritical marks*, in which we set some diacritical marks over others. We use the same interface (**Anchor Attachment**), the only difference being that we select two glyphs of type "mark". Warning: although the interface is the same, the lookup is of a separate type; thus we cannot mix "mark on a base glyph" rules with "mark on a mark" rules.

- *Diacritical marks on ligatures*, in which we take the glyph for a ligature and define as many anchors for it as the ligature has components, so that we can attach diacritical marks to it. VOLT's approach is rather funny. The positioning window displays as many anchors as there are components in the ligature. We select one of the components through the **Component** pull-down menu and move the corresponding anchor, still using the same diacritical mark. In this case, it behooves us to lock the anchor for the diacritical mark by checking **Lock 2nd Anchor**; otherwise chaos may result.

- *Cursive attachment* (**Cursive Attachment**), in which we join the "exit point" of each glyph to the "entry point" of the following one. Once again, the interface is not very intuitive and deserves a few words of explanation.

We might have expected to define two anchors for each glyph,[7] one for entry and one for exit. But that is not so. VOLT's procedure requires that anchors be defined by the *interaction of the two glyphs*, not on a single glyph. Thus in the positioning area we have two glyphs (of which only the second can be moved) and only one anchor. This anchor is at once the *anchor for the exit point of the first glyph* and the anchor for the *entry point of the second glyph*. The names of these anchors are required to be entry and exit.

The proofing window

The *proofing window* (see §14-9) is one of VOLT's best features, as it allows us to test the behavior of an OpenType font in a very detailed manner. First we choose the script and the language. Next we enter a string of glyphs, *using glyph names separated by spaces*. We check the features to be tested. VOLT highlights the lookups used by these features.

An OpenType rendering engine will read the string of glyphs once for each lookup, in the order in which the lookups appear. VOLT does the same, and we can follow its progress glyph by glyph, lookup by lookup, with buttons like those of an audio CD player. The **Complete** button will finish reading the string of glyphs, and the **Restart** button will start again from the beginning.

Finally, in the case of a lookup for alternate substitution, we can test the different versions of a glyph by entering the corresponding numerical values in the **Alternate** input area.

---

[7] FontForge, for instance, operates this way; see page 577.

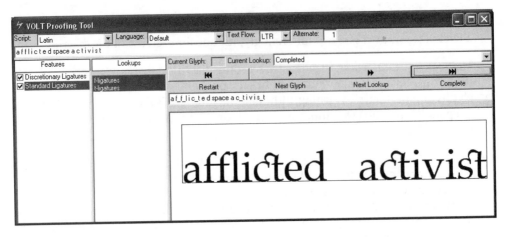

Figure 14-9: The proofing window in VOLT.

Managing OpenType Tables in FontForge

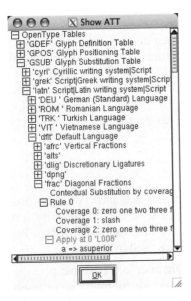

Once again, FontForge offers us a perspective rather different from those of the other software systems, this time with regard to OpenType tables. There is no language to learn, unlike in FontLab; everything is managed through menus and windows, which may be considered an advantage by those readers who are put off by programming. At the same time, FontForge does not share VOLT's elitism; it agrees without hesitation to read the OpenType tables already present in a font. Conversely, the tables written by FontForge are standard OpenType tables that can be read by any other software.

One peculiarity of the interface: only contextual tables can be edited *globally*; by contrast, rules for positioning and substitution are *attached to the glyphs*. For instance, to add a single substitution rule to the letter 'f', we select its glyph in the font window and define this rule through the corresponding tab in the **Glyph Info** window. Rules are thus *scattered* throughout the set of glyphs, which may be practical for small projects but can pose problems of organization for large projects in which there are hundreds or even thousands of OpenType rules to manage.

Nevertheless, we can get a synthetic view of the OpenType and AAT features through View>Show ATT (see figure opposite). But this window allows us only to inspect the data, not to modify them.

Another peculiarity of FontForge is that anchors are managed in a way very different from that of VOLT (and one closer to what we hope to have one day in FontLab): we define anchors, whether for diacritical marks or for cursive attachment, in the glyph window. Thus we have a clear and precise view of the anchors defined for each glyph, and we can use them to construct positioning rules.

One last peculiarity, which is not the least of them: FontForge *short-circuits the notion of a lookup*. To FontForge, a feature contains rules directly, with no intermediate hierarchical level. When we define a new rule, we attach it to a feature, not to a lookup, as is done in VOLT and in the OpenType file format. Never mind: the user is at least presented with some technical details, and the result is often strictly the same.

Anchors

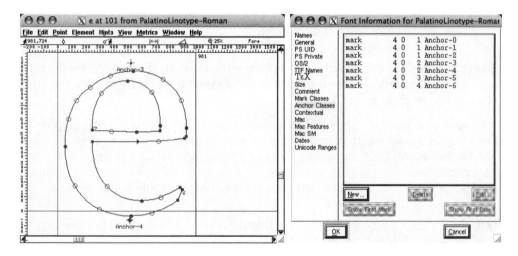

Figure 14-10: Two anchors defined in the glyph window. Right: the anchor-class window.

As can be seen in Figure 14-10, FontForge allows us to set named anchors in the glyph window. To set a named anchor, we must have defined its class beforehand. That is done at the level of the entire font in the **Element>Font Info** window, tab **Anchor Classes**. Clicking on **New** opens a window for creating anchor classes. In this window, we specify the name of the class—a strictly internal name that will be displayed next to the anchor in the glyph window—the OpenType feature (**Tag**) to which the anchor is attached, the scripts to which it applies, and, finally, its type: **Default** (mark on a base glyph or mark on a ligature), **Mk–Mk** (mark on a mark), or **Cursive** (an anchor for a cursive attachment).

The feature to which we attach the anchor class calls for some explanation. FontForge is well aware that we can create any features we wish but that, at the end of the day, only certain features recognized by the major software packages have any chance of ever being used. That is why FontForge offers us six predefined features (see page 577 for more information):

- "Above-base mark positioning" (abvm), i.e., automatic positioning of diacritics that appear above a letter. This feature is enabled by default.

- "Below-base mark positioning" (blwm), the counterpart of the preceding for marks that appear below a letter. This feature is also enabled by default.

- "Mark positioning" (mark), which combines the previous two. Enabled by default.

- "[Diacritical] mark-to-mark positioning" (mkmk), the possibility of positioning diacritical marks over other diacritical marks. Enabled by default.

- "Cursive attachment" (curs), for joining letters in cursive scripts, such as Arabic or calligraphic Latin.

- "Required feature" (RQD), a feature with no precise semantics that is nonetheless required for the given script and language.

Most of the time our choice will be made from mark, mkmk, and curs. Note: for the class to be defined and available for use in other windows, it is necessary to close the Font Info window by clicking on OK.

Once we have defined the glyph's class, we can create an instance of it in the glyph window. We perform a contextual click where we wish to place it and then select the entry Add Anchor Point. Doing so opens the Anchor Point Info window, where we can select the anchor's class from the pull-down menu. In each menu entry, we can see the feature's tag (first) and the anchor's name (last). We select the anchor's role in this window:

- Is the anchor for a diacritical mark, so that the mark can be attached to a base glyph? If so, we check Mark.

- Is the anchor for a ligature? Then we check Base Lig. In this case, we must also specify the component index in the corresponding input area. (If a ligature is composed of n letters, the *component index* is the sequential number of each component, between 0 and $n-1$).

- Is the anchor for a base glyph? Then we check Base Glyph.

- Is the anchor for a diacritical mark, so that the mark can be attached to another diacritical mark? Then we check Base Mark.

- Finally, is the anchor for the entry or exit point of a cursive attachment? Then we check CursEntry or CursExit, respectively.

According to the type of anchor class that we choose, some of the choices will be disabled because they are inapplicable.

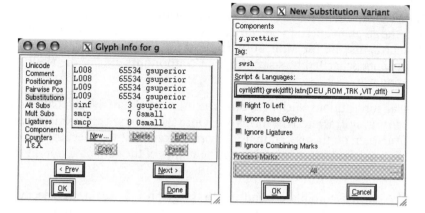

Figure 14-11: Left: the glyph window, "single substitution" tag. Right: the window for a new single substitution.

Noncontextual Substitutions

In FontForge, we distinguish two types of substitutions: those that are independent of the context and those that are contextual. The former are made at the glyph level, through the **Glyph Info** window. The latter are defined by way of the former at the same time as contextual positionings, through the **Font Info** window.

Let us examine the various cases of *noncontextual* substitutions:

- *Single* substitutions, such as replacing the glyph g with another glyph, g.prettier. We make a contextual click[8] on the box for the first glyph in the font window, and from the menu that appears we select **Glyph Info**. In this window, as can be seen in Figure 14-11, there are tabs for all types of noncontextual substitutions.

  To create a single substitution, we click on the **Glyph Info>Substitutions>New** button. A window entitled **New Substitution Variant** then appears, in which we indicate the target glyph and the tag for the feature to which we wish to associate this substitution (Figure 14-11, right).

  On the pull-down menu for selecting feature tags, FontForge presents an *enormous* list of predefined features: all the predefined OpenType and AAT features are found there. Thus, if the substitution aims to replace a lowercase letter with a small capital, we select **Lowercase to Small Capitals**, etc.

  In the window for new substitutions, we can also select the script(s) and language(s) to which the substitution applies. Finally, we can choose to disregard base glyphs, ligatures, or diacritical marks.

---

[8] Henceforth we shall use the term *contextual click* for a right-click under Unix and Windows and for a click with a modifying key under Mac OS X. In Mac OS X, the modifying key associated with the right-click is selected in the preferences of *X11* or *XDarwin*.

- *Multiple* substitutions, such as to replace the ligature f_f_t with its components. We select the glyph in question and do exactly as for simple substitutions, with just two differences: first, we use Mult Subs tab instead; second, we enter the names of the components, separated by spaces, in the Components area of the New Multiple List window.

- *Alternate* substitutions, such as to offer the user a choice of the glyphs a.old, a.odd, a.pretty, a.ugly as alternate forms of a. Once again, we select the original glyph (a), and from then on the procedure is the same, except that we select the tab Alt Subs for this type of substitution and enter the names of the variant glyphs in the input area of the New Alternate List window.

- *Ligatures*, such as to replace f and i with the glyph f_i. Again, we select the glyph f_i, go to the Ligatures tab, and enter the glyph names of its components in the appropriate area of the New Ligature window.

Thus FontForge's interface is peculiar in that it sometimes starts with the input of the substitution and sometimes with the output. For instance, in the case of a *multiple substitution*, we start with the *original* and enter the names of the glyph's components in the multiple-substitution window; conversely, for a *ligature*, we start with the *target* glyph— that is, the ligature itself—and enter the names of the ligature's components in the same input area. For the former, the names are the names of the *glyphs produced*; for the latter, they are the *glyphs that produce* the ligature.

Another peculiarity, found throughout FontForge, is that we must always associate a feature tag with our substitutions at the time that we define them. To associate the same substitution with more than one feature, we must redefine it.

Contextual substitutions will be described later, together with contextual positionings.

Noncontextual Positionings

FontForge uses a rather different approach for managing simple and pairwise positionings, cursive attachments, diacritical marks, etc. For positionings, we proceed as with substitutions, using special tabs in the Glyph Info window. For cursive attachments and the various operations connected to diacritical marks, we use anchors, as described on page 577.

Here are the various types types of noncontextual positionings:

- Positioning of a *single glyph*, where we specify that a glyph is to be moved horizontally and/or vertically. We select the glyph in the font window and request the Glyph Info window. There we select the Positionings tab and click on New. The *New Position Variant* window (Figure 14-12) opens, wherein we can select the horizontal and vertical offsets from the origin (ΔX, ΔY) and from the end of the displacement vector (ΔXAdvance, ΔYAdvance). These four numbers are the data for the glyph's positioning. We have good control over both the point at which the active glyph will be rendered

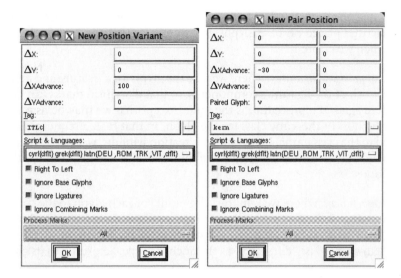

Figure 14-12: The windows for simple (left) and pairwise (right) positionings.

(using its origin) and the point at which the *following* glyph will be rendered (using the displacement vector). Next, as always, we select the tag for the feature with which the positioning is associated and the relevant script and language, and we specify whether the positioning should disregard base glyphs, ligatures, and/or diacritical marks.

- Positioning of a *pair of glyphs*, where we specify that the members of certain pairs of glyphs are to be moved horizontally and/or vertically. The procedure is the same, except that the tab in the **Glyph Info** window is entitled **Pairwise Pos** and that the *New Pair Position* window (Figure 14-12) that appears is slightly richer. Specifically, here we are positioning not *one* but *two* glyphs. We must therefore indicate, in addition to what is needed for a simple positioning, which glyph is the second (the entry **Second Glyph**) and supply the data for its positioning (the origin and the displacement vector). These are the only differences between the *simple* and *pairwise* positioning windows. Note that horizontal kerning is a very special case of a pairwise positioning: the case in which the only value changes is the ΔXAdvance of the first glyph, i.e., its set-width.

- *Combining diacritical marks*, for which we define marks, to be matched up by the rendering engine, on both the base glyphs and the diacritics. This is done using anchors of the same class for both diacritics and base glyphs. The features to which the positioning is associated, the script, and the relevant language are chosen through the definition of the anchor's class, under **Font Info>Anchor Classes**.

- *Multiple diacritical marks*, where we place diacritics on other diacritics. We proceed as with diacritics placed on base glyphs, but we specify that the anchor class is of type Mk-Mk when we create it.

- *Diacritical marks on ligatures*, where we take the glyph for a ligature and define an anchor for each of the ligature's components, so that diacritical marks can be attached to it. Here again the procedure is the same, except that we may occasionally create several anchors of the same class for the glyph. In that case, a sequential number is attached to the class name. In the anchor-creation window, we specify that the glyph is a ligature, and we enter the sequential number of the letter to which the anchor corresponds.

- *Cursive attachment*, where we join the "exit point" of each glyph to the "entry point" of the one that follows. Thus we must create two anchor classes, which we can call "entry" and "exit". When creating an instance of an anchor on the glyph, we choose either "CursEntry" or "CursExit" as the anchor's type, according to its class.

Contextual positionings are described in the following section, together with contextual substitutions.

Contextual Substitutions and Positionings

Let us move on to contextual transformations. Here we use the Font Info window, which is independent of any glyphs. In this window, we select the Contextual tab, which contains subtabs corresponding to the various types of contextual transformations (see Figure 14-13 [a]).

Whether for a simple, chained, or reverse chaining contextual transformation, the definition procedure is the same. We select the appropriate tab and click on New. The usual window opens (Figure 14-13 [b]), with the tag for the feature to which the transformation will be associated and our choices to respect or disregard base glyphs, ligatures, and diacritical marks.

Once these choices have been made, another window opens, one with many tabs. We use the Prev and Next buttons to move from tab to tab. The first tab (Figure 14-13 [c]) asks us to choose one of three ways to display the transformation: do we wish to use individual glyphs, glyph classes, or coverage tables (see §D.9.1.3)? *Coverage tables* are the most practical choice, with the fewest limitations.

Suppose then that we have decided to display our substitution or our positioning in a *coverage table*, which is the most attractive option. The second tab in the window (Figure 14-13 (d)) then displays the contextual transformation in a very abstract manner. To understand it, let us first answer one question: what are contextual substitutions and positionings, whether chained or not?

We begin with a *match*—the string of n glyphs that the rendering engine will recognize in order to launch the transformation. Let this string be denoted $M = M_0, \ldots, M_{n-1}$. A

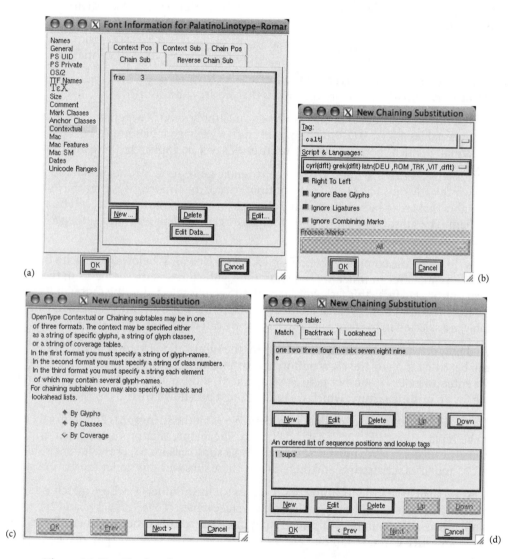

Figure 14-13: The first four steps for defining a chained contextual substitution.

substitution consists of replacing some of the glyphs in M; a positioning consists of moving them. Suppose that we have a substitution (the logic for positionings is exactly the same) and that we wish to replace the glyphs M_i and M_j. Only these two glyphs will be modified; all the others are there to "set the scene", forming the *context*. The indexes of the glyphs to be substituted are i and j. How can we perform this substitution? By means of noncontextual substitutions: *single* ones, *multiple* ones, and *ligatures*.

Now let us increase the complexity a bit. We have said that we are going to display our substitution through the use of coverage tables. That means that the $M_0, \ldots, M_{n-1}$ that we just saw are no longer glyphs but rather sets of glyphs $M_k = \{m_{k,0}, \ldots, m_{k,i_k}\}$. The same is true of M_i and M_j, which are the glyphs that we are substituting.

To describe a substitution of this kind, we can simply specify which are the glyphs in coverage tables $M_0, \ldots, M_n$, which indexes in the coverage tables are to be substituted, and, finally, which (noncontextual) substitutions will be applied to these indexes.

That is what FontForge does. We list the coverage tables, one by one, in the top part of the window (Figure 14-13 (d)). In the bottom part of the window, we enter the *indexes* in the table that are to be substituted and the tags for the substitutions that will be applied to them. The substitutions must therefore have been defined in advance—for *each* glyph in the coverage table concerned.

How do we define coverage tables? By clicking on **New**, just below the match's box, we open an input area in which we can enter the glyph names of the elements in the table. Two buttons facilitate this task: **Set** takes all the glyphs selected in the font window and inserts them into our coverage table; **Select** does the opposite: all the elements in the table are selected in the font window, so that we can check our glyph selections.

And how do we enter the indexes and tags for the substitutions to be applied? As easily as can be: by clicking on the **New** button at the bottom. In the little window that appears, we enter an index (a number between 0 and $n-1$, if the match contains n glyphs) and a tag for an existing feature, which we select from a pull-down menu.

Let us take the example of ordinal numbers. We want the strings 1st, 2nd, 3rd, 4th, etc., to be replaced by "1ˢᵗ", "2ⁿᵈ", "3ʳᵈ", "4ᵗʰ", etc. The feature that produced superscripts is usually called sups. We must first define simple substitutions to set the letters 's', 't', 'n', 'd', 'r', and 'h' as superscripts and then classify these substitutions under the feature sups.

Next we shall have to define four classes: a class for the number '1', whose match is 1st or 1th (in the case of 11, 111, etc.), with three coverage tables: "[one]", "[s t]", and "[t h]";[9] similar classes for numbers '2' and '3', and one class for the other numbers, for which there are three coverage tables: "[zero four five six seven eight nine]", "[t]", and "[h]".

For the first of these classes, we shall enter in the first input area:

---

[9] That may cause a problem, since we transform not only "1ˢᵗ" and "1ᵗʰ" but also "1ˢʰ" and "1ᵗᵗ". But who would ever write those? They do not exist in English.

```
one
s t
t h
```

Thus there are three sets of glyphs, and those that will be substituted are the second and the third sets; i.e., those for superscripts 1 and 2. Then, in the second input area, we enter:

```
1 'sups'
2 'sups'
```

We proceed similarly for the second and third class. For the fourth class, we enter in the first input area:

```
zero four five six seven eight nine
t
h
```

and, in the second input area:

```
1 'sups'
2 'sups'
```

Now let us examine chained contextual transformations. The procedure is the same: we select the tab Contextual>Chain Sub or the tab Contextual>Chain Pos in the Font Info window, and in the same manner we reach the window in which we have entered the match. Except that now there are two extra tabs at our disposal: Backtrack and Lookahead.

The idea is as follows. We still have the same match, $M = M_0, \ldots, M_{n-1}$; but this time, when the rendering engine detects this match, it will also compare the glyphs that appear before and after it. The backtrack will be a string P of glyphs (or coverage tables) that must appear before the match in order for the transformation to take place. Likewise, the lookahead, F, must appear after the match; otherwise the transformation will not occur. The reader may be wondering why we do not say that the concatenation of P, M, and F is just one big match. After all, it is not the whole match that is to be transformed but just some of its glyphs. What difference does it make if the match is made larger?

There is a major difference that occurs not at the level of the transformations themselves but rather at the level of the overall rendering. When the rendering engine reads the string and detects a match for a contextual transformation, the match is "swallowed" by the engine and cannot interact further with the rest of the string. For example, if a hypothetical match ended with 'f' and were followed by 'i', these letters could not form the ligature "fi". If, however, the 'f' is part of the lookahead, this problem will not occur, since the lookahead "belongs to the future": it has not yet been "read" when the transformation takes place. After the transformation, the lookahead will be read as if nothing had happened.

Thus chained contextual transformations allow us to reduce the match to a minimum number of glyphs, often only those that are actually substituted or positioned, and to leave the remained to the backtrack and the lookahead.

Let us take as our example of a chained transformation a chained contextual positioning: the one for the string "V.A.V." that we have already mentioned several times in this book. We need to move the 'V' closer to the period that precedes it, but only if that period is in turn preceded by an 'A'. To kern the period and the 'V', we must first define a (non-contextual) pairwise positioning. Thus we select the "period" glyph (which is named period) and click on **New** in the window **Glyph Info>Pos**. In the window for defining a simple positioning, we specify a ΔXAdvance of -300 and attach this positioning to a new tag, e.g., skrn.

Now that we have defined the positioning, we must incorporate it into its context by defining a chained contextual positioning. To do so, we click on **New** in the **Font Info> Contextual>Chain Pos** window. Then we attach the positioning to the kern (horizontal kerning) feature. Next, in the new window that opens, we choose to display the positioning as coverage tables (Figure 14-13 [c]) and click on **Next**. This brings us to the window for entering the match, the backtrack, and the lookahead.

In our case, one idea would be to take "A.V" as the match, but it turns out to be more desirable to restrict ourselves to the period '.' and to use 'A' as the backtrack and 'V' as the lookahead. Accordingly, we select the appropriate tabs and enter the strings period, A, and V, just as in the example for a contextual substitution. Finally, we must specify which feature will be applied, and to which glyph, when the conditions specified in the context are satisfied. To this end, we choose the index 0 to the string (after all, the match has only one glyph) and specify skrn (which we have previously defined for this purpose) as the feature to execute. Nothing remains but to record our entries by clicking on OK, and voilà!

Reverse chaining contextual substitutions are defined in the same way, with the single difference that we select the tab by this name in the **Font Info** window. The reader will find more information on the reasons for these very exotic substitutions in §D.9.4.7 of this book.

Managing AAT Tables in FontForge

Up to now we have seen how the two main software packages (FontLab and FontForge), as well as another piece of software that specializes in this task (VOLT), manage Open-Type tables. But OpenType is not the only way to enrich a TrueType font. Recall that in parallel with the work by Microsoft and Adobe on TrueType Open and OpenType, Apple developed the TrueType GX format, which was latter rechristened AAT. Currently AAT fonts can be used only under Mac OS X, but they are no less interesting for that. The magnificent font *Zapfino*

itself is reason enough for us to examine the possibilities of AAT fonts. The contextual character of the Arabic and Indian fonts of the Mac OS X operating system is also managed entirely by AAT.

One detail that is not insignificant: while OpenType fonts can be based on TrueType or PostScript CFF outlines, AAT fonts can be based only on TrueType outlines.

In §D.11.5.1 of this book, we provide a rather exhaustive technical description of AAT tables. In this section, we shall discuss only the insertion of these tables into TrueType fonts.

For the moment, only FontForge has seriously confronted the problem.[10] The problem is in no way trivial, as AAT tables use *finite automata* to perform substitutions or contextual positionings. A finite automaton is a method that can be illustrated more easily with diagrams, by drawing bubbles and arrows on a sheet of paper, than through the user interface of software, through its menus, buttons, and input areas.

Not to mention that AAT also offers variable fonts, in a format similar to and slightly more powerful than Multiple Master.

Let us now describe, as simply as possible, FontForge's user interface for creating AAT tables.

Choosing between OpenType and AAT

No, this section will not present arguments for or against these two font formats; it will instead give some very important information about fonts generated by FontForge.

When we generate a font, we select the font format on the pull-down menu in the dialog box for saving files. Whether we wish to generate an OpenType or an AAT font, we select **TrueType** (or **TrueType (Mac dfont)** under Mac OS X). Under the pull-down menu, there is a button labeled **Options**. Clicking on this button brings up a window with a number of checkboxes. Those of interest to us are **Apple** and **OpenType**. To obtain AAT tables in the generated font, we must check the first box. If we do, we are wise to uncheck the second box, thanks to certain possible incompatibilities.

---

[10] Doubtless because VOLT comes directly from Microsoft, a company with no interest in promoting AAT, and because FontLab will probably first cover the OpenType features completely before addressing AAT.

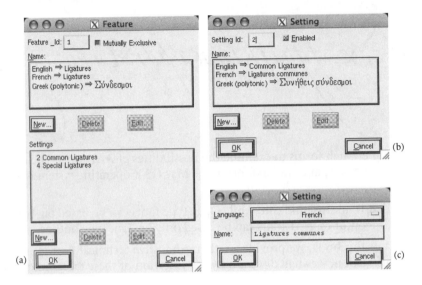

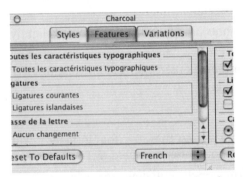

Figure 14-14: Editing the names of AAT features and selectors.

Features and selectors

Like OpenType, AAT also uses *features*, but it enriches them by adding a new concept: *selectors*. A selector is a series of properties that the user will enable or disable at the same time as the feature. For example, in the *WorldText* window shown opposite, several features and selectors for the font *Charcoal* are shown. The English version of the software was used here, but since we chose **French** from the pull-down menu for language, the names of the features and selectors are given to us in French. The example illustrates another clear advantage of AAT fonts: the names of the features are *contained within the font*. For instance, the choice of features available to the user is no longer the province of the software; it is now the font's responsibility. We can devise new features (and new selectors); they can be used immediately in all Mac OS software.

FontForge allows us to edit the names of features and selectors in any language. In Figure 14-14 (a), we have selected the feature **Ligatures** (from the font *Zapfino*); FontForge displays a list of all the translations of this name. In the bottom part of the window, we see the names of the selectors, in French. Using the windows shown in Figure 14-14 (b) and (c), we can modify existing translations or add new ones.

It is important to understand that *only the names* are defined at this step. No information about the features or selectors is given, with one exception: when we modify a selector (window 14-14 [b]), we can check the box **Enabled** so that the selector will be enabled by default when the font is selected.

How, then, can we define the properties of these features and selectors, with such beautifully defined names? In fact, the crucial data in the three windows in Figure 14-14 are the small numbers that appear in the **Feature _Id** and **Setting Id** input areas. These are the numbers that we shall later use to identify the pair (feature, selector).

One last detail about feature names before we move on to AAT's finite automata. In **File>Preferences>Mac** we have a tab allowing us to modify the default names of Apple's predefined features (see §D.11.5.1 for a detailed description) and a table of mappings between AAT features and their OpenType counterparts. This table will be used when FontForge has to convert an AAT font to OpenType or vice versa.

Managing AAT's Finite Automata in FontForge

To the reader who is not familiar with the concept of finite automata, we highly recommend reading section §D.13.1 of this book. She will find a plethora of examples using the same conventions and notations as the AAT tables.

Let us summarize the contents of that section. A *finite automaton* consists of three tables: a *table of states*, a *table of inputs*, and a *table of classes*. States are the different situations in which the automaton may find itself. Classes are the different categories of glyphs that we use. Inputs are pairs ("new state", "action"). Actions are the operations that we perform on glyphs.

For instance, we start from a default state (there are even two of them in AAT: state 0 is called "beginning of document", and state 1 is called "beginning of line"). We remain in the initial state as long as we have only glyphs that do not cause a state change. One fine day we encounter a glyph from another class. We then check the table of inputs to see what we are to do in the current state, in the presence of this new glyph. The table of inputs tells us that, for the given state and the given glyph class, we must move to a certain other state and, possibly, perform a certain action. The actions depend on the contextual table. For a morx table, there are five types of actions: rearrangements of glyphs, contextual substitutions, ligatures, simple substitutions, and insertions of glyphs. In the kern, for kerning, there is another action: contextual kerning.

Let us take a real-world example so as to give a better illustration of the technique of finite automata in AAT: the example of most ordinal numerals in English (4th, 5th, etc.). We begin by defining three states: the "INITIAL" state, the "DIGITS" state and the "T_FOUND" state. We start in the "INITIAL" state. When we write a digit, we switch to the "DIGITS" state. When the following glyph is also a digit, we remain in the "DIGITS" state. When the following glyph is a 't', we go into the "T_FOUND" state. If the next glyph is an 'h', we replace 'th' with '[th]' and return to the initial state. If the next glyph is not an 'h', we leave both the 't' and that glyph as they are and return to INITIAL state. For a human, the best way to describe a finite automaton is to reach for a good old pencil and a sheet of paper, with which to draw arrows and bubbles—which is what we have done below:

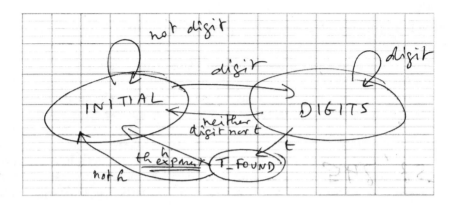

Then, when the diagram is complete, all the bubbles and arrows have been drawn, and we have run through all the possibles paths, we must transcribe the diagram into the three tables that we have mentioned (states, inputs, and classes). And that is where Font-Forge comes in: it gives us an interface for entering the three tables.

Let us go to Font Info>Mac SM (for "Mac State Machines"). This tab has four subtabs, which correspond to four operations[11] requiring finite automata: *rearrangement of glyphs, contextual substitution, insertion,* and *kerning.*

We shall examine them one by one. Let us start with the rearrangement of glyphs.

Rearrangement of glyphs

This is a very interesting transformation of the string of glyphs, as it has no counterpart in OpenType. Specifically, in OpenType it is the Uniscribe driver that manages the rearrangement of glyphs: for example, this driver places Indian vowels before a list of consonants.

The idea behind the rearrangement of glyphs is as follows. We read a string $G = g_1, \ldots, g_n$ of glyphs, move from state to state, and at some point we decide to *mark* a glyph; call it g_i. We continue reading until we reach another glyph, g_j, which will be the "initiator" of the transformation. At that point, the substring $g_i, \ldots, g_j$ will be run through the mill, and some glyphs will be permuted. *Which* glyphs depends on a parameter that is given when the initiator is reached: the simplest cases are those in which g_i moves to the end and those in which g_j moves to the beginning. The more complex cases are those in which the four glyphs $g_i, g_{i+1}, g_{j-1}, g_j$ are permuted in different ways, while the string in the middle, $g_{i+2}, \ldots, g_{j-2}$, remains unchanged.

Let us now see how FontForge allows us to enter a transformation of this sort.

Take the example given, which may seem pointless to the Eurocentric user but in fact simulates a transformation that is found in almost all the scripts of India: when there is a sequence of consonants without vowels that is followed by an 'r', the glyph for the 'r' will

---

[11] Note that one operation is missing from the morx table: ligatures. They are converted to OpenType contextual ligatures when an AAT font is opened and converted back to AAT ligatures upon saving.

be placed at the beginning of the string of consonant glyphs. For instance, the Unicode characters "KGPTHr" will produce a series "rKGPTH" of glyphs. Here, then, is what we want: that an 'r' that appears after any number of occurrences of the letters 'K', 'G', 'P', 'T', and 'H' be moved to the beginning of that group of letters.

Let us attempt to think in terms of finite automata. The initial state is that of "beginning of document" or "beginning of line". As long as we are reading characters other than consonants, we remain in the initial state. But as soon as we read a consonant, we know that an 'r' may eventually appear and force a permutation. Thus we go to the "waiting for an 'r'" state, which we can also call the "consonants" state. Once we are in the "consonants" state, we remain there as long as we keep reading consonants. But that state is left as soon as anything other than a consonant or an 'r' occurs: we then move back to the initial state. Finally, if an 'r' appears, we also return to the initial state, but this time we first launch the permutation. One question arises: how can we know exactly where to place the 'r'? Because we took care to mark the location when we moved from the initial state to the "consonants" state. Thus we shall say that the 'r' will go just after the *last* mark in the text. That's right: the "last" one, since each consonant in the text will cause a transition to the "consonants" state and will thus make a mark, but only the last mark is of interest to us.

Let us summarize what we have seen. We have three classes: consonants ('K', 'G', 'P', 'T', etc.), the letter 'r', and everything else. We have two states: the initial state and the "consonants" state. We have two ways to leave the initial state: when we read a consonant (and thus move to the "consonants" state after marking the location), and when we read any other glyph (and thus remain in the initial state). We have three ways to leave the "consonants" state: when we read a consonant (and thus remain in the same state), when we read an 'r' (in which case we return to the initial state after permuting the glyphs), and when we read a glyph of another type (and thus return to the initial state).

Graphically, the procedure can be shown as two bubbles (for the two states), two arrows going out of the first bubble, and three arrows going out of the second. Here is the diagram in question:

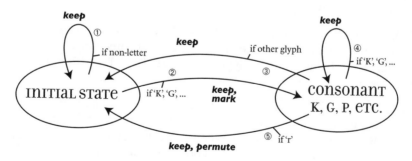

Now let us convert the diagram for use with FontForge's interface. First of all, we must create an AAT feature. To do so, we go to Element > Font Info > Mac Features and click on New. In the window that appears, we enter the number of the feature and its name, in at least one language (it is politically correct to enter the name in multiple languages).

Likewise for the selector: we enter the number and, in at least one language, the name. We can also check the **Enabled** box. After this step, the feature exists—but it does not yet do anything. Make note of the numbers assigned to the feature and the selector: 5 and 1.

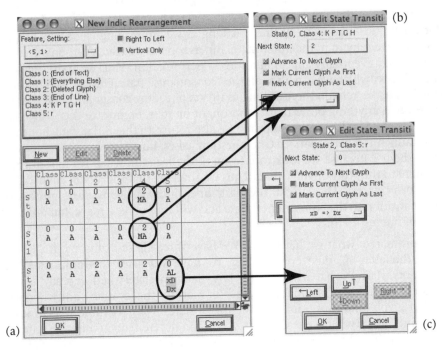

(a)

Figure 14-15: (a), The input window for the class and state tables for a rearrangement of glyphs in AAT; (b) and (c), the input windows for the entries (state 0, class 4) and (state 2, class 5).

Then we select the **Mac SM** tab and choose the **Indic** subtab. We click on **New**, and window 14-15 (a) comes up.

At the top, we enter the numbers of the feature and the selector: <5,1>. Below, we go into the glyph classes that we shall use. The first four classes are predefined in AAT, and Font-Forge displays them by default. We shall go into the "K P T G H" and "r" classes by clicking on **New**.

Next comes the most delicate operation. We must fill in the state table, which appears at the bottom. For the moment, there are only the two initial states: 0 ("beginning of document") and 1 ("beginning of line"). When we designed the automaton, we provided only one bubble for the initial state; but that does not matter, as in our example the two initial states will have exactly the same behavior. On the other hand, we do need a new state, for the state that we have called "consonants". How do we reach that state? When the automaton reads an element in the class "K P T G H", i.e., class 4. Thus it is from the box "class 4, state 0" that we shall move to the new state, which does not yet exist. Let us click on this box!

A window for editing the state transition (see §14-15 [b]), i.e., the shift from one state to another, appears. In this window, we must enter the number of the target state, which in our case is 2. As if by magic, state 2 appears in the table. Let us also perform the same operation for the box "class 4, state 1". We then obtain the arrow ② of our diagram. Do not forget to check the box **Mark Current Glyph As First**. Thus the consonant that brought us to the "consonants" state and that must necessarily be the first glyph is so marked.

Next, we shall click on the box "class 4, state 2": we are then in "consonants" state, and there is a new consonant that has been read. Thus we remain in this state. Here we must absolutely not check the box for the "first glyph"!

Finally, the most interesting box: "class 5, state 2". This is where an 'r' appears, after any number of consonants. Here we must mark the glyph as being the "last" so that it will initiate the permutation operation. Next, from the pull-down menu, we select the permutation that we desire from the following list of choices: Ax => xA, xD => Dx, ... ABxCD => DCxBA. This bizarre notation can be explained as follows: A is the first glyph, B is the second (if any), D is the last, C is the next-to-last (if any), and x is the string that appears in the middle, which can be arbitrarily long. In our case, we want the permutation xD => Dx, since we are taking the 'r', which is the last glyph, and placing it at the beginning.

We have just finished defining the finite automaton. Note, incidentally, that unlike OpenType features, AAT features allow us to use strings of arbitrary length (within the limits of a line of text, as the shift to a new line always returns us to the initial state). In OpenType, we would need a separate substitution for *each string length*.

Contextual substitutions

Now let us proceed to another type of operation: contextual substitution. Here the goal is to replace certain glyphs with others, according to context, through the use of a finite automaton. Once again we shall take a typical example of finite automata that cannot be implemented in OpenType: fractions. In OpenType, we must specify the numerator and the denominator of a fraction separately. Here we shall write an AAT transformation that will convert the digits before the slash into the numerator and those after the slash into the denominator—*however many digits there be*!

What are our glyph classes? On the one hand, we have "digits" (the glyphs that will be put into the numerator or the denominator); on the other hand, we have the "slash" (which will initiate the change from numerator to denominator). And what are our states? Starting in the initial state, as soon as we detect a digit, we switch to the "numerator" state. Then, as soon as we detect a slash, we switch to the "denominator" state, and we remain there as long as we keep reading digits. Finally, after the last digit, we return to the initial state. In addition, if in the "numerator" state we read a glyph that is neither a digit nor a slash, we also return to the initial state:

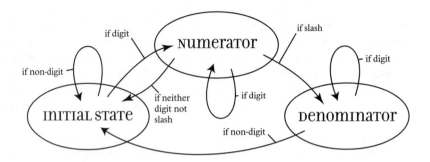

Now all that we have to do is to implement the finite automaton. We shall first create an AAT feature under **Element>Font Info>Mac Features**, just as in the previous section. Let <11,2> be its identifier.

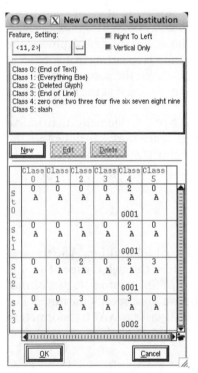

In the editing window for contextual substitutions, we shall then enter the data for the three tables. Let us start with the class table: after the four default classes (0–3), we shall define a class 4 (the digits, zero one two three four five six seven eight nine) and a class 5 (the slash, slash). Next, we shall fill in the relevant boxes in the table of inputs. Let us first take class 4 (the digits): when we encounter a digit in the initial state, we switch to a new state, which will be state 2 (which we just called "numerator"). At the same time, we replace the glyph for the number with its superscript version.

Then we must indicate the simple substitution that will produce superscript digits. This substitution must be defined for each digit. We shall therefore select, in the font window, the glyph for the digit zero and, in **Glyph Info>Substitutions**, we shall create a new substitution by specifying the name of the superscript zero—say, zero.superscript. There is one technical detail that we absolutely must respect: we must choose "-- **Nested** --" as the script/language on the pull-down menu. The feature tag may be anything; for instance, G001.

Next we create a new simple substitution in the same way: that for the subscript form, which we shall call G002. These two operations should be repeated for all the digits.

Now let us return to the table of inputs. We had been in class 4 (the digits). When we come upon a digit in state 0 (or state 1), we move to state 2 ("numerator") after replacing the digit with its superscript version. Let us then click on the box (state 0, class 4). In the window that appears, we indicate that the new state is 2 and that the substitution that applies to the current glyph is G001.

In this window, we also see a box to check (**Mark Current Glyph**) and an input area for the feature tag, entitled **Mark Subs**. What is the purpose of these? Let us digress for a moment to explain the usefulness of marking. We have seen that the matches for OpenType transformations can have contexts before and after the current glyph. Thus we can replace a glyph when it is followed by certain other glyphs. But it is hard to see how to do so when using a finite automaton: after all, when we are in a position to say that one glyph is followed by certain others, it is too late to modify the glyph; we have already passed it by. That is where marking comes into play. We mark a glyph that may later be subject to transformation, and when the appropriate context arises, we request that a substitution be applied to the glyph that we have marked.

Let us return from this digression to the table of inputs. The box "state 1, class 4" is in every way identical to the preceding one. So is state 2, since any digit that appears when we are in state 2 is also subject to a substitution, and we move on to the next glyph. To exit state 2, we need to encounter a slash. Let us now handle class 5 (the slash). The only box of interest to us is "state 2, class 5": it sends us to state 3 ("denominator"). There is no need to apply a substitution, unless, of course, there is a special glyph in the font for a slash that was specifically designed for oblique fractions.

Only state 3 remains. The only interesting box is "state 3, class 4", where we stay in state 3 and replace the digit with its subscript form (tag G002).

This concludes the writing of the contextual substitution.

Insertion

Insertion is an AAT feature that has no analogue in OpenType—other than a few simple cases of insertion that can be achieved through multiple substitutions. The goal is to insert some glyphs between the marked glyph and the current glyph, just as if the user had entered them. But beware: the glyphs that appear are not characters; *they do not exist* in the file. Does the operating system consider them as real glyphs? Can we find them by searching for a string? The author is doubtful. They should therefore be used sparingly: using an insertion to replace the author's initials with his full name would be clever but potentially dangerous. Instead, we should set things up so that the inserted glyphs are of less importance or, at a minimum, cannot possibly be mistaken for characters. Here are two typical examples:

insertion of *kashida*   ligature   split insertion

At the left, we have an insertion of a *kashida*, which is a connecting stroke between Arabic letters. The result is inferior typography, but often there is no better solution. After all, true long strokes that connect Arabic letters must be curves, and that is already beyond the capabilities of most typesetting systems. In any event, the *kashida* has one peculiarity: it is not a letter in its own right but a deformation of a letter. If we obtain *kashidas* by adding glyphs, that fact should not be evident to the user. In particular, the user should not be able to *select* a *kashida* with the cursor.

The example on the right, by contrast, is that of the Cambodian script, in which vowels are often split into two: one part remains in the logical (and phonetically correct) location of the vowel, and the other part is moved before the group of consonants, just like the Indian 'r' in our example of rearrangement.

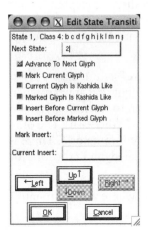

Thus the left side of the glyph becomes detached and, at least in the technical sense, becomes a glyph in its own right.

How will this "phantom" glyph interact with the user? Is it possible to select it with the cursor? That depends, of course, on the operating system; but one thing is certain: we cannot apply the same rules as for the *kashida*. Specifically, the latter are joined to the current glyph, but in the Cambodian script the glyph to be inserted is quite far from the current glyph. What, then, shall we do?

AAT solves this problem very simply by saying: in the first case, we shall say that the inserted glyph(s) behave like the *kashida*. We must specify this behavior when we define the insertion, both for the current glyph and for the marked glyph (which could behave differently).

We must also specify which glyphs are to be inserted and where to put them. In fact, we have the possibility of inserting different strings of glyphs before or after the marked glyph and before or after the current glyph.

All of these choices are presented to us in the interface for editing transitions in Font-Forge. In the **Mark Insert** and **Current Insert** input areas, we enter the strings of glyphs to insert, respectively, after the marked glyph (or before the marked glyph, if **Insert Before Marked Glyph** is checked) or after the current glyph (or before the current glyph, if **Insert Before Current Glyph** is checked). The glyphs to be inserted are described by their names separated by spaces, as we did above for glyph classes. We can insert up to 31 glyphs.

Kerning

Apple wanted to be innovative and offer kerning for eight glyphs *at the same time*. That certainly covers our celebrated string "S.A.V.", and many other more complicated situations. How does it work? The window for inputs appears, just as with any other AAT finite automata, with the single difference that there is no possibility of choosing a feature or a selector: Apple considers that kerning "transcends" features and that it should always be enabled by default. Likewise, for Apple, there is only one way to perform kerning, and therefore the notion of a selector does not apply.

What do we do, then? We fill in the glyph classes, as usual. The state-transition window allows us to enter four pieces of data, including the two classic ones: what is the next state? and should we process the current glyph immediately or wait until we reach the new state? The checkbox **Push Current Glyph** allows us to store a series of glyphs (up to eight). These glyphs are retained in memory so that they can be "popped". When *n* glyphs are popped, *n* − 1 kerning values are applied to them *simultaneously*. The kerning values are entered in the input area at the bottom.

Each of these kerning values is therefore a path on which we have gone through as many states as there are glyphs in the string to be kerned: to kern A.V, we have the classes A (and Agrave, Lambda, etc.), period (and comma, etc.), and V (and W, etc.). When we read an A, we leave the initial state for state 2, and we place an A on the stack. When we read a period, we leave state 2 for state 3 and place period on the stack. When we read a V, we leave state 3 to return to the fold by popping the three glyphs and applying to them the kerning values 0 - 400.

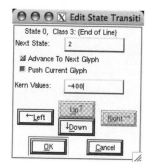

Bitmap Font Formats

Without a doubt, bitmap font formats are things of the past. Aside from a few visionaries such as Luc Devroye [117], who dreams of the *perfect rendition* of a font in bitmap form with a pixel having the size of a *molecule of ink* (!), few people give serious consideration to bitmap fonts today, since all operating systems, without exception, have switched to vector fonts.

Yet bitmap fonts are practical for display on screen. First, they are rendered more cleanly: as much as we sing the praises of vector fonts, a good, sturdy bitmap font is more efficient than the most beautiful *Aldine* for displaying text on the screen as it is typed, especially at a small size. Moreover, bitmap fonts are easy to modify and adapt to changing needs. Creating a new glyph takes less than a minute; modifying it is a matter of a few clicks to enable or disable a handful of pixels.

Bitmap fonts can always be useful in any application oriented towards reading on a screen rather than towards printing, such as the Unix console that we use every day but hardly ever print out.

Next, there are also bitmap fonts that go with vector fonts. An intelligent operating system can take advantage of them to display certain actual sizes optimally while using vector fonts for printing.

Below we shall examine the most common bitmap font formats. Most of them are surprisingly simple, unlike those for vector fonts.

A.1   The Macintosh World

A.1.1   The FONT Format

In 1984, the first Macintosh was already equipped with 17 fonts, some of which, such as *Venice*, *Athens*, and *Cairo*, rather quickly left the scene; others, such as *Chicago* (which was replaced by

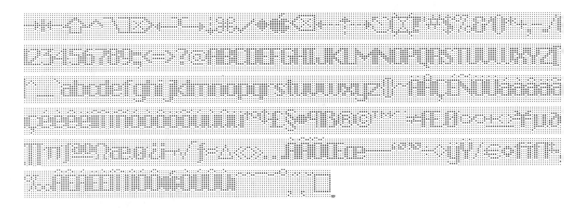

Figure A-1: The global image of the font Chicago, which was used on the Macintosh's menus for more than 15 years. It is an up-to-date version of the font, as we can see that the euro sign has been included.

Charcoal to give the Mac's desktop a new look), stayed around for a while; finally, two of them have survived to the present, becoming vector fonts along the way: *Geneva* and *Monaco*.

These fonts were all resources of type FONT. The "Macintosh Programmer's Guide" (*Inside Macintosh* [49, p. I-227]) of the era explains the structure of these resources in great detail. Here is a brief description: A FONT resource is a series of pairs of bytes in little-endian order that consists of the following:

- *Global parameters*: the "type of font" (monospaced or proportional), the positions of the first and last glyphs in the table, the maximum set-width, the "maximum kern"[1]), the number of pixels below the baseline, the width and height of the bounding box, a pointer to the table of set-widths, the leading (i.e., the number of pixels to add between lines of glyphs), and the width of the font's global image (see below).

- The *global image*: the concatenation of all the glyphs into a single—very long—bitmap image (see Figure A-1). Apple requires us not to leave any space between the glyphs. The pixels of this image are grouped into lines of the same length, running from top to bottom, which means that, to obtain a glyph, we must read its first line and then make a leap equal to the width of the global image to find its second line, and so on.

- A table of pointers to the origins of the glyphs in the global image.

- A table of offsets of the lower left pixel of the glyphs with respect to the origin, as well as the values of the displacement vectors.

For instance, a program that wants to display an italic '*f*', whose terminal may extend a few pixels beyond the origin, will go to the table of pointers to find the origin of the '*f*' in the

---

[1] The term "kern" here is used in an unexpected way: here it refers to the number of pixels that appear *to the left of the origin* of the displacement vector. This sense corresponds to what kerning meant in the days of metal type: that part of the character that extended beyond its parallelepiped to appear over the preceding parallelepiped or the following one.

global image, and then to the table of offsets to find out how much it should move to the left *before* beginning to draw any pixels, and, at the same time, how many pixels it should move forward *after* drawing the pixels. Clean and simple.

A.1.2 The NFNT Format

A short time later, when Apple realized that it would be convenient to have several point sizes of the same bitmap font, a new type of resource was introduced: the FOND resource (see §6). This is a "font family" resource that dispatches to the different bitmap fonts that are available. Since FONT resources were stand-alone resources, a new name was given to this new type of resources in order to avoid any confusion: henceforth FONT resources that belonged to a FOND family would be called NFNT ([50, p. IV-35, 43]). Apple took advantage of the change to add two optional tables to the end of the resource: a new table of displacement vectors and a table of glyph heights.

A.1.3 Color

In 1986 [51, p. V-181], after the release of the incredibly sexy Macintosh II and its wonderful color screen, a new type of resource was added to FOND and NFNT: the fctb (font color table). We have the choice of four levels of color: 1 (black and white), 2 (four colors or gray levels), 4 (16 colors), and 8 (256 colors, which at the time was considered the height of luxury). Whatever the number of colors may be, it always refers to indexed colors: specifically, the fctb resource makes the connection between the indices of the colors and their actual RGB values (in a space of 2^{48} possible colors, since each value of red, green, or blue is a 16-bit number!).

The reader must surely be wondering, "But, if implementing beautiful colored fonts was technically possible, why were we never inundated with them?" Well, Apple's intention was not so much to provide "beautiful colored fonts" as to accelerate access to fonts by making available a system of bitmap images already adapted to the level of colors on the screen. In other words, black and white would remain black and white; only the image would be larger, since there would be 2, 4, or even 8 bits per pixel.

In any event, we can create such fonts, whether to speed up processing or to add gray levels, a possible colored background, or actual colors. To do so, we must merely ensure that the fcbt resource has the same number as the NFNT resource and that a number of flags are enabled in the latter's "font type".

A.2 The DOS World

A.2.1 The CPI Format

The DOS font format is CPI (for "Code Page Information", in the Microsoft sense; see page 45). The peculiarity of the CPI fonts is the fact that they contain several fonts, arranged first by code page, then by type size.

They are console fonts, therefore monospaced; what is more, they have a constant width equal to 8 pixels (which is equal to 8 bits, or 1 byte). Usually three sizes are found: 8, 14, and 16 pixels. Each font contains exactly 256 glyphs.

The structure of CPI fonts [91] is quite natural: there is a global heading, then the file is divided into sections corresponding to code pages (each with its own heading), themselves subdivided into subsections corresponding to the various available sizes, and each subsection again has its own heading and, finally, the bitmap data for the size in question.

The global heading is fixed:

```
ff 46 4f 4e 54 20 20 20 00 00 00 00 00 00 00 00
01 00 01 17 00 00 00 01 00
```

except for the last two bytes, which indicate the number of code pages supplied in the file (in this case, just one; the number 1 is written in little-endian order).

Next comes a section for each code page, with the following heading:

- a fixed 2-byte number: 00 1c; a 4-byte pointer to the heading of the following code page (or ff ff ff ff); a 2-byte number with the value 1 (screen font) or 2 (printer font); an 8-byte ASCII string to indicate the type of screen/printer (for example, "EGA   "); the Microsoft code-page number, written as 2 bytes: 437 (United States), 850 ("multilingual"), 863 (Canadian French), etc.; 6 null bytes; a 4-byte pointer to the next font heading, or else 0; a fixed 2-byte number: 00 01;[2] a 2-byte number: the number of fonts belonging to this code page; the total size of these fonts.

Next come the fonts belonging to this code page. Each one is preceded by a font heading: one byte to indicate the size (6, 8, 14, or 16), and 5 fixed bytes (00 00 00 01 00).

Finally come the bitmap data, glyph by glyph and line by line. As each line contains pixels, therefore 8 bits, it occupies exactly 1 byte. Each glyph therefore occupies as many bytes as the size of the font.

A.3   The Windows World

The malicious say that there is a connection between the names FNT of Microsoft and NFNT of Apple, as well as between Microsoft's FON and Apple's FOND. That is not so: aside from the fact that both cases combine a single bitmap font with a font "family", their approaches have very little in common.

A.3.1   The FNT Format

A.3.1.1   Bitmap FNT Fonts

FNT is a format for individual bitmap fonts. The latest update of this format dates to 1991, which was before the advent of the TrueType format; but it already gives us a foretaste of the parameters that we shall see a few years later in the TrueType fonts.

The reason is that the FNT fonts of Windows, unlike Apple's NFNT fonts, are crawling with global parameters of all kinds [45].

---

[2] The font format described here is that of MS-DOS and PC-DOS. There are also CPI fonts for the DR-DOS and Novell-DOS operating systems. Their format differs in significant ways from the one described here; in particular, the number in question here takes the value 2.

- "Typographical" parameters: the optical size (!); the vertical and horizontal resolutions for which the font was designed; the number of pixels above the baseline; two types of leading (*internal* leading, which can include accents or other marks, and *external* leading, which must be left white); the presence of italics, underscoring, or strikethrough; the weight (on a scale between 1 and 1,000, with 400 being the average value); the size of the grid on which the glyphs were designed; the average set-width; the maximum set-width; the font's name.

- Parameters for "organization": the version of the format (2 for fonts meant for Windows 2 and 3 for fonts meant for Windows 3 and later); the font's type (bitmap or vector); the font's copyright notice; the positions of the first glyph and the last glyph in the font table; the font's "character set number" (8 bits); the (very rough) classification of the font ("roman", "swiss" [i.e., sans serif], "modern" [i.e., monospaced], "script", "ornamental", and "don't care"); finally, the "default glyph", which is the glyph displayed when a glyph that does not exist in the font is requested.

- A parameter for interaction with typesetting software, which affects characters rather than glyphs: the character that the software is supposed to use as a word delimiter. This character is the space by default, and that is how the font tells the software how to divide the text into words.

- Parameters for managing a glyph's width and height. A font is said to be of "type ABC"[3] if three types of data are provided for each glyph: "A" equals the left side bearing, "B" equals the width of the glyph's bounding box, "C" equals the right side bearing. In this way, A + B + C yields the glyph's offset vector. The heading contains the maximum values of these three quantities.

- Some low-level computer-related parameters: the total size of the file; the number of bytes in each line of the bitmap image; a pointer to the font's name; a pointer to the name of a peripheral; the "absolute machine address" (i.e., an address within the computer's RAM, a highly volatile piece of data!) of the bitmap image; an internal pointer to this same image; a number of flags indicating whether the font is monospaced/proportional and/or of "type ABC" and/or of color level 1, 4, 8, or outright RGB; a pointer to the table of colors; and, finally, the name of the output peripheral, if the font is intended for a specific peripheral device.

After these parameters comes a table of widths (possibly broken down into three quantities: A, B, C) and pointers to the bitmaps of the glyphs and to the font's bitmap image.

Note that the pixels are organized in a way different from that of Apple's bitmap fonts. Specifically, the glyphs are stored within the image in sequential order: the pixels of glyph n all occur between those of glyph $n-1$ and those of glyph $n+1$. But each glyph is not necessarily filled in from top to bottom for its entire width; rather, columns of a fixed width (given as a parameter in the font's heading) are used.

---

[3] We can only admire the imagination of the developers at Microsoft who came up with this name, which has absolutely nothing to do with what it represents.

A.3.1.2 Vector FNT fonts

There are also "vector" FNT fonts, but the author, *despite his many efforts*, has not been able to find documentation for them. They are outline fonts: only the outlines are displayed; they are not filled in. The thickness of the outline depends on the display device; usually it is one pixel, giving these fonts very thin strokes. Three of these fonts have survived in Windows 2000 and XP: *Modern, Roman,* and *Script.*

A.3.2 The FON Format

Since 1992 [304], Windows has used the concept of *resources*, which are similar to the resources of the Mac and of X Window. Resources are compiled by a special tool that reads a resource-description file (extension .rc) and a number of binary files needed to create the resources.

Thus the FNT files examined above become "font resources"; for that purpose, we need only prepend to them a *resource heading*. By grouping several of these resources together and adding to them a "font directory" resource, we obtain a FON file.

A.4 The Unix World

A.4.1 The PSF Format of Linux

The acronym PSF stands for "PC Screen Font". This font format is peculiar to Linux and is used only for monospaced fonts meant for on-screen display. It was defined in 1989 by Peter Arvin for his DOS font editor, *fontedit.* Later adopted by Linus Torvalds for Linux, it was supplemented with Unicode tables in 1994 and, finally, was updated in version 2 of 1999.

Version 1 of the PSF format is of a childlike simplicity. It begins with a 4-byte heading, in which the first 2 bytes are fixed (0x3604), the third contains three flags (does the font contain 256 or 512 glyphs? does it have a Unicode table? does this table contain *character sequences*?[4]), and the fourth contains the height of the glyphs in pixels. Next come the bitmap images of all the glyphs, described in the following manner: the width being fixed at 8 pixels (one byte), each glyph is described row by row, and thus needs as many bytes as there are pixels in its height.

The heading in Version 2 of the PSF format is slightly longer (32 bytes, or even more), since this version considerably extends the preceding one: the number of glyphs is arbitrary (encoded as 4 bytes), and the height and width of the glyphs are configurable. Here is this heading (made up of eight 4-byte numbers):

- A fixed value (0x72b54a86)

- The version (0x00)

- The size of the heading (to allow for later versions with longer headings)

---

[4] By *Unicode character sequences*, we mean a Unicode character followed by at least one combining character.

- Flags (only one is used at present: does the font have a Unicode table?)

- The number of glyphs

- The number of bytes used for each glyph

- The maximum number of rows of pixels for each glyph

- The maximum set-width of a glyph, in pixels

To calculate the number of bytes used for each glyph, we take the glyph's width in pixels, round it to obtain whole bytes, and multiply by the number of rows.

A.4.1.1 The Unicode table

The most attractive property of PSF fonts is without a doubt the possible presence of a Unicode table, to the point that we have developed the habit of assigning the extension .psfu to PSF fonts that have a Unicode table and .psf to those that do not. We shall see that there are tools for equipping PSF fonts with Unicode tables.

The Unicode table immediately follows the bitmap image of the final glyph. Its structure is as follows: There are as many entries as glyphs. Each entry consists of:

1. Zero, one, or more Unicode characters, represented either in UCS-16LE (2 bytes, little-endian) for version 1 of PSF or in UTF-8 for version 2.

2. Zero, one, or more Unicode sequences. The characters are represented in the same way as in (1). Each sequence is preceded by a "sequence initiator" (0xfffe in version 1 of PSF, 0xfe in version 2).

3. An entry terminator (0xffff in version 1 of PSF, 0xff in version 2).

Thus, for example, the glyph 'Ÿ' might have the following entry in a Unicode table (PSF Version 1):

0x0178	LATIN CAPITAL LETTER Y WITH DIAERESIS
0x03ab	GREEK CAPITAL LETTER UPSILON WITH DIALYTIKA
0xfffe	sequence initiator
0x0059 0x0308	LATIN CAPITAL LETTER Y followed by COMBINING DIAERESIS
0xfffe	sequence initiator
0x03a5 0x0308	GREEK CAPITAL LETTER UPSILON followed by COMBINING DIAERESIS
0xffff	entry terminator.

To obtain the entry in Version 2 of PSF, represent the Unicode characters in UTF-8 and replace the initiators and terminators with the corresponding one-byte values.

The utilities *psfaddtable* and *psfgettable*, which are included in practically every Linux distribution, allow the user to add the Unicode table to a PSF font and to retreive the table from the font. The text-based version of the required Unicode table (or the table thus obtained) is in the following format: For each glyph, one line of text is written, which includes some integers—the first number, written in decimal, octal (preceded by a 0), or hexadecimal (preceded by 0x) notation, indicates the glyph's position in the font, and the other numbers (in U+hhhh notation) indicate the corresponding Unicode characters. When there is a sequence, the base character is separated from the combining characters with commas. Lines beginning with a crosshatch (#) are comments.

For example, the line corresponding to the sample entry that we gave above would be

```
# Y WITH DIAERESIS
0x0178 U+0178 U+03ab U+0059,U+0308 U+03a5,U+0308
```

The utility *psfstriptable* will delete the Unicode table from a PSF font.

A.4.2   The BDF Format

As astonishing as this may seem, the BDF format, which is the basis for practically all Unix fonts, was defined by Adobe, a company that we do not usually associate with this operating system. BDF is a doubly deceptive acronym: the 'F' stands not for "font" but for "format", and the 'B' stands not for "binary" but for "bitmap": "bitmap distribution format" (yes, you read it correctly: the word "font" does not appear).

According to the first paragraph of the documentation [8], this format was intended to be nothing more or less than "easily understandable by both humans and machines". Indeed, what is the most striking is the fact that everything is written in pure ASCII, according to the "keyword/values" schema, with one keyword per line.

The global structure of the font is in no way surprising: first come the global parameters, then come the descriptions of the glyphs. The most important keys in the first section are the following:

- STARTFONT followed by the version number of the format: either 2.2 (the latest official version, dating to March 22, 1993) or 2.3 (an extension of the BDF format by Microsoft to support glyphs with a gray scale, [349]).

- FONT followed by the name of the font. This name, according to Adobe, must be identical to the font's PostScript name, if one exists.

- SIZE followed by three numbers: the actual size and the horizontal and vertical resolutions of the device for which the font was designed.

  Note that in version 2.3 of these fonts, this keyword takes a fourth parameter: the number of bits per pixel (1, 2, 4, and 8, corresponding to 2, 4, 16, or 256 gray levels).

- FONTBOUNDINGBOX followed by four numbers: the font's bounding box.

- METRICSSET followed by a number selected from 0, 1, and 2. Here is what the numbers mean: 0, which is the default value, indicates that the font is horizontal; 1 indicates a vertical font; and in the case of 2, the font can be used in both directions.

- SWIDTH, SWIDTH1, DWIDTH, DWIDTH1, VVECTOR: the default metrics (see below for their descriptions).

- ENDFONT, the end of the file.

Aside from these properties defined in the BDF specification, a font can contain an arbitrary number of "properties", which are *any* keywords followed by values. It is good practice to use for those properties those of the *X logical font description* XLFD (see Chapter 8, page 222). Specification 2.1 of BDF [354] even recommends the use of the properties FONT_ASCENT, FONT_DESCENT, and DEFAULT_CHAR.

These global properties of the font must be surrounded by the lines STARTPROPERTIES (followed by the number of properties) and ENDPROPERTIES.

Next comes the section for the description of the glyphs, which begins with a CHARS line (followed by the number of glyphs) and ends with the line ENDFONT.

Each glyph contains the following keywords:

- STARTCHAR followed by the name of the glyph. Adobe recommends the use of the same glyph name or CID number as in PostScript fonts.

- ENCODING followed by one or two numbers. Here Adobe shows itself viciously lacking in political correctness by favoring its own font encoding, *Adobe Standard* (see page 660), a font encoding known not to contain any accented letters. If the glyph in question belongs to the Adobe Standard set of glyphs, then the keyword ENCODING is followed by its position in this table; if, however, the glyph is not present in that set, the keyword is followed by the number −1 and then the position of the glyph in the other encoding. Note that we are never allowed to specify the name of the other encoding, whose only shortcoming is that it is not Adobe Standard.

- ENDCHAR, the end of the glyph's description.

and two types of metric properties (see Figure A-2):

1. Metric properties at the pixel level:

   - DWIDTH, followed by two whole values: the coordinates of the glyph's primary displacement vector (called "horizontal" in the specifications). As a vector, it can, in principle, be at an angle rather than strictly horizontal. Nonetheless, Adobe persists in calling it "horizontal". This displacement vector starts from the glyph's primary origin.

   - DWIDTH1, followed by two whole values: the coordinates of the glyph's "vertical" displacement vector. As in the previous case, verticality can be relative. This vector starts from the glyph's secondary origin, which is used for vertical typesetting.

   - BBX, followed by four whole values (BBw, BBh, BBxo, BByo): a "bounding box" whose definition is different from that of the bounding boxes of PostScript fonts. In the present case, we first write the width and the height of the glyph's envelope, then the horizontal and vertical offsets of its lower left pixel relative to the origin.

   - VVECTOR, followed by two whole values: the coordinates of the vector that starts at the primary origin and ends at the secondary origin.

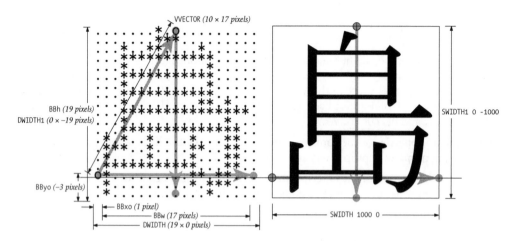

Figure A-2: BDF's vision of the bitmap and vector versions of a single ideographic character, with all the associated metric properties.

2. Metric properties established on a grid of 1,000 × 1,000 units (similar to that of the PostScript fonts):

   - SWIDTH, the equivalent of DWIDTH, but with the greater precision of the new grid
   - SWIDTH1, the equivalent of DWIDTH1

The mixing of values in pixels with "abstract" values is bound to make display or printing more precise when the screen or printer has a higher resolution than the font. Even better, if the bitmap font is accompanied by a vector font, and therefore the values SWIDTH and SWIDTH1 are those of the widths of the vector glyphs, then the typesetting software can work on two levels: it can use DWIDTH (or DWIDTH1) for display on screen with the bitmap font and SWIDTH (or SWIDTH1) to define with precision the PostScript code sent to the printer, which will use the corresponding vector font.

Finally comes the glyph's bitmap image:

   - BITMAP, on a line by itself, followed by as many lines of text as the glyph contains rows of pixels. Each line contains the values of the pixels encoded as hexadecimal numbers, to which we add null bits (at the right) to obtain full bytes.

     For example, if we have the row ..**.* (6 pixels), and therefore the binary value 001101, we add two zeroes at the right, 00110100, to obtain the hexadecimal number 0x34.[5]

     Note that if the font format used is 2.3, the pixels in the image can be at a gray scale (2, 4, or 8 bits per pixel: 4, 16, or 256 gray levels). In this case as well, we write the bits as hexadecimal numbers. For instance, the same number 0x93 = 10010011 can, according

---

[5] The advantage of this notation is that with a little Perl program like while (<>) { s/([0-9A-F][0-9A-F])/sprintf("%08b", hex($1))/ge ; tr/01/.*/ ; print ; } we can convert the hexadecimal numbers into series of dots and asterisks, as in Figure A-2.

to the number of gray levels, represent 8 black-and-white pixels *..*..**, or 4 pixels at 4 gray levels (with the values 2, 1, 0, 3), or 2 pixels at 16 gray levels (9, 3), or 1 pixel at 256 gray levels (147).

A.4.3   The HBF Format

The acronym HBF comes from *Hanzi Bitmap Font*, where "hanzi" is the transcription of 漢字, which means "Chinese character", a name used not only in Chinese but also in Japanese, Korean, and old Vietnamese for the ideographic characters common to these languages (with a few minor differences). HBF [296, 295] was developed by four Chinese researchers (one from Hong Kong and three from the United States) in order to optimize the use of disk space and memory by storing in separate files, which could be loaded into memory or not, as the application required.

The idea is very simple: since the glyphs of the ideographic scripts all have exactly the same dimensions, we can eliminate the bounding boxes and other data on width, height, etc. Even better, since the bitmap image of each glyph occupies exactly t bits, we can include all the glyphs, concatenated together, in a single image file: the nth glyph will appear at position nt in the file.

But the positions of the glyphs in the font table are not always contiguous; on the contrary, many East Asian encodings include structures in subblocks that contain the glyphs. For example, the Taiwanese encoding Big5 contains two subblocks: 0x40-0x7e and 0xa1-0xfe; any 2-byte code outside these subblocks is not valid in the encoding. This property is supported in the HBF format through the following keywords:

- HBF_START_BYTE_2_RANGES, followed by a whole number: the number of valid subblocks;

- HBF_BYTE_2_RANGE, followed by a range of hexadecimal numbers in uppercase (for example, 0x40-0x7E): one such block;

- HBF_END_BYTE_2_RANGES, the end of this section;

- Note that the same keywords with a 3 in place of the 2 are provided for 3-byte encodings.

But, again, not all the valid positions will necessarily contain glyphs. We must therefore be more precise and determine which parts of these subblocks actually contain glyphs. That is what HBF does, through the use of the following keywords:

- HBF_START_CODE_RANGES, followed by a whole number: the number of contiguous sections with glyphs.

- HBF_CODE_RANGE, followed by a range of hexadecimal numbers in uppercase, a filename, and a whole number. This is the most important keyword in HBF: the range designates the positions of the glyphs contained in the file, the number indicates the position of the offset of the first glyph in the range, starting at the beginning of the file. Thus, by writing

```
HBF_CODE_RANGE 0xA140-xA3E0 spcfont.24 0
HBF_CODE_RANGE 0xA440-xC67E stdfont.24k 0
HBF_CODE_RANGE 0xC940-xF9FE stdfont.24k 388872
```

we employ two fonts (spcfont.24 and stdfont.24k), of which the second contains contiguous glyphs, with the exception of a hole (the glyphs from 0xc67f to 0xc93f are missing); thus we invoke this file twice, the second time with an offset directly addressing glyph 0xc940.

- HBF_END_CODE_RANGES, the end of the section.

The other keywords in HBF are:

- HBF_START_FONT, followed by the version of the format (currently 1.1): it replaces the STARTFONT keyword of BDF.

- HBF_CODE_SCHEME, followed by the name of the encoding being used. The values provided are GB2312-1980 (Chinese); Big5 (Taiwanese); Big5 ETen 3.10 (the Big5 encoding with additions by the Taiwanese company ETen 倚天資訊); CNS11643-92pi, with i between 1 and 7 (Taiwanese), Unicode 1.1 (the only one available at the time), JISX0208-1990 (Japanese), and KSC5601-1987 (Korean).

- HBF_BITMAP_BOUNDING_BOX, followed by four whole values: a stricter version of BDF's FONTBOUNDINGBOX (see [296, section "Bounding Boxes"]).

- HBF_END_FONT: the end of the file.

Note that this bitmap font format can be used only for monospaced fonts, such as ideographic fonts. The reduction in space is impressive: a Chinese font at 24×24 pixels takes up 550 kB in HBF (of which 1.6 kB is for the HBF specification file and the rest is for bitmap image files), 961 kB in PCF, and 1.935 MB in BDF.

A.4.4   The SNF, PCF, and ABF Formats

The SNF font format (for "Server Normal Format"), which has been consigned to history, was the first attempt at "compressing" BDF fonts, until Version X11 R4 of X Window. Its peculiarity was that it depended on the platform (byte format, size of numbers, etc.). Thus there were as many different SNF formats as manufacturers of Unix workstations: NCD, Hewlett-Packard, IBM, DEC, SCO, Sun Microsystems, and so forth. Rather than converting SNF formats among themselves, the method used was to go through the BDF format by decompiling (with the *snftobdf* utility) and recompiling (*bdftosnf*).

The X Consortium took advantage of the change from X11 R4 to R5 in 1991 to change its font format radically. Since the biggest drawback of the SNF format was that it depended on the platform and was therefore not portable, what was more natural than to adopt a new *portable* format that nonetheless remained *compiled*? PCF, accordingly, stands for *Portable Compiled Font*. To obtain PCF fonts, we can use the tools *pcftobdf* and *bdftopcf*.

When Adobe finally took up the BDF format, in 1992, it wanted to issue its own version of a binary format associated with it. The result was ABF (for "Adobe Binary Font").

We shall not describe the internal structure of these three formats: they contain no more or fewer data than the BDF fonts that were used to create them; the information is merely stored in a more compact manner.

As for the SNF format, a description is given in issue 2 of the journal *The X Resource* [251]. For more information, one may also consult the source code of the X 11 R 6.4 distribution—more specifically, the modules for reading SNF fonts [46].

For the PCF format, the situation is a bit better, since, beyond the corresponding source-code modules [285], which are, after all, the final authority, there is also the attempt of George Williams [350] to describe the format.

Finally, the ABF format, given its origins, is the only one that is perfectly described in a publicly available document, an Adobe technical note [3]. Yet, while there are clearly a great many SNF fonts and vastly more PCF fonts in the world, the author has never seen a single ABF font.

A.4.5   The RAW and CP Formats

To bring the section on Unix to a close, let us discuss two obsolete formats that have long since been forgotten: RAW and CP.

RAW has at least one big point in its favor: it is *the simplest* bitmap font format. It contains only the bitmap images of the glyphs, without any sort of heading or escape character!

Here is a little riddle: if there is no heading, how on earth does the system know how to find a given glyph in the font? Answer: the width of the glyphs is always 8 pixels. There are always exactly 256 glyphs. If the height of each glyph is h pixels, the file necessarily contains $8 \times 256 \times h$ bytes. Conversely, if the size of the file is T, the height, h, of the font is necessarily $\frac{T}{8 \times 256}$, and the ith glyph appears in position $i \times 8 \times h$ in the file. Elementary, my dear Watson!

The CP format is another story altogether. Yann Dirson (of Debian) [120] has called it an "awful thing" and a "horror". It is a stripped-down version of DOS's CPI format with a unique code page (see §A.2.1). A CPI font ordinarily contains multiple code pages (in the Microsoft sense; see page 45) of fonts. The *codepage* utility (whose name could lead to confusion) will extract as many fonts from the CPI file as there are code pages. For example, if we assume that we have a CPI file ega.cpi and that we execute

```
codepage ega.cpi -a
```

we will obtain the fonts 850.cp, 437.cp, and so on for each code page contained in the CPI file. These fonts can then be used as Linux console fonts by running them through the utility *setfont*.

A.5   The T_EX World

Appendix B of this book deals with the real and virtual metric data of T_EX and Ω. But T_EX long used bitmap fonts, compiled from font descriptions written in the METAFONT programming language (see Appendix F). In this section, we shall discuss the bitmap formats defined by Knuth and his students for the needs of T_EX.

A.5.1 The PXL and CHR Formats

Unlike humans, who learn languages as they grow up, METAFONT was born speaking several languages, which she later forgot. For instance, in 1983, METAFONT[6] was able to produce fonts in FNT (nothing to do with the Windows FNT format; these were fonts for the Xerox Graphics Printer), VNT (for the Varian Versatec printer), ANT (Alphatype CRS), RST (Canon), OC (Dover), and WD (PrePress).

It quickly became clear that it would be more practical to have a single bitmap format and to generate the data on the fly from this generic format, whether the task be on-screen display or printing. That became a reality in November 1981, when David Fuchs announced the PXL font format [145].

The PXL format (the abbreviation comes from the word *pixel*) is a variable-width bitmap format without compression: the glyphs are described by bitmap images, and at the end of the file there is a table of metric data. PXL had two main drawbacks: a font could contain no more than 128 glyphs, and the lack of compression made the size of these files substantial for large type sizes or high-resolution printers.

Just as TFM and VF (see Appendix B) can be converted to a human-readable format and vice versa without loss of data, PXL can be converted to one such format, by the name of CHR (a poorly chosen name, as it comes from "*character*", whereas *glyphs* are being discussed here). As we frequently do in this book when a "humanized" format exists, we are going to employ this format here instead of the binary format, which is of interest to no one but the machine. The utilities for converting PXL to CHR and vice versa are *pxtoch* and *chtopx*.

The CHR format contains a global heading followed by descriptions of glyphs, each of them preceded by a glyph heading. Here is an example of a global heading for the font *Computer Modern Roman*, 10 points, generated for a 360-DPI printer:

```
Font file info  :
Number of char  :128
Checksum        :1274110073
Magnification   :1800
Design size     :10485760
Directory ptr   :4547
Pixel Id        :1001
Max height      :50
Max width       :49
```

A few words of explanation:

- Since 200 DPI is, in a sense, the "default" resolution of the system, we can say that a 360-DPI font is a "standard font" to which we have applied a magnification factor of 1.8. The value of *magnification* is this factor multiplied by 1,000.

---

[6] We are referring, of course, to METAFONT78, the ancestor of the current METAFONT, which was written in the proprietary language of the SAIL system. The interested reader can find all the SAIL files for the TeX and METAFONT projects in [43].

- The *design size* is expressed in 2^{20}-ths of an American printer's point; in our case, we have a value of 10,485,760, which, when divided by 2^{20}, gives us 10 points.

- *Directory ptr* is a pointer to a table of metric data in the PXL file; this information is useless, as *chtopx* recalculates the pointer.

- *Pixel Id* is the signature of this version of the font format.

And here is the complete description of the glyph 'a':

```
chrcode          :141         .....******..........
height           :24          ...**.....***........
width            :22          ..*........****......
right            :22          .****......***.......
left             :1           .*****.....****......
depth            :2           .*****......****.....
x offset         :-           .*****......****.....
y offset         :22          ..***.......****.....
tfm width        :524290      ............****.....
raster width     :24          ............****.....
internal width   :22          .........********....
right kerning    :22          ......****...****....
top              :1           ....***......****....
bottom           :24          ..****.......****....
data row count   :24          ..***........****....
-+                            .****........****....
                             ****.........****...*
                             ****.........****...*
                             ****.........****...*
                             ****.........*****..*
                             ****.........*****..*
                             .****......*..****..*.
                             :..****....*...*******.
                             ....******......****..
```

In the header, *chrcode* gives the position of the glyph in the table, in octal notation. *tfm width* gives the width of the glyph in the corresponding TFM file; it is calculated in 2^{20}-ths of an American printer's point.

In the image shown beneath the heading, the characters - and : are the projections of the glyph's origin onto the coordinate axes. The character +, on the other hand, indicates the point $(-1, -1)$ in the bitmap image (whose origin is the upper left corner).

A.5.2 The GF Format

When Donald Knuth set about rewriting TEX and METAFONT in Pascal-WEB, he also addressed the problem of bitmap fonts. Drawing his inspiration from DVI (the format for "generic" page description), he created a format for "generic" fonts that is structured like a DVI file.

This format is called GF (for "generic font") [216, pp. 484-489], and it remains to this day the output format of METAFONT.

A GF file contains *operators* and *values* thereof; each operator is represented in the file by a 1-byte value (which the reader will find in [216, pp. 484-489]). Globally, the file consists of a preamble, the description of the glyphs, and a postamble.

The preamble is as follows: the *pre* operator, followed by two parameters, the second being a string of comments less than 256 characters long and the first being the string's length, stored in a one-byte value.

Each glyph description begins with a *boc* operator and ends with an *eoc*. The *boc* operator takes six parameters: the glyph's position in the table (4 bytes: thus there can be 4 billion glyphs in a font, the world record!), a pointer to the glyph in the same position in the previous plane, which takes the value −1 if the plane does not exist,[7] and then the dimensions of the grid containing the glyph.

Now we have come to the description of a glyph. At any moment there is a "current color": white or black. Here are some of the most important operators:

- The operator *paint_0* permutes the current color.

- The operators from *paint_1* to *paint_63* paint the following 1 to 63 pixels in the current color and then switch from black to white or from white to black.

- The operator *skip0* moves to the following line and changes the current color to white.

- The operator *skip1*, followed by a 1-byte number *n*, skips *n* rows and switches to white.

- The operator *new_row_0* skips a row and changes to black.

- The operators from *new_row_1* to *new_row_164* move to the following line, skip from 1 to 164 pixels, and switch to black.

- The operator *xxx1*, followed by two parameters (the second of which is a string of fewer than 256 characters and the first of which is the length of this string), is a "special", i.e., an external block of code that can be read and processed by certain software (for example, it might contain PostScript code).

- The operator *yyy1*, followed by a 4-byte number, is used by METAFONT to incorporate into the code for a glyph the numbers of the points defined in the code.

Finally, the postamble, which begins with a *post* operator followed by nine parameters. These nine parameters include the font's optical size, a checksum, the proportions of the pixels (if

---

[7] An explanation is in order. Years before the valiant developers of Ω set about implementing them, Knuth had already planned for fonts with more than 256 glyphs. But to him a font of that sort would be useful only for the ideographic languages, and it is well known that all the glyphs in those languages have the same dimensions. Thus he dreamed of a GF font with several "planes" of 256 glyphs, all of them obeying a single TFM file with 256 positions. The parameter in question in the GF file is used to leap from one plane to another. The least that we can say is that these fonts were never really implemented, so the parameter has very seldom been used. There is another operator, *boc1*, which eliminates this parameter by assuming that it has the value −1.

they are not square), and the dimensions of the global grid that incorporates all the grids of the glyphs.

The *post* operator is followed by a series of *char_loc* operators, which point to the start of each glyph's description in the file. These operators take five parameters: the glyph's position in the table; the coordinates of the glyph's displacement vector;[8] the exact set-width of the glyph, as defined in the TFM file; and, finally, the pointer to the *boc* operator at the beginning of the glyph's description.

The postamble ends with a *postpost* operator followed by a pointer to *post*, a number indicating the version of the format, and as many instances of 0xdf as needed to make the size of the file a multiple of 4 bytes.

Thus we can see that the GF format is very different from all the bitmap formats of the era, and even from those of today. We can raise questions about the efficiency of the process: on the one hand, the interpretation of the operators requires processing that is too complex for direct display; on the other hand, the compression achieved by these operators may be attractive at the level of each row, but nothing is done for identical rows that are repeated. Nevertheless, that remains fertile ground for experimentation.

The program *gftype* allows for debugging GF fonts by generating a human-readable list of the operators used to describe each glyph. Here, for example, are the beginning and end of the description of the glyph 'a' in the font *Computer Modern Roman* 10:

```
4101: beginning of char 97: 2<=m<=27 0<=n<=23
(initially n=23) paint (5)9
4109: newrow 3 (n=22) paint 2(7)4
4113: newrow 2 (n=21) paint 4(8)3
4117: newrow 2 (n=20) paint 5(8)3
4121: newrow 2 (n=19) paint 5(8)4
4125: newrow 2 (n=18) paint 5(9)4
4129: newrow 4 (n=17) paint 1(11)4
4133: newrow 16 (n=16) paint 4
4135: newrow 16 (n=15) paint 4
4137: newrow 16 (n=14) paint 4
4139: newrow 9 (n=13) paint 11
4141: newrow 6 (n=12) paint 5(5)4
...
4179: newrow 0 (n=4) paint 5(10)5(4)1
4185: newrow 1 (n=3) paint 4(10)5(4)1
4191: newrow 1 (n=2) paint 5(8)1(1)5(2)2
4199: newrow 3 (n=1) paint 4(5)2(3)7
4205: newrow 5 (n=0) paint 7(7)4
4209: eoc
```

---

[8] Note that the displacement vector may be vertical, or even oblique, whereas TEX moves only horizontally while setting type.

```
.<--This pixel's lower left corner is at (2,24) in METAFONT coordinates
      *********
    **         ****
    ****        ***
    *****        ***
    *****        ****
    *****         ****
       *          ****
                  ****
                  ****
                  ****
             **********
       *****      ****
      *****       ****
      ****        ****
      ****        ****
     *****        ****
    *****         ****    *
    *****         ****    *
    *****         ****    *
    *****         *****   *
     ****         *****   *
    *****       * ***** **
     ****    ** *******
       *******      ****
.<--This pixel's upper left corner is at (2,0) in METAFONT coordinates
```

In the code, the numbers at the beginning of each line refer to positions in the file, and newrow * refers to a *new_row_** operator that begins a new row and leaves a certain number of pixels white. In addition, paint refers to a series of *paint_** operators, where the numbers in parentheses are white pixels and the other numbers are black pixels.

Unfortunately, *gftype*, as its name suggests, is not a tool for conversion *without loss of information* but rather a tool for *debugging*. It is not possible to capture its output and generate a GF font from it.

Another very appealing tool (and, for some people, the major attraction of the GF format) is *gftodvi*. Provided that we have used the METAFONT command labels for all the points on the outline and that we have generated a GF file with a strictly positive value to the proofing value and a sufficiently high resolution, *gftodvi* will produce, from the GF file alone, a DVI file with as many pages as there are glyphs in the font. On each page, we find a rather large and very precise copy of the glyph on which all the "labeled" points are also identified. And if there are points that are too close to existing points, a list of them is shown separately, with their coordinates relative to the nearest points.

In Figure A-3 we see the glyph 'a' of the font *Computer Modern Roman* at an optical size of 10, the result of the following manipulations:

METAFONT output 2003.07.28:2342 Page 27 Character 97 "The letter a"

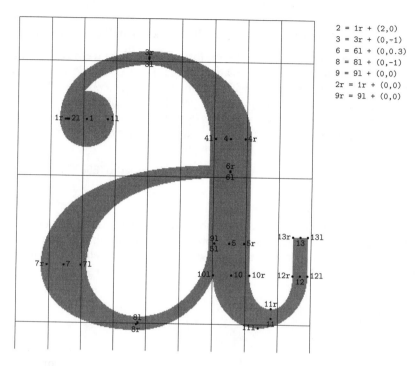

```
2 = 1r + (2,0)
3 = 3r + (0,-1)
6 = 61 + (0,0.3)
8 = 81 + (0,-1)
9 = 91 + (0,0)
2r = 1r + (0,0)
9r = 91 + (0,0)
```

Figure A-3: A page from the DVI file produced by gftodvi from the font Computer Modern Roman 10, at 5,203 DPI.

```
mf "\mag:=2; input cmr10"
gftodvi cmr10.5203gf
dvips -D 300 -p 27 -l 27 -E cmr10.dvi
```

(Because no mode is indicated, METAFONT has used the *proofing* mode, which usually produces fonts at 2,602 DPI. Thanks to mag:=2, we have achieved a resolution of 5,203 DPI. Next, *gftodvi* produced a DVI file cmr10.dvi, of which we have converted only page 27, corresponding to the glyph 'a', to EPS. The parameter -D 300 of *dvips* is present for this reason: in the DVI file, a very special font by the name of gray is used to achieve the gray shading effect. For Figure A-3, which, in any case, was going to be reduced for inclusion in this book, using the gray font at a very high resolution turned out to be pointless; thus we imposed a resolution of 300 DPI for this font. This restriction does not affect the other fonts on the page, which are all vector fonts.)

A.5.3   The PK Format

The latest in the saga of bitmap formats for T_EX, PK was announced to the world by Tom Rokicki (student of Knuth and developer of *dvips*) in 1985 [306, 305]. PK solves the main problems of the GF format: its complexity and its size. The description of a glyph is no longer a series of operators that must be interpreted but a pre-structured block of code, similar to the other bitmap font formats. What distinguishes PK from the other formats studied in this chapter is the fact that it is *compressed* (incidentally, the acronym PK comes from *packed*).

The method of compression chosen for the PK format is simple and efficient: average compressions of 60 to 65 percent over GF files are achieved. It is RLE (*run-length encoding*) compression, and its principle is very simple: if there are, for example, 57 black pixels, instead of 57 bits (= almost 8 bytes), we write the number 57 (which can be encoded with 6 bits) followed by the black pixel (1 bit), which saves us 50 bits. But the question is: are there often glyphs with so many consecutive pixels? The answer is no, and that is why the RLE compression used in the PK format is adapted to the needs of each glyph.

Here is how it is done. (Warning: The description of the format in [306, 305] is a bit hard to understand.)

- We have seen that the GF format encodes the rows of a glyph as a series of numbers that indicate alternately the number of black pixels and white pixels. Here we shall go a bit farther: we shall also encode repeated rows while concatenating all the rows into one. For instance, if the glyph

```
. . . . . . .***. . . . . .
. . .***. . .***. . .
. . .***. . .***. . .
. . . . . . .***. . . . . .
```

is encoded

```
(6) 3 (6)
(3) 3 (3) 3 (3)
(3) 3 (3) 3 (3)
(6) 3 (6)
```

in GF (the numbers in parentheses being the white pixels), then in PK it will be (6) 3 (9) [1] 3 (3) 3 (9) 3 (6), where the [1] means that the current row is repeated once. To understand this notation, let us proceed step by step. First of all, we detect the repeated rows:

```
. . . . . . .***. . . . . .
. . .***. . .***. . .  [1]
. . .***. . .***. . .
. . . . . . .***. . . . . .
```

Next, we describe the first row and the beginning of the second, up to the first transition between black and white on the line that will be repeated:

```
. . . . . . .***. . . . . .
. . .
```

That already gives us (6) 3 (9), and it is at that point that we insert the information on the repetition of a row [1]. Henceforth we act as if the repeated row did not exist (we are between the third and fourth pixels of the second row):

```
......***......
...***...***...
......***......
```

and thus we continue with 3 (3) 3 (9) 3 (6).

- Now that we have a new representation of the glyph ((6) 3 (9) [1] 3 (3) 3 (9) 3 (6)), we must merely encode it in RLE.

- We decide to work not at the level of bytes or bits but at the level of nybbles (4 bits). We can see that we have two types of information to encode: the repetition of rows, and the number of black (or white) pixels in sequence. Already we need a kind of flag to indicate which type of information will follow.

- Since a nybble consists of 4 bits, it can take values between 0 and 15. We therefore decide that the value 15 indicates that the current line is repeated once ([1] in the glyph's representation). Moreover, the value 14 of the nybble, followed by a "packed number" N (we shall see what it is below), means that the current row is repeated N times (= [N]).

- All that remains is to encode the pixels, and that is where the procedure turns interesting. We can say that the value 1 of the nybble means "1 pixel"; the value 2, "2 pixels"; etc. But we can also say that we are switching to bytes and that the first nybble is in fact multiplied by 16 and added to the second one. The first method is efficient for encoding small values; the second will be more efficient for large ones. We decide to use both, but then the question arises: when do we switch from the "1-nybble" schema to the "2-nybble" one (or to one for even more nybbles)?

  Rokicki answered this question by giving an algorithm (by Knuth) that calculates a "magic" number: the value beyond which we move from 1 to 2 nybbles, and which gives the best compression. Rokicki's idea was to recalculate this number for *each glyph*.

  For instance, if M is the magic number for the current glyph, the sequences of 1 to M pixels will be encoded as a single nybble (whose value is between 1 and M), and sequences of $M + 1$ to $(13 - M) * 16 + M$ pixels will be encoded as 2 nybbles (the first of which will take the values between $M + 1$ and 13). Finally, the value 0 of the nybble will be used for sequences of more than $(13 - M) * 16 + M$ pixels, which will be encoded with "packed" numbers.

- What is a "packed" number? Here the principle is the same as in the UTF-8 encoding: we use "escape sequences" to indicate the number of nybbles to follow. The escape sequences are null nybbles: 1 null nybble indicates that there are 2 nybbles to follow, 2 null nybbles indicate that there are 3 nybbles to follow, and so forth.

Let us point out that if we apply the method above to our example (supposing that the magic number is greater than or equal to 9), we obtain 6 3 9 F 3 3 3 9 3 6, thus 10 nybbles (5 bytes). Since the PXL format would have required 48 bits (6 bytes) for the same bitmap, we can see that the gain is not huge. For even smaller glyphs (or glyphs without repetition), compression in RLE could even be negative. In that case, the PK format allows the glyph to be represented in PXL. When that occurs, the "magic number" is equal to 14.

Thus we see that everything has been done so that the bitmap for each glyph will be encoded as efficiently as possible, by choosing the "magic number" on the fly and even abandoning compression when it does not have the desired result.

In conclusion, here is a description of the PK format itself:

- The principle of GF (itself borrowed from the DVI format) is used: there are operators and their values. Only the operators *xxx* ("specials"), *yyy*, *pre*, and *post* are retained from the GF format. Placing *xxx* or *yyy* inside glyphs is prohibited.

- Each glyph is represented in the manner described above and is preceded by a heading.

- This heading contains the following parameters: the "magic number", the length of the glyph's description (including the heading), the glyph's position in the table, the set-width (drawn from the TFM file), the horizontal displacement vector, the width and height of the glyph's image, the horizontal and vertical offsets of the image relative to the origin. Each of these values takes up 1 byte (except the TFM set-width, which takes 3). If the values of these parameters are larger, longer forms of headings may be employed.

- The first byte of the heading plays a special role: its first nybble contains the "magic number" (which is 14 if the glyph is encoded in PXL), the next bit indicates whether the glyph begins with a black or a white pixel, and the bits after that indicate whether the short version of the heading or one of the longer versions is being used.

A.5.4 Fonts or Images? Both!

One interesting application of the PK format is the utility *bm2font*, by Friedhelp Sowa, developed between 1989 and 1993. The goal is to segment an image (GIF, TIFF, PCX, etc.) into small square blocks and to store these blocks in a font as glyphs. That may seem incongruous to us today, but in the late 1980s, when the PostScript language was not as common as it is today, there was a big problem of compatibility between DVI drivers and image formats. By creating a PK font instead of an image, we were assured of having printed output, though the quality be inferior. Whereas if we supplied a bitmap to a driver that did not know how to interpret it, we had no chance of producing an image.

The photos of Ernestine and Danae above were processed by *bm2font* from TIFF images at gray levels and at a resolution of 300 DPI. Each image is built up from 12 glyphs distributed over two PK fonts. Here are the command lines that were used:

```
bm2font -b1 -fernestine -x8 ernestine.tif
bm2font -b1 -fdanae -x8 danae.tif
```

in which -b1 reduces the number of gray levels by half in order to brighten the image, -fernestine causes the creation of font files and TeX files named ernesti* and danae* (because of the limitations on the length of DOS filenames), and -x8 indicates the number of bits per pixel (here there are 8 bits, yielding $2^8 = 256$ gray levels). There is a range of other options that the reader will find in the documentation for the tool [319].

A.6 Other Less Common Bitmap Formats

Other bitmap formats exist. Usually they are connected to hardware manufacturers. For instance, the Hewlett-Packard printers, at one time, used a font format called *HP Soft Font* [176, Chapter 7], with the file extensions .sfp ('p' for "portrait") and .sfl ('l' for "landscape"). Why did we need two different formats for portrait mode and landscape mode? Because these printers' page-description language (called "PCL") did not by default support the automatic rotation of glyphs when we switched from one printing format to the other. Being accustomed to the PostScript language, we no longer think about problems of this kind.

A.7 Whoever Can Do More Can Also Do Less

Finally, some vector formats can also be used to contain bitmap fonts. That is the case for PostScript Type 3 and TrueType, OpenType, and AAT fonts.

PostScript Type 3 fonts are used, for example, by *dvips* to incorporated TeX's PK fonts into PostScript code. *dvips* generates temporary fonts in which the operator BuildChar uses the operator imagemask, which takes a bitmap in the form of a hexadecimal string and displays it (§C.2).

TrueType, OpenType, and AAT fonts often contain bitmaps for the most common sizes for on-screen display. These bitmaps are managed by the tables EBLC and EBDT (called bloc and bdat in AAT) and EBSC. See §D.7 for a detailed description of these tables.

B

T_EX and Ω Font Formats

B.1   TFM

The TFM format (for "T_EX font metrics") was defined in 1980 by Lyle Ramshaw, a student of Knuth, and remains today the only font format recognized by T_EX. Only in recent years have extensions of T_EX finally used other font formats: TrueType and OpenType.

TFM is a binary format, but there is a human-readable form called PL (for "property list"). In this book, we have adopted the principle of showing only the "humanized" form of a font format whenever it exists, provided that conversion from binary to legible format and vice versa can be done without loss of information.

To convert from TFM to PL, we have a tool: *tftopl*, written by Leonidas Guibas in 1978. When used in one of the following ways:

```
tftopl cmr10 > cmr10.pl
tftopl cmr10.tfm cmr10.pl
```

it will convert the font cmr10.tfm, wherever it is found on the disk, to the PL format and store this representation of the font in the file cmr10.pl in the current directory. This manipulation would be useless if the antidote did not exist: the opposite tool *pltotf*, which restores our font to its binary form. This tool is used as follows:

```
pltotf cmr10
pltotf cmr10.pl othername.tfm
```

In the first case, a file by the same name as the PL file and with extension .tfm will be created in the current directory, whereas in the second case we explicitly provide the names of these files.

The principle of the PL file syntax is very simple: there are *expressions*, which have the following form:

```
(KEYWORD VALUE)
```

where KEYWORD is a keyword and VALUE is its value, which may be another keyword, a set of keywords and numeric values, or another expression (again in parentheses). The keywords are written in uppercase letters, as computer code was written 20 years ago, in the era of Fortran IV and IBM 360/370 assembly language. Here is a short extract of a hypothetical PL file:

```
(FAMILY HYPOTHETICAL)
(FACE F MIE)
(CODINGSCHEME ASCII)
(DESIGNSIZE D 10)
(COMMENT THIS EXAMPLE IS PURELY)
(COMMENT HYPOTHETICAL)
(FONTDIMEN
   (SLANT R .25)
   (SPACE R .33)
   (SHRINK R .17)
   (STRETCH R .17)
   (XHEIGHT R 0.4)
   (QUAD R 1.0)
   )
(LIGTABLE
   (LABEL C f)
   (LIG C i 0 0)
   (STOP)
   (LABEL C i)
   (KRN C f R 0.05)
   (STOP)
   )
(CHARACTER C f
   (CHARWD R 0.3)
   (CHARHT R 0.7)
   )
(CHARACTER C i
   (CHARWD R 0.278)
   (CHARHT R 0.67)
   )
(CHARACTER O o
   (CHARWD R 0.488)
   (CHARHT R 0.7)
   )
```

Inserting a carriage return after each expression is not required, nor is leaving three spaces at the beginning of every line when we are inside an expression. We have presented the code in this way because *tftopl* does so.

One detail of the syntax: numbers are always preceded by a letter selected from the following: R (real), O (octal), H (hexadecimal), D (decimal). When we refer to the code point of an ASCII character other than the parentheses, we can also write C followed by the character itself. Example: C i is the number 105.

From a glance at this code, we can see that the file is divided into four sections:

- Global declarations

- Font parameters

- Kerning pairs and ligatures

- Metric properties of the glyphs

B.1.1 Global Declarations

Below we shall give the complete list of available keywords, but note that only one is really useful to TeX: DESIGNSIZE.

Here is the complete list of keywords and their official interpretations:

- CHECKSUM, followed by a 4-byte whole number, is a checksum used to confirm the physical integrity of the file.

- DESIGNSIZE, followed by a whole number between 0 and 2,048, is the font's design size, expressed in American printer's points.

- DESIGNUNITS, followed by a positive real number, indicates the correspondence between the abstract units used in the PL file and the design size (which is a dimension from the real world, as it is expressed in American printer's points). Its default value is 1.0, which means that to find a real dimension it is necessary to multiply the abstract dimension by the design size. To have abstract units equal to those of the PostScript Type 1 fonts, it would be sufficient to take (DESIGNUNITS R 1000) (because the unit of a PostScript font is one-thousandth of the design size).

  The simplest choice is to leave DESIGNUNITS equal to 1. We quickly acquire the habit of interpreting (WIDTH R 0.7) as "width of seven-tenths of the design size".

- CODINGSCHEME, FAMILY, FACE: three data that are obsolete, no longer used.

B.1.2 Font Parameters

Unlike the preceding section, this one is very interesting, as the font's global behavior depends on it. It contains the font's global parameters, which can be as numerous as 255 (in current implementations of TeX), but only the first 22 parameters have special names. Among them, the first seven [which correspond to the \fontdimens that we saw in the section on configuring NFSS] are used in text fonts. The others are used only with mathematical fonts. Here are the meanings of the first seven parameters:

- SLANT specifies the slope, expressed as the tangent of the angle—in other words, the horizontal displacement at a height of 1 point. This value is used when TEX places an accent over a letter so that the accent will remain centered over the letter's axis, which in this case is oblique.

- SPACE specifies the ideal interword space, i.e., the space used to set type in the font in question in the absence of any constraints imposed by justification.

- STRETCH specifies the maximum stretching allowed for the interword space.

- SHRINK specifies the maximum shrinking allowed for the interword space.

- XHEIGHT specifies the font's "x-height", i.e., the height of the lowercase letters. This information is used by TEX for the placement of accents over letters. By way of example, let us assume that the XHEIGHT of a font is x and that we wish to place an accent over a letter of height $x' > x$. We will therefore move the accent up by the amount of $x' - x$. We have direct and very elegant access to the value of this parameter through the dimension ex.

- QUAD specifies the size of the font's em. We have access to it through the dimension em.

- EXTRASPACE applies primarily to the Anglo-Saxon and German typographic traditions. Within these traditions, it involves an increase of the interword space whenever this space comes after a punctuation mark that ends a sentence. When more space is inserted after a sentence-final punctuation mark, the reader's eye can more easily detect the beginnings of sentences and can more easily distinguish periods used in abbreviations, which are not followed by extra space. This practice is not observed in France; indeed, TEX even calls the command that disables this property \frenchspacing.

The next 15 parameters are named NUM1 (or DEFAULTRULETHICKNESS), NUM2 (or BIGOPSPAC-ING1), NUM3 (or BIGOPSPACING2), DENOM1 (or BIGOPSPACING3), DENOM2 (or BIGOPSPACING4), SUP1 (or BIGOPSPACING5), SUP2, SUP3, SUB1, SUB2, SUPDROP, SUBDROP, DELIM1, DELIM2, and AXIS-HEIGHT. They are indispensable for mathematical fonts and serve to manage the composition of glyphs into two-dimensional mathematical constructions, such as fractions, superscripts and subscripts, extensible delimiters, etc.

We can also use the keyword PARAMETER D followed by an integer between 1 and 255 to indicate any parameter.

B.1.3   Kerning Pairs and Ligatures

The rules for the interactions of glyphs with each other appear in this table. Two glyphs that are set side by side can attract or repel each other: this information constitutes a *kerning pair*. They can also become "very close" to each other and form a new glyph: a *ligature*. They can also remain intact but give birth to a new glyph that appears between them: we call that approach, and some variations on the theme, *smart ligatures*.

All these operations are carried out within the expression (LIGTABLE *operations*). They are classified according to the first glyph in the kerning pair or ligature. Each of these initial glyphs is represented by an expression (LABEL *glyph*). At the end of all these operations affecting a given glyph, we find the expression (STOP). For example, if a period or comma following the letter 'f' should be moved 1.5 points closer to the letter, we write:

```
(LIGTABLE
   (LABEL C f)
   (KRN C . R -.15)
   (KRN C , R -.15)
   (STOP)
   )
```

In the code above, we can already see the kerning operation, represented by the keyword KRN. This glyph is followed by the second glyph in the pair and the amount of kerning requested: a negative amount when we move glyphs closer together, a positive one when we move them farther apart. Two points must be noted:

- Once kerning has been performed, the second letter of the kerning pair is "free" and can take part in other kernings or ligatures.

- If we request both kerning and a ligature between two letters, the one that appears first in the file will be executed.

Let us now move on to ligatures. The operation for a simple ligature, LIG, is written as follows:

```
(LIGTABLE
   (LABEL C f)
   (LIG C f H 13)
   (LIG C i H 14)
   (LIG C l H 15)
   (STOP)
   )
```

In the code above, the glyph pairs "ff", "fi", and "fl" are replaced by other glyphs (in hexadecimal positions 13, 14, 15) that represent the ligatures 'ff', 'fi', and 'fl'. When a new glyph is inserted, it is granted the same rights as the glyphs explicitly inserted by the user, and it in turn takes part in the formation of other ligatures or kerning pairs. For example, to obtain an 'ffi', we first form the ligature "f + f = ff" and then "ff + i = ffi". That means that forming a ligature of n glyphs requires, in addition to the ligature itself, $n - 2$ intermediate positions in the glyph table.

Now let us discuss "smart" ligatures. What distinguishes "smart" ligatures from "simple" ligatures is the fact that we preserve the old glyphs when inserting the new one. We write /LIG/ if we wish to preserve both glyphs and place the new one in the middle, /LIG if we wish to preserve only the first glyph, and LIG/ if we wish to preserve only the second.

Smart ligatures allow us to save space in the glyph table. Let us take an example. Suppose that, in a rather exotic font, we wish to have two types of apostrophes: one used after capitals, the other used after lowercase letters. Suppose that the latter is the rule and the former is the exception. Then in the box for the apostrophe there will be a "lowercase apostrophe". We need another code point for the glyph of the "uppercase apostrophe". If we used only simple ligatures, we would need 26 new glyphs: one for each combination of an uppercase letter and a special apostrophe. Not to mention the accented letters.

With smart ligatures, however, it is sufficient to use /LIG: in this case, the uppercase letter remains intact, and only the apostrophe changes. No extra box in the table is required.

Having reached this point, we may well wonder what happens after the replacement. Does the new glyph, or even the old glyphs kept intact, take part in the formation of new kerning pairs or ligatures? For instance, in the preceding example, supposing that we wrote 'A' ', the apostrophe would become an "uppercase apostrophe"; but can it also be kerned with the letter 'A'? That is very desirable indeed. But there is also the risk of an infinite loop: if xy produces xy' and there is a ligature between x and y' that brings us back to the starting point, xy, a few iterations will certainly cause the software to crash. Noticing that the question of the "time of availability" of the glyphs used to form a ligature does not have only one answer, Knuth provided for all the possible cases:

- /LIG: we replace the first glyph and examine the possible kerning pairs and ligatures that the newly inserted glyph might form with the second, before examining those that the second glyph might form with the glyph that follows it.

- /LIG>: we replace the first glyph and continue with the possible kerning pairs and ligatures of the second glyph with the one that follows.

- LIG/: we replace the second glyph and examine the possible kerning pairs and ligatures of the first glyph (kept intact) with the newly inserted glyph, and then those of the second glyph with the one that follows.

- LIG/>: we replace the second glyph and continue with the possible kerning pairs and ligatures that the second glyph might form with the one that follows.

- /LIG/: we insert a new glyph between the first and the second and then examine first the kerning pairs and ligatures that the first glyph forms with the new one, then those that the new glyph (or whatever it became, if it was in turn replaced by something else) forms with the second, and then those that the second forms with the one that follows.

- /LIG/>: we insert a new glyph between the first and the second and then examine first the kerning pairs and ligatures that the new glyph forms with the second, then those that the second forms with the one that follows.

- /LIG/>>: we insert a new glyph between the first and the second and then examine the possible kerning pairs and ligatures of the second glyph with the one that follows.

It is evident that the potential of smart ligatures remains yet unexplored: very few fonts use them, and their complexity is due more to Knuth's penchant for thoroughness than to any real need. The most common criticism of smart ligatures is that they are inseparably tied to the font and cannot be enabled or disabled according to context. For example, about 15 years ago, the author developed an Arabic font in which contextual analysis was managed entirely by smart ligatures. But in view of the rigidity of this approach and the problems he encountered, he was quite happy to abandon the approach altogether and perform the same operations with ΩTPs [170], which are filters internal to $Ω_1$, and later with $Ω_2$ internal modules. The difference between these approaches corresponds to the difference between AAT and OpenType fonts: in the former case, the font itself manages contextual analysis without leaving many opportunities for intervention to the typesetting software; in the latter case, software modules (including the rules for contextual analysis) and the software are responsible for applying them, and sophisticated software may allow for all kinds of interventions by the user.

But let us return to smart ligatures. One peculiarity of TeX relative to other typesetting systems is that the interword space is not a glyph but an offset. What, then, should be done to define ligatures between a "normal" glyph and a space? For instance, in some decorative fonts there is an 'e' with a longer curve, used at the end of a word. If the word is followed by a punctuation mark, we can write a ligature between the letter 'e' and that mark; but what can be done if it is followed by a space, when the space *is not* a glyph? The same question arises for ligatures at the beginning of a word.

This possibility is covered—in a somewhat awkward way, it must be admitted—at least for ligatures at the end of a word. To define a ligature at the beginning of a word, we write

```
(LABEL BOUNDARYCHAR)
    etc.
    (STOP)
```

Everything is fine up to this point. It is the ligatures at the end of a word that are problematic. We must define a glyph as being the "word boundary", using the expression (BOUNDARYCHAR *glyph*). This glyph may be an empty box that is used only to convey the abstract concept of "word boundary". But it may also be an actual glyph. The same ligatures and kerning pairs will apply in both cases. If there is an empty box in the font, that box can play the role of "word boundary", and the problem will not arise. But in most font encodings of the TeX world—T1, T2, etc.—no box is left empty; thus we must select a "real" glyph that will never be used as such. One stopgap is to use the glyph for a combining accent (code points 0 to 12 in the T1 encoding), which will never be placed next to another glyph but will only be placed above or below another glyph by means of the \accent primitive. But that means that we have long since left the realm of elegant programming and taken up hacking. Once again, these problems are handled better by Ω and its internal filters, which are closer to the original text and the Unicode characters than to the typeset result, the fonts, and the glyphs.

B.1.3.1 Optimizing operations

In the table of kerning pairs and ligatures, another layer of complexity comes on top of the complexity inherent in simple and smart ligatures: the optimization of operations. There are historical reasons for that: it must be borne in mind that this file format dates from the 1970s and that every byte of memory saved represented a non-negligible savings. Thus everything was done to make the table of kerning pairs and ligatures as small as possible. Here are some of the strategies for optimization:

- If two or more glyphs behave the same way towards the following glyphs with respect to kerning, they are listed together. For example, in cmr10, we find the code:

```
(LABEL C F)
  (LABEL C V)
  (LABEL C W)
```

```
(KRN C o R -.083334)
(KRN C e R -.083334)
(KRN C u R -.083334)
(KRN C r R -.083334)
(KRN C a R -.083334)
(KRN C A R -.111112)
(LABEL C K)
(LABEL C X)
(KRN C O R -.027779)
(KRN C C R -.027779)
(KRN C G R -.027779)
(KRN C Q R -.027779)
(STOP)
```

which means that the letters 'F', 'V', and 'W' behave the same way relative to the letters 'o', 'e', 'u', 'r', 'a', 'A', 'O', 'C', 'Q', and 'R'. Moreover, the letters 'K' and 'X' behave the same way as the preceding, but only towards the last four letters: 'O', 'C', 'Q', and 'R'. Without optimization, we would need 48 lines to describe the same kerning pairs; here, however, we have only 16. That represents compression of 75 percent.

- Now suppose that two glyphs behave in the same way towards a great many other glyphs, except in one case. And suppose that in that case there are two distinct nonzero kerning pairs or two distinct ligatures. The format shown above assumes that the "partners" of one glyph form a subset of the "partners" of the other. That is not the case here. To cope with this situation, Knuth introduced the operation (SKIP *integer*), which allows us to skip a given number of operations.

Let us take an example. Suppose that we have an 'f' and an 'ſ' (long 's'). These two letters have the same kerning pairs with, for example, the period and the comma. But they form different ligatures with the letter 'i'. Suppose that we have placed the 'ſ' in the box for the 's'. We want the following operations:

```
(LABEL C s)
    (KRN C . R -.1)
    (KRN C , R -.1)
    (LIG C i H 0)
    (STOP)
    (LABEL C f)
    (KRN C . R -.1)
    (KRN C , R -.1)
    (LIG C i H 1)
    (STOP)
```

where we have placed the ligature 'ſi' in code point 0 and the ligature 'fi' in code point 1. How can we optimize this code? The first step is to write:

```
(LABEL C s)
    (LIG C i H 0)
    (LABEL C f)
```

```
(LIG C i H 1)
(KRN C . R -.1)
(KRN C , R -.1)
(STOP)
```

In this code, it is the fourth line that causes a problem, when we start reading from the first line: specifically, we are concerned with the long 's', and we discover that there are two ligatures, the second of which has nothing to do with it. Thus we introduce a SKIP just after the second line:

```
(LABEL C s)
   (LIG C i H 0)
   (SKIP D 2)
   (LABEL C f)
   (LIG C i H 1)
   (KRN C . R -.1)
   (KRN C , R -.1)
   (STOP)
```

In this way, when we start reading from the first line, we skip from the third line directly to the sixth and thus avoid the problematic ligature.

One can imagine software tools that carry out these optimizations. The fact that they do not exist after almost 25 years, since the TFM format was created, perhaps shows that this optimization is no longer really indispensable.

B.1.4   *The Metric Properties of Glyphs*

We have reached the most important and, at the same time, the simplest part: the metric properties of each glyph. These properties are four in number, plus two "gadgets". Here are the four metric properties:

- CHARWD: the glyph's set-width.

- CHARHT: its height.

- CHARDP: its depth, i.e., the vertical dimension of the part located below the baseline.

- CHARIC: its italic correction, i.e., the amount of kerning to perform when the glyph is set "up against a wall". For example, let us take an italic 'f' followed by an upright bracket: "*f*]". The result is rather catastrophic and calls for kerning: "*f*]". But this kerning is technically not possible, as the two glyphs belong to different fonts and nothing yet has been done for executing kerns or ligatures between glyphs of different fonts. Thus the software must add a bit of space, at a higher level. But how much space? After all, if instead of the 'f' there had been a 'g' (also italic), the problem would not have occurred. This datum is the letter's "italic correction", and it is one of the four dimensions of each TeX glyph.

The two "gadgets" are the following:

- NEXTLARGER, followed by a reference to another glyph in the font. In mathematical typography, we have some constructions that assume the size of the expression that they enclose,[1] such as roots and large delimiters, for example. The approach is quite impressive: specifically, we can have any number of predefined sizes of these objects. We must merely arrange them in order and include within each one a reference to the one that immediately follows. T_EX will then run through this linked list of glyphs and stop at the one that is closest to the desired size. The author used this property to produce expanding parentheses and braces in some 30 different sizes in the *yhmath* package [162].

- We all know that mathematicians can never be satisfied. However large the predefined symbols may be, there will always be even larger mathematical constructs. There as well, T_EX anticipated the problem: beyond a certain point, it offers symbols *built up from basic components*. For example, to produce a huge brace, we need only take the top part, the notch in the middle, and the bottom part, and then insert small vertical strokes between these pieces. Since any number of vertical strokes may be used, our brace can be arbitrarily large. That is defined in the TFM file as follows (example drawn from the font cmex10.tfm):

```
(CHARACTER O 71
    (CHARWD R 0.888891)
    (CHARDP R 0.900009)
    (VARCHAR
        (TOP O 71)
        (MID O 75)
        (BOT O 73)
        (REP O 76)
        )
    )
```

where TOP, MID, and BOT denote, respectively, the glyph placed at the top, in the middle, and at the bottom of the extensible delimiter and REP denotes that will be repeated as much as necessary in both the top and bottom parts of the delimiter. This approach may seem limited at first glance, but it yields quite acceptable results for the usual delimiters; for more aesthetically satisfactory delimiters, we can always resort to METAFONT to produce larger sizes and store them either in section 0x80-0xFF of the font table or directly in an Ω font that may contain up to 65,536 glyphs—which is what the *yhmath* package does.

B.2   OFM

The OFM format (for "Ω font metrics") was defined by John Plaice and the author in 1994. It is an extension of the TFM format. The only difference (and it is important) is that the maximum number of glyphs grows from 256 to 65,536 and that the maximum number of kerning pairs and ligatures grows from 2^{16} to 2^{32}. The human-readable file format associated with the OFM binary format is called OPL (= "Ω properties list"). The tools that convert OFM to OPL and OPL to OFM are, respectively, *ofm2opl* and *opl2ofm*.

---

[1] Michael Spivak, in his book *The Joy of T_EX* [321], full of nasty allusions, speaks of "things that grow".

B.3 VF

The VF format (= "virtual font") was proposed by Knuth in 1990. It was immediately implemented by *dvips* and many other DVI drivers. We have already explained the advantages and disadvantages of virtual fonts in Sections 9 and 9. Here we shall present their structure.

Let us recall the principle behind virtual fonts: the idea is to replace, within a DVI file, a glyph in a virtual font with more interesting DVI code that for various reasons cannot be produced by TeX. This code can be as short as the simple naming of another glyph or as long as an entire page.

As with TFM files, VF also have a human-readable counterpart, the format VPL (for "virtual properties list"), which is what we shall describe here. The VPL file format is an extension of the PL file format: it contains the same expressions and also a few others that are specific to virtual fonts.

Note that every virtual font must be accompanied by a TFM font with the same metrics, for the very simple reason that TeX can read only TFM files. We can easily obtain the real font associated with a virtual font: all that we have to do is switch to VPL and delete all the expressions specific to the VPL format; we then obtain a PL file that we can then convert to TFM.

The new expressions are of two types: those placed in the preamble, which apply to the entire font, and those found within each glyph, which describe the DVI code that will ultimately replace it. The global expressions are font definitions:

- (MAPFONT D *number* ...), which defines a font and associates with it an internal number. This expression contains a series of expressions, defined below.

- (FONTNAME *string*), the name of the corresponding TFM file (without the extension). This font may be real or virtual; if it is virtual (i.e., if there is a VF file by the same name), *dvips* will follow the references until it finds a real font (unless it gets stuck in an infinite loop).

- (FONTAREA *string*), the name of the directory in which the font is stored. By all means avoid this expression, which makes the font dependent upon the local file system.

- (FONTCHECKSUM *4-byte integer*), the checksum of the TFM font.

- (FONTAT R *real number*), the magnification factor requested (where R 1.0 is the factor 1, unlike in TeX, where the factor must be divided by 1,000).

- (FONTDSIZE R *real number*), the requested optical size of the font. Changing this value apparently has no effect on anything.

And here are the instructions that we can include in each glyph:

- (MAP ...), the expression that is placed under CHARACTER and that contains all the others.

- (SELECTFONT D *number*) selects the font whose number is *number*, defined in advance, as the active font. This font will remain active until the next SELECTFONT. The font selected by default is the one defined first in MAPFONT.

- (PUSH) stores the current coordinates in the DVI and places these coordinates on a stack.

- (POP) retrieves the coordinates from the stack and makes them the current coordinates.

- (MOVERIGHT *real number*) moves to the right.

- (MOVELEFT *real number*) moves to the left.

- (MOVEUP *real number*) moves upwards.

- (MOVEDOWN *real number*) moves downwards.

- (SETCHAR *glyph*) sets the glyph *glyph* in the active font.

- (SETRULE *height width*) sets a black box of the given dimensions.

- (SPECIAL *string*), a "special", i.e., an island containing arbitrary code.

- (SPECIALHEX *series of bytes in hexadecimal notation*). Within the SPECIAL instruction there is a problem of protection. Specifically, how can we include a closing parenthesis in any "special" that occurs, when the closing parenthesis is what terminates the expression? The solution (a bit awkward, but radical) is to write the entire special in hexadecimal notation. For example, to obtain the equivalent of \special{ps:(hi\)) show}, we would have to write (SPECIALHEX 70 73 3A 28 68 69 5C 29 29 20 73 68 6F 77).

We can see that every DVI instruction can be incorporated within a VF glyph. There is also a very basic tool for creating virtual fonts, written by Eberhard Mattes (the developer of the long-famous emT_EX) and called *qdtexvpl* (for "quick and dirty T_EX to VPL") [249], which does the opposite: we write a T_EX file containing the T_EX commands that correspond to each virtual glyph, then compile this file to obtain a DVI file, and *qdtexvpl* reads the DVI file, extracts the DVI codes corresponding to each glyph, and produces a VPL file containing these instructions.

B.4   OVF

The OFM format was defined by John Plaice and the author in 1994, for $Ω_1$ (version 1.* of Ω). It is an extension of the TFM format. The only difference with VF (and it is important) is that the maximum number of glyphs grows from 256 to 65,536 and that the maximum number of kerning pairs and ligatures grows from 2^{16} to 2^{32}. The human-readable file format associated with the OFM binary format is called OPL (for "Ω properties list"). The tools that convert OFM to OPL and OPL to OFM are, respectively, *ofm2opl* and *opl2ofm*.

C

PostScript Font Formats

Since its appearance in 1985, the year in which the first laser printer (the Apple *LaserWriter*) came onto the market, the PostScript language has conquered the computer world, in everything from the industrial production of printed material to office management and the personal printing of documents. In this chapter, we shall describe the various PostScript font formats: Type 1, of course, but also Type 3, Type 42, Type 0, CID, Multiple Master, and the very recent CFF/Type 2.

Before beginning to describe these font formats, we shall start with a brief introduction to the PostScript language—an introduction that is essential for understanding the syntax of the language used in fonts as well as the nature of the objects being manipulated. This introduction has no pretensions to thoroughness; after all, the specification of the PostScript language [24] contains no fewer than 912 pages, and very dense ones at that! Instead, our goal will be merely to give the basic information that is needed in order to understand what follows. The reader eager to obtain more information on the PostScript language may consult three books by Adobe (the red [24], blue [22], and green [20] books); there are also many introductory books [303, 318, 250], and some works focused on the PostScript capabilities of certain printers, such as the *LaserWriter* [52, 182].

C.1   *Introduction to the PostScript Language*

PostScript is an *interpreted* programming language, in the sense that it does not involve a step for compilation: the printer or the rendering software reads the PostScript code and executes it at the same time. The goal of the PostScript language is to describe a page for the purpose of printing or display:[1] an abstract description of the page (made up of mathematical objects)

---

[1] We have seen people use the PostScript language to do calculations, but that remains in the realm of the anecdotal.

is supplied to the PostScript interpreter. When an entire page has been described, it is then printed out, and execution continues with the following page.

The objects that can be manipulated are straight lines, cubic Bézier curves (see Appendix G), shapes whose outlines are made of straight lines or cubic Bézier curves, and, finally, fonts (whose glyphs are also made of—straight lines and cubic Bézier curves).

C.1.1   Syntax

PostScript may seem strange to those accustomed to languages such as C and Java. First of all, it is a language written in *reverse Polish notation*: to perform an operation, we first write the operands and then the operator ("2 2 +" instead of "2 + 2"). Next, it is a language based on a *stack*: we are not required to write declarations that end with a special character, as in other languages. In PostScript, we write data, and these data are automatically placed on a stack; then we write operators, and the operators pop the data from the stack, and possibly push others onto the stack.

Here is a simple example of a block of PostScript code:

```
40 60 add 2 div sqrt round
```

and here is an interpretation: we place the numbers 40 and 60 onto the stack; add then adds them and leaves 100 on the stack; we push a 2 onto the stack; the div operator takes the objects 100 and 2 and performs the division $\frac{100}{2}$; thus it leaves 50 on the stack; then sqrt calculates the square root and leaves $\sqrt{50}$ on the stack; round then rounds this number and leaves on the stack the final result: 7.

As the example shows, to understand how a block of PostScript code works, we must think *in terms of the stack*, always being aware of which data appear where on the stack and knowing what effect each operator has on the stack's data.

The peculiarities of the PostScript language do not end there. The objects[2] manipulated by the PostScript language can be of various types: *integer, real number, string, name* (a name is a word that cannot be interpreted as a number; a name designates an executable object, *unless it is preceded by a slash*), *operator, table* (a series of objects, placed within brackets), *procedure* (a series of objects, placed within braces, that can be executed), *dictionary* (a series of keyword/value pairs, where the keyword is a name and the value can be any object), *file, boolean* (true or false), etc.

The representation of strings obeys a few rules:

- They are written in ASCII and placed within parentheses. Certain characters must be protected: \n (*newline*), \r (carriage return), \t (tab), \b (backspace), \f (form feed), \\ (backslash), \(and \) (parentheses), \123 to obtain the character whose decimal code is *123*.

---

[2] PostScript's "objects" have nothing to do with those of object-oriented programming. We have preserved the name in accordance with the official specification, and also to avoid less elegant choices such as "thing" or "gizmo".

- Or they are written in hexadecimal (and thus need not be protected). We write the hexadecimal code in lowercase letters and enclose it in brackets: `<6561737920746F2072656164>`.

Any object can be pushed onto the stack or popped off the stack.

A table, a procedure, or a dictionary can contain objects of all types, mixed together. For instance, the following table `[ 1 true [ /foo pop ] (hello) ]` contains a number, 1; a boolean, `true`; a subtable (itself containing a nonexecutable name, `/foo`, and an operator, `pop`); and a string, `(hello)`.

C.1.2 The System of Coordinates

We work on a Cartesian plane whose origin is the lower left corner of the page (and thus the x-axis points to the right and the y-points upward). Lengths are measured in units called *PostScript points*. A PostScript point is equal to $\frac{1}{72}$ of an inch (approximately 0.3528 mm). It is therefore slightly larger than the American printer's point, which is equal to $\frac{1}{72.27}$ of an inch (approximately 0.3515 mm), but smaller than the Didot point (approximately 0.376 mm).

C.1.3 The current transformation matrix

The *current transformation matrix* (CTM) allows us to change the system of coordinates at any time. The reader will certainly have used vector-design software before: we use it to define a shape, and then we can enlarge the shape, turn it, scale it homogeneously or heterogeneously, etc. In the PostScript language, these operations are also possible, but there is a slight difference of a philosophical nature: it is not the shape that changes but rather the *system of coordinates in which it is expressed*. For example, instead of saying "I am drawing twice as large", we say "Henceforth my units of length will be twice as large"; instead of saying "I am drawing my shape at a 45° angle", we say "I am rotating my system of coordinates 45°"; thus the same PostScript code can generate infinitely many different shapes, according to the properties of the selected system of coordinates. In the case of fonts, this approach allows us to preserve the definition of the glyphs and set them at any size and at any angle: only the system of coordinates changes.

But how do we indicate a change to the system of coordinates?

A bit of mathematics: a *linear transformation* of the Euclidean plane is a function $(x,y) \mapsto (ax+by+t_x, cx+dy+t_y)$, where $(x,y) \in \mathbb{R}^2$ and a,b,c,d,t_x,t_y are real numbers. A linear transformation can thus be written as a system of two linear equations in two variables:

$$x' = ax+by+t_x$$
$$y' = cx+dy+t_y$$

and we say then that it is characterized by the six parameters (a,b,c,d,t_x,t_y).

We all know from our high-school math courses (and if we have forgotten, it is easy enough to verify) that *translation*, *scaling*, and *rotation* are linear transformations and that we can use matrix notation to describe them. For instance:

$$\begin{pmatrix} x \\ y \end{pmatrix} \mapsto \begin{pmatrix} x+t_x \\ y+t_y \end{pmatrix}, \quad \begin{pmatrix} x \\ y \end{pmatrix} \mapsto \begin{pmatrix} s_x x \\ s_y y \end{pmatrix}, \quad \begin{pmatrix} x \\ y \end{pmatrix} \mapsto \begin{pmatrix} x\cos\theta - y\sin\theta \\ x\sin\theta + y\cos\theta \end{pmatrix}$$

are, respectively, a translation of (t_x, t_y), a scaling of (s_x, s_y), and a rotation of the axes by the angle θ.

Thus we can say that translation is the *sum* of the matrix $\binom{x}{y}$ with the matrix $\binom{t_x}{t_y}$, whereas scaling and rotation are the *products* of the matrix $\binom{x}{y}$ with the matrices $\left(\begin{smallmatrix} s_x & 0 \\ 0 & s_y \end{smallmatrix}\right)$ and $\left(\begin{smallmatrix} \cos\theta & -\sin\theta \\ \sin\theta & \cos\theta \end{smallmatrix}\right)$. In the former case, we *add* matrices; in the latter, we *multiply* them.

That is quite a nuisance if we wish to find a general way to describe linear transformations, one that applies to translations just as it applies to scaling and rotations. After all, these three transformations are the most important operations performed by vector-design software.

Fortunately, mathematicians have found a way to solve the problem. Rather than going into the details of the theory,[3] let us go straight to the method that is used in practice: instead of working with two-row matrices to indicate a point in space, which seems logical since the Euclidean plane is two-dimensional, we shall work with three-row matrices, in which the third row always contains the value 1.

Scaling and rotations thus become multiplications by 3×3 matrices, as follows:

$$\begin{pmatrix} s_x & 0 & 0 \\ 0 & s_y & 0 \\ 0 & 0 & 1 \end{pmatrix}, \quad \begin{pmatrix} \cos\theta & -\sin\theta & 0 \\ \sin\theta & \cos\theta & 0 \\ 0 & 0 & 1 \end{pmatrix}.$$

And the pleasant surprise is that translation also becomes a *multiplication* by a 3×3 matrix, namely:

$$\begin{pmatrix} 1 & 0 & t_x \\ 0 & 1 & t_y \\ 0 & 0 & 1 \end{pmatrix}.$$

What could be more natural, then, than to say that we *model transformations of the plane* with matrices?

$$M = \begin{pmatrix} a & b & t_x \\ c & d & t_y \\ 0 & 0 & 1 \end{pmatrix},$$

where the parameters (a, b, c, d, t_x, t_y) are precisely those of the linear transformation with which we started. The transformation of a point (x, y) of the plane is therefore the product of this point, considered as the matrix $\binom{x}{y}{1}$, by the transformation matrix M.

Even better, suppose that we carry out a series of operations (translations, scalings, rotations) with the matrices $M_1, M_2, \ldots, M_n$. The result will be an operation whose matrix M is the product of the matrices $M_1 M_2 \cdots M_n$. Even other operations, such as reflection about an axis, can be expressed in this manner.

---

[3] For the reader with a mathematical background, the method involves switching from the plane $\mathbb{R}^2$ to the projective plane $\mathbb{P}^2$. The latter is the quotient of $\mathbb{R}^3 \setminus \{(0,0,0)\}$ by the equivalence relation $(x, y, z) \cong (x', y', z') \iff (x', y', z') = r(x, y, z)$ for $r > 0$. If $z \neq 0$, since all values of $r(x, y, z)$ correspond to the same point in projective space, we can take $r = 1/z$ and write this point as $(x, y, 1)$. That is exactly what we do. For more practical details, consult [246, p. 21]; the theory is admirably described in a course by the unforgettable professor Rémi Goblot [149, 150].

Let us leave the platonic world of mathematics and come back down to earth. It is for all these reasons that the PostScript language uses the methods that we have just examined. In our code, we shall use the notation $[a\ b\ c\ d\ tx\ ty]$ to represent a transformation by the matrix $\begin{pmatrix} a & b & t_x \\ c & d & t_y \\ 0 & 0 & 1 \end{pmatrix}$.

As we have just seen, some special cases of linear transformations are:

- *Translation*: $[1\ 0\ 0\ 1\ tx\ ty]$

- *Scaling*: $[sx\ 0\ 0\ sy\ 0\ 0]$

- *Rotation* by the angle θ: $[c\ s\ \text{-}s\ c\ 0\ 0]$ (where $c = \cos\theta$ and $s = \sin\theta$)

PostScript considers that every object is governed at any time by a transformation, whose matrix is the *current transformation matrix*. Thus, between the coordinates that appear in our code and what appears on paper or on the screen, we always pass through the current transformation, whether we are drawing an outline or filling one in. That is equivalent to the change of system of coordinates that we have just described.

It remains to be seen how we can manipulate this CTM within code. We can:

- Initialize it, using the operator `initmatrix`).

- Give it a new value (with the operator $[a\ b\ c\ d\ tx\ ty]$ `setmatrix`).

- But the most elegant approach is certainly to multiply it by another transformation matrix. The operator that does so is `concat`.[4] Thus we can write, for example, $[1\ 0\ 0\ 1$ $100\ 100]$ `concat` to set the current transformation with a translation of the system of coordinates by 100 units to the right and 100 units upwards.

- There are simplified versions of `concat` for the three most important operations:

    - Translation by (t_x, t_y) PostScript units: `tx ty translate`
    - Scaling by the horizontal factor s_x and the vertical factor s_y: `sx sy scale`
    - Rotation by the angle θ: `θ rotate`

Since matrix multiplication is not commutative, it is obvious that the result will be different if the order of these operations changes.

C.1.4 Paths

We use two mathematical objects to *draw*: *straight lines* and *cubic Bézier curves* (Appendix G). The straight line between the starting point (x_0, y_0) and the ending point (x_1, y_1) is the function:

$$t \mapsto (1-t)\begin{pmatrix} x_0 \\ y_0 \end{pmatrix} + t\begin{pmatrix} x_1 \\ y_1 \end{pmatrix}$$

$$[0,1] \to \mathbb{R}^2$$

---

[4] Do not be surprised by the name: Adobe calls the product of matrices "concatenation".

The cubic Bézier curve with starting point (x_0, y_0), *control points* (x_1, y_1) and (x_2, y_2), and ending point (x_3, y_3) is the function:

$$t \mapsto (1-t)^3 \begin{pmatrix} x_0 \\ y_0 \end{pmatrix} + 3t(1-t)^2 \begin{pmatrix} x_1 \\ y_1 \end{pmatrix} + 3t^2(1-t) \begin{pmatrix} x_2 \\ y_2 \end{pmatrix} + t^3 \begin{pmatrix} x_3 \\ y_3 \end{pmatrix}$$

$$[0, 1] \to \mathbb{R}^2$$

If f_1, f_2 are functions of these kinds (straight lines or cubic Bézier curves) in which the ending point of the first coincides with the starting point of the second, their *concatenation* is the function:

$$t \mapsto \begin{cases} f_1(t), & \text{if } x \in [0, \frac{1}{2}[\\ f_2(t), & \text{otherwise, with } \lim_{t \to \frac{1}{2}} f_1(t) = f_2(1) \end{cases}$$

$$[0, 1] \to \mathbb{R}^2$$

We use the term *path* for the concatenation of any number of straight lines and cubic Bézier curves. Here are some of the PostScript operators that produce paths:

- To trace a path, one must first initialize it (in other words, create a *current path*). That is done with the newpath operator. After this operator has been invoked, the *current point* is no longer defined. Before using any other operation, we must define it by using an *absolute displacement*.

- moveto is the operator for this purpose: by writing x y moveto, we set the current point to (x, y). This operator does not draw anything.

- There are also operators for *relative displacement*: x y rmoveto. There is nothing magical about them; the displacement is simply performed *relative to* the previous current point, rather than in an absolute way.

- Along the lines of moveto and rmoveto, there are the operators x y lineto and x y rlineto, which draw straight lines using the previous current point as the starting point.[5]

- Likewise, there are the operators curveto and rcurveto, which produce cubic Bézier curves:

  - If $\begin{pmatrix} x_c \\ y_c \end{pmatrix}$ is the current point before the operator is executed, x1 y1 x2 y2 x3 y3 curveto will draw the Bézier curve with starting point $\begin{pmatrix} x_c \\ y_c \end{pmatrix}$, control points $\begin{pmatrix} x_1 \\ y_1 \end{pmatrix}$ and $\begin{pmatrix} x_2 \\ y_2 \end{pmatrix}$, and ending point $\begin{pmatrix} x_3 \\ y_3 \end{pmatrix}$.

  - x1 y1 x2 y2 x3 y3 rcurveto, however, will draw the Bézier curve with the same starting point but with control points $\begin{pmatrix} x_c + x_1 \\ y_c + y_1 \end{pmatrix}$ and $\begin{pmatrix} x_c + x_2 \\ y_c + y_2 \end{pmatrix}$ and ending point $\begin{pmatrix} x_c + x_3 \\ y_c + y_3 \end{pmatrix}$.

---

[5] Note that lineto, unlike moveto, will not *initialize* the current point. Therefore, after a newpath, we must perform a moveto to obtain a current point before drawing anything.

① newpath
② 100 50 moveto
③ 0 50 50 75 100 100 rcurveto
④ -100 0 rlineto
⑤ 2 setlinewidth
⑥ stroke

① newpath
② 200 50 moveto
③ 100 0 rlineto
④ 0 100 rlineto
⑤ 0 -25 -50 -50 -100 -50 rcurveto
⑥ closepath
⑦ 0.8 setgray
⑧ fill

Figure C-1: Examples of PostScript code: tracing a path, filling a shape.

- *thickness* setlinewidth specifies the thickness of the current path in PostScript points. Note that the thickness 0 is in fact one pixel (thus it is invisible to the naked eye, if the printer is of high resolution).

- A colored path, specified by *t* setgray (gray level, with *t* between 0 and 1, where 0 is white and 1 is black), *r v b* setrgbcolor (a three-color specification: red, green, blue), or *c m j n* setcmykcolor (a four-color specification: cyan, magenta, yellow, black).

- All the operators above are used only to construct an abstract path. Nothing is actually drawn until we use the operator stroke. This operator has the effect of newpath and will initialize a new current path.

On the left side of Figure C-1, we can see an example of a PostScript path.

C.1.5 Shapes

A shape is drawn by filling in an outline or multiple outlines. An *outline* is a *closed* path, in the sense that the starting and ending points coincide.

In fact, this condition is not sufficient for the PostScript language: it is necessary to close a path explicitly, using the closepath operator. If the extremities of the path actually do coincide, this operator will have no visual effect. Otherwise, it will draw a straight line between the extremities.

Above we mentioned the *inside* of an outline. This notion, so intuitive to the human,[6] is not at all obvious to the computer. When a shape is built up from several outlines that intersect or that are contained one inside another, what is the "inside" of the shape? And even if it is made of only one outline, that outline could well intersect itself, leaving our intuition about inside and outside on shaky ground.

The PostScript language provides two rules for calculating the inside of a shape (only the first of which is used in Type 1 fonts, as we shall see below):

1. The *nonzero winding number rule*: to determine whether a point is inside or outside the shape, trace a ray from the point to infinity. Ensure that the ray does not pass through any point at which paths intersect and is not tangent to any path. (If by bad luck it happens

---

[6] Incidentally, some geometric constructions, such as the Möbius strip and the Klein bottle, prove that the concepts of inside and outside are in no way trivial.

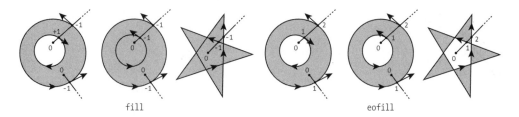

Figure C-2: Examples of filling according to the nonzero winding number rule (the three figures at the left) and the even–odd rule (the three figures at the right).

to violate this condition, adjust it by some epsilon to bring it into compliance.) Let $n = 0$. Suppose that we are standing on the ray and that we start walking from its point of origin to infinity. Every time we encounter a curve or a straight line belonging to the shape that *runs from right to left*,[7] we will decrement n by 1. In the opposite case, we will increment n by 1. If, at the end, n is zero, we declare that the point is outside the shape; otherwise, it lies inside the shape (see Figure C-2, left).

2. The *even–odd rule*: we perform the same manipulation, but this time we merely increment n, irrespective of the direction of any curve or line segment that we encounter. If at the end n is odd, then the point lies inside the curve; if n is even, the point lies outside the curve (see Figure C-2, right).

The first method is more powerful, since it makes use of the direction of the paths.

The fill operator fills the current closed path with the current color, using the nonzero winding number rule to decide what is inside the curve and what is outside. The eofill does the same but uses the even–odd rule.

C.1.6   Bitmap Images

Vector operations (tracing, filling, typesetting) are certainly important, but it is also perfectly possible to include bitmap images in the description of a PostScript page. The image format is specific to the PostScript language (and therefore is neither JPEG nor TIFF nor any other bitmap format in the industry). A bitmap image is incorporated into a PostScript page through the use of the image operator, which reads the following parameters on the stack:

width height depth matrix source image

where *width* and *height* are the image's dimensions in pixels, *depth* is the number of bits per color (1, 2, 4, 8, or 12), *matrix* is the transformation matrix being applied to the image, and *source* is either a procedure (which manages the image dynamically), a string, or a file (which may be compressed with LZW, RLE, CCITT, etc.) [24, pp. 129–156].

---

[7]   A more rigorous way to describe this situation is to say that if we take a point of reference orthonormal to $\mathbb{R}^3$ whose first unit vector, $\vec{i}$, lies on the ray (and points to infinity), the second unit vector, $\vec{j}$, lies on the tangent to the curve at the point of intersection (and points in the direction of the curve), and the third unit vector, $\vec{k} = \vec{i} \wedge \vec{j}$, points to the reader (we apply the famous "right-hand rule").

The image operator will draw an image with its own colors. But now let us imagine that the image is not an ordinary image but a glyph in bitmap form (like those contained in bitmap fonts). In this case, we do not want our glyph to have *a set color*; we want it to be able to assume the *active color* from the context. That can be done with a variant of image by the name of imagemask:

> width height polarity matrix source imagemask

The image produced is of depth 1, and its color depends on the context; an image of this kind is called a "mask", whence the name of the operator. The parameter *polarity* enables us to obtain the "negative" of a glyph (the values of all the pixels are inverted). This is the operator that is used by *dvips* in Type 3 bitmap fonts.

C.1.7   Managing the Stack, Tables, and Dictionaries

To place an item on the stack, we merely … write it. If we want to get rid of it, we can use pop, which deletes the top item from the stack. The exch operator swaps the first and second entries on the stack. dup duplicates the top item on the stack. count returns the number of items contained on the stack, and clear deletes them all. These are simple operators. Now let us look at two operators for stack management that are a bit more complex:

> xn ... x1 x0 n index

The index operator retrieves the number n from the pile, descends $n + 1$ levels below that number, and places a copy of element *xn* (found at that position) on the top of the stack. Example: a b c d e 3 index leaves the stack as a b c d e b.

> xn ... x1 n j roll

The roll retrieves the numbers j and n, then performs j cyclic permutations of n entries: *xn* … *x1*. Example: a b c d e 4 2 roll leaves the stack as a d e b c.

To place an element into a table, we have the put operator. This operator takes three arguments: the table, the index of the new element, and the new element. For instance, [a b c] 1 d put returns [a d b c]. (Counting starts at 0!) The get operator takes a table and an index as its arguments and returns the corresponding element in the table: [a b c] 2 get returns c. And length returns the length of the table.

As in any other self-respecting programming language, we can define variables in PostScript as well. But given the nature of the language, "definition" has a rather peculiar meaning here: defining a variable with the def operator means, in fact, *creating a new entry in the current dictionary*. Thus, by writing /foo 2 def, we can say that the interpreter should henceforth systematically replace foo with 2, but we can also say that we are going to create a new entry in the current dictionary, with the keyword foo and the value 2.

To create a new dictionary, we use the dict operator, which takes as its argument a whole number: the size of the dictionary. The reader will notice that the *name* of the dictionary appears nowhere. How is that possible? Heavens! Let us not forget that we are always *in* a dictionary (the *current dictionary*) and that we need only define the dictionary that we wish to create as an entry in the current dictionary. The key for this entry will be the dictionary's name. For example, if I write:

```
/foo
10 dict
def
```

I create a dictionary of size 10 and call it foo. The begin operator, with a dictionary as its argument, makes that dictionary the *current dictionary*; in other words, it places it on the top of the *dictionary stack*. And end performs the opposite operation: it pops the current dictionary. For example, to add entries to the dictionary foo, I can write:

```
foo begin
/bar (abc) def
end
```

After these operations, the dictionary foo contains an entry—bar—, whose value is (abc). Another way to write the same operation is:

```
foo /bar (abc) put
```

To look up a value in a dictionary, we use get:

```
foo /bar get
```

If we do not know in which dictionary a given entry is contained, we use load:

```
/bar load
```

The interpreter will then search through all the dictionaries (in the order in which they appear on the dictionary stack) until it finds an entry whose keyword has this name.

To delete an entry from a dictionary, we use undef (which takes as its arguments a dictionary and a keyword). To check whether an entry exists in a dictionary, we use either known (which takes as its arguments a dictionary and a keyword) or where (which takes as its argument a keyword). The former returns a boolean; the latter returns the dictionary containing the keyword, together with the boolean true, or simply the boolean false, if the entry cannot be found in any dictionary.

Before concluding this section, let us discuss a somewhat technical operator that nevertheless often appears in fonts and thus should be well understood. It is the bind operator. It takes a procedure as its argument and returns the same procedure. Its effect is to take all the operators in the procedure and replace them with their values, if any. For example, if an operator is the name of a procedure (in technical terms, a keyword in the current dictionary whose value is a procedure), the name is replaced by the procedure itself. For example, suppose that we have defined increase as follows:

```
/increase { 1 add } def
```

In other words, increase is a procedure with the effect of adding 1 to the item on top of the stack. If we now write

```
/temporary { increase } def
/stable { increase } bind def
```

then both temporary and stable are procedures whose effect is the same as increase. What is the difference? temporary will have the behavior of increase: if we redefine the latter, the former will also change. stable will have the behavior not of increase but of 1 add, since bind first replaced increase by its value before def was executed. The action of bind is recursive. Thus we really do process the procedure thoroughly and avoid the risk of depending on the value of any intermediate variable. Accordingly, the behavior of stable will never change [unless a virus changes the behavior of add, which would be a great nuisance indeed].

C.1.8 Font Management and Typesetting

Since this subject is the emphasis of our book, we shall discuss it in somewhat more detail.

In the PostScript language, a font (whatever its type) is a *dictionary*. Fonts are stored in a larger dictionary called the *font directory*. When we ask the printer to produce a list of the available fonts, it is the contents of this dictionary that are explored, and the font names displayed are those contained in this dictionary.

For example, to use the font Palatino-Roman, when it is already present in the font directory, at an actual size of 24 PostScript points, we write:

```
/Palatino-Roman findfont 24 scalefont setfont
```

which means that we place the keyword for the font onto the stack, and it is then popped by the findfont operator, which places the dictionary of the corresponding font onto the stack. Next, we place the number 24 onto the stack; the scalefont pops the font's dictionary and the number, and then places a new font dictionary onto the stack: the glyphs are scaled for setting type at 24 PostScript points; finally, the setfont operator takes the font dictionary off the stack and makes it the *active font*.

The scalefont operator affects only the actual size of the glyphs.

We can also distort the glyphs in a more flexible way by modifying the font's transformation matrix (whose initial value is part of the font dictionary, as we shall soon see). By writing:

```
/Palatino-Roman findfont [21.6 0 0 24 0 0] makefont setfont
```

we multiply the font's current transformation matrix by $\begin{pmatrix} 21.6 & 0 & 0 \\ 0 & 24 & 0 \\ 0 & 0 & 1 \end{pmatrix}$, which will yield glyphs with a "horizontal size" of 21.6 and a "vertical size" of 24 PostScript points—that is, a 24-point font condensed 90 percent.

To produce the time-honored string "Hello, world!", we can write:

```
200 200 moveto (Hello, world!) show
```

The first moveto is needed so that we will be well *inside* the page (the current point is by default (0,0), i.e., the lower left corner of the page). The show operator will typeset the preceding

Voici du texte

(Voici du texte) show

Voici du texte

5 0 (Voici du texte) ashow

Voici du texte

(Voici du texte) [10 0 ... 10 0] xyshow

Voici du texte

0 5 116 (Voici du texte) widthshow

Figure C-3: The show *and three of its variants:* ashow *(letterspacing),* xyshow *(equalizing the set-widths of all the glyphs), and* widthshow *(the glyph 't' has a slanted width vector). We can see clearly that PostScript does not manage kerning automatically: the glyphs 'V' and 'o' are a bit too far apart.*

string in the active font (and the data on the current font also include the actual size, as we saw above).

There are several variants of the show operator:

- *string table* xyshow retrieves two numbers from the table for every character in the string. These are the coordinates of each glyph's width vector. Thus we can set type with metrics totally different from the font's original metrics.

- *string table* xshow is analogous to xyshow except that only one number is retrieved for each character, since the width vector is horizontal and this number is its length.

- *string table* yshow is similar, but with a vertical width vector.

- *cx cy char string* widthshow is a very unusual operator. It sets the string with the font's original set-widths, except for the occurrences of the glyph *char*, which will be set with the width vector (*cx, cy*). That is most useful for changing the interword space, by modifying the width of glyph 32 (the space). It goes without saying that this operator is so crude that we strongly discourage its use.

- *ax ay string* ashow letterspaces glyphs (i.e., inserts space between them) in a uniform manner. The string will be typeset, but with the vector (*ax, ay*) added to each glyph's width vector. Note that this approach to letterspacing is also discouraged because it does not take kerning pairs into account—which is no surprise, as kerning pairs are not among the data contained in the font dictionary but are found in an auxiliary file (the AFM file; see §C.3.7).

- *cx cy char ax ay string* awidthshow is a combination of the widthshow and ashow operators.

C.1.9   The Image Model and the Graphics State

Let us review. To fill in a page, we perform four types of operations:

- We *draw* lines or Bézier curves (with the stroke operator).

- We *fill* the *insides* of shapes whose outlines are made up of lines and Bézier curves (with the `fill` operator).

- We *incorporate* bitmap images (with the `image` operator).

- We *typeset* glyphs taken from fonts (with the `show` operator).

These operations imply the existence of several parameters that are updated by the various operators and that have, at any time, a "current" value: the current transformation matrix, the coordinates of the current point, the current color, the current path, the current stroke thickness, the current font, etc. All these values make up what we call the "graphics state".

We can save the current graphics state and return to it at any time, using the operators gsave and grestore. In fact, there is a stack for graphics states: thus we can save many of them and recover them one by one in the order opposite that in which they were stored.

We can also create a "graphics state object" and place it on the stack of operands, using the save operator. We can return to this graphics state at any time by using restore, which retrieves a graphics state object from the stack.

C.1.10   Structured Comments (DSCs)

We have quickly come to realize that describing a page through the use of an interpreted programming language may not always be the best strategy, especially if the software that reads the code must retain it in memory, ensure that certain resources are present, or retrieve them before processing the document, etc. That becomes all the more critical when the software is interactive, as, for example, is *ghostscript*, which displays a PostScript document for viewing: when we view a document, we have the desire to change from page to another, to move ahead several pages, or even to back up. How can we do so if there is no marker in the document that says "Here is where page 135 begins", "This document requires the font *Throhand-Roman*", "This document requires 42 megabytes of memory", etc.?

But how can we introduce this data without imposing in some way upon the authors of PostScript code? After all, we live in a democracy, and PostScript neither more nor less than a programming language; each person has the right to prepare her PostScript documents as she sees fit, as long as the printed result satisfies her. When we raise questions of this sort, the solution is often to employ *metadata*. And the only metadata provided by the syntax of the PostScript language are *comments*. Adobe therefore declared that a self-respecting PostScript document must contain several comments of a special type, called "Document Structuring Conventions" (DSCs). And Adobe took itself so seriously that the specification of these DSCs [4] runs to no fewer than 109 pages! Adobe requires, among other things, that a certain subset of the DSCs be respected if a document is to be considered *DSC-compliant*.

We shall give a few examples and several DSCs related to fonts.

First of all, every DSC-compliant PostScript document must begin with the following line:

```
%!PS-Adobe-.0
```

If you believe that the '3' here represents the level of the PostScript language, you are wrong! It refers to version 3 of the DSCs.

This initial line is at the same time an exception to the general rule that says that all DSC comments begin with *two* percent signs. For example, the level of the PostScript language can indeed be indicated by a DSC: %%LanguageLevel: 2; the document's bounding box is given by %%BoundingBox: 0 0 135 579; the virtual memory required for a resource is given by %%VMUsage: 56000; the date of a document's creation is given by %%CreationDate: 4 Apr 1998; and so on.

In some cases, the software that produces the PostScript code happens to be genuinely unable to include some data in the DSCs. Imagine, for example, the case of a scientific software package that draws clouds of points from data on nuclear particles that pass through a membrane. This drawing occurs in real time, and therefore the software has no way to know, at the beginning of the file, what the final bounding box will be. In that case, we can write (atend) instead of the data and include the same DSC comment with the correct values at the end of the document. The instruction (atend) (note: just one 't'!) asks the interpreter to wait until the end of the file to read the data in question.

The DSCs that will concern us below are those related to *resources*. PostScript categorizes resources into several types, and we shall examine those of the types font and encoding.

If a document requires a font (for example, *Palatino-Roman*) that is not included in the PostScript code, the following DSC can be used in the preamble to the file:

    %%DocumentNeededResources: font Palatino-Roman

Somewhere in the file (before the corresponding findfont operator), we shall write an instruction to include this resource:

    %%IncludeResource: font Palatino-Roman

Note one peculiarity of the syntax: if we have to refer to multiple fonts, we shall write the keyword only once per line. We can change lines with the comment %%+. Example:

    %%IncludeResource: font Foo-Roman Foo-Italic Foo-Bold Foo-BoldItalic
    %%+ font Foo-Ciccio Foo-Franco Foo-Laurel Foo-Hardy

Be careful about one detail of some importance. When we ask for a resource to be included, the request is made of the PostScript interpreter. If this interpreter is located in a printer, the resource (the font) must be stored there as well. It is then what we call a *resident font*. Do not suppose that the printer will go looking for the font on your computer's disk drive; it is much too late for that!

If the font is not resident, it behooves us to include it in the PostScript code. In this case, we use the DSC:

    %%DocumentSuppliedResources: font Palatino-Roman

in the preamble. Next, we incorporate the code for the font (in PFA format, if the font is of Type 1) into the PostScript file, surrounded by the following DSCs:

```
%%BeginResource: font Palatino-Roman
... the font ...
%%EndResource
```

The operation shown above will have the effect of temporarily loading the font into memory, i.e., only while the current document is being printed.

Now suppose that we wish to load the font into memory permanently. To do so, we create a special PostScript document [6, pp. 12–13] that will contain a rather special DSC comment:

```
%!PS-Adobe-.0
%%BeginExitServer: 0
serverdict begin
    0 exitserver
%%EndExitServer
%%BeginResource: font Palatino-Roman
... the font ...
%%EndResource
```

followed by the font, as a PostScript resource. What does this comment mean? What is the zero (0) that appears twice? Well, it is important to know that a printer, for its own security, encloses all the PostScript documents that it receives (its "print jobs") between the operators save and restore. Thus whatever atrocities we ask it to print, it emerges in its virgin state at the end of every print job, just as it was when it was first used.

That is all very well, but the system administrator, as the printer's legal guardian, must still be able to modify its "permanent state". To do so, he needs a password (also assigned by the administrator when he installed the printer). The 0 in the code above is the default password (administrators often do not bother to change this password).[8] The exitserver operator takes the password off the stack; if it is correct, the operator breaks the infinite cycle of save and restore and arranges for the document that follows to be able to make lasting changes to the printer's virtual memory.

But let us return to the DSCs. A document of several pages that aims to be DSC-compliant should include DSC comments of the type:

```
%%Page: 37 15
```

at the beginning of the description of each page. (The first number is the number of the physical page; the second is the page number.) We can then be a bit more precise about resources and say that a certain resource is used on the current page. Smart software will then be able to load fonts as they are needed for the page that it is currently displaying. The corresponding DSC comment is:

```
%%PageResources: font Palatino-Roman
```

---

[8] We may well wonder why system administrators, usually so passionate about security, do not have the habit of changing the printer's password. The answer may be that the effects of this "permanent configuration"—if it is made within the printer's virtual memory, as is usually the case—last only until the printer is next rebooted. The situation is different when one or more hard disks are connected to the printer.

Finally, every DSC-compliant file ends with the DSC comment %%EOF (end of file).

Now that we have finished this brief introduction to the PostScript language, we can examine the PostScript font formats.

C.2   Type 3 Fonts

We shall first describe Type 3 fonts, as they are the closest to the standard PostScript language that we have just described. In fact, the glyphs in these fonts are defined by arbitrary PostScript operators: everything is permitted, including drawing, filling, including bitmaps, and even typesetting with other fonts. In theory, any PostScript page could become a single glyph in a Type 3 font.[9] But then why, despite this immense power, have Type 3 fonts been an unprecedented commercial flop? Why do we find hardly any at all in the world, be they free or commercial?

Simply because we must not confuse the *typesetting of text* with *graphical design*. In typesetting, we use the graphical elements of fonts, i.e., their glyphs. These are characterized by three properties: their high degree of repetition (which calls for the optimization of resources), their small size, and the uniformity of their strokes. The first property (repetition) is managed very well by all types of fonts, thanks to the structure of the font dictionary. The last two properties, on the other hand, present a significant problem. If most of the capital letters have predominantly vertical strokes, the aesthetic tradition would have these strokes be of the same thickness within a single font. The printer must therefore know that it must assign the same number of pixels to each of these strokes, whatever their position or the orientation of the glyphs on the page may be. Worse yet, if we change sizes, the number of pixels in a "generic" vertical stroke will also change, but the condition of uniformity remains the same: within a single font, *the vertical strokes must have the same thickness*, period!

That requirement exceeds the capabilities of PostScript operators: indeed, while we can ask the printer to draw a stroke with precision, we cannot ask it how many pixels it used for that stroke so that we can store the number and reuse it for the following stroke. And even if we could do so, it would greatly slow down an operation that should be the most natural and the fastest in the world: the typesetting of a simple document.

Type 3 fonts are thus unable to ensure uniform rendering of the glyphs; the result is a poorly printed document, unless the printer has very high resolution, where the difference of a single pixel is invisible to the naked eye.

Given their enormous shortcomings, how can Type 3 fonts be useful?

They allow us to do things that Type 1 fonts cannot handle: we can use them for dynamic fonts, random fonts, fonts in color or with gray levels, bitmap fonts, etc. We shall give a few examples below.

Now let us describe these fonts. A Type 3 font is a dictionary containing the following entries:

- A few global parameters:

---

[9] The reader will recognize here the principle behind the SVG fonts and, in part, that of the virtual fonts of TeX.

- FontType, equal to 3.

- FontMatrix, containing the transformation matrix that allows us to switch from the font's system of coordinates to that of the PostScript page. If we draw glyphs on grids of 1,000 units, this matrix will be the one for scaling by a factor of one thousandth: [0.001 0 0 0.001 0 0]. Thus 1,000 units of the font will become 1,000 thousandths of a PostScript point on the page. This quantity will then be multiplied by the actual size: if we are setting type at 10 points, the 1,000 units of the font will become 10 PostScript points, or one em.

- FontBBox, the bounding box of all the glyphs in the font.

- FontName, the font's name, often used to store the font in the global font dictionary.

- FontInfo, a dictionary of less-important data on the font.

- LanguageLevel, the level (1 or 2) of the PostScript language being used.

- The font encoding: a table of 256 glyph names. Every unused position in the table must contain the name .notdef (the only name that is allowed to begin with a period).

- Most important of all, a procedure named BuildChar and possibly another named BuildGlyph.

What do BuildChar and BuildGlyph do?

When the PostScript sets a string using a Type 3 font and the font has a BuildGlyph procedure, it will apply this procedure to all the characters in the string. For each byte representing a character, the interpreter must go through the font's encoding to retrieve the *glyph's name*; it will place it on the stack. Next, it will push the font dictionary onto the stack. Finally, it will push the BuildGlyph operator, which will pop the name and use it to draw the glyph.

The BuildGlyph operator belongs to level 2 of the PostScript language. If it is not defined in the font, the interpreter will fall back on the BuildChar operator, which is required at all levels of the PostScript language. BuildChar will not go through the encoding to retrieve the glyph's name; it will use only the glyph's position in the font table. Which means that a font that contains only BuildChar cannot easily change encodings. That is why Adobe asks developers to use a "real" BuildGlyph, and a "phony" BuildChar that invokes it, as follows:

```
/BuildChar {
    1 index /Encoding get exch get
    1 index /BuildGlyph get exec
} bind def
```

The entry Encoding, which is a table, is retrieved from the font dictionary. From this table, we read the entry whose position is supplied as a parameter, which is the name of the glyph that we desire. We push this name onto the stack, push the font dictionary onto the stack, and, finally, retrieve the BuildGlyph procedure from the font dictionary and execute it.

Usually (but this is not at all mandatory) we create a dictionary that contains one procedure per glyph—a procedure whose name coincides with that of the glyph. Next, we arrange for BuildGlyph to execute the procedure whose name is given as a parameter.

Note also that `BuildGlyph` and `BuildChar`, before drawing anything, must both supply to the PostScript interpreter the glyph's width and bounding box, using the `setcachedevice` operator. This operator retrieves six entries from the stack: two values for the width (horizontal and vertical) and four values for the bounding box. At the same time, the interpreter will try to place the image of this glyph in the font's cache in order to speed up any subsequent access to the glyph. For internal reasons, when we use `setcachedevice`, we are not allowed to modify the current color[10] or to incorporate a bitmap by means of the `image` operator. In that case, we can use the `setcharwidth` operator, which supplies only the width of the glyph and does not attempt to place the glyph in the cache (and therefore has no need to know its bounding box, which is used only to allocate memory for the caching of the glyph).

To achieve a better understanding of the structure of Type 3 fonts, we shall examine a real-world case: the Type 3 version of the font *Computer Modern Roman 10*, generated by Graham Toal in 1990. This font does not contain a `BuildGlyph` but only a `BuildChar`. On the other hand, it contains three different dictionaries: one for the widths, another for the bounding boxes, and a third for the glyphs' outlines. The names of the glyphs are of no interest: they are formed with the prefix `char` and the position of the glyph in the table, expressed as a decimal number. These same names are used as keywords in the three dictionaries as well as in the encoding table.

Here are the font's global parameters:

```
/FontType 3 def
/PaintType 0 def
/FontMatrix [.001 0 0 .001 0 0] def
/FontBBox [- - 1006 747] def
/UniqueID 1034 def
```

and here is the encoding table:

```
/Encoding [
/char0 /char1 /char2 /char3
/char4 /char5 /char6 /char7
...
/char124 /char125 /char126 /char127
/.notdef /.notdef /.notdef /.notdef
...
/.notdef /.notdef /.notdef /.notdef
] def
```

which stops at 127 because the *Computer Modern Roman 10* font (OT1 encoding) contains only 128 glyphs, plus the pseudoglyph `.notdef`.

Here are the three dictionaries:

---

[10] The outside of the glyph is considered *transparent*. For example, when we set type in a color, we use only one color, that of the interior of the shapes. What is forbidden when we use `setcachedevice` is the explicit use of two or more colors other than "transparent", which is nothing but the absence of color.

```
/Metrics 129 dict dup begin
  /.notdef 0 def
  /char0 621 def
  /char1 830 def
...
  /char126 499 def
  /char127 499 def
end def
/BBox 129 dict dup begin
  /.notdef [0 0 0 0] def
  /char0 [33 0 578 679] def
  /char1 [45 0 782 703] def
...
  /char126 [84 570 408 665] def
  /char127 [103 565 394 668] def
end def
/CharacterDefs 129 dict dup begin
  /.notdef {} def
  /char0 {
    33 679 moveto
    549 679 lineto
...
    33 679 lineto
    closepath
  } def
...
  /char127 {
    333 667 moveto
    390 680 422 594 362 569 curveto
...
    93 558 82 655 141 667 curveto
    closepath
  } def
end def
```

and, finally, here is the heart of the font, the BuildChar procedure:

```
/BuildChar {
  0 begin
    /char exch def
    /fontdict exch def
    /charname fontdict /Encoding get char get def
    fontdict begin
      /Metrics charname get 0
      /BBox charname get aload pop
        setcachedevice
      /CharacterDefs charname get exec
```

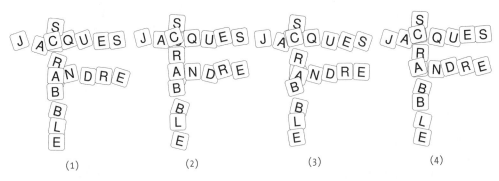

Figure C-4: The font Scrabble, by Jacques André [32]. Four consecutive printings of the same document, with slight random displacements of the letters. Here is the code that produced these three words: 2   8 moveto (JACQUES) show 4 6 moveto (ANDRE) show 4 9 moveto (scrabble) show. We can notice two things: (a) the capital letters are set horizontally and the lowercase letters are set vertically; (b) the system of coordinates is such that the numbers given as arguments to moveto are the coordinates of the first letter of the word according to the game Scrabble.

```
        eofill
    end
  end
} def
```

where we first read the position of the desired glyph and store it in the variable char, and then read the font dictionary, which we store in fontdict. Next we define the procedure charname as fontdict /Encoding get char get (which pushes the font dictionary onto the stack, extracts from it the value of the entry Encoding, which is a table, and finally retrieves the glyph's name from its position in this table). Then we make the font dictionary the active dictionary, extract from it the entry corresponding to the glyph's name in the dictionary Metrics and then in the dictionary BBox (since the bounding box is a table, we retrieve the elements from the table with aload pop), and finally execute the corresponding entry in the dictionary CharacterDefs. The latter constructs an outline, which we fill with eofill.

The example font shown above is neither a masterpiece of elegance nor an original and innovative application of Type 3 fonts; it is simply an ordinary text font with the distinction of being a real-world example.

The other examples of Type 3 fonts that we find are either pedagogical or experimental.

For instance, in [24, p. 341], we find a font whose glyphs are a square and a triangle; in [22, pp. 219 and 223], we have a similar font as well as a bitmap font; in [303, p. 41], we have a font whose glyphs are random strokes; and so forth.

As for experimental fonts, Jacques André and Irène Vatton [42] have created a font of extensible mathematical symbols with automatic optical correction; Jacques André once again, but this time with font designer Christian Delorme [37], has created a font called *Delorme* whose glyphs are "contextual", in the sense that they can build automatic ligatures without requiring these ligatures to be predefined; finally, this same Jacques André [32] has written the code for a Type 3 font for the game of Scrabble, shown in Figure C-4. [33] gives a good description of these experimental fonts.

Unfortunately, there is less and less software that is compatible with Type 3 fonts. Acrobat displays them poorly in PDF files, and *xpdf* refuses to display them at all. Only *ghostscript* seems to display them decently, which is to be expected, as this software can display any PostScript code. As for creating, modifying, and editing these fonts, the situation could not be worse: no software recognizes them, which is not surprising. The only software that could even partly process Type 3 fonts was *Metamorphosis*, from the now-defunct company Altsys. *Metamorphosis* would directly convert simple Type 3 fonts, and when that proved impossible, it would connect to a PostScript printer, download the font, and retrieve its outlines from the printer in order to produce from it a Type 1 font. Having seen *Metamorphosis* in action, the author can confirm that that was indeed possible, but it must be admitted that the Type 1 fonts so generated almost always required manual corrections. One could imagine passing through a rendering at a very large size and an automatic vectorization of the bitmaps obtained from *ScanFont* or *potrace* (see Chapter 12), but the automation of this procedure has never turned out to be necessary, doubtless because of the small number of Type 3 fonts that are actually available.

C.3 Type 1 Fonts

In this section, we shall describe *the most widely available fonts on Earth* (at least if we extrapolate from office-automation software, where TrueType seems to be the leader). Incidentally, Adobe has managed—God knows how—to make the structure of these fonts an *ISO standard!* It is part 3, "Glyph Shape Representation",[11] of ISO standard 9541, *Information Technology—Font Information Interchange*, of May 1, 1994 [195].

The structure of these fonts is quite close to that of Type 3, with a few exceptions of considerable importance:

- First, Type 1 fonts do not use the standard PostScript operators to describe outlines; instead, they use a smaller set of special operators.

- Second, they have a number of tools for optimizing rasterizations (the famous hints).

- Finally, they are binary, encoded, and encrypted.

A Type 1 font consists of four components:

- The "public dictionary" (global parameters written in plain text in the font)

- The "private dictionary" (encoded and encrypted parameters that mainly affect the optimization of the rasterization)

---

[11] Reading this specification is a real thrill since one finds in it all the properties of Type 1 fonts—and even a few hints on the internal workings of the black box that is the Type 1 font renderer—properties described in a much more serious style than the Adobe specification [21]. One feels that Adobe has put a big effort into rewriting the specification in ISO's jargon. Note that the name "Adobe" does not appear anywhere and that the name "PostScript" appears just once in a footnote in the appendix on compatibility with existing software.

- Subroutines (procedures used in the descriptions of outlines)

- The descriptions of the outlines (also encoded and encrypted), called *charstrings*

C.3.1   Before We Begin: the Format of the File that Contains the Font

A Type 1 font is a dictionary that we shall describe in the following section. First, however, here is a bit of information on the format of the file that contains this PostScript dictionary.

Under Unix and Windows, there are two types of Type 1 files: PFB and PFA. The 'PF' shared by these two types comes from *PostScript Font*, and the letters 'B' and 'A' mean "binary" and "ASCII", as often happens.

In a PFA file [6, p. 7], the last three parts (private dictionary, subroutines, descriptions of outlines) are encoded in the form of a long hexadecimal string with 512 copies of the character 0 at the end, followed by the operator cleartomark.[12]

The PFB file [6, p. 9] has adopted a more pragmatic attitude. The encoded and encrypted part (private dictionary, subroutines, descriptions of outlines) is written in binary, while the public dictionary remains in ASCII. But how, then, can we know where the binary part begins and thus exactly which part of the file must be decoded and decrypted? The solution is very simple. The PFB format assumes that there are two types of data in a PFB font: (1) PostScript code in ASCII, and (2) encoded and encrypted binary data. Any block of text of type 1 or 2 is preceded by a 6-byte header of which the first byte is always 0xA0, the second is always of type (0x01 or 0x02), and the last four represent the size of the block in the form of a 4-byte big-endian number. And the file ends with the two bytes 0xA003.

On the Macintosh, an equivalent system has been adopted. The PostScript code for a font is stored in a resource group of type POST. The identification numbers of these resources must begin with the number 501 and be sequential. The resources must not be processed in the same way by the interpreter: it is the first byte of the resource that indicates to the interpreter how it must proceed. There are four cases [6, p. 8]: (1) if the first byte is 01, the data are in ASCII; (2) if it is 02, the data are binary; (3) if it is 03, the resource indicates the end of the font file; finally, (4) if it is 00, it is a comment that will not be sent to the interpreter.

Since the PFB, PFA, and "POST resource" formats are strictly equivalent, from the point of view of the data contained in them, there are tools for switching from one to another [175]: *t1ascii* (from PFB to PFA), *t1binary* (from PFA to PFB), *t1mac* (from PFB or PFA to Macintosh resources), and *t1unmac* (from Macintosh resources to PFB or PFA). In the last two cases, Macintosh resources in the "AppleSingle", "AppleDouble", "MacBinary", or "BinHex" format are manipulated.

Note that the PFB format is very fragile: specifically, the beginning of the file (aside from the first six bytes) suggests that it is a text file, and text editors too often have the habit of

---

[12] Its raison d'être is that, when the interpreter decodes the hexadecimal part, it may skip over the nonzero characters and "swallow" some of the zeroes. It is not important to know how many zeroes are thus used, since one of the last operators to be decoded is mark, which inserts a mark. The cleartomark returns to that mark, and everything runs smoothly.

converting newlines between the original format of the font (which could be for the Macintosh, Unix, or Windows) and the format of the current platform. But we know that Windows uses 2 bytes to encode newlines (0x0A followed by 0x0D) where the Macintosh and Unix use only 1. A modification of this kind, which is harmless enough in a document in text format, will immediately corrupt the file, since the length of the block of text will no longer be the same, thus making the header incorrect.

Last but not least, a word on what is to come. Just as elsewhere in this book, rather than discussing the binary structure of the Type 1 font format, we are going to describe the "human-readable version" of the format. This code cannot be used directly by the computer; there are tools for converting it to PFB or PFA and vice versa. The tools in question [175] are *t1disasm* (which converts PFB to "plain text") and *t1asm* (which converts "plain text" to PFB or PFA). No loss of information occurs among the PFB, PFA, and "plain text" formats: they are three different representations of the same data.

C.3.2 The Public Dictionary

The public dictionary contains seven obligatory entries:

- FontType, equal to 1.

- FontMatrix, containing the transformation matrix that allows us to switch from the font's system of coordinates to that of the PostScript page. If we draw glyphs on grids of 1,000 units, this matrix will be that of scaling by a factor of one-thousandth: [0.001 0 0 0.001 0 0]. Thus 1,000 units of the font will become 1,000 thousandths of a PostScript point on the page. This quantity will then be multiplied by the actual size: if we are setting type at 10 points, the 1,000 units of the font will become 10 PostScript points, or one em.

- FontBBox, the bounding box of all the glyphs in the font.

- Encoding, the font's encoding; in other words, a table of size 256 whose elements are names of glyphs (or the name of the pseudoglyph .notdef, if one or more positions are unused). The position of a glyph name in this table (counting starts at 0) is the position of the corresponding glyph in the encoding. See §C.3.3 for more information on the glyph names recognized by Adobe. Two encodings are predefined in Adobe's implementations of PostScript: StandardEncoding (Figure C-5) and ISOLatin1Encoding (ISO 8859-1; see page 36).

- PaintType, equal to 1 if the outlines are to be filled (or to 2 if the outlines are to be drawn, which we strongly discourage).

- Private, a dictionary of internal information used to optimize the rasterization of the glyphs.

- CharStrings: a dictionary whose keywords are the names of glyphs and whose values are descriptions of the outlines of glyphs.

There may also be up to four optional entries:

- FontName, the name of the font, which is often used to store the font in the global font dictionary.

- FontInfo, a dictionary of optional data:

  - FamilyName, the name of the "font family". Adobe gives us no instructions, other than the obvious fact that fonts belonging to the same font family must have the same value of FamilyName.

  - FullName, the long version of the font's name, meant only for the human reader.

  - Notice, the font's copyright message.

  - Weight, the font's weight, in free form.

  - Version, the version of the font, in free form.

  - ItalicAngle, the slope of the font in degrees, in the trigonometric direction (i.e., counterclockwise).

  - isFixedPitch, a boolean value (true or false)—is the font monospaced?

  - UnderlinePosition and UnderlineThickness, the vertical offset and thickness of the underline.

- UniqueID, a unique identifier for the font, between 0 and $2^{24} - 1$ (see below).

- XUID (for "eXtended Unique Identifier"), a table of numbers, of which the first is the identifier of the "organization" and the others are freely assigned by this organization (see below).

A few words on the unique identifiers. As poetic as the concept of a "unique identifier" may seem—are we humans not in quest of a "unique identifier" all our lives?—the utility of these identifiers is quite concrete: when the interpreter caches rasterized glyphs, these glyphs are "marked" by their glyph names and the unique identifier of the font to which they belong. The absence of a unique identifier is not a serious problem: there would simply be more glyphs in the cache, which would slow printing down slightly and require a little more virtual memory. But an incorrect assignment of a unique identifier (for example, two fonts with the same identifier) could lead to catastrophes. And, unfortunately, some font-design software (such as *Fontographer*) has the infuriating habit of assigning the same "unique" identifier to all the fonts that it produces. Thus it is the responsibility of the font's creator to assign a truly unique number to the font.

How to do so? In the beginning it was done either by choosing at random a number between 4 million (inclusive) and 5 million (exclusive)—after all, if the number selected is that large, the probability that another font in the same document will have the same number is very small—or by contacting Adobe to obtain an "official" number.

Things got better with the introduction of "extended" unique identifiers (with the unpronounceable acronym XUID). An extended identifier is a PostScript table containing whole numbers. The idea is brilliantly simple: the first number is assigned by Adobe to an "organization", and all the other numbers are assigned by the "organization". To register as an "organization", one must first obtain an Adobe Solutions Network (ASN) account and then register the "organization's" name through Adobe's web site, at https://partners.adobe.com/asn/

tech/idreg/xuid/index.jsp). For example, ENST-Bretagne has the XUID 1039. Once this formality has been completed, the "organization" adds other numbers without justifying them or explaining them to anyone; it must merely ensure that they are unique. Adobe delegates the responsibility for uniqueness to the "organizations". We have written the word "organization" in quotation marks in this paragraph because there is no control over the registration of "organizations": it is entirely possible to make one up. There is also no procedure for searching for the individual behind an XUID number: confidentiality is preserved. All that we have is Adobe's guarantee that the XUID number is unique, which is quite a lot in itself.

C.3.3   Encodings for Type 1 Fonts

The most common encodings for Type 1 fonts are *Adobe Standard* and *Adobe Expert*. The first has the peculiarity of not containing any accented letters: the font may well contain information on combining letters and accents, but these combinations do not appear in the encoding. The second contains glyphs that are used more in desktop publishing than in office automation, hence the name "expert": the small capitals; the ligatures "ff", "ffi", "ffl"; the old-style figures; and so forth. One slight inconsistency: while *Standard* contains no accented letters, *Expert* does contain accented small capitals. The reader will find the tables for these two encodings, illustrated with Monotype's font *Columbus*, in Figures C-5 and C-6.

In the previous section, we saw that the encoding of a Type 1 font is a table of 256 strings that are either .notdef (if the position is empty) or glyph names, for which a description must exist in the font. Everything is fine up to that point. But we may well ask ourselves the reasonable question: how to select the glyph names?

Like any good programmer (according to Larry Wall [343], a good programmer must be lazy), let us first ask another question: before we get bogged down in almost metaphysical problems, does the choice of the glyph's name matter at all?

Ten years ago, the answer would have been *no*. What does it matter whether the glyph name for the glyph "É" is Eacute or foo, as long as the glyph is rendered correctly on the page? Indeed, if the glyph's final destination is a sheet of paper, the glyph name is of no importance.

But things have changed since Adobe introduced the PDF file format [28]. Through programs like Acrobat, *xpdf*, etc., we do more than just *read* a document: we *interact* with it. This interaction may be a search, an indexing operation, or any other operation. But when, for example, we search for a string in a document, we are searching for *characters*, not for *glyphs*. Thus the software must be able to match the characters with the glyphs.

The encoding table of a PostScript Type 1 font can contain at most 256 entries. The way to refer to these 256 glyphs in PostScript code is the same as always: in the strings that we typeset using show (or its avatars), we use either ASCII characters or notations of the type \123 (the glyph found in octal code point 123 in the encoding). No reference—really, none at all—is made to the glyph's semantics. Thus there is no way to recover the character to which this glyph belongs.

To work around that problem, Adobe came up with the following idea: *the correspondence between characters and glyphs will be established by means of glyph names.* The idea is at once brilliant and absurd. Brilliant, because the glyph names are the only information that we are assured of having for each glyph; absurd, because the correspondence between characters and

Figure C-5: The Adobe Standard font encoding (font Monotype Columbus)

	00	01	02	03	04	05	06	07	08	09	0A	0B	0C	0D	0E	0F
0_																
1_																
2_		!	"	#	$	%	&	'	(	)	★	+	,	–	.	/
3_	0	1	2	3	4	5	6	7	8	9	:	;	<	=	>	?
4_	@	A	B	C	D	E	F	G	H	I	J	K	L	M	N	O
5_	P	Q	R	S	T	U	V	W	X	Y	Z	[	\	]	^	_
6_	'	a	b	c	d	e	f	g	h	i	j	k	l	m	n	o
7_	p	q	r	s	t	u	v	w	x	y	z	{	|	}	~	
8_																
9_																
A_		¡	¢	£	⁄	¥	ƒ	§	¤	'	"	«	‹	›	fi	fl
B_		–	†	‡	·		¶	•	‚	„	"	»	…	‰		¿
C_		`	´	ˆ	˜	¯	˘	˙	¨		˚	¸		˝	˛	ˇ
D_		—														
E_		Æ		ª					Ł	Ø	Œ	º				
F_		æ				ı			ł	ø	œ	ß				

Figure C-5: The Adobe Standard font encoding, illustrated with the font Monotype Columbus.

Figure C-6: The Adobe Expert font encoding (font Monotype Columbus Expert)

	00	01	02	03	04	05	06	07	08	09	0A	0B	0C	0D	0E	0F
0_				˙												
1_																
2_		!	"		$	$	&	'	(	)	‥	·	,	–	·	/
3_	O	I	2	3	4	5	6	7	8	9	:	;	'	—	·	?
4_	a	a	b	¢	d	e				i			l	m	n	o
5_			r	s	t		ff	fi	fl	ffi	ffl	(		)	^	
6_	`	A	B	C	D	E	F	G	H	I	J	K	L	M	N	O
7_	P	Q	R	S	T	U	V	W	X	Y	Z	₵	1	Rp	~	
8_																
9_																—
A_		i	¢	Ł			Š	Ž	‥	˘	ˇ		·			
B_			–	-			‹	°	›				¼	½	¾	¿
C_	⅛	⅜	⅝	⅞	⅓	⅔			°	1	2	3	4	5	6	7
D_	8	9	0	1	2	3	4	5	6	7	8	9	¢	$	·	'
E_	À	Á	Â	Ã	Ä	Å	Æ	Ç	È	É	Ê	Ë	Ì	Í	Î	Ï
F_	Ð	Ñ	Ò	Ó	Ô	Õ	Ö	Œ	Ø	Ù	Ú	Û	Ü	Ý	Þ	Ÿ

Figure C-6: The Adobe Expert font encoding, illustrated with the font Monotype Columbus Expert.

glyphs may be more complex than what a measly string (representing a glyph name) could ever represent.

Nevertheless, such was Adobe's decision, and the program *Acrobat Distiller* (which converts PostScript files to PDF) follows this approach.

Here is what Adobe decided in regard to glyph naming (still with the aim of achieving a correspondence between glyphs and Unicode characters) [27]:

- First of all, some glyphs already have names that were assigned by Adobe, either because they are included in one of Adobe's font encodings or because they have been given names from Association for Font Information Interchange (AFII), an initiative that still exists as the ISO 10036 standard [29]. These names are mandatory, and the file [25] contains the list of corresponding Unicode characters (a list called AGL, for "Adobe Glyph List", by the initiated).

- If the glyph is not on the AGL but corresponds, say, to Unicode character 0xABCD on the basic plane (16-bit characters), it will have the name uniABCD.

- If the glyph is not on the AGL but corresponds, say, to Unicode character 0xABCDEF on one of the higher planes (characters beyond 16 bits), it will have the name uABCDEF.

- If there are several variants of the glyph, each of them will have a name from those described above, followed by a period and a string of characters (capital letters, lowercase letters, digits). Example: a.gothic, uni0137.alt3.

- In addition to the conventions listed above, if the glyph does not correspond to a single Unicode character but is instead a ligature, we write the names of the ligature's constituents, separated by underscores. For instance, the glyph for the ligature 'ft' will have the name f_t. Note: we can have variants of ligatures but not ligatures of variants. In other words, f_t.gothic has a meaning, but f.gothic_t does not; the latter would be interpreted as "the variant gothic_t of the glyph f.

Note that some software (such as *FontStudio* and *Fontographer*) does not know about these conventions and does not accept glyph names containing an underscore or a period (with the exception of the pseudoglyph .notdef).

C.3.4   The Private Dictionary

Now we are entering the dark cave that is the encoded and encrypted part of Type 1 fonts. Recall that we shall present the data in the form of "plain text" and that the tools *t1disasm* and *t1asm* [175] allow us to convert from plain text to the formats PFB/PFA and vice versa.

The private dictionary contains various and sundry global parameters whose purpose is to optimize the rasterization of the glyphs. As the optimization mechanism is, in a way, a "black box", the role of font creator/optimizer is very limited: we provide a certain set of data to the PostScript processor and hope that they will be used judiciously.

We can divide the entries of the private dictionary into five categories.

Figure C-7: The relevant heights, with overshoot, of a number of glyphs in various scripts (Latin, Arabic, Hebrew, Armenian). The font is Omega Serif.

C.3.4.1   Relevant heights

The question arises: what are the most relevant heights of the glyphs? If the font is a Latin one, a number of candidates occur to us immediately: the height of the capital letters, the height of the lowercase letters with or without ascenders, the baseline, the depth of the descenders, etc. For a Hebrew or Chinese font, the relevant heights are certainly different. On the one hand, owing to certain optical effects, a letter whose uppermost part is curved will be slightly taller than the letters that are flat on the top: for instance, an 'O' will be slightly taller than a 'Z' (at the same point size and in the same font). The difference between the two (the height of the horizontal line tangent to the upper curve of the 'O' and the height of the 'Z') is called *overshoot*.

The private dictionary can contain the height of the baseline and up to six relevant heights above the baseline and five relevant heights below it. For each of these heights and depths, we also specify any overshoot that may exist. The alignment zones thus established must not overlap; there is even a minimum distance between them that must be respected. Below a certain number of pixels, the processor will align the glyphs whose heights fall into the same alignment zone. It is even possible to do so for different fonts belonging to the same "family": each font need only know the relevant heights/depths of the "family's" default font.

We have explained the principle; now let us move on to the representation of this data in PostScript code, which does not win any medals for simplicity:

- The y-coordinates of the relevant heights and the overshoot values, starting with the baseline, are given in the entry `BlueValues` in the form of an expanding table of integers. For example, if the baseline is at 0, the maximum overshoot is -10, the height of the 'Z' is 700, and the height of the 'O' is 710, then we have two zones: `/BlueValues [-10 0 700 710] def`.

- The y-coordinates of the relevant depths are shown in the same way in the entry `OtherBlues`.

- Similar to `BlueValues` and `OtherBlues` are `FamilyBlues` and `FamilyOtherBlues`, which contain the corresponding values for the default font in the font "family".[13]

---

[13] Quite frankly, we may well wonder what the use of this information is. They would be meaningful if we could use the "individual" values in a document that employed only one font and the "family" values in a document containing glyphs from many members of the font "family". In the first case, priority would go

- The entry BlueScale allows us to specify when the processor will *stop aligning* the pixels that fall within the alignment zone. The value of this entry is given by the following formula: if we want alignment to stop at point size *p* (for a 300-DPI printer), then the value of BlueScale will be $\frac{p-0.49}{240}$.

- Using BlueScale gives us alignment up to a certain point size and "normal" behavior beyond that point. The entry BlueShift allows us to manage overshoot for sizes beyond BlueScale. If a given overshoot at a size greater than BlueScale exceeds BlueShift, the rendering engine will be forced to represent it with at least one pixel. The idea is to regularize the overshoot. Suppose that the letter 'O' has upper and lower overshoot values of 5 pixels and that, on the grid that we are using, only one of these overshoot values yields a pixel. If we set BlueShift equal to 5 (its value is 7 by default), the rendering engine will produce identical numbers of pixels for each overshoot value, irrespective of the grid.

Only BlueValues is required (but its value may perfectly well be an empty table).

C.3.4.2   Revelant stroke thicknesses

Just as we were able to select the most relevant heights in a font, we can also specify to the rendering engine the most relevant thicknesses of the horizontal and vertical strokes. For example, we can indicate the thickness of the downstrokes of the capital letters (that of the 'I'), the lowercase letters (that of the 'l'), the numerals (that of the '1'), etc. We can indicate up to 12 horizontal thicknesses and as many vertical ones. If the glyph is slanted, we measure the thickness perpendicular to the stroke's central axis.

In our code, we write /StdHW [*thickness*] def for the most important thickness of a horizontal stroke and /StemSnapH [*th1 th2* ...] def, which will contain the 12 most important thicknesses of horizontal strokes (including the thickness given in StdHW), in ascending order. For the thicknesses of vertical strokes, we use StdVW and StemSnapV, in the same manner.

One technical note from Adobe [5] is completely dedicated to these four entries in the private dictionary.

C.3.4.3   Parameters specific to ideographic scripts

The glyphs of the ideographic characters may be among the most complex in the world: there can be as many as 30 or so strokes in each one, and the glyphs pose a real challenge to rendering engines, whether for printed output or on-screen display.

Adobe offers two methods for addressing this situation:

1. First, we have the possibility of artificially magnifying the representation of a glyph if its complexity requires. The entry ExpansionFactor is a real number indicating the amount of expansion allowed for the glyphs in the font: giving it a value of 0.3 means that the glyph can be magnified by 30 percent. The default value of this entry is 0.06.

---

to the accuracy of the rendering; in the second case, it would go to consistency between members of the same family. But is the PostScript processor capable of knowing that several fonts of the same family are used within the same document? The author has serious doubts.

2. Second, a special mechanism was established at the level of each glyph's description to indicate the glyph's counters (white areas). We shall return to this subject in the section on the description of glyphs, §C.3.6.2.

One question remains: How does the rendering engine know whether or not the current font is an ideographic one? Adobe asks us to indicate the answer with the following code:

```
/LanguageGroup 1 def
/RndStemUp false def
```

C.3.4.4   Miscellaneous parameters

The entry `/ForceBold  true  def` tells the rendering engine that the font is boldface and that the rendering should thus be "fat" (so that the difference between the font and a lighter version will be immediately noticeable).

The following entries, with the values shown, must be included "for historical reasons":

```
/MinFeature{16 16} noaccess def
/password 5839 def
```

Do not be surprised, dear reader, by the following code at the beginning of the private dictionary:

```
/-|{string currentfile exch readstring pop}executeonly def
/|-{noaccess def}executeonly def
/|{noaccess put}executeonly def
```

It defines the three operators `-|`, `|-`, and `|`, which are later used in the code for the font. The purpose of this maneuver is to improve the legibility of the code. In some cases, these three operators are named `RD`, `ND`, and `NP`. This code is required.

C.3.4.5   Subroutines and "other subroutines"

Subroutines are blocks of code used in glyph descriptions. These blocks of code must end with the operator `return`. The space saved through the judicious use of subroutines can be enormous. They are stored in an entry in the private dictionary, called `Subrs`. There is no limit on the number of subroutines, but the first five (from 0 to 4) are reserved by Adobe:

```
dup 0 { 3 0 callothersubr pop pop setcurrentpoint return } |
dup 1 { 0 1 callothersubr return } |
dup 2 { 0 2 callothersubr return } |
dup 3 { return } |
dup 4 { 1 3 callothersubr pop callsubr return } |
```

The code shown above is not the actual code executed by the PostScript interpreter when it encounters one of these subroutines. On the contrary, it is merely a stopgap—the code to be executed by interpreters that do not know the secret meaning of these subroutines.

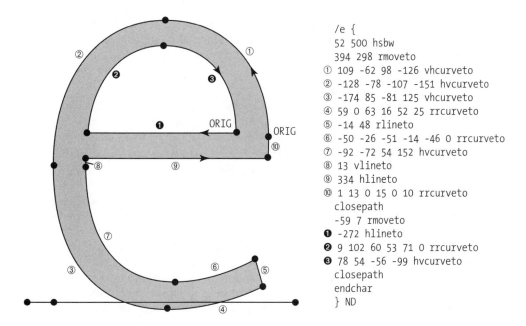

```
/e {
  52 500 hsbw
  394 298 rmoveto
① 109 -62 98 -126 vhcurveto
② -128 -78 -107 -151 hvcurveto
③ -174 85 -81 125 vhcurveto
④ 59 0 63 16 52 25 rrcurveto
⑤ -14 48 rlineto
⑥ -50 -26 -51 -14 -46 0 rrcurveto
⑦ -92 -72 54 152 hvcurveto
⑧ 13 vlineto
⑨ 334 hlineto
⑩ 1 13 0 15 0 10 rrcurveto
  closepath
  -59 7 rmoveto
❶ -272 hlineto
❷ 9 102 60 53 71 0 rrcurveto
❸ 78 54 -56 -99 hvcurveto
  closepath
  endchar
} ND
```

Figure C-8: The description of the glyph 'e' in the font The Sans Mono Condensed Light, by Luc[as] de Groot.

There is another type of subroutine, one that is less interesting for the font designer because he usually cannot modify them. These subroutines—whose name, "other subroutines", shows a severe lack of imagination—are written in the ordinary PostScript language, not in the more limited language of Type 1 fonts. They are stored in the entry OtherSubrs in the private dictionary.

The entry OtherSubrs is optional unless we are using this format's advanced features, which are *flex*, hint replacement, and the control of counters. Subrs is also optional unless Other-Subrs is being used.

C.3.5 Glyph Descriptions

Glyph descriptions are contained in the dictionary CharStrings (which is at the same level as Private, in the font's global dictionary). The keyword for an entry in this dictionary is a *glyph name*, one assigned according to Adobe's conventions (see §C.3.3). The value of an entry in this dictionary is the description of the glyph in question—a description given in a language similar to PostScript but highly constrained: only 25 operators in all. A description of this sort is called a *charstring* (from the dictionary's name). We shall later see that the Type 2 font format includes more sophisticated *charstrings*, with some 30 additional operators.

Below we shall briefly describe the most important operators. The curious reader will find a complete description of all the operators in [21, 10].

The first operator in a glyph description must be hsbw (the abbreviation of *horizontal side-bearing [and] width*). This operator takes two arguments: the left side-bearing (the distance between the origin of the abstract box containing the glyph and the leftmost point of the glyph) and the set-width (the glyph's width vector). It defines the current point as the glyph's left side-bearing. Nevertheless, it does not initialize a path. There is an extended version of this operator: sbw allows for the definition of a side-bearing and a set-width that need not be horizontal.

To begin to draw, we must first initialize a path. That is done with an operator that effects movement. There are three such operators: one for arbitrary movement (rmoveto, two arguments), one for horizontal only (hmoveto, one argument), and one for vertical (vmoveto, one argument). The arguments are always relative: they express motion from the current point.

We can draw straight lines or cubic Bézier curves starting at the current point. For the former, we use three operators that are similar to the ones used for movement: rlineto (two arguments: the offset of the ending point relative to the starting point), hlineto (one argument: the horizontal offset), vlineto (one argument: the vertical offset); for the latter, we use the arguments rrcurveto (six arguments), hvcurveto, and vhcurveto. The operator rrcurveto has two 'r's in its name because it is doubly relative: specifically, the six arguments express the offset of the first control point relative to the starting point, the offset of the second control point relative to the first, and the offset of the ending point relative to the second control point. The other two operators are used for special cases in which the tangent line at the starting point is horizontal and that at the ending point vertical, and vice versa.

The closepath operator (no arguments) closes a path. Unlike the homonymous operator in the PostScript language, this one really does require us to close the path with an operator that completes the drawing; in other words, we must make sure that the starting and ending points of the path are identical. closepath will only check the validity of a path that has already been closed. Finally, endchar (no arguments) terminates the glyph's description. In Figure C-8, the reader can see a real example of a glyph description.

The remaining operators concern subroutines and hints. Subroutines are called through callsubr, which takes one argument: the number of the subroutine in question. The code inside a subroutine is made up of any Type 1 operators and must end with a return. "Other subroutines" are called through callothersubr, in the same manner.

C.3.6 Individual Hints

"Individual" hints are part of the description of each glyph. A hint is a piece of data, intended for the rendering engine, whose aim is to optimize the glyph's rasterization. We have already seen two types of "global" hints, i.e., those defined at the level of the entire font, or even at the level of a font "family": the relevant stroke thicknesses (§C.3.4.2) and the alignment zones (§C.3.4.1). Adobe calls Type 1 hints *"declarative"*, in the sense that a font designer is asked to *declare* the peculiarities and essential strokes of the font's glyphs, and Adobe then manages, in its own way, to make as much use as possible of these declarations.[14]

At the level of the description of a given glyph, we must first indicate which are the relevant horizontal and vertical strokes. That is done by specifying their coordinates. We use the operator hstem to indicate a relevant horizontal stroke. This operator takes two arguments:

---

[14] But Adobe cannot guarantee that the rasterization will be perfect, nor can the font's designer clearly see the cause-and-effect relationships that these hint declarations entail: everyone is swimming in an artistic haze, with the peace of mind that everything has been done to make the rendering as good as possible.

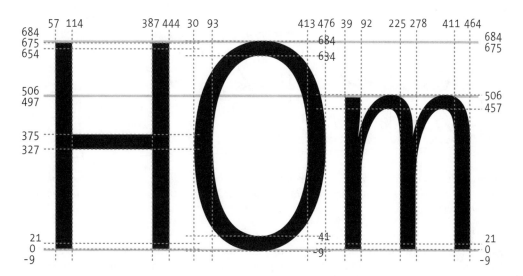

Figure C-9: Potential hints for the letters 'H', 'O', and 'm'. The gray zones are the font's alignment zones.

the lower y-coordinate of the stroke (calculated from the left side-bearing) and the stroke's thickness. Similarly, the vstem is used to indicate a relevant vertical stroke, and its two arguments are the left-hand x-coordinate (calculated from the left side-bearing) and the stroke's thickness. In the 'H' in Figure C-9, for example, the code for the hints of the vertical strokes and the horizontal bar would be:

```
57 57 vstem 387 57 vstem 327 48 hstem
```

In the same figure, we see the font's alignment zones: the one for the baseline (at 0), the one for the height of the lowercase letters (at 480), and the one for the height of the capitals (at 675). These zones are well defined, but they do not suffice for aligning the 'H' with the other letters. Specifically, an individual hint is needed in order for the alignment to take place. In the case of the letter 'O', we have natural horizontal hints: the stroke thicknesses of the 'O' at its two vertical extremes. The letter 'H' does not have any visual characteristic that can serve as an "anchor" for horizontal hints linked to the two alignment zones. Thus we use "ghost hints", which will apply to the inside of the alignment zones and, as Adobe has decreed, will have a thickness of 21 units:

```
0 21 hstem 654 21 hstem
```

For the letter 'O', there is no need for a ghost hint; everything works naturally:

```
30 63 vstem 413 63 vstem - 50 hstem 634 50 hstem
```

The letter 'm' is special—not only because we want the three downstrokes to have the same width, but also because we want the white spaces between them to have the same width.

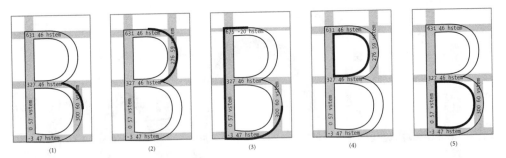

Figure C-10: An example of replacing four hints in the letter 'B'. Image 1 shows the initial situation; images 2 to 5 show the situation after each hint replacement. The thickest stroke is the one drawn in each configuration of hints.

Adobe has introduced a new operator for this purpose: vstem3 (the '3' doubtless means that the hint applies to three downstrokes). This operator takes the six arguments that three consecutive vstem operators would have taken, reading from left to right:

```
39 53 225 53 411 53 vstem3
```

There is an hstem3 for analogous situations with horizontal strokes (for instance, the Greek letter 'Ξ').

C.3.6.1 *Technical peculiarities of hints*

In this section, we shall discuss two properties of hints that can prove very useful for improving the rendering of glyphs: *hint replacement* and *flex*.

Let us begin with hint replacement. The problem is the following: *hints cannot be superimposed*. In the case of simple letters, such as 'H', 'O', or 'm', that does not happen. But consider the letter 'B': often the top part of this letter is slightly smaller than the bottom part, but not so much that the vertical hint for the one will not touch that of the other. We see an example in Figure C-10: the hint for the bottom part should be 300 60 vstem and the one for the top part, 276 59 vstem; but we cannot have both at the same time, because they touch. What, then, should we do?

The makeshift solution given by Adobe [21, pp. 69–71] [234, p. 5] is as follows: we start by drawing the contours, and at certain times we change the configuration of the hints; i.e., we erase them all and we redefine them in a way that is optimal for the part of the outline that we are preparing to draw.

Here is an example from the real world: the hinting of the letter 'B' by FontLab. We begin at the beginning: after the operator hsbw, which initializes the glyph description, we supply an initial series of hints and draw part of the letter (see part 1 in Figure C-10):

```
/B {
    82 500 hsbw
    - 47 hstem 327 46 hstem 631 46 hstem
```

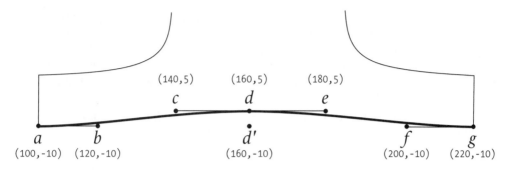

Figure C-11: An example of flex formed by two cubic Bézier curves, abcd and defg. The point of reference is d'.

```
0 57 vstem 300 60 vstem
360 196 rmoveto
0 90 - 57 - 14 rrcurveto
```

In parallel, we create a subroutine (here it bears the number 5), into which we place the second series of hints:

```
dup 5 {
    - 47 hstem 327 46 hstem 631 46 hstem
    0 57 vstem 276 59 vstem
return
} NP
```

In the code for the glyph, we call this subroutine in the following manner (yes, most bizarre):

```
5 1 3 callothersubr pop callsubr
```

The hints are then replaced, and we can draw part 2 of the glyph as follows:

```
70 26 36 62 0 71 rrcurveto
98 - 63 - vhcurveto
```

We continue in this manner three more times to draw parts 3, 4, and 5 of the glyph. Since configuration 4 is identical to configuration 2, we can reuse subroutine 5. Configuration 3 is different from 1 and from 5: FontLab uses a ghost hint, 675 -20 hstem, to align the top part of the glyph, instead of using the regular hint for the top of the vertical stroke, 631 46 hstem.

Flex [21, §8.3] is a mechanism that manages curves in the shape of horizontal or vertical Gaussian bell curves. It works only for very flat curves (20 units at the most). The ideal application of *flex* is at the bottom of serifs (see Figure C-11).

The most important things to know are the conditions that are necessary for a *flex* to be usable. There are five of these conditions. Let us describe them using the example in Figure C-11:

(1) there must be exactly two cubic Bézier curves, *abcd* and *defg*, to be drawn; (2) the endpoints, *a* and *g*, must have the same x-coordinate or the same y-coordinate; (3) line *ce* must be parallel to line *ag*; (4) if *d'* is the projection of *d* onto *ag*, then the distance *dd'* must be less than or equal to 20 units; and (5) the variable BlueShift in the private dictionary must be strictly greater than *dd'*. Point *d'* is called the *point of reference*, because all the coordinates are rewritten with respect to it.

Flex is expressed in the code in a rather obscure way. Suppose that the usual code for the curves would have been:

```
100 - rmoveto
20 0 20 15 20 0 rrcurveto
20 0 20 - 20 0 rrcurveto
```

The final code is the following:

```
100 - rmoveto
1 callsubr
60 0 rmoveto 2 callsubr
- 0 rmoveto 2 callsubr
20 15 rmoveto 2 callsubr
20 0 rmoveto 2 callsubr
20 0 rmoveto 2 callsubr
20 - rmoveto 2 callsubr
20 0 rmoveto 2 callsubr
50 220 - 0 callsubr
```

Here we find a call to subroutine 1, which initiates the process; as many rmoveto instructions and calls to subroutine 2 as there are points between the first control point of the first curve and the ending point of the second; a call to subroutine 0 with three arguments: the first of them, very important, is the size, in hundredths of a pixel, below which this pair of Bézier curves becomes a straight line—the last two are the absolute coordinates of the ending point of the *flex*.

C.3.6.2 *"Counter control"*

Adobe soon noticed that the problems of the letters 'm' and 'Ξ' look trivial when we start to set type in other alphabets—in particular, using ideographic languages such as Chinese, Japanese, and Korean. For instance, the ideographic character 事 (*koto*, "fact, matter"), which already has no fewer than six horizontal strokes, is eighteenth on the list of the most frequent characters in the Japanese language [155]. And the character 書 (*sho*, "write"), with its eight horizontal strokes, is 166th. Not to mention exceptional cases, such as 驫 (*kyō*, "horses"), which is made up of three copies of 馬 (*uma*, "horse"), and 警 (*kei*, "alert"), which are true challenges for printers and readers alike.

To address this problem, Adobe introduced a special hint [10] in 1994 for Chinese/Japanese/ Korean glyphs: "counter control". It involves describing the *counters*, which are the *white spaces between horizontal or vertical strokes*. For simple glyphs such as 目 (*moku*, "eye") and

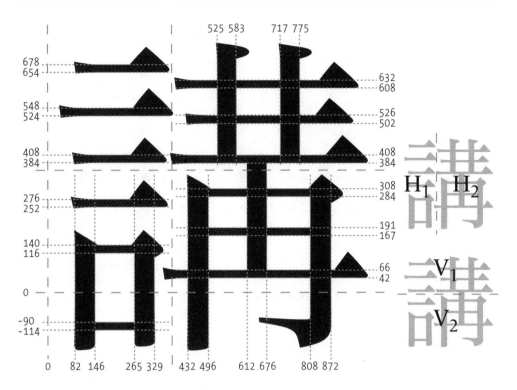

Figure C-12: The "counter controls" of PostScript Type 1 fonts, illustrated on the glyph 講 (kō, "oration").

皿 (*sara*, "dish"), it is sufficient to give the coordinates of these famous counters in order to obtain a good rendering, *dixit* Adobe.

But things become more complicated when the glyph contains several zones with different counters. Take the example in Figure C-12: we have the glyph 講 (*kō*, "oration"), which has two zones of horizontal counters ("H_1" and "H_2") and two zones of vertical counters ("V_1" and "V_2"). The problem is as follows: Suppose that the rendering is done so that the strokes in zone H_1 are rendered properly; then if those in zone H_2 follow the model of those in zone H_1, the glyph will be deformed. We must be able to treat each of the two parts of the glyph independently, as if they were two different glyphs. That is what we do, and here is how:

Let us begin with the horizontal counters of 講. There are five of them in zone H_1, and we can identify them as follows: we give the y-coordinate of the bottom part of the lowest stroke (-114) and the successive thicknesses of the strokes and counters, proceeding from bottom to top (24 206 24 112 24 108 24 116 24 106 24), which gives us 12 altogether. Let us proceed in the same way for zone H_2: there are also five counters, but they are arranged differently, as follows: 42 24 101 24 93 24 76 24 94 24 82 24. We also have two zones for vertical counters: V_1 (525 58 134 58, going from left to right) and V_2 (82 58 119 58 103 58 312 58).

We might have expected a handy operator that would take all these values as arguments. But there is none.[15] After a series of technical transformations of no great interest, which is explained in [10, pp. 13–14], the counter controls are finally declared with the following code:

```
24 93 24 76 24 94 24 106 - 2 525 58 192 - 82
58 119 58 103 58 370 - 22 12 callothersubr
2 - 24 206 24 112 24 108 24 116 24 130 - 42 24
101 16 13 callothersub
```

In conclusion, let us note that the *order of the zones* need not be from bottom to top or from left to right. In fact, it is the order of their *graphical priority*: we put the most graphically important part first. If the interpreter has to choose between rendering one or the other of these zones correctly, the decision will favor the one that was declared first.

C.3.7   AFM Files

Before proceeding to the other PostScript font formats, let us briefly discuss a type of file that accompanies practically all PostScript fonts: the AFM file (for "Adobe font metrics") [12]. The AFM file is a set of generic and platform-independent metrics from which we can generate PFM files under Windows or FOND resources on the Macintosh. This approach is similar to that of BDF files, which make up the "generic bitmaps" from which we can easily produce other bitmap formats that are more efficient and more appropriate for the various platforms.

There is another very important property that AFM files share with BDFs: they are quite legible to the human eye. We might even say that they were meant to be read by humans, so much so that the separators and other notational apparatus found in programming languages are all absent. An AFM file is just a sequence of keywords and values. The overall structure of an AFM file is also very simple. It is divided into four parts: the heading, the metric properties of the glyphs, data on letterspacing and kerning, and composite glyphs.

An AFM file is entirely contained between the lines StartFontMetrics 3.0 and EndFontMetrics. The number that follows StartFontMetrics is the version of the AFM format: currently we are at version 4.1, but the examples given by the specification [12] still use version 3.

The header of an AFM file contains a number of keywords that represent part of the data contained in the Type 1 font or that add new data:

- FontName (required), the name of the font, as used with the findfont operator of the PostScript language.

- FullName, a version of FontName that is less strict and intended only for the human reader.

- FamilyName, the name of the font "family".

- Weight, the font's weight, in a free form.

- FontBBox, the bounding box of all the glyphs in the font.

- Version, the font's version, which is taken from the data contained in the font.

---

[15] In fact, it will not appear until the *charstrings* of Type 2.

- Notice, the copyright notice.

- EncodingScheme, the font's encoding, if it has a name recognized by Adobe, or FontSpecific, in the general case.

- CharacterSet is a little more specific than the font's encoding: AdobeStandardLatin, AdobeStandardCyrillic, etc. There is no default value.

- Characters, the number of glyphs in the font.

- VVector (required if the font is set in two directions), the coordinates of the vector that connects the origin of the first direction of writing to the origin of the second. If this keyword is present, that indicates that the vector is shared by all the glyphs.

- IsFixedV takes the value true if the keyword VVector above is defined and the value false otherwise.

- CapHeight, the height of the capitals.

- XHeight, the height of the lowercase letters without ascenders.

- Ascender, the height of the lowercase letters with ascenders.

- Descender, the depth of the lowercase letters with descenders.

- StdHW and StdVW: the entries of the same name in the font's private dictionary.

- MetricsSets, the number of possible directions of writing: 0 (by default), horizontal; 1, vertical; 2, both.

Depending on the value of MetricsSets, we have one or two sections StartDirection i ... EndDirection, where i can take the values 0 and 1. Each such section (which is implicit if MetricsSet is missing or has the value 0) contains the following entries:

- UnderlinePosition, the y-coordinate of the center of the underline, if any

- UnderlineThickness, the thickness of the underline, if any

- ItalicAngle, the slope of the font, measured in degrees in the trigonometric direction (thus negative for the usual italic Latin fonts)

- CharWidth, followed by two numbers—the coordinates of the glyph's width vector, if that width vector is common to all the glyphs, as is the case for some ideographic fonts

- IsFixedPitch, true if CharWidth exists, false otherwise

Now we come to the section for the metric properties of each glyph. This section is delimited by the entries StartCharMetrics i ... EndCharMetrics, where i is the number of glyphs described in the section. Each glyph is described in the form of a line containing keyword/value pairs separated by semicolons, as shown:

```
C 131 ; WX 599 ; N Eacute ; B 33 0 549 923 ;
```

Here is the list of possible keywords:

- C, followed by an integer, indicates the glyph's position in the current encoding, -1 if none. Note that we can also use hexadecimal numbers: the keyword becomes CH, and the hexadecimal number, written in uppercase letters, is placed within < and > (e.g., CH <91F8>).

- WX, the horizontal part of the glyph's width vector, if there is only one direction of writing. If there are two directions of writing, we use the keywords WOX and W1X.

- WY, the vertical part of the glyph's width vector, if there is only one direction of writing, otherwise WOY and W1Y. There are also W, WO, and W1, followed by two numbers, which combine the two coordinates of the different width vectors.

- VV, followed by two numbers: the coordinates of the vector that connects the origin of the first direction of writing to the origin of the second.

- N, followed by a string: the glyph's name.

- B, followed by four numbers: the glyph's bounding box.

- L, followed by two strings: a ligature. For instance, N f ; L i fi ; means that the glyph f followed by the glyph i produces the glyph fi.

Then come the data on kerning, placed between StartKernData and EndKernData. We distinguish two types of data: *letterspacing* (i.e., the overall expansion or contraction of the distance between the glyphs) and *individual kerning pairs* (i.e., the drawing together or moving apart of specific pairs of letters).

Letterspacing values are placed between the keywords StartTrackKern i ... EndTrackKern, where i is the number of letterspacing values to follow.

Letterspacing values are distinguished by their *degree*: an integer that is positive if we are moving glyphs apart and negative if we are drawing them together. The degree 0 is the absence of letterspacing.

Each letterspacing value is described by a keyword

```
TrackKern d p k P K,
```

where the parameters are numeric values: d is the degree; p, a small point size; k, the letterspacing corresponding to p; P, a large point size; and K, the letterspacing corresponding to P. For any point size between p and P, letterspacing will be interpolated; for any point size outside this interval, letterspacing will remain constant.

The reader will have noticed that something very interesting has happened here. For the first time in the whole chapter, we have come upon a metric property of PostScript fonts that *is not independent of the point size*. Thus, rather than saying that letterspacing is the same at every point size of the font, we have established limits beyond which letterspacing becomes constant.

Longtemps, je me suis couché de bonne heure. Parfois, à peine ma bougie éteinte, mes yeux se fermaient si vite que je n'avais pas le temps de me dire : Je m'endors. Et, une demi-heure après, la pensée q
Longtemps, je me suis couché de bonne heure. Parfois, à peine ma bougie éteinte, mes yeux se fermaient si vite que je n'avais pas le temps de me dire : Je m'endors. Et, une demi-heure
Longtemps, je me suis couché de bonne heure. Parfois, à peine ma bougie éteinte, mes yeux se fermaient si vite que je n'avais pas le temps de me dire : Je m'endors. Et,
Longtemps, je me suis couché de bonne heure. Parfois, à peine ma bougie éteinte, mes yeux se fermaient si vite que je n'avais pas le temps de me dire : Je m
Longtemps, je me suis couché de bonne heure. Parfois, à peine ma bougie éteinte, mes yeux se fermaient si vite que je n'avais pas le temps de me dire :
Longtemps, je me suis couché de bonne heure. Parfois, à peine ma bougie éteinte, mes yeux se fermaient si vite que je n'avais pas le tem
Longtemps, je me suis couché de bonne heure. Parfois, à peine ma bougie éteinte, mes yeux se fermaient si vite que je n'avais p
Longtemps, je me suis couché de bonne heure. Parfois, à peine ma bougie éteinte, mes yeux se fermaient si vite que je n
Longtemps, je me suis couché de bonne heure. Parfois, à peine ma bougie éteinte, mes yeux se fermaient si vite q
Longtemps, je me suis couché de bonne heure. Parfois, à peine ma bougie éteinte, mes yeux se fermaient si
Longtemps, je me suis couché de bonne heure. Parfois, à peine ma bougie éteinte, mes yeux se fermaie
Longtemps, je me suis couché de bonne heure. Parfois, à peine ma bougie éteinte, mes yeux se fe
Longtemps, je me suis couché de bonne heure. Parfois, à peine ma bougie éteinte, mes yeux
Longtemps, je me suis couché de bonne heure. Parfois, à peine ma bougie éteinte, mes ye
Longtemps, je me suis couché de bonne heure. Parfois, à peine ma bougie éteinte, me
Longtemps, je me suis couché de bonne heure. Parfois, à peine ma bougie éteinte,
Longtemps, je me suis couché de bonne heure. Parfois, à peine ma bougie étein
Longtemps, je me suis couché de bonne heure. Parfois, à peine ma bougie é
Longtemps, je me suis couché de bonne heure. Parfois, à peine ma bougie
Longtemps, je me suis couché de bonne heure. Parfois, à peine ma bou
Longtemps, je me suis couché de bonne heure. Parfois, à peine ma b
Longtemps, je me suis couché de bonne heure. Parfois, à peine ma

Longtemps, je me suis couché de bonne heure. Parfois, à peine ma bougie éteinte, mes yeux se fermaient si vite que je n'avais pas le temps de me dire : Je m'endors. Et, une demi-he
Longtemps, je me suis couché de bonne heure. Parfois, à peine ma bougie éteinte, mes yeux se fermaient si vite que je n'avais pas le temps de me dire : Je m'e
Longtemps, je me suis couché de bonne heure. Parfois, à peine ma bougie éteinte, mes yeux se fermaient si vite que je n'avais pas le temps de me dire : Je m'e
Longtemps, je me suis couché de bonne heure. Parfois, à peine ma bougie éteinte, mes yeux se fermaient si vite que je n'avais pas le temps de
Longtemps, je me suis couché de bonne heure. Parfois, à peine ma bougie éteinte, mes yeux se fermaient si vite que je n'avais pas le temps de
Longtemps, je me suis couché de bonne heure. Parfois, à peine ma bougie éteinte, mes yeux se fermaient si vite que je n'avais pas le t
Longtemps, je me suis couché de bonne heure. Parfois, à peine ma bougie éteinte, mes yeux se fermaient si vite que je n'avais p
Longtemps, je me suis couché de bonne heure. Parfois, à peine ma bougie éteinte, mes yeux se fermaient si vite que je n
Longtemps, je me suis couché de bonne heure. Parfois, à peine ma bougie éteinte, mes yeux se fermaient si vite q
Longtemps, je me suis couché de bonne heure. Parfois, à peine ma bougie éteinte, mes yeux se fermaient si
Longtemps, je me suis couché de bonne heure. Parfois, à peine ma bougie éteinte, mes yeux se fermaie
Longtemps, je me suis couché de bonne heure. Parfois, à peine ma bougie éteinte, mes yeux se fe
Longtemps, je me suis couché de bonne heure. Parfois, à peine ma bougie éteinte, mes yeux
Longtemps, je me suis couché de bonne heure. Parfois, à peine ma bougie éteinte, mes ye
Longtemps, je me suis couché de bonne heure. Parfois, à peine ma bougie éteinte, me
Longtemps, je me suis couché de bonne heure. Parfois, à peine ma bougie éteinte,
Longtemps, je me suis couché de bonne heure. Parfois, à peine ma bougie éteint
Longtemps, je me suis couché de bonne heure. Parfois, à peine ma bougie éte
Longtemps, je me suis couché de bonne heure. Parfois, à peine ma bougie é
Longtemps, je me suis couché de bonne heure. Parfois, à peine ma bougie
Longtemps, je me suis couché de bonne heure. Parfois, à peine ma bou
Longtemps, je me suis couché de bonne heure. Parfois, à peine ma bo

Figure C-13: Two examples of letterspacing in the font Times-Roman for sizes between 5 and 15.5. In the first case, letterspacing varies with the point size throughout its magnitude: TrackKern 1 5 0.5 15.5 1.55. *In the second case, letterspacing remains constant below 8 points and above 12 points:* Track-Kern 1 8 0.8 12 1.2.

We can request that letterspacing remain constant below 5 PostScript points and above 240 points. By making that specification, we give the values of letterspacing at its extremes. The value of letterspacing for an intermediate point size is calculated by interpolation from the extremes. In other words, if at every point size below p the letterspacing is k and if at every point size below P it is K, then for $c \in [p, P]$ the letterspacing will be $\frac{(K-k)(c-p)}{P-p} + k$.

Note that nothing prevents us from taking inordinately large values of P and ridiculously small ones of p in order to keep letterspacing from becoming constant in a document. For example, a specification such as

```
TrackKern 10 1 0.1 65535 6553
```

is entirely possible and will produce letterspacing of one point at point size 10, two points at point size 20, and so on.

Now we have come to the kerning pairs, which, most of the time, are the only interesting material in an AFM file. They are placed in a section `StartKernPairs` *i* ... `EndKernPairs`, where *i* is the number of kerning pairs to follow. If there are two directions of writing, there will also be two sections, `StartKernPairs0` *i0* ... `EndKernPairs` and `StartKernPairs1` *i1* ... `EndKernPairs`.

Each pair is written on a line of the type KPX *nom1* *nom2* *k*, where *nom1* and *nom2* are the names of the glyphs in the pair (in the logical order, thus independent of whether we are writing from left to right or from right to left) and *k* is the amount of kerning—positive if we are moving the glyphs apart, negative if we are drawing them closer together. Example:

    KPX F comma -

There are variants of KPX: KPY for vertical kerning, and KP for kerning with two coordinates.

It may happen that some glyphs have no names. In that case, we use their positions in the encoding, written as hexadecimal numbers, and the keyword becomes KPH. Since KPH is a variant of KP, it must be followed by two numbers: the coordinates of the kerning vector. Example:

    KPH <305A> <3002> - 0

which expresses (horizontal) kerning between the ideographic character '字' and the ideographic period, '。', provided that these glyphs have been encoded according to Unicode.

We have come to the final section, the one for composite characters. It supplies complementary data that are ofter indispensable to a Type 1 font, especially if the font does not contain any glyphs for accented letters.....

This section is delimited by the keywords `StartComposites` *i* ... `EndComposites`, where *i* is the number of composite glyphs in the font. The description of a glyph of this type takes up one line, which consists of the keyword CC followed by the name of the glyph and the number, *c*, of its components, then *c* instances of the keyword PCC. Each instance of PCC is followed by the name of the glyph for the component and the coordinates of its width vector. For instance, if the glyph "circumflex accent" in the font was designed for the letter 'e', it may be moved to the right when it is placed over a 'w' (as is done in Welsh) or upward when it is placed over an 'E'. Here is an example of a composite glyph:

    CC Eacute 2 ; PCC E 0 0 ; PCC acute 195 224 ;

Note that a composite glyph must also appear in the section on the glyphs' metric properties, even though its position in the encoding is often -1, as, for example, in the font encoding `AdobeStandardEncoding`.

This concludes the description of the AFM font format. There are other keywords that are specific to Type 0, CID, or Multiple Master fonts. We shall present them gradually in the description of these font formats.

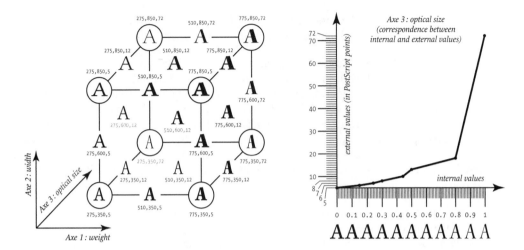

Figure C-14: The eight master designs of the glyph 'A' in the font Adobe Kepler MM, together with several intermediate glyphs. Next to each glyph, we can read the triplets of values for the parameters. The glyph whose values are 510, 600, 12 appears in the middle of the cube and is, in a sense, the average value of the glyph 'A' in this font.

C.4   Multiple Master Fonts

The idea is very simple. A *master* is an outline of a master design, which is most often designed by a human. The computer can interpolate two or more master designs to obtain arbitrary intermediate outlines called *instances*. Thus we have not only a single glyph for every character but an infinite number[16] of instances, described by their coefficients of interpolation from some number of master designs.

We can have up to 16 master designs in a Multiple Master font, and they can be organized around four *axes of interpolation*. Each axis of interpolation is defined by two master designs placed at extreme locations. We can also decide that certain master designs will appear not at the extremities of an axis but at "intermediate positions" along a given axis.

Here we have a practical example: the font *Adobe Kepler MM* is a Multiple Master font with three axes, respectively called "weight", "width", and "size". In the left part of Figure C-14, we see the three axes of the font represented in Cartesian form. The encircled glyphs take on the extreme values and are therefore master designs.

Now let us look at the technical side. Multiple Master fonts have a well-deserved reputation for being quite complex. Here is some information that will help us to understand Adobe's strategy:

1. According to the nature of the axes that have been defined, some properties remain fixed and others vary. For instance, in the case of *Adobe Kepler MM*, the property ItalicAngle remains equal to 0, regardless of the instance. It is a *fixed* property. But we can easily

---

[16] In computer science, the term "infinity" means "a very large number".

imagine a Multiple Master font with one axis for the slope; in that case, the property would be *variable*. Thus it is helpful to distinguish the two types of properties in the font.

2. Suppose that a Multiple Master font is sent to an aging PostScript interpreter that does not know beans about Multiple Master. Instead of getting a stupid PostScript error and an aborted print job or rendering on screen, would it not be preferable to make do with even a "standard" instance of the font? To that end, Adobe ensures that all the variable data appear twice in a Multiple Master font file: the first time, they take only one value, which corresponds to a canonical "standard" instance; the second time, they appear as tables with as many values as there are master designs. We can therefore hope that the obsolete PostScript interpreter will be content with the first values and will ignore the second.

3. Finally, one little additional complication that is very useful: there are two "spaces" for the values of the parameters: "external" values, defined by the font's designer (*design values*), which may have some typographic semantics (for example, in Figure C-14, the units of the third axis are true PostScript points for the optical size); and internal (*blend values*), which always fall between 0 and 1. Adobe's brilliant idea was to say that the correspondence between the design values and the blend values is not linear but *piecewise linear*!

Let us explain. The font *Adobe Kepler MM* offers optical sizes between 5 and 72. Fonts grow like humans: the difference (in design) between 6 and 12 points can be enormous, whereas between 66 and 72 it is certainly much smaller. Thus it would be stupid to split up the interval $[0, 1]$ evenly across sizes running from 5 to 72. On the other hand, it would be much more prudent to devote a large portion of this interval to text sizes and to leave a small portion for sizes used in titles. That is what Adobe did: as the right side of Figure C-14 shows, the blend values between 0 and 0.5 roughly correspond to the optical sizes from 5 to 13; then the section between 0.5 and 0.8 corresponds to the sizes from 13 to 18, and only the remaining fifth of the interval is dedicated to sizes beyond 18.

Now we shall see how these data are represented in PostScript code.

A Multiple Master font is, above all, a Type 1 font. Thus it includes a FontInfo dictionary. We shall store all the "fixed" values in this dictionary. To them we shall add three entries:

1. BlendAxisTypes, a table containing the names of the axes. Example:

   /BlendAxisTypes [/Weight /Width /OpticalSize] def ;

2. BlendDesignPositions, a table containing a subtable for each master design. Each subtable contains the coordinates of the master design, according to the axes. For instance, in the font *Adobe Kepler MM*, we have

   /BlendDesignPositions [[0 0 0] [1 0 0] [0 1 0]
   [1 1 0] [0 0 1] [1 0 1] [0 1 1] [1 1 1]] def

   i.e., the eight vertices of the cube in Figure C-14. If some of the master designs are intermediate values rather than extreme ones, that will be seen from their coordinates, which assume values between 0 and 1.

3. `BlendDesignMap`, a table containing a subtable for each axis. Each subtable contains sub-subtables that are the coordinates of the points that define the linear (or piecewise-linear) relationship between design values and blend values. Most of the time, we find here only the extreme design values. In *Adobe Kepler MM*, for example, the first two subtables of `BlendDesignMap` are `[[275 0][775 1]]` and `[[350 0][850 1]]`, which means that the design values of the first axis (weight) range from 275 to 775 and that those of the second axis (width) range from 350 to 850. The third subtable of this font is more complex: it contains eight correspondences between design values and blend values (see Figure C-14), which gives us a linear relationship in seven pieces. Here is this table: `[[5 0][6 0.15][7 0.24][8 0.30][10 0.44][13 0.50][18 0.80][72 1]]`.

These three entries are of capital importance, since they define the system of instances globally. Now let us move on to the "variable" data. At the same level as `FontInfo`, there is a small dictionary called `Blend`. There are three entries in this dictionary: `FontBBox`, `FontInfo`, and `Private`. In each of them we find the customary subentries of Type 1 fonts, except that here everything is done in a *table*, with one element for each master design. For instance, the `FontBBox` of the font *Adobe Kepler MM* is:

```
/FontBBox {{- - - -} {- - - - }
{- - - -} {- - - - }
{1052 1155 1291 1429} {693 816 1103 1183 }
{866 892 925 925} {798 850 854 871 }} def
```

Here we see eight bounding boxes, for the eight master designs[17] (in the order in which they are defined in `BlendDesignPositions`).

One little detail that has irritated plenty of people: When we define the `Blend` dictionary, we are not in "private territory". Indeed, we are still in the public part of the font, and the private part is usually found in the encrypted binary section. Thus we write:

```
/Blend 3 dict dup begin
/FontBBox{{- ... }}def
/FontInfo 14 dict dup begin ... end readonly def
/Private 14 dict def
end def
```

and leave it at that, without giving any more information about the `Private` dictionary. Later, this dictionary will be filled in with values. Let us take an example, drawn from the font *Adobe Kepler MM*. There are six alignment zones in the font, which therefore means 12 values in `BlueValues`. Here is the `BlueValues` entry in the private dictionary of `Blend`:

```
/BlueValues[
[ - - - - - - - - - ][ 0 0 0 0 0 0 0 0]
[ 630 630 654 654 642 642 655 654 ][ 652 652 676 676 664 664 677 676 ]
```

---

[17] We have used braces here instead of brackets because `FontBBox` is considered to be a procedure rather than a table; thus instead of using a table of tables, we have a procedure of procedures.

```
[ 425 427 430 426 413 413 413 413 ][ 447 449 452 448 435 435 435 435 ]
[ 609 609 631 632 613 613 636 634 ][ 626 626 650 650 625 625 650 650 ]
[ 655 655 679 679 673 667 705 679 ][ 672 672 701 699 683 677 715 692 ]
[ 598 602 622 627 604 599 614 626 ][ 598 602 622 627 604 599 614 626 ]
] def
```

We see that each number has indeed become a table of eight numbers. In some cases, these numbers are identical. That is of no importance: what matters is that we do indeed have a value for each master design.

Now let us examine another type of data: that for the standard instance. Specifically, a Multiple Master font must contain various data on a privileged instance. To find out which instance this is, we have three entries[18] at the level of Blend:

1. DesignVector, which is a table of numbers containing as many entries as there are axes. These numbers are the design values of the instance.

2. NormDesignVector, which is a table of numbers (between 0 and 1) with as many entries as there are axes. These numbers are the blend values of the instance.

3. WeightVector, which is a table of numbers (between 0 and 1) with as many entries as there are master designs. These numbers indicate the *weight* of each master design in creating the instance. The total of these numbers must be equal to 1.

The font's private dictionary (the entry Private, at the same level as CharStrings) is the one for the standard instance. Thus an interpreter that cannot understand the font's interpolation properties can still continue by using the properties of the standard instance, which are quite consistent with those of ordinary Type 1 fonts.

Last but not least, we have come to the glyph descriptions. We shall not go into the details here. The principle is as follows: We have the most standard operators of Type 1. But instead of supplying fixed numeric arguments to them, we multiply the number of arguments by the number of master designs and send this mass of data through certain subroutines (numbers 14 through 18) that will interpolate them and give the operators the exact number of arguments that they are expecting—no more, no fewer. Here is an example, drawn from the font *Adobe Kepler MM*, of what has happened to the extremely simple rlineto operator, which ordinarily takes two arguments (the coordinates of the ending point of the line that is to be drawn):

```
6 38 - 0 0 - - - - 8 0 15 - - - - - 8 15 callsubr
rlineto
```

There are indeed 2 × 8 arguments supplied to subroutine 15, which will deduce two arguments from them according to the selected instance of the font and then supply these arguments to the good old rlineto operator for Type 1 fonts.

---

[18] The entries DesignVector and NormDesignVector do not appear in the Multiple Master specifications [10], but they are indeed used in various Adobe fonts. We shall describe them as if they were part of the specifications.

We cannot refrain from emphasizing once more the great weakness of Multiple Master fonts, which becomes apparent here: all the instances share the same operators; only the values change. Be the instances of a single glyph ultra-bold or extra-light, be they as wide as a sumo wrestler or as thin as a statue by Giacometti, be they used in titles spanning five columns or for the subscripts of variables appearing in footnotes, they always have exactly the same number of Bézier curves, in the same order and in the same arrangement. That requires unprecedented discipline on the part of font designers and often results in aesthetic compromises.

C.4.1 Using Multiple Master Fonts in the PostScript Language

Ultra-technical though the innards of Multiple Master fonts may be, their use in the PostScript language is of a childlike simplicity. As explained in [10, §3.7] and [7, §5], we use the same findfont operator, which will track down the instantiation of the font in a transparent manner. But how does it know the values of the parameters of the font instance? Quite simply, from the name of the font.

Specifically, the font's name is followed by an underscore and one numerical value for each axis in the font, these values also being separated by underscores.[19] For example, to obtain the instance 385 575 10 of the font *Adobe Kepler MM*, whose FontName is KeplMM, we simply write:

```
KeplMM_385_575_10 findfont
```

C.4.2 The AMFM file

Every Multiple Master is ordinarily[20] accompanied by an AMFM file (for "Adobe Multiple [Master] Font Metrics"). The format of this file is an extension of the AFM file format; it is described in [12, §6].

To show that it is AMFM rather than AFM, the file begins with StartMasterFontMetrics 4.1 and ends with EndMasterFontMetrics.

In the preamble to the AMFM file, we find the same global data on the font as in an AFM file: FullName, FontName, FamilyName, Weight, Notice, Version, IsFixedPitch, etc.

Next, some global data reminiscent of Multiple Master:

- Masters, followed by the number of master designs.

- Axes, followed by the number of axes.

- BlendDesignPositions, BlendDesignMap, BlendAxisTypes, with exactly the same values as in the font itself.

---

[19] Slight variations on this syntax are possible; see [7].

[20] We criticize Adobe for not supplying the AMFM files for the Multiple Master fonts. A high-ranking official at Adobe with whom the author raised this question said in reply that "the true solution would be to create software that does not need an AFM file"—an answer that clearly shows Adobe's reversal in the direction of OpenType. In any event, to obtain an AMFM file, one need only open and save the font in FontLab. For reasons of compatibility with older operating systems, the extension that FontLab appends to AMFM files is .amm.

- WeightVector, the description of the standard instance, with the same values as in the font itself.

- For each axis, a StartAxis on one line, followed by an AxisLabel with the name of the axis and an AxisType with the type of the axis (by "type", Adobe means a keyword selected from Weight, Width, and OpticalSize), and, finally, an EndAxis.

- A list of "primary" fonts, which are the instances corresponding to the master designs and the standard instance. The keyword StartPrimaryFonts is followed by the number of those fonts. Next, for each font, there is a keyword PC followed by the design values of the instance's axes (required), and possibly a keyword PL followed by the instance's labels (see [7, Appendix B]) and a keyword PN followed by a human-readable font name. A semicolon comes at the end of this list of values. The list of "primary" fonts ends with EndPrimaryFonts.

Finally, for each master design there is a section StartMaster ... EndMaster containing the font names (FullName, FontName, FamilyName), the version (Version), and, most important of all, the WeightVector of each master design (which is made up entirely of 0s and 1s if it is at a vertex of the cube but may contain values between 0 and 1 if it is an "intermediate" master design).

C.5   Type 42 Fonts

Ever since version 2013, PostScript interpreters have contained a TrueType rendering engine. This engine allows for direct rendering of glyphs found in TrueType fonts, without first going through a conversion to PostScript (which would be catastrophic, since the nature of the curves is different and the hints in the two systems have absolutely nothing to do with each other). The only problem is communication: how to transfer data from a TrueType font to the TrueType rendering engine inside a PostScript interpreter? To this end, Adobe introduced *Type 42* [13].

The reader surprised by this sudden switch from small numbers (Types 0, 1, 2, 3...) to the number 42 will understand once he has read *The Hitchhiker's Guide to the Galaxy*, by Douglas Adams [2], a gem of British science fiction and British humor, and a must for those who wish to learn about hacker culture. In this book, the number 42 is of central importance, as it represents the "answer to the Ultimate Question of Life, the Universe, and Everything".[21]

Type 42 combines the PostScript and TrueType formats into one. Does it solve the problems of these two formats? Not really. A Type 42 must rather be considered as a wrapper for a

---

[21] In fact, according to Adams, an extraterrestrial race designed a supercomputer called *Deep Thought* to find the answer to the Ultimate Question of Life, the Universe, and Everything. After seven and a half million years, *Deep Thought* proclaimed that the answer is "42". Thus we noticed that the answer is worthless if we do not know the question. *Deep Thought* therefore designed an even more enormous computer to find the question, after 10 million years of calculations. This computer is Earth, it is powered by mice, and humanity's reason for being is to feed the mice. But five minutes before fulfilling its mission, Earth was destroyed to make room for an intergalactic highway.
Ken Lunde, in [240, p. 280], even gives the name of the person who is responsible for assigning the number 42 to this type of font: Kevin Andresen, an employee of Xerox. Apparently all the computers used by his team had names drawn from this book, and their network printer was called *Forty-Two*.

TrueType font—a wrapper that is used to send the data to the TrueType processor through the PostScript language, much as we send a letter through the postal service in an envelope that the recipient rips open because she is concerned mainly with the letter's contents.

Nevertheless, it is worth while to study format 42 in order to observe Adobe's efforts to supply a minimum of data on the font's glyphs to the PostScript interpreter—data to which the PostScript interpreter has no direct access because they are stored inside the TrueType code, which is a sort of black box.

Before we begin, one small detail that could cause big problems if neglected: the current transformation matrix is [1 0 0 1 0 0], which means that the units used in the font are not divided by 1,000, as is the case for Type 1 fonts. Thus one must be careful to use the correct units when writing values such as the set-width, the left side-bearing, the thickness of the underline, etc.

Now we shall describe the dictionary entries that are either new or different from those of Type 1:

- The entries PaintType (was the glyph produced by filling or by drawing outlines?) and StrokeWidth (the stroke width, if the glyph was drawn with outlines) are required. Recommended values: /PaintType 0 def /StrokeWidth 0 def.

- Here an element in the dictionary CharStrings contains not a glyph description but a number. This number is the index of the glyph in question within the TrueType tables loca (table of pointers to the glyph descriptions, which are stored in the table glyf) and hmtx (table of horizontal set-widths). This approach is quite interesting: it completely short-circuits the table cmap, and therefore the TrueType font encoding.

- The (optional) dictionary Metrics contains the left-hand side-bearings and the set-widths of the glyphs: the keywords are glyph names, and the values are tables containing two numbers [24, §5.9.2]. There can also be tables with four numbers, which will be the two numbers just mentioned followed by their vertical counterparts.

- Likewise, if we have defined the direction 1 (vertical) in the font, we can have a second dictionary, Metrics2, with the side-bearings and widths for that direction.

- Most important of all: the entry sfnts contains the data for the TrueType font in the form of binary or hexadecimal strings. In fact, the value of sfnts is a table containing one or more strings: it is necessary because strings in PostScript cannot contain more than 65,535 characters. Thus the TrueType code is cut into pieces, which become the elements of a table.

Finally, an entry that is very interesting but apparently not universally construed in the same way by all PostScript interpreters: GlyphDirectory. The idea is as follows: It is all very well to have an entire TrueType font at one's disposal, but if we actually need only a few glyphs from the font, what is the point of loading the *entire* font? The GlyphDirectory dictionary contains separate TrueType descriptions for each glyph. An intelligent (well, *very* intelligent) PostScript driver can reconstruct a TrueType font with only the glyphs that it desires and deliver that font to the TrueType processor as if nothing had happened. Better yet, the description can begin with the glyph's metrics (set-width, left side-bearing). For that purpose, the entry MetricsCount must have the value 2 or 4 (see [13, §5.7]).

C.6   Type 0, or OCF, Fonts

This font format is an example of a bad business strategy. In order to make it possible to set type in the languages of East Asia without extending the Type 3 or Type 1 fonts to support more than 256 glyphs, Adobe decided to use hierarchical fonts with several levels, in which references to characters are dispatched by a central file to subfonts, which ultimately yield very ordinary Type 3 or Type 1 fonts. These fonts were called "composite fonts", and the entry for the font type in the FontInfo dictionary took the value 0. Apparently Adobe did not immediately release precise and comprehensive specifications; as a result, several Asian companies tried to "guess" the specifications (through reverse engineering) and delivered fonts that were more or less similar but not always compatible. Adobe subsequently developed a more powerful font format, known as CID, and immediately declared the Type 0 fonts null and void. The "composite" fonts were then given a new name: OCF (for "original composite fonts"), where "original" was a synonym for "obsolete". To this day, Adobe has never stopped denigrating OCF and singing the praises of CID. Most Asian foundries issue their fonts in both OCF and CID. (One wonders why, if CID is so much better.)

Now let us examine the description of OCF, based on a bit of information published by Adobe.

We have already said that OCF fonts are those whose FontType entry takes the value 0.

The first problem that arises concerns the typesetting operator show: how does it handle ideographic languages? Seeking a simple approach, Adobe used the same show operator as for the Western languages, but its complexity greatly increased at the font level. To set type in Chinese, for example, one would apply the show operator to strings represented by one, two, or even three bytes, in different encodings. The show operator was expected to adopt completely different behavior according to the representation of the characters and the encoding of the text data, while the font remained the same.

In fact, just the opposite is done: the font must be adapted to the text data, and show determines how it is to behave from the type of the OCF font being used. Thus it will use a special method, according to the font, to interpret the strings. The interpreting procedure will yield pairs of integers: *subfont number* plus *glyph number*. Using these numbers, the interpreter will finally find the correct glyph in the correct subfont of the OCF font.

Thus there are two important aspects, independent of the OCF font: the aspect of "character mapping" and the aspect of the "hierarchical organization of the fonts".

C.6.1   Character Mapping

Character mapping refers to describing the various methods that are available for representing ideographic characters in the form of one or more bytes. Here is the general schema. Each Type 0 font must contain three required entries:

- FMapType, an integer between 2 and 9 that indicates how strings are to be interpreted in PostScript code. By applying the correct method, the PostScript interpreter will obtain pairs of integers consisting of a "subfont number" and a "glyph number".

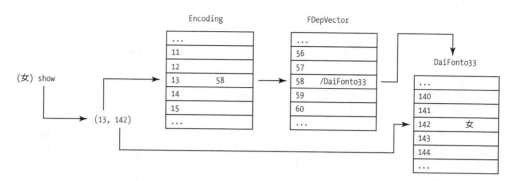

Figure C-15: How OCF fonts work: the show *operator supplies a pair of integers "subfont number plus glyph number"; by means of the subfont number, an index for the subfont is obtained from the table* Encoding*; by means of the subfont index, the name of the subfont is obtained from the table* FDepVector*; finally, by means of the subfont name and the glyph number, the much-desired glyph (here,* 女*, that is, onna, or "woman") is obtained.*

- Encoding, a table of integers. The interpreter uses the "subfont number" above as an index into this table to obtain a whole number that is the "subfont index". (Do not confuse the "subfont number" and the "subfont index"!)

- FDepVector, a table of subfont dictionaries that represents all the descendants of the "root" font. The interpreter uses the "subfont index" above as an index into this table[22] to obtain and load the correct subfont dictionary.

Only one question remains: how to interpret the "glyph numbers" obtained by interpreting the strings in the PostScript code? That depends on the type of the target subfont. If it is of Type 1, 3, or 42, it represents the glyph's position in the subfont table. We need merely go to the Encoding dictionary of the target subfont to obtain the corresponding glyph name. If the target subfont is a CID (types 9 to 12), it is a CID identifier; we shall see those in the following section, which is dedicated to CIDs.

All that remains is to describe the different methods for representing strings. Here they are:

- FMapType equal to 2 ("8/8 mapping"): show reads two bytes per character, the first being the subfont number, the second being the glyph number. This is what is used, for example, for the JIS and EUC encodings.

- FMapType equal to 3 ("escape mapping"): we have the concepts of "current subfont" and "escape character". The escape character is given by another entry (optional, by default 0xFF) in the font, called EscChar. At the beginning of the string, the current subfont is number 0. The show operator reads bytes, and if it finds an escape character, then the following byte is the subfont number of the new current subfont. Otherwise, it is a glyph number.

---

[22] One may well ask why it is necessary to go through two distinct tables to obtain the subfont dictionary. Could FMapType not supply the correct subfont dictionary number directly? The answer is that the procedure allows the same font, with just a change to the Encoding table, to be used for several compatible encodings. For example, an OCF font can be used in JIS, Shift-JIS, or EUC, and the Encoding table plays a pivotal role.

- FMapType equal to 4 ("1/7 mapping"): a byte is read; its first bit gives the subfont number, and the other bits give the glyph number. The result is rather paltry: two fonts of 128 glyphs each. We would be better off with a single font of 255 glyphs.

- FMapType equal to 5 ("9/7 mapping"): a 16-bits number is read (the most significant byte comes first). The first 9 bits represent the subfont number and the remaining 7 bits represent the glyph number. Thus we can have up to 512 fonts of 128 glyphs each.

- FMapType equal to 7 ("double escape mapping"): an extension of escape mapping, described above. If an escape character is followed by a second escape character, a third byte is read. The subfont number will then be the value of the byte plus 256. With this value of FMapType, we can have as many as 512 fonts (but the strings may be longer, since there will be more escape characters).

- FMapType equal to 8 ("shift mapping"): also an extension of escape mapping. Here, however, there are two escape characters, corresponding to the entries ShiftIn (by default 15) and ShiftOut (by default 14), and only two subfonts are possible, numbers 0 and 1. The first escape character switches to subfont 1; the second takes us back to subfont 0.

There are also two more sophisticated ways to represent characters: SubsVector and CMap.

The SubsVector method corresponds to an FMapType equal to 6. It uses the value of the entry SubsVector to describe the method of representation. Suppose that the number of bytes per character in our method of representation is n. The value of SubsVector is a hexadecimal string whose first byte is equal to $n - 1$: an initial byte with the value 0x00 means that show will read one byte at a time, 0x001 means that it will read two bytes at a time, and so on. Next come as many n-byte groups as there are subfonts. Each of these groups is a number whose value is the maximum number of glyphs in the subfont. For example, the "8/8 mapping" method uses two bytes per character, the first being the subfont number (thus a maximum of 256 fonts), the second being the glyph number (thus a maximum of 256 glyphs). The corresponding SubsVector string would be 01 followed by 256 repetitions of 0100.

Finally, the method CMap corresponds to an FMapType equal to 9 and works only in Level 3 PostScript. It assumes that a CMap dictionary exists within the font and that it is the dictionary used for finding a subfont number and a glyph number, in the fashion of CID fonts (see the following section). By means of this method, we can use methods specific to CID fonts, even if the root font is not explicitly CID.

The rules to observe when we create Type 0 fonts with several levels of embedding (the root font refers to composite fonts, which in turn refer to other fonts) are quite complex. The reader will find them in [24, pp. 363–364].

C.6.2   The ACFM File

As the reader will have guessed, the 'C' in ACFM comes from "composite". ACFM is a special metric file for composite fonts. Just as with AMFM, we do not find the metrics of individual glyphs in an ACFM file, only general data about the subfonts of the OCF font.

An ACFM file is enclosed within a section StartCompFontMetrics ... EndCompFontMetrics. The entry Descendents gives the number of subfonts provided in the OCF font. After the usual global entries (FontName, FontBBox, Version, etc.) come several entries specific to OCF: EncodingScheme, MappingScheme, EscChar, CharacterSet, Characters, and IsBase-Font, which take the same values as their counterparts in the font.

Then follows a section StartDescendent *min max* ... EndDescendent for each subfont. The values *min* and *max* give the values of the characters in the original string that correspond to the glyphs in the subfont. For each subfont, there are the usual global entries (FontName, FontBBox, Version, etc.) and the entry IsBaseFont, which here takes the value true. We can also have global glyph metrics: in ideographic fonts there is often a CharWidth 500 0, which means that *all* of the glyphs in the font have a set-width of 500 units.

Clearly the description of an OCF font in an ACFM file is only the tip of the iceberg. It is also necessary to have an AFM file for each subfont.

C.7 CID Fonts (Types 9–11, 32)

The idea behind CID fonts is very simple. Over the past 10 years, Adobe has defined *"character collections"* (incorrectly named *character collections*, although they concern glyphs, not characters), containing numbered glyphs: typically we have one character collection for traditional Chinese glyphs, another collection for simplified Chinese glyphs, a collection of Korean glyphs, a collection of Japanese glyphs, etc. CIDs are fonts whose glyphs have no names but are described in relation to a character collection.

A member of a character collection is identified by a number called "CID" (*glyph identifier*), whence the name of this type of font: the glyphs are identified by the CID numbers of a given character collection.

For a CID font, at least two files (or two PostScript resources) are needed:

- The first is called *CMap* (for "character map"), and it establishes the correspondence between characters (as read by the PostScript show operator) and glyphs, in a character collection. Thus it is a somewhat peculiar font encoding: instead of using glyph names as its basis, as do the Type 1 font encodings, it uses CID—i.e., the glyph numbers in a given character collection.

- The second is called *CIDFont*, and it is a sort of Type 1 font with up to 65,536 glyphs that are indexed not by glyph names but by CID numbers.

The traditional findfont operator establishes the connection between CIDFont and CMap: put together, these data form a CID font. Thus we can have arbitrary fonts with arbitrary encodings:[23] the font encoding becomes a separate file, and the merging of the font encoding and the part of the font that contains the glyphs is done automatically when the font is declared in PostScript code.

Below we shall describe CMap and CIDFont files/resources separately. The official specification is found in [11], but [24, pp. 364–370] and [9] are also good introductions to the subject.

---

[23] The concept is not far removed from that of *virtual* fonts in TEX: the font defined by findfont can borrow glyphs from all sorts of fonts (Type 1, Type 3, CID, etc.), in any encoding. The difference is that a virtual font can also combine multiple glyphs into one, which is not possible with the CMap.

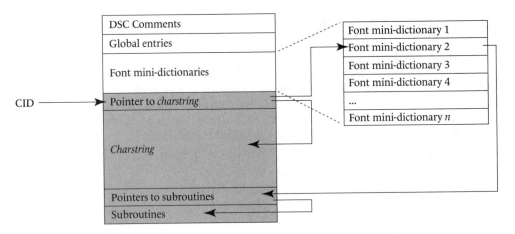

Figure C-16: The overall structure of a CIDFont file (of CID type 0) and the path that must be followed to obtain the data needed for rendering the glyph. The starting point is the datum for the CID number.

C.7.1   CIDFont

The CIDFont file exists in four flavors, identified by their CID type number but also by their "traditional" type number (the same type as for fonts of Type 0, Type 1, Type 3, etc.). Here are these four flavors:

- CID type 0, or "Type 9": the glyphs are described by *charstrings*, as in "Type 1"

- CID type 1, or "Type 10": the glyphs are described by BuildGlyph procedures, as in "Type 3"

- CID type 2, or "Type 11": the glyphs are described by TrueType code, as in "Type 42"

- CID type 4, or "Type 32": the glyphs are bitmaps

Be careful not to confuse "CID type 0" ("Type 1" CID) with "Type 0" (OCF) or "CID type 1" ("Type 3" CID) with "Type 1".

To understand the structure of a CIDFont file, let us recall what a Type 1 font is: global data ("public" and "private"), including the encoding, subroutines, and a set of glyph descriptions.

In the case of CIDs, the encoding is absent (because the glyph name is replaced by the CID identifier to which we have access through a simple table of pointers), and the glyph descriptions do not change. This situation may pose a problem: the "global" data may not be sufficiently global. Specifically, if in a font we mix Latin letters and Chinese ideographs, it is unlikely that the same hinting parameters or the same subroutines will be optimal for both. Thus it would be more desirable to classify the glyphs into a number of sets that share the same characteristics and to create for each set a "mini–font dictionary" containing the set's "private" parameters and subroutines. By "mini–font dictionary", we mean a structure similar to a Type 1 font dictionary, but without the encoding, subroutines, and glyph descriptions. Then each glyph identifier (CID) will be associated with one of these mini–font dictionaries.

When the CMap asks the CIDFont to draw a glyph by supplying the glyph's CID, the interpreter will first look up the CID's entry in a table (see Figure C-16). This table will supply two things: a pointer to the glyph's description, and a number for the corresponding mini–font dictionary. For rendering the glyph, the glyph description is not sufficient: the code for the subroutines, which are also contained in the binary section, is also required. The mini–font dictionary provides a pointer to the table of subroutines, which in turn supplies pointers to the subroutines themselves.

The structure of a CIDFont file is quite simple: there are a few structured comments, a few global entries, a few mini–font dictionaries corresponding to the different types of glyphs in the CID font, and an enormous binary section containing descriptions of the glyphs *en masse*, which sometimes occupies up to 99.9 percent of the space in a CIDFont file.

The section for structured comments in a CIDFont resembles the following code:

```
%!PS-Adobe-.0 Resource-CIDFont
%%DocumentNeededResources: ProcSet (CIDInit)
%%DocumentSuppliedResources: CIDFont (WadaMin-Regular)
%%IncludeResource: ProcSet (CIDInit)
%%BeginResource: CIDFont (WadaMin-Regular)
%%Title: (WadaMin-Regular Adobe Japan1 1)
%%Version: 3.002
```

In the `Title` field, we have the font name followed by three pieces of data that define the character collection with which it is associated (see below).

Next come some global entries that stem from the Type 1 font entries—`FontBBox`, `FontInfo`, etc.—as well as a few entries specific to CID fonts. Of the latter, a few are used for identification:

- `CIDFontType`: the CID type.

- `CIDFontName`: the font name.

- `CIDSystemInfo`: a subdictionary containing three entries of crucial importance. These entries define the character collection with which the font is associated:

  - `Registry`: the name of the organization that defined the character collection.

  - `Ordering`: the name of the language, followed by a number to cover the possibility of having multiple character collections for the same language.

  - `Supplement`: an integer indicating the version of the "supplement". A *supplement* is a batch of glyphs defined at a given moment. Glyph collections are built up from successive supplements. A CID, once defined, cannot be deleted or replaced, but new CIDs can be defined as often as we wish.

- `CIDFontVersion`: the font's version.

Here is an example of entries used for identification:

```
20 dict begin

/CIDFontName /WadaMin-Regular def
/CIDFontVersion 3.002 def
/CIDFontType 0 def

/CIDSystemInfo 3 dict dup begin
  /Registry (Adobe) def
  /Ordering (Japan1) def
  /Supplement 1 def
end def

/FontBBox [ - - 1023 900 ] def
/UIDBase 2483200 def
/XUID [1 11 2483200] def
/FontInfo 5 dict dup begin
  /Notice (\050c\051 Copyright 1996 Adobe Systems
    Incorporated. All rights reserved.) readonly def
  /FullName (WadaMin-Regular) readonly def
  /FamilyName (WadaMin-Regular) readonly def
  /Weight (Medium) readonly def
  /FSType 4 def
end readonly def
```

Next there are four more technical entries that are indispensable for entering the binary section. To understand them, we need only give the description of this block. It begins with a table of fixed-length records. Each of these records is divided into two parts: the first part contains the number of a mini–font dictionary, and the second contains a pointer to the start of a *charstring*, calculated as the offset of bytes from the beginning of the binary section. The length, in bytes, of these two sections is given by the entries FDBytes and GDBytes. The records correspond to consecutive CID numbers. The first record corresponds to the CID number given by the entry CIDMapOffset. The number of records is given by the entry CIDCount, which is the fourth and last of the "technical" entries. Example:

```
/CIDMapOffset 0 def
/FDBytes 1 def
/GDBytes 3 def
/CIDCount 8286 def
```

Finally, there are the mini–font dictionaries. These contain the usual entries of a Type 1 font—BlueValues, BlueScale, BlueFuzz, BlueShift, StdHW, StdVW, StemSnapH, StemSnapV, etc.—as well as three entries specific to CID fonts that give access to subroutines. Once again, it is important to know that the code for the subroutines in the binary section is preceded by a table of records of fixed length. The entry SubrMapOffset is a pointer to the record corresponding to subroutine 0 in the current mini-dictionary, SubrCount gives the number of records, which is the number of subroutines that apply to this mini-dictionary, and SDBytes gives the length of each record in bytes. Each record contains a pointer to the beginning of the code for a subroutine. Counting always begins at 0. There are no "other subroutines" (*OtherSubr*), because these are defined in the global private dictionary of the CIDFont file.

The mini-dictionaries are subentries of the entry FDArray:

```
/FDArray 5 array
dup 0

14 dict            %beginning of mini-dictionary 0
begin
/FontName /WadaMin-Regular-Alphabetic def
/FontType 1 def
/FontMatrix [ 0.001 0 0 0.001 0 0 ] def
/PaintType 0 def

/Private 18 dict dup begin %beginning of private section
  /MinFeature{16 16}def
  /BlueValues [ - 0 800 806 550 575 ] def
...
  /SubrMapOffset 33148 def
  /SDBytes 3 def
  /SubrCount 119 def
end def                     %end of private section

currentdict end %end of mini-dictionary 0

put
dup 1

14 dict            %beginning of mini-dictionary 1
  begin
  /FontName /WadaMin-Regular-Dingbats def
...
def
```

Thus we see that while the font name used in our example[24] is *WadaMin-Regular*, the names of the mini-dictionaries consist of the same name followed by -Alphabetic and -Dingbats. In this same CID font, there are three other mini-dictionaries: -Generic, -Kana, and -Kanji.

Finally, after the final def of the entry FDArray, comes the binary section. This section is preceded by a call to the procedure StartData, which takes two values: a string that is either (Binary) or (Hex) (if the latter, the data are encoded in hexadecimal), and a number indicating the exact length of the binary data. The keyword StartData must be followed by a space. The first byte after the space is the first byte of the data. At the end of the data, three structured comments conclude the file with a flourish:

---

[24] It is a Japanese font freely distributed by Adobe [23].

```
%%EndData
%%EndResource
%%EOF
```

Last but not least, one very important piece of data: the binary section contains no global parameters, only *charstrings* and subroutines, which can be read as needed. There is no need to keep all this data in memory. The PostScript will therefore keep the global parameters and the mini-dictionaries in memory and will leave the binary section on disk, thus allowing Chinese/Japanese/Korean to be typeset on printers with very little RAM available.

C.7.2   CMap

A CMap file is an ASCII file that defines the correspondence between a character encoding and a character collection. There are two types of CMap files: "abstract" ones, which make no reference to a given font, and "concrete" ones, which invoke one or more fonts and thus allow for combining the glyphs of multiple fonts.

Let us begin with "abstract" CMap files. A file of this kind begins with a few structured comments, an identification block, and a number of tables that contain the correspondences between characters in the input and CIDs in the output, etc.

The block of DSC structured comments is typical:

```
%!PS-Adobe-.0 Resource-CMap
%%DocumentNeededResources: ProcSet (CIDInit)
%%DocumentNeededResources: CMap (90ms-RKSJ-H)
%%IncludeResource: ProcSet (CIDInit)
%%IncludeResource: CMap (90ms-RKSJ-H)
%%BeginResource: CMap (90ms-RKSJ-V)
%%Title: (90ms-RKSJ-V Adobe Japan1 2)
%%Version: 11.001
%%EndComments
```

Note that lines 2 and 4 indicate that the current CMap (90ms-RKSJ-V) is based on another CMap, called 90ms-RKSJ-H. The difference between the two is that 90ms-RKSJ-H contains the glyphs for horizontal kanji ideographs, whereas 90ms-RKSJ-V (less often used) contains only the specifically vertical glyphs and shares the vast majority of its glyphs with the first (which are thus both horizontal and vertical). In this case, we will find the operator usecmap at the beginning of the file, as follows:

```
/90ms-RKSJ-H usecmap
```

to load the data from the other CMap file.

The identification block contains the following entries:

- CIDSystemInfo, a dictionary containing three subentries—Registry, Ordering, Supplement—which are strictly the same as for the CIDFont

- CMapName, followed by the name of the CMap

- CMapVersion, followed by the version expressed in the form of a rational number

- CMapType, equal to 1

- possibly an XUID, similar to that of the Type 1 fonts

- WMode, followed by 0 if the direction of writing is horizontal, and 1 if it is vertical

Here is an example, again drawn from the same CMap:

```
/CIDSystemInfo 3 dict dup begin
  /Registry (Adobe) def
  /Ordering (Japan1) def
  /Supplement 2 def
end def
/CMapName /90ms-RKSJ-V def
/CMapVersion 11.001 def
/CMapType 1 def
/XUID [1 10 25344] def
/WMode 1 def
```

Next begin the tables of correspondences. As a general rule, each table foo is delimited by the operators beginfoo and endfoo. The operator beginfoo is preceded by the number of entries in the table. A table can contain at most 100 entries; if more are needed, we start a new table of the same type.

The first table, codespacerange (CID), indicates the set of *valid* characters—i.e., those that we expect to read in the input. It turns out to be crucial for knowing whether we should read 1, 2, 3, or 4 bytes in the input in order to obtain one character. For example, the codespacerange of the Shift-JIS encoding is

```
4 begincodespacerange
  <00> <80>     % JIS X 0201- Roman
  <8140> <9FFC> % The first 16-bit block
  <A0> <DF>     % Half-width katakana
  <E040> <FCFC> % The second 16-bit block
endcodespacerange
```

which means that we can expect to read single bytes between 0x00 and 0x80, or between 0xA0 and 0xDF. But if we ever come upon a byte between 0x81 and 0x9F, or between 0xE0 and 0xFC, we will read a second byte, and the two bytes together will form the character from the input.

The most important table is the one that matches characters with CIDs. For practical reasons, these tables come in two types: one for ranges of consecutive characters and CIDs (cidrange), and one for isolated characters (cidchar). Example:

```
2 begincidrange
  <20> <7F>     132
  <A20> <A7F>   847
endcidrange

2 begincidchar
  <80> 247
  <FFFD> 3972
endcidchar
```

In this example, we match the consecutive characters between 0x20 and 0x7F with the same number of consecutive CIDs, starting with CID 132 (and therefore ending with CID 240; there is no need to write it explicitly). Next, we match the interval [0xA20, 0xA7F] to the CIDs [847, 955]. Finally, the second table allows us to match the characters 0x80 and 0xFFFD directly with the CIDs 97 and 3972. Reminder: hexadecimal numbers can be recognized by the fact that they are enclosed in angle brackets.

What happens if the input contains a character for which there is unfortunately no CID in the font? Remember that in Type 1 fonts we must always have a glyph called .notdef, which takes care of such situations. Here, however, we can have a different glyph according to the range in which the character appears. Those glyphs are configured in the table notdefrange, by which ranges of characters are matched to CIDs. Example:

```
1 beginnotdefrange
  <A1> <DF> 1
endnotdefrange
```

which maps the characters between 0xA1 and 0xDF (in the Shift-JIS encoding, these are the half-width katakana ｶﾀｶﾅ; compare the full-width katakana, カタカナ) to CID 1. Everything that is not listed is mapped to CID 0. What is the benefit of this operation? If we leave aside for the moment any possible kerning, all the ideographs have the same set-width. Some of them are condensed and have half the width of the others. If the glyph for substitution has the same width as the missing glyph, the document's layout will be preserved, despite the substitution of glyphs.

Finally, we can indicate the font's current transformation matrix with the operators begin-usematrix *[...]* endusematrix.

C.7.3   *Rearrangement of a CID font*

Now let us discuss the "concrete" CMap fonts [11, §6]. The problem that must be solved is the following: when we write, for example, in Japanese, we merrily mix four types of script. These scripts are the kanji (漢字) ideographs of Chinese origin, the syllabic scripts hiragana (ひら がな) and katakana (カタカナ), and the altered Latin script r o m a j i. "Altered", in the sense that the Latin letters must obey the same rules for set-width as the ideographs: thus they will be of full width or of half width, even if that seems a l i t t l e b i z a r r e t o u s W e s t e r n e r s. A self-respecting Japanese CID font will necessarily contain the glyphs required for these four types of script.

Now suppose that we wish to mix our kanji with the kana of another font and with the Latin letters of yet another font. The visual result is certainly promising, but we will have to change the font, using the mouse, every two or three characters from the beginning of the document to the end, which means thousands of times. Could we do so without losing our mental health? Not likely.

Once again approaching TEX's concept of *virtual fonts*, Adobe offers another type of CMap file, with explicit indication of the fonts being used. The procedure is called *font rearrangement*, and we can use it to combine any number of fonts of any type (Type 0, Type 1, Type 3, Type 42, or CIDFont). Each font can have its own current transformation matrix and can also be scaled, translated, rotated, or reflected.

The syntax is very simple: first, we use the operator beginrearrangedfont to define the new font and to indicate the fonts on which it will be based. This operator takes the name of the font as its first argument and a table containing the names of the base fonts as its second argument. Example:

```
/Jun101-Light-K-G-R-pv-RKSJ-H
[ /Jun101-Light-pv-RKSJ-H
  /Palatino-Roman
  /ShinseiKai-CBSK1-pv-RKSJ-H
  /FutoGoB101-Bold-pv-RKSJ-H
  /FutoMinA101-Bold-pv-RKSJ-H
  /HSMinW3Gai30
] beginrearrangedfont
```

In the first position (position 0), we have the original font; then, in any order, come the fonts from which we are going to borrow glyphs. For example, in position 1, we have the font Palatino-Roman, which is of Type 1. The rearranged font should be regarded as a variant of font 0, which thus is of paramount importance; in particular, font 0 must be a CID font.

The usefont operator takes the font number in the table as its argument. But since up to now we have seen only cidrange and cidchar tables that return CID numbers, which non-CID fonts do not have, we need a new type of table: the bfrange and bfchar tables ("bf" comes from "base font") match up ranges of characters or isolated characters with glyph names or code points in the font's encoding.

For example, by writing:

```
1 usefont

1 beginbfrange
<30> <39> <30>
endbfrange

2 beginbfchar
<5C> yen
<7F> <7F>
endbfchar
```

we replace the digits, the yen sign, and the mysterious character 0x7F in *Jun101-Light-83pv-RKSJ-H* with those from *Palatino-Roman*.

We can use the operators beginusematrix *[...]* endusematrix with a different value for each base font. We write the number of the font as the argument to the operator beginusematrix:

```
1 beginusematrix
  [1.1 0 0 1.1 0 0]
endusematrix
```

Here we scale the glyphs from the font *Palatino-Roman* up by a factor of 110 percent.

One last small detail: to ensure the successful inclusion of all the files needed for the PostScript project, we should also include a number of structured comments at the beginning of the file, as shown:

```
%!PS-Adobe-.0 Resource-Font
%%ADOResourceSubCategory: RearrangedFont
%%DocumentNeededResources: procset CIDInit
%%+ font Jun101-Light-pv-RKSJ-H
%%+ font Palatino-Roman
%%+ font ShinseiKai-CBSK1-pv-RKSJ-H
%%+ font FutoGoB101-Bold-pv-RKSJ-H
%%+ font FutoMinA101-Bold-pv-RKSJ-H
%%+ font HSMinW3Gai30
%%IncludeResource: procset CIDInit
%%IncludeResource: font Palatino-Roman
%%IncludeResource: font HSMinW3Gai30
%%BeginResource:Font Jun101-Light-K-G-R-pv-RKSJ-H
%%Version: 1
```

C.7.4   The AFM File for the CID Font

Unlike OCF fonts, which have their own AFM file format called ACFM, the CID fonts use ordinary AFM files. Only two differences reveal that the font is a CID font: an entry IsCIDFont, which takes the value true, and the fact that there are numbers instead of glyph names.

C.7.5   Using a CID Font

Last but not least, how do we use a CID font in a PostScript file?

We simply use the classic findfont operator and specify as its argument a CIDFont name followed by *two hyphens* and a CMap name [11, Appendix B]:

```
WadaMin-Regular--ms-RKSJ-V findfont
```

There could hardly be a simpler approach. If the font is a rearranged font, we use the name of its CMap.

C.8   Type 2/CFF Fonts

Type 2 and CFF fonts are the *ne plus ultra* of Adobe font technology. There has never been a Type 2 font or a CFF font.[25] If the reader finds these two sentences contradictory, she does not know Adobe very well. Let us clarify the matter (as much as we can): "Type 2" [15] is not a type of font but a type of *charstring*—in other words, a type of glyph description. The *charstrings* of traditional Type 1 fonts were of Type 1, without being aware of it. Now we have *charstrings* of Type 2, which are more powerful and more efficient.

CFF (for "compact font format") [14] is not a font format either, despite its name. It is a way to compress existing font formats, in particular the two most successful formats: Type 1 fonts and CIDs.

Wait! We are not finished. When we compress Type 1 or CID fonts, Adobe requires us to use *charstrings* of Type 2. Can we use the result as an alternative to traditional fonts? Is it a new type of font? Not at all! The only way to use a CFF font is *within an OpenType font*, in the form of a CFF table.

Thus both Type 2 and the CFF format were created to make PostScript fonts easier to incorporate into an OpenType font structure.[26] There has been a precursor to this: at some time, in the early days, it was possible to insert a complete Type 1 PostScript font in a special, nowadays obsolete, TrueType table called typ1. On the Mac, such a font looks like any other TrueType font (a font suitcase containing a **sfnt** resource), it is only by investigating the tables contained in the TrueType structure that one discovers the existence of PostScript data. Once extracted, the PostScript data can be saved in a PFA file and used normally.

C.8.1   The Compact Font Format

This format is a different way to write code in binary, more powerful than the approach of Type 1 fonts. Fortunately, the tool TTX, used to display OpenType fonts in a human-readable form, can also handle CFF code. In this book, we have decided to (re)present TrueType and OpenType code using TTX; and CFF will be no exception. Thus we shall focus on CFF as represented by TTX rather than looking at the actual binary data.

TTX is based on XML. What we usually consider to be an entry in a PostScript dictionary becomes an XML element here. If the value of the entry is a number or a string, it is represented in TTX by a value attribute. If it is a subdictionary, we obtain an XML subelement. Only *charstrings* are always represented as PostScript code.

Here is an example of a CFF table as seen through TTX:

```
<CFF>
<CFFFont name="ComputerModern-Regular">
  <version value="002.000"/>
  <Notice value="Copyright (c) Selwyn Hollis."/>
```

---

[25] With the possible exception of a few fonts woven on the spot into the PDF files produced by Acrobat Distiller. We have learned that FontForge will henceforth produce CFF fonts without an OpenType wrapper.

[26] That also explains why we did not mention Type 42 when we mentioned the "most successful font formats" two paragraphs earlier: incorporating a TrueType font into a PostScript font that was in turn incorporated into an OpenType font would be befitting of the Marquis de Sade.

```
    <Copyright value="Computer Modern typefaces..."/>
    <FullName value="ComputerModern Regular"/>
    <FamilyName value="ComputerModern"/>
    <Weight value="Regular"/>
    <isFixedPitch value="0"/>
    <ItalicAngle value="0"/>
    <UnderlinePosition value="-"/>
    <UnderlineThickness value="40"/>
    <PaintType value="0"/>
    <CharstringType value="2"/>
    <FontMatrix value="0.001 0 0 0.001 0 0"/>
    <UniqueID value="4113773"/>
    <FontBBox value="- - 1195 940"/>
    <StrokeWidth value="0"/>
    <Encoding value="0"/>
    <Private>
<BlueValues value="- 0 431 448 514 528 652 666 680 705"/>
<OtherBlues value="- -"/>
<BlueScale value="0.36364"/>
<BlueShift value="7"/>
<BlueFuzz value="1"/>
<StdHW value="31"/>
<StdVW value="25"/>
<StemSnapH value="22 25 31 40"/>
<StemSnapV value="25 66 69 83"/>
<ForceBold value="0"/>
<LanguageGroup value="0"/>
<ExpansionFactor value="0.06"/>
<initialRandomSeed value="0"/>
<defaultWidthX value="500"/>
<nominalWidthX value="673"/>
<Subrs>
  <CharString index="0">
hvcurveto
- - - - - - - - rlinecurve
- callsubr
23 43 2 36 hhcurveto
31 26 callgsubr
...
  </CharString>
</Subrs>
  </Private>
  <CharStrings>
<CharString name=".notdef">
  endchar
</CharString>
```

```
<CharString name="A">
  - callgsubr
  457 - hstem
  - callsubr
  endchar
</CharString>
...
  </CharStrings>
</CFFFont>

<GlobalSubrs>
  <CharString index="0">
rmoveto
- 4 27 - 47 hhcurveto
21 61 14 81 hvcurveto
56 - - vlineto
...
  </CharString>
  ...
</GlobalSubrs>
</CFF>
```

There can be several CFF fonts in a CFF table: they are represented by CFFFont elements. Their subelements correspond to entries in the Type 1 (or CID, as the case may be) font dictionary. There is one new element: CharStringType, which takes the value 2.

Each of the fonts may have its own local subroutines (the element Subrs), but there can also be global subroutines (the element GlobalSubrs). The glyph descriptions are found in the element CharStrings. Under a subroutine (be it local or global) or under CharStrings (with an 's'), we find CharString elements (without the 's'). In the case of subroutines, these elements contain an attribute index, which makes their order explicit. In the case of glyph descriptions, they have an attribute name, whose value is the glyph's name. But beware: appearances are deceiving. It is TTX that assigned the names to the glyph descriptions, using a number of internal tables, in order to make it easier for us to read the XML document. The correspondence is not so direct; in fact, in an OpenType font, the glyphs are obtained by their indices in a table, not by their names.

In any event, the XML representation of a CFF table seems cleaner than the representation in text format of a Type 1 font, and that is no accident. For instance, the attentive reader will have noticed that this font does not have any "other subroutines"; thus we have managed to avoid that nightmare dating back to the 1980s: PostScript code that was hard to understand, that could not be modified, and that, finally, was part of the system of that "black box" known as the rendering engine for Type 1 fonts. Also missing are the obscure but obligatory entries such as MinFeature and password. Good riddance!

Let us now move on to the syntax of the *charstrings* of Type 2.

C.8.2   *The charstrings of Type 2*

In the transition from *charstrings* of Type 1 to those of Type 2, Adobe killed three birds on one stone:

1. Clean-up. All the constructions with uncertain syntax (hstem3, *flex*, hint replacements, counter controls) now have their own elegant and concise operators. In addition, irritating operators such as callothersub were eliminated.

2. Compression. Much was done to reduce the size of the code.

3. Innovation. There are new features: oblique *flex*, more arithmetic operations, and even a random-number generator.

The general schema of a *charstring* of Type 2 is as follows: First, we give the glyph's set-width, not followed by any operator. Next come, in order, the horizontal hints, the vertical hints, the counter controls, and the hint replacements. Finally, one movement operator, followed by a closed path. If there are other paths, they must be preceded by a movement operator.

Before moving on to the description of the operators, let us take note of one striking peculiarity of the new syntax: the operators are *polymorphic*, in the sense that they can read a variable number of arguments and change their behavior accordingly. A simple example: the rlineto operator usually takes two arguments: the coordinates of the ending point of the line that is to be drawn. In fact, we can supply up to 24 pairs of arguments (a limit imposed by the implementation; see [15, Appendix B]), and it will be executed as many times. Similarly, most operators also accept a variable number of arguments; their behavior changes according to rules that are sometimes quite elaborate.

Here is a brief description of the most important operators. The reader will find a detailed description in [15, §4].

Let us begin with the simplest case: movement operators. There are three of them: one for arbitrary movement (rmoveto, two arguments), one for horizontal movement (hmoveto, one argument), and one for vertical movement (vmoveto, one argument). The arguments are always relative: they express movement relative to the current point.

We can draw straight lines or cubic Bézier curves starting from the current point. For the former, we use three operators, just as for movement: rlineto (two arguments: the offset of the ending point relative to the starting point), hlineto (one argument: the horizontal offset), vlineto (one argument: the vertical offset); for the latter, we can use the operator rrcurveto (six arguments). This operator has two 'r's in its name because it is doubly relative: specifically, the six arguments express the offset of the first control point relative to the starting point, the offset of the second control point relative to the first, and the offset of the ending point relative to the second control point. There are four "abbreviated" forms of this operator, according to the tangents of the starting and ending points: hhcurveto (four arguments, horizontal tangents), hvcurveto (four arguments, horizontal and vertical tangents), hvcurveto (four arguments, vertical and horizontal tangents), hhcurveto (four arguments, vertical tangents). There are also two operators that combine Bézier curves and line segments: rcurveline (eight arguments) draws first a curve and then a line; rlinecurve does the opposite.

There are several arithmetic operators: abs (absolute value), add (addition), sub (subtraction), div (division), neg (change of sign), random (generation of a random rational number in the interval $(0, 1]$), mul (multiplication), sqrt (square root). Some logical operators and tests: and, or, not, eq (tests whether two numbers are equal; returns 0 or 1), a b c d ifelse (returns a if $a \leq b$, otherwise b). There are also some operators for stack management: drop (discards an element from the stack), exch (swaps the top two elements on the stack), dup (duplicates the top element on the stack), n index (replaces n with the nth element below it), n j roll (makes j cyclic permutations of the n elements below).

There are also 32 areas in memory for temporarily storing numerical values (at the level of a *charstring*). We store them with put and retrieve them with get. That has never been necessary in PostScript, since we can simply place the values on the stack and retrieve them when we need them. But most of the operators for *charstrings* of Type 2 reset the stack after their execution; thus another way for storing useful numerical values is needed.

Finally, endchar (with no arguments) ends the description of a glyph.

The remaining operators are for subroutines, *flex*, and hints. Subroutines are called with callsubr (or callgsubr, if the subroutine is a global one), which takes one argument: the number of the subroutine in question. The code inside a subroutine is constructed from any Type 2 operators and must end with a return or an endchar if the *charstring* ends with the subroutine in question.

The flex operator takes no fewer than 13 arguments: the coordinates (relative to the current point) of the starting point, the control points, and the ending points of the two curves, and, at the end, the threshold, expressed in hundredths of a pixel, below which the curves are so flat that they become a straight line. If we use the notation of Figure C-11 (§C-11), the arguments are the relative coordinates of points b, c, d, e, f, and g; and if the threshold is T, the distance dd' must be smaller than T hundredths of a pixel for the curves to become straight. Note once again that the restrictions imposed on Type 1 *flex* (horizontal or vertical orientation, etc.) have been removed, and we can have *flex* at any angle. There are also the abbreviated versions flex1, hflex, and hflex1 for the cases in which the curves have horizontal tangents.

C.8.2.1   *Hints in charstrings of Type 2*

We have come to hint management, whose syntax is much simpler than that of Type 1 *charstrings*. The methods used for hints are exactly the same (simple hints, ghost hints, hstem3, hint replacement, counter control), but the way to represent them in code is much cleaner.

First, all the hints are declared at the *beginning of the charstring*, irrespective of whether some of them overlap. They are declared from left to right (or from bottom to top), relative to their left (or lower) edges. No other hint can be declared later. The operators hstem and vstem are used to declare hints, unless there is at least one hint replacement in the glyph; in that case, the operators hstemhm and vstemhm are used instead.

Hints always have a positive thickness, with the exception of ghost hints, which have a thickness of -20 (when the desired alignment is towards the right/top) or -21 (when the alignment is towards the left/bottom).

Now suppose that we have declared our horizontal and vertical hints. If some hints overlap, we must be able to enable and disable some of them while the glyph is being drawn (see

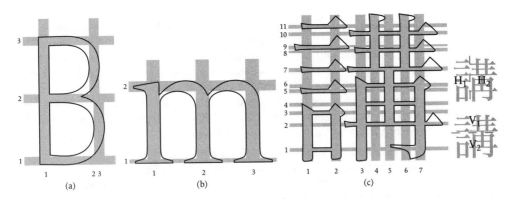

Figure C-17: Hint management in charstrings of Type 2. From left to right: hint replacement, counter control for three downstrokes, counter control for 11 horizontal and 7 vertical strokes.

Figure C-10). Here is how we proceed: we associate a bit with each hint; the bit will have the value 1 if the hint is enabled, otherwise 0. These bits aligned in order (horizontal hints first) form a number with as many bytes as necessary: we pad it with zeroes to obtain complete bytes. This number is called the *hint mask*. The hintmask operator, *followed*[27] by the hint mask, will enable the hint indicated in the mask. This operator, and it alone, may appear anywhere in the code for the *charstring*.

Let us examine the example in Figure C-17 (a): there are three horizontal hints and three vertical hints. Of the latter, hints 2 and 3 touch. Thus we must enable hint 2 at one time and hint 3 at another. There are therefore two masks: 11011100, which is the number 220, and 10111100, which is 188. By writing hintmask 220 and hintmask 188, we switch from one configuration of enabled hints to the other. Note that there is only one hintmask, which manages horizontal and vertical hints at the same time.

The management of counter controls is similar: the strokes on the two sides of each counter must have hints; we create a mask by enabling the hints corresponding to them. The operator cntrmask, followed by this mask, declares a set of counter controls. Unlike hintmask, the cntrmask operators all appear at the *beginning* of the *charstring*, before the first drawing instruction. In Figure C-17 (c), we see the ideograph 講 (*kô*, "oration"), which has 11 horizontal hints and 7 vertical hints. We must therefore define the two horizontal zones H_1 and H_2 and the two vertical zones V_1 and V_2. Thus we shall use the operator cntrmask twice, combining the first and second horizontal and vertical zones. The horizontal hints of zone H_1 are 1, 3, 5, 7, 9, 11; the others are in zone H_2. Likewise, the vertical hints of zone V_1 are 4 and 6, and those of zone V_2 are 1, 2, 3, 5, 7. The two corresponding masks are therefore 10101010101000101000000 (11,182,720) and 010101010101110101000000 (5,594,432).

As with Type 1, counter control works only if LanguageGroup has the value 1; otherwise we can still use cntrmask, but only with three strokes: we have the functionality of the old operators hstem3 and vstem3, which is useful for the letters 'm' and 'Ξ'. For example, in Figure C-17 (b) we have the letter 'm', whose three downstrokes have the hints 1, 2, and 3. The mask of cn-

---

[27] Warning! Arguments usually precede their operators; hintmask is an exception.

trmask will therefore be 11111 (31). This mask is unique, since there is only one zone, and therefore all the hints can be enabled at the same time.

The TrueType, OpenType, and AAT Font Formats

Microsoft is not the only company that wants to take over the world. To a smaller degree, Adobe also sought to control the world of printing during the years 1987 through 1989, i.e., when its PostScript language first met with success. That was a source of no little worry to the two giants of the day (Apple and Microsoft), who started looking for another system for rendering fonts on screen. The two companies joined forces to develop one such system and thus break free of Adobe. Apple was supposed to be in charge of the fonts, and Microsoft was responsible for the engine for rendering graphics. The product that Microsoft promised to Apple was called *TrueImage*. But TrueImage never saw the light of day. For its part, Apple had a number of projects in hand. One project, called *Royal*, by a Finnish engineer named Sampo Kaasila, was selected and delivered to Microsoft.

Microsoft renamed it: "TrueType" was a better match for "TrueImage". In March 1991, Apple released a preliminary version of TrueType as a plug-in for its Mac OS 6. Microsoft took one year longer to incorporate TrueType into Windows 3.1 in 1992 [258]. The beginnings of TrueType under Windows were difficult because Kaasila, working with Apple, naturally wrote the code for 32-bit machines, whereas Windows 3.1 was still at 16 bits. These problems were not really resolved until 1995, with the release of Windows 95. During the 1990s, Mac OS and Windows equipped their respective operating systems with TrueType fonts exclusively. At the same time, both Apple and Microsoft were working independently on extensions to TrueType.

Apple had a great deal invested in *TrueType GX* ('GX' for "graphics extended") [54, 55], a technology that added several new features to TrueType, notably for the typesetting of East Asian scripts. Apple adopted the approach of *finite automata*, where contextual analysis is done through *states*. The rendering engine is considered to be in a certain state, the current state, at any moment. It can move from one state to another according to the glyphs that it is processing; conversely, it can process glyphs differently according to the current state.

It goes without saying that GX technology never really has won the hearts of the "specialists" in graphic design and publishing—Quark and Adobe. After all, if the fonts are too intelligent, there is less work for the desktop publishing software, thus there are fewer reasons to buy it. Not to mention that both Quark and Adobe have for ages been issuing their software in Windows and Macintosh versions, with the same functionality, at least in theory. But GX exists only for Mac OS—one more reason not to invest in this technology. To exorcise this commercial failure, the name "TrueType GX" was abandoned, and the technology was rechristened AAT (for "Apple advanced typography"). AAT is an integral part of Mac OS X.

Microsoft has done work on *TrueType Open* [259]. This technology also addresses East Asian scripts, but only through the use of the *context*. In other words, the shape of a glyph depends on the glyphs that precede it and those that follow it. The more precise the context described in the font, the smarter the transformation of the glyphs can be. TrueType Open was developed jointly with Adobe.[1] To fill the gap between TrueType and PostScript, Adobe provided for the inclusion of PostScript data in TrueType fonts, within a special table called CFF (see Appendix C). Finally, "TrueType Open" (a name that reminds us a bit too much of the tennis championship known as the "U.S. Open") was renamed "OpenType".

In this chapter, we shall describe, in order, the basic TrueType format, the OpenType extensions, and the AAT extensions. This description will be facilitated by the fact that the data in a TrueType font are stored in *tables*. Since each table has a very specific role, the data contained therein are clearly classified (unlike those of PostScript fonts, where everything is jumbled together). In TrueType there are required tables and optional tables; and OpenType and AAT have additional tables of their own. In addition, the TrueType file format is a tolerant one: the rendering engine, be it for TrueType, OpenType, or AAT, collects the data that it requires from only the tables that it recognizes; the presence of other tables, ones that it may not recognize at all, does not bother it in the least. Even better, every font developer can define new tables and include them in fonts. If the fonts in question are meant to be distributed, the new table names can be registered with Apple (for AAT) or with the OpenType Consortium (for OpenType). The discussion forum opentype@topica.com, which is followed by officials at Adobe and Microsoft, is the ideal place to discuss proposals for new tables.

Before we continue with the description of TrueType tables, one little word on the wonderful tool TTX, which allows us to manipulate these fonts in a user-friendly manner far removed from the binary editors, pointers, checksums, and all the other things that are the daily bread of low-level programmers but that need not concern font designers.

D.1 TTX: TrueType Fonts Represented in XML

Unlike PostScript fonts, TrueType is a completely binary font format. The system of tables is technically efficient precisely because the TrueType file teems with *pointers* to the tables and, beyond that, to entries within the tables. By following pointers, software that recognizes the

---

[1] Such is the ballet of alliances and rivalries: at the end of the 1980s, it was Microsoft and Apple against Adobe; a decade later, it is Microsoft and Adobe against Apple. In 2010, we may perhaps see an alliance of Apple and Adobe against Microsoft, if the first two have not been bought out by the third in the meantime.

structure of the tables will thus very quickly find the data that it needs. It is a clean, rapid, and efficient approach. At the same time, however, it is rather badly designed for humans. Unlike PostScript fonts, in which one can read and even modify the code through a conversion with *t1disasm* and *t1binary*, these fonts cannot be handled by a human who does not have a binary editor and a great deal of patience.

To bridge this gap, font designer Just van Rossum, brother of the famous creator of the Python language, Guido van Rossum, developed a free tool in 2001, called TTX ('TT' for "TrueType" and 'X' for "XML"), which converts TrueType into a human-readable format, the file format also being called TTX. The most attractive feature of this tool is that it also performs the *opposite* operation just as easily: from a TTX file, it can generate another TrueType font that is identical to the original. Thus we can say that TTF and TTX are *equivalent*, in the sense that they contain the same data.

Following the general principle on which this book was organized, we shall describe TTX in this appendix rather than TTF: thus we shall be able to focus on the essential, leaving aside all the boring issues of pointers, offsets, short and long numbers, signed and unsigned numbers, etc.

Even better, the TTX format is based on the XML markup system. Thus a TrueType font becomes an XML document, a TrueType table becomes an XML element, the entries in the table become subelements or attributes, etc. This approach makes the hierarchy of the data in a TrueType font even clearer. Do not worry if you are not familiar with XML: here we shall use only the rudiments of the system. In fact, we shall use it merely as a syntax for representing data.[2] On page 345 in Chapter 10, we give a brief introduction to this syntax in the scope of an introduction to the SVG fonts, which are also described in XML.

Now let us talk about the program TTX [307].

There are binary versions for Mac OS 9 and Windows; for other systems, it is a simple matter to obtain the source code and compile it oneself.[3]

To convert `foo.ttf` into `foo.ttx`, we write:

```
ttx foo.ttf
```

Likewise, for the opposite conversion, from TTX to TTF:

```
ttx foo.ttx
```

Note that the TTX file is often more than 10 times larger than the original TTF. The command-line option `-l` gives us a list of the tables in the font; for instance, TTX generates the following list for the OpenType font *Palatino Linotype*:

---

[2] In particular, there will be no DTD, no schemas, no validation, no XSL transformation, no advanced XML techniques.

[3] To do so, one must also obtain the numpy library for numerical calculations [63], and then the source code in Python. To install Python libraries, one goes into the top-level directory of the uncompressed source code and runs `python setup.py install` while logged in as root.

```
ttx -l pala.ttf
Listing table info for "pala.ttf":
    tag     checksum    length    offset
    ----    ----------  -------   -------
    BASE    0x7b5692db       86    483316
    DSIG    0x6edef86c     5360    501476
    GDEF    0x4106d6ad     1078    483404
    GPOS    0x8193c0a3    13096    484484
    GSUB    0x9e8956bf     3648    497580
    JSTF    0x58023ab0      248    501228
    LTSH    0x0d0716a6     1332     27072
    OS/2    0x7db7af65       96       536
    PCLT    0x5f35eba2       54    483260
    VDMX    0xfaaee43a     3002     28404
    cmap    0x5bd843ef     8882     12872
    cvt     0x03bf08d3     1260     37316
    fpgm    0x1c783cd8     1432     35884
    gasp    0x00180009       16       632
    glyf    0x2a83b1cb   397836     71868
    hdmx    0x463cb359    27980     43888
    head    0xd1e333a7       54       412
    hhea    0x12870cbc       36       468
    hmtx    0x54010411     5312     38576
    kern    0x4d914fd6      906    482352
    loca    0x123a1952     5316     21756
    maxp    0x0ee612f2       32       504
    name    0xe1785cd3    12221       648
    post    0xbffb3888    12647    469704
    prep    0x053578ed     4475     31408
```

The tables are presented in alphabetical order (first uppercase letters, then lowercase), and the checksum, length, and pointer to the start of the table is also given in each entry.

Other interesting options:

- The option -s allows us to store each table in a separate file. There will be as many files pala.B_A_S_E_.ttx,[4] pala.D_S_I_G_.ttx, pala.G_D_E_F_.ttx, ... , as there are True-Type tables and also a coordination file pala.ttx containing a list of the generated files. The opposite procedure is, of course, also possible. One must merely ensure that all the files are in the same directory.

---

[4] The reader must be wondering why TTX inserts underscores into the tables' names. The answer is very simple. The case of the ASCII characters that make up a table name is significant: BASE, base, baSe, etc., must not be mixed up. But not all operating systems are sufficiently advanced to distinguish uppercase and lowercase letters. Therefore, TTX's approach involves saying "we shall place an underscore *before* a lowercase letter and *after* a capital. Thus the three examples that we just gave would become B_A_S_E_, _b_a_s_e, _b_aS__e; the names are unambiguous, even under primitive operating systems such as MS-DOS, without naming names.

- If we write -t followed by a table name, only that table will be extracted. To obtain multiple tables, we use this option multiple times. Warning: do not forget any space characters that occur in the table name. Example: `ttx -t "cvt " pala.ttf`.

- -x followed by a table name: do not extract the table in question. To specify multiple tables, use this option several times. The same precautions apply.

D.2 TrueType Collections

A *TrueType collection* (TTC) [258] is a file with the extension `.ttc` that contains a set of True-Type fonts that share some tables. The header of a file of this sort is also a TrueType table, named `ttcf`. What is interesting about a TTC relative to the individual TTFs that it contains is the fact that the TTFs can share a large part of their resources. For example, recall that the Japanese language has four scripts: the kanji (漢字) ideographs, of Chinese origin; the hiragana (ひらがな) and katakana (カタカナ) syllabaries; and the "modified" Latin script ｒｏｍａ ｊ ｉ. Thus we can easily imagine Japanese fonts that share the kanji but contain different kana or different Latin letters.[5] Given that the kanji make up perhaps 95 to 99 percent of the total volume of the glyph descriptions, it would be strictly redundant to have the same kanji in multiple Japanese fonts. In a TTC, we can set things up so that the same table of glyphs (for all the glyphs, including the different versions of kana) is used in different ways, which is equivalent to providing several TrueType fonts.

TTX processes TTCs by converting the fonts that they contain into separate TTX files, then combining all of these files into a TTC once again. Optimizations of the structure are performed automatically: every time TTX comes across two tables with the same checksum, it considers them to be data shared by different fonts in the collection. Thus it is necessary to make sure that the tables are strictly identical (with cut-and-paste operations, if necessary). For instance, by running:

```
ttx msmincho.ttc
```

we obtain `msmincho1.ttx`, `msmincho2.ttx`, and `msmincho3.ttx`. Conversely, when we run:

```
ttx -collect msmincho1.ttx msmincho2.ttx msmincho3.ttx -o msmincho.ttc
```

the three fonts are assembled into a TTC collection.

D.3 General Overview of TrueType Tables

The tables of a TrueType, OpenType, or AAT font are identified by a *tag*, which must be a string of four ASCII characters (possibly including spaces, but only at the end of the string). Tags that are entirely in lowercase are the private hunting ground of Apple. It was doubtless

---

[5] We have already seen this sort of situation during the rearrangement of a CID font (§C.7.3). It shows that each font system tries to solve this problem, inherent in the Japanese language, as well as it can. The same problem arises every time scripts are mixed: in Korean, for example, we can combine hangul (한글) and hanja (漢字), etc.

in response to that that the OpenType-specific tables, as we shall see, use tags consisting of uppercase letters only.

There are some tables that are required in every TrueType font, therefore also in OpenType and AAT fonts:

- cmap (mapping between characters and glyphs, §D.4.2).

- head (header, §D.4.3).

- hhea (header for the horizontal metrics, §D.4.4).

- hmtx (horizontal metrics, §D.4.4).

- maxp (maximum profile, §D.4.5).

- name (table of names, §D.4.6).

- OS/2 (information related to OS/2 and Windows, §D.4.7). Microsoft considers it mandatory, but Apple does not.

- post (information that is useful when the font is used in a PostScript environment, §D.4.8).

Next, everything depends on whether the glyph descriptions are written in TrueType or in PostScript. In the first case, there are five other tables that must not be missing:

- cvt (table of control values, §D.5.3)

- fpgm (font program, §D.5.3)

- glyf (glyph descriptions, §D.5.2)

- loca (pointers to the glyph descriptions, §D.5.1)

- prep (program of control values, §D.5.3)

In the second case, which is the one seen in Appendix C, §C.8, where the OpenType font contains a PostScript CFF font with Type 2 *charstrings*, there are two required tables:

- CFF [OpenType] (PostScript CFF font, §D.6.1)

- VORG [OpenType] (coordinates of the origins of the glyphs for vertical typesetting, §D.6.2)

Note that in the earliest versions of OpenType there were two other tables: MMSD (Multiple Master supplementary data) and MMFX (Multiple Master font metrics), which contained information on PostScript Multiple Master fonts. These were abandoned in version 1.3, and we shall not describe them.

Some tables manage bitmap fonts:

- EBDT (bitmap data, §D.7.1), an extension of bdat [AAT]

- EBLC (pointers to bitmap data, §D.7.1), an extension of bloc [AAT]
- EBSC (data on the scaling of bitmaps, §D.7.2)
- bhed [AAT] (the head table, which was renamed only to show that the font is a bitmap font, §D.7.3)

A few other optional tables:

- DSIG [OpenType] (digital signature, §D.8.1)
- gasp (fitting to the grid, §D.8.2)
- hdmx (horizontal metrics relative to the rendering device, §D.8.3)
- kern (kerning, §D.8.4)
- LTSH (linear threshold, §D.8.3)
- PCLT (data for the PCL 5 printer, §D.8.7)
- VDMX (vertical metrics relative to the rendering device, §D.8.5)
- vhea (header for vertical metrics, §D.8.6)
- vmtx (vertical metrics, §D.8.6)

Finally, let us discuss the TrueType extensions as such. These are "advanced" OpenType and AAT tables:

- BASE [OpenType] (table of the different baselines, §D.9.2)
- GDEF [OpenType] (various definitions, §D.9.6)
- GPOS [OpenType] (glyph positionings, §D.9.3)
- GSUB [OpenType] (glyph substitutions, §D.9.4)
- JSTF [OpenType] (justification, §D.9.5)
- acnt [AAT] (attachment of accents, §D.11.1)
- avar [AAT] (variation of the axes, §D.12.2)
- bsln [AAT] (different baselines, §D.11.2)
- cvar [AAT] (variation of the control values, §D.12.4)
- fdsc [AAT] (font descriptors, §D.11.3)
- feat [AAT] (features of the font, §D.11.5)
- fmtx [AAT] (font metrics, §D.11.4)

- fvar [AAT] (font variation, §D.12.1)

- gvar [AAT] (glyph variation, §D.12.3)

- just [AAT] (justification, §D.13.3)

- lcar [AAT] (ligature caret, §D.11.6)

- morx [AAT] (table of metamorphosis, §D.13.2, formerly mort)

- opbd [AAT] (optical boundaries, §D.11.7)

- prop [AAT] (properties, §D.11.8)

- trak [AAT] (leading, §D.11.9)

- Zapf [AAT] (various data on the glyphs, §D.11.10)

There are also private tables, which are not part of the specifications for OpenType or those for AAT, such as the following:

- The table VTT, incorporated into a TrueType font with Microsoft's tool *VTT (Visual True-Type)* [262]

- The tables TSID, TSIP, TSIS, and TSIV, incorporated into a TrueType font with Microsoft's tool VOLT [266]

- The tables Silf, Gloc and Glat, by Graphite: another extension of TrueType, developed by the Summer Institute of Linguistics [184]

- And doubtless other applications unknown to the author

Below we shall describe the tables in the following order:

- First, the required tables that are shared by everybody: the "kernel" of the TrueType fonts (§D.4).

- Next, the basic tables that are specific to TrueType-style glyph descriptions (§D.5).

- The OpenType tables, specific to PostScript glyph descriptions (§D.6).

- The tables specific to bitmap fonts (§D.7).

- The various and sundry optional tables (§D.8).

- Finally, the most interesting part: the tables for "advanced typography". First, those defined by Microsoft and Adobe in OpenType (§D.9).

- Next, those defined by Apple in AAT, starting with the general tables (§D.11).

- The AAT tables for font variation (§D.11).

- Finally, the AAT tables with finite automata (§D.11).

Note that in both systems (OpenType and AAT) there is the notion of *feature*, and in both cases the respective instances present quite long lists of *predefined features*. We shall describe these predefined features in §D.10.2 for OpenType and in §D.11.5.1 for AAT.

Recall that in this appendix we shall describe the TrueType tables as represented in XML by TTX: thus we shall speak of XML elements, names, and values of attributes, etc. If the reader does not feel at ease with the jargon of the XML syntax, now would be the ideal time to reread the introduction to XML on pages 345 through 349 of this book.

It is time to begin, at the beginning—with the tables that are indispensable for every True-Type font.

D.4   The Kernel of the TrueType Tables

These are the tables defined and used since the first version of TrueType.

Before describing them, let us say a few words about the global structure of TTX documents. The global element of these XML documents is `ttFont`:

```
<ttFont sfntVersion="\x00\x01\x00\x00" ttLibVersion="2.0b2">
```

This element contains two attributes:

- `sfntVersion`, the version of the TrueType format. Fortunately, we are still at version 1 of TrueType, despite the extensions made by OpenType and AAT. Yet the value of this attribute has a peculiar appearance in the example below. In fact, it is the rational number 1.0 written with 32 bits, of which the first 16 bits contain the integer part and the other 16 contain the fractional part: 0x00010000. Here this number is written as a sequence of four bytes, `\x00\x01\x00\x00`.

- `ttLibVersion`, the version of TTX—a very useful value, as TTX is an evolving system and no one can guarantee that the format of a TTX document will not change in the future.

Now we shall describe the different elements that are found in a TTX document and that correspond to the tables of the kernel of TrueType.

D.4.1   The GlyphOrder Table

There is no `GlyphOrder` table; indeed, how could there have been one? The name, containing more than four letters, is not in any way compliant with the TrueType specifications! Yet, in a TTX document, it is the first element after `ttFont`:

```
<GlyphOrder>
  <GlyphID id="0" name="missing"/>
  <GlyphID id="1" name=".null"/>
  <GlyphID id="2" name="nonmarkingreturn"/>
```

```
    <GlyphID id="3" name="A"/>
    <GlyphID id="4" name="B"/>
    <GlyphID id="5" name="C"/>
    <GlyphID id="6" name="D"/>
    <GlyphID id="7" name="E"/>
    ...
    <GlyphID id="1326" name="uni1EF9"/>
    <GlyphID id="1327" name="uni20A0"/>
  </GlyphOrder>
```

What is this table? It is, in fact, a great service that TTX has done for us. In a binary TrueType font, when we refer to glyphs, we always do so through their *numbers*. For example, in a kerning pair for 'A' and 'C', we refer to the glyphs by their respective numbers: 3 and 5. If the same thing were done in a TTX document, we would be obliged to search constantly through the tables in order to find out *which* glyphs are 3 and 5. TTX thus generously takes the initiative of assigning *unique names* to the glyphs and referring to them by these names. This operation is not without risks: how can TTX know which name to assign to each glyph? Obviously there are some indications, but TTX may nonetheless make a mistake. Never mind: even if TTX goes astray, the worst that can happen is that the human reader will err in the interpretation of a glyph. That will not affect the *internal structure* of the font in any way, since the names vanish upon conversion to TTF and become anonymous numbers once again. In other words, the binary TTF font will be the same regardless of the names that TTX gives to the glyphs.

Thus this table is indispensable to the "humanization" of the TrueType font.

D.4.2   The cmap Table

Do not confuse this table with the CMap files of the CID fonts (which are written with the capital letters "CM"). This table contains mappings of the glyphs in the font to the characters in various *encodings*. Here is an example:

```
  <cmap>
    <tableVersion version="0"/>
    <cmap_format_4 platformID="0" platEncID="3" version="0">
      <map code="0x20" name="space"/><!-- SPACE -->
      <map code="0x21" name="exclam"/><!-- EXCLAMATION MARK -->
      <map code="0x22" name="quotedbl"/><!-- QUOTATION MARK -->
      <map code="0x23" name="numbersign"/><!-- NUMBER SIGN -->
      ...
      <map code="0xfb05" name="uniFB05"/><!-- LATIN
        SMALL LIGATURE LONG S T -->
      <map code="0xfb06" name="uniFB06"/><!-- LATIN SMALL LIGATURE ST -->
      <map code="0xfffc" name="uniFFFC"/><!-- OBJECT
        REPLACEMENT CHARACTER -->
    </cmap_format_4>
    <cmap_format_6 platformID="1" platEncID="0" version="0">
      <map code="0x0" name=".null"/>
```

```
            <map code="0x1" name="missing"/>
            <map code="0x2" name="missing"/>
            ...
            <map code="0xfe" name="ogonek"/>
            <map code="0xff" name="caron"/>
          </cmap_format_6>
          ...
      </cmap>
```

The map elements match the code point code of a given encoding to the glyph indicated by the attribute name. When there is no glyph associated with a code point in the encoding, either the corresponding map element is omitted or the glyph name missing is used. The cmap contains many subtables, which are represented by cmap_format_* subelements and correspond to the different encodings of the font.

The format of the subtable will vary according to the type of the encoding: small encodings will have subtables in which all the code points are represented, while 16-bit encodings will have subtables with only those code points for which a glyph exists. Even 32-bit encodings are supported (for example, Unicode with surrogates, or the higher planes of Unicode 3.2 and later versions).

There are seven formats for subtables, corresponding to seven different elements in TTX:

Format	TTX	Peculiarities
0	cmap_format_0	Anonymous 8-bit font encoding: all the positions from 0x00 to 0xff must be represented by <map> elements.
2	cmap_format_2	Mixed 8-bit/16-bit font encoding. This is used for some ideographic encodings, in which some bytes represent characters while other bytes must be followed by a second byte, the two jointly forming one 16-bit character. This subtable must not contain any holes: all the valid characters must be represented.
4	cmap_format_4	A 16-bit font encoding that may contain holes.
6	cmap_format_6	A lighter version of the preceding: a character encoding in any contiguous zone in the 16-bit table.
8	cmap_format_8	The equivalent of 2, but in 16-bit/32-bit. This subtable is ideal for Unicode surrogates.
10	cmap_format_10	The equivalent of 6, but in 32-bit: any contiguous zone in the 32-bit table.
12	cmap_format_12	The most powerful of all: the equivalent of 4, but in 32-bit. Ideal for Unicode with the higher planes.

The reader must have thought of one fundamental question: if each subtable corresponds to a font encoding, where does its name appear? Nowhere, unfortunately. To find it, we have only the values of the attributes platformID and platEncID. There are three possibilities for the former: 0 = Unicode, 1 = Macintosh, 3 = Windows. Here are the possibles values for the latter, according to the value of the former:

- If platformID is 0 (Unicode), then platEncID can take the following values: 0 (default), 1 (version 1.1), 3 (version 2 or later). We therefore recommend 0 or 3.

- If platformID is 1 (Macintosh), then platEncID can take the following values: 0 (Roman, *i.e*, the Latin alphabet for the countries of Western Europe), 1 (Japanese), 2 (traditional Chinese), 3 (Korean), 4 (Arabic), 5 (Hebrew), 6 ("monotonic" Greek), 7 (Russian), 8 (all sorts of symbols), 9 (Devanagari), 10 (*Gurmukhi*), 11 (Gujarati), 12 (Oriya), 13 (Bengali), 14 (Tamil), 15 (Telugu), 16 (Kannada), 17 (Malayalam), 18 (Sinhala), 19 (Burmese), 20 (Khmer), 21 (Thai), 22 (Lao), 23 (Georgian), 24 (Armenian), 25 (simplified Chinese), 26 (Tibetan), 27 (Mongolian), 28 (Geez), 29 (Old Cyrillic), 30 (Vietnamese), 31 (Sindhi), 32 (not interpreted). Each case refers to the corresponding Macintosh encoding.

- If platformID is 3 (Windows), then platEncID can take the following values: 0 (symbols), 1 (Unicode), 2 (Shift-JIS, Japan), 3 (GB, People's Republic of China), 4 (Big5, Taiwan), 5 (Wansung, precomposed encoding, Korea), 6 (Johab, non-precomposed encoding, Korea), 10 (UCS-4, i.e., 32-bit Unicode).

For example, the font *Palatino Linotype* contains the following 6 cmap subtables: 4/0/0, (i.e., format 4, platform 0, encoding 0 = Unicode version 2 and later), 6/1/0 (Macintosh, Latin alphabet, Western Europe), 6/1/6 (Macintosh, "monotonic" Greek), 6/1/7 (Macintosh, Russian), 6/1/29 (Macintosh, Old Cyrillic), 4/3/1 (Windows, Unicode). Note that the tables 4/0/0 and 4/3/1 are identical in every respect.

Finally, Apple requests that the subtables that correspond to a given language also have a language attribute, whose value is drawn from Apple's table of language identifiers [56, Chapter 6].

The cmap table is indispensable for communication between the font and the operating system, which knows about nothing but characters. But the problem is that some glyphs do not belong to any character and others belong to the same character. As we shall see, a large number of resources are put into service so that we can make use of these glyphs, either by going beyond the cmap table or by supplementing it.

D.4.3   *The head Table*

The font's global header, with 17 entries. Here is an example:

```
<head>
  <!-- Most of this table will be recalculated by the compiler -->
  <tableVersion value="1.0"/>
  <fontRevision value="1.0"/>
  <checkSumAdjustment value="0x10AE3726"/>
  <magicNumber value="0x5F0F3CF5"/>
  <flags value="00001000 00011011"/>
  <unitsPerEm value="2048"/>
  <created value="Mon Jan 29 10:11:20 1996"/>
  <modified value="Tue Jun  8 10:02:55 1999"/>
  <xMin value="-"/>
  <yMin value="-"/>
```

```
  <xMax value="2907"/>
  <yMax value="2150"/>
  <macStyle value="00000000 00000000"/>
  <lowestRecPPEM value="9"/>
  <fontDirectionHint value="2"/>
  <indexToLocFormat value="1"/>
  <glyphDataFormat value="0"/>
</head>
```

A few interesting subelements:

- flags contains 16 flags that cover all sorts of things: for example, bit 0 means that the baseline is at $y = 0$, bit 8 means that the font is subject to a morx metamorphosis table (and therefore is an AAT font), bit 13 means that the font has been optimized for ClearType on-screen display technology, etc.

- unitsPerEm defines the grid for the glyphs: it is the number of abstract units per em. Maximum possible value: 16,384. The most common value is 2,048 for TrueType fonts and 1,000 for PostScript.

- xMin, yMin, xMax, yMax: the bounding box for all the glyphs that do contain outlines (in other words, empty glyphs do not have a bounding box, which may seem obvious, but we may as well state it).

- macStyle, six flags that indicate the font's "Quickdraw style" (bit 0, bold; bit 1, italic; bit 2: underlined; bit 3, outline; bit 4, shadowed; bit 5, condensed; bit 6, extended).

- lowestRecPPEM: the size (expressed in pixels!) below which the font is no longer legible.

- fontDirectionHint: a global hint about the direction in which the glyphs are typeset. Possible values: 0 (left-to-right and right-to-left), 1 (left-to-right only), 2 (left-to-right and neutral, such as the space and the period), -1 and -2 (the opposites of 1 and 2: right-to-left only, and right-to-left and neutral).

D.4.4   The Tables hhea and hmtx

The table hhea contains global data for horizontal typesetting. Like head, it also contains 17 subelements. Here is an example:

```
<hhea>
  <tableVersion value="1.0"/>
  <ascent value="1499"/>
  <descent value="-"/>
  <lineGap value="682"/>
  <advanceWidthMax value="2861"/>
  <minLeftSideBearing value="-"/>
  <minRightSideBearing value="-"/>
  <xMaxExtent value="2907"/>
```

```
        <caretSlopeRise value="1"/>
        <caretSlopeRun value="0"/>
        <caretOffset value="0"/>
        <reserved0 value="0"/>
        <reserved1 value="0"/>
        <reserved2 value="0"/>
        <reserved3 value="0"/>
        <metricDataFormat value="0"/>
        <numberOfHMetrics value="1328"/>
      </hhea>
```

A few interesting subelements:

- ascent and descent: the height of the ascenders and the depth of the descenders.

- lineGap: the leading recommended for this font, minus the height of the ascenders and the depth of the descenders.

- advanceWidthMax, the maximum width vector.

- minLeftSideBearing and minRightSideBearing: the minimum values of the left and right side-bearings. Warning: when we say "minimum", we do not mean an absolute value! Glyphs that extend beyond their abstract boxes have negative side-bearings. Here, then, we are looking for the greatest amount of overhang.

- xMaxExtent is the maximum horizontal extent of the glyph.

- The entries caretSlopeRise, caretSlopeRun, and caretOffset pertain to the mouse's cursor: they are the coordinates of the vector for the direction towards which it is pointing. As an example, the cursor will be vertical for the values 1 and 0; for 0 and 1, it will be horizontal; but it may very well be slanted (for an italic font, for instance). The third parameter indicates a possible horizontal offset of the cursor. This value will be primarily for highlighting: we wish to ensure that the entire body of each glyph will be contained in the highlighted area, even if the font is heavily sloped.

- numberOfHMetrics refers to the following table: hmtx. It is the number of entries in that table.

The table hmtx is one of the simplest that exist: for each glyph, it contains the values of the width vector and the left side-bearing. Here is how it is represented in TTX:

```
      <hmtx>
        <mtx name=".null" width="0" lsb="0"/>
        <mtx name="A" width="1593" lsb="35"/>
        <mtx name="AE" width="1933" lsb="0"/>
        <mtx name="AEacute" width="1933" lsb="0"/>
        <mtx name="AEacutesmall" width="1503" lsb="10"/>
        . . .
```

```
    <mtx name="zeta" width="1022" lsb="82"/>
    <mtx name="zsuperior" width="597" lsb="6"/>
</hmtx>
```

Note that there are counterparts of tables hhea and hmtx that are used for vertical typesetting: they are the optional tables vhea and vmtx (see §D.8.6).

D.4.5   The maxp Table

The name maxp comes from "maximum profile". This table contains data that are useful to the processor during allocation of the memory required to process a font. This table contains 15 entries. Here is an example:

```
<maxp>
    <!-- Most of this table will be recalculated by the compiler -->
    <tableVersion value="0x10000"/>
    <numGlyphs value="1328"/>
    <maxPoints value="180"/>
    <maxContours value="16"/>
    <maxCompositePoints value="166"/>
    <maxCompositeContours value="9"/>
    <maxZones value="1"/>
    <maxTwilightPoints value="0"/>
    <maxStorage value="27"/>
    <maxFunctionDefs value="75"/>
    <maxInstructionDefs value="0"/>
    <maxStackElements value="2382"/>
    <maxSizeOfInstructions value="4475"/>
    <maxComponentElements value="3"/>
    <maxComponentDepth value="1"/>
</maxp>
```

A few interesting subelements:

- tableVersion takes the value 0x10000 if the font contains TrueType glyph descriptions. If it is a CFF font, the value of this entry must be 0x5000.

- numGlyphs, the number of glyphs. This is the only entry in the table (along with tableVersion) for the CFF fonts.

- maxPoints and maxContours: the maximum numbers of points and contours for simple glyphs.

- maxCompositePoints and maxCompositeContours: the maximum numbers of points and contours for composite glyphs.

- maxComponentElements: the maximum number of components in composite glyphs.

- `maxComponentDepth`: can the components themselves be composite glyphs, and to what depth? 1 means that the components are simple glyphs.

- The other entries concern TrueType instructions, i.e., the assembly language that is used for optimizing the rendering of the glyphs. We shall examine it in detail in Appendix E.

D.4.6 *The name Table*

This table is a gem of political correctness on the part of Apple and Microsoft: we can provide a certain amount of information in 150 different languages (including, among others, Breton, Esperanto, and even Latin[6]). Here is an extract of this table:

```
<name>
  <namerecord nameID="0" platformID="0" platEncID="3" langID="0x0">
    Copyright 1981-, 1989,1993, 1998 Heidelberger...
  </namerecord>
  <namerecord nameID="1" platformID="0" platEncID="3" langID="0x0">
    Palatino Linotype
  </namerecord>
  <namerecord nameID="2" platformID="0" platEncID="3" langID="0x0">
    Regular
  </namerecord>
  ...
</name>
```

This table contains only `namerecord` elements. Each of these elements is associated with a platform, an encoding, and a language. We find the same approach as for the `cmap` table, which uses the same attributes `platformID` and `platEncID`, with the same values (see §D.4.2). What is new here is the language (attribute `langID`). The language identifiers depend on the platform. For example, for the "Unicode" platform (`platformID` equal to 0), there are none. For the "Macintosh" platform (`platformID` equal to 1), there are some 150 identifiers, described in [264]. For the "Windows" platform (`platformID` equal to 3), there are some 135 identifiers: 0x0409 is American English, 0x040c is French, etc.

We have seen how to indicate the language of a record. Now let us give a list of the records provided in the specification:

- 0: the copyright notice.

- 1: the name of the font family.

- 2: the "style", which is what must be added to the name of the font family (1) to obtain the name of the font (4).

---

[6] The reader may be wondering of what use a description of the font in *Latin* can be. Well, today there are still admirers of this language, which was still heard in Catholic churches 50 years ago. Note that in Finland, that European Union member country renowned for the humor of its residents, there is a state-run radio station [288] that has been broadcasting the news in Latin every week for more than 15 years! A Finnish jazz group even released a CD entitled *Variationes Horatianae Iazzicae*, with songs in Latin, to celebrate the bimillennial anniversary of the death of Horace.

- 3: the unique identifier (UID) of the font.

- 4: the complete name of the font.

- 5: the version of the font, in a very strict format, which follows: the string Version followed by a primary version number, a period, and a secondary version number (the numbers must be between 0 and 65535).

- 6: the PostScript name of the font. This information must appear twice, with the following value of the attributes: platform 1, encoding 0, language 0; and platform 3, encoding 1, language 0x0409.

- 7: the trademark.

- 8: the name of the foundry.

- 9: the name of the designer.

- 10: a description of the font (at most 65,536 characters).

- 11: the URL of the foundry.

- 12: the URL of the designer.

- 13: a description of the license. The OpenType specification includes the following exhortation: "This field should be written in plain language, not legalese". We may well wonder whether that exhortation is itself legal.

- 14: the URL for the license.

- 16: a "family name" that can be used by Windows in menus that list fonts.

- 17: a "style name" that can be used by Windows in menus that list fonts.

- 18: a "family name" that can be used by the Macintosh in menus that list fonts.

- 19: a sample of text; for example, a *pangram*.[7]

- 20: a CID font name, with the CMap component. The notes in 6, above, also apply to the values of the parameters for this record.

---

[7] A pangram, from the Greek πᾶν ("all") and γράμμα ("letter"), is a sentence containing *all* the letters in a given alphabet. For example, in English, "The quick brown fox jumps over the lazy dog"; in French, *Portez ce vieux whisky au juge blond qui fume* ("Take this old whisky to the blond judge who is smoking"); in German, *Franz jagt im komplett verwahrlosten Taxi quer durch Bayern* ("Franz chases straight across Bavaria in a completely run-down taxi"); in Russian, *в чащах юга жил-был цитрус... да, но фальшивый экземпляръ!* ("Once upon a time there was a citrus in the bushes of the south—yes, but a fake one!") [358]; in Greek, *γαζίες καὶ μυρτιὲς δὲν θὰ βρῶ πιὰ στὸ χρυσαφὶ ξέφωτο* ("No more shall I see acacias or myrtles in the golden clearing") [137], etc.

D.4.7   The OS/2 Table

The name of this table is deceptive: one is likely to think that it applies only to the little-distributed and rather peculiar operating system known as IBM OS/2. That is not so, for this table applies above all to another operating system, much more widely used, by the name of Windows. While hhea is a table intended primarily for the Macintosh, OS/2 assembles some data from that table for the Windows environment.

It has a record number of entries: 37! Here is an example of the table:[8]

```
<OS_2>
  <version value="2"/>
  <xAvgCharWidth value="912"/>
  <usWeightClass value="400"/>
  <usWidthClass value="5"/>
  <fsType value="00000000 00001000"/>
  <ySubscriptXSize value="1285"/>
  <ySubscriptYSize value="1230"/>
  <ySubscriptXOffset value="0"/>
  <ySubscriptYOffset value="0"/>
  <ySuperscriptXSize value="1285"/>
  <ySuperscriptYSize value="1230"/>
  <ySuperscriptXOffset value="0"/>
  <ySuperscriptYOffset value="560"/>
  <yStrikeoutSize value="120"/>
  <yStrikeoutPosition value="530"/>
  <sFamilyClass value="260"/>
  <panose>
    <bFamilyType value="2"/>
    <bSerifStyle value="4"/>
    <bWeight value="5"/>
    <bProportion value="2"/>
    <bContrast value="5"/>
    <bStrokeVariation value="5"/>
    <bArmStyle value="5"/>
    <bLetterForm value="3"/>
    <bMidline value="3"/>
    <bXHeight value="4"/>
  </panose>
  <ulUnicodeRange1 value="11100000 00000000 00000011 10000111"/>
  <ulUnicodeRange2 value="01000000 00000000 00000000 00010011"/>
  <ulUnicodeRange3 value="00000000 00000000 00000000 00000000"/>
  <ulUnicodeRange4 value="00000000 00000000 00000000 00000000"/>
  <achVendID value="LINO"/>
  <fsSelection value="00000000 01000000"/>
```

---

[8] The reader will notice that the global element in this TTX table is OS_2, not OS/2, a name that is not suitable for XML, as it contains a slash.

```
<fsFirstCharIndex value="32"/>
<fsLastCharIndex value="65532"/>
<sTypoAscender value="1499"/>
<sTypoDescender value="-"/>
<sTypoLineGap value="682"/>
<usWinAscent value="2150"/>
<usWinDescent value="613"/>
<ulCodePageRange1 value="00100000 00000000 00000001 10011111"/>
<ulCodePageRange2 value="00000000 00000000 00000000 00000000"/>
<sxHeight value="925"/>
<sCapHeight value="1405"/>
<usDefaultChar value="0"/>
<usBreakChar value="32"/>
<usMaxContext value="3"/>
</OS_2>
```

A few interesting entries:

- version: today we are at version 3.

- xAvgCharWidth, the average width of all the glyphs (except those that have a zero width).

- usWeightClass, the font's weight, an even number of hundreds between 100 (very light) and 900 (very bold). Usual value: 400.

- usWidthClass, the font's width, an integer between 1 (ultra-condensed) and 9 (ultra-extended). Usual value: 5.

- fsType, a very important entry, as it determines whether the font is protected, whether it can be incorporated into a publicly distributed document, and, if so, under what conditions. Sixteen flags are available. If they are all disabled, there is no restriction on including the font within documents. Here are the meanings of some of the other bits:

  - Bit 1: if it is enabled, and if it is the only bit enabled (the value of fsType thus being 0x0002), then the font is under a strict license: it may not be incorporated into a document in any way!
  - Bit 2: if it is enabled, the font may be installed temporarily on other systems, but only for the purposes of reading and printing (as is the case, for example, in PDF documents);
  - Bit 3: like the preceding, but the font may also be used for editing (as is the case, for example, with fonts included in Word documents);
  - Bit 8: this flag, if enabled, prohibits the use of partial fonts.[9]
  - Bit 9: if this flag is enabled, only the bitmaps contained in the font may be included in a document.

---

[9] Yet partial fonts are a good thing, as they are less bulky and better protected against piracy: what would a pirate do with a font half of whose glyphs were missing?

- ySubscriptXSize, ySubscriptYSize, ySuperscriptXSize, ySuperscriptYSize: the horizontal and vertical sizes of the font's subscripts and superscripts (the two sizes are kept separate in case we should wish to stretch or shrink the superscripts and subscripts to achieve an optical correction).

- ySubscriptXOffset, ySubscriptYOffset, ySuperscriptXOffset, ySuperscriptYOffset: the horizontal and vertical offsets of the subscripts and superscripts. As for the horizontal offset, the typesetting software would be better off using the bounding box of each glyph: examples such as A^2 (superscript too far to the right) and f^2 (superscript too far to the left) show that this offset *cannot* be the same for every glyph. As for the vertical offset, the situation is a bit better, but TrueType forgot the case in which we have *both* a superscript *and* a subscript. In this case, it is better to separate the subscripts from the superscripts. Just compare x^0x_0 and x_0^0: the subscript is higher in the former than in the latter. This detail, of course, escaped the notice of TrueType.

- yStrikeoutPosition and yStrikeoutSize: the position and thickness of the strikethrough bar, if any.

- sFamilyClass and Panose, with their subelements: the IBM (derived from ISO 9541-5) and Panose-1 classifications of the font. These are described in Chapter 11 of this book, starting on page 416.

- ulUnicodeRange1 (bits 0–31) to ulUnicodeRange4 (bits 96–127), a sequence of 128 flags, of which the first 92 correspond to Unicode tables. The list of tables is given in [264]. The question that arises is "Is the font *operational* for this or that Unicode table?" For example, if bit 70 is enabled, it is claimed that one can set type in Tibetan with this font.

- achVendID, a string of four ASCII characters that identifies the foundry. The list of foundries appears in [270]; there are already 240!

- fsSelection, the Windows counterpart for the entry macStyle in the head table: seven flags that describe the font. In order, starting with bit 0: italic, underlined, white on black, outline, strikethrough, bold, average weight and width.

- usFirstCharIndex and usLastCharIndex, the first and last Unicode code points for which the font contains a glyph.

- sTypoAscender, sTypoDescender, and sTypoLineGap: entries that are oddly similar to ascent, descent, and lineGap in the hhea table but that should not necessarily be so precise or so closely tied to the vagaries of the glyphs' outlines. Windows supposedly uses these values to find the ideal parameters for layout; thus we have a certain degree of artistic freedom.

- usWinAscent and usWinDescent, once again, are for ascenders and descenders, but here their definition is clear: they are the font's vertical extrema, taken from the bounding box.

- ulCodePageRange1 and ulCodePageRange2, a sequence of 64 flags representing the font's compatibility with the same number of Microsoft code pages:

Bit	Code page	Name
0	1252	Latin 1
1	1250	Latin 2
2	1251	Cyrillic
3	1253	Greek ("monotonic")
4	1254	Turkish
5	1255	Hebrew
6	1256	Arabic
7	1257	Windows for the Baltic states
8	1258	Vietnamese
16	874	Thai
17	932	JIS/Japan
18	936	Chinese, simplified
19	949	Korean, Wansung
20	950	Chinese, traditional
21	1361	Korean, Johab
29		*MacRoman*
30		OEM
31		Symbols
48	869	IBM Greek
49	866	MS-DOS Russian
50	865	MS-DOS Nordic
51	864	Arabic
52	863	MS-DOS Canadian French
53	862	Hebrew
54	861	MS-DOS Icelandic
55	860	MS-DOS Portuguese
56	857	IBM Turkish
57	855	IBM Cyrillic
58	852	Latin 2
59	775	MS-DOS Baltic
60	737	Greek (ex 437 G)
61	708	Arabic (ASMO 708)
62	850	Latin 1
63	437	United States

- sxHeight and sCapHeight, what the designer considers the height of the lowercase letters and the capitals to be.

- usDefaultChar and usBreakChar: what is the Unicode substitution character (the character whose glyph is displayed when we ask the font to display a character that it does not support), and what is the Unicode character that separates the words in a sentence of running text? The latter is a very bad idea, for it actually depends on the script. For example, the words in Thai are not separated, and we may use the Unicode character 0x200B (ZERO WIDTH SPACE) to indicate their boundaries. A font may contain glyphs for several scripts; which one should it favor over the others?

- Finally—and here again we have a mixed bag—usMaxContext indicates the maximum length of the context in the advanced OpenType tables. For instance, if the font contains an 'ffi' ligature, it will usually have a ligature feature ffi → 'ffi' and therefore a *context string* (see §D.9.4.4) ffi of length 3. If this is the longest ligature, its length will be the value of this entry.

D.4.8   The post Table

In Appendix C, §C.5, we saw that to transfer TrueType data to a TrueType processor hidden deep in the bowels of a PostScript printer, we can employ a PostScript Type 42 font. But creating that font requires a certain amount of data, and it is easier to collect them into a table made for the purpose than to go rummaging all over the font. The post table is devoted to the task. Here is an example:

```
<post>
  <formatType value="2.0"/>
  <italicAngle value="0.0"/>
  <underlinePosition value="-"/>
  <underlineThickness value="120"/>
  <isFixedPitch value="0"/>
  <minMemType42 value="0"/>
  <maxMemType42 value="0"/>
  <minMemType1 value="0"/>
  <maxMemType1 value="0"/>
  <psNames>
    <!-- This file uses unique glyph names based on the information
         found in the 'post' table. Since these names might not be unique,
         we have to invent artificial names in case of clashes. In order to
         be able to retain the original information, we need a name to
         ps name mapping for those cases where they differ. That's what
         you see below. -->
  </psNames>
  <extraNames>
    <!-- following are the name that are not taken from the standard
      Mac glyph order -->
    <psName name="missing"/>
    <psName name=".null"/>
    <psName name="nonmarkingreturn"/>
    <psName name="Abreve"/>
```

```
    <psName name="Aringacute"/>
    ...
    <psName name="uni1EF9"/>
    <psName name="uni20A0"/>
  </extraNames>
</post>
```

There have been five successive versions of this table (1, 2, 2.5, 3, and 4), of which 2.5 is obsolete and deprecated. The first nine entries are common to all the versions:

- formatType, the version.

- italicAngle to isFixedPitch correspond to the entries in the PostScript dictionary of the same name, which is found in every PostScript font (Appendix C).

- minMemType42 and minMemType42 correspond not to PostScript entries but to DSC comments (see §C.1.10). They are the minimum and maximum amounts of virtual memory to allocate to reading the font. There are two values because processors are often quite clever and set resources aside when they are shared by several fonts: the maximum value covers the situation in which no resource is shared, and the minimum value is for the case in which everything that can be shared already has been shared.

- minMemType1 and minMemType1 are similar, but they are applied when the TrueType font is converted to PostScript Type 1 (the only solution that was available before Type 42).

One big problem remains: in a PostScript font, the glyphs have names. That is *not* the case in a TrueType font, although TTX gives us the illusion of glyph names because of its pseudotable GlyphOrder. Yet some software, such as *Adobe Acrobat*, needs these names. It would therefore be good if we could supply them rather than leaving them to be guessed from the cmap table. And indeed it is in their strategies for naming glyph that the successive versions of this table differ.

In version 1, for example, the glyphs were assumed to be named according to a list of 258 glyphs supplied by Apple [56, table post]. It is not very politically correct to favor in this manner the Latin alphabet as used for the languages of Western Europe, but such questions did not often arise at the time. In version 2, an explicit name is given to each glyph (other than those on the list in version 1). Version 3 declares that there are no predefined glyph names. Let us cite the OpenType specification [264, Chapter 6]: "The printing behavior of this format on PostScript printers is unspecified, except that it should not result in a fatal or unrecoverable error." Finally, version 4 (AAT only) is for composite fonts, in which the only way to refer to a glyph is through its index. In this case, the post table provides a glyph index for each glyph in the font (this information comes from the numGlyphs entry in the table maxp), and in the same order.

The reader must have noticed that what we have just stated in the previous paragraph is not necessarily reflected in the XML code for the example of a post table in TTX. That comes from the fact that this information is duplicated in the GlyphOrder table (see §D.4.1), which plays exactly the same role: it matches names with glyphs. The element psNames contains the possible exceptions—cases in which the name given in GlyphOrder does not correspond to the PostScript glyph name. Finally, the element extraNames is for informational purposes only; it contains the glyph names that are not on Apple's famous list.

D.5   The Tables That Pertain
to TrueType-Style Glyph Descriptions

We have already mentioned that an OpenType font can be of either of two types: it can contain glyph descriptions written in TrueType, or it can contain PostScript CFF code with Type 2 *charstrings*. In this section, we shall concern ourselves with the tables that pertain to the first case. TrueType and AAT fonts must necessarily be of this type.

D.5.1   The loca Table

In a binary TTF file, loca is a table of pointers to glyph descriptions in the glyf table (pointers calculated with reference to the start of the glyf table). This table does not belong in a TTX document (this is precisely the sort of calculations that we avoid by converting to XML). We find merely

```
<loca>
  <!-- The 'loca' table will be calculated by the compiler -->
</loca>
```

Isn't that beautiful?

D.5.2   The glyf Table

This table is often the bulkiest one in a TrueType font. It is certainly the most important one, as it contains the descriptions of the contours of the glyphs, and a font without glyphs is like a forest without trees. Here is an example of the glyf table: the letter 'A' from the font *Palatino Linotype*:

```
<glyf>
  ...
  <TTGlyph name="A" xMin="35" yMin="-" xMax="1545" yMax="1487">
    <contour>
      <pt x="44" y="-" on="1"/>
      <pt x="35" y="0" on="1"/>
      <pt x="35" y="52" on="1"/>
      ... 43 similar lines ...
      <pt x="363" y="0" on="0"/>
      <pt x="266" y="0" on="1"/>
      <pt x="156" y="0" on="0"/>
    </contour>
    <contour>
      <pt x="500" y="553" on="1"/>
      <pt x="1006" y="553" on="1"/>
```

```
         <pt x="755" y="1156" on="1"/>
       </contour>
       <contour>
         <pt x="803" y="1487" on="1"/>
       </contour>
       <contour>
         <pt x="780" y="-" on="1"/>
       </contour>
       <instructions><assembly>
           NPUSHB[ ]   /* 40 values pushed */
           51 24 20 20 58 6 51 1 11 13 51 1 83 61 51 1 237 51 1 123
           51 251 51 2 11 51 203 51 2 19 12 51 1 30 51 40 23 27 72 16
           ... 366 lines of code ...
           SDB[ ]
           DELTAP1[ ]
           CALL[ ]
       </assembly></instructions>
     </TTGlyph>
     ...
   </glyf>
```

The structure is very simple: there is a TTGlyph element for each glyph. Each of these elements has the following attributes: the glyph's name (name) and its bounding box (the xMin, yMin, xMax, and yMax attributes).

Next, there is one contour element for each distinct closed contour in the glyphs. Each contour includes points, which are represented by point elements. The point element has three attributes: the coordinates of the point (x and y) and an indication of whether the point lies on the contour or is a control point (see Appendix G). The on attribute takes the value 1 if the former and 0 if the latter. That may seem simplistic, but owing to the structure of B-splines, these data are sufficient to describe a TrueType glyph contour.

Note that there are always two more points than are required. These last two points are auxiliary: they are the origin of the coordinate system and the far end of the width vector. They are sometimes called "phantom points". Using these two points, we can very conveniently obtain two vital data: the glyph's set-width and offset relative to the origin.[10] In addition, as we shall see in Appendix E, these points can be moved under the control of TrueType instructions. For instance, the left side-bearing and the glyph's set-width can also be generated, quite naturally, by instructions—something inconceivable under PostScript, where the set-width is not influenced by hints at all.

The astute reader may have noticed that in the example of the letter 'A' above, after the two "genuine" contours of the letter 'A', which are the external and internal contours, there are two "false" contours that contain only one point each. These are the markers that we shall use in the OpenType advanced typographic tables. In this example, they are markers for placing an accent above the letter and an accent below.

---

[10] In PostScript Type 1 *charstrings*, these same two data are given by the first command in the glyph description, named hsbw. TrueType puts these data at the end of the list of points.

After the last contour or component element comes an instructions element, which contains the *TrueType instructions* for optimizing the glyph's rasterization. These are written in an assembler-type language in which the TrueType hints are described; we shall describe this language in Appendix E.

D.5.2.1 Composite glyphs

Aside from the glyphs with genuine contours, we also have, here just as in the AFM files for PostScript fonts or in TEX's virtual fonts, the concept of a *composite glyph*, which is a set of references to other glyphs, each of them positioned with a certain offset. This feature of TrueType is often used to create glyphs for accented letters, except, of course, when the accents for the various letters differ slightly and thus must be designed separately. Here is an example of a composite glyph, the letter 'É' in the same font:

```
<TTGlyph name="Eacute" xMin="73" yMin="-" xMax="1165" yMax="1894">
  <component glyphName="E" x="0" y="0" flags="0x214"/>
  <component glyphName="Acute" x="470" y="0" flags="0x14"/>
  <instructions><assembly>
      NPUSHB[ ]  /* 29 values pushed */
      3 159 94 1 223 94 1 94 5 3 16 94 1 160 94 176 94 2 0 94 16 94 2 0 94
      94 53 53 37
      ... 8 lines of code ...
      DELTAP2[ ]
      DELTAP3[ ]
      SHC[1]
  </assembly></instructions>
</TTGlyph>
```

Thus there is one component element for each component of the composite glyph. Each component element takes four attributes: the name of the glyph in question, the coordinates of the offset, and a number (flags) that is in fact a sequence of 16 flags of no great interest (we can give the value 0x214 to the first component and 0x14 to the others without much worry; there are more details in [56, 264]).

D.5.3 The Tables fpgm, prep, and cvt

The tables fpgm and prep contain global TrueType instructions (which, therefore, are not attached to any specific glyph). These instructions are executed when the first glyph in the active font is typeset (for fpgm) and every time the type size or the current transformation matrix is changed (for prep). Examples of these tables:

```
<fpgm>
  <assembly>
    NPUSHB[ ]  /* 47 values pushed */
    74 73 72 71 70 59 58 57 54 51 50 49 48 47 46 45 44 43 42 41 39
    31 30 29 28 27 26 25 24 22 21 20 19 18 17 15 14 13 12 11 8 3 2
    ... 1357 lines of code ...
```

```
      POP[ ]
      EIF[ ]
      ENDF[ ]
    </assembly>
  </fpgm>

  <prep>
    <assembly>
      NPUSHB[ ]  /* 17 values pushed */
      223 224 22 23 28 212 213 22 23 28 123 124 22 27 123 124 25
      PUSHW[ ]  /* 1 value pushed */
      ... 1449 lines of code ...
      12
      SWAP[ ]
      WS[ ]
    </assembly>
  </prep>
```

The table cvt contains the values of global variables, which are used by the instructions (see §D.8.5). Here is an example:

```
  <cvt>
    <cv index="0" value="1481"/>
    <cv index="1" value="0"/>
    <cv index="2" value="0"/>
    ...
    <cv index="627" value="1067"/>
    <cv index="628" value="1539"/>
    <cv index="629" value="1427"/>
  </cvt>
```

D.6 The TrueType Tables That Affect PostScript-Style Glyph Descriptions

D.6.1 The Table CFF

The table CFF contains a PostScript CFF font with Type 2 *charstrings*. We have described this type of table in Appendix C, §C.8.

D.6.2 The Table VORG

This table was born from a small gap in the TrueType structure. When we want to calculate a glyph's offset, we know that the starting point of the width vector is the point $(0,0)$ and that the table hmtx contains the magnitude of the vector. All, then, is well.

But here we find ourselves in utter political incorrectness: that approach works only for horizontal movement, and not everyone in the world uses horizontal movement only. What happens if we move vertically? Well, there is, of course, the table vmtx, which contains the magnitude of the vertical width vector.

But what is that vector's starting point? Without that information, we cannot compute its ending point. Fortunately, the coordinates of the starting point and the ending point appear in the table glyf: they are the last two points described in the table, the *phantom points*.

Yes, but OpenType fonts with a CFF table do not have a glyf table! Where, then, shall we find even the height of the starting point of the width vector?

We have a hard way and an easy way to go about it. The hard way involves interpreting the *charstring* and calculating the vertical extrema of all the Bézier curves. The easy way is to use the VORG table.

This table has only one piece of information to offer us: the y-coordinate of the glyph's vertical origin. Here is an example of this type of table:

```
<VORG>
    <majorVersion value="1"/>
    <minorVersion value="0"/>
    <defaultVertOriginY value="878"/>
    <numVertOriginYMetrics value="2"/>
    <VOriginRecords>
      <VOriginRecord>
        <glyphName value="A"/>
        <vOrigin value="800"/>
      </VOriginRecord>
      <VOriginRecord>
        <glyphName value="AE"/>
        <vOrigin value="900"/>
      </VOriginRecord>
      ...
    </VOriginRecords>
</VORG>
```

In this table we find the version (major and minor components), a default value for the ordinate of vertical origins, the number of exceptions to this rule, one VOriginRecord subelement for every different vertical origin of the default value. Each of these subelements contains a glyph name and the value of the ordinate of that glyph's vertical origin.

D.7   *Bitmap Management*

D.7.1   *The Tables EBLC and EBDT (Alias bloc and bdat)*

Every effort was made so that TrueType fonts could contain bitmaps, together with—or instead of—vector contours. We have seen in Appendix A that a number of bitmap formats have appeared in the past 20 years and that some of them turned out to be better suited than others to certain situations. For instance, there are fonts with multiple sizes of glyphs, others with only one size, monospaced and proportional fonts, etc. The fact that ideographic fonts containing thousands, even tens of thousands of glyphs are monospace fonts is a decisive factor: when there are tens of thousands of glyphs, every single bit saved in the glyph descriptions is important; thus such fonts will not be described in the same way as alphabetic fonts, in which each letter may in principle have a different width.

TrueType had an ingenious idea: a font can be "multiformat"; i.e., we divide its glyphs into a number of blocks, and for each block we use the appropriate bitmap font format. If many glyphs have the same metrics, we store those metrics separately and declare that they apply to all of the glyphs in the block in question. If they have different metrics, those metrics will be stored with the glyphs.

Thus there are different sizes of bitmap fonts and, for each size, different font formats, which are applied to collections of glyphs in different blocks. TrueType provides two tables: one (EBLC) classifies the glyphs, the other (EBDT) contains the bitmaps. Thus the system that needs a bitmap glyph will first go to the table EBLC; there it will find a subtable corresponding to the desired size (measured in pixels per em), and that subtable will lead it to a table containing collections of glyphs. There it will learn the block to which the glyph corresponds and that block's format; according to the format, it will find the metrics at that very location in the EBLC table or else in the glyph descriptions, in the EBDT table. Finally, the EBLC table will provide the system with the exact address of the glyph description in the EBDT table, and voilà!

Here is an example of the tables EBLC and EBDT:

```
<EBLC>
  <tableVersion version="2.0"/>
  <numSizes value="4"/>
  <bitmapSize ppemX="9" ppemY="9">
    <numberOfIndexSubTables value="1"/>
    <colorRef value="0"/>
    <hori>
      <ascender value="7"/>
      <descender value="0"/>
      <widthMax value="9"/>
      <caretSlopeNumerator value="0"/>
      <caretSlopeDenominator value="0"/>
      <caretOffset value="0"/>
      <minOriginSB value="0"/>
      <minAdvanceSB value="0"/>
      <maxBeforeBL value="7"/>
      <minAfterBL value="0"/>
    </hori>
    <vert>
      <ascender value="0"/>
      <descender value="0"/>
      <widthMax value="0"/>
      <caretSlopeNumerator value="0"/>
      <caretSlopeDenominator value="0"/>
      <caretOffset value="0"/>
      <minOriginSB value="0"/>
```

```
                <minAdvanceSB value="0"/>
                <maxBeforeBL value="0"/>
                <minAfterBL value="0"/>
            </vert>
            <startGlyphIndex value="1"/>
            <endGlyphIndex value="256"/>
            <bitDepth value="1"/>
            <flags value="1"/>
            <indexSubTables>
                <indexSubTable firstGlyph="1" lastGlyph="256"
                  indexFormat="1" imageFormat="2" imageDataOffset="4">
                    <hexdata>
                        00000000 0000000d 00000019 00000026
                        00000032 00000040 0000004d 0000005a
                        00000067 00000074 00000080 0000008e

                        ...

                        00000e66 00000e73 00000e81 00000e8e
                        00000e9b 00000ea8 00000eb5 00000ec3
                        00000ed0 00000edd 00000eea 00000ef7
                    </hexdata>
                </indexSubTable>
            </indexSubTables>
        </bitmapSize>
    </EBLC>

    <EBDT version="00020000">
        <hexdata>
            08092422 595555ff 1c2b0807 0108094c
            06080702 0809252a 0aa92011 3c080800

            ...

            9834c0b5 a9560809 01080908 552f152a
            c3fe541e 08080108 0908bfaa aeb17b9d
        </hexdata>
    </EBDT>
```

The exact structure of the EBLC table is as follows:

- At the highest level, there are just two pieces of information: the version (tableVersion) of the table (currently 2), and the number of bitmap fonts that it contains (numSizes). In TrueType jargon, a bitmap font is called a *strike*. For each *strike* there is a bitmapSize element, whose attributes ppemX and ppemY give its size: the number of pixels per em, horizontally and vertically.

- Inside a bitmapSize we find, first, some global data, including metrics and other data; and, second, a subelement that will contain tables of pointers to the glyphs' bitmaps.

- The global data that we find in a bitmapSize are the following:

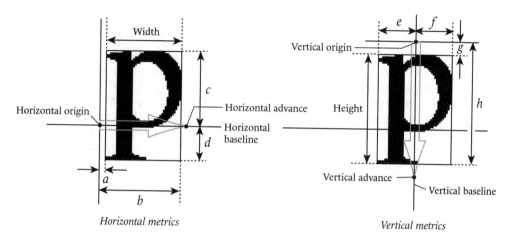

Figure D-1: The horizontal and vertical metrics of a bitmap glyph in an EBLC table. To avoid giving incomprehensible names, we have used the letters a, ..., h for some measurements that we shall use later.

- The number of tables of pointers (numberOfIndexSubTables). Specifically, for each bitmap font, we can have several blocks of glyphs, in different formats. And these tables of pointers can also be in formats different from the bitmaps—which yields many possible combinations, and therefore as many potential pointers.

- The depth of the bits (between 1 for black-and-white and 8 for 256 gray levels) and the color mode: for Microsoft, this value must always be 0; for Apple, it can be 0 (a standard black-and-white font), 1 (a black-and-white font, but with more bits per pixel, so that it can be displayed without interpolation on devices with a greater depth of bits), or 2 (a color font or a font with gray scales).

- The indices of the first and last glyphs (startGlyphIndex, endGlyphIndex).

- A flag, flags, to indicate whether the glyphs are horizontal (value 1) or vertical (value 2). A word of explanation is needed: of the formats for tables of poiners, there are some with "short metrics" and others with "long metrics". "Long metrics" support two directions of writing. "Short metrics" support only one, and it must be the same for the entire font—which is why we have this flag that is relevant only to "short metrics".

- Two subelements, called sbitLineMetrics in TrueType jargon, that contain global horizontal (hori) and vertical (vert) metrics. These are the metrics that come into play if the chosen format for the table of pointers is "without metrics" (a method well suited to the ideographic scripts, in which tens of thousands of glyphs have the same metrics). These metrics contain the following subelements: the height of the ascenders (ascender) and the depth of the descenders (descender); the maximum width of the glyph (widthmax); the slope and offset of the caret (caretSlopeNumerator, caretSlopeDenominator, and caretOffset); according to Figure D-1, in the horizontal case, the minimum value of a (minOriginSB), the minimum value of b (minAdvanceSB), the maximum value of c (maxBeforeBL), and the minimum value of d (minAfterBL); in the vertical case, the minimum value of g (minOriginSB), the

minimum value of *h* (minAdvanceSB), the maximum value of *e* (maxBeforeBL), and
the minimum value of *f* (minAfterBL).[11]

- An element indexSubTables, containing a subelement indexSubTable (without
  an 's') for each block of glyphs in the strike. Each indexSubTable element has four
  attributes: the index of the first glyph in the block (firstGlyph), the index of the
  last glyph (lastGlyph), the format number of the table of pointers (indexFormat),
  the format number of the bitmap data (imageFormat), and, finally, the offset
  (imageDataOffset) of the description of the first glyph in the EBDT table—an offset
  computer starting from the beginning of the table. Then comes the table of pointers,
  in the form of hexadecimal data.

All that remains is to describe the various formats for the table of pointers. Some of them
contain metrics; others do not. Here they are:

- Format 1: the simplest format. The glyphs' bitmaps are of variable size. Each position
  between firstGlyph and lastGlyph has a 4-byte pointer into the EBDT table, even if there
  is no corresponding glyph (in which case the pointer points to the end of the last glyph
  that exists before the positions that precede the current position).

- Format 2: the format specific to ideographic scripts. All the bitmap images for glyphs are
  of the same size. This format is not at all similar to the previous one. In particular, instead
  of the block of code in hexadecimal, the following elements appear:

```
<indexSubTable firstGlyph="1" lastGlyph="256"
   indexFormat="2" imageFormat="2" imageDataOffset="4">
   <imageSize value="81"/>
   <height value="7"/>
   <width value="0"/>
   <horiBearingX value="9"/>
   <horiBearingY value="0"/>
   <horiAdvance value="0"/>
   <vertBearingX value="9"/>
   <vertBearingY value="0"/>
   <vertAdvance value="0"/>
</indexSubTable>
```

where the entries have the following meanings, as shown in Figure D-1: height (height),
width (width), *a* (horiBearingX), *c* (horiBearingY), horizontal advance (horiAdvance), *e*
(vertBearingX), *g* (vertBearingY), vertical advance (vertAdvance).

These measurements are called "big metrics" in TrueType jargon because they contain
information about the horizontal *and* vertical directions; they are also used in the EBDT
table when the bitmaps are accompanied by metrics, as in Format 1, above. There are also
the "small metrics" (used only in the EBDT table); for them, we have the entries BearingX,

---

[11] Note: Here we have used the letters *a*, ... , *h* to denote measurements, rather than giving those
measurements' names. The Microsoft and Apple specifications assign quite disconcerting names to these measurements: for example, *c* is called horiBearingY, i.e., "horizontal side-bearing on the *y*-axis (!). The reader's
mental well-being seemed more important to us than the need to assign a name to absolutely everything.

BearingY, and Advance, which have the meaning of horiBearingX, etc., when the flags entry that we saw above has the value 1 and the meaning of vertBearingX, etc., when that entry has the value 2.

- Format 3 is identical to Format 1, except that only 2 bytes are used for each pointer. Thus the format takes up less space, but the EBDT can be no larger than 64 kilobytes.

- Format 4 solves the problem of sparse blocks—those that have a few glyphs at the beginning and a few more several thousand positions later. With a table of Format 1 or Format 2, we would have to include useless pointers for all the intermediate positions. Here we have the number of glyphs, in the form of the additional attribute numGlyphs in the indexSubTable element. Next, in a hexadecimal block, we have, for each glyph that actually exists in the EBDT table, its index (2 bytes) and its position in the table (also 2 bytes).

- Format 5 combines formats 4 (sparse tables) and 2 (glyphs of identical size). In it, therefore, appear the element imageSize and the "big metrics" of Format 2, together with the attribute numGlyphs of Format 4. The hexadecimal block that follows contains the indices of the glyphs that actually exist, encoded as 2-byte values.

Note that formats 4 and 5 of the table of pointers can be used only within EBLC, not within bloc (the Apple table corresponding to EBLC). That is the only difference between EBLC and bloc.

Now let us move on to the description of the EBDT table. In TTX, its appearance is quite deceptive: just a block of hexadecimal data. At the beginning of this block is a 4-byte version number; all the rest is merely bitmap data. What, then, can we say about these bitmap data? Well, we can describe their structure, even though TTX does not give us any more help. We thus find ourselves forced to make recourse to the good old-fashioned method of counting bytes, which we have used for most other bitmap formats (Appendix A) but have elegantly avoided when describing the other TrueType tables, thanks to TTX.

The contents of the EBDT table are divided into several subblocks, each of which can be in another format. When we are inside the EBDT table, there is no way to know where each subblock begins; only the EBLC table contains that information.

There are nine formats for subblocks in EBDT:

- Format 1: for each glyph, we have first a series of "small metrics" (5 bytes) and then the bitmap data, aligned on 1-byte boundaries (in other words, when a row of pixels ends within a byte, we pad the byte with bits having the value zero). Aligning the images on 1-byte boundaries gives us access to the glyphs a few milliseconds faster.

- Format 2: as above, except that the alignment is performed even within the bytes. In other words, the data contain only the pixels that appear within the glyph's bounding box; no padding bits are used.

- Format 3 is obsolete.

- Format 4 (used only in bdat tables) uses Huffman compression. This is a first, since, as we saw in Appendix A, no other bitmap font format than TeX's PK format is *compressed*. The Huffman compression [255, pp. 61–71] of a string composed of symbols drawn from a certain set of symbols involves creating a binary tree (a tree in which each node that is not a leaf has exactly two children) corresponding to the frequency of the symbols in the string. The most common symbol will therefore be at the top of the tree, and the least frequent symbols will appear at the leaves. Since each node has exactly two children, we can say that these children correspond to the numbers 0 and 1. The path that connects the root of the tree to any given leaf is therefore a binary number. The larger this number, the less common the corresponding symbol. We replace the symbols in the string with these binary numbers, and the compression is finished.

  This method of compression is quite efficient because the most frequent symbols are replaced by very few bits. To decompress a string, we first read the tree and then read the data bit by bit, following along in the tree: every time we reach a leaf, we replace the bits read with the symbol in question. This extremely simple method of compression, developed by Daniel Huffman in 1952 [185], is applied here by taking two sets of symbols: the groups of black pixels and the groups of white pixels. We build a separate tree for each group. We read the bits and interpret them alternately as belonging to the first or the second tree.

  In this type of subblock, we have, first of all, three pointers (of 4 unsigned bytes each) to the tree of white pixels, the tree of black pixels, and the start of the data; next come these three types of data, in the same order.

- Format 5 contains no metrics: the glyphs are assumed to have the same metrics, therefore the same number of pixels. The rows of pixels are aligned on bits (within the bytes).

- Format 6 is like Format 1, but the glyphs have "big metrics" (a useful format when glyphs are to be used horizontally and vertically).

- Format 7 is the combination of 2 and 6 (alignment on bits, with "big metrics").

- Formats 8 and 9 contain *composite* glyphs. The principle is the same as for the composite glyphs in AFM files (see §C.3.7) or TeX's virtual fonts (see §B.3): we take n glyphs, each of which may be displaced in both directions, and create a new glyph from them. For example, we can combine the glyph "acute accent" with the glyph 'e' to obtain an 'é'. We can have as many glyphs as we please, and each of them can in turn be a composite.

  The data of Format 8 are structured as follows: First, a set of "small metrics" for the composite glyph, followed by the number of components. Next, for each glyph, its glyph code and its horizontal and vertical offsets, encoded as one signed byte (an offset can be between −127 and +128 pixels).

  Format 9 is similar, but its metrics are "big."

Note that Format 4 can be used only in bdat tables and that Formats 8 and 9 can be used only in EBDT tables.

這本書寫得十分好用了很合當的例子我十分欣賞

這本書寫得十分好用了很合當的例子我十分欣賞

這本書寫得十分好用了很合當的例子我十分欣賞

這本書寫得十分好用了很合當的例子我十分欣賞

Figure D-2: Comparison of a line of Chinese text rendered at 12 pixels per em and 24 pixels per em (by a rather poor rendering engine), then enlarged from 12 to 24 by means of the EBSC table. Finally, the same text in a vector font.

D.7.2   The EBSC Table

Suppose that you have just finished designing the 7,000 bitmap glyphs of a fine Chinese font at the sizes of 9 and 12. Your boss then comes to you and asks for size 18 as well, due tomorrow! Panic sets in! It is in these difficult moments that the EBSC table comes to the rescue: thanks to it, we can request that a new size be generated from an existing one. The procedure in question involves scaling bitmaps and rounding to the nearest pixel. We can thus obtain size 18 in a flash, simply by scaling size 12 up by 150 percent. Unfortunately, the quality of the resulting font is very much in doubt, but could we expect anything better?

The EBSC table has the following structure:

```
<EBSC>
  <tableVersion version="2.0"/>
  <numScales value="1"/>
  <bitmapScale ppemX="18" ppemY="18"
    substitutePpemX="12" substitutePpemY="12">
    <hori>
      <ascender value="12"/>
      <descender value="0"/>
      <widthMax value="11"/>
      <caretSlopeNumerator value="0"/>
      <caretSlopeDenominator value="0"/>
      <caretOffset value="0"/>
      <minOriginSB value="0"/>
      <minAdvanceSB value="0"/>
      <maxBeforeBL value="12"/>
      <minAfterBL value="0"/>
    </hori>
    <vert>
      <ascender value="0"/>
      <descender value="0"/>
      <widthMax value="0"/>
```

```
        <caretSlopeNumerator value="0"/>
        <caretSlopeDenominator value="0"/>
        <caretOffset value="0"/>
        <minOriginSB value="0"/>
        <minAdvanceSB value="0"/>
        <maxBeforeBL value="0"/>
        <minAfterBL value="0"/>
      </vert>
    </bitmapScale>
  </EBSC>
```

Here we recognize the elements hori and vert from the EBLC table (see §D.7.1).

D.7.3   The bhed Table

The bhed table is used by Apple alone. It is identical to the head table and replaces that table when the font has no vector contours but only bitmaps. A font containing bhed must, first of all, also contain bloc and bdat tables and, second, must not contain head or glyf tables.

D.8   Some Other Optional Tables

We shall leap all over the place in this section, since we shall describe all the optional True-Type tables that are not "advanced tables" (in the sense of OpenType and AAT).

D.8.1   The DSIG Table

The DSIG table (OpenType only) contains a *digital signature* of the font. The principle of digital signatures is as follows: the font's designer or vendor registers with a provider of digital signatures (such as VeriSign, Cybertrust, or another) and obtains two "keys": a private key and a public key. Using the private key, she produces the font's *digital signature*. Operating systems and other software that uses fonts will read the public key and use it to *authenticate* the font. In other words, they check that it does indeed correspond to the original data.

OpenType accepts PKCS#7 digital signatures with an X.509 certificate [308, 187].

TTX shows the contents of the DSIG table in the form of hexadecimal data, but at the same time it warns the user that the table will no longer be valid after conversion to TTF.

Microsoft freely distributes a tool [256] that digitally signs OpenType and TrueType fonts. The tool is free, *but* the certificate provided by VeriSign [339] costs the considerable *annual* sum of more than $430. And take note: before committing yourself, consider that you will never be able to stop your annual subscription if you do not want your users to be confronted with warning messages about a revoked certificate! We may well ask who are the greater crooks: font pirates or authenticators.[12]

---

[12] Fortunately, books such as *Web Security, Privacy & Commerce* [147] show us how to create certificates ourselves.

D.8.2 The gasp Table

The name *gasp* is the acronym of *grid-fitting and scan procedure*. It is a small table whose purpose is to tell the system how to render the glyphs at different point sizes. Here is one such table:

```
<gasp>
  <gaspRange rangeMaxPPEM="8" rangeGaspBehavior="2"/>
  <gaspRange rangeMaxPPEM="16" rangeGaspBehavior="1"/>
  <gaspRange rangeMaxPPEM="65535" rangeGaspBehavior="3"/>
</gasp>
```

The gasp element contains several gaspRange elements. The attribute rangeGaspBehavior indicates the method for rendering; it may take the following values:

- 0: use neither TrueType instructions TrueType nor gray levels.

- 1: use TrueType instructions but not gray levels.

- 2: use gray levels but not TrueType instructions.

- 3: use both TrueType instructions *and* gray levels.

The idea is that we are often better off using gray levels when setting type at small sizes; at moderate sizes, we benefit more from using instructions; at large sizes, we can use both; and at very large sizes, we need neither instructions nor gray levels. The attribute rangeMax gives the maximum value of each interval; the intervals are arranged in increasing order. In the example above, therefore, we start with gray levels (up to 8 pixels per em), then we move on to instructions (up to 16 pixels per em), and finally we combine the two. The maximum size is encoded as a 2-byte value in the TTF file; therefore, 65,535 is the largest value allowed for this attribute.

The gasp table can be used only with TrueType glyphs; it does not work in OpenType/CFF fonts.

D.8.3 The Tables hdmx and LTSH

Do not confuse hdmx with its near cousin hmtx. Both tables contain horizontal widths; the only difference is that the widths in hmtx (a required table) are expressed in TrueType units while those of hdmx (an optional table) are expressed in pixels.

According to Microsoft, what is useful about the hdmx is that it relieves the system from having to perform scaling and rounding operations for every size of glyphs in the hmtx table. We may well wonder whether the savings in time and CPU cycles is really significant enough to justify another table. In any event, these tables do exist, and have existed since the beginning.

In its binary form, this table contains subtables corresponding to the different sizes supported. Each subtable contains indices for glyphs and the corresponding widths.

TTX, on the other hand, displays this table in a much more convenient manner. Here, for example, is an hdmx table as presented by TTX:

```
<hdmx>
  <hdmxData>
    ppem:       9  10  11  12  13  14  15  16  17  18  19  ... 100 ;

    .notdef:    9  10  11  12  13  14  15  16  17  18  19  ... 100 ;
    .null:      0   0   0   0   0   0   0   0   0   0   0  ...   0 ;
    A:          8   7   8   8   9  10  10  11  12  12  13  ...  68 ;
    AE:        10  10  11  12  12  14  15  16  17  18  19  ...  99 ;
    AEacute:   10  10  11  12  12  14  15  16  17  18  19  ...  99 ;
    ...
  </hdmxData>
</hdmx>
```

Here we have omitted the sizes between 19 and 100 so that the code will fit on the page. The first line indicates the sizes (there are 31 in all); the following lines show the widths corresponding to these sizes for each glyph. Microsoft asks us to include at least the following sizes in the table: 11, 12, 13, 15, 16, 17, 19, 21, 24, 27, 29, 32, 33, 37, 42, 46, 50, 54, 58, 67, 75, 83, 92, and 100.

Note that there is also a VDMX table (see §D.8.5); but it is quite different from hdmx, as it does not provide the (vertical) widths for each glyph in the font, only their extreme values.

The astute reader will certainly have noticed that the letter 'A' is narrower at 10 points than at 9. How can that be possible? There is only one plausible explanation: δ instructions. The font's designer specified that the last auxiliary point (the glyph's width) at size 10 be moved to the left; thus the width is smaller than that of the preceding size, for which no δ instruction has been given. That, by the way, is one of the raisons d'être for this table: without it, the rendering engine would be required to apply all the TrueType instructions before making a decision about the width of a given glyph.

In Figure D-3, we see the widths of the letter 'A' in *Verdana* as they are given in the font's hdmx table. Although there is still a bit of chaos at the smallest sizes, we see that the distribution becomes almost linear beyond 50 points, which is to be expected, since the effect of TrueType instructions becomes less marked at large sizes. If the distribution is linear, there is no need for the hdmx: we merely apply a simple rule of three and round to the nearest pixel. But how do we know at what point the distribution becomes linear?

Instead of placing these crucial data into the hdmx table, the inventor of TrueType decided to create a new table for this purpose, LTSH (unpronounceable acronym of *linear threshold*). This table contains the size in pixels per em beyond which the widths in pixels follow a linear distribution (aside from rounding). Here is an example:

```
<LTSH>
  <yPel name=".notdef" value="1"/>
  <yPel name=".null" value="1"/>
  <yPel name="A" value="50"/>
  <yPel name="AE" value="51"/>
  <yPel name="AEacute" value="51"/>
  <yPel name="Aacute" value="50"/>
```

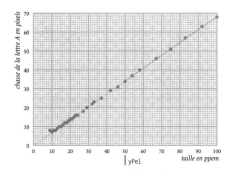

Figure D-3: The distribution of the sizes in pixels of the letter 'A' from the font Verdana, as a function of point size, expressed in pixels per em. The data come from the font's gasp table.

```
<yPel name="Abreve" value="50"/>
...
<yPel name="z" value="17"/>
<yPel name="zacute" value="17"/>
<yPel name="zcaron" value="17"/>
<yPel name="zeta" value="13"/>
</LTSH>
```

The reader may be astonished to see that the threshold for the letter 'A' and its variants is only 50 or 51 pixels per em, whereas it is 17 pixels per em for the letter 'z'. That is due to the fact that the definition of this threshold is slightly more complex. For a size to be considered the "threshold", at least one of the following two conditions must obtain beyond that size:

- The width as calculated by linear extrapolation coincides with the width after rendering.

- The difference between these two widths is less than 2 percent, but in this case the threshold cannot be lower than 50 pixels per em.

In our example, the letter 'z' is apparently stable enough to meet the first condition, whereas 'A' is less stable and thus has a higher threshold (which just happens to be 50, the minimum value in the second condition).

The values in the gasp table that exceed the LTSH threshold are useless.

D.8.4   The kern Table

The kern table was hit with the full force of the *font war* fought by Microsoft, Apple, and Adobe. It differs greatly according to the context (TrueType, OpenType, or AAT) and applies only to fonts with TrueType glyph descriptions (and not, for example, to OpenType/CFF fonts).

As the name suggests, the purpose of this table is to manage kerning between glyphs.

Here is an example:

```
<kern>
  <version value="0"/>
  <kernsubtable coverage="1" format="0">
    <pair l="A" r="S" v="-"/>
    <pair l="A" r="T" v="-"/>
    <pair l="A" r="U" v="-"/>
    <pair l="A" r="V" v="-"/>
    <pair l="A" r="W" v="-"/>
    <pair l="A" r="Y" v="-"/>
    ...
    <pair l="z" r="oslash" v="-"/>
    <pair l="z" r="q" v="-"/>
  </kernsubtable>
</kern>
```

The first element is the version of the table. In the binary version of this table, we have already seen a disagreement among the companies mentioned—one that borders on provocation. Everyone agrees that the table begins with a header containing two numbers: the version number and the number of subtables. That is quite customary, as most TrueType tables begin the same way. Yes, but for Microsoft these numbers are encoded as two-byte values, whereas for Apple they are encoded with four bytes (as if kerning tables with more than 65,536 subtables were anticipated). Result: an incompatibility between the two variants of the kern table—one that renders the tables for one system useless on the other. Apple backed down in order to compensate for this ridiculous situation, and today AAT can detect the origin of the table and read both the version with 2 bytes and the one with 4.

Aside from the difference in the "version" field, there is also a difference in value: 0 for True-Type and OpenType, 1 for AAT.

Then come some kernsubtable elements. These are subtables, and there can be several of them, in different formats. The format attribute is the format of the table: OS/2 accepts only Format 0; the OpenType specification OpenType describes formats 0 and 2, but Microsoft declares in another document [265] that only Format 0 is recognized by Windows. Finally, Apple accepts formats 0, 1, 2, and 3.

The coverage attribute contains a series of flags that are also victims of this skirmish: for Microsoft, the first flag, when set, indicates that the kerning pairs are horizontal; the second flag indicates that the subtable contains "minimal data" (we shall see what these are); the third indicates that the kerning pairs are applied perpendicularly to the direction of the text (*cross stream*); and the fourth indicates that the values of this table's kerning pairs replace those of the preceding tables.

Apple, on the other hand, recognizes neither the "minimal data" nor the replacement of the kerning values. To Apple, the first flag is set if the pairs are vertical (!), the second indicates *cross stream*, the third indicates that the different subtables belong to AAT font *variations* (see the fvar and gvar tables of AAT).

What is "minimal data"? The concept is quite confused: the OpenType specification declares that the values of the same kerning pairs taken from the different subtables are added together; to keep the final result from becoming unreasonably large, the specification provides subtables containing only the "minimal data", which reduces the waste. In any case, Microsoft makes this concept obsolete by imposing the restriction that there be only one subtable in a kern table in an OpenType font.

D.8.4.1   The kern subtables common to OpenType and AAT

The most widely used subtable is that of Format 0. It is also the one that we see in the sample code above. It contains pair subelements, each of which has three attributes: the glyph on the left (l), the glyph on the right (r), and the kerning value (v). There could hardly be a simpler approach.

Format 2 sorts the glyphs into different *classes* according to their behavior with respect to kerning. For instance, we can say that the kerning applied to 'AV' will also apply to 'ÂV', 'ÁV', 'ÀV', etc. The glyphs 'A', 'Â', 'Á', and 'À' will therefore be placed into the same class. This approach is convenient but can be disastrous in certain cases: for example, 'fè' must not be kerned in the same way as 'fe'.

TTX does not process the tables of Format 2; it represents them as hexadecimal data.

D.8.4.2   The kern subtables specific to AAT

Let us begin with a table of Format 3, which is an improved version of Format 2. The reader is certainly familiar with the technique of *value indexing*, which is used, for example, in the GIF graphics format, in which instead of giving the true value of each pixel, that value is stored in a table, and the pixel is represented by the index of its value into the table. The benefit is that when a pixel in an image with 16.7 million colors required three bites, if the image has fewer than 256 colors, a single byte for the index of the color is sufficient. The image is thus one third the size.

The same applies here: we index the kerning values on the assumption that there will be at most 256 different values. We also assume that there is a maximum of 256 classes for the glyph at the left and the same number for the glyph at the right. Thus the entire table is encoded as single bytes rather than as two-byte values, as with the tables of Format 2. Other structural optimizations make this formate more efficient (in both memory space and CPU time necessary for processing) than Format 2.

Format 1 is the *ne plus ultra* of kerning: Apple uses a *finite automaton*, just as with the morx and just tables. In this regard, we invite the reader to read the introduction to finite automata for AAT fonts in the relevant section (§D.13.1).

Here the actions of the finite automaton serve (1) to place the glyphs onto a special stack, called the *kerning stack*; (2) to retrieve the glyphs from that stack while applying a certain amount of kerning to each. The benefit is that the stack may contain up to eight glyphs: thus we can kern as many as eight glyphs *simultaneously*.

The English-speaking, or merely Eurocentric, reader may wonder why anyone would want to kern eight glyphs simultaneously. Indeed, eight is a rather high number, but we can easily find triplets of glyphs that give a different result if we kern them pairwise. For example, the result will be different if the upper part of the glyph on the left protrudes to the right, the opposite is true of the glyph on the right, and the glyph in the middle is rather low.

To find an example of one such triplet, let us take the *Vlaamse Aikido Vereniging* (Flemish Aikido Union), or V.A.V. The reader's eye will have caught the problem: when we write 'VAV', the letters are correctly kerned; but when periods appear between these letters, the distance between the period and the letter preceding it is too great. That is very much to be expected, since when examining the pair '.A' we are no longer aware that the period is preceded by a 'V' (and similarly for the second period). What if there were a different letter before the period? The designer of the font used in this book, Jean François Porchez, handled the most extreme case (for example, two 'V's in a row: 'V.V') and moved the period as far from the 'V' as necessary for the pair of glyphs in question to be correctly kerned. His decision was perfectly logical, but it causes problems for the opposite extreme: 'V.A' and 'A.V'. How, then, can we obtain 'VA' and 'A.V'?

This sort of adjustment is supported by Format 1 of the kern table—a format that is, as you will recall, reserved for AAT, i.e., for Mac OS X.

Here is an example of a table of this type. We begin with the header:

```
<kern>
  <version value="1"/>
  <kernsubtable coverage="1" format="1">
    <stateSize value="7"/>
```

Next come the table of classes:

```
<classes>
  <class value="0">
    <glyph name=".notdef"/>
    <glyph name=".null"/>
    ...
    <glyph name="zerowidthjoiner"/>
  </class>
  <class value="1">
    <glyph name="A"/>
    <glyph name="B"/>
    ...
    <glyph name="Z"/>
  </class>
  ...
</classes>
```

the table of states:

```
<states>
  <state value="0">
    <entry class="0" value="2"/>
    <entry class="1" value="0"/>
    ...
    <entry class="7" value="2"/>
```

```
      </state>
      <state value="1">
        <entry class="0" value="2"/>
        <entry class="1" value="0"/>
        ...
        <entry class="7" value="0"/>
      </state>
      ...
    </states>
```

the table of entries (or "arrows leading into a state"):

```
  <entries>
    <entry value="0" newState="0" flags="0x8000" action="0"/>
    <entry value="1" newState="2" flags="0x8000" action="0"/>
    <entry value="2" newState="0" flags="0x0000" action=""/>
    ...
    <entry value="5" newState="0" flags="0x8000" action="2"/>
  </entries>
```

and, finally, the table of actions:

```
  <actions>
        <action value="0">
          <eol/>
        </action>
        <action value="1">
          <kern value="682"/>
          <eol/>
        </action>
        <action value="2">
          <flag value="0x8000"/>
          <eol/>
        </action>
      </actions>
    </kernsubtable>
  </kern>
```

These four tables are the four ingredients of a finite automaton: classes, states, entries, and actions. In class, the glyphs are classified according to their behavior. A state contains, for each class, the entries corresponding to the arrows that leave the state in question. The "entries" are pairs (ε, α): the action α associated with the arrow leading into state ε. For instance, an entry entry contains a "new state" value (newState) and a value for the action action. There is one other attribute: flags. This attribute supplements the action: it is a set of flags describing the behavior of the processor while it performs the action. Finally comes the element actions, which contains the actions: each action is a sequence of kerning values or flags, terminated by an end-of-list marker, eol.

If the actions seem complicated in this syntax, that is because, according to the size of the kerning stack, they can contain up to eight kerning values, which will be applied to the eight glyphs read from the stack.

D.8.5   *The VDMX Table*

The VDMX table is in no way a "vertical version" of the hdmx table (and doubtless it is precisely to avoid this sort of misunderstanding that its name is written in full capitals). It does not contain the vertical widths in pixels of all the glyphs, only their extreme values. Here is an example:

```
<VDMX>
  <version version="0"/>
  <ratRanges>
    <ratRange bCharSet="1" xRatio="1" yStartRatio="1" yEndRatio="1">
      <records startsz="8" endsz="255">
        <record yMax="7" yMin="-" yPelHeight="8"/>
        <record yMax="9" yMin="-" yPelHeight="9"/>
        <record yMax="10" yMin="-" yPelHeight="10"/>
        <record yMax="11" yMin="-" yPelHeight="11"/>
        ...
        <record yMax="233" yMin="-" yPelHeight="254"/>
        <record yMax="233" yMin="-" yPelHeight="255"/>
      </records>
    </ratRange>
  </ratRanges>
</VDMX>
```

The version can take the value 0 or 1, but Microsoft recommends version 1. The element ratRanges ("ranges of ratios") contains some ratRange values corresponding to the different ratios of width to height. The meaning of the bCharSet attribute depends on the version: if the version is 0, a bCharSet of 0 means that the record data of the ratRange have been calculated for all the glyphs; a bCharSet of 1 means that only the "proper" glyphs (those belonging to the Windows ANSI encoding for Western European languages) have been used in the calculations. For version 1, the meanings are, generally speaking, just the opposite.

The xRatio attribute is the numerator, and yStartRatio and yEndRatio are the extreme values of the range of denominators of the fractions that make the ratios compatible with the current ratRange.

The records element (with an 's') contains the entries to this table (startsz and endsz indicate the extreme sizes in pixels per em). Each record (without an 's') corresponds to a size in pixels per em. The attributes yMax and yMin indicate the maximum and minimum values of the glyphs' heights.

The data in this table will help the system to calculate the ideal leading for a given font without first rendering all the glyphs in the font.

D.8.6   The Tables vhea and vmtx

The vhea table is the spitting image of its horizontal counterpart, hhea. What are left and right side-bearings in the latter become upper (the vertical distance between the vertical origin and the upper extremity of the glyph) and lower (the distance between the lower extremity and the vertical set-width) side-bearings in the former. Here is an example:

```
<vhea>
  <tableVersion value="1.0"/>
  <ascent value="1024"/>
  <descent value="-"/>
  <lineGap value="0"/>
  <advanceHeightMax value="0"/>
  <minTopSideBearing value="0"/>
  <minBottomSideBearing value="0"/>
  <yMaxExtent value="0"/>
  <caretSlopeRise value="0"/>
  <caretSlopeRun value="0"/>
  <reserved0 value="0"/>
  <reserved1 value="0"/>
  <reserved2 value="0"/>
  <reserved3 value="0"/>
  <reserved4 value="0"/>
  <metricDataFormat value="0"/>
  <numberOfVMetrics value="247"/>
</vhea>
```

There is a version 1.1 of this table, in which the three dimensions ascent, descent, and line-Gap, which can ordinarily be calculated from the glyph descriptions, are replaced by the "noble" values vertTypoAscender, vertTypoDescender, and vertTypoLineGap. These are the vertical counterparts of the entries sTypoAscender, sTypoDescender, and sTypoLineGap, which are found in the OS/2 table. The idea is that the entries that contain the word "typo" are chosen by the font's (human) designer and do not strictly correspond to measurements made within the font. We can thus avoid the risk of having an excessively large or small value caused by an isolated glyph of secondary importance.

The vmtx table is as simple as its cousin hmtx: it contains the vertical set-width and the top side-bearing for each glyph in the font. Here is an example:

```
<vmtx>
  <mtx name=".notdef" height="256" tsb="65"/>
  <mtx name="A" height="128" tsb="43"/>
  <mtx name="Alpha" height="256" tsb="43"/>
  <mtx name="B" height="128" tsb="45"/>
  <mtx name="Beta" height="256" tsb="42"/>
  ...
  <mtx name="y" height="128" tsb="104"/>
```

```
        <mtx name="z" height="128" tsb="104"/>
        <mtx name="zero" height="128" tsb="43"/>
        <mtx name="zeta" height="256" tsb="42"/>
    </vmtx>
```

Here tsb comes from *top side-bearing*. There is a short version of this table for fonts in which many glyphs are of the same width (such as ideographic fonts), which cuts the size of the table down by half. If the font contains numGlyphs glyphs (a value drawn from maxp) and the table vhea contains a numberOfVMetrics that is different from numGlyphs, then the first numberOfVMetrics glyphs in the vmtx table have *both* a vertical set-width *and* a top side-bearing; the remaining glyphs have only top side-bearings, their set-widths being equal to that of the last glyph with a stated set-width.

D.8.7   The PCLT Table

This table provides data for the Hewlett-Packard printers that use the PCL 5 language. It is interesting to note that the original specification for TrueType [258] states that this table is "highly recommended", the OpenType specification [264] states that its use in fonts containing TrueType glyph descriptions is "strongly discouraged", and the AAT specification [56] ignores it outright. Thus it is a *controversial* table, to say the least. Here is an example of this table:

```
    <PCLT>
        <version value="1.0"/>
        <fontNumber value="1292025634"/>
        <pitch value="569"/>
        <xHeight value="1062"/>
        <style value="0"/>
        <typeFamily value="16602"/>
        <capHeight value="1466"/>
        <symbolSet value="0"/>
        <typeface value="M Arial          "/>
        <characterComplement value="ffffffff003ffffe"/>
        <fileName value="ARLRO0"/>
        <strokeWeight value="0"/>
        <widthType value="0"/>
        <serifStyle value="64"/>
        <reserved value="0"/>
    </PCLT>
```

Here is a very brief description of the key entries. (The reader will find more detailed information in [264].)

- fontNumber and typeFamily: identifiers for the font and the font "family" that also identify the foundry.

- pitch: the set-width of the whitespace. (The whitespace in some software is a glyph representing the Unicode character SPACE.)

- `xHeight` and `capHeight`: the height of the lowercase and uppercase letters, in TrueType units.

- `style`, a number that combines three characteristics of the font: the type of stroke filling (plain, hollow, shadowed, etc.), the set-width (regular, condensed, extended, etc.), and the slope (upright, slanted forward, slanted backward).

- `symbolSet`: what we usually call *character set*, i.e., the set of glyphs contained in the font.

- `typeface`: the name of the font as it appears on the printer's LCD display. It must be mentioned that neither Microsoft nor Adobe gave any thought to this sort of feature.

- `characterComplement`: a series of flags that indicate this font's compatibility with several encodings. In theory there are 64 possibilities, but only 10 are actually defined.

- `fileName`: the suggested filename. Six uppercase characters, which brings us back to the glorious era of MS-DOS filenames—and even earlier, since MS-DOS supported eight-character filenames.

- `StrokeWeight`: the font's weight, ranging from −7 ("ultra-light") to 4 ("extra-bold").

- `WidthType`: the font's set-width, ranging from −5 ("ultra-compressed") to 3 ("extra-extended"). The specification states that this value "The values are not directly related to those in the appearance with field of the style word above", with no further comments.

- `serifStyle`: the style of serifs, presented as a list of names, with neither comments nor examples.

D.9 *The OpenType Advanced Typographic Tables*

In this section, we shall describe the tables BASE, GDEF, GPOS, GSUB, and JSTF, which make up the major artillery of the OpenType format. They are called *advanced typographic tables*, not to be confused with AAT (*Apple advanced typographic tables*), which we shall see in the following section, §D.11.

D.9.1 *Important concepts*

D.9.1.1 *Script, language, feature, lookup*

In the advanced typographic tables, we use the concepts of *script* and *language*. OpenType considers that the behavior of a font should differ according to its script, and sometimes even according to the language being used. Of course, this is an enormous simplification of what actually happens in the real world, but we can accomplish quite a lot even with this simplification.

More original are the concepts of *feature* and *lookup*. In an interactive context, the font's user selects those of the font's features that she wishes to apply. Some features can be enabled automatically when the font is selected. Each feature includes a number of *lookups* in the string being typeset. Each of these *lookups* can, according to the string being typeset, contain some operations: positionings or glyph substitutions, etc.

The system works in the following way: the user selects the script and possibly the language (otherwise the default language will be used); the software shows the available features; the user decides to apply some of them to a block of text; each feature contains some *lookups*, all of which are applied to the block of text; each *lookup* contains a number of rules for positioning or substitution that depend on the string being set, and the first rule that matches the conditions imposed is the one that will be executed.

For example, in a Latin font, we declare the Latin script and select English as the default language. In this font there is a feature called liga (the names of features are like the names of TrueType tables: they contain four Latin letters; see §D.10.2 for a description of many of the predefined features). Inside this feature we define a lookup that will handle the "f-ligatures" ('fi', 'ff', etc.). Within this lookup we write the rules "f + i → fi", etc. The user informs the software that he is using the Latin alphabet and the English language. The software informs the user that the liga feature is available. The user selects the word "afflict" and enables liga. The software consults the feature, which supplies a list of the lookups to execute—in this example, the lookup for the f-ligatures. The lookup in question applies substitution rules. The word is converted to "afflict" (with the 'ffl' ligature), and the task is complete.

In this entire example, order is important only for the rules inside the lookup. Indeed, the specification does not state whether the lookups are executed in a given order (and even if they were, the high muckamucks at Adobe declared that their software would execute the lookups on the OpenType list in the order that it deemed best). Conversely, the order of the rules is crucial: in the word "afflict", if the rule "f + l → fl" were placed before the rule "f + f + l → ffl", the latter rule would never be executed, and the word would be set as "afflict" (with the 'fl' ligature but not the 'ffl' ligature).

Lookups are usually applied to all the glyphs in the input string, but we have the possibility of limiting their scope to certain types of glyphs. In the GDEF table, we classify the glyphs into four classes: base glyphs, diacritical marks, ligatures, and components of composite glyphs. Each lookup has a number called LookupFlag that is, as its name suggests, a series of flags. The flags contained in this number allow us to apply lookups in a selective manner, ignoring certain types of glyphs. For instance, suppose that in our font (say, *Monotype Garamond* italic) we have a ligature "*eta*" but also wish to use it with an acute accent and a circumflex accent ("*étâ*") or with two circumflex accents ("*êtâ*", as in the French verb form "nous prêtâmes"). To do so, we will arrange for the lookup for ligatures to ignore any accents that appear between the letters and to create the ligature first. Then the accents will be set by a special lookup whose purpose is to position accents over the constituents of a ligature. Here are the meanings of the flags in LookupFlag:

- The first bit, when enabled, indicates that the script is of the Urdu type, in which the text is typeset at an angle and the last glyph in the word must appear *on the baseline*. This flag seems extremely specialized, but for the specific case of Urdu it is of pivotal importance (see §D.9.3.4).

- The second, third, and fourth bits, when enabled, tell the lookup to ignore base glyphs, ligatures, and diacritical marks, respectively.

- The last eight bits tell the lookup to ignore not all diacritical marks, but a certain type (see §D.9.6)

D.9.1.2   Device tables

Another innovation that characterizes the OpenType advanced typographic tables: *device tables*, so called because they adapt the font data to given resolutions for rendering. We have already dealt with tables whose purpose is to avoid the need to use TrueType instructions. For example, the hdmx table contains the values of set-widths as they stand after the instructions have been executed. Device tables generalize this idea. We take any dimension (for example, the x-coordinate of a point) and indicate the variations that that dimension has at different sizes—variations expressed in pixels per em. As this approach recalls that of the δ instructions (see §E.2.4), these values are called *δ values*. Here is an example of a *device table*:

```
<XAdvDevice>
  <StartSize value="9"/>
  <EndSize value="19"/>
  <DeltaFormat value="1"/>
  <DeltaValue value="[1, 0, 0, 0, 0, 0, 0, 0, 0, 0, -]"/>
</XAdvDevice>
```

where the sizes from 9 to 19 pixels per em are considered and the δ correction is zero everywhere but at the ends of the interval, where it takes the values 1 and −1. That means that at sizes between 10 and 18, the calculation of the dimension in question from the value in abstract TrueType units gives good results. Only for the values 9 and 19 is it necessary to correct the calculation, as indicated.

D.9.1.3   Coverage tables

Another important concept: there is a general method for selecting the glyphs that will be subjected to positioning or substitution, the *coverage table* for an operation. The selected glyphs are placed into a Coverage element. This element takes a single attribute: Format. There are, in fact, two formats for the Coverage element, but one can look in vain for the difference between these two formats in the XML code produced by TTX: in both cases, Coverage contains a list of glyphs in the form of Glyph elements. TTX displays both formats in the same manner, leaving us with a difficult decision for the choice of format. It is enough to note that Format 1 is better suited to short or sparse lists while Format 2 is better suited to series of glyphs with contiguous identifiers. Here is an example of a coverage table as shown by TTX:

```
<Coverage Format="2">
  <Glyph value="A"/>
  <Glyph value="B"/>
  <Glyph value="C"/>
  ...
  <Glyph value="uni1EF8"/>
  <Glyph value="uni1EF9"/>
  <Glyph value="uni20A0"/>
</Coverage>
```

Coverage tables are nothing more than lists of glyphs. Their benefit is that their binary form can be accommodated to the nature of the lists that contain them. For example, if the indices of the glyphs in question are contiguous, we can use a coverage table that contains only the extreme values of these indices; if, however, the list of indices is sparse, we can use a type of table adapted to sparse lists. For each type of list of glyphs, there is an appropriate coverage table. But TTX glosses over these differences by showing us only what is essential: the glyphs contained in the list.

D.9.2   The BASE Table

Let us begin our tour of the OpenType advanced typographic tables with the most basic one: the BASE table. This table aims to solve the problem of the different baselines that various scripts have. The reader will certainly have noticed that we cannot always use the same base-line when mixing scripts. Here are three well-known examples:

I'm based 日本語の文字です ཨཐེསཁརཕོངུས

Here we see the Latin, ideographic Chinese (and Japanese hiragana syllabary), and Tibetan scripts. The baseline for the ideographs, i.e., the bottom edge of the abstract square in which each glyph is drawn, is traditionally placed slightly lower than the baseline of the Latin script. As for Tibetan, its baseline is actually at the top (as with various other scripts of northern India, as well as Hebrew).

We shall apply the principles of OpenType: first the *script*, then the *language*, and finally the *features* (there are no *lookups*). There is another classification at a level higher than *script*: the *direction of writing*.

Here is an example of a BASE table, the one for the font *Palatino Linotype*, which contains Latin, Greek, and Cyrillic glyphs but not Chinese or Tibetan ones:

```
<BASE>
  <Version value="1.0"/>
  <HorizAxis>
    <BaseTagList>
      <!-- BaseTagCount=3 -->
      <BaselineTag index="0" value="hang"/>
      <BaselineTag index="1" value="ideo"/>
      <BaselineTag index="2" value="romn"/>
    </BaseTagList>
    <BaseScriptList>
      <!-- BaseScriptCount=3 -->
      <BaseScriptRecord index="0">
        <BaseScriptTag value="cyrl"/>
        <BaseScript>
          <BaseValues>
            <DefaultIndex value="2"/>
            <!-- BaseCoordCount=3 -->
            <BaseCoord index="0" Format="1">
              <Coordinate value="1405"/>
```

```
            </BaseCoord>
            <BaseCoord index="1" Format="1">
              <Coordinate value="-"/>
            </BaseCoord>
            <BaseCoord index="2" Format="1">
              <Coordinate value="0"/>
            </BaseCoord>
          </BaseValues>
          <!-- BaseLangSysCount=0 -->
        </BaseScript>
      </BaseScriptRecord>
      <BaseScriptRecord index="1">
        <BaseScriptTag value="grek"/>
        <BaseScript>
        ...
        </BaseScript>
      </BaseScriptRecord>
      <BaseScriptRecord index="2">
        <BaseScriptTag value="latn"/>
        <BaseScript>
        ...
        </BaseScript>
      </BaseScriptRecord>
    </BaseScriptList>
  </HorizAxis>
</BASE>
```

The structure of this table is quite complex. First of all, it must be understood that this table contains *baseline systems*, on the one hand, and *scripts*, on the other. The baseline systems in the example above are hang for hanging scripts, ideo for ideographic scripts, and romn for alphabetic scripts. The scripts are cyrl (Cyrillic), grek (Greek), and latn (Latin). For each script, we do two things: first, we indicate the most appropriate baseline system; second, we supply the offsets needed for switching from this baseline system to each of the other baseline systems.

Thus, if we take cyrl as the "dominant script" (if we write in Russian, for example), the table tells us that the romn baseline (that for the Western languages) is the default line and that the baseline for Tibetan, for example, will be set at a height of 1,405 TrueType units relative to the Western baseline.

Now let us examine a sample BASE table in more detail. It contains:

- Two higher-level elements: HorizAxis (the horizontal direction) and VertAxis (the vertical direction).

- Below them, two elements: BaseTagList and BaseScriptList, described here.

- BaseTagList contains one BaselineTag for each baseline system.

- `BaseScriptList` contains `BaseScriptRecords`, which correspond to the `BaseTagLists`. Each `BaseScriptRecord` contains the name of a script (`BaseScriptTag`) and a `BaseScript` element.

- `BaseScript` contains, first of all, the default baseline for the script: it is in the `Default-Index` element.

- Next, it contains the coordinates for the offset required to switch from the default base-line of the dominant script to another baseline: `BaseCoord` has an `index` attribute that connects it to a `BaselineTag` element and gives us the corresponding baseline system. It contains a subelement, `Coordinate`, which is the y-coordinate (or the x-coordinate, if we are setting type vertically) of the baseline.

We had to go through all these steps before coming to something concrete: the y-coordinates of the baselines. And we might have hoped that the work would end there, but, alas, the designers of OpenType are merciless. Therefore let us continue: the element `BaseCoord` also contains an attribute `format`, which can take the values 1, 2, or 3. Indeed, there are three ways to express the exact position of the baseline in question:

1. The simplest is to give its x-coordinate in TrueType units. That is what we see in the ex-ample.

2. Format 2 involves additionally supplying a glyph and a point on the glyph's contour. This is a warning for the case in which the TrueType instructions transform the glyph in such a way that the "uninstructed" baseline is no longer correct. Thus we supply a glyph (which could be an actual glyph or one designed only for use in this manipulation) and a point on the glyph, and the TrueType processor will use the position of this point, *after* the instructions have been executed, to obtain the baseline.

3. If the reader had imagined that Format 2 was the *ne plus ultra* of establishing the baseline, she was mistaken. Format 3 uses a *device table* (see above, §D.9.1). Thus the processor has direct access to the number of pixels between two baselines, which is calculated very precisely and stored in the device table.

We have now dissected the example. But the specification of the BASE table goes even further. Aside from the baselines, the *bounding boxes* of the glyphs are also of interest when we calcu-late the spacing between lines. In the horizontal case, we are concerned with the upper and lower edges of the box for all the glyphs in the font. We call it *MinMax*. Unlike the baselines, *MinMax* also depends on the current language and the current features.

Therefore we can continue our example by adding the following code within the element `BaseScript` and after the last `BaseValues`:

```
<DefaultMinMax index="0"/>
<BaseLangSysRecord index="0">
  <BaseLangSysTag value="RUS"/>
  <MinMax>
    <MinCoord value="-"/>
```

```
      <MaxCoord value="1861"/>
      <FeatMinMaxRecord>
        <FeatureTableTag value="smcp"/>
        <MinCoord value="-"/>
        <MaxCoord value="1861"/>
      </FeatMinMaxRecord>
      <FeatMinMaxRecord>
        <FeatureTableTag value="ital"/>
        <MinCoord value="-"/>
        <MaxCoord value="1851"/>
      </FeatMinMaxRecord>
    </MinMax>
  </BaseLangSysRecord>
```

Suppose that we are in the `cyrl` (Cyrillic) script. We select a language, in this case Russian (RUS), and supply the extrema of the glyphs for that language. It is `MinMax` that contains these extrema, in the form of the two elements `MinCoord` and `MaxCoord`. But the extrema can vary according to the selected features. That is why `MinMax` can also contain `FeatMinMaxRecord` subelements (for "record of minima and maxima with features"), in which we specify the features (here `smcp` means "small capitals" and `ital` means "italics"). One may ask what happens when we use several features at the same time. The answer does not appear in the specification, but probably the system will take the maximum values for the selected features.

D.9.2.1 Types of baselines predefined for the BASE table

The OpenType specification defines seven types of baselines, with their respective *tags*:

- `romn`: the baseline for the alphabetic scripts. (The name is politically incorrect because it comes from the word "Roman", whereas not all alphabetic scripts are derived from that of the Romans.)

- `math`: the central axis of the mathematical symbols.

- `hang`: the baseline of "hanging" scripts, such as certain scripts of India (Devanagari, for instance), Tibetan, and also ancient Hebrew.

- `ideo` and `idtp`: the lower and upper baselines of the ideal ideographic square.

- `icfb` and `icft`: the lower and upper baselines for ideographic alignment, also known as *ICF parameters* (for "ideographic character face").

The last four deserve some explanation: on the one hand, there is the *ideal ideographic square*, one em wide; on the other hand, there is the *square for ideographic alignment*, a square concentric with the previous one but smaller. This square is used for aligning Japanese glyphs. This property of glyphs recalls the `opbd` table of AAT (§D.11.7) or the `opbd` feature of Open-Type (§D.10.2.1), where the concern is with the edges of the glyph when it is aligned at the beginning of a line. Here is an example of these two types of squares:

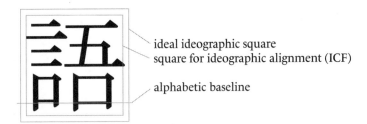

ideal ideographic square
square for ideographic alignment (ICF)

alphabetic baseline

The reader should not be surprised that we are speaking here of "squares", whereas when presenting the description of the types of baseline we spoke only of lower and upper *lines*. Let us not forget that both horizontal and vertical baselines are defined in the BASE table. In the definitions above, lower and upper become left and right when we set type vertically. By combining the lines icfb and icft (or ideo and idtp) for the two directions, we do indeed obtain a rectangle. And the age-old philosophy of the Chinese script requires this rectangle to be a square, symbol of balance and perfection.

Finally, let us note that associating the *lower* baseline with the *left* baseline (and the opposite for the *upper* baseline) when switching from horizontal to vertical typesetting is a good choice for the ideographic languages, in which vertical lines are written from right to left, but a poor choice for Mongolian, in which vertical lines are written from left to right—and for which the equivalent of the *lower* baseline would rather be the *right* baseline.

D.9.3   The GPOS Table

The GPOS table manages the positioning of the glyphs. Its applications are numerous: they range from simple kerning to the positioning of diacritical marks, the positioning of diacritical marks over other diacritical marks, typesetting at an angle in Urdu, and many others.

This table shares with the others its schema for organizing data: we start with a script (*script*) and possibly a language; then we select one or more features (*features*), and the features lead us to a number of *lookups*. These *lookups* are of nine types, and we shall study them by starting with the simplest ones.

D.9.3.1   Scripts and features

The sample GPOS table that we show here is from the font *Palatino Linotype*. Note that this table is enormous: 9,560 lines of XML code.

The table begins with a Version element and the list of scripts offered (ScriptRecord), which is contained within the element ScriptList. Let us take the code for the Latin script:

```
<GPOS>
  <Version value="1.0"/>
  <ScriptList>
    <ScriptRecord index="2">
      <ScriptTag value="latn"/>
      <Script>
        <DefaultLangSys>
          <ReqFeatureIndex value="65535"/>
```

```
      <!-- FeatureCount=3 -->
      <FeatureIndex index="0" value="3"/>
      <FeatureIndex index="1" value="4"/>
      <FeatureIndex index="2" value="0"/>
    </DefaultLangSys>
    <!-- LangSysCount=4 -->
    <LangSysRecord index="0">
      <LangSysTag value="DEU "/>
      <LangSys>
        <ReqFeatureIndex value="65535"/>
        <!-- FeatureCount=3 -->
        <FeatureIndex index="0" value="3"/>
        <FeatureIndex index="1" value="4"/>
        <FeatureIndex index="2" value="0"/>
      </LangSys>
    </LangSysRecord>
    <LangSysRecord index="1">
      <LangSysTag value="ROM "/>
      <LangSys>
        <ReqFeatureIndex value="65535"/>
        <!-- FeatureCount=3 -->
        <FeatureIndex index="0" value="3"/>
        <FeatureIndex index="1" value="4"/>
        <FeatureIndex index="2" value="0"/>
      </LangSys>
    </LangSysRecord>
    <LangSysRecord index="2">
      <LangSysTag value="TRK "/>
      <LangSys>
        <ReqFeatureIndex value="65535"/>
        <!-- FeatureCount=3 -->
        <FeatureIndex index="0" value="3"/>
        <FeatureIndex index="1" value="4"/>
        <FeatureIndex index="2" value="0"/>
      </LangSys>
    </LangSysRecord>
    <LangSysRecord index="3">
      <LangSysTag value="VIT "/>
      <LangSys>
        <ReqFeatureIndex value="65535"/>
        <!-- FeatureCount=4 -->
        <FeatureIndex index="0" value="3"/>
        <FeatureIndex index="1" value="4"/>
        <FeatureIndex index="2" value="5"/>
        <FeatureIndex index="3" value="0"/>
      </LangSys>
```

```
            </LangSysRecord>
          </Script>
        </ScriptRecord>
```

Under `ScriptRecord` we have a `ScriptTag`, which contains the name of the script in question (here, `latn`), and a `Script` element containing data on the languages that share this script.

In our example, we find one `DefaultLangSys` element for the "default language"—i.e., the behavior of the font when the language is not specified—and four `LangSysRecord` elements for four languages written in the Latin alphabet: `DEU` (German), `ROM` (Romanian), `TRK` (Turkish), `VIT` (Vietnamese).

The difference between `DefaultLangSys` and `LangSysRecord` is that the latter contains a `LangSysTag` element with information on the name of the language and a `LangSys` element that contains the features, whereas `DefaultLangSys` contains only features.

Now we come to the features attached to each language. There is one that is privileged: `ReqFeatureIndex`, the required feature. It is the only feature that is enabled automatically, without interaction with the user. It must be a feature inextricably tied to the language in question. If there is no such feature, we set `value` equal to `0xffff`.

Next comes a list of features, or rather pointers to descriptions of features, which appears in another branch of the XML document, under the element `FeatureList`. It is the `value` attribute that gives the identifier of the feature in question. In our example, for instance, when we set type in the default language, in German, in Romanian, or in Turkish, we have access to the features 3, 4, and 0. We shall see below that these are the features `subs` (subscripts), `sinf` (scientific subscripts), and `kern` (kerning). In addition, when we set type in Vietnamese, we have access to feature 5, `mark` (positioning of diacritical marks).

Now let us continue with the code for the features:

```
    <FeatureList>
      <!-- FeatureCount=6 -->
      <FeatureRecord index="0">
        <FeatureTag value="kern"/>
        <Feature>
          <!-- LookupCount=1 -->
          <LookupListIndex index="0" value="0"/>
        </Feature>
      </FeatureRecord>
      <FeatureRecord index="1">
        <FeatureTag value="kern"/>
        <Feature>
          <!-- LookupCount=1 -->
          <LookupListIndex index="0" value="1"/>
        </Feature>
      </FeatureRecord>
      <FeatureRecord index="2">
        <FeatureTag value="kern"/>
```

```
      <Feature>
        <!-- LookupCount=1 -->
        <LookupListIndex index="0" value="2"/>
      </Feature>
    </FeatureRecord>
    <FeatureRecord index="3">
      <FeatureTag value="subs"/>
      <Feature>
        <!-- LookupCount=1 -->
        <LookupListIndex index="0" value="3"/>
      </Feature>
    </FeatureRecord>
    <FeatureRecord index="4">
      <FeatureTag value="sinf"/>
      <Feature>
        <!-- LookupCount=1 -->
        <LookupListIndex index="0" value="4"/>
      </Feature>
    </FeatureRecord>
    <FeatureRecord index="5">
      <FeatureTag value="mark"/>
      <Feature>
        <!-- LookupCount=4 -->
        <LookupListIndex index="0" value="5"/>
        <LookupListIndex index="1" value="6"/>
        <LookupListIndex index="2" value="7"/>
        <LookupListIndex index="3" value="8"/>
      </Feature>
    </FeatureRecord>
  </FeatureList>
```

This branch of the document contains the *lookups* associated with each feature. Each FeaturereRecord contains, first of all, a name (FeatureTag), and then a Feature element that contains value pointers to lookups called Lookup. These lookups are found in another branch of the document, the one that appears under LookupList.

The other 98.6 percent of the table is found under LookupList: the list of *lookups*. This element contains the well-known Lookups to which the features point. Each Lookup contains, first, a LookupType (the type of the lookup; there are nine in the GPOS table), and then a LookupFlag (see §D.9.1.1).

Here is the beginning of a LookupList:

```
  <LookupList>
    <!-- LookupCount=9 -->
    <Lookup index="0">
      <LookupType value="2"/>
      <LookupFlag value="8"/>
```

The lookup in question is thus of type 2, and the flag `LookupFlag` indicates that we should disregard combining marks.

Below we shall examine the types of lookups one by one.

D.9.3.2   Lookup type 1: positioning of a single glyph

This type involves positioning a single glyph, as, for example, when creating a superscript or a subscript, centering parentheses better when setting type in small capitals, centering mathematical signs better when using old-style figures, etc. Here is an example of its use:

(BACH) (BACH) (BACH)

We see the word "BACH" with regular parentheses, the same word in small capitals with the default parentheses, and, finally, small capitals with the parentheses corrected. It is incredible how much better the result became when we simply moved the parentheses downward a few points.

Here is the code for moving the parentheses:

```
<Lookup index="0">
  <LookupType value="1"/>
  <LookupFlag value="0"/>
  <!-- SubTableCount=1 -->
  <SinglePos index="0" Format="1">
    <Coverage Format="1">
      <Glyph value="parenleft"/>
      <Glyph value="parenright"/>
    </Coverage>
    <ValueFormat value="2"/>
    <Value YPlacement="-"/>
  </SinglePos>
</Lookup>
```

The `SinglePos` element corresponds to the type of lookup that we are examining: the *positioning of a single glyph*. It contains a coverage table, which in turn contains the glyphs for the parentheses. Next, it contains an element for a *formatted value*. This is a peculiarity of the GPOS table: to represent a positioning value, we use the `Value` element, which can take eight attributes:

- `XPlacement`, for horizontal positioning of the glyph

- `YPlacement`, for vertical positioning of the glyph

- `XAdvance`, for a modification to the glyph's horizontal set-width

- YAdvance, for a modification to the glyph's vertical set-width

- XPlaDevice, a pointer to a *device table*, for horizontal positioning of the glyph

- YPlaDevice, a pointer to a *device table*, for vertical positioning of the glyph

- XAdvDevice, a pointer to a *device table*, for a modification to the glyph's horizontal set-width

- YAdvDevice, a pointer to a *device table*, for a modification to the glyph's vertical set-width

Moreover, to make it easier for the processor to read these attributes, we include, before the first Value, a ValueFormat element. The value attribute of this element contains a series of eight flags that indicate which attributes will subsequently be used.

D.9.3.3 Lookup type 2: positioning of a pair of glyphs

The *positioning of a pair of glyphs* is not simply a sophisticated way to talk about *kerning*. This operation goes much further, as each of the two glyphs can be moved separately, and in any direction. Here is one example of this type of table:

```
<Lookup index="2">
  <LookupType value="2"/>
  <LookupFlag value="8"/>
  <!-- SubTableCount=1 -->
  <PairPos index="0" Format="1">
    <Coverage Format="1">
      <Glyph value="A"/>
    </Coverage>
    <ValueFormat1 value="4"/>
    <ValueFormat2 value="0"/>
    <!-- PairSetCount=2 -->
    <PairSet index="0">
      <!-- PairValueCount=1 -->
      <PairValueRecord index="0">
        <SecondGlyph value="T"/>
        <Value1 XAdvance="-"/>
      </PairValueRecord>
    </PairSet>
    <PairSet index="1">
      <!-- PairValueCount=0 -->
    </PairSet>
  </PairPos>
</Lookup>
```

We see here that the type of the lookup is indeed 2. This lookup is represented by a PairPos element, for which there are two distinct formats. The first (as in the example) uses a coverage table for the first glyph and then one PairSet element for each element in the coverage table.

In each PairSet element, we find a PairValue element for each kerning pair with the same first glyph. Each PairValue contains, first, a Glyph, which gives us the second glyph, and usually two elements Value1 and Value2, which are *formatted values*—the positionings of each of the two glyphs in the kerning pair. Needless to say, Value2 usually is lacking, since we usually change the spacing of the first glyph rather than moving the second.

The second format for PairPos uses glyph *classes*. Here is an example of one such element:

```
<Lookup index="3">
  <LookupType value="2"/>
  <LookupFlag value="8"/>
  <!-- SubTableCount=1 -->
  <PairPos index="0" Format="2">
    <Coverage Format="1">
      <Glyph value="A"/>
      <Glyph value="Aacute"/>
    </Coverage>
    <ValueFormat1 value="68"/>
    <ValueFormat2 value="0"/>
    <ClassDef1 Format="2">
      <ClassDef glyph="A" class="1"/>
      <ClassDef glyph="Aacute" class="1"/>
    </ClassDef1>
    <ClassDef2 Format="2">
      <ClassDef glyph="T" class="1"/>
    </ClassDef2>
    <!-- Class1Count=1 -->
    <!-- Class2Count=1 -->
    <Class1Record index="0">
      <Class2Record index="0">
        <Value1 XAdvance="-">
          <XAdvDevice>
            <StartSize value="15"/>
            <EndSize value="24"/>
            <DeltaFormat value="1"/>
            <DeltaValue value="[-, 0, 0, 0, 0, 0, 0, 0, -, -]"/>
          </XAdvDevice>
        </Value1>
      </Class2Record>
    </Class1Record>
  </PairPos>
</Lookup>
```

In the example, we see the lookup type (LookupType), the series of flags (LookupFlag; see §D.9.1.1), the coverage table (Coverage), and the *formatted values* (ValueFormat1 and Value-Format2), which did not exist in Format 1. But rather than addressing the glyph pairs right off the bat, we first define glyph *classes*: for instance, the ClassDef1 element contains a ClassDef for each initial glyph in the pair; ClassDef2 contains the glyphs that appear second. Each ClassDef contains the glyph name and the class, in the form of attributes.

Once the classes have been defined, there are some kerning pairs, which are classified in the following manner: the element Class1Record contains Class2Record subelements for all the pairs whose first glyph is in a class given by its index attribute. Class2Record contains a *formatted value*.

In the example above, we first see a pair between classes 1 and 0. Class 1 is that of the letter 'A' and similar glyphs ('Á', for example, is in the same class). Class 0 is the class for all the glyphs that do not have a ClassDef (not surprisingly, that includes thousands of glyphs). The value of the positioning is 0, which is not surprising, as if we wished to kern the letter 'A' with *every* glyph, we would be better off changing its width; that would take less time to calculate. Thus it is a phony Class2Record.

What follows is more useful: a kerning pair between the classes 1 and 4. Class 1 is still the class for the letter 'A'; Class 4 is for the letter 'V' and similar glyphs. The amount of kerning requested comes from a device table: the exact value is -195 TrueType units, but there are also 10 δ values, which cover the sizes between 15 and 24 pixels per em. The corrections concern the extreme values: at 15, 23, and 24 pixels per em, one additional pixel of kerning is needed. At and above 25 pixels per em, we leave the decision to the processor, which will transform the 195 TrueType units into pixels and round them.

D.9.3.4 *Lookup type 3: cursive attachment*

In school, children are taught to connect their

letters, and what a child can do at school, a computer should also be able to do. But how can we be sure that the stroke that emerges from the letter 's', for example, and the one that leads into the letter 'c' will actually coincide? Up to now, font designers needed damn good organization to make all the letters join up correctly. Lookup type 3 turns this task into child's play.

Here is a table of this type:

```
<Lookup index="4">
  <LookupType value="3"/>
  <LookupFlag value="8"/>
  <!-- SubTableCount=1 -->
  <CursivePos index="0" Format="1">
    <Coverage Format="1">
      <Glyph value="a"/>
      <Glyph value="b"/>
      <Glyph value="c"/>
    </Coverage>
    <!-- EntryExitCount=1 -->
    <EntryExitRecord index="0">
      <EntryAnchor Format="1">
        <XCoordinate value="1425"/>
        <YCoordinate value="654"/>
```

```
        </EntryAnchor>
        <ExitAnchor Format="2">
          <XCoordinate value="1425"/>
          <YCoordinate value="654"/>
          <AnchorPoint value="34"/>
        </ExitAnchor>
      </EntryExitRecord>
    </CursivePos>
  </Lookup>
```

Each glyph has an *entry anchor* and an *exit anchor*. The processor will match the exit anchor of one glyph up with the entry anchor of the following glyph. Provided that all these anchors are at the same height, this method drastically simplifies the development of a cursive font.

Let us look more closely at the sample code. After the usual LookupType and LookupFlag, we have an element CursivePos. This element contains, first, a coverage table containing glyphs, and then an EntryExitRecord element for each glyph. Each of these elements contains the data for the glyph's entry anchors (EntryAnchor) and exit anchors (ExitAnchor). There are three ways to define these anchors:

- Format 1: we provide merely the point's x-coordinate (XCoordinate) and y-coordinate (YCoordinate).

- Format 2: like Format 1, but a point on the glyph's contour is also supplied. Coordinates are sufficient for preliminary calculations, but when the time comes to render the glyphs in question, the point will be much more precise, because any instructions that are present could move it *in extremis*.

- Format 3: even more powerful than Format 2. We still supply precise coordinates, but we also add device tables for each of the point's coordinates. Thus the last word will no longer go to the TrueType instructions but to the designer, who determines the exact number of pixels at each size.

Let us recall the primordial role played by the first bit in the LookupFlag in this very special lookup: if it is enabled, then for each "word" (the software decides what constitutes a "word"), we first set all the glyphs by matching up their entry and exit anchors, and then we move the entire word so that the *last* glyph will lie on the baseline. If the bit is disabled, the first glyph will be placed on the baseline, as usual, and the others will deviate from it according to the angle between the entry and exit anchors. We have given two examples of the use of this bit in Figure D-4.

D.9.3.5   *Lookup type 4: diacritical marks*

In Europe, èšþĕçîåłÿ íf ôñé íṣ ä ğŗĕâţ àdṁîŕëṛ ỗf ḋîåćŕïṭịcạĺ m̄åŕk̂ŝ, like the author, one often complains that Americans do not pay enough attention to the needs of our languages, with their accents and other oddities. That era has been definitively reversed: thanks to Type 4 lookups, we can place *any diacritical mark* on *any letter*. And not in just any way: we can indicate this type of positioning with a great deal of precision.

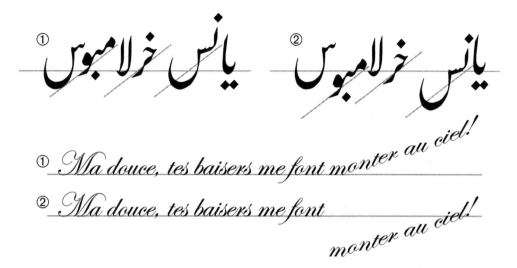

Figure D-4: Two examples of the use of the lookup flag for cursive attachment. First example: in the Urdu script, groups of connected letters (written from right to left, don't forget!) must end on the baseline. Case 1: bit enabled, correct typesetting; case 2: bit disabled, poor typesetting (going off in every direction).
Second example: a figurative use of typeset text: letters "sent flying". Case 1: bit disabled, correct typesetting; case 2: bit enabled, poor typesetting (the letters seem to be climbing out of the basement; the image is spoiled).

The principle is simple and powerful: each diacritical mark has a point of attachment; the diacritical marks are arranged into several *classes* according to their behavior; each "base" glyph has a point of attachment for each class of diacritical marks. We select a base glyph and a diacritical mark, and the processor bends over backwards to make us happy by matching the correct point of attachment on the base glyph with that of the diacritical mark.

Here is an example of one such table:

```
<Lookup index="5">
  <LookupType value="4"/>
  <LookupFlag value="0"/>
  <!-- SubTableCount=1 -->
  <MarkBasePos index="0" Format="1">
    <MarkCoverage Format="1">
      <Glyph value="dotaccent"/>
    </MarkCoverage>
    <BaseCoverage Format="1">
      <Glyph value="A"/>
      <Glyph value="E"/>
    </BaseCoverage>
    <!-- ClassCount=2 -->
    <MarkArray>
      <!-- MarkCount=1 -->
```

```
            <MarkRecord index="0">
              <Class value="1"/>
              <MarkAnchor Format="2">
                <XCoordinate value="0"/>
                <YCoordinate value="-"/>
                <AnchorPoint value="12"/>
              </MarkAnchor>
            </MarkRecord>
          </MarkArray>
          <BaseArray>
            <!-- BaseCount=1 -->
            <BaseRecord index="0">
              <BaseAnchor index="0" Format="2">
                <XCoordinate value="803"/>
                <YCoordinate value="1487"/>
                <AnchorPoint value="52"/>
              </BaseAnchor>
              <BaseAnchor index="1" Format="2">
                <XCoordinate value="780"/>
                <YCoordinate value="-"/>
                <AnchorPoint value="53"/>
              </BaseAnchor>
            </BaseRecord>
          </BaseArray>
        </MarkBasePos>
      </Lookup>
```

After the usual LookupType and LookupFlag, we find the element MarkBasePos. This element has a very simple structure: first come some coverage tables for the diacritical marks and the base glyphs; then come the coordinates of the points of attachment for the diacritical marks; finally, there are similar coordinates for the base glyphs.

The coverage tables are exactly the same as the ones that we have already seen; the only difference is that here, since we have two types of tables, we have named the corresponding elements MarkCoverage (*mark* for "diacritical mark") and BaseCoverage.

In the global element MarkArray that follows, there is a MarkRecord subelement for each glyph in MarkCoverage. Each MarkRecord corresponds to a diacritical mark. The first piece of data that it contains is the diacritical mark's *class*, obtained through the Class element. The coordinates of the point of attachment of a diacritical mark are given in the MarkAnchor element, which immediately follows the Class element. MarkAnchor is of the same type as the EntryAnchor of the preceding type of lookup; thus there are three different formats: either we give only the precise coordinates (format 1) or we also add a point on the glyph's contour (format 2) or we even add device tables for each of the point's two coordinates (format 3). In the example, the MarkAnchor is of format 2.

Finally, in BaseArray, there are BaseRecord elements, which correspond to the base glyphs as these are listed in BaseCoverage. Each BaseRecord contains a BaseAnchor for each class of diacritical marks.

In the example, for instance, there are two classes of diacritical marks: class 0 corresponds to accents placed *above* the letter (the acute accent acutecomb, the grave accent gravecomb, etc.), and class 1 is for those placed *beneath* the letter (the underdot dotbelowcomb). Thus there is the same number of BaseAnchor elements in each BaseRecord, corresponding to the points of attachment of each class of diacritical marks. The class is given by the attribute index. The position of the point of attachment BaseAnchor is given in the same way as that of MarkAnchor: once again, there are three formats (coordinates alone, a point on the contour, device tables).

We see in the example that the points of attachment for the letter 'A' are $(803, 1487)$ for upper accents and $(780, -60)$ for lower accents. We can see that, contrary to the visual impression that is left, the axes for upper and lower accents do not coincide, since their x-coordinates differ by 23 TrueType units. The difference is doubtless attributable to the fact that the letter's design is not strictly symmetrical.

It can be seen that this table can be used to combine diacritical marks and base glyphs arbitrarily. All that is necessary is to supply the corresponding points of attachment for each glyph and create multiple glyphs for each diacritical mark in case the diacritical mark should have several possible behaviors. For example, the diacritical marks "dot above a letter" and "dot below a letter" must come from different glyphs, even if the contour of the dot is the same and we could have simply moved the dot in order to switch from one diacritical mark to the other. The reason is connected to the fact that each diacritical mark belongs to only one class and can be attached to only one point of attachment on the base glyph.

D.9.3.6 *Lookup type 6: multiple diacritical marks*

Whether in Vietnamese, in the International Phonetic Alphabet, or in Greek with the lengths of the syllables marked, we sometimes need multiple diacritical marks. For instance, in the following line of Vietnamese text:[13]

Kìa, Ngài đến giữa những đám mây, mọi mắt sẽ trông thấy

there are no fewer than three letters with double accents: the letter 'e' with the circumflex and acute accents, the letter 'a' with the breve and the acute accent, and the letter 'a' with the circumflex and acute accents. That is due to the fact that, on the one hand, the letters 'â', 'ă', 'ê', and 'ô' are considered basic letters of the alphabet and, on the other hand, the *tone* of every vowel has to be indicated with a diacritical mark. The four vowels that already bear diacritical marks thus end up with two diacritics.

We could, of course, design these double accents for Vietnamese and thus avoid the problem of multiple diacritical marks. But for purposes such as the International Phonetic Alphabet, in which there is a plethora of diacritical marks that can appear together on the same base glyph, we simply cannot cover every possibility. Furthermore, any software that claims to be Unicode-compatible must be able to set any characters followed by any series of combining characters. Thus there is a genuine problem, and lookup type 6 is less useless than it might have seemed at first glance.

---

[13] Revelation 1:7: "Behold, He cometh with clouds; and every eye shall see Him", set in *Stempel Schneidler*, from the Neufville Digital Foundry, adapted for Vietnamese by the author.

From a technical point of view, we find the same structure as for lookup type 4. The difference is that here, instead of having tags that begin with Mark (diacritical mark) and Base (base glyph), there are tags that begin with Mark1 (diacritical mark) and Mark2 (diacritical mark that plays the role of base glyph). Here, for example, is the TTX code for the lookup that produces the double accents of Vietnamese:

```
<Lookup index="6">
  <LookupType value="6"/>
  <LookupFlag value="0"/>
  <!-- SubTableCount=1 -->
  <MarkMarkPos index="0" Format="1">
    <Mark1Coverage Format="1">
      <Glyph value="grave"/>
      <Glyph value="acute"/>
      <Glyph value="tilde"/>
      <Glyph value="caron"/>
      <Glyph value="dotaccent"/>
    </Mark1Coverage>
    <Mark2Coverage Format="1">
      <Glyph value="circumflex"/>
      <Glyph value="breve"/>
    </Mark2Coverage>
    <!-- ClassCount=1 -->
    <Mark1Array>
      <!-- MarkCount=1 -->
      <MarkRecord index="0">
        <Class value="1"/>
        <MarkAnchor Format="1">
          <XCoordinate value="0"/>
          <YCoordinate value="170"/>
        </MarkAnchor>
      </MarkRecord>
    </Mark1Array>
    <Mark2Array>
      <!-- Mark2Count=1 -->
      <Mark2Record index="0">
        <Mark2Anchor index="0" Format="1">
          <XCoordinate value="0"/>
          <YCoordinate value="-"/>
        </Mark2Anchor>
      </Mark2Record>
    </Mark2Array>
  </MarkMarkPos>
</Lookup>
```

The Mark1Record elements thus contain the points of attachment for the "secondary" accents and a class value for each. The Mark2Record elements contain the different points of attachment for the "base" accents, according to the class of the "secondary" accent (given by the index attribute).

D.9.3.7 Lookup type 5: diacritical marks on ligatures

ʰA QⱯⵜE ESͳÉⵜɪQⱸ ᴅE ⵜE ꜰONE EST ꜞNᴅᴇNꞮABʰE, MᴬꞮS

"The aesthetic quality of this font is undeniable, but"—but we need some accents. The font used here is *Prestige*, by the foundry Présence Typo, located in Hautes-Alpes (France). This font contains a great many ligatures, all of them quite beautiful. The only problem is that no accents are provided. Yet the *Lexique des règles en usage à l'Imprimerie nationale* [48] does indeed call for accents in French. Doubtless the accents were omitted because the composition of ligatures and accents would have necessitated thousands of additional glyphs. That is where OpenType comes to the rescue.

Table 5 is devoted to diacritical marks placed on ligatures. How can we put an acute accent over the ligature 'ᴙ' in the French word "ESTHÉTIQUE"? or an acute accent over the ligature 'ᴺ' in the word "INDÉNIABLE"?

Technically, this type of lookup also draws its inspiration from Type 4, but here the tags beginning with Base are replaced with Ligature tags. In addition, there is a level below LigatureArray in the hierarchy: *components of the ligature*. Thus there is no LigatureRecord but rather a LigatureAttach containing ComponentRecords that correspond to the components. Here is an example of one such subtable:

```
<Lookup index="7">
  <LookupType value="5"/>
  <LookupFlag value="0"/>
  <!-- SubTableCount=1 -->
  <MarkLigPos index="0" Format="1">
    <MarkCoverage Format="1">
      <Glyph value="dotaccent"/>
      <Glyph value="grave"/>
      <Glyph value="acute"/>
      <Glyph value="tilde"/>
      <Glyph value="caron"/>
    </MarkCoverage>
    <LigatureCoverage Format="1">
      <Glyph value="X"/>
      <Glyph value="Y"/>
    </LigatureCoverage>
    <!-- ClassCount=2 -->
    <MarkArray>
      <!-- MarkCount=1 -->
      <MarkRecord index="0">
        <Class value="1"/>
        <MarkAnchor Format="2">
          <XCoordinate value="0"/>
```

```
            <YCoordinate value="-"/>
            <AnchorPoint value="12"/>
          </MarkAnchor>
        </MarkRecord>
      </MarkArray>
      <LigatureArray>
        <!-- LigatureCount=1 -->
        <LigatureAttach index="0">
          <!-- ComponentCount=1 -->
          <ComponentRecord index="0">
            <LigatureAnchor index="0" Format="2">
              <XCoordinate value="803"/>
              <YCoordinate value="1487"/>
              <AnchorPoint value="52"/>
            </LigatureAnchor>
            <LigatureAnchor index="1" Format="2">
              <XCoordinate value="780"/>
              <YCoordinate value="-"/>
              <AnchorPoint value="53"/>
            </LigatureAnchor>
          </ComponentRecord>
        </LigatureAttach>
      </LigatureArray>
    </MarkLigPos>
  </Lookup>
```

Thus we divide the ligature into several hypothetical components. In each of these components, we insert one point of attachment for every class of diacritical marks. These points of attachment are LigatureAnchors and, like other types of lookups in the GPOS table, they can be represented in three different ways (format 0: the coordinates only; format 1: the coordinates and a point on the contour; format 2: the coordinates and two device tables for them). The element ComponentRecord, which contains the poins of attachment, corresponds to a component of the ligature. It is contained in a LigatureAttach, which corresponds to a ligature.

Note that the OpenType font merely supplies to the typesetting software the data necessary for the positioning of the diacritical mark; the software must be able to detect the presence of a ligature even when accents are present, which is no easy task. For instance, if the software knows that the characters LATIN CAPITAL LETTER T, LATIN CAPITAL LETTER H, and LATIN CAPITAL LETTER E automatically form a ligature, it must also be aware that an 'E' with an acute accent, 0x00C9 LATIN CAPITAL LETTER E ACUTE can be decomposed into LATIN CAPITAL LETTER E followed by 0x0301 COMBINING ACUTE ACCENT (OXIA, TONOS) and that a ligature should still be formed, through the use of the mechanism for accenting ligatures in the GPOS table.

To conclude this section, one small detail about an unforeseen problem: given that the 'E' in the ligature 'Ǝ' is reversed, the acute accent placed on this letter should be reversed as well. But the reversed acute accent has a name: it is called a grave accent. Positioning should therefore be followed by a substitution, as is done in the GSUB table.

D.9.3.8 *Lookup type 7: contextual positioning*

The two types of lookups that follow are, in a sense, "virtual" lookups, since they direct the processor to other lookups. Here is their purpose: they search for a certain set of strings of glyphs (called *context strings*), and when one of these strings is found, a given lookup from types 1 to 6 is applied to each glyph in the string. The role of the lookup for contextual positioning is therefore to recognize the model string of glyphs and indicate which lookup must be applied to each glyph in the string.

The overall procedure is as follows: As we have already seen, the user selects a script and a language; the operating system then offers some features. The user chooses one of the features, and that action triggers a series of lookups. Each lookup in turn contains a series of positioning rules: context strings and numbers of the lookups to apply to each of their glyph. Warning: while all the lookups for a given feature are executed, only the first matching context string in the lookup will cause the positioning of a glyph.

For example, to illustrate contextual kerning, let us revisit the example that we gave in the kern table, Format 1 (§D.8.4.2): the problematic string "S.A.V.", in which we wish to kern the period and the 'V'. Here is how we shall present the problem: we select 'A.V' (i.e., A, period, and V) as the context string, and we request kerning of −400 units between the glyphs period and V. Here is the code for the "virtual" lookup:

```
<Lookup index="8">
  <LookupType value="7"/>
  <LookupFlag value="0"/>
  <!-- SubTableCount=1 -->
  <ContextPos index="0" Format="1">
    <Coverage Format="1">
      <Glyph value="A"/>
    </Coverage>
    <!-- PosRuleSetCount=1 -->
    <PosRuleSet index="0">
      <!-- PosRuleCount=1 -->
      <PosRule index="0">
        <!-- GlyphCount=3 -->
        <!-- PosCount=1 -->
        <Input index="0" value="period"/>
        <Input index="1" value="V"/>
        <PosLookupRecord index="0">
          <SequenceIndex value="1"/>
          <LookupListIndex value="5"/>
        </PosLookupRecord>
      </PosRule>
    </PosRuleSet>
  </ContextPos>
</Lookup>
```

This code first creates a coverage table for the first glyph in the context string: the one that concerns us is A. Next, there is one PosRuleSet for each glyph in the coverage table. A PosRuleSet contains all the context strings that begin with the corresponding letter in the coverage table. Each context string corresponds to a `PosRule` element.

This element contains `Input` elements corresponding to the other glyphs in the string of glyphs. Finally, we have one `PosLookupRecord` for each lookup that is to be applied. The subelements `SequenceIndex` and `LookupIndex` indicate the index of the glyph to which the lookup will be applied, together with the number of that lookup: in our case, we shall apply lookup number 5 to glyph 1 (i.e., the period, since counting starts at 0).

Which lookup will number 5 be? Easy: it is a lookup for single glyph positioning (see §D.9.3.2) in which we shall reduce the period's width by 400 TrueType units. Here it is:

```
<Lookup index="5">
  <LookupType value="1"/>
  <LookupFlag value="0"/>
  <SinglePos index="0" Format="1">
    <Coverage Format="1">
      <Glyph value="period"/>
    </Coverage>
    <ValueFormat value="4"/>
    <Value index="0" XAdvance="-"/>
  </SinglePos>
</Lookup>
```

We have just described Format 1 of the Type 7 lookup. There are two additional formats: Format 2 is richer, since it uses glyph classes rather than individual glyphs. Thus our context string becomes a "meta-string". Not only 'A.V' but also 'Á.V' and 'À.V' and 'Â.V', and even 'A.W' and perhaps 'A.T', 'A.Y', etc. We need only declare that the glyphs 'A', 'Á', 'À', and so on are part of the same class; likewise for 'V', 'W', 'T', 'Y', etc.

The code for this lookup is slightly more elaborate, since after `Coverage` we insert a table of class definitions that is in every way identical to that of lookup 2, format 2 (see §D.9.3.3):

```
<Lookup index="9">
  <LookupType value="7"/>
  <LookupFlag value="0"/>
  <!-- SubTableCount=1 -->
  <ContextPos index="0" Format="2">
    <Coverage Format="1">
      <Glyph value="A"/>
      <Glyph value="Agrave"/>
      <Glyph value="Aacute"/>
    </Coverage>
    <ClassDef Format="2">
      <ClassDef glyph="A" class="1"/>
      <ClassDef glyph="Aacute" class="1"/>
      <ClassDef glyph="Agrave" class="1"/>
      <ClassDef glyph="V" class="3"/>
```

```
          <ClassDef glyph="W" class="3"/>
          <ClassDef glyph="period" class="2"/>
        </ClassDef>
        <!-- PosClassSetCount=4 -->
        <PosClassSet index="0">
          <!-- PosClassRuleCount=0 -->
        </PosClassSet>
        <PosClassSet index="1">
          <!-- PosClassRuleCount=1 -->
          <PosClassRule index="0">
            <!-- GlyphCount=3 -->
            <!-- PosCount=1 -->
            <Class index="0" value="2"/>
            <Class index="1" value="3"/>
            <PosLookupRecord index="0">
              <SequenceIndex value="1"/>
              <LookupListIndex value="0"/>
            </PosLookupRecord>
          </PosClassRule>
        </PosClassSet>
        <PosClassSet index="2">
          <!-- PosClassRuleCount=0 -->
        </PosClassSet>
        <PosClassSet index="3">
          <!-- PosClassRuleCount=0 -->
        </PosClassSet>
      </ContextPos>
    </Lookup>
```

Thus we see that the coverage table Coverage also contains the other glyphs in the same class as 'A'. Next comes the class table, ClassDef1, and that is where each glyph is associated with one class, and only one. Next, PosClassSet contains all the meta–context strings that begin with the class given by the index attribute (class 0 being the default class—the one that includes all the glyphs that do not belong to any other class).

In our example, obviously, the only PosClassSet of interest to us is the one for class 1: those context strings whose first glyph is in class 1.

Inside the PosClassSet we find the same data as in Format 1. The only difference is that here, instead GlyphIDs, there are Classes: it is the list of classes that makes up our context string (which is a string not of glyphs, but of classes of glyphs).

Let us point out that Format 2, as flexible as it may seem, suffers from a few drawbacks. These drawbacks are due primarily to the fact that each glyph can belong to only one class. Suppose then that we are interested in the context strings "ATA", in which the first 'A', but not the second, can also be an 'À'. On the other hand, the second 'A' can also be an 'Â'. How can we define the classes in question? We cannot. The only solution is to use Format 1 and explicitly write out all the permitted combinations of glyphs.

Or we can use Format 3, which has a different approach. To avoid the problem that we just mentioned, we use not *classes* but *coverage tables*. Thus a context string becomes a string of coverage tables. The main difference is that we are free to put the same glyph into more than one coverage table—something that is not possible with classes.

Here is the same example, this time in Format 3:

```
<Lookup index="10">
  <LookupType value="7"/>
  <LookupFlag value="0"/>
  <!-- SubTableCount=1 -->
  <ContextPos index="0" Format="3">
    <!-- GlyphCount=3 -->
    <!-- PosCount=1 -->
    <Coverage index="0" Format="1">
      <Glyph value="A"/>
      <Glyph value="Agrave"/>
      <Glyph value="Aacute"/>
    </Coverage>
    <Coverage index="1" Format="1">
      <Glyph value="period"/>
    </Coverage>
    <Coverage index="2" Format="1">
      <Glyph value="V"/>
      <Glyph value="W"/>
      <Glyph value="Y"/>
    </Coverage>
    <PosLookupRecord index="0">
      <SequenceIndex value="1"/>
      <LookupListIndex value="0"/>
    </PosLookupRecord>
  </ContextPos>
</Lookup>
```

The structure of this Lookup is quite different. First of all, there is no PosRuleSet or PosClass-Set here. Next, we have not just one Coverage entry but one for each glyph in the context string. Finally, we need only supply a PosLookupRecord for each glyph that could be moved by another lookup, and the task is done.

This format for lookup 7 is so powerful that the reader must be wondering why we still retain Format 2. Yet there are cases in which Format 2 is much more powerful. For example, all the context strings in Format 3 have exactly the same length. For instance, it is impossible a string of three glyphs and a string of four glyphs at the same time—something that can be done with Format 2.

D.9.3.9   Lookup type 8: extended contextual positioning

Now we come to the *ne plus ultra* of positioning: *extended contextual positioning*. But in what way can it be "extended"? Can we leave the plane to extend the positioning into space? Of course not. In fact, it is the *context* that is "extended". In lookup type 7, we would indicate a string of glyphs, and when that string occurred in a document, it became the context. Within this context, we would move certain glyphs. Here we still have the concept of a context string; but when that string occurs, we can also examine what happens before and after it.

Let us put ourselves in the position of the processor. We read glyph codes and render the corresponding glyphs. Suddenly we encounter an extended context string, "ABC". Processing it entails (a) having retained the preceding glyphs (those that we had just set before "ABC") in memory, retrieving them, and checking whether or not they match another string of glyphs that we call the *backtrack*; (b) being able to move forward and examine what will follow, without setting the glyphs but instead merely checking whether the following glyphs match another string of glyphs that we call the *lookahead*.

Why should we do such a thing? Because the glyphs in the context string can no longer be used for other lookups. Suppose that our context string is "TAT" and that another 'A' comes after this string. We would have wanted kerning between the second 'T' and the 'A' to follow. But it is too late: the formatting is ruined, because the string "TAT" was used whole in a certain operation, even if only the first or the second glyph was moved. Once this lookup has been finished, the string disappears from circulation, and kerning with what follows can no longer be performed.

By using an extended context, on the other hand, we can take as a context string only the glyph that is to be moved. What occurs before that string will be the *backtrack*; what occurs after the string will be the *lookahead*.

Here is our example of a lookup of type 7, rewritten in type 8:

```
<Lookup index="11">
  <LookupType value="8"/>
  <LookupFlag value="0"/>
  <!-- SubTableCount=1 -->
  <ChainContextPos index="0" Format="1">
    <Coverage Format="1">
      <Glyph value="period"/>
    </Coverage>
    <!-- ChainPosRuleSetCount=1 -->
    <ChainPosRuleSet index="0">
      <!-- ChainPosRuleCount=1 -->
      <ChainPosRule index="0">
        <!-- BacktrackGlyphCount=1 -->
        <Backtrack index="0" value="A"/>
        <!-- InputGlyphCount=2 -->
        <Input index="0" value="period"/>
        <!-- LookAheadGlyphCount=1 -->
        <LookAhead index="0" value="V"/>
        <!-- PosCount=1 -->
        <PosLookupRecord index="0">
          <SequenceIndex value="0"/>
          <LookupListIndex value="0"/>
```

```
        </PosLookupRecord>
      </ChainPosRule>
    </ChainPosRuleSet>
  </ChainContextPos>
</Lookup>
```

What has changed? The elements ContextPos (the type of lookup), PosRuleSet (the set of rules), and PosRule (a rule) have become ChainContextPos, ChainPosRuleSet, and Chain-PosRule; only the name has changed. On the other hand, two elements have been added at the same level as Input: Backtrack and LookAhead. These two elements contain glyphs listed in a certain order. This order is the logical order of the glyphs in the lookahead for LookAhead and the order opposite that of the lookahead for Backtrack. For example, if we wish to move the string "DEF" only if it is preceded by "ABC" and followed by "GHI", the lookahead will be in the order 'G', 'H', and 'I'; conversely, the backtrack will be in the opposite order: 'C', 'B', 'A'. That is due to the fact that the glyphs are placed on a stack; when they are popped, they will necessarily be in the order opposite to that in which they were pushed.

We have not yet discussed formats. Type 8 also offers three formats. There is nothing surprising about that: the formats are the same as for type 7. First we take individual glyphs (Format 1); then we extend Format 1 by taking glyph classes (Format 2); finally, we extend it in a different way by taking coverage tables for glyphs. The advantages and disadvantages of the three formats are the same as for type 7: Format 1 is simple and precise but may be quite long when there are many glyphs; Format 2, which is suited to very precise and distinct categories of glyphs, allows us to save a great deal of space by defining glyph *classes*, and we can use these classes to write the context string, the backtrack, and the lookahead; Format 3 uses coverage tables rather than classes, which has the advantage that we can use the same glyph in different ways, since it can appear in several coverage tables at the same time—which is not true of classes.

Here is our example of code, rewritten in Format 2:

```
<Lookup index="12">
  <LookupType value="8"/>
  <LookupFlag value="0"/>
  <!-- SubTableCount=1 -->
  <ChainContextPos index="0" Format="2">
    <Coverage Format="1">
      <Glyph value="period"/>
    </Coverage>
    <BacktrackClassDef Format="2">
      <ClassDef glyph="A" class="1"/>
      <ClassDef glyph="Aacute" class="1"/>
      <ClassDef glyph="Agrave" class="1"/>
    </BacktrackClassDef>
    <InputClassDef Format="2">
      <ClassDef glyph="period" class="1"/>
    </InputClassDef>
```

```
      <LookAheadClassDef Format="2">
        <ClassDef glyph="V" class="1"/>
        <ClassDef glyph="W" class="1"/>
      </LookAheadClassDef>
      <!-- ChainPosClassSetCount=2 -->
      <ChainPosClassSet index="0">
        <!-- ChainPosClassRuleCount=0 -->
      </ChainPosClassSet>
      <ChainPosClassSet index="1">
        <!-- ChainPosClassRuleCount=1 -->
        <ChainPosClassRule index="0">
          <!-- BacktrackGlyphCount=1 -->
          <Backtrack index="0" value="1"/>
          <!-- InputGlyphCount=2 -->
          <Input index="0" value="1"/>
          <!-- LookAheadGlyphCount=1 -->
          <LookAhead index="0" value="1"/>
          <!-- PosCount=1 -->
          <PosLookupRecord index="0">
            <SequenceIndex value="0"/>
            <LookupListIndex value="0"/>
          </PosLookupRecord>
        </ChainPosClassRule>
      </ChainPosClassSet>
    </ChainContextPos>
  </Lookup>
```

In the first part, we define the classes for the backtrack (BacktrackClassDef), the context string (InputClassDef), and the lookahead (LookAheadClassDef). Next, within the element ChainPosClassSet corresponding to class 1, the class for the period in the context string, there is a rule named ChainPosClassRule. This rule operates on the backtrack 'A' (Backtrack), the context string '.' (Input), and the lookahead 'V' (LookAhead). The PosLookupRecord has not changed, except that the '.' now appears at index 0, since it is the only glyph in the context string.

Note that the coverage table is concerned only with the first glyph in the context string (not with the first glyph in the backtrack, even though the backtrack, as its name suggests, logically precedes the context string).

One important note: In type 7, we saw that defining classes is quite constraining. If the same glyph occurs multiple times in the context string, it must have the same behavior each time, since it can belong to only one class—the class that was part of the context string, not the glyph itself. This constraint still exists in type 8, but it is greatly lightened by the fact that the classes for the backtrack, the context string, and the lookahead are defined separately. Thus there are fewer chances of having the same glyph with different behavior.

In any event, we have now come to Format 3 of type 8. As in type 7, here again we use coverage tables. Here is our perennial example of "A.V", written in Format 3:

```
<Lookup index="13">
  <LookupType value="8"/>
  <LookupFlag value="0"/>
  <!-- SubTableCount=1 -->
  <ChainContextPos index="0" Format="3">
    <!-- BacktrackGlyphCount=1 -->
    <BacktrackCoverage index="0" Format="1">
      <Glyph value="A"/>
    </BacktrackCoverage>
    <!-- InputGlyphCount=1 -->
    <InputCoverage index="0" Format="1">
      <Glyph value="period"/>
    </InputCoverage>
    <!-- LookAheadGlyphCount=1 -->
    <LookAheadCoverage index="0" Format="1">
      <Glyph value="V"/>
    </LookAheadCoverage>
    <!-- PosCount=1 -->
    <PosLookupRecord index="0">
      <SequenceIndex value="0"/>
      <LookupListIndex value="0"/>
    </PosLookupRecord>
  </ChainContextPos>
</Lookup>
```

What is there to say? This lookup is simple and powerful: we can take as many glyphs as we wish for the backtrack, the context string, or the lookahead, and we can choose a coverage table for each glyph in these three strings. In short, we enjoy total freedom. The coverage tables for the glyphs in the backtrack are called BacktrackCoverage; those in the context string, InputCoverage; finally, those in the lookahead, LookAheadCoverage. The PosLookupRecord is not changed.

D.9.3.10   *Lookup type 9: an extension*

Having seen the epitome of power in tables 7 and 8, one may well ask apprehensively: "what could there be in table 9?". Do not worry. Suppose that you wish to make a hole in the fence on the other side of your yard and that the power cord for your drill is not long enough. What do you do? You use an extension cord. Type 9 is exactly the same thing: an extension.

One thing that we have not mentioned—since TTX allows us to avoid this sort of banal detail—is the fact that in the GPOS table there are often pointers to lookups and that these pointers are always 2-byte values. That means that a subtable for a lookup can never be more than 64 kilobytes from the start of the table. That seems reasonable at first glance because the font itself is often smaller than 64 kB.

But imagine that we have a super-font with thousands of glyphs, each of which behaves differently. The developer would have to create thousands of classes or coverage tables, and the threshold of 64 kB would quickly be surpassed. Type 9 comes to the rescue. It has a 4-byte pointer, and we can therefore point to data as far as $2^{32} = 4$ gigabytes from the start of the table. The lookup of type 9 is thus the "local representative" of the more distant lookup: we place the former less than 64 kB from the start of the table and point to it when we need to use the latter.

D.9.4   The GSUB Table

The GSUB table manages glyph substitution. Its applications are numerous: it can be used to replace one glyph with another in a certain context given by the *feature*, to choose from among several variants of the same glyph, to form ligatures (or, conversely, to decompose them), to perform contextual analysis, etc.

It shares with the other tables its schema for organizing data: we start with a script (*script*) and possibly a language; then we choose one or more features (*features*), which lead us to a number of lookups. These lookups are of seven types, and we shall study them by starting with the simplest ones.

D.9.4.1   Lookup type 1: simple substitution

This is the simplest case: if the feature is enabled, a given glyph is systematically replaced by another. For example, when we select the "small capitals" feature, the lowercase letters are replaced with small capitals. Here is the beginning of the GPOS table followed by an example of one such lookup, drawn from the font *Palatino Linotype*:

```
<GSUB>
  <Version value="1.0"/>
  <ScriptList>
    <!-- ScriptCount=3 -->
    <ScriptRecord index="0">
      <ScriptTag value="cyrl"/>
      <Script>
        <DefaultLangSys>
          <ReqFeatureIndex value="65535"/>
          <!-- FeatureCount=8 -->
          <FeatureIndex index="0" value="0"/>

          ...

          <FeatureIndex index="5" value="5"/>
          <FeatureIndex index="6" value="6"/>
          <FeatureIndex index="7" value="7"/>
        </DefaultLangSys>
        <!-- LangSysCount=0 -->
      </Script>
    </ScriptRecord>
    <ScriptRecord index="1">

    ...

    </ScriptRecord>
    <ScriptRecord index="2">

    ...

    </ScriptRecord>
```

```
</ScriptList>
<FeatureList>
  <FeatureRecord index="5">
    <FeatureTag value="subs"/>
    <Feature>
      <!-- LookupCount=1 -->
      <LookupListIndex index="0" value="9"/>
    </Feature>
  </FeatureRecord>
  ...
</FeatureList>
<LookupList>
  ...
  <Lookup index="9">
    <LookupType value="1"/>
    <LookupFlag value="0"/>
    <SingleSubst index="0" Format="2">
      <Substitution in="a" out="asuperior"/>
      <Substitution in="ae" out="aesuperior"/>
      ...
      <Substitution in="zero" out="zeroinferior"/>
    </SingleSubst>
  </Lookup>
</LookupList>
</GSUB>
```

where we also see the sections ScriptList and FeatureList, which are identical to those that
have already been described in the section on the GPOS table (see §D.9.3.1).

The lookup is also arranged as in the GPOS table: first its type (LookupType), then the usual
LookupFlag (see §D.9.1.1). Next, there is a Substitution element for each substitution: the
in attribute contains the name of the original glyph, and out contains the name of the glyph
that we obtain in its place. There could hardly be anything simpler.

The reader must have noticed that the SingleSubst element also has a Format attribute,
which has not been mentioned yet. Indeed, there are two formats for lookups of type 1. The
first assumes that the identification numbers of the target glyphs have a fixed offset relative
to the original glyphs. Thus we supply, in the TTF file, the original numbers and the offset,
and the processor immediately finds the target glyphs. The second format is more general: it
contains a coverage table for the original glyphs and a table of the corresponding glyphs to be
substituted. In any case, TTX flattens all that and shows us only the Substitution elements;
thus there is no need to worry about the choice of format and its implementation.

D.9.4.2   Lookup type 2: multiple substitution

It is relatively rare to replace one glyph with several. The font *Nafees Nasta'leeq* [1], for example, uses this mechanism to replace an Arabic glyph by its base part and its dots (see
Figure D-5). Do not forget that after going through the GSUB table we must still go through

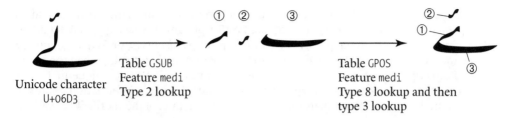

Figure D-5: *The glorious fate of the character 06d3 ARABIC LETTER YEH BARREE WITH HAMZA ABOVE: first it becomes a glyph; then the glyph is replaced (through a type 2 lookup) by the three glyphs above; finally, the three glyphs are repositioned by a number of lookups. The feature in question is medi—i.e., the letter's medial form. Thus the whole process involves moving from the isolated form (which represents the original Unicode character) to the medial form by decomposing the glyph into three parts for greater flexibility.*

GPOS; therefore, we can very precisely reposition the glyphs generated through the multiple substitution in question.

Here is an example of a multiple substitution. The code has been taken from the font *Nafees Nasta'leeq*.

```
<Lookup index="2">
  <LookupType value="2"/>
  <LookupFlag value="1"/>
  <!-- SubTableCount=1 -->
  <MultipleSubst index="0" Format="1">
    <Coverage Format="2">
      <Glyph value="uni0628"/>
      <Glyph value="afii57506"/>
    </Coverage>
    <!-- SequenceCount=2 -->
    <Sequence index="0">
      <!-- GlyphCount=2 -->
      <Substitute index="0" value=".notdef#49"/>
      <Substitute index="1" value=".notdef#714"/>
    </Sequence>
    <Sequence index="1">
      <!-- GlyphCount=2 -->
      <Substitute index="0" value=".notdef#49"/>
      <Substitute index="1" value=".notdef#716"/>
    </Sequence>
  </MultipleSubst>
</Lookup>
```

The element that corresponds to lookup type 2 is MultipleSubst. For now, there is only one format. It is followed by a coverage table for the original glyph. For each element in the coverage table, there is a Sequence element, which contains the glyphs with which that glyph is to be replaced. They are given in the desired order. Do not be astonished by glyph names as bizarre as .notdef#716: the font may happen to be a pure TrueType font, and its developers may not have provided an adequate PostScript name for each glyph. After all, in a TrueType font we refer to glyphs by their numbers (*glyph identifiers*, or GlyphIDs), not by their names. When TTX tried to give names to these poor nameless glyphs, it had to use the default PostScript name (.notdef); and since glyph names must also be unique in TTX, it added a number to each nameless glyph that it encountered. Just for information: there are 962 glyphs in this font, no fewer than 790 (!) of which have names of the .notdef#123 variety.

D.9.4.3   *Lookup type 3: variant selection*

In the discussion of characters and glyphs, we said that a character can be represented by thousands of glyphs. But who takes on the responsibility of representing all those glyphs? Most will be in the various fonts, which come from different designers from different countries, different eras, and different contexts. But some may appear in the same font or, at a minimum, in the same font family. For example, are the glyphs 'ᴀ', '*A*', and '**A**', not variants of 'A'?

We have acquired the habit of separating roman from small capitals, italics, and bold in separate fonts, just as formerly we had schools for girls and schools for boys. But the fact of separating them imposed numerous limitations: no kerning between glyphs from different fonts; no word division in words containing letters from several fonts; no searching or indexing, since a font change is data that settles inside a word like a foreign body. The problem of an italic letter followed by an upright bracket (as in "[*horrid*]"), for which TᴇX invented the concept of *italic correction*, would not have existed if the two glyphs '*d*' and ']' had been present in the same font.

Not to mention those cases in which a little silliness is desired: actual collections of variants of the same glyph, as in the case of the fonts *AmpersandsOne* and *AmpersandsTwo*, which together have no fewer than 202 variants of the ampersand (Figure D-6).

Now that we have demonstrated the attraction (or the pleasure) in having several variants of the same glyph in the same font, let us see the technique for implementing variants. The lookup of type 3 offers us the possibility of associating any number of variants with a glyph. What is spectacular is not the lookup itself (which is very simple) but the way that software uses it. By enabling a glyph in the document and bringing up the contextual menu, we obtain a list of all the variants. Faced with this splendid list, we truly have an embarrassment of riches.

Here is an example of one such lookup, drawn from the font *Palatino Linotype*:

```
<Lookup index="3">
  <LookupType value="3"/>
  <LookupFlag value="0"/>
  <!-- SubTableCount=1 -->
  <AlternateSubst index="0" Format="1">
    <AlternateSet glyph="s">
      <Alternate glyph="longs"/>
    </AlternateSet>
  </AlternateSubst>
</Lookup>
```

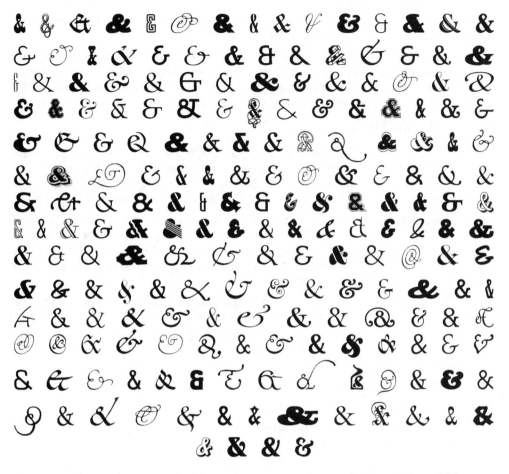

Figure D-6: The 202 (!) ampersands of the two fonts AmpersandsOne and AmpersandsTwo, by the American foundry CastleType. In these fonts we find everything, from the sublime to the horrible.

We could hardly do anything simpler. The element AlternateSubst contains all the cases of glyphs with variants. Each AlternateSet contains one such glyph and its variants. The original glyph is given by the glyph attribute of the element AlternateSet. This element can contain any number of Alternate elements, which represent the variants. Once again, it is the glyph attribute that contains the name of the corresponding glyph.

The little example of code above is for the 's' and the "long s". Although one would never have guessed, this example contains a whole page of German history. If Hitler had not banned the Gothic script in 1941 (see page 403) and if the Americans in 1945 had not considered this script to have a Nazi character, the Germans would probably still be writing in gothic, and therefore with a "long s". But since History—"with a capital *H*", as Georges Pérec said—decided otherwise, the "long s", banned from the living languages, has been condemned to be a "variant", a relic of the past, a bad memory. This lookup, obeying the hist (for "historic") feature, replaces the 's' that we know and love with a "long s".

This lookup has only one format. Once again, the reader will be happy to know that TTX enormously simplifies life by offering us these data in a very simple fashion. The binary table in a TTF is more complex, since it contains a coverage table and another table with subtables for variants that correspond to the entries in the coverage table.

D.9.4.4   Lookup type 4: ligatures

"Et ouais, ça va, je les souffle, mes bougies ! — Ffffffffff !" (Michel Albertini, *Les Merdi-coles*, 1998, 173.)" This extract from the *Dictionnaire des onomatopées* [131, p. 214] contains the longest ligature that the author has ever seen. Unfortunately, in the book in question, it is not properly typeset,[14] and we have the impression of seeing a series of six classic "ff" ligatures…

But there are more realistic cases as well. Contemporary typesetting makes frequent use of ligatures, be they '', 'fi', 'fl', 'ff', 'ffi', 'ffl', the Flemish 'ij', or the Scandinavian 'æ', etc. And in the Arabic script and the scripts of India, there are literally hundreds of ligatures. Ligatures have always been cosseted by typographers, to the point that a special issue of the journal *Cahiers GUTenberg* is dedicated to them [38].

Let us talk technically now: how do we encode ligatures in a GSUB table? In view of the title of this section, the answer is not surprising: we use a type 4 lookup.

Here is the code for one such lookup, drawn from the font *Palatino Linotype*:

```
<Lookup index="4">
  <LookupType value="4"/>
  <LookupFlag value="0"/>
  <!-- SubTableCount=1 -->
  <LigatureSubst index="0" Format="1">
    <LigatureSet glyph="I">
      <Ligature components="J" glyph="IJ"/>
    </LigatureSet>
    <LigatureSet glyph="Ismall">
      <Ligature components="Jsmall" glyph="IJsmall"/>
    </LigatureSet>
    <LigatureSet glyph="f">
      <Ligature components="f,i" glyph="ffi"/>
      <Ligature components="f,l" glyph="ffl"/>
      <Ligature components="f,t" glyph="fft"/>
      <Ligature components="f,b" glyph="ffb"/>
      <Ligature components="f,h" glyph="ffh"/>
      <Ligature components="f,k" glyph="ffk"/>
      <Ligature components="i" glyph="fi"/>
      <Ligature components="l" glyph="fl"/>
      <Ligature components="f" glyph="ff"/>
```

---

[14] It is surprising that a publisher as prestigious as *Presses Universitaires de France* did not take the trouble of asking a font designer to create a duodectuple 'f'. We may well wonder where French publishing is headed!

```
                <Ligature components="t" glyph="ft"/>
                <Ligature components="b" glyph="fb"/>
                <Ligature components="h" glyph="fh"/>
                <Ligature components="k" glyph="fk"/>
                <Ligature components="j" glyph="fj"/>
            </LigatureSet>
            <LigatureSet glyph="i">
                <Ligature components="j" glyph="ij"/>
            </LigatureSet>
            <LigatureSet glyph="t">
                <Ligature components="t" glyph="tt"/>
            </LigatureSet>
        </LigatureSubst>
    </Lookup>
```

We have refrained from shortening this code because it also gives us the full list of ligatures in the magnificent font that is *Palatino Linotype*: those that we have already mentioned, but also 'ft', 'fb', 'fh', 'fk', 'fj', 'ff', 'ffb', 'ffh', 'ffk', the 'IJ',[15] the 'ij', the 'ɪ', and the 'tt'. The code is very simple: the LigatureSubst contains all the rules for this lookup; for each initial letter in the ligature there is a LigatureSet (whose glyph attribute contains the letter in question). Finally, within each LigatureSet there is one Ligature for each ligature beginning with the same letter. Each Ligature takes a components attribute, which contains the other glyphs from which the ligature is built up, and the glyph attribute contains the name of the glyph that represents the ligature. Note in this regard that the glyph names given here do not correspond to those suggested by Adobe; indeed, according to Adobe's rules, the glyph name of a ligature is built up from the names of the components, separated by underscores. For example, the glyph name of the 'ff' ligature should be f_f_t (see §C.3.3).

D.9.4.5 Lookup type 5: contextual substitutions

Just as with lookups 7 through 9 in the GPOS table, lookups 5 through 7 in the GSUB table are "virtual", in the sense that the refer the processor to other lookups, from types 1 through 4. A number of strings of glyphs, called *context strings*, are available, and when one of these strings occurs, a certain lookup is applied to each of its glyphs. The role of the lookup for contextual substitution is therefore to recognize the model string of glyphs and to indicate which lookup should be applied to each glyph in the string.

The procedure is the same as for the contextual lookups in GPOS: the user selects a script (*script*) and a language (*language*); the software then offers a number of features (*features*). The user selects a feature, and that launches a series of lookups. Each lookup in turn contains a series of substitution rules: context strings and lookup numbers to apply to each of the glyphs.

---

[15] Notice here a major error in appreciation: the reader will observe that this list contains neither an 'œ' nor an 'æ', which is quite correct, since both glyphs represent linguistic, not aesthetic, ligatures. In other words, in French, the 'o' and the 'e' are not necessarily connected: consider the word "moelleux"; likewise, the 'æ' in the Scandinavian languages is a genuine separate letter, not a common ephemeral ligature between the 'a' and the 'e'. The error lies in the fact of including in this list the Dutch ligature 'ij'; indeed, this ligature is not obligatory in this language. There are words, in particular foreign words such as "bijou" that do not take this ligature. Thus it does not belong in this table.

Warning: although each of the lookups for a given feature is executed, only the first matching context string in the lookup invokes a glyph substitution.

To illustrate contextual substitution, let us take the case of the old-fashioned form of the ampersand: '&c.'. Here is the code for the lookup that will use "etc." as a context string and replace the first two glyphs with an ampersand:

```
<Lookup index="5">
  <LookupType value="5"/>
  <LookupFlag value="0"/>
  <!-- SubTableCount=1 -->
  <ContextSubst index="0" Format="1">
    <Coverage Format="1">
      <Glyph value="e"/>
    </Coverage>
    <!-- SubRuleSetCount=1 -->
    <SubRuleSet index="0">
      <!-- SubRuleCount=1 -->
      <SubRule index="0">
        <!-- GlyphCount=4 -->
        <!-- SubstCount=1 -->
        <Input index="0" value="t"/>
        <Input index="1" value="c"/>
        <Input index="2" value="period"/>
        <SubstLookupRecord index="0">
          <SequenceIndex value="0"/>
          <LookupListIndex value="8"/>
        </SubstLookupRecord>
      </SubRule>
    </SubRuleSet>
  </ContextSubst>
</Lookup>
```

In this code, we find the lookup type (5) and the lookup's flag (0). The element containing the rules for substitution is ContextSubst. Above we see Format 1 of this element. It begins with a coverage table for the first glyph. Next there is a SubRuleSet for each glyph in the coverage table. Each SubRuleSet contains the rules that begin with the same glyph, which are given in the coverage table. A rule of that kind is a SubRule element that in turn contains a GlyphCount (the total number of glyphs in a context string), an Input (a list of Glyph glyphs), a SubstCount (the number of substitutions to perform), and a SubstLookupRecord for each substitution to perform.

The subelement SequenceIndex in SubstLookupRecord gives the position of the glyph to which the current substitution in the string is to be applied. Here a great deal of attention is required, for unlike the PosLookupRecords that we saw in §D.9.3.8, the number of glyphs can vary throughout the process. For instance, if the first SubstLookupRecord is of type 2 (multiple substitution), there will be more glyphs after the substitution than before it. Conversely, if it is of type 4 (ligature), there may be fewer glyphs.

Let us take an example. Suppose that we wish to abuse the word "rifle" in the following manner: first, we decompose the glyph 'i' into a "dotless i" (duly positioned by a GPOS lookup that will subsequently be executed); next, we replace the glyphs 'f' and 'l' with the glyph 'fl'. What will the values of SequenceIndex be?

Counting starts at zero; therefore, the glyph 'i' is in position 1. But after the first rule has been executed, our string of glyphs is 'r', 'ı', dot, 'f', 'l', 'e'. The 'f' is therefore in position 3, not position 2, as it was before.

Let us return to our example of substitution, '&c.' Here is the type 4 lookup that will produce the ligature "e + t → &":

```
<Lookup index="8">
  <LookupType value="4"/>
  <LookupFlag value="0"/>
  <!-- SubTableCount=1 -->
  <LigatureSubst index="0" Format="1">
    <LigatureSet glyph="e">
      <Ligature components="t" glyph="ampersand"/>
    </LigatureSet>
  </LigatureSubst>
</Lookup>
```

Now let us move on to the other type 5 lookup formats: formats 2 and 3. For the reader who has read the description of lookups 7 and 8 of the GPOS table, there is no surprise: while Format 1 is the simplest (a coverage table for the first glyph, explicit choices for the other glyphs), Format 2 uses glyph classes, and Format 3 uses coverage tables for all the glyphs. Thus we extend the possibilities for formats in two different ways. In the case of Format 2, it is sufficient to define the class of each glyph; according to those classes, the processor will select the substitution rule to use. This format is very practical when there are glyphs with well-defined and quite distinct behaviors: they belong to as many classes as there are behaviors. The Arabic contextual forms, for example, are examples of classes: a glyph cannot be initial and medial at the same time. Format 3, conversely, is very convenient when there are sets of glyphs that we wish to combine in order to make substitutions; but Format 3 also has drawbacks, such as the fact that the context strings must all be of the same length.

Here is the same example of a substitution, in Format 2:

```
<Lookup index="6">
  <LookupType value="5"/>
  <LookupFlag value="0"/>
  <!-- SubTableCount=1 -->
  <ContextSubst index="0" Format="2">
    <Coverage Format="1">
      <Glyph value="e"/>
    </Coverage>
    <ClassDef Format="2">
      <ClassDef glyph="c" class="3"/>
```

```
                    <ClassDef glyph="e" class="1"/>
                    <ClassDef glyph="period" class="4"/>
                    <ClassDef glyph="t" class="2"/>
                 </ClassDef>
                 <!-- SubClassSetCount=1 -->
                 <SubClassSet index="0">
                    <!-- SubClassRuleCount=1 -->
                    <SubClassRule index="0">
                       <!-- GlyphCount=4 -->
                       <!-- SubstCount=1 -->
                       <Class index="0" value="2"/>
                       <Class index="1" value="3"/>
                       <Class index="2" value="4"/>
                       <SubstLookupRecord index="0">
                          <SequenceIndex value="0"/>
                          <LookupListIndex value="8"/>
                       </SubstLookupRecord>
                    </SubClassRule>
                 </SubClassSet>
              </ContextSubst>
           </Lookup>
```

We see that the element ContextSubst always contains the same coverage table for the same glyph. But here it is immediately followed by a class definition table: we start counting from 1 because class 0 is the default class for the glyphs in the font. Next, there are several SubClass-Sets, which contain the substitution rules that begin with the same class; the class number is given by the index attribute. Within a SubClassSet, there is a SubClassRule for each substitution rule beginning with a glyph in the class in question. GlyphCount gives the total number of glyphs in the context string. It is followed by a list of classes that describes the string in question. Finally, there is a series of SubstLookupRecord containing the numbers of the lookups to execute, each of them associated with a position in the string of classes. The usual caveat applies: since the number of glyphs is subject to change for each lookup, we must calculate the position every time, taking account of the strings produced by the preceding lookups.

Finally, here is the same example in Format 3:

```
           <Lookup index="7">
              <LookupType value="5"/>
              <LookupFlag value="0"/>
              <!-- SubTableCount=1 -->
              <ContextSubst index="0" Format="3">
                 <!-- GlyphCount=4 -->
                 <!-- SubstCount=1 -->
                 <Coverage index="0" Format="1">
                    <Glyph value="e"/>
                 </Coverage>
                 <Coverage index="1" Format="1">
```

```
            <Glyph value="t"/>
          </Coverage>
          <Coverage index="2" Format="1">
            <Glyph value="c"/>
          </Coverage>
          <Coverage index="3" Format="1">
            <Glyph value="period"/>
          </Coverage>
          <SubstLookupRecord index="0">
            <SequenceIndex value="0"/>
            <LookupListIndex value="8"/>
          </SubstLookupRecord>
        </ContextSubst>
      </Lookup>
```

The form is much simpler because there is no rearrangement according to the first letter in the context string. Thus there is a coverage table, Coverage, for each position in the context string (here the context strings are all of the same length). The SubstLookupRecords are exactly the same as in all other formats.

D.9.4.6 *Lookup type 6: extended contextual substitutions*

Just as in the GPOS table, we extend contextual substitutions by adding *backtracks* and *lookaheads*. For those that have not read the section describing the type 8 lookup of the GPOS table (§D.9.3.9), let us put ourselves in the position of the processor: we read glyph codes and render the corresponding glyphs. Suddenly the extended context string "ABC" occurs. Processing it entails (a) having retained the preceding glyphs (those that we had just set before "ABC") in memory, retrieving them, and checking whether or not they match another string of glyphs that we call the *backtrack*; (b) being able to move forward and examine what will follow, without setting the glyphs but instead merely checking whether the following glyphs match another string of glyphs that we call the *lookahead*.

When the backtrack, the context string, and the lookahead match the string of glyphs that is being typeset, the substitution is performed.

The existence of the backtrack and the lookahead seems to complicate the situation, but this complication is far from being gratuitous. On the contrary, it allows us to shorten the context string as much as possible and to leave the backtrack and the lookahead available for other purposes. For instance, in the previous example, we can be more precise and require a space before the 'e' in "etc." Then the space will be the backtrack, and "c." will be the lookahead. Here is the corresponding code:

```
<Lookup index="8">
  <LookupType value="6"/>
  <LookupFlag value="0"/>
  <!-- SubTableCount=1 -->
  <ChainContextSubst index="0" Format="1">
    <Coverage Format="1">
      <Glyph value="e"/>
```

```
      </Coverage>
      <!-- ChainSubRuleSetCount=1 -->
      <ChainSubRuleSet index="0">
        <!-- ChainSubRuleCount=1 -->
        <ChainSubRule index="0">
          <!-- BacktrackGlyphCount=1 -->
          <Backtrack index="0" value="space"/>
          <!-- InputGlyphCount=3 -->
          <Input index="0" value="e"/>
          <Input index="1" value="e"/>
          <!-- LookAheadGlyphCount=2 -->
          <LookAhead index="0" value="c"/>
          <LookAhead index="1" value="period"/>
          <!-- SubstCount=1 -->
          <SubstLookupRecord index="0">
            <SequenceIndex value="0"/>
            <LookupListIndex value="1"/>
          </SubstLookupRecord>
        </ChainSubRule>
      </ChainSubRuleSet>
    </ChainContextSubst>
  </Lookup>
```

The substitution rules are contained in the element `ChainContextSubst`. This element contains a coverage table for the first glyph in the context string (note: it is indeed the context string, not the backtrack) and then a `ChainSubRuleSet` for each glyph in the coverage table. Each `ChainSubRuleSet` contains the rules corresponding to the context strings whose first glyph is the glyph in question. Each of these rules is contained in a `ChainSubRule`.

So far, the structure resembles that of the lookups of type 5. But at this point there are six new elements: the length of the backtrack (`BacktrackGlyphCount`) and its glyphs in the opposite order (`Backtrack`), the length of the context string (`InputGlyphCount`) and its glyphs (`Input`), and finally the length and glyphs of the lookahead (`LookAheadGlyphCount`, `LookAhead`). The `SubstLookupRecord` that follows is identical to the lookup of type 5: it contains, on the one hand, the position of the glyph, or the substring of glyphs, to which the rule is to be applied within the context string, and on the other hand the number of the lookup to apply to the glyph or substring of glyphs.

The example above uses Format 1 of the lookup of type 5. Once again, just as in the preceding type of lookup and the type 8 lookup of the GPOS table (§D.9.3.9), we have a Format 2 that uses glyph classes and a Format 3 that uses coverage tables for all the glyphs in the backtrack, the context string, and the lookahead, with the advantages and disadvantages explained above.

Here is the code for the same example, rewritten in Format 2:

```
  <Lookup index="9">
    <LookupType value="6"/>
    <LookupFlag value="0"/>
```

```
<!-- SubTableCount=1 -->
<ChainContextSubst index="0" Format="2">
  <Coverage Format="1">
    <Glyph value="e"/>
  </Coverage>
  <BacktrackClassDef Format="2">
    <ClassDef glyph="space" class="1"/>
  </BacktrackClassDef>
  <InputClassDef Format="2">
    <ClassDef glyph="e" class="1"/>
    <ClassDef glyph="t" class="2"/>
  </InputClassDef>
  <LookAheadClassDef Format="2">
    <ClassDef glyph="c" class="1"/>
    <ClassDef glyph="period" class="2"/>
  </LookAheadClassDef>
  <!-- ChainSubClassSetCount=1 -->
  <ChainSubClassSet index="0">
    <!-- ChainSubClassRuleCount=1 -->
    <ChainSubClassRule index="0">
      <!-- BacktrackGlyphCount=1 -->
      <Backtrack index="0" value="1"/>
      <!-- InputGlyphCount=3 -->
      <Input index="0" value="1"/>
      <Input index="1" value="2"/>
      <!-- LookAheadGlyphCount=2 -->
      <LookAhead index="0" value="1"/>
      <LookAhead index="1" value="2"/>
      <!-- SubstCount=1 -->
      <SubstLookupRecord index="0">
        <SequenceIndex value="0"/>
        <LookupListIndex value="1"/>
      </SubstLookupRecord>
    </ChainSubClassRule>
  </ChainSubClassSet>
</ChainContextSubst>
</Lookup>
```

Here we have defined separate classes for each of the three strings. And here is the same example in Format 3:

```
<Lookup index="10">
  <LookupType value="6"/>
  <LookupFlag value="0"/>
  <!-- SubTableCount=1 -->
  <ChainContextSubst index="0" Format="3">
    <!-- BacktrackGlyphCount=1 -->
```

```
      <BacktrackCoverage index="0" Format="1">
        <Glyph value="space"/>
      </BacktrackCoverage>
      <!-- InputGlyphCount=2 -->
      <InputCoverage index="0" Format="1">
        <Glyph value="e"/>
      </InputCoverage>
      <InputCoverage index="1" Format="1">
        <Glyph value="t"/>
      </InputCoverage>
      <!-- LookAheadGlyphCount=2 -->
      <LookAheadCoverage index="0" Format="1">
        <Glyph value="c"/>
      </LookAheadCoverage>
      <LookAheadCoverage index="1" Format="1">
        <Glyph value="period"/>
      </LookAheadCoverage>
      <!-- SubstCount=1 -->
      <SubstLookupRecord index="0">
        <SequenceIndex value="0"/>
        <LookupListIndex value="1"/>
      </SubstLookupRecord>
    </ChainContextSubst>
  </Lookup>
```

Here we have a coverage table for each glyph in the three strings.

D.9.4.7 *Lookup type 8: reverse chaining contextual substitutions*

This is a variant of type 6 that was developed specially for Urdu. What is so unusual about this script? Well, it is a variety of the Arabic script that is unique in the world because it is written diagonally, at the level of the individual word. The lines of text run from right to left, but each word[16] begins at the upper right and ends at the left on the baseline. Thus each word has its own little baseline, as can be seen in the few words below, which are set in the font *Nafees Nast'aliq* [1]:

But how is this script so different from the others that it needs a type of lookup all to itself? After all, it is only a variant of the Arabic script, and for that script there has never been a need for a lookup of type 8.

---

[16] In fact, each *connected* part of a word. In the Arabic script, there are letters that have only two forms: the isolated form and the final form. When those letters are placed within a word, they break it into several parts. The letters within each part are connected. The same is true in Urdu: each connected part of a word is written diagonally.

Well, if the Arabic script can be considered *cursive*, that is even more true of Urdu. The letters take more forms than the four forms (isolated, initial, medial, final) of the script, even though only four forms exist from a grammatical point of view. In the example below, the same letter *beh* has been typed multiple times: first (starting at the right) by itself, then as two, three, four, five, and six copies of the letter *beh*. The reader may admire the different forms that this letter takes as it connects—to itself:

Let us now try to dissect the last of these strings of glyphs:

At the right we see the same word, but with the letters disconnected. Thus we see that we have a final form, ①; an initial form, ⑥; and no fewer than four medial forms, ② through ⑤. Of the medial forms, the first, ②, is a "pre-final" form; it is used to attach the preceding letters to the final consonant. The second, ③, is the right half of the fourth, ⑤; it is used to attach the preceding letters to the pre-final consonant. Things become more regular starting from the third form: if we had continued to write *beh*, we would have had an infinite sequence of ④ and ⑤. Finally, the initial, ⑥, is a slight variant of ④, the difference being that its lead-in stroke is pointed, since it is a lead-in stroke, not a connecting one.

Now let us observe the evolution of the forms as we gradually add *behs*. Form ② first appears in the third word (the one with three *behs*) and then remains stable. Form ③ first appears in the fourth word and then remains stable. Indeed, by comparing these words, we can see that the word is built up *from left to right*: the end of the word remains stable, and the beginning of the word changes, moving higher and higher.

We have just said that words are built up from left to right. This is why it is quite natural that the lookup of type 8 processes the string from left to right.

The author knows one other example of a script in which words are built up from left to right even though writing runs from right to left: biblical Hebrew with the Masoretic signs, for which he was the first to develop a typesetting system [158].

But let us leave the fragrant spheres of the East and return to our lookup.

There is only one format for this lookup: Format 1 (which is, however, actually Format 3 of the lookups of types 5 and 6). And the lookups invoked by substitution rules must necessarily be simple substitutions.

Here is the code for one such example:

```
<Lookup index="11">
  <LookupType value="8"/>
  <LookupFlag value="0"/>
  <!-- SubTableCount=1 -->
  <ReverseChainSingleSubst index="0" Format="1">
    <Coverage Format="1">
      <Glyph value="e"/>
      <Glyph value="eacute"/>
    </Coverage>
    <!-- BacktrackGlyphCount=1 -->
    <BacktrackCoverage index="0" Format="1">
      <Glyph value="space"/>
    </BacktrackCoverage>
    <!-- LookAheadGlyphCount=3 -->
    <LookAheadCoverage index="0" Format="1">
      <Glyph value="t"/>
    </LookAheadCoverage>
    <LookAheadCoverage index="1" Format="1">
      <Glyph value="c"/>
    </LookAheadCoverage>
    <LookAheadCoverage index="1" Format="1">
      <Glyph value="period"/>
    </LookAheadCoverage>
    <!-- GlyphCount=2 -->
    <Substitute index="0" value="E"/>
    <Substitute index="1" value="Eacute"/>
  </ReverseChainSingleSubst>
</Lookup>
```

This example, as hypothetical as it is useless, will replace 'e' (or 'é') with 'E' (or 'É') if the letter is preceded by a space and followed by 'tc.'.

D.9.4.8   Lookup type 7: an extension

As in the case of GPOS, it may happen that a table will exceed 64 kB. In this case, the various pointers in the table will no longer point to the data that that table contains. Therefore, as with lookup 9 of the GPOS table, we use a special lookup that serves as an "extension": its only role is to point to a lookup that appears further on. The processor will follow the pointer of a lookup of type 7, which is a 32-bit value that can thus manage tables as large as 4 gigabytes. Fortunately, TTX masks these fastidious details, which are due to the inadequacies of the TrueType format.

D.9.5   The JSTF Table

Here is the verse "All things were made by him; and without him was not any thing made that was made" (John 1:3), set in a font very close to that of Gutenberg (the font *Historical English Textura*, which is part of the splendid collection of historical fonts from the American foundry Hoefler):

𝔒mnia per ipfum facta funt: et fine ipfo factum eft nichil.

(The spelling *nichil*, with a 'ch', is that of Gutenberg.)

And here is the same verse presented after applying the same ligatures and abbreviations that Gutenberg used for this verse in the Göttingen Bible [280]:

𝔒m̄ia p ipm facta funt: ꝗ fine ipo factum eft nichil.

The difference is clear: the text is 15 percent narrower. The ligatures and abbreviations are indisputably a good way to achieve fine control over the widths of words. They can be used to improve the management of interword spaces. To do so, however, one must be able to "enable" or "disable" them dynamically, according to the requirements of each line of text.

The JSTF table goes in that direction: it gives the typesetting software the means to expand or reduce the width of certain words in order to obtain the best interword spaces. To that end, three strategies are employed: extenders, GPOS and GSUB lookups, and specific JSTF lookups.

D.9.5.1   Extenders

In the first strategy, certain glyphs are designated as *extenders*. An extender is a glyph whose purpose is to expand the text. The typical example is the Arabic *kashida*, or "connecting stroke", which is used to expand words. This stroke is fundamental to the Arabic script, whether for emphasizing letters by spreading them apart (that is done in poetry) or for achieving good justification, since word division is not allowed.

The only problem is that typesetting systems very often define the *kashida* as a straight horizontal line segment—doubtless because it is easier to draw a straight line than to calculate a curve with the correct properties in real time. In the example below, we see what a real connecting stroke should be:

In this example, typeset with the superb font *Decotype Naskh* by the Dutch company Decotype [271], we have marked with arrows the locations at which a connecting stroke occurs.

An Arabic font must indeed be very modern for rectilinear extenders to work. One such example appears below: it shows the same line as above, this time set in a "journalistic" font. It goes without saying that the author does not consider the line below a masterpiece of typography.

قِيــلَ لَهُـــمْ ءَامِنُـــواْ كَمَآءَامَـــنَ النَّـــاسُ قَالُـــواْ أَنُؤْمِـــنُ كَمَـــآءَامَـــنَ

But let us return to the JSTF table. Here is the code for one JSTF table, inspired by the font *Arial Unicode*:

```
<JSTF>
  <Version value="1.0"/>
  <!-- JstfScriptCount=1 -->
  <JstfScriptRecord index="0">
    <JstfScriptTag value="arab"/>
    <JstfScript>
      <!-- JstfLangSysCount=1 -->
      <JstfLangSysRecord>
        <JstfLangSysTag value="ARA"/>
        <JstfLangSys>
          <ExtenderGlyph>
            <!-- GlyphCount=5 -->
            <ExtenderGlyph index="0" value="afii57440"/>
            <ExtenderGlyph index="1" value="afii57391"/>
            <ExtenderGlyph index="2" value="afii57440-"/>
            <ExtenderGlyph index="3" value="afii57440-"/>
            <ExtenderGlyph index="4" value="afii57440-"/>
          </ExtenderGlyph>
        </JstfLangSys>
      </JstfLangSysRecord>
    </JstfScript>
  </JstfScriptRecord>
</JSTF>
```

The element JstfScriptRecord contains the rules associated with a given script, whose name JstfScriptTag contains: arab, for the Arabic script. Next, as in other OpenType advanced typographic tables, comes the level of specialization, which involves separating the rules according to the current language. There may be an element DefJstfLangSys for the "default language" and a JstfLangSysRecord for each language in which extenders are used. Within the JstfLangSysRecord is the name of the language (JstfLangSysTag)—here, the Arabic language. Next, there is an element JstfLangSys, which contains the rules for justification: in this case, the definitions of the extenders.

The glyphs that are extenders are indicated in the value attributes of the ExtenderGlyph elements. In the example above, they are five connecting strokes (*kashida*) of different widths.

D.9.5.2   GPOS and GSUB lookups

The second strategy, infinitely more powerful than the first, involves the judicious application of lookups taken from the two main OpenType tables: GPOS (positionings) and GSUB (substitutions). Thus we are free to become modern-day Gutenbergs and define a series of ligatures or rearrangements of glyphs (as in the font *Prestige*, seen in §D.9.3.7) that will either reduce or increase the widths of words.

Here is how this table works. We divide the lookups into *priority levels*. As the priority level gradually increases, the effect of the selected lookups must be more pronounced. The type-setting software recognizes the shortage or excess of space between the words and applies the groups of lookups one after the other, according to increasing priority level. This operation is repeated until the shortage or excess of space has been corrected.

Note that the lookups of the different priority levels are independent and that their effects are not cumulative. For instance, if at extender level 1 we have designated the decomposition of the triple ligatures 'ffi' (into 'f' and 'fi') and 'ffl' (into 'f' and 'fl'), and at level 2 we break up all the "f-ligatures", we must include the lookups for the triple ligatures in the description of level 2. That allows us to change the method of expansion or contraction completely when moving from one level to another.

But it also introduces a major risk. Suppose that at priority level 1 we use the "f-ligatures" (which are rather infrequent) and at level 2 we use variants of the letter 'e' (which is the most common letter in English). Statistically, in a line of text, we have a much greater chance of finding an 'e' than of finding an "f-ligature". Unless, of course, the text that we are typesetting is *La disparition* [289], by Georges Perec.[17] No one can guarantee that priority level 2 will give better results than priority level 1. But not to worry: after all, that is a problem for the typesetting software, which confirms once again the principle of the OpenType fonts: *the font proposes, the software disposes.*

Let us now see how these software levels appear in code. Each priority level is contained in a JstfPriority element. This element can contain 10 subelements: five for shrinkage and five for extension. For both shrinkage and extension, we can enable or disable an operation, and the lookups can appear in the GPOS table or the GSUB table. By combining choices in this way, we obtain the eight subelements: their names begin with Shrinkage or Extension, continue with Enable or Disable, and end with GPOS or GSUB. The two remaining subelements are described in the following section (§D.9.5.3).

Here is an example of code drawn from the font *Palatino Linotype*:

```
<JstfPriority index="1">
  <ShrinkageEnableGSUB>
    <!-- LookupCount=2 -->
    <GSUBLookupIndex index="1" value="4"/>
    <GSUBLookupIndex index="0" value="12"/>
  </ShrinkageEnableGSUB>
  <ExtensionDisableGSUB>
    <!-- LookupCount=2 -->
    <GSUBLookupIndex index="1" value="4"/>
    <GSUBLookupIndex index="0" value="12"/>
  </ExtensionDisableGSUB>
</JstfPriority>
```

Here the priority level is 1, which offers only enabling and disabling of shrinkage through the GSUB lookups. Lookups 4 and 12 of the GSUB table are enabled. By checking to see what these lookups look like, we see that lookup 4 is indeed the one that produces all the Latin ligatures (the f-ligatures, but also the Flemish 'ij', etc.); incidentally, we have described it on page 786.

---

[17] A 300-page book from 1969 that does not contain the letter 'e' even once (although an urban legend claims that one, and only one, letter 'e' lies hidden in the text). [Translator's note: An English translation by Gilbert Adair, *A Void* [291], observes the same constraint.] Perec shows how a letter can disappear without leaving a void in the book. Somewhat like his parents, who disappeared quite suddenly—on the front lines and at Auschwitz. Perec struck again in 1972 with *Les Revenentes* [290], a 137-page novel with no vowel other than 'e'.

We expected this type of lookup. On the other hand, lookup 12 is much more enigmatic: it is for the substitution of the glyphs 'Ş' and 'ş', which are used in Turkish or, with a comma in the place of the cedilla, in Romanian. But whether written with a cedilla, a comma, or no diacritical mark at all, these glyphs always have exactly the same set-width. We may therefore wonder what the purpose of this lookup is, especially since the font's designer, if he was Turkish or Romanian, would certainly be chagrined to see these glyphs change their nationality at random.

As for "substitutions made for justification", it can never be said too much: they must be *handled with care*. The reader should not forget that the software enables and disables substitution lookups haphazardly, according to the distribution of spaces in each line. A text in which there is an 'ffi' ligature on one line while the ligature is broken on the following line is a poorly typeset text, irrespective of the marvelous technology that helped to optimize the spacing.

In order for this operation to succeed, the presence or absence of ligatures or glyph variants must not affect the legibility of the text in any way. Gutenberg succeeded with his great many ligatures, used in a rather arbitrary manner. In a way, he also trained the reader's eye not to pay attention to ligatures or glyph variants. That is a more difficult goal to achieve in a long Latin text in which the only ligatures that occur are f-ligatures.

On the other hand, ligatures and variants often have semantic significance. In German, for example, a ligature is broken up when its glyphs straddle two constituents of the word: *Auflage* ("edition") is set without a ligature because it is a word made up of *auf* and *Lage*; the word *fliegen* ("to fly"), however, should be written with a ligature. Here, therefore, it is out of the question to take action for the purposes of justification if the meaning that the ligature or its absence has would be sacrificed.

The same is true of variants. The example below

shows us very beautiful Arabic typesetting (using the font *Decotype Naskh*) in which we have marked the variant ⌐ of the Arabic letter *kaf* with a solid arrow and two beautiful connecting strokes (*kashida*) with hollow arrows. This calligraphic variant of *kaf* has often been used for justification. But Vlad Atanasiu, in his dissertation on Ottoman calligraphy [61, Chapter 12], teaches us that this glyph has been known since the thirteenth century as the "*kaf* of impiety", doubtless because calligraphers copying out the Koran used it in particular to write the word *kufr* (= "impiety") in order to stigmatize impious persons. And the history of this glyph does not stop there: since the regular *kaf* is used in the Sindhi language for the sound 'gk', the *kaf* of impiety is used in that language for the sound 'k'. That is how a glyph, even one with so bad a reputation, managed to hit the jackpot and become a character: U+06AA ARABIC LETTER SWASH KAF.

Therefore, be careful: do not use a glyph substitution for purposes of justification unless you are sure that the modification thus made to the text concerns only a character of a purely graphical nature that has no cultural or semantic repercussions.

D.9.5.3 JSTF lookups

This strategy is less spectacular than the previous one, but safer. It involves using lookups that are in every respect similar to those of the GPOS table (contextual lookups are excluded). But how do they differ from the ShrinkageEnableGPOS, etc., of the previous section?

There is one difference: size. Up to now, OpenType tables have always supplied *exact* values (for offset, positioning, etc.). If a lookup specified an offset of 500 TrueType units, then enabling the lookup would cause an offset of 500 units—no more, no fewer.

In the case of JSTF lookups, the software is allowed to use a value (for offset, positioning, etc.) *less than or equal to* the value specified. That approach allows very fine and flexible control of spacing.

Let us discuss the technical details. As their name suggests, JSTF lookups are described in the JSTF table itself. They are found in ShrinkageJSTFMax and ExtensionJSTFMax elements (the two elements that were missing from the previous section). Here is an example of those lookups, drawn from the font *Palatino Linotype*:

```
<JstfPriority index="2">
  <ShrinkageJstfMax>
    <!-- LookupCount=1 -->
    <Lookup index="0">
      <LookupType value="1"/>
      <LookupFlag value="0"/>
      <!-- SubTableCount=1 -->
      <SinglePos index="0" Format="1">
        <Coverage Format="1">
          <Glyph value="space"/>
        </Coverage>
        <ValueFormat value="4"/>
        <Value XAdvance="350"/>
      </SinglePos>
    </Lookup>
  </ShrinkageJstfMax>
  <ExtensionJstfMax>
    <!-- LookupCount=1 -->
    <Lookup index="0">
      <LookupType value="1"/>
      <LookupFlag value="0"/>
      <!-- SubTableCount=1 -->
      <SinglePos index="0" Format="1">
        <Coverage Format="1">
          <Glyph value="space"/>
        </Coverage>
```

```
            <ValueFormat value="4"/>
            <Value XAdvance="550"/>
          </SinglePos>
        </Lookup>
      </ExtensionJstfMax>
    </JstfPriority>
```

In this example, a lookup of type 1 (positioning of a single glyph) is applied to the glyph space, which is the whitespace character. The lookup involves changing the space's width: in the first instance, it is reduced by 350 units; in the second, it is increased by 550 units. Since the width of this pseudoglyph is 512 units (information that we have in the table htmx), the code above tells the software that the space character can vary between $512 - 350 = 162$ and $512 + 550 = 1,062$ units during typesetting.

And here, by way of information, is the priority level immediately above:

```
    <JstfPriority index="3">
      <ShrinkageJstfMax>
        <!-- LookupCount=1 -->
        <Lookup index="0">
          <LookupType value="1"/>
          <LookupFlag value="0"/>
          <!-- SubTableCount=1 -->
          <SinglePos index="0" Format="1">
            <Coverage Format="2">
              <Glyph value="A"/>
              <Glyph value="B"/>
              <Glyph value="C"/>
              ... 1319 lines ...
              <Glyph value="uni1EF8"/>
              <Glyph value="uni1EF9"/>
              <Glyph value="uni20A0"/>
            </Coverage>
            <ValueFormat value="1"/>
            <Value XPlacement="-"/>
          </SinglePos>
        </Lookup>
      </ShrinkageJstfMax>
      <ExtensionJstfMax>
        <!-- LookupCount=1 -->
        <Lookup index="0">
          <LookupType value="1"/>
          <LookupFlag value="0"/>
          <!-- SubTableCount=1 -->
          <SinglePos index="0" Format="1">
            <Coverage Format="2">
              <Glyph value="A"/>
```

```
          <Glyph value="B"/>
          <Glyph value="C"/>
          ... 1319 lines ...
          <Glyph value="uni1EF8"/>
          <Glyph value="uni1EF9"/>
          <Glyph value="uni20A0"/>
        </Coverage>
        <ValueFormat value="1"/>
        <Value XPlacement="10"/>
      </SinglePos>
    </Lookup>
  </ExtensionJstfMax>
</JstfPriority>
```

Here we take all the glyphs in the font and apply to them the same type 1 lookup: a reduction or expansion of the set-width by 10 units. It is too little to be visible to the naked eye; therefore this technique cannot be called *letterspacing*. But is it effective? Let us take a typical line: 60 glyphs, 12 spaces. By multiplying the increase by 60 and dividing it by 12, we find that each space can thus be reduced by 50 units. That is a negligible amount in comparison to the previous lookup, in which the changes to the spaces could be 11 (!) times larger. But the visual result is certainly better, since the space is distributed among the glyphs, albeit in homeopathic doses.

D.9.6   The GDEF Table

We have now come to the last OpenType advanced typographic table. It is an auxiliary table, a space in which we store certain data that will be useful to the other tables. In this table, which is something of a hodgepodge, we find four types of data:

- An arrangement of all the glyphs in the font into four *classes*: "base glyph", "ligature", "combining glyph", and "glyph component". Knowing the class to which a given glyph belongs is useful for (among other things) applying the famous LookupFlag that appears in every lookup and that we have only briefly discussed up to now.

- A list of all the glyphs that have points of attachment, together with these points. This list allows the software to prepare itself and not be caught by surprise when a lookup suddenly asks it to attach a diacritical mark to a glyph.

- A list of the positions of the cursor inside ligatures. Specifically, if the font contains a ligature, the user must not be prevented from selecting with the mouse those letters that make up the ligature. To do so, he must be able to place the cursor inside a ligature, and the software must know the most appropriate location. This table gives the possible cursor positions for each ligature in the font.

- Finally, an arrangement of all the "combining glyphs" into different classes, so that a lookup, through the use of the LookupFlag, can ignore one of them.

Here is an example of a GDEF table (drawn from the font *Palatino Linotype*). First, the subtable for glyph classes:

```
<GDEF>
  <Version value="1.0"/>
  <GlyphClassDef Format="2">
    <ClassDef glyph=".null" class="1"/>
    <ClassDef glyph="A" class="1"/>
    <ClassDef glyph="AE" class="2"/>
    ... 9 lines ...
    <ClassDef glyph="Acute" class="3"/>
    <ClassDef glyph="Acutesmall" class="3"/>
    ... 1181 lines ...
    <ClassDef glyph="zerotext" class="1"/>
    <ClassDef glyph="zeta" class="1"/>
    <ClassDef glyph="zsuperior" class="1"/>
  </GlyphClassDef>
```

This subtable is contained in a GlyphClassDef element. Each glyph is represented by a Class-Def subelement whose attributes glyph and class indicate, respectively, the glyph's name and class. Ordinarily there are four classes: 1 (base glyph), 2 (ligature), 3 (diacritical mark), and 4 (glyph component, like the two parts of the 'j', for example). In the example above, only the first three are present.

Next comes the list of glyphs that have points of attachment (those points being given in a coverage table), together with the list of these points, classified by glyph:

```
<AttachList>
  <Coverage Format="1">
    <Glyph value="A"/>
    <Glyph value="E"/>
    <Glyph value="I"/>
    ... 24 lines ...
    <Glyph value="acutecomb"/>
    <Glyph value="tildecomb"/>
    <Glyph value="hookabovecomb"/>
  </Coverage>
  <!-- GlyphCount=30 -->
  <AttachPoint index="0">
    <!-- PointCount=2 -->
    <PointIndex index="0" value="52"/>
    <PointIndex index="1" value="53"/>
  </AttachPoint>
  ...
  <AttachPoint index="29">
    <!-- PointCount=1 -->
    <PointIndex index="0" value="32"/>
  </AttachPoint>
</AttachList>
```

This subtable is contained in an `AttachList` element. In it we find, first of all, a coverage table containing the glyphs of interest to us. Next, for each of these glyphs, there is an `AttachPoint` element containing the `PointIndex` point numbers. These are the points of attachment of each glyph.

Next comes the list of positions of the cursor within the ligatures:

```
<LigCaretList>
    <Coverage Format="1">
      <Glyph value="AE"/>
      <Glyph value="OE"/>
      <Glyph value="ae"/>
      ... 36 lines ...
      <Glyph value="AEsmall"/>
      <Glyph value="OEsmall"/>
      <Glyph value="IJsmall"/>
    </Coverage>
    <!-- LigGlyphCount=42 -->
    <LigGlyph index="0">
      <!-- CaretCount=1 -->
      <CaretValue index="0" Format="1">
        <Coordinate value="1010"/>
      </CaretValue>
    </LigGlyph>
    ...
    <LigGlyph index="40">
      <!-- CaretCount=1 -->
      <CaretValue index="0" Format="2">
        <CaretValuePoint value="45"/>
      </CaretValue>
    </LigGlyph>
    <LigGlyph index="41">
      <!-- CaretCount=1 -->
      <CaretValue index="0" Format="3">
        <Coordinate value="645"/>
        <DeviceTable>
          <StartSize value="9"/>
          <EndSize value="19"/>
          <DeltaFormat value="1"/>
          <DeltaValue value="[1, 0, 0, 0, 0, 0, 0, 0, 0, 0, -]"/>
        </DeviceTable>
      </CaretValue>
    </LigGlyph>
  </LigCaretList>
</GDEF>
```

This list is contained within a `LigCaretList` element. In it, we find a coverage table containing the glyphs that we declared as ligatures (class 2) in `GlyphClassDef`. Next come `LigGlyph` elements, one for each glyph in the coverage table. Each `LigGlyph` contains `CaretValue` elements corresponding to the various positions of the cursor.

The `CaretValue` elements can be of three different formats (which are, with one slight difference, identical to the three formats of the elements `EntryAnchor`, etc.; see §D.9.3.4): Format 1 indicates that only the x-coordinate (or the y-coordinate, if the direction of the text is vertical) of the cursor's position is given; Format 2 indicates that not the x-coordinate or the y-coordinate[18] but a point on the glyph's contour is given, which has the benefit that we can track the development of the contour under the influence of TrueType instructions and that the cursor's position will take account of those instructions; finally, Format 3, the most powerful of all, includes the x-coordinate (or the y-coordinate) and that coordinate's device table.

Finally, the subtable of classes for combining glyphs:

```
<MarkAttachClassDef Format="2">
    <ClassDef glyph="Acute" class="1"/>
    <ClassDef glyph="Acutesmall" class="1"/>
    <ClassDef glyph="Breve" class="1"/>
    ... 40 lines ...
    <ClassDef glyph="dotbelowcomb" class="2"/>
    ... 25 lines ...
    <ClassDef glyph="uni1FFD" class="1"/>
    <ClassDef glyph="uni1FFE" class="1"/>
    <ClassDef glyph="vrachy" class="1"/>
</MarkAttachClassDef>
```

It is the spitting image of the `GlyphClassDef` subtable, except for the name of the global element, which is `MarkAttachClassDef`. The specification gives no indication of the choice of classes of combining glyphs. Here we have adopted a very simplistic classification: 1 for accents placed above a letter, 2 for those placed below. We could also use a classification similar to that of combining characters in Unicode (see page 127).

The last eight bits of the `LookupFlag` in a lookup can take the value of a class of combining glyphs. The combining glyphs of that class will then be ignored by the lookup.

D.10   Predefined Features, Languages, and Scripts

D.10.1   Predefined Languages and Scripts

The OpenType specification defines tags for scripts and languages. Here is the list of scripts:

---

[18] There is one slight difference. In the case of `EntryAnchor` and `ExitAnchor`, Format 2 included *both* the x-coordinate or y-coordinate *and* the number of the point on the contour. Here only the point on the contour is used.

Arabic	arab	Georgian	geor	Mongolian	mong
Armenian	armn	Greek	grek	Ogham	ogam
Bengali	beng	Gujarati	gujr	Oriya	orya
Bopomofo	bopo	Gurmukhi	guru	Runic	runr
Braille	brai	Hangul	hang	Sinhalese	sinh
Burmese	mymr	Hangul Jamo	jamo	Syriac	syrc
Byzantine music	byzm	Hebrew	hebr	Tamil	taml
Canadian syllabics	cans	Hiragana	kana	Telugu	telu
Cherokee	cher	Kannada	knda	Thaana	thaa
CJK Ideographic	hani	Katakana	kana	Thai	thai
Cyrillic	cyrl	Khmer	khmr	Tibetan	tibt
Default	DFLT	Lao	lao	Yi	yi
Devanagari	deva	Latin	latn		
Ethiopian	ethi	Malayalam	mlym		

And here is the list of languages, following ISO 639-2 [191]:

Abkhazian	ABK	Greek, Modern (1453–)	GRE/ ELL	Nyankole	NYN
Achinese	ACE	Greenlandic	KAL	Nynorsk, Norwegian	NNO
Acoli	ACH	Guarani	GRN	Nyoro	NYO
Adangme	ADA	Gujarati	GUJ	Nzima	NZI
Adygei	ADY	Gwicht'in	GWI	Occitan (post-1500)	OCI
Adyghe	ADY	Haida	HAI	Oirat	XAL
Afar	AAR	Haitian	HAT	Ojibwa	OJI
Afrihili	AFH	Haitian Creole	HAT	Old Bulgarian	CHU
Afrikaans	AFR	Hausa	HAU	Old Church Slavonic	CHU
Afro-Asiatic (Other)	AFA	Hawaiian	HAW	Old Newari	NWC
Ainu	AIN	Hebrew	HEB	Old Slavonic	CHU
Akan	AKA	Herero	HER	Oriya	ORI
Akkadian	AKK	Hiligaynon	HIL	Oromo	ORM
Albanian	ALB/ SQI	Himachali	HIM	Osage	OSA

Alemani	GSW	Hindi	HIN	Ossetian	OSS
Aleut	ALE	Hiri Motu	HMO	Ossetic	OSS
Algonquian languages	ALG	Hittite	HIT	Otomian languages	OTO
Altaic (Other)	TUT	Hmong	HMN	Pahlavi	PAL
Amharic	AMH	Hungarian	HUN	Palauan	PAU
Angika	ANP	Hupa	HUP	Pali	PLI
Apache languages	APA	Iban	IBA	Pampanga	PAM
Arabic	ARA	Icelandic	ICE/ ISL	Pangasinan	PAG
Aragonese	ARG	Ido	IDO	Panjabi	PAN
Aramaic	ARC	Igbo	IBO	Papiamento	PAP
Arapaho	ARP	Ijo	IJO	Papuan (Other)	PAA
Araucanian	ARN	Iloko	ILO	Pedi	NSO
Arawak	ARW	Inari Sami	SMN	Persian	PER/ FAS
Armenian	ARM/ HYE	Indic (Other)	INC	Persian, Old (ca. 600– 400 BC)	PEO
Aromanian	RUP	Indo-European (Other)	INE	Philippine (Other)	PHI
Artificial (Other)	ART	Indonesian	IND	Phoenician	PHN
Arumanian	RUP	Ingush	INH	Pilipino	FIL
Assamese	ASM	Interlingua (International Auxiliary Language Association)	INA	Pohnpeian	PON
Asturian	AST	Interlingue	ILE	Polish	POL
Athapascan languages	ATH	Inuktitut	IKU	Portuguese	POR
Australian languages	AUS	Inupiaq	IPK	Prakrit languages	PRA
Austronesian (Other)	MAP	Iranian (Other)	IRA	Provençal	OCI
Avaric	AVA	Irish	GLE	Provençal, Old (to 1500)	PRO

Avestan	AVE	Irish, Middle (900–1200)	MGA	Punjabi	PAN
Awadhi	AWA	Irish, Old (to 900)	SGA	Pushto	PUS
Aymara	AYM	Iroquoian languages	IRO	Quechua	QUE
Azerbaijani	AZE	Italian	ITA	Rajasthani	RAJ
Bable	AST	Japanese	JPN	Rapanui	RAP
Balinese	BAN	Javanese	JAV	Rarotongan	RAR
Baltic (Other)	BAT	Judeo-Arabic	JRB	Reserved for local use	QAA–QTZ
Baluchi	BAL	Judeo-Persian	JPR	Rhaeto-Romance	ROH
Bambara	BAM	Kabardian	KBD	Romance (Other)	ROA
Bamileke languages	BAI	Kabyle	KAB	Romanian	RUM/RON
Banda	BAD	Kachin	KAC	Romany	ROM
Bantu (Other)	BNT	Kalaallisut	KAL	Rundi	RUN
Basa	BAS	Kalmyk	XAL	Russian	RUS
Bashkir	BAK	Kamba	KAM	Salishan languages	SAL
Basque	BAQ/EUS	Kannada	KAN	Samaritan Aramaic	SAM
Batak (Indonesia)	BTK	Kanuri	KAU	Sami languages (Other)	SMI
Beja	BEJ	Kara-Kalpak	KAA	Samoan	SMO
Belarusian	BEL	Karachay-Balkar	KRC	Sandawe	SAD
Bemba	BEM	Karelian	KRL	Sango	SAG
Bengali	BEN	Karen	KAR	Sanskrit	SAN
Berber (Other)	BER	Kashmiri	KAS	Santali	SAT
Bhojpuri	BHO	Kashubian	CSB	Sardinian	SRD
Bihari	BIH	Kawi	KAW	Sasak	SAS
Bikol	BIK	Kazakh	KAZ	Saxon, Low	NDS
Bilin	BYN	Khasi	KHA	Scots	SCO
Bini	BIN	Khmer	KHM	Scottish Gaelic	GLA

Bislama	BIS	Khoisan (Other)	KHI	Selkup	SEL
Blin	BYN	Khotanese	KHO	Semitic (Other)	SEM
Bokmål, Norwegian	NOB	Kikuyu	KIK	Sepedi	NSO
Bosnian	BOS	Kimbundu	KMB	Serbian	SCC/SRP
Braj	BRA	Kinyarwanda	KIN	Serer	SRR
Breton	BRE	Kirdki	ZZA	Shan	SHN
Buginese	BUG	Kirghiz	KIR	Shona	SNA
Bulgarian	BUL	Kirmanjki	ZZA	Sichuan Yi	III
Buriat	BUA	Klingon	TLH	Sicilian	SCN
Burmese	BUR/MYA	Komi	KOM	Sidamo	SID
Caddo	CAD	Kongo	KON	Sign languages	SGN
Carib	CAR	Konkani	KOK	Siksika	BLA
Castilian	SPA	Korean	KOR	Sindhi	SND
Catalan	CAT	Kosraean	KOS	Sinhala	SIN
Caucasian (Other)	CAU	Kpelle	KPE	Sinhalese	SIN
Cebuano	CEB	Kru	KRO	Sino-Tibetan (Other)	SIT
Celtic (Other)	CEL	Kuanyama	KUA	Siouan languages	SIO
Central American Indian (Other)	CAI	Kumyk	KUM	Skolt Sami	SMS
Chagatai	CHG	Kurdish	KUR	Slave (Athapascan)	DEN
Chamic languages	CMC	Kurukh	KRU	Slavic (Other)	SLA
Chamorro	CHA	Kutenai	KUT	Slovak	SLO/SLK
Chechen	CHE	Kwanyama	KUA	Slovenian	SLV
Cherokee	CHR	Ladino	LAD	Sogdian	SOG
Chewa	NYA	Lahnda	LAH	Somali	SOM
Cheyenne	CHY	Lamba	LAM	Songhai	SON
Chibcha	CHB	Lao	LAO	Soninke	SNK

Chichewa	NYA	Latin	LAT	Sorbian languages	WEN
Chinese	CHI/ ZHO	Latvian	LAV	Sotho, North-ern	NSO
Chinook Jargon	CHN	Letzeburgesch	LTZ	Sotho, Southern	SOT
Chipewyan	CHP	Lezghian	LEZ	South Amer-ican Indian (Other)	SAI
Choctaw	CHO	Limburgan	LIM	South Ndebele	NBL
Chuang	ZHA	Limburger	LIM	Southern Altai	ALT
Church Slavic	CHU	Limburgish	LIM	Southern Sami	SMA
Church Slavonic	CHU	Lingala	LIN	Spanish	SPA
Chuukese	CHK	Lithuanian	LIT	Sranan Togo	SRN
Chuvash	CHV	Lojban	JBO	Sukuma	SUK
Classical Nepal Bhasa	NWC	Low German	NDS	Sumerian	SUX
Classical Newari	NWC	Low Saxon	NDS	Sundanese	SUN
Coptic	COP	Lower Sorbian	DSB	Susu	SUS
Cornish	COR	Lozi	LOZ	Swahili	SWA
Corsican	COS	Luba-Katanga	LUB	Swati	SSW
Cree	CRE	Luba-Lulua	LUA	Swedish	SWE
Creek	MUS	Luiseño	LUI	Swiss German	GSW
Creoles and pidgins (Other)	CRP	Lule Sami	SMJ	Syriac	SYR
Creoles and pidgins, English-based (Other)	CPE	Lunda	LUN	Tagalog	TGL
Creoles and pidgins, French-based (Other)	CPF	Luo (Kenya and Tanzania)	LUO	Tahitian	TAH

Creoles and pidgins, Portuguese-based (Other)	CPP	Lushai	LUS	Tai (Other)	TAI
Crimean Tatar	CRH	Luxembourgish	LTZ	Tajik	TGK
Crimean Turkish	CRH	Macedo-Romanian	RUP	Tamashek	TMH
Croatian	SCR/HRV	Macedonian	MAC/MKD	Tamil	TAM
Cushitic (Other)	CUS	Madurese	MAD	Tatar	TAT
Czech	CZE/CES	Magahi	MAG	Telugu	TEL
Dakota	DAK	Maithili	MAI	Tereno	TER
Danish	DAN	Makasar	MAK	Tetum	TET
Dargwa	DAR	Malagasy	MLG	Thai	THA
Dayak	DAY	Malay	MAY/MSA	Tibetan	TIB/BOD
Delaware	DEL	Malayalam	MAL	Tigre	TIG
Dhivehi	DIV	Maldivian	DIV	Tigrinya	TIR
Dimili	ZZA	Maltese	MLT	Timne	TEM
Dimli	ZZA	Manchu	MNC	Tiv	TIV
Dinka	DIN	Mandar	MDR	tlhIngan-Hol	TLH
Divehi	DIV	Mandingo	MAN	Tlingit	TLI
Dogri	DOI	Manipuri	MNI	Tok Pisin	TPI
Dogrib	DGR	Manobo languages	MNO	Tokelau	TKL
Dravidian (Other)	DRA	Manx	GLV	Tonga (Nyasa)	TOG
Duala	DUA	Maori	MAO/MRI	Tonga (Tonga Islands)	TON
Dutch	DUT/NLD	Marathi	MAR	Tsimshian	TSI
Dutch, Middle (ca. 1050–1350)	DUM	Mari	CHM	Tsonga	TSO
Dyula	DYU	Marshallese	MAH	Tswana	TSN
Dzongkha	DZO	Marwari	MWR	Tumbuka	TUM
Eastern Frisian	FRS	Masai	MAS	Tupi languages	TUP

Efik	EFI	Mayan languages	MYN	Turkish	TUR
Egyptian (Ancient)	EGY	Mende	MEN	Turkish, Ottoman (1500–1928)	OTA
Ekajuk	EKA	Mi'kmaq	MIC	Turkmen	TUK
Elamite	ELX	Micmac	MIC	Tuvalu	TVL
English	ENG	Minangkabau	MIN	Tuvinian	TYV
English, Middle (1100–1500)	ENM	Mirandese	MWL	Twi	TWI
English, Old (ca. 450–1100)	ANG	Miscellaneous languages	MIS	Udmurt	UDM
Erzya	MYV	Mohawk	MOH	Ugaritic	UGA
Esperanto	EPO	Moksha	MDF	Uighur	UIG
Estonian	EST	Moldavian	MOL	Ukrainian	UKR
Ewe	EWE	Mon-Khmer (Other)	MKH	Umbundu	UMB
Ewondo	EWO	Mongo	LOL	Undetermined	UND
Fang	FAN	Mongolian	MON	Upper Sorbian	HSB
Fanti	FAT	Mossi	MOS	Urdu	URD
Faroese	FAO	Multiple languages	MUL	Uyghur	UIG
Fijian	FIJ	Munda languages	MUN	Uzbek	UZB
Filipino	FIL	N'Ko	NQO	Vai	VAI
Finnish	FIN	Nahuatl	NAH	Valencian	CAT
Finno-Ugrian (Other)	FIU	Nauru	NAU	Venda	VEN
Flemish	DUT/NLD	Navaho	NAV	Vietnamese	VIE
Fon	FON	Navajo	NAV	Volapük	VOL
French	FRE/FRA	Ndebele, North	NDE	Votic	VOT
French, Middle (ca. 1400–1600)	FRM	Ndebele, South	NBL	Wakashan languages	WAK
French, Old (842–ca. 1400)	FRO	Ndonga	NDO	Walamo	WAL
Friulian	FUR	Neapolitan	NAP	Walloon	WLN

Fulah	FUL	Nepal Bhasa	NEW	Waray	WAR
Ga	GAA	Nepali	NEP	Washo	WAS
Gaelic	GLA	Newari	NEW	Welsh	WEL/ CYM
Galician	GLG	Nias	NIA	Western Frisian	FRY
Ganda	LUG	Niger-Kordofanian (Other)	NIC	Wolof	WOL
Gayo	GAY	Nilo-Saharan (Other)	SSA	Xhosa	XHO
Gbaya	GBA	Niuean	NIU	Yakut	SAH
Geez	GEZ	No linguistic content	ZXX	Yao	YAO
Georgian	GEO/ KAT	Nogai	NOG	Yapese	YAP
German	GER/ DEU	Norse, Old	NON	Yiddish	YID
German, Low	NDS	North American Indian	NAI	Yoruba	YOR
German, Middle High (ca. 1050– 1500)	GMH	North Ndebele	NDE	Yupik languages	YPK
German, Old High (ca. 750– 1050)	GOH	Northern Frisian	FRR	Zande	ZND
Germanic (Other)	GEM	Northern Sami	SME	Zapotec	ZAP
Gikuyu	KIK	Northern Sotho	NSO	Zaza	ZZA
Gilbertese	GIL	Norwegian	NOR	Zazaki	ZZA
Gondi	GON	Norwegian Bokmål	NOB	Zenaga	ZEN
Gorontalo	GOR	Norwegian Nynorsk	NNO	Zhuang	ZHA
Gothic	GOT	Nubian languages	NUB	Zulu	ZUL
Grebo	GRB	Nyamwezi	NYM	Zuni	ZUN
Greek, Ancient (to 1453)	GRC	Nyanja	NYA		

D.10.2   Predefined Features

In this section, we shall describe the 123 features that are predefined in the OpenType specification and cataloged by Microsoft. We have subdivided them into four categories:

- General features, those specific to the Latin script

- Features specific to the Semitic scripts

- Features specific to the scripts of India and Southeast Asia

- Features specific to the ideographic scripts

Please note that this classification is arbitrary and very rough. For example, it includes Latin fonts with initial, medial, and final glyphs, but such fonts are rare; conversely, every Arabic font is required, by the very nature of the Arabic script, to include those forms. That is why Arabic fonts have been classified in the section for the Semitic languages.

D.10.2.1   General features, or those specific to the Latin script

- aalt (*access all alternatives*): show the user all the variants of a given glyph.

- abvm (*above-based mark [positioning]*): supports placing a diacritical mark on a base glyph, possibly one that already bears other diacritical marks. Should be enabled by default.

- afrc (*alternative fractions*): automatically yields fractions with a horizontal bar. Not to be confused with frac: afrc replaces '3/4' with '$\frac{3}{4}$', while frac replaces it with '¾'. Should be disabled by default.

- blwm (*below-base mark [positioning]*): place a diacritical mark below a base glyph, possibly one that already bears other diacritical marks. Should be enabled by default.

- blws (*below-base substitutions*): replace a base glyph bearing a lower diacritical mark with a ligature when appropriate. Should be enabled by default.

- calt (*contextual alternatives*): replace a glyph with one of its variants that is more appropriate in the context. Should be enabled by default.

- case (*case-sensitive forms*): replace the glyphs for punctuation marks with other glyphs that are better suited to capital letters and "modern" digits; also replace old-style figures with modern figures.

- clig (*contextual ligatures*): replace certain glyphs with a ligature, if the context is appropriate. Should be enabled by default.

- cpsp (*capital spacing*): add a bit more space between the letters for type set in full capitals. Should be enabled by default.

- cwsh (*contextual swash*): replace a glyph with one of its calligraphic variants that is more appropriate in the given context. If more than one variant is available, the interface may present a palette of glyphs to the user.

- c2pc (*petite capitals from capitals*). Warning: font designers have invented a new type of letters—small capitals that are smaller than small capitals. To distinguish these letters from small capitals, they have given them the pseudo-French name *petite capitals*. This feature converts capitals into petite capitals.

- c2sc (*small capitals from capitals*): converts capitals into small capitals.

- dlig (*discretionary ligatures*): replace a string of glyphs with a ligature upon the express request of the user. Example: in Japanese, one writes ㌖ for キロメートル (*kiromeetoru*, or "kilometer"), ㍿ for 株式会社 (*kabushiki-gaishya*, or "corporation"), etc.

- frac (*fractions*): replace a number followed by a slash and another number with a fraction written with a slanted bar. Example: "3/4" is replaced with ¾. This feature calls the two internal features numr and dnom in order to produce the numerator and the denominator. Should be disabled by default.

- hist (*historical forms*): uſe, for example, the long 'ſ'. Handle with care, becauſe the uſe of this letter is often contextual (there is no long 'ſ' at the end of a word) or even grammatical (in German the long 'ſ' is not written at the end of a conſtituent of a word: "Eſel", but "Ausgabe"). The feature is more general and affects all the hiſtorical forms of the letter. Should be diſabled by default.

- hlig (*historical ligatures*): use a number of obsolete ligatures. It is up to the designer to decide which ligatures are "current" and which are "obsolete". Should be disabled by default.

- ital (*italics*): switch to italics. It is an *excellent idea* to have roman and italic glyphs in the same font: it allows for kerning between the two!

- jalt (*justification alternative*): show the user some glyph variants (wider or narrower letters that are intended to improve justification.

- kern (*kerning*): enable kerning. Should be enabled by default for horizontal typesetting.

- liga (*standard ligatures*): produce the standard ligatures, such as 'fi' and 'fl'.

- lnum (*lining figures*): replace old-style figures with modern figures.

- locl (*localized forms*): tailor the glyphs to the selected language. In certain scripts, such as Cyrillic, the ways of writing a given letter vary from one country behind the former Iron Curtain to another. Another example: in German the umlaut is written lower than the French diaeresis; compare "äöü" (German) and "äöü" (French). This difference is certainly due to the fact that French gives precedence to the other accent marks, with which the diaeresis must be aligned: "äéöèüê". This feature produces forms tailored to the active language. Should be enabled by default.

- mark (*mark positioning*): places diacritical marks on the glyphs. Should be enabled by default.

- mgrk (*mathematical Greek*): use the glyphs for Greek letters that are better suited to mathematics than to Greek text. Warning: using special letterforms for Greek mathematics is a habit peculiar to the English-speaking countries. Traditionally the French use the letters from Greek text faces in formulae as well. See [163] for a series of examples.

- mkmk (*mark-to-mark positioning*): supports the placing of diacritical marks over other diacritical marks. Should be enabled by default.

- nalt (*alternate annotation forms*): show the user a list of "annotated" letters or digits—i.e., those enclosed in circles or boxes, written white on black, etc.

- onum (*oldstyle figures*): replace modern figures with old-style figures.

- opbd (*optical bounds*): a feature that plays the same role as the opbd table in AAT (see §D.11.7), i.e., to align the glyphs according to their contours rather than their abstract boxes (their origin, at the left, and their set-width, at the right). It calls two internal features: lfbd (when the glyph appears at the beginning of a line) and rtbd (when it comes at the end of a line).

- ordn (*ordinals*): cause the number to be interpreted as an ordinal rather than as a cardinal. In other words, replace '2' with '2ⁿᵈ' in English, '2ᵉ' in French, '2.' in German, '2oς' in Greek, etc. Use in moderation: the font is unable to decide whether what follows is masculine or feminine. Thus how can we obtain '1ᵉʳ' and '1ʳᵉ' in French? The situation is even more complicated in Greek because ordinals are declined: '2oς', '2ou', '2ω', '2ov', '2ε', etc. Therefore, do not rely on the font to choose the right form!

- ornm (*ornaments*): help the user to enter ornamental glyphs. Two different approaches are covered: either the user enters a bullet and the system shows him a palette of ornamental glyphs (which is appropriate for interactive use) or the user enters ASCII characters that the system proceeds to replace with ornamental glyphs according to a given transcription.

- pcap (*petite capitals*) replace lowercase letters with "petite capitals" (special small capitals that are smaller than the ordinary small capitals), which we saw above in the discussion of the feature c2pc.

- pnum (*proportional figures*): use figures whose set-widths may be unequal; the approach is more aesthetically appealing but less useful when setting bills or balance sheets, where the figures absolutely must be aligned.

- rand (*randomize*): the font is supposed to contain some slightly different glyphs that the system can select at random when this feature is enabled. The author cannot resist pointing out that in PostScript it is the printer that performs this selection: in particular, that is how the fonts *Punk* [41], *Beowolf* [86], and *Tekla* [118] work.

- rlig (*required ligatures*): produce only the strictly essential ligatures—for instance, in Arabic, the *lam-alif* ﻻ or the special *lam-lam-ha* that is used to write the name of Allah (الله). Should be enabled by default.

- salt (*stylistic alternatives*): obtain variants that cannot be classified either as historical or as calligraphic.

- sinf (*scientific inferiors*): replaces figures at text size with figures at a smaller size that are moved downward for use as subscripts.

- size (*optical size*): this feature is a notorious hack to enter information on optical size into a font. Adobe asks us to include this feature in a GPOS table, but without associating it with any lookup. This table contains the optical size and perhaps also the ranges of optical sizes at which the font may be used.

- smcp (*small capitals*): replace lowercase letters with small capitals. Not to be confused with c2sc, which replaces capitals with small capitals.

- ss01 to ss20 (*stylistic sets 1–20*): gives the user another way to obtain variant glyphs.

- subs (*subscript*): replaces a glyph at text size with the same glyph as a subscript. Not to be confused with sinf, which places the glyph in subscript position—i.e., slightly below the baseline.

- sups (*superscript*): replaces a glyph at text size with the same glyph as a superscript.

- swsh (*swash*): presents a palette for selecting calligraphic variant glyphs.

- titl (*titling*): replaces ordinary capitals with capitals customized for use in titles.

- tnum (*tabular figures*): replaces proportional figures with glyphs of uniform space, which are more suited for use in accounting, in which the figures must be aligned.

D.10.2.2 *Features specific to the Semitic scripts*

- curs (*cursive positioning*): connects the letters in the cursive scripts, such as Arabic.

- falt (*final glyph on line alternatives*): select a variant glyph adapted for use at the end of a line.

- fin2 and fin3 (*terminal form #2/#3*): these features are used only to change the shape of the Syriac letter *alaph* in the *Serto* script when this letter is preceded by *dalath* or *rish*, with or without a dot.

The reader must be wondering what could justify two features that apply to only one letter.

Here is the situation. In the Syriac *Serto* script, the letter *alaph* can have two isolated forms: the curvilinear shape ¦ and the upright shape ƒ. The author has long attempted (see [160]) to find the rules that determine how this letter is to be written. Here are his conclusions: (a) the curvilinear form is used at the beginning of a word and the final form in the middle and at the end of a word; (b) the curvilinear form is used in the middle or at the end of a word when it is preceded by the letter *rish* (ȷ), *dalath* (ȷ), or *waw* (ᴏ). All is well so far. But the author has found several exceptions in the dictionaries: *oar* ܐܐܪ "air", *diabol* ܕܝܘ "devil", *daro* ܩܪܒ "combat", etc. Therefore the form that this letter should take is by no means clear, and it is better to have a feature that supports easy switching from one form to the other.

- fina (*terminal forms*): select a glyph variant suited for use at the end of the word. Essential in Arabic, where the final form of a letter is obtained.

- init (*initial forms*): select a glyph variant suited for the beginning of a word. Essential in Arabic, where the initial form of a letter is obtained.

- isol (*isolated forms*): select a glyph variant suited for an isolated letter. Essential in Arabic, where the isolated form of a letter is obtained.

- medi (*medial forms*): select a glyph variant adapted to a letter in the middle of a word. Essential in Arabic, where the medial form of a letter is obtained.

- med2 (*medial form #2*): change the glyph for the letter *alaph* in the *Serto* script when the preceding letter cannot be connected to it. Should be enabled by default.

- mset: place diacritical marks over Arabic letters. This feature applies only to Microsoft fonts under Windows 95.

- rtla (*right-to-left alternatives*): replaces left-to-right glyphs with their right-to-left counterparts. For example, the parentheses, brackets, braces, and other delimiters will be shown in mirror image.

D.10.2.3 *Features specific to the scripts of Inda and Southeast Asia*

- abvf (*above-base forms*): In scripts such as Khmer, there are often vowels in two parts, of which one is anteposed (placed to the left of the consonant to which the vowel applies) and the other is placed over the consonant in the manner of a diacritical mark. The second of these two components is the one produced by this feature. For example, according to Unicode notation, the vowel *oe* in Khmer is written ៊ែ; applying it to the consonant *cho* ឆ yields ឆ៊ែ. The feature abvf allows us to obtain the part ˜ of this vowel. Should be enabled by default.

- abvs (*above-base substitutions*): replaces a base glyph bearing an upper diacritical mark with a ligature, when appropriate. Should be enabled by default.

- akhn (*akhand* = "unbreakable" in Hindi) produces the independent ligatures for every context in the scripts of India. In Devanagari, for example, when a *ka* (क) with no vowel is followed by a *ssa* (ष), the ligature *kssa* (क्ष) is obtained; likewise, when a *ja* (ज) with no vowel is followed by a *nya* (ञ), the ligature *jnya* (ज्ञ) is obtained. Should be enabled by default.

- blwf (*below-base forms*): obtain the subscript form of a consonant in a consonant complex. In Khmer, for example, if the consonant *nno* ណ with no vowel is followed by *nyo* (ញ), the latter assumes its subscript form, and the overall result is ណ្ញ (*nnnyo*). Should be enabled by default.

- dist (*distances*): manages distances between the glyphes in the languages of India.

- half (*half forms*): produces the half-forms of the Indian consonants. What is a half-form? In the languages of India, the consonants by default include an inherent short vowel 'a' (thus the written form "prtk" is pronounced "parataka"). When several consonants with no intervening vowel must be pronounced, a number of orthographic subterfuges are used to indicate the absence of an inherent vowel. One of these subterfuges is the "half-form": only half of the consonant is written. Examples: in Devanagari, the half-form of the consonant *ja* (ज) is ज़; that of the consonant *kha* (ख) is ख़, and so forth.

- haln (*halant forms*): replace an Indian consonant with its special form lacking an inherent vowel. In Devanagari, for example, the form of *nga* (ङ) that lacks a vowel is written ङ्. It involves the mere addition of a *virama* (्), but specially designed glyphs are often used, for aesthetic reasons.

- nukt (*nukta*): In the scripts of India, a diacritical mark called *nukta*. The role of this sign, which is shaped like a dot, is to indicate a new letter whose pronunciation differs from that of the original letter. For example, the letter *ka* (क) becomes *qa* (क़) when this sign is applied to it, and that is what this feature does. That said, since Unicode does provide letters with *nukta*, the author believes that the responsibility for producing them lies with the keyboard rather than the font.

- pref (*pre-base forms*): In the languages of India and Southeast Asia, there are letters that are placed before a group of consonants even though they logically (and phonetically) come afterwards. This feature allows us to obtain the anteposed form of a letter. For example, Khmer has the consonant *ro* (រ) (not to be confused with the vowel *e* [ɨ]). The consonant *cho* (ឈ) without a vowel, followed by *ro* (រ), yields ឈ្រ (*chro*): *ro* here has assumed its anteposed form. Should be enabled by default.

- pres (*pre-base substitutions*): like the feature pref, except that a ligature is produced between the two glyphs, rather than simply a more appropriate form of the first glyph. For example, the consonant *nga* (ङ) with no vowel, followed by the consonant *ma* (म), gives the spectacular form ङ्म (*ngma*).

- pstf (*post-base forms*): In the languages of India and Southeast Asia, some letters have a special form when they follow a group of consonants. This feature produces that form.

- psts (*post-base substitution*): like the feature pstf, except that a ligature of the two glyphs is produced rather than merely a more appropriate form of the second glyph.

- rphf (*reph form*): In the languages of India and Southeast Asia, this feature produces the special form of a consonant preceded by the letter 'r' (with no vowel). For example, *ra* (र) with no vowel, followed by *ka* (क), yields *rka* (र्क), and that is what this feature does.

D.10.2.4 *Features specific to the ideographic languages*

- ccmp (*glyph composition/decomposition*): decompose a glyph in order to reconstitute it in a way more suited to interaction with other glyphs, diacritical marks, etc. For example, separate the dots of the Arabic letters and replace them as indicated in the GPOS table, or, even more spectacularly, produce Korean syllables from hangul letters (see the ljmo feature).

- expt (*expert forms*). No, this has nothing to do with Adobe's "Expert" font encodings; it is a set of Japanese ideographic glyph variants [239] that are needed in printing but that are not covered by Unicode.

- fwid (*full widths*): write w i t h   l e t t e r s   a s   w i d e   a s   t h e   i d e o g r a p h s. This "modified" Latin script is quite useful in the ideographic countries for aligning Latin, Cyrillic, and Greek letters with ideographs. Should be disabled by default.

- hkna (*horizontal kana alternatives*): use kana that were specially designed for horizontal typesetting. Should be disabled by default.

- hngl (hangul): replace Chinese ideographs with the Korean phonetic hangul script. For instance, 漢字 will become 한글, etc. Since the choice is not always unique, the application should be able to offer the user a list of the possible choices.

- hwid and halt (*half width* and *alternative half widths*): set type in half-width characters in the ideographic languages—either in "modified Latin" as illustrated by these few words or in katakana ｶﾀｶﾅ. The halt offers the user a second list of possible glyphs.

- jp78, jp83, jp90 (*JIS78/JIS83/JIS90 forms*): offer the user some variants of ideographic glyphs that are based on the JIS C 6226-1978, JIS X 0208-1983, and JIS X 0208-1990 standards. These features aim to make up for the shortcomings of Unicode: when the ideographic glyphs were unified, it was not possible to envision all the variants of each glyph. But in some branches of publishing, such as dictionaries, history, and geography, these variants are indeed needed. To use them, one selects the nearest Unicode character and employs features of this type to obtain the desired variant. See [239] for more details.

- ljmo, vjmo, tjmo (*leading, vowel, trailing jamo*). The Korean hangul script works as follows: a *syllable* is made from a group of consonants, a possible group of vowels, and a possible second group of consonants. These three groups of letters are combined in an ideographic square. Example: the consonant 'p' (ㅂ) followed by the vowel 'ŏ' (ㅓ) and the consonant 'm' (ㅁ) produces the syllable 'pŏm' (범). In general, all of the syllables required for modern Korean are supplied in Unicode and also in fonts. But to write Old Korean, one must sometimes combine letters explicitly. The features ljmo, vjmo, and tjmo are used to give each group of letters its status of "first group of consonants", "group of vowels", "second group of consonants". Finally, through the feature ccmp, these three groups are combined into one syllable. As an example (specially concocted by the author according to [267]), let us take as the first group of consonants the letters 'p' (ㅂ), 's' (ㅅ), and 't' (ㅌ), and apply the feature ljmo to it; then let us take the group of vowels 'o' (ㅗ) and 'ye' (ㅒ) and apply vjmo to it; finally, let us take as the second group of consonants 'l' (ㄹ), 'm' (ㅁ), and 'h' (ㅎ) and apply the feature tjmo to it. In conclusion, let us apply the feature ccmp to the full set of eight letters, bake for a few milliseconds, and observe the result: the astonishing syllable *pstoyelmh* (ꥲꥲ)!

- nlck (*NLC kanji forms*): like the features expt, jp78, jp83, and jp90, this one yields Japanese ideographic glyph variants.

- pwid and palt: (*proportional [alternate] widths*): When we set text in the Latin alphabet within an ideographic context, this feature switches from full—width Latin letters or half-width Latin letters to the Latin letters that we know and love—i.e., letters with "proportional widths". The "alternative" feature gives us a variant of these glyphs.

- qwid (*quarter widths*): set type in quarter-width characters in the ideographic languages—using either "modified Latin" as illustrated by these few words or katakana カタカナ. For timid authors.

- ruby (*ruby notation forms*): *Ruby* characters, or *furigana*, are phonetic (or other) annotations used in Japanese, notably to enable children and adolescents to read books with ideographs that they have not yet learned at school. Here is an example of ideographs with *ruby* characters: 日本語の文字 (*nihon-go-no moji*, "Japanese characters"). Given the small size of these glyphs, we are wise to use variants that have been optically customized, and that is what this feature does: it chooses glyph variants that are suited for use as *ruby* characters.

- smpl (*simplified forms*): replace the traditional forms of Chinese and Japanese ideographs with simplified forms.

- tnam (*traditional name forms*): offers a range of traditional Japanese ideographs that are variants of the selected ideograph. These variants are used especially for proper names, especially surnames.

- trad (*traditional forms*): replace the simplified forms of Chinese and Japanese ideographs with their traditional forms. If necessary, offer the user a selection of various choices.

- twid (*third widths*): compose type in the ideographic languages at one third of the standard width—using either "modified Latin" as illustrated by these few words or katakana カタカナ. For authors less timid than those who use quarter-width characters, but timid nonetheless.

D.11   General AAT Tables

Apple [56] has defined 17 TrueType tables that for now are used only under Mac OS X. These tables are known by the name "AAT" (= *Apple Advanced Typography*). We shall divide them into three groups.

The first group, to which this section is devoted, contains eight various and sundry tables. The second group, with five tables, is dedicated to fonts *with variation*, a concept close to Multiple Master. Finally, the third group, with four tables, contains the big guns of the AAT tables—i.e., tables for positioning, substitution, and justification; they use finite automata to do their task, which makes them very powerful—and very difficult to design.

But let us begin with the relatively simple tables: acnt, bsln, fdsc, feat (with the list of predefined AAT features), lcar, opbd, prop, trak, and Zapf.

D.11.1   The acnt Table

This table's name comes from the word "accent". In fact, it is a table for describing composite glyphs, in the same vein as AFM files (§C.3.7) or the virtual fonts of TEX (§B.3). Composite glyphs consist of a base glyph (here called the *primary glyph*) and one or more combining glyphs (here called *secondary glyphs*). The table contains the names of the glyphs in question and their relative positions.

Rather than giving a global offset for the combining glyph (as in AFM files or TEX virtual fonts), the acnt table adopts a more efficient strategy that is also closer to the type 4 lookups of the GPOS table: a point on the base glyph's contour and a point on the combining glyph's contour are selected, and the second glyph is moved so that the points coincide.

The benefit of this method is that it takes into account the TrueType instructions that may move the points in question. It thus offers better control over the positioning of diacritical marks at any size.

Here is an example of one such table:

```
<acnt>
  <Version value="1"/>
  <Glyph value="Aacute" format="0">
    <primaryGlyph value="A"/>
    <secondaryGlyph index="0" value="acute">
      <primaryAttachmentPoint value="24"/>
      <secondaryAttachmentPoint value="7"/>
    </secondaryGlyph>
  </Glyph>
  ...
</acnt>
```

The acnt element contains an element for the version and one Glyph element for each composite glyph in the table. Each Glyph element has two attributes: value, which gives the name of the composite glyph, and format, which is 0 if there is only one diacritical mark or 1 if there are more than one.

The Glyph element contains an element primaryGlyph, whose value attribute gives the name of the base glyph, and one secondaryGlyph for each glyph that combines with the baes glyph to form the composite glyph. Each secondaryGlyph takes a value attribute, which contains the name of the combining glyph and has two elements: the numbers of the points of attachment on the base glyph (primaryAttachmentPoint) and the combining glyph (secondaryAttachmentPoint). The number of the point of attachment on the base glyph is repeated in each secondaryGlyph, for the simple reason that this point can be different for each combining glyph.

D.11.2   The bsln Table

This table's name comes from the word *baseline*. It attempts to solve the same problem as the BASE table of OpenType: the possibility of having several baselines, according to the type of script. The figure below (taken from page 754):

I'm based 日本語の文字です ཡཆེསཁརལྦུ࿐

illustrates the situation for the BASE table of OpenType. In it, we see three types of script (Latin, ideographic, Tibetan), with three different baselines. Here, in the case of bsln, the approach to the ideographic script is different: the ideographic baseline is considered to run *through the middle of the glyphs*. Therefore we have redrawn this figure with regard to the bsln table:

Here we see:

1. English, for the "Latin" baseline (number 0).

2. Japanese typeset so as to be consistent with the English, i.e., moved slightly downward. Since the baseline here is considered to run through the middle of the glyphs, the baseline appears at the location indicated in the figure. This baseline (number 2) is called the "ideographic baseline".

3. More Japanese, this time on the Latin baseline. Here the baseline that runs through the middle of the ideographs (number 1) is called the "central ideographic" line. This baseline is used in documents containing nothing but ideographs (or characters assimilated to ideographs—do not forget that Asian fonts and encodings contain Latin glyphs and characters, respectively, that have the exact dimensions of the ideographs and that are typeset in the same way).

4. Tibetan, using a "hanging" baseline (number 3).

What is missing from this figure is a fifth "baseline", the axis for the vertical centering of mathematical symbols: '$=$', '$+$', '$-$', '$*$', '$\otimes$', '$\oplus$', '$\circ$', etc.

AAT supposes that we can, in theory, have up to 32 baselines. But do not plan to define any others: only the five described above are permitted; the other 27 are reserved by Apple.

There are four formats for the bsln table: in Format 0, the baselines apply to all the glyphs in the font and are defined by y-coordinates expressed in TrueType units; in Format 1, they are again defined by y-coordinates but can take different values for each glyph; in Format 2, they are defined with points on the contour of a model glyph and take the same value for every glyph; finally, Format 3 combines formats 1 and 2: the baselines are defined by points on the contour of a model glyph and can take different values for each glyph.

Here is an example of a bsln table of format 0:

```
<bsln>
  <Version value="1"/>
  <baselines format="0">
    <defaultBaseline value="0"/>
```

```
      <deltas>
        <delta index="0" value="0"/>
        <delta index="1" value="352"/>
        <delta index="2" value="352"/>
        <delta index="3" value="705"/>
        <delta index="4" value="352"/>
      </deltas>
    </baselines>
  </bsln>
```

After the customary Version, we find a baselines element, which contains the data for the table. Its format attribute gives the table's format. In baselines, we find an element default-Baseline. This element allows us to select the font's default baseline. Since we are using Format 0, the rest of the content of baselines is a single element: deltas. This element contains the descriptions of the different baselines. These descriptions consist of delta (with no 's') elements whose value attributes are the distances between the lines in question and the default baseline. (The name "delta" comes from the fact that the values are not absolute coordinates but rather offsets from the default value).

Format 1 adds, after the end of the deltas, a Glyphs element, like this:

```
<Glyphs>
  <Glyph value="A" baseline="0"/>
  <Glyph value="B" baseline="0"/>
  <Glyph value="C" baseline="0"/>
  ...
</Glyphs>
```

This element contains, in the form of attributes, the glyph names and baselines associated with each glyph. The value of the baseline attribute corresponds to the value of the index attribute of the element delta.

Format 2 resembles Format 0, but instead of delta elements there are ctlPoint elements:

```
<bsln>
  <Version value="1"/>
  <baselines format="2">
    <defaultBaseline value="0"/>
    <stdGlyph value="P"/>
    <ctlPoints>
      <ctlPoint index="0" value="34"/>
      <ctlPoint index="1" value="35"/>
      <ctlPoint index="2" value="35"/>
      <ctlPoint index="3" value="36"/>
      <ctlPoint index="4" value="35"/>
    </ctlPoints>
  </baselines>
</bsln>
```

But it is not enough to give the numbers of points on the contour: we must also specify the glyph in which the points appear. That is the role of the element stdGlyph. The value attributes of the ctlPoint elements contain the numbers of points on the contour of the glyph in question. Finally, Format 3 contains in addition the Glyphs element that we saw in Format 1.

D.11.3   The fdsc Table

The idea behind this table, whose name is an abbreviation of *font descriptor*, is to classify the font so that a suitable substitute can be found. For example, the user selects a block of text in the font and specifies a different font family. The system will then select the individual fonts from that font family that most closely match the characteristics of the text itself.

The table is a small one: it merely supplies some general information on the font—information that also appears in part in OS/2, head, and elsewhere. Here is an example of this table:

```
<fdsc>
  <Version value="1"/>
  <descriptors>
    <descriptor tag="wght" value="0.8"/>
    <descriptor tag="wdth" value="1.0"/>
    <descriptor tag="slnt" value="0"/>
    <descriptor tag="opsz" value="10"/>
    <descriptor tag="nalf" value="3"/>
  </descriptors>
</fdsc>
```

The descriptors element contains descriptor elements (with no 's'). Each descriptor contains *one piece of data on the font*; it has a "name", which is the value of the tag, and a value. Here are the descriptors defined by Apple: wght is the font's weight relative to the standard weight of the "font family" (1 by default), wdth is the font's width relative to the standard width (1 by default), slnt is the slant (measured clockwise in degrees), opsz is the optical size (in American printers' points), and nalf is a classification of the font as "alphabetic" (value 0), "dingbats" (1), "pi characters" (i.e., symbol fonts such as *Symbol*; value 2), "fleurons" (3), "decorative borders" (4), "international symbols" (5), "mathematical symbols" (6). The specification provides no other explanation in the specification on the difference between "pi characters" and "mathematical symbols" or on the meaning of "international symbols" (are they internationally recognized symbols, such as the pictograms that we see in airports, or simply the glyphs of non-Latin scripts?).

D.11.4   The fmtx Table

One more small table that makes up, to some extent, for the absence of the concept of "device table" that we have in OpenType. The question at issue here is "The tables head, OS/2, etc., give us explicit values; what would happen if the TrueType instructions changed these values for certain font sizes?"

In the OpenType context, we had "device tables". AAT offers something simpler: We select a glyph as our model. For each relevant dimension in the font, we select a point on the model glyph whose x-coordinate or y-coordinate will serve as a reference for us. Then the relevant dimensions of interest to us will develop according to the wishes of the TrueType instructions. Note that this model glyph may very well be an ad hoc glyph whose only reason for existence is to be a model for the behavior of other glyphs—an attitude worthy of the Tibetan monks.

Here is an example of one such table:

```
<fmtx>
  <Version value="1"/>
  <glyphIndex value="X"/>
  <horizontalBefore value="15"/>
  <horizontalAfter value="17"/>
  <horizontalCaretHead value="29"/>
  <horizontalCaretBase value="29"/>
  <verticalBefore value="15"/>
  <verticalAfter value="19"/>
  <verticalCaretHead value="31"/>
  <verticalCaretBase value="29"/>
</fmtx>
```

The element glyphIndex gives us the model glyph. We shall use the points on this glyph and their offsets under the influence of the instructions in order to obtain the dimensions of interest to us. There are eight of them: horizontalBefore indicates the height of the ascenders, horizontalAfter indicates the depth of the descenders, horizontalCaretHead indicates the size of the cursor, horizontalCaretBase indicates its depth. The word "horizontal" is a bit jarring because its values represent both height and depth; in fact, its name refers rather to the *direction of typesetting*. The same concepts exist in vertical typesetting; the names of the corresponding elements begin with vertical. Note that when we say "height of ascenders" and "depth of descenders" we refer not to the exact values but rather to values given by the designer that are used for the management of leading.

D.11.5   The feat Table

Could it be rivalry between Apple and Adobe/Microsoft? Or proof that *universal truth* exists? Whatever the case may be, it is a fact that both OpenType and AAT share the concept of a *feature*. We described the features of OpenType in §D.10.2; in this section, we shall describe the features of AAT.

But AAT features have two flagrant disadvantages, and we may as well mention them right away: AAT features are *flexible* and *easy to use*. Specifically, AAT features have *selectors*: series of properties specific to each, which the user enables or disables upon selecting the feature. On the other hand, their names are not vulgar four-letter ASCII strings, like those of the OpenType features, but namerecords from the name table—which means that the designer can translate the name of a feature into every language and script in the world! OpenType can only dream of such richness.[19]

---

[19] The reader must be wondering why the author is so hostile. Well, first of all, what he is exhibiting is not hostility but anger. And the reason is as follows: the fact that OpenType features are described by four-letter

But before describing the features, let us say a few words about the `feat` table, whose role is to list their names.

Here is an example of one such table:

```
<feat>
  <Version value="1"/>
  <FeatureNames>
    <!-- featureNameCount=3 -->
    <FeatureName nameIndex="260" index="0" code="0"
                 exclusiveSettings="0" defaultSetting="0">
      <!-- nSettings=1 -->
      <Setting code="0" nameIndex="261"/>
    </FeatureName>
    <FeatureName nameIndex="262" index="0" code="3"
                 exclusiveSettings="1" defaultSetting="0">
      <!-- nSettings=1 -->
      <Setting code="0" nameIndex="268"/>
      <Setting code="3" nameIndex="264"/>
      <Setting code="4" nameIndex="265"/>
    </FeatureName>
    ...
  </FeatureNames>
</feat>
```

The element that follows `Version` and that contains all the data is `FeatureNames`. It contains a `FeatureName` (with no 's') for each feature that exists in the font. Each `FeatureName` has five attributes: its number (`index`); the number of the corresponding namerecord in the `name` table that contains the name of the feature (`nameIndex`); the feature's "code"—i.e., its number in the official list of Apple features that we shall present below (`code`); an indication of whether or not the selectors for the feature should be exclusive (`exclusiveSettings`), the difference being that if they are exclusive, the user interface will represent them with *radio buttons*, and if they are not exclusive, they will be represented with *checkboxes*; and the number of the selector that is enabled by default (`defaultSetting`).

Each `FeatureName` contains a `Setting` element for each selector. A `Setting` selector is described by three attributes: `index` gives its number among the feature's selectors; `code` gives its number in the official list of AAT features, which we shall see below; and `nameIndex` gives the number of the namerecord in the `name` table that contains its name, in all possible and imaginable languages.

---

tags, which by definition are incomprehensible to the ordinary user; Adobe has used this fact as an excuse for including only a few predefined features in the user interface to *Adobe InDesign*, thus completely and inexorably disregarding all the marvelous features that the designer might have included in a font.

In this book, we have learned how to create fonts with new features; yet *Adobe InDesign* does not allow us to use those features, simply because it considers their four-letter names unseemly. And that situation is likely to continue, because OpenType makes *no provision* for assigning to these unfortunate features names that are more legible and better adapted to localizable user interfaces. As if the name had not existed since the very beginning of the TrueType format. Therefore, long live AAT!

Let us move on now to the comprehensive list of AAT features, as of late 2006. (On its web site, Apple has warned us that the list is a "dynamic list", but the last update was made in May 1998.).

D.11.5.1 The AAT features

For each feature, we present below its "official" name (in fact, it is the name given in the code for Apple's API [58]) and its code number.

The selectors with an `On` in their name are always accompanied by opposite selectors that disable the property in question. For example, a selector called `SomethingOnSelector` (code n) is always accompanied by a selector `SomethingOffSelector` (code $n+1$), which we shall omit in the following discussion.

- `AllTypographicFeaturesType` (code 0): *all the features*. This is "all or nothing". There is only one selector:

    - `AllTypeFeaturesOnSelector` (code 0): all the features are enabled.

- `LigaturesType` (code 1): *ligatures*. Certain types of ligatures are enabled. Here are the selectors:

    - `RequiredLigaturesOnSelector` (code 0): enables the ligatures that are absolutely necessary for the active language, such as simple connections of Arabic letters.

    - `CommonLigaturesOnSelector` (code 2): enables the most common ligatures, such as the f-ligatures for the Latin alphabet.

    - `RareLigaturesOnSelector` (code 4): enables the less common ligatures, such as 'ft' or 'yy'.

    - `LogosOnSelector` (code 6): enables the ligatures that produce logos: for example, the font may systematically replace "O'REILLY" with the logo of this illustrious publishing house, **O'REILLY**®.

    - `RebusPicturesOnSelector` (code 8): according to the dictionary, a *rebus* is *a pictographic character that designates an object by its shape or by the sound associated with the word that it depicts*. This selector enables rebuses.

    - `DiphthongLigaturesOnSelector` (code 10): enables "diphthongs", i.e., the letters 'Æ', 'Œ', etc.

    - `SquaredLigaturesOnSelector` (code 12): enables the ligatures used in the ideographic scripts, such as ㌖ (*kiromeetoru*, or "kilometer"), ㍿ (*kabushiki-gaisha*, or "corporation"), ㏘ ("8:00 PM"), ㏝ ("the 16th day of the month"), etc.

    - `AbbrevSquaredLigaturesOnSelector` (code 14): another type of ideographic ligatures that packs Latin letters like sardines into the famous ideographic square. Here are some typical examples: ㎢, ㏒, ㎒, ㎭, etc.

    - `SymbolLigaturesOnSelector` (code 16): enables ligatures that have become symbols, such as '℔', the symbol for the *pound* (approx. 453 grams), etc.

- `CursiveConnectionType` (code 2): *cursive script with connected letters*. Applies to both Arabic and calligraphic Latin scripts. Its selectors:

- UnconnectedSelector (code 0): everything is disconnected
- PartiallyConnectedSelector (code 1): some, but not all, letters are connected
- CursiveSelector (code 2): all the letters that can be connected are connected

• LetterCaseType (code 3): *change of case*, for scripts that do have this property (the Latin, Greek, Cyrillic, Armenian, and old Georgian alphabets). The selectors correspond to the various types of case that are available:

- UpperAndLowerCaseSelector (code 0): uppercase and lowercase letters are mixed, and the user's choice of case is respected
- AllCapsSelector (code 1): everything is shown in capitals
- AllLowerCaseSelector (code 2): everything is shown in lowercase letters
- SmallCapsSelector (code 3): everything is shown in small capitals
- InitialCapsSelector (code 4): everything is shown in lowercase letters except the first letter of each word, which is changed to uppercase (thanks to finite automata, we can define with a great deal of precision what is a word and what is not)
- InitialCapsAndSmallCapsSelector (code 5): everything is shown in small capitals except the first letter, which is changed to uppercase

• VerticalSubstitutionType (code 4): *choice of glyph for vertical typesetting*. When type is set vertically, some glyphs change their shape. For instance, the parentheses, brackets, braces, and other delimiters are turned 90 degrees. There is only one selector:

- SubstituteVerticalFormsOnSelector (code 0): selects the glyphs customized for vertical typesetting

• LinguisticRearrangementType (code 5): *rearrangement of glyphs for grammatical reasons*. In some languages of India or Southeast Asia, the glyphs are not displayed in their logical or phonetic order. In the example below:

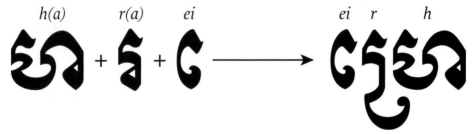

This is set in the Khmer font *Moul*, which was designed by the author [159]. The consonants *h(a)* and *r(a)*, and the vowel *ei*, are shown at the left. At the right, the three letters combined yield *hrei* phonetically, although graphically the *ei* comes first and is followed by *r(a)* and then *h(a)*. This is the sort of behavior that this feature controls. There is only one selector:

- LinguisticRearrangementOnSelector (code 0): enables the grammatical rearrangement of the glyphs

- NumberSpacingType (code 6): *choice of monospaced digits.* This feature allows us to choose between digits of variable width and digits of fixed width. The latter are useful in tables of numbers, in which all figures must be aligned. Two selectors:

  - MonospacedNumbersSelector (code 0): digits of fixed width.

  - ProportionalNumbersSelector (code 1): digits of variable width.

  - ThirdWidthNumbersSelector (code 2): digits of two-thirds width: 1, 2, 3, 4.

  - QuarterWidthNumbersSelector (code 3): digits of one-quarter width: 1, 2, 3, 4. This is extremely narrow. Of what good is it? Perhaps it can be used to display astronomical numbers: "I won ⦀⦀⦀⦀ cents in the lottery!"

- SmartSwashType (code 8): *management of calligraphic variants.* When these selectors are enabled, the context will enable or disable certain calligraphic glyph variants. Five selectors:

  - WordInitialSwashesOnSelector (code 0): enables the variants at the beginning of a word (once again, the finite automata allow us to define precisely which glyphs form words)

  - WordFinalSwashesOnSelector (code 2): ditto, but at the end of a word

  - LineInitialSwashesOnSelector (code 4): ditto, but at the beginning of a line

  - LineFinalSwashesOnSelector (code 6): ditto, but at the end of a line

  - NonFinalSwashesOnSelector (code 8): enables the variants that do not occur at the end of a word

- DiacriticsType (code 9): *display of diacritical marks.*

  - ShowDiacriticsSelector (code 0): the marks are displayed as usual

  - HideDiacriticsSelector (code 1): the marks are completely hidden

  - DecomposeDiacriticsSelector (code 2): rather than combining them with letters, they are shown at the side, as independent glyphs

- VerticalPositionType (code 10): *management of superscripts and subscripts.* The name "vertical position" may lead one astray: in fact, it refers to converting a glyph into a superscript or a subscript, as the font allows. The selectors:

  - NormalPositionSelector (code 0): neither superscripts nor subscripts

  - SuperiorsSelector (code 1): superscripts

  - InferiorsSelector (code 2): subscripts

  - OrdinalsSelector (code 3): like a superscript, but often it requires something else, such as the Spanish ª and º

- FractionsType (code 11): *automatic fractions.* There are two techniques for obtaining beautiful fractions: either predefined glyphs for fractions are used, or the fraction bar is combined with superscript and subscript digits to construct the fraction.

  - NoFractionsSelector (code 0): no automatic construction of fractions

- VerticalFractionsSelector (code 1): uses the font's precomposed fractions
- DiagonalFractionsSelector (code 2): fractions obtained with a superscript, a fraction bar, and a subscript

• OverlappingCharactersType (code 13): *prevents collisions*. This features helps us to prevent collisions of glyphs with protruding elements. Only one selector:

- PreventOverlapOnSelector (code 0): prevents collisions

• TypographicExtrasType (code 14): *automatic application of typographic conventions* . Some software already handles this: for example, to obtain an em dash, the user enters two hyphens, and the software automatically performs the substitution. Here are the selectors for this feature:

- HyphensToEmDashOnSelector (code 0): two hyphens yield an em dash.
- HyphenToEnDashOnSelector (code 2): a hyphen between two spaces or between two digits becomes an en dash.
- SlashedZeroOnSelector (code 4): use a zero with a slash through it (as is done in some fonts used to display computer code in order to distinguish the zero from the letter 'O', but there is a risk of confusion with the empty set, ∅, and the Scandinavian Ø).
- FormInterrobangOnSelector (code 6): The year 1962 saw the birth of not only the author but also a bizarre punctuation mark: the *interrobang* [320], shown here: '‽'. This feature replaces the strings !? and ?! with this beast.
- SmartQuotesOnSelector (code 8): replaces computer-style quotation marks (also known as "straight quotes" or "double quotes") with proper English quotation marks.
- PeriodsToEllipsisOnSelector (code 10): replaces the string "..." with an ellipsis as used in English-language typography.

• MathematicalExtrasType (code 15): *assistance with mathematical typesetting*. Automated typesetting mechanisms specializing in mathematical typesetting. Here are the selectors:

- HyphenToMinusOnSelector (code 0): a hyphen between two spaces or between two digits becomes a mathematical minus sign.
- AsteriskToMultiplyOnSelector (code 2): an asterisk between two spaces is replaced by the multiplication sign, ($\times$). Handle with care, since the asterisk is also (rarely, it is true) used in mathematics as an operator.
- SlashToDivideOnSelector (code 4): the slash between two spaces becomes the division sign, ($\div$).
- InequalityLigaturesOnSelector (code 6): replaces the strings '<=' and '>=' with the symbols '$\leq$' and '$\geq$'. A funny choice, since, to the author's eye, '<=' symbolizes implication ($\Leftarrow$) rather than inequality ($\leq$); but never mind.
- ExponentsOnSelector (code 8): the digit that follows the ASCII caret (^) becomes a superscript. This is similar to TEX's convention for superscripts; but then why can we not have the same thing for subscripts by using an underscore?

- OrnamentSetsType (code 16): *selection of special glyphs.* This feature dates from the dark days before Unicode. In that era, it was very difficult to select nonalphabetic glyphs. Apple thus had the following idea: in a font of dingbats or any other font, the glyphs should be accessible by entering alphabetic characters, and the characters A–Z, etc., are converted into symbols, dingbats, and so on according to the selector chosen. Here are the selectors:

  - NoOrnamentsSelector (code 0): no special glyphs
  - DingbatsSelector (code 1): a set of dingbats, or miscellaneous symbols
  - PiCharactersSelector (code 2): a set of "pi" glyphs, which are symbols used in various contexts (cartography, hotel management, military medals, etc.)
  - FleuronsSelector (code 3): a set of fleurons
  - DecorativeBordersSelector (code 4): a set of decorative borders and lines
  - InternationalSymbolsSelector (code 5): a set of internationally recognized symbols (road signs, safety, etc.)
  - MathSymbolsSelector (code 6): mathematical symbols

- CharacterAlternativesType (code 17): *choice among the variants of a glyph.* The software should provide one selector for each variant of a given glyph. Only one selector is predefined:

  - NoAlternatesSelector (code 0): no variants

- DesignComplexityType (code 18): *choice of calligraphic level.* A calligraphic font may have several variants of each glyph that are arranged as more or less calligraphic forms. The examples below are drawn from the different levels of the font *Zapfino*:

  - DesignLevel1Selector (code 0):

    abcdefghijklmnopqrstuvwxyz

  - DesignLevel2Selector (code 1):

    abcdefghijklmnopqrstuvwxyz

  - DesignLevel3Selector (code 2):

    abcdefghijklmnopqrstuvwxyz

– DesignLevel4Selector (code 3):

abcdefghijklmnopqrstuvwxyz

– DesignLevel5Selector (code 4):

a bcde fghijklmn o pqrstuvwxyz

– DesignLevel6Selector (code 5):

a bcde fghijklmn opqrstuvwxyz

– DesignLevel7Selector (code 6):

abcde fghijklmn opqrstuvwxyz

– DesignLevel8Selector (code 7):

abcde fghijklmnopqrstuvwxyz

– DesignLevel9Selector (code 8):

abcdefghijklmnopqrstuvwxyz

- StyleOptionsType (code 19): *choice of "style"*. For this purpose, "style" means glyphs for titling, engraved glyphs, illuminated glyphs, etc. The selectors:

  - NoStyleOptionsSelector (code 0): no "style"

  - DisplayTextSelector (code 1): glyphs customized for large sizes

  - EngravedTextSelector (code 2): glyphs set in relief, as if engraved in stone

  - IlluminatedCapsSelector (code 3): illuminated glyphs, as in mediaeval illuminated manuscripts, or like the beautiful romantic dropped capitals of the nineteenth century

  - TitlingCapsSelector (code 4): capitals customized for use in titles

  - TallCapsSelector (code 5): very tall capitals

- CharacterShapeType (code 20): *choice of glyph for a CJK character* (where CJK means "Chinese, Japanese, Korean"). We know that Unicode unified the Chinese, Japanese, and Korean ideographs. But when there are several glyphs to represent an ideographic character, we need a way to gain access to those glyphs, since there will always be a need for particular variants in the different areas of human knowledge: geography, history, surnames, etc. This feature allows us to select a glyph according to its membership in a set of predefined glyphs. The selectors:

  - TraditionalCharactersSelector (code 0): traditional Chinese ideographs (Taiwan, etc.)

  - SimplifiedCharactersSelector (code 1): simplified Chinese ideographs (People's Republic of China)

  - JIS1978CharactersSelector (code 2): Japanese ideographs, according to JIS C6226-1978

  - JIS1983CharactersSelector (code 3): ditto, but according to JIS X 0208-1983

  - JIS1990CharactersSelector (code 4): ditto, but according to JIS X 0208-1990

  - TraditionalAltOneSelector (code 5) to TraditionalAltFiveSelector (code 9): Chinese ideographs, sets 1 to 5

  - ExpertCharactersSelector (code 10): Japanese ideographs, according to the Fujitsu FMR set of glyphs

- NumberCaseType (code 21): *choice of digit shapes*. Do not be surprised by the name of this feature. It refers not to the "case of the digits" but rather to old-style and modern figures:

  - LowerCaseNumbersSelector (code 0): old-style figures

– `UpperCaseNumbersSelector` (code 1): modern figures

- `TextSpacingType` (code 22): *choice of glyph spacing.* This feature is especially useful for CJK ideographs. Selectors:

    – `ProportionalTextSelector` (code 0): proportional spacing

    – `MonospacedTextSelector` (code 1): monospaced

    – `HalfWidthTextSelector` (code 2): half width

    – `NormalTextSelector` (code 3): default spacing

- `TransliterationType` (code 23): *phonetic transcription of ideographs.* Chinese ideographs are used in both Japan and Korea, but so are scripts that are specific to those two countries. Japan uses kana: hiragana for Japanese words and katakana for foreign words; Korea uses hangul. All three are examples of syllabic scripts that are therefore purely phonetic. In addition, Japan also uses the Latin script (officially recognized as the country's fourth script). This feature allows us to switch from one script to another or to give the possible solutions for switching from the Chinese ideographs in the Korean language to hangul.[20] Here are the selectors:

    – `NoTransliterationSelector` (code 0): no phonetic transcription

    – `HanjaToHangulSelector` (code 1): Korean ideographs to hangul; for example, 再會 (*chae-hoe*, "meeting") → 재회

    – `HiraganaToKatakanaSelector` (code 2): hiragana to katakana; for example, はらら んぶす → ハララ ンブス

    – `KatakanaToHiraganaSelector` (code 3): katakana to hiragana; for example, ハララ ンブス → はららんぶす

    – `KanaToRomanizationSelector` (code 4): kana to Latin script; for example, はららん ぶす → *hararanbusu* (the author's name, pronounced in a Japanese style)

    – `RomanizationToHiraganaSelector` (code 5): Latin script to hiragana; for example, *hararanbusu* → はららんぶす

    – `RomanizationToKatakanaSelector` (code 6): Latin script to katatana; for example, *hararanbusu* → ハララ ンブス

    – `HanjaToHangulAltOneSelector` (code 7) to `HanjaToHangulAltThreeSelector` (code 9): Korean ideographs to hangul, alternative selections 1 to 3

- `AnnotationType` (code 24): *encircled glyphs, glyphs in parentheses, etc.* Selectors:

    – `NoAnnotationSelector` (code 0): no annotation

    – `BoxAnnotationSelector` (code 1): glyphs inside boxes

    – `RoundedBoxAnnotationSelector` (code 2): glyphs in boxes with rounded corners

    – `CircleAnnotationSelector` (code 3): encircled glyphs

    – `InvertedCircleAnnotationSelector` (code 4): ditto, but white on black

---

[20] See [171, p. 161] for an attempt at the automatic transcription into kana of the Chinese ideographs of the Japanese language.

- ParenthesisAnnotationSelector (code 5): glyphs in parentheses
- PeriodAnnotationSelector (code 6): glyphs followed by a period
- RomanNumeralAnnotationSelector (code 7): numbers written as Roman numerals
- DiamondAnnotationSelector (code 8): glyphs inside diamonds
- InvertedBoxAnnotationSelector (code 9): glyphs inside boxes, white on black
- InvertedRoundedBoxAnnotationSelector (code 10): glyphs inside boxes with rounded corners, white on black

- KanaSpacingType (code 25): *choice of kana spacing. Kana* are the Japanese phonetic script. Since aesthetically they look different from the kanji (Japanese characters of Chinese origin), they are sometimes handled differently. In particular, one can choose to set them "Western-style"—i.e., with variable widths—while keeping the ideographs enclosed in their perfect ideographic square. Selectors:

  - FullWidthKanaSelector (code 0): "Chinese-style" typesetting of the kana—i.e., at a fixed width
  - ProportionalKanaSelector (code 1): "Western-style" typesetting of the kana (with variable widths)

- IdeographicSpacingType (code 26): *choice of ideographic spacing.* We can extend the principle of the previous feature to the ideographs of Chinese origin (*han* in Chinese, kanji in Japanese, *hancha* in Korean). There are three options:

  - FullWidthIdeographsSelector (code 0): "Chinese-style"—i.e., at a fixed width
  - ProportionalIdeographsSelector (code 1): "Western-style" (with variable widths)
  - HalfWidthIdeographsSelector (code 2): "economically"—i.e., at half width

- CJKRomanSpacingType (code 103): *width of Latin letters in an ideographic context.* We have already seen what happens to our poor Latin letters in the hands of our East Asian colleagues, a s i n t h i s s a m p l e o f t e x t. Here is how to manage the width of this "modified Latin" script:

  - HalfWidthCJKRomanSelector (code 0): half width, as in this sample of text
  - ProportionalCJKRomanSelector (code 1): normal typesetting
  - DefaultCJKRomanSelector (code 2): the default choice
  - FullWidthCJKRomanSelector (code 3): full-width Chinese typesetting, l i k e t h i s

- UnicodeDecompositionType (code 27): *choice of Unicode decomposition.* If the font does not contain a certain glyph, we attempt to decompose the Unicode character with which it is associated. We can decompose it in the canonical manner or in compatibility mode:

  - CanonicalCompositionOnSelector (code 0): canonical decomposition
  - CompatibilityCompositionOnSelector (code 2): compatibility mode. Example: suppose that the glyph 'Ŀ', which is needed for the Catalan digraph "Ŀl" does not exist; then it will be replaced with an 'l' followed by a mathematical centered dot (as in $a \cdot b$).

- RubyKanaType (code 28): *Japanese annotation*. In Japanese, there is a custom of annotating the ideographs with small glyphs placed above them. Most of the time, these small glyphs are kana, and therefore the annotation is a phonetic transcription intended for children and teenagers who do not yet have the education needed to read kanji directly. Example: 日本語の文字 (*nihon-go-no moji*, "Japanese characters"). These annotations are called *furigana*, or *ruby*. Note that it is essential, from a typographic point of view, that ruby characters be set in a font that has been optically corrected and customized for their small size; otherwise the difference in the stroke thicknesses between the ruby characters and the base characters will be intolerable. Two selectors:

  - NoRubyKanaSelector (code 0): without ruby characters
  - RubyKanaSelector (code 1): with ruby characters

- CJKSymbolAlternativesType (code 29): *choice of CJK symbols*. The "CJK symbols" are the equivalent of our punctuation marks for the ideographic languages. They can have different variants. Selectors:

  - NoCJKSymbolAlternativesSelector (code 0): no variants (default glyphs only)
  - CJKSymbolAltOneSelector (code 1) to CJKSymbolAltFiveSelector (code 5): variants 1 to 5

- IdeographicAlternativesType (code 30): *ideographic variants*. More variants of ideographs:

  - NoIdeographicAlternativesSelector (code 0): default glyphs
  - IdeographicAltOneSelector (code 1) to IdeographicAltFiveSelector (code 5): variants 1 to 5

- CJKVerticalRomanPlacementType (code 31): *behavior of Latin glyphs during vertical typesetting*.

  - CJKVerticalRomanCenteredSelector (code 0): centered
  - CJKVerticalRomanHBaselineSelector (code 1): aligned on the horizontal baseline

- ItalicCJKRomanType (code 32): *italics in CJK context*. Ideographic fonts usually do not have any italic Latin letters. The user who wishes to obtain italic letters may use this feature (if the font does include italics):

  - NoCJKItalicRomanSelector (code 0): no italics in an ideographic context
  - CJKItalicRomanSelector (code 1): italic Latin letters in an ideographic context

D.11.6   The lcar Table

The lcar table (*ligature caret*) addresses the problem of placing the mouse's cursor over ligatures. If a font contains ligatures and therefore replaces individual glyphs with large glyphs containing several components (i.e., ligatures), that must not be done at the expense of interaction with the user. Specifically, if the user typesets the word "afflicted" and wishes to select the string 'fli', a problem immediately arises, since 'ffl' is only one glyph: how can we select one part of the glyph with the mouse?

The lcar table comes to the rescue: for each ligature, it gives the number of components and the possible values of the position of the cursor to place between the components. In the case of 'ffl', for instance, lcar will advise the system that there are three components (and therefore two possible positions for the cursor to be placed within the ligature) and will give the system the x-coordinates of these cursor positions (or their y-coordinates, if we are setting type vertically). lcar fulfills the same role as the LigCaretList subtable of the OpenType table GDEF.

It exists in two formats: in Format 0, the x-coordinates of the cursor positions are given explicitly in TrueType units; in Format 1, points on the glyph's contour are furnished to the system. The second case is more powerful, since it takes into account any TrueType instructions that are present, which may play an important role at a low resolution.

Here is an example of this table, in Format 0:

```
<lcar>
  <Version value="1"/>
  <LigCaretClassEntries format="0">
    <LigCaretClassEntry index="0">
      <distance index="0" value="239"/>
      <distance index="1" value="475"/>
    </LigCaretClassEntry>
    ...
  </LigCaretClassEntries>
  <Glyphs>
    <Glyph value="f_f_l" class="0"/>
    ...
  </Glyphs>
</lcar>
```

After the usual Version element, we have two other elements: LigCaretClassEntries contains the different combinations of cursor positions, with no reference to glyphs, which we call caret classes; Glyphs contains glyphs, with reference to *caret classes*. In LigCaretClass-Entries, there is a LigCaretClassEntry for each class. It contains distance elements, which represent the cursor positions. Their value value (or class) attributes contain glyph names (or numbers of caret classes).

And here is an example of this table, in Format 1:

```
<lcar>
  <Version value="1"/>
  <LigCaretClassEntries format="1">
    <LigCaretClassEntry index="0" format="1">
      <ctlPoint index="0" value="50/>
    </LigCaretClassEntry>
    ...
  </LigCaretClassEntries>
  <Glyphs>
    <Glyph value="f_r" class="0"/>
```

Ô *ma douce dulcinée*

γλυκειά μου ὕπαρξη, φῶς μου

du ewig Weibliches

ziehst mich hinan

Ô *ma douce dulcinée*

γλυκειά μου ὕπαρξη, φῶς μου

du ewig Weibliches

ziehst mich hinan

Figure D-7: *A trilingual and tri-fontal love poem (the fonts, in order: the sublime Zapfino, by Hermann Zapf; equally sublime, for fonts of its kind, Δεκαεξάρια τῆς κάσσας ["Sixteen-point [letters] taken from the case"] by Tereza Tranaka-Haralambous; and Monotype Modern italic). Left: default typesetting, with simple line changes and justification according to the letter's point of origin. Right: the same typesetting, but with the use of the opbd table: the verses are aligned better.*

```
        ...
    </Glyphs>
  </lcar>
```

Instead of `distance` elements, we have `ctlPoint` elements, whose value element contains the number of a point on the glyph's contour. That means, of course, that all the glyphs in the same class must have the same point on the contour at the same location, which requires some attention when designing the glyph.

D.11.7   The opbd Table

This table is quite original and deserves a beautiful love poem (Figure D-7). Its name is the unpronounceable abbrevation of *optical bounds*. It solves one simple, but fundamental, problem. We know that all glyphs have side-bearings (i.e., the space on each side of the glyph). These side-bearings are as indispensable as the rules of courtesy in human society: without them, the glyphs would touch, yielding an illegible jumble.

Thus side-bearings are a good thing. But what happens when we wish to *align* glyphs, such as at the beginning of the line? Stupid typesetting software will not align the *glyphs*, only their *points of origin*. If the side-bearings of all the glyphs were the same, that approach would effectively align the glyphs. But who can guarantee that the side-bearings will indeed be the same? Figure D-7 shows that the side-bearings in different fonts may indeed be quite different—especially when roman and italic are mixed.

The opbd table supplies the glyphs' "optical bounds"—i.e., the coordinates of the abstract box that will ultimately be used for alignment. Software must be quite intelligent to be able to say "I am aligning at the left; therefore I shall take the left edge of the abstract box in opbd as the left part of the glyph and use its usual box for the other edges".

The reader will have observed that we could just as well take the glyph's bounding box. That is only partly true: the font's designer may have wished to disregard a part of the glyph. For example, the letter 'd' at the beginning of the third line in the figure could have been aligned not according to its ascender but according to its lower part. No software in the world can be as intelligent as the designer, nor as capable of foreseeing this detail. Thus it is quite useful to have in the font a piece of data, distinct from the bounding box, that will be used for this purpose.

Here is an example of the opbd table:

```
<opbd>
   <Version value="1"/>
   <bounds format="0">
      <Glyph value="A" left="-" top="15" right="0" bottom="0"/>
      <Glyph value="C" left="-" top="5" right="55" bottom="-"/>
      ...
   </bounds>
</opbd>
```

Once again, there are two formats for this table: in format 0, we use coordinates in TrueType units; in Format 1, we use the numbers of points on the contour. The bounds element contains Glyph glyphs. Each Glyph has five attributes: the glyph name (value) and the left (left), top (top), bottom (bottom), and right (right) optical bounds. The vertical limits are used when we set type in that direction.

The values given are the amounts by which the glyph must be displaced so that it will reach its optical bounds. The same table in Format 1 would yield:

```
<opbd>
   <Version value="1"/>
   <bounds format="1">
      <Glyph value="A" left="32" top="41" right="-" bottom="-"/>
      <Glyph value="C" left="36" top="37" right="38" bottom="39"/>
      ...
   </bounds>
</opbd>
```

Here the values are the numbers of points on the contour. The software must therefore align those points in order to achieve optimal alignment. A value of -1 means that no correction of the alignment is necessary for that side of the glyph. Note that there is a predefined OpenType feature that bears the same name and plays the same role as the opbd table of AAT.

D.11.8 The prop Table

"Zounds!" This table, whose name comes from "property", gives us certain data on the glyphs, some of those data inspired in part by the *Unicode properties* of the characters to which the glyphs belong. For example, the table tells us whether a glyph is "floating" (in the sense that it has zero width and that the software has to place it in the right spot); whether it must be set in the margin (like the quotation marks that begin this paragraph[21]); whether it should be inverted when we switch from left-to-right typesetting to right-to-left typesetting or vice versa,

---

[21] Whose presence justifies the unexpected exclamation at the beginning of the paragraph.

as with the left parenthesis, which becomes a right parenthesis, etc.; where appropriate, the identity of its mirror-image *alter ego*;[22] whether the current glyph is "physically attached" to the glyph at its right—in other words, if the two glyphs are playing Romeo and Juliet, the software must not do anything that would separate them or move them apart, even by the slightest amount; finally, the Unicode directionality class (see page 142) of the character to which the glyph belongs.

Here is an example of one such table:

```
<prop>
   <Version value="3"/>
   <properties>
      <defaultGlyph floater="0" hangLeft="0" hangRight="0"
             mirrored="0" mirrorGlyph="A" attachRight="0"
             directionalityClass="0"/>
      <Glyph value="A" floater="0" hangLeft="0" hangRight="0"
             mirrored="0" mirrorGlyph="A" attachRight="0"
             directionalityClass="0"/>
      <Glyph value="parenleft" floater="0" hangLeft="0" hangRight="0"
             mirrored="1" mirrorGlyph="parenright" attachRight="0"
             directionalityClass="11"/>

      ...
   </properties>
</prop>
```

The properties element contains Glyph elements corresponding to the different glyphs and a defaultGlyph element that supplies the values of the glyph's properties that do not appear on the list. For each of these elements, there are eight attributes (seven for defaultGlyph, since it does not have a glyph name): the glyph's name (value); an indication of whether it hangs in the left margin (hangLeft) or the right margin (hangRight); an indication of whether it is mirrored (mirrored), and, if appropriate, the name of the glyph that is its mirror image (mirrorGlyph); an indication of whether the glyph is "physically" attached to the glyph at its right (attachRight); and, finally, the Unicode directionality class of the character to which the glyph belongs (directionalityClass).

These data are indeed very useful, but reality is often a bit more complex: for example, the accents and breathing marks of the Greek language (which are placed before capital letters, as in the word "Ελληνας) must be set in the margin, but *only* at the beginning of a paragraph or a verse. But this table does not accommodate the fact that a glyph may change its properties according to its context.

D.11.9   The trak Table

This table manages global letterspacing. Its name comes from *tracking*, just as with the Track-Kern entries of the AFM files (see §C.3.7). Here is an example of one such table:

---

[22] Warning: we use the glyph's number to find the mirror-image glyph, but there is a catch—the offset between the two glyphs must not exceed 15. Apple asks that glyphs that are mirror images of each other appear *consecutively* in the font in order to avoid the problem of their being located too far apart.

```
<trak>
  <Version value="1"/>
  <tracking format="0">
    <horizData>
      <!-- nTracks=3 -->
      <trackEntry index="0" value="-" nameIndex="15">
        <!-- nSizes=2 -->
          <track size="12" value="-"/>
          <track size="24" value="-"/>
      </trackEntry>
      <trackEntry index="1" value="0" nameIndex="16">
        <!-- nSizes=2 -->
          <track size="12" value="0"/>
          <track size="24" value="0"/>
      </trackEntry>
      <trackEntry index="2" value="1" nameIndex="17">
        <!-- nSizes=2 -->
          <track size="12" value="50"/>
          <track size="24" value="20"/>
      </trackEntry>
    </horizData>
    <vertData>
      <!-- nTracks=0 -->
    </vertData>
  </tracking>
</trak>
```

In the tracking element, which contains all the data, we find a horizData for horizontal typesetting and a vertData for vertical typesetting. In each of these two cases, there are several trackEntry elements, which correspond to different levels of predefined letterspacing. Each level has an integer value value (0 for the absence of letterspacing, negative for tightly spaced text, positive for loosely spaced text) and a name. Apple exhibits political correctness: the name of the level of letterspacing is not a bland four-letter *tag* (like the names of OpenType features) but an entry in the name table, which, as we know, contains names and other short texts in all the languages into which the font's designer wished to translate them! The value of nameIndex is therefore a number of the entry namerecord in the name table (see §D.4.6).

The element trackEntry contains several track entries, which are values of letterspacing in TrueType units (the value attribute), for a given actual size (the size attribute, in American printers' points). In our example, for instance, there is negative letterspacing, whose English name could have been "tight spacing"; it involves reducing the widths of the glyphs by 15 units at 12 points and by 7 units at 24 points. For every size other than 12 and 24, the value of letterspacing will be interpolated (or extrapolated, as the case may be).

Note that this table is rather simplistic, for several reasons. First of all, letterspacing is sometimes "semantic"; i.e., it is deliberately requested by the author in order to highlight a block of text—a technique that replaces italics in some typographic traditions. Semantic letterspacing is used in Russian, gothic German, Greek, etc. But in this case [163, 164] we move only the *letters* apart, not the punctuation marks! That is, unfortunately, impossible with the trak table. Another shortcoming: the actual values of letterspacing are given only at an actual size in points. But we should be able to force letterspacing by one pixel more or fewer, for example, depending on the resolution of the display or printing device. Here, a structure like the device table of the OpenType tables would be quite suitable for giving the values of letterspacing in pixels, according to the *size* of the glyphs.[23] But as the proverb says, *faute de chien, on emmène le cabri à la chasse*; in other words, we must make do with what we have.

D.11.10   The Zapf Table

The name of this table is inspired by the name of a great font designer who shall remain nameless here. He is a member of the very small group of famous people such as Bach, Kant, Hugo, Zola, Dalí, Tati, etc., whose names contain only four letters. (Bill Gates fell just short of membership in this group of immortals.)

The aim of this table is both ambitious and praiseworthy: it is there for nothing more or less than giving order to the chaos that reigns when we switch from characters to glyphs. Mr. Zapf (not to name names) is the great Oracle who answers the existential questions about each glyph: "where do I come from?", "which is my character?", "what had to happen to bring me into being?", "which other glyphs resemble me?", "how did the holy Designer describe me?", "by what name do others identify me?" It is a pity that there is no Zapf table for human beings.

Let us talk concretely. The Zapf table collects a range of data about each glyph. Here they are:

- Some Unicode characters that can yield the glyph (which are, therefore, its potential fathers).

- Some strings of characters that describe the glyph. Each of these strings is of a certain type, as shown:

  - type 0: a string, nothing more
  - type 1: the glyph's "Apple name"
  - type 2: the glyph's name, according to Adobe's specifications (see §C.3.3)
  - type 3: the glyph's AFII name (§C.3.3 and [29])
  - type 4: the Unicode description of the glyph
  - type 64: the glyph's CID number (see §C.7), if it is a Japanese ideograph
  - type 65: ditto, if it is a traditional Chinese ideograph
  - type 66: ditto, if it is a simplified Chinese ideograph
  - type 67: ditto, if it is a Korean ideograph

---

[23] Do not confuse "size" and "point size": the size is given in pixels per em, whereas the point size is given in American printers' points. To convert from one to the other, one must know the resolution: the glyphs of a font at size 9, when displayed on a screen with 72 pixels per inch, will have a point size of $\frac{9}{72} = 0.125$ inches = 9.03374 American printers' points; the same glyphs displayed at 96 ppi will have an effective point size of 6.7753 points!

- type 68: a namerecord entry number in the name table; this entry should allow the designer to describe, in every language supported, the history of all the versions of the glyph

- type 69: another namerecord number, this time used to write the designer's name

- type 70: as above, but a longer name (…)

- type 71: as above, for the designer to explain the glyph's usage

- type 72: as above, for the designer to place the glyph in the historical context of typography (for example, "this 'd' was cut by Claude Garamond on December 24, 1534, the memorable day when his friend Antoine Augereau was burned at the stake in Maubert Square" [105])

- The glyph's membership in a group of glyphs. The *groups* are defined in the same table; they consist of a namerecord number that contains the group's name, and several glyphs belonging to the group. Among these groups, there may be some that are *groups of groups*—sets of references to groups of glyphs. That may happen when a glyph belongs to more than one group.

- Last but not least, an indication of whether the glyph is the result of the application of a set of AAT features, in a certain context. Let us explain: We have seen, in the description of the feat table (§D.11.5), that AAT offers several *features*, each of which has its own *selectors*. To obtain a given glyph, we must, if necessary, enable certain selectors for some of these features, and also be in a given context—e.g., at the beginning of a line. Here is a list of the possible contexts:[24]

  - 0: not in any context

  - 1, 2, 4: beginning, middle, or end of line

  - 8, 16, 32: beginning, middle, or end of word

  - 64, 128: numerator or denominator of a fraction

All those things (features, selectors, context) are stored in the Zapf table.

Here is the first part of a Zapf table:

```
<Zapf>
  <Version value="1"/>
  <GlyphInfos>
    <GlyphInfo value="A" GroupInfo="0" FeatureInfo="-">
      <unicodes>
        <!-- n16BitUnicodes=1 -->
        <unicode value="0041"/>
      </unicodes>
```

---

[24] Bizarrely enough, these contexts are the values of flags, yet, contrary to the way in which flags are usually employed, it is not possible to enable several of these flags at the same time—something that the author considers absurd: if a word consists of only one glyph, then the glyph appears at the beginning of the word, in the middle, and at the end. And the glyph may also very well occur at the end of the line…

```
    <kindNames>
      <!-- nNames=2 -->
      <kindName kind="2" value="A"/>
      <kindName kind="4" value="LATIN CAPITAL LETTER A"/>
      <kindName kind="69" value="18"/>
    </kindNames>
  </GlyphInfo>

  ...
</GlyphInfos>
```

We see here that the list GlyphInfo of glyphs is contained within a GlyphInfos (with an 's') element, which makes up the first part of the table. Each GlyphInfo has three attributes: the glyph name (value), the number of the associated group of glyphs (GroupInfo, an element that appears in the second part; it can also represent a group of groups), and the number of a list of features (FeatureInfo; this list appears in the third part of the table).

In a GlyphInfo element, there are two subelements: unicodes, which contains several Unicode characters to which the glyph belongs, each of them represented by a unicode (with no 's') element, and kindNames, which contains a number of strings that describe the glyph.

Each string is represented by a kindName element, of which the kind attribute describes the meaning and the value attribute contains the string itself. Above, we presented the list of possible values of kind and the associated meanings. In the snippet of code, we see three cases: when kind is equal to 2, it is the glyph's Adobe name (A); when kind is equal to 4, it is the Unicode name of the glyph (LATIN CAPITAL LETTER A); and when kind is equal to 69, it is the number of a namerecord, in the name table, that contains the name of the glyph's designer.

Here is the second part of our example:

```
<GroupInfos>
  <GroupInfo index="0" nameIndex="19" isSubdivided="0">
    <!-- nGlyphs=26 -->
    <Glyph value="A"/>
    <Glyph value="B"/>

    ...
    <Glyph value="Z"/>
  </GroupInfo>
  <GroupInfo index="1" nameIndex="20" isSubdivided="0">
    <!-- nGlyphs=6 -->
    <Glyph value="a"/>
    <Glyph value="e"/>

    ...
    <Glyph value="y"/>
  </GroupInfo>
  <GroupInfo index="2" nameIndex="21" isSubdivided="0">
    <!-- nGlyphs=20 -->
    <Glyph value="b"/>
    <Glyph value="c"/>
```

```
    ...
    <Glyph value="z"/>
  </GroupInfo>
    ...
  <GroupInfoGroup index="7" nameIndex="22">
    <!-- nGroups=2 -->
    <GroupInfo ref="1"/>
    <GroupInfo ref="2"/>
  </GroupInfoGroup>
    ...
</GroupInfos>
```

This part contains the definitions of groups of glyphs, which are contained in GroupInfos elements. Each GroupInfo contains merely a list of glyphs. In addition, it has three attributes: its number (index), the number of the associated namerecord in the name table (nameIndex), and a flag indicating whether it is a subdivision of a larger group (in which case isSubdivided takes the value 1).

In the example, we also see a *group of groups*, GroupInfoGroup. It contains not glyphs but references to groups of glyphs, in the form of GroupInfo elements whose ref attribute contains the number of the group in question.

Finally, here is the third part of our example:

```
<FeatureInfos>
    <FeatureInfo index="0" context="0">
      <!-- nAATFeatures=3 -->
      <Feature value="1" selector="4"/>
      <Feature value="8" selector="2"/>
      <Feature value="8" selector="6"/>
    </FeatureInfo>
      ...
  </FeatureInfos>
  <OTTags>
    <!-- nOTTags=2 -->
    <tag value="hist"/>
    <tag value="ss07"/>
  </OTTags>
</Zapf>
```

This part contains a list of features and a given context. If the glyph GlyphInfo, through the attribute FeatureInfo, refers to this list of features, it is thanks to them that it was possible to typeset it.

The element FeaturesInfo contains a FeatureInfo (with no 's') for each list of features. Each FeatureInfo contains a context attribute that gives the context (according to the list presented above). It contains Feature elements, each of which represents an AAT feature; more precisely, there are a feature number (the value attribute) and a selector number (selector). See §D.11.5.1 for a list of the features and their selectors.

Finally, the element OTTags is an attempt at reconciliation with the OpenType world. Let us quote the author of this table, David Opstad: "When I designed the 'Zapf' table I explicitly wanted to provide for OpenType as well as AAT, for a more harmonious future" (private communication of September 24, 2003). The tag subelements of OTTags contain the tags for the OpenType features that are required in order to obtain the glyph in question. That assumes a mixed OpenType/AAT table, for which we are still waiting.

D.12   The AAT Tables for Font Variation

The principle of *font variation* is close to that of the Multiple Master fonts: we define several "axes of variation" and take a few points in the space formed by these axes—in other words, several combinations of the values of these axes. Example: if we define the *weight* and the *optical size* as axes, and if the weights range from -1 to $+1$ and the optical sizes range from 6 to 72, we can take the combinations $(0, 10)$ = weight 0 and optical size 10, $(-1, 10)$, $(+1, 10)$, $(-1, 6)$, $(+1, 72)$, etc. To each of these pairs of values, there corresponds a version of the font.

In the case of Multiple Master, we made the distinction between *master designs* and *intermediate values*. That means that a designer could focus on several specific designs and let the system perform the requisite interpolations on the positions of the points to yield all the other possible variants.

Here the situation is slightly more complex. The master designs still exist, but they can differ for each glyph. Therefore a glyph that never varies will be described only once. The glyphs that vary only slightly will have only a few master designs. Those with many details will have more master designs. It is a genuine miracle if the processor manages to cope with all these values and generate a reasonable rendering.

D.12.1   The fvar Table

Almost all the tables in this section, which is devoted to font variation, have a name that ends in var. Here it is fvar ("font variation"). Later we shall see variations of axis (avar), glyph (gvar), and table of control values (cvar).

The fvar table contains definitions of axes and predefined instances. It is quite simple: we define the names, the extreme values, and the default values of the axes, and then we give the values (on the axes) of the predefined instances. Here is an example of the first part of this table:

```
<fvar>
  <Version value="1"/>
  <sfntVariations>
    <!-- axisCount=2 -->
    <sfntVariationAxis index="0" flags="0">
      <axisTag value="wght"/>
      <minValue value="0.5"/>
      <defaultValue value="1.0"/>
      <maxValue value="2.0"/>
      <nameIndex value="256"/>
```

```
        </sfntVariationAxis>
        <sfntVariationAxis index="1" flags="0">
          <axisTag value="wdth"/>
          <minValue value="0.5"/>
          <defaultValue value="1.0"/>
          <maxValue value="2.0"/>
          <nameIndex value="257"/>
        </sfntVariationAxis>
      </sfntVariations>
```

In this example, we define two axes, sfntVariationAxis, which we place within an sfnt-Variations element. Each sfntVariationAxis has a zero-valued flags attribute and five subelements:

- axisTag: the tag, or the four-letter ASCII name of the axis: we have the choice of wght (weight), wdth (width), or slnt (slant).

- opsz, the optical size.

- The minimum value (minValue), default value (defaultValue), and maximum value (maxValue) of the axis.

- The record number, namerecord, of the name table, stored in the subelement nameIndex.

Thanks to the name table, we can give each axis a human-readable name—in every language in the world (something that is pitifully lacking from the Multiple Master fonts).

In the example above, we have defined two axes: weight and width. These two axes can take values between 0.5 and 2, and their common default value is 1.

Here is the second part of this table:

```
      <sfntInstances>
        <!-- instanceCount=3 -->
        <sfntInstance index="0" flags="0">
          <nameIndex value="258"/>
          <coords>
            <coord index="0" value="0.5"/>
            <coord index="1" value="1.0"/>
          </coords>
        </sfntInstance>
        <sfntInstance index="1" flags="0">
          <nameIndex value="258"/>
          <coords>
            <coord index="0" value="2.0"/>
            <coord index="1" value="1.5"/>
          </coords>
        </sfntInstance>
```

```
<sfntInstance index="2" flags="0">
  <nameIndex value="258"/>
  <coords>
    <coord index="0" value="2.0"/>
    <coord index="1" value="0.5"/>
  </coords>
</sfntInstance>
</sfntInstances>
</fvar>
```

Here there are four font instances—i.e., four pairs of values of axes (we say pairs because each font has only two axes). The instances are represented by sfntInstance elements contained in an sfntInstances (with an 's') element. Each sfntInstance instance has a zero-valued flags attribute, a subelement nameIndex that points back to a name of the instance in the name table, and an element coords that contains the values of the axes for the instance. The coords element, in turn, contains a coord subelement for each axis. Each of them contains a value (the value attribute), the value of that coordinate on the axis.

D.12.2   The avar Table

The avar table is a very small table based on a simple idea: why should the interpolation of the coordinates of points on the contour be linear as we move along an axis? Indeed, it would be attractive to be able to interpolate the points in a manner other than mere linear interpolation. Unfortunately, the AAT processor does not afford us the luxury of arbitrary interpolation, but it nevertheless does allow one thing: *piecewise linear* interpolation.

Let us take an example. Suppose that the values of an axis (for example, the axis for optical size) range from 6 to 72. The user selects the correct value through a user interface that offers, for example, a sliding bar to select a value between these two extremes:

But if the values are represented linearly, that means that for values between 6 and 12 points, which are, incidentally, the most important ones, one must be extremely precise to place the triangle in the correct location:

That calls for the precision of a watchmaker, whereas the rest of the sliding bar is underused. Therefore we can do as follows: we can set aside half of the bar for the values between 6 and 12, the next quarter for the values between 12 and 24, and the remaining quarter for the values between 24 and 72:

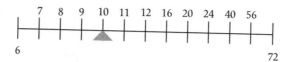

This is a much more rational approach that allows for precision where it is most needed, by sacrificing other areas in which precision is less important.

That is exactly what the avar table does. It associates *values on an axis* with the *user's values*. Between two pairs of values so linked, interpolation is linear. On the sample bar that we presented above, the associated pairs are $(0,6)$, $(\frac{1}{2},12)$, $(\frac{3}{4},24)$, $(1,72)$.

Here is an example of one such table:

```
<avar>
  <Version value="1"/>
  <!-- axisCount=2 -->
  <axis index="0">
    <!-- pairCount=4 -->
    <pair index="0" from="0" to="6"/>
    <pair index="1" from="0.5" to="12"/>
    <pair index="2" from="0.75" to="24"/>
    <pair index="3" from="1" to=72/>
  </axis>
  <axis index="1">
    <!-- pairCount=2-->
    <pair index="0" from="-" to="-"/>
    <pair index="1" from="1" to="1"/>
  </axis>
</avar>
```

Its structure is very simple. There is one axis element for each axis. Each axis element contains pair elements that represent pairs of values: the from attribute contains the "user's value" (in our case, the subdivision of the bar), and the to attribute contains the value on the corresponding axis. In our example, we have taken the case shown by the bar as our axis 0 and the identity between the user values and the axis values for our axis 1.

Note that the very same technique (piecewise linear interpolation) is also applied in Multiple Master fonts—in the BlendDesignMap entry of the PostScript dictionary (see §3). In Multiple Master jargon, the user values are called *design values* and are defined by the font's designer; the axis values are called *blend values* and always lie between 0 and 1. Aside from these insignificant differences, the technique is exactly the same.

D.12.3   The gvar Table

The gvar table contains the data needed to transform the glyphs according to the different axes of variation. These data are in fact offsets from points on the contour; but it is necessary to decide, for each glyph, *which points* are to be modified and *for which axis values* the required

This is font Skia. "Skia" in Greek means "shadow".
This is font Skia. "Skia" in Greek means "shadow".
This is font Skia. "Skia" in Greek means "shadow".
This is font Skia. "Skia" in Greek means "shadow".
This is font Skia. "Skia" in Greek means "shadow"
This is font Skia. "Skia" in Greek means "shadow
This is font Skia. "Skia" in Greek means "shadov
This is font Skia. "Skia" in Greek means "shado
This is font Skia. "Skia" in Greek means "shado
This is font Skia. "Skia" in Greek means "shad

Figure D-8:   The font Apple Skia and its variations along the wght axis.

offsets are to be given explicitly (whereas for the other axis values, the system will perform the necessary interpolations to obtain appropriate glyphs).

The structure of this table is relatively simple, at least when it is represented in TTX (whereas its binary version is a bit of a nightmare for the programmer, doubtless because of the large number of optimizations found within it).

It is divided into two main sections: the definition of the *n*-tuples of axis values (where *n* is the number of axes), and the provision of offsets from the points for each glyph in the font. Here is an example of the first section:

```
<gvar>
  <Version value="1"/>
  <header axisCount="2" flags="0"/>
  <sharedCoordinates>
    <!-- globalCoordCount=4 -->
    <sharedCoord index="0">
      <coord index="0" value="-.0"/>
      <coord index="1" value="0.0"/>
    </sharedCoord>
    <sharedCoord index="0">
      <coord index="0" value="1.0"/>
      <coord index="1" value="0.0"/>
    </sharedCoord>
    <sharedCoord index="0">
      <coord index="0" value="0.0"/>
      <coord index="1" value="-.0"/>
    </sharedCoord>
    <sharedCoord index="0">
      <coord index="0" value="0.0"/>
```

```
          <coord index="1" value="1.0"/>
       </sharedCoord>
    </sharedCoordinates>
```

Here we assume that there are two axes; therefore, the "*n*-tuplets" are pairs. The header element contains the number of axes (which must be the same as in the fvar table). Next comes the element sharedCoordinates, which contains pairs of predefined axis values. In a Multiple Master font, it corresponds to coordinates of the master designs. Here we have the possibility of defining other pairs of "private" axis values for individual glyphs.

Each sharedCoordinate (with no 's') corresponds to a pair of values shared by all the glyphs. It contains a coord element for each axis in the font. The value attribute contains the value of the "coordinate" for the axis in question.

In the first section, therefore, we have defined the axis values that are available to all the glyphs. But nothing compels any glyph to use these values; indeed, it can add others or even replace these values outright.

Here is the second part of the table:

```
<Glyphs>
    <Glyph value="A" index="0">
      <sharedPointNumbers>
        <!-- pointcount=10 -->
        <pointNumber index="0" value="0"/>
        <pointNumber index="1" value="1"/>
        ...
        <pointNumber index="8" value="8"/>
        <pointNumber index="9" value="9"/>
      </sharedPointNumbers>
      <tuples sharedPointNumbers="1">
        <!-- tupleCount=4 -->
        <tuple index="0">
          <sharedCoord index="0"/>
          <deltas>
            <xDelta index="0" value="169"/>
            ... 12 lignes semblables ...
            <xDelta index="13" value="0"/>
            <yDelta index="0" value="86"/>
            ... 12 lignes semblables ...
            <yDelta index="13" value="0"/>
          </deltas>
        </tuple>
        <tuple index="0">
          <sharedCoord index="1"/>
          ...
        </tuple>
        <tuple index="0">
```

```
        <sharedCoord index="2"/>
        ...
      </tuple>
      <tuple index="0">
        <sharedCoord index="3"/>
        ...
      </tuple>
    </tuples>
  </Glyph>
  ...
</Glyphs>
</gvar>
```

There is a Glyph element for each glyph in the font. For each of these elements, there are two types of information: the numbers of the points on the contour that are to be offset, and the offsets of these points for each pair of axis values.

The numbers of points on the contour are contained in the element sharedPointNumbers. That is hardly surprising: there is a pointNumber element for each point that may be modified; the value attribute contains the numbers of these points.

Let us point out once again that these points are shared by all the master designs but that each master design may also use its own "private" points. Finally, one important detail: here we list only the points on the contour that are of interest to us, but the font will give the offsets for four additional points. These points, called "phantom points", are the origin of the glyph, its set-width (these points have already been given in the description of the contour), its vertical origin, and its "vertical set-width" (i.e., the ending point of the displacement vector during vertical typesetting). Do not be astonished that the example above describes 10 points but then lists 14 offsets!

Next comes a rather bulky element called tuples. This name deserves a brief explanation. American hackers love to create new names (as we have already seen with *byte* and *nybble*). The word *tuple* comes from the common ending of words "sextuple", "septuple", "octuple", etc.

The tuples element (with an 's') contains the different pairs of axis values selected for the glyph. In this example, there are four pairs of predefined values. There is a tuple element (with no 's') for each of the axis values. Any "personalized" pair of axis values will be contained in a subelement of tuple that is called embeddedCoord. In the example above, there are only predefined values; they are indicated by sharedCoord elements, which refer (through the index attribute) to elements of the same name that appear directly under gvar.

A tuple may refer to shared points on the contour (contained in sharedPointNumbers), or it may define its own points on the contour (called "private point numbers" and included in privatePointNumbers). In any event, it contains, after sharedCoord (or embeddedCoord), the offsets corresponding to these points. These offsets are represented by two series of elements: xDelta (horizontal offsets) and yDelta (vertical offsets).

Note that this specification unfortunately gives explicit offset values and does not support specifying them as points (to take the effects of any TrueType instructions into account) or as "device tables", as is done in OpenType.

In any case, we enjoy a great deal of flexibility for defining different master designs for each glyph; thus the system is undeniably powerful. And, last but not least, since the disappearance of the Multiple Master fonts, the AAT fonts with variation tables *are now the only "dynamic" fonts on the market*, if we exclude fonts created in the form of computer programs, such as those written in METAFONT.

D.12.4   The cvar Table

The cvar table is constructed in the same way as gvar, but in the place of numbers of points on the contour, there are numbers of CVT entries (values of the control table; see the cvt table). Recall that the CVT entries are global values (at the level of the entire font) used in TrueType instructions for the glyphs. The control values are used to store certain characteristics of the font: the heights of the ascenders, the thicknesses of the strokes, the widths of the serifs, etc.

For each *n*-tuplet of axis values in fvar and gvar—in other words, for each choice of master design—cvar contains a set of offsets from control values, which are customized for the master designs. For example, if stroke thickness varies, the value of the corresponding entry in the CVT table should do so as well.

Here is an example of the cvar table:

```
<cvar>
  <Version value="1"/>
  <cvtEntries>
    <!-- cvtCount=10 -->
    <cvtEntry index="0" value="17"/>
    <cvtEntry index="1" value="24"/>
    ...
    <cvtEntry index="8" value="137"/>
    <cvtEntry index="9" value="249"/>
  </cvtEntries>
  <tuples>
    <!-- tupleCount=4 -->
    <tuple index="0">
      <deltas>
        <delta index="0" value="169"/>
        <delta index="1" value="0"/>
        <delta index="2" value="0"/>
        <delta index="3" value="169"/>
        <delta index="4" value="1"/>
        ...
      </deltas>
    </tuple>
    <tuple index="0">
      <sharedCoord index="1"/>
      ...
    </tuple>
```

```
        <tuple index="0">
          <sharedCoord index="2"/>
          ...
        </tuple>
        <tuple index="0">
          <sharedCoord index="3"/>
          ...
        </tuple>
      </tuples>
  </cvar>
```

We see here the two main elements: cvtEntries, which contains the relevant entry numbers in the CVT table, and tuples, which contains a tuple subelement (with no 's') for each master design (*n*-tuplets of axis values). Each tuple contains a deltas element (with an 's'), which in turn contains delta subelements (with no 's') corresponding to the cvtEntry entries in cvtEntries. Each delta is an offset (contained in the value attribute) from the corresponding CVT entry.

D.13   AAT Tables with Finite Automata

In this section, we shall describe the big guns of the AAT tables: those used as finite automata to perform positionings, substitutions, and justification. They are the tables morx (the new version of the mort table) and just: they play the same role as the tables GPOS/GSUB and JSTF in OpenType. Before we confront the formidable morx table, let us say a few words about *finite automata*.

D.13.1   Finite Automata

A *finite automaton* is a way to represent certain simple programs. In our case, we shall describe in this manner the program that reads the string of glyphs for a line of text and then displays the glyphs. A program of this type may be in one or more *states*. *Being in a given state* means that the program reacts in a certain manner when it reads the glyphs, and that this manner is always the same for the same glyph; in other words, if in state *A* the program replaces an a with a b, then that will always be the case, however many times the letter a occurs, as long as the program remains in that state. The program's reaction consists of performing an *action* (leaving the glyph as it is, modifying it, replacing it, moving it, etc.) and possibly changing states. When the program changes state, we say that a *transition* has occurred. The automaton is called "finite" because this type of program has only a finite number of possible states, therefore only a finite number of transitions.

In Figure D-9, we see two examples of finite automata. Let us take case (a). We shall consider the following problem: describing the automaton that will keep the first letter in a string, add a period to it, and hide the rest. In this way, we car replace personal names with initials: thus "John Fitzgerald" becomes "J. F."

The ellipses in the figure symbolize the possible states. For example, at time *t*, there are two possibilities: we are either *outside* a word (the "initial state") or *inside* one ("inside a word"). When the first glyph arrives, we are always in the initial state. If the glyph is not a letter,

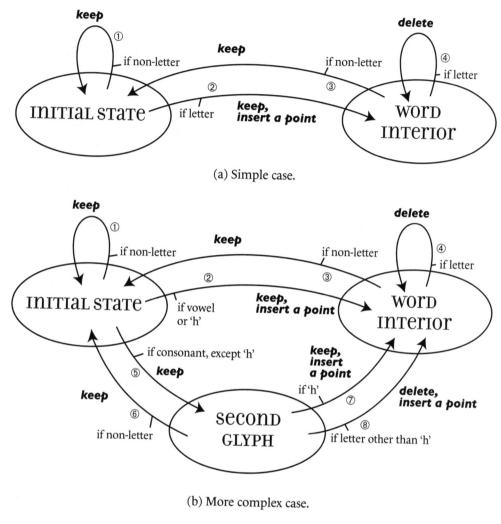

(a) Simple case.

(b) More complex case.

Figure D-9: Two examples of finite automata.

we preserve it and stay within the same state (arrow ①). When a letter arrives, we perform an action: we retain the letter and append a period to it; at the same time, we change states (arrow ②), and then we are in the state "inside a word". Thus we find ourselves in the ellipse at the right. Once again, there are two cases. If the following glyph is a letter, that means that we are still inside a word. We therefore hide the letter and remain in the state (arrow ④). If a nonletter arrives, we retain it (our marching orders did not ask us to delete nonletters) and return to the initial state (arrow ③).

It is important to understand the concepts represented in Figure D-9. The ellipses are *states*. The arrows are *transitions*. The words set in bold italic *Gill* are the *actions* that accompany the transitions. The tests of style—"if a letter" and "if not a letter"—are the *conditions* required for an action to occur. We say that there are *classes* of glyphs: in the initial state, the classes are "letter" and "nonletter". The same is true of the state "inside a word".

To understand the structure of this diagram, the reader is advised to go through the intellectual exercise of saying "I am the string Raymond; what will happen to me if I pass through this automaton?"

Having established our terminology and our basic concepts, let us make our problem slightly more complex. The automaton shown in Figure D-9 (a) may satisfy most of our friends, but it will leave others unhappy: Philippe, Christian, Thierry, Kharostani, Dharmaputtra, Xhiang-Go, and many other individuals whose names begin with a consonant followed by an 'h'. For their names, we are accustomed to writing two letters, not just one, as an abbreviation: 'Ph.', 'Ch.', 'Th.', etc. Of course, this convention has no effect on names that begin with an 'H', since 'Hh' can never occur.

How does this convention affect what we have done? First observation: if the first letter is not a consonant, then there is nothing to change. That is the condition that arrow ② will handle: it is no longer "if a letter" but rather "if a vowel or 'h' ". The case of the vowels and 'h' is therefore settled. Now, if the first letter is a consonant (other than 'h'), a new arrow, ⑤, leaves from the initial state and goes to a new state that we shall call "second glyph". Thus we have processed the first glyph, which is a consonant (other than 'h'), and we are preparing to process the second. Three cases must be handled: (1) the character is not a letter, and so we return to the initial state (arrow ⑥); (2) the character is the letter 'h', and so we preserve the letter and append a period to it (arrow ⑦); (3) the letter is not an 'h', and so we omit the glyph but still insert a period (something that was not done during action ⑤, unlike action ②).

Here, then, is how we have extended our automaton to take account of the new condition that represents the nature of the second letter.

For those of our readers who have previously programmed in *lex* (a very widely used lexical parser), the automaton in our example would be written as follows:

```
%{
%}

%x INSIDE_A_WORD
%x SECOND_GLYPH

%%

[BCDFGKLMNPQRSTVWX]     { ECHO; GOTO SECOND_GLYPH; }
[A-Z]                   { ECHO; printf("."); GOTO INSIDE_A_WORD; }
<SECOND_GLYPH>[h]       { printf("h."); GOTO INSIDE_A_WORD; }
<SECOND_GLYPH>[a-z]     { printf("."); GOTO INSIDE_A_WORD; }
<SECOND_GLYPH>.|\n      { ECHO; GOTO 0; }
<INSIDE_A_WORD>[a-z]    { }
<INSIDE_A_WORD>.|\n     { ECHO; GOTO 0; }
.|\n                    { ECHO; }

%%
```

```
int yywrap (void) { return 1; }

void main (void) { yylex(); }
```

In this code, the part before %% declares the states other than the initial state. The lines between the two instances of %% correspond to the arrows in our example. At the left, we have the patterns to match, possibly preceded by a state in which we must be. When the patterns are checked, the first match will be retained. Thus we place the pattern [BCDFGKLMNPQRSTVWX] first: it means that we are searching for a *consonant* (other than 'h', which is not in the list). The second pattern is [A-Z], or all the capital letters. Since the consonant did not match the first pattern, if we find a consonant at this point, it will necessarily be a vowel or an 'H'. The pattern in the eighth line is . | \n, which means "any character": we can use it because this line comes at the end and thus matches any character that the other patterns rejected. We shall not go into the details of the code here, for we wished merely to give the reader the chance to compare the two (the figure and the code) and understand that they are two ways to represent the same thing: the finite automaton.

But let us return to the case of interest to us: AAT fonts. We have already given two ways to represent a finite automaton, and here is a third: by writing three tables. These three tables are the *state table*, the *entry table*, and the *class table*. Where are we headed with these tables? It should be clear: we are going to store a finite automaton in a TrueType table. Thus we shall use neither diagrams nor Lex code to achieve our goal. The approach of using three tables is the only one that is appropriate.

How do we write these three tables? The approach is both easy and ingenious. The first table is the *class table*: the glyphs are classified according to the conditions for applying a given action. In our example, the classes are the consonants (other than 'h'), the vowels, the letter 'h', and the nonletters.

The second table is the *entry table*. Here the word "entry" is not used in the sense of "dictionary entry" but rather in the sense of "act of entering". We might have called it a *table of entering arrows*, but that is a bit too Western for our tastes. In any event, it is used to catalog all the combinations of actions and the targets of the transitions—in other words, *the state to which each arrow points and the action associated with it*.

Finally, the third, and most important, table is the *state table*. The columns correspond to classes, and the rows correspond to states. The cells contain "entries", in the sense of the previous table.

Let us review. To implement the automaton in Figure D-9, we need the following ingredients:

- The ovals; that is, the states. We have them: they are the rows in the state table.

- The arrows; that is, the following information: where does the arrow start? under which condition? where does it lead? which action is associated with it? Here are the answers:

    - Where does the arrow start? We have this information in the state table, since we know that we have a given transition arrow for a given class and a given state.

    - Under which condition? Once again, this information is in the state table, since we know that a given arrow will start from a given state for a well-defined set of classes. This set of classes is our starting condition.

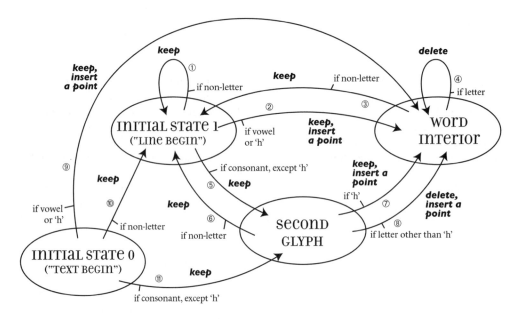

Figure D-10: The second example of a finite automaton, with an additional initial state.

- Where does it lead? The entry table answers this question. The state table gives us a reference to the entry table, and an entry contains, among other things, a "target state", which is where the corresponding arrow leads.
- Which action is associated with it? This is the other piece of information contained in an entry, within the entry table.

In these tables we have all the information needed to implement the diagram. It can be shown that the converse is also true: the tables can be constructed from the diagram. The two representations are therefore equivalent.

Now we shall describe, by way of an example, the tables associated with the automaton in Figure D-9 (b). But there is a problem: Apple imposes on us not one initial state, but two: the *start of text* and the *start of line*. Specifically, when text is selected with the mouse, if the start of the selection is at the beginning of the line, state 1 will be the initial state; otherwise state 0 will be.

Thus we have to add complexity to our diagram once again. The reader can examine the new automaton in Figure D-10. We have had to make the following modifications. The former "initial state" is now called *initial state 1 ("start of line")* (the quotation marks around "start of line" are there to remind us that we are handling not only the start of a line, but much more as well: we are in this state whenever we are not within a word); there is a new state called *initial state 0 (start of text)*; when we are in this state, three windows to the future are opened: if we have a consonant, it is retained, and we move to the *second glyph*; if we have a vowel, it is retained, and we move directly to the state *inside a word*; finally, if we have a nonletter, it is retained, and we move to *initial state 1*. Thus the new state is one in which everything flows out but nothing flows in—which is to be expected, since the text has only one starting point, just as there is only one birth (in the corporal sense, of course) in a person's life.

We shall denote the state *inside a word* as 2 and the state *second glyph* as 3.

Here is the class table (the numbers from 0 to 3 are reserved by Apple):

Description	Class
Consonants (other than 'h')	4
Vowels	5
The letter 'h'	6
Nonletters (default case)	7

We have four different actions; let us number them: "retain" (or "do nothing") will be action 0, "delete" will be action 1, "retain, insert a period" will be action 2, and "delete, insert a period" will be action 3. Thus the entry table looks like this:

Entry number	Arrow	New state	Action
0	①	1	0
1	②	2	2
2	④	2	1
3	⑤	3	0
4	⑧	2	3

The reader must have noticed that there are fewer entries than arrows in Diagram D-10. That is because the arrows ①, ③, ⑥, ⑩, and ②, ⑦, ⑨, and ⑤, ⑪ end in the same states and are associated with the same actions. Thus each of these groups gives rise to only one entry. The ingenuity of this table is that only the distinct combinations of a new state and an action are cataloged.

Finally, the state table:

States	Classes							
	0	1	2	3	4	5	6	7
Initial 0	0	0	0	0	3	1	1	0
Initial 1	0	0	0	0	3	1	1	0
Inside a word (2)	0	0	0	0	2	2	2	0
Second glyph (3)	0	0	0	0	4	4	1	0

What can we conclude from the table above? First, that states 0 and 1 have exactly the same behavior (their rows are identical). Second, that the nonletters are ignored during processing (their column contains only zeroes). Third, that when we leave state 0 or state 1, the letter 'h' is considered a vowel (since 'Hh' never occurs). Fourth, and last, that Figure D-10 is more verbose than all the tables together!

After this introduction to finite automata, we are ready to describe the AAT tables that use this technique. Note that we have already encountered a finite automaton previously: it was used in subtable 1 of the `kern` table (§D.8.4.2), a subtable specific to AAT.

D.13.2   The morx Table (Formerly mort)

The `mort` table has shuffled off this mortal coil. It has been dead since Apple replaced it with the table `morx` (for "mort extended"). The `morx` table is nothing but version 2 of `mort`; why, then, was it necessary to change the name? As often happens in the course of human history, the `morx` was born because of a regrettable mistake: Apple noticed, when it was already too late to change anything, that the system's code did not check the version of the `mort` table after a change of font. Every new version of this table will therefore be misunderstood, poorly received, and disrespected by the system, with more or less severe consequences—failure to display the font, or perhaps even a revolt by the system, leading to a total crash. The only solution for avoiding this cascade of horrors was to assign a new name to the second version of `mort`: specifically, `morx`.

Let us now see how `morx` works. We have already seen that AAT has the concept of *feature*, just like OpenType. But rather than using lookups, as OpenType does, AAT offers a system based on *supply and demand*. In a `morx` table, we define some features and some operations (called "subtables" in AAT jargon). The link between the two is a 4-byte number N that is used as a series of 32 flags. The `morx` table—more precisely, a substructure of it that is called a string—establishes the default value of N, which we shall call N_d.

Suppose that that the user selects a section of text and chooses n features. Let F_1 be the first feature selected. This feature has two numbers that are specific to it: $F_{1,e}$ and $F_{1,d}$. We shall perform a logical AND and a logical OR between these values and N_d. The new value of N, which we shall designate N_1, will be $N_1 = (N_d \text{ AND } F_{1,d}) \text{ OR } F_{1,e}$. Likewise, if F_2 is the second feature selected, we have $N_2 = (N_1 \text{ AND } F_{2,d}) \text{ OR } F_{2,e}$, and so forth. After all the AND and OR operations corresponding to the n features selected, we obtain a number N_n, which we denote N'.

Now we can begin to carry out the operations, in the order established in the font. Each operation i has a signature in the form of a series of flags, S_i, of its own. We perform a logical AND: $N' \text{ AND } S_i$. If the result is nonzero, we perform the operation.

This method is extremely flexible. First of all, it is the font's designer who decides which features and which selectors for those features will come into play in setting up the series of flags N. If 32 flags are not enough (which happens when there are many features and/or selectors), we create other "chains", with new default values and new features.

But the most interesting characteristic of this method is that the features and operations are independent—what we have called "supply and demand". The features establish the number N', which is a sort of "mission statement". Next, the operations, one by one, compare their signatures to this "mission statement". If the result is nonzero, the operation will take place; otherwise, it will give way to the following operation. The last operation is an empty one that merely returns control to the system.

On the other hand, we see the importance of the number N_d: even before the user chooses a single feature, several operations have already been preselected. For example, we can declare that certain ligatures are required by default. The user can always disable them, but they will be enabled by default. And it is easy to change a font's default behavior: one merely changes the number N_d of the corresponding string in the morx table.

The code for the morx table is therefore subdivided, as one would expect, into two sections: a section that describes the features and one that describes the operations (or "subtables"). Here is an example of the first section, drawn from the font *Skia*:

```
<morx>
  <Version value="2"/>
  <!-- nChains=2 -->
  <chain index="0" defaultFlags="\x00021449">
    <features>
      <!-- nFeatureEntries=30 -->
      <featureTable index="0">
        <type value="15"/>
        <setting value="2"/>
        <enableFlags value="\x00040000"/>
        <disableFlags value="\xffffffff"/>
      </featureTable>
       <featureTable index="1">
        <type value="15"/>
        <setting value="0"/>
        <enableFlags value="\x00080000"/>
        <disableFlags value="\xffffffff"/>
      </featureTable>
      ...
    </features>
```

After the usual Version, there is a chain element. The "chain" is a subdivision of morx that is of no great interest: its only reason for being is the fact that the number N that contains the flags is of a limited size and can contain no more than 32 flags. When the font's needs surpass these 32 flags, we fill up the first N, write the corresponding features and operations, and then start a new chain with a new N, and so forth, until we have covered all the flags required for our superfont.

The chain element has two attributes: index (its number) and defaultFlags, which contains the number N_d (i.e., the default values of the 32 flags) written in hexadecimal form. Within chain, we have the features: several featureTable elements, each of them having four subelements:

- Its "type" (type). Here one must not assume that the "type" has anything to do with the feature's behavior. It is simply a link to the feat table, which we redirect to the name table, which contains the names of the features in every language. This information allows for displaying the feature's name on the software's user interface and for grouping the corresponding selectors together.

- Its "selector" (setting). Each feature has selectors; here, we give the value desired. Once again, this information is used only for displaying the selector in question on the user interface. Recall that the feat table contains a piece of information on the exclusivity of the selectors: if the selectors are exclusive, they are displayed as radio buttons; otherwise, they are displayed as checkboxes.

- The numbers enableFlags and disableFlags, which will modify the current value of N as follows: first, we perform an AND with disableFlags; then an OR with enableFlags, which is what we noted above: $N_{i+1} = (N_i \text{ AND } F_{1,d}) \text{ OR } F_{1,e}$.

  But why do we need *both* an AND *and* an OR? Suppose that we have two sets of ligatures, A and B. Then we have two flags: 01 for A and 10 for B, the default value being 00. We select the string of text and apply set A of ligatures: in order for the number to become 01, we need an OR: 00 OR 01 = 01. The enableFlags for A will then be 01. But now suppose that B must disable A because the designer does not want both sets of ligatures to be used at the same time. If the enableFlags for B is 10 and we perform 01 OR 11, we obtain 11, which means that both sets of ligatures are enabled. Thus we also need a disableFlags for B, which will be 10. By computing 11 AND 10, we obtain 10, which is B, not A ∪ B.

  Now we are better equipped to understand the meanings of the names enableFlags and disableFlags. We enable *our own flags* and disable *the flags for other features*—i.e., those that we wish to exclude.

Now let us examine the operations. It is they that will serve the needs created by the features. Each operation comes in turn, quite humbly, and compares its signature S_i with the number N'. If the result of S_i AND N' is nonzero, the operation will be executed. If not, it will forever hold its peace (well, until the next group of glyphs is examined by the font).

Operations can be of five *types*. Here, and here only, the "types" are actually significant. No longer are we in the realm of features, where everything is oriented towards the user interface. Here we dive in, and what is important is the *transformation of glyphs* that we have to perform. There are five types of transformations, which differ from one another in fundamental ways:

- Type 0, a change in the order of the glyphs, called "Indian rearrangement", since it applies most of all to the languages of India.

- Type 1, glyph substitution according to the previous glyph, pompously called "contextual substitution".

- Type 2, ligatures (from 1 to 16 glyphs!).

- Type 4, glyph substitution pure and simple, even more pompously called "noncontextual glyph substitution".

- Type 5, insertion of between 1 and 31 glyphs, according to context.

These types (except type 4) have in common the fact that they occur within the scope of a finite automaton. The differences among the corresponding finite automata lie mainly in the actions that they perform. Below, we shall examine the first type in detail, and then present only the ways in which the other types differ from it.

D.13.2.1 Operations of type 0: changing the order of the glyphs

As a finite automaton, this operation is described in TTX in the form of three tables: the class table, the state table, and the entry table (or table of "in-bound arrows"). Before we begin to describe the classes, here is the preamble from an operation of type 0, drawn from the font *Monotype Devanagari*, which was furnished standard with Mac OS 8.5 but was dropped from later versions of Mac OS:

```
<IndicRearrangementSubtable index="0">
  <coverage value="\x0000"/>
  <subFeatureFlags value="\x00000001"/>
  <stateSize value="11"/>
```

The element that contains the data for this operation is `IndicRearrangementSubtable`. The first three subelements are

- `coverage`, a number that consists of three flags and the type of the operation. The flags are \x8000 (if the flag is enabled, the operation applies only to vertical typesetting; if it is disabled, the operation applies only to horizontal typesetting), \x4000 (a very important flag: if it is enabled, the string of glyphs is red *starting from the end!*), \x2000 (a flag that allows us to cancel the choice indicated by flag \x8000: if it is enabled, the operation applies to both horizontal and vertical typesetting).

- `subFeatureFlags`, the signature S_i of this operation, which will be compared (through a logical AND operation) with N' to determine whether the operation should be performed or not.

- `stateSize`, the size in bytes of a row in the state table; in other words, the number of classes.

Once it has read these lines, the AAT processor already knows whether it should perform the operation or not, and, if necessary, in which direction it should read the glyphs.

Now let us continue with the class table:

```
<classes>
  <!-- nbClasses=11 -->
  ...
  <class value="1">
    <glyph name="edeva"/>
    <glyph name="aideva"/>
    ...
  </class>
  ...
  <class value="5">
    <glyph name="rvocalicdeva"/>
  </class>
  ...
</classes>
```

The classes element contains a class subelement for each class. Each of these subelements contains some glyphs, identified by their names. No surprise there.

The state table is just as simple:

```
<states>
  <!-- nbStates=10 -->
  <state value="0">
    <entry class="0" value="0"/>
    <entry class="1" value="0"/>
    ...
    <entry class="10" value="0"/>
  </state>
  ...
  <state value="10">
    <entry class="0" value="6"/>
    <entry class="1" value="6"/>
    ...
    <entry class="5" value="6"/>
  </state>
</states>
```

For each state state in states (with an 's'), there is an entry entry for each class. Each entry contains, in the form of attributes, the number of the class (class) and the number of the corresponding entry (value).

Finally, the entry table (or table of "in-bound arrows"):

```
<entries>
  <!-- nbEntries=12 -->
  <entry value="0" newState="0"/>
  <entry value="1" newState="2" markFirst="1"/>
  <entry value="2" newState="0" markLast="1" verb="1"/>
  <entry value="3" newState="3"/>
  <entry value="4" newState="4"/>
  <entry value="5" newState="5" markLast="1"/>
  <entry value="6" newState="0" dontAdvance="1" verb="4"/>
  <entry value="7" newState="6" markLast="1"/>
  <entry value="8" newState="7"/>
  <entry value="9" newState="9" markLast="1"/>
  <entry value="10" newState="8"/>
  <entry value="11" newState="0" markLast="1" verb="4"/>
</entries>
```

The entries element contains the entry elements that correspond to the entries. Each entry contains, in the form of attributes, its number (value), the state into which the arrow leads (newState), and the action. But things turn complicated here. To describe the action, we use several attributes, which vary from one type of operation to another.

Here are the attributes specific to an operation of type 0:

- markFirst, whose value can be 0 or 1 (if the attribute is omitted, its value is 0). The action consists of marking the current glyph as being the first to be rearranged.

- markLast is similar, but the current glyph is the last of the glyphs to be rearranged; in other words, this operation initiates rearrangement.

- verb, a number between 0 and 15 that indicates the nature of the rearrangement (see below).

- dontAdvance, whose value can be 0 or 1; this attribute appears in all operations and means that we must perform the requested action, change state, and then act as if we have not yet processed the glyph and read it again.

Now all that we have left to describe is the rearrangement itself (the verb attribute). To do so, we shall use the following notation: '1', '2', '3', '4' will be four glyphs that we are going to rearrange, and 'XYZ' will be a string of one or more glyphs that appear among the candidates for rearrangement and that will not be modified. For example, if the string 'abcd' becomes 'dbca', we can say that '1' is 'a', '2' is 'd', and 'XYZ' is 'bc'. Here are all the possible cases of rearrangement and the associated values of verb:

verb	Before	After	verb	Before	After
0	-	-	8	1-XYZ-2-3	2-3-XYZ-1
1	1-XYZ	XYZ-1	9	ditto	3-2-XYZ-1
2	XYZ-1	1-XYZ	10	1-2-XYZ-3	3-XYZ-1-2
3	1-XYZ-2	2-XYZ-1	11	ditto	3-XYZ-2-1
4	1-2-XYZ	XYZ-1-2	12	1-2-XYZ-3-4	3-4-XYZ-1-2
5	ditto	XYZ-2-1	13	ditto	3-4-XYZ-1-2
6	XYZ-1-2	1-2-XYZ	14	ditto	4-3-XYZ-1-2
7	ditto	2-1-XYZ	15	ditto	4-3-XYZ-2-1

Let us mention an undeniable benefit of finite automata that becomes clear here. What we have denoted "XYZ" in the table above is an arbitrarily long string of glyphs. For instance, we can "mark" a glyph, move forward, and much farther along find its "companion" for permutation. Irrespective of what we read between the two glyphs, we can always apply a rearrangement between them, according to the table. That is one thing that would be hard to do in OpenType, since all of the patterns for strings in OpenType are of a fixed length.

An example: in the scripts of India and Southeast Asia, when consonants occur consecutively without any intervening vowels, we speak of "consonant complexes". These complexes can sometimes include as many as six or seven consonants. When the last consonant of a complex is an 'r', the 'r' will appear graphically at the beginning of the string. Thus here is a typical type of situation that an AAT operation of type 0 allows us to solve: we mark the first consonant after a vowel or a nonletter, we accumulate consonants, and when we encounter an 'r', it is placed *before* the marked consonant, irrespective of the distance traversed and the glyphs that have been set in the meantime.

D.13.2.2 Operations of type 1: contextual substitution

By contextual substitution, we mean the substitution of two glyphs (possibly separated by a string of glyphs) by two other glyphs. The first of the two will be "marked", and when we reach the second, the two will be replaced with two other glyphs, provided that we are still in the right state. We may also change only one of the glyphs. And there is symmetry between the "marked" glyph (which comes first) and the "active" glyph (which comes second), since we can read the glyphs from start to finish or from finish to start, according to the value of flag 0xx4000 in coverage.

An example: in the font *Apple Skia*, there is a feature that assists with entering mathematics. When we enter an asterisk (∗) surrounded by spaces or digits, the asterisk is replaced with a multiplication sign (×). That does not occur when the asterisk is between two letters, for example. How does this substitution work? There are four states. When we are in the initial state and a digit or a space is read, we switch to state 2 (which we could describe as the "state for waiting for an asterisk"). In state 2, when an asterisk is encountered, we mark it and change to state 3 (which could be described as the "state in which we have just read an asterisk"). There are two ways to get out of state 3: if the following glyph is neither a space nor a digit, we return to state 0, and the game is over; conversely, if the following glyph is a space or a digit, we replace the asterisk with the multiplication sign and return to state 2 to wait for another possible asterisk.

From the point of view of TTX's code, this operation is only slightly different from the previous one. The global element is ContextualGlyphSubstitutionSubtable. The class, state, and entry tables are the same, with only one small difference: the entry entries have their specific attributes, which describe the actions connected to contextual substitution. These actions are

- setMark (0 or 1), which marks the current glyph.

- dontAdvance (0 or 1), as in the previous operation.

- substituteMarkedGlyph, whose value is the name of a glyph. When this attribute takes a nonzero value, the marked glyph is to be replaced by the glyph in question. If the attribute is omitted, the marked glyph cannot be modified.

- substituteCurrentGlyph is the same, but for the current glyph.

For example, suppose that we have the string 'f', 'i', and that we would like to replace the first glyph with "fi" and the second with an empty glyph. That is a very practical way to obtain a ligature. When we come upon an 'f', we mark it. Next, when the 'i' is read, we replace the marked glyph (i.e., the 'f') with "fi" and the current glyph (i.e., the 'i') with the empty glyph (for example, the glyph .null).

D.13.2.3 Operations of type 2: ligatures

In the preceding type of operation, we saw how to obtain simple ligatures. Type 2 is much more powerful and, as it happens, more complex. Specifically, this operation uses a stack of glyphs onto which all the marked glyphs are placed as components of the ligature. Then it will pop the series of glyphs and will perform several replacements. The size of the stack is 16; therefore, we can obtain ligatures with up to 16 components!

The global element for this operation is LigatureSubstitutionSubtable. Its code is richer than that of the previous operations. First of all, entry has, once again, its own attributes: setComponent (whose value is 0 or 1), to indicate whether the current glyph is a component of the ligature; dontAdvance, as in the preceding types; ligature, to indicate the name of the glyph for the ligature that will replace the last of these marked glyphs.

Here is an example of the entries table, drawn from the font *Skia*:

```
<entries>
  <!-- nbEntries=12 -->
  <entry value="0" newState="0" setComponent="0"/>
  <entry value="1" newState="2" setComponent="1"/>
  <entry value="2" newState="1" setComponent="0"/>
  <entry value="3" newState="2" setComponent="0"/>
  <entry value="4" newState="3" setComponent="1"/>
  <entry value="5" newState="0" setComponent="1" ligature="fi"/>
  <entry value="6" newState="0" setComponent="1" ligature="fj"/>
  <entry value="7" newState="0" setComponent="1" ligature="fl"/>
  <entry value="8" newState="0" setComponent="1" ligature="ft"/>
  <entry value="9" newState="0" dontAdvance="1" ligature="ff"/>
  <entry value="10" newState="3" setComponent="0"/>
  <entry value="11" newState="0" setComponent="1" ligature="ffi"/>
  <entry value="12" newState="0" setComponent="1" ligature="ffl"/>
</entries>
```

We can see that for the ligatures 'fi', 'fj', 'fl', and 'ft', which are "terminal", there is an entry whose new state is the initial state (0), whose setComponent has the value 1 (and therefore its second glyph—'i', 'j', 'l', 't'—is indeed a component), and whose ligature has a nonempty value. This is the simple case.

Now let us see what happens for triple ligatures. When an 'f' occurs, we are in state 2. When a second 'f' occurs, we move to state 3 via entry 4. This entry tells us that the second 'f' is indeed a component, but nothing more than that. At that point, three cases are possible:

1. What follows is an 'i'. We then move to state 0 via entry 11. This entry concludes the process.

2. What follows is an 'l'. We do as for the 'i', but using entry 12.

3. What follows is neither an 'i' nor an 'l'. Ordinarily we would say "OK, we'll set the 'ff' and return to the starting point". But things are not so simple: after the second 'f', we are in state 3. The following glyph takes us to state 0. But suppose that the next glyph is

another 'f'. After that 'f' we will again be in state 0, whereas ordinarily after an initial 'f'
we would be in state 2 to prepare for a possible ligature! Thus we have skipped a step: the
switch from state 3 to state 0 caused us to skip state 2, where we should be. That is why
we use the attribute dontAdvance. We thus act as if we had not seen the 'f' and proceed to
examine it again. In the meantime, however, we have switched to state 0, and therefore
the 'f' will move us back to state 2, and everything works as it should.

D.13.2.4   *Operations of type 5: insertion of glyphs*

The aim of this operation is to insert glyphs before or after the marked glyph or the current
glyph. There are two types of *inserted glyphs*: those that are attached to the preceding or following glyph, and those that lie at a certain distance and seem to be independent of the glyph
that caused their insertion. The canonical examples are, for the first case, the connection of
Arabic letters, and, for the second, the Khmer "split vowels":

                insertion of *kashida*   ligature   split insertion

The actual difference between these two types of inserted glyphs is at the level of text selected
by the user. In the first case, the glyphs cannot be dissociated from the current glyph—that is,
the one that caused them to appear. In the second case, they attach themselves to the marked
glyph. For example, in the case of the split vowels, the following phenomenon occurs: a group
of consonants 'BCD' followed by the vowel 'aA' becomes 'aBCDA', where 'DA' is a new glyph
that replaces 'D' and 'a' attaches itself to 'B'. The possible selections that the user can make
within 'aBCDA' are therefore 'aB', 'C', and 'DA'. On the other hand, in the case of Arabic, if
'kml' becomes 'k__m__l', the possible selections are 'k__', 'm__', and 'l'.

We can insert up to 31 glyphs before or after the marked glyph, and the same number before
or after the current glyph.

In TTX, the global element for this operation is GlyphInsertionSubtable. The TTX code for
this operation is slightly richer than the code for the previous operation: while the class and
state tables are the same, the entry tables include entry entries that, for the first time, can
have content. Indeed, up to now, we have placed the value for a substitution or a ligature in
an entry attribute. In this case, however, there is a variable number of glyphs to insert; thus
we cannot forgo the introduction of new XML elements. The entry element can contain two
elements: currentInsertList (a list of glyphs to insert before or after the current glyph) and
markedInsertList (likewise, but before or after the marked glyph). For its part, entry has
the following attributes:

- value: its number.

- newState: the new state that is reached when we follow this arrow.

- setMark: mark the current glyph.

- dontAdvance: act as if the glyph has not been processed and process it again after changing
  state.

- `currentIsKashidaLike` (0 or 1): do the glyphs inserted before or after the current glyph behave like the *kashida* (1), or more like "split" vowels (0)?

- `markedIsKashidaLike` (0 or 1): the same, but for the marked glyph rather than the current glyph.

- `currentInsertBefore` (0 or 1): should glyphs be inserted before (1) or after (0) the current glyph?

- `markedInsertBefore` (0 or 1), the same, but for the marked glyph.

- `currentInsertCount` (from 0 to 31): how many glyphs shall we insert before or after the current glyph?

- `markedInsertCount` (from 0 to 31): the same, but for the marked glyph.

Each of `currentInsertList` and `markedInsertList` can contain up to 31 `Glyph` elements, for which the `value` attribute contains the glyph's name.

D.13.2.5   Operations of type 4: simple glyph substitution

We have left this operation for last because it is in a way the "poor sibling" of the operations: it is not a finite automaton but rather a table of correspondences between replaced glyph and replacement glyph:

```
<NonContextualGlyphSubstitutionSubtable index="0">
  <coverage value="\x2004"/>
  <subFeatureFlags value="\x00000001"/>
  <substitutions>
    <!-- nSubstitutions=10 -->
    <substitution from="zero" to="zerooldstyle"/>
    <substitution from="one" to="oneoldstyle"/>
    <substitution from="two" to="twooldstyle"/>
    <substitution from="three" to="threeoldstyle"/>
    <substitution from="four" to="fouroldstyle"/>
    <substitution from="five" to="fiveoldstyle"/>
    <substitution from="six" to="sixoldstyle"/>
    <substitution from="seven" to="sevenoldstyle"/>
    <substitution from="eight" to="eightoldstyle"/>
    <substitution from="nine" to="nineoldstyle"/>
  </substitutions>
</NonContextualGlyphSubstitutionSubtable>
```

Apart from the horribly long name of the global element (`NonContextualGlyphSubstitutionSubtable`), there is no surprise here: we find `coverage` (the nature of the operation) and `subFeatureFlags` (the number S_i that is used to determine whether or not this operation is to be executed), just as in the other tables. Immediately afterwards comes an element `substitutions` that contains `substitution` elements (with no 's'). Each `substitution` has two attributes that contain glyph names: from for the original glyph and to for the glyph that is obtained after the substitution.

The sample code above is for the operation that switches from "modern" to old-style digits.

D.13.3 The just Table

No, it is not the given name of the author of TTX, Just van Rossum. As with the JSTF table in OpenType, the just table in AAT manages the optimization of the *justification* of lines. We shall see that the developers of AAT had a whale of a time with this one. With it, we can do things as simple as changing the interword space or as complex as using font variation to expand or contract certain specified glyphs.

Like the other tables, this one begins with a version element and a format element, which have fixed values. It contains one or two JustificationTable elements, according to the direction of typesetting (horizontal or vertical), which is given by the attribute of the same name:

```
<just>
  <Version value="1"/>
  <Format value="0"/>
  <JustificationTable direction="h">
```

The table is divided into three parts:

- The table of justification classes
- The quantitative table
- The qualitative table

Let us start with the first of these.

D.13.3.1 The table of justification classes

These classes assign to each glyph in the string a class that will manage its behavior with respect to justification. It is clear that the same glyph may behave differently according to its position in the string: we can more easily expand the left side-bearing of the letter 'a' if it appears at the beginning of a word; otherwise, the expansion will be what we call *letterspacing*, which not everyone fancies. Therefore, we absolutely cannot use a simple class table in which each glyph name is associated with a *fixed* and *unchanging* class value.

The solution that AAT proposes is to *use a finite automaton* to assign justification classes. Here we must be careful not to confuse the *glyph classes of the finite automaton* (the class table is an indispensable ingredient of any finite automaton) with the *justification classes*. Here is the code for one such finite automaton:

```
<justClassTable>
  <stateSize value="9"/>
  <classes>
```

```
    <!-- nbClasses=9 -->
    ...
    <class value="1">
      <glyph name="a"/>
      <glyph name="b"/>
      ...
      <glyph name="z"/>
    </class>
    ...
  </classes>
  <states>
    <!-- nbStates=4 -->
    <state value="0">
      <entry class="0" value="0"/>
      <entry class="1" value="0"/>
      ...
      <entry class="8" value="0"/>
    </state>
    ...
  </states>
  <entries>
    <!-- nbEntries=13 -->
    <entry value="0" newState="0"/>
    ...
    <entry value="4" newState="3" currentClass="3"/>
    ...
  </entries>
</justClassTable>
```

This code is no different from that of the other finite automata that we have seen up to now. The global element is justClassTable, and, as always, the entry elements have a certain number of attributes that are specific to this finite automaton:

- setMark (0 or 1): mark the current glyph.

- dontAdvance (0 or 1): act as if the glyph had not been processed and read it again after changing state.

- markClass (between 0 and 255): the justification class of the marked glyph.

- currentClass (between 0 and 255): the same, but for the current glyph.

Thus we can say that we assign to 'a' class 35 if it is at the beginning of a word and if it is followed by an 'f': to do so, we will mark an 'a' that occurs after a nonletter by using setMark, and then we will watch for the appearance of an 'f', and when the 'f' does appear, we will give markClass the value 35: thus class 35 will be assigned not to the 'f' that we have just read but to the preceding 'a'. Of course, nothing stops us from assigning a class to the 'f' at the same time and/or marking it before continuing.

At this point, we have assigned justification classes to our glyphs in the most intelligent way possible. Now we need to make use of them.

D.13.3.2   *The quantitative table*

What we have blandly called the "quantitative table" has a very cool English name: *width delta clusters*. Here is where the classes are associated with quantitative behaviors. In other words, this is where we decide *how much* we can expand or contract a glyph, whether to do so at the left or at the right, and what the global priority of this operation will be. In the following table (the "qualitative table"), we shall decide *how* the glyph will fill in the extra space that we have given it, or how it will squeeze into the more limited space that we have allotted.

Here is an example of a quantitative table:

```
<widthDeltaClustersTable>
  <widthDeltaCluster>
    <widthDeltaPair index="0" justClass="0"
      beforeGrowLimit=".5" beforeShrinkLimit="0"
      afterGrowLimit=".5" afterShrinkLimit="0"
      growUnlimitedGap="1" shrinkUnlimitedGap="1"
      growPriority="2" shrinkPriority="2"/>
    ...
  </widthDeltaCluster>
</widthDeltaClustersTable>
```

The global element is `widthDeltaClustersTable`, which contains `widthDeltaClusters`, which in turn contain `widthDeltaPairs`. The latter are the elements that match up a justification class (`justClass`) with a certain number of quantitative properties:

- `beforeGrowLimit` and `afterGrowLimit`, expressed in ems: how much we can expand the width (the width vector) of this class of glyphs at the *left* (or at the *top*, if we are setting type vertically) or at the *right* (or *bottom*).

- `beforeShrinkLimit` and `afterShrinkLimit`, expressed in ems—the same, but for reducing the width.

- `growUnlimitedGap` and `shrinkUnlimitedGap` (0 or 1): should the values of the attributes *`GrowLimit` and *`ShrinkLimit` be considered "infinite", thus giving us carte blanche to do anything?

- `growPriority` et `shrinkPriority` (between 0 and 3): the priority that we assign to this instance of expansion or narrowing. Four possible cases:

  - Value 0: "*kashida* priority". This is the highest priority. *Kashida*s are there to absorb all the extra interword space, and they can be used excessively. (This type of straight *kashida* does not necessarily yield good typographical results; see §D.9.5.1).

  - Value 1: "whitespace priority". This is the priority for interword spaces. This priority is assigned to the pseudoglyphs "space", "unbreakable space", etc.

  - Value 2: the default case for the glyphs that are somehow involved in justification.

– Value 3: "zero priority". The exceptional case for glyphs that should not be involved in justification. We can also create a justification class with zero values for expansion and narrowing; the result will be the same.

Now we know to what extent we can play with the width of each glyph in our string. All that we need to know is *how*, and that is what we shall see in the following section.

D.13.3.3 The qualitative table

This involves associating with a justification class several possible actions. These actions will be performed in order until justification is complete. The global element for this table is `postcompTable`. It contains one or more `glyphActionRecords`, which in turn contain `glyphActions`. Each `glyphAction` is therefore a justification action; it has two parameters, given by their attributes: the justification class to which it applies (`class`) and the type of action to perform (`type`).

Here is a typical example:

```
<postcompTable>
  <glyphActionRecord index="0">
    <glyphAction index="0" class="35" type="0">
    ...
    </glyphAction>
  </glyphActionRecord>
</postcompTable>
```

All that we need to know is the content of `glyphAction`: it depends on the action's type. Here are the various types that are available:

- Type 0: *ligature decomposition*. We decide to decompose some ligatures in order to expand some words slightly. This approach should be used with care, since we must refrain from disturbing the reader's eye by setting an 'fi' in one place and an 'fi' in another—not to mention committing semantic blunders by decomposing ligatures in German, since that is done only for compound words (see the discussion in §D.9.5.2). Example:

```
<glyphAction index="0" class="35" type="0">
  <decomposition lowerLimit=".25" upperLimit=".25" order="3">
    <Glyph index="0" value="f"/>
    <Glyph index="1" value="f"/>
    <Glyph index="2" value="i"/>
  </decomposition>
</glyphAction>
```

We see that `glyphAction` (which is of type 0) contains a subelement `decomposition` that has three attributes. Among them, `lowerLimit` and `upperLimit` give the minimum and maximum values, expressed in ems, for which the ligature will be decomposed; `order` gives a relative order for the choice of ligatures to break up: when the software must choose among various ligatures to break up, it will use this number to do the job in the optimal order.

On the other hand, glyphAction contains some Glyphs, which are those into which the ligature will be decomposed.

- Type 1: *glyph insertion*. Here we merely insert a glyph that will be distorted horizontally to fill the space that we ask it to fill. Here is an example:

```
<glyphAction index="1" class="35" type="1">
  <addGlyph value="kashida"/>
</glyphAction>
```

The addGlyph element contains the name of a glyph to insert, in the form of a value of the value attribute.

- Type 2: *intelligent glyph insertion*. Here we do a bit better than in type 1: we set a limit, measured in ems, for the width. If adding the glyph in question causes the limit to be exceeded, we replace the original glyph (the one whose justification class spawned this action) with another glyph. The idea is that if we add a very long *kashida*, we may just as well take a wider version of the original glyph, which could only improve the aesthetic result. Thus we try to salvage what we can and replace *kashida*s (which, by definition, are typographically unpleasant) with specially designed wider forms of letters. Here is an example of one such action:

```
<glyphAction index="2" class="35" type="2">
  <addGlyph value="kashida"/>
  <substGlyph threshhold="1.5" value="swashnoon"/>
</glyphAction>
```

A new element is found in the addGlyph of type 1: substGlyph. Here we call for replacing the original glyph with the one given in the value attribute of substGlyph, if and only if the value of the extra space required is greater than the treshhold attribute, expressed in ems.

- Type 3: *glyph stretching*. We stretch the glyph horizontally to fill the space available. The element glyphAction is empty in this case, since no extra information is needed.

- Type 4: *glyph stretching managed by font variation*. This is the high-tech version of type 3: rather than blindly stretching a glyph, we use an *axis of variation* in the font to obtain the same result in a *neat* manner. Example:

```
<glyphAction index="4" class="35" type="4">
  <ductileGlyph variationAxis="duct" minimumLimit="0.7"
    maximumLimit="2.0" noStretchValue="1.0"/>
</glyphAction>
```

Here we are using ductileGlyph, which has four attributes:

- variationAxis, which answers the question "which axis is the axis of variation?" In the example, we can take wdth, the axis for widths; but the AAT specification allows us to create an axis on the fly, called duct.

- minimumLimit and maximumLimit, which give the extreme values at which variation is still permitted.

- Finally, noStretchValue, which gives the value at which variation is not allowed. Its default value is 1.

- Type 5: *repeated insertion of a glyph*. In types 1 and 2, we added only one glyph to the string in order to optimize justification. Type 5 allows us to insert any number of copies of the same glyph. Example:

```
<glyphAction index="1" class="35" type="5">
  <addGlyph flags="0" value="kashida"/>
</glyphAction>
```

As in type 1, the addGlyph contains the name of the glyph to be inserted, in the form of a value of the value attribute.

E

TrueType Instructions

TrueType instructions have the same purpose as PostScript hints: the optimization of the bitmap rasterization of glyphs. That is why people often speak of "TrueType hints"—a false term that loses the meaning of "hint", which is "indication", "suggestion". There is a fundamental difference between the strategies for optimizing rasterization that the PostScript and TrueType fonts use. In the former, the font's designer gives a few indications to the PostScript interpreter, *in the hope that his wishes will be granted*. What he provides are nothing but indications: a few relevant dimensions, such as the height of the lowercase letters and the thickness of the strokes, and a few strokes that he would like to have rendered in the same way. These data are supplied to the "black box" that is the interpreter, and one can only hope that they will be used appropriately. But there is no guarantee as to the final result—only the promises of Adobe, balanced by a few arguments such as "if you give us the correct hints, we'll give you a good optimization", which could also be interpreted as "if the optimization is poor, the hints you gave us were incorrect; don't blame us!"

TrueType's strategy is different: one provides some *clear and precise* instructions to the True-Type processor and expects that they will be applied. A set of instructions is a program, written in a syntax similar to assembly language. This approach is also more democratic, since anyone can write his own TrueType rendering engine: all that is required is to follow the instructions to the letter, according to the descriptions given in the specifications of Microsoft and Apple. We have much more control, but also much more responsibility. But before we begin, we must learn and master the programming language.

You may be wondering why you should bother to learn this language if there are tools for producing TrueType glyphs with instructions in an interactive graphical manner, as we demonstrated abundantly in Chapter 13. Such tools do indeed exist, but it must be acknowledged that it is far harder to create interactive tools for writing code in TrueType instructions than for designing glyphs in TrueType. To design glyphs, one need only place the points in the right places and indicate whether they are points on the curve or control points. That can be done on the screen through the use of the mouse. But how can instructions be represented graphically? Our programming language includes variables, subroutines, tests, loops—in short, series of instructions that are executed in a certain order, which depends on the context. All that we can expect from a graphical utility is one window for writing code and another in which we can watch the result unfold step by step, instruction by instruction, as in the IDEs for traditional programming languages. That is the approach adopted by FontForge (see page 546). Other software, such as FontLab, page 520, or Visual TrueType, page 529, offers us the possibility of indicating certain operations in a graphical manner. The software will take our indications and turn them into a program of TrueType instructions. Here only a subset of the language's features is available to us, but often it is better to let the software instruct the font automatically, through what we call *autohinting*.

In this appendix, we shall attempt to refute the claim of Luc Devroye [116], who said that "If you are not a computer scientist with at least a B average from MIT, you can forget about understanding the TrueType specs." TrueType instructions have a reputation for being complex and incomprehensible; it is time to shatter that reputation and show that, while there is indeed a certain amount of complexity, there is also quite a bit of logic and common sense.

The main reason for the apparent complexity of TrueType instructions is the logic of assembly languages. In a third-generation programming language, such as C or Pascal, one writes commands (which have names) followed by their parameters. There are, of course, global variables; the commands have access to them, and thus the result of a command often depends as well on parameters other than those formally supplied; but that is something that we can avoid when programming as we should. And it does not cost a great deal of computational time to supply the same parameter three or four times to three consecutive commands.

In the language for TrueType instructions, we wish to avoid repetition. For instance, if two consecutive commands must operate on the same point, we prefer to keep that point in memory and write only the commands. That need gave rise to the concept of a *reference point*: being a reference point means that the given point will be used by several consecutive instructions. If the same point is used by several consecutive instructions, there will be fewer instructions to execute than if we were required to rewrite the point's number each time.

On the basis of this reflection, we turn *reference points* (there are three of them!) into a true method. Most instructions use reference points and assign new values to them. For example, when we write instructions, there is, behind the scenes, a ballet of reference points that is performed, without any evidence of it in the code. We have restored this ballet of reassignments of points in the *comments* to the samples of code presented a bit later in this appendix.

Let us consider a metaphor. When we learn to drive, we learn to pay attention to a relatively large amount of information at the same time (the vehicle's direction, its speed, the other vehicles, the rear-view mirror, the clutch, the pedestrians, the presence of any police officers, and so on). The same is true of TrueType instructions: to understand them, we must constantly keep in mind the current reference points, the current vectors, the stack and the storage area, the zones, etc.

We hope that this appendix will show the reader how all these elements interact and that it will reveal the full potential of TrueType instructions.

The primary bibliographic references are the specifications of Microsoft [258] and Apple [56], as well as a few introductory texts [102, 263, 59].

E.1   Basic Concepts

We shall briefly review the most important concepts of TrueType instruction: reference points, freedom and projection vectors, the interpreter's stack and the instruction stream, and a few less important concepts such as zones, the cut-in, etc.

E.1.1   Interpreter's Stack, Instruction Stream

Let us begin at the beginning. Just as in the PostScript language, there is a *stack* for the interpreter, on which the instructions place their arguments to be read by other instructions. But unlike the PostScript language, not everything is placed on this stack systematically. For, alongside the stack, there is also the *instruction stream*. The instructions themselves are thus not on the interpreter's stack; only the data generated by the commands are found there. But there are also hard-coded data in the font that appear in the instruction stream. There are instructions whose role is to retrieve values from the instruction stream and place them on the interpreter's stack.

We work on a plane containing a number of points: the starting points, control points, and ending points of the Bézier curves, which form the glyph's various contours, and which are given in the font's glyf table, before the section dedicated to TrueType instructions. In this table, we provide each point's coordinates and indicate whether the point lies *on* the curve or *off* it—i.e., whether it is a *control point*.

The task involves modifying the points' coordinates to adapt them to the grid of pixels being used. We can even convert a point on the curve into a control point and vice versa, but that is rather uncommon (and can have quite drastic consequences).

E.1.2   Reference Points

For reasons explained in the previous section, we have three *reference points*: rp_0, rp_1, rp_2. These points are used as parameters to the instructions. We say that "this instruction takes rp_0 and does that with it", etc. The instruction MIRP[ ], for example, retrieves two numbers from the interpreter's stack, but it also uses the point rp_0. After its execution, the points rp_1 and rp_2, and sometimes even rp_0, have different values. Thus we observe reassignments of values, carried out in the background, that have a decisive effect on the program's execution.

E.1.3   Freedom and Projection Vectors

Let us now discuss vectors. We *measure* and *modify* distances between points; to do so, we switch to *polar coordinates*: instead of saying that we "move this much horizontally and that much vertically", we say that we "move this much in a given direction", called the *freedom vector*. To measure distances, we proceed in the same way: we measure not the direct distance between two points but the distance between their projections onto an axis. The direction of that axis is the *projection vector*, which is not necessarily the same as the freedom vector.

These two vectors are used together. If I say "to go from p to p' I move point p a distance of d", that actually means "I move point p in the direction of the freedom vector as much as necessary for the projection of pp' onto the projection vector to be d". Of course, the two vectors cannot be orthogonal, else we would have infinite amounts—amounts that the computer, unlike mathematicians, does not appreciate.

Here are some useful techniques.

E.1.4   Table of Control Vectors and Storage Area

There are two ways of setting values aside for subsequent reuse: either storing them in the control value table (CVT), a data structure contained in the TrueType table cvt, or storing them in the *storage area*. The storage area is temporary, and its effect is limited to the current glyph, whereas the CVT is shared by all the glyphs in the font.

E.1.5   Touched and Untouched Points

We have the concepts of *touched* and *untouched* points. A "touched point" is a point whose position has been modified by an instruction. What is useful about untouched points is that there is a magical instruction that corrects their positions by performing interpolation on the positions of the touched points, as well as any necessary rounding. In other words, this instruction (named IUP[]) will restore the shape of a glyph that our instructions may have seriously altered. There is a way to "untouch" touched points so that they can be processed by IUP[].

E.1.6   Minimum Distance and Cut-In

Another interesting notion is that of *minimum distance*. It ensures us that between two points there will always be a space of at least 1 pixel, come what may. For example, in an 'o' there will always be a hole in the middle, no matter what the point size, because the hole is a property *sine qua non* of the letter (which would become an ordinary bullet without it). There is also an amount called the *cut-in*. It is a threshold below which two coordinates are equated at the pixel level. It resembles the blue values of PostScript and allows for establishing a certain degree of uniformity among the glyphs. At the same time, when the difference between two points exceeds that threshold, it can be taken to be a *relevant difference*—an aesthetic characteristic of the font. For example, a font that deliberately chooses to make the two downstrokes of the 'H' uneven in height, like the 'H' in the very funny font Garamouche of the P22 foundry, which claims to be the hypothetical work of an intoxicated Garamond, should have a cut-in less than the difference between the downstrokes, else the difference may be eliminated.

E.1.7   Twilight Zone and Zone Pointers

To create "temporary" points that will not ultimately effect the glyph's contour, we double our workspace: there will be a real workspace and one for scratch work. In TrueType jargon, these two workspaces are called *zones*. The "scratch" workspace is also called the "twilight zone", after the famous American science-fiction series by Rod Serling broadcast from 1959 to 1964 and from 1970 to 1973.

Let us make the situation a bit more complex. We have three numbers—zp_0, zp_1, zp_2—that are *zone pointers*. They take the value 0 or 1, depending on whether they point to the "real" zone or the "twilight" zone. The instructions will use one, two, or even three points: we say that the first point used is in zone zp_0 and that the first and second, if they occur, are in zones zp_1 and zp_2. For example, if we want the next instruction to take its third point from zone 1, we merely change the value of zp_2 to 1 just before executing the instruction. The principle is the same for reference points: in a high-level language, we would have said that the "zone number of the third point" is one of the function's parameters, given each time it is needed; here, we agree by convention that the instruction *always* takes its third point from zone zp_2, and before executing the instruction we set zp_2 to the correct value.

E.2 Instructions

The language for TrueType instructions is an assembly language; that is, a language very close to the processor (in this case, the processor for TrueType fonts). In this language, concepts such as strings do not exist: everything is done with numbers.

E.2.1 Instructions for Managing the Stack and Storage Area

The following instructions allow for managing the interpreter's stack:

- NPUSH[], PUSHB[], NPUSHW[] et PUSHW[] take several entries from the instruction stream and place them onto the interpreter's stack.

- DUP[] copies the element on the top of the stack.

- POP[] deletes it.

- CLEAR[] deletes the entire stack.

- SWAP[] exchanges the first two elements on the stack.

- DEPTH[] returns the depth of the stack.

- Both CINDEX[] and MINDEX[] retrieve a number n from the top of the stack and then copy (CINDEX[]) or move (MINDEX[]) the nth element on the stack to the top position.

- Finally, ROLL[] performs a cyclic permutation of the top three elements on the stack.

We have access to a number of places in the "storage area" (their exact number is given in the font's maxp table—more specifically, in the maxStorage entry of that table). The instruction RS[] retrieves the position number from the stack and returns the value stored at that position. The instruction WS[] retrieves a value and a position number: it places the value at the stated position. The storage area is temporary, and it lasts only as long as the glyph is being processed.

We have another way to store data: the CVT. The CVT contains all the relevant metric information for the font (height of the capitals and of the lowercase letters, thicknesses of characteristic strokes, etc.); but these data bear neither names nor comments. The author of the instructions must therefore know what corresponds to each entry in the CVT. The CVT is initialized by the processor when the font is loaded into memory, using the font's cvt table.

There is a basic difference between the CVT and the storage area: the storage area can hold any numeric values, whereas the CVT holds only measurements (heights, thicknesses, etc.). But there are two ways to view measurements: abstractly, through the use of abstract units based on the font's grid, and concretely, using pixels, according to the font's actual size and the resolution of the display device. The CVT *always gives us values in pixels*. For instance, the instruction RCVT[] takes a CVT entry number from the stack and returns the value of the corresponding entry, in pixels.

We can also *write* in the CVT. There are two instructions for doing so, according to the nature of the data that we wish to record: if the data is in abstract units, we use the instruction WCVTF[]; if it is in pixels, we use WCVTP[]. Both instructions take a value and a CVT entry number off the stack and write the value of the CVT entry in question.

E.2.2   *Managing Vectors, Zones, and Reference Points*

In this section, we shall concern ourselves with another category of instructions: those for setting up our working tools, i.e., the freedom vectors and projection vectors, the "real" and "twilight" zones, and the three reference points.

Let us begin with the two vectors. There are four ways to define them:

1. Using the stack: SFVFS[] and SPVFS[] retrieve two values, y and x, from the stack. These are the normalized coordinates of the freedom vector and the projection vector, respectively. Warning! These numbers are expressed in "$F_{2.14}$", which means 2 bits for the integer part and 14 bits for the decimal part; the coordinates must be *normalized*, which is to say that $\sqrt{x^2 + y^2} = 0\text{x}4000$, where 0x4000 is nothing but the number 1 written in "$F_{2.14}$".

2. Using two points on the plane. To do so, we use the instructions SFVTL[0] and SPVTL[0], which take two point numbers, a_1 and a_2, from the stack. The direction of the freedom vector or the projection vector, respectively, will be that of the vector connecting the points p_{a_1} and p_{a_2}.

   There are variants of these instructions: SFVTL[1] and SPVTL[1] define a *perpendicular* freedom vector or projection vector connecting the points p_{a_1} and p_{a_2}. It is as if the vector produced by SFVTL[0] or SPVTL[0] were rotated 90 degrees, in the trigonometric sense (counterclockwise).

3. Parallel to one axis of the system of coordinates: SFVTCA[0] and SPVTCA[0] make the freedom and projection vectors, respectively, point upwards (the y-axis); with SFVTCA[1] and SPVTCA[1], they point to the right (the x-axis).

4. With respect to each other: when the instruction SFVTPV[] is used, the freedom vector will take the direction of the projection vector. The inverse operation (which corresponds to the hypothetical instruction SPBTFV[]) does not exist.

The coordinates of the freedom and projection vectors are retrieved by means of the instructions GFV[] and GPV[]), respectively.

Finally, to change the values of the reference points rp_0, rp_1, and rp_2, we use the instructions SRP0[], SRP1[], and SRP2[]. These retrieve the number of a point from the stack and make it the new reference point. Likewise, the instructions SZP0[ ], SZP1[ ], and SZP2[ ] retrieve a zone number (0 for the "real" zone and 1 for the "twilight" zone) from the stack and consequently change the values of the zone pointers zp_0, zp_1, and zp_2. If you wish to give the same value to all three pointers at the same time (thus saving a few thousandths of a second in processing time), the instruction SZPS[ ] is made for you; it works just like the others.

E.2.3 Moving Points

We have reached the end of the line: moving points, be they points on the contour or control points. It is by *moving points* that we manage to adapt a contour to the grid of pixels.

Let us begin with the simple cases. We obtain the "coordinate" of a point by using the instruction GC[0], which retrieves the number of a point from the stack. The reader must be wondering which coordinate is meant by "the coordinate". After all, we are on a plane, and the points are defined by *pairs of coordinates*. Heavens, have we forgotten the *projection vector*? GC[0] gives us the value of the projection of the point in question onto the projection vector. In other words, if the projection vector is horizontal, that will be the abscissa; if it is vertical, we will obtain the ordinate; and so on.

Now suppose that several points have already been moved. The processor still keeps in memory the coordinates of the original points. We can obtain them through the use of a variant of GC[0], called GC[1].

How, then, do we *move* a point? A simple way is to use the instruction SCFS[ ]. It takes a distance *d* and the number of a point from the stack and moves the point in question by that distance. Once again, the reader who has not yet fully understood the logic of the True-Type instructions may be wondering: "moving a point—fine, but in which direction?" In the direction of the freedom vector, of course! That, incidentally, is why it is called the "freedom vector": because that is the only direction in which we are *free* to move the point. Can we then say that we move by *d* in the direction of the freedom vector? Not really, because if we say that, we forget about the other vector—the projection vector. What actually happens is that we move as much as is necessary (in the direction of the freedom vector) so that the projection of the move onto the projection vector will be equal to *d*.

The instruction MD[0] allows us to measure the "distance" between two points. It takes the numbers of two points from the stack and returns the distance between the points (along the projection vector) in pixels. The variant MD[1] of this instruction yields the distance between the original positions of the points—those given in the glyf table before the TrueType instructions were applied.

Mimicry is not always a praiseworthy attitude in life. But when we move points, it very often happens that we wish to move several of the points on the contour in the same way as the other points. For example, if we decide to move the lower left point of the downstroke of a letter 'I', we should move the upper right point similarly, or the left side of the downstroke will no longer be parallel with the right side.

There are three instructions—SHP[0], SHC[0], SHZ[0]—that move, respectively, a single point, all the points of a contour, and all the points in a zone by the same amount as reference point rp_2 was previously moved. These three instructions take the number of a point, a contour, or a zone, respectively, off the stack. The contour numbers are simply obtained from the order in which the contours are defined in the glyf table (counting from 0). The variants SHP[1], SHC[1], and SHZ[1] of these three instructions uses reference point rp_1 instead of rp_2.

Now, let us move on to the most complex and most useful instructions: MDAP[], MDRP[], MIAP[], and MIRP[]. These instructions move a point. In the case of the instructions whose names begin with "MD" ('D' for "direct"), the number of a point to be moved is retrieved from the stack. In the case of the instructions whose names begin with "MI" ('I' for "indirect"), the motion will be made with respect to a value in the CVT; thus first a CVT entry number is retrieved, and then the number of a point to be moved. Thus we have "direct" and "indirect" moves.

But there are also "absolute" moves (MDAP[], MIAP[]) and "relative" moves (MDRP[] and MIRP[]). In the former, we set the point at absolute coordinates, which are retrieved from either the stack or the CVT; in the latter, the move will be relative to reference point rp_0.

The instructions above are never used in isolation but are always accompanied by a set of flags: MIRP[10110], MDAP[1], etc. The meanings of these flags always depend on the instruction.

Let us examine all that more closely. The instruction MIRP[] ("indirect relative move") takes an entry number from the CVT and the number of a point from the stack. Suppose that the value of the entry in the CVT is d and that the point to be moved is p. The instruction will move p so that it stands at the distance d from reference point rp_0. So far there has been nothing especially complicated: we take a piece of relevant metric data (for example, the thickness of a stroke) from the CVT, we designate as reference point rp_0 a point of interest to us, and we move a second point so that its distance from the reference point is precisely the relevant metric datum that we retrieved.

Complications arise when we begin to enable the flags. When bit 2 is enabled,[1] the processor will apply the cut-in. That means that it will measure the distance between rp_0 and p, and then compare it with d; if the difference between the two is below a certain value, it will move the point so that the distance between rp_0 and p will be exactly d; otherwise, it *will not move* the point. This value is called the cut-in value; by default, it is equal to $\frac{17}{16}$ of a pixel, but its value can be changed at any time through the instruction SCVTCI[]. Next—and this is very important—the processor will round the position of p according to the current rounding method.

Let us review. If flag 2 is enabled, we are asking the processor to make a certain distance equal to a "relevant" value—a value general and important enough to be stored in the CVT. If our original distance is close enough to the relevant value, the processor will do so; otherwise it will completely ignore our request. But in any case, whether or not the distance has changed, it will round the point that we are moving. By rounding the pixel value of a point, we set the point on the edge of a pixel, *irrespective of the location of the contour relative to the grid of pixels*. In other words, the behavior of pixels that we obtain is independent of the vagaries of placing a glyph on the screen or on a printed page, and that is indeed the goal of the hinting process.

---

[1] TTX labels the flags from left to right; thus "bit 2", which in the usual binary notation (10110) is the third digit from the *right*, is in our case the third digit from the *left*. TTX made that decision; we cannot do anything about it.

If flag 1 is enabled, the principle of *minimum distance* applies. This principle states that the points in question (here, p and rp_0) must be distinct; in other words, the distance between them must be at least one pixel.

Finally, if flag 0 is enabled, then after the move, point p becomes the new reference point rp_0 and can therefore be reused in other operations of this kind. Thus we have series of MIRP[ ] instructions in which the point p of one instruction becomes the rp_0 of the following one—which is not surprising, as that means that the points are corrected in order, that the correction of one point depends on that of the previous point, and so on.

The instruction MIAP[ ] ("indirect absolute move") is similar to MIRP[ ], but in this case we do not use rp_0. We retrieve a piece of relevant data from the CVT table and place the point p at the corresponding coordinate. There is only one flag: MIAP[1] applies the cut-in and rounds the result; MIAP[0] does nothing.

The instruction MDRP[ ] ("direct relative move") is an instruction for "re-establishing correct distances". Specifically, a point p is moved so that its distance from the point rp_0 is the initial distance (before any moves) between p and rp_0. The method of cut-ins applies. In addition, if flag 2 of this instruction's parameter is enabled, the position of p is rounded. Flag 1 will enable the constraint of the maximum distance.

We see that the difference between "direct" and "indirect" moves lies in the fact that the first is a move according to a given value (which is retrieved from the CVT or the stack), whereas the second is merely a synchronization of moves: if rp_0 has moved from its initial position, then p will move in the same manner. In both cases, we go through a step involving a cut-in and rounding. The cut-in ensures that the equalization is intended and does not represent the loss of one of the letter's relevant characteristics: if the difference between the values before and after correction is less than the cut-in, there has been an error due to the pixel grid, and the correction is carried out; if the difference exceeds the cut-in, that difference is necessitated by the letter's shape and should be preserved (if it survives the subsequent step of rounding).

Only one instruction remains to be described: MDAP[ ]. It is a fine philosophical puzzle: if 'D' means that the amount of the move comes from the difference between the original contour and the modified contour, and if 'A' means that it is not a distance between two points on the contour but the coordinates of a single point, what can MDAP[ ] mean? Well, it is very simple: it does nothing at all. Even though there is an 'M' (for "move") in its name, MDAP[ ] does not move anything. If its only flag is enabled, this instruction will merely round point p.

Note that after the instructions MIRP[ ] and MDRP[ ], the point rp_1 will take the value of the previous rp_0 and the point p will become the new rp_2. If their flag 0 is enabled, then p will also become the new rp_0. In addition, following the instructions MIAP[ ] and MDAP[ ], the point p becomes the new rp_0 and the new rp_1. This is the "ballet" of reference points to which we alluded above.

We have two other ways to move points: *alignment* and *interpolation*.

Alignment involves *making the distance between two points zero*. Taken outside the context of the TrueType instructions, this phrase would have no meaning: everyone knows that two points located at a distance of zero are much more than merely aligned—they are identical! Alas, do not forget that we are in a context quite different from the Euclidean geometry that we learned at school. Remember that all distances are measured along the axis of projection; thus there may well be points whose distance from each other is zero but that are not identical: they need only lie on the same line perpendicular to the axis of projection. And "being on the same line" is synonymous with "being aligned".

The instruction ALIGNPTS[] does just that: it takes the numbers of two points from the stack and moves the corresponding points in such a way that their projections onto the projection vector are identical. Therefore they are aligned relative to a line perpendicular to the projection vector.

ALIGNRP[] goes a bit further: it aligns not only a pair of points but any number of points. Specifically, there is a variable for the graphics state, named *loop*. Its default value is 1, but it can be changed through the instruction SLOOP[]. What does it have to do with ALIGNRP[]? Well, the latter takes *loop* elements from the stack—the numbers of *loop* points to be aligned with rp_0. Thus we can align a heap of points with a single instruction. After this instruction has been executed, the variable *loop* is reset to its default value, namely 1.

The instruction ISECT[] moves a point p so that it falls at the intersection of two straight lines. It retrieves from the stack the four points that make up the two line segments, and then the point p. If the segments are parallel, the point p is placed at the center of mass of the parallelogram thus formed.

There is also an instruction for interpolation: IP[]. It takes a point p off the stack and moves it so that the ratio of its distances to reference points rp_1 and rp_2 is the same as in the original contour. In other words, if $d(p_a, p_b)$ is the distance between p_a and p_b, and if the prime mark denotes the initial positions, we are asking that $\frac{d(p,rp_1)}{d(p,rp_2)} = \frac{d(p',rp_1')}{d(p',rp_2')}$.

This instruction is very powerful because it allows us to recover the ratios between the initial distances (i.e., those before the instructions were executed) in a very simple way. For example, suppose that a point lies halfway between the edges of a letter's downstroke. We have just moved those edges, and we want the point in question to be moved so that it still lies halfway between them. If we take a projection vector perpendicular to the edges, then every point on one of the edges is projected onto the same point on the projection vector. Thus it suffices to take a point on each edge, make reference points rp_1 and rp_2, and then apply IP[] to the point in question. As if by magic, it will again appear in the middle of the downstroke.

And, speaking of magic, we have now come to the magical instructions IUP[0] and IUP[1]. They interpolate *all* the untouched points: IUP[0] performs horizontal interpolation and IUP[1] performs vertical interpolation. An *untouched point* is a point to which no instruction for movement has been applied. The usual approach is to proceed in three steps: first we move certain important points individually, and very carefully; then we use IP[] to interpolate some other, less important, points; at the end, we correct all the other points *en masse* with a single stroke of our magic wand, through the use of the IUP[] instructions.

What, then, shall we do if we also wish to interpolate a point that is unlucky enough to have been touched? For that purpose, there is the instruction UTP[], which will "untouch" a point.

Thus the IUP[] instructions allow us to rectify all the points in between the relevant points that we have so abundantly moved; they are among the most frequently used instructions, and the most spectacular.

E.2.4 δ Instructions

The pretty name of *δ instruction* comes from the fact that the letter 'δ' is often used for infinitesimal increments. We can consider δ-instructions as *exceptions to the rule*—the rule being all the moves performed by the instructions that we have seen up to this point. The reader may reply that the instructions in question are *already* exceptions to the rule, which is the glyph's regular contour. By modifying the contour to adapt it to the pixel grid, we have already created an "exception": an exceptional contour tailored to the present situation. True, but that contour, as exceptional as it may be, is nonetheless based on instructions *independent of the sizes of the glyphs*. The same instructions will be applied (with more or less success) whether the glyph is rendered at 5, 10, 15, or 50 pixels, whether on screen or on paper. We can only hope that the validity of the instructions for movement will ensure an ideal rendering at all sizes.

Unfortunately, that is not always the case. Sometimes we must make slight corrections that apply only to a specific size: those are *δ instructions*. There are two kinds of δ instructions: "DELTAP", which apply to points on the contour, and "DELTAC", which apply to entries in the CVT.

We use two variables for a graphics state (*delta_base* and *delta_shift*) to specify, with as much precision as possible, how large the correction should be and at which sizes it should be applied. Thus there are *two* quantitative data to supply to a δ instruction: the magnitude of the correction and the size at which it is applied.

The life of the TrueType instructor would be much easier if the δ instructions could simply retrieve these two pieces of data from the stack. Unfortunately, in order to make our code more compact, we are required to compress these two pieces of data into a single 8-bit number. This poor number must indicate *both* the exact size at which the correction is to be applied *and* the magnitude of the correction itself. The font's size (in pixels per em) may vary between, say, 5 and 250; the correction may be on the order of one-sixteenth of a pixel, or half a pixel. How can we pack all this information into a tiny byte, which will never have more than 8 bits?

We shall divide this famous byte right down the middle, into two nibbles. The first nibble is devoted to the font size to which the correction will be applied. A nibble contains 4 bits, and that corresponds to 16 numeric values; thus we have an interval of 16 consecutive sizes at our disposal. That is not very many. Through the use of three different instructions (DELTAP1[], DELTAP2[], DELTAP3[], and likewise for DELTAC1[], etc.), we can have three intervals of 16 sizes, which is to say one large interval of 48 consecutive sizes, which is more reasonable. Next, everything depends on the size at which we start counting: if we start counting from 5 pixels, we can cover all sizes between 5 and 52 pixels per em; if we start at 9, we will have the interval between 9 and 56 pixels per em; and so on. The minimum size is stored in the graphics state variable *delta_base*, whose value can be changed at any time with the instruction SDB[]. For instance, if we specify that *delta_base* has the value 5, DELTAP1[] will cover the sizes between 5 and 20, DELTAP2[] will cover those between 21 and 36, and DELTAP3[] will cover those between 37 and 52 pixels per em. That is our makeshift solution for font sizes. Conversely, if we know that we want size α, we first figure out in which interval it lies, according to the value of *delta_base*, and then we subtract from α the smallest value in that interval. Since each interval is of size 16, the difference will necessarily be less than 16; therefore, it can be encoded in one nibble.

Let us now move on to the magnitude of the correction. Here we have not whole values but fractions of a pixel. To get the greatest use out of the four little bits that we have on hand, we shall use another graphics state variable, called *delta_shift*. It indicates the precision in the form of a power of two. If *delta_shift* has the value 4, we will have a precision of $\frac{1}{2^4}$, i.e., one-sixteenth of a pixel. Accordingly, we distribute the possible values of our 4 bits according to the following table, which gives us the value of the numerator:

Value of the nibble	0	1	2	3	4	5	6	7	8	9	10	11	12	13	14	15
Numerator		-8	-7	-6	-5	-4	-3	-2	-1	1	2	3	4	5	6	7	8

where the denominator is 2 to the power *delta_shift*. We change the value of *delta_shift* with the instruction SDS[ ].

A practical example: we wish to move point 13 to the left by seven thirty-seconds of a pixel at the size of 17 pixels per em. Suppose that, for whatever reason, *delta_base* is equal to 5. Since $17 - 5 = 12$, we are in the scope of DELTAP1[ ], and the first nibble of our byte will have the value 12 (in binary, 1100). As for the magnitude, in order to work with thirty-seconds of a pixel, we must have *delta_shift* equal to 5. Since -8 thirty-seconds corresponds to 0000 and $+8$ corresponds to 1111, it follows that 7 corresponds to 1110. Taken together, these two nibbles form the byte 11001110, which is the number 206. There, then, is the argument to DELTAP1[ ]. And the requirement that the correction be made to the left can be handled very quickly: we merely set the freedom vector to point in that direction.

The example above works because we requested a correction of less than 8 times *delta_shift*. If we had wanted a correction of 31 thirty-seconds, for example, it would not have been possible. We would have had to approximate that fraction by a fraction whose numerator is less than 8: the best that TrueType could do for us would be $\frac{7}{8}$, with a *delta_shift* of 3. Thus the greater the correction, the lower its precision; that is what always happens when we are required to compress information into a fixed number of bits.

E.2.5   Tests and Logical and Arithmetic Functions

There is an "if/else/end" test structure, which works as follows: The IF[ ] instruction retrieves an entry from the stack. If the entry is nonzero, the test has the value true, and the following instructions will be executed. If the entry is zero, the interpreter proceeds to the next ELSE[ ] or EIF[ ] (= "end of test"). It then executes the instructions that follow.

To prevent some instructions from being executed, we can skip them with the instruction JMPR[ ] (from "jump relative"), which takes a number n from the stack and moves forward as many instructions in the instruction stream. We can also combine a test and a jump, with JROT[ ] ("jump relative if true") and JROF[ ] ("jump relative if false"), which take two numbers, b and n, from the stack and move forward n instructions if b is nonzero or zero, respectively.

There is a heap of logical and arithmetic functions. To describe them, let us suppose that the top two elements on the stack are a_1 and a_2:

- LT[ ] ("strictly less than") places 0 on the stack if $a_1 < a_2$ and 1 otherwise.

- LTEQ[ ] ("less than or equal") places 0 on the stack if $a_1 \leq a_2$ and 1 otherwise.

- GT[ ] and GTEQ[ ] are the "greater-than" counterparts of LT[ ] and LTEQ[ ].

- EQ[ ] and NEQ[ ] test for equality and inequality, respectively.

- EVEN[ ] and ODD[ ] test for evenness and oddness, respectively.

- AND[ ] and OR[ ] are the logical operations AND and OR.

- NOT[ ] is logical negation.

- ADD[ ], SUB[ ], MUL[ ], and DIV[ ] are the four arithmetic operations $a_1 + a_2, a_1 - a_2, a_1 a_2, \frac{a_1}{a_2}$. The calculations are performed on numbers in "$F_{26.6}$" format, i.e., 26 bits for the integer part and 6 bits for the decimal part.

- ABS[ ] is absolute value, and NEG[ ] changes the sign.

- FLOOR[ ] and CEILING[ ] round up and down, respectively.

- MAX[ ] and MIN[ ] return the larger and the smaller, respectively, of a_1 and a_2.

E.2.6   Definitions of Subroutines and New Instructions

In the tables cvt and fpgm of a TrueType font, we can define *subroutines* of instructions (which can subsequently be called by the code of any glyph) and even *new instructions*.

To define a block of code as a subroutine, we surround it with the instructions FDEF[ ] ("subroutine definition") and ENDF[ ] ("end of subroutine definition"). FDEF[ ] will take a number off the stack, which will be the number of the subroutine. To call the subroutine, we place that same number onto the stack and execute the instruction CALL[ ]. We can also use the instruction LOOPCALL[ ] ("iterative call to a subroutine"), which takes two numbers off the stack: the first is the subroutine's number, and the second is the number of times that we wish to execute the subroutine.

Each TrueType instruction is represented by a 1-byte number. To define a new instruction that will represent a certain block of code, we must find a number that does not correspond to any instruction. Then we place that number on the stack and surround the new instruction's block of code by the instructions IDEF[ ] ("instruction definition") and ENDF[ ].

The instruction IDEF[ ] was introduced to ensure upward compatibility for the anticipated addition of new instructions. Suppose that Microsoft and Apple decided to introduce a new instruction COFFEE[ ] that would turn a coffee maker on every time we wrote a certain glyph that represented a coffee bean. What would current processors do when they encountered this instruction? To keep them from crashing, we can give this instruction a phony definition by using IDEF: a processor that knows the real COFFEE[ ] instruction would skip the redefinition; other processors would apply the phony definition, and the problem would be solved.

But that has in fact never happened: in the 15 years that TrueType has existed, never once has a new instruction been introduced!

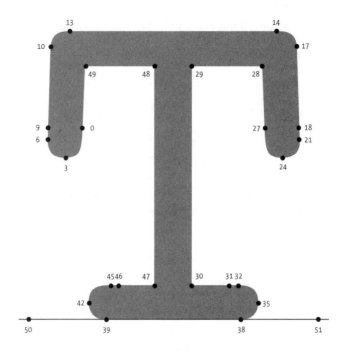

Figure E-1: The 'T' of the TrueType font Courier, by Apple/Bistream. The control points are not indicated.

E.3   Some Examples

Here are a few examples that will, the author hopes, show concretely how the instructions described in the previous section are used.

E.3.1   The 'T' in the Font Courier

Here we have the font *Courier* v. 4.0d2, which belongs to Apple and Bitstream and is part of the Mac OS X operating system. More precisely, it is the font "*Courier* with rounded caps", not to be confused with Adobe's *Courier* font, which is much lighter and has square terminals.

This letter has many points (52!) but few instructions, and those instructions are easy to understand. There are no δ instructions. Below we show the actual code, with no simplification or other changes.

In Figure E-1, the reader can see the letter whose instructions we shall examine. We have indicated the positions of the points that lie on the contour and those of the auxiliary points: the origin (50) and the ending point of the displacement vector (51).

Here are the letter's instructions, as represented by TTX. We have added in comments (C-style, not XML-style, as we are using assembly-language syntax) the numbers that the instructions retrieve from the stack and the values of the reference points rp_0, rp_1, and rp_2 that the instructions leave after their execution. This data turns out to be *indispensable* for understanding how the instructions work. Here is the complete code; below we shall examine it line by line:

```
<instructions><assembly>
    NPUSHB[ ]
    28 27 0 49 10 17 13 27 21 18 9 6 0 6 28 24 3
    48 28 185 13 228 45 30 196 38 39 45 47 42 32
    38 29 35 14 18 17 3 27 21 13 10 9 3 6 0 27 49
    21 72 35 71 29 0 49 6 72 29 15 42 71 47 50
    SRP0[ ]          /* 50.         rp0=50 */
    MDRP[10100]      /* 47.         rp0=47, rp1=50, rp2=47 */
    MIRP[00100]      /* 71, 42.     rp2=42 */
    MIRP[01100]      /* 15, 29.     rp2=29 */
    MIRP[10100]      /* 82, 6.      rp0=6, rp2=6 */
    MIRP[01100]      /* 49, 0.      rp1=6, rp2=0 */
    SRP0[ ]          /* 29.         rp0=29 */
    MIRP[00100]      /* 71, 35.     rp1=29, rp2=35 */
    MIRP[10100]      /* 72, 21.     rp0=21, rp2=21 */
    MIRP[01110]      /* 49, 27.     rp1=21, rp2=27 */
    SRP1[ ]          /* 0.          rp1=0 */
    SRP2[ ]          /* 6.          rp2=6 */
    SLOOP[ ]         /* 3 */
    IP[ ]            /* 13, 10, 9 */
    SRP1[ ]          /* 21.         rp1=21 */
    SRP2[ ]          /* 27.         rp2=27 */
    SLOOP[ ]         /* 3 */
    IP[ ]            /* 17, 18, 14 */
    SRP1[ ]          /* 35.         rp1=35 */
    SRP2[ ]          /* 29.         rp2=29 */
    IP[ ]            /* 38 */
    IP[ ]            /* 32 */
    SRP1[ ]          /* 42.         rp1=42 */
    SRP2[ ]          /* 47.         rp2=47 */
    IP[ ]            /* 45 */
    IP[ ]            /* 39 */
    IUP[1]
    SVTCA[0]
    MDAP[1]          /* 38.         rp0=38, rp1=38 */
    MIRP[01110]      /* 196, 30. rp1=38, rp2=30 */
    SHP[0]           /* 45 */
    MIRP[11110]      /* 228, 13. rp0=13, rp2=13 */
    MIRP[01110]      /* 185, 28. rp1=13, rp2=28 */
    SHP[0]           /* 48 */
    MDRP[00110]      /* 3.          rp2=3 */
    SHP[0]           /* 24 */
    SRP1[ ]          /* 28.         rp1=28 */
    SLOOP[ ]         /* 6 */
    IP[ ]            /* 0, 6, 9, 18, 21, 27 */
    SRP2[ ]          /* 13.         rp2=13 */
```

```
    IP[ ]           /* 17 */
    IP[ ]           /* 10 */
    IUP[0]
</assembly></instructions>
```

How many numbers can a human (the reader, the author, anyone else) retain in memory? Two dozen? At the beginning of the code, we ask the processor to retain 63 numbers in memory (!), through the use of the instruction NPUSHB[]:

```
NPUSHB[ ]
28 27 0 49 10 17 13 27 21 18 9 6 0 6 28 24 3
48 28 185 13 228 45 30 196 38 39 45 47 42 32
38 29 35 14 18 17 3 27 21 13 10 9 3 6 0 27 49
21 72 35 71 29 0 49 6 72 29 15 42 71 47 50
```

This clearly shows that the code was not written to be read by a human. Never mind: writing the numbers retrieved by each instruction at the side makes the code perfectly legible, however many instructions were placed on the stack at the start of the program.

The code that follows can be divided into two parts: the first concerns horizontal modifications to the contour; it ends with the instruction IUP[1], which is a global interpolation in the horizontal direction. The second part deals with vertical modifications and ends with IUP[0].

Let us begin at the beginning. After NPUSHB[] and the 63 numbers placed on the interpreter's stack, the code continues with an SRP0[]:

```
    SRP0[ ]         /* 50.      rp0=50 */
```

which takes the number 50 off the stack. This instruction sets auxiliary point 50 (the glyph's origin) as reference point rp_0.

Next come the instructions to move the point. The first instruction is an MDRP[]:

```
    MDRP[10100]   /* 47.      rp0=47, rp1=50, rp2=47 */
```

i.e., a *direct* move. It applies to point 47, which appears on the left edge of the main downstroke. Recall that the purpose of this instruction is to restore the original distance between reference point rp_0 (currently 50) and the point in question, and then to round the point. Here there is nothing to restore (since neither 50 nor 47 has been modified); thus we merely round the position of point 47 and set it at the edge of a pixel. When we have also applied this correction to point 48, which also lies on the left edge of the downstroke, this stroke will have the same thickness as all the other downstrokes of letters in the font. Note that after this instruction, point 50 becomes rp_1 and point 47 becomes rp_2. Since its first bit is enabled, point 47 becomes the new rp_0, and therefore we shall use that point as we continue to "correct" other points.

Next, we address the lower left serif. We have an MIRP[] instruction:

```
    MIRP[00100]   /* 71, 42.  rp2=42 */
```

which takes the numbers 71 and 42 off the stack; it will therefore use CVT number 71 (whose value is 266, as seen in the cvt table) and point 42. What about MIRP[], which is an instruction for *indirect* movement? It will cause the distance between point 42 (which in our case is the end of the serif) and reference point rp_0 (point 47: the left edge of the main downstroke) to be equal to entry 71 in the CV.

We have just solved one of the font's mysteries: the role of entry 71 in its CVT! This entry, whose value is 266, is the width of a horizontal serif. There is a very good chance that the letters 'Y' and 'I' use the same CVT entry. The reader must now be feeling the same shivers that Einstein felt when he discovered the laws of general relativity—perhaps on a smaller scale, but, after all, everything is relative.

As it exits the stage, this instruction leaves us in the following situation: point 47 has become rp_1 and point 42 has become rp_2. Since flag 0 of the latter instruction is disabled, the point rp_0 has not changed, and therefore is still 47—i.e., the left edge of the main downstroke. The MIRP[] instruction that comes next:

```
MIRP[01100]   /* 15, 29.  rp2=29 */
```

takes CVT entry number 15 and point 29 off the stack. Point 29 is on the right edge of the downstroke! Conclusion: though you would never have guessed, CVT entry 15 (whose value is 156) contains the font's *stroke thickness*. It is not surprising that that value is one of the first in the CVT (which has 328 values in all): for an "Egyptian" font—one whose stroke width is constant—it is of capital importance!

The last MIRP[] had bit 0 disabled; therefore, the point rp_0 still has not changed. What else can we correct with our celebrated point 47? We have already corrected the length of the serif and the thickness of the downstroke. What remains? Well, the horizontal bar of the letter 'T'! It is still an important property because without a horizontal bar there can be no letter 'T'; even Ernestine (the author's elder daughter) knew that already at the age of five. Next comes an MIRP[] instruction:

```
MIRP[10100]   /* 82, 6.   rp0=6, rp2=6 */
```

which will use CVT entry 82 and point 6: the left edge of the letter. Well, 82 is not far from 71, but it is quite far from 15; thus we might reasonably assume that these CVT entries are specific to the letter 'T'. They are for correcting the distance the left edge of the downstroke and the letter's left side. Surprise: this MIRP[] instruction has its bit 0 enabled! Point 6 therefore becomes the new reference point rp_0.

Why? Because the left side of the letter is also the left edge of the left vertical serif. And now we must make sure that the thickness of this serif is correct. We shall try to correct the position of point 0 by using point 6: indeed, the following MIRP[] instruction:

```
MIRP[01100]   /* 49, 0.   rp1=6, rp2=0 */
```

makes use of point 0 and a CVT entry—this time, entry 49 (whose value is 141).

The astute reader must be wondering why we should use a CVT entry other than 15. Have we not said that 15 contains the stroke's thickness? Answer: yes, 15 contains the stroke's thickness, but who said that the stroke thickness of an "Egyptian" font is always *exactly* the same? And what about artistic license? Here, then, is the inside scoop on the font in question: just as Marilyn was not a true blonde, this font is not a true "Egyptian"!

After this instruction, an SRP0[ ]:

```
SRP0[ ]        /* 29.        rp0=29 */
```

forces us to change our reference point: our new rp_0 is the point 29—i.e., the right edge of the main downstroke. Up to now we have been handling the left side, but now we are moving over to the right. Fortunately, everything is symmetric. The three instructions that follow:

```
MIRP[00100]    /* 71, 35.   rp1=29, rp2=35 */
MIRP[10100]    /* 72, 21.   rp0=21, rp2=21 */
MIRP[01110]    /* 49, 27.   rp1=21, rp2=27 */
```

are MIRP[ ] instructions applied to the points 35 (the right edge of the serif, with CVT entry 71, as we just saw), 21 (the right side of the letter, CVT entry 72), and 27 (the left edge of the right serif, CVT entry 49 for the distance between 21 and 27). Since points 35, 21, and 27 are the symmetric counterparts of points 42, 6, and 0, there is nothing surprising: we use the same CVT entries as before.

We have finished our "relevant" corrections; now we need to modify all the other points to match. What does that mean, exactly? Well, the entire upper left part of the letter must be modified according to the corrections made to 0 and 6. The entire upper right part must be modified according to the changes made to 21 and 27. What are the points on the upper left part? There are, for example, 9, 10, and 13. We shall use the instruction IP[ ], applied to these three points, to perform interpolation:

```
SRP1[ ]        /* 0.         rp1=0 */
SRP2[ ]        /* 6.         rp2=6 */
SLOOP[ ]       /* 3 */
IP[ ]          /* 13, 10, 9 */
```

The first two (SRP1[ ] and SRP2[ ]) change points 0 and 6 to rp_1 and rp_2. Next, SLOOP[ ] takes the number 3 off the stack and assigns that value to the variable *loop*. That variable is used by IP[ ], which takes three points off the stack: the points 13, 10, and 9. The effect of an IP[ ] instruction is to correct the positions of the points that we supply to it, with respect to two reference points rp_1 and rp_2: thus we have just corrected points 13, 10, and 9. The four lines of code that follow:

```
SRP1[ ]        /* 21.        rp1=21 */
SRP2[ ]        /* 27.        rp2=27 */
SLOOP[ ]       /* 3 */
IP[ ]          /* 17, 18, 14 */
```

do the same for the points 17, 18, and 14 (rp_1 being 21 and rp_2 being 27).

Next, we deal with the serif:

```
SRP1[ ]      /* 35.      rp1=35 */
SRP2[ ]      /* 29.      rp2=29 */
IP[ ]        /* 38 */
IP[ ]        /* 32 */
```

Points 35 and 29 become, respectively, rp_1 and rp_2. We first interpolate point 38 (through the first instruction IP[ ], which interpolates only a single point, since *loop* has become equal to 1 again) and then point 32 (through the second IP[ ] instruction).

The reader must be wondering why we use repeated IP[ ] instructions rather than a single instruction that interpolates *loop* points all at once. The answer is simple: we wish to interpolate two points, and therefore we must place 2 onto the stack, perform an SLOOP[ ], and then perform an IP[ ]—that makes *three* operations, whereas performing an IP[ ] and then another IP[ ] makes only *two* operations. Thus we have saved a whole microsecond of processing time!

We have just processed the right side of the horizontal serif; now let us do the same for the left side:

```
SRP1[ ]      /* 42.      rp1=42 */
SRP2[ ]      /* 47.      rp2=47 */
IP[ ]        /* 45 */
IP[ ]        /* 39 */
```

Points 42 and 47 become rp_1 and rp_2, and then we interpolate points 45 and 39.

There are a few other points that have not been corrected: in particular, all the control points, which have not even been indicated in Figure E-1. We shall correct *all* these points with the magical instruction IUP[1]:

```
IUP[1]
```

which performs horizontal interpolation for everyone, or at least for the points that have been "touched". And that concludes the horizontal corrections to this letter.

The next instruction:

```
SVTCA[0]
```

makes the two vectors vertical. Henceforth we shall think "vertically".

The vertical corrections follow the same schema: an MDAP[ ]:

```
MDAP[1]      /* 38.      rp0=38, rp1=38 */
```

makes absolute corrections to the position of point 38, which is the bottom of the letter. Next:

```
MIRP[01110]  /* 196, 30. rp1=38, rp2=30 */
```

point 30 is corrected relative to 30, through the use of CVT entry 196 (whose value is 141, which is indeed the same as 49, the thickness of the vertical serif). Thus we have corrected the lower serif. Next, with 30 as our reference point rp_2, we execute an SHP[0] instruction:

```
SHP[0]        /* 45 */
```

applied to point 45. That means that we move the point in question as much as reference point rp_2 was moved.

That move was necessary because when we corrected the distance between points 38 and 30, we corrected only the right side of the serif. By requiring that 45 do the same as 30, we maintain the thickness of the serif and the vertical downstroke.

Next comes an MIRP[ ]:

```
MIRP[11110]  /* 228, 13. rp0=13, rp2=13 */
```

which uses CVT entry 228 (value: 1,186) and is applied to point 13. This point lies on the letter's top edge; the current point rp_0 is 38, which is at the bottom of the letter. One would never have guessed, but CVT entry 228 contains the *height of the capital letters*, at least those that have no overshoot. Furthermore, by looking at the bounding boxes of the capital letters, we can see that most of them are of height 1,186. The last MIRP[ ] therefore corrects the letter's height; we can say that it is the equivalent of a *blue zone* in the hints of PostScript Type 1 fonts.

Since the last MIRP[ ] has its flag 0 enabled, reference point rp_0 changes and becomes point 13. Next comes another MIRP[ ]:

```
MIRP[01110]  /* 185, 28. rp1=13, rp2=28 */
```

which will correct point 28 (the lower edge of the horizontal bar) relative to the top of the letter. Then an SHP[0]:

```
SHP[0]        /* 48 */
```

will apply the same correction as for the last rp_2 (which was 28) to point 48, which is also on the lower edge of the horizontal bar, but at the other end of the downstroke. Thus we obtain an optimal horizontal bar.

Now we handle the vertical serifs. The MDRP[ ] that comes next:

```
MDRP[00110]  /* 3.        rp2=3 */
```

requests that the point 3 that appears at the end of the left serif be corrected in the same way as the current point rp_0, which is 13: the upper edge of the horizontal bar. Next follows an SHP[0]:

```
SHP[0]        /* 24 */
```

which applies the same correction to point 24, on the end of the other serif. That concludes the correction of the serifs.

We have now handled all the "relevant" points as well as we can. Now is the time to perform interpolation, and we shall do so in a big way: six (!) points will be interpolated at one stroke. They are the points 0, 6, 9, 18, 21, and 27. These points form the top parts of the serifs. They shall be interpolated relative to the current points rp_1 and rp_2, which are 28 (the lower part of the horizontal bar) and 3 (the end of the vertical serif):

```
SRP1[ ]      /* 28.      rp1=28 */
SLOOP[ ]     /* 6 */
IP[ ]        /* 0, 6, 9, 18, 21, 27 */
```

Finally, we also interpolate points 10 and 17 relative to 28 and 13:

```
SRP2[        /* 13.      rp2=13 */
IP[ ]        /* 17 */
IP[ ]        /* 10 */
```

i.e., relative to the two edges of the horizontal bar. And we are ready to launch the great magical instruction IUP[0]:

```
IUP[0]
```

which will interpolate everything—at least all the points that have not been "touched". And that concludes the program for this glyph's instructions.

We have seen that the strategy adopted in this example is as logical as it is natural: we correct the positions of the points by starting with the most important ones; we proceed by basing the correction of each point on that of another point that has already been corrected; when we correct the most relevant points, we make some local interpolations to correct other, less important, points, that appear in the same context; finally, when all of the smart operations have been completed, we run one great big massive interpolation to correct all of the points that have not been corrected with ready-made instructions.

E.3.2 The 'O' from the Font Verdana

We have examined a letter from a font by Apple/Bitstream; now let us look at a font by Microsoft: *Verdana*, a font that is part of Windows XP and that was specifically designed for display on screen.

The instructions for this letter are few:

```
<instructions><assembly>
  NPUSHB[ ]
    4 0 4 6 11 12 11 18 23 0 23 6 25 12 25
    18 87 1 87 5 83 7 95 11 88 13 88 17 95
    19 83 23 16 118 9 121 21 2 27 52 21 2
```

```
33 52 9 10 24 21 3 115 37 15 37 1 15 37
31 37 63 37 3 30 21 15 104 36
SRP0[ ]        /* 36.            rp0=36 */
MIRP[10110]    /* 104, 15.       rp0=15, rp1=36, rp2=15 */
MIRP[01101]    /* 21, 30.        rp1=15, rp2=30 */
DELTAP1[ ]     /* 3, 37, 63, 37, 31, 37, 15 */
DELTAP1[ ]     /* 1, 37, 15 */
SRP0[ ]        /* 37.            rp0=37 */
MIRP[10110]    /* 115, 3.        rp0=3, rp1=37, rp2=3 */
MIRP[01101]    /* 21, 24.        rp1=3, rp2=24 */
SVTCA[0]
MIAP[1]        /* 10, 9.         rp0=9, rp1=9 */
MIRP[01101]    /* 52, 33.        rp1=9, rp2=33 */
MIAP[1]        /* 2, 21          rp0=21, rp1=21 */
MIRP[01101]    /* 52, 27         rp1=21, rp2=27 */
DELTAP1[ ]     /* 2, 21, 121, 9, 118 */
IUP[1]
IUP[0]
SVTCA[1]
DELTAP1[ ]    /* 16, 23, 83, 19, 95, 17, 88, 13, 88,
                  11, 95, 7, 83, 5, 87, 1, 87, 18, 25,
                  12, 25, 6, 23, 0, 23, 18, 11, 12, 11,
                  6, 4, 0, 4 */
</assembly></instructions>
```

Yet they are quite efficient. As we see above, a few δ instructions appear among them.

Let us begin at the beginning. In Figure E-2, the reader can see the glyph that we shall examine. Let us point out, in passing, the interesting optical illusion that can be seen on the contour: we have the impression that points 28 and 26 are slightly higher than point 27, yet they are in fact perfectly aligned! The same is true of the points 32-33-34, and vertically for 29-30-31 and 35-24-25.

First of all, we shall place 66 numbers on the interpreter's stack:

```
NPUSHB[ ]
4 0 4 6 11 12 11 18 23 0 23 6 25 12 25
18 87 1 87 5 83 7 95 11 88 13 88 17 95
19 83 23 16 118 9 121 21 2 27 52 21 2
33 52 9 10 24 21 3 115 37 15 37 1 15 37
31 37 63 37 3 30 21 15 104 36
```

Next, after the instruction:

```
SRP0[ ]        /* 36.            rp0=36 */
```

our first reference point, rp_0, becomes the point 36. It is the first auxiliary point and therefore the origin of the glyph. Next comes an MIRP[ ] instruction:

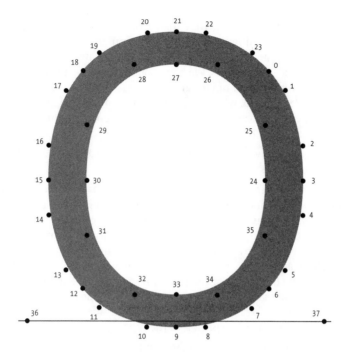

Figure E-2: The 'O' from the TrueType font Verdana, by Microsoft.

```
MIRP[10110]   /* 104, 15.       rp0=15, rp1=36, rp2=15 */
```

which for is CVT entry number 104 and point 15. The value of the CVT entry is 115; point 15 is at the left boundary of the glyph. Thus we place that boundary at the edge of a pixel.

Since this instruction's bit 0 is enabled, reference point rp_0 changes and becomes point 15.

Next comes another MIRP[]:

```
MIRP[01101]   /* 21, 30.       rp1=15, rp2=30 */
```

This time it is for point 30, which lies exactly opposite point 15, on the other side of the stroke. The value of the CVT entry in question (entry 21) is 206. Thus it represents the thickness of the stroke.

After these two MIRP[] instructions, we have corrected the left side of the letter. That does not leave us with a beautiful letter 'O', but it is a good start.

Before continuing, we have two δ instructions for special cases:

```
DELTAP1[ ]    /* 3, 37, 63, 37, 31, 37, 15 */
DELTAP1[ ]    /* 1, 37, 15 */
```

The first is a DELTAP1[]; therefore, it pertains to the range of sizes between 9 (the current value of *delta_base*) and 25 points.

We can see that the three applications of the δ instruction affect the same point: point 37. That is not just any point: it is the ending point of the displacement vector. Thus we are correcting its position in three different cases, which correspond to the attribute values 63, 31, and 15. Let us proceed to "decode" these values. We have not changed the default value of *delta_shift*; thus it is still 3. These numbers in binary are 00111111, 00011111, and 00001111. Thus the lower nibbles are still 1111, or 15, which is the maximum magnitude for this *delta_shift*: $\frac{8}{8}$ of a pixel. The three upper nibbles are 0011 (3), 0001 (1), and 0000 (0); thus we are applying this modification to the sizes of 9, 10, and 12 pixels per em.

Apparently this δ correction was not enough for size 9, as we apply a second δ instruction to the same point, 37, for a new move of $\frac{8}{8}$ of a pixel.

The reader must be wondering why we are going to such pains to correct the position of point 37 when that point is not on the contour and no pixel is found there. Apart from the fact that the correction allows us to modify the glyph's width according to its size, the question is answered in part by the subsequent instructions: specifically, we are now adjusting the right side of the glyph, and we start by making this famous point 37 our reference point rp_0. By starting on the right to adjust the right side of our glyph, we mirror, in a way, the operations that we carried out at the beginning of the program to correct the left side of the glyph. The only difference: for the left side, we left point 36 where it was (the instruction SRP[] does nothing but a rounding operation), whereas on the right side we are applying several δ instructions to "configure" point 37 according to the type size.

Next, we correct the position of point 3 (the rightmost limit of our contour) relative to point 37 by performing:

```
SRP0[ ]     /* 37.          rp0=37 */
MIRP[10110] /* 115, 3.      rp0=3, rp1=37, rp2=3 */
```

The CVT entry used is 115 (value 114, thus one unit less than the left side). Once we have corrected this point, which appears at the right edge of the stroke, we expect to correct the left edge as well.

And we do indeed. Since reference point rp_0 has been set to point 3, which we have just corrected, we now have an MIRP[]:

```
MIRP[01101] /* 21, 24.      rp1=3, rp2=24 */
```

applied to point 24. This point appears right across from point 3. No surprises with regard to the CVT entry chosen: it is entry 24, the same one used for the pair of points 15, 30. That confirms our assumption that entry 24 contains the *stroke thickness* for this type of letter.

After that instruction, an SVTCA[0]:

```
SVTCA[0]
```

switches to the vertical mode. Let us mention that Apple, in the previous example, first interpolated all the untouched points before switching to vertical mode. Microsoft has chosen to do so afterwards.

The MIAP[] instruction:

```
MIAP[1]       /* 10, 9.        rp0=9, rp1=9 */
```

places a point at a coordinate given by the CVT entry. Here it is point 9, which is the lowest point on the glyph, and the CVT entry in question is 10 (value: -31). The conclusion is easy: entry 10 of the CVT is nothing but the overhang of this font, or at least the overhang used by some glyphs in the font (the lowercase letters may have a smaller overhang). Thus we round this position by possibly applying the cut-in.

The reader must have guessed what comes next: we shall correct the stroke's thickness by addressing point 33.

That is indeed right. The MIRP[ ] instruction that follows:

```
MIRP[01101]  /* 52, 33.       rp1=9, rp2=33 */
```

corrects the (vertical) position of this point by using CVT entry number 52. Surprise! this CVT entry has the value 171, which is noticeably smaller than the one that we used for the "horizontal" thickness of the stroke. Thus we have just discovered a subtlety of the font: *near the horizontal tangent, the curves are 15 percent thinner than near the vertical tangent.*

Next we address the upper part of the letter. In the horizontal case, we first handled the left side and then corrected auxiliary point 37 to continue from right to left and correct the right side.

Here the situation is different: the height of our letter is "standard", since it is simply the *height of the uppercase letters with overshoot.* Thus we shall act as if the lower part of the letter did not exist, and go on to point 21 (the top of the letter) with an MIAP[ ] instruction:

```
MIAP[1]       /* 2, 21         rp0=21, rp1=21 */
```

using CVT table entry number 2 (value: 1,520). The fact that it is the *second* entry in the CVT table shows the importance and general application of this value.

Finally—no surprise—an MIRP[ ]:

```
MIRP[01101]  /* 52, 27         rp1=21, rp2=27 */
```

moves us from point 21 to point 27 through CVT entry 52, the same one that we used in the lower part of the letter.

Nonetheless, there is a δ instruction:

```
DELTAP1[ ]    /* 2, 21, 121, 9, 118 */
```

It applies to points 21 and 9 (the boundaries of the letter). The attributes are 121 (01111001) and 118 (01110110). The lower nibbles are 1001 (9) and 0110 (6); thus the corrections are small ones of $\frac{2}{8}$ and $-\frac{2}{8}$, which is to say a quarter of a pixel upwards for point 21 and the same amount downwards for point 9. These corrections are applied to the same size: 16 pixels per em.

Now that we have finished the most important changes, the time has come to play "Harry Potter" and launch our two magical instructions:

```
IUP[1]
IUP[0]
```

which will interpolate all the points that we have not yet mentioned.

That could have been the last of the instructions. But it seems that there are still some other horizontal δ corrections to perform. Thus we switch to horizontal mode with:

```
SVTCA[1]
```

and issue no fewer than 16 (!) δ instructions:

```
DELTAP1[ ]    /* 16, 23, 83, 19, 95, 17, 88, 13, 88,
                 11, 95, 7, 83, 5, 87, 1, 87, 18, 25,
                 12, 25, 6, 23, 0, 23, 18, 11, 12, 11,
                 6, 4, 0, 4 */
```

applied to points 23, 19, 17, 13, 11, 7, 5, 1 (which are the control points for the slanted external tangents) and 18, 12, 6, 0 (which are the points on the curve for the same tangents). The corrections that we have requested take the values 83 ($-\frac{5}{8}$ of a pixel, size 14), 95 (1 pixel, size 14), 88 ($\frac{1}{8}$ of a pixel, size 14), 87 ($\frac{7}{8}$ of a pixel, size 14), 25 ($\frac{2}{8}$ of a pixel, size 10), 23 ($-\frac{1}{8}$ of a pixel, size 10), 11 ($\frac{4}{8}$ of a pixel, size 9), 4 ($-\frac{4}{8}$ of a pixel, size 9). In other words, the corrections to the control points apply only to size 14, whereas the corrections to the points on the curve apply to sizes 10 and 9.

We can also understand why we waited until the end to make these corrections: it is because all these points are "untouched" points, and only after global interpolation instructions have been used do they assume their definite positions. A δ correction is a precise, localized operation; to interpolate a point *after* performing the δ correction would be in contradiction to the precision and specificity of this operation.

METAFONT *and Its Derivatives*

Donald Knuth is an incurable perfectionist. He considered the issue of fonts when he decided to create a programming language for typesetting his books on programming. While he was at it, he decided to resolve the question of fonts once and for all by creating the ultimate programming language for creating all possible and imaginable fonts in the same logical, efficient way.

That was 1979. The programming language in question is METAFONT. In 1983, a second version of the software was released to improve the language. That is the version that we use today.

In the same year, 1983, John Warnock of Adobe was working on the PostScript language. That language was the ideal complement to TeX, since a DVI file produced by TeX could then be very profitably converted to PostScript. But the PostScript language, and even more the PDF format, signed the death warrant for METAFONT, at least in its current form.

Knuth's philosophy was to say that the rendering of glyphs was best handled by the central processing unit, since it could interpret the METAFONT language and construct perfect glyphs according to as many parameters as necessary. Having multiple printers is no problem: we merely tell METAFONT which printer we wish to use, and it applies the correct parameters. PostScript's philosophy is different: according to PostScript, the printer should have a rendering engine intelligent enough to render any glyph according to the parameters provided. We send the printer some contours, and it fills them with pixels.

Each approach has its advantages and disadvantages. We saw those of PostScript in Appendix C, where we discussed that language. Let us now examine those of METAFONT.

METAFONT is extremely powerful for describing glyphs and even for describing their rendering. METAFONT does not work with contours, since glyphs have a certain dynamic that completely defies description by contours. For example, consider the ampersand, (&): it consists of a single stroke that goes down, up, and down again. Described in this way, the glyph has a visual logic, and that logic can be used for its optical correction (i.e., its adaptation to different optical sizes), its adaptation to the characteristics of the printer or the screen, and even to its rasterization. The same glyph described by a PostScript contour no longer has any dynamics: the contour does not even know that the strokes *cross*; thus it cannot tell that the strokes on the two sides of an intersection must match up graphically. It is for such reasons that there has never been a satisfactory way to create dynamic glyphs in PostScript.

The disadvantages of METAFONT are practical in nature. METAFONT must come between the "abstract document" and the output device. But that goes against the principle of *electronic documents*. An electronic document downloaded from the Web must be suitable for printing anywhere, which means that METAFONT would have to be installed on every machine, that fonts written in METAFONT (thus readily susceptible to piracy) would have to accompany the document, and that the user would have to have a perfect knowledge of the technical characteristics of his printer in order to share them with METAFONT. Not to mention that the designer of METAFONT fonts would have to handle all possible and conceivable cases of printers and screens in her code. Of course, if the industry had given METAFONT a slightly warmer reception, we could imagine printers equipped with compilers for the language, and also a form of PostScript that would incorporate METAFONT code to send it to the printer. We could imagine Acrobat with a built-in METAFONT rendering engine that would perform the rendering in real time. But that is nothing but fiction: the industry did not welcome META-FONT and did not deliver any support for it.

Nonetheless, we present METAFONT in this book, albeit only in the appendix, because there is still a glimmer of hope. In the past few years, several attempts to "revive" this marvelous language have come to light. METATYPE1 is a project that uses a language similar to METAFONT to create PostScript Type 1 fonts, and METATYPE is another whose purpose is to produce TrueType fonts. Thus we can consider not the METAFONT software but the METAFONT *programming language* as a tool for "contemporary" font design. The possibilities of METAFONT as a programming language go far beyond those of other font-design software. Only one thing is missing: an interactive approach. But there is a good chance that the coming years will bring us an interactive font editor that would work as a front end to the METAFONT language. Stay tuned!

In the following text, the reader will find a very brief description of the language, based on the personal experience of the author, who made his debut in the TeX community in the late 1980s by designing Gothic, Arabic, Hebrew, Greek, and other fonts, always in METAFONT.

F.1   The METAFONT *Programming Language*

F.1.1   *Basic Concepts*

There is a fundamental peculiarity of the METAFONT language that distinguishes it from all other languages for graphical description: it takes *initiatives*. More precisely, METAFONT has an inherent notion of "beauty", and if we give it enough room for maneuver, it will draw curves that it considers "beautiful".

Let us take an example. Suppose that we have a line segment *AB* and that we ask a graphic artist to draw a curve from point *A*, with a tangent perpendicular to the segment, that ends at point *B*, once again perpendicularly to the segment. In the absence of other information, what will he draw? We have no idea. But we know what METAFONT will do: it will draw a *semicircle of diameter AB*. Any other language for graphical description, such as PostScript or SVG or CGM, would have stopped and made the ironic and condescending remark "insufficient data", worthy of the famous "Illogical, Captain!" that the noted Vulcan frequently uttered to the helpless human Captain Kirk. But since Kirk always won in the end, thanks to his human qualities and despite his illogicality, METRFONT always manages to draw "beautiful" curves, despite the lack of data supplied by its human operator.

We have just said "despite the lack of data". We could go further: most of the time it is "thanks to the lack of data". Indeed, the author has often noticed that supplying fewer data to METR-FONT produces a more beautiful curve.

But how does METRFONT conceive of "beauty"?

In his article "Mathematical Typography" [215], drawn from a presentation of January 4, 1978, Knuth defined the notion of the *most pleasing curve*, abbreviated "MPC". After a description of the mathematical models of letters created by Dürer, Tory, Pacioli, Jaugeon, etc., he gives six principles for the MPC that passes through *n* given points: *invariance* (if the points of an MPC are rotated or translated, we obtain another MPC), *symmetry* (a cyclic permutation of the points does not change the result), *extensibility* (if we add a new point that is already on the MPC, the new curve is an MPC identical to the previous one), *locality* (the curve between two points z_i and z_{i+3} depends only on the four points $z_i, \ldots, z_{i+3}$), and *roundness* (if four given points are consecutive points on a circle, then the MPC is that circle). He then shows that these conditions cannot all be respected at the same time but that we can work reasonably well by sacrificing one principle, and the principle that he chose to sacrifice was extensibility. In other words, if, starting with an MPC, we add a point that is already on the curve, the new MPC may not be the same.

It was his thesis student, John Hobby [177], who put this theory into practice, using cubic Bézier curves (see Appendix G). Thus whenever we ask METRFONT to draw a curve, it always starts out as an MPC. But, of course, we can also impose constraints on it, and if we do badly enough, the "most pleasing curve" may well turn out not to be pleasing at all.

METRFONT introduced an important concept, in the absence of Bézier curves and the PostScript language: the concept of *pens*. A pen is a shape of which a given point—which we shall call the "center", even though it is not necessarily the center of the shape—moves along a Bézier curve. The pixels that it blackens are those that have been touched by the shape at a given moment during its trajectory. It is very important to understand that even though the center of the pen follows a Bézier curve, the contour of the blackened surface need not be made of Bézier curves!

That is the main difficulty in converting from METRFONT to a type of font based on contours. In the absence of a precise mathematical solution, we must make do with methods for the autotracing of surfaces to obtain PostScript or TrueType contours from METRFONT glyphs. At least no risk is involved, since we can arbitrarily enlarge the bitmaps produced by METR-FONT—which leaves the autotracing software no excuse for drawing the contour badly.

One important concept is *mode*. By mode, we mean the characteristics of a printing or display device: its resolution, any additional blackening of pixels that may be required, the need to preserve the overshoot of rounded letters, the need to correct sharp corners by adding pixels, etc. These technical data may sometimes be difficult to understand, but we must have them in order to produce fonts that are perfectly suited to the device. As early as 1991, Karl Berry undertook the monumental task of compiling modes for all printers and all displays; the result is a file called modes.mf that is part of every TEX distribution. The reader should find what he needs in that file; if not, the file explains how to test a printer in order to obtain the correct values of the parameters.

Another essential notion: what are our base units? We have already seen in this book that both PostScript and TrueType used abstract systems of coordinates connected to the real world by transformation matrices. METAFONT is fundamentally different: *it works with pixels!*

But then we can legitimately raise the question: are we to use explicit values of pixels to describe a glyph? Of course not. That is where the magic of the programming language comes in. When we describe a glyph, we use variables that play the role of abstract units. But we are the ones who get to define those variables. The connection with the real world is made in a very clever way. There are two types of dimensions: *sharp dimensions* and plain old dimensions. Sharp dimensions are followed by a crosshatch. Thus by writing 1dd#, we request a true Didot point, whatever the optical size or resolution of the font may be. Conversely, when we say 1dd, we obtain a number, which is the number of pixels that correspond to 1dd# for the optical size of the font and the resolution of the current mode.

That allows us to work on two levels. First we define the parameters in sharp dimensions, and when we have all the parameters that we need, we switch to pixel mode and ask METAFONT to calculate the values of these parameters in pixels. From that point on, we work with those values through the use of variable names, etc.

F.1.2   The Basics: Drawing and Filling

The reader will certainly have noticed that the METAFONT logo uses a font designed just for it. For the TEX logo, we can use any font we please; we must merely make sure to move the 'E' correctly. For the METAFONT logo, however, we are required to use the *Logo* font.

We write METAFONT code in files with the extension ".mf". METAFONT will read these files and produce a GF font (see §A.5.2) and a TFM font (see §B.1). To produce the font, META-FONT first reads a configuration file, which gives the values of some parameters; then it reads a number of files that contain descriptions of glyphs; finally, it reads files with data on kerning, etc. This order is not fixed, but it is the most practical. Like TEX, METAFONT also has some predefined instructions, called *primitives*. The primitives are rarely used; instead, we tend to use the high-level instructions defined in a file called *format*. Currently the most commonly used format is plain.

To run METAFONT, we enter on the command line the name of the executable file, the name of the format (preceded by an at sign), the name of the mode, and the name of the "source" file, which is to say the file that contains the values of the parameters and that will trigger the reading of all the other files. The name of the font produced will be that of the source file.

But for very technical reasons, the syntax of this command line is quite peculiar. To specify the plain format, the mode cx (which corresponds to the Canon printing engine, which is embedded in the Apple LaserWriter printers), and the source file cmr10.mf, we write:

```
mf "&cm \mode:=cx; input cmr10"
```

where the backslash indicates that we are already supplying METAFONT code rather than a filename.

Now we are at a point at which we may ask: what does one write in a METAFONT file?

The basic syntax of METAFONT is much more approachable than that of TeX, for the simple reason that it includes practically no text data, just instructions. And since there is nothing but instructions, we are not required to protect those instructions, and everything is much easier to do. Thus everything works as in an ordinary programming language: there are expressions that end with a semicolon, and they contain instructions and parameters. Depending on the situation, the parameters may be sharp dimensions or abstract numbers that designate pixels.

For example, the expression

```
z1=(50,50);
```

creates a variable z1 and assigns the value (50,50) to it. A few words of explanation are in order: By writing x1=50; y1=50; we define the coordinates of point '1'. They may be written with 'x' and 'y' for abscissas and ordinates or with 'z' (the symbol for complex numbers in mathematics) to designate both coordinates at the same time. Conversion from 'x' and 'y' to 'z' and vice versa happens automatically.

The system of coordinates used by METAFONT is as follows: the origin of the coordinates coincides with the origin of the glyph, and the units of the coordinate system are pixels. Thus by writing (50,50), we obtain a point 50 pixels to the right of the origin and 50 pixels above it.

It behooves us to start out within the perspective of creating glyphs. To that end, here are two instructions that "enclose" the code for the description of a given glyph:

```
beginchar(65,10pt#,10pt#,0pt#);
% the code for the glyph goes here
endchar;
bye
```

The instruction beginchar is a macro-command (or "macro") that initializes METAFONT so that it is ready to draw a glyph. Between parentheses, we write the parameters for the macro, which are four in number: the glyph's position in the font table (an abstract number; in this case, 65), the set-width (in "sharp dimension"; here, 10 American printers' points), and the height and depth of the box containing the glyph. A semicolon terminates the expression.

The second line in the sample code begins with a percent sign; that line is a comment. The third line is the endchar command, which terminates the code for the glyph's description. The last line tells METAFONT that the program ends at that location. If we omit that line, METAFONT will switch to interactive mode and await additional instructions from the user.

What, then, shall we write for the glyph's description? We have seen how to define points through the use of explicit coordinates in pixels. But since the number of pixels depends on the resolution and we want our glyph to be independent of the resolution, we shall define a utility variable u, which will serve as our "base unit". The value that we shall assign to this variable is not of great importance. Let us take, for example, the equivalent of a point in pixels:

```
u#=1pt#; define_pixels(u);
```

By writing u#=1pt#;, we define a "sharp" version of our variable—i.e., one that uses amounts from the real world. In this case, its value is one American printers' point.

Next, by writing define_pixels(u#), we request the creation of a variable u whose value is the equivalent in pixels of u#. Here is where the conditions of rendering—mode, resolution, size of pixels, etc.—come into play. Henceforth the value of u is a certain number (most likely a rational one) of pixels. We do not know that number, but we shall use it to define the glyph. Here is the brilliance of MET∧FONT: we do not define the variable u; rather, we define u# and ask MET∧FONT to convert it to u according to the current size and mode.

MET∧FONT does the same for the three dimensions of the abstract box that contains the glyph: using the "sharp" data that we provide, it defines the three variables w, h, and d, which are the width, the height, and the depth of the glyph, expressed in pixels.

Thus, by writing:

```
z1=(.5w,0);
```

we define a point z1 that appears in the middle of the glyph's width and on the baseline.

Defining points is very useful, but it is time to blacken a few pixels—by drawing something pretty, if possible. That is done in two different ways: by *drawing* or by *filling*.

The first approach is that of the pencil or the paintbrush: we move our imaginary drawing tool, and it leaves a mark on the page. That mark depends on the shape of the tool. The second approach is that of the PostScript and TrueType fonts: we define a contour and fill it in black. We can also combine the two approaches, by drawing a closed curve and then filling it.

Let us begin with drawing. To do so, we must first define the tool with which we intend to draw. That is done through the instruction pickup followed by a description of the *pen*. There are several types of pens: the most important are circular pens, defined by pencircle; rectangular pens, defined by pensquare; and "razor" pens, defined by penrazor.

When we write:

```
pickup pencircle;
```

MET∧FONT will take a circular pen as the active pen. But what is its size? Since we have not specified the size, the pen will be of diameter 1, i.e., one pixel. That is a rather poor choice, as at a high resolution that poor little pixel is not visible to the naked eye. To specify the size of a pen, we *transform* the default pen. We shall see that the *transformation operators* that we shall apply to pens can in fact be applied to any MET∧FONT object. Here are some of these operators:

- scaled, followed by a dimension, scales an object. There are two variants: xscaled changes only the horizontal scaling factor, and yscaled changes the vertical one.

- rotated, followed by an angle (an abstract number), rotates an object through the angle specified.

Thus to obtain a round pen of thickness 0.4pt (four-tenths of an American printers' point), we write

```
pickup pencircle scaled 0.4pt;
```

Now we are ready to draw. By writing:

```
z1=(.5w,0); z2=(.5w+2u,0);
z3=(.5w+2u,2u); z4=(.5w,0);
draw z1--z2--z3--z4--cycle;
```

we obtain a square of side 2u. The double hyphen means that we are drawing a straight line between the two points. The instruction cycle closes the contour.

We can rewrite the code above as a sequence of relative moves:

```
z1=(.5w,0); z2=z1+(2u,0);
z3=z2+(0,2u); z4=z3+(-2u,0);
draw z1--z2--z3--z4--cycle;
```

The result is the same, but the way of describing the path is a little more intuitive.

Before continuing with the drawing of curves, let us play around by modifying the pen. Let us take an elliptical pen with a major axis of 0.6pt and a minor axis of 0.3pt that is turned 30 degrees and use it to draw the same square:

```
pickup pencircle xscaled 0.6pt
    yscaled 0.3pt rotated 30;
z1=(.5w,0); z2=z1+(2u,0);
z3=z2+(0,2u); z4=z3+(-2u,0);
draw z1--z2--z3--z4--cycle;
```

The outline is already more interesting. And now let us take a "razor" pen, 0.6pt wide, that is slanted 45 degrees:

```
pickup penrazor xscaled 0.6pt
    rotated 45;
z1=(.5w,0); z2=z1+(2u,0);
z3=z2+(0,2u); z4=z3+(-2u,0);
draw z1--z2--z3--z4--cycle;
```

Now is the time to move on to curves. By writing two periods (".. ") instead of two hyphens ("--"), we obtain *curves* instead of *line segments*. Let us apply the double period to two points, using a slightly smaller circular pen:

```
pickup pencircle scaled 0.2pt;
z1=(.5w,0); z2=z1+(-3u,0);
draw z1..z2..cycle;
```

Surprise! We obtain a circle, yet we never specified that that was the shape that we wanted. What happened?

The expression z1..z2..cycle must be read as a whole: we start from z1 and return to the same point, passing through z2 as well. In the absence of other instructions, METAFONT drew the MPC (most pleasing curve) that passes through z1, z2, and z1 again: it is simply a circle of diameter z1z2 that is drawn counterclockwise, starting from z1 and moving up and to the left.

The circle is certainly the most perfect shape, according to Eastern philosophers. But unless we are designing a *Futura* or an *Avant Garde*, we will need other shapes as well. How can we modify this basic shape?

The first thing that we can do is to impose an initial direction other than the vertical. We indicate the direction that a curve takes when leaving a point through the use of an expression in braces that is placed after the point in question. This expression can be a point or even a primary direction (up, down, right, left), or it can be the keyword dir followed by an angle in degrees.

For example, if we write z1{dir45}, the path will leave point z1 at an angle of 45°. Here an angle of 0° corresponds to a direction that starts out towards the right (to the east, on a map); thus 45° corresponds to a departure to the right and upwards (to the northeast).

In the circle that we obtained by default, the departure from point z1 was vertical, which corresponded to an angle of 90°. Let us request an angle of 120°:

```
pickup pencircle scaled 0.2pt;
z1=(.5w,0); z2=z1+(-3u,0);
draw z1{dir120}..z2..cycle;
```

From this result, we can draw several conclusions. First, when we say "cycle", we return to the initial point, but not necessarily with the initial angle. Second, by modifying an angle in the northern half of the cycle, we also modify the southern half; specifically, the angle of approach to the point z2 has changed, and therefore also the angle of departure from that point, and that is what changed the part of the curve that lies below the baseline.

Another way to modify the curve involves adding *tension*. The default value for tension is 1. Let us use a tension of 1.5 between z2 and cycle—in other words, in the bottom half of the curve:

```
pickup pencircle scaled 0.2pt;
z1=(.5w,0); z2=z1+(-3u,0);
draw z1{dir120}..z2..tension1.5..cycle;
```

Result: the lower half is tighter; the angles of approach to and departure from point z2 have changed.

Now let us combine curves and straight lines. Let us define a point z3 below the baseline and ask METAFONT to produce a curve between z1 and z2 and straight lines to connect z2, z3, and again z1:

```
pickup pencircle scaled 0.2pt;
z1=(.5w,0); z2=z1+(-3u,0);
z3=z1+(-1.5u,-2u);
draw z1..z2--z3--cycle;
```

A new surprise awaits us: the curve z1..z2 takes its simplest form, that of a straight line. Conclusion: when we approach z2 with a curve and depart with a straight line, there is no smooth connection between the two.

Now let us add a third hyphen between z2 and z3. Here is what we obtain:

```
pickup pencircle scaled 0.2pt;
z1=(.5w,0); z2=z1+(-3u,0);
z3=z1+(-1.5u,-2u);
draw z1..z2---z3--cycle;
```

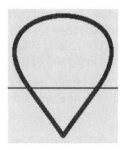

How could we have obtained this head of an extraterrestrial? Because three hyphens are a short way to say ..tension infinity..; thus we replaced a straight line segment with a curve, but one of infinite tension. In this way, we obtain *both* the look of a straight line *and* a smooth connection to the curve that precedes it.

What happens if we also replace the segment z3--cycle with a curve of infinite tension? The result is deceptive: nothing changes, because we are making contradictory demands of METAFONT. If z3---cycle is of infinite tension, it has the shape of a line segment. But then it cannot form a smooth connection with z2--z3. Therefore METAFONT drops the smooth connection and produces the same drawing for us.

Up to now we have seen the syntax of various lines that we can draw. Without being aware of it, we have created a data structure that is very important in METAFONT, that of the *path*. We can define a variable for a path with the keyword path and assign as its value an expression similar to the one that we just saw:

```
path p; p=z1..z2---z3;
```

Later, we can use the variable p in a drawing instruction: draw p;. If we have two paths, p and q, for which the end of the former coincides with the start of the latter, we can merge them with an ampersand (&). Thus draw p & q; will draw the concatenation of the two paths.

A path need not be closed. But if it is closed, we can *fill* it, using the fill command:

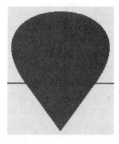

```
z1=(.5w,0); z2=z1+(-3u,0);
z3=z1+(-1.5u,-2u);
fill z1..z2---z3--cycle;
```

Here we encounter a fundamental difference between METAFONT and PostScript or True-Type. In the latter, pixels can be either black or white, and applying black on black yields white. In METAFONT, however, pixels are weighted. When they are of weight 0, they are white. When we add a layer of black, the weight of the pixels is increased by 1; thus they become black. When we add other layers of black, the weight increases; but as long as it remains positive, the pixels will appear black.

The opposite command exists: unfill reduces the weight of a pixel. In the code below, we shall define a second path inside the first and apply an unfill to it:

```
z4=(.5w-.5u,0); z5=z4+(-2u,0);
z6=z4+(-u,-1.5u);
unfill z4..z5---z6--cycle;
z1=(.5w,0); z2=z1+(-3u,0);
z3=z1+(-1.5u,-2u);
fill z1..z2---z3--cycle;
```

Note that we have deliberately "emptied" the path before "filling" it. After the unfill, the pixels contained in the first path have a weight of −1. With the fill that followed, they were assigned a weight of 0 and thus remained white.

The undraw command will "undraw" a path; that is, it will draw a path with a negative weight. The commands filldraw and unfilldraw will draw and fill (or undraw and unfill) at the same time. As simpler versions of draw and undraw, there are drawdot and undrawdot, which draw or undraw a single point.

Now we shall try, as an exercise, to draw a circle inside a square. To obtain a square, we can define points as follows:

```
z1=(0.5w-.5u,0); z2=(0.5w+1.5u,0);
z3=(0.5w+1.5u,3u); z4=(0.5w-.5u,3u);
```

But there is also a more elegant way. We can define the points' coordinates separately, according to the *logic* of a horizontal square. For example, we can begin by observing that points 1 and 2 are at the same height, as are points 3 and 4, and that the height is known in each case:

```
y1=y2=0; y3=y4=3u;
```

Next, we can say that points 1 and 4, and also points 2 and 3, have the same x-coordinate:

```
x1=x4; x2=x3;
```

Next, we can say that the square is symmetric about the bisector of the glyph's width:

```
.5(x1+x2)=.5w;
```

Finally, we have the fact that it is a square; that is, its horizontal side is equal to its vertical side:

```
x2-x1=y4-y1;
```

The advantage of this way of expressing the points is that the length of the square's side appears only once (when we say y3=y4=3u). Simply changing that one value will change the size of the square automatically. And it will still remain centered relative to its set-width.

The syntax used above is an algebraic syntax. The equal sign does not have the same function as in other programming languages. Specifically, when we write $x1=$x4; in the Perl language, for example, that means that the variable $x1 takes the value of the variable $x4. Here that is not the case, for when we write x1=x4, neither of the two variables has a known value yet. Using an algebraic syntax means that METAFONT will consider the expressions written above as linear equations. When there is an equation for every variable, it will solve the linear system and obtain values for those variables.

Let us return to our exercise. We shall draw the circle using a "calligraphic" pen—one that is elliptical and turned at an angle. The circle will touch the square at the midpoints of the sides. To express the fact, for example, that point z5, which is the starting point of the circle, is halfway between z1 and z2, we can use the following notation:

```
z5=.5[z1,z2];
```

Instead of the .5, we can use any rational number. Writing a 0 gives us the first point; writing a 1, the second.

Here, then, is an initial attempt to obtain a circle in the square:

```
pickup pencircle scaled 0.1pt;
y1=y2=0; y3=y4=3u; x1=x4; x2=x3;
.5(x1+x2)=.5w; x2-x1=y4-y1;
draw z1--z2--z3--z4--cycle;
pickup pencircle xscaled 0.5pt
yscaled 0.1pt rotated 45;
z5=.5[z1,z2]; z6=.5[z2,z3];
y8=y6; x7=x5; y7=y3; x8=x1;
draw z5..z6..z7..z8..cycle;
```

Seeing the result, we cannot really say that the circle lies *within* the square, as it slightly exceeds the square's bounds. Indeed, it is the *center* of the pen that touches the square, and we wanted the *edges* of the pen to touch it.

But when we draw a curve, it is the center of the pen that we manipulate. How can we know the exact coordinates of the pen's edges?

METAFONT has a very practical notation for that: by writing top z1, we obtain the uppermost point of the pen whose center is placed on the point z1. If top is the top, we also have bot (the bottom), rt (the right side), lft (the left). We can also combine them: bot lft z2 is the lower left edge of the pen whose center is at the point z2.

We shall use these operators to draw our circle within the square:

```
pickup pencircle scaled 0.1pt;
y1=y2=0; y3=y4=3u; x1=x4; x2=x3;
.5(x1+x2)=.5w; x2-x1=y4-y1;
draw z1--z2--z3--z4--cycle;
pickup pencircle xscaled 0.5pt
yscaled 0.1pt rotated 45;
bot z5=.5[z1,z2]; rt z6=.5[z2,z3];
y8=y6; x7=x5; top y7=y3; lft x8=x1;
draw z5..z6..z7..z8..cycle;
```

Before moving on to the next important concept, *pen strokes*, let us do one exercise by way of review: we shall draw the yin–yang symbol as elegantly as possible.

We shall use a width of 8 points and leave side-bearings of 1 point on each side. The outer circle of the symbol will be drawn with a pen whose thickness is $\frac{1}{3}$ of a point, and it must descend by 1 point below the baseline:

```
beginchar(110,8pt#,8pt#,0pt#);
pickup pencircle scaled 0.2pt;
x3=x1=.5w; y2=y4=.5[y1,y3];
bot y1=-1pt;
w-rt x2=lft x4=1pt;
y3-y1=x2-x4;
draw z1..z2..z3..z4..cycle;
endchar;
```

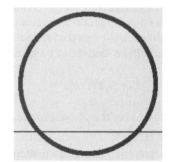

Next, we shall fill in the left side:

```
beginchar(110,8pt#,8pt#,0pt#);
pickup pencircle scaled 0.2pt;
x3=x1=.5w; y2=y4=.5[y1,y3];
bot y1=-1pt;
w-rt x2=lft x4=1pt;
y3-y1=x2-x4;
draw z1..z2..z3..z4..cycle;
fill z3{left}..z4..z1{right} &
z1{left}.. .5[z1,z3]{right}
..z3{left} ..cycle;
endchar;
```

Finally, we must draw the points that symbolize the birth of the new yin in the yang and the new yang in the yin. To do so, we can go back to drawing mode, but first we select a pen whose size is that of the dot. Since the centers of these dots are known, we need only draw a dot with the pen and "undraw" one for the upper part, and our work is done:

```
beginchar(110,8pt#,8pt#,0pt#);
pickup pencircle scaled 0.2pt;
x3=x1=.5w; y2=y4=.5[y1,y3];
bot y1=-1pt;
w-rt x2=lft x4=1pt;
y3-y1=x2-x4;
draw z1..z2..z3..z4..cycle;
fill z3{left}..z4..z1{right} &
z1{left}.. .5[z1,z3]{right}
..z3{left} ..cycle;
draw z1..z2..z3..z4..cycle;
pickup pencircle scaled 1pt;
drawdot .25[z1,z3];
undrawdot .75[z1,z3];
endchar;
```

F.1.3 More Advanced Concepts: Pen Strokes and Parameterization

Let us not delude ourselves: the "pens" that we described in the previous section are poor tools for the graphic designer. How can we draw beautiful things with a pen that changes neither its shape nor its angle of inclination? The letters that we design in that way will be singularly dull, artificial, boring.

To account for that problem, METAFONT introduced another concept: *pen strokes*. This time the logic is different. We shall work with "razor" pens and define a number of *pen positions*. A pen position includes both the coordinates of its center and the width and angle of the pen.

Suppose, for example, that we define two points z1=(6u,0) and z2=(2u,0). We place a pen of width 1u and angle 60° on the first point. On the second, we place a pen of width 2u and angle 120°. To do so, we use the macro penpos, followed by three arguments: the position number, the width of the pen, and the angle of the pen position.

METAFONT will then calculate the position of the extremities of these pen positions. They are denoted z1l (left extremity of point z1), z1r (right extremity of point z1), etc. It is important to understand here that "left" and "right" here are defined from the point of view of someone who is standing on the pen position.

Now, to draw the pen stroke that goes between these two positions, we use the keyword penstroke, and the suffix e for each of the positions. That suffix indicates that we are referring not to the point at the center of the position but rather to the whole pen position. Only one thing remains: defining the initial direction. If the position of pen 1 has an angle of 60°, it makes sense that the initial direction be perpendicular to the pen's angle; it will therefore be $60+90=150°$. Here is the result:

```
z1=(6u,0); z2=(2u,0);
penpos1(1u,60); penpos2(2u,120);
penstroke z1e{dir150}..z2e;
```

All of the tricks of the previous section can be applied here: directions, tension, the keyword `cycle`, triple hyphens. Furthermore, we are not required to state the coordinates of the center of a pen position immediately. We can very well define the position and give its coordinates only at the last minute. But flexibility has its limits: the values of the arguments of the `penpos` macro may not be unknown when the position is defined. When we write `penpos1(width,angle)`, the values of `width` and `angle` must be known.

To achieve a better understanding of the vast possibilities that METAFONT's concept of pen stroke offers us, we shall examine an example from the real world, step by step. We shall write the code for the following glyph, which is inspired by the 'n' of the font *Vendôme*:

The first step is to place the pen positions at the correct locations. We need to capture the *dynamics* of the letter. To get a better feeling for these dynamics, let us consider some questions: What would happen if these parameters changed? If the letter became lighter or bolder? What are its relevant strokes? What are the strokes that will remain the same irrespective of the values of the parameters?

After due reflection, the author came to the conclusion that the the most relevant pen positions might be the following:

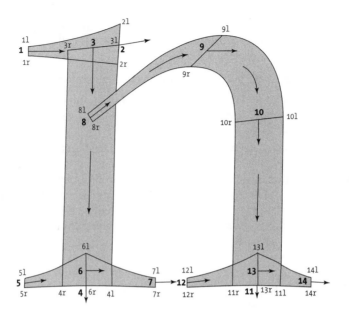

Let us analyze this configuration. The letter includes a downstroke on the left, an arch that starts from the inside of the left-hand downstroke and ends in the right-hand downstroke, two serifs on the baseline, and a head serif on the left-hand downstroke. Among these elements, the most important are the two downstrokes and the arch. We can start with those. The left-hand downstroke corrects pen positions 3 and 4. It is slightly curved. The location of pen position 4 seems clear. But at what height should we place position 3?

If we set positions 9 and 10 at those precise locations, it is because they are where the edges of the arch are horizontal and vertical, respectively. By taking measurements, we find that the center of pen 9 is at the same height as that of pen 1, which is the starting point of the head serif. But let us not forget that our letter does not appear in isolation: it is part of a font; and in that font, as in any Latin font, there is a relevant height, that of the lowercase letters, which we call the *x-height*. It turns out that the left edge of pen 1 appears at the x-height. If z9l is slightly higher, that is because we have overshoot.

Without even being aware of it, we have been performing *parameterization*. We have already established two parameters for the font: the height of the lowercase letters and the amount of overshoot. There are four other parameters that appear very clearly in our construction: the thickness of the downstroke, which is that of pens 4 and 11; the thickness of the upstroke, which is that of pen 8; the thickness of the tips of the serifs (pens 1, 5, 7, etc.), and the "inside" thickness of the serifs (pens 6 and 13). These are the parameters that will determine the behavior of our glyph. We shall call them stem, join, serif_tip, serif_ht. Likewise, we shall use x_height for the x-height and oo for the overshoot.

But let us go back to our analysis. Using arrows, we find the (hypothetical) motion made by the calligrapher who drew this letter. Why was z8 placed at the midpoint of the left downstroke? After all, what difference would it make if we placed farther to the left or the right, as long as it lies within the downstroke? Because we cannot know the thickness of the heavy stroke in advance. If we place z8 too far to the right, it may lie outside the downstroke if that stroke is too light. If we place z8 too far to the left, it may become exposed if the downstroke is light. By placing it in the middle, we make sure that the arch will always begin within the downstroke.

That is also why we place z3 on the hypothetical curve that connects z1 to z2.

Now let us begin writing code. First, we must define our parameters. To that end, we have the instruction `numeric`, whose role is to define simple numeric variables:

```
numeric x_height, oo, stem, join, serif_tip, serif_ht;
```

There is another instruction, `pair`, to define points—pairs of numeric values—but we do not need it here. Next, we shall give provisional values to these parameters. To obtain an initial set of values, we can place an ordinary sheet of tracing paper, with a grid marked in millimeters, over the letter's sketch and take some measurements. Here are some of the values obtained in this manner:

```
x_height=5.1u; oo=.2u;
stem=1.1u; join=.2u;
serif_tip=.2u; serif_ht=.7u;
```

Now let us address the left-hand downstroke. Although we will be more malevolent later on, we can begin by using a measured value taken from our graph paper as the x-coordinate of pen 4. On the other hand, close examination reveals that the serifs are slightly flared. Let us use the name `delta` (a value that is very small but not zero) for the heights of points z4 and z11:

```
numeric delta; delta=.033u;
z4=(1.6u,delta);
```

As for point z3, we would like to control the angle of the downstroke. Let us use `offset` for the offset between the x-coordinates of points z3 and z4, and let us give it the provisional value of `0.125u`. Thus we need only write:

```
numeric offset; offset=.125u;
x3=x4+offset; y3r=x_height;
```

Before drawing the downstroke, we need to define pen positions 3 and 4. For pen 4, this is easy:

```
penpos4(stem,180);
```

On the other hand, pen 3 is not perfectly horizontal. Thus we shall construct this pen position from the data that we have. We already know the locations of x3 and y3r. It would be interesting to have a horizontal projection of our pen that is equal to `stem`:

```
x3l-x3r=stem;
```

Finally, we can say that the difference in height between z3l and z3r is half of serif_tip:

```
y3l-y3r=.5serif_tip;
```

Thus it has turned out to be unnecessary to write penpos3: we found the pen position by calculating the coordinates of points z3r and z3l. Nonetheless, METAFONT cannot read our minds; we do have to tell it that z3 lies halfway between points z3l and z3r:

```
z3=.5[z3l,z3r];
```

To draw the stroke, we have only to specify the direction in which to start. For now, we can allow METAFONT to choose the starting direction; we shall merely state that point z4 must be approached vertically:

```
penstroke z3e..{down}z4e;
```

And here is the result:

```
beginchar("n",7pt#,6pt#,0pt#);
u#=1pt#; define_pixels(u);
numeric x_height, oo, stem,
join, serif_tip, serif_ht;
x_height=5.1u; oo=.2u;
stem=1.1u; join=.2u;
serif_tip=.2u; serif_ht=.7u;
numeric delta; delta=.033u;
z4=(1.6u,delta);
numeric offset; offset=.125u;
x3=x4+offset; y3r=x_height;
penpos4(stem,180);
x3l-x3r=stem;
y3l-y3r=.5serif_tip; z3=.5[z3l,z3r];
penstroke z3e..{down}z4e;
endchar;
```

A great deal of code for just one stroke, but it will be much easier from now on! Now let us draw the connecting stroke and the second downstroke. We shall use graph paper to measure the x-coordinate of z11; its y-coordinate will be the same as that of z4. But let's be wicked: since we measured the x-coordinate of z4 from the glyph's origin, let us measure that of z11 from the glyph's set-width. In this way, the glyph is tied to the dimensions of the abstract box that contain it.

```
x11=w-.65u; y11=y4; penpos11(stem,180);
```

As for points z8r and z10r, we can see that they are at the same height, which is seven-tenths of the x-height:

```
y10=y8=.7x_height;
```

We want the angle of segment z11--z10 to be the same as that of segment z4--z3. To that end, we shall use a keyword that is very important in METAFONT, the keyword whatever. The expression:

```
z10-z11=whatever*(z3-z4);
```

can be interpreted as "the vector $\overrightarrow{z_{10}z_{11}}$ is a scalar multiple of the vector $\overrightarrow{z_3z_4}$", which means that they "have the same direction". Thus we need only give the height of z10 to establish the exact position of that point. We have already given the height of z10r; now we must give the characteristics of pen position 10. For consistency's sake, we can decide that this pen will have the same width and angle as pen 3:

```
z10l-z10r=z3l-z3r; z10=.5[z10l,z10r];
```

We now have pens 10 and 11; let us proceed for 9 and 8. What will the width of pen 9 be? We do not yet know. But we can say that it must be proportional to both 10 (i.e., the parameter stem) and 8 (the parameter join). It is sufficient to indicate where this value lies between join and stem. Using measurements from our graph paper, we find that the width of 9 is .87[join,stem] and that its angle is −136°:

```
penpos9(.87[join,stem],-);
```

We have already determined the height of z9l:

```
y9l=x_height+oo;
```

but what is its x-coordinate? That is a delicate question, because the aesthetic quality of the arch depends on that x-coordinate. Since the widths of the pens can vary according to the values of the parameters, we should reason in terms of a "skeleton" stroke. Thus we shall define the x-coordinate of the center of pen z9 according to those of points z8 and z10:

```
x9=.68[x8,x10];
```

On the other hand, we may suppose, for simplicity's sake, that z8 lies on the line connecting z3 and z4:

```
z8=whatever[z3,z4];
```

Now all that remains is to determine the width and the angle of pen 8. First, what is the starting angle of the arch? We can measure it, of course; in the figure, it is 37°. But that angle will change if the width of the glyph changes. It would be more appropriate to say that the line tangent to the arch at initial point z8 must intersect the (hypothetical) extension of the right-hand downstroke at a given height:

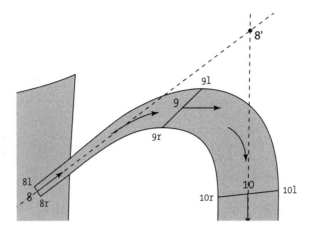

By defining point z8' and allowing the stroke that starts from z8 to head in the direction of that point, we have a way of starting our arch *independently* of the letter's set-width. Here is how we can define z8':

```
z8'=whatever[z11,z10]; y8'=6.33u;
```

Pen 8 must be perpendicular to the direction z8--z8':

```
penpos8(join,angle(z8'-z8)-);
```

All that remains is to draw the stroke:

```
penstroke z8e{z8'-z8}..z9e{right}..z10e..{down}z11e;
```

And here is the result:

```
beginchar("n",7pt#,6pt#,0pt#);
... previous code ...
x11=w-1.65u; y11=y4; penpos11(stem,180);
y10=y8=.7x_height; z8=whatever[z3,z4];
z10-z11=whatever*(z3-z4);
z10l-z10r=z3l-z3r; z10=.5[z10l,z10r];
penpos9(.87[join,stem],-136);
y9l=x_height+oo;
x9=.68[x8,x10];
z8'=whatever[z11,z10]; y8'=1.25x_height;
penpos8(join,angle(z8'-z8)-90);
penstroke z8e{z8'-z8}..z9e{right}..
z10e..{down}z11e;
endchar;
```

We can see that we may have allowed METAFONT a bit too much freedom: the arch and the right-hand downstroke are a bit too soft; we wanted something tighter. Let us adjust the tension between 8 and 9 and replace z10e..z11e with a curve of infinite tension:

```
beginchar("n",7pt#,6pt#,0pt#);
... previous code ...
x11=w-1.65u; y11=y4; penpos11(stem,180);
y10=y8=.7x_height; z8=whatever[z3,z4];
z10-z11=whatever*(z3-z4);
z10l-z10r=z3l-z3r; z10=.5[z10l,z10r];
penpos9(.87[join,stem],-136);
y9l=x_height+oo;
x9=.68[x8,x10];
z8'=whatever[z11,z10]; y8'=1.25x_height;
penpos8(join,angle(z8'-z8)-90);
penstroke z8e{z8'-z8}..tension 1.5..
z9e{right}..z10e---z11e;
endchar;
```

The result is already much more acceptable. Now let us add the head serif to the left-hand downstroke. We see that we shall need a new parameter: the width of the serif. Our model glyph has serifs of highly varying width; we shall take one of them as a parameter, and the others will have values proportional to it. Let us take the left serif of the right-hand downstroke as our starting point and define serif as:

```
    numeric serif; serif=x11r-x12=1u;
```

A measurement from our graph paper shows us that x7-x4l is also equal to serif. On the other hand, x3r-x1=.95serif, x4r-x5=.9serif, and x14-x11l=.8serif. Therefore, we have:

```
    x7-x4l=serif; x3r-x1=.95serif; x4r-x5=.9serif; x14-x11l=.8serif;
```

Now we need to set pen positions 1 and 2. Here is the data that we already know:

```
    y1=y3; penpos1(serif_tip,-); z2=z3l;
```

But that does not give us the angle of pen 2. That angle must be equal to the starting angle of the stroke connecting positions 3 and 4. What is that angle? We do not know, because we have allowed METAFONT to choose it. By writing:

```
    penstroke z3e..{down}z4e;
```

we have only decided that the angle at the end of the stroke must be vertical. How, then, can we find the angle that we need? If METAFONT chose it, then METAFONT must know what it is. Indeed, there is a command, named direction, that gives us the direction that a path has at a given moment.

Let us pause briefly to explain this command. We have seen that METAFONT has a data structure called the "path". A path is obtained by drawing Bézier curves (or straight line segments) that go through several points. If there are $n+1$ points, $z_0, z_1, \ldots, z_n$, we say that at time t, we are at point z_i. And at time $t' \in [t, t+1]$, we are somewhere between z_t and z_{t+1}.

The `direction` command takes as its arguments a time *t* and a path. It returns the direction of the path at the specified time.

In our case, the path is none other than:

```
z3l..{down}z4l
```

and the time, for simplicity's sake, is that of the start of the path, namely 0. The path's direction at time 0 is:

```
direction 0 of (z3l..{down}z4l)
```

But to define a pen position, we need an *angle*, not a direction. Never fear: the `angle` command will give us the angle of a direction:

```
angle(direction 0 of (z3l..{down}z4l))
```

and we can therefore define pen position 2 as follows:

```
penpos2(1.25serif_ht,direction 0 of (z3l..{down}z4l));
```

We draw the head serif in this way:

```
penstroke z1e{right}..z2e;
```

Here is the result:

```
beginchar("n",7pt#,6pt#,0pt#);
... previous code ...
numeric serif; serif=x11r-x12=1.55u;
x7-x4l=serif; x3r-x1=.95serif;
x4r-x5=.9serif; x14-x11l=.8serif;
y1l=y3l; penpos1(serif_tip,-90); z2=z3l;
penpos2(1.25serif_ht,angle(direction 0
of (z3l..{down}z4l)));
penstroke z1e{right}..z2e;
endchar;
```

Only the serifs remain. The code is simple:

```
penpos5(serif_tip,-); penpos7(serif_tip,-);
penpos12(serif_tip,-); penpos14(serif_tip,-);
penpos6(serif_ht,-); penpos13(serif_ht,-);
y5r=y7r=y12r=y14r=0; z6r=z4; z13r=z11;
penstroke z5e{right}..z6e & z6e..{right}z7e;
penstroke z12e{right}..z13e & z13e..{right}z14e;
```

And here is the result:

```
beginchar("n",7pt#,6pt#,0pt#);
... previous code ...
penpos5(serif_tip,-90); penpos7(serif_tip,-
90);
penpos12(serif_tip,-90);penpos14(serif_tip,-
90);
penpos6(serif_ht,-90); penpos13(serif_ht,-
90);
y5r=y7r=y12r=y14r=0; z6r=z4; z13r=z11;
penstroke z5e{right}..z6e &
z6e..{right}z7e;
penstroke z12e{right}..z13e &
z13e..{right}z14e;
endchar;
```

But what would happen if serif became so large that the space between the downstrokes was not wide enough to hold the two half-serifs? We do not want the serifs to overlap. On the contrary, we would like for a safe distance to be preserved between z7 and z12—a distance of .2u, let us say.

For that purpose, we shall use two of METAFONT's other features: (re)assignments and tests. The following code tests whether the sum of x7-x4, .2u, and x11-x12 exceeds the letter's aperture (i.e., x11-x4). If that is the case, we redefine the values of x12 and x7:

```
if (x7-x4+.2u+x11-x12 > x11-x4):
x7:=.5[x4,x11]-.1u;
x12:=.5[x4,x11]+.1u; fi
```

Here, by way of review, is the code for this letter 'n', which has enabled us to explore quite a few of METAFONT's features:

> **beginchar**$(110, 7pt^{\#}, 6pt^{\#}, 0pt^{\#})$;
> $u^{\#} = 1pt^{\#}$; **define_pixels**(u);
> **numeric** *x_height, oo, stem, join, serif_tip, serif_height, delta, offset*;
> *x_height* $= 5.1u$; *oo* $= .2u$; *stem* $= 1.1u$; *join* $= .2u$;
> *serif_tip* $= .2u$; *serif_height* $= .7u$; *delta* $= .033u$; *offset* $= .125u$;
> $z_4 = (1.6u, delta)$; *penpos*$_4(stem, 180)$;
> $x_3 = x_4 + offset$; $y_{3r} = x\_height$;
> $x_{3l} - x_{3r} = stem$; $y_{3l} - y_{3r} = .5serif\_tip$; $z_3 = .5[z_{3l}, z_{3r}]$;
> **penstroke** $z_{3e} .. \{down\}z_{4e}$;
>
> $x_{11} = w - 1.65u$; $y_{11} = y_4$; *penpos*$_{11}(stem, 180)$;
> $y_{10} = y_8 = .7x\_height$; $z_8 = whatever[z_3, z_4]$;
> $z_{10} - z_{11} = whatever * (z_3 - z_4)$;
> $z_{10l} - z_{10r} = z_{3l} - z_{3r}$; $z_{10} = .5[z_{10l}, z_{10r}]$;
> *penpos*$_9(.87[join, stem], -136)$; $y_{9l} = x\_height + oo$; $x_9 = .68[x_8, x_{10}]$;
> $z_{8'} = whatever[z_{11}, z_{10}]$; $y_{8'} = 1.25x\_height$;

$penpos_8(join, \text{angle}(z_{8'} - z_8) - 90)$;
penstroke $z_{8e}\{z_{8'} - z_8\}$ .. tension 1.5 .. $z_{9e}\{right\}$ .. z_{10e} -- z_{11e};

numeric $serif$; $serif = x_{11r} - x_{12} = 1u$;
$x_7 - x_{4l} = serif$; $x_{3r} - x_1 = .95serif$; $x_{4r} - x_5 = .9serif$; $x_{14} - x_{11l} = .8serif$;
$y_{1l} = y_{3l}$; $penpos_1(serif\_tip, -90)$; $z_2 = z_{3l}$;
$penpos_2(1.25serif\_height, \text{angle}(\textbf{direction } 0 \textbf{ of}(z_{3l} .. \{down\}z_{4l})))$;
penstroke $z_{1e}\{right\}$ .. z_{2e};

if $(x_7 - x_4 + .2u + x_{11} - x_{12} > x_{11} - x_4)$:
$x_7 := .5[x_4, x_{11}] - .1u$;
$x_{12} := .5[x_4, x_{11}] + .1u$; **fi**

$penpos_5(serif\_tip, -90)$; $penpos_7(serif\_tip, -90)$;
$penpos_{12}(serif\_tip, -90)$; $penpos_{14}(serif\_tip, -90)$;
$penpos_6(serif\_height, -90)$; $penpos_{13}(serif\_height, -90)$;
$y_{5r} = y_{7r} = y_{12r} = y_{14r} = 0$; $z_{6r} = z_4$; $z_{13r} = z_{11}$;

penstroke $z_{5e}\{right\}$ .. $z_{6e} \& z_{6e}$ .. $\{right\}z_{7e}$;
penstroke $z_{12e}\{right\}$ .. $z_{13e} \& z_{13e}$ .. $\{right\}z_{14e}$;
endchar;

The formatting of the code above was done by a pretty-printer for METAFONT code, known as *mft*. This utility converts METAFONT code into TEX code with a rather refined layout that, unfortunately, can be compiled only under the plain format. There is a LATEX package called *mftinc* that allows code produced by *mft* to be included in a LATEX document, as we did above.

The reason that we used so many parameters in the METAFONT code above is to have the ability to play with them. Let us try some tests.

First of all, we can have fun modifying the thickness of the downstroke (the stem parameter). For example, we can start with stem=join and go up to stem=2.2u, which is twice the standard value.

To do so, we shall create a test font in which the first 64 glyphs will be variants of the one that we have just designed. We shall use the following code:

```
input modes.mf;
mode_setup;
font_size 10pt#;
font_quad 18pt#;
font_normal_space 6pt#;

u#=1pt#; define_pixels(u);

numeric i;
for i=0 step 1 until 63:

beginchar(i,7pt#,6pt#,0pt#);
...
```

```
stem=(i/63)[join,2.2u];
...
endchar;

endfor
bye
```

And we shall generate the font by writing:

```
mf "\mode:=linoone; proofing:=0; mag:=1.5; input testfont;"
gftopk testfont.1905gf
```

A few words of explanation: The mode linoone is for the Linotype phototypesetters that were used to make the plates for this book; since that mode has a resolution of 1,270 ppi and the font used in the test is a 15-point font, the file generated by METAFONT has a resolution of 1,905 points. In the METAFONT code, we first call for the reading of the file modes.mf, which contains the definition of the linoone mode; then we perform mode_setup to establish the conversion from "true" units to units in pixels; then we give some of the font's metric parameters: the type size, the size of the em, and the width of the normal space.

Next, we define a numeric variable i and create a loop using that variable, with an increment of 1, running from 0 to 63. Finally, instead of writing stem=1.1u in the code, we write stem=(i/63)[join,2.2u], which means that we go from the value of the connecting stroke to 2.2u in 64 steps.

And here is the result:

Note that we have modified only one parameter and that properly increasing the glyph's weight would also have required the modification of the other parameters at the same time.

Let us run another test: we shall modify the glyph's set-width. We wish to emphasize that it is not merely a matter of reducing the image's horizontal scaling factor. We shall modify the set-width while leaving all the stroke thicknesses unchanged. Here is the result:

n n n n n n n n n n n n n n n
n n n n n n n n n n n n n n n

Let us continue the torture session to which we are subjecting this innocent glyph. We shall make this font into a mechanistic font worthy of those of the nineteenth century. To do so, we shall increase the thickness of the ends of the serifs—that is, the parameter serif_tip.

In doing so, we notice that we have not taken all the necessary precautions. In particular, we wrote the following in our code: serif_tip=.2u; serif_ht=.7u;. What will happen if serif_tip becomes larger than serif_ht? To prevent that eventuality, let us replace the line with:

```
serif_tip=.2u; serif_ht=max(serif_tip,.7u);
```

Now serif_ht is always *at least* as large as serif_tip. One other change to make: as the serifs become larger, it is also desirable to thicken the letter's connecting stroke slightly. Here we shall take connecting strokes whose thickness is at least half that of the tips of the serifs: join=max(.2u,.5serif_tip);. Here is what we get once these precautions have been taken:

n n n n n n n n n n n n n n
n n n n n n n n n n n n n n
n n n n n n n n n n n n n n
n n n n n n n n n n n n n n

Finally, we can play with the lengths of the serifs—the serif parameter. Let us draw glyphs for which the serif parameter ranges from 0 to 1.5 times the usual serif:

n n n n n n n n n n n n n n
n n n n n n n n n n n n n n
n n n n n n n n n n n n n n
n n n n n n n n n n n n n n

F.1.4   *Optimizing the Rasterization*

In Chapter 13, we saw the different techniques that PostScript and TrueType fonts use to optimize the rasterization at a low resolution, whether on the screen or in printed output. What does METAFONT do?

As we shall see in this section, METAFONT goes far beyond the other formats in this area. The reason is very simple. We have already mentioned that in METAFONT code we work with pixels. Thus optimization is merely a matter of checking whether the values of the different dimensions are whole (not just rational) and that the dimensions that traditionally cause problems, such as stroke thicknesses, are equal. Unlike PostScript fonts, our METAFONT fonts have no need of hints, as we have complete control over the rendering; and unlike TrueType, METAFONT does not use obscure assembly instructions but rather a genuine high-level programming language.

Let us examine several examples to see how METAFONT optimizes the rendering. First, let us take the most classic case, that of the letter 'H'. To check the rendering of this glyph at low resolution, we shall use the utility *gftype* (see §A.5.2). Here is what we obtain for METAFONT mode epsdrft at a resolution of 72 ppi:

```
autorounding:=0;
smoothing:=0;

u#=2pt#; define_pixels(u);

beginchar("H",14pt#,12pt#,0pt#);
pickup pensquare scaled 1u;
lft bot z1=(1u,0);
x2=x1; top y2=h;
x3=w-x1-.666u; y3=y1; x4=x3; y4=y2;
z5=.5[z1,z2]; z6=.5[z3,z4];
draw z1--z2; draw z3--z4; draw z5--z6;
endchar;
```

We see that what we feared did indeed come to pass: the downstroke on the left is not of the same thickness as the downstroke on the right. We must admit that we did in fact deliberately create this catastrophe: we explicitly asked METAFONT not to optimize the rendering automatically, by setting the parameters autorounding and smoothing to zero.

The solution is easy: METAFONT has an instruction called round that rounds the value given as its argument. Here, the values x1 and x3 have not been rounded; thus let us change our code to:

```
autorounding:=0;
smoothing:=0;

u#=2pt#; define_pixels(u);

beginchar("H",14pt#,12pt#,0pt#);
pickup pensquare scaled 1u;
lft bot z1=round(1u,0);
x2=x1; top y2=h;
x3=round(w-x1-.666u); y3=y1; x4=x3; y4=y2;
z5=.5[z1,z2]; z6=.5[z3,z4];
draw z1--z2; draw z3--z4; draw z5--z6;
endchar;
```

That did not work. Indeed, we were very clumsy: on the left we rounded the left side of the pixel, and on the right we rounded the center of the pixel. It is not surprising that the result was poor. To correct it, we must round the pixels on both sides. Thus we shall write:

```
rt x3=round(w-lft x1-.666u);
```

which does indeed give the correct result:

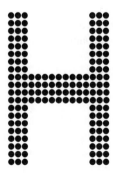

```
autorounding:=0;
smoothing:=0;

u#=2pt#; define_pixels(u);

beginchar("H",14pt#,12pt#,0pt#);
pickup pensquare scaled 1u;
lft bot z1=round(1u,0);
x2=x1; top y2=h;
rt x3=round(w-lft x1-
.666u); y3=y1; x4=x3; y4=y2;
z5=.5[z1,z2]; z6=.5[z3,z4];
draw z1--z2; draw z3--z4; draw z5--z6;
endchar;
```

Now let us take a more complex case, that of the letter 'T'. We shall draw it in a rather peculiar way in order to force an asymmetric rendering:

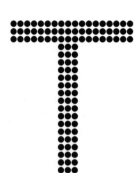

```
beginchar("T",11.8pt#,12pt#,0pt#);
pickup pensquare scaled .9u;
bot z1=(.5w-.33u,0);
x2=x1; top y2=top y3=top y4=h;
lft x3=0; rt x4=w-.66u;
draw z1--z2; draw z3--z4;
endchar;
```

Indeed, we have 8 pixels on the left and only 7 on the right. What to do?

We can start by noticing that since the error in the rendering came from the rounding of (w-.66u), that error cannot be more than 1 pixel at the most. Thus we can compare the number of pixels in the horizontal stroke to the right and to the left of the stem. If the number on the right is larger, we shall subtract a pixel from it; if the number on the left is larger, we shall do the opposite.

Here is the code, along with the result, which is good:

```
beginchar("T",11.8pt#,12pt#,0pt#);
pickup pensquare scaled .9u;
lft bot z1=(round(lft .5w-.33u),0);
x2=x1; top y2=top y3=top y4=h;
lft x3=0; rt x4=w-.66u;
if (round(lft x1)-round(lft x3) >
    round(rt x4)-round(rt x1)):
    x4 := x4+1; fi
if (round(lft x1)-round(lft x3) <
    round(rt x4)-round(rt x1)):
    x4 := x4-1; fi
draw z1--z2; draw z3--z4;
endchar;
```

This code is somewhat inelegant. It is easier to use a macro defined by Knuth to solve problems of this kind: change_width. The idea is that we want what is left of the glyph's set-width, after we have taken a pixel from the downstroke, to be an even number of pixels. If that is not the case, we add or subtract a pixel, as needed, so as to be closer to the unrounded value.

Adding or subtracting a pixel changes the parity of the set-width and solves the problem.

To avoid such problems from the start, we can define "correct amounts in pixels for the active pen". Explanation: if we define, for example, sidebearing as the left side-bearing, then there is no point in rounding its value, since if we place the center of a pen on the point z1=(sidebearing,0), it is the left edge of the pen, not its center, that will be rounded.

Thus we should lft z1=(round(lft sidebearing),0). A more elegant way to write it is:

```
z1 = (good.x sidebearing,0);
```

Even better, we can define the pixel version of sidebearing# as a "correct value":

```
define_good_x_pixels(sidebearing);
```

After that, the value of sidebearing is correct, for the active pen, in the sense that lft sidebearing is a round number.

A case similar to that of 'T': the point of the letter 'V'. A naive approach would be to write:

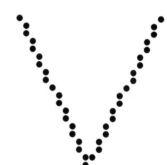

```
beginchar("V",13pt#,12pt#,0pt#);
pickup pencircle scaled .3u;
lft top z1=(0,h); rt top z3=(w,h);
z2=(.5w-eps,good.y 0);
draw z1--z2--z3;
endchar;
```

But the point is not symmetrical. Why not? Because the row of pixels immediately above the point contains two pixels. Aside from the point, the rest of the letter is symmetrical. Thus we have the same number of pixels on each side. Conclusion: the problem comes from the fact that the sum of all the pixels is an even number. Thus we shall adopt Knuth's solution: we shall check whether the total width of the letter is an even number of pixels, and, if it is, we shall use the change_width command.

To check whether a number is even, we merely take half of the number and compare it with its rounded version. If the two are equal, the original number is even. Here, then, is the code, together with the results obtained:

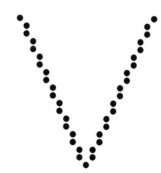

```
beginchar("V",13pt#,12pt#,0pt#);
pickup pencircle scaled .3u;
if (.5w = round(.5w)): change_width; fi
lft top z1=(0,h); rt top z3=(w,h);
z2=(.5w-eps,good.y 0);
draw z1--z2--z3;
endchar;
```

Note that the change_width method works because the letter's width in pixels is directly related to the set-width.

Let us take one last example, a more complicated one: that of the letter 'O'. Our first attempt will be to write:

```
beginchar("O",10pt#,12pt#,0pt#);
pickup pencircle scaled .3u;
lft z1=(0,.5h);
z2=(.5w,0); x4=x2; y4-y2=x3-x1;
rt z3=(w,.5h);
draw z1..z2..z3..z4..cycle;
endchar;
```

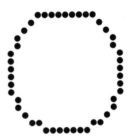

We see that there are far more pixels at the bottom than at the top. The problem comes from the fact that at the bottom of the letter we placed the center of the pen on the baseline, whereas at the top we really do not know exactly what is going on, since y4-y2=x3-x1 has no reason to be round. We could, of course, round that amount, but doing so would not ensure that the letter would turn out symmetrical; indeed, it would not, as can be seen below:

```
beginchar("O",10pt#,12pt#,0pt#);
pickup pencircle scaled .3u;
lft z1=(0,.5h);
z2=(.5w,0); x4=x2; rt x3=w;
y4-y2=round(x3-x1); y3=.5h;
draw z1..z2..z3..z4..cycle;
endchar;
```

What we need is to rewrite the code so that y2 and y4 are "correct" for the current pen, and then y1 will then simply be defined as half of the distance between them. Here is what we shall do, together with the result that we obtain:

```
beginchar("O",11.8pt#,12pt#,0pt#);
pickup pencircle scaled .333u;
lft x1=0;
z2= (.5w,good.y 0); x4=x2;
rt x3=w; y4=good.y (y2+x3-x1);
y3=y1=.5[y2,y4];
draw z1..z2..z3..z4..cycle;
endchar;
```

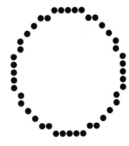

Quite a success!

F.2   The Computer Modern Family of Fonts

When Knuth developed TeX, his goal was to be able to typeset his own books. But to do so he needed a font—nay, an entire family of fonts, with a "typewriter" version (for computer code) and all the mathematical symbols that he wanted. He needed to find a reasonably neutral typeface that would be suitable for any type of text, yet one that was also sophisticated enough to demonstrate the possibilities of the METAFONT language. And, if possible, an American typeface. After some investigation, Knuth decided to focus on the "legible" typefaces from the turn of the twentieth century, an in particular on *Monotype Modern*. He found several designs of *Modern*, including one produced by Monotype's American branch, the typeface *Modern 8A*. This is the typeface that he used as a basis for designing what was to become one of the most widely used typefaces on the planet, at least in the academic world: *Computer Modern*.

In this section, we shall very quickly present the structure of this family of fonts, which greatly exceeds in its complexity everything else that has ever been designed in METAFONT, before or since. To be sure, some people may say that this complexity was somewhat gratuitous and that Knuth wished to face the challenge of a single program that could generate roman type, italic type, slanted type, "typewriter" type, sans serif type, calligraphic type—all in every weight and every optical size. Was it really necessary? Let the reader decide. In any event, as the inseparable companion of TeX, this font family has traveled the world and has even been extended to other scripts, as we shall see in §F.2.2.

Another peculiarity of this font family is that it is perhaps the only one in the world whose code has been *published in book form*. Specifically, the fifth, and last, volume of Knuth's *Computers & Typesetting* series is entitled *Computer Modern Typefaces*. It presents the METAFONT code for this font family, illustrated and documented. Not surprisingly, that code takes up no fewer than 588+xvi pages!

But first, a few words about the general structure of *Computer Modern*.

F.2.1   General Structure

The original distribution of *Computer Modern* included 128 files, of five types:

- Parameter files: cmr10.mf, cmr12.mf, etc. These files contain the appropriate values of the parameters for each font variation. Their names indicate the type and optical size of the font. These are the files that METAFONT reads first.

- Driver files: roman.mf, textit.mf, etc. These are the files that will drive the rest of the font-generation process. They are invoked by the parameter files, and they in turn invoke the other required files. There are only eight of them, for the eight font "categories": roman, titling, extended ASCII, small capitals, italic, mathematical italic, mathematical symbols, extensible mathematical symbols.

- Program files: romanu.mf, itall.mf, etc. These contain descriptions of the glyphs, arranged according to their type. For example, there is a file for the lowercase Latin letters, another for the italics, another for the lowercase Greek letters, another for punctuation, and so forth.

- A "base" file: cmbase.mf. It contains the definitions of all of the subroutines required to describe the glyphs. It is the only file that is read by all the fonts; it contains neither glyph descriptions nor values of parameters but only indispensable chunks of code.

- Test files: 3test.mf, 6test.mf. These files display several styles of the same glyph on the screen so that the designer can test the effect of his code on several values of the parameters at the same time.

But exactly which fonts does this family contain?

As can be seen in Figures F-1 and F-2, the original distribution, described in [219], contained 75 fonts:

- Roman, cmr, in optical sizes ranging from 5 to 17 points. Size 5 is intended for superscripts of superscripts, and size 17 is intended for titles. Knuth never was a fan of superlatives, unlike Caslon and Bodoni; therefore, this family does not contain a size 72 or a size 96.

- Slanted type, cmsl, in 8, 9, 10, and 12 points. "Slanted" type is an invention of Knuth that serves to distinguish the statement of a theorem, set in slanted type, from mathematical variables, which are set in italic.

- Extended bold, cmbx, in sizes ranging from 5 to 12 points. This is the default version of bold; the nonextended version is seldom used. Versions for slanted (cmbxsl) and italic (cmbxti) also exist, but only in 10 points.

- "Typewriter" type, cmtt, in 8, 9, 10, and 12 points. This font is without a doubt Knuth's greatest success; it is infinitely more beautiful than the ubiquitous *Courier*.

- Four variants of "typewriter" type: slanted (cmsltt), italic (cmitt), small capitals (cmtcsc), and variable width (cmvtt), only in 10 points.

- "Extended typewriter", cmtex, in 8, 9, and 10 points. The parameters for these fonts are the same as for cmtt, but they contain special glyphs: some Greek letters, some mathematical symbols, etc. The number of glyphs per font was limited to 128 at the time, and the addition of a few new glyphs called for the creation of a new font. These glyphs did, in fact, exist on the experimental keyboard used by Knuth, a keyboard that the author was fortunate enough to see before it was sent to the Computer Museum in Boston.

- Sans serif (cmss), in sizes from 8 to 17.

- Slanted sans serif (cmssi), also in sizes from 8 to 17.

- Two variants of weight and width in sans serif type: condensed semi-bold (cmssdc) and extended bold (cmssbx), in 10 points only.

- A mammoth font called cminch (because the capitals are one inch high) that is in fact an extended bold sans serif of 72.27 points. This font contains only capitals and digits, and it is used primarily for the numbers and letters of the chapters in *The T_EXbook* and *The METAFONTbook*, which were the inspiration for the chapter numbers and letters in the book that you are now reading, which was also set with T_EX but in the font *Le Monde Livre*, by Porchez. The font cminch does not mention its size because that size is fixed.

cmr17 : AaBbCcDdEeFfGgHhIiJjKkLlMmNnOoPpQq
cmr12 : AaBbCcDdEeFfGgHhIiJjKkLlMmNnOoPpQqRrSsTtUuVvWwX
cmr10 : AaBbCcDdEeFfGgHhIiJjKkLlMmNnOoPpQqRrSsTtUuVvWwXxYyZz01234
cmr9 : AaBbCcDdEeFfGgHhIiJjKkLlMmNnOoPpQqRrSsTtUuVvWwXxYyZz0123456789Aa
cmr8 : AaBbCcDdEeFfGgHhIiJjKkLlMmNnOoPpQqRrSsTtUuVvWwXxYyZz0123456789AaBbCcDd
cmr7 : AaBbCcDdEeFfGgHhIiJjKkLlMmNnOoPpQqRrSsTtUuVvWwXxYyZz0123456789AaBbCcDdEeFfG
cmr6 : AaBbCcDdEeFfGgHhIiJjKkLlMmNnOoPpQqRrSsTtUuVvWwXxYyZz0123456789AaBbCcDdEeFfGgHhIiJjKk
cmr5 : AaBbCcDdEeFfGgHhIiJjKkLlMmNnOoPpQqRrSsTtUuVvWwXxYyZz0123456789AaBbCcDdEeFfGgHhIiJjKkLlMmNn

cmsl12 : AaBbCcDdEeFfGgHhIiJjKkLlMmNnOoPpQqRrSsTtUuVvWwX
cmsl10 : AaBbCcDdEeFfGgHhIiJjKkLlMmNnOoPpQqRrSsTtUuVvWwXxYyZz01234
cmsl9 : AaBbCcDdEeFfGgHhIiJjKkLlMmNnOoPpQqRrSsTtUuVvWwXxYyZz0123456789A
cmsl8 : AaBbCcDdEeFfGgHhIiJjKkLlMmNnOoPpQqRrSsTtUuVvWwXxYyZz0123456789AaBbCcD

cmbx12 : AaBbCcDdEeFfGgHhIiJjKkLlMmNnOoPpQqRrSsTt
cmbx10 : AaBbCcDdEeFfGgHhIiJjKkLlMmNnOoPpQqRrSsTtUuVvWwX
cmbx9 : AaBbCcDdEeFfGgHhIiJjKkLlMmNnOoPpQqRrSsTtUuVvWwXxYyZz
cmbx8 : AaBbCcDdEeFfGgHhIiJjKkLlMmNnOoPpQqRrSsTtUuVvWwXxYyZz0123456
cmbx7 : AaBbCcDdEeFfGgHhIiJjKkLlMmNnOoPpQqRrSsTtUuVvWwXxYyZz0123456789Aa
cmbx6 : AaBbCcDdEeFfGgHhIiJjKkLlMmNnOoPpQqRrSsTtUuVvWwXxYyZz0123456789AaBbCcDdE
cmbx5 : AaBbCcDdEeFfGgHhIiJjKkLlMmNnOoPpQqRrSsTtUuVvWwXxYyZz0123456789AaBbCcDdEeFfGgHhI

cmtt12 : AaBbCcDdEeFfGgHhIiJjKkLlMmNnOoPpQqRrSsTtUuVvWwXxYyZz
cmtt10 : AaBbCcDdEeFfGgHhIiJjKkLlMmNnOoPpQqRrSsTtUuVvWwXxYyZz0123456789A
cmtt9 : AaBbCcDdEeFfGgHhIiJjKkLlMmNnOoPpQqRrSsTtUuVvWwXxYyZz0123456789AaBbCcDdEe
cmtt8 : AaBbCcDdEeFfGgHhIiJjKkLlMmNnOoPpQqRrSsTtUuVvWwXxYyZz0123456789AaBbCcDdEeFfGgHhIiJ
cmsltt10 : AaBbCcDdEeFfGgHhIiJjKkLlMmNnOoPpQqRrSsTtUuVvWwXxYyZz012345678
cmvtt10 : AaBbCcDdEeFfGgHhIiJjKkLlMmNnOoPpQqRrSsTtUuVvWwXxYyZz0
cmtex10 : AaBbCcDdEeFfGgHhIiJjKkLlMmNnOoPpQqRrSsTtUuVvWwXxYyZz0123456789
cmtex9 : AaBbCcDdEeFfGgHhIiJjKkLlMmNnOoPpQqRrSsTtUuVvWwXxYyZz0123456789AaBbCcDdE
cmtex8 : AaBbCcDdEeFfGgHhIiJjKkLlMmNnOoPpQqRrSsTtUuVvWwXxYyZz0123456789AaBbCcDdEeFfGgHhIi

cmss17 : AaBbCcDdEeFfGgHhIiJjKkLlMmNnOoPpQqRr
cmss12 : AaBbCcDdEeFfGgHhIiJjKkLlMmNnOoPpQqRrSsTtUuVvWwXxYyZ
cmss10 : AaBbCcDdEeFfGgHhIiJjKkLlMmNnOoPpQqRrSsTtUuVvWwXxYyZz0123456789
cmss9 : AaBbCcDdEeFfGgHhIiJjKkLlMmNnOoPpQqRrSsTtUuVvWwXxYyZz0123456789AaBbCc
cmss8 : AaBbCcDdEeFfGgHhIiJjKkLlMmNnOoPpQqRrSsTtUuVvWwXxYyZz0123456789AaBbCcDdEeFfG

cmssi17 : AaBbCcDdEeFfGgHhIiJjKkLlMmNnOoPpQqR
cmssi12 : AaBbCcDdEeFfGgHhIiJjKkLlMmNnOoPpQqRrSsTtUuVvWwXxYy
cmssi10 : AaBbCcDdEeFfGgHhIiJjKkLlMmNnOoPpQqRrSsTtUuVvWwXxYyZz012345678
cmssi9 : AaBbCcDdEeFfGgHhIiJjKkLlMmNnOoPpQqRrSsTtUuVvWwXxYyZz0123456789AaBbC
cmssi8 : AaBbCcDdEeFfGgHhIiJjKkLlMmNnOoPpQqRrSsTtUuVvWwXxYyZz0123456789AaBbCcDdEeFf
cmssdc10 : AaBbCcDdEeFfGgHhIiJjKkLlMmNnOoPpQqRrSsTtUuVvWwXxYyZz0123456789A
cmssbx10 : AaBbCcDdEeFfGgHhIiJjKkLlMmNnOoPpQqRrSsTtUuVvWwXxYyZz0

Figure F-1: The fonts of the original Computer Modern distribution, 1/2.

CMINCH A

cmssq8 : AaBbCcDdEeFfGgHhIiJjKkLlMmNnOoPpQqRrSsTtUuVvWwXxYyZz0123456789
cmssqi8 : AaBbCcDdEeFfGgHhIiJjKkLlMmNnOoPpQqRrSsTtUuVvWwXxYyZz0123456789
cmdunh10 : AaBbCcDdEeFfGgHhIiJjKkLlMmNnOoPpQqRrSsTtUuVvWwXxYyZz01
cmbxsl10 : AaBbCcDdEeFfGgHhIiJjKkLlMmNnOoPpQqRrSsTtUuVvWw
cmb10 : AaBbCcDdEeFfGgHhIiJjKkLlMmNnOoPpQqRrSsTtUuVvWwXxYyZz01234
cmff10 : AaBbCcDdEeFfGgHhIiJjKkLlMmNnOoPpQqRrSsTtUuVvWwXxYyZz0123456789AaBbCcDdEeF
cmfib8 : AaBbCcDdEeFfGgHhIiJjKkLlMmNnOoPpQqRrSsTtUuVvWwXxYyZz01
cmti12 : AaBbCcDdEeFfGgHhIiJjKkLlMmNnOoPpQqRrSsTtUuVvWwX
cmti10 : AaBbCcDdEeFfGgHhIiJjKkLlMmNnOoPpQqRrSsTtUuVvWwXxYyZz012345
cmti9 : AaBbCcDdEeFfGgHhIiJjKkLlMmNnOoPpQqRrSsTtUuVvWwXxYyZz0123456789Aa
cmti8 : AaBbCcDdEeFfGgHhIiJjKkLlMmNnOoPpQqRrSsTtUuVvWwXxYyZz0123456789AaBbCcD
cmti7 : AaBbCcDdEeFfGgHhIiJjKkLlMmNnOoPpQqRrSsTtUuVvWwXxYyZz0123456789AaBbCcDdEeF
cmmi12 AaBbCcDdEeFfGgHhIiJjKkLlMmNnOoPpQqRrSsTtUuVvWw
cmmi10 AaBbCcDdEeFfGgHhIiJjKkLlMmNnOoPpQqRrSsTtUuVvWwXxYyZz0123
cmmi9 AaBbCcDdEeFfGgHhIiJjKkLlMmNnOoPpQqRrSsTtUuVvWwXxYyZz0123456789
cmmi8 AaBbCcDdEeFfGgHhIiJjKkLlMmNnOoPpQqRrSsTtUuVvWwXxYyZz0123456789AaBbCc
cmmi7 AaBbCcDdEeFfGgHhIiJjKkLlMmNnOoPpQqRrSsTtUuVvWwXxYyZz0123456789AaBbCcDdEe
cmmi6 AaBbCcDdEeFfGgHhIiJjKkLlMmNnOoPpQqRrSsTtUuVvWwXxYyZz0123456789AaBbCcDdEeFfGgHh
cmmi5 AaBbCcDdEeFfGgHhIiJjKkLlMmNnOoPpQqRrSsTtUuVvWwXxYyZz0123456789AaBbCcDdEeFfGgHhIiJjKk
cmbxti10 : AaBbCcDdEeFfGgHhIiJjKkLlMmNnOoPpQqRrSsTtUuVvWw
cmmib10 AaBbCcDdEeFfGgHhIiJjKkLlMmNnOoPpQqRrSsTtUuVvWw
cmitt10 : AaBbCcDdEeFfGgHhIiJjKkLlMmNnOoPpQqRrSsTtUuVvWwXxYyZz012345678
cmu10 : AaBbCcDdEeFfGgHhIiJjKkLlMmNnOoPpQqRrSsTtUuVvWwXxYyZz
cmff10 : AaBbCcDdEeFfGgHhIiJjKkLlMmNnOoPpQqRrSsTtUuVvWwXxYyZz012
CMCSC10 : AABbCcDdEeFfGgHhIiJjKkLlMmNnOoPpQqRrSsTtUuVvWwX
CMTCSC10 : AABbCcDdEeFfGgHhIiJjKkLlMmNnOoPpQqRrSsTtUuVvWwXxYyZz01234567
cmsy10 : A⊣B⌊C⌋D⌈E⌉F{G}H⟨I⟩JⱩK∥L≀M↕N∖O℘P√QURVSʃTⱵUⱶVⱵWⱵ⅄X§Y†Z‡/
cmsy9 : A⊣B⌊C⌋D⌈E⌉F{G}H⟨I⟩JⱩK∥L≀M↕N∖O℘P√QURVSʃTⱵUⱶVⱵWⱵ⅄X§Y†Z‡/∞∋Ə△▽
cmsy8 : A⊣B⌊C⌋D⌈E⌉F{G}H⟨I⟩JⱩK∥L≀M↕N∖O℘P√QURVSʃTⱵUⱶVⱵWⱵ⅄X§Y†Z‡/∞∋Ə△▽∃A⊣B
cmsy7 : A⊣B⌊C⌋D⌈E⌉F{G}H⟨I⟩JⱩK∥L≀M↕N∖O℘P√QURVSʃTⱵUⱶVⱵWⱵ⅄X§Y†Z‡/∞∋Ə△▽∃A⊣B⌊C⌋D
cmsy6 : A⊣B⌊C⌋D⌈E⌉F{G}H⟨I⟩JⱩK∥L≀M↕N∖O℘P√QURVSʃTⱵUⱶVⱵWⱵ⅄X§Y†Z‡/∞∋Ə△▽∃A⊣B⌊C⌋D⌈E⌉F{G}
cmsy5 : A⊣B⌊C⌋D⌈E⌉F{G}H⟨I⟩JⱩK∥L≀M↕N∖O℘P√QURVSʃTⱵUⱶVⱵWⱵ⅄X§Y†Z‡/∞∋Ə△▽∃A⊣B⌊C⌋D⌈E⌉F{G}H⟨I⟩J
cmbsy10 : A⊣B⌊C⌋D⌈E⌉F{G}H⟨I⟩JⱩK∥L≀M↕N∖O℘P√QURVSʃTⱵUⱶVⱵW
cmex10 : Ⅱ⌢⟨⟩⌣⊔⊓ ʃʃ⊙⊙⊕⊕⊗⊗Σ√Π√ʃ√⋃⋂⊎∧∨

Figure F-2: The fonts of the original Computer Modern distribution, 2/2.

- A "Dutch" sans serif font (i.e., one with a very large x-height), "sans serif quotation" (cmssq), and its italic (cmssqi), used by Knuth for the wonderful quotations that appear at the end of each chapter of his books. Only in 8 points.

- "Dunhill" (cmdunh), a typeface with capitals and lowercase letters that have very tall ascenders, whose name refers to the logo of the famous brand of cigarettes. Only in 10 points.

- Bold non-extended (cmb), an anemic version of cmbx.

- A "funny" font (cmff, the 'f' coming from *funny*), whose italic version (cmfi) has a positive slope whereas the upright version has a backslant. Only in 10 points.

- An experimental typeface, "Fibonacci", so called because the values of its parameters were all derived from the series of numbers devised by this famous mathematician. It is, of course, a joke, but the result is not necessarily unattractive. In 8 points only, because 10 is not a Fibonacci number, but 8 is. Other permissible sizes: 5, 13, 21, 34 ...

- Text italic (cmti), in sizes from 7 to 12 points.

- Mathematical italic (cmmi), slightly wider than text italic, and with no kerning pairs (since in mathematical mode the distances are generated in a different way). In sizes from 5 to 12 points. There is also a bold version of this font (cmmib), in 10 points only.

- "Upright italic" (cmu), which uses the glyphs for the italic letters, but with a zero slope. Only in 10 points. Not very satisfying.

- Small capitals (cmcsc), in 10 points only.

- Mathematical symbols (cmsy), in sizes from 5 to 10 points. There is also a bold version (cmbsy), in 10 points only.

- Extensible mathematical symbols (cmex), i.e., the large delimiters, the large operators, and everything else that either is very large or must be built up from components. In 10 points only.

To generate a font of the *Computer Modern* family, one need only give the values of its 62 parameters. We have illustrated in Figure F-3 some of the ways in which they are used. Here is a list of them, in the order in which they appear in the parameter files:

- u: the "base unit", used primarily to define the widths of the glyphs. The smaller this parameter is, the narrower the letters will be.

- width_adj: an empirical parameter for "correction" that is added to certain widths.

- serif_fit: the side-bearings of lowercase letters with serifs.

- cap_serif_fit: the side-bearings of capitals with serifs.

- letter_fit: a value that is added systematically to all side-bearings.

- body_height: the height of the parentheses, brackets, and other large symbols.

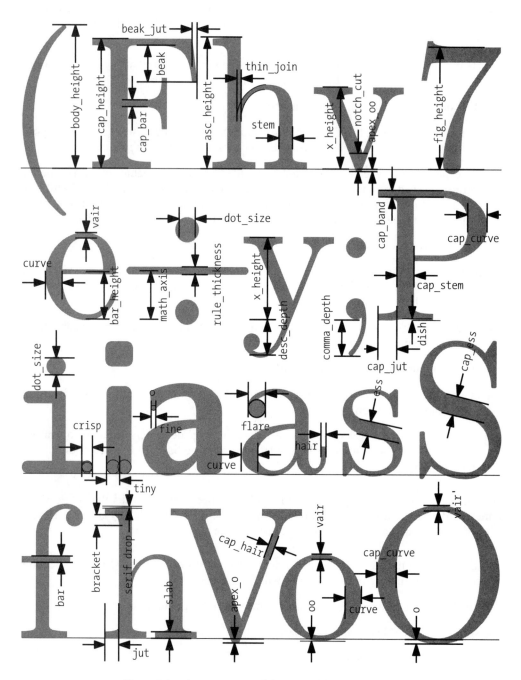

Figure F-3: The parameters of the Computer Modern fonts.

- asc_height: the height of the ascenders.

- cap_height: the height of the capitals.

- fig_height: the height of the digits.

- x_height: the height of the lowercase letters.

- math_axis: the height of the mathematical axis of symmetry; that is, the axis relative to which such symbols as $<> \div = + - \oplus \otimes$, etc., are centered.

- bar_height: the height of the cross-stroke of the 'e'. Knuth admits that this parameter was an excess and recommends that it always be kept between 50 percent and 55 percent of the x_height.

- comma_depth: the depth of the bottom of the comma.

- desc_depth: the depth of the descenders.

- crisp: the diameter for the rounded ends of serifs. It is zero for roman, but it is clearly visible for "typewriter type".

- tiny: the diameter of the rounded ends of the fundamental strokes (such as the down-strokes of sans serif letters, for example).

- fine: the diameter of the more tightly rounded corners, such as that of the terminal of the sans serif 'a'.

- thin_join: a very thin stroke thickness, used internally. For example, the thickness of the beginning of the second downstroke of the roman 'h'.

- hair: the horizontal thickness of the connecting strokes of the lowercase letters.

- stem: the thickness of the thick upright strokes of the lowercase letters.

- curve: the thickness of the thick curved strokes of the lowercase letters.

- ess: the thickness of the stem of the lowercase 's' at its center of gravity.

- flare: the diameter of the ball terminals of 'a' and 'c' (that of 'f' is .8[stem,flare]).

- dot_size: the diameter of the dot on the 'i' and, for that matter, of any dot. In Figure F-3, we see that the dots on the division sign ($\div$) are thicker than those of the 'i' and the ';', yet all of these dots use the dot_size parameter. The difference is due to the pen used to draw and fill the dot: for the former, it is a pen of thickness rule_thickness; for the latter, it is a pen of thickness fine.

- cap_hair: the horizontal thickness of the connecting strokes of the capitals.

- cap_stem: the thickness of the thick upright strokes of the capitals.

- cap_curve: the thickness of the thick curved strokes of the capitals.

- `cap_ess`: the thickness of the stem of the capital 's' at its center of gravity.

- `rule_thickness`: the thickness of the strokes of the "geometrical" symbols, such as the mathematical symbols '$<$', '$>$', '$\div$', '$=$', '$+$', '$-$', '$\oplus$', '$\otimes$', etc.

- `dish`: the height of the arch in the serifs.

- `bracket`: the height of the serif's bracket, which is to say the distance between the height of the point at which we leave the letter's stem and the height of the serif's bar.

- `jut`: the width of the serif of a lowercase letter (measured from the edge of the letter's stem).

- `cap_jut`: like `jut`, but for the capitals.

- `beak_jut`: for slanted serifs, such as the one on the upper arm of the 'F', the horizontal projection of the slanted part.

- `beak`: the height of a slanted serif, measured from the internal boundary of the cross stroke.

- `vair`: the vertical thickness of the connecting strokes of the lowercase letters.

- `notch_cut`: the vertical distance between the inner and outer points of the 'v'.

- `bar`: the thickness of the crossbar of the 'f'.

- `slab`: the thickness of the serifs.

- `cap_bar`: the thickness of the crossbars of the letters 'E', 'F', 'G', and 'H'.

- `cap_band`: likewise, but for the letters 'A', 'B', 'D', 'P', and 'R'. In most cases, `cap_bar` is equal to `cap_band`.

- `cap_notch_cut`: the vertical distance between the inner and outer points of the 'V'.

- `serif_drop`: the obliqueness of the upper half-serifs of the letters 'b', 'd', 'h', 'i', 'j', 'k', 'l', 'm', 'n', 'p', 'r', and 'u'.

- `stem_corr`: a parameter for correcting `stem`. By subtracting this parameter from `stem`, we obtain `stem'`; likewise for `cap_stem'`.

- `vair_corr`: a parameter for correcting `vair`. By adding the two, we obtain `vair'`.

- `apex_corr`: a parameter for correcting `apex`, used, for example, for the apex of the 'A'.

- `o`: the overshoot of the round strokes of the capital letters. From `o` we calculate `oo`, the overshoot of the round strokes of the lowercase letters.

- `apex_o`: the overshoot of the apexes of the capital letters. From `apex_o` we calculate `apex_oo`, the overshoot of the apexes of the lowercase letters.

- `slant`: the slant.

- fudge: a multiplicative factor for correcting thicknesses, used, for example, for the 'v' in the "typewriter" fonts.

- math_spread: the distance between the bars of the equal sign at small point sizes.

- superness: the curvature of the round letters. It is this parameter that enables us to distinguish the letter 'O' from the zero '0' in the "typewriter" font.

- superpull: the thinning of the strokes of the round letters.

- beak_darkness: the coefficient for filling the serifs: nonzero for roman, zero for "typewriter".

- ligs: a whole number that indicates the number of ligatures to include in the font.

- square_dots: a boolean value that indicates whether the dots are round (roman) or square (sans serif).

- hefty: a boolean value that indicates whether we want to lighten the strokes or not.

- serifs: a boolean value that indicates whether want to have serifs or not.

- monospace: a boolean value that indicates whether the font is monospace or not.

- variant_g: a boolean value that indicates whether the 'g' is of the roman ('g') or italic ('*g*') variety.

- low_asterisk: a boolean value that indicates whether the asterisk is low (the mathematical symbol '∗') or high (the editorial symbol '*').

- math_fitting: a boolean value that indicates whether or not we want spacing that has been customized for the mathematical mode.

To those, of course, are added the name of the font, its optical size, its metric parameters (see §B.1.2), and the choice of driver file.

In 1986, John Sauter [311] developed an extended version of the *Computer Modern* parameter files; people began to refer to the "Sauterized" versions of the fonts. In Sauter's version, the fonts can be generated at any optical size. If we request an optical size that already exists in Knuth's original distribution, we obtain exactly the same font. If, however, we request a different size, the original values are interpolated so as to generate the font on the fly. Generating fonts in this way could not be easier. Suppose that we wish to obtain the font cmitt at 17.28 points. We create a file cmitt1728.mf that contains only one line of code:

```
design_size:=17.28; input b-cmitt
```

F.2.2   Extensions

From the beginning, Knuth invited the friends of TeX and METAFONT to extend *Computer Modern* to other languages and other alphabets. Extensions were not long in coming.

Starting in 1981 [236], Hermann Zapf designed mathematical fonts for the American Mathematical Society; they are implemented in his *AMSTeX* package. These fonts are programmed in METAFONT78, and the code has never been made public. In 1985 [67, 68], the AMS supplemented these fonts with additional mathematical symbols and some Cyrillic fonts. Only in 1995 were the fonts rewritten in METAFONT82, improved, and publicly released as META-FONT source code [31].

In 1988, Silvio Levy [238] developed a Greek version (in the *hapla* style) of *Computer Modern*:

$$ΑΒΓΔΕΖΗΘΙΚΛΜΝΞΟΠΡΣΤΥΦΧΨΩ$$

$$αβγδεζηθικλμνξοπρσςτυφχψω$$

Unfortunately, the parameters work only for roman; there are neither italic nor sans serif nor "typewriter" fonts. In 1989, the author and his friend Klaus Thull [172] (known by the pseudonym Mahilata Shamaya) added small capitals and the glyphs needed for Greek numeration.

In 1989, in an article in the journal *TUGboat* [174], Doug Henderson explained how to obtain *Computer Modern* fonts as contours.

In 1990, at the meeting of the TeX Users Group in Cork, Ireland, a new font encoding, called the "Cork encoding" (or T1), was adopted. This encoding, which is a mixture of ISO 8859-1 and 8859-2, was quickly implemented by Norbert Schwarz and Jörg Knappen [212, 213], in the *DC* font family. Most of the glyphs are combinations of glyphs from *Computer Modern* (letters and accents, etc.), but a few new glyphs were also designed: the *thorn*, the *edh*, etc. Finally, in 1997, Jörg Knappen [214] renamed this font family *EC*.

In 1991, Dean Guenther and Janene Winter, of Washington State University, developed a LaTeX package for typesetting the International Phonetic Alphabet [153, 286]. Unfortunately, the METAFONT code is of poor quality. The situation was corrected in 1996 when Fukui Rei [302] issued his own system, of excellent quality, for typesetting in the International Phonetic Alphabet.

In that same year, 1991, Mícheál Ó Searcóid [315] designed a Gaelic *Computer Modern* font, *EIAD*:

$$ᴀbḃċċ́ᴅḋėꝼꝼ́ᵹᵹ́ḣiᴌmṁṅoρʀꜱṡċťu$$

$$ᴀbḃċċ́ᴅḋėꝼꝼ́ᵹᵹ́ḣiᴌmṁṅoρꝗꝗ́ťu$$

In 1993, Jörg Knappen [211] developed an extension of *Computer Modern* for the African languages that use the Latin alphabet and for certain languages not supported by *DC*: Maltese, Esperanto, etc. These fonts are called *FC*.

In 1996, at the TeX Users Group meeting in Moscow, Olga Lapko [227] presented a new family of *Computer Modern* Cyrillic fonts that were of higher quality than those of the AMS and that contained enough glyphs for all of the languages, including the Asian ones, that use the Cyrillic alphabet. These fonts are called *LH*:

$$АБВГДЕЁЖЗИЙКЛМНОПРСТУФХЦЧШЩЪЫЬЭЮЯѲѴ$$

абвгдеёжзийклмнопрстуфхцчшщъыьэѣюяѳѵ

In 1998, Walter Schmidt [314] noticed that the sans serif font of *Computer Modern* was used mainly as a supplementary typeface for roman but was ill suited for use on its own. He released *CM Bright*, a lighter sans serif font that is appropriate for running text:

ABCDEFGHIJKLMNOPQRSTUVWXYZ

abcdefghijklmnopqrstuvwxyz

Starting in 2000, Hàn Thế Thành [328, 327] designed *Computer Modern* fonts for Vietnamese, the *VN* fonts.

In 2001, Alan Hoenig [181] tried to adapt the parameters of *Computer Modern* to *Monotype Modern*. The result, called *Modernized Modern*, is very interesting:

ABCDEFGHIJKLMNOPQRSTUVWXYZ

abcdefghijklmnopqrstuvwxyz

F.3 MetaFog

Over the past 20 years, there have been several attempts to produce PostScript or TrueType fonts from METAFONT code, the first of them doubtless being that of Shimon Yanai and Daniel Berry [355], who developed a program called *mf2ps* that converted METAFONT surfaces into PostScript Type 1 contours. The code for this software (which is in fact a *change-file* for METAFONT—i.e., a file for adding Pascal code to METAFONT and modifying that code) can be found on the CTAN servers (http://www.ctan.org), but it is difficult to compile today, as it depends on a library of subroutines peculiar to Sun that dates from the years 1990 to 1991.

Richard Kinch, in his *TrueTEX* system [210], offered a program (for Windows only) called *Meta-Fog* [209] that converts METAFONT code into TrueType contours.

The process is quite complex:

1. We begin by compiling the METAFONT sources with METAPOST (!). The latter produces a file for each glyph in the font. We assemble the glyphs into a ZIP archive.

2. We launch *MetaFog* on those glyphs through the use of an AWK script. *MetaFog* produces two types of glyph-description files: *reduced* ones (those that have valid contours) and *nonreduced* ones (in which the contours of the different METAFONT pen strokes have not been merged). It is the filename that differs: for example, _065.eps is a reduced file, and _065u.eps is a nonreduced file.

3. We open the nonreduced files in the program *weed* (Figure F-4). This program is a type of glyph editor in which we can do only one thing: separate the Bézier curves that will be part of the glyph's contour from those that will not. We do so by clicking on them. It is quite entertaining to see the glyph take its shape amidst a heap of useless curves.

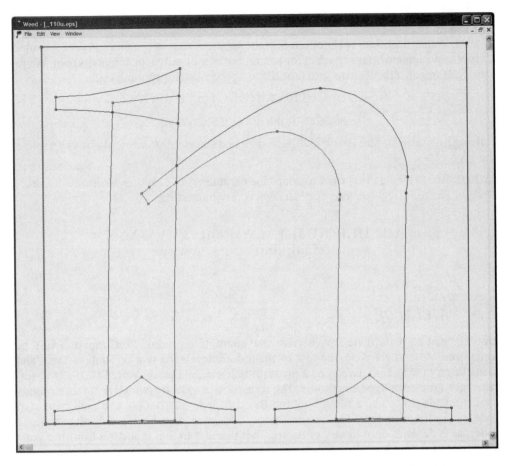

Figure F-4: The window of weed, where we see the META̸FONT glyph that we designed in §F.1.3.

4. Finally, one last script collects the files produced by *weed* into a TTF font. *MetaFog* includes quite a few "administrative" scripts: those that calculate the metrics, manage the encoding, etc.

Richard Kinch used *MetaFog* to produce the Computer Modern TrueType fonts that accompany *TrueTEX*. The result is excellent. In fact, Kinch was the only one to do serious work on the mathematical calculation of the curves that envelop the META̸FONT strokes. He gives an overview of his calculations in [209].

The tragedy is that these calculations, with which we could have created splendid fonts, remain prisoner to *MetaFog*, a program that does indeed do an admirable job of "vectorizing" META̸FONT code but that is in general of such abominably complex structure that it would give any programmer nightmares—and that is, alas, inaccessible to nonprogrammers. We can only hope that Richard will manage in the coming years to convert this chaotic set of scripts into a true software package; that will be a great breakthrough for the TEX/METAFONT community and a wonderful tool for all font designers.

The reader who is eager to encourage Richard to work towards this goal can send him email at kinch@truetex.com.

F.4 METATYPE1 *and Antykwa Półtawskiego*

In 1999, three Poles—Bogusław Jackowski, Janusz Nowacki, and Piotr Strzelczyk—shocked the TEX world by issuing a new family of fonts, *Antykwa Półtawskiego* (see §F.4.3), completely programmed in METATYPE1 [198].

In this section, we shall discuss the tool METATYPE1. By developing the tool together with the fonts produced by it, as Knuth had done with METAFONT and the *Computer Modern* fonts, the three Poles showed that the tool is of genuine practical interest. Let us also mention that in 2003 [197], Bogusław Jackowski and Janusz Nowacki produced *Computer Modern* fonts with METATYPE1, but not simply by rereading the METAFONT code; in fact, they started with PostScript Type 1 fonts and converted them to METATYPE1 code. Next, they cleaned the code up and fitted it with accents for the Latin languages. This is an interesting application of METATYPE1, even though it does not allow us to produced arbitrary *Computer Modern* fonts.

F.4.1 *Installing and Using* METATYPE1

While METAFONT does not require any installation, since it has been included in every TEX distribution since the 1980s, things are different for METATYPE1. What is METATYPE1, technically speaking?

It is a set of tools, the most important of which is METAPOST, a program derived from META-FONT, also written by Knuth's student John Hobby, that produces graphics in Encapsulated PostScript [179]. Jackowski and his colleagues wrote special routines in the METAPOST language to generate fonts and also wrote a postprocessor in the AWK language (the ancestor of Perl).

To install METATYPE1, one must have METAPOST, which, fortunately, is included in most TEX distributions, as well as *gawk* (the GNU implementation of AWK). One also needs the *t1utils* (which were described on page 233; see also [175]) to convert from PFB to human-readable PostScript code and vice versa. To create PFM files (which are required if we wish to use the PostScript fonts under Windows), we also need Perl. Finally, to obtain the documentation, we also need the tool *mft*, which is a pretty-printer for METAFONT and METAPOST code.

To install METATYPE1 under Windows, one downloads the installation from ftp://bop.eps.gda.pl/pub/metatype1/ and places the scripts (files with the extension .bat) into a directory listed in the PATH.

Under Unix or Mac OS X, installation is similar. The files can be downloaded from CTAN (http://www.ctan.org/tex-archive/systems/unix/mtype13); they were ported to Unix by Włodzimierz (Włodek) Bzyl. The scripts have slightly different names (without the 1 and the .bat extension). They must be placed somewhere where the system can find them when it looks for an executable file.

Whether under Windows or Unix, the files with the extension .mp (which are files of META-POST code), including the one that appears in extra, must be placed in a directory accessible to METAPOST. Do not forget to rebuild the TEX file-finding base by running *mktexlsr* or by performing the corresponding operation in the current TEX distribution.

Once the scripts have been installed, one must open mt1set.bat (or mt1set under Unix) in a text editor and modify the value of the environment variable METATYPE1. This is the absolute path of the directory that contains the METATYPE1 scripts.

Another detail: The Poles use a special version TEX called mex. Some TEX distributions contain it, but not all. In the script mkfont1.bat (or mkfont), it is mex that is invoked. If you do not have it available, replace the line:

```
mex $FNAME.tex
```

with:

```
tex "&plain $FNAME.tex"
```

METATYPE1 offers three scripts (written in the AWK language) to the user:

- mt1set.bat (or *mt1set* under Unix), a script that initializes the environment variable METATYPE1; it must be launched at the start of the session.

- mkfont1.bat (or *mkfont* under Unix), takes as its argument the name of a file of font parameters. This name must contain the extension .mp. It is the system's main script; it will launch METAPOST as well as the AWK scripts and the required *t1utils* binaries.

- mkproof.bat (or *mkproof* under Unix), a script that launches the pretty-printer *mft* and a number of other utilities to produce an attractively presented version of META-POST code.

To use METATYPE1, we change to the directory containing the font files to be processed—let us call it bar.mp—and run the script mkfont1.bat (or mkfont under Unix):

```
mkfont1.bat bar
```

Warning: Do not write the extension .mp of the METAPOST file! METATYPE1 then does the rest, and in a few moments we find ourselves with a PFB font.

F.4.2   Syntactic Differences from METAFONT

The authors of METATYPE1 did everything they could to smooth out the syntactic differences between METAFONT and METAPOST; nonetheless, there remain some major differences due to the PostScript Type 1 output format, which has needs other than those of the GF bitmap fonts traditionally produced by METAFONT.

We shall illustrate these differences by translating the code for our pseudo-*Vendôme* sample letter 'n' into METATYPE1.

First of all, we need a special package of macros, called fontbase.mp. Thus we begin our code with:

```
input fontbase;
```

Next, we need to define the unit u that we have used so much for describing distances. In METAFONT we would have first defined a "true unit" u# of one American printer's point; then we would have converted it into pixels to obtain u. Here we give the value of u directly in PostScript font units:

```
u:=100;
```

A PostScript Type 1 font needs some metadata. These are supplied by macros whose names begin with pf_:

```
pf_info_familyname "Pseudo-Vendome";
pf_info_fontname "Pseudo-Vendome-Regular";
pf_info_weight "Normal";
pf_info_version "1";
pf_info_capheight 7u;
pf_info_xheight 5.1u;
pf_info_space 3u;
pf_info_author "Yannis Haralambous, for 'Fonts & Encodings'";
pf_info_encoding "AdobeStandard";
pf_info_creationdate;
```

The last of these, pf_info_creationdate, may be given with no argument. In that case, the data given to the font will be the date and hour of compilation.

Having given these global data, we can now begin the font:

```
beginfont;
```

One peculiarity that stems from a choice made by Jackowski and his colleagues: there is no longer a beginchar macro that gives both the code for the glyph and its abstract dimensions. We use several types of macros:

```
wd.n=7u;
ht.n=6u;
dp.n=0u;
encode("n")(110);
introduce "n"(utilize)(0);
```

In the code above, we first see that the dimensions of the box containing the glyph have been dissociated from the glyph's description. Thus we can place these dimensions in another file; they will become, in a sense, the font's metric parameters.

The encode command produces the PostScript font encoding—a problem that did not exist under METAFONT, where it was sufficient for each glyph to have a position in the table (i.e., a number between 0 and 255). The encode command takes two arguments: the *PostScript name* of the glyph and the glyph's position in the font encoding.

The introduce command is quite peculiar. It takes four arguments:

1. The glyph's name.

2. A string that may be either `utilize` or `store`, or both: `utilize+store`. "Utilize" means to create a glyph in the font; "store" means to create a global path variable `glyph.name`, where name is the glyph's name—a path that will be used in other glyphs. In this way, the glyph for the comma, for example, can be used to produce the apostrophe, the English and German quotation marks, etc.

3. A number 0 or 1. If 1, the glyph in question is slanted when the font is oblique; if 0, the glyph remains unchanged, irrespective of the slant. For example, the mathematical symbols '$+$', '$\oplus$', '$\otimes$', '$\div$', etc., are never slanted.

4. A string that is in fact the name of the future EPS file, which is used when we create a file of documentation for the font. The EPS file is supposed to contain a bitmap image that can be compared with the vector contour. Thus if we wish to simulate a typeface from scans, we can directly compare the scans and the contours, using FontLab masks.

As a result, `beginglyph` takes only one argument, the name of the glyph:

```
beginglyph("n");
```

The first task is to initialize the variables that correspond to the abstract dimensions of the glyph, something that METAFONT would do automatically:

```
w:=wd.n; h:=ht.n; d:=dp.n;
```

Now we are ready to write the code for the glyph's description.

The first peculiarity of METATYPE1: we do not use pens. As Richard Kinch said [209, p. 236], "Algebra tells us that stroking a 3rd degree polynomial curve (the ellipse approximated by Bézier curves) along a 3rd degree polynomial curve (the Bézier curve of the stroked path) results in a 6th degree envelope curve." Neither METAFONT nor METAPOST knows how to solve polynomials of this kind; we have to abandon pens and restrict ourselves to filling operations.

Fortunately, we can still use the *pen strokes* of METAFONT, which, in fact, are nothing but filling operations that give us the illusion of working with pens. And in any event, we used nothing but pen strokes in our example of the letter 'n'. Thus this specific sample of code should be compatible with METATYPE1. Indeed, we can make a first attempt by taking the glyph's METAFONT code as it stands, with no changes. Result: there are no syntax errors, but some parts of the glyph do not appear! Why?

Because we have run into another serious constraint: the filling operations that we do *must never have tangent points*. Let us explain. It often happens that our pen strokes intersect. But a glyph in a PostScript Type 1 font is a contour with no intersections. Thus we must *merge* the contours for the different pen strokes. To do so, we must find the points at which the curves intersect. But that is possible only if we are working with isolated points. If two contours share part of a Bézier curve, or if their intersection is in fact a point at which the two curves touch, it is impossible to merge them.

If the mountain will not come to Mohammed, Mohammed must go to the mountain. In other words, since we cannot force METATYPE1 to merge our pen strokes properly, we have to write them in such a way that they will not come into contact.

Let us examine our glyph as we divided it up in order to write the METAFONT code:

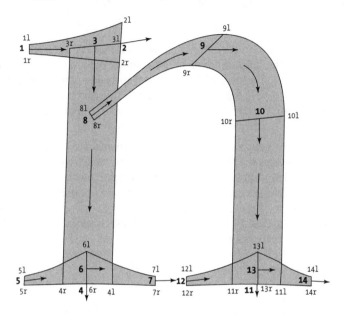

There are three spots that cause a problem; we have drawn them with a heavy line:

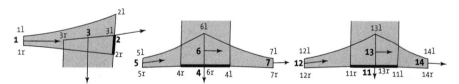

In the case of z2--z2r (left), the problem is that this stroke is common to the curve z2l--z2r..z4l{down} at pen position z2 of the stroke z1e{right}..z2e. Thus the two contours are identical there. One possible solution is to replace the pen stroke with a filling operation:

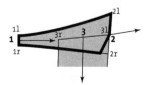

Thus we must find a point on the path z1r{right}..z2r that is quite close to z2 and then draw the part of the path between z1r and our point, and between our point and z2. Then there will be no more problem with paths that coincide.

To find this "nameless" point, we shall use the subpath command of METAFONT (and of METAPOST), which gives us a subpath from a given path. Here, then, is how we write the path that is shown with a heavy line:

```
fill subpath(0,0.9) of (z1r{right}..z2r)--z2--z2l..
z1l{left}--cycle;
```

Explanation: subpath (a command present in METAFONT) takes four arguments: the "times" of departure and arrival, the keyword of, and the original path. By "time" we mean the parameter for the path's development, which begins at 0 and takes whole values for each Bézier curve on the path. Here we have only one Bézier curve; thus the point at time 0 on the path is z1r and the point at time 1 is z2r. By choosing a time of arrival of 0.9, we come quite close to the right edge of the downstroke without actually reaching it.

The two other problematic cases are the feet of the downstrokes. The curve for the serif z5r..z6r{right}..z7r is tangent to pen position z4r--z4l; the same goes for position z11r--z11l on the other serif. Here the solution is much easier: we merely move the pen positions up slightly, making sure that they still remain within the area of the serifs. Since the parameter serif_ht can take on very small values, it behooves us to define the height of z4 and z11 with respect to that parameter. In addition, we must not forget delta, which gives us the height of the serif's arch. Here is a possible solution:

```
y4=delta+.25serif_ht; y11=delta+.25serif_ht;
```

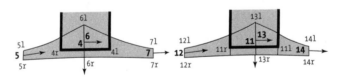

Now let us continue with the syntactic differences between the languages. Under METAFONT, one merely writes penstroke to draw the pen stroke. Under METATYPE1, one does not draw the strokes directly; one keeps all the pen strokes in memory in order to merge them at the end and fill the global contour. Thus we create a table stroke[] of paths and fill in its elements one by one.

Here is the glyph's code at the point that we have reached:

```
save stroke_; path stroke_[];

numeric x_height, oo, stem, join, serif_tip, serif_ht, delta, offset;
x_height=5.1u; oo=.2u; stem=1.1u; join=.2u;
serif_tip=.2u; serif_ht=.7u; delta=.033u; offset=.125u;
z4=(1.6u,.5serif_ht); penpos4(stem,180);
x3=x4+offset; y3r=x_height;
x3l-x3r=stem; y3l-y3r=.5serif_tip; z3=.5[z3l,z3r];

stroke_2:=penstroke z3e..{down}z4e;
```

```
x11=w-.65u; y11=y4; penpos11(stem,180);
y10=y8=.7x_height; z8=whatever[z3,z4];
z10-z11=whatever*(z3-z4);
z10l-z10r=z3l-z3r; z10=.5[z10l,z10r];
penpos9(.87[join,stem],-); y9l=x_height+oo; x9=.68[x8,x10];
z8'=whatever[z11,z10]; y8'=1.25x_height;
penpos8(join,angle(z8'-z8)-);

stroke_3:=penstroke z8e{z8'-z8}..tension 1.5..z9e{right}..z10e---z11e;

numeric serif; serif=x11r-x12=1u;
x7-x4l=serif; x3r-x1=.95serif; x4r-x5=.9serif; x14-x11l=.8serif;
y1l=y3l; penpos1(serif_tip,-); z2=z3l;
penpos2(1.25serif_ht,angle(direction 0 of (z3l..{down}z4l))+eps);

stroke_4:=subpath(0,0.9) of (z1r{right}..z2r) -- z2 -- z2l..z1l{left}--cycle;

if (x7-x4+.2u+x11-x12 > x11-x4):
x7:=.5[x4,x11]-.1u;
x12:=.5[x4,x11]+.1u; fi

penpos5(serif_tip,-); penpos7(serif_tip,-);
penpos12(serif_tip,-); penpos14(serif_tip,-);
penpos6(serif_ht,-); penpos13(serif_ht,-);
y5r=y7r=y12r=y14r=0; z6r=(x4,delta); z13r=(x11,delta);

stroke_5:=penstroke z5e{right}..z6e & z6e..{right}z7e;
stroke_6:=penstroke z12e{right}..z13e & z13e..{right}z14e;
```

In this code, we have defined five pen strokes (with indices from 2 to 6). We have omitted index 1 for a reason: the command find_outlines, which merges the contours, and which we shall employ later, uses index 1 to store the result of the merger of the contours.

Now we shall gradually merge the contours:

```
find_outlines(stroke_4, stroke_2)(stroke_);
find_outlines(stroke_1, stroke_3)(stroke_);
find_outlines(stroke_1, stroke_5)(stroke_);
find_outlines(stroke_1, stroke_6)(stroke_);
```

Now the contour for the entire glyph is stored in stroke_1. The command that actually draws the contour is:

```
Fill stroke_1;
```

The 'F' in Fill is capitalized to distinguish the command from the fill command of META-FONT.

If our glyph had counters, we would use the unFill command to write a contour in the opposite direction, inside the first contour, which would produce the required "holes".

At this stage we are not yet finished; we still have to specify the set-width of the PostScript glyph and terminate the description of the glyph and the font:

```
fix_hsbw(w,0,0);
endglyph;
endfont.
```

The command fix_hsbw takes three arguments: the set-width of the glyph and the sidebearings. The latter will form the abstract box that contains the glyph.

Ordinarily we include here the definitions of any hints. Thus we write:

```
fix_vstem(foo)(stroke_1);
fix_hstem(bar)(stroke_1);
```

for a horizontal stem of thickness foo or a vertical stem of thickness bar. But there are no vertical or horizontal stems in our example (because the two downstrokes of the letter 'n' are slightly slanted); thus it is not possible to define hints for this particular case.

And here is the result:

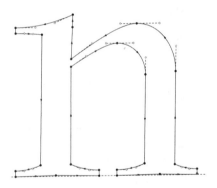

The PostScript image above was produced by the documentation module of METATYPE1. Here, in its entirety, is the code, pretty-printed by *mft*, that enabled us to obtain the font containing this single glyph:

```
input fontbase;
u := 100;
pf_info_familyname"Pseudo-Vendome";
pf_info_fontname"Pseudo-Vendome-Regular";
pf_info_weight"Normal";
pf_info_version"1";
pf_info_capheight_{7u};
pf_info_xheight_{5.1u};
```

$pf\_info\_space_{3u}$;
pf_info_author"Y. Haralambous for 'Fonts & encodings'";
$pf\_info\_encoding$"AdobeStandard";
$pf\_info\_creationdate$;
beginfont

$wd\_n = 7u$; $ht\_n = 6u$; $dp\_n = 0u$;
$encode($"n"$)($ASCII "n"$)$;
$introduce$"n"$(utilize)(0)()$;
$beginglyph($"n"$)$;
$w := wd\_n$; $h := ht\_n$; $d := dp\_n$;
save $stroke\_$; **path** $stroke\_[]$;

numeric x_height, oo, $stem$, $join$, $serif\_tip$, $serif\_height$, $delta$, $offset$;
$x\_height = 5.1u$; $oo = .2u$; $stem = 1.1u$; $join = .2u$;
$serif\_tip = .2u$; $serif\_height = .7u$; $delta = .033u$; $offset = .125u$;
$z_4 = (1.6u, .5serif\_height)$; $penpos_4(stem, 180)$;
$x_3 = x_4 + offset$; $y_{3r} = x\_height$;
$x_{3l} - x_{3r} = stem$; $y_{3l} - y_{3r} = .5serif\_tip$; $z_3 = .5[z_{3l}, z_{3r}]$;

$stroke\_2 :=$ **penstroke** z_{3e} .. $\{down\}z_{4e}$;

$x_{11} = w - 1.65u$; $y_{11} = y_4$; $penpos_{11}(stem, 180)$;
$y_{10} = y_8 = .7x\_height$; $z_8 = whatever[z_3, z_4]$;
$z_{10} - z_{11} = whatever * (z_3 - z_4)$;
$z_{10l} - z_{10r} = z_{3l} - z_{3r}$; $z_{10} = .5[z_{10l}, z_{10r}]$;
$penpos_9(.87[join, stem], -136)$; $y_{9l} = x\_height + oo$; $x_9 = .68[x_8, x_{10}]$;
$z_{8'} = whatever[z_{11}, z_{10}]$; $y_{8'} = 1.25x\_height$;
$penpos_8(join, $ angle$(z_{8'} - z_8) - 90)$;

$stroke\_3 :=$ **penstroke** $z_{8e}\{z_{8'} - z_8\}$ .. tension 1.5 .. $z_{9e}\{right\}$ .. z_{10e} --- z_{11e};

numeric $serif$; $serif = x_{11r} - x_{12} = 1u$;
$x_7 - x_{4l} = serif$; $x_{3r} - x_1 = .95serif$; $x_{4r} - x_5 = .9serif$; $x_{14} - x_{11l} = .8serif$;
$y_{1l} = y_{3l}$; $penpos_1(serif\_tip, -90)$; $z_2 = z_{3l}$;
$penpos_2(1.25serif_height, $ angle$($**direction** 0 **of** $(z_{3l}$ .. $\{down\}z_{4l})) + eps)$;

$stroke\_4 :=$ **subpath**$(0, 0.9)$ **of** $(z_{1r}\{right\}$ .. $z_{2r})$ -- z_2 -- z_{2l} .. $z_{1l}\{left\}$ -- cycle;

if $(x_7 - x_4 + .2u + x_{11} - x_{12} > x_{11} - x_4)$:
$x_7 := .5[x_4, x_{11}] - .1u$;
$x_{12} := .5[x_4, x_{11}] + .1u$; **fi**

$penpos_5(serif\_tip, -90)$; $penpos_7(serif\_tip, -90)$;
$penpos_{12}(serif\_tip, -90)$; $penpos_{14}(serif\_tip, -90)$;
$penpos_6(serif\_height, -90)$; $penpos_{13}(serif\_height, -90)$;
$y_{5r} = y_{7r} = y_{12r} = y_{14r} = 0$; $z_{6r} = (x_4, delta)$; $z_{13r} = (x_{11}, delta)$;

$stroke\_5 :=$ **penstroke** $z_{5e}\{right\}$ .. z_{6e} & z_{6e} .. $\{right\}z_{7e}$;
$stroke\_6 :=$ **penstroke** $z_{12e}\{right\}$ .. z_{13e} & z_{13e} .. $\{right\}z_{14e}$;

$find\_outlines(stroke\_4, stroke\_2)(stroke\_)$;

antpr17 : AaBbCcDdEeFfGgHhIiJjKkLlMmNnOoPpQqRrSs
antpr12 : AaBbCcDdEeFfGgHhIiJjKkLlMmNnOoPpQqRrSsTtUuVvWwXxYyZ
antpr10 : AaBbCcDdEeFfGgHhIiJjKkLlMmNnOoPpQqRrSsTtUuVvWwXxYyZz01234567
antpr8 : AaBbCcDdEeFfGgHhIiJjKkLlMmNnOoPpQqRrSsTtUuVvWwXxYyZz0123456789AaBbCcDdEeFf
antpr6 : AaBbCcDdEeFfGgHhIiJjKkLlMmNnOoPpQqRrSsTtUuVvWwXxYyZz0123456789AaBbCcDdEeFfGgHhIiJjKkLlMmNnOoPpQq

antpri17 : AaBbCcDdEeFfGgHhIiJjKkLlMmNnOoPpQqRr
antpri12 : AaBbCcDdEeFfGgHhIiJjKkLlMmNnOoPpQqRrSsTtUuVvWwXxY
antpri10 : AaBbCcDdEeFfGgHhIiJjKkLlMmNnOoPpQqRrSsTtUuVvWwXxYyZz01234
antpri8 : AaBbCcDdEeFfGgHhIiJjKkLlMmNnOoPpQqRrSsTtUuVvWwXxYyZz0123456789AaBbCcDdE
antpri6 : AaBbCcDdEeFfGgHhIiJjKkLlMmNnOoPpQqRrSsTtUuVvWwXxYyZz0123456789AaBbCcDdEeFfGgHhIiJjKkLlMmNnOo

antpb17 : AaBbCcDdEeFfGgHhIiJjKkLlMmNnOoPpQ
antpb12 : AaBbCcDdEeFfGgHhIiJjKkLlMmNnOoPpQqRrSsTtUuVvWw
antpb10 : AaBbCcDdEeFfGgHhIiJjKkLlMmNnOoPpQqRrSsTtUuVvWwXxYyZz0
antpb8 : AaBbCcDdEeFfGgHhIiJjKkLlMmNnOoPpQqRrSsTtUuVvWwXxYyZz0123456789AaBbCc
antpb6 : AaBbCcDdEeFfGgHhIiJjKkLlMmNnOoPpQqRrSsTtUuVvWwXxYyZz0123456789AaBbCcDdEeFfGgHhIiJjKkLlMmNn

antpbi17 : AaBbCcDdEeFfGgHhIiJjKkLlMmNnOoPpQ
antpbi12 : AaBbCcDdEeFfGgHhIiJjKkLlMmNnOoPpQqRrSsTtUuVvWw
antpbi10 : AaBbCcDdEeFfGgHhIiJjKkLlMmNnOoPpQqRrSsTtUuVvWwXxYyZz01
antpbi8 : AaBbCcDdEeFfGgHhIiJjKkLlMmNnOoPpQqRrSsTtUuVvWwXxYyZz0123456789AaBbCcD
antpbi6 : AaBbCcDdEeFfGgHhIiJjKkLlMmNnOoPpQqRrSsTtUuVvWwXxYyZz0123456789AaBbCcDdEeFfGgHhIiJjKkLlMmNnO

Figure F-5: The fonts of the Antykwa Półtawskiego distribution, v.0.52.

find_outlines(*stroke*$_{-1}$, *stroke*$_{-3}$)(*stroke*_);
find_outlines(*stroke*$_{-1}$, *stroke*$_{-5}$)(*stroke*_);
find_outlines(*stroke*$_{-1}$, *stroke*$_{-6}$)(*stroke*_);

Fill$_{stroke\_1}$;

fix_hsbw(*w*, 0, 0);
endglyph;
endfont

F.4.3   Antykwa Półtawskiego

The *Antykwa Półtawskiego* font family is based on a Polish typeface designed in the 1920s by a great Polish typographer, Adam Półtawski (1881–1952). According to Nowacki [281], this typeface was used in almost half of all works printed in Poland before the era of phototype-setting and the computer. We have shown all the optical sizes and styles of this typeface in Figure F-5.

Technically, this font is organized in a simpler and perhaps more rational way than *Computer Modern*. There are five types of files:

- Driver files (extension .mp). These are the files that we invoke. Their names are those of the fonts that they generate: *antpr* (roman), *antpi* (italic), *antpb* (bold), and *antpbi* (bold italic), at 6, 8, 10, 12, and 17 points. They contain calls to the other required files.

- Parameter files (extension .par). These have the same names as the driver files and contain the specific values of the parameters for each font, including all the set-widths and the encode and introduce commands for all the glyphs. There are also a file antp.par of global parameters and a file ap_names.mp containing the PostScript names of the glyphs.

- Files of general METAPOST subroutines. There is only one: ap_lego.mp, its name being inspired by the Lego brand of toys, since the code for the glyphs in *Antykwa Półtawskiego* is based on the principle of building blocks.

- Glyph-description files, which contain the METAPOST code for the capital letters, the lowercase letters, the digits, the mathematical symbols, the Greek letters, etc.

- Files of kerning pairs. There is only one: antp.lkp.

All of these are amply documented; we merely run the script mkproof1.bat (or *mkproof* under Unix) to produce the TeX file of documentation. This documentation even contains the EPS images of the glyphs; after all, METAPOST creates PostScript code, so we may as well take advantage of it to produce the automatically generated documentation.

In Figure F-6, we have shown the main parameters for the glyphs in the *Antykwa Półtawskiego* font family. Here they are:

- beak_gap: the offset between the outer two arms of the 'E'.

- beak_ht: the height of the serif on an upper or lower arm (on the letters 'E', 'F', etc.).

- beak_wd: the filling width of the serif on an upper or lower arm (on the letters 'E', 'F', etc.).

- depth_ogonek: the depth of the ogonek.

- depth: the depth of the descenders (the letters 'g', 'p', 'y', etc.).

- dot_size: the theoretical diameter of the dots ("theoretical" because the dots are in fact either hexagons or octagons).

- equal_shift: the distance between the axis of symmetry and the middle of a stroke of the equals sign.

- horn_ht: the height of the serif on the middle bar of the 'E'.

- horn_wd: the width for filling the serif on the middle bar of the 'E'.

- hstem_ogonek: the maximum vertical thickness of the ogonek.

- lc_crook_ht: the height of the serif on the upper terminal of the 'c'.

- lc_crook_shift: the offset of the serif on the upper terminal of the 'c'.

- lc_height: the height of the lowercase letters.

- lc_overshoot: the overshoot of the round strokes of the lowercase letters.

- lc_serif_jut: the width of the serifs of the lowercase letters.

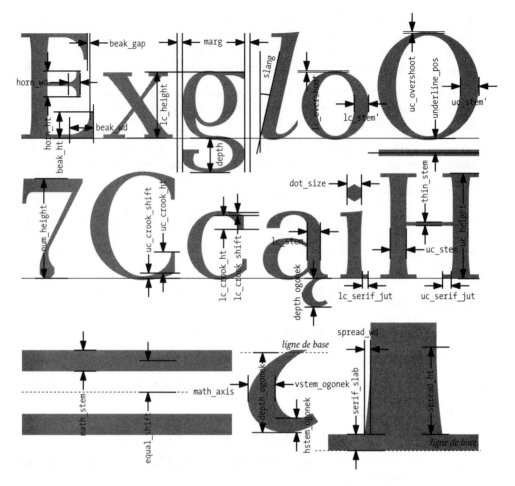

Figure F-6: The parameters of the Antykwa Półtawskiego font family.

- `lc_stem'`: the thickness of the thick curved strokes of the lowercase letters.

- `lc_stem`: the thickness of the thick upright strokes of the lowercase letters.

- `marg`: the standard side-bearings of the glyphs.

- `math_axis`: the height of the horizontal axis of symmetry of the mathematical symbols.

- `math_stem`: the stroke thickness of the "geometrical" mathematical symbols.

- `num_height`: the height of the digits.

- `serif_slab`: the thickness of the serifs.

- `slang`: the angle of the italic glyphs (**N.B.**: this is λ in METAFONT, but here it is the angle $\phi = \tan(\lambda)$).

- spread_ht: the height of the point at which the vertical stem begins to reach a serif.

- spread_wd: the width of the vertical stems.

- thin_stem: the width of the connecting strokes.

- uc_crook_ht: the height of the serif on the terminal of the 'C'.

- uc_crook_shift: the offset of the serif on the terminal of the 'C'.

- uc_height: the height of the capitals.

- uc_overshoot: the overshoot of the round strokes of the capitals.

- uc_serif_jut: the width of the serifs of the capitals.

- uc_stem': the thickness of the thick curved strokes of the capitals.

- uc_stem: the thickness of the thick upright strokes of the capitals.

- underline_pos: the depth of the underscore. There are no underscored letters in the font, but this information is part of the standard font dictionary of PostScript Type 1 fonts.

- vstem_ogonek: the maximum horizontal thickness of the ogonek.

The development of the *Antykwa Półtawskiego* font family continues, and future years will certainly add other styles and glyphs to the ones that we have today.

G

Bézier Curves

G.1 History

We can hardly imagine the connection between the splendid curves of a font like *Monotype Garamond* and the hood of a Renault. Yet both consist of curves, and in both cases the production process (whether the final product be a Type 1 font or a piece of metal) went through a phase of computer-assisted design.

But how were car bodies designed before the computer era? Engineers made models out of wood or plaster and approached the desired result through successive approximations. Developing one model after another was neither rapid nor efficient. Pierre Bézier (1910–1999), an engineer at Renault since 1933, started doing research on computer science in 1960 to find a system for modeling curves, or even surfaces, that would be easy to compute and also easy for the human to manipulate.

The curves that bear his name satisfy these conditions. But he was not the only one to work on these techniques. There were also Paul de Casteljau, an engineer at Citroën, and Birkhoff, Garabedian, and de Boor, at General Motors, in the United States. Bézier's work gave us the curves, which today are known around the world because they are at the heart of every computer-assisted design system; de Casteljau's work gave us the algorithm that we shall see below; Boor and his colleagues worked on *B-splines* ('B' as in "Bézier"), a more refined version of Bézier curves.

In the text that follows, we shall present the main properties of the Bézier curves. This text was inspired primarily by [246].

G.2 Bézier Curves

To draw a straight line with graphic-design software, it is usually sufficient to click once with the mouse to select the starting point and once again to select the ending point.

These two points define the line segment perfectly: it is a linear function—i.e., a first-degree polynomial—and is therefore defined by two points.

We would like to be able to do the same thing with curves: click to obtain the starting point and the ending point, and then use an intuitive means, accessible even to those with the most severe case of technophobia, to modify the curve and obtain the precise curve that we want from the infinite range of curves that can be drawn between two points.

That is precisely what Bézier curves do: they are third-degree polynomials and are therefore defined by four points. We already have two of those points: the starting point and the ending point; we need only define the two that remain. We call those two points the *control points*. In most software packages like *Illustrator* and *CorelDraw*, we click once to obtain the starting point, then drag the mouse to obtain the first control point, release the mouse button, move, click again to obtain the ending point, and drag the mouse again to obtain the second control point. How do we know where to place the last of these? Well, as soon as we have indicated the ending point, the software begins to draw a Bézier curve, which changes dynamically as we drag the mouse to set the second control point. Thus we watch the curve develop, and we stop as soon as it is optimal.

Later we can come back and change the location of the first control point. By playing with the two control points, we almost always manage to find the desired curve, whether it be a new curve that we have just created and that evaluate according to our aesthetic criteria or a curve that must be as close as possible to a model that we see behind the screen.

Drawing Bézier curves in this way is so intuitive and efficient that it has become second nature to graphic artists and industrial designers. And no one wonders anymore how the computer can be so powerful—and especially how it could have been so powerful in the late 1980s, when Adobe Illustrator v.1 came out—to display a mathematical curve, a third-degree polynomial, that changes, moves, and leaps about in real time while following the hand of the designer. Does the computer solve a third-degree equation every millisecond? It would not be able to do so!

What happens, then? What mystery lies hidden behind these polynomials that makes them so easy to represent graphically on a computer, even the clunkiest one? Let us push the envelope farther: just as Hercules always found himself faced with two new heads whenever he cut a head off the Hydra at Lerna, whenever we "cut" a Bézier curve with the software's "scissors" tool, we *instantly* find ourselves with two new Bézier curves, yet the path covered by these two curves is exactly the same as that covered by the original one. How is that possible? And how could the computer have calculated the coordinates of the control points of these new curves in a fraction of a second?

The solution to this mystery lies in the algorithm of de Casteljau, which we shall describe in this chapter. It is unfortunate that the name of Paul de Casteljau is less well known that that of Bézier, since the curves of the latter would be of little interest without the algorithm of the former.

In the following text, we shall present the mathematical bases of the technique of Bézier curves, which are indispensable to anyone who wishes to manipulate the curves in any way other than with a mouse and a screen.

G.2.1 Definition and Interesting Properties

DEFINITION. — Let z_0, z_1, z_2, z_3 be elements of $\mathbb{R}^2$. Then the *cubic Bézier curve* with starting point z_0, ending point z_3, and control points z_1 and z_2 is:

$$b(t) = (1-t)^3 z_0 + 3t(1-t)^2 z_1 + 3t^2(1-t)z_2 + t^3 z_3$$

for $t \in [0,1]$.

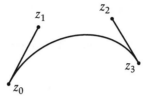

INTERESTING PROPERTIES. — (1) *Control points lie on the lines tangent to the starting and ending points.*

(2) *Bézier curve b lies completely within the polygon $z_0 z_1 z_2 z_3$.*

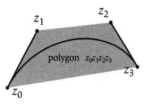

(3) *Let A be an affine transformation (for example, a rotation, reflection, translation, or scaling operation). Then the image of b under A is equal to the Bézier curve defined by the points $A(z_0), A(z_1), A(z_2), A(z_3)$.*

COMMENTS. — Property 1 makes the drawing of the curves more intuitive. Property 2 ensures us that the entire curve will remain within the visible area of the screen if the four points that define it lie in that area: after all, who would want to see curves that could fly off to infinity at any time? Finally, property 3 implies that design software can very easily torture Bézier curves by moving them, rotating them, reflecting them, and scaling them up or down. That is because software in fact transforms only four points. The calculation of the curve is then done by the famous algorithm of de Casteljau, once the four new points have been established. Applying an affine transformation to four points is not really a great feat of numerical computation.

PROOF OF THE PROPERTIES. — (1) We need only derive b:

$$b'(t) = 3[t^2 z_0 + t(2-3t)z_1 + (1-4t+3t^2)z_2 - (1-t)^2 z_3];$$

therefore $b'(0) = 3(z_2 - z_3), b'(1) = 3(z_0 - z_1)$. In other words, the slopes of the lines tangent to the curve at the points $t = 0$ (the starting point) and $t = 1$ (the ending point) are parallel to the vectors $\overrightarrow{z_0z_1}$ and $\overrightarrow{z_2z_3}$, respectively. Since the tangent lines are parallel to the vectors, and since each has a point in common with them, the vectors therefore lie on the tangents, and so do the points z_1 and z_2.

(2) The inside of the polygon $z_0z_1z_2z_3$ is the set of points:

$$\lambda_0z_0 + \lambda_1z_1 + \lambda_2z_2 + \lambda_3z_3, \text{ where } \sum\lambda_i = 1 \text{ and } \lambda_i \geq 0.$$

It is sufficient to prove that $\lambda_0(t) = t^3, \lambda_1(t) = 3(1-t)t^2, \lambda_2(t) = 3(1-t)^2t, \lambda_3(t) = (1-t)^3$; then the two properties above will be confirmed for every $t \in [0,1]$. Three lines of calculation of no great interest.

(3) If $z = (x,y)$ is the representation of $z \in \mathbb{R}^2$ in Cartesian coordinates, an affine transformation A can, by definition, be written:

$$A(x,y) = (\alpha x + \beta y + \gamma, \delta x + \varepsilon y + \zeta).$$

We wish to show that $A(b(t)) = (1-t)^3A(z_0) + 3t(1-t)^2A(z_1) + 3t^2(1-t)A(z_2) + t^3A(z_3)$.

Let us simplify by writing $b(t) = \sum_{i=0}^{3}b_i(t)z_i$ and then proceed:

$$A(b(t)) = A\left(\sum_{i=0}^{3}b_i(t)z_i\right)$$

$$= \left(\alpha\sum_{i=0}^{3}b_i(t)x_i + \beta\sum_{i=0}^{3}b_i(t)y_i + \gamma, \delta\sum_{i=0}^{3}b_i(t)x_i + \varepsilon\sum_{i=0}^{3}b_i(t)y_i + \zeta\right).$$

But we just proved in Property 2 that $\sum_{i=0}^{3}b_i(t) = 1$ for all t. We can therefore multiply γ and ζ by this expression:

$$A(b(t)) = (\alpha\sum_{i=0}^{3}b_i(t)x_i + \beta\sum_{i=0}^{3}b_i(t)y_i + \gamma\sum_{i=0}^{3}b_i(t), \delta\sum_{i=0}^{3}b_i(t)x_i$$

$$+ \varepsilon\sum_{i=0}^{3}b_i(t)y_i + \zeta\sum_{i=0}^{3}b_i(t)).$$

And we can remove $\sum_{i=0}^{3}b_i(t)$ from the expression: $A(b(t)) = \sum_{i=0}^{3}b_i(t)\cdot(\alpha x_i + \beta y_i + \gamma, \delta x_i + \varepsilon y_i + \zeta) = \sum_{i=0}^{3}b_i(t)\cdot A(x_i,y_i)$. QED

G.2.2   de Casteljau's Algorithm

THEOREM. — *Let z_0, z_1, z_2, z_3 be elements of $\mathbb{R}^2$ and let $b(t)$ be the cubic Bézier curve defined on $[0,1]$ by these points. We shall define a set of points in the plane $\{z_{i,j}(t) \mid 0 \leq j \leq 3, 0 \leq i \leq 3-j\}$ as follows:*

$$z_{i,0}(t) = z_i \text{ for all } 0 \leq i \leq 3 \text{ and all } t \in [0,1]$$

$$z_{i,1}(t) = (1-t)z_{i,0}(t) + tz_{i+1,0}(t) \text{ for all } 0 \leq i \leq 2$$

$$z_{i,2}(t) = (1-t)z_{i,1}(t) + tz_{i+1,1}(t) \text{ for all } 0 \leq i \leq 1$$

$$z_{0,3}(t) = (1-t)z_{0,2}(t) + tz_{1,2}(t).$$

Therefore $b(t) = z_{0,3}(t)$.

PROOF. — We need only replace $z_{i,j}(t)$ with their values:

$$z_{0,1}(t) = (1-t)z_0 + t z_1$$
$$z_{1,1}(t) = (1-t)z_1 + t z_2$$
$$z_{2,1}(t) = (1-t)z_2 + t z_3$$

and therefore:

$$z_{0,2}(t) = (1-t)[(1-t)z_0 + t z_1] + t[(1-t)z_1 + t z_2]$$
$$z_{1,2}(t) = (1-t)[(1-t)z_1 + t z_2] + t[(1-t)z_2 + t z_3]$$

which gives:

$$z_{0,3}(t) = (1-t)\big[(1-t)[(1-t)z_0 + t z_1] + t[(1-t)z_1 + t z_2]\big]$$
$$+ t\big[(1-t)[(1-t)z_1 + t z_2] + t[(1-t)z_2 + t z_3]\big]$$
$$= (1-t)^3 z_0 + 3t(1-t)^2 z_1 + 3t^2(1-t)z_2 + t^3 z_3$$
$$= b(t). \quad \text{QED}$$

COMMENTS. — de Casteljau's algorithm can be represented graphically as follows:

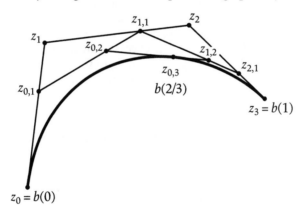

where we have chosen to determine the point $b(\frac{2}{3})$ graphically. The point $z_{0,1}$ lies at $\frac{2}{3}$ of the distance between z_0 and z_1. The same goes for $z_{1,1}$ and $z_{2,1}$. We draw the line segments $z_{0,1}z_{1,1}$ and $z_{1,1}z_{2,1}$. Then we find the points $z_{0,2}$ and $z_{1,2}$, which are $\frac{2}{3}$ of the distance between the endpoints of the line segments. We draw the segment $z_{0,2}z_{1,2}$. It must necessarily be tangent to the Bézier curve. The point of intersection of this segment with the curve is $b(\frac{2}{3})$.

G.2.3 Subdivision of Bézier Curves

DEFINITION. — Let $b(t)$ be a Bézier curve and let κ be in $[0,1]$. Then $b(t)$ is subdivided into two Bézier curves $b_{\text{start}}(t) = b(\kappa t)$ and $b_{\text{end}}(t) = b(\frac{t-\kappa}{1-\kappa})$.

THEOREM. — *Let z_0, z_1, z_2, z_3 be in $\mathbb{R}^2$ and let b be the cubic Bézier curve defined on $[0,1]$ by those points. Let κ be in $[0,1]$. Let b_{start} and b_{end} be the two Bézier curves obtained by subdividing b at the* point $b(\kappa)$. Let $z_{0,1}, z_{1,1}, z_{2,1}, z_{0,2}, z_{1,2}$ be the points obtained by applying de Casteljau's algorithm to the curve b.

Then the points $z_{0,1}$ and $z_{0,2}$ are the control points of b_{start}, and the points $z_{1,2}$ and $z_{2,1}$ are the control points of b_{end}.

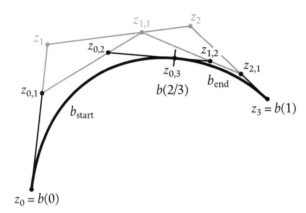

COMMENTS. — The mystery is solved: here is how the software instantly knows the control points of the new Bézier curve obtained by "cutting" the old Bézier curve into two pieces. As soon as we click on a point z on the curve, the software calculates the value t of that point through the *bisection* method: it takes $b(\frac{1}{2})$ and checks whether the point z lies in the polygon formed by the four points of b_{start} or b_{end}. According to the result, the curve is subdivided again, and the the software determines in which polygon the point lies, and so forth. By continuing in this manner, it can calculate the value of t for which $b(t) \approx z$ with ever greater precision.

PROOF. — By performing the calculations of de Casteljau's algorithm on the point κ, we find:

$$z_{0,1} = (1 - \kappa)z_0 + \kappa z_1$$
$$z_{0,2} = (1 - \kappa)[(1 - \kappa)z_0 + \kappa z_1] + \kappa[(1 - \kappa)z_1 + \kappa z_2]$$
$$z_{0,3} = (1 - \kappa)\big[(1 - \kappa)[(1 - \kappa)z_0 + \kappa z_1] + \kappa[(1 - \kappa)z_1 + \kappa z_2]\big]$$
$$+ \kappa\big[(1 - \kappa)[(1 - \kappa)z_1 + \kappa z_2] + \kappa[(1 - \kappa)z_2 + \kappa z_3]\big].$$

Suppose that the theorem is true. Then we have:

$$b_{\text{start}}(t) = (1 - t)^3 z_0 + 3t(1 - t)^2 z_{0,1} + 3t^2(1 - t)z_{0,2} + t^3 z_{0,3}.$$

Make the substitutions:

$$b_{\text{start}}(t) = (1 - t)^3 z_0 + 3t(1 - t)^2[(1 - \kappa)z_0 + \kappa z_1]$$
$$+ 3t^2(1 - t)\big[(1 - \kappa)[(1 - \kappa)z_0 + \kappa z_1] + \kappa[(1 - \kappa)z_1 + \kappa z_2]\big]$$
$$+ t^3\Big[(1 - \kappa)\big[(1 - \kappa)[(1 - \kappa)z_0 + \kappa z_1] + \kappa[(1 - \kappa)z_1 + \kappa z_2]\big]$$
$$+ \kappa\big[(1 - \kappa)[(1 - \kappa)z_1 + \kappa z_2] + \kappa[(1 - \kappa)z_2 + \kappa z_3]\big]\Big].$$

We need only check that this expression is equal to:

$$b(\kappa t) = (1 - \kappa t)^3 z_0 + 3\kappa t (1 - \kappa t)^2 z_1 + 3\kappa^2 t^2 (1 - \kappa t) z_2 + t^3 \kappa^3 z_3.$$

Simply carry out the calculations term by term. A full page of calculations of no great interest.

Bibliography

[1] Atif Aamir. Nafees Nasta'leeq, 2003. http://www.crulp.org/nafeesNastaleeq.html

[2] Douglas Adams. *The Hitchhiker's Guide to the Galaxy*. Pan Books, 1979.

[3] Adobe Developer Support. *Adobe Binary Screen Font Files Specification v. 2, Technote 5006*, 1992. http://partners.adobe.com/asn/developer/pdfs/tn/5006.ABF_Spec.pdf

[4] Adobe Developer Support. *PostScript Language Document Structuring Conventions Specification, Technote 5001*, 1992. http://partners.adobe.com:80/asn/developer/pdfs/tn/5001.DSC_Spec.pdf

[5] Adobe Developer Support. *The StemSnap Hint Operator for Type 1 Font Programs*, 1992. http://partners.adobe.com:80/asn/developer/pdfs/tn/5049.StemSnap.pdf

[6] Adobe Developer Support. *Supporting Downloadable PostScript Language Fonts, Technote 5040*, 1992. http://partners.adobe.com/asn/developer/pdfs/tn/5040.Download_Fonts.pdf

[7] Adobe Developer Support. *Font Naming Issues, Technote 5088*, 1993. http://partners.adobe.com/asn/developer/pdfs/tn/5088.FontNames.pdf

[8] Adobe Developer Support. *Glyph Bitmap Distribution Format (BDF) Specification v. 2.2, Technote 5005*, 1993. http://partners.adobe.com/asn/developer/pdfs/tn/5005.BDF_Spec.pdf

[9] Adobe Developer Support. *CID-Keyed Font Technology Overview, Technote 5092*, 1994. http://partners.adobe.com:80/asn/developer/pdfs/tn/5092.CID_Overview.pdf

[10] Adobe Developer Support. *Type 1 Font Format Supplement, Technote 5015*, 1994. http://partners.adobe.com:80/asn/developer/pdfs/tn/5015.Type1_Supp.pdf

[11] Adobe Developer Support. *Adobe CMap and CIDFont Files Specification, Technote 5014*, 1996. http://partners.adobe.com:80/asn/developer/pdfs/tn/5014.CMap_CIDFont_Spec.pdf

[12] Adobe Developer Support. *Adobe Font Metrics File Format Specification v. 4.1, Technote 5004*, 1998. http://partners.adobe.com/asn/developer/pdfs/tn/5004.AFM_Spec.pdf

[13] Adobe Developer Support. *The Type 42 Font Format Specification, Technote 5012*, 1998.
`http://partners.adobe.com:80/asn/developer/pdfs/tn/5012.Type42_Spec.pdf`

[14] Adobe Developer Support. *The Compact Font Format Specification, Technote 5176*, 2000.
`http://partners.adobe.com:80/asn/developer/pdfs/tn/5176.CFF.pdf`

[15] Adobe Developer Support. *The Type 2 Charstring Format*, 2000. `http://partners.`
`adobe.com:80/asn/developer/pdfs/tn/5177.Type2.pdf`

[16] Adobe Developer Support. Adobe-Japan1-6 character collection for CID-keyed fonts,
technote 5078. Technical report, Adobe Systems Inc., 2004. `http://partners.adobe.`
`com/public/developer/en/font/5078.Adobe-Japan1-6.pdf`

[17] Adobe Systems. Adobe Type Manager Deluxe. `http://www.adobe.com/products/atm/`
`main.html`

[18] Adobe Systems.   Adobe Type Manager Light. `http://www.adobe.com/products/`
`atmlight/main.html`

[19] Adobe Systems. Adobe Type Reunion Deluxe. `http://www.adobe.com:80/products/`
`atm/atr.html`

[20] Adobe Systems.   *PostScript Language Program Design*.   Addison-Wesley, 1988.
`http://partners.adobe.com/asn/tech/ps/download/samplecode/ps_psbooks/`
`GreenBook.zip`

[21] Adobe Systems. *Adobe Type 1 Font Format, version 1.1*. Addison-Wesley, 1990. `http:`
`//partners.adobe.com:80/asn/developer/pdfs/tn/T1_SPEC.PDF`

[22] Adobe Systems.   *PostScript Language Tutorial and Cookbook*.   Addison-Wesley, 1990.
`http://partners.adobe.com/asn/tech/ps/download/samplecode/ps_psbooks/`
`BlueBook.zip`

[23] Adobe Systems. `WadaMin-Regular` CIDFont file, 1996. `ftp://ftp.oreilly.com/pub/`
`examples/nutshell/cjkv/adobe/samples`

[24] Adobe Systems. *PostScript Language Reference Manual*. Addison-Wesley, 3rd edition,
1999. `http://partners.adobe.com/asn/developer/pdfs/tn/PLRM.pdf`

[25] Adobe Systems. Adobe glyph list, 2002. `http://partners.adobe.com:80/asn/tech/`
`type/glyphlist.txt`

[26] Adobe Systems. CMaps for PDF 1.4 CJK fonts, 2003. `http://partners.adobe.com/`
`asn/acrobat/technotes.jsp`

[27] Adobe Systems. Unicode and glyph names, 2003. `http://partners.adobe.com:80/`
`asn/tech/type/unicodegn.jsp`

[28] Adobe Systems. *PDF Reference: Version 1.6*. Addison-Wesley, 5th edition, 2004.
`http://partners.adobe.com/asn/acrobat/docs/File_Format_Specifications/`
`PDFReference.zip`

[29] AFII. *Registration Authority for Font-Related Objects*, 2001. http://www.glocom.ac.jp/iso10036/

[30] Jean Alessandrini. Nouvelle classification typographique: Codex 1980. *Communication et Langages*, 43:35–56, 1979.

[31] AMS. AMSFonts, 1995. http://www.ams.org/tex/amsfonts.html

[32] Jacques André. The Scrabble font. *The PostScript Journal*, 3(1):53–55, 1990.

[33] Jacques André. *Contribution à la création de fontes en typographie numérique, Habilitation à diriger des recherches*. PhD thesis, Université de Rennes 1, IFSIC, 1993.

[34] Jacques André. Lucida, a-t-elle un gros œil ? *La Lettre GUTenberg*, 5:24–26, 1997. http://www.gutenberg.eu.org/pub/GUTenberg/publicationsPDF/lettre5.pdf

[35] Jacques André. De Pacioli à Truchet, trois siècles de géométrie pour les caractères. In *Actes du treizième colloque Inter-IREM d'Histoire et d'Épistémologie des mathématiques*, 2000. http://www.univ-irem.fr/commissions/epistemologie/colloques/co00.htm

[36] Jacques André. Histoire d'@, histoire d'Œ. Rumeurs, traitement de textes et enseignement. In *Traitement de texte et production de documents, INRP, Octobre 2004*, pages 19–34, 2004. http://jacques-andre.fr/japublis/dida/andrej.htm

[37] Jacques André and Christian Delorme. Le *Delorme*: un caractère modulaire et dépendant du contexte. *Communication et Langages*, 86:65–76, 1990.

[38] Jacques André et al. Ligatures et caractères contextuels, *Cahier GUTenberg 22*, 1995. http://www.gutenberg.eu.org/publications/cahiers/48-cahiers22.html

[39] Jacques André et al. La fonte du jour: Vendôme. *La Lettre GUTenberg*, 16:16–20, 1999. http://www.gutenberg.eu.org/pub/GUTenberg/publicationsPDF/lettre16.pdf

[40] Jacques André, Roger Hersch, et al. Workshop on font design systems (Sophia-Antipolis, 18–19 mai 1987), 1987.

[41] Jacques André and Victor Ostromoukhov. Punk: de METAFONT à PostScript. *Cahiers GUTenberg*, 4:23–28, 1989. http://www.gutenberg.eu.org/pub/GUTenberg/publicationsPDF/4-ostromoukhov.pdf

[42] Jacques André and Irène Vatton. Dynamic optical scaling and variable-sized characters. *Electronic Publishing—Origination, Dissemination, and Design*, 7(4):231–250, 1994.

[43] Anonymous. Archives of the SAIL (*Stanford Artificial Intelligence Laboratory*) project, 1966-1990. http://z.baumgart.org/saildart/prog/SYS/index.html

[44] Anonymous. *Introduction à la calligraphie chinoise*. Éditions du centenaire, Paris, 1983.

[45] Anonymous. Font-file format. Technical report, Microsoft Knowledge Base, 199? http://support.microsoft.com/default.asp?scid=KB;en-us;q65123

[46] Anonymous. snfstr.h and snfread.c, taken from X11 R6.4 source code, 1998. http://ftp.x.org/pub/

[47] Anonymous.   PFM file format, 2000. `http://homepages.fbmev.de/bm134751/pfm_fmt_en.html`

[48] Anonymous. *Lexique des règles typographiques en usage à l'imprimerie nationale.* Imprimerie Nationale, 2002.

[49] Apple Computer. *Apple Inside Macintosh, Volume I.* Addison-Wesley, 1985. `http://developer.apple.com/techpubs/mac/pdf/MoreMacintoshToolbox.pdf`

[50] Apple Computer. *Apple Inside Macintosh, Volume IV.* Addison Wesley, 1985. `http://developer.apple.com/techpubs/mac/pdf/MoreMacintoshToolbox.pdf`

[51] Apple Computer. *Apple Inside Macintosh, Volume V.* Addison Wesley, 1986. `http://developer.apple.com/techpubs/mac/pdf/MoreMacintoshToolbox.pdf`

[52] Apple Computer. *LaserWriter Reference.* Addison-Wesley, 1988.

[53] Apple Computer. *Guide to Macintosh Software Localization.* Addison-Wesley, 1992.

[54] Apple Computer. *TrueType GX Font Formats*, 1993.

[55] Apple Computer. *QuickDraw GX Typography.* Addison-Wesley, 1994. `ftp://ftp.apple.com/developer/Technical_Publications/Archives/QDGX_Typography.sit.hqx`

[56] Apple Computer. *The TrueType Reference Manual*, 1996. `http://developer.apple.com/fonts/TTRefMan/index.html`

[57] Apple Computer. Installable keyboard layouts, 2002. `http://developer.apple.com/technotes/tn2002/tn2056.html`

[58] Apple Computer.   SFNT file layout structures and constants, *in* macos x, 2002. `/System/Library/Frameworks/ApplicationServices.framework/Versions/A/Frameworks/ATS.framework/Versions/A/Headers/SFNTLayoutTypes.h`

[59] Apple Computer.   Instructing fonts, 2003. `http://developer.apple.com/fonts/TTRefMan/RMO3/Chap3.html`

[60] Apple Computer. *Using and Managing Fonts in Mac OS X, A Guide for Creative Professionals*, 2003. `http://205.134.180.85/UsingFontsinMacOSX.pdf`

[61] Vlad Atanasiu. *Le phénomène calligraphique à l'époque du sultanat mamluk.* PhD thesis, École pratique des Hautes Études, Section des Sciences historiques et philologiques, 2003. `http://atanasiu.freesurf.fr/thesis/atanasiu2003phd.pdf`

[62] Peter Bain and Paul Shaw. *Blackletter: Type and National Identity.* Princeton Architectural Press, 1998.

[63] Paul Barrett et al.   Numerical Python, 2000. `http://sourceforge.net/projects/numpy`

[64] Dieter Barron. *ttftot42*, 1999. `http://ftp.giga.or.at/pub/nih/ttftot42/`

[65] Benjamin Bauermeister. *A manual of Comparative Typography: The PANOSE System*. Van Nostrand Reinhold, 1988.

[66] Benjamin Bauermeister. Panose classification guide - numeric specifications for classification of fonts in the panose typeface matching system. Technical report, Elseware Corporation, 1992.

[67] Barbara Beeton. Mathematical symbols and cyrillic fonts ready for distribution. *TUGboat*, 6(2):59–63, July 1985.

[68] Barbara Beeton. Mathematical symbols and cyrillic fonts ready for distribution (revised). *TUGboat*, 6(3):124–128, November 1985.

[69] Barbara Beeton. METAFONT mode_def settings for various TeX output devices. *TUGboat*, 8(1):33–33, 1987.

[70] Barbara Beeton. Update: METAFONT mode_def settings for TeX output devices. *TUGboat*, 8(2):132–134, 1987.

[71] Gábor Bella and Yannis Haralambous. Fontes intelligentes, textèmes et typographie dynamique. *Document Numérique*, 9:167–216, 2006.

[72] Bob Bemer. How ASCII got its backslash, 2002. http://www.bobbemer.com/BACSLASH.HTM

[73] A. Berdnikov, O. Lapko, M. Kolodin, A. Janishevsky, and A. Burykin. Cyrillic encodings for LaTeX 2ε multi-language documents. *TUGboat*, 19(4):403–416, 1998.

[74] Tim Berners-Lee, R. Fielding, U.C. Irvine, and L. Masinter. *Uniform Resource Identifiers (URI): Generic Syntax, RFC 2396*. IETF, 1998. http://www.ietf.org/rfc/rfc2396.txt

[75] Karl Berry. Filenames for fonts. *TUGboat*, 11(4):517–520, 1990.

[76] Karl Berry. modes.mf, a collection of METAFONT mode_def's, 2005. http://www.ctan.org/tex-archive/fonts/modes/modes.mf

[77] Karl Berry and Kathryn A. Hargreaves. GNU font utilities, v. 0.6, 1992. http://www.math.utah.edu/docs/info/fontu_toc.html

[78] Karl Berry and Olaf Weber. kpathsea *library, version 3.5.4*, 2005. http://www.tug.org/teTeX/tetex-texmfdist/doc/programs/kpathsea.pdf

[79] Tom Bishop and Richard Cook. A specification for cdl *Character Description Language*. Technical report, Wenlin, 2003. http://www.wenlin.com/cdl/cdl_spec_2003_10_31.pdf

[80] Tom Bishop and Richard Cook. Character description language cdl: The set of basic CJK unified stroke types. Technical report, Wenlin, 2004. http://www.wenlin.com/cdl/cdl_strokes_2004_05_23.pdf

[81] Bitstream. TrueDoc. http://www.bitstream.com/categories/developer/truedoc/index.html

[82] Lewis Blackwell. *Twentieth-Century Type*. Yale University Press, 2004 (revised edition).

[83] Gérard Blanchard. *Pour une sémiologie de la typographie*. PhD thesis, École des hautes études en sciences sociales, 1980.

[84] Gérard Blanchard. *Aide au choix de la typo-graphie*. Atelier Perrousseaux, 2001.

[85] Gérard Blanchard et al. *Pour une sémiologie de la typographie*. Rémy Magermans, 1979.

[86] Erik van Blokland and Just van Rossum. Random code—the Beowulf random font. *The PostScript Journal*, 3(1):8–11, 1990.

[87] Andrew Boag. Typographic measurement: a chronology. *Typography Papers*, 1:105–121, 1996.

[88] Bert Bos, Hakon Wium Lie, Chris Lilley, and Ian Jacobs (eds.). *Cascading Style Sheets, level 2. CSS2 Specification*. W3C, 1998. http://www.w3.org/TR/REC-CSS2

[89] René Bouvard. *Notions de typographie orientale*. Éditions de l'École Estienne, 1893.

[90] Jim Breen. The EDICT project, 1991-2003. http://www.csse.monash.edu.au/~jwb/edict.html

[91] Andries Brouwer. *Font Formats Recognized by the Linux kbd Package*, 2002. http://www.win.tue.nl/~aeb/linux/kbd/font-formats.html

[92] Max Bruinsma. The erotics of type, 2000. http://www.xs4all.nl/%7emaxb/erotype.html

[93] Ian Caldwell and Dustin Thomason. *The Rule of Four*. The Dial Press, 2004.

[94] Harry Carter. *A view of early typography up to about 1600*. Hyphen Press, 2002.

[95] Juliusz Chroboczek. *mkfontscale - Create an Index of Scalable Font Files for X*. http://www.xfree86.org/current/mkfontscale.1.html

[96] Marcel Cohen, Jean Sainte Fare Garnot, et al. *L'écriture et la psychologie des peuples, XXIIᵉ semaine de synthèse*. Armand Colin, 1963.

[97] Collectif. *De plomb, d'encre & de lumière. Essai sur la typographie & la communication écrite*. Imprimerie nationale Éditions, 1982.

[98] Collectif. *Les caractères de l'Imprimerie nationale*. Imprimerie nationale Éditions, 1990.

[99] John Collins and Bob Thomas. *Coding of Outline Fonts: PFR Specification (Version 1.3)*. Bistream, 2005. http://www.bitstream.com/font_rendering/pdfs/pfrspec1.3.pdf

[100] François Colonna. Hypnerotomachia polophili, 1499. http://mitpress.mit.edu/e-books/HP/

[101] Agfa Compugraphic. Intellifont scalable typeface format, 1992.

[102] Vincent Connare. Basic hinting philosophies and TrueType instructions, 1997. http://www.microsoft.com/typography/hinting/tutorial.htm

[103] Robin Cover. Language identifiers in the markup context. Technical report, OASIS, 2002. http://xml.coverpages.org/languageIdentifiers.html

[104] Dan Crevier, Richard Northcott, Abbey Kazuya, and Ayumi Kimura. UniDict, 1999. http://www.enfour.co.jp/unidict/e/manual.html

[105] Anne Cuneo. *Le maître de Garamond*. Stock, 2003.

[106] Peter Daniels and William Bright. *The World's Writing Systems*. Oxford University Press, 1996.

[107] John Davies, Dieter Fensel, and Frank van Harmelen. *Towards the Semantic Web: Ontology-Driven Knowledge Management*. John Wiley & Sons, 2003.

[108] Mark Davis. Unicode Standard Annex #24. script names. Technical report, Unicode Consortium, 2003. http://www.unicode.org/reports/tr24

[109] Mark Davis and Martin Dürst. Unicode Standard Annex #15. Unicode normalization forms. Technical report, Unicode Consortium, 2003. http://www.unicode.org/reports/tr15

[110] Mark Davis and Markus Scherer. Binary-Ordered Compression for Unicode, 2001. http://oss.software.ibm.com/icu/docs/papers/binary_ordered_compression_for_unicode.html

[111] Michael Dawson. *Python Programming for the Absolute Beginner*. Thomson Course Technology, 2003.

[112] Luc[as] de Groot. *MoveMeMM*, a porno font, 1996. http://www.fontfabrik.com/lucfuse.html

[113] Michael S. de Laurentis. PANOSE 2.0 white paper. Hewlett-Packard document EWC-92-0015h, 1993. http://www.w3.org/Fonts/Panose/pan2.html

[114] Jacques Derrida. *De la grammatologie*. Les Éditions de Minuit, 1967.

[115] Jacques Derrida. *Signature événement contexte, dans Marges de la philosophie*. Les Éditions de Minuit, 1972.

[116] Luc Devroye. TrueType versus Type 1, 2001. http://cg.scs.carleton.ca/~luc/ttvst1.html

[117] Luc Devroye. Font formats, talk given at EuroTEX 2003, ENST Bretagne, Brest, 2003.

[118] Luc Devroye and Michael McDougall. Random fonts for the simulation of handwriting. *Electronic Publishing—Origination, Dissemination, and Design*, 8(4):281–294, 1995. http://cajun.cs.nott.ac.uk/compsci/epo/papers/volume8/issue4/ep129ld.pdf

[119] DiamondSoft. Font Reserve for Macintosh, Font Reserve for Windows, Font Reserve Server. http://www.diamondsoft.com/products/index.html

[120] Yann Dirson. The CP file format. Technical report, Debian, 1998. http:
//www.ambienteto.arti.beniculturali.it/cgi-bin/dwww?type=file&location=
/usr/share/doc/console-tools/file-formats/cp

[121] Mark Douma. dfontifier, 2003. http://homepage.mac.com/mdouma46/dfont/dfont.
html

[122] DTL. FontMaster, 1995. http://www.fontmaster.nl/english/

[123] Duden. *Rechtschreibung der deutschen Sprache und der Fremdwörter.* Bibliographisches
Institut Mannheim, 1961.

[124] Albrecht Dürer. *On the Just Shaping of Letters.* Dover, 1917, reprint 1965.

[125] Martin Dürst. Coordinate-independent font description using Kanji as an example.
Electronic Publishing—Origination, Dissemination, and Design, 6(3):133–143, 1993.

[126] Martin Dürst, François Yergeau, Richard Ishida, Misha Wolf, and Tex Texin. W3C working draft. character model for the World Wide Web 1.0. Technical report, W3C, 2003.
http://www.w3.org/TR/charmod/

[127] David Earls. *Designing Typefaces.* RotoVision, 2002.

[128] Julia Ecklar. *Kobayashi Maru.* Star Trek, 1989.

[129] David Eisenberg. *SVG.* O'Reilly France, 2003. http://www.oreilly.fr/catalogue/
SVG.html

[130] em2 Solutions. Glyphgate. http://www.glyphgate.com/info/

[131] Pierre Enckell and Pierre Rézeau. *Dictionnaire des onomatopées.* puf, 2003.

[132] Extensis. Suitcase for Macintosh, Suitcase for Windows, Suitcase Server. http://www.
extensis.com/fontman/

[133] Carl Faulmann. *Das Buch der Schrift enthaltend die Schriftzeichen und Alphabete aller
Zeiten und aller Völker des Erdkreises.* Druck und Verlag der kaiserlich-königlichen Hof-
und Staatsdruckerei, Wien, 1880.

[134] Jon Ferraiolo, Jun Fujisawa, and Dean Jackson (eds.). *Scalable Vector Graphics (SVG) 1.1
Specification.* W3C, 2003. http://www.w3.org/TR/SVG11/

[135] Gabriel Valiente Feruglio. Modern Catalan typographical conventions. *TUGboat*,
16(3):329–338, 1995.

[136] James Février. *Histoire de l'écriture.* Payot, 1995.

[137] Dimitrios Filippou. Διαγωνισμὸς ἑλληνικοῦ παγγράμματος: τὰ ἀποτελέσματα. *To
Eutupon*, 9:57–59, 2002. http://ocean1.ee.duth.gr/eutupon/eutupon9.pdf

[138] Jim Flowers and Stephen Gildea. *X Logical Font Description Conventions, version 1.5.*
Digital Equipment Corporation, 1994. http://www.xfree86.org/current/xlfd.pdf

[139] FontLab. TransType, 1999-2003. `http://www.fontlab.com/html/transtype.html`

[140] FontLab. FontLab Studio – next-generation pro font editor, 1999-2006. `http://fontlab.com/Font-tools/FontLab-Studio/`

[141] FontLab. FontLab 5 user manual, 2006. `http://www.font.to/downloads/manuals/FLS5MacManual.zip`

[142] Fournier, le jeune. *Manuel typographique, utile aux gens de lettres & à ceux qui exercent les différentes parties de l'Art de l'Imprimerie.* Imprimé par l'Auteur, rue des Postes, 1764, facsimile réédité en 1995.

[143] Jeffrey Friedl. *Mastering Regular Expressions.* O'Reilly France, 3rd edition, 2006. `http://www.oreilly.com/catalog/regex3/index.html`

[144] Adrien Frutiger. *Type Sign Symbol.* ABC Edition, 1999.

[145] David Fuchs. The format of PXL files. *TUGboat*, 2(3):8–12, 1981.

[146] Jim Fulton. *xfd - Display All the Characters in an X Font.* `http://www.xfree86.org/4.3.0/xfd.1.html`

[147] Simon Garfinkel. *Web Security, Privacy & Commerce.* O'Reilly, 2nd edition, 2001. `http://www.oreilly.com/catalog/websec2/index.html`

[148] Roudzéro Sergeïevitch Gilyarevskii and Vladimir Sergeïevitch Grivnin. *Определитель языков мира по письменностям (Language identification through its writing system).* Издательство восточной литературы, Москва, 1960.

[149] Rémi Goblot. Algèbre Géométrique, polycopié de cours donné à l'Université de Lille I, 1982-83.

[150] Rémi Goblot. *Thèmes de géométrie: Géométrie affine et euclidienne — agrégation de mathématiques.* Dunod Masson, 1998.

[151] Danny Goodman. *Dynamic HTML. The Definitive Reference.* O'Reilly, 2e edition, 2002. `http://www.oreilly.com/catalog/dhtmlref2/`

[152] David Gourley and Brian Totty. *HTTP: The Definitive Guide.* O'Reilly, 2002. `http://www.oreilly.com/catalog/httptdg/index.html`

[153] Dean Guenther and Janene Winter. An international phonetic alphabet. *TUGboat*, 12(1):149–156, 1991.

[154] Max Hall. *An Embarrassment of Misprints: Comical and Disastrous Typos of the Centuries.* Fulcrum Publishing, 1995. `http://www.amazon.com/exec/obidos/tg/detail/-/1555912028/qid=1101141316/sr=1-4/ref=sr_1_4/102-1069734-0297715?v=glance&s=books`

[155] Jack Halpern. *The Kodansha Kanji Learner's Dictionary.* Kodansha International, 1999.

[156] Tereza Haralambous and Yannis Haralambous. Characters, glyphs and beyond. In *Proceedings of the Glyph and Typesetting Workshop, Kyoto, Japon*, 2003. http://omega.enstb.org/yannis/pdf/kyoto-tereza.pdf

[157] Yannis Haralambous. The DVR and DVX formats, specifications and tools. http://omega.enstb.org/yannis/dvi2dvr

[158] Yannis Haralambous. *Tiqwah*, a typesetting system for biblical Hebrew, based on TEX. In *Proceedings of the Fourth International Colloquium "Bible and Computer: Desk and Discipline, The impact of computers on Bible Studies," Amsterdam, 1994*, pages 445–470. Honoré Champion Éditeur, 1994. http://omega.enstb.org/yannis/pdf/biblical-hebrew94.pdf

[159] Yannis Haralambous. Typesetting Khmer. *Electronic Publishing—Origination, Dissemination, and Design*, 7(4):197–215, 1994.

[160] Yannis Haralambous. *Sabra*, a Syriac TEX system. In *Proceedings of SyrCOM-95, the 1st International Forum on Syriac Computing, Washington DC 1995*, pages 3–24, 1995. http://omega.enstb.org/yannis/pdf/syriac96.pdf

[161] Yannis Haralambous. Tour du monde des ligatures. *Cahiers GUTenberg*, 22:69–80, 1995. http://omega.enstb.org/yannis/pdf/ligatures.pdf

[162] Yannis Haralambous. Large brackets and accents: the *yhmath* package. *TUGboat*, 6(1):6–8, 1996. http://tug.ctan.org/cgi-bin/getFile.py?fn=/usergrps/uktug/baskervi/bask6_1.pdf

[163] Yannis Haralambous. From Unicode to typography, a case study: the Greek script. In *Proceedings of the 14th International Unicode Conference, Boston 1999*, pages b.10.1–b.10.36, 1999. http://omega.enstb.org/yannis/pdf/boston99.pdf

[164] Yannis Haralambous. Druckſatz in gebrochenen Schriften. In *Proceedings of the DANTE 2000 Conference*, 2000. http://omega.enstb.org/yannis/pdf/dante2000.pdf

[165] Yannis Haralambous. Unicode et typographie : un amour impossible. *Document Numérique*, 6(3-4):105–137, 2002. http://omega.enstb.org/yannis/pdf/docnum.pdf

[166] Yannis Haralambous. Οἱ ἀναφορὲς τῶν μονοτονιστῶν στὸν Βιλαμόβιτς καὶ στὸν Γεώργιο Χατζιδάκι (*References of monotonists to Wilamowitz and to Georgios Hadzidakis*). Ὁ μικρὸς ἀστρολάβος, Εὐθύνη, 2007. http://www.polytoniko.org/haralambous.php

[167] Yannis Haralambous and Gábor Bella. Injecting information into atomic units of text. In *Proceedings of the ACM Symposium on Document Engineering, Bristol*, 2005.

[168] Yannis Haralambous and Gábor Bella. Open-belly surgery in Ω_2. *TUGboat*, 27(1):91–97, 2006.

[169] Yannis Haralambous et al. Homepage of the citizen's movement for the re-introduction of the polytonic system. http://www.polytoniko.gr

[170] Yannis Haralambous and John Plaice. Multilingual typesetting with Ω, a case study: Arabic. In *Proceedings of the International Symposium on Multilingual Information Processing, Tsukuba 1997*, pages 137–154. ETL Japan, 1997. http://omega.enstb.org/yannis/pdf/tsukuba-arabic97.pdf

[171] Yannis Haralambous and John Plaice. Traitement automatique des langues et composition sous Ω. *Cahiers Gutenberg*, 39-40:139–166, 2001. http://omega.enstb.org/yannis/pdf/metz2001.pdf

[172] Yannis Haralambous and Klaus Thull. Typesetting modern Greek with 128 character codes. *TUGboat*, 10(3):354–359, 1989.

[173] Doug Henderson. Update: METAFONT mode_def settings for TeX output devices. *TUGboat*, 8(3):268–270, 1987.

[174] Doug Henderson. Outline fonts with METAFONT. *TUGboat*, 10(1):36–38, 1989.

[175] Lee Hetherington and Claire Connelly. Type 1 utilities version 1.28, 2003. http://www.lcdf.org/~eddietwo/type/#t1utils

[176] Hewlett Packard. *PCL 5 Printer Language Technical Reference Manual*, 1992. http://h20000.www2.hp.com/bc/docs/support/SupportManual/bpl13210/bpl13210.pdf

[177] John D. Hobby. *Digitized Brush Trajectories*. PhD thesis, Stanford University, 1985. http://cm.bell-labs.com/who/hobby/thesis.pdf

[178] John D. Hobby and Gu Guoan. A Chinese meta-font. *TUGboat*, 5(2):119–136, 1984.

[179] Alan Hoenig. Introducing METAPOST. *TUGboat*, 16(1):45–45, 1995.

[180] Alan Hoenig. Virtual fonts, virtuous fonts. *TUGboat*, 18(2):113–121, 1997.

[181] Alan Hoenig. Modernizing Computer Modern. *TUGboat*, 22(3):216–219, 2001.

[182] David A. Holzgang. *Programming the LaserWriter*. Addison-Wesley, 1991.

[183] Gerard J. Holzmann and Björn Pehrson. The first telegraphs. http://labit501.upct.es/ips/libros/TEHODN/ch-2-1.5.html

[184] Martin Hosken and Sharon Correll. Extending TrueType for Graphite. Technical report, Summer Institute for Linguistics, 2003. http://scripts.sil.org/cms/sites/nrsi/media/GraphiteBinaryFormat_pdf.pdf

[185] David A. Huffman. A method for the construction of minimum-redundancy codes. *Proceedings of the IRE*, 40:1098–1101, 1952.

[186] IANA. Character sets, 2004. http://www.iana.org/assignments/character-sets

[187] IETF. Public-key infrastructure X.509 (PKIX). http://www.ietf.org/html.charters/pkix-charter.html

[188] Bitstream Inc. Bitstream Speedo font file format, 1993. http://www.bitstream.com/fonts/support/speedo_fonts.html

[189] Insider Software.   FontAgent. http://www.insidersoftware.com/products/
      fontagentpro/

[190] ISO 3166/MA. ISO 3166-1:1997 Codes for the representation of names of countries and
      their subdivisions — Part 1: Country codes, 1974-1997. http://www.iso.ch/iso/en/
      prods-services/iso3166ma/02iso-3166-code-lists/list-fr1-semic.txt

[191] ISO 639 Joint Advisory Committee. ISO 639, codes for the representation of names of
      languages — part 2: alpha-3 code, 2003. http://www.loc.gov/standards/iso639-2/

[192] ISO/ECMA. 7-bit coded character set, 1991. http://www.ecma-international.org/
      publications/standards/Ecma-006.htm

[193] ISO/ECMA. Ecma-35/iso 2022 character coded structure and extensions techniques,
      1994.   http://www.ecma-international.org/publications/standards/Ecma-035.
      htm

[194] ISO/IEC. *Information Technology — Font Information Interchange, Part 1: Architecture
      ISO/IEC 9541-1:1991(E)*, 1991. http://www.iso.ch/iso/fr/CatalogueDetailPage.
      CatalogueDetail?CSNUMBER=17280

[195] ISO/IEC.   *Information Technology — Font Information Interchange, Part 3: Glyph
      Shape Representation ISO/IEC 9541-3:1994(E)*, 1994. http://www.iso.ch/iso/fr/
      CatalogueDetailPage.CatalogueDetail?CSNUMBER=17280

[196] ISO/IEC. International register of coded character sets to be used with escape se-
      quences, 2003. http://www.itscj.ipsj.or.jp/ISO-IR/

[197] Bogusław Jackowski and Janusz Nowacki. Accents, accents, accents... — enhancing CM
      fonts with "funny" characters. In *Proceedings of the 24th Annual TUG Meeting, Waikoloa,
      Hawai'i*, 2003.

[198] Bogusław Jackowski, Janusz Nowacki, and Piotr Strzelczyk. Antykwa Półtawskiego: a
      parameterized outline font. *MAPS*, 25:86–102, 2000.

[199] Alan Jeffrey and Rowland McDonnell. *fontinst* - font installation software for TEX, 1998.
      http://www.tug.org/applications/fontinst/

[200] Alan Jeffrey, Sebastian Rahtz, Ulrik Vieth, and Lars Hellström. *fontinst*, a utility for font
      installation, 1993. http://www.tug.org/applications/fontinst/

[201] Tom Jennings. ASCII: American Standard Code for Information Infiltration, 2001.
      http://www.wps.com/projects/codes/index.html

[202] Brian Jepson and Ernest E. Rothman. *Mac OS X for Unix Geeks*. O'Reilly, 2002. http:
      //www.oreilly.com/catalog/mosxgeeks/

[203] Erik A. Johnson. FONT→NFNT FONT→NFNT, 1991. http://www.mirror.ac.uk/
      collections/hensa-micros/local/mac/converters/font_to_nfnt.hqx%5Bpeek%5D

[204] Nadine Kano. *Developing International Software for Windows 95 and Windows NT*. Mi-
      crosoft Press, 1995.

[205] Albert Kapr. *Fraktur: Form und Geschichte der gebrochenen Schriften*. Schmidt, 1993.

[206] Peter Karow. *Typeface Statistics*. URW Verlag, 1993.

[207] Peter Karow. *Font Technology, Description and Tools*. Springer, 1994.

[208] Sakasai Katsumi 逆井克己. 日本文字組版 *(Typesetting in Japanese Characters)*. 日本印刷新聞社, 1999.

[209] Richard Kinch. MetaFog: Converting METAFONT shapes to contours. *TUGboat*, 16(3):233–243, 1995.

[210] Richard Kinch. TrueTEX software, 1995-2000. http://www.truetex.com/

[211] Jörg Knappen. Fonts for Africa: the fc-fonts. *TUGboat*, 14(2):104–106, 1993.

[212] Jörg Knappen. Release 1.2 of the *dc*-fonts: Improvements to the European letters and first release of text companion symbols. *TUGboat*, 16(4):381–387, 1995.

[213] Jörg Knappen. The *dc* fonts 1.3: Move towards stability and completeness. *TUGboat*, 17(2):99–101, 1996.

[214] Jörg Knappen. Ankündigung: Die ec-Schriten 1.0 sind da! *Technische Komödie*, 4/96:8–9, 1997.

[215] Donald E. Knuth. Mathematical typography. *Bulletin of the American Mathematical Society (new series)*, 10:337–372, 1979.

[216] Donald E. Knuth. METAFONT: The Program, volume D of *Computers and Typesetting*. Addison-Wesley, Reading, MA, USA, 1986.

[217] Donald E. Knuth. *The TEXbook*, volume A of *Computers and Typesetting*. Addison-Wesley, Reading, MA, USA, 1986.

[218] Donald E. Knuth. *The METAFONTbook*, volume C of *Computers and Typesetting*. Addison-Wesley, Reading, MA, USA, 1986.

[219] Donald E. Knuth. *Computer Modern Typefaces*, volume E of *Computers and Typesetting*. Addison-Wesley, Reading, MA, USA, 1986.

[220] Donald E. Knuth. Virtual Fonts: More Fun for Grand Wizards. *TUGboat*, 11(1):13–23, 1990.

[221] Donald E. Knuth. *Digital Typography*. CSLI Publications, 1999.

[222] Donald E. Knuth and Pierre MacKay. Mixing right-to-left texts with left-to-right texts. *TUGboat*, 8(1):14–25, 1987.

[223] Eddie Kohler. LCDF typetools, 2003. http://www.lcdf.org/type/

[224] Helmut Kopka and Patrick W. Daly. *Guide to LATEX*. Addison-Wesley, 4th edition, 2003.

[225] Jukka Korpela. Soft hyphen (SHY) — a hard problem?, 1997-2002. http://www.cs.tut.fi/~jkorpela/shy.html

[226] Jukka Korpela. Character histories: notes on some ASCII code positions, 2000. http: //www.cs.tut.fi/~jkorpela/latin1/ascii-hist.html

[227] Olga G. Lapko. Full Cyrillic: How many languages? *TUGboat*, 17(2):174–180, 1996.

[228] Alexander Lawson. *Anatomy of a Typeface*. Hamish Hamilton, London, 1990.

[229] Azzeddine Lazrek. Aspects de la problématique de la confection d'une fonte pour les mathématiques arabes. *Cahiers GUTenberg*, 39-40:51–62, 2001. http://www.gutenberg. eu.org/pub/GUTenberg/publicationsPDF/39-lazrek.pdf

[230] Azzeddine Lazrek. *Vers un système de traitement du document scientifique arabe*. PhD thesis, University Cady Ayyad, Marrakech, 2002.

[231] Liane Lefaivre. *Leon Battista Alberti's Hypnerotomachia poliphili*. MIT Press, 1997.

[232] Mark Leisher. The XmBDFEd BDF font editor, 2001. http://crl.NMSU.Edu/ ~mleisher/xmbdfed.html

[233] Dave Lemke and Keith Packard. *xfs, X Font Server*. http://www.xfree86.org/4.3.0/ xfs.1.html

[234] David Lemon. Basic Type 1 hinting. Technical report, Adobe Systems Inc., 1999. http: //www.pyrus.com/downloads/hinting.pdf

[235] Leterror. robofog, 1999. http://www.letterror.com/code/old/robofog/index.html

[236] William J. LeVeque. Font development at the AMS. *TUGboat*, 2(2):39–40, July 1981.

[237] Noah Levitt. gucharmap, resisting the worldwide hegemony of english!, 2003. http: //gucharmap.sourceforge.net/

[238] Silvio Levy. Using Greek fonts with TEX. *TUGboat*, 9(1):20–24, April 1988.

[239] Ken Lunde. Accessibility of unencoded glyphs. In *Proceedings of the 13th Unicode Conference, San José, 1998*. Unicode Consortium, 1998. http://www.unicode.org/iuc/iuc13/ a10/paper.pdf

[240] Ken Lunde. *CJKV Information Processing*. O'Reilly, 1st edition, 1999. http://www. oreilly.com/catalog/cjkvinfo/

[241] Mark Lutz and David Asher. *Introduction à Python*. O'Reilly France, 2000. http://www. oreilly.fr/catalogue/lpython.html

[242] Charles E. MacKenzie. *Coded Character Sets, History and Development*. The Systems Programming Series. Addison-Wesley, 1980.

[243] James Macnicol. *type1inst*. ftp://sunsite.unc.edu/pub/Linux/X11/xutils/ type1inst-0.6.1.tar.gz

[244] Macromedia. Fontographer, 1995-2003. http://www.macromedia.com/software/ fontographer/

[245] Ladislas Mandel. *Écritures, miroir des hommes et des sociétés*. Atelier Perrousseaux, 1998.

[246] Duncan Marsh. *Applied Geometry for Computer Graphics and CAD*. Springer Undergraduate Mathematics Series. Springer, 1999.

[247] Alex Martelli. *Python in a Nutshell*. O'Reilly, 2003.

[248] Bernard Marti. *Télématique. Techniques, normes, services*. Dunod, 1990.

[249] Eberhard Mattes. Quick and dirty TEX to VPL, 1993. http://www.ctan.org/tex-archive/fonts/utilities/qdtexvpl/

[250] Henry McGilton and Mary Campione. *PostScript by Example*. Addison-Wesley, 1992.

[251] Dinah McNutt and Miles O'Neal. The X administrator: Font formats and utilities. *The X Resource*, 2(1):14–34, 1992.

[252] W. Scott Means and Elliotte Rusty Harold. *XML in a Nutshell, manuel de référence*. O'Reilly France, 3rd edition, 2004. http://www.oreilly.com/catalog/xmlnut3/index.html

[253] Philip Meggs. *Revival of the Fittest: Digital Versions of Classic Typefaces*. North Light Books, 2000.

[254] Eric Meyer. *CSS: The Definitive Guide*. O'Reilly, 3rd edition, 2006. http://www.oreilly.com/catalog/csstdg3/index.html

[255] John Miano. *Compressed Image File Formats*. ACM Press - SIGGRAPH Series. Addison-Wesley, 2000.

[256] Microsoft. Digital signatures. http://www.microsoft.com/typography/developers/dsig/default.htm

[257] Microsoft. Font Properties Extension. http://www.microsoft.com/typography/property/property.htm

[258] Microsoft. *TrueType 1.0 Font Files, Technical Specification, version 1.66*, 1995. http://www.microsoft.com/typography/tt/ttf_spec/_toc.doc

[259] Microsoft. *Welcome to TrueType Open*, 1997. http://www.microsoft.com/typography/tt/ch1.htm

[260] Microsoft. Visual TrueType resources, sample fonts, 1999. http://www.microsoft.com/typography/tools/vttfont.htm

[261] Microsoft. 1-year license agreement for Microsoft Visual TrueType tool, 2000. http://www.microsoft.com/typography/tools/vttlicen.htm?fname=%20&fsize=

[262] Microsoft. Visual TrueType, 2000. http://www.microsoft.com/typography/tools/vtt.htm

[263] Microsoft. Hinting and production guidelines specification, 2002. http://www.microsoft.com/typography/developers/delivery/hinting.htm

[264] Microsoft. *The OpenType Specification, v. 1.4*, 2002. http://www.microsoft.com/typography/otspec/default.htm

[265] Microsoft. Recommendation for OpenType fonts, 2002. http://www.microsoft.com/typography/otspec/recom.htm

[266] Microsoft. Visual OpenType Layout Tool, 2002. http://www.microsoft.com/typography/developers/volt/default.htm

[267] Microsoft. Features for the Korean Hangul script, 2003. http://www.microsoft.com/typography/otfntdev/hangulot/features.htm

[268] Microsoft. Microsoft Keyboard Layout Creator, 2003. www.microsoft.com/globaldev/tools/msklc.mspx

[269] Microsoft. Web Embedding Font Tool, 2003. http://www.microsoft.com/typography/web/embedding/weft3/default.htm

[270] Microsoft. Microsoft typography registered vendors, 2007. http://www.microsoft.com/typography/links/links.aspx?type=vendor&part=1

[271] Thomas Milo. Decotype, Support for Authentic Arabic, 1998. http://diwww.epfl.ch/w3lsp/conferences/ridt98/decotype.html

[272] Frank Mittelbach and Rainer Schöpf. A new font selection scheme for TEX macro packages — the basic macros. *TUGboat*, 10(2):222–238, 1989.

[273] Stanley Morison. *Pacioli's Classic Roman Alphabet*. Dover, 1933, reprint 1994.

[274] Shigeki Moro. Surface or essence: beyond character model set. In *Proceedings of the Glyph and Typesetting Workshop, Kyoto, Japon*, 2003. http://coe21.zinbun.kyoto-u.ac.jp/ws-type-2003.html.en

[275] Morrison Soft Design. Font Doctor. http://www.morrisonsoftdesign.com/fd_mac.html

[276] James Mosley and *al. Le Romain du Roi. La typographie au service de l'État, 1702-2002*. Musée de l'imprimerie, 2002.

[277] Stephen Moye. *Fontographer: Type by Design*. Hungry Minds, 1995.

[278] Neuber Software GbR. Typograf. http://www.neuber.com/typograph/

[279] Han-Wen Nienhuys. mftrace. scalable PostScript fonts for METAFONT, 2003. http://www.xs4all.nl/~hanwen/mftrace/

[280] Nordsächsische Staats- und Universitätsbibliothek Göttingen. The Göttingen Gutenberg Bible. http://www.gutenbergdigital.de/gudi/eframes/

[281] Janusz M. Nowacki and Bogusław Jackowski. Antykwa Toruńska: An electronic replica of a Polish traditional type. *TUGboat*, 19(3):242–243, 1998.

[282] Tobias Oetiker, Hubert Partl, Irene Hyna, and Elisabeth Schlegl. *The Not So Short Intro-duction to LATEX 2ε, or LATEX 2ε in 138 minutes*, 4.22 edition, 2007. http://www.ctan.org/tex-archive/info/lshort/english/lshort.pdf

[283] Oscar Ogg. *Three Classics of Italian Calligraphy: Arrighi, Tagliente, Palatino*. Dover, 1953.

[284] P22 Type Foundry. P22 online, 2003. http://www.p22.com

[285] Keith Packard. pcf.h and pcfread.c, taken from X11 R6.4 source code, 1998. http://ftp.x.org/pub/

[286] Anshuman Pandey. Using the WSU International Phonetic Alphabet, 1992. http://www.ctan.org/tex-archive/fonts/wsuipa/

[287] Minje Byeng-sen Park. *Histoire de l'imprimerie coréenne des origines à 1910*. Maisonneuve & Larose, Paris, 2003.

[288] Tuomo Pekkanen, Reijo Pitkäranta, et al. Nuntii latini, 1999. http://www.yle.fi/fbc/latini/index.html

[289] Georges Pérec. *La disparition*. Julliard, 1969.

[290] Georges Pérec. *Les revenentes*. Julliard, 1972.

[291] Georges Perec. *A Void*. Verba Mundi, 2005.

[292] Toby Phipps. Unicode technical report #26. compatibility encoding scheme for UTF-16: 8-Bit (CESU-8). Technical report, Unicode Consortium, 2002. http://www.unicode.org/unicode/reports/tr26

[293] François Pinard. Free recode package, 1999. http://recode.progiciels-bpi.ca/

[294] Joerg Pommnitz. *ttmkfdir*. http://freshmeat.net/projects/ttmkfdir/?topic_id=850

[295] Man-Chi Pong 龐文治, Fung Fung Lee 李楓峰, Ricky Yeung 楊振富, and Yongguang Zhang 張永光. Han character font sharing across incompatible bitmap file formats. Technical Report HKUST-CS94-5, The Hong Kong University of Science and Technology, 1994. http://www.ibiblio.org/pub/packages/ccic/software/info/hbfa.html

[296] Man-Chi Pong 龐文治, Fung Fung Lee 李楓峰, Ricky Yeung 楊振富, and Yongguang Zhang 張永光. *Hanzi Bitmap Font (HBF) File Format Version 1.1*, 1994. http://www.ibiblio.org/pub/packages/ccic/software/info/HBF-1.1/

[297] René Ponot. Classification typographique. *Communication et Langages*, 81:40–54, 1989.

[298] Peter Prymmer. Perl and EBCDIC? *The Perl Journal*, 2(4), October 1997. http://www.foo.be/docs/tpj/issues/vol2_4/tpj0204-0005.html

[299] Valerie Quercia and Tim O'Reilly. *X Window System User's Guide*. O'Reilly, 1993. http://www.oreilly.com/catalog/v3m/

[300] Erik T. Ray. *Learning XML*. O'Reilly, 2nd edition, 2003. http://www.oreilly.com/ catalog/learnxml2/index.html

[301] Red Hat.   Cygwin user's guide, 2003. http://www.cygwin.com/cygwin-ug-net/ cygwin-ug-net.pdf.gz

[302] Fukui Rei.   *TIPA*: A system for processing phonetic symbols in LaTeX.   *TUGboat*, 17(2):102–114, 1996.

[303] Glenn C. Reid. *Thinking in PostScript*. Addison-Wesley, 1990.

[304] Floyd Rogers. Win32 binary resource formats. Technical report, Microsoft, 1992. http: //www.powerbasic.com/files/pub/docs/RESFMT.ZIP

[305] Tomas Rokicki. Packed font file format. *TUGboat*, 6(3):115–120, 1985.

[306] Tomas Rokicki. GFtoPK, v. 2.3, 1990. http://www.ctan.org/tex-archive/systems/ knuth/mfware/gftopk.web

[307] Guido van Rossum.   TTX, from OpenType to XML and back, 2001. http:// sourceforge.net/projects/fonttools/

[308] RSA Laboratories. *PKCS-7: Cryptographic Message Syntax Standard, v. 1.5*, 1993. ftp:// ftp.rsasecurity.com/pub/pkcs/ascii/pkcs-7.asc

[309] Geoffrey Sampson. *Writing Systems*. Stanford University Press, 1985.

[310] Ferdinand de Saussure and Roy Harris. *Course in General Linguistics*. London: Duck-worth, 1983.

[311] John Sauter. Building Computer Modern Fonts. *TUGboat*, 7(3):151–152, 1986.

[312] Bob Scheifler and David Krikorian. *xset - User Preference Utility for X*. http://www. xfree86.org/4.3.0/xset.1.html

[313] Markus Scherer and Mark Davis.   Unicode Technical Note #6. BOCU-1: MIME-Compatible Unicode Compression.   Technical report, Unicode Consortium, 2002. http://www.unicode.org/notes/tn6/

[314] Walter Schmidt. The Computer Modern Bright family of fonts, 1998. http://www. ctan.org/tex-archive/help/Catalogue/entries/cmbright.html

[315] Mícheál Ó Searcóid. The Irish alphabet. *TUGboat*, 12(1):139–148, 1991.

[316] Peter Selinger. potrace. transforming bitmaps into vector graphics, 2003. http:// potrace.sourceforge.net

[317] Raymond Seroul and Silvio Levy. *A Beginner's Book of TeX*. Springer, 1995.

[318] Ross Smith. *Learning PostScript, a Visual Approach*. Peachpit Press, 1990.

[319] Friedhelm Sowa.   bm2font, 1993. http://vega.rz.uni-duesseldorf.de/sowa/ bm2font/

[320] Penny Spector. The interrobang: A twentieth century punctuation mark, 2001. http: //www.interrobang-mks.com/

[321] Michael Spivak. *The Joy of TEX: A Gourmet Guide to Typesetting With the AMS-TEX Macro Package*. American Mathematical Society, 2ᵉ edition, 1990.

[322] Siegfried H. Steinberg. *Five Hundred Years of Printing*. Oak Knoll Press, 1996.

[323] Sumner Stone. ITC Classics: *ITC Bodoni*. http://www.itcfonts.com/fonts/classics. asp?nCo=AFMT&sec=fnt&art=bodoni

[324] Ralph R. Swick and Mark Leisher. *xfontsel - Point and Click Selection of X11 Font Names*. X Consortium, 1989. http://www.xfree86.org/4.0.2/xfontsel.1.html

[325] Adobe Systems. OpenType feature file specification, v. 1.4, 2003. http://partners. adobe.com/asn/tech/type/otfdk/techdocs/OTFeatureFileSyntax.jsp

[326] Péter Szabó. TEXtrace, 2001. http://www.inf.bme.hu/~pts/textrace/

[327] Hàn Thế Thành. Making type 1 fonts for Vietnamese. In *Proceedings of the 24th Annual TUG Meeting, Waikoloa, Hawai'i*, 2003.

[328] Hán Thê Thánh. Vietnamese TEX and LATEX support, 2000. http://www.ctan.org/ tex-archive/language/vietnamese/vntex/

[329] The Apache Software Foundation. *Batik SVG Toolkit*. http://xml.apache.org/batik/ index.html

[330] The FreeType Project. FreeType & patents, 2003. http://www.freetype.org/patents. html

[331] Bhavani Thuraisingham. *XML Databases and the Semantic Web*. CRC Press, 1st edition, 2002. http://www.crcpress.com

[332] Geofroy Tory. Champ fleury. Au quel est contenu Lart & Science de la deue & vraye Proportiõ des Lettres Attiques, quõ dit autremẽt Lettres Antiques, & vulgairement Lettres Romaines proportionnees selon le Corps & Visage humain, 1529.

[333] Adam Twardoch and Andreas Eigendorf. Unofficial FontLab 4.5 Python reference, 2003. http://dev.fontlab.net/flpydoc/

[334] Unicode Consortium. Code charts (PDF version), 2006. http://www.unicode.org/ charts/

[335] Unicode Consortium. *The Unicode Standard. Version 5.0*. Addison Wesley, 5th edition, 2006. http://www.unicode.org/book/aboutbook.html

[336] Daniel B. Updike. *Printing Types, their History, Forms, and Use*. Harvard University Press, 2ᵉ edition, 1937.

[337] R. H. van Gent. Islamic-western calendar converter. http://www.phys.uu.nl/~vgent/ islam/islam_tabcal.htm

[338] Just van Rossum and Erik van Blokland. Bleifrei!, 1992-2001. http://www.letterror. com/catalog/bleifrei/index.html

[339] VeriSign. VeriSign digital ID for Microsoft Authenticode technology, 2000. ttps:// digitalid.verisign.com/developer/help/mscs_intro.htm

[340] Michel Villandry. Brest, Ouessant. *Parages*, 2000. http://www.parages.ens.fr/n1/ 15.html

[341] Vladimir Volovich. CM-Super font package, version 0.3.3, 2002. ftp://ftp.vsu.ru/ pub/tex/font-packs/cm-super/

[342] Maximilien Vox. *Faisons le point*. Larousse, 1963.

[343] Larry Wall, Tom Christiansen, and Jon Orwant. *Programming Perl*. O'Reilly, 3^e edition, 2000.

[344] Martin Weber.   AutoTrace. converts bitmap to vector graphics, 1998. http:// autotrace.sourceforge.net/

[345] Heinz Wendt. *Sprachen*. Fischer Taschenbuch Verlag, 1987.

[346] Andrew West.   BabelMap, 2002-2006. http://www.babelstone.co.uk/Software/ BabelMap.html

[347] Ken Whistler and Mark Davis.   Unicode technical report #17. character encoding model.   Technical report, Unicode Consortium, 2000. http://www.unicode.org/ unicode/reports/tr17

[348] George Williams.   PostScript font utilities, 2001. http://bibliofile.mc.duke.edu/ gww/FreeWare/MyToys.html

[349] George Williams. *Extensions to Adobe's BDF for Greymap Fonts*, 2002. http://pfaedit. sourceforge.net/BDFgrey.html

[350] George Williams.   *Format for X11 PCF Bitmap Font Files*, 2002. http://pfaedit. sourceforge.net/pcf-format.html

[351] George Williams. Fondu – a set of programs to interconvert between Mac font formats and PFB, TTF, OTF and BDF files on unix, 2003. http://fondu.sourceforge.net/

[352] George Williams. PfaEdit, an outline font editor, 2003. http://pfaedit.sourceforge. net/overview.html

[353] Misha Wolf, Ken Whistler, Charles Wicksteed, Mark Davis, Asmus Freytag, and Markus Scherer.   Unicode Technical Report #6. a standard compression scheme for Unicode.   Technical report, Unicode Consortium, 2003. http://www.unicode.org/ unicode/reports/tr6

[354] X Consortium. *Bitmap Distribution Format, v. 2.1*, 1997. ftp://ftp.x.org/pub/R6.6/ xc/doc/hardcopy/BDF/bdf.PS.gz

[355] Shimon Yanai and Daniel M. Berry. Environment for translating METAFONT to PostScript. *TUGboat*, 11(4):525–541, 1990.

[356] Candy Yiu, Wai Wong, and Kelvin Ng. Typesetting rare chinese characters in LaTeX. *TUGboat*, 24(3):582–588, 2003. http://www.tug.org/TUGboat/Articles/tb24-3/wong.pdf

[357] Dimitar Zhekov. *fontconv*, 2003. http://www.is-vn.bg/hamster/jimmy-en.html

[358] Maxim Zhukov. A Russian pangram, 2001. http://gmunch.home.pipeline.com/typo-L/articles/tsitrus.html

General Index

The names of fonts are shown in sans serif type.

Index of Persons

About the Author

Yannis Haralambous was born in Athens (Greece) in 1962. He moved to France in 1979 to study at the Université de Lille I, where in 1990 he completed his doctoral dissertation in pure mathematics. After a brief period at INALCO and several years of self-employment, in 2001 he joined the faculty of ENST Bretagne, in Brest (Brittany), where he teaches computer science. He does his research in the fields of digital typography (especially for the languages of East Asia), internationalization, and the electronic book. He has been the co-developer of Ω, a successor to TEX, now merged into the very promising luaTEX.

He is married to Tereza (who is, among other things, an excellent font designer). Together they have two daughters: Ernestine Chloé Hélène (*1998) and Danaé Elsa Catherine 英子 (*2004), whose photos are shown on page 620 for the reader's appreciation. Apart from typography, his chief passion is so-called "classical" piano music (from Bach to Hindemith, including Schumann, Debussy, and Poulenc along the way), especially chamber music.

Colophon

This book was prepared in XML with the XⱯTEX DTD, using the *BBEdit* editor. It was typeset and laid out using the Ωšystem on an Apple PowerBook G4 running MacOS X 10.4.6. The fonts employed are *Le Monde Livre*, by Jean François Porchez, for the body text; *The Sans Mono Condensed*, by Luc[as] de Groot, for the computer code; *Mantegna Italic*, by Philip Bouwsma, for the dedication; and more than a hundred other fonts, for the various examples. The list of bibliographic references was generated by BibTEX under *BibDesk*; the indexes, by *makeindex*. The illustrations were prepared in *Adobe Creative Suite*. The Latin text in the dedication comes from the student song *Gaudeamus Igitur* and means "Where be those who ere our day graced the world we live in?"

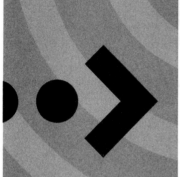

O'REILLY®

Fonts & Encodings

This reference is a fascinating and complete guide to using fonts and typography on the Web and across a variety of operating systems and application software. *Fonts & Encodings* shows you how to take full advantage of the incredible number of typographic options available, with advanced material that covers everything from designing glyphs to developing software that creates and processes fonts.

The era of ASCII characters on green screens is long gone, and industry leaders such as Apple, HP, IBM, Microsoft, and Oracle have adopted the Unicode Worldwide Character Standard. This only solves part of the problem, as a multitude of font standards and tools remain between the numeric character codes and their presentation. This book explores how those pieces fit together.

- Part I introduces Unicode, with a brief history of codes and encodings, including ASCII. Learn about the data that accompanies each Unicode character, and how Unicode deals with normalization, the bidirectional algorithm, and the handling of East Asian characters.

- Part II discusses font management, including installation, tools for activation/deactivation, and font choices for three different systems: Windows, Mac OS, and the X Window System (Unix).

- Part III deals with the technical use of fonts in two specific cases: the TeX typesetting system (and its successor, Ω, which the author co-developed) and web pages.

- Part IV presents the history of typefaces, and then examines methods for classifying fonts: Vox, Alessandrini, and Panose-1, which is used by Windows and the CSS standard. Learn about existing tools for creating (or modifying) fonts, including FontLab and FontForge, and become familiar with OpenType properties and AAT fonts.

- The appendixes explain a variety of standards and tools in depth, exploring bitmap font formats, TeX formats, PostScript formats, TrueType/OpenType and AAT, including tutorials in TrueType instructions, Metafont language, and Bézier curves.

Nowhere else will you find the valuable technical information that software developers, web developers, and graphic artists need to know to get typography and fonts to work properly.

Yannis Haralambous is the founder of Atelier Fluxus Virus, a company specializing in the high-quality typesetting of books with specific requirements, such as dictionaries and critical editions. Since 2001 he has taught computer science at ENST Bretagne in Brest (Brittany, France).

P. Scott Horne, who translated this book from French, is a former software developer with experience in localization and internationalization. He is also a typographer fluent in English, French, Spanish, Chinese, and Latin.

www.oreilly.com

US $59.99   CAN $71.99
ISBN-10: 0-596-10242-9
ISBN-13: 978-0-596-10242-5

55999

9 780596 102425

Free online edition
with purchase of this book.
Details on last page.